THE BLUE GUIDES

ENGLAND
SCOTLAND
IRELAND
WALES AND THE MARCHES
LONDON
MUSEUMS AND GALLERIES OF LONDON
OXFORD AND CAMBRIDGE
THE CHANNEL ISLANDS
MALTA
GREECE
ATHENS AND ENVIRONS
CRETE
CYPRUS
BOSTON AND ENVIRONS
NEW YORK
EGYPT
ISTANBUL
PORTUGAL
PARIS AND ENVIRONS
LOIRE VALLEY, NORMANDY, BRITTANY
NORTHERN ITALY
SOUTHERN ITALY
ROME AND ENVIRONS
SICILY
FLORENCE
VENICE
HOLLAND
SPAIN: THE MAINLAND
BELGIUM AND LUXEMBOURG
MOSCOW AND LENINGRAD

BLUE GUIDE

NEW YORK

Carol von Pressentin Wright

Atlas of Manhattan, maps and plans

Ernest Benn Limited
London

W. W. Norton & Company Inc.
New York

FIRST EDITION 1983

Published by Ernest Benn Limited
12 Norwich Street, London, EC4A 1EJ
& Sovereign Way, Tonbridge, Kent, TN9 1RW

© Ernest Benn Limited 1983

Printed in Great Britain

Published in the United States of America by
W. W. Norton & Company Inc.
500 Fifth Avenue, New York, N.Y. 10110

ISBN *Cloth* 0 510–01660–X   0 393–01559–9 (U.S.A.)
ISBN *Paper* 0 510–01659–6   0 393–30011–0 (U.S.A.)

Acknowledgements

I would like to thank first of all Susan E. Benn and Timothy Benn who made this job possible in the first place. Many people have made the job easier, more pleasant, or both: Estelle Girard, Brooklyn Botanic Garden; Joan Ingles, Metropolitan Museum of Art; Doreen Lown, Lincoln Center for the Performing Arts; Canon Jonathan L. King, Cathedral of Saint John the Divine; Margaret Lo Vero, New York Botanical Garden; Paul Stanton and James Cade, Urban Park Rangers; Arthur Lindo, Brooklyn Museum; Thomas Young and Edward Ryan, Saint Patrick's Cathedral; Frank Papay, Jr, Department of Parks and Recreation; Mitzi Bhavnani, Miriam Johnson, and Herbert Kurz, American Museum of Natural History; Ellen F. Rosebrock; Woody Lee, and John Harrison.

The black and white route maps are based on maps provided by the City of New York Department of City Planning. The *AIA Guide to New York City* by Norval White and Elliot Willensky (revised edition), New York, 1978) is the indispensable starting point for anyone writing about New York.

For services gratefully received but of a less institutional nature, I would like to thank Itie Caldwell, George Kinsley, and especially, Jean Mitchell Taylor. Paul Langridge and Tom Neville have been the most patient of editors. Even closer to home I would like to thank Fred Wright for his support—financial, moral, and other—and Catherine Wright who has endured significant inconvenience for the sale of this book.

CONTENTS

I BOROUGH OF MANHATTAN / NEW YORK COUNTY

II BOROUGH OF THE BRONX / BRONX COUNTY

III BOROUGH OF BROOKLYN / KINGS COUNTY

MAPS

GROUND PLANS

INTRODUCTION

This book attempts to present 'the real New York' in all its multiplicity to the visitor or even the resident. Most tourists focus their energies on a few areas—the Theater District, Wall St and the World Trade Center, the United Nations, Rockefeller Center, the Statue of Liberty, and the major museums which are fully covered here. But also included are the places in between—residential areas, ethnic neighbourhoods, areas less often seen but equally interesting to the curious visitor. Walking tours cover Manhattan's most interesting neighbourhoods and the major sights in the outer boroughs—the Bronx Zoo, the Brooklyn Botanic Garden, Brooklyn Heights, etc. Points of interest inconvenient for the pedestrian have been organised in gazetteer form: for these the visitor will need either a car or a lot of time and a good map. In describing the city, I have tried to suggest both how it looks now and how it got that way.

Restaurants and hotels have been covered for the sake of convenience and completeness but not bars, clubs, or night spots, mainly because of their transitory nature; to make up for this lack I have suggested sources of information about entertainment.

Approaches to New York

By air: Most international and many domestic flights arrive at **John F. Kennedy International Airport,** known as JFK, facing Jamaica Bay in the S.E. section of the borough of Queens, about 15 miles from midtown Manhattan (an hour's drive under reasonable traffic conditions). The airport is a complex of terminals serving more than 80 airlines, some of which have their own passport control and customs offices, though many international flights are channelled through the International Arrivals Building.

La Guardia Airport, also in Queens but on the East River about 8 miles (half an hour) from midtown, serves shorter domestic flights. There is a two-level Main Terminal and a satellite terminal with shuttle flights to Washington and Boston.

Newark International Airport, near Newark Bay in New Jersey is about 16 miles (45 minutes under normal driving conditions) from midtown. Some international flights originate and terminate there, and its location makes it useful to passengers whose destination is on Manhattan's West Side.

Transportation to and from airports. TAXIS operate between midtown and all airports. Fares for destinations within the city from JFK, La Guardia, and Newark airports are metered (approximately $25 to JFK, $18 to La Guardia, and $35 to Newark) and cover all passengers up to four (five in the large Checker cabs) and all luggage except for trunks (50¢ surcharge) but passengers must pay the tolls for bridges or tunnels. Fares to Newark Airport are twice the meter amount plus tolls. Passengers to destinations other than midtown Manhattan should agree upon the fare with the driver before departing. A 50¢ surcharge is in effect in some taxis at some times and this information will be posted inside the cab. During peak hours a dispatcher may organise taxi traffic but most of the time passengers must hail their own cabs; New Yorkers are assertive in this respect. Only yellow cabs are licensed by the city and they operate at the airports from designated taxi stands. Do not take taxis whose drivers solicit business from the sidewalk; foreigners have been grossly over-charged and sometimes intimidated by taxi hustlers. Taxi drivers are required legally to stay inside their cabs except to help with luggage, etc. They will expect a tip of 15–20%.

EXPRESS BUS SERVICE operates between all airports and midtown. *JFK*: Coaches of Carey Transportation, Inc. operate between all airport terminals and the East Side Airlines Terminal (37th St and First Ave) at intervals of about half an hour (slightly more frequent in peak hours). Service begins at 5.20 a.m. and continues until 12.30 a.m. From the East Side Airlines Terminal to JFK, service begins at 5 a.m. and continues more or less at half-hourly intervals until the last coach at 1.10 a.m. Fare, $5·00. Carey also provides service from the East Side Airlines Terminal to 41st St and Park Ave (near Grand Central Terminal) and to the Port Authority Bus Terminal; for further information, tel: 995–4700.

La Guardia Airport is also serviced by Carey Transportation, Inc., whose coaches run between the airport and the East Side Airlines Terminal (see above). The service begins at 6.50 a.m. and runs at 20 minute or half hour intervals through the day and evening until 12.30 a.m. Coaches make one stop at Park Ave and 41st St near Grand Central Terminal until 10.40 p.m. when they go directly to the East Side Airlines Terminal. Service from the East Side Airlines Terminal to La Guardia Airport runs at 20 minute or half hourly intervals from 6 a.m. until midnight. The fare is $3·50; for information call 632–0500. For information about free service connecting 41st St/Park Ave to the East Side Airlines Terminal and about the free shuttle between the Port Authority Bus Terminal and the East Side Airlines Terminal, see description under JFK Airport.

Newark International Airport: Transport of New Jersey provides express motorcoach service between all terminals of the airport and the Port Authority Bus Terminal (platform #35) at Eighth Ave and 41st St in Manhattan. Buses run at 20 minute or half hour intervals from 5.45 a.m. until the last coaches at 12.30 a.m. and 1.15 a.m. Reduced service on weekends. The fare is $2·25. For information tel: in New York 1–800–526–4515 or in New Jersey, 1–800–772–2222. (The 800 indicates a toll-free number.) Newark International Air-port-New York City Mini Bus Service operates between the airport and midtown hotels in Manhattan from 7 a.m. to 1 a.m. at about half hourly intervals during the week; reduced service on weekends: special service for late night flights. For information call 586–8280. The fare is $9·00.

The **JFK Express** or **'Train to the Plane'** is a special bus-subway combination operating between JFK and several stops in midtown Manhattan. To use this service to get to New York from the airport, follow the signs (a blue circle with a white airplane) to the nearest bus stop from where an air-conditioned bus takes you to the subway portion of the ride. The subway makes eight stops: Jay St/Borough Hall in Brooklyn, Broadway/Nassau in the Wall St area of Manhat-tan, Chambers St near the World Trade Center, West 4th St in Greenwich Village, and along Sixth Ave at 34th St, 42nd St, 50th

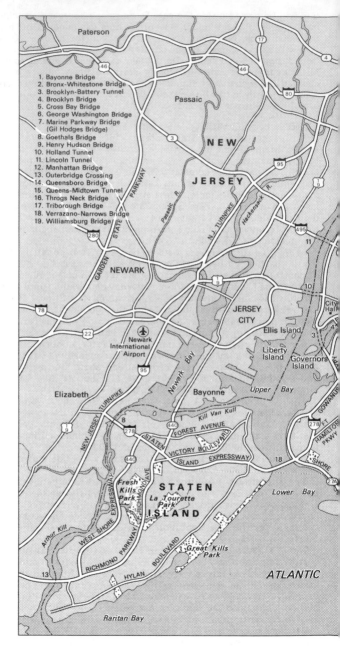

1. Bayonne Bridge
2. Bronx-Whitestone Bridge
3. Brooklyn-Battery Tunnel
4. Brooklyn Bridge
5. Cross Bay Bridge
6. George Washington Bridge
7. Marine Parkway Bridge
   (Gil Hodges Bridge)
8. Goethals Bridge
9. Henry Hudson Bridge
10. Holland Tunnel
11. Lincoln Tunnel
12. Manhattan Bridge
13. Outerbridge Crossing
14. Queensboro Bridge
15. Queens-Midtown Tunnel
16. Throgs Neck Bridge
17. Triborough Bridge
18. Verrazano-Narrows Bridge
19. Williamsburg Bridge

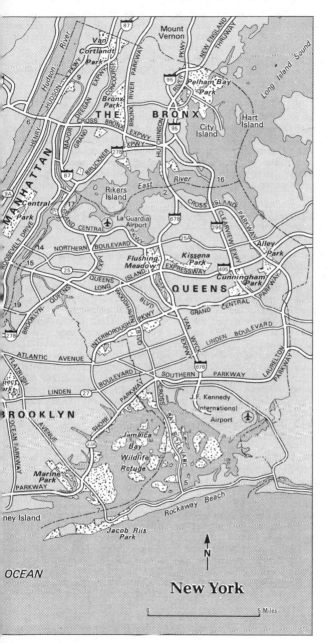

New York

N

0   5 Miles

St/Rockefeller Center, and 57th St. The $5·00 fare covers both parts of the ride; coming from the airport pay the bus conductor; going to the airport pay 75¢ (a token) to enter the subway and the remainder to the bus conductor. The service operates daily between 5 a.m. and midnight at approximately 20-minute intervals. No porter service is available. Running time should be about 90 minutes, but allow plenty of leeway.

HELICOPTER SERVICE: New York Helicopter, based at the East 34th St Heliport on the East River (tel: 895–1695 in New York or –800–645–3494 from out of state) flies to Newark ($45), La Guardia ($28), and Kennedy ($39) Airports. Fares are considerably reduced if you have a continuing flight with one of the participating domestic or foreign airlines. Flights take about 10 minutes, unless there is a stopover at one airport en route to another, and leave the airports or heliport at about 40-minute intervals between about 8 a.m. and 6.30 p.m.

Car Rentals. Avis, Hertz, and other major car rental companies maintain offices at the airports. For information call these companies or consult your airline or travel agent.

Parking. All airports maintain large parking lots or structures for long- and short-term parking.

Public transportation to suburban areas: The following carriers provide transportation from JFK and La Guardia to outlying areas on a regular basis and maintain facilities within the airports:
Long Island (Nassau and Suffolk Counties): Long Island-Airports Limousine (516) 433–2277 or (212) 656–7000. *Westchester County* (New York): Airport Transportation Services (914) 968–7000 or (212) 655–4400. *Orange and Sullivan Counties* (upstate New York): Shortline Flight Catcher Coach (201) 529–3666. *Bergen County* (suburban New Jersey): Fugazy Continental of N.J. (212) 247–8383 or Shortline Flight Catcher Coach (201) 529–3666. *Fort Dix and McGuire Air Force Base, Mercer, Middlesex and Burlington Counties, Philadelphia* (outlying New Jersey areas and Pennsylvania): Salem Limousine (212) 656–4511. *Fairfield and New Haven Counties* (Connecticut): Connecticut Limousine (212) 656–8128.

By train: The main railroad stations are *Pennsylvania Station* between Seventh and Eighth Aves, 31st–33rd Sts, and *Grand Central Terminal* at Park Ave and 42nd St. Connections between the terminals must be made on foot (about one mile), by public transportation, or by taxi. The easiest public transportation from Grand Central is the M4 bus (downtown on Fifth Ave two blocks W. of Grand Central) which goes directly to Penn Station. To get from Penn Station to Grand Central, take the M4 bus across 32nd St and up Madison Ave to 42nd St. It is also possible to take the shuttle subway to Times Square and the IRT Broadway–7th Ave (trains 1, 2, 3) to Penn Station, though this route is not recommended to novices with luggage since the Times Square subway station is vast and bleak. Taxis cruise outside both train stations.

By bus: The main terminal is the *Port Authority Bus Terminal* at Eighth Ave and 41st St, recently expanded and renovated. There are local bus and subway connections within the station and taxis cruise along Eighth Ave. The immediate neighbourhood, a sinkhole of pornography and vice, is no place to linger.

By car: New York drivers are aggressive and impatient but generally predictable. Traffic can be maddening both along the avenues and on the crosstown streets, and to the uninitiated the city's alternate side of the street parking regulations (parking allowed on one side one day, on the other side the next day) can seem byzantine in their complexity. Parking garages are expensive. If you are staying at a hotel, check with the doorman about nearby facilities.

New York roads are pocked with potholes, some of them impressive in their dimensions, which jolt the innards of the cars and drivers who go over them. Parking tickets are expensive and in places meter maids lurk awaiting the expired meter and pounce upon the delinquent car with alacrity. Cars towed from a zone marked 'tow away zone' are taken to a West Side pier and impounded; it costs at least $65 in cash to retrieve such a vehicle.

Getting Around the City

Walking is the best way to see any city and is generally safe in New York if you use common sense. During the day you can walk almost anywhere, especially with a friend, and at night you can certainly stroll around busy streets. Avoid high crime areas—Eighth Ave around 42nd St, Harlem, the South Bronx. Do not wander in the parks after dark unless attending a concert or other activity and even then stick with the crowds; do not wander alone in the isolated, remote parts of parks at any time (be cautious of Central Park above 100th St). Stick to busy streets and avoid blind building entrances. Do not display money or jewellery; keep bus or subway fares handy so you do not have to dig publicly in wallet or handbag to find change. Be alert to your surroundings and look confident.

Manhattan's grid system makes it easy to find your way around N. of about 14th St. Avenues run north and south and are either named (Park, Lexington) or numbered. Sixth Ave, officially the Avenue of the Americas, is still Sixth Ave to most New Yorkers. Broadway runs diagonally from the N.W. to the S.E. Traffic on most avenues flows in one direction, with alternate avenues running N. and S., though there are exceptions to this rule. Streets run east and west and are numbered E. or W. of Fifth Ave with the smallest numbers closest to Fifth Ave; thus 42 E. 72nd St lies E. of Fifth Ave but fairly close to it. Traffic on even-numbered streets generally goes east and on odd-numbered streets goes west, though again there are exceptions. Major crosstown streets with two-way traffic are 14th St, 34th St, 42nd St, 57th St, and 72nd St. Transverses cross Central Park at 65/66th St, 79th/80th St, and 96th/97th St. Below 14th St the grid system does not exist and streets are laid out unsystematically, reflecting their historical development. Uptown means north; downtown means south; crosstown means either east or west. Lower Manhattan lies S. of about 34th St; midtown is from about 34th–86th St, and upper Manhattan is the rest stretching up to the Bronx border.

To find the nearest cross street on any avenue in Manhattan, take the address number, cancel the last digit, divide by two and add or subtract the key number below. **Example:** Where is 500 Fifth Ave? Cancel the last 0, and divide 50 by 2. To 25 add the key number 18 to get 43. No. 500 Fifth Ave is near 43rd St.

First Ave.	Add 3.
Second Ave.	Add 3.
Third Ave.	Add 10.
Fourth Ave.	Add 8.
Fifth Ave.	
Up to 200	Add 13.
200 to 400	Add 16.
400 to 600	Add 18.
600 to 775	Add 20.
775 to 1286	Eliminate the last digit; do not divide by 2; instead, subtract 18.
1286 to 1500	Add 45.
above 2000	Add 24.
Sixth Ave.	Subtract 12.
Seventh Ave.	Add 12.
Above 110th St.	Add 20.
Eighth Ave.	Add 10.
Ninth Ave.	Add 13.
Tenth Ave.	Add 14.
Amsterdam Ave.	Add 60.
Broadway	Subtract 30.
Columbus Ave.	Add 60.
Lexington Ave.	Add 22.
Madison Ave.	Add 26.
Park Ave.	Add 35.
West End Ave.	Add 60.
Central Park West	Divide number by 10 and add 60.
Riverside Drive	Divide number by 10 and add 72.

Taxis: The city fleet has more than 11,700 cabs; yellow taxis are licensed and regulated by the New York City Taxi and Limousine Commission, and may be identified by their colour and the medallion in the rear window. Rates, which cover up to four passengers (five in the large Checker cabs) are posted on the door and are currently (1982) $1·00 for the first $^{1}/_{9}$ mile and 10¢ for each additional $^{1}/_{9}$ mile; a 50¢ surcharge, perhaps temporary, is added to fares of some cabs and this information is plainly posted in the cab. Fares to destinations outside the city should be agreed upon before starting. There are a few taxi stands within the city, but most cabs cruise looking for passengers. The lighted sign on top of the car indicates whether the cab is available. To enquire about lost objects, tel: 825–0416; to register complaints, tel: 825–0420 (you must have either the taxi identification number from the lighted roof panel or the driver's identification number posted inside the cab).

Unlicensed 'gypsy' cabs operate in the outer boroughs and sometimes in Manhattan; they are unregulated, painted colours other than yellow, often have 'livery' license plates, and are not recommended to visitors.

Buses are relatively cheap, moderately reliable, and pleasant except during rush hours when they are exasperatingly slow. You must have exact change (no bills) or a subway token (available at toll booths in the subway stations) to board. Since many stores will refuse to give change without a purchase, it is wise to stock up on tokens.

Official bus route maps and schedules are available at the Information Booth on the main concourse in Grand Central Station. A single ride costs 75¢ and a transfer (free, ask the driver when you board) enables you to change to a second bus whose route crosses yours. Buses stop on demand about every two blocks going up- and downtown and every block crosstown. To signal your desire to get off, press the tape on the bus wall or, on older buses, pull the bell cord. Most buses run on a 24-hour schedule with reduced service at night.

Subways are the fastest but not the most pleasant way to get around. The trains run 24 hours a day across a 238-mile route (458 stations) in four boroughs (excluding Staten Island). The fare is 75¢ or a token (available in booths inside the stations). Maps are posted inside the stations and also in the cars but many of the latter have been stolen or defaced by vandals. Free system maps are available at the Information Booth in Grand Central Station, the Convention and Visitors Bureau at Columbus Circle, and sometimes in token booths. Routes to outlying areas can be complicated and confusing, but it is easy to travel up- and downtown along major avenues. Rush hours are crowded and unpleasant, best avoided by those unnerved by crowds. If possible ride the bus instead of the subway late at night, except in company; if you must take the subway, ride in the car with the conductor or, better yet, transit policeman.

SUBWAY SAFETY: The New York subway system has a reputation for crime and filth which is not undeserved. Stations have been vandalised, cars sprayed with graffiti, platforms are smelly and filthy in many stations. In 1981 there were 15,812 felonies in the transit system including 13 murders, but it is also true that more than three million travellers ride the system daily and survive. Use common sense; be alert to your surroundings; stay with other people; don't go down empty stairwells or ride in empty cars; don't lean over the edge of the platform; if in doubt stay near the conductor who has a telephone, as does the attendant at the toll booth.

Tourist Information. The best source of information is the New York Convention and Visitors Bureau at Columbus Circle (tel: 397–8222), open Mon–Fri, 9–6; Sat and Sun, 10–6. The bureau offers subway and bus maps, listings of hotels and restaurants, seasonal calendars of events, brochures about points of interest. The Information Center at Times Square is open 9–6 seven days.

For schedules of weekend special events, guided tours, street fairs, etc, check the Friday edition of the 'New York Times'. Both 'New York Magazine' and 'The New Yorker' (issued weekly) have listings of films, concerts, plays, opera, ballet, sporting events, museum and gallery shows, and night-life. The Sunday edition of the 'New York Times' contains weekly listings of a similar nature as well as capsule restaurant reviews.

Information for British Visitors. You must have a valid passport and a U.S. visa which can be put only in the 10-year kind of passport. Get the visa from the U.S. Embassy, Visa and Immigration Department, 24 Grosvenor Sq., London W1 (tel: 01–499 3443). Vaccination certificates are not normally required.

INSURANCE. Health care is astronomically expensive in the U.S. and British visitors should seriously consider insuring themselves against accidents and illness. Contact Europ Assistance, 252 High St, Croydon CRO 1NF (tel: 01–680 1234).

CUSTOMS. Visitors over the age of 21 may bring in 200 cigarettes, 3 lbs of tobacco or 50 cigars and 1 litre of alcohol as well as duty-free gifts whose value does not exceed $100. Do not bring in fruits, plants, seeds, or meat and meat products, firearms, marijuana or other illegal drugs.

HOTELS. Do not come to New York without a hotel reservation unless you are adventurous and do not mind pounding the pavement. There are generally no hotel booking services in airports or train stations in the U.S. HBI-HOTAC, Globegate House, Pound Lane, London NW10 (tel: 01–451 2311) can reserve rooms for individuals or for businesses at any of about 60 New York hotels.

TOURIST INFORMATION. In London contact the State of New York Division of Tourism, 35 Picadilly, London W1 (tel: 01–734 7282) by telephone or post; they can supply printed information about tourism in New York. See also the section on Information for sources in New York.

TRAVEL AGENTS. Visitors wishing to avoid the inconvenience of making arrangements should contact a travel agent, preferably a reputable member of the Association of British Travel Agents, who for a fee will make airplane and other travel arrangements, book hotel rooms, arrange tours, etc. American travel agents will also perform these services, often but not always without a fee.

Hotels

Hotels in New York are not inexpensive by the standards of other American cities and they are often full; reserve a room in advance. The New York Convention and Visitors Bureau (2 Columbus Circle, New York, N.Y. 10019, tel: 397–8222) publishes a list of hotels in the city with current prices as well as a Directory of Vacation Packages, indicating special weekend or seasonal rates; available on request. The following list has been extracted from the Visitors Bureau publication and is offered with the reminder that inflation will undoubtedly have affected the rates.

Luxury Hotels: Double room with bath well over $100.

	Address and zip code	Telephone
Berkshire Place	21 E. 52nd St, 10022	753–5800
Hotel Carlyle	35 E. 76th St, 10021	744–1600
Grand Hyatt, New York	Park Ave at Grand Central, 10017	883–1234
Harley of New York	214 E. 42nd St, 10017	490–8900
Helmsley Palace	455 Madison Ave at 50th St, 10022	888–7000
Loews Drake, a Swissôtel	440 Park Ave at 56th St, 10022	421–0900
Marriott's Essex House	160 Central Park South, 10019	247–0300
Park Lane	36 Central Park South 10019	371–4000
Parker Meridien	118 W. 57th St, 10019	245–5000
Pierre	Fifth Ave at 61st St, 10021	838–8000
Plaza	Fifth Ave at 59th St, 10019	759–3000
Regency	540 Park Ave at 61st St, 10021	759–4100
St. Regis-Sheraton	2 E. 55th St at Fifth Ave, 10022	753–4500
United Nations Plaza	1 U.N. Plaza, 44th St and First Ave, 10017	355–3400
Waldorf-Astoria	Park Ave at 50th St, 10022	355–3000

Expensive Hotels: Double room with bath over $100.

Alrae	37 E. 64th St, 10021	744–0200
American Stanhope	995 Fifth Ave at	
	81st St, 10028	288–5800
Dorset	30 W. 54th St, 10019	247–7300
Elysee	60 E. 54th St, 10022	753–1066
Halloran House	641 Lexington Ave at	
	49th St, 10017	755–4000
Inter-Continental New		
York, formerly the		
Barclay	111 E. 48th St, 10017	755–5900
Lowell	28 E. 63rd St, 10021	838–1400
Mayfair Regent	610 Park Ave at	
	65th St, 10021	288–0800
Mayflower	15 Central Park West	
	at 61st St, 10023	265–0060
Navarro	112 Central Park South,	
	10019	757–1900
New York Hilton	1335 Ave of the Americas	
	at 53rd St, 10019	586–7000
St. Moritz	50 Central Park South,	
	10019	755–5800
San Carlos	150 E. 50th St, 10022	755–1800
Sheraton Russell	45 Park Ave at 37th	
	St, 10016	685–7676
Tuscany	120 E. 39th St, 10016	686–1600
Vista International	3 World Trade Center	938–9100
Warwick	65 W. 54th St, 10019	247–2700

Moderate Hotels: Double room between $50–$100.

Abbey Victoria	7th Ave at 51st St,	
	10019	246–9400
Adams	2 E. 86th St, 10028	744–1800
Algonquin	59 W. 44th St, 10036	840–6800
Barbizon Plaza	106 Central Park South,	
	10019	247–7000
Bedford	118 E. 40th St, 10016	697–4800
Best Western Skyline		
Motor Inn	725 10th Ave, 10019	586–3400
Blackstone	50 E. 58th St, 10022	355–4200
Century-Paramount	235 W. 46th St at	
	Broadway, 10036	246–5500
Consulate	224 W. 49th St, 10019	246–5252
Doral Inn	49th–50th St on	
	Lexington Ave, 10022	755–1200
Doral Inn Park Avenue	70 Park Ave at 38th	
	St, 10016	687–7050
Edison	228 W. 47th St, 10036	246–5000
Empire	63rd St & Broadway,	
	10023,	265–7400
Executive	237 Madison Ave at	
	38th St, 10016	686–0300
George Washington	23 Lexington Ave at	
	23rd St, 10010	475–1920
Gorham	136 W. 55th St, 10019	245–1800
Gramercy Park	2 Lexington Ave at	
	21st St, 10010	475–4320
Henry Hudson	353 W. 57th St, 10019	265–6100
Holiday Inn–Coliseum	440 W. 57th St, 10019	581–8100
Holiday Inn–Staten	1415 Richmond Ave, S.I.,	
Island	10314	698–5000
Howard Johnson's Motor	8th Ave & 51st St,	
Lodge	10019	581–4100
Kitano	66 Park Ave at 38th	
	St, 10016	685–0022

Lexington	511 Lexington Ave at	
	48th St, 10017	755–4400
Loews Summit	569 Lexington Ave at	
	51st St, 10022	752–7000
Lowell	28 E. 63rd St, 10021	838–1400
Madison Towers	22 E. 38th St, 10016	685–3700
Middletowne–Harley	148 E. 48th St, 10017	755–3000
Milford Plaza	270 W. 45th St, 10036	869–3600
New York Sheraton	56th St & 7th Ave, 10019	247–8000
New York Statler	401 Seventh Ave at	
	33rd St, 10001	736–5000
Prince George	14 E. 28th St, 10016	532–7800
Ramada Inn of New York		
City	8th Ave & 48th St, 10019	581–7000
Roger Smith	501 Lexington Ave at	
	47th St, 10017	755–1400
Roosevelt on Madison	45th St & Madison Ave,	
Ave	10017	661–9600
Royalton	44 W. 44th St, 10036	730–1344
Salisbury	123 W. 57th St, 10019	246–1300
Seymour	50 W. 45th St, 10036	840–3480
Shelbourne–Murray Hill	303 Lexington Ave at	
	37th St, 10011	689–5200
Sheraton Centre	7th Ave at 53rd St,	581–1000
	10019	
Sheraton City Squire	51st St & 7th Ave, 10019	581–3300
Shoreham	33 W. 55th St, 10019	247–6700
Taft	777 Seventh Ave at	
	50th St, 10019	247–4000
Tudor	304 E. 42nd St at	
	Second Ave, 10017	986–8800
Wellington	55th St & 7th Ave,	
	10019	247–3900
Wentworth	59 W. 46th St, 10036	719–2300
Windsor Harley	100 W. 58th St, 10019	265–2100
Wyndham	42 W. 58th St, 10019	753–3500

Inexpensive Hotels: Double Room for Less than $50.

Clinton	19 W. 31st St, 10001	279–4017
Diplomat	108 W. 43rd St, 10036	921–5666
Earle	Washington Square	
	Park, N.W., 10011	777–9515
Grand Union	34 E. 32nd St, 10016	683–5890
Lenox	149 W. 44th St, 10036	221–3722
Mansfield 5th Ave	12 W. 44th St, 10036	944–6050
Penn Terminal	215 W. 34th St, 10001	947–5050
Piccadilly	227 W. 45th St, 10036	246–6600
Pickwick Arms	230 E. 51st St, 10022	355–0300
President	234 W. 48th St, 10036	246–8800
Remington	129 W. 46th St, 10036	221–2600
Rio	132 W. 47th St, 10036	757–3870
Seville	Madison Ave at 29th St,	
	10016	532–4100
Stanford	43 W. 32nd St, 10001	563–1480
Times Square Motor		
Hotel	255 W. 43rd St, 10036	354–7900
Townhouse Forty Four	120 W. 44th St, 10036	582–3900
Wales	1295 Madison Ave at 92nd	
	St, 10028	876–6000

Special Hotels: In addition to the regular commercial hotels there are special hotels available only to certain visitors.

YMCAS. The *YMCA–Sloane House*, 356 W. 34th St, New York 10001, tel: 760–5850, located near Ninth Ave, accepts both men and women and is popular with students and Europeans. Rooms (some double rooms for couples) are simple but some have private bath. Enquire about weekly rates. To reserve, send the price of one night's stay to the residence director. The *YMCA–Vanderbilt Branch*, 224 E. 47th St, New York 10017, tel: 755–2410, located between Second and Third Aves, is also 'co-ed', has shared bath facilities, a swimming pool, gymnasium, cafeteria, and laundromat. One night's deposit required to reserve; write or call residence director. The *Westside Y*, 5 W. 63rd St, New York 10023, tel: 787–4400, near Lincoln Center, is the most attractive but accepts women only if they are students (identification required) staying for a semester. Men may reserve by the day or week; a few rooms have private bath. The extensive facilities—cafeteria, two swimming pools, sauna—and good location make this YMCA very popular; write to the residence director for reservations well in advance.

Students aged 21 or older arriving in the summer may rent rooms at *International House of New York*, 500 Riverside Drive, New York 10027 (tel: 678–5000) near Columbia University. During the year International House is a student residence, mostly for foreign students though some from Columbia and Barnard live there, and has a low-cost cafeteria, study rooms, and other facilities associated with dormitory life. Bathrooms are communal.

There are several hotels reserved. *Allerton House*, 130 E. 57th St, New York 10022 (tel: 753–8841), near Lexington Ave, accepts only women, with most rooms occupied by permanent residents who tend to be older women. The *Martha Washington*, 29 E. 29th St, New York 10016 (tel: 689–1900), belongs to the same category and is quite inexpensive.

Restaurants

Because of the sheer impossibility of one person's visiting all the restaurants worthy of consideration, this list has been compiled from restaurant guides, personal recommendations, and newspaper reviews. It attempts to include the city's most famous, established restaurants, a wide variety of ethnic restaurants, and a number of restaurants located conveniently for the walking tours in the *Guide*. The brief descriptions are intended not as reviews—there is no restaurant on the list that some critic has not praised—but as aids to the visitor, since a list of names only seems of little value.

Those restaurants categorised as very expensive will charge $40 or more for a three-course meal excluding alcoholic beverages; expensive restaurants fall into the $25–35 range; moderate restaurants should run from $15–25 and inexpensive restaurants less than $15. The tax on restaurant meals is currently $8^{1}/_{4}\%$. In most restaurants lunches are somewhat less expensive than dinners. Most but not all establishments accept the major credit cards. Make reservations at weekends for all restaurants and at any time for the more expensive ones. Call ahead in summer since many restaurants close for vacation.

Also included is a list of restaurants in the outer boroughs, which are all moderately priced unless otherwise indicated.

Many Manhattan restaurants are concentrated in midtown or on the East Side above 59th St. Ethnic restaurants, with the exception of the more expensive Italian and Chinese restaurants, tend to be clustered in the old neighbourhoods—Little Italy, Chinatown, Yorkville (German and Slavic), and the Lower East Side (Jewish). There are Greek restaurants on Eighth Ave in the 40s and for some reason Thai restaurants in the same area. Indian restaurants can be found on E. 6th St as well as in the Indian district on Lexington Ave in the high 20s. Brooklyn's Atlantic Ave near Court St has Lebanese and other Arab restaurants while Astoria in Queens has Greek ones. Japanese restaurants are concentrated in midtown, near the business district.

The list is selective and no slight is intended to restaurants not included.

Lower Manhattan

Lower Manhattan is not known for its restaurants. The lunch crowd can be overwhelming so eat early or late if possible.

The Big Kitchen. One World Trade Center, concourse level (938–1153). Fast food complex with deli, health food, ice cream, sandwiches; attractive but no frills; crowded at lunch. Inexpensive.

Bridge Cafe. 279 Water St near Dover St (227–3344). Small pub-tavern with pressed-tin ceiling, American and continental food emphasising vegetable dishes. Moderate.

Cheese and Wine Restaurant. 153 Chambers St (tel: 732–0752). Restaurant on the second floor above Cheese of All Nations Shop. Open weekdays only, for lunch 11.30–2.00. Moderate.

Fraunces Tavern. 54 Pearl St at Broad St (269–0144). Reconstructed 18C house; famous for history, not food. Closed Sat, Sun. Moderate.

Market Dining Rooms and Bar. One World Trade Center, concourse level (938–1155). Market setting; American food. No lunch Sat. Expensive.

Petrosino. 100 Greenwich St, S. of World Trade Center (227–5398). Long-time fish restaurant with wide selection. Mon–Fri, last seating 6.15 p.m. Moderate.

Sloppy Louie's. 92 South St in South St Seaport area (952–9657). Seafood; very informal with long communal tables; bring your own beer, wine. No reservations. Lunch only, Mon–Fri. Inexpensive.

Sweets. 2 Fulton St, near Fulton Fish Market (825–9786 or 344–9189). Unprepossessing restaurant in landmark building (scheduled for renovation); fresh, traditional American seafood dishes. Lunch and early dinner (until 8.30), Mon–Fri; closed July and holidays. Moderate.

Windows on the World. 107th floor, One World Trade Center (938–1111). Stunning view, international food, run as a club for weekday lunch (surcharge for non-members); good, but uneven, food. Best bargain is Sun buffet (see *Brunch*). Very expensive.

Zum Zum. 74 Broad St at Marketfield St (997–1369). A chain restaurant with wursts, soup, and beer. Inexpensive.

Chinatown

Most restaurants in Chinatown notably lack refinements of decor, with bare Formica tables, fluorescent lights, and paper napkins constituting the main decorative elements. Toilet facilities are rudimentary. However, the food is often excellent and inexpensive. You can bring your own beer and wine to those restaurants lacking liquor licenses. Many do not take reservations.

BoBo. $20^1/2$ Pell St (962–9458). Fine Cantonese cooking; bring your own wine; popular restaurant; will take reservations. Inexpensive.

Canton. 45 Division St near Market St (226–9173). Large restaurant, seafood specialties, minimal decor; beer sold, but bring your own wine, liquor. Reservations for large groups. Closed Mon. Moderate.

Chi Mer. 11–12 Chatham Square (267–4565). Attractive; serves Cantonese, Szechuan, Mandarin, Hunan dishes. Inexpensive.

Foo Joy. 13 Division St near Catherine St (431–4931). Fukien cuisine, seafood; spicy but not fiery hot. Inexpensive.

Hee Seung Fung. 46 Bowery near Canal St (374–1319). Chinatown's largest selection of dim sum (point at what you want); also Cantonese food; Chinese decor, bustling. Dim sum served 7a.m.–5p.m. Moderate.

Hong Fat. 63 Mott St (962–9588). Popular noodle house. Open until 5 a.m. Inexpensive.

Home Village Restaurant. 20 Mott St (964–0380). Modern, two-story restaurant; large menu; bring own liquor or beer. Moderate.

Hwa Yuan Szechuan Inn. 40 E. Broadway near Market St (966–5534). Szechuan cuisine, hot and spicy. Inexpensive.

Phoenix Garden. 46 Bowery near Elizabeth St, in the arcade (962–8934). Modest surroundings; sophisticated Cantonese food; bring your own beer, wine. Closed Mon. Inexpensive.

Say Eng Look. 5 E. Broadway near Chatham Square (732–0796). Shanghai cuisine; very popular but no reservations. The name means Four Five Six, a winning dice combination in Chinese gambling games. *Four Five Six* (964–5853) at 2 Bowery (corner of Doyers St) is a branch of the same restaurant with a similar menu. Inexpensive.

Wo Hop. 15 and 17 Mott St near Chatham Square (962–8617). Cantonese noodle shop serves noodles with pork, chicken, vegetable toppings. No. 15 open until 5 a.m.; No. 17 open around the clock. Inexpensive.

Yun Luck Rice Shoppe. 17 Doyers St near Pell St (571–1375). Superior Cantonese food; fluorescent and Formica decor; highly rated by food critics. Inexpensive.

Little Italy

Most of the Italians are gone from Little Italy but the restaurants remain, augmented by a number of new ones that have arrived with the neighbourhood *rinascimento*.

Angelo's. 146 Mulberry St near Grand St (966–1277). Pasta, zuppa di pesce, Neapolitan specialities. Closed Mon. Moderate.

Ballato. 55 E. Houston St near Mott St (226–9683). Modest exterior; good Italian food. Closed Sun and during July Aug. Expensive.

Benito's (I and II). 174 Mulberry St (226–9007) and 163 Mulberry St (226–9012); between Broome and Grand Sts. Rustic; Sicilian and S. Italian food. Closed Sun. Moderate.

Florio's. 192 Grand St between Mott and Mulberry Sts (226–7610). Fine pizza in small, sit-down restaurant. Inexpensive.

Il Cortile. 125 Mulberry St, between Hester and Canal Sts (226–6060). N. and S. Italian dishes, handsome restaurant with tile floors, pressed tin ceiling. Expensive.

Luna's. 112 Mulberry St (226–8657). Lively and popular spot for Neapolitan cuisine. Moderate.

Puglia. 189 Hester St near Mulberry St (226–8912). Informal, popular; hearty Sicilian fare in large portions; long communal tables. Closed Mon. Inexpensive.

Umberto's Clam House. 129 Mulberry St at Hester St (431–7545). Famous seafood restaurant; counter for quick service; outdoor tables in season. Mafia boss Joey Gallo was murdered here in true gangland style. Inexpensive.

Vincent's Clam Bar. 119 Mott St at Hester St (226–8133). Informal; features pasta and seafood with special hot sauces. Inexpensive.

Cafes and Pastry Shops

Caffè Biondo. 141 Mulberry St between Grand and Hester Sts (226–9285).

Caffè Primavera. 51 Spring St at Mulberry St (226–8421).

Caffè Roma. 385 Broome St between Mulberry and Mott Sts (226–8413).

Ferrara's. 195 Grand St between Mott and Mulberry Sts (226–6150).

Lower East Side / East Village
Restaurants here reflect their surroundings—far from affluent, ethnically oriented. Those in the Cooper Square neighbourhood are somewhat more modern, attracting a young, artistic clientele.

Baltyk. 12 First Ave at 1st St (260–4809). Polish; family style. Inexpensive.

Colonnades. 432 Lafayette St near Astor Place in Colonnade Row (473–8890). Informal, attractive; theatrical crowd. American-continental menu. Weekday lunch, dinner every day. Moderate.

Garden Cafeteria. 165 E. Broadway at Rutgers St (254–6962). Famous Jewish dairy cafeteria and dining room; fish, omelettes, sandwiches, blintzes. Closed Fri after sundown and Sat. Inexpensive.

Hisae's Place. 35 Cooper Square between 5th and 6th Sts (228–6886). Attractive; continental food with Japanese overtones. Dinner only Mon. Moderate.

Indian restaurants on E. Sixth St. E. of 2nd Ave. In this block are more than a half dozen small, informal Indian restaurants, most run by members of the same family. Among them: *Shah Bagh.* 329 E. Sixth St (475–9499); *Romna.* 322 E. Sixth St (673–4718); *Mitali.* 334 E. Sixth St (533–2508); *Anar Bagh.* 338 E. Sixth St (533–2177).

Lady Astor's. 430 Lafayette St near Astor Place (228–7888). Continental food, Victorian ambience. Moderate.

McSorley's Old Ale House. 15 E. Seventh St near 3rd Ave (473–8800). Old-fashioned bar with sawdust on floors, memorabilia on walls; sandwiches, daily specials, ale. Lunch only. Inexpensive.

Phebe's Place. 361 Bowery at E. 4th St (473–9008). Actors' hangout; hamburgers, chicken, American food. Inexpensive.

Ratner's. 138 Delancey St between Norfolk and Suffolk Sts (677–5588). Famous Jewish dairy restaurant with large menu. Inexpensive.

Sammy's Roumanian Restaurant. 157 Chrystie St near Delancey St (673–0330). Good Jewish restaurant with Roumanian meat dishes, boiled beef, sausages (karnatzlach); avuncular waiters. Moderate.

Second Avenue Delicatessen. 156 Second Ave at 10th St (677–0606). Jewish deli (claimed by supporters to be the city's best) renowned for its pastrami; kosher, no dairy dishes. Moderate.

SoHo
The SoHo renaissance brought an abundance of eating places from modest cafés to chic French restaurants serving haute cuisine. This list is minimal.

Berry's. 180 Spring St at Thompson St (226–4394). Small café; omelettes, grilled dishes. Moderate.

Broome Street Bar. 363 Broome St at W. Broadway (925–2086). Pub-like atmosphere; young, noisy crowd. Hamburgers on pitta bread, omelettes, quiche; weekend brunch. Inexpensive.

Chanterelle. 89 Grand St at Greene St (966–6960). Nouvelle cuisine, chic, graceful decor in old building. Closed Sun and Mon. Very expensive.

Cupping Room Café. 359 W. Broadway between Grand and Broome Sts (925–2898). Salads, sandwiches, desserts; good weekend brunch. Moderate.

Elephant and Castle. 183 Prince St near Sullivan St (260–3600). Casual but sophisticated branch of Greenwich Village restaurant; omelettes and egg dishes, quiche, hamburgers. Moderate.

Greene Street. 103 Greene St between Prince and Spring Sts (925–2415). Old building, exposed brick walls, plants; continental food; live music in evenings. Expensive.

Odeon. 145 W. Broadway at Thomas St (233–0507). Nouvelle cuisine in the old warehouse district; 1940s ambience. No lunch Sat. Expensive.

Oh-Ho-So. 395 W. Broadway near Spring St (966–6110). Cantonese food and American desserts in American style restaurant. Moderate.

SoHo Charcuterie. 195 Spring St at Sullivan St (266–3545). One of SoHo's first restaurants during the revival period; charcuterie in front with take-out counter; dining room behind. French food. Expensive.

Greenwich Village

Arnold's Turtle. 51 Bank St between W. 4th and Bleecker Sts (242–5623). Small, casual, vegetarian restaurant; soups, sandwiches, casseroles. Inexpensive.

Black Sheep. 342 W. 11th St (741–9772). Bohemian, romantic; French country cooking. Two seatings at dinner, 7 and 9. Expensive.

Captain's Table. 410 Sixth Ave near W. 9th St (473–0670). Established village restaurant; seafood, clams, oysters. Closed Mon. Moderate.

Coach House. 110 Waverly Place near Sixth Ave (777–0303). Elegant, fine American and European food. Top honours with restaurant critics. Handsome inn-like setting. Closed Mon, dinner only. Very expensive.

Da Silvano. 260 Sixth Ave near Bleecker St (982–0090). Italian storefront restaurant, interesting daily specialities, fine pasta; al fresco dining in season. Expensive.

El Rincón de Espana. 226 Thompson St near Bleecker St (475–9891). Spanish restaurant featuring paella, seafood dishes. Dinner only. Inexpensive.

El Coyote. 774 Broadway at 9th St (677–4291). Rustic cantina; Tex-Mex food, including generous combination platters. Inexpensive.

Elephant and Castle. 68 Greenwich Ave between W. 11th and W. 12th Sts (243–1400). Small and popular; omelettes, quiche, hamburgers. Moderate.

Front Porch. 253 W. 11th St at W. 4th St (675–8083). Casual small restaurant; soups, sandwiches, homemade desserts. Moderate.

Jane Street Seafood Cafe. 31 Eighth Ave at Jane St (243–9237). New England charm; clam chowder, broiled seafood. Dinner only, closed Sun. Moderate.

John's Pizzeria. 278 Bleecker St near 7th Ave (242–9529). Only whole pizzas; often crowded; the pizza is famous. Inexpensive.

La Tulipe. 104 W. 13th St near Sixth Ave (691–8860). Stylish small French restaurant, nouvelle cuisine; in renovated brownstone. Closed Mon; dinner only. Very expensive.

Ray's Original Pizza. Sixth Ave at W. 11th St (243–2253). A stand-up pizzeria with a few tables; whole pies or by the slice. A contender for the city's best. Inexpensive.

Trattoria da Alfredo. 90 Bank St at Hudson St (929–4400). Small popular café, known for pastas, bring your own wine; must reserve for dinner. Closed Tues, no lunch Sun. Moderate. Also run by the same management are the *Caffè da Alfredo* (17 Perry St near 7th Ave (989–7028; bring your own wine) and the *Tavola Calda da Alfredo,* 285 Bleecker St near 7th Ave (924–4789).

Gramercy Park/Murray Hill: East Side, 14th–42nd Sts

Ararat. 4 E. 36th St (686–4622). Armenian and middle eastern cuisine; handsomely decorated. Closed Sun in summer. Moderate.

East Bay. 491 First Ave at 29th St (683–7770). Sandwiches, blintzes, daily specials. Inexpensive.

El Parador. 325 E. 34th St. (679–6812). Small popular Mexican-Spanish restaurant. Closed Sun. Moderate.

Hakubai. 66 Park Ave at 38th St in Hotel Kitano (686–3770). Quiet, authentic Japanese restaurant. Moderate.

Hee Seung Fung. 578 Second Ave between 31st–32nd Sts (689–6969). Chinese dim sum lunch, also Cantonese food from the menu; newer branch of the Chinatown restaurant of the same name. Moderate.

Jack's Nest. 310 Third Ave near 23rd St (260–7110). Soul food (pork chops, ribs, fried flounder, candied yams); informal with booths and Formica tables, juke box. Moderate.

Mimosa. 153 E. 33rd St between Lexington and Third Aves (685–2595). Small attractive French café; crêpes, quiche. Inexpensive.

Mon Paris. 111 E. 29th St near Park Ave (683–4255). Posh decor; fine French food. No lunch Sat, closed Sun. Expensive.

Pastrami & Things. 297 Third Ave near 23rd St (683–7185). Jewish deli with counter and dining room; renowned pastrami. Inexpensive.

Reuben's. 244 Madison Ave near 38th St (867–7800). Delicatessen, birthplace of the legendary Reuben sandwich. Inexpensive.

Sal Anthony's. 55 Irving Place near 17th St (982–9030). Large, handsome, Italian restaurant; pasta, eggplant (aubergine) dishes. Expensive.

Z. 117 E. 15th St between Park Ave S. and Irving Place (254–0960). Greek food; taverna decor. Closed Mon. Inexpensive.

Chelsea/Penn Station: West Side 14th–40th Sts

Chelsea Commons. 463 W. 24th St (929–9424). Hamburgers and simple dishes. Moderate.

Dubrow's Cafeteria. 515 Seventh Ave between 37th–38th Sts (221–6775). Classic garment district cafeteria with Jewish emphasis and better than average food. Closed Sat at 8 p.m., Sun. Inexpensive.

Empire Diner. 210 Tenth Ave at 22nd St (243–2736). Art Deco interior; simple food. Open 24 hours. Moderate.

Healthworks. 12 E. 36th St (686–0401). Salads, yogurt, light attractive dishes; informal setting. Inexpensive.

Madison Square Garden, immediate vicinity: *Brew Burger* in One and Two Penn Plaza. *Burger King* on 33rd St near 7th Ave. *Charley O's at the Garden* in 9 Penn Plaza between 7th and 8th Aves (947–0222). Pub atmosphere; full bar. Closed Sun. *Toots Shor* at 233 W. 33rd St (279–8150). Classic bar for the sporting set, steak and chops. Closed weekends except during major Garden sporting events. Expensive.

Manganaro's Hero-Boy. Ninth Ave between 37th–38th Sts (947–7325). In the Ninth Ave market district; no atmosphere but famous for overstuffed hero sandwiches. Closed Sun, closed 7.00 p.m. other days. Inexpensive.

Old Garden Restaurant. 15 W. 29th St (532–8323). American food in a former antique shop. Moderate.

Paddy's Clam House. 215 W. 34th St between 7th and 8th Aves (244–9123). Fish, clams, oysters in a favorite restaurant for habitues of Macy's and Madison Square Garden. Inexpensive.

Pesca. 23 E. 22nd St off 5th Ave (533–2293). Seafood of Italian-Portuguese persuasion, attractive restaurant. Expensive.

Smokey's Real Pit Barbecue. 239 Ninth Ave at 24th St (924–8181). Cafeteria with hickory smoked chicken, spare ribs, beef. No lunch Sat, Sun. Inexpensive.

Variations. 358 W. 23rd St between 8th and 9th Aves (691–1559). Intimate supper club with piano music, continental food. Moderate.

West Boondock. 114 Tenth Ave near 16th St (929–9756). Home cooked soul food and jazz in comfortable restaurant. Dinner only Sat and Sun. Inexpensive.

Broadway, Theater District: West Side, 42nd–57th Sts

Backstage. 318 W. 45th St near Eighth Ave (581–8447). Before or after the show; piano bar; chicken, prime ribs, American food. Moderate.

Bangkok Cuisine. 885 Eighth Ave at 53rd St (581–6370). Atmospheric Thai restaurant. Closed Sun. Inexpensive.

Cabana Carioca. 123 W. 45th St between 6th–7th Aves (581–8088). Colourful upstairs Brazilian restaurant; feijoada, black bean dishes. Inexpensive.

Café de France. 330 W. 46th St between 8th–9th Aves (586–0088). French food; inexpensive for the district. Moderate.

Carnegie Delicatessen. 854 Seventh Ave at 56th St (757–2245). Famous deli, corned beef, pastrami. Open 24 hours. Inexpensive.

Charley O's. 33 W. 48th St between 5th and 6th Aves (582–7141). Irish pub atmosphere, popular bar, simple fare, Irish stew, corned beef. Moderate.

El Tenampa. 304 W. 46th St between 8th–9th Aves (840–9398). Small, modest Mexican restaurant; good food. Inexpensive.

Fuji. 238 W. 56th St between Broadway–7th Ave (245–8594). Restful dining room; well prepared Japanese food. Closed Sun, dinner only Sat. Moderate.

Gardenia Club. 482 W. 43rd St at 10th Ave in Manhattan Plaza (594–8402). Romantic upstairs dining room; international cuisine; chicken specialities. Moderate.

Joe Allen's. 326 W. 46th St between 8th–9th Aves (581–6464). Casual restaurant; theatre clientele; hamburgers, and simple food. Popular at show time. Moderate.

Landmark Tavern. 626 Eleventh Ave near 47th St (757–8595). Irish pub; hearty, traditional food, soda bread. Open until midnight. Moderate.

Little Afghanistan. 106 E. 43rd St near 6th Ave (921–1676). Middle Eastern–Indian cuisine: lamb, eggplant, kebabs; music. Closed Sun, weekday lunch, dinner Mon–Sat. Moderate.

Molfetas. 307 W. 47th St near 8th Ave (840–9594). Greek restaurant-cafeteria; lamb dishes, stuffed grape leaves. Moderate.

Pantheon. 689 Eighth Ave near 43rd St (664–8294). Popular Greek restaurant. Moderate.

Patsy's Restaurant. 236 W. 56th St between 6th–7th Aves (247–3491). Neapolitan cuisine in friendly, simple surroundings. Closed Mon. Expensive.

Raga. 57 W. 48th St (747–3450). Beautiful restaurant, serving highly acclaimed Indian food. Dinner only Sat, Sun. Expensive.

Russian Tea Room. 150 W. 57th St near 7th Ave (265–0947). Favoured by musicians, theatrical clientele; lively atmosphere, a landmark; Russian food. Expensive.

Seafare of the Aegean. 25 W. 56th St (581–0540). Handsome, outstanding seafood restaurant. Expensive.

Sardi's. 234 W. 44th St between 7th–8th Aves (221–8440). Famous for the theatrical clientele rather than the food. Expensive.

Tout Va Bien. 311 W. 51st St between 8th–9th Aves (974–9051). Small bistro; French food. Closed Sun. Moderate.

"21". 21 W. 52nd St off Fifth Ave (582–7200). Haunt of businessmen (lunch) celebrities, and celebrity watchers. Steak, continental cuisine. Very expensive.

Siam Inn. 916 Eighth Ave near 55th St (489–5237). Attractive restaurant, good Thai food. Inexpensive.

Chain restaurants and restaurants suitable for children:
B.O.S.S. Broadway at 44th St, Broadway at 53rd St, Broadway at 57th St (563–7440, all locations). Salads, sandwiches, hamburgers; a step up from fast food. Inexpensive.

Bun and Burger. 16 W. 48th near Fifth Ave (586–3231).

Burger King. 45th St at Sixth Ave (575–9137).

La Crêpe. 158 W. 44th St just E. of Broadway (246–5388). Inexpensive.

Magic Pan Creperie. 1409 Sixth Ave between 57th–58th Sts (765–5080). Pre- and post-theatre menu. Hungarian food and French crêpes. Inexpensive.

Nathan's Famous. 1482 Broadway at 43rd St (594–7455). Hot dogs, french fries, egg roll, pizza and other Coney Island food transported to Broadway; huge restaurant with bright plastic decor. Inexpensive.

Midtown East: 42nd–59th Sts

Akbar. 475 Park Ave at 58th St (838–1717). Romantically decorated N. Indian restaurant; tandoori dishes. Dinner only Sun. Moderate.

Auberge Suisse. 153 E. 53rd St near Lexington Ave (421–1420). Small restaurant; modern decor; Swiss food. No lunch Sun. Expensive.

Chalet Suisse. 6 E. 48th St (355–0855). Established restaurant, country inn decor; Swiss food; fondue. Closed Sat and Sun. Expensive.

Christ Cella. 160 E. 46th St near 3rd Ave (697–2479). Recognised as one of New York's two finest restaurants for steak and beef; continental cuisine. Closed Sat, Sun during July–Aug. Very expensive.

Four Seasons. 99 E. 52nd St near Park Ave (754–9494). Famous decor changes seasonally as does the menu; continental cuisine. Pre-theatre dinner (5–7) and grill room less expensive. Closed Sun. Very expensive.

Gloucester House. 37 E. 50th St (755–7394). Seafood restaurant; comfortable surroundings; no meat or chicken. Very expensive.

Hatsuhana. 17 E. 48th St near Fifth Ave (355–3345). Small, busy authentic Japanese restaurant; seafood, sushi. Closed Sun; no lunch Sat. Moderate.

Il Nido. 251 E. 53rd St near Second Ave (753–8450). Fashionable, handsome restaurant with fine N. Italian food. Closed Sun. Expensive.

La Côte Basque. 5 E. 55th St (688–6525). Fine French haute cuisine; handsome opulent dining room. Closed Sun. Very expensive.

La Grenouille. 3 E. 52nd St near 5th Ave (752–1495). Superb French haute cuisine in a beautiful, stylish restaurant. Closed Sun and holidays. Very expensive.

Le Chantilly. 106 E. 57th St near Park Ave (751–2931). Pretentious, but highly rated for its French haute cuisine. Dinner only Sat, closed Sun. Very expensive.

Le Cygne. 53 E. 54th St near Fifth Ave (759–5941). Fine French haute cuisine in deluxe surroundings; rather formal. Dinner only on Sat, closed Sun and Aug. Very expensive.

Le Madrigal. 216 E. 53rd St near Third Ave (355–0322). Attractive restaurant; traditional French haute cuisine. No lunch Sat, closed Sun. Very expensive.

Les Tournebroches. 153 E. 53rd St near Park Ave (935–6029). In the Citicorp Building; simple French food. Closed Sun. Expensive.

Lutèce. 249 E. 58th St between 2nd–3rd Aves (752–2225). Superb French cuisine in lovely, former townhouse; many think it is New York's finest French restaurant. Closed Sun, no lunch on weekends, closed Sat in summer. Very expensive.

Madras Woodlands. 310 E. 44th St near 2nd Ave (986–0620). Highly rated South Indian vegetarian cuisine. Closed Tues. Moderate.

Nanni. 146 E. 46th St near Lexington Ave (697–4161). Fine N. Italian cuisine; excellent pasta dishes, in lively, noisy restaurant. Closed Sun. Expensive.

Oyster Bar & Restaurant. Grand Central Station, 42nd St near Vanderbilt Pl., lower level (599–1000). Tiled and vaulted rooms deep in the station; counter for quick service; fresh fish, many varieties of oysters in season. Closed weekends. Moderate.

Palace. 420 E. 59th St near 1st Ave (355–5150). Famous for its prices, with $100+ prix fixe dinners; food is reputedly fine but not as extraordinary as the prices and the table appointments. Closed Sun, dinner only, reservations required. Very expensive.

Palm. 837 Second Ave at 45th St (687–2953). Superb food; sawdust on the floors, simple surroundings; rated one of the city's two best steak houses. Very crowded at dinner, no reservations. Closed Sun, no weekend lunch. Very expensive.

Peng Teng's. 219 E. 44th St near 3rd Ave (682–8050). Pleasant Chinese decor; dim sum lunch Sat and Sun; fine food. Moderate.

Shinbashi. 280 Park at 48th St (661–3915). Japanese restaurant with rock garden; well-prepared familiar specialities. Dinner only Sat, closed Sun. Expensive.

Sichuan Pavilion. 322 E. 44th St (986–3775). Highly acclaimed Chinese restaurant in cheerful, attractive rooms. Moderate.

Take-Zushi. 11 E. 48th St near 5th Ave (755–6534). Upstairs restaurant; fine sushi and sashimi. Moderate.

Upper East Side, Yorkville: 59th St and North

Box Tree. 242 E. 50th St (758–8320). Intimate, pretty restaurant; French food; small menu; reservations essential; specify front room. No credit cards. No lunch weekends. Very expensive.

Cafe Geiger. 206 E. 86th St (734–4428). Pastry shop in front, German restaurant behind. Moderate.

Chez Pascal. 151 E. 82nd St near Lexington Ave (249–1334). French food in intimate restaurant. Dinner only; closed Sun. Very expensive.

Casa Brazil. 406 E. 85th St near 1st Ave (288–5284). Inviting small restaurant in townhouse, serving excellent feijoada Wed nights; continental food other days; bring own beer or wine. Dinner only, closed Sun. Very expensive.

Csarda. 1477 Second Ave at 77th St (472–2892). Home-style Hungarian restaurant with hearty cooking. Dinner only. Moderate.

Elaine's. 1703 Second Ave at 88th St (534–8103). Famous more for the clientele—writers, journalists, assorted celebrities—than for the food (mostly Italian) or the service. Expensive.

Gibbon. 24 E. 80th St (861–4001). Spacious, pleasant, Japanese food with French influence. Dinner only Sun. Very expensive.

Greener Pastures. 117 E. 60th St near Park Ave (832–3212). Imaginative salads, health food, vegetarian dishes. Inexpensive.

Il Monello. 1460 Second Ave near 76th St (535–9310). Fine N. Italian food, pasta, seafood; pleasant, quiet atmosphere. Closed Sun. Expensive.

La Petite Ferme. 973 Lexington Ave at 71st St (249–3272). French food, well-prepared; provincial atmosphere. Closed Sun. Very expensive.

Le Plaisir. 969 Lexington Ave at 70th St (734–0400). Elegant; fine nouvelle cuisine with Oriental influence. Closed Sun. Very expensive.

Maxwell's Plum. First Ave and 64th St (628–2100). The classic East Side bar and restaurant; elaborate art nouveau decor, ambitious menu. Expensive.

Pancho Villa's. 1501 Second Ave at 78th St (650–1455). Mexican food; sidewalk cafe. Inexpensive.

Parioli Romanissimo. 1466 First Ave at 77th St (288–2391). Small N. Italian restaurant with highly reputed cannelloni. Closed Sun and Mon. Expensive.

Pinocchio. 170 E. 81st St near 3rd Ave (650–1513). Small, family-run restaurant; home-style Italian cooking. Dinner only; closed Mon. Moderate.

Rao's. 455 E. 114th St at Pleasant Ave (534–9625). Tiny, but favoured by those who know; S. Italian home cooking; rough East Harlem neighbourhood formerly Italian, now Hispanic; drive or take a cab and have the host call you one for the return trip. Moderate.

Red Tulip. 439 E. 75th St near 1st Ave (734–4893). Picturesque Hungarian restaurant with lively clientele and robust country cooking. Dinner only, closed Mon. Moderate.

Ruc. 312 E. 72nd St near 2nd Ave (650–1611). Czech restaurant with folkloric decor; East European specialities including roast duck. Moderate.

Sahib. 222 E. 86th St between 2nd–3rd Aves (535–6760). Indian restaurant with tandoori specialities. Moderate.

Sign of the Dove. 1110 Third Ave at 65th St (861–8080). Handsome East Side townhouse restaurant with its own devotees who like it better than food critics do. Very expensive.

Soomthai. 1490 Second Ave at 78th St (570–6994). Small, busy restaurant, with very good Thai food. Moderate.

Tip Top. 1489 Second Ave between 77th–78th Sts (650–0723). Small, undecorated, family Hungarian restaurant; good food, very good value. Closed Tues. Inexpensive.

Vasata. 339 E. 75th St (650–1686). Pleasant Czech restaurant known for roast duck and paprikasch specialties. Closed Mon, dinner only Tues–Sat. Moderate.

Vienna '79. 320 E. 79th St near 2nd Ave (734–4700). Highly acclaimed sophisticated restaurant with Austro-German food, fine desserts. Dinner only. Expensive.

Lincoln Center: West Side, 59th–72nd St

Cafe des Artistes. 1 W. 67th St off Central Park West (877–3500). Howard Chandler Christy murals; romantic 1930's decor; French and continental food. Expensive.

Cafe La Fortuna. 69 W. 71st St near Central Park West (724–5846). Pastries, ice cream, espresso. Open late.

Dan Tempura House. 2018 Broadway at 71st St (877–4969). Short on atmosphere, good tempura, seafood. Inexpensive.

Dmitri. 152 Columbus Ave at 67th St (787–7306). Greek and continental cuisine, convivial neighbourhood restaurant. Dinner only Sat, Sun. Moderate.

Genghiz Khan's Bicycle. 197 Columbus Ave at 69th St (595–2138). Turkish cooking with nightly Turkish music. Moderate.

Lenge Japanese Restaurant. 202 Columbus Ave at 69th St (874–8278). Japanese cuisine; American ambience; quick service. Dinner only Sun. Moderate.

Los Panchos. 71 W. 71st St near Columbus Ave (864–9378). Outdoor tables in season; Mexican food in pleasant surroundings; life-sized stuffed burro at the bar. Moderate.

Milestone. 70 W. 68th St near Columbus Ave (874–3679). Popular, family-run restaurant; American food with continental overtones. Dinner only; closed Sun and Mon. Moderate.

Perretti. 270 Columbus Ave at 72nd St (362–3939). Busy neighbourhood Italian restaurant; pizza. Inexpensive.

Sushiko. 251 W. 55th St between Columbus and Amsterdam Aves (245–9315). Pleasant Japanese restaurant with sushi bar. Closed Sun, dinner only Sat. Moderate.

Victor's Café. 240 Columbus Ave at 71st St (595–8599). City's best Cuban restaurant; sidewalk cafe. Moderate.

Ying. 220 Columbus Ave at 70th St (724–2031). Pleasant Chinese restaurant; Szechuan and other specialities. Inexpensive.

Restaurants suitable for children near Lincoln Center:
La Crêpe. Broadway and 67th St (874–6900). Chain restaurant with more than 100 kinds of crêpes; quick service. Inexpensive.

Snow White Restaurant. 989 Eighth Ave near 58th St (765–3719). Coffee shop with dishes chosen eclectically from world's cuisines: bagels, chili, souvlaki. Inexpensive.

Upper West Side: 72nd St and North

Anita's Chili Parlor. 287 Columbus Ave at 74th St (595–4091). Chili, Mexican food; eat in or take out. Inexpensive.

Balcony. 2772 Broadway at 107th St (864–8505). Hamburgers, sandwiches, etc; glassed-in sidewalk cafe. Moderate.

Dobson's. 341 Columbus Ave at 76th St (362–0100). Hamburgers, seafood, quiche; oak floors, brick walls, and plants. Moderate.

Empire Szechuan Gourmet. 2574 Broadway at 97th St (663–6980). Spicy and not-so-spicy Szechuan and Hunan fare in modest surroundings. Inexpensive.

Fine & Schapiro. 138 W. 72nd St (877–2874). Delicatessen, sandwiches; within walking distance of Lincoln Center. Inexpensive.

Green Tree Hungarian Restaurant. 1034 Amsterdam Ave at 111th St (864–9106). Hungarian, family style restaurant near Columbia. Closed Sun. Moderate.

J. G. Melon West. Amsterdam Ave at 76th St (877–2220). West Side branch of trendy hamburger, sandwich restaurant. Moderate.

Museum Cafe. 366 Columbus Ave at 77th St (799–0150). Burgers, steak, sandwiches, fish; pleasant atmosphere; near Museum of Natural History. Moderate.

Poletti's. 2315 Broadway at 84th St (580–1200). Italian; homemade pasta. Expensive.

Ruelles. 321 Columbus Ave at 75th St (799–5100). Eclectic continental food in attractive cafe; near Museum of Natural History. Expensive.

Sylvia's. 328 Lenox Ave near 126th St (534–9414). Luncheonette (open also for dinner) noted for soul food in Harlem; not the best neighbourhood, drive if possible. Closed Sun. Inexpensive.

Tavern-on-the-Green. 40 W. 67th St in Central Park (873–3200). Beautiful surroundings, average food; continental menu; touristic. Expensive.

Terrace. 400 W. 119th St near Morningside Drive (666–9490). At the top of Columbia's Butler Hall; fine view; French food; romantic atmosphere. Expensive.

Brunch

A New York institution served Sunday and in some restaurants also on Saturday, brunch consists of light lunch or fancy breakfast dishes and drinks. Prices may be somewhat cheaper than at standard workday meals. Make reservations several days in advance. Some hotels also serve brunch; notable are the Algonquin, the Berkshire, the Carlyle, and the Plaza.

Berry's. 180 Spring St at Thompson St in SoHo (226–4394). Sat 12–3; Sun 11–4. Moderate.

Cafe des Artistes. 1 W. 67th St near Central Park West (877–3500). Sun 11–3. Expensive.

Elephant and Castle. 183 Prince St near Sullivan St in SoHo (260–3600); 58 Greenwich Ave between W. 11th–W. 12th Sts in the Village (243–1400). Sun 10–5. Moderate.

Hors d'Oeuvrerie. N. Tower of the World Trade Center (938–1111). A more economical way to enjoy the view than dining in Windows on the World. Sun 12–3. Expensive.

La Gauloise. 502 Sixth Ave at 12th St in the Village (691–1363). Art Deco cafe-brasserie. Sun 12–4. Moderate.

Maxwell's Plum. 1182 First Ave at 64th St (628–2100). Sat 12–5, Sun 11.30–5. Expensive.

Mme Romaine de Lyon. 32 E. 61st St near 5th Ave (758–2422). Temple of the omelette, more than 600 varieties. Sat, Sun 11–3. Moderate.

Museum Cafe. 336 Columbus Ave at 77th St (799–0150). 11.30 onward, daily. Inexpensive.

Odeon. 145 W. Broadway at Thomas St near SoHo (233–0507). Sun 12–4. Expensive.

Oenophilia. 473 Columbus Ave at 83rd St (580–8127). Attractive restaurant with classical guitarist. Sun 12–3.30; must reserve two days in advance. Expensive.

Rainbow Room. 65th Floor of the RCA Building, 30 Rockefeller Plaza (757–8970). Stupendous view, big crowds, so-so food. Sun 11.30–3; reservations essential. Expensive.

SoHo Charcuterie. 195 Spring St at Sullivan St (226–3545). Sun 11–5. Expensive.

Village Green. 531 Hudson St (255–1650). Wood-burning fireplaces; brass and pewter. Sun 12–4. Inexpensive.

Windows on the World. 1 World Trade Center (938–1111). A good time to see this spectacular room. Sun buffet 12–7.30. Expensive.

Open Late

These restaurants serve a complete meal until at least midnight. Hamburger places and pubs serve later.

The Balcony. 2772 Broadway at 107th St (864–8505). Burgers. Open until 2 a.m. Thurs–Sat; until midnight the rest of the week. Moderate.

Boodles. 1478 First Ave at 77th St (628–0900). Attractive restaurant with popular bar, big hamburgers. Open until 2 a.m. except Mon. Moderate.

Broome Street Bar. 363 W. Broadway at Broome St in SoHo (925–2086). Burgers on pitta bread; simple food. Open until 2.15 a.m. Inexpensive.

Cafe San Martin. 1458 First Ave near 76th St (288–0470). Lively, authentic Spanish restaurant. Moderate.

Elephant and Castle. 183 Prince St near Sullivan St (260–3600). See entry under SoHo.

Elmer's. 1034 Second Ave at 54th St (751–8020). Prime beef and steak; minimal gentility; hefty portions. Expensive.

Four Seasons. 99 E. 52nd St (754–9494). After theatre prix-fixe supper. See entry under Midtown East. Closed Sun. Expensive.

Hanratty's. 732 Amsterdam Ave at 96th St (864–4224) or 1754 Second Ave at 92nd St (289–3200). Hamburgers and simple fare, Irish bar. Open until midnight Sun–Tues, until 1 a.m. Wed–Sat. Inexpensive.

Home Village Restaurant. 20 Mott St in Chinatown (964–0380). See entry under Chinatown.

Joanna. 18 E. 18th St (675–7900). Brasserie in an old warehouse building. Eclectic menu. Moderate.

La Chaumière. 310 W. Fourth St near Bank St (741–3374). Small, friendly; French provincial menu. Moderate.

Mortimer's. 1057 Lexington Ave at 75th St (861–2481). Upper East Side restaurant; American-continental food. Late night supper, Tues–Sun, midnight supper midnight–2.30. Moderate.

Odeon. 145 W. Broadway at Thomas St (233–0507). Late night supper, 12.30–2.30. See entry under SoHo. Expensive.

Régine's. 502 Park Ave at 59th St (826–0990). Disco with restaurant. Closed Sun. Expensive.

Sardi's. 234 W. 44th St (221–8440). See entry under Times Square/Theater District.

Serendipity. 225 E. 60th St (838–3531). Ice cream parlor with Tiffany-type shades; hamburgers, ice cream concoctions. Open until 2 a.m. Sat; other days 1 a.m. Expensive for what it is.

Spring Street Bar and Restaurant. 162 Spring St at W. Broadway in SoHo (431–7637). Popular spot with fine burgers. Open until 1.45 a.m. Moderate.

"21". 21 W. 52nd St (582–7200). Famous clientele, excellent steak and steak tartare. Closed Sun. Very expensive.

Uzic's. 1442 Third Ave near 82nd St (744–8020). Popular cafe-restaurant; Italian specialties. Expensive.

W.J. Flywheel. 359 Second Ave at 21st St (473–8908). Pub-restaurant with big burgers and good service. Open until 12.30 a.m. Moderate.

Restaurants with Views

Anna's Harbor Restaurant. 565 City Island Ave, City Island, Bronx (885–1373). Large restaurant with good Italian seafood and a view of docks and water (reserve table with view). Moderate.

Beekman Towers Hotel. First Ave at 49th St (355–7300). Glass-enclosed terrace on roof; music, drinks, and snacks. No meals. Moderate.

Rainbow Room. RCA Building, 30 Rockefeller Plaza (757–9090). Classic Art Deco room with wonderful view, uneven service, uneven food. Enjoy the view from the cocktail lounge or at Sun brunch.

River Cafe. 1 Water St, Brooklyn (522–5200). Glorious view of the harbour, Statue of Liberty, and East River bridges; ambience better than food; simple dishes are best. Expensive.

The Terrace. Butler Hall, 400 W. 118th St at Morningside Drive, near Columbia University. Fine view of Hudson River and city; good food with French accent; sometimes live chamber music. Expensive.

Tavern-on-the-Green. Central Park off Central Park West, near 67th St (873–3200). Lovely decor—mirrors, brass, crystal, wood—in park setting; stick to simplest fare. Expensive.

Top of the Park. Gulf and Western Plaza, between Broadway and Central Park West. N. of 60th St (333–3800). Tourist attraction; inspiring view, uninspired food; consider trying the cocktail lounge. Closed Sun. Expensive.

Top of the Six's. 666 Fifth Ave between 52nd–53rd Sts (757–6662). Good view, and a good spot for cocktails; uninteresting food; hors d'oeuvres served with cocktails Mon–Fri 5–7. Closed Sun. Expensive.

Windows on the World. 1 World Trade Center, 107th Floor (938–1111). Stunning room, stunning view; food of uneven quality. It is possible to enjoy the view from the Hors d'Oeuverie lounge with drinks and international snacks at less expense. Reservations far in advance for Windows on the World; go early or late to Hors d'Oeuverie to avoid waiting. Very expensive.

Restaurants in the Bronx

In City Island: *Sammy's Fish Box Restaurant,* 41 City Island Ave (885–0920). *The Lobster Box,* 34 City Island Ave (885–1952). *The Sea Shore,* 591 City Island Ave (885–9849). *Anna's Harbor Restaurant,* 565 City Island Ave (885–1373), expensive. *Thwaites Inn,* 536 City Island Ave (885–1023). *Note:* weekend evenings in the summer restaurants are crowded.

In Belmont (near the zoo): *Mario's,* 2342 Arthur Ave near 186th St (583–1188), moderately expensive. *Dominick's,* 2335 Arthur Ave (733–2807), a bar with a few tables in front. *Ann & Tony's,* 2407 Arthur Ave (364–8250). *Full Moon Pizzeria,* 602 E. 187th St (584–3451).

Near Van Cortlandt Park: *Stella d'Oro,* 5806 Broadway near 238th St (548–2245), Italian family-style. **In Baychester** (near Co-op City): *Il Boschetto,* 1660 E. Gun Hill Rd at Tiemann Ave (379–9335). **In Throg's Neck:** *Amerigo's,* 3587 E. Tremont Ave (824–7766).

Restaurants in Brooklyn

On Atlantic Ave (Arab and Near Eastern restaurants): *Son of Sheik*, 165 Atlantic Ave between Clinton and Henry Sts (625–4203). *Sindbad*, 172 Atlantic Ave (624–9105). Numerous other inexpensive restaurants; bring your own wine or beer.

In Fulton Ferry: *River Cafe*, 1 Water St (522–5200); see entry under Restaurants with Views. **In Coney Island:** *Gargiulo's*, 2911 W. 15th St (266–0906), famous Italian seafood restaurant. **In Brooklyn Heights:** *Jimmy's*, 36 Joralemon St (858–3018), Italian. *Old Hungary*, 142 Montague St (625–1649). *Cafe Galleria*, 174 Montague St (625–7883). **In Downtown Brooklyn:** *Gage & Tollner*, 372 Fulton St at Jay St (875–5181); seafood in handsome 19C restaurant, expensive. *Lisanne*, 448 Atlantic Ave at Nevins St (237–2271); French, closed Mon, expensive.

In Williamsburg: *Peter Luger Steak House*, 178 Broadway (387–7400), expensive. **In Clinton Hill:** *Joe's Place*, 264 Waverly Ave (622–9244). **Near Prospect Park:** *Raintree*, Prospect Park West at 9th St (768–3723).

Restaurants in Queens

In Astoria (Greek restaurants): *Kalyva*, 36–15 Ditmars Blvd between 36th–37th Sts (932–9229). *The Neptune Diner*, 31–05 Astoria Blvd at 31st St (278–4853). *Rumeli Taverna*, 33–04 Broadway, between 33rd–34th Sts (278–7553). All are moderately priced. Pastry and coffee shops: *Omonoia*, 32–30 Broadway (274–6650). *Hbh*, 29–28 30th Ave (274–1609). *Hilton Zaxaroplasteion*, 22–06 31st St (274–6399). *Lefkos Pyrgos*, 22–85 31st St (932–4423).

In Flushing: *Kalpana*, 42–75 Main St (939–0500); Indian restaurant. **In Forest Hills:** *Buonavia*, 101–19 Queens Blvd between 67th Ave–67th Drive (275–6743); Italian family restaurant, closed Mon. *Caesar's*, 97–12 63rd Rd near 97th St (459–2828). *La Stella*, 102–11 Queens Blvd (459–9511), closed Mon.

Restaurants in Staten Island

Many museums and sights are oriented toward the community and do not provide eating facilities. There are more than enough fast food restaurants on Hylan Blvd and in the Staten Island Mall (Richmond Ave at Richmond Hill Rd). **Near the zoo:** *Forest Inn Restaurant*, 834 Forest Ave not far from Broadway; snacks, plain food (727–6060). **In New Dorp:** *Mauro's*, 121 Roma Ave off New Dorp Lane near the beach; moderately priced Italian restaurant; closed Mon (351–8441). **Near South Beach:** *Top o' the Mast*, 1177 Hylan Blvd near Parkinson Ave; moderately priced seafood restaurant (981–9191). **Near Great Kills Park:** *Carmen's*, 750 Barclay Ave near Arden Ave overlooking Raritan Bay; Mexican food; moderately expensive (984–9786). **In the Staten Island Mall** (K Mart Plaza, S. of the main mall): Jade Island, 2845 Richmond Ave, Chinese food (761–8080).

Sightseeing Services

The Quarterly Calendar of Events published by the New York Convention & Visitors' Bureau contains an inclusive list of commercial sightseeing services. Copies are available at the bureau's two information centres: Two Columbus Circle (9–6, Mon–Fri) and in Times Square (42nd St between Broadway and Seventh Ave, S. side of street), open 9–6, seven days.

Visitors with limited time might wish for an overall tour by boat, bus, or helicopter. Among the better known are:

Circle Line Sightseeing, three-hour cruises around Manhattan Island with commentary. Boats leave from Pier 83 at the foot of W. 43rd St at frequent intervals during warm weather. Adults, $7; children under 12, $3·50. Tel. 563–3200 for sailing schedule.

The Island Helicopter Corp., located at the foot of 34th St at the East River offers rides daily from 9 a.m.–9 p.m. Prices start at $12 for a seven-minute, 16-mile ride, giving a vista of midtown, the United Nations, and the East Side skyline. Minimum of two passengers required (895–5372 or 683–4575).

The Gray Line offers a choice of ten bus tours, starting with two $7 tours (Lower Manhattan including Chinatown and Upper Manhattan including Harlem) which last about two hours. The four-and-a-half-hour all day tour costs $10·50 and includes a visit to the top of either the Empire State Building or the World Trade Center. Terminal at Eighth Ave and 53rd St (397–2600).

Crossroads Sightseeing at 701 Seventh Ave (47th St) has two-hour uptown or downtown tours ($6·75) as well as longer tours (half- or full day, $9·75 or $16·25) including visits to the Empire State Building and the Statue of Liberty (581–2828).

Saturdays and Sundays the New York City Transit Authority runs its **Culture Buses** over two routes every 20 min. from 9 a.m.–6 p.m. The buses pass the city's most important monuments and interesting neighbourhoods, and riders may get on and off as they wish at no extra cost. *Loop I* circles N. in Manhattan from the 30s and passes the United Nations, Empire State Building, Metropolitan Museum, Frick Collection, and Columbia University among other places. *Loop II* circles south from 42nd St and passes the World Trade Center, Chinatown, Greenwich Village, Wall Street, Little Italy, and the South Street Seaport as well as several locations in Brooklyn. The fare is $2·50. For further information call 330–1234, the Transit Authority number, usually maddeningly difficult to reach, or request a schedule at the Columbus Circle or Times Square information centers.

Specialised tours include guided visits by bus as well as walking tours, demanding more energy but offering greater rewards.

Art Tours of Manhattan, 33 E. 22nd St (254–7682), offers tours with visits of SoHo, museums, galleries, artists' studios, and/or private collections.

The *Penny Sightseeing Company* has three-hour bus tours of Harlem (10 a.m., Mon and Thurs at $7 per person; 11 a.m., Sat at $8 per person) that leave from 303 W. 42nd St and journey to the Cathedral of St. John the Divine as well as the Schomburg Collection and the main sights of Harlem. Call 247–2860.

Lou Singer offers unscheduled Brooklyn tours to churches, elegant old homes, and clubs. Minimum group size is eight people at $15 each. He will pick up visitors at Second Ave and 41st St or other Manhattan locations; call him at 875–9084 between 6–9 p.m.

Backstage on Broadway, a commercial tour, offers visits to Broadway behind the scenes. Adults $4; students $3. 228 W. 47th St Call 575–8065. Those interested in the theatre might also enjoy a *Radio City Music Hall tour* at

Rockfeller Center (Sixth Ave at 50th St), offered every half-hour from 10 a.m. to noon and again at 4 and 4.30; admission, $3·95; reservations required, 246–4621.

The *Municipal Arts Society* offers three-hour walking tours emphasising history and architecture, on Sundays during warm months. Tours touch on such areas as Manhattan's Gold Coast (the mansions of Fifth Ave), New York's First Suburb (Greenwich Village), and City on the River (Lower Manhattan). For information and schedule, call 935–3969. Tours cost $3.

The *Museum of the City of New York* sponsors occasional unusual tours generally with a historical emphasis; call 534–1672 for information.

Weekends during warm weather the *Urban Park Rangers* frequently offer free tours through Central Park. The walks may focus either upon Central Park as a model of urban planning and park design or upon its natural history. For information: 397–3156.

Holidays in New York (152 W. 58th St) offers inexpensive ($4 per person) half-day walking tours of such areas as Greenwich Village, Chinatown, Little Italy, and the municipal center. For information and reservations: 765–2515.

Walking Tours Unlimited (310 W. 47th St, Suite 6–J) offers $5 and $6 guided visits with such itineraries as 'East River Views' (Beekman Place, Tudor City, the United Nations), City Hall and the municipal district, lower Broadway and the Battery. Night tours are also available starting at 7 p.m. and costing $22–35 depending on the entertainment. Information: 581–9638.

Theatre

The theatre in New York can be divided into three categories: Broadway, Off Broadway, and Off Off Broadway. Proximity to or distance from Broadway in these terms, however, is not merely geographical but also economic and artistic. The Broadway theatre represents the Establishment, the center of commercial theatre in America. Its houses are located mainly north of Times Square between about 43rd and 53rd Sts; most are large, seating more than a thousand spectators. They have given rise to a special genre, the Broadway Production, usually large in scale, expensive in details of production, star-studded in personnel, and popular in appeal.

The Off Broadway movement may have originated in the years around World War I when such groups as the Provincetown Players and the Washington Square Players burst upon the scene in Greenwich Village, but it truly began to flourish in the early 1950s, notably with Jose Quintero's production in 1952 of Tennessee Williams' 'Summer and Smoke', which had failed four years earlier on Broadway but which became the first major theatrical success south of 42nd Street in thirty years. According to Actors' Equity, Off Broadway is defined by an exclusion clause that relegates its theatres (necessarily holding fewer than 300 spectators) to areas outside the regular Times Square theatre district, but which permits smaller work crews and lower wages, hence allowing for experimentation and less expensive productions. Artistically Off Broadway suggests a place where new actors and directors can work, where new work can be discovered, where Broadway failures can be resuscitated, and where theatre companies may develop continuity and consistent artistic policies.

As Off Broadway became more successful commercially and less innocent, the Off Off Broadway movement began to flourish, filling the spot that Off Broadway occupied in its early days. Historians trace its beginnings to Alfred Jarry's 'King Ubu' which opened in the Take 3 coffeehouse in Greenwich Village in 1960 or to Ellen Stewart's Cafe La Mama which opened in a cellar on East 12th St the same year. Geographically Off Off Broadway productions usually occupy non-theatrical buildings—lofts, churches, coffeehouses—all over the city. Plays tend to be headily experimental or to deal with themes too explosive for Broadway. Companies may be amateur or amateurish, but one of the principles of the movement is to preserve the intimacy between a playwright and his work, where the author may participate in all parts of a production, free from the demands of commercial success. Off Off Broadway productions appeal to a young, artistically daring audience that includes students, artists, and theatrical people interested in getting in at the ground floor.

Tickets: Tickets to Broadway and many Off Broadway productions may be purchased at the box office or from ticket brokers who add a $2 or $3 surcharge to the ticket price. Telephone ticket services are *Chargit* (944–9300) for holders of major credit cards, or *Ticketron* (977–9020); both charge additional fees. Half-price tickets available the day of performance may be purchased at TKTS (Times Square Ticket Center) at W. 47th St. and Broadway or downtown at 100 William St (see pp252–3 for schedule). Prices of Broadway shows range from about $17 to $40. Off Broadway tickets are cheaper with top prices at about $20·00; Off Off Broadway events are still less expensive.

The Sunday Arts and Entertainment Guide of 'The New York Times', 'The New Yorker' magazine, and 'New York' magazine offer fairly complete listings of current shows and theatrical events.

Broadway Theatres

Alvin	250 W. 52nd St	757–8646
	(B'way–Eighth Ave)	
Ambassador	215 W. 49th St	541 6490
	(B'way–Eighth Ave)	
Belasco	111 W. 44th St	354–4490
	(Sixth–Seventh Aves)	
Booth	222 W. 45th St	246–5969
	(B'way–Eighth Ave)	
Broadhurst	235 W. 44th St	247–0472
	(B'way–Eighth Ave)	
Broadway	1681 Broadway	247–3660
	(52nd–53rd Sts)	
Brooks Atkinson	256 W. 47th St	245–3430
	(B'way–Eighth Ave)	
Century	235 W. 46th St	354–6644
	(B'way–Eighth Ave)	
Circle in the Square	1633 Broadway	581–0720
	(50th–51st Sts)	
Cort	138 W. 48th St	489–6392
	(Sixth–Seventh Aves)	
Edison	240 W. 47th St	757–7164
	(B'way–Eighth Ave)	
Ethel Barrymore	243 W. 47th St	246–0390
	(B'way–Eighth Ave)	
Eugene O'Neill	230 W. 49th St	246–0220
	(B'way–Eighth Ave)	
Forty-Sixth St	226 W. 46th St	246–0246
	(B'way–Eighth Ave)	

Golden	252 W. 45th St (B'way–Eighth Ave)	246–6740
Imperial	249 W. 45th St (B'way–Eighth Ave)	265–4311
Little	240 W. 44th St (B'way–Eighth Ave)	221–6425
Longacre	220 W. 48th St (B'way–Eighth Ave)	246–5639
Lunt-Fontanne	205 W. 46th St (B'way–Eighth Ave)	586–5555
Lyceum	149 W. 45th St (Sixth–Seventh Aves)	582–3897
Majestic	245 W. 44th St (B'way–Eighth Ave)	246–0730
Mark Hellinger	237 W. 51st St (B'way–Eighth Ave)	757–7064
Martin Beck	302 W. 45th St (Eighth–Ninth Aves)	246–6363
Minskoff	Broadway at 45th St	869–0550
Music Box	239 W. 45th St (B'way–Eighth Ave)	246–4636
Nederlander	208 W. 41st St (Seventh–Eighth Aves)	921–8000
New Apollo	234 West 43rd St (B'way–Eighth Ave)	921–8558
Palace	B'way at 47th St	757–2626
Plymouth	236 W. 45th St (B'way–Eighth Ave)	730–1760
Royale	242 W. 45th St (B'way–Eighth Ave)	245–5760
St. James	246 W. 44th St (B'way–Eighth Ave)	398–0280
Shubert	225 W. 44th St (B'way–Eighth Ave)	246–5990
Uris	1633 B'way (50th–51st St)	586–6510
Virginia, formerly ANTA	245 W. 52nd St (B'way–Eighth Ave)	977–9370
Winter Garden	1634 B'way (50th–51st St)	245–4878

Off Broadway Theatres

Actors Playhouse	100 Seventh Ave S.	691–6226
American Place *Theatre*	111 W. 46th St	247–0393
Astor Place Theatre	434 Lafayette St	254–4370
Chelsea Theater Center	407 W. 43rd St	541–8394
Cherry Lane Theatre	38 Commerce St	989–2020
Circle in the Square *(Downtown)*	159 Bleecker St	254–6330
Circle Repertory Co.	99 Seventh Ave S.	924–7100
Colonnades Theatre *Lab*	428 Lafayette St	673–2222
CSC Repertory	136 E. 13th St	477–5808
Manhattan Theatre Club	321 E. 73rd St	472–0600
Public Theater	425 Lafayette St	598–7150
Ridiculous Theatrical *Company*	1 Sheridan Square	260–7137
Roundabout/Stage One	333 W. 23rd St	242–7800
Roundabout/Stage Two	307 W. 26th St	242–7800
Sullivan Street Playhouse	181 Sullivan St	674–3838
Theater of Saint *Peter's Church*	*Lexington Ave at 54th* St	751–4140

| *Theatre de Lys* | 121 Christopher St | 924–8782 |
| *Village Gate* | Bleecker and Thompson St | 475–5120 |

Off Off Broadway Theatres

There are over two hundred Off Off Broadway theatres scattered throughout the city. Most are small, seating fewer than 100 spectators, and many offer productions only on certain days of the week. For information about Off Off Broadway events, telephone the Off Off Broadway Alliance (tel: 757–4473), Mon–Fri, 10–6. The Alliance, 162 W. 56th St, also publishes a free listing of theatres by neighbourhood.

Amusements

Concerts, Dance and Opera

The Brooklyn Academy of Music (BAM), 30 Lafayette St, Brooklyn (636–4100) has a full schedule of music, dance, and drama events through the winter season. The *Brooklyn Center for the Performing Arts at Brooklyn College* (BCBC), Nostrand Ave and Ave H, Brooklyn (434–1900) also offers a concert season. At the *Brooklyn Museum*, Eastern Pkwy and Washington Ave, Brooklyn (638–5000) Sun afternoon concerts are held in the sculpture garden during nice weather.

Carnegie Hall, 154 W. 57th St, (247–7459) is the city's best-loved concert hall both for its acoustics and its tradition. Such orchestras as the Chicago, the Philadelphia, and the Boston symphonies perform here as well as instrumental soloists and recitalists from the top ranks of internationally famous artists—both classical and popular. Less well-known artists appear at *Carnegie Recital Hall.*

City Center, 131 W. 55th St (246–8989), the home of the New York City Ballet before it moved to Lincoln Center, is still known as a center of dance. The Alvin Ailey American Dance Theater, the Joffrey Ballet, the Paul Taylor Dance Company, and the Dance Theater of Harlem appear regularly, while the summer season is usually devoted to foreign companies.

The largest facility in the city for music and dance is LINCOLN CENTER FOR THE PERFORMING ARTS, Broadway at 64th St (877–1800). *Alice Tully Hall* (362–1911) is the home of chamber music concerts and recitals requiring a moderately intimate theatre. *Avery Fisher Hall* (874–2424) is the home of the New York Philharmonic, and the Mostly Mozart Festival; it also hosts visiting orchestras and famous soloists including jazz musicians. The *Metropolitan Opera* (580–9830) is the home of the nation's premier opera company, the American Ballet Theater, and visiting ballet companies. The opera season runs from late Sept through mid-April, and the ballet season, divided into two, runs from Oct through Nov and from mid-April through June. The *New York State Theater* (870–5570) is the home of the New York City Opera Company, a 'starless' company whose casts feature young American singers, and of the New York City Ballet whose fame is due largely to artistic director

George Balanchine. The opera season under the direction of former diva Beverly Sills runs from late Feb to early May and from early Sept to mid-Nov. The ballet season runs from mid-Nov to the end of Feb, with performances of the 'Nutcracker' (write for tickets far in advance) taking up December.

The *Juilliard Theater* (799–5000) where Juilliard students, orchestras, dance, and theatre groups perform, presents a wide range of free concerts, usually Fri evenings at 8.30. Call the school for a schedule.

Also in Lincoln Center is the *Library and Museum of the Performing Arts*, 111 Amsterdam Ave at 65th St, a branch of the New York Public Library. During the winter season (Sept–June) there are almost daily performances of solo and chamber music, dance, film, and drama. Tickets are free and can be picked up an hour before the performances which begin at 4 p.m. on weekdays and at 2.30 on Saturdays.

Tickets for Lincoln Center events are available by mail (order a month ahead), at the box office, and at most Ticketron outlets.

In addition to the Met and The New York City Opera the *Amato Opera Theatre, Inc.*, 319 Bowery (228–8200) and the *Bel Canto Opera Company*, 30 E. 31st St in the Madison Avenue Baptist Church (535–5231) offer student and semi-professional productions. *The Light Opera of Manhattan*, 334 E. 74th St (861–2288), known to its devotees as LOOM, offers a season of Gilbert and Sullivan operettas, and the confections of Strauss, Lehar, and other light-hearted composers.

Some museums offer concert series with well-known soloists or chamber groups. Notable among them is the *Metropolitan Museum of Art*, Fifth Ave at 82nd St (570–3949). The *Museum of the City of New York*, Fifth Ave at 103rd St (534–1672), offers free Sun afternoon concerts from Oct–May, and the *New-York Historical Society*, 107 Central Park West (873–3400), also has free Sun programmes, Nov–April. *The Frick Collection*, 1 E. 70th St (288–0700) has chamber music concerts during the winter.

Two other halls offering concert series are the *92nd St YM-YWHA* on Lexington Ave (427–6000), whose programme includes a young artists' series, chamber music, opera, and instrumental soloists. The programming of *Abraham Goodman House*, 129 W. 67th St (362–8719) is even more adventurous, including the work of lesser known composers, choral music, unusual ensembles (the Chinese Music Ensemble of New York, the Music Project) as well as more conventional fare.

Church music. *Trinity Church* (tel: 285–0872) at Broadway and Wall St presents organ concerts at noon on weekdays. *St. Bartholomew's Episcopal Church*, Park Ave at 51st St (tel: 744–2500), sometimes offers Sun afternoon choral concerts, usually at 4.00. *St. Peter's Lutheran Church* in the Citicorp Building, Lexington Ave at 54th St (tel: 935–2220), has an extensive jazz programme which includes a regular Jazz Vespers at 5.00 on Sun. Chamber groups give occasional noontime weekday concerts in *St. Paul's Chapel*, Broadway at Fulton St (tel: 285–0874) and the *Fifth Avenue Presbyterian Church* at 55th St (tel: 247–0490) sponsors frequent Sun concerts. Uptown at the *Riverside Church*, Riverside Drive at 122nd St (tel: 749–7000), are carillon concerts Sat noons. Telephone the churches for further information.

Movie theatres are located all over the city. Seats cannot be reserved and there are usually long lines in front of popular, first-run movies. Patrons buy their tickets and then get into the line; be prepared to arrive at least half an hour to 45 minutes before the show (call the box office or check the newspaper for times) if you wish to get a good seat. The most expensive movie theatres are the East Side first-run houses where tickets cost $5 and up (one price for the entire house). Slightly cheaper are the neighbourhood theatres which show films that have already had some exposure; some of the theatres have been divided to show more than one film at a time, an architectural feature usually apparent in the theatre's name: Lincoln Plaza 1, 2, and 3; R.K.O. Century Cinerama 1 and 2, Quad Cinema. The better theatres in the Times Square area show popular adventure films or comedies while the less savoury ones offer movies featuring sex and violence. In addition to the museums which have film programmes (the Whitney and the Museum of Modern Art are outstanding in this respect), several commercial theatres have established themselves as revival houses. Notable are the *Agee Room*, 144 Bleecker St (473–8306), the *Bleecker St Cinema*, 144 Bleecker St (674–2560), the *Carnegie Hall Cinema*, 7th Ave at 57th St (757–2131), *Cinema Village*, 22 E. 12th St (924–3363), the *8th St Playhouse*, 52 W. 8th St (674–6515), the *Regency*, Broadway at 67th St (724–3700), the *Thalia*, Broadway at 95th St (222–3370), and the *Theatre 80 St. Marks*, 80 St. Marks Place (254–7400). The *Anthology Film Archives* in SoHo at 80 Wooster St is the most arcane of these establishments, offering little-known and esoteric films to its demanding clientele: for information tel: 226–0010.

The most important film event in the city is the *New York Film Festival* at Lincoln Center (usually late Sept to mid-Oct), where foreign and American films deserving of special attention get their first American showing. 'The New Yorker' and the Sun edition of 'The New York Times' have short reviews of current films.

Art exhibitions. Most museums are open Tues–Sat, 10–5 and Sun, 12–5. The Museum of Modern Art is the only major museum open on Mon. Galleries, like museums, are usually open Tues to Sat from around 10 to 11 in the morning until 5 or 6 in the afternoon; many close for part of the summer.

Spectator sports. New York has professional baseball, football, basketball, hockey, and soccer teams as well as enjoying the presence of important tennis tournaments and track and field meets.

BASEBALL. The season runs from early April to Oct with New York's two teams, the Yankees and the Mets, each playing about 75 home games (many at night). The Yankees occupy Yankee Stadium in the Bronx (tel: 293–6000) while the Mets play at Shea Stadium, Queens (tel: 672–3000). Tickets are usually easy to get and are available at Ticketron outlets throughout the city (call 977–9020 for the branch nearest you).

To reach Yankee Stadium by SUBWAY, take the IRT Lexington Ave (train 4) uptown to 161st St/River Ave or the IND Sixth Ave (D train) to the same stop.

BY CAR: Major Deegan Expwy to Grand Concourse; Grand Concourse N. to 161st St, turn l. to Stadium. Car parking available; traffic is usually heavy just before game time.

The handsome modern stadium is in a borderline neighbourhood and the fans sometimes get extremely vocal.

Shea Stadium is in the Flushing Meadows-Corona Park area of Queens.

SUBWAY: IRT Flushing line (train 7) to the Willets Point/Shea Stadium stop.

CAR: Grand Central Pkwy or Northern Blvd to Flushing Meadow Park; follow signs to Shea Stadium.

BASKETBALL. The season begins in Oct and ends in April. The New York Knicks play at Madison Square Garden; for ticket information call the Garden (564–4400).

SUBWAY: IRT Broadway–7th Ave (train 1, 2, 3) or IND Eighth Ave (train A, CC, or E) to Penn Station.

BUS: M4 downtown on Fifth Ave or any downtown bus with a transfer to the 34th St crosstown bus.

PARKING: Numerous nearby, expensive parking lots.

Rabid fans may also want to see the New Jersey Nets, formerly of New York, who now play in Piscataway, N.J.; for information call (201) 935–8888.

In March the National Invitational Tournament for top college basketball teams is held in Madison Square Garden. For information call 563–8000.

BOXING. Once the highest shrine of boxing, Madison Square Garden still hosts prize fights, though they lack their former prestige. The Amateur Golden Gloves tournament is held here annually in Jan or Feb; tel: 563–8000 for information.

FOOTBALL. The two New York teams, the Jets and the Giants, play in Shea Stadium and the New Jersey Meadowlands respectively. The season runs from Sept–Jan but the Jets do not play any home games until after the completion of the baseball season. For Jets ticket information, call Shea Stadium (672–3000). For information about public transportation, check the listing under Baseball, New York Mets.

The Meadowlands Sports Complex, home of the Giants and the Cosmos (soccer) is located on Route 3 in East Rutherford, New Jersey. To get there by car take the Lincoln Tunnel from Manhattan and follow Rte 3 west to exit 16. Buses run to the stadium from the Port Authority Bus Terminal on game days. For ticket information call (201) 935–8222. (To reach this number from a New York telephone you must dial the digit '1' before the area code.) Pre-game traffic is inevitably heavy so allow extra time.

HORSE RACING. Aqueduct Racetrack in Ozone Park, Queens (season Oct–Dec, Feb–May) and Belmont Racetrack in Elmont on Long Island just over the Queens border (season June–July, Aug–Oct) offer thoroughbred racing. The Belmont Stakes in June is the final leg of the Triple Crown for three-year-olds after the Kentucky Derby and the Preakness Stakes. For ticket information and post time for both tracks call the New York Racing Association, tel: 641–4700.

TRANSPORTATION TO AQUEDUCT. SUBWAY: IND Special Race Track Express from 42nd St IND Station at 8th Ave. Service begins approximately two hours before first race.

BY CAR: Take Belt Pkwy toward Kennedy Airport and follow signs for Aqueduct.

EXPRESS BUS SERVICE from 41st St and Seventh Ave. For information tel: 641–4700, ext. 306.

TRANSPORTATION TO BELMONT. SUBWAY: IND Sixth Ave (E and F train) to Parsons Blvd. Or BMT Jamaica Ave train (J train) to 160th St/Jamaica Ave. Special bus service from both stations to the track. Express bus service from 41st St and Seventh Ave. For information tel: 641–4700, ext. 306.

ICE HOCKEY. The New York Rangers play at Madison Square Garden from Oct–April. For ticket information, telephone the Garden (564–4400). For travel information see the entry under Basketball, New York Knicks. The New York Islanders, a suburban team, play in the Nassau Coliseum in Uniondale, Long Island. For information call (516) 794–4100.

SOCCER. The New York Cosmos play from April–Aug at the Meadowlands in New Jersey. For directions to the stadium, see the entry under Football, New York Giants. Ticket information is available by calling 265–8600 in New York.

TENNIS. The major event, the U.S. Open Tennis Championships, are played in late Aug–early Sept at the National Tennis Center in Flushing Meadows, Queens. For ticket information, tel: 592–8000. Tickets for the semi-finals and the finals are usually sold out well in advance but it is easy to get tickets for the earlier rounds when more matches are played on a single day. The West Side Tennis Club in Forest Hills, Queens, former host of the U.S. Open, now holds a men's tournament in the spring before the Wimbledon championships (tel: 268–2300). The Grand Prix Masters Tournament, a major men's indoor event, is held in Madison Square Garden (tel: 564–4400) in Jan and in recent years the final of the women's winter tour has taken place in the Garden (same telephone number) in late March.

TRACK AND FIELD. Madison Square Garden annually hosts the Wanamaker Millrose Games in late Jan or Feb. Call 563–8000 for schedule.

Participant sports. Most public parks have playing fields for such sports as baseball, football, and frisbee. In Central Park the athletic fields are S. of 66th St on the West Side and N. of the Reservoir in the centre of the park.

BICYCLING. During weekends, on holidays, and during most non-rush hours weekdays, traffic is banned from Central Park roads except the crosstown transverses. In the park itself bicycles are for rent at the Loeb Boathouse for a modest fee (April–Oct) but you must leave a substantial deposit and identification (call the boathouse, 772–7020, for details).

Commercial rental shops near the park are Gene's Bicycles, 242 E. 79th St between Second and Third Aves (tel: 249–9218), Angelo's Bicycle Service, 140 W. 83rd St between Columbus and Amsterdam Aves (tel: 362–1122), and Bicycle Renaissance, 505 Columbus Ave at 84th St (tel: 724–2350).

Near Prospect Park in Brooklyn are Dixon's Bicycle Shop, 792 Union St near Seventh Ave (tel: 636–0067) and the Prospect Park Bicycle Shop, 494 Flatbush Ave near Empire Blvd (tel: 284–6936).

Fishing. Boats leave daily during the warm months for fishing excursions from Sheepshead Bay (call the Bay End Dock Co., 332–5863) and City Island (Jack's Bait and Tackle, 885–2042).

Golf. The city has a surprising number of public golf courses with green fees ranging from $5–$7. Telephone ahead to find out approximately how long a wait to expect.

BROOKLYN: Dyker Beach, 86th St and 6th Ave (836–9722); Marine Park, 2880 Flatbush Ave (338–7113). BRONX: Mosholu-Booth, Jerome Ave at Holly Lane (822–4845); Pelham-Split Rock, City Island and Pelham Bay Pkwy West (885–0838); Van Cortlandt, Broadway near 242nd St (543–4595). QUEENS: Clearview in Bayside, 202-12 Willets Point Blvd (229–2570); Douglaston Park in Douglaston, Commonwealth Blvd and Marathon Pkwy (224–6566); Forest Park in Ridgewood, Interboro Pkwy and Main Drive (296–2442); Kissena Park in Flushing, N. Hempstead Turnpike and Fresh Meadows Rd (445–3388). STATEN ISLAND: Latourette, Forest Hill Rd in Latourette Park (351–1889); Silver Lake, Victory Blvd and Park Rd (447–5686); South Shore, Huguenot Ave (984–0108).

Ice Skating. The most beautiful and memorable place to skate, especially during the Christmas season, is at Rockefeller Center, open from about Nov–March (tel: 757–6230). Telephone ahead for schedule as there are several skating sessions daily and the admission price applies only to one session. The rink is open from 9 a.m. until 11.30 p.m. and is often very crowded.

Indoor rinks include Sky Rink in Manhattan, 450 W. 33rd St (tel: 695–6555) between Ninth and Tenth Aves, open all year, which features live organ music Mon and Tues evenings and ice disco on weekends; skate rental. In Queens, the New York City Building at the World's Fair site in Flushing Meadows-Corona Park (tel: 271–1996) offers skating sessions, Wed–Sun in season. In the Bronx, the Riverdale Ice Skating Center, Broadway and 236th St (543–6460) has morning and afternoon sessions and some evening sessions with disco skating including a disk jockey to spin records; skate rental available.

Outdoor rinks (generally open Nov–March) include the Wollman Rink in Central Park (360–8260), now closed for renovation but expected to open in 1983; call for schedule and rates; also in Central Park, Lenox Ave and 110th St is the Lasker Memorial Rink; telephone 397–3142 for schedule and rates. In Prospect Park the Kate Wollman Memorial Rink is open in season daily except Mon with continuous skating Tues–Thurs 8 a.m.–8 p.m. and weekends, 10 a.m.–10 p.m.; call 965–6561. On Staten Island there is outdoor skating at the Staten Island War Memorial Rink, Clove Lakes Park, Wed–Sun; tel: 720–1010.

Ponds and lakes: The pond in Central Park near the 73rd St entrance from Fifth Ave has winter skating, weather permitting. The water level is lowered to a depth of one foot to provide safety and to promote early freezing of the surface. Other free skating ponds in the city are in Crotona Park Lake and Van Cortlandt Park Lake (Bronx), Prospect Park near Ocean Ave and Lincoln Rd (Brooklyn), Alley Pond Park in Queens Village, Bowne Park in Flushing, Brookville Park in Rosedale, and Tilly Memorial Park in Jamaica (Queens). On Staten Island are Allison Pond in New Brighton, Clove Lakes Park in West Brighton, and Wolfe's Pond Park in Prince's Bay. To find out whether the ice is thick enough (5 inches) to permit skating call the Department of Parks and Recreation: in Manhattan, 397–3100; in the Bronx, 822–4711; in Brooklyn, 965–6511; in Queens, 520–5311, and in Staten Island, 442–7640.

Racquetball. Many clubs are private; among the better known public ones are the Manhattan Squash and Racquetball Club at two locations, 41 W. 42nd St (tel: 869–8969) and 60 W. 65th St (tel: 496–9200) and the St. George Health and Racquet Club, 43 Clark St in Brooklyn Heights (tel: 625–0500). Check the Yellow Pages of the telephone book for additional listings.

Riding: If you wish to ride in Central Park, contact the Claremont Riding Academy, 175 W. 89th St between Columbus and Amsterdam Aves (tel: 724–5100). In Brooklyn near Prospect Park Culmit Stables, 51 Caton Place off Coney Island Ave near Park Circle (tel: 438–8849) rents horses for the park while the Jamaica Bay Riding Academy, 7000 Shore Pkwy (tel: 531–8949) is located near the Gateway National Recreation area. In Staten Island are the Clove Lake Stables, 1025 Clove Rd (tel: 448–1414) near the park of that name and in the Bronx, the Van Cortlandt Park Stables, Broadway and W. 254th St (549–6200).

ROLLER SKATING. Both roller skating and roller disco currently enjoy great popularity. Skaters in Central Park gather W. of the Mall opposite about 70th St. You may rent skates in the park at Good Skates near the Sheep Meadow (tel: 535–1080). Indoor rinks in Manhattan include the Roxy Roller Rink, 515 W. 18th St between Tenth and Eleventh Aves (tel: 675–8300), the Metropolis Roller Skate Club, 241 W. 55th St (tel: 586–4649), Wheels Disco Roller Rink at 75 Christopher St in the Village (tel: 675–3913) and Village Skating at 15 Waverly Place also in the Village (tel: 677–9690).

Running. The New York Road Runners Club, 9 E. 89th St (tel: 860–4455) sponsors the New York Marathon in Oct (places filled far ahead) as well as less ambitious races in Central Park on weekends during seasonable weather. 'The Road Runner's Guide to New York City', by Patti Hagan with Joe Cody (New York, 1979), issued in paperback, offers succinct and useful descriptions of routes for runners in the five boroughs.

The route of the New York Marathon begins in Ft Wadsworth, Staten Island, crosses the Verrazano-Narrows Bridge, angles across the Bay Ridge, Sunset Park, Gowanus, and Park Slope sections of Brooklyn before continuing N. through downtown Brooklyn and Williamsburg to Greenpoint. The course passes through the Long Island City area of Queens, over the Queensboro Bridge, N. Along First Ave in Manhattan through East Harlem and makes a brief foray through the South Bronx. After crossing the 138th St Bridge over the Harlem River, the course turns S. again for the homestretch, down Fifth Ave through Harlem and through Central Park, to the Plaza Hotel, across Central Park South and up to the Tavern-on-the-Green on the West Side of the park.

Squash. Squash clubs open to the public in Manhattan are the Fifth Ave Racquet Club, 404 Fifth Ave (tel: 599–3120); the Manhattan Squash Club, 41 W. 42nd St (tel: 869–8969); Park Ave Squash and Racquet Club, 3 Park Ave (tel: 686–1085); Town Squash, 151 E. 86th St (tel: 860–8630); and the Turtle Bay Racquet Club, 541 Lexington Ave (tel: 838–2102).

Tennis: The Parks Department maintains public courts for city residents, open mid-April–Oct; seasonal pass available at the Arsenal. Visitors may obtain daily passes at the Central Park Courts (currently $4) which entitle the holder to one hour of tennis on any city-owned court (list available from the Parks Dept in the Arsenal).

The Central Park courts are popular and often involve a wait; others on the list may be less well-maintained.

Privately owned, commercial courts, more expensive in the winter and during prime time, in Manhattan include: Crosstown Tennis, 14 W. 31st St (tel: 947–5780); East Side Tennis Ltd, 177 E. 84th St (tel: 472–9114); Gramercy Tennis and Racquetball Club, 708 Sixth Ave near 23rd St (tel: 691–0110); Manhattan Plaza Racquet Club, 450 W. 43rd St (tel: 594–0554); Randalls Island Indoor Tennis, Parks Dept Field House, Randalls Island (tel: 534–4845); Tennis Club Grand Central in Grand Central Terminal (tel: 867–3841); Wall Street Racquet Club, Wall St at the East River (tel: 952–0760). Be sure to call first to check prices and make reservations.

Courts in the outer boroughs are considerably less expensive. The most famous facility is the U.S.T.A. National Tennis Center, Flushing Meadows (tel: 592–8000) where the national championships are played.

Swimming: The Parks Dept operates a number of city pools, indoor and outdoor, and while inexpensive they can often be very crowded. Many are located in poorer neighbourhoods for the benefit of local residents. Among the more appealing are the John Jay Pool on York Ave and 77th St near the East River (tel: 397–3159) and the East 23rd St Pool at First Ave and the F.D.R. Drive (tel: 397–3184).

Two YMCAs with fine recreational facilities are the Westside Y at 5 W. 63rd St (tel: 787–4400) with pools, a running track, exercise rooms, handball, squash, and racquetball courts, and a sauna, and the Vanderbilt YMCA, 224 E. 47th St between Second and Third Aves (tel: 755–2410), also with a pool, gym, and sauna.

Beaches. New York is not known for its beaches but there are several within striking distance. Of the city public beaches probably the nicest is *Manhattan Beach* in Brooklyn, just E. of Coney Island.

PUBLIC TRANSPORTATION: Take the Sixth Ave. IND (D train) to the Sheepshead Bay stop and transfer to the B1 bus E. to Manhattan Beach. Or walk from the subway stop. Changing rooms and toilets at Oriental Blvd. Tel: 965–6589.

Coney Island and *Orchard Beach* are also accessible by public transportation but are less attractive: for directions check under the main entries.

Across Jamaica Bay is JACOB RIIS PARK, part of the Gateway National Recreation Area and operated by the National Park Service, a definite advantage.

PUBLIC TRANSPORTATION: Take the IND Far Rockaway line (A train) to Broad Channel; change to the Rockaway Park A train and get off at Beach 116th St, the last stop. From here either hike E. to the park (about a 15 minute walk) or take the Q22 bus.

CAR: Take the Belt Parkway east to the Flatbush Ave South exit and continue across the Marine Parkway (Gil Hodges) Bridge to the park. Large parking lot (fee).

The beach is over a mile long and is frequented in various areas by family groups, homosexuals, and teenagers or young adults. In the easternmost bays there is some nude sunbathing.

Further out on Long Island is JONES BEACH STATE PARK, Wantagh, probably the best public beach in the U.S.; tel: (516) 785–1660, with a 5$^{1}/_2$ mile beach, boardwalk, a pool, refreshment stands, toilet facilities, rental boats, and athletic fields.

PUBLIC TRANSPORTATION: The Long Island Rail Road offers round-trip train-bus service during the summer from Penn Station with a change to the bus at Freeport (tel: 739–4200 for further information). The last shuttle bus leaves Jones Beach at 12.30 a.m. Also available in the summer are buses from the Port Authority Bus Terminal (41st St and Eighth Ave) which run more or less continuously on weekday mornings from 9.30 to 11 a.m. and from 8.00 to 9.30 on weekend mornings (tel: 564–8484).

BY CAR: Take the Long Island Expwy or the Southern State Pkwy to the Meadowbrook State Pkwy and follow the signs to the parking lots. Go early in the day to avoid traffic jams and waits at the parking lots which are closed when filled.

During the summer the Jones Beach Marine Theater offers evening performances of Broadway musicals and family entertainment.

Gardens. Contrary to the popular opinion that New York is completely surfaced with unrelieved expanses of asphalt, several lovely gardens flourish within the city limits. Most impressive are the *Brooklyn Botanic Garden* and the *New York Botanical Garden* in the Bronx, both worth the attention of anyone interested in flora. Other gardens are the *Conservatory Gardens* in Central Park off Fifth Ave at 105th St with seasonal plantings, the *Queens Botanical Garden* in Flushing, and the gardens at the *Wave Hill Center for Environmental Studies* in Riverdale. The *Cloisters*, the medieval branch of the Metropolitan Museum of Art, has arcaded walks leading around thoughtfully planted central courtyards as well as landscaped grounds (at their best in spring and autumn). The *Bartow-Pell Mansion* in Pelham Bay Park (Bronx) is maintained by the International Garden Club and has a well-kept garden with a fine view of the sound. Smaller gardens are the biblical garden at the *Cathedral of Saint John the Divine*, the plantings at the *Abigail Adams Smith House* and the *Morris-Jumel Mansion*, and the *Channel Gardens* at Rockefeller Center with seasonal plantings.

Specialised Museums: The following list groups museums by content. Check 'The New York Times', 'New York' or 'The New Yorker' magazines for changing exhibitions of particular interest.

American 18–19C Painting	City Hall, the Governors' Room; Metropolitan Museum of Art; Museum of the City of New York; New-York Historical Society; Brooklyn Museum
Architecture	Museum of Modern Art (collection shown in changing exhibits); Urban Center; Brooklyn Museum (architectural ornaments); Institute for Art and Urban Resources: P.S. 1 (Queens).
Bibles	Bible House; Interchurch Center.
Black Art and Culture	African-American Institute; Schomburg Center for Research in Black Culture (changing exhibits); Studio Museum in Harlem; New Muse Community Museum (Brooklyn).
Books and Manuscripts	Grolier Club; New York Public Library; Pierpont Morgan Library.
Ceramics	American Craft Museum (changing exhibitions); Asia Society Galleries; Cooper-Hewitt Museum; Frick Collection; Hispanic Society of America; Metropolitan Museum of Art; Brooklyn Museum.
Coins, Medals	American Numismatic Society

Costume	Fashion Institute of Technology; Metropolitan Museum of Art; Brooklyn Museum.
Crafts	American Craft Museum I and II; American Museum of Natural History; Cooper-Hewitt Museum; Museum of American Folk Art; Museum of the American Indian.
Decorative Arts	American Craft Museum I and II; Cooper-Hewitt Museum; Metropolitan Museum of Art; Museum of the City of New York; Museum of Modern Art; New-York Historical Society; Brooklyn Museum.
Ethnic Exhibits	African-American Institute; Afro-Arts Cultural Centre, Inc.; American Museum of Immigration; American Museum of Natural History; Asia Society Gallery; Black Fashion Museum; Center for Inter-American Relations; China House Gallery; French Institute/Alliance Française; Hispanic Society of America; INTAR Latin American Gallery; Japan House; Jewish Museum; Korean Cultural Service; El Museo del Barrio; Museum of the American Indian; Puerto Rican Museum for the Arts; Ukrainian Institute of America; Ukrainian Museum; Brooklyn Museum.
European Art 15–19C	Frick Collection; Metropolitan Museum of Art; Brooklyn Museum.
Fire-fighting	Fire House; Museum of the City of New York; New-York Historical Society.
Furniture	Abigail Adams Smith House; City Hall, The Governor's Room; Fraunces Tavern Museum; Frick Collection; Metropolitan Museum of Art; Morris-Jumel Mansion; Museum of the City of New York; New-York Historical Society; Old Merchant's House; Theodore Roosevelt Birthplace; Bartow-Pell Mansion (Bronx); Brooklyn Museum; Bowne House (Queens).
Graphic Arts	American Institute of Graphic Arts; Metropolitan Museum of Art; Museum of Modern Art.
Jewish Art and History	Educational Alliance; Jewish Museum; Yeshiva University Museum; YIVO Institute for Jewish Research; Ferkauf Museum at International Synagogue (Queens).
Maritime History	Museum of the City of New York; South Street Seaport Museum; City Island Historical Nautical Museum (Bronx); Harbor Defense Museum (Brooklyn); National Maritime Historical Society/Fulton Ferry Museum (Brooklyn).
Medieval Art	The Cloisters; Metropolitan Museum of Art.
Modern Art	Guggenheim Museum; Metropolitan Museum of Art; Museum of Modern Art; Whitney Museum of American Art.

Musical Instruments	Metropolitan Museum of Art; Songwriters' Hall of Fame.
New York History	Abigail Adams Smith Museum; Castle Clinton National Monument; Dyckman House; Federal Hall National Memorial; Fraunces Tavern Museum; Morris-Jumel Mansion; Museum of the City of New York; New-York Historical Society; Old Merchant's House; Theodore Roosevelt Birthplace; South Street Seaport Museum; Museum of Bronx History/Valentine Varian House (Bronx); Van Cortlandt Mansion and Museum (Bronx); Lefferts Homestead (Brooklyn); Long Island Historical Society (Brooklyn); New Muse Community Museum (Brooklyn); New York Public Transit Exhibit (Brooklyn); Bowne House (Queens); Flushing Quaker Meeting House (Queens); King Manor (Queens); Kingsland House (Queens); Queens Museum; Conference House (Staten Island); Richmondtown Restoration (Staten Island).
Oriental Art	Asia Society Galleries; China House Gallery; Japan House Gallery; Korean Cultural Service; Metropolitan Museum of Art; Brooklyn Museum; Jacques Marchais Center of Tibetan Art (Staten Island).
Period Rooms	Abigail Adams Smith House; Fraunces Tavern Museum; Frick Collection; Metropolitan Museum of Art; Morris-Jumel Mansion; Museum of the City of New York; New-York Historical Society; Old Merchant's House; Theodore Roosevelt Birthplace; Van Cortlandt Mansion (Bronx); Lefferts Homestead (Brooklyn); Brooklyn Museum; Bowne House (Queens).
Photography	French Cultural Service; International Center of Photography; Midtown Y Gallery; Museum of Modern Art.
Science and Technology	American Museum of Natural History; Con Edison Energy Museum; Manhattan Laboratory Museum (children), Museum of Holography; New York Hall of Science (Queens)
Television	The Kitchen (video art); Museum of Broadcasting.
Theatre	Library and Museum of the Performing Arts; Museum of the City of New York (changing exhibitions); Theater Museum.
Toys	Aunt Len's Doll and Toy Museum; Museum of the City of New York.

Calendar of Events

For daily schedule, further information, rain dates, etc tel: 755–4100. The following calendar gives a general picture of events that recur from year to year, though there are variations in times of celebrating some holidays, opening exhibitions, and other activities. The Friday 'New York Times' carries schedules of weekend events; the New York Convention and Visitors' Bureau at Columbus Circle and the Visitors' Information Center in Times Square have quarterly calendars with detailed listings and information about parades.

JANUARY
Conventions and shows held annually in January include the *National Boat Show* and the *Greater New York Auto Show*, both currently held at the N.Y. Coliseum but scheduled to move to the new Convention Center near 30th St after its completion.
Masters Tennis (men), Madison Square Garden, tel: 564–4400.
Winter Antiques Show, Seventh Regiment Armory, Park Ave at 67th St, tel: 288–0200.
Chinese New Year, celebrated in Chinatown at the end of Jan or early Feb. Parades, demonstrations of martial arts, fireworks on New Year's eve (11.30–1 a.m.), banquets in Chinese restaurants. For information call the Chinese Community Center, tel: 397–8222.
Ice Capades at Madison Square Garden.

FEBRUARY
National Antiques Show at Madison Square Garden.
New York City Opera season opens, late Feb, at New York State Theater, Lincoln Center.
Westminster Kennel Club Dog Show, Madison Square Garden.
Washington's Birthday sales at stores in all boroughs, around 22 Feb.
Track and field events at Madison Square Garden; Wanamaker Millrose Games, A.A.U. National Track and Field Championships.

MARCH
Championships of women's winter tennis circuit, Madison Square Garden.
St. Patrick's Day Parade, 17 March, Fifth Ave, from 44th–86th St. Bands, marchers from Ireland and elsewhere. This year the police successfully curbed the excessive conviviality of former years. Reviewing stand at 65th St.
Ringling Bros. and Barnum & Bailey Circus, Madison Square Garden. The day before the first performance a *Parade of Circus Animals* (10 a.m.) marches from the railroad siding, Twelfth Ave and 34th St to the Garden.
Greek National Day Parade, 25 March or a Sat near that date, Fifth Ave from 59th to 79th St. School bands, floats, Greek music.

APRIL
Circle Line boat trips begin season (until Nov) circumnavigating Manhattan.
Easter floral displays at Channel Gardens in Rockefeller Center and at Brooklyn Botanic Garden and New York Botanical Garden in the Bronx.

Easter Parade on Fifth Ave at noon Easter Sunday; informal parade near St. Patrick's Cathedral.

Baseball season opens for Yankees and Mets.

New York City Ballet spring season opens, State Theater in Lincoln Center, through June.

Ellis Island tours begin.

Hudson River Day Line begins excursion to Bear Mountain State Park and the U.S. Military Academy at West Point; Pier 81, foot of W. 41st St, tel: 279–5151.

MAY

Bronx Day, Van Cortlandt Park.

Brooklyn Heights Promenade Art Show, on the Esplanade from Remsen to Clark St, one weekend early or mid-May.

Ninth Avenue International Festival, Ninth Ave from 37th–57th Sts, 11 a.m.–7 p.m. A large street festival celebrating ethnic groups living on or near Ninth Ave. Food—Italian, Greek, Philippine, Chinese, etc—and entertainment. Two-day festival usually in mid-May.

Norwegian Constitution Day Parade on weekend nearest 17 May in Bay Ridge (Brooklyn) from 67th–90th St.

Belmont Racetrack opens.

Spring flower show at the World Trade Center.

Armed Forces Day Parade, Fifth Ave, 96th–62nd Sts, usually the third Sun in May.

Beaches open officially on Memorial Day, last weekend in May.

American Ballet Theater at the Metropolitan Opera, Lincoln Center, early May through June.

Washington Square Outdoor Art Show, Greenwich Village, weekends, noon-sundown, late May to early June.

JUNE

Metropolitan Opera performances in parks, all five boroughs.

Summergarden concerts at the Museum of Modern Art, Fri and Sat evenings in the sculpture garden.

Rose shows at the New York Botanical Garden in the Bronx and the Queens Botanical Garden in Flushing.

Salute to Israel Parade, Fifth Ave, 57th–86th St.

Feast of St. Anthony of Padua, Sullivan St south of Houston St in Little Italy, early to mid-June. Italian street fair, 6 p.m. to midnight. Procession with image of the saint carried through the streets.

Jewish Festival on Lower East Side, E. Broadway between Rutgers and Grand Sts, 10 a.m.–9 p.m., usually the second Sun.

Belmont Stakes at Belmont Racetrack, Elmont, Long Island.

Guggenheim Concerts, outdoor band concerts in Damrosch Park, Lincoln Center, evenings 8–10, late June through Aug, several nights a week.

Puerto Rican Day Parade, Fifth Ave, 44th–86th St, usually first Sun in June, 11 a.m.

Shakespeare in the Park, Delacorte Theater, Central Park at 81st St. Tickets distributed 6.15 day of performance, one per person, line forms in early afternoon, tel: 535–5630.

Newport Jazz Festival in New York. Late June; famous jazz festival with performances in various halls, tel: 787–2020.

Museum Mile Celebration, Fifth Ave, between 82nd and 105th Sts. Museums stay open late, special exhibitions and events.

52nd Street Festival, Sun in mid-June. Street fair with crafts, entertainment, food, jazz bands.

St. Paolino Festival, N. 8th St and Havemeyer St in Williamsburg, Brooklyn. Italian street festival, late June–mid-July. Procession to Our Lady of Mt Carmel Church with men carrying a large monument.

JULY

American Crafts Festival, Lincoln Center Plaza, 11 a.m.–9 p.m., usually the first two weekends.

Brooklyn Arts and Culture Association (BACA) Theater-in-the-Back, at the Brooklyn Museum; performances Sat evenings and Sun afternoon and evening, July and Aug, tel: 783–4469.

Summer Festival at Sailors Snug Harbor Cultural Center, Staten Island; concerts, exhibitions, tel: 448–2500.

Harbor Festival celebrations, end of June through July 4. Events at Battery Park, in the rivers, etc. Parade of ships in the Hudson River, band concerts, hot air balloons, etc. Festival climaxes on 4 July with a half-hour spectacle of fireworks provided by Macy's from barges in the Hudson River, 79th–125th Sts, 9 p.m.

Mostly Mozart Festival at Lincoln Center, Avery Fisher Hall.

Feast of Our Lady of Pompeii in Greenwich Village on Carmine St near Bleecker St, evenings for about a week in late July.

AUGUST

New York Philharmonic concerts in major parks.

Harlem Week, usually the last week in Aug. Parades, art exhibitions, dance contests, sports clinics taught by prominent athletes, tours of Harlem landmarks.

Lincoln Center Out-of-Doors, summer events through the end of the month.

Belmont Racetrack autumn season, end of Aug to mid-Oct.

SEPTEMBER

Washington Square Outdoor Art Show, usually the first two or three weekends in Sept, noon–sundown.

Richmond County Fair, early Sept, grounds of Richmondtown Restoration, Staten Island, 10–5; only true county fair in the city.

Governor's Cup Race, sailing boat race, Battery Park to Verrazano Bridge and back; Sat in mid-Sept, noon–4, tel: 930–0281.

West Indian-American Day Carnivale in Brooklyn. Labor Day weekend with parade on Mon, 11–6 along Eastern Parkway from Utica Ave to the Brooklyn Museum. Floats, extravagant costumes, West Indian music, dancing in the streets, food.

Baseball season ends (unless World Series is played in New York). *Football season* begins.

Feast of San Gennaro in Little Italy on Mulberry St between Houston St and Washington Square Park, noon–midnight, about 10 days in mid-Sept. Street fair, food and games, procession with saint's image carried through the streets, tel: 226–9546.

U.S. Open Tennis Championships at National Tennis Center in Queens. Afternoon and evening matches, early Sept.

Lincoln Center New York Film Festival, late Sept to early Oct, tel: 369–1911.

Steuben Day Parade, third weekend, Sat or Sun, Fifth Ave, 61st–86th St, noon. Bands, floats, costumed folk dancers march to honour Baron von Steuben who assisted Washington during the Revolutionary War.

Metropolitan Opera and *New York City Opera seasons* open, Lincoln Center. Concert season opens at major halls.

Atlantic Antic, Atlantic Ave from the East River to Flatbush Ave in Brooklyn, Sun in late Sept, 11 a.m.–6 p.m. Arab bazaar with food, music, belly dancing, sometimes camel rides.

OCTOBER

Ice skating begins at Rockefeller Center, late in month or early Nov.

New York Rangers ice hockey season begins, Madison Square Garden.

New York Knicks basketball season begins, Madison Square Garden.

Mayor's Schooner Cup Race, South Street Seaport, usually first Sat, 10 a.m., tel: 766–9078.

Pulaski Day Parade, Fifth Ave, 26th–52nd Sts, 5 Oct or nearest Sun, noon.

Hispanic American Day Parade, Fifth Ave, 44th–79th Sts, Sun mid-month, noon.

Columbus Day Parade, Fifth Ave, 44th–86th St, 11.30 a.m., with Italian-American groups, bands.

New York Marathon, 26·2 mile race through the five boroughs, third Sun in Oct. Begins at Verrazano Bridge, 10.30 a.m., and finishes at Tavern-on-the-Green in Central Park.

Aqueduct Racetrack autumn season, Oct–Dec, Aqueduct Racetrack, Ozone Park, Queens.

NOVEMBER

National Horse Show, Madison Square Garden, early in month.

New York City Ballet autumn season opens, State Theater, Lincoln Center.

Thanksgiving Parade, Thanksgiving Day (last Thurs in month), Central Park West from 77th–59th St, down Broadway to Macy's at 34th St. Floats, bands, giant helium-filled balloons representing cartoon characters, etc. When the parade reaches Macy's Santa Claus arrives, opening the Christmas season.

Radio City Music Hall Christmas spectacular begins, tel: 246–4600.

Hayden Planetarium Christmas show begins, tel: 873–8828.

DECEMBER

Holiday celebrations include *Christmas tree lightings* at Rockefeller Center, City Hall, other borough halls. Consult the newspaper for schedule. *Chanuka candle lighting* at City Hall. *Carol singing* along Fifth and Park Aves. *Brass choirs* at Rockefeller Center.

Christmas windows along Fifth Ave. Especially: B. Altman & Co. (34th St), Lord & Taylor (39th St), Saks Fifth Ave (50th St), F.A.O. Schwartz (58th St). The tree and illuminated angels in the Channel Gardens at Rockefeller Center attract large crowds, especially at night. Office buildings on Park Ave below 50th St often have lavish displays.

Richmondtown Christmas festival at Richmondtown Restoration, Staten Island, early Dec, tel: 351–9414.

Yuletide Festival, Wave Hill in the Bronx, early Dec, tel: 549–2055.

Large Christmas tree with 18C Neapolitan carved angels and crèche figures in Medieval Sculpture Hall, Metropolitan Museum of Art. *Special holiday displays* usually at the Cloisters, Jewish Museum, Museum of the City of New York.

New Year's Eve in Times Square, recommended for those undaunted by celebratory crowds. At midnight a Big Apple, formerly a ball, descends from the former Times Tower. In Central Park there are *midnight fireworks* and a *midnight run* sponsored by the New York Roadrunners Club.

Children's Activities

Museums. For complete information, hours, etc, check the main entry listed in the index.

American Museum of Natural History, Central Park West at 79th St. Animal dioramas, anthropology exhibits, films most Sats at 2 p.m., Discovery Room. Tel: 873–4225.

Brooklyn Children's Museum, 145 Brooklyn Ave in the Crown Heights section of Brooklyn. Fine children's museum with participatory exhibits on technology, natural history, human culture. Tel: 735–4432.

Hayden Planetarium, Central Park West at 81st St. Skyshows weekday and weekend afternoons; model of solar system, slide presentation, blacklit gallery. Tel: 873–8828.

Manhattan Laboratory Museum, 314 W. 54th St. Children's museum with participatory exhibits on art, nature, technology; special events. Tel: 765–5904.

Metropolitan Museum of Art Junior Museum, Fifth Ave at 81st St on the ground floor of the Metropolitan. Gallery talks, workshops, special exhibitions geared to introducing young people (ages 5–15) to art. For schedule and further information tel: 879–5500, ext. 3932.

Museum of the American Indian, Broadway at 155th St. Largest collection of Indian artifacts in the world. Tel: 283–2420.

Museum of the City of New York, Fifth Ave near 103rd St. Dioramas of early New York, multi-media exhibition, dolls, toys, dollhouses. Tel: 534–1672.

New York Fire House, 258 Spring Street. Scheduled to open in December 1982. Display of antique fire fighting equipment, educational programme on fire safety. The new museum will combine the present collection at the Home Insurance Company with that of the city fire department formerly housed at 104 Duane St.

New York-Historical Society, 170 Central Park West at 77th St. Early American toys, carriages, sleighs, fire trucks, period rooms. Tel: 873–3400.

New York Hall of Science, 111th St and 48th Ave in Flushing Meadows-Corona Park, Queens. Closed for renovation until 1983. Former displays have included a Space Park with full-scale models of U.S. rockets and spacecraft, scale-model of the city's water and sewage disposal systems, model of Williamsburg Bridge, exhibits on astronomy, amateur radio, the metric system, weather. Expanded museum will include a planetarium. Tel: 669–9400.

Staten Island Children's Museum, 15 Beach St. Changing participatory exhibits on the arts, humanities, science; tours, workshops, Sun performances. Tel: 273–2060.

Ukrainian Museum, Second Ave at 12th St. Workshops on egg decoration and other crafts. Call for schedule: 228–0110.

Just opened (4 July, 1982) is the decommissioned aircraft carrier 'Intrepid', refitted as a museum. Pier 86 on the Hudson River at 46th St. Tel: 245–0072.

Aquarium and Zoos

New York Aquarium, Boardwalk and West 8th St, Coney Island, Brooklyn. Whales, seals, penguins, shark tank, electric eel shows; dolphin and sea lion shows daily, May–Sept. Tel: 266–8500.

Barrett Park Zoo (Staten Island Zoo), 613 Broadway near Clove Rd, Staten Island. Zoo set in an 8-acre park, famous for its reptiles, also offering Children's Zoo with farm animals, colony of vampire bats. Tel: 442–3100.

Bronx Zoo, officially the New York Zoological Park, Southern Blvd and 185th St, Bronx. Large (252-acre), handsomely maintained zoo with more than 3000 animals, many in open expanses of land, fine Children's Zoo, monorail ride, cable car ride, World of Birds. Tel: 220–5100.

Central Park Zoo, Fifth Ave at 64th St. Small (5-acre) urban zoo with penguins, polar bears, sea lions, monkeys, red pandas. It is being redesigned with glassed and moated enclosures. Tel: 360–8213.

Prospect Park Zoo, Flatbush Ave and Empire Blvd, Brooklyn. Small zoo with camels, zebras, bears, lions; Children's Zoo. Tel: 965–6560.

Queens Zoo, 111th St and 56th Ave, Flushing Meadow-Corona Park, Queens. Small-scale modern zoo, pleasant if you are in the neighbourhood.

Tall Buildings with Observation Decks. For further information, hours, prices, etc. check main entry in index.

World Trade Center, Two World Trade Center (Church St, N. of Liberty St). Enclosed deck on 107th floor; world's highest open air-viewing platform, open weather permitting. Tel: 466–7377.

Empire State Building, Fifth Ave at 34th St, Observatories on 86th and 102nd floors. Tel: 736–3100. On the concourse level, one floor down from the main lobby is the Guinness World Records Exhibit Hall, with video presentations, models, replicas, photographs, of amusing and freakish world records. Tel: 947–2335.

Rockefeller Center Observation Roof in the RCA Building, 50th St just W. of the skating rink. Tel: 489–2947.

Boat Rides

Statue of Liberty Ferry, Battery Park to Liberty Island. Often crowded, go early. For information tel: 732–1236; ticket office, tel: 269–5755.

Staten Island Ferry, from South Ferry. Good views of the Statue of Liberty, Lower Manhattan skyline, Governors Island, harbour traffic. Ride is about half an hour each way.

Circle Line, Pier 83, foot of W. 43rd St at Hudson River. Three-hour tour (perhaps too long for smaller children) around Manhattan, April–Nov. Tel: 563–3200.

Puppet Shows and Story Hours: Children's Entertainment

Barnes & Noble, downtown store, Fifth Ave at 18th St, free puppet shows Sun, 11 a.m. and 12.30 p.m. Tel: 675–5500.

Big Apple Circus, 1 East 104th St, shows June–Sept. Tel: 369–5110.

Bill Baird's Marionette Theater, 59 Barrow St in Greenwich Village. Tel: 989–7060.

F.A.O. Schwartz, Fifth Ave at 58th St, puppet shows of fairy tales and original stories, Mon–Fri, 2.30 p.m. Free. Tel: 644–9400.

New York Public Library, branch libraries, including the *Donnell Library Center*, 20 W. 53rd St, (tel: 621–0636) and the *Library for the Performing Arts at Lincoln Center*, 111 Amsterdam Ave at 65th St (tel: 870–1633), have story hours, puppet shows, filmstrips, often on Sat. Call ahead for schedule.

Restaurants for Children. New York has branches of the major fast food chains: McDonald's, Burger King, Steak and Brew, Chock Full O'Nuts, and Zum Zum, a chain specialising in Germanic sandwiches, wursts and sauerkraut. There is a branch of Nathan's Famous (hot dogs and other fast food) at Broadway and 43rd St. There is still one Automat in New York, at 42nd St and Second Ave, not outstanding for the food but for the way it is dispensed. Taco Rico, a Mexican fast food chain, has branches around the city as does the Magic Pan, whose shops feature omelettes and crêpes. The Autopub in the General Motors Building on Fifth Ave between 58th–59th Sts has booths disguised as antique cars (the food is expensive for what you get) and caters to a youthful clientele.

Useful Information

Emergency telephone numbers

Fire, police, ambulance	911
Dentist	679–3966
after 8 p.m.	679–4172
Poison Control Center	764–7667
Rape Crisis Center	233–3000
Crime Victims' Hotline	577–7777
Physician	
Doctors' Referral Service	745–5900
Doctors on Call	238–2100
House Calls	238–1800

Useful telephone numbers.

Time	976–1616
Weather	976–1212
Parks and special events	755–4100
New York Report (recorded information on daily events)	999–1111
Travel information (buses and subways)	330–1234
Traffic report	976–2323
All-night pharmacy, Kaufman's, Lexington Ave at 50th St	755–2266.

Telephones. Public pay telephones take nickels, dimes, and quarters. Deposit 10¢ for a local call, listen for the dialling tone, and dial the seven digit number. The area code for all boroughs is 212 but should not be dialled from telephones within New York City. If you expect to be talking long and don't have much change, tell the person you are calling the number of your pay phone so that he or she may return the call when your time has elapsed.

To make a direct long distance call within the U.S., dial the digit '1' + the three digit area code + the local number. To dial an operator assisted long distance call (credit card calls, collect calls), dial 0 + the area code + the local number: the operator will come on the line.

To reach the operator, dial 0. For information in Manhattan, dial 411 from Manhattan telephones. For information in the other boroughs (except the Bronx, dial 411) from Manhattan, dial 555–1212. For information throughout the U.S. dial 1 + area code + 555–1212.

The city emergency number is 911.

Daylight Saving Time. During the summer months from the last Sun in April to the last Sat in Oct, clocks are advanced by one hour. Eastern Standard Time is five hours earlier than Greenwich Mean Time.

Business hours in offices are usually 9–5, Mon–Fri. Most department stores and speciality shops open at 10, though pharmacies, food stores, etc open earlier. Many larger stores are open until 9 on Thurs evenings. Banks are open regularly 9–3, sometimes later one day a week, and sometimes on Sat a.m. from 9–12.

Holidays. Legal holidays are New Year's Day (1 Jan), Lincoln's Birthday (12 Feb), Washington's birthday (22 Feb, but celebrated on or near this date), Easter Sunday, Memorial Day (30 May, celebrated on or near this date), Independence Day (4 July,) Labor Day (first Mon in Sept), Columbus Day (12 Oct, celebrated on or near this date), Veterans' Day (11 Nov), Thanksgiving (fourth Thurs in Nov), Christmas (25 Dec). Some holidays are moved to a Mon or Fri to make a three-day weekend. Many businesses are closed on the major Jewish holidays, Passover (March or April), Rosh Hashanah (Sept or Oct) and Yom Kippur (Sept or Oct). Some shops are open on Sun.

Money. U.S. currency follows the decimal system with one dollar equal in value to 100 cents. Coins presently in circulation are the penny (1¢), a copper-coloured coin, and the silver-coloured nickel (5¢), dime (10¢), quarter (25¢), half dollar (50¢), and Susan B. Anthony dollar, a coin about the size of a quarter, recently issued and not very popular. Paper notes come in denominations of one, two (uncommon), five, ten, twenty, fifty, and one hundred dollars.

Post offices. The two main post offices in New York are the General Post Office on Eighth Ave at 33rd St (open weekdays 8–6, Sat 8–2, and Sun 9–5) and the Grand Central Post Office, Lexington Ave at 45th St (open weekdays 8–6, Sat 8–2, and Sun 11–3). Branch post offices are located throughout the city; look in the telephone book under United States Government, Postal Information; they are generally open from 9–5 on weekdays, and Sat mornings, 9–12. Mail boxes are on street corners; many hotels will perform postal services.

Climate. New York has a temperate climate but can be very cold in winter when the icy wind whips down the canyonlike streets and very hot in summer when heat radiates off pavements and buildings. With the exception of the subway, however, most public facilities are air-conditioned. The most pleasant seasons are late spring and autumn. The U.S. National Weather Service offers the following statistics (Celsius in parentheses):

	Ave Max. Temp.	Ave Min. Temp.	Ave Precip.
January	39° (4)	26° (−3)	2·71 in
February	40° (4)	27° (−3)	2·92
March	48° (9)	34° (1)	3·73
April	61° (16)	44° (7)	3·30
May	71° (22)	53° (12)	3·47
June	81° (27)	63° (18)	2·96
July	85° (29)	68° (20)	3·68
August	83° (28)	66° (19)	4·01
September	77° (25)	60° (16)	3·27
October	67° (19)	51° (11)	2·85
November	54° (12)	41° (5)	3·76
December	41° (5)	30° (−1)	3·53

Clothing. Most better restaurants expect men to wear jackets and ties, though many will lend them to unprepared visitors. Raincoats are useful in spring and autumn. Layered clothing is most appropriate in summer when air conditioning can be chilly or in winter when some restaurants and public places are overheated. Short skirts and shorts on women may elicit unpleasant remarks. Wear comfortable shoes for touring since there is little respite from the hard pavements.

Tipping. In restaurants the usual tip is 15% (twice the tax added at the end of the bill), though more is expected for superior service. Give 50¢ to coat check attendants except where signs forbid tipping. Room service waiters and taxi drivers should also receive at least 15% (no less than 25¢ for cab drivers); bellhops will expect 50¢–$1 per suitcase at hotels depending on the suitcase and the hotel. Porters in airports expect $1, more if you have large amounts of luggage.

Alcoholic beverages. Liquor stores are open daily except Sun, holidays, and election days when the polls are open. Beer is sold in grocery stores and delicatessens except on Sun mornings. The legal drinking age is 18. Bars may remain open until 4 a.m.

Toilets are not easy to find in New York. Public facilities are often dirty and unattended. Restaurants are usually unwilling to let non-customers use their restrooms. Try department stores, museums (especially free ones), some hotel lobbies, some major tourist attractions (Rockefeller Center in the RCA Building, United Nations, etc), train and bus stations.

Consulates and Foreign Government Information Services.
Australia, 636 Fifth Ave (tel: 245–4000).
Belgium, 50 Rockefeller Plaza (tel: 586–5110).
Canada, 1251 Sixth Ave (Ave of the Americas; tel: 586–2400).
France, 934 Fifth Ave (tel: 535–0100).
Irish Republic, 580 Fifth Ave (tel: 245–1010).
Italy, 690 Park Ave (tel: 737–9100).
Netherlands, 1 Rockefeller Plaza, (tel: 246–1429).
New Zealand, 630 Fifth Ave (tel: 586–0600).
South Africa, 425 Park Ave (tel: 838–1700).
Switzerland, 444 Madison Ave (tel: 758–2560).
United Kingdom, 845 Third Ave (tel: 752–5747).
West Germany, 460 Park Ave (tel: 940–9200).

Shopping is surely a major tourist attraction and, for some New Yorkers, a hobby. Department stores are known for their wide range of goods and services and offer convenience and ambience but not bargain prices. The most famous are: *Bloomingdale's*, 59th St at Lexington Ave, *Saks Fifth Ave* at 50th St, *Bonwit Teller*, 57th St between Fifth and Madison Aves, *Henri Bendel*, 57th St between Fifth and Sixth Aves; *Lord & Taylor*, Fifth Ave at 39th St; *Bergdorf*

Goodman, 57th St and Fifth Ave, and *B. Altman*, Fifth Ave at 35th St. Less luxurious are *Alexander's*, Lexington Ave between 58th–59th Sts; *Orbach's*, 34th St between Fifth and Sixth Aves; and *Macy's*, Herald Square, 34th St at the intersection of Broadway and Sixth Ave.

Most shopping areas are in midtown though some outlying districts are known for special commodities. Along Fifth Ave from about 44th to 59th St are boutiques, jewellery stores, shoe stores, and other luxury establishments interspersed with tourist traps selling electronic goods, oriental rugs, cameras, and 'artworks'. Although Fifth Ave around 34th St is no longer the fashionable center it formerly was, several fine stores—*B. Altman*, *Lord & Taylor*, and *W. & J. Sloane & Co.* (furniture), have chosen to remain there. Boutiques line Madison Ave from about 44th St through the 70s and into the 80s (high fashion clothes, books, shoes, accessories, fancy foods), with *Brooks Brothers* (44th St), a bastion of conservative haberdashery, as the southernmost outpost of the strip. Lexington and Third Aves also have shops and boutiques though they are not generally as elegant as those lining Fifth and Madison Aves. Dealers in musical instruments can be found on 45th St between Sixth and Seventh Aves and also on 48th St in the same crosstown block. There are antique (and junk) shops in the 30s on Second and Third Aves as well as on Columbus Ave in the low 80s. Camera stores, notably *Willoughby's* at 110 W. 32nd St, are clustered in the low 30s W. of Seventh Ave while shops with notions (haberdashery), trimmings, millinery supplies, and similar paraphernalia can be found in the garment district (mid-to high 30s around Seventh Ave).

While 47th St just of Fifth Ave is 'Diamond Street', the premier jewellers are on Fifth Ave itself: *Tiffany's* at 57th St, *Harry Winston* at 56th St; *Van Cleef & Arpels* in Bergdorf Goodman (57th St), and *Cartier's* at 52nd St.

Visitors interested in the other end of the shopping spectrum should try the Lower East Side where women's clothing, shoes, handbags, fabrics, and similar articles cost considerably less than they do uptown; try bargaining to lower the price even more. Since most merchants are Jewish, most shops close on Sat but remain open on Sun, the busiest day. Orchard St, with its outdoor displays of goods, is the center of the district. Greenwich Village and SoHo both have boutiques with fashionable and occasionally outrageous clothing, and SoHo offers a concentration of art galleries as well.

Most stores are open from 10 to around 6 daily and may remain open later one evening. The best source of information about shopping is the Yellow Pages of the telephone book which comes in two versions, one for consumers and one for businesses. 'New York' magazine publishes a weekly column with notices of special sales and events.

Bookstores. Among the larger chain stores are *Barnes and Noble*, with two branches on Fifth Ave, one at 18th St and an uptown store near 48th St (tel: 255–8100); *Brentano's*, 586 Fifth Ave near 47th St (757–8600); *Doubleday Bookshop*, 724 Fifth Ave near 56th St (397–0550), and *B. Dalton*, 666 Fifth Ave at 52nd St (247–1740). *Rizzoli International Bookstore*, 712 Fifth Ave near 56th St (397–3705) and *Scribner's*, 597 Fifth Ave near 48th St (486–4070) with its landmark facade and elegant interior are less harried and less geared to the best seller trade than the chain stores. The *Gotham*

Book Mart, 41 W. 47th St (757–0367) is a literary landmark (see p264), well-stocked with poetry and books from small presses. *Urban Center Books*, 457 Madison Ave near 51st St (935–3595) in the N. wing of the Villard Houses, has a fine collection on architecture and urban design.

Specialised shops away from the Fifth Avenue book district: *Argosy*, 116 E. 59th St near Madison Ave (753–4455), old maps, Americana, used books, and first editions; *The Ballet Shop*, 1887 Broadway near 63rd St (581–7990); *Batcave Comic Book Store*, 351 E. 82nd St between Second and First Aves (570–2453); *Books & Co.*, 939 Madison Ave near 74th St (737–1450); *China Books & Periodicals*, 125 Fifth Ave at 18th St (677–2650), books from the People's Republic; *The Complete Traveller*, 199 Madison Ave at 35th St (679–4339) and *Traveller's Bookstore*, 22 W. 52nd St (664–0995), guidebooks and maps; *Djuna Books*, 154 W. 10th St between Sixth and Seventh Aves (242–3642), books for, about, and by women; *Drama Book Shop*, 150 W. 52nd St between Sixth and Seventh Aves (582–1037), *Eeyore's Books for Children*, 2252 Broadway near 80th St (362–0634); *Four Continent Book Corp.*, 149 Fifth Ave at 21st St (533–0250), Russian and other imported books; *Hacker Art Books*, 54 W. 57th St (757–1450); *Julius Levin*, 1391 Madison Ave at 97th St (289–3167), medical books; *Madison Ave Bookshop*, 833 Madison Ave near 69th St (535–6130), a small, elegant East Side bookshop; *Mason's Bookshop*, 789 Lexington Ave near 61st St (832–8958), occult books and books on astrology; *Murder Ink*, 271 W. 87th St between Columbus and Amsterdam Aves (362–8905), or *The Mysterious Book Shop*, 129 W. 56th St W. of Sixth Ave (765–0900), books on murder, crime, espionage; *Oscar Wilde Memorial Bookshop*, 15 Christopher St near Greenwich Ave (255–8097) books by and about homosexuals; *Jaap Rietman*, 167 Spring St near Thompson St in SoHo (966–7044); *Quinion Books*, 541 Hudson St near Perry St (989–6130), cookbooks and drama books; *Sky Books International*, 48 E. 50th St (688–5086), books on aviation and military history; *Strand Bookstore*, 828 Broadway at 12th St (473–1452), thousands of used books at bargain prices; *Supersnipe Comic Book Euphorium*, 1617 Second Ave at 84th St (879–9628); *Samuel Weiser*, 740 Broadway near 8th St (777–6363), books on astrology, the occult, and oriental religions; *Witkin Gallery*, 41 E. 57th St (355–1461), photographic books; *Wittenborn Art Books*, 1018 Madison Ave near 79th St (288–1558).

Chronology

1524   Giovanni da Verrazano, working for Francis I of France, explorers New York bay and the North American coastline.

1525   Esteban Gomez explores what was probably the Hudson River for Charles V of Spain.

1609   Henry Hudson, seeking a water route to the orient for the Dutch East India Company, explores the harbour and sails upriver to the site of Albany.

1613   Adriaen Block and crew overwinter in lower Manhattan building a new ship after their first, the 'Tyger', burns.

1614   Block explores Long Island Sound, discovers Block Island, and makes the first map of Manhattan.

1624   Thirty Dutch and Walloon families sent by the Dutch West India Company settle in New Netherland, a territory reaching from the Delaware to the Connecticut River.

1625   First permanent settlement made in lower Manhattan and named New Amsterdam.

1626   Governor General Peter Minuit purchases Manhattan Island from the Indians for 60 guilders (estimated at $24).

1628   First church (Dutch Reformed) founded with arrival of its first minister.

1633   First church built at site of 39 Pearl St.

1636   Settlers Jacques Bentyn and Adrianse Bennett buy land from the Indians in Brooklyn near Gowanus Creek. Jacobus Van Corlaer buys Corlaer's Hook.

1638   First ferry line established from Fulton Ferry in Brooklyn to about Dover St in Manhattan. Earliest Manhattan land grant given to Andries Hudd in what is now Harlem.

1639   Jonas Bronck, a Dane, buys part of the Bronx from the Indians. David de Vries and others settle Staten Island, but are driven out by Indians.

1642   Religious tolerance of New Amsterdam attracts dissidents from New England including John Throgmorton (Throg's Neck) and Anne Hutchinson (Hutchinson River).

1643   Indian uprisings in New Amsterdam, New Jersey, and Staten Island; they continue intermittently until 1655.

1645   First permanent settlement in Queens at Vlisingen (Flushing).

1647   Peter Stuyvesant becomes governor.

1653   New Amsterdam receives charter establishing the municipal government. Peter Stuyvesant builds a fortified wall, river to river, at the present latitude of Wall St, to keep out the British, trading rivals of the Dutch.

1654   First permanent Jewish settlement. Asser Levy and 22 others arrive, fleeing persecution in Brazil.

1655   Flatbush Dutch Reformed Church founded, Long Island's first.

1661   First permanent settlement on Staten Island at Oude Dorp. Bowne House built in Flushing.

1664   The British capture New Amsterdam without a fight and rename it after James, Duke of York, brother of King Charles II.

1665   Thomas Willett becomes first mayor of New York.

1667 Treaty of Breda, closing a second Anglo-Dutch war, confirms Britain's possession of New Netherland.

1673 The Dutch capture New York, again without a fight, and rename it New Orange.

1674 Treaty of Westminster makes New York British once again.

1676 Canal on Broad St filled.

1682 Jews establish cemetery (still there) at Chatham Square.

1686 The Dongan Charter—first British charter—gives city a form of municipal government that remains until modern times.

1689 King James II facing rebellion abdicates and flees to France. Jacob Leisler leads uprising against the British in New York.

1693 Frederick Philipse builds Kingsbridge across Harlem River joining Manhattan Island to the mainland.

1713 First Staten Island ferry.

1725 First newspaper, the 'New-York Gazette' founded by William Bradford.

1729 First synagogue of Congregation Shearith Israel built on Beaver St.

1732 First theatre opens near present Maiden Lane.

1733 John Peter Zenger publishes the 'New-York Weekly Journal', an anti-government paper.

1734 Zenger jailed for slander and issues of his paper publicly burned.

1735 Zenger acquittal establishes freedom of the press.

1754 King's College, now Columbia University, founded near Trinity Church as city's first college.

1762 Samuel Fraunces, buys DeLancey house, opens Tavern.

1763 French and Indian War closes with Treaty of Paris, confirming English control of North America.

1765 Stamp Act. Congress meets with delegates from nine colonies in New York and denounces British policies of taxation.

1766 Stamp Act repealed in England. St. Paul's Chapel dedicated; oldest remaining church in New York. Roger Morris House built, now Morris-Jumel mansion in Harlem.

1767 Townshend Acts, named after British Chancellor of Exchequer, increase taxes and restrict colonial self-government. Although repealed three years later they fuel anti-British sentiment.

1776 Declaration of Independence marks beginning of Revolutionary War. British occupy Brooklyn after Battle of Long Island and take control of all Manhattan by November 17.

1783 Treaty of Paris concludes Revolutionary War as Britain recognises independence of the 13 colonies. British army leaves New York.

1784 New York City becomes the capital of the state and nation.

1787 Erasmus Hall Academy opens in Flatbush, Brooklyn.

1789 U.S. Constitution ratified. George Washington takes oath as nation's first President in Federal Hall on Wall St.

1790 Federal capital moves to Philadelphia. First census puts city population at 33,000.

1791 Yellow fever epidemic stimulates development of Greenwich Village.

1792 Buttonwood Agreement leads to formation of New York Stock Exchange.

1794 City buys Bellevue, an East River estate, and opens contagious disease hospital.

1796 Robert Fitch tests experimental steamboat on Collect Pond.
1797 Albany becomes state capital. Washington Square purchased as a potter's field.
1798 Yellow fever epidemic claims 2086 lives.
1799 Aaron Burr founds Manhattan Company to provide drinking water but clause in charter allows him also to found bank.
1800 Alexander Hamilton builds the Grange.
1801 Brooklyn Navy Yard founded.
1803 Cornerstone laid for present City Hall. Yellow fever epidemic.
1806 First New York free school opens.
1807 Robert Fulton demonstrates steamboat 'Clermont' on the Hudson River.
1810 Fulton opens steam ferry service to New Jersey.
1811 John Randel, Jr heads group of commissioners who plan New York's rectilinear street grid, known as the Commissioner's Plan or Randel Survey.
1812 City Hall opens. U.S. declares war on Britain; port suffers in trade war and is fortified against possible British attack.
1814 Treaty of Ghent ends War of 1812.
1816 Village of Brooklyn incorporated on site of present downtown Brooklyn.
1820 New York becomes nation's largest city, with population of 123,706.
1823 City buys site of Bryant Park for another potter's field.
1825 Erie Canal opens, greatly enhancing the importance of New York as a port and making it the gateway to the midwest.
1827 State legislature ends all slavery in New York state.
1828 Washington Square Park laid out in old potter's field.
1829 Large reservoir built on 14th St at the Bowery, one of the numerous stop-gap measures aimed at solving the city's water problems.
1831 New York University founded as University of the City of New York. Gramercy Park laid out.
1832 New York and Harlem Railroad, a horsecar line, opens along the Bowery and Fourth Ave from Prince St to 14th St as city's first railroad.
1834 Village of Brooklyn incorporated as City of Brooklyn.
1835 'Great Fire' destroys 674 buildings near Hanover and Pearl Sts.
1837 Business panic in which city losses total some $60 million. New York and Harlem Railroad reaches Harlem. First steam locomotives added in 1839.
1841 St. John's College, now Fordham University, founded in the Bronx.
1842 Croton Aqueduct brings water to city; stored in reservoir on site of Bryant Park. John Jacob Astor founds Astor Library. Charles Dickens visits the city.
1843 Potter's field established on Randall's Island.
1846 Potato famine in Ireland swells immigration. Tensions between Catholics and Protestants arise over such issues as aid to parochial schools.
1847 Madison Square Park laid out, replacing old potter's field.
1848 Political uprisings increase immigration from Germany.
1849 Free Academy (chartered 1847), the precursor of City College,

opens on Lexington Ave at 23rd St. Astor Place Riot demonstrates incompetence of police force.

1850   P.T. Barnum organises concert with Jenny Lind at Castle Garden. Giuseppe Garibaldi arrives in Staten Island during period of exile.

1851   'New York Daily Times', now 'New York Times', begins publication. Hudson River Railroad links New York and Albany.

1852   William Marcy 'Boss' Tweed begins political career as alderman of Seventh Ward.

1853   State legislature authorises Central Park. World's Fair held at Crystal Palace in Bryant Park.

1855   Castle Garden becomes immigrant station. Construction of large numbers of inhumane tenements leads to tenement reform movement; first model tenement built on Elizabeth and Mott Sts.

1856   City buys land for Central Park.

1857   Another financial panic.

1858   Vaux and Olmsted chosen to design Central Park; work is begun. Fire destroys Crystal Palace. Macy's founded.

1859   Cooper Union opens. State legislature authorises Prospect Park. Otis passenger elevator installed in Fifth Avenue Hotel.

1860   City's population, 312,710 in 1840, reaches 813,669, including large numbers of immigrants.

1861   Civil War begins.

1862   The 'Monitor', an ironclad ship designed by John Ericsson, launched in the Greenpoint section of Brooklyn.

1863   Draft Riots against conscription into the Union Army (those who could pay a $300 fee were exempted) paralyse the city for three days.

1865   Civil War ends. Municipal fire fighting system replaces volunteer companies.

1867   Prospect Park opens in Brooklyn. First tenement house law attempts to set standards for ventilation, sanitation, and room size.

1868   Andrew H. Green proposes consolidation of boroughs. First elevated railroad opens on Greenwich St from the Battery to Cortlandt St, a cable system with both moving and stationary engines.

1869   Rutherford Stuyvesant builds city's first known apartment house on E. 18th St. Potter's field moved to Hart's Island where it remains today. Jay Gould and Jim Fisk corner the gold market.

1870   Work begins on Brooklyn Bridge. First building with passenger elevators (Equitable Life Assurance Building at 120 Broadway; burned 1912). Joseph Warren Beach opens pneumatic subway under Broadway from Warren to Murray Sts. Ninth Ave El reaches 30th St.

1871   Grand Central Depot opens. Boss Tweed arrested, closing a period during which city government reached a low point of inefficiency, corruption, and moral squalor.

1873   Financial panic.

1874   P.T. Barnum opens Hippodrome at Madison Square. Part of the Bronx annexed to New York City.

1877   Alfred Tredway White opens model tenement houses in

Brooklyn. Museum of Natural History opens at its present site.

1878 Sixth Ave El opens from Rector St to Central Park.

1879 'Dumb bell' tenement plan by James F. Ware wins competition for model tenement sponsored by magazine. Plan condemned by tenement reformers but widely adopted.

1880 Sixth Ave El reaches 155th St. Metropolitan Museum of Art opens. Broadway illuminated by Brush electric arc lamps.

1882 Thomas Edison opens generating plant at 257 Pearl St, making electricity commercially available.

1883 Brooklyn Bridge opens. Metropolitan Opera opens on Broadway between 39th–40th Sts (demolished 1967).

1885 Elevated railway opens in Brooklyn.

1886 Statue of Liberty inaugurated on Bedloe's (now Liberty) Island. Elevated railway joins Manhattan and Bronx.

1888 Great Blizzard. First building with steel skeleton erected, Tower Building at 50 Broadway.

1890 Madison Square Garden, designed by Stanford White, opens at the N.E. corner of Madison Square.

1891 Carnegie Hall opens. New York Botanical Garden opens in the Bronx.

1892 Immigration station opens on Ellis Island.

1895 Harlem Ship Canal opens along Harlem River with channel dug south of Spuyten Duyvil Creek. Rest of Bronx annexed to New York City.

1898 Greater New York created by joining the five boroughs under a single municipal government. Population of 3·4 million makes it the world's second largest city behind London (4 million).

1899 Bronx Zoo opened. Brooklyn Children's Museum established. Croton Reservoir in Bryant Park razed.

1900 Subway construction begins. Blacks begin moving to Harlem. Census shows tenements house 70% of city's population.

1901 Tenement House Law institutes 'New Law' tenements, superceding dumb bell plan. Macy's opens on Broadway.

1903 Williamsburg Bridge opens, making N. Brooklyn accessible to the poor of the Lower East Side.

1904 IRT subway opens from City Hall to W. 145th St.

1905 Municipal Staten Island ferry opens, with 5¢ fare.

1906 Harry K. Thaw, deranged Pittsburgh millionaire, shoots architect Stanford White on the roof of Madison Square Garden.

1908 East River subway tunnel between Bowling Green and Joralemon St links Manhattan and Brooklyn. First Hudson Tube, the McAdoo Tunnel, links Manhattan and Hoboken, New Jersey. IRT Broadway line reaches Kingsbridge section of the Bronx.

1909 Queensboro and Manhattan Bridges open.

1910 Pennsylvania Station opens.

1911 Triangle Shirtwaist Co. fire kills 145. Brooklyn Botanic Garden opens.

1913 The present Grand Central Terminal opens. The Armory Show at the 69th Regiment Armory introduces New York to 'modern art'.

1916 Nation's first zoning resolution enacted, dividing city into residential and commercial areas and restricting height and bulk of buildings.

1923 'Setback' law restricting configuration of tall buildings enacted.

1925 Columbia University and Presbyterian Hospital join to form Medical Center at 168th St and Broadway. Madison Square Garden at Madison Square demolished.

1927 Holland Tunnel (for vehicular traffic) opens between New York and New Jersey.

1928 Cornell University and New York Hospital join forces as New York Medical Center, York Ave, and E. 70th St. Goethals Bridge and Outerbridge Crossing open linking Staten Island and New Jersey.

1929 Stock Market crashes; Great Depression begins.

1931 Empire State Building and George Washington Bridge open. Floyd Bennett Field opens as city's first municipal airport. Bayonne Bridge opens linking Staten Island and New Jersey.

1932 Mayor James J. ('Beau James') Walker resigns after Seabury Investigations reveal rampant corruption.

1933 Fiorello La Guardia elected mayor. IND subway opens to Queens.

1934 New York City Housing Authority formed to plan and enact low-rent housing and slum-clearance projects.

1935 Work begins on East River Drive.

1936 Triborough Bridge opens. First Houses (Avenue A at E. 3rd St) open.

1938 La Guardia's City Charter of 1936 goes into effect centralising municipal power and giving full legislative authority to City Council.

1939 North Beach Airport opens; soon renamed after La Guardia. New York Worlds's Fair of 1939–40 opens in Flushing Meadow Park, Queens.

1940 Queens-Midtown Tunnel opens, linking mid-Manhattan and Queens. Brooklyn Battery Tunnel begun.

1941 U.S. enters World War II. New York becomes important as major Atlantic port. Brooklyn Navy Yard operates at full capacity.

1945 World War II ends. Army bomber crashes into Empire State Building. United Nations charter passed.

1946 U.N. selects New York as permanent headquarters. Army plane crashes into Bank of Manhattan Co. building's 58th floor.

1947 Rockefellers donate $5·8 million site of U.N. headquarters. Stuyvesant Town, middle-income housing for returning war veterans and their families, is built by Metropolitan Life Insurance Co. along East River Drive, 14th–20th Sts.

1948 Subway and bus fares rise to 10¢. New York International Airport (opened 1942) greatly expanded; now called Idlewild.

1950 Brooklyn Battery Tunnel opens after construction delay caused by war. City population at all-time high: 7,891,957. Mayor William O'Dwyer, on the verge of exposure for corruption and links with organised crime, is appointed ambassador to Mexico by fellow Democrat, President Harry Truman.

1952 Lever House opens, first of glass-box skyscrpapers. Transit Authority established.

1954 Robert F. Wagner elected mayor. Decline of older American cities begins in mid-late 1950s. Puerto Rican immigration increases as does influx of poor blacks.

1956 Ebbets Field sold as housing site. Brooklyn Dodgers move to Los Angeles.

1957 Fair Housing Law outlaws racial discrimination. Manhattantown scandal reveals housing project sponsors have failed to develop site while pocketing tenants' rents.

1959 Ground broken for Lincoln Center.

1960 World Trade Center proposed at estimated cost of $250 million. Completion of Chase Manhattan Bank marks beginning of construction boom in lower Manhattan.

1961 New zoning law offers incentives for public amenities, plazas, arcades.

1962 Philharmonic Hall, now Avery Fisher Hall, opens as first building of Lincoln Center for the Performing Arts.

1963 Pennsylvania Station demolished despite protests.

1964 Race riots in Harlem and Bedford-Stuyvesant. World's Fair of 1964–65 opens in Flushing Meadows, Queens. Fair plagued by financial difficulties and controversy but attracts 51 million visitors. Verrazano-Narrows Bridge opens, ending relative isolation of Staten Island.

1965 Landmarks Preservation Commission established to save city's architectural heritage. New laws allow increased Asian, Greek, Haitian, Dominican, etc immigration. First power blackout.

1966 Ground broken for World Trade Center.

1968 City teachers strike in battle over school decentralisation an issue with racial overtones.

1971 Football Giants move to New Jersey.

1973 Construction of Twin Towers at World Trade Center completed. Welfare Island renamed Roosevelt Island, as redevelopment begins.

1974 City's financial position worsens, as loss of middle class and departure of businesses erode tax base while social services increase.

1975 Cash flow problems and inability to sell more municipal bonds bring city to verge of insolvency. Federal government staves off default on city notes by offering loans. South Bronx becomes symbol of urban despair as 13,000 fires break out in 12 sq. mile area.

1977 Power blackout, 25 hours, results in widespread looting, vandalism.

1978 Radio City Music Hall saved from demolition. Supreme Court decision preserves Grand Central Terminal in its present form. 'Herald Tribune' ceases publication. Federal government gives city $1·65 billion in long-term loan guarantees.

1980 Census shows sharp decline in city's white population, moderate increase in black population, and substantial increase in Hispanic population. Blacks and Hispanics account for 48·1% of city's population.

1981 City re-enters long-term municipal bond market.

1982 Morosco and Helen Hayes Theatres demolished despite protest as Portman Hotel project begins in Times Square.

I BOROUGH OF MANHATTAN / NEW YORK COUNTY

To many people New York is synonymous with Manhattan, a slender island 12·5 miles long, 2·5 miles wide, with a total area of 22·6 square miles, which means that Peter Minuit who reputedly paid the Indians $24 for it, got it for a little more than a dollar a square mile. It is the third largest borough in population (1,427,533, a drop of 7·3% in the last decade) behind Brooklyn and the Bronx, and the smallest in size. City Hall, the center of the borough politically if not geographically, lies at a latitude of 40° 42' 26" and a longitude of 74° 0' 23". Its highest altitude is about 268 ft and its lowest, sea level.

Topographically there remain only a few vestiges of Manhattan's appearance before the Dutch came. Southern Manhattan is flat, a coastal plain lying over a fairly shallow stratum of Manhattan schist, the bedrock on which its skyscrapers stand. Again in midtown bedrock lies close to the surface, supporting a second great concentration of towering buildings. A large pond near City Hall, swampy ground in the West Village and near Turtle Bay, as well as streams and rivers have been drained, channelled underground, or filled in as progress demanded so that Manhattan from the Battery to Central Park is uniform and undistinguished, with the exception of a few small hills like Murray Hill.

In its more northerly areas however some traces of the past remain, the outcroppings of Manhattan schist in Central Park, the occasional hills and dips that include Carnegie Hill on the upper East Side, the valley of W. 125th St slashing diagonally across the regular north–south street grid, the two ridges extending from N. Manhattan between which lies the valley of Broadway, an old road which follows an Indian path.

Manhattan is encircled by rivers, the Hudson (once called the North River) on the W., the East River, actually a tidal inlet from Long Island Sound on the E., and the Harlem River on the N.E., part of which, the Harlem Ship Canal on the N., is an artificial channel dug at the end of the 19C to facilitate navigation.

The island was settled from S. to N., with its oldest neighbourhoods in what is today called Lower Manhattan. The first settlement was near Battery Park and the Financial District, a residential area for the Dutch, had already begun to assume some public functions after the British took over in 1664. North of it are the Civic Center, Chinatown, and Little Italy, the two latter areas the home of a large immigrant population toward the end of the 19C. South of Houston St is SoHo, once the industrial outpost of Little Italy but more recently a center of the city's artistic life, whose industrial buildings have been converted to studios and apartments and have in the past decade attracted boutiques, restaurants, and establishments similar to those in Greenwich Village directly to its N. The upper reaches of the Lower East Side, once a home of immigrants largely from Eastern Europe, became the East Village during the late 1960s, home of many young people who represented what was then called the Counterculture.

South of midtown are Chelsea, Gramercy Park, Herald Square, and Murray Hill, all once finer residential districts than they are now. Times Square, as every tourist knows, is in midtown at the S. edge of the theatre district.

On the East Side in midtown are the United Nations and Rockefeller Center, as well as an important business district which includes banks, corporate headquarters, the advertising industry on Madison Ave, the long stretch of fine Park Ave apartment houses, and the commercial glitter of Fifth and Madison Aves.

Central Park divides the East Side from the West Side above 59th St. The former includes the elite neighbourhoods of Sutton Pl. and Beekman Pl., the more arriviste apartments, bars, and restaurants of Second and First Aves, and Yorkville, once an uptown immigrant neighbourhood for Germans, Czechs, and Hungarians, now growing daily more fashionable and expensive. Above 96th St lies East Harlem, once largely Italian, now known as El Barrio or Spanish Harlem. On the West Side is Lincoln Center for the Performing Arts, a cultural mecca whose presence has catalysed the upgrading of Amsterdam and Columbus Aves. Central Park West and Riverside Drive are the finest residential areas on the West Side, with their fine views of greenery and the Hudson River respectively. North of 96th St are several large urban renewal projects. Above the park and 110th St are Harlem, Morningside Heights (home of Columbia University), Hamilton Heights (home of C.U.N.Y., the City University of New York), and Upper Manhattan, consisting of the neighbourhoods of Washington Heights and Inwood, both residential. The Cloisters in Fort Tryon Park is the major cultural institution in Upper Manhattan. Across the Harlem River, physically attached to the Bronx, is Marble Hill, politically a part of Manhattan, to which it was joined before the digging of the Harlem Ship Canal.

1 Statue of Liberty and Ellis Island

Boats for the Statue of Liberty and Ellis Island leave from the ferry station at the foot of Battery Park; to reach Battery Park, see transportation information prefacing Rte 2. Although the islands are close together no boat currently serves both.

The STATUE OF LIBERTY FERRY leaves every hour on the hour all year from 9–4, with additional sailings during the summer and on weekends in spring and early autumn; for schedule information call 269–5755. Adults $2·25; children under 12 years, $0·50. The round trip takes about 45 minutes, while the entire visit including the ascent of the statue and a visit to the Museum of Immigration requires about 2 $^1/_2$ hours. Restrooms and refreshments are available on the island; picnicking is prohibited. Since the trip is very popular in pleasant weather, it is advisable to go early in the day. For additional information about the museum or statue call 732–1286.

The ELLIS ISLAND FERRY departs daily April–October at 9.30, 11.30, 1.30, and 3.30; it is wise to check sailing times near the beginning or end of the season by calling 269–5755. Adults $2·50; children under 12 years, $1·25. The visit, including the tour of the island, requires about 2 hours. There are no tourist facilities on Ellis Island.

The ****Statue of Liberty** (dedicated 1886, sculptor Frédéric Auguste Bartholdi), probably the most famous piece of sculpture in America, stands in towering majesty on Liberty Island in direct view of ships entering the Upper Bay. A gift of the people of France, the figure stands on a handsome pedestal, donated by the American public,

Her head is surrounded by a radiant crown, while her feet step forth from broken shackles; in her uplifted right hand is a torch, her left holds a tablet representing the Declaration of Independence on which is inscribed the date July 4, 1776.

History. The inspiration for the Statue of Liberty, originally called 'Liberty Enlightening the World', comes primarily from two men: Édouard-René Lefebvre de Laboulaye (1811–83), a noted jurist, professor, and authority on U.S. Constitutional history, and Frédéric Auguste Bartholdi (1834–1904), a sculptor of monumental ambitions. Laboulaye and his followers saw in a jointly sponsored Franco-American project the opportunity to further their ambitions for a new French republic by identifying their nation's destiny and history with that of the United States, at the time the pre-eminent modern republic and a nation destined to emerge as a major power. Laboulaye proposed a monument in 1865 and introduced Bartholdi to the project, which became the crown of his career.

Yearning to create a work of colossal scale, Bartholdi in 1867–69 was contemplating a monumental lighthouse for the mouth of the Suez Canal, a female figure bearing an upraised torch and symbolising 'Progress', or 'Egypt Carrying Light to Asia'. In 1871 he travelled to America to proselytise for the Liberty project and selected Bedloe's Island (renamed Liberty Island in 1956) for its site, an inspired choice in an era when almost all foreigners reached New York by ship. Although Bartholdi based the Statue of Liberty on his Suez lighthouse, he drew on other models, notably the face of his mother, a stern, commanding woman who deeply influenced her son, and Delacroix's painting (1830), 'Liberty Leading the People to the Barricades'. The statue's iron skeleton was devised by Alexandre Gustave Eiffel (1832–1923), whose reputation before the statue and the later Eiffel Tower rested with his iron trusswork railway bridges.

The French people, through a series of benefits, individual contributions and

Enlarging Liberty's hand (1876–81). Bartholdi's clay model of the statue was enlarged in three stages to full scale. The sculptor, bareheaded in foreground, modified the form each time as increased size created unexpected visual effects. (New York Public Library)

finally a public lottery raised about $400,000 for the statue, which was constructed in Paris by the firm of Gaget, Gauthier, et Cie. It was completely assembled outside Bartholdi's workshops; the construction scaffolding was removed and the figure formally presented to the United States on 4 July 1884; the scaffolding was re-erected, the statue dismantled, crated, and shipped. On 28 October 1886 President Grover Cleveland dedicated it during spectacular ceremonies climaxed by fireworks and the unveiling of its face. It soon became a tourist attraction, a symbol of hope offered to immigrants by the New World, and eventually a symbol for the United States itself.

As such it has been the target of extremist groups: in 1965 four terrorists attempted to blow off the head and arm holding the torch; and in 1971 a group of Vietnam veterans occupied it for a few days as a war protest.

The ferry docks at the W. side of **Liberty Island,** formerly known as Bedloe's Island after Isaac Bedloe who acquired it in 1667 from the English colonial governor.

Before the Revolution it was used as a quarantine station, particularly for smallpox epidemics, and from 1746–57 it was owned by Archibald Kennedy (see p80) who summered there. The U.S. government acquired it in 1800 to build Fort Wood (1808–11), designed by Col Jonathan Williams who also planned Castle Williams on Governors Island and Fort Gibson on Ellis Island. Named after a now obscure hero of the War of 1812, the fort later served as a Civil War recruitment camp and an ordnance depot; in 1877 it was donated by the government to the Liberty project. Originally the statue's pedestal rested upon a platform enclosed by the star-shaped bastions of the fort; the base, however, has been considerably altered to accommodate the Museum of Immigration.

From the boat dock the statue's scale is impressive: height of statue alone, 151 ft; pedestal, 89 ft; height of torch above sea level, 305 ft; weight, 225 tons; waist measurement, 35 ft; width of mouth, 3 ft; index finger length, 8 ft.

The figure's size imposes technical difficulties which Eiffel solved with great ingenuity. He devised an interior framework consisting of a heavy central iron pylon supporting a lightweight system of trusswork that reaches out toward the interior surface of the statue. The hammered copper 'skin' of the figure, only $^3/_{32}$ of an inch thick, is bound together in sections by iron straps and joined to the trusswork in such a way that it 'floats' at the ends of hundreds of flexible attachments and can thus accommodate both thermal changes and winds buffeting its large surface area.

A broad mall leads from the water to the **pedestal,** designed by Richard Morris Hunt and constructed of strongly rusticated blocks of Stony Creek granite and concrete. The 40 shields ringing the pedestal above the portals were meant to carry the coats-of-arms of the then 40 states.

The cornerstone was laid in 1884, but construction was halted for lack of funds. In 1885 publisher Joseph Pulitzer launched a fundraising campaign, partly to promote his financially troubled New York 'World', and partly because he sincerely respected the Liberty project. By August 1885, he had raised over $100,000, mostly in modest donations, while quadrupling the circulation of his newspaper.

INTERIOR. Within the base of the statue (open 9–5, free admission) a stairway leads from the lobby to a balcony level (restrooms and telephones); on the left of the balcony and one flight up is the **American Museum of Immigration** (open daily 9–5, free admission), opened in 1972 in the expanded base of the statue (cornerstone laid 1962). The exhibits, organised chronologically and by nationality, present the full panorama of American immigration, beginning with the 'immigration' of the American Indians from Asia and ending with

The Statue of Liberty under construction in Paris
(1881–84). The statue was completely assembled outside
sculptor Bartholdi's studio and presented ceremoniously
to the U.S. ambassador before being dismantled and
shipped. (New York Public Library)

a series of historical posters. The displays consist largely of photographs, articles brought by immigrants, and dioramas showing the contributions of different national groups; recorded lectures further explain the exhibits.

Accessible from the museum level is a promenade on the ramparts of Fort Wood, with placards along the way describing the statue's environs. On the right of the balcony is the Statue of Liberty Story Room, with exhibits explaining the construction and installation of the statue. Here also is a placard with Emma Lazarus' famous sonnet (1883), 'The New Colossus'.

Although she came from a comfortable, sheltered background and had little actual knowledge of conditions in Eastern Europe, Emma Lazarus was stirred by the plight of the Jews persecuted by Czar Alexander III. She saw in Bartholdi's statue a symbol for the freedom that would draw millions of immigrants to this country and contributed the poem to a contest as part of the fund-raising efforts for the pedestal.

The *entrance to the pedestal* is at the left of the Emma Lazarus placard. Stairways ascend (167 steps) to the top of the pedestal (also accessible by elevator, 10¢ for visitors over 16 years); a spiral stairway continues another 171 steps to the crown from which there are beautiful views of the harbour. The torch, although structurally sound, has been closed to visitors since 1916 because its only access is via a narrow 42-ft ladder. Since the climb from the foot to the crown is equivalent to 12 stories, visitors with physical difficulties are urged not to attempt it. **Note:** the statue will be closed for renovation in 1984.

*Ellis Island, originally a low-lying sandbar of about 3 acres now enlarged by landfill to 27·5 acres, lies about a mile S.W. of Battery Park in the Upper Bay. It is the site of the *former United States Immigration Station* and since 1965 has been part of the Statue of Liberty National Monument. The turreted, vaguely Byzantine, brick and limestone buildings (1898; Boring & Tilton) are unrestored and in places dangerously dilapidated so that visitors may not wander around unescorted, but National Park Service guides lead an excellent tour (about 1 hour, considerable stair climbing and walking involved) of the baggage room, registry hall, medical and legal rooms, and other facilities of the main station, now furnished with token pieces of the original furniture. In bleak and cavernous rooms—their plumbing and electrical fixtures stripped by vandals, their walls and ceilings peeling from the damp sea air—the guides illuminate the experience of the more than 12 million immigrants who passed through the building on their way to a new life.

History. The Indians called Ellis Island *Kioshk* (Gull Island); the Dutch bought it in 1630, named it Little Oyster Island, and then ceded it to a patroon—a sort of feudal landowner—who also held title to what is now Hoboken, Staten Island, and Jersey City, but never left Amsterdam to enjoy his territories. During much of the 18C the British called it Bucking Island (etymology unknown), though for a period after 1765 it was known as Anderson's or Gibbet Island, in honour of a pirate named Anderson who was hanged there. At the time of the Revolution it was owned by Samuel Ellis (died 1794), who owned a farm in New Jersey, sold general merchandise in Manhattan, and leased out part of the island to a fisherman's tavern. After his death, the federal government acquired it (1808) from his heirs for an exorbitant $10,000 to build a fort. Like the three other fortifications built at about this time (see p73), it was intended to protect the city from a British naval invasion in the War of 1812, but saw no action. Named Fort Gibson in 1814 after an officer killed in the battle of

Fort Erie, it is the only one of the four harbour fortifications of which no trace remains. From 1835–90 it served as an ammunition dump, threatening nearby New Jersey residents with the possibility of being accidentally blown up.

In 1890 when the federal government took over the immigration service, Ellis Island was designated as the site of the main receiving station almost by default. The army did not want immigrants on Governors Island; New Yorkers did not want them on Manhattan, where they were more vulnerable to local swindlers anyhow; and the public considered the use of Bedloe's Island, already the site of the Statue of Liberty, an outrage, sculptor Auguste Bartholdi calling such a proposal a 'downright desecration.' The station, therefore, was built on Ellis Island; primarily constructed of Georgia pine, it opened in 1892 on acreage approximately doubled by landfill. Five years later it burned to the ground, fortunately without loss of lives, but with the destruction of the immigration records from 1855–90, which had been stored in the former powder magazines.

In 1898 the firm of Boring & Tilton began to construct a new station, while the immigration service returned to the Barge Office in Battery Park, where it had been temporarily housed in 1890–91. The new fireproof buildings opened on 17 December 1900 and that day received 2251 immigrants. Inside the station federal inspectors processed the immigrants, detaining those who would be physically or mentally handicapped in earning a living, weeding out paupers, criminals, prostitutes, the insane, and those suffering from contagious diseases or professing such beliefs as anarchy or polygamy. Persons not admitted were either detained (20%) until their cases could be resolved or deported (2%), and so were housed and fed in the dormitories, hospitals, and dining halls.

Until 1902 when President Theodore Roosevelt appointed as Commissioner of Immigration a former Wall Street lawyer, William Williams, immigrants were often abused, robbed, and improperly inspected, concessionaires who operated the food, laundry, baggage, and currency exchange services enriched themselves illegally at the expense of both the immigrants and the government. After Williams' reforms, problems arose primarily from overcrowding. In 1907, the peak year of immigration, 1,285,349 people entered the United States, of whom, 1,004,756 came through Ellis Island, approximately twice the number the station was designed to handle since the architects had unfortunately based their plans on pre-1898 statistics.

The heavy influx continued until 1915 when World War I closed trans-Atlantic shipping. During the war Ellis Island served as a detention center for enemy aliens and for immigrants waiting to be deported. In the period of isolationism and racism that followed the war, immigration never reached its earlier level; a series of laws passed in the 1920s imposed an overall annual ceiling (first 358,000, later only 164,000) as well as quotas for particular nationalities, discriminating against Latins, Slavs, and Jews. Under the National Origins Act (1924) immigrants were processed in their own countries and thereafter Ellis Island became gradually underused and increasingly expensive to run and maintain. Sporadically the government found uses for it—detaining war criminals and enemy aliens during World War II, screening the political beliefs of immigrants, visitors, and foreign seamen seeking shore leave in the United States during the McCarthy era in the early 1950s.

In 1954 the last detainee, a Norwegian sailor who had jumped ship, was released; the station closed and the island was vacated. The buildings were put up for sale to the highest bidder with the stipulation that the government approve of the use to which the island be put. The highest bid in 1956 was $201,000 by would-be developers of a luxury facility called 'Pleasure Island', including a hotel, convention hall and museum. Later proposals included a Bible college, a gambling casino, and a mental institution. Gradually, however, the government became more aware of the island's historical importance and in 1965 it became a National Monument, a few months before a new immigration law was passed abolishing the national origins quotas of the 1920s. In 1970 militant American Indians tried to occupy it to dramatise the destruction of the native population by European immigrants. Later a group of blacks landed, cleared undergrowth, and began renovating some of the smaller buildings, avowing their aim of creating a rehabilitation center for drug addicts and convicts; they were granted a five year permit to use buildings on the hospital side of the slip. In 1976 the island opened to visitors.

Ellis Island is actually two rectangular land masses separated by a ferry slip (created c. 1890) and joined by a narrow neck of man-made land. In the slip is the rotting hulk of the old *ferryboat 'Ellis Island'* (built 1904), which plied the harbour for more than 50 years. Abandoned when the station closed in 1954, the ferry sank in August 1968, before plans to preserve her could come to fruition. Directly behind the slip is the *Immigrant Building* (erected 1934?) to house detained entering aliens, thus segregating them from the criminal and undesirable deportees who constituted much of the island's population in the 1930s; since the volume of immigration fell off at this time, the building was never used for its original purpose. To the left of the slip is the hospital island, formerly divided by a second slip into two separate islands. Near the ferry slip are the pavilions of the *General Hospital* (opened 1902). On the far side of the island are the buildings of the *Contagious Disease Hospital* (completed 1909). The slip between the two hospital islands was filled during the 1920s and landscaped in the 1930s to provide a recreation area for patients; it is now densely overgrown.

To the right of the slip is the original island, now enlarged by landfill, upon which stand the main *Immigrant Receiving Station*, the Baggage and Dormitory Building, the restaurant and laundry building, and the power plant.

The largest and most impressive of the group, the Immigrant Receiving Station (385 ft long, 165 ft wide, corner towers 100 ft tall) is constructed of brick laid in Flemish bond and trimmed with limestone. The two-story arched windows (duplicated on the other side of the structure) once served as doorways, from which a sheltering roof ran to the slip. The Registry Hall on the second story (200 × 100 × 56 ft) was designed to handle 5000 immigrants per day. The Guastavino tile ceiling was installed after 1916, when explosions of ammunition stockpiled on nearby New Jersey wharves damaged the earlier roof. The red tile floor was laid at the same time, replacing asphalt. Until 1911 the interior of the hall was divided by iron pipes into a series of pens resembling a cattle run.

2 Lower Manhattan and Battery Park

SUBWAY: IRT Broadway-7th Ave (train 1) to South Ferry. IRT Lexington Ave (train 4 or 5) to Bowling Green. BMT RR train to Whitehall St.

BUS: M1, M6, or M15 to South Ferry. Culture Bus Loop II (weekends and holidays) to Stop 28.

New York City owes its historic supremacy among American cities to its closeness to the sea, and nowhere within its boundaries are these ties more obvious than at the S. tip of Manhattan where the East and Hudson Rivers converge and flow into New York Bay.

The **former U.S. Custom House** (1907; Cass Gilbert, DL), just S. of Bowling Green at the foot of Broadway, occupies the probable site of New York's first permanent European settlement.

In 1624 the Dutch ship 'Nieu Nederlandt' deposited eight men on what is now Governors Island and continued upstream to locate other settlers at the present site of Albany. These men, sponsored by the Dutch West India Company, were joined the following year by six families who brought with them the livestock, seeds, and tools necessary for subsistence farming. The settlers moved to the S. shore of Manhattan, where they built rude shelters and a fort to protect themselves from the Indians, who though initially friendly inevitably became hostile later on.

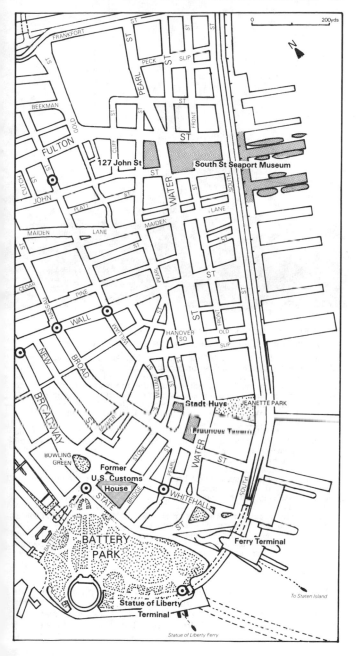

Tugboat 'Watuppa' against the skyline of lower Manhattan (1936). (Museum of the City of New York)

The original fort, built in 1626 and named Fort Amsterdam, was a simple affair consisting of a blockhouse protected by a cedar palisade. As the town grew and alternately fell under the jurisdiction of the Dutch, the British, the Dutch again, and the British once more, the fort was strengthened and appropriately renamed. The last such structure, called Fort George after the reigning British monarch, remained until after the Revolution when it was torn down (1789) to make way for Government House, a building intended as the residence for the nation's President.

Since New York's hopes to become the nation's permanent capital city did not materialise, Government House was demoted to serving as the mansion for the state governor until the state capital was moved to Albany in 1796. The mansion now became a hotel, the Elysian Boarding House, and then served briefly as a custom house until it was severely damaged by a fire in 1815 and demolished. A row of six elegant brick houses replaced it, serving first as residences and then, as commerce invaded this residential area, as offices of the principal shipping companies, conferring on the street its nickname, Steamship Row.

Meanwhile the customs service had moved to Wall St, first to the old Federal Hall, later to the building now occupied by Citibank, but as the 19C progressed, these facilities became inadequate. In 1892 the U.S. Treasury bought this plot of land and announced an architectural competition for a new Custom House. Cass Gilbert, although less famous than some of the other contestants, won the competition with a design that symbolised the commercial greatness of the nation and of the city.

EXTERIOR. The Custom House facade is a triumph of Beaux-Arts exuberance, boldly adorned with emblems of commerce and the sea. In the window arches are heads of the eight 'races' of mankind: Caucasian, Hindu, Latin, Celtic, Mongolian, Eskimo, Slavic, and African. Above the cornice statues representing twelve great com-

mercial nations of history stare down on the vicissitudes of Broadway, while the head of Mercury, Roman god of commerce, crowns
the capital of each of the 44 Corinthian columns encircling the
building. Over the main entrance a heroic cartouche by Karl Bitter
(1867–1915) bears the arms of the United States.

Gilbert commissioned the immense statues of *The Four Continents*
by Daniel Chester French (1850–1931), best known for his statue of
Abraham Lincoln in the Lincoln Memorial. The four limestone
sculptures, resting on pedestals at the ground floor level of the
building, honour commercial ties that reach to the four corners of the
globe; from left to right they represent Asia, America, Europe, and
Africa.

Asia, shown as the mother of religions, sits withdrawn in contemplation, a small
Buddha on her lap, a serpent-wreathed lotus in her right hand, a cross behind
her. On one side a tiger glares into her face; on the other are three figures in
attitudes of suffering and suppliance, while the skulls of the dead rest beneath
her feet. *America* looks confidently outward, surrounded by symbols of the
New World and its vitality: the wheel of commerce, the torch of liberty, the
sheaf of corn suggesting fertility. The Aztec serpent Quetzalcoatl underfoot, the
Mayan glyphs on the throne, and the Indian peering over her shoulder signify
the original cultures of America. In contrast *Europe*, robed in a Grecian gown,
sits enthroned among the achievements of the past: the open book, the globe,
the ship's prow, the section of the Parthenon frieze decorating the pedestal.
Leaning against her shoulder from the back is a mysterious draped figure,
perhaps representing History. *Africa*, a continent as yet unrealised, slumbers
heavily between a sphinx and a lion; behind her, a darkly shrouded figure of
uncertain significance contributes to the mystery of the composition.

INTERIOR. Since the U.S. Customs Service moved to the World
Trade Center in 1973, the building has been a challenge to planners
seeking new uses for it. The main entrance leads into a fine hallway,
enhanced by marbles of different colours quarried in Europe and the
United States. At either end of the hall is a spiral staircase that
mounts the entire height of the building. To the right of the main
entrance off the hallway is a room richly panelled in oak with an
elaborately worked ceiling, once intended for the U.S. Secretary of
State when he visited the city in a ceremonial capacity. In the center
of the main floor is the great rotunda (135 × 85 ft, 48 ft high) with its
oval skylight, now unfortunately painted over on the inside and
tarred over on the outside (to conform to blackout regulations during
World War II). Constructed of 140 tons of tile and plaster (no steel),
it was engineered by Rafael Guastavino, whose tilework also
appears in such disparate structures as the Cathedral of St. John the
Divine and Grand Central Station. Just below the dome are frescoes
by Reginald Marsh, painted in 1937 in a period of weeks. The eight
smaller vertical panels, painted to resemble niches, display the
figures of early explorers of America; the eight larger trapezoidal
panels depict the progress of an ocean liner as it enters New York
harbour, docks, and unloads its cargo and passengers (including the
movie star Greta Garbo, who is shown being interviewed by the
press).

The small plot of greenery just N. of the main facade of the Custom
House is BOWLING GREEN PARK, the city's first park. During the
Dutch colonial period, this area was an open place at the S. end of
'De Heere Wegh' ('the Main Street', now Broadway) and was used as
a cattle market; hence the name of Marketfield Street, a block east.
Later the area became a parade ground and still later a bowling
green, leased in 1733 to several citizens for the annual fee of one

peppercorn per year. The *Bowling Green Fence* (DL) was built in 1771 to keep the park from collecting 'all the filth and dirt in the neighborhood' and to protect an equestrian statue of George III, which had been erected in 1766.

The statue, which depicted the king clad in a Roman toga and crowned with a laurel wreath, met an inglorious end on 9 July 1776, when a crowd of patriots, roused to energetic zeal by the public reading of the Declaration of Independence, tore it down and dismembered it. The pieces of the gilded lead statue were melted down and made into bullets which, according to legend, killed 400 British soldiers during the Revolution. The fence has survived better than the statue, although the crowd made off with the ornaments which originally capped the fence posts.

LOWER BROADWAY has several commercial buildings interesting either for their architectural detail or for their historical associations with an era when transatlantic shipping dominated the neighbourhood. No. 1 Broadway (on the W. side of the Bowling Green at Battery Place) occupies the site of the *Archibald Kennedy House* (1771–1882), which was used by George Washington and General Howe during their respective periods of residence in New York during the Revolutionary War. The building next door (11 Broadway), built in 1898 (W.G. Audsley) has amused architectural critics for its eclecticism, the 'Egyptian' style pylons on the ground level, the materials and forms of the early Chicago School on the upper stories. A little further N. at 25 Broadway is the former *Cunard Building* (1921; Benjamin Wistar Morris). Behind the Renaissance facade with its arched entranceways and attractive second story colonnade lies one of the city's great interiors, reputedly inspired by Raphael's Villa Madama in Rome. Inside the doors, the vaulted vestibule has ornate ceilings by Ezra Winter and a tall wrought-iron gate by Samuel Yellin. The room beyond, now housing the drab bureaucratic apparatus of the U.S. postal service, once proclaimed the romance of steamship travel in a manner suitable to a company that owned the 'Queen Mary' and the 'Queen Elizabeth'. A dome, 65 ft high, rises loftily above the octagonal chamber (185 × 74 ft) formerly called the Freight Distribution Hall. The ceiling designs, again by Ezra Winter, were executed by Italian craftsmen brought in for the work; the pendentives supporting the dome are covered with frescoes depicting the ships of Columbus (S.E.), Sir Francis Drake (N.E.), John Cabot (N.W.), and Leif Ericson (S.W.) The maps of world steamship routes on the N. and S. walls were designed by Barry Faulkner.

Across the street at 26 Broadway is the former *Standard Oil Building* (1922; Carrère & Hastings). The facade of this elegant office building curves to follow the contour of Broadway, but the tower, best seen from Battery Park, is aligned with the north–south orientation of the streets and buildings further uptown; obviously the architects had the skyline in mind when they planned the tower, which terminates in a structure designed like an oil lamp, concealling a chimney. Oil lamps also adorn the facade around the principal entrance, and when Standard Oil had its offices here a bust of John D. Rockefeller stood on the pedestal in the lobby; although the statue is gone, his name and the names of other illustrious company executives adorn the marble walls.

Return S. along Broadway to **Battery Park,** whose name recalls a row of cannons which defended the original fort and stood near the present sidewalk W. of the Custom House. Situated on filled land, the park is a pleasant place to escape the shadows and canyons of the financial district and serves as a lunchtime refuge for office workers as well as a restful haven for sailors temporarily or permanently idle in the port of New York. It offers spectacular views of the harbour and a group of monuments recalling New York's maritime and commercial history. In winter, however, the winds sweeping across it diminish its pleasures, while giving some inkling of the hardships the early settlers must have endured.

Near the intersection of State Street, Bowling Green, and Battery Place just outside the fence is the BATTERY PARK CONTROL HOUSE (1904–05; DL), the original entrance and exit for the Bowling Green station of the Lexington Avenue IRT. As the only kiosk remaining from the city's first subway and a fine example of the influence of the École des Beaux-Arts, this little building is being restored as part of the Bowling Green renovation. Designed by the firm of Heins & La Farge, better known as first architects of the Cathedral of St. John the Divine, its monumental quality achieved despite its small scale suggests the city's pride in its new subway system.

The flagpole near the park entrance is the *Netherlands Memorial Monument*, given to the city in 1926 by the people of Holland as a token of affection for their forebears who founded New York. The flagpole base bears a map of Manhattan in Dutch times and a representation of the Indian receiving $24 for the island (see p85) as well as a presentation inscription. Between the flagpole and Castle Clinton stretches the Eisenhower Mall, its grassy strip containing a Cor-Ten (weathering) steel statue by Chuck Ginnever entitled *Peace* (1970).

About half way down the mall, a path leads off behind the hedges to the right toward a bronze *statue of John Ericsson* (1893; Jonathan Scott Hartley), known to students of American naval history as the designer of the ironclad ship 'Monitor', whose clash with the Confederate frigate 'Merrimac' off Hampton Roads, Virginia, in 1862 marked the beginning of the end for wooden warships.

Castle Clinton (open Sept–Dec and March–May, Mon–Fri, 9–5; June–Aug, daily, 9–5; free; tel: 344–7220), now administered by the National Park Service of the US. Department of the Interior, is the most important structure in the park.

The original fort, first named the West Battery, was situated on an island about 200 ft from the mainland and connected to it by a wooden causeway with a drawbridge. It came into existence during the period of tensions preceding the War of 1812. Because the British practice of impressing American seamen into the British navy and the consequent attacks on American ships had made the nation aware of the vulnerability of its coastline, New York, virtually defenceless at the time, began the construction of four forts: Fort Wood on Bedloes (now Liberty) Island, Fort Gibson on Ellis Island, Castle Williams on Governors Island, and the West Battery here. Built from plans by John McComb, Jr, one of New York's earliest native architects, this fort along with Castle Williams reflected the early 19C conception of coastal defences, paired fortifications facing one another across a strategic waterway. The walls facing the harbour were pierced by a row of 28 cannons; those facing the land housed powder magazines and officers' quarters. Completed in 1811, the West Battery was untested during the war and fired its guns only for target practice and on commemorative occasions.

After the war it was renamed Castle Clinton after De Witt Clinton, who served during a long and distinguished career as both mayor of the city and governor of the state. In 1824, however, it was renamed again, this time Castle Garden; planted about with flowers and shrubbery, it opened as a place of entertainment, the top of the eight-foot thick sandstone walls serving as a promenade while the officers' quarters became a bar and refreshment room. Delighted audiences watched band concerts, balloon ascensions, fireworks, and scientific demonstrations (Samuel F.B. Morse's 'wireless telegraph' was the most famous) and enjoyed gaping at famous people who were publicly received here—for example the Marquis de Lafayette and Andrew Jackson. In 1845 a roof was added and Castle Garden became a theatre for more serious cultural fare. Perhaps the hall enjoyed its greatest night on 11 September 1850 when P.T. Barnum staged the American debut of Jenny Lind, the 'Swedish Nightingale', before a wildly enthusiastic sellout crowd of more than 6000 people.

In 1855, after more than a quarter of a century as a theatre, Castle Garden closed its doors to the American public and reopened them to the immigrants streaming in from abroad. By this time the land between the island and Manhattan had been filled, and the immigrant depot had to be fenced off from the rest of the area to exclude the swindlers who lurked in the area to prey on the linguistic and economic bewilderment of the new arrivals. The station, which provided medical care, fair currency exchange, and reliable information about jobs, housing, and travel to the interior, welcomed more than eight million people between 1855–89 when the Immigration Service became a function of the federal government.

Castle Garden was remodelled once more in 1896, this time by the firm of McKim, Meade & White, to open as the New York Aquarium, its tanks at first containing specimens from local waters. In the 1940s, despite the immense popularity of the aquarium, it appeared that this historic building was destined for the scrap heap. Robert Moses, then Commissioner of Parks, determined to raze the aquarium building perhaps as an act of revenge for the defeat of his proposed Brooklyn-Battery Bridge Crossing. A group of concerned citizens fought in Washington and in the courts to save the old fort. World War II gave them extra time, since all the heavy wrecking equipment was tied up in the war effort, and in 1946 Congress declared Castle Clinton a National Monument. By then the roof, much of the two-story facade and the great doors had been destroyed, but the walls at least remained.

Enter through the main gate. On the right side of the passageway is a small museum offering displays of the building during its various reincarnations; on the left is a reconstruction of the officers' quarters. The passageway opens into a circular courtyard surrounded by the massive walls of the fort which, on the inside, are faced with brick. At various points around the perimeter, recorded talks explain the history of the building.

Follow the path (counterclockwise direction) that encircles Castle Clinton. About a third of the way around, between the fortress and the Fireboat Station, is a *plaque commemorating Emma Lazarus*, who wrote the famous sonnet, 'The New Colossus', as part of the fund-raising effort for the pedestal of the Statue of Liberty (see p74).

Along the shoreline runs the *Admiral George Dewey Promenade*, with a spectacular *panorama of New York Harbor: from left to right, Brooklyn Heights, Governors Island (now a military reservation), Staten Island in the distance, Liberty Island with the Statue of Liberty, Ellis Island, and the New Jersey coastline behind it. At the N. end of the promenade on *Pier A* is the Fireboat Station (1885; DL). The pier rests on a complex underwater foundation of concrete blocks, arches, granite sections, and iron girders, and is one of the oldest piers remaining in the Hudson River. The tower, originally used as a lookout, now holds a clock donated in 1919 by Daniel Reid, one of the founders of U.S. Steel, to commemorate servicemen who died in World War I. The clock tolls the hours in ships' bells.

The promenade leads S. along the shoreline. Beyond Castle Clinton and a few yards inland from the promenade walkway is the *monument to Giovanni da Verrazano*, a Florentine explorer employed by the king of France, who in 1524 became the first known European to sail into New York Harbor. He wrote an enthusiastic description of his surroundings and of the Indians who welcomed him and claimed the land for France; four years later he set out on a fatal voyage either to South America or to the Carribean, where he is said to have been killed and eaten by cannibals. The bronze statue (1909; Ettore Ximenes) was donated by a group of Italian-American citizens who timed their presentation for the Hudson-Fulton Festival to point out that Verrazano got here 85 years before Henry Hudson. The female figure in front of the granite base represents Discovery, a sword in her right hand, formerly a torch in her left, the book of History at her feet.

At about the same time that Verrazano arrived, Esteban Gómez, a Portuguese explorer sailing for Spain, also reached the harbour, but Spain like France seems to have been indifferent to the new territory. In 1609, however, when Henry Hudson looking for a northwest passage to the orient on behalf of the Dutch East India Company explored the river as far as the site of Albany, the Dutch realised the potential of the new land for the fur trade. In 1613 Adraien Block, a Dutch trader, became the first European to spend any time on Manhattan, for his ship the 'Tyger' burned and he and his crew were forced to overwinter while constructing a new ship for their return. The timbers of the 'Tyger' were discovered in the Hudson River in 1904 during excavations for the subway. Block is also credited with exploring the Connecticut coast, discovering Long Island and Block Island, and naming Hell Gate, a treacherous stretch of water in the East River.

A little further S. and further inland is the *Wireless Operators' Memorial*, dedicated to those radio operators who perished at sea, the most famous of whom was Jack Phillips, radioman of the 'Titanic' which struck an iceberg and sank on the night of 14–15 April 1912.

Continue S. to the *East Coast War Memorial*, with its great bronze eagle (dated 1961) staring out to sea; sculptor Albino Manca claims that he modelled the eagle on pigeons he saw in Washington Square, though the resemblance seems slight. The eight marble pylons bear the names of 4596 Americans who perished in Atlantic coastal waters during World War II. Between the war memorial and the ferry terminal at the S. tip of the park is the *U.S. Coast Guard Memorial*, an eight-foot bronze statue of two guardsmen supporting an injured comrade. The statue (sculptor, Norman M. Thomas) financed by individual $1 contributions from Coast Guard personnel, was erected in 1947 after a controversy as to its artistic merit. (The concrete structure nearby is a ventilator for the Brooklyn-Battery Tunnel) On the W. side near the rear of the terminal for the Statue of Liberty ferries is a *bust of John Wolfe Ambrose* (1936; Andrew O'Connor), planner of the Ambrose ship channel, which opened in 1899, the year of its designer's death. The new channel, both deeper and shorter than its predecessor, reduced accidents and made the harbour accessible to larger ships, including the great luxury liners of the coming decades.

Tickets for the Statue of Liberty and Ellis Island ferries (see Rte 1) may be purchased at the terminal here. There is a public restroom near the playground to the E. of the ferry terminal.

Follow the path leading out of the park toward the E., past the Marine Flagpole. Just inside the fence is the *Oyster Pasty Cannon*, discovered during excavations and believed to have been part of the original battery that protected the fort in pre-Revolutionary times.

Continue along the path past the cannon and take the first exit from the park. Directly opposite at the S.E. corner of Bridge and State Streets is the *Seamen's Church Institute* (1969; Eggers & Higgins), a tall building whose tower ends in an elongated cross. The institute, which started in 1834 as a floating chapel in the East River, first occupied a sort of houseboat tied up at the foot of Pike Street; later it was moved to a building on South Street whose memorial to the victims of the 'Titanic' disaster is now part of the South Street Seaport Museum (see p90).

Organised to meet the needs of active merchant seamen, the institute, an agency of the Episcopal Church, offers a range of recreational and educational facilities for seamen. The cafeteria on the second floor is inexpensive and open to the public. On the first and second floors a collection of nautical artifacts includes bells salvaged from shipwrecks, photographs, prints, and ship models. Herman Melville (1819–91), author of 'Moby Dick' and himself a sea wanderer, was born approximately at the site of this building.

South of Peter Minuit Plaza are two ferry stations. The new one belongs to the *Staten Island Ferry*, the main commuting link between the boroughs of Richmond and Manhattan, one of New York's greatest cheap tourist attractions (see p597). To the left of the unattractive modern terminal is the BATTERY MARITIME BUILDING (1909; DL), at 11 South St, a fine old relic of the days when numerous ferries plied the East River. Constructed of sheet steel and painted green to imitate *verdigris* (compare the Statue of Liberty whose copper sheeting has weathered to its grey-green colour), it is elaborately decorated in the Beaux-Arts style of the period, with rivets, lattice work, rosettes, and marine designs. The great open-mouthed arches on the water side should be seen from the river, against the severely rectilinear background of the surrounding skyscrapers.

The *Governors Island ferry* leaves from this terminal; public access to the island is limited.

Next door to the S. at 7 State Street is the Rectory of the Shrine of the Blessed Elizabeth Ann Seton (originally the *James Watson House*; DL), the only survivor of the time when State Street was an elegant residential street. Designed in two sections (E. wing 1793, W. wing 1806), it has been attributed to John McComb, Jr. The details of the facade (the interior has been altered) reflect its Georgian and Federal heritage: the marble plaques in the brickwork, the oval windows on the W. wall, the splayed lintels above the rectangular windows. Its most distinctive feature, however, is the curved wooden portico which follows the street line; the tapered Ionic columns above the ground level are said to be made from ships' masts. Recognising the architectural importance and almost miraculous survival of the building, the present owners restored it in 1965 using a print in 'Valentine's Manual' of 1859.

The Blessed Elizabeth Ann Seton (1774–1821), the first American-born saint (canonised in 1975), founded the first order of nuns in the United States and was instrumental in establishing the Catholic parochial school system.

Across State Street to the S.E. is a small triangular park which contains a *monument to New York's first Jewish immigrants*, a group of Sephardic refugees fleeing persecution in Brazil seeking refuge in Holland. Their ship was seized by pirates, but luckily for the refugees the pirate ship was overtaken a few days later by a French frigate whose captain charged them for a voyage to Amsterdam but treacherously brought them to New Amsterdam instead. Their ship arrived in September 1654 and despite Peter Stuyvesant's opposition the Jews were granted permission to remain and to engage in commerce. South of the park is Peter Minuit Plaza, named after the Dutch governor who in 1626 made the most famous real estate deal in the city's history, purchasing the island of Manhattan from the Indians for 60 guilders, a sum worth $24 according to traditional rates of exchange.

At or near the present intersection of State and Whitehall Streets stood Peter Stuyvesant's town house, built in about 1657 and renamed Whitehall by the first English governor of New York, Sir Edmund Andros. Before landfill pushed the shoreline outward, the area was a small peninsula projecting into the harbour.

Return along Whitehall St to Water St for a view of some of the new skyscrapers which have radically altered the historic skyline. Two of the most visible are *1 New York Plaza* (1969; William Lescaze & Assocs) facing Water St between Whitehall and Broad Sts, an office building with a branch of the Chase Manhattan Bank, and *4 New York Plaza* (1968; Carson, Lundin & Shaw) across Broad St to the east, which contains offices, computers, and data-processing equipment for the Manufacturers Hanover Trust.

The former, with its recessed, picture frame windows, has been nicknamed the 'waffle iron', and singled out by architectural critics as a particularly unhappy example of modern architecture. The latter, although aesthetically more pleasing, has evoked such descriptions as 'behemoth', 'bulky brick brown fort', and 'monolith'. Like the other new office towers in the area, these buildings are the products of a construction boom that began in lower Manhattan in the late 1950s and continued through the 1960s, culminating in the building of the World Trade Center, which opened for tenants in the early 1970s.

The effects of the boom have not been entirely salubrious. One estimate reckons that some 40 million square feet of rentable office space have been added to lower Manhattan since 1956, glutting the market, placing severe financial pressures on smaller and older buildings, and straining the fragile network of public services, particularly mass transit. The brick and granite warehouses and small houses that once graced Front and Water Streets have been ruthlessly destroyed. The contours of the streets have been altered in the interests of efficiency and profit; Front Street has practically been obliterated S. of Wall Street, absorbed into the 'superblocks' that have allowed developers to erect ever larger buildings.

In an effort to make up for neighbourhoods destroyed by these tall buildings and to make the streets more attractive to pedestrians, the city passed the Zoning Resolution of 1961 offering a financial incentive to builders who provided street-level public facilities. For every square foot of 'plaza' space, the builder was allowed an additional 10 square feet of floor area up to an increase of 20% of the size of the building. Unfortunately the law did not have significant design requirements, and many of the plazas built south of Canal Street suggest that building owners wished to discourage public use, to make their plazas merely reflect a given corporate image. After this became apparent, the city passed an amendment to the Zoning Resolution requiring certain design features (like trees and seating) and amenities (like shopping facilities) to attract pedestrians.

From the corner of State and Whitehall Sts, walk a block E. along Water St (the eastward extension of State Street) to Broad Street. During the Dutch colonial period. BROAD STREET ('de Heere Gracht') was a canal for drainage and shipping, which reached to the present site of Exchange Place. The British filled it about 100 years before the Revolution, since it had become polluted and smelly, but the extra width of Broad St remains as a reminder of the former canal.

Walk one block inland along Broad St to the corner of Pearl St.

Pearl St, once on the shore of the East River, was named from the opalescent shells that lined the beaches. At Bridge St, which joins Pearl St at this intersection, stood the first bridge across the Broad St canal.

On the S.E. corner of Broad and Pearl Streets is the Fraunces Tavern, the most famous of a group of notable old buildings, the FRAUNCES TAVERN BLOCK, one of the few full blocks of 18 and 19C buildings to have escaped the successive downtown building booms.

Built on land filled in about 1700, it originally stood at the center of the city, containing both residential and commercial buildings. As East River shipping approached its zenith between the War of 1812 and the Civil War, land values rose making residential property too expensive to maintain, and the area became strictly commercial. Later, as shipping moved into the Hudson River during the closing decades of the 19C, the area deteriorated but remained relatively untouched. The block was threatened in the most recent construction boom, but since several of the buildings belong to the Sons of the Revolution, acquisition by developers was difficult; although prospective developers did acquire some land in the block, the boom faltered and collapsed before their plans could come to fruition.

The **Fraunces Tavern** at 54 Pearl St is a reconstruction (1907; William Mersereau; DL) of a mansion built in 1719 for Stephen (or Etienne) De Lancey. Unfortunately only a section of Holland brick in the W. wall remains of the original house, and since no graphic records of it are known to exist, the reconstruction is based largely on guesswork. An advertisement of 1781 offering it for sale, however, mentions '9 spacious rooms plus 5 bedchambers, 13 fireplaces, . . . and an exceeding good kitchen, and a spring of remarkable fine water therein'.

The De Lanceys, one of New York's wealthy and powerful early families, remained loyal to the king during the Revolution and suffered the confiscation of their property for this lack of political foresight. Even before the war, however, the house had become a warehouse and then a tavern owned by Samuel Fraunces, a West Indian of French and black ancestry, who purchased the property and opened it in 1763 as the Queen's Head Tavern.

Fraunces' abilities earned him the position of chief steward to George Washington, and his tavern subsequently became the scene of several significant events. In November 1783 De Witt Clinton gave a celebratory dinner to commemorate the evacuation of the British. Later in the same year Washington bade farewell to his officers in the Long Room and retired temporarily to private life. The tavern also witnessed the founding of the organisation that evolved into the New York Chamber of Commerce (1768).

During the 19C the building deteriorated along with the rest of the neighbourhood, becoming at its nadir a hotel for transients; after being badly burned several times (1832, 1837, 1852), it remained in a disreputable state until its purchase (1904) by the Sons of the Revolution, who restored it to its present condition.

The ground floor contains a restaurant (remarkable more for its historical associations than its fare) and the two stories above house a small museum (open Mon–Fri, 10.00–4.00, free; tel: 425–1778) with artifacts from the Revolutionary period and mementos of George Washington's Farewell Dinner, as well as an exhibit explaining the history and reconstruction of the building.

Across Pearl St toward the E. end of the block stood the original Dutch *Stadt Huys* or City Hall. The building began as a tavern in about 1641, a five-story gabled structure right at the water's edge, but was converted to the Town Hall when New Amsterdam was granted its municipal charter in 1653. It served not only as a meeting place, but as a jail, a debtors' prison, courthouse, and public warehouse. The British demolished the building in 1699, but part of the foundation was incorporated in a succeeding building. In 1968, the firm of Lehman Brothers purchased a 54,000 square foot plot containing the suspected site of the old *Stadt Huys* and generously paid for archaeological excavations. Two years later researchers uncovered parts of a wall and staircase (the jail was known to have been in the basement) as well as fragments of pottery, nails, clay pipes, and pieces of Dutch roofing tile.

Continue along Pearl St; turn left at COENTIES ALLEY. The name Coenties (Dutch *Coentje*) is either a nickname for Conraet or a combined form of Conraet and Antje; in any case Conraet and Antje Ten Eyck lived nearby and Conraet ran a tannery on Broad St. Follow Coenties Alley until it ends at Stone Street, so named because it was the first paved street in the city (1658). According to tradition, the wife of Stephanus Van Cortlandt the brewer (the street was first called Brouwers St) disliked the dust raised by passing vehicles and got her husband to have the situation improved. The present stones were laid in the 19C and are called Belgian blocks because they were supposedly invented there.

Follow Stone St to Mill Lane, the first intersection on the left, named after a large windmill built by the Dutch in 1626 which stood on the approximate site of Mill Lane and Mill St (now called S. William St).

Used primarily for grinding grain, it had a meeting room on the second story which was rented to the city's first Jewish congregation, Shearith Israel, starting sometime in the 1680s. Two millstones from the original mill can be seen in the Spanish & Portuguese Synagogue on Central Park West and W. 70th St. In 1729 the congregation, many of whose members were descendants of those refugees from Brazil who had arrived in 1654, purchased land S. of the mill for 100 pounds plus a loaf of sugar and a pound of tea. Here, at the site of 26 S. William St, they built their first permanent synagogue.

Continue along Stone Street to HANOVER SQUARE. Named after the English royal family of the Georges, Hanover Square was once a public common in an elegant residential neighbourhood. Its most notorious resident was William Kidd, the sea captain hanged in England in 1701 for piracy, who was nonetheless one of the city's most respected citizens and a contributor to Trinity Church. At the end of the 17C the area was the city's first Printing House Square, and a plaque on the building at 3 Hanover St records the publication in 1725 of New York's first newspaper, the 'New-York Gazette', published weekly by William Bradford whose grave can be seen in Trinity Churchyard. Bradford had come from England to Philadelphia in 1682 and in 1693 moved to New York, bringing with him the city's first printing press.

The plaque also mentions Hanover Square as the center of the *Great Fire of 1835*, the most devastating of a number of serious fires that plagued the city in the early 19C.

On the night of 17 December, a gas explosion rocked the area; fed by stockpiles of dry goods and chemicals, the blaze quickly raged out of control and spread to neighbouring buildings, whipped by winter winds. Firemen who rushed to the scene braving a subzero temperature found that their hoses quickly froze. Merchants hurried to rescue their stock, piling it in the streets, but by noon the next day the fire had destroyed all of Hanover Square, taking with it the stacked merchandise. By the time the blaze burned itself out, slowed by the thick masonry walls on Wall St in one direction and blocked by the river in the other, it had destroyed over 20 acres and more than 650 buildings, including all the Dutch colonial structures remaining in downtown New York.

The park is being renovated; when it is finished the *statue of Abraham de Peyster* (1896; George Edwin Bissell), which stood for a long time in Bowling Green Park, will be erected here. Commissioned by the de Peyster family, the bronze statue depicts their famous ancestor (1658–1728), a wealthy merchant and tireless public servant who served as alderman, mayor, chief justice of the colony and acting governor.

India House, at 1 Hanover Sq. on the S.W. side of the square, is a beautiful old brownstone built between 1851–54 (Richard Carman?; DL) for the Hanover Bank. One of the finest buildings in the Italianate style surviving in the city, India House is important both as a reminder of the elegance to which 19C commercial life could aspire (subsequent tenants were the New York Cotton Exchange and W.R. Grace and Company, the shipping firm) and as a prototype for the New York brownstone rowhouse. Noteworthy architectural details taken over by the rowhouse builders and sometimes repeated with monotonous regularity are the columns flanking the doorway and supporting a cornice and balustrade, the pediments over the first and second floor windows (segmental arches above the former, triangular above the latter), and the roof cornice supported by brackets. India House now belongs to a private men's club.

Walk along Hanover Square toward the East River. Diagonally across Water St is a large office building known by its address, *55 Water Street* (1972; Emery Roth & Sons), occupying a four-block 'superblock', a zoning concession its builders won by constructing Jeannette Park on the S. side of the building. The outdoor escalator leads to a rather forbidding plaza with a good view of the river and the Brooklyn waterfront.

At one time the upper plaza was to have been linked with Manhattan Landing, a colossal building project to extend from the South Street Seaport to Whitehall St and to include 6 million square feet of office space, 9500 units of luxury housing, a new Stock Exchange building, a hotel, a marina, an indoor sports complex, and a large parking garage. These facilities on the fringe of the Financial District would stand on landfill and on platforms extending 500 ft into the East River to the present pierhead line, a fact that accounted somewhat for the staggering price tag, some $1·2 billion, attached to the project. During the city's fiscal crisis, which grew acute during the depression year 1974–75, the project was shelved.

Jeannette Park, squeezed between 55 Water Street and its equally gigantic neighbours downtown, is now a stepped plaza, paved in brick and studded with small pieces of modern sculpture. Once it was a favourite haunt of stranded seamen, a tree-shaded park occupying the land created when Coenties Slip was filled in the late 19C. Named after the ship 'Jeannette', which took part in the tragic polar expedition of 1879–81, the park was trapezoidal and its walkway outlined the shape of a bell.

Return to the intersection of Water St and Old Slip, one block north.

Walk toward the waterfront along Old Slip. The *East River slips* (Old Slip, Burling Slip, Coenties Slip, and others) were originally docking areas for ships. As the coastline was pushed further out by landfill the slips were dredged to provide adequate draft and breakwaters were built further out in the river. Eventually the rectangular slips were filled, but their outlines remain in the shape of these streets.

In the middle of Old Slip sits the *former First Precinct Police Station* (1909; Joseph and Richard Howland Hunt; Dl.), designed to resemble a fortified Italian Renaissance palazzo. Across the slip (between Old Slip, South, and Front Sts) is the *United States Assay Office* (1930; James A. Wetmore), a five-story granite building with an impressive chimney. Within the building (not open to the public), gold and silver bullion is refined and uncurrent and mutilated coins are melted into bars to be sold as scrap to refiners.

Just inland from the Assay Office (across Front St) is *77 Water Street* (1970; Emery Roth & Sons), one of the more successful of the new office towers, with a pleasant and whimsical plaza. The seating, fountains, sculpture, and candy store attract pedestrians who daily enjoy the area and occasionally make nuisances of themselves wading in or drinking the water, soliciting, and littering.

At the four corners of the plaza stand four pieces of sculpture all dated 1969. In the N.E. is *City Fountains* by Victor Scallo. *Helix* by Rudolph de Harak in the N.W. is made of 120 stainless steel squares, each an inch thick, placed on top of each other in such a way that they create the illusion of a continuous spiral. George Adamy's work *Month of June* stands in the S.E. In the S.W. is a kind of sculptural joke called *Rejected Skin*, executed by William Tarr and inspired by some pieces of aluminum sheeting intended for use on the building, rejected because of imperfections, taken to a scrap yard and compacted. It has been praised as excellent and dismissed as 'rubbish', which it literally is. As Melvin Kaufman, the builder, pointed out when he conceived of the sculpture, the piece poses the question that while admittedly art can be trash, is it possible for trash to be art?

Further N. on Water St near the intersection of Pine St is an elegant building formerly called 88 Pine Street, now renamed *Wall Street Plaza*, presumably a more impressive address. On its small plaza stands a two-part stainless steel sculpture (1974) by Yu Yu Yang, consisting of an L-shaped vertical slab with a circular opening facing a polished, mirrorlike disc (diameter, 12 ft, weight, 4000 lbs). The work is a *Memorial to the Queen Elizabeth I*, the Cunard liner which burned in Hong Kong harbour; a nearby tablet recalls the history of the ship.

Whatever its address, the building (1973; I.M. Pei & Assocs), clad in white aluminum and glass, has been much admired, receiving an award from the American Institute of Architects for its 'classical purity'.

Continue N. on Water St. In Feb 1982, during construction of the building at 175 Water St near John St, an 18C merchant ship was discovered 15 ft below ground.

It was brought to shore some time after 1746, the date on a ceramic top found below its decks, before the coastline was pushed outward by landfill. Archaeological workers discovered thousands of small items—mostly dishes and bottles—on the western part of the site and in mid-January hit a solid wall along the lot's eastern edge, which in time they realised was the hull of an 85-by-26 ft ship with a rounded bow. Since building construction was already delayed a month by the archaeological work, only one side of the ship was removed from the site.

The building known simply as *127 John Street* (along Water St between John and Fulton Sts) is another modern building (1969; Emery Roth & Sons) with amusing artifacts to attract pedestrians. The plaza, planned by Corchia-de Harak Assocs, features an immense digital clock, a sculptural phone both (1972; Albert Wilson) with cut-out figures, and a neon tunnel.

Continue to Fulton St and turn right (E.). In the triangle formed by the intersection of Water and Fulton Sts is the *Titanic Memorial*, originally erected on top of the former Seamen's Church Institute in memory of those who went down with the Titanic. Follow Fulton St toward the East River.

The **South Street Seaport Museum** is a collection of historic buildings—counting houses, saloons, hotels, warehouses—restored ships, exhibition galleries, and shops in an area around Fulton St on the East River, once a major shipping center. The area is being restored in connection with a commercial development that will include shops, restaurants, offices, and other commercial activities, as well as expanding the facilities of the museum.

The piers, shops, and galleries are open 11–6 daily, except Thanksgiving, Christmas, and New Year's Day, though ship hours may be curtailed during winter. Admission to exhibition vessels, $2·50 for adults, $1·25 for students; children under six and senior citizens, free; tel: 766–9020 or, on weekends, 766–9066.

SUBWAY: IRT Broadway-Seventh Ave (trains 2, 3) to Fulton St; IRT Lexington Ave (trains 4, 5) to Fulton St; IND Eighth Ave (A train) to Broadway/Nassau. BMT Nassau St lines (J and M trains) to Fulton St or BMT Broadway local (RR train) to Cortlandt St.

BUS: M15 (via Second Ave) to Fulton St.

History. From the first days of settlement until the years after the Civil War, the city's maritime activity focused on the East River, actually an arm of the sea lying on the lee side of Manhattan and less affected than the Hudson River by ice floes, flooding, and the battering of the prevailing westerlies. During the early 19C Fulton St became a major thoroughfare leading to the Fulton Ferry which made the crossing to Brooklyn starting in 1816. The Fulton Market opened in 1822, first a produce market for farmers in Brooklyn and on Long Island, eventually a fish market. When the Erie Canal opened in 1825 industrial and farm products from the midwest began pouring into New York for export, and during its first year of existence 500 new shipping firms came into existence. The China trade, spearheaded by the firm of A.A. Low on Burling Slip (now John St) and the California trade both increased activity on South St. After the Civil War, however, the area fell into slow decline as steamships superceded the beautiful clippers and trade moved to the deepwater docks on the Hudson.

In the mid-1960s concerned citizens began working to save the old port which had become a backwater and miraculously still had a large number of 19C buildings intact, though decayed. Chartered in 1967, the South Street Seaport Museum began acquiring the historic buildings and collecting a fleet of ships, some like those that once rested at anchor in the port, others that worked in New York harbour. In 1979 the city approved a plan to merge museum interests with major commercial development and at present large scale restoration and construction are in progress. Included in the project, undertaken by the Rouse Company, are: restoration of the buildings of Schermerhorn Row, construction of a new Marketplace Building (bounded by South, Fulton, Front, and Beekman Sts), construction of a pavilion on Pier 17 with restaurants and shops, construction of an exhibition building on John St at South St which will serve as an introduction gallery to the Seaport, and restoration of the Tin Building (1907) on the waterfront at Pier 17, the oldest structure still occupied by the Fulton Fish Market.

The commercial development of the area has been welcomed by some who feel it will revitalise the neighbourhood and provide the museum with needed income, but castigated by others who believe that developers are sacrificing a fragile historical area to commercial enterprise disguised as preservation and that if successful the development will bring congestion, traffic, noise, chaos, and high prices to one of the last parts of the city to escape them.

EXHIBITION VESSELS are docked at Piers 15 and 16, and when the present restoration is completed in 1983 it is hoped that five vessels will be ready for boarding, all with exhibits of historical interest. The 'Wavertree' (1885) is a square-rigged, iron-hulled ship built in England to carry jute from India to Europe; she was dismasted rounding Cape Horn in 1910 and towed to a remote backwater where a slick of lanoline from a nearby slaughterhouse greased and preserved her hull. The 'Peking' is a four-masted bark (1911) from Hamburg, Germany, one of the last sailing ships built for commercial purposes. The 'Lettie G. Howard' (1893), a Gloucester fishing schooner, is typical of many that formerly brought their catches to the Fulton Fish Market. Built in 1907, the 'Ambrose lightship' marked the entrance to the Ambrose Channel (see p83) until replaced at that station in 1932. Other ships are the steam lighter 'New York Central No. 29' (1912) and the 'Maj. Gen. William H. Hart', a steam ferryboat launched in 1925 which ended her career on the Governors Island run.

The 1885 schooner, 'Pioneer', takes the public on sails in the harbour during warm months; call 766–9076 for reservations, schedule, and information.

GALLERIES AND SHOPS will change considerably as restoration and development continues. Among the familiar landmarks will be the *Seaport Gallery*, 215 Water St (tel: 766–9040) with changing exhibitions on nautical life (open Tues–Sun, 11–5); *Bowne & Co., Stationers*, at 211 Water St (tel: 766–9048), a printing museum whose antique presses are still in commercial operation; and the *Steamship Model Room and Museum Offices* at 203 Front St (tel: 766–9020), open 9.30–5.30 weekdays. There will be shops in Schermerhorn Row and in the Marketplace Building, whose 60,000 square ft of retail space will enclose also fish market stalls. The Seaport Store will be located in a museum building at the N.W. corner of South St and John St (Burling Slip).

Another major museum space is planned for the Inter City Fish Building on Beekman St between Water and Front Sts, built in 1914 as a warehouse. In addition to the museum library and facilities for conservation, the building will have collections of scrimshaw, nautical folk art, maps, charts, and early navigational equipment.

Architecturally the most interesting buildings in the seaport area are those known as SCHERMERHORN ROW (2–18 Fulton St, 91–93 South St, and 195–197 Front St) on the block bounded by John, Front, Fulton, and South Sts. The buildings (1811–12; DL) were built by Peter Schermerhorn as warehouses and counting houses on water-lots (land between the extremes of high and low tide) granted to him by the city under the condition that he fill them. The row originally consisted of 12 red brick buildings in the conservative Georgian-Federal style with brownstone-quoined doors (one remains at 2 Fulton St), wide shop windows, wrought-iron balconies, and steeply pitched slate roofs. The upper floors, with the exception of some roof and window changes, remain much in their original form though the ground floor facades were altered several times as fashion demanded. The row is being restored with historical accuracy to the point of time they best represent today. Sweets and Sloppie Louie's, two of the city's most famous seafood restaurants, are currently located in Schermerhorn Row.

Walk around the block to the S. from Fulton to John St, formerly known as Burling Slip between Front St and South St. Although the slip was filled in 1835, its original shape remains, giving the street its unusual width. At 167–171 John St is the *former A.A. Low & Co.* (1850) whose builder pioneered the China trade, maintaining a fleet of clipper ships: the 'Montauk', the 'Houqua', the 'Oriental', and mundanely, the 'N.B. Palmer', named after one of the firm's captains. The building has cast-iron piers that once sported Corinthian capitals; the upper floors, now covered with stucco, are faced with brownstone.

Across the street is the *Baker, Carver, and Morrell Ship Chandlery* at 170–176 John St (1840; DL), a handsome Greek Revival commercial building, perhaps the last survivor of the type. Less elegant examples of the period had the upper stories faced with brick; this one has granite from top to bottom.

For a detailed guide to the architecture of the area, read Ellen Fletcher Rosebrock's *Walking Around in South St* (1975), available at the Seaport bookstore.

3 The Financial District

SUBWAY: IRT Broadway-7th Ave local (train 2) to Rector St. IRT-Lexington Ave local (trains 4, 5) to Wall St. BMT subway (RR train) to Rector St.

BUS: Bus M6 (Broadway and Seventh Ave) to Rector St. Culture Bus Loop II (weekends and holidays) to Broadway-Rector St.

CAR PARKING: Battery Parking Garage (between Washington and Greenwich Sts, metered municipal parking). World Trade Center Parking Garage (under World Trade Center).

Wall Street, symbol of money and power, is a small street only about a third of a mile long, running between Broadway and the East River. The imposing buildings give it a monumental quality,

Once a wall reached from river to river, erected (1653) during Peter Stuyvesant's tenure, to protect the Dutch town from incursions by its British neighbours to the north. Fortunately for the townspeople the wall was never needed for defence, since it suffered the indignities frequently attendant upon municipal projects. The original plan called for a palisade to be made of whole tree trunks sharpened and driven into the ground, but perhaps because of bureaucratic bungling or perhaps because of simple laziness on the part of the builders, the wall was eventually constructed of planks instead. These proved overpoweringly attractive to homeowners as sources of firewood or lumber for household repairs, and so in 1699 the wall was torn down as useless by the British who didn't need it for defence anyhow. Wall Street still has a wall, though now it is made of the facades of banks and office towers and is therefore more institutional, more permanent (though the gap at 40 Wall shows that it is not eternal), and less responsive to the needs of the individual citizen than was its predecessor.

Visit the Financial District weekdays during business hours when the streets are crowded and busy; restaurants are very crowded during the lunch hour, so it is wise to eat early or late.

*Trinity Church. At the head of Wall St. on Broadway stands Trinity Church, once the loftiest building in the neighbourhood, now overshadowed by gigantic office buildings. Although modest in size

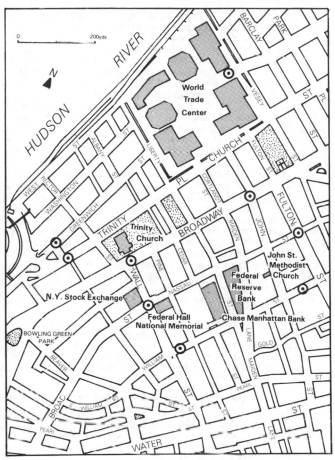

and conception, Trinity Church (1846; Richard Upjohn; DL) is probably New York's most famous church because of its dramatic setting. It is also one of the wealthiest as befits a parish situated in a district so unabashedly devoted to Mammon.

The wealth of the parish stems from the original land grant made in 1705 by Queen Anne, which included land west of Broadway between Fulton and Christopher Sts, an impressive chunk of lower Manhattan. Although the parish no longer owns the entire parcel, the endowment has been skillfully invested and in the early 1970s earned an income of some $5 million a year; the land in the (2^1/2 acre) graveyard alone is worth millions, considering the value of real estate in the area. Less lucrative but more picturesque were the rights extended to the church to take over all unclaimed shipwrecks and stranded whales.

The present church is the third on the site. The first, finished in 1697, was an attractive stone building facing the river, paid for by all citizens of the colony who were taxed for the construction costs regardless of religious preference. The most famous contributor to the building fund was William Kidd, who was one of New York's most respected citizens before his career as a privateer ended ignominiously on the gallows in 1701. The church burned in the Great Fire of 1776 during the British occupation and remained in ruins until long after the Revolution. A second church had to be demolished in 1839 after a heavy snowfall compromised the roof.

The building now occupying the site was completed in 1846 (architect Richard Upjohn) and belongs to the Gothic Revival tradition, although its 'Gothic' quality pertains to the decoration rather than to the structure. In a medieval church, the buttresses along the nave would support the high walls against the outward thrust of the stone roof vaults, a structural safeguard unnecessary here since the vaults are made of plaster and hung from wooden roof trusses, more or less like any plaster ceiling. Nevertheless, the Gothic elements (the flying buttresses, the stained glass windows, the Gothic tracery, and the medieval inspiration of the sculpture) impressed and pleased 19C New Yorkers. The use of brownstone on the facade, however, drew criticism, since until the construction of Trinity Church brownstone had been an inexpensive material generally used as a cheap substitute for marble, granite, or limestone. But since Trinity was a wealthy parish even in 1839 when the building was being planned, the choice was probably made for aesthetic rather than financial reasons. The Romantic Movement, making itself felt in architecture as well as the other arts, favoured the use of dark building materials, which were considered more 'picturesque' and more 'natural'—that is, more like the colours of the landscape—than lighter coloured marble or granite.

The doors of the church, modelled after the famous Ghiberti doors on the Baptistery in Florence, were designed by Richard Morris Hunt and donated by William Waldorf Astor. Karl Bitter, who won the competition for the construction, executed the main doors whose panels illustrate the theme 'Thou didst open the Kingdom of Heaven to all believers.'

The north doors, by J. Massey Rhind, depict scenes from the lives of men delivered from trouble and brought to places of rest. The south doors, by Charles H. Niehaus, present scenes from the history of Manhattan and of Trinity Church. The stained glass window is by the architect. The All Saints Chapel on the north aisle was built in 1913 by architect Thomas Nash. The addition on the south side contains a small museum with communion silver and other articles of religious and historical importance to the parish. (Museum open Mon–Fri: 10.30–12, 12.30–3.30; Sat: 10.30–3.30; Sun: 12.30–3.30; free; tel: 285–0872.)

The building is 79 ft wide and 166 ft long; the tower including the spire stands 280 ft above the ground. The first 'ring of bells' was received from London in 1797 and is the oldest in New York. Originally the bells were to be swung, but since no tradition of bell ringers exist in the United States, the bells are now stationary, their clappers connected to a ringing case in a room below the belfry, so that tunes can be played on them.

The church sits in a beautiful *Graveyard, one of the few unpaved spots in the Financial District, a pleasant place to wander and meditate, though visitors are advised not to feed the pigeons and not to traffic in drugs. Some of the gravestones are quite old and beautiful, their incised frizzle-haired angels and hourglasses reminding onlookers of mortality and what lies beyond. The oldest belongs to Richard Churcher who died at the age of five in 1681.

Others are more elaborate, marking the burial places of renowned figures: Robert Fulton, whose 'Clermont' proved that steamboat travel was economically viable, Alexander Hamilton, William Bradford, the publisher of the 'New York Gazette' (see p87), and Captain James Lawrence, whose nautical tombstone brings to mind his famous remark about not giving up the ship. Near the Broadway sidewalk is the burial place of Charlotte Temple, a young lady of genteel background who was seduced and abandoned by a British officer and immortalised in a long but popular novel by Sarah Haswell Rowson. 'Charlotte, a Tale of Truth' was published in 1791 in London, reprinted in Philadelphia in 1794, and quickly went through 160 editions. The impressive graveyard cross in the center of the northern portion of the cemetery is a monument to the memory of Caroline Webster Astor, queen of New York society at the turn of the century (see pp256,297). At the northeast corner of the plot is a large and very Gothic tribute to the Martyrs of the American Revolution, who died while imprisoned by the British in a sugarhouse (see p120).

Walk up Broadway as far as Thames St. The *Trinity and U.S. Realty Buildings* at 111 and 115 Broadway (1906; Francis H. Kimball) are two fine examples of early 20C Gothic skyscrapers. The Gothic decoration continues inside the lobbies, which have polychromed ceilings, sculptured corbels, and elaborate tracery around the elevators.

Diagonally across the street at 120 Broadway, the *Equitable Building* demonstrates what a skyscraper should not be. In order to maximise the available rental space and hence the owners' profit, the Equitable Building rises 40 stories without setback, filling almost the entire site and darkening the sidestreets and the windows of adjacent buildings (this problem has been alleviated somewhat by the setback of the new Marine Midland Bank to the north; Pine St, however, is still dark and gloomy). The negative impact of the building (completed 1915; architect Ernest R. Graham) spurred the city the following year to pass the **Zoning Resolution of 1916.**

This was a law that required buildings above a certain height to set back from the building line. The amount of setback required by this Zoning Resolution was determined by running an imaginary plane, the 'sky exposure plane', up from the center of the street at a predetermined angle and requiring the profile of the building to remain within this boundary. The setback regulation explains the 'wedding cake' silhouette of so many early skyscrapers. If carried to its logical conclusion, this regulation would mean that very tall buildings, like the Empire State Building, would end either in pyramids or in tiny cubes, but a further provision of the law stated that after setbacks had reduced the building size to 25% of the site, the tower could rise straight up. In 1961 the earlier zoning law was amended in significant ways. First the size of tower allowed to rise straight up without stepping back was enlarged from 25% to 40% of the site. Second, the law established absolute limits on building size. Third, the law offered builders a bonus for including plaza space in their designs (see p35).

At 100 Broadway near the corner of Wall St is the present *Bank of Tokyo* (1895; Bruce Price), with a row of allegorical stone ladies above the ground floor by J. Massey Rhind who did the north doors on Trinity Church. Although the present owners have remodelled the building, the lobby still contains its original elaborate ceiling and columns.

1 Wall St is the IRVING TRUST COMPANY (1932; Voorhees, Gmelin & Walker, with an addition in 1965), a fine 1930s skyscraper whose exterior detail emphasises its verticality and whose setbacks

illustrate the provisions of the 1916 Zoning Resolution. The curtain wall is designed to suggest fabric folds and is incised with a fabric pattern. The large windows which appear at the top of the faceted tower open into a lounge (not open to the public) with a high faceted ceiling. The Wall St lobby contains wonderful Art Deco mosaic decoration by Hildreth Meière in tones of gold, flaming red, and orange.

The *New York Stock Exchange at 8 Broad St (1903; George B. Post), like Federal Hall and the Citibank building, is a financial district 'temple', dating from the period after the World's Columbian Exhibition, when classical architecture was expected for all important public buildings. The sculpture on the pediment is by J.Q.A. Ward and Paul W. Bartlett, and depicts *Integrity Protecting the Works of Man*. The central figure, Integrity, is seen stretching out her arms protectively toward figures that represent the various activities and industries pursued by humanity—a farmer and his wife, an industrial worker, a prospector. The group was designed by Ward, who was elderly at the time, and modelled primarily by Bartlett.

History of the Exchange: Shortly after the end of the American Revolution, the Congress sitting in Federal Hall issued about $80 million in bonds to pay for the war debt. A central marketplace became necessary for these securities, and after a few years of informal trading outdoors and in coffeehouses, a group of 24 brokers got together and drew up the 'Buttonwood Agreement' (17 May, 1792), which marks the formal beginnings of the New York Stock Exchange. The name of the document commemorated a buttonwood or sycamore tree on the north side of Wall St between William and Pearl Sts near which the brokers used to meet (a tree stands in front of the present Stock Exchange in memory of the origins of the organisation). The Stock Exchange gained greater importance from its role in financing the War of 1812 and from selling bonds for the Erie Canal (opened 1825) and moved into a rented room in the Merchants Exchange Building. During this period (1842–54) two sessions were held each day, conducted by the call system; the president of the exchange read off the names of the different issues, pausing after each so that the brokers could make their transactions. Since each member had a regular chair during these proceedings, membership became known as having a 'seat' on the exchange. The New York Stock Exchange achieved even greater power financing the Civil War, and in 1865 it moved to a new building at 10–12 Broad St, which it purchased five years later.

The period from the close of the Civil War to the beginning of World War I was one of great industrial and geographical expansion, the era when the great American fortunes were made, and men like Gould, Harriman, Morgan, and Vanderbilt fought one another for financial domination. Their struggles were marked by stock market panics, by failures of banks and other institutions, and by the ever greater acquisition of wealth by the victors. World War I brought prosperity to Wall St, and the market rose to staggering heights until the most famous crash, the crash of October 1929, which was followed by the nation's most severe depression. As a result of the crash and depression, the Securities and Exchange Commission was formed in 1934 to attempt governmental regulation of the Stock Exchange. There are now 1366 members, the maximum permitted by law. The most recently sold seat brought $50,000; the highest sold cost $625,000 in 1929, and the lowest $17,000 in 1942.

THE VISIT: The New York Stock Exchange is open to visitors weekdays from 10.00 until 4.00; visitors' entrance at 20 Broad St. Exhibits on the third floor include a film, lectures, and visual presentations showing the history of the Exchange, the workings of the stock market, and related subjects. Although the Visitors' Gallery was closed for a while after someone placed a tear gas bomb in the ventilating system in 1933, the public is now admitted to the gallery though visitors are asked to deposit packages and cases. Guides point out the various activities taking place on the apparently chaotic trading floor and explain the functions of the annunciator boards, the ticker tape, and the trading posts.

The *Morgan Guaranty Trust Company* at 23 Wall St (1913; Trowbridge & Livingston; DL) was the bank of J. Pierpont Morgan, who more than any other single man epitomised Wall St, power, and the rapacious acquisition of wealth. The Wall St facade still bears traces of a tragic and unsolved explosion that occurred in 1920, killing 33 passersby and injuring 400 others. At first, the explosion was believed to be part of a diabolical anarchist plot; another more innocent but rather fantastic theory attributes it to the ignorance of the junk dealer parked outside the bank who somehow mistook the sticks of dynamite in his wagon for sash weights and inadvertently set them off. The building itself is elegant and severe, belonging to the same classic, eclectic tradition that inspired the First National City Bank (now Citibank) down the street (see p292 for architectural background).

Across the street at 26 Wall St is *Federal Hall National Memorial (1842; Town & Davis with John Frazee; DL), one of the finest Greek Revival buildings in the city and one of New York's most important historic sites, although unfortunately the important historic events that took place here predate the present building.

Museum open June–Aug: daily 9–5; Sept–May: Mon–Fri, 9–5; free; tel: 264–8711. Telephones and rest rooms; no eating facilities. Exhibits include dioramas and artifacts relating to the history of the building and site, including models of the building in its various incarnations, memorabilia relating to Washington's inauguration, the Zenger trial, and New York during the Revolutionary War period.

HISTORY. In the early 18C the British City Hall (begun 1699; demolished 1812), the successor to the Dutch *Stadt Huys* stood on this site. In that building, John Peter Zenger, the argumentative publisher of the 'Weekly Journal', was tried in 1735 for libelling the Royal Governor, William Cosby. Zenger's lawyer argued that the criticism Zenger had printed was true, and hence could not be called 'seditious libel'; the jury acquitted Zenger, establishing a precedent for freedom of the press, that would later be reaffirmed in the Bill of Rights.

Thirty years later the Stamp Act Congress, a group of 27 delegates from nine of the thirteen colonies, met in the building to declare their indignation at the Stamp Act, a fund-raising plan to help defray the cost of maintaining a British army in the colonies. The delegates worked out a statement of principle asserting that Americans should enjoy the same rights and privileges accorded to British citizens living in Britain and should not be taxed without their consent.

After the Revolution the Congress met here, first under the Articles of Confederation, but later under the present U.S. Constitution. George Washington was inaugurated here in 1789, more or less on the spot where J.Q.A. Ward's statue (1883) stands today. The President took the oath of office on the second floor balcony, wearing what was for the period a simple suit; it was made of brown cloth manufactured in Connecticut and its choice reflected Washington's desire to encourage local industry.

Well-to-do citizens had contributed $32,000 to renovate the building for the occasion, and Pierre L'Enfant, later one of the principal planners of Washington, D.C., directed the remodelling. The hall was renamed Federal Hall in honour of New York's prestigious position as the nation's capital, although this preeminence did not last long since the federal government was moved to Philadelphia in 1790. Too small to serve again as the seat of local government, Federal Hall began to decline and was eventually sold at auction for scrap, bringing in only a paltry $425.

In its place arose the present building, a Greek Revival temple with Doric columns carved from Westchester county marble and a rotunda inside. It functioned as the U.S. Custom House and later as one of the six government sub-treasuries; one of the vaults concealed behind an innocuous looking door is on view in the rotunda. In 1939 Congress designated the building as a National Historic site, and in 1955 it came under the jurisdiction of the National Park Service;

The steps on the Wall St side serve as a kind of informal outdoor theatre for office workers during the lunch hour; entertainments range from Salvation Army brass choirs, pantomime artists, prophets of doom or enlightenment, to more formal dance and dramatic troupes.

Next door is the *Seamen's Bank for Savings*, which incorporates the facade, the foundations and the bullion vaults of its predecessor, a United States Assay Office built in 1919 by York & Sawyer. The bank thus provides a successful example of architectural preservation and adaptation in a city where demolition is an omnipresent threat.

The original Seamen's Bank had as one of its goals the inculcation of thrift in sailors who were all too ready to squander their wages on the transient pleasures available to them when they reached port. The bank contains a collection of ship models, antique coin banks, scrimshaw, and other nautical artifacts (open Mon–Fri, 8.30–5.30).

In 1826 a Greek Revival building designed by Martin E. Thompson occupied this site, functioning as a bank and later as a U.S. Government Assay Office. When the building was torn down in 1915, its marble facade was dismantled and eventually incorporated in the American Wing of the Metropolitan Museum of Art (see p351).

At 40 Wall St is *Manufacturer's Hanover Trust*, a building originally occupied by the Bank of Manhattan (1929; H. Craig Severance & Yasuo Matsui). Planned as the world's tallest building during a period when architects were exercising secrecy and cunning to build higher than their competitors, this building never broke the record; the builders of the Chrysler Building surreptitiously added a stainless steel spire to their structure, previously 2 ft shorter than 40 Wall St, to become victors in the contest—at least until the completion of the Empire State Building. The pyramidal tower and spire atop this bank make it a familiar part of the downtown skyline. For the history of the Bank of Manhattan, see p100.

At 48 Wall St is the *Bank of New York* (1927; Benjamin Wistar Morris), whose top, a Georgian style cupola, makes it another familiar skyline landmark. Founded by Alexander Hamilton in 1784 it is the oldest commercial bank in the country (see the plaques on the west corner describing its beginnings and the original Wall St wall).

Across the street at 55 Wall St is **Citibank** (formerly the First National City Bank), one of Wall St's most famous buildings remarkable for having been constructed in two separate stages. The first section (1842; Isaiah Rogers; DL), a three-story Ionic temple with an imposing domed central hall, belongs to the same period and the same architectural tradition as Federal Hall. The 16 granite columns, quarried in Quincy, Mass, were hauled up Wall St by 40 teams of oxen, to make an impressive facade for the building, which first served as the new Merchants Exchange, replacing the one destroyed in the Great Fire of 1835. Later used as the Custom House, the building was remodelled by the firm of McKim, Mead & White in 1907 when the Custom House at Bowling Green opened (see p76). The architects doubled the volume of the building by adding the upper stories, which are surrounded by a tier of Corinthian columns.

Walk around the block to the N. to *70 Pine Street* (1932; Clinton & Russell), another building famous for its top, a Gothic crown with a slender spire. Before the buildings across the street were demolished, 70 Pine St was attached to one of them by an aerial bridge on the sixteenth floor and hence gained the more prestigious address, 60 Wall Tower. Now that 60 Wall St is gone, the excuse for the address is gone also.

Near the east entrance on Pine St is a large model of the building itself. During the 1920s and 30s, designers made considerable use of sculptural models, and it is possible that the architect, having gone to so much trouble to construct the model, had it installed here (there is another on the Cedar St side). Formerly the Cities Service Building, 70 Pine St has a fine Art Deco lobby, with brown and beige tones of marble, polished aluminum decoration, and Egyptian-looking elevator doors.

Return to Wall St. On the N.W. corner of Wall and Water Sts is the *site of the Tontine Coffee House*, where members of the infant New York Stock Exchange transacted business before the organisation had an official residence.

Turn right on William St. At *No. 20 Exchange Place* is another skyscraper which holds a recognizable place in the skyline. Completed in 1931, the building was originally planned with an elaborate top, which went by the wayside after the crash of 1929. It still has fine Art Deco detailing inside and out. There are gargoyles high on the facade and plaques depicting some of the most famous coins in history. Further down the street at 56 Beaver St is the former *Delmonico's Restaurant*. Sitting imposingly on its triangular plot, the building remains an elegant reminder of its distinguished past when it was one of the most highly acceptable places to dine and to be seen. The original Delmonico's opened here in 1827 and was among the first restaurants to offer the public the delights of fine continental cuisine.

Although New Yorkers were at first cautious about foreign food, the Delmonico brothers were eventually successful and in 1846 opened a second establishment, a hotel and restaurant at 25 Broadway. This building, roughly on the site of the present Bowling Green Post Office, was elaborately furnished (rooms cost $10 to $60 per month) and gave its owners 'a new and indisputable claim to immortality', according to a contemporary newspaper review.

Further down South William St is *Mill Lane*, whose name commemorates the presence of a flour mill erected by the Dutch West India Company. Upstairs a large loft used as a public meeting place served also as the first house of worship in the community. William St, incidentally, takes its name from one of the early settlers, William

Beekman, whose family also donated its name to Beekman St, near City Hall, and Beekman Place further uptown. The block of S. William St between Mill Lane and Broad St is rather curious, with coffee shops and night clubs of the apparently transient variety installed on the ground floors of buildings whose facades are imitation Dutch or English: nevertheless, because the street is narrow and crooked, the neighbourhood retains some of the flavour of an older New York. Walk back to the intersection of Wall and William Sts, and continue N. on William St.

The **Chase Manhattan Bank** (1960; Skidmore, Owings & Merrill) was a trendsetting building in many ways. First, its very presence here is testimony to the bank's decision in the late 1950s to remain downtown when the financial community appeared to be on the brink of flight uptown. By electing to remain, the Chase Manhattan encouraged other firms to do likewise and thus stimulated the present growth of the area. Second, the building became the first example in lower Manhattan of the International Style, a style characterised by severe, slablike forms of glass and steel with equally severe, unembellished surfaces. The designers of the bank were also the first in the area to provide a plaza for pedestrians, a gratuitous act at the time, since the building predates the Zoning Resolution of 1961.

History. The Chase Manhattan Bank is the successor to the Chase Bank (named after Salmon P. Chase, Secretary of the Treasury under Abraham Lincoln and originator of the national banking system) and the Manhattan Company, formed by Aaron Burr among others. In 1799 Burr and a group of investors organised the **Manhattan Water Company,** whose apparent intent was to supply the city with an adequate, safe water supply. Included in the group's charter was an unobtrusive clause which gave the investors the right to form a bank and engage in various financial activities. Although the Manhattan Water Company did lay several miles of wooden pipe to carry water, its primary interest quickly became banking—and maybe always had been. Alexander Hamilton claimed that Burr used his banking privileges to enhance his political career, and this vociferous and sustained criticism of the bank was yet another source of hostility between the two men.

Though bold and imaginative when it was built, the PLAZA is not entirely successful, partly because the terrain slopes downhill at the north end, making the plaza inaccessible from Liberty St, partly because it offers such a large expanse of pavement. Isamu Noguchi's sunken *Japanese garden* does provide some relief from the inhospitality of the concrete, with its undulating floor, trickling water, and black basalt rocks brought from Japan by the sculptor. Originally the fountain was to contain fish, but they had to be rescued from the deleterious effects of air pollution and from people's irrepressible desire to throw coins into fountains.

The rocks were dug from the bed of the Uji River near Kyoto, where centuries of erosion shaped them into their present distinctive forms. Each rock, weighing from 1·5 to 7·5 tons, was hoisted into position under the sculptor's supervision and is now supported by a poured concrete base. A fountain of 45 vertical pipes near the center of the pool produces various effects, from a massive spray to a mere bubbling.

In 1972 the owners installed the sculpture, *Group of Four Trees* by Jean Dubuffet a 43-ft, 25-ton fabrication supported by a steel skeleton and constructed of fibreglass, aluminum, and plastic resin materials the artist hoped would withstand the city's toxic environment; the polyurethane paint used on the surface is essentially the same kind used to paint lines on streets.

The work has been called handsome, humane, amusing, and ominous; and critics have been quick to point out the ironic juxtaposition of an institution that epitomises the moneyed 'establishment' in this country and a work by an artist who styles himself antibourgeois and anticultural, and claims the influence of children, criminals, and psychotics.

The bank building itself is 813 ft tall, has six underground levels and 60 stories above ground. Excavation began in 1957 but took 20 months since bedrock lay some 25 ft below layers of sand and muck which had to be hardened with chemicals before the site could be blasted. The vault, which weighs 985 tons, reaches down 90 ft below street level and occupies 35,000 square ft of floor space. It is anchored in bedrock to keep it from being washed away in the event of a tidal wave, surely an unlikely occurrence but not an unprecedented one, since such a disaster occurred in 1807.

Close to the Chase Manhattan are several important old and new buildings connected with business and banking. Across Nassau St at 140 Broadway the designers of the Chase Manhattan came up with the architecturally superior *Marine Midland Bank Building* (1967; Skidmore, Owings & Merrill), a smooth, dark building that soars straight up without setbacks (it occupies 40% of its site; the rest is plaza). On the Broadway side stands Isamu Noguchi's red steel and aluminum '*Cube*' (1973), a 28-ft outdoor sculpture that required a building permit because it is an enclosed mass. At 65 Liberty St, the CHAMBER OF COMMERCE OF THE STATE OF NEW YORK (1901; James B. Baker; DL) is a fine remnant of the Beaux-Arts tradition, unusual because of the assymetrical placement of the entrace. Originally three large sculptural groups graced the facade between the columns, but the damage inflicted by air pollution and pigeons forced their removal.

The Chamber of Commerce, founded in 1768 in the Fraunces Tavern (p86), is an organisation primarily concerned with commercial growth within the city and state; in the past it has supported such projects as the Erie Canal, the Atlantic cable, and the development of the rapid transit system.

At *55 Liberty Street* (1909; Henry Ives Cobb) is an attractive early skyscraper with Gothic details, now converted to apartments.

THE FEDERAL RESERVE BANK (1924; York & Sawyer; DL) fills the entire block north of the Chase Manhattan with its massive institutional stolidity. Philip Sawyer, the architect, had studied in Italy, and his design obviously reflects his admiration for the fortified palaces of the great Renaissance families whose wealth and power made them institutions in their own right. The Strozzi Palace in Florence is the principal model for the bank, and the superbly crafted wrought iron lanterns flanking the doorway are almost exact replicas of their Florentine predecessors. Executed by Samuel Yellin (who was responsible for the wrought iron work in the Cunard Building on lower Broadway), they are considered outstanding examples of the work of a master craftsman.

Beneath the imposing bank are five levels containing offices and bullion vaults, where gold from foreign countries is stored. International transactions can be consummated by simply moving the gold from one vault to another without its ever getting above ground. Free tours of the building are available by advance request; call the Public Information Office at 791–6130.

North of the Federal Reserve Bank (intersection of William St and Maiden Lane) is the *Home Insurance Company* with a small plaza and a plaque recording Thomas Jefferson's residence on the site.

At 100 William St is a building for which the 1961 Zoning Resolution was amended so that the owners could provide a covered gallery with shops instead of the usual open plaza and still qualify for the bonus floor area.

Around the corner to the W. on John St (between William and Nassau Sts) is the JOHN STREET METHODIST CHURCH, which in the midst of continual worldly change has steadfastly occupied this property from 1768. It is the oldest Methodist society in the country. The present building (1841; DL) is the third on the site and an early example of the Italianate style. The wide board flooring, entrance stairway, pews, and light brackets along the balcony were preserved from an earlier building of 1817, demolished when John St was widened.

The first congregation, composed primarily of Irish Methodist immigrants who had come to this country in the early 1760s, was led by Philip Embury and Barbara Heck. Mrs Heck, Embury's cousin, came home one day to find her husband, brother, and friends gambling at cards in her kitchen; shocked at such social laxity, she broke up the game (one early illustration shows her tossing the cards into the fire), and entreated her cousin to assume the duties of local preacher, since he had served in that office in Ireland. Embury began preaching at his home in 1766, but when his living room became too crowded, the group rented the upper story of a Rigging Loft to hold their services. In 1768 the Society purchased this property on John St, and Embury drew up plans for the original chapel, a stone building faced with plaster, which he literally helped build.

One of the early sextons of the church was Peter Williams, a black man whose parents were slaves of a wealthy family living on Beekman St. Williams was converted to Christianity and became sexton of Wesley Chapel, as the first church was called. When his owner returned to England after the Revolution, the Church trustees bought him privately for 40 pounds, thinking it embarrassing for a well-known Christian to be sold publicly at auction. He repaid his purchase price over a period of years and was formally emancipated in 1785; he then went into the tobacco business, prospered, and eventually founded the Mother Zion Church, the first Black Methodist church in New York.

In the basement of the present church are articles dating back to this period; among them the first altar rail, a clock sent by John Wesley, Embury's Bible and lectern.

Walk down John St to Broadway. Go left on Broadway to Liberty St.

At the N.W. corner of Liberty St and Broadway is *One Liberty Plaza*, the U.S. Steel Building, (1972; Skidmore, Owings, & Merrill). The building is notable primarily because it replaced the famous SINGER BUILDING (1908; Ernest Flagg) which was the tallest building in the world for eighteen months and is still the tallest building ever to be demolished. While the Singer Building was beautiful and much prized by architectural critics and city historians, it did not provide enough office space to keep up with rising real estate values in the area, and in 1964 the land on which it stood was sold to U.S. Steel for $30 million. The architects designed a speculative office tower which, to maximise the rentable floor space, occupied most of the block. In order to conform with zoning regulations they devoted the land across the street to park space.

There is an exhibition in the lobby of the building called the 'Money Tree', which explains the flow of funds in the U.S. economy, and gives the passing investor an opportunity to watch the tickers from the New York and American Stock Exchanges. (Open Monday–Friday, 9.00–5.00, free.)

Across Cortlandt Street from the north side of One Liberty Plaza is the *East River Savings Bank*, a fine Art Deco building of the 1930s, with a panoramic mural of the East River and its environs as they appeared in 1935 (artist Dale Stetson).

*The World Trade Center

SUBWAY: IRT Broadway–7th Ave, (train 1) to Cortlandt St. IND, Eighth Ave (trains A, AA, or E) to Chambers St. BMT Broadway local (train RR) to Cortlandt St.

BUS: Bus 10 (Eighth Ave and Central Park West) or Culture Bus B:88.

Dominating the neighbourhood with its huge twin towers, its five acre plaza, and surrounding buildings is the **World Trade Center** (1976; Minoru Yamasaki and Assocs; Emory Roth and Sons). Although the idea of a centralised facility which would bring together businesses and government agencies involved in international trade had been bandied about since the end of World War II, the World Trade Center was seriously proposed in 1960 and made possible by legislation enacted in 1962. It opened for business in 1970, some ten years and (according to recent estimates) some $700 million later.

Developed by the Port Authority of New York and New Jersey, the Trade Center houses more than 600 businesses and trade organisations including importers, freight handlers, the U.S. Custom House, steamship lines, and international banks.

CONSTRUCTION OF THE WORLD TRADE CENTER: Like Battery Park, much of the Trade Center stands on man-made land, once the bed of the Hudson River.

During excavation for the Hudson tube in this vicinity in 1904, construction workers came across some of the charred timbers of the 'Tyger', a trading ship captained by Adriaen Block that burned in the harbour in 1613. Block and his followers, hardy and inventive men that they were, spent the winter in New York and built themselves another vessel, the 'Onrust' ('Restless') which carried them back to Holland. The relics from the 'Tyger' can be seen at the Museum of the City of New York.

For construction workers the presence of landfill meant that bedrock was buried some 70 ft below layers of silt, sand, and rubble; normal excavation methods might therefore result in the sinking of neighbouring streets with disastrous effects on surrounding buildings. Furthermore the land, like all New York underground, was infiltrated by fire alarm cables, sewer lines, water pipes, telephone and electrical cables, steam pipes, and, most difficult of all, the Hudson tubes and terminal, all of which had to be relocated while maintaining service. The engineers for the project chose a method for excavating the basement walls which had never been used in the United States, the slurry trench method. As material was dug out for the basement walls, bentonite slurry, a sloppy mixture of clay and water, was piped into the trench, making conventional shoring unnecessary. When the trench was completed, a steel cage was lowered into the slurry to form the skeleton of that section of the wall; concrete was poured into the bottom of the trench and the slurry was pumped out by a pipe into the next section to be excavated.

Once the basement perimeter walls were built, the site itself could be excavated. During this period of construction, the railroad tubes beneath the site were exposed and placed in protective cradles so that the trains could continue to run. The excavated dirt and rubble was dumped into the Hudson behind a retaining wall forming New York's newest filled land, 23·5 acres between Rector and Cortlandt Sts.

Structurally the twin towers represent an innovation in skyscraper technology. Unlike conventional skyscrapers whose inner steel skeleton carries the weight (but rather like the masonry wall buildings of the late 19C), the towers have load bearing walls. The only interior steel columns are in the elevator cores, an arrangement which permits maximum interior space but which also cuts down on possible arrangements and sizes of windows.

Much of the material in the towers was prefabricated—the outer walls and the floor sections, for example—so the task of lifting all these pieces to greater and greater heights provided considerable lunchtime interest to office workers and sidewalk superintendents. On top of each tower stood four kangaroo cranes, presumably named from their ability to 'jump' upward whenever the walls reached the height at which they were working. When the time came, diesel driven hydraulic jacks lifted the 200-ton cranes about 30 ft higher to a new position astride the construction. At the end of the job, each crane dismantled and lowered the one next to it. The last crane raised a guy derrick from the street and assembled it. The derrick took apart the crane and lowered it. Finally the derrick itself was dismantled and brought down by freight elevator.

THE BUILDINGS: The World Trade Center is a complex of six buildings surrounding a five-acre plaza. The most famous are the two towers (One and Two World Trade Center), each 1350 ft tall, having 104 elevators, 21,800 windows, and an acre of rentable space per floor. The hotel (Three World Trade Center) is a 20 story building serving international businessmen, tourists, and other people with ties to downtown New York. The United States Custom House (Six World Trade Center) handles the services relating to import and export that used to be transacted in the building at Bowling Green.

In the lobby of the new building are exhibits on smuggling (where not to hide contraband items) and photographs and documents relating to the port of New York. (Open Monday–Friday, 9.00–4.00, free.)

The two Plaza Buildings (Four and Five World Trade Center) will serve as product display areas and trading places for four leading New York commodities exchanges. The Trade Center also offers various trade and information services to tenants and visitors.

FACTS ABOUT THE BUILDINGS: Since the windows of the towers cannot be opened, and since buildings so large obviously pose certain dangers to their inhabitants, the interior environment is controlled by a central computer with 6500 sensors that feed it information about the temperature, humidity, water and power needs; the computer is to deal with breakdowns and malfunctions before they become emergencies.

The maximum permissible sway was determined by carrying out a series of experiments in a Eugene, Oregon, optometrist's office, where subjects who thought they were getting free eye examinations were treated to various amounts of sway to determine what they could tolerate. A maximum of 11 inches of slow or damped sway was deemed acceptable. There is enough aluminum sheeting on the outside of the towers for 9000 houses. Every day building occupants generate 50 tons of garbage (the maximum take-off weight of a Boeing 737). It is estimated that at full occupancy 2 25 million gallons of water will be required per day, and 2·25 million gallons of raw sewage will be produced. The building requires enough electricity to power a city of about 40,000 inhabitants. An estimated 43,000 more commuters per day must use neighbourhood transit facilities.

Critical reaction to the buildings has been mixed. Some beholders have bemoaned the intrusion of these large rectangular buildings on the old familiar skyline. Others have found them beautiful, and the buildings have received various architectural commendations and awards. Yet the environmental impact of the center cannot be denied. Any complex of buildings serving an estimated 50,000 workers and 80,000 visitors per day on a 16-acre site obviously puts heavy additional stresses on city facilities which were already overloaded. The position of those who oppose the buildings was perhaps best stated by Lewis Mumford, an elder statesman of American architectural and urban affairs: 'Tall buildings are outmoded concepts. This is Victorian thinking. Skyscrapers have always been put up for reasons of advertising and publicity. They are not economically sound or efficient . . . the Trade Center's fate is to be ripped down as nonsense.'

OUTDOOR SCULPTURE AT THE WORLD TRADE CENTER: Like other recently built plazas, the World Trade Center plaza is graced by several pieces of sculpture, all of them rather monumental in keeping with the scale of the project. In the center of the main plaza is a bronze, broken-surfaced *Globe* by Fritz Koenig, designed to revolve slowly in the central fountain. Between the twin towers is a work by James Rosati, entitled *Ideogram*; made of polished stainless steel, it is about 24 ft high and 28 ft long. Near the main entrance is the largest free-standing stone carving of modern times, a highly polished asymmetrical work of black granite by sculptor Masayuki Nagare.

Nagare as a child was apprenticed in Japan to a number of traditional craftsmen, including a swordmaker; after World War II he travelled throughout his country, finding work as an itinerant woodworker and stone craftsman, eventually developing as one of his country's leading artists, whose work though modern reflects his attachment to traditional materials.

Not visible from the central plaza is Alexander Calder's 25-ton stabile, *Three Red Wings*, installed on the west side of the North Tower.

FACILITIES: On the concourse level below the plaza (enter via 5 World Trade Center on Vesey St) are a number of fast food establishments, serving good and relatively inexpensive food. (Open weekdays from 7.00 a.m. to 7.00 p.m.; Saturdays until 5.00 p.m.) On the top of One World Trade Center is an elegant and expensive restaurant with spectacular views. There is a snack bar on the Observation Platform at Two World Trade Center. The underground concourse also includes a drugstore, banks, and other shopping facilities and provides access to subways and the railroad tubes. There is a subterranean parking garage for some 2000 cars.

Observation Deck: The observation deck on the 107th floor of Two World Trade Center offers stunning views of the city, the harbour, New Jersey, and Long Island. (Open daily, 9.30–4.30. Adults $1·70; children $·85. Snack bar and rest room facilities.) The observation deck has an attractive display on the history of world trade. An escalator to the outdoor observation platform is open when wind and weather permit.

Like the Brooklyn Bridge and the Empire State Building, the World Trade Center has attracted its share of publicity seekers. The most famous is Phillip Petit, the French aerialist, who shot a rope across the gap between the two towers with a crossbow and then walked across the rope. His signature is preserved on the outdoor deck of the Observation Platform. In July 1975 an unemployed construction worker from Queens parachuted from the top of the Trade Center to call attention to the plight of the world's poor. And in May 1977 George Willig, a mountaineer and toy factory employee, gained notoriety by scaling the outside of the South Tower using special equipment he had designed to fit the tracks of the window washing apparatus. When Willig arrived at the top some $3^1/2$ hours after he began the ascent, the city charged him with 'intentionally, willfully and wrongfully scaling and climbing the South Tower of the World Trade Center' and threatened him with a $250,000 civil suit. On the advice of the mayor, the suit was dropped, and the city amicably settled for a fine of $1·10, a cent per floor, and a promise to refrain from a repeat performance.

BATTERY PARK CITY, the country's largest planned urban development project, will eventually arise from the construction site along the river west of the World Trade Center. The developers have created a 100-acre site about a mile long by removing obsolete and abandoned piers and filling the area with material partly dug up in the World Trade Center excavation. Plans call for three large office towers, apartment buildings providing housing for 45,000 people (a resident population for the financial district now deserted when everyone goes home at 5.00), as well as shops and services. An esplanade will surround the project, once more giving people pedestrian access to the river from which they have been cut off by piers and heavy traffic.

4 Park Row, City Hall and the Civic Center

SUBWAY: IRT Broadway–Seventh Ave (train 1) to Cortlandt St, or IRT Broadway–Seventh Ave (train 2 or 3) to Fulton St/William St. IRT Lexington Ave (train 4 or 5) to Fulton St/Broadway. IND Eighth Ave (A train) to Broadway/Nassau. BMT Broadway local (RR train) or Nassau St line (J or M train) to Fulton/Nassau Sts.

BUS: M1 (via Fifth Ave and Broadway), M6 (via Broadway), M15 (via Park Row), or M102 (via Third and Lexington Aves). Culture Bus, Loop II, stop 26 (weekends and holidays).

Facing Broadway between Fulton, Church, and Vesey Sts is **St. Paul's Chapel and Churchyard** (1766; Thomas McBean; tower and steeple added 1794, James C. Lawrence; DL), built as a subsidiary chapel of Trinity Church to accommodate worshippers in outlying areas of the city. As the oldest church in the city, a beautiful example of Georgian architecture, and the site of the service following George Washington's inauguration as President, it has particular interest.

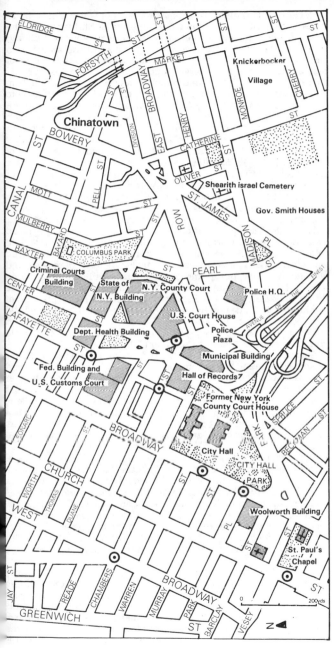

EXTERIOR. Designed by Thomas McBean of whom almost nothing is known, St. Paul's shows the influence of St. Martin's in the Fields, London, though executed in rather homely native building materials. The masonry of rough Manhattan schist was quarried on the site of the graveyard and cut into blocks about the size of cobblestones. An early observer reports that its original colour was reddish-grey, though time and pollution have darkened it. The trim is of smooth brownstone. When the church was built it faced W. to the river, but as Broadway became an important thoroughfare, a portico and entrance were added on that side, although the location of the altar made a central entrance impossible. On the E. porch with its fluted Ionic columns is *the tomb and monument of Brigadier General Richard Montgomery*, mortally wounded in the Battle of Quebec, 25 Dec 1775, 'after a series of successes amidst the most discouraging difficulties', as his epitaph points out. The monument by sculptor Jean-Jacques Caffieri pays tribute to his martial skill and the cause of freedom: on the right of the obelisk are a Phrygian cap (given to freed Roman slaves), broken swords, and a club of Hercules with a ribbon inscribed, 'Libertas Restituta' ('Liberty Restored').

INTERIOR. The light interior, painted in white and gold, is graced by a row of slender Corinthian columns supporting a barrel vaulted ceiling. The chancel wall has a beautiful Palladian window glazed with clear glass. The Waterford crystal chandeliers, organ case, and elaborately carved pulpit and communion rail all date from before the Revolution. Over the pulpit are three feathers, the emblem of the Prince of Wales. Pierre L'Enfant, best known as city planner of Washington D.C., designed the gilded wooden sunburst behind the altar. At the rear of the church is a memorial to John Wells (died 1823), a well-known lawyer, the earliest known (1824) marble portrait bust by an American sculptor (John Frazee).

Spared by the Fire of 1776 as old Trinity Church was not, St. Paul's Chapel became the most prominent Anglican church in the city and was used by George Washington following his inauguration at Federal Hall. The pew where he worshipped, originally canopied, is preserved in the N. aisle; in the S. aisle is the Governor's Pew, reserved first for royal governors, now for the state governor. It is a tribute to the church that during the British occupation while others became stables, prisons, and hospitals, St. Paul's Chapel served British officers as their own house of worship.

At the rear of the church is a *burial ground* with gravestones of moderately prominent early New Yorkers (the most famous were buried in Trinity churchyard). Among them: George Frederick Cooke (died 1812), a famous English actor whose monument was financed by Edmund Kean, an even more famous English actor; Etienne-Marie Bechet Sieur de Rochefontaine (died 1814), who fought in the American Revolution and emigrated to New York after the execution of Louis XVI; and Thomas Addis Emmet (died 1827), Irish patriot and lawyer exiled from British territory after serving a prison term for treason.

Return to Broadway. Just S. of the church (S.W. corner of Broadway and Fulton St) is the *American Telephone and Telegraph Building* (1917; William Welles Bosworth), at 195 Broadway, a building with more columns than any other building anywhere (eight tiers of Ionic, one tier of Doric). Evelyn Beatrice Longman's statue, 'The Genius of the Telegraph', formerly adorned the roof and will be installed in the new A.T. & T. headquarters on Madison Ave when that building is completed. In the lobby (open during business hours) are a plaque memorialising the inventor of the telephone, Alexander Graham Bell, and a bronze and marble sculptural work by Chester Beach entitled 'Service to the Nation'. Its central figure, wearing head-phones, his hair electrified by lightning bolts, is posed before a map of the U.S., its prominent cities linked by long distance telephone wires.

Walk N. past Fulton St, named after Robert Fulton, entrepreneur of the steamboat, and Vesey St, named after William Vesey, first rector of Trinity Church. Barclay St, the next one uptown, takes its name from the second rector, Henry Barclay, shown on one of the panels of the S. doors in Trinity Church preaching to the Indians.

Turn left into Vesey St. At 14 Vesey St between Broadway and Church Sts, is the *New York County Lawyers' Association* (1930; Cass Gilbert; DL), a white marble and limestone neo-Georgian building. At 20 Vesey St just beyond is the *Garrison Building* (1906; Robert D. Kohn; DL), home of the 'New York Evening Post' between 1907 and 1930. Look at the colophons of famous early printers on the spandrels between windows and the elaborate Art Nouveau top. The four statues represent the 'Four Periods of Publicity' and are by Gutzon Borglum, best known for his gigantic portrait heads of American Presidents at Mt Rushmore in N. Dakota, and Estelle R. Kohn, wife of the architect.

Continue W. (away from Broadway). At 140 West St between Barclay and Vesey Sts (1926; Voorhes, Gmelin & Walker) is the *New York Telephone Company Building*, admired for its arcaded side-walk along Vesey St (originally a shopping arcade), and for the lavish Art Deco ornament on the exterior—plant forms, aborigines, bells (symbol of the telephone company). During business hours it is possible to visit the lobby with its ceiling paintings and hand-wrought elevator doors, but visitors are not allowed beyond the security desk.

Continue N. to Barclay St, turn right and walk back toward Broadway. *St. Peter's Roman Catholic Church*, at 22 Barclay St on the S.E. corner of Church St (1838; John Haggerty and Thomas Thomas; DL) is one of several Greek Revival churches remaining in Lower Manhattan and is historically interesting as Manhattan's oldest Roman Catholic church, standing on the site of its predecessor, the first Catholic church in the city. Since the regulations outlawing Roman Catholicism in Britain applied to the U.S. during the colonial period it was not until 1785 that the congregation was able to purchase this land from Trinity Parish and lay the cornerstone for the original building. Architecturally the church is interesting because it uses granite for the facade rather than the softer, more easily carved brownstone. The Ionic portico with six massive columns has a low wood-framed pediment containing a central niche with a statue of St. Peter holding the keys to the eternal kingdom.

Return to Broadway. The *Transportation Building*, 225 Broadway between Vesey and Barclay Sts, occupies the *site of the Astor House Hotel* (demolished 1915). Built (1836) by John Jacob Astor in his declining years, it was the city's first famous hostelry, including among its conveniences gaslight and bathing facilities on every floor, a luxury unknown at the time even in the finest mansions. By 1870 fashion had deserted lower Broadway and the Astor House began receiving mercantile visitors and a few older people who remembered its happier days.

Continue uptown. The ***Woolworth Building** at 233 Broadway between Barclay St and Park Pl was the tallest building in the world when completed (1913; Cass Gilbert), eclipsed in 1929 by the tower at 40 Wall St and in 1930 by the Chrysler Building.

History. The Woolworth Building was officially opened at 7.30 in the evening of 24 April 1913 by President Woodrow Wilson in Washington, who received a signal from a telegrapher and pressed a button that illuminated 80,000 light bulbs in the tower in New York. A band on the 27th floor broke into the 'Star Spangled Banner' and the 800 notables gathered for a banquet broke into sustained applause. The Rev. S. Parkes Cadman, known for the fullness of his prose, remarked that the building inspired 'feelings too deep even for tears. [He] looked upon it and at once cried out, "The Cathedral of Commerce".' The nickname stuck, though modern admiration is more subdued.

F.W. Woolworth, its builder, enjoyed a classic 19C American rags-to-riches career, starting out as a farm boy and beginning his life's work clerking in a general store.

During this apprenticeship Woolworth became convinced that customers would patronise a store where they could see and even finger the merchandise and where they did not have to haggle over prices with intimidating clerks. After a few false starts he proved himself right in a grand way, opening his first successful five-and-ten cent store in 1879 and enlarging it eventually into a chain of stores which then permitted him to buy in quantity and offer the consumer better prices. By 1913 he was able to pay $13,500,000 in cash for his building.

While Woolworth was occasionally cautious to the point of penury in small business matters, he enjoyed living luxuriously in his mansion on the N.E. corner of 80th St and Fifth Ave, which had a large organ on the second floor complete with lighting and sound effects—lightning, thunder, and torrential rains. He disdained all forms of exercise and, as his portraits suggest, indulged his preference for rich fare including over-ripe bananas of which he was especially fond.

The care and attention which Woolworth devoted to the smallest detail of his building (he personally picked out the bathroom fixtures and the mail chutes), the extravagant expenditures for beautiful materials and fine craftsmanship, and the gradiose conception of the whole make the building a monument to its owner's career.

EXTERIOR. The building which covers the entire site, predating the 1916 zoning restrictions (see p95) rises about 300 ft straight up from the street, its verticality emphasised by the light-coloured piers which rise in an unbroken line straight to the top of the main section. The tower then soars another 400 ft, ending in a light, delicate crown surrounded by four small towers (total height, 792 ft). At street level around the elaborate doorway arch are beautifully carved figures of young men and women performing various jobs, the work necessary, according to some observers, to earn the money they need to shop at Woolworth's. Above the second floor are masks representing four centers of civilisation—Europe, Africa, Asia, and American—a motif Gilbert used earlier on the Custom House at Bowling Green. On the 26th, 49th, and 51st floors are gargoyles representing frogs, bats, and pelicans and other creatures. The final crown is a delicate Gothic confection surrounded by flying buttresses and pinnacles recently regilded with gold leaf.

INTERIOR. More than the facade, the interior betrays Woolworth's uninhibited love of spectacle. The walls are covered with golden-toned marble quarried on the Isle of Skyros; the vaulted mosaic ceilings in blue, green, and gold have bird and flower patterns which are intended to recall the mosaics of Ravenna. In the side hallways at the mezzanine level, visible from the main lobby, are murals by C. Paul Jennewein representing 'Commerce' and 'Labor' (S. and N. respectively). At the end of the entrance corridor is a grand marble staircase with an elaborately carved marble balustrade further ornamented with gilded metal work.

The only relief in all this magnificence (neither Gilbert nor Woolworth was known for a sense of humour) is offered by a set of sculpted figures beneath the arches leading to the lateral hallways near Broadway. These statues depict Woolworth and some of his builders in appropriate postures. Woolworth clutches a big nickel; Cass Gilbert peers through a pince-nez at a large model of the building (currently missing); Lewis E. Pierson, president of the Irving Bank, first tenant of the building, gazes at a stock ticker tape; Edward Hogan, the renting agent, negotiates a rental; Gunvald Aus, the structural engineer, checks the measurement of a girder.

Woolworth's office on the 24th floor has been converted into a small museum (open during business hours) with photographs and memorabilia of his career and a selection of furniture demonstrating his fascination with Napoleon.

Cross City Hall Park to the intersection of Broadway and Park Row. Between 1842–65 P.T. Barnum's American Museum occupied the S.E. corner of Broadway and Ann St, delighting or deceiving the public with such exhibits as a Feejee Mermaid, a bearded lady whom the skeptical found unladylike, and General Tom Thumb, a midget from Bridgeport, Connecticut. The museum burned in 1865 and Barnum went on to organise the 'Greatest Show on Earth', a circus that opened in Brooklyn in 1871. James Gordon Bennett's marble New York Herald Building (1866) succeeded the museum, home of a famous newspaper with a distinguished history; the Herald Building was town down to make way for the predecessor of the present Western Electric Building.

PARK ROW. In its earliest days Park Row was a center of theatrical activity in the city. The Park Theatre, New York's most famous early playhouse, which faced a small street parallel to Park Row still known as Theatre Alley, saw the comings and goings of such notable performers as Edmund Kean, Edwin Booth, and Fanny and Charles Kemble. It first opened in 1798, and though burned and refurbished several times, remained open until 1848 when a final fire and the changing character of the neighbourhood closed it forever. Thereafter Park Row became the center of the city's newspaper industry, close to City Hall (political news) and close to the slums of the Lower East Side (sensational, human interest stories). In its prime 'Newspaper Row', as the street was known, ran from Ann St to Chatham Square and was divided by the approaches to the Brooklyn Bridge into a N. section for the foreign language press and a S. section which belonged to the great New York dailies.

History. In one grand row facing City Hall Park stood buildings housing four of the city's greatest papers: Joseph Pulitzer's 'New York World', Charles Anderson Dana's 'New York Sun', the 'New York Tribune', founded by Horace Greeley, and the 'New York Times', revitalised by Adolph Ochs. William Randolph Hearst's 'New York American' and 'New York Evening Journal' spewed forth their successful blend of saccharine and vitriol from offices on William St, and until 1906 the 'Evening Post', once headed by William Cullen Bryant, stood on the S.E. corner of Broadway and Fulton St. When Joseph Pulitzer died in 1911, there were 14 daily newspapers in the city, 12 of which were published on Park Row.

The *Potter Building* (1883; Nathan G. Starkweather) at 38 Park Row on the N.E. corner of Beekman St, converted to apartments in 1979, was designed to be totally fireproof since its predecessor had burned in 1882. Named after its developer, real estate investor Orlando B. Potter, it is constructed of brick, iron, and stone, with elaborate cast-iron work on the first two stories.

At 41 Park Row between Beekman and Spruce Sts is a building now belonging to Pace University, the former *New York Times Building* (original building, 1857; considerably enlarged and altered, 1889; George B. Post; altered again, 1905; Robert Maynicke). The first home (1858–1904) of the 'Times' was both imposing (its height of more than 80 ft gave it a grand panoramic view) and elegant, with plate glass windows on the ground level, elaborately frescoed walls and marble floors, its luxury starting a trend in newspaper buildings which until then had humbly reflected the status of the industry. It was also fireproof, surviving the blaze that destroyed its neighbour in 1882.

Continue N. on Park Row. The area N. of Nassau and Spruce Sts and Park Row once was known as *Printing House Square*, although the ramps to the Brooklyn Bridge now occupy much of the former open space. A *statue of Benjamin Franklin* (1872; Ernst Plassman) stands amidst the traffic as a reminder of the time when the printing industry dominated the neighbourhood. He holds a copy of the 'Pennsylvania Gazette', which he published from 1730–48.

The New Building of *Pace University* stands to the E., bounded by Nassau, Frankfort, Gold, and Spruce Sts (1970; Eggers & Higgins). Founded in 1906 as an accounting school, Pace University now offers courses in the arts and sciences, education and nursing, as well as business. On the facade facing Park Row is a sculptural relief of welded copper by Henri Nachemia entitled 'Brotherhood of Man'.

Cross the street to **City Hall Park,** the closest thing New York has to a commons or town green. In Dutch times it was a cow pasture; later it stood at the intersection of the two main arteries of British New York—Broadway which led N. along the W. side of town to the village of Bloomingdale, and the Boston Post Road which followed a route up the present East Side.

History. During the colonial period the Commons or Fields served as a parade ground and a public gathering place. Later it served as the site of numerous public protests, several riots, and occasional celebrations. In 1911 an oak was planted in front of City Hall to commemorate the Leisler Rebellion (1689–91), an early political clash between a faction supporting the British royal governors and a party with more local loyalties. Jacob Leisler, leader of the rebellion, was hanged for treason somewhere near the present park, though he was later exonerated and his followers freed from prison.

On the W. lawn of City Hall is a *monument to the Liberty Poles*, which were erected in the years preceeding the Revolution by the Sons of Liberty, a group of tradesmen, workers, and army veterans who felt themselves discriminated against because of their colonial origins.

The Liberty Boys, as they were also called, harassed the British government and propagandised against taxation policies, erecting five successive Liberty Poles as symbols of protest and as rallying points for demonstrations and meetings. The poles were decorated at the top with an emblem saying 'Liberty' and protected at the bottom by iron hoops which made it more difficult to chop them down, and had an intentionally provocative effect, since the Sons of Liberty erected them in sight of the British barracks and then taunted the troops officially stationed in the city to protect the colonists.

Near Broadway in the park is a bronze *statue of Nathan Hale* (1893; Frederick MacMonnies), a school teacher from Connecticut who joined the militia and volunteered to penetrate the British lines and gather information about troop movements in occupied New York.

He was captured, but when asked for his last words before being hanged uttered the statement that ensured his place in the textbooks of American history: 'I regret that I have but one life to lose for my country.' The location of the gallows is unknown but a plaque on the N. side of Vanderbilt Pl. at 44th St claims the honour. For a while historians favoured a location at First Ave and 46th St near the British military headquarters but recent scholars favour 63rd St and First Ave.

The statue depicts Hale as a handsome youth (he was 21 when executed) in a romantic attitude of defiance, his arms and ankles bound with ropes. This portrayal represents MacMonnies' conception of Hale's appearance which one of his contemporaries describes as 'above the common stature . . . his shoulders of moderate breadth, his limbs straight and very plump', a description which would certainly have produced a less appealing statue.

On the E. side of City Hall is a bronze *statue of Horace Greeley* (1890; John Quincy Adams Ward) showing the famous newspaperman sitting casually in a bronze upholstered chair with bronze fringes, a newspaper draped over his right knee. Greeley founded the 'New York Tribune' and guided it to a position of eminence. Famous also for his advice to an unknown fortune seeker. 'Go West, young man', Greeley is known to have been careless about his dress and personal appearance, a quality Ward has caught in the statue.

*City Hall (1802–11; Joseph Mangin and John McComb, Jr; DL) is the dominant building in the park.

Open without charge Mon–Fri, 10.00–3.00. The public may visit the Governor's Room and the Rotunda. On days of public hearings the Board of Estimate Chamber and the Council Chamber are open. Tel: 566–5700.

Small by comparison with the buildings surrounding the park, City Hall is one of New York's architectural jewels, elegant, gracefully proportioned, and attractively situated. Oddly enough the building has not always been treasured and only within the past two decades has it been restored from a condition of shabby neglect.

History. The present City Hall is the third building to house the municipal government following the *Stadt Huys* on Pearl St (see p87), and the 18C City Hall on Wall St that later became Federal Hall (see p97). When it became obvious in 1800 that the city government needed a new home, a site was chosen and a design competition announced. John McComb, Jr and Joseph Mangin, two architects already well established in New York, took the prize of $350, for which (plus construction costs estimated at a half million dollars) the city got one of its outstanding public buildings.

The cornerstone for City Hall was laid in 1803 and though the building was not completed until 1812, it officially opened on 4 July 1811. Delays caused by a yellow fever epidemic, labour disputes, and financial difficulties held up the work. McComb, who supervised the construction, got $6 per day; John LeMaire, a French artisan, got $4 per day for his work as master stonecarver, while the labourers received something between $1 and $1·50. The marble, more than 35,000 cubic ft, quarried in West Stockbridge, Mass, came to what nowadays seems a reasonable $35,000.

Like most older buildings in New York, City Hall has led a precarious existence, first threatened in 1833 when the City Council considered selling it to the Federal Government for use as a Custom House. In 1858, during the celebration of the completion of the Atlantic Cable, the fireworks became too exuberant and the cupola burned along with John Dixey's wooden statue of 'Justice'. Also destroyed were the roof and parts of the upper stories including much of the Governor's Room. By 1895 the building had so deteriorated that it was considered an offence to the sight and a menace to health; consequently a committee of eminent architects undertook to demolish the building and replace it with something more modern, a scheme fortunately blocked by public outcry. Between 1907–20 Mrs Russell Sage contributed $65,000 for renovation, and architect Grosvenor Atterbury undertook to restore first the Governor's Room and later (1912–13) the Rotunda including the dome of the cupola which had been replaced following the 1858 fire and then damaged again by another blaze touched off by a careless workman in 1917. In 1956, at a cost of $2 million, the most recent renovation was completed, that of the facade. The original marble and brownstone, by then badly decayed, were stripped off and replaced by Alabama limestone and Missouri red granite. Plaster casts were made of exterior sculptural details, and after the old stone was chipped away, a new veneer of stone about 4 inches thick was anchored to the old. The N. side of the building, originally faced in brownstone because the city fathers wished to save money and felt that the N. facade was safely out of sight, was now covered with limestone.

City Hall has seen its share of ceremony and pageantry, both joyous and mournful. In the 19C it was used as a place for entertaining visiting celebrities, including the Prince of Wales (later Edward VII) who visited in 1860 and the Grand Duke Alexis of Russia, who was received there in 1871. Other less exalted people have been honoured: astronauts, ballplayers, aviators, and politicians. Ulysses S. Grant, General William J. Worth, and Abraham Lincoln lay in state there. Indeed Lincoln's funeral was one of the great ceremonial event's in the city's history. A large catafalque was built at the top of the grand staircase and the entire Rotunda was draped in black; in the two days of the ceremony, 120,000 New Yorkers walked past the coffin to see the remains of a man they had greeted with less respect on his only previous visit to the city.

EXTERIOR: For the best view of the facade approach the building from the S., along the central path of the park.

City Hall is an elegant example of the Federal style modified by a decided French influence, perhaps the contribution of Mangin, a French emigré, who is thought to have been the principal designer of the exterior. This influence appears particularly in the long rows of windows gracefully ornamented with pilasters and swags instead of the usual more severe classical orders and in the general disposition of the building. The tower, however, belongs to the native tradition, as does the design of the interior, probably McComb's inspiration.

Like many other classical buildings, City Hall is designed in tripartite form, both vertically and horizontally. Architecturally the most important section of City Hall is the central block, its prominence signalled by the wide flight of steps at the entrance, the round-headed doors and windows (considered in classical architecture to be nobler than square-headed ones), the columns—freestanding and Ionic on the first floor, attached and Corinthian on the second—and, of course, the attic, clock tower and cupola above. The dome is decorated with floral garlands and crowned by John Dixey's statue of Justice, originally executed in wood (1812), but destroyed during the fire of 1858 and replaced by the present copper replica during the 1910s.

The base, of red granite, a darker and coarser stone than the veined limestone used on the upper stories, is laid in large rusticated building blocks, effectively making the lower story look heavy and rugged in contrast with the smoothly finished and lighter coloured upper stories. The ground floor, which contains private offices (of the mayor and the president of the City Council) has a smooth facade with Ionic columns and pilasters. The second story, which houses the great public rooms (the City Council and Board of Estimate chambers as well as the Governor's Room), is more elaborate: pilasters and columns are of the Corinthian order; windows are taller; ceilings are higher. In the curved spaces above the windows are sculpted medallions with garlands of acorns and oak leaves, a motif frequently used in the decoration of public buildings to symbolise strength and incorruptibility.

INTERIOR: *Ground floor.* The walls of the lobby are still covered with the original white Massachusetts marble that once adorned the facade. To the right of the entrance is a bronze copy (1857) of a *bust of George Washington* made from a marble original by Jean-Antoine Houdon in 1787; the original, in the state capitol at Richmond, Va., is based on life casts Houdon made during a visit to the United States in 1785. The mayor's office is at the end of the left corridor; the office of the president of the City Council on the right. Beyond the lobby is the **Rotunda,** with its beautiful circular staircase. In the center of the Rotunda supported by ten marble fluted Corinthian columns is a dome with a clear glass oculus opening into the tower. The design for this domed space is probably McComb's and has an antecedent in the plan of Wardour House (Wiltshire, England) designed by James Paine.

Second floor. To the E. of the Rotunda on the second floor is the *City Council Chamber,* designed in about 1898 when the five boroughs were joined to make Greater New York, a union commemorated by the low-relief sculpture in the corners of the ceiling. The plaster statue of Thomas Jefferson is a copy of an original bronze (1833) by Pierre-Jean-David d'Angers, a student of Houdon. The ceiling painting, 'New York Receiving the Tributes of the Nation' (1903), is by Taber Sears, George W. Breck, and Frederick C. Martin.

On the W. side of the building the *Board of Estimate Chamber* resembles a courtroom of the Federal period. At the W. end is a semi-circular dais where the members of the board sit elevated above the public for whom white bench pews with mahogany trim are provided. An elaborate canopy with red hangings enhances the mayor's chair. The chandeliers are from the Civil War period. In niches on the walls are marble busts of two of the nation's outstanding chief justices of the Supreme Court, both by John Frazee, often called America's first native portrait sculptor: John Jay (chief justice 1789–95) and John Marshall (chief justice 1790–1852).

At the head of the stairs is the **Governor's Room.** Originally it was set aside as an office for the state governor when he visited the city and the two flanking rooms were occupied by the Comptroller and the Grand Jury. However, when these rooms were rebuilt after the fire of 1858, the Governor's Room was joined to the other two, making a suite.

The *portraits in the room belong to the city historical collection and include on permanent display twelve of the thirteen paintings by *John Trumbull* commissioned by the city. The portrait of George Washington on the W. wall shows the general on Evacuation Day (24 November 1783) standing by his horse, with a background view of Bowling Green and the Upper Bay. Over the opposite mantle is his portrait of George Clinton, Brigadier General in the American army, with the Hudson River highlands in the background. Other Trumbull portraits, mainly of mayors and governors, were acquired in two groups; the first, from 1805, includes Governor John Jay, Secretary of the Treasury Alexander Hamilton, and Mayors James Duane, Richard Varick, and Edward Livingston, The second group of Trumbull portraits, acquired in 1808, includes Governors Morgan Lewis and Daniel D. Tompkins, and Mayor Marinus Willett. Trumbull painted the portrait of Mayor Jacob Radcliff in 1816. The portrait of Peter Stuyvesant is a copy by Trumbull of an earlier painting. The frames for the 1805 and 1808 commissions were made by John LeMaire, the chief carver for the building.

The furniture displayed consists of chairs, desks, and tables made for City Hall at the time of its completion. The high backed upholstered settees have been attributed to Duncan Phyfe although without documentation. The writing table used by George Washington is an earlier piece, dating from the period when Federal Hall on Wall St was the nation's capitol.

The New York City Art Commission occupies the *attic floor*, once an apartment for the housekeeper. Consisting of ten unsalaried commissioners plus the mayor, the Art Commission acts as a watchdog of aesthetic quality, reviewing designs for bridges, monuments and arches, schools, courthouses and other public buildings as well as artworks placed in parks and other public places. In the entrance hall just off the Rotunda is a heroic bronze copy by Louis Noel of a statue (1828) of George Washington by Pierre-Jean-David d'Angers.

The Paintings in City Hall: The collection of paintings began in 1790 when New York enjoyed its brief moment as capital city of the nation. The Common Council, then the chief legislative body of the city, commissioned John Trumbull to paint the portraits of George Washington and George Clinton, the state's first governor. Again in 1805 the Council commissioned a group of portraits of governors and mayors who had served since the Revolution, and after the War of 1812 the group requested a series of portraits commemorating some of the heroes of that struggle. The tradition of adding portraits of governors and mayors was continued through the mayorality of Fiorello La Guardia (1934–45) when it was stopped, and subsequent portraits have been gifts. Thus the series constitutes a gallery of famous New York politicians, a few of whom have risen to national prominence; it further gives an impression of changing styles of portraiture during the 19C. Especially noteworthy are the portraits by Trumbull and the first generation of post-Revolutionary artists—*John Wesley Jarvis, Thomas Sully, Samuel F.B. Morse, John Vanderlyn, Samuel L. Waldo, George Catlin,* and *Rembrandt Peale.*

Since it is impossible to give a room by room tour of the portraits because with the exception of the paintings by Trumbull in the Governor's Room, they have no permanent location, they are grouped below by painter.

John Trumbull (1756–1843): In addition to the portraits in the Governor's Room, the collection contains a portrait of DeWitt Clinton (acquired in the group of 1805). *John Wesley Jarvis* (1781–1839): Commodore William Bainbridge, General Jacob Brown, Commodore Isaac Hull, Commodore Thomas MacDonough, Commodore Oliver Hazard Perry, and General Joseph G. Swift. *Thomas Sully* (1783–1872): General Jonathan Williams and Commodore Stephen Decatur. *Samuel L. Waldo* (1783–1861): General Alexander Macomb, Mayor Cadwallader C. Colden, and John McComb, Jr, architect of City Hall. With his partner William Jewett, Waldo also painted Mayor Stephen Allen. *John Vanderlyn* (1775–1839): President James Monroe, General Andrew Jackson, Mayor Philip Hone, Governor Joseph C. Yates, and President Zachary Taylor. *Samuel F. B. Morse* (1791–1872): Mayor William Paulding, Christopher Columbus, and the Marquis de Lafayette, a picture which usually hangs in the City Council Chamber. *George Catlin* (1796–1872): DeWitt Clinton. *Rembrandt Peale* (1778–1860): James Kent. Later portraits include works by Charles Wesley Jarvis, Henry Inman, Charles L. Elliott, William Page, Thomas Hicks, Robert W. Weir, and William H.

Powell. Of particular interest among the later portraits are the painting of Grover Cleveland by *Eastman Johnson* (1824–1906) and that of Governor John A. Dix by *Anna Lea Merritt* (1844–1930).

N. of City Hall in the park facing Chambers St is the former **New York City Courthouse** (1872; John Kellum) known familiarly as the *Tweed Courthouse* because William M. 'Boss' Tweed and his 'Ring' stole spectacular amounts of money from the city during its construction.

History. In 1858 the city Board of Supervisors agreed to a preliminary expenditure of $250,000 for a much-needed new criminal courthouse, and the cornerstone was laid in Dec 1861. By the time the building reached completion 10 years later, the cost had risen to somewhere between $12 and $13 million—the exact figures were concealed during the ensuing scandal—and it is estimated that Tweed and his cronies absconded with about two-thirds of the money. Their system involved having contractors pad their accounts and then kick back to the politicians most of the difference between what the work actually cost and what the city paid for it. Thus a plasterer named Andrew J. Garvey appeared in the records as receiving $45,966·89 for a single day's work, eventually being dubbed by the press the 'Prince of Plasterers'. Although the Tweed Ring fleeced the city in other ways, the disclosure of cost overruns during the construction of the courthouse precipitated Tweed's exposure, downfall, and ultimate imprisonment.

Tweed, who rose from humble beginnings to become wealthy, powerful, and famous through the machinery of Tammany Hall, the most powerful organisation within Democratic party politics, never held a high city office himself, but was a kingmaker who profited from the position of his friends in high places. His fall, however, was swift and spectacular, and he died in prison, poor and friendless in 1876.

EXTERIOR. The building is a three-story flat-roofed structure of Massachusetts marble, formerly white but now weathered to a dark grey. In the rear is an addition (1880) by Leopold Eidlitz. At one time a grand stairway on the Chambers St side led to the doors, but when the street was widened in 1955 the staircase was removed leaving a blank wall the entire width of the portico and a full story high. Along with the building which has been poorly maintained, this inhospitable entrance makes the courthouse more forbidding than it would otherwise be. In the mid-1970s it was scheduled for demolition but the high cost of taking it down plus resistance by preservationists have temporarily saved it, although as a symbol of municipal graft it can hardly endear itself to those in power. Some restoration has been done on the beautiful rotunda (not presently open to the public).

Continue through the park to *Chambers St* which runs along the N. side of the courthouse, named after John Chambers, an 18C lawyer and official of Trinity Church.

Turn left. On the N.E. corner of Broadway and Chambers St is the *former A.T. Stewart Marble Palace* (1846; John B. Snook and Joseph Trench), once an elegant department store proudly leading architectural fashion, later the home of the 'New York Sun', now a city-owned office building with an uncertain future.

History. Alexander Turney Stewart's store did for merchandising at the upper end of the economic scale what F.W. Woolworth's 5- and-10¢ stores did for it at the lower end of the spectrum, bringing together many different types of merchandise under a single roof, selling clothing in fixed sizes at fixed prices to free shoppers from the uncertainties and psychological demands of bargaining. In addition Stewart saw the need to make shopping itself an entertainment, and to this end built the Marble, Palace.

EXTERIOR. The building is an early example of the Italianate style which replaced Greek Revival as the dominant architectural fashion in the city. In its day it was much admired for its palatial dimensions, beautiful white marble facade, and elegant details (note the classical masks in the keystones over the second story windows). When it opened there were slender Corinthian columns on the ground floor with large plate glass display windows between, whose dimensions were so large that Stewart had to order the sheets of glass from France. By 1862, however, fashionable society had begun shopping further uptown and Stewart moved up Broadway to a new palace, the Cast Iron Palace, between Ninth and Tenth Sts, retaining this store as a warehouse. Stewart had a mansion on Fifth Ave at 34th St, a $3 million extravagance that set the standard for younger generations of millionaires.

Walk E. (away from Broadway) on Chambers St to Centre St. At 31 Chambers St (N.W. corner of Centre St) is the *Surrogate's Court*, also known as the *Hall of Records* (1899–1911; John R. Thomas and Horgan & Slattery; DL). Like the Woolworth Building with which it is roughly contemporary, the Surrogate's Court was built as a monument, and the impulse of civic pride that inspired the design is expressed in the elegance and costliness of both the facade and the interior. Originally it was intended to function as a repository for municipal records and as a surrogate's court administering trusts and guardianships, but since the building has been used more and more by the court, the name was officially changed from Hall of Records to Surrogate's Court in 1963.

EXTERIOR. Faced with white granite quarried in Maine, the facade is lavishly ornamented with sculpture appropriate to the building's first function as a guardian of records and documents. Flanking the Chambers St entrance are two sculptural groups by *Philip Martiny*: New York in Revolutionary Times represented by a proud female figure wearing a helmet and grasping a torch and globe, and (right) New York in Its Infancy, a woman wearing a feathered headdress and holding a document and books. The frieze above the portico carries eight figures representing prominent early New Yorkers including Peter Stuyvesant (third from left) and DeWitt Clinton (third from right). The cornice figures facing Reade and Centre Sts represent the arts, professions, and industries. Two additional figures were removed to the New York County Court House in Foley Square during alterations in 1959.

INTERIOR (open during business hours): The walls of the Foyer are faced with yellow-toned Siena marble. Above the doorways at each end of the rooms are sculptural groups by *Albert Weinert*: (E. door), The Consolidation of Greater New York and (W. door), Recording the Purchase of Manhattan Island. On the ceiling is a mosaic by *William de Leftwich Dodge*, a Paris-trained artist known for his murals; it is organised into a series of panels depicting Greek and Egyptian deities and includes corner figures of Greek gods whose functions touch those of the building: Themis (Justice), Erinys (Retribution), Penthos (Sorrow), and Ponos (Labour). On the end walls are mosaics also by Dodge entitled Searching the Records and Widows and Orphans Pleading Before the Judge of the Surrogate's Court. Above the central landing of the grand staircase in the lobby is a stucco relief of the seal of New York City upon whose shield are the sails of a windmill; between the sails are beavers and flour barrels, both important facets of the early economy of the colony. A sailor and an Indian support the shield which rests on a horizontal laurel branch bearing the date 1664, the year the British captured New Amsterdam and gave it the name New York.

Also of interest are the fifth floor *North and South Court Rooms*. The South Court Room is finished in Santo Domingo mahogany, giving it a rich, almost sombre appearance. Fireplaces are of red Numidian marble with elaborate overmantels whose decoration includes a winged blindfolded head of Justice above a wreathed shield. The North Courtroom panelled in quarter-sawn English oak has fireplaces of olive green Easton marble and decorations of a military nature (helmets, ancient weapons, etc) as well as the conventional scales of justice.

At the N.W. corner of Reade and Centre Sts stood the Manhattan Water Tank (demolished during the early years of the 20C), originally made of iron plates and eventually enclosed within a building. It was built by Aaron Burr's Manhattan Water Company, a business venture whose real aim was to secure a charter for the Manhattan Bank, now part of the Chase Manhattan Bank. The water came from the nearby Collect Pond (now drained) and was brought through wooden pipes, samples of which may be seen at the New-York Historical Society.

The **Civic Center,** focus of the city's government, lies N. of City Hall around Foley Square and consists of a collection of buildings constructed from the turn of the century to the present according to changing architectural fashions. Numerous comprehensive plans for development of the area have been devised, but none has been carried out until very recently beyond the construction of a single building. The location itself was chosen almost by default, the boggy ground making the neighbourhood unsuitable for high-rise commercial construction, and the nearby seedy neighbourhoods making it unattractive for anything else.

One of the main landmarks of the Civic Center is the **Municipal Building** (1914; McKim, Mead & White; DL) located on the E. side of Centre St at Chambers St, a pivotal building designed on the one hand to complement City Hall to its S. and on the other to set the style for other buildings in Foley Square to the N. Applauded as a great civic skyscraper and an example of the Eclectic style at its grandest, it replaces the former Staats-Zeitung Building, home of the most important German language newspaper in the city.

EXTERIOR. Like other early skyscrapers, the Municipal Building is divided horizontally into an elaborate base (impressive to the pedestrian), a simple central tower, and a monumental top planned to take a conspicuous place in the skyline. The central arch in the ground level colonnade formerly straddled Chambers St, forming a monumental gateway to the slums of the Lower East Side, but now acts as a grand entrance to Police Plaza. Above the colonnade are shields with the insignia of Amsterdam, Great Britain, New York City, and New York State. The winged figures flanking the arch represent Guidance (left) and Executive Power (right). The panels over the smaller arches are (left) Civic Duty, which shows the City conferring the law upon its citizens and (right) Civic Pride, depicting the citizens returning the fruits of their labours to the city. Above, relief medallions depict Progress (left) and Prudence (right). Crowning the building is *Adolph Weinman*'s 25-ft statue, Civic Fame, garbed in flowing robes and holding a bouquet and crown. Made of copper hammered over a steel frame, the statue stands 582 ft above the street, was installed in 1914, and was regilded in 1974.

INTERIOR. Walk through the central arch to see the coffered

ceiling and the bronze ornamental work inside the lobby. On the S. side of the building is an arcade with a vaulted ceiling, making the subway entrance there one of the most imposing in the city. The building contains various city offices and the *Marriage Chapel* where couples who wish to get married 'at City Hall' take their vows.

Walk through the central arch to **Police Plaza,** one of the few areas within the Civic Center resulting from comprehensive architectural planning. Bounded by the remnants of a former warehouse district on the E., by the entanglements of the Brooklyn Bridge approaches on the S., and by existing municipal buildings and irregular streets in other directions, the site recommended itself to planners only because the city could conveniently purchase its many small land parcels at a reasonable price. The three-acre multi-level plaza paved in brick has such pedestrian amenities as benches, a small waterfall, outdoor sculpture, and historical artifacts. The central sculpture of five interlocking oxidised steel discs by *Bernard (Tony) Rosenthal* (1974) is entitled '5 in 1' and is said to symbolise the five city boroughs. Each disc weighs 15,000 lbs and is 20 ft in diameter and 10 inches thick. Its installation caused adverse comment, perhaps because it appeared merely rusty at the time and one correspondent to the 'New York Times' likened it to the 'rusty propeller of a supertanker', but since then its weathering steel has taken on a dark red-brown colour.

Beyond the Municipal Building on the S. side of the plaza is the *Rhinelander Sugar House Prison Window Monument.* During the 18C one of the city's prime industries was distilling rum for which raw sugar was a principal ingredient. The Rhinelander Sugar Warehouse built (1763) on the corner of Rose (formerly the name of the S. extension of Madison St) and Duane Sts served this purpose until the British occupation during the Revolutionary War when it became a prison for American soldiers. The sugar house was razed in 1892 but a window was incorporated in the Rhinelander Building (1895) which stood here until it was demolished (1968) for Police Plaza. Behind Police Headquarters are five Ionic Columns from the Rhinelander Building.

Look N. from the plaza. *Southbridge Towers* (1969; Gruzen & Partners), at Gold, Frankfort, Water, and Fulton Sts, is a middle-income cooperative housing project. The *Beekman Downtown Memorial Hospital* at Spruce, Gold, Beekman, and William Sts (1971; Skidmore, Owings & Merrill) is the major medical facility in the area. Look toward the bridge. N. of it are the *Murry Bergtraum High School for Business Careers* (1976; Gruzen & Partners) at 411 Pearl St on the S. corner of Madison St, whose three cylindrical towers house heavy service equipment which could not be installed in the basement because of the questionable solidity of the old landfill beneath the site. Nearby is a *New York Telephone Company building* (1976) which houses automatic switching equipment. Beneath the plaza is a municipal parking garage with space for 407 cars. *The Avenue of the Finest* runs past the S. side of the plaza, named to honour the city's police force.

Police Headquarters (1973; Gruzen & Partners) dominating the plaza and bounded by Park Row, Pearl, Henry, and New Sts, is a 15-story, $58-million building of brick and reinforced concrete, its ground level containing an auditorium, meeting rooms, and prisoner-holding and interrogation rooms. On the wall behind the information desk is a brick abstract design by Josef Twirbutt. Above the ground level are offices and a communications center where a computer records the 18,000 average daily incoming calls and remembers the locations of available patrol cars. An underground parking garage accommodates 155 police cars and the rooftop has an emergency helicopter pad.

Between Police Headquarters and St. Andrews Church is the *U.S. Courthouse Annex* (1975; Gruzen & Partners) between Park Row, Duane, and Pearl Sts, really two buildings straddling an old power substation of the subway which could not be relocated. The S. part houses the U.S. Attorney's Building; the N. Part contains the Federal Metropolitan Correctional Center, one of the most technologically advanced detention centers in the nation; the windows of unbreakable glass have a built-in alarm system.

Between the Annex and St. Andrew's Church is *Cardinal Hayes Place*, named after Patrick Joseph Cardinal Hayes (died 1938), born nearby, altar boy at the old St. Andrew's Church, archbishop of New York (from 1919) and cardinal (from 1924).

St. Andrew's Church (1939; Maginnis & Walsh, Robert J. Reilly) stands facing the plaza between Cardinal Hayes Pl. and Duane St. It bears the coats of arms of Pope Pius XI (central door) and Cardinal Hayes (side doors), both holding office when the church was consecrated. The present building replaces an earlier one known as Carroll Hall, which became the first Church of St. Andrew, ministering to the Catholic immigrants pouring into this neighbourhood in the mid-19C. In 1900, when the printing industry dominated the area, the church began offering a Printer's Mass at 2.30 a.m., for newsmen and other late night workers, making St. Andrew's the first work-centered parish in the city.

East of the Civic Center lies CHATHAM SQUARE, formerly the S.E. boundary of Chinatown. Follow Cardinal Hayes Pl. to Worth St; turn right and follow Worth St to Chatham Sq. Between Worth St and Park Row (170 Park Row) are the *Chatham Towers apartments* (1965; Kelly & Gruzen), admired by architectural critics, and across Park Row between St. James Pl., Pearl, and Madison Sts (185 Park Row), the *Chatham Green apartments* (1961; Kelly & Gruzen), with their undulating brick wall and exposed access galleries.

On the E. side of Chatham Sq. is a neighbourhood once considered part of the Lower East Side, now becoming an extension of an expanding Chinatown. During the early years of the 19C, however, it was a prosperous area, home of successful merchants and ships' captains, a few of whose homes and churches still remain.

Cross the square to St. James Pl. and follow it a block to James St, barely more than an alley. At 32 James St between St. James Pl. and Madison St is *St. James (Roman Catholic) Church* (1837; attrib. Minard Lafever; DL), a brownstone Greek Revival building. The facade has two central columns placed between flanking walls, an arrangement known formally as 'distyle in antis'. The only ornaments are rosettes on the door lintels and a carved scroll and anthemion above the central doorway.

A plaque on the doors of the Hall of St. James School across the street announces that Alfred E. Smith received his only formal education here. Smith, born at 174 South St and raised on Oliver St, rose from these lowly beginnings to become a social reformer, four-time governor of the state, and Democratic candidate for President in 1928. He is also remembered in the *Governor Alfred E. Smith Houses* (1952; Eggers & Higgins), between South, Madison, and Catherine Sts and St. James and Robert F. Wagner, Sr Places, a public housing project.

Return along St. James Pl. Between James and Oliver Sts is the *First Shearith Israel Graveyard*, (1683–1828; DL), the earliest surviving burial ground of the city's first Jewish congregation, Shearith Israel ('Remnant of Israel') which dates from 1654 (see p419). The earliest stone dates from 1683. As the congregation moved uptown following the general development of the city, it established two other cemeteries, one at W. 11th St and another at W. 21st St. The burial place used by the congregation before they purchased this plot of land can no longer be located.

Continue along St. James Pl. to Oliver St and turn right. Follow it to 12 Oliver St at the N.W. corner of Henry St. *The Mariners' Temple* (1842; Minard Lafever; DL), formerly the Oliver St Church, was originally built by a Baptist congregation to serve the spiritual needs of sailors docked in New York and continued as a social mission through the 19C, allowing various immigrant groups to use the church until they could construct their own. After the turn of the century its social work focused on the homeless derelicts of the Bowery. The Mariners' Temple, roughly contemporary with the St. James Church nearby, is constructed of stone laid in random courses, plastered over (where visible to the street), and grooved with false joints to give it the smooth appearance characteristic of the Greek Revival style.

Follow Henry St to Catherine St and turn right; continue two blocks to Monroe St. The huge housing project bounded by Catherine, Market, Monroe, and Cherry Sts is *Knickerbocker Village* (1934; Van Wart & Ackerman) completed during the Depression and replacing a notorious slum. Unfortunately the rental fees of $12·50 per room per month priced the apartments out of reach of former slum dwellers who then had to find other slum housing. Despite its high density—500 units per acre as opposed to the average New York City Public Housing figure of 80–100 units per acre—the project is well-maintained and successful.

Follow Monroe St to Market St and turn left. At 51 Market St between Monroe and Madison Sts is the *former William Clark House* (1824; DL), one of the few remaining Federal houses in the city, unusual for its four stories. Built in an age when handwork was costly, it has a simple facade but an elaborate doorway, with an eight-panelled door flanked by fluted Ionic columns and leaded glass sidelights; above is a leaded glass fanlight and a moulded elliptical arch. The main floor is raised above street level over a high basement, an architectural feature inherited from the Dutch, whose houses in Holland were elevated against the threat of floods. In New York this raised first floor made possible a basement entrance to the kitchen, sorely needed in a city generally lacking service alleys, and conferred added elegance upon the first floor entrance. The stairway leading to the main door, called a 'stoop' from the Dutch 'stoep', has a wrought iron railing, a typical detail of the Federal style.

Continue up Market St to the N.W. corner of Henry St. The *Sea and Land Church* at 61 Henry St, also called the *First Chinese Presbyterian Church*, and formerly the Market Street Church (1817; DL), resembles St. Paul's Chapel in several ways: it is built of local building materials, has brownstone quoins and trim, rubble masonry, steep gabled ends, and a square tower (though without a spire). In its proportions it is simple and austere and has unusually tall side windows for a church of the period ending in pointed arches that predate the Gothic Revival period by about two decades.

Nearby, between Market and Catherine Sts at 48 Henry St is the *Chinatown Mission* (1830), originally built as a subsidiary chapel of Trinity Church and later the Church of Our Saviour. The houses have carving around the doorways and a roof balustrade apparently from a Georgian country house.

Continue along Henry St to Catherine St; turn right and follow Catherine St into Chatham Sq. Take Park Row along the W. side of the square to Pearl St; turn right and continue to Foley Square.

Foley Square, formed by the intersection of Duane, Lafayette, Pearl, and Centre Sts, is considered the focal-point of the Civic Center.

History. Until the beginning of the 19C the square lay beneath the waters of the Collect (from Dutch 'kolch' designating any small body of water) or Freshwater Pond. Known for its depth (60 ft) and the purity of its water, the spring-fed pond drained W. into the Hudson and much of the land on that side was low marshland called the Lispenard Meadows. In the 18C tanners settled in the area because the water supply was essential to their business, but in 1730 Anthony Rutgers, a landowner, petitioned the city for the swamp and pond which he then began to drain, much to the distress of the tanners. The city gained title to the pond in 1791. In 1796 John Fitch tested a prototypical steamboat on its waters, a vessel driven by paddlewheels and screw propellers. Though successful technologically, the boat never achieved the fame of Robert Fulton's 'Clermont' which steamed up the Hudson in 1807 and Fitch eventually abandoned his craft in the pond and left the city.

Around 1800 the city began filling the pond and draining the Lispenard Meadows. By 1807 cartloads of dirt and garbage were being dumped into the pond, eventually rising to form a foul-smelling island some 12–15 ft above the water. In 1809 Canal St was laid out and a sewer built beneath it to drain the springs which formerly fed the pond. By 1811 the pond had disappeared altogether.

The offensive odours, the sinking of neighbourhood land still undermined by springs, and the encroachment of the dry goods trade into nearby streets made the area undesirable for people who could afford to live elsewhere. By the early 19C it was a slum, inhabited by freed slaves, immigrants, and other poor people. By 1840 it had become notorious for crime, its worst section called Five Points at the intersection of Park, Baxter, and Worth Sts. The area was so filthy that it offended even the experienced eye and benumbed olfactory organs of native New Yorkers. Houses, mostly of wood, were rotten and overcrowded, with people packed into windowless basements and relegated to back buildings hastily erected in dark rear yards by greedy landlords.

A central feature of Five Points was the Old Brewery, on part of the site of the present County Court House, a squalid building once used for making beer but by the mid-19C home to some 1200 people. In 1852 the Ladies' Home Missionary Society bought it and eventually replaced it with the Five Points Mission and House of Industry, a nursery school with about 400 students and boarders. Before demolishing the building, however, the ladies with remarkable skill at public relations opened the brewery for tours, allowing middle class visitors who were becoming increasingly curious about the seamier side of life to see just how the poor lived.

Foley Square is named after Thomas F. Foley (died 1923), Tammany politician considered a kingmaker though never an important office holder himself. He was born in the Williamsburg section of Brooklyn and entered politics by way of the saloon business, moving his saloons closer to the center of the city as he moved closer to the center of power. Foley was influential in helping Al Smith become governor and in keeping William Randolph Hearst, who had attacked him in his newspapers, from becoming governor or U.S. senator.

Walk along the E. side of Foley Square, whose buildings have been built up so that their friezes are level with that of the Municipal Building. The *U.S. Courthouse* (1936; Cass Gilbert and Cass Gilbert, Jr; DL) at the S.E. corner of Pearl St is joined to its Annex in Police Plaza by a pair of covered aerial bridges. Like the Municipal Building it is a tall office tower (32 stories) with classical details and a memorable top, a gold pyramid. Like the County Courthouse to its N. it presents to Foley Square a heroic portico (Corinthian columns 50 ft high). The building houses the U.S. District Court and the Federal Court of Appeals.

On the N.E. corner of Pearl St at Foley Square is the *New York County Courthouse* (1926; Guy Lowell; DL) home of the New York State Supreme Court. Guy Lowell, a Boston architect, won the architectural competition for the building with plans for a circular structure, later altered to the present hexagonal plan. The grand portico in the Roman Corinthian style is three columns deep and about 100 ft wide. The carving in the tympanum above the portico (sculptor Frederick W. Allen) shows Justice with Courage and Wisdom. Atop the pediment are statues representing Law (center) flanked by Truth and Equity. The niches of the porch have two female figures (Philip Martiny) removed from the Surrogate's Court on Chambers St. The figure with a shield and the city coat of arms (left) is Authority, while her companion (right), resting her foot upon a bundle of records, is said to represent Justice.

INTERIOR. In the center of the building is a saucer dome supported on Corinthian columns of Tennessee marble. Ceiling frescoes by Attilio Pusterla depict famous monuments in the history of jurisprudence. The central oculus, originally open to the sky, is now protected against the elements and, presumably, the pigeons. Beneath the dome is a circular design in coloured marble with bronze figures representing the signs of the zodiac.

Look across Foley Square to the W. side. The *U.S. Federal Building and Customs Courthouse* (1967; Alfred Easton Poor, Kahn & Jacobs; Eggers & Higgins) stand between Duane and Worth Sts facing a plaza paved with old Belgian blocks salvaged from the city streets. The smaller cube-like building houses the Customs Court; the taller with its odd-looking windows has U.S. government offices.

On the N. edge of the square are two buildings in the Art Deco style of the 1930s. *The State of New York Building* (1930; Sullivan W. Jones & William E. Haugaard) on the N.E. corner of Worth and Centre Sts has a classic frieze and sculptured cornice. The *Department of Health Building* (1936; Charles B. Meyers) on the N.W. corner of the same intersection has a moulding bearing the names of great men of medicine.

Continue past the front of the Department of Health Building to Lafayette St and turn right (N.). Between Catherine Lane and Leonard St is the former *New York Life Insurance Co. Building* (1870; Griffith Thomas; remodelled in 1895; McKim, Mead & White), whose front is at 346 Broadway. The two clock towers originally had cupolas and a great iron globe with an eagle on top once graced the Broadway side. Today the clocktower (enter from 108 Leonard St) houses the *Institute for Art and Urban Resources* (13th floor; open Wed–Fri, 1–6; Sat, 10–6; free; tel: 233–1096 or 784–2084), a gallery with studio and exhibition space for contemporary artists.

Continue N. on Lafayette St. At 60 Lafayette St between Leonard and Franklin Sts is the *Family Court of New York City* (1975; Haines Lundberg & Waehler), shaped like a cube partially sheered off or one surface. It is faced with grey granite, highly polished on the sides of the cube, rough and unfinished on the recessed surfaces. A statue (1975) entitled 'Three Forms' by Roy Gussow stands before the entrance.

Across the street and parking lot (100 Centre St between Leonard and White Sts) looms the grim bulk of the New York City *Criminal Courts Building* (1939; Harvey Wiley Corbett), formerly the Manhattan Detention Center for Men, better known as 'The Tombs'.

The name originated with an earlier prison (1836–38) officially known as 'The Halls of Justice' and constructed in the Egyptian Revival style with trapezoidal windows, lotus columns, and emblems of the sun god. The old prison acquired the name 'The Tombs' partly because of the funeral associations of the architectural style and partly because of its dismal function and appearance, made even gloomier by the site—a hollow so deep that the massive prison walls hardly rose above the level of Broadway some hundred yards to the W. This 'Tombs' served as the city jail until 1893 when a second prison, Romanesque Revival in style but still called 'The Tombs' replaced it. The present building is the third generation of penal institutions on the site.

Built in the Art Moderne or Art Deco style of the 1930s with ziggurat-shaped towers, and cast aluminum detail, it is laid out in four main blocks with the northernmost containing the prison cells while the others have offices and courtrooms. Originally it was a short-term detention facility for prisoners awaiting trial, but as preliminary detention periods lengthened, the prison became overcrowded and inadequate; in 1970 it witnessed a violent riot and in 1974 the Men's House of Detention was moved to its present site on Rikers Island.

North of the parking area at 111 Centre St on the S.W. corner of White St is the *Municipal and Civil Court Building* (1960; William Lescaze & Matthew Del Gaudio), a plain white marble cube with a vertical stripe of windows down the S. facade. On the E. side are granite reliefs by William Zorach; on the W. facade is Joseph Kiselewski's relief depicting Justice flanked by an infant and a serpent.

Walk N. to White St, turn left and walk one block W. to *Engine Company No. 31* (1895; Napoleon Le Brun; DL) at 87 Lafayette St on the N.E. corner of White St. Built like a French Renaissance château with a steep slate roof, a corner turret, assorted dormers, and crestings of metal and stone, the building evokes a time when firefighting was a dangerous sport. It was also a showcase of technology, offering such modern features as automatic stall latches that released the horses at the sound of the alarm. It is presently used as the Chinatown Service Center.

5 Chinatown and Little Italy

SUBWAY: IRT Lexington Ave Local (train 6) to Canal St. Walk four blocks E. on Canal St and two blocks S. on Mott St to Chatham Sq. BMT via Broadway (train N or RR) to Canal St. Walk E. five blocks to Mott St and S. to Chatham Sq. (two blocks).

BUS: M1 or M6 (downtown) via Broadway to Worth St; walk E. to Chatham Sq (5 blocks counting on the N. side). M15 (downtown) via 2nd Ave to Chatham Sq. M101 or M102 (downtown) via Lexington and Third Aves to Chatham Sq (Bowery and E. Broadway). Culture Bus, Loop II, Stop 31; walk S. on the Bowery to Chatham Sq.

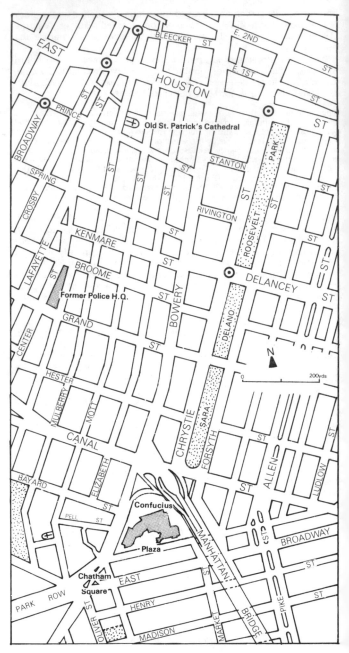

For the visitor, Chinatown—traditionally bounded by Canal, Worth, and Baxter Sts and the Bowery—is the city's most vibrant ethnic enclave, its narrow, crowded streets still redolent with the fragrance of the Far East. For the 22,000 people living in and around Chinatown, it is a ghetto, plagued by poverty, overcrowding, and physical deterioration. Most Chinatown housing is substandard, though rents are low; most business space is also substandard, though commercial rents are high. Since 1965 when immigration laws were liberalised annulling the Exclusion Acts of 1882, Chinatown has witnessed a population explosion, with an estimated 10–15 thousand immigrants settling in New York yearly, putting stress on both the physical and social fabric of Chinatown. But unlike the city's other ghettos where physical deterioration is matched by a decay of the spirit, Chinatown remains hopeful and relatively free of crime, its businesses thriving and its institutions still coping with the social problems caused by the new immigrants.

Sunday is Chinatown's busiest day as former residents return to visit and Chinese from all over the greater metropolitan area come to purchase supplies. It is at its most brilliant during the Chinese New Year celebration (first full moon after 21 Jan), when masked dragon dancers parade through the streets amid the din and sulphurous fumes of exploding firecrackers and restaurants offer festive banquets.

Chinese Restaurants: In old Chinatown, a nine block area, it has been estimated that there are 461 businesses of which 130 are restaurants, making food supply Chinatown's most important trade. At the turn of the century when laws in many states prohibited the Chinese from entering occupations in which they would compete with Caucasians, the restaurant business was one of the few open areas. Early Chinese restaurants catered to a Chinese clientele, generally immigrant men without wives and families, but after 1890 the Caucasian trade became acceptable, led by journalists from nearby Park Row. Because most Chinese immigrants were Cantonese—one study estimates that 60% came from Toishan, a small district near Canton—most restaurants were at first Cantonese in style, but after World War II when refugees from all over China remained in America, it became possible to find restaurants specialising in the cooking of Canton, Shantung, Szechuan, and Hunan.

In addition to regional restaurants, different kinds of Chinese restaurants serve different gustatory needs. First, there are numerous 'regular' Chinese restaurants, serving a complete menu. For lunch, there are dim sum parlours, offering what can best be described as dumplings—noodle doughs wrapped in various shapes around meat or vegetable stuffings and either steamed or fried. Some dim sum restaurants have no menu; the waiters carry around trays with the dishes and the diner simply asks for (or points at) what he wants. Another lunch or snack restaurant is the noodle shop, where the staple is either noodles—in soup or with meat and vegetables—or congee, a thick soup made of a little rice cooked for a long time in a lot of water and garnished with fish or meat. Noodle shops draw a Chinese clientele and are simple in appearance, as well as inexpensive. Rice houses—small, economical, lunch counter restaurants—offer rice topped with meat and vegetables and also serve plain, home-style fare. Coffee shops, offering Chinese buns, almond cookies, steamed sponge cake, and some sweet types of dim sum, have become convenient places for a snack.

Begin at CHATHAM SQUARE. Before population pressures caused Chinatown to overflow its traditional boundaries, Chatham Sq marked the border between Chinatown on the W. and the Lower East Side to the E. Park Row, St. James Pl., Oliver St, East Broadway, Catherine St, Division St, the Bowery, Doyers St, Mott St, and Worth St all empty into this congested, hectic intersection. On one of the traffic islands is the *Kim Lau Memorial* (1962; Poy G. Lee), an arch with a pagoda-style top dedicated to Americans of Chinese ancestry who died in defence of freedom and democracy. On another traffic island E. of the arch is a branch of the Manhattan Savings Bank, brightly painted and topped with a traditional curved roof. Most of the buildings in Chinatown are loft buildings or Old Law Tenements, and only recently has there been an effort to make Chinatown architecturally 'Chinese'.

Look across Chatham Sq to the S.W. where a new 11-story office building has been constructed with aid from a city tax incentive programme. The building (uncompleted at the time of writing) is expected to draw as tenants Chinese doctors, lawyers, accountants, and insurance agents who serve local residents as well as the large number of Chinese who live outside Chinatown but come here seeking ethnically orientated professional services.

Walk E. into East Broadway, once part of the Jewish ghetto, now ethnically Chinese. At No. 11 E. Broadway is the _Pagoda Theater_ which shows Chinese movies, many imported from Hong Kong, often with romantic and melodramatic plots; a few sample titles suggest their flavour: 'Poison Rose and the Bodyguard', 'Fish and Guts', 'The Lotus Triangle', 'Who Will Be My Boyfriend?' Across the street at No. 26 E. Broadway is the Tak Yan Tong Co., one of Chinatown's medicinal herb shops, which offers dried deer antlers, sea horses, ginseng, and starfish as well as more familiar herbs and teas to a clientele primarily of older immigrants who adhere to traditional remedies. The _Chatham Square Branch of the New York Public Library_, once the intellectual territory of Jewish immigrants, now offers oriental readers a large selection of Chinese language books. Continue along E. Broadway to the _Sun Sing Chinese Theater_ (75 E. Broadway) under the approach to the Manhattan Bridge, Chinatown's opera house until 1950 when it was converted to a movie theatre. Turn left on Market St just before the bridge and walk a block to Division St, so named because it marked the division between the farms of James De Lancey and Henry Rutgers in pre-Revolutionary New York. At one time the area now occupied by the street was used as a rope walk, where strands of hemp were twisted into rope.

On the N. side of the street is CONFUCIUS PLAZA (1976; Horowitz & Chun), the first new housing built in the Chinatown area since Chatham Towers (1965) on Park Row. The project includes PS 124 Manhattan, an elementary school, as well as 764 apartments, 20% of which are reserved as low income housing. All the apartments were let before completion of the building and there is now a long waiting list, understandable since overcrowding is a dominant fact of life in Chinatown, and immigration now far outpaces residential construction.

Continue back along Division St past the apartment complex. Oddly enough, the benign bronze _statue of Confucius_ facing Chatham Square at Division St and the Bowery aroused a flurry of controversy when presented (1976) to the city by the Chinese Consolidated Benevolent Association. At the time Confucius had fallen into disfavour in the People's Republic of China for the traditional and authoritarian nature of his teachings, and Chinatown residents who followed the party line found the philosopher a poor representative of China's cultural heritage.

Continue around Confucius Plaza, past the shops facing the Bowery; cross the Bowery at the traffic light opposite Bayard St; turn left and walk downtown one block. On the S.W. corner of the Bowery and Pell St (18 Bowery) is the *Edward Mooney house*, the city's oldest rowhouse (1785–89; DL), now containing an off track betting parlor, whose clientele lounges around on the sidewalk waiting the race results. Mooney, a merchant, meat wholesaler, and, ironically, amateur racehorse breeder, built the house on land that once belonged to Tory James De Lancey, who had to forfeit his property and flee the country at the end of the Revolutionary War.

Dating from the beginning of the Federal period, the house is Georgian in its proportions (three full stories with a gambrel roof and a finished loft beneath it) and in its details: the fine door hood, the lintels with splayed keystones, the quarter-round and round-headed windows facing Pell St. The generous number of windows reveals Mooney's wealth, since glass had been manufactured in the middle colonies only since c. 1740 and was an expensive commodity.

Turn right into Pell St, named after John Pell, a prosperous butcher in pre-Revolutionary days. At No. 16 Pell St (the door says No. 13) is the headquarters of the Hip Sing Association or tong.

The Chinese, like other immigrant groups, drawn together by shared customs and language as well as shared problems, became a close-knit community, forming self-help organisations to help them adapt to an alien culture. The tongs, as these associations were called, soon became involved in vice, especially prostitution, gambling, and opium dealing, and eventually came into conflict with one another. Tong wars, fought mainly by hired assassins wielding either guns or cleavers (hence the term hatchetmen), were luridly exploited by the American press, so that for years Chinatown bore the image of sinister crimes and exotic sins. Today the tongs have become merchants' associations which exercise influence mainly among the older Chinese.

Turn left into DOYERS ST, named after Anthony H. Doyer, a distiller. The crooked, narrow street was originally a cart lane leading to the distillery at the S. end (No. 5–7 Doyers St).

The bend in Doyers St was once known as 'Bloody Angle', recalling a tong war around the turn of the century during which the Hip Sings battled the On Leongs. On the site of the present Post Office at No. 6 Doyers St stood the Chatham Club where Irving Berlin, known in those days as Isidore Baline, waited at table. Across the street at No. 5–7 Doyers St is the site of the original Chinese Opera House, which stood here until 1910 when it was acquired for a mission run by Tom Noonan, an ex-convict who dispensed charity to the Bowery bums until his death in 1935.

Follow Doyers St to the Bowery. On the S.W. corner of the intersection is a house remaining from 1809 when Anthony Doyers built it as one of four. Just N. of this intersection (turn left) is the *Olliffe's Apothecary* at No. 6 Bowery. It is the oldest apothecary shop in the city (1803) and though it still bears the sign of W.M. Olliffe, it is now run by a Chinese druggist. Turn around and walk down the Bowery to Mott St, named after Joseph Mott, another prosperous pre-Revolutionary butcher. Mott also ran a tavern at what is now 143rd St and Eighth Ave, which served as Washington's headquarters before he moved into the Morris-Jumel Mansion (see pp396-7).

Turn right into **Mott St,** Chinatown's main street. At No. 8 Mott St stood (c. 1875) New York's first Chinese mercantile establishment run by one Wo Kee.

The identity of New York's first Chinese resident is not known, but as early as the 1850s a few Chinese came from San Francisco, most of whom found work as street corner cigar sellers or as sandwich sign carriers. As racial hostilities increased on the west coast, more Chinese immigrants came east, settling in this area, known then as the Plow and Harrow district after a tavern of that name founded in the 17C. Wo Kee's shop and others like it that soon opened on Mott St became sources of Chinese groceries and medicines as well as social centers on Sundays, where immigrants—generally men without families—could receive mail, socialise, and eat in restaurants.

Continue along Mott St. Just beyond Park St is the CHURCH OF THE TRANSFIGURATION (1801; DL) at No. 25 Mott St, built as the Zion Episcopal Church and now serving a Roman Catholic parish. Like the nearby Sea and Land Church on Henry St (see p122), this modest rubblestone building belongs to the Georgian tradition with its triangular pediment and simple tower but has pointed arch windows, unusual in a church of this period. The copper clad spire was added in 1868.

Continue along Mott St. The amusing telephone booths with their pagoda tops were inspired by a similar design in San Francisco. Some of Chinatown's larger vegetable and fish stores are along Mott St, which still remains the east coast supply center of Chinese foodstuffs.

In the building at No. 41 Mott St is the New York branch of Lee's Federal Credit Union, not precisely a tourist attraction but an indication of the kind of development that is taking place in Chinatown. Mr K.L. Lee of Washington, D.C., once president of the Lee Family Association, formed the credit union in an effort to get older immigrants to work together with younger, Americanised Chinese. Knowing that many of the non-English speaking elders had money which was not deposited in banks and that many younger, non-Chinese speaking people needed money to start new businesses, Lee persuaded the one group to deposit their capital in a credit union so that it could be put into circulation. He then had to persuade the younger group that a credit union under the auspices of a family association would be run democratically instead of patriarchically.

At No. 62 Mott St is the headquarters of the CHINESE CONSOLI-DATED BENEVOLENT ASSOCIATION, the oldest and best-known of Chinatown's leadership groups, with 59 family associations represented. Family or clan associations were originally formed as social agencies for people of the same surname—Lee, Chen—providing for the aged and for widows, acting as employment agencies, organising social functions, and aiding illiterate or non-English speaking immigrants. The *Chinese School* (opened 1915) in the same building has worked to transmit and preserve Chinese culture, and now enrolls more than 3000 students, many of whom come from outlying towns to learn Chinese. At No. 64B Mott St is the *Eastern States Buddhist Temple of America*, dimly lit and perfumed with incense.

Continue along Mott St to Canal St. On the S.W. corner of the intersection is the *Chinese Merchants' Association* (1958) at No. 85 Mott St. The building, a colourful but inauthentic mixture of western and oriental architectural features, houses a group that evolved from the On Leong tong.

CANAL ST, once the N. border of Chinatown, has recently seen the resurgence of the garment industry at a time when clothing manufacture is declining throughout the city as a whole. Many loft buildings here are leased by apparel contractors who hire predominantly women, especially recent immigrants with language difficulties that bar them from other jobs, and older women who do the lighter tasks.

Turn left on Canal St and walk one block W. to MULBERRY ST, the spine of **Little Italy,** an ethnic enclave dating from the 1880s but whose population dramatically increased between 1890 and 1924 before restrictive laws staunched immigration. Nowadays Little Italy is fighting a war of attrition as its population ages and dwindles and as younger, richer families leave for the suburbs. Before the city killed the proposed Lower Manhattan Expressway in 1968 (see p163), Little Italy reached its nadir, with sagging real estate values and morale, abandoned buildings, and a withering economic base. However the resurgence of SoHo to the W., the immigration of Chinese businesses N. of Canal St, and the efforts of local community leaders have combined to give Little Italy new life and hope.

FESTIVALS: Little Italy is at its most colourful during its two principal festivals when old residents return to mingle with crowds of tourists. The *Feast of St. Anthony of Padua*, held evenings during the first two weeks of June, centers on Sullivan St (tel: SP7–2755 for information). The *Feast of San Gennaro* around the week of 19 Sept (tel: CA6–9546) centers on Mulberry St. Images of the saints are carried through the streets and at night arcades of lights turn the neighbourhood into a carnival offering games of chance, balloons and souvenirs, and such earthy delights as Italian sausage and *zeppole*, a kind of deep fried cake dusted with powdered sugar.

Walk N. on Mulberry St. At Nos 132–138 Mulberry St between Hester and Grand Sts is a subtle trompe l'oeil *mural* by Richard Haas (1976); the warehouse wall has been painted to depict imaginary stores whose facades incorporate real details from the wall beneath. At No. 140 Mulberry St is the Società San Gennaro, Napoli e Dintorni, sponsors of the saint's annual festival. At No. 142 Mulberry St is the Sun Mee Company, a spillover from Chinatown, behind whose innocuous walls bean sprouts grow in an artifically induced tropical climate. Paolucci's Restaurant (No. 149 Mulberry St) occupies the original *Stephen van Rensselaer House* (1816; DL). A lonely survivor among the tenements of the block, this Federal house has been painted green and white but still retains its original dormers.

Turn left at Grand St. At No. 165 Grand St on the S.E. corner of Centre St is the *former Odd Fellows Hall* (1849; J.B. Snook), an immense brownstone pile with a mansard roof, once the home of a fraternal organisation, now unused and badly deteriorating.

N. of it at No. 240 Centre St is the **former Police Headquarters** (1909; Hoppin & Koen; DL), whose grand scale, trapezoidal shape, and Baroque ornateness set it apart from the surrounding tenements and loft buildings. The main entrance on Centre St is embellished by a large New York coat of arms and five statues representing the five boroughs. There are plans to remodel this dramatic building, empty since the police department moved to its present headquarters in 1973, as a community center or a hotel.

Along its E. facade runs CENTRE MARKET PL. named after the old Centre Market, known for its beautiful flowers, once atop a high hill. The diagonal course of the street was dictated by the boundaries of the 18C Bayard farm.

Go N. to Broome St where one of the few bishop's crook lamp posts remains on the S.W. corner of the intersection (see p164). Turn right and walk E. Visible from the corner of Mott and Broome Sts is *Engine Company 55* of the City Fire Department (1898; R.H. Robertson) at No. 363 Broome St, a fine Renaissance Revival firehouse.

Turn left and walk N. on Mott St two blocks to Prince St. On the S.W. corner is OLD ST. PATRICK'S CONVENT AND GIRLS' SCHOOL (1826; DL), an unusually large Federal building with brownstone trim, its handsome doorway framed with slender Corinthian columns and with a fanlight (now filled with stained glass).

Across Prince St is OLD ST. PATRICK'S CATHEDRAL (1815; Joseph F. Mangin; DL), begun in 1809 and finished six years later after the War of 1812 interrupted the work. Until the present St. Patrick's was completed in 1879, this was the cathedral church of the see of New York, and as such was an important, albeit oddly designed building, altered after a fire in 1866 so that its present appearance only hints at what it once looked like. Above the present sheered-off Gothic facade was once a balustrade above which was a central pointed window framed by a broken pediment and topped off by a spire, the oddness of the whole explainable by the fact that this was America's second Gothic Revival church (the first was the Chapel of St. Mary's Seminary in Baltimore dating from 1807) and architect Mangin (designer of classically beautiful City Hall) was experimenting with an unfamiliar style.

At No. 256–258 Mott St is the *former Fourteenth Ward Industrial School* (1888; Vaux and Radford), later the Astor Memorial School, a Gothic Revival reminder of Little Italy's past as an immigrant slum, now converted by charitable organisations like the Children's Aid Society to fill the gap between the tenement and the public school, gathering in street children and teaching them the rudiments of citizenship as well as reading and writing.

Walk around to the rear of St. Patrick's on Mulberry St. In the graveyard (usually locked) lie the remains of Pierre Toussaint (1766–1853), born into slavery in Haiti, known for his ministrations to the poor and plague-stricken. The Gothic Revival interior of the church (entrance on Mulberry St) is unremarkable, except that it is worth noting that the columns supporting the roof are made of cast-iron. N. of the church on Mulberry St is *St. Michael's Chapel* (c. 1850; DL), a small, oddly isolated brownstone and brick church completed from designs by James Renwick.

Continue N. on Mulberry St toward Houston St. On the W. side, between Jersey and Houston Sts, is the *Puck Building*, an imposing brick Romanesque Revival commercial building (1885; addition 1892; Albert Wagner) which has long served the printing industry, first as the home of the humour magazine 'Puck', today as the plant of the Superior Printing Ink Company. At the corner of Houston St and above the main entrance on Lafayette St are figures of Puck, top-hatted and cherubic, by Caspar Buberl (died 1889), who immigrated from Bohemia.

The nearest uptown subways are the IRT Lexington Ave local (train 6) at Bleecker and Lafayette Sts or the IND Sixth Ave (B,D, or F trains) at Broadway and Lafayette St. There are uptown buses on the Bowery (M101 and M102), on Lafayette St (M1) and on W. Houston St (M5, via Sixth Ave). Downtown buses run on Broadway (M1, M6) and the Bowery (M101 and M102).

6 Lower East Side

SUBWAY: IND F train to East Broadway-Canal St.

BUS: M15 (First and Second Ave) or M9 (Ave B from Union Square to Chatham Square). Culture Bus Loop II (weekends and holidays) to Stop 14.

Sunday is a good day to visit the Lower East Side, since shops and markets are open and lively; many are closed on Saturday, the Jewish Sabbath. Many churches and synagogues in the area are closed except during services because of vandalism.

The Lower East Side is not one of New York's finer neighbourhoods and has not been so for over 150 years. It lacks famous landmarks, fine buildings, museums, and appealing shops (although it is a good place for bargain hunters). Instead its interest lies in its past, and visiting the area becomes an exercise in urban archaeology: the visitor with an historical imagination must look through layers of peeling paint and past shattered windows to see the once proud synagogue, or try to visualise from the crumbling tenements what life must have been like within their walls for the immigrants who lived and laboured there. There are many traces of the past: the jewellery shops near the Manhattan Bridge approach remain from a time when the area had an active outdoor diamond market; the stores selling bedclothes on Grand St near Allen St survive from the old bed linens market in the Romanian district. The former presence of the Second Avenue El can be detected from the old powerhouse at the intersection of Allen and Division Sts. There are also human survivors, some of the original immigrants now elderly and mostly poor, sometimes still clinging to old country dress and ways.

History. In the 18C, much of what is now the Lower East Side belonged to the city's great landowning families, the Rutgers and the De Lanceys. The Rutgers settled E. of Division St and the De Lanceys until the conclusion of the American Revolution held the land W. of Division St to the East River, and had a mansion between the present Delancey and Rivington Sts on what is now Chrystie St. After the war the area still remained semi-rural, with pleasant homes and considerable open space. By 1800, however, the city had spread as far N. as Cherry St, and Federal and Greek Revival row houses began to be built to house the newly prosperous merchants and sea captains who lived in these neighbourhoods because of their proximity to the center of the shipping industry on South St.

By 1850 the pressures of immigration were beginning to be felt, and the Lower East Side was starting to deteriorate socially. The former captains' mansions on East Broadway were becoming shops; the slums of Five Points (see p123) were boiling over into Cherry St, and the area surrounding the present Brooklyn Bridge was becoming crowded and undesirable. The once quiet streets began to witness the violence of street gangs who harrassed respectable citizens, and single family row houses were being sold off for a quarter of their value in the '20s and '30s.

The ethnic makeup of the district was also shifting. Between 1846 and 1860, large numbers of Irish immigrants forced out of Ireland by the potato blight, poverty, and political oppression, sought relief in the United States and many settled in the Lower East Side, at least until the next wave of immigration swept them out. Many joined the building and maritime trades and later became municipal workers, policemen, firemen, and eventually politicians and lawyers. At mid-century a large group of Germans, both Jews and gentiles, also arrived, a group that included skilled workers and craftsmen, who actively pursued their trades, forming trade unions and working-men's associations. They became Americanised with relative ease and took their places in society as merchants, jewellers, clothing manufacturers, furriers, professionals, and even bankers.

In 1881, however, revolutionary terrorists assassinated Czar Alexander II of Russia, and in the pogroms and repressive political actions that followed, a wave of Russian and east European Jewish immigration began that entirely changed the character of the Lower East Side and still affects the ethnic balance of New York. Between 1881 and 1914 almost 2 million Jews came to the United States, many of whom settled at least temporarily in the Lower East Side. After the end of World War I until the immigration quotas were imposed in 1924, another group arrived. In general the Jews who came were young; they intended to resettle permanently; they included a higher proportion of women and children than other immigrant groups. Those who arrived after 1900 tended to be better educated, more highly skilled than earlier settlers.

The life in store for them was not what the myth of America, the golden land, had led many to believe: much was demanded, little

Sweat shop in a Ludlow St tenement, about 1889. Jacob Riis's photographs of tenement life remain a testament to the hardships endured by the city's immigrant poor and to the photographer's crusading spirit. (Jacob Riis Collection, The Museum of the City of New York)

was given in return. Immigrants had to show great endurance to accept the constant crowding and lack of privacy that awaited them in the tenements, the pitiful wages that their jobs offered. They had to endure boredom and loss of identity, the inability to communicate, and the ensuing family crises, as the young quickly adapted to the New World and rejected the traditions of their parents. Coping with all these difficulties demanded the heroic expenditure of both physical and psychological energy, and naturally everyone did not survive. Many immigrants were reduced to resignation and fell prey to physical and mental illness, especially tuberculosis (the worst tenement areas were called 'lung blocks' and claimed mortality rates twice as high as the rest of the city) and depression; suicide was not uncommon. Some turned to crime, although studies indicate that most of these criminals were native born, the children of the immigrants; and that, ghetto crimes tended to be fraudulent rather than violent.

Most of the Jewish immigrants found work either peddling or in the 'needle trades', virtually the only choices open to the uneducated poor. Neither was pleasant. Peddling was heavy work that bent the back and broke the spirit, with endless trudging door to door to meet scorn, rejection, pity, and hostility from anti-Semitic groups. Peddling from a pushcart was perhaps easier although even these men were harrassed by children, by the police, by gentiles.

Since the skills demanded by the 'needle trades' could be learned quickly and since English was unnecessary, many immigrants, both male and female, worked in the garment factories or sweatshops of the district. They could be forced by starvation wages into working a 12- or 14-hour day under the most miserable conditions: the machines were powered by foot treadles; the pressing irons weighed as much as 25 lbs; lighting, ventilation, and toilet facilities were pitifully inadequate. Wages were low: in 1911, fewer than 30% of the male workers who had come from east Europe after 1905 earned more than $12·50 per week. Women and children eked out the family income at home by sewing, making paper flowers, and shelling nuts.

The anguish of these immigrants awoke the compassion of reformers, some of them co-religionists like Lillian Wald, others non-sectarian humanitarians like Jacob Riis. American social work began on the Lower East Side, and early settlement houses included the Neighborhood Guild, founded in 1886 by a small group of middle class Christians who trucked their belongings down to the Lower East Side to live by the people they proposed to serve. Other social agencies were the Henry Street Settlement, the University Settlement, and the Educational Alliance, all of which are active today.

Following a long cultural tradition, the Jews also helped each other. Various ethnic or local groups formed *landsmanshaftn* to offer each other financial and social support. They formed labour unions in the various trades and a central organisation called the United Hebrew Trades (1888). Often risking personal injury, immigrant workers both male and female went out on strike and not infrequently had to prove their physical courage in the face of threats from thugs hired to intimidate them. Women at home 'organised' in other ways: the members of the Ladies Anti-Beef Trust, for example, instituted a meat boycott and poured kerosene over extortionately priced kosher beef.

Another bright spot in the general greyness of the slums was the intellectual life which the immigrants, despite the rigours of their working hours, carried on with undiminished passion. Lower East Side cafés became informal institutions where they could discuss socialism, industrialism, Zionism, literature, and drama. Agencies like the Educational Alliance offered lecture series, and after the turn of the century there were libraries, whose reading rooms were filled to capacity nightly. Jewish workers read Tolstoy and Goethe during their lunch breaks, and companies of Jewish actors began occupying the theatres of the Bowery and Second Ave north of Houston St.

Here one could see such luminaries as Jacob Adler and Boris Tomashevsky who first performed in rather rough comedies and gaudy melodramas and later in serious translations and adaptations of the works of Shakespeare, Ibsen, and Goethe. Among the actors and performers who rose from the ghetto theatres to the brighter lights uptown were Eddie Cantor, Fannie Bryce, Sophie Tucker, Al Jolson, and George Jessel.

Although the Biblical injunction against graven images traditionally had made Jews suspect of the fine arts, a number of men who eventually became important American artists stepped over the invisible boundaries into what was essentially a gentile field of endeavour. While the Yiddish poet or playwright merited cultural respect no matter how poor, the painter or sculptor bore the double burden of poverty and indifference or suspicion. Among the artists who overcame these difficulties mainly through inflexible will were Jo Davidson, Jacob Epstein, William Gropper, William Zorach, Raphael Soyer, and Max Weber. Oddly enough, the Educational Alliance began to offer art classes in the 1880s (although it dropped them as a luxury in 1905 when the pressures of immigration had begun to mount), and the roll of alumni is studded with famous names: Leonard Baskin, Louise Nevelson, Ben Shahn, and Mark Rothko.

The Lower East Side was also a hotbed of political activity with clubs and organisations mostly of left wing persuasions meeting in the cafés and in the meeting halls. The more successful of these put out their own propaganda and the most successful of these left wing publications was the 'Jewish Daily Forward', but there was also the Yiddish Communist daily, 'Freiheit', and Emma Goldman's anarchist 'Mother Earth', as well as periodicals like the 'Yidisher Kemfer', which had a labour Zionist point of view. The titles of these journals reflect the aspirations of their writers: 'Yidisher Kemfer' (the Jewish Fighter), the 'Naye Lebn' (the New Life), the 'Naye Land' (the New World), and 'Tsukunft' (the Future).

The socialists of the Lower East Side had their victories at the polls, electing Meyer London (1871–1922) to Congress in 1914, 1916, and 1920 and putting three socialist assemblymen in office in 1918. Morris Hillquit (1869–1933), a leader of the American Socialist Party, ran for mayor of New York in 1917 and attracted 145,332 votes, five times those garnered by the previous socialist candidate.

The highwater mark of immigration came in the early years of the 20C, when the Lower East Side ghetto suffered a population density of more than 700 people per acre. But while new arrivals were pressing at the barricades of Ellis Island, established residents were beginning to move on. They went out to Brooklyn across the Brooklyn, Williamsburg and Manhattan Bridges which opened in 1883, 1903, and 1909 respectively. They took the elevated railway up to the Bronx starting in 1896 or rode the new subway through the tunnel under the Harlem River (1905) or to Brooklyn (1908). Harlem itself had a burgeoning Jewish community in 1900, and by 1910 the 'Jewish Daily Forward' was bemoaning that this once green and lovely town had become airless, foul, and tenement ridden.

The immigration law of 1924 virtually stopped all new arrivals from Eastern Europe and as the existing population drained away through the newly opened portals, the area became less crowded and also less vital. The first synagogues were abandoned in the 1930s. Today the population is approximately 35% Jewish, 35% Puerto Rican, 8% Black, 17% Chinese and 5% other (Italian, Ukranian, Polish, and Indian). Year by year the Jewish population dwindles as the remaining Jews, mostly elderly and poor, move out if they can afford it or grow older and die here if they cannot. Several large public housing developments were constructed after the close of World War II, but many tenements still remain. While many synagogues have either been torn down or sold to new Christian congregations, reversing the trend of the early years of the century, others remain, deserted, crumbling, often besieged by hostile and ethnically alien neighbours. The social agencies continue their work in the face of inadequate funding (though everything in New York seems to be inadequately funded at the present time).

Observers look back, almost nostalgically, at an era that will never return, and from this distance what was a time of misery and dislocation for many seems attractive and almost quaint. And yet the problems facing the new immigrants and the new ghetto dwellers—poverty, poor housing, cultural alienation, the language barrier, and lack of job opportunities—are essentially those the Jews encountered. The people come and go; the slum remains.

The **Educational Alliance** (197 E. Broadway), organised in 1889 and named in 1893, was one of the most important early agencies formed to help the massive influx of East European Jews adapt to the bewildering, alien culture of America. Founded by a group of German-Jewish philanthropists, many of them immigrants themselves, who had arrived a generation earlier, prospered, and moved out of the ghetto (if they had ever lived there), the Alliance started as a merger of three organisations: the Aguilar Free Library Society, the Young Men's Hebrew Association, and the Hebrew Free School Association. It proposed to bring education to the ignorant, recreation to the weary, and, most important, knowledge of American institutions and language to the foreigner, for the 'uptown' Jews, as the German philanthropists came to be known, saw Americanisation as the key to self-reliance and freedom from want.

The Alliance held classes for immigrant children to prepare them for the public school system and gave courses in English and civics to adults to ready them for naturalisation. It showed movies about American history and held Legal Holiday parties (on the 4th of July, Lincoln's Birthday, and so on) which naturally had educational as well as celebratory aspects. It opened a library before the free public system was organised, and offered a broad programme of courses for interested adults: art, Greek and Roman history, botany, electricity and physics, piano, violin, and mandolin lessons, stenography, American history, book-keeping. It presented lectures which probed moral, philosophical, and literary topics. It ran social clubs for children and a children's theatre, where aspiring actors and actresses could participate in plays like 'Little Lord Fauntleroy' and 'The Tempest'. It provided a gymnasium and facilities for taking showers, an important service in a tenement-ridden slum where bathtubs were rare. Children could escape the heat, filth, and crowding of an East Side summer by attending an Alliance camp. Wives deserted by their husbands, a common problem in this stressful society, could find legal assistance from Yiddish-speaking lawyers. Mothers could buy pasteurised milk from a dispensary on the roof, which in 1896 recorded an average daily attendance of 4600.

While the Alliance provided services sorely needed by the immigrant community, it still remained something of a source of distress to the people who used it, and relations between the 'uptown' and 'downtown' Jews were prickly for a long time. The assimilated uptowners found the new immigrants backward, 'oriental', and slovenly, people who needed lessons in hygiene as well as English. The 'greenhorns', or new immigrants, found the German Jews condescending and insensitive to their natural desire to perpetuate their native, east European culture. Yet despite such strains, the Alliance survived to make life better for many.

Today it carries on its work, although those who use its facilities are Puerto Rican, Chinese, and black as well as Jewish. Its annual budget of over $1·8 million comes from the Federation of Jewish

Philanthropies of New York, and from federal, state, and city grants, from foundations and from fees.

The Alliance helps the aged poor by making home visits, providing escort services, and offering consumer education. It schedules trips and programmes of cultural enrichment for the increasingly isolated population of elderly Jews still in the district. Since half the population of the Lower East Side still lives in tenements dating from the 19C, the Alliance offers special services to families living in these slum buildings including mental health services. It has a day care center, an alcoholism programme, a programme for runaway young people, a programme for the mentally retarded, and a programme directed at local street groups of boys and girls alienated from society and using drugs.

Across E. Broadway in the park is the SEWARD PARK BRANCH OF THE NEW YORK PUBLIC LIBRARY (192 E. Broadway), founded in 1910 as one of the early branches of the public system. It ministered to the intellectual hunger of the immigrants by offering a large collection of books in Yiddish, and frequently long lines formed at the door as people waited to get in.

The nearby Chatham Square branch also served the immigrant community and recorded in 1903 that books in English were being borrowed at the rate of 1000 per day.

SEWARD PARK, created from land acquired in 1897 and opened officially in 1903, is named after William H. Seward (1801–72), governor of the State of New York. U.S. Senator, and eventually Secretary of State under Abraham Lincoln.

Across the street from the park is the **Jewish Daily Forward Building.** Although the newspaper is now published uptown on East 33rd St, this building at 175 E. Broadway was long the home of the most influential Yiddish daily newspaper. It was founded in 1897 and after a few years of floundering began to rise under the guidance of Abraham Cahan (1860–1951).

Cahan, himself an immigrant from Lithuania, dictated the editorial policy of the paper, which focused on the whole spectrum of immigrant Jewish experience. Intimate in tone, straightforward in diction, socialist in political leaning, the 'Forward' told of the everyday events of the Lower East Side and described the minutiae of Jewish life. Cahan wrote about the prostitution of Allen St, about the iniquities of bosses who imposed unbearable working conditions; his paper explained baseball to the greenhorn and offered advice on the proper use of the pocket handkerchief. Although he carried lurid and sensational stories, he also presented high quality fiction and serious essays. The most famous feature of the paper, the *Bintel Brief* (Bundle of Letters), was a column in which readers unburdened themselves of the personal problems confronting them in their new homeland. The topics covered are an index of the miseries of immigrant life. A mother writes that her adult daughter ridicules the old country modes of dress, speech, and even cooking (alienation between parents and children was a common source of grief during a time when parents clung to old ways and children eagerly embraced the new). A father worries because his daughters hang around with street boys, no better than gangsters, but since both parents work from dawn to nightfall they cannot chaperone their children. A sick and penniless woman fears that her children will be taken away from her and perhaps forcibly converted to Christianity.

The newspaper naturally had its enemies. Cahan was criticised as vulgarly anti-intellectual and degradingly commercial; his paper, according to the intellectual component of the community, had the mind of a child and the lusts of a grown scoundrel. Today it is the only surviving Yiddish daily, claiming a readership of about 50,000, less than a quarter of its peak circulation in 1924.

Continue along E. Broadway to RUTGERS STREET which honours one of early New York's illustrious families, whose original landowner Hendrick Rutgers had a farm stretching from Division St to the East River. The Rutgers mansion, built in 1754, occupied the city block bordered by Cherry, Jefferson, Monroe, and Clinton Sts and remained there until 1875 when it was razed in favour of tenements and sweatshop loft buildings.

Although it is not the province of this book to recommend restaurants or shops, several have been included on this route because they suggest something of the culture of this section of New York. The GARDEN CAFETERIA (intersection of Rutgers St and E. Broadway) is such a place, serving Jewish specialties—blintzes, borscht, fish, dairy, and vegetable dishes. The mural on the E. wall recalls the time when an artisans' market flourished in what is now Seward Park. People wishing to hire the services of a carpenter or plasterer, for example, came here in the morning and bargained for his services.

Visible from the entrance to the cafeteria is *St. Teresa's Roman Catholic Church* (141 Henry St), originally built as a Presbyterian Church in 1841 but purchased by the Roman Catholic Church in 1863 to serve the growing population of Irish Catholics. As the ethnic balance of the Lower East Side continues to shift, the congregation does also, and the church now offers services in Spanish and Chinese as well as English.

NATHAN STRAUS SQUARE, at the intersection of E. Broadway and Canal St, honours the Jewish philanthropist and businessman perhaps best remembered for his campaign to provide pasteurised milk to city children.

Straus (1848–1931) made his fortune in the R.H. Macy & Co. department store and went on to devote his energies and that fortune to the welfare of the city and its people. He was park commissioner between 1889–93 and president of the Board of Health in 1898. In 1923 he was chosen by popular vote as the New Yorker who had done the most for the city during its first 25 years as Greater New York.

The marble column in the square commemorates servicemen from the Lower East Side who gave their lives during the two World Wars.

Walk W. on Canal St. The former *Yarmulowsky's Bank* (S.W. corner of Canal and Orchard Sts) was one of a number of small private Jewish banks that came into existence when financial conditions eased enough for local residents to save a few dollars. Unfortunately for the depositors, several of these home-grown institutions failed, taking with them the savings painfully culled from sweatshops, factories, and small businesses.

The Yarmulowsky bank was founded at the beginning of the period of heaviest Jewish immigration and lasted until August 1914, when the state banking superintendent closed it because of its 'unsound' condition, with assets of $654,000 and liabilities of $1,703,000. On 5 August of that year, 2000 people demonstrated in front of the bank, and a month later an angry crowd of about 500 swarmed around the entrance of Yarmulowsky's apartment, while he and his family scurried to safety over the rooftops. Yarmulowsky was given a suspended sentence for mismanaging the bank's assets, and the depositors, who eventually did recover some of their losses, learned to be wary of such local institutions.

The ornate clock and lettering above the corner entrance proclaim the original function of the building, which dates from around 1895.

Walk W. on Canal St. The building at 5 Ludlow St formerly belonged to the *Independent Kletzker Brotherly Aid Society* and served both as a synagogue and the center for the group's mutual-aid activities. The Kletzker Society (founded 1892), an organisation of immigrants from the Polish village of Kletsk, was one of an estimated 3–6000 of such *landsmanshaftn* which existed on the Lower East Side at the turn of the century. Besides providing such real services as making burial and funeral arrangements and visiting the sick, these groups also had a social function. Through them people could enjoy the company of their countrymen; they could keep in touch with developments in the old country and find relief from the pressures of the new. It is easy to understand why immigrants, uprooted from the soil that had nurtured their parents and grandparents, formed these organisations. It is equally easy to see why the *landsmanshaftn* did not attract their children who had no special love for little places like Chortkov, Kletsk, or Prszemisl, and indeed would rather forget their foreignness as soon as possible.

Continue W. on Canal St to Eldridge St. Turn left (south). Although several low-income and middle-income cooperative housing projects have been constructed on the Lower East Side since the close of World War II, there are many **19C tenements** still standing. These buildings, constructed for the purpose of exploiting all available space to swell the owner's profits, were one of the horrors of immigrant life. They can be classified as pre-Old Law (before 1879), Old Law (1879–1901), or New Law (after 1901) tenements; and in general, the earlier buildings were darker, more dangerous, and

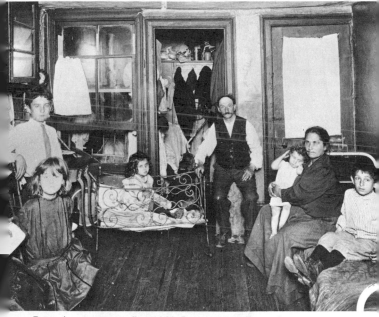

Room in a tenement flat, 1910. Despite the efforts of Jacob Riis and others, tenement reform came slowly and many Old and New Law tenements still remain on the Lower East Side. (Jacob Riis Collection, The Museum of the City of New York)

more primitive than later ones, since each successive law laid new restrictions on greedy landlords and builders. The row of tenements at 15–21 Eldridge St was built after the enaction of the Old Law; the small building across the street at 18 Eldridge St was built before the Old Law.

The tenement became a fact of life starting in about 1850, when the migrations of German, Irish, and N. European people became significant. In that year one Silas Wood built a 'model' tenement on Cherry St, between Roosevelt St and Franklin Square, 'with the design of supplying the labouring people with cheap lodging.' His tenement, named Gotham Court, was made of brick and was five stories high, with about 144 apartments each containing two rooms. Six years after its completion, it housed over a thousand tenants and had become such a scandal that a Health Commission Committee inspecting the sanitary conditions of the basement had to retreat, their untried sensibilities assaulted by the foul air. The visit of the committee did not improve conditions, however, since by 1863 there was a row of privies in the cellar used by the community at large and occasionally flushed out by the public water supply.

In 1867 the city passed an act that promised improvement, but lacked methods of enforcement and was therefore feeble. Technically landlords were required to provide fire escapes and to connect toilets with sewers instead of cesspools, but for every requirement the law provided a loophole, and so the tenements remained filthy firetraps.

The next attempt at amelioration came in 1878 when Henry C. Meyers advertised in his magazine, 'Plumber & Sanitary Engineer', for a design that would best fit the standard New York 25 × 100 ft lot, simultaneously affording the greatest safety and convenience to the tenant and the greatest profit for the landlord. In a situation like this, it is not the landlord whose interests will be neglected, and the prize-winning design soon became synonymous for all that was miserable in tenement design. Reformer Jacob Riis called James E. Ware's 'dumbbell' plan hopeless: two tenements were constructed side by side with a narrow airshaft, often only a foot or so wide, between them, which gave the buildings their characteristic dumbbell shape, but provided virtually no air or light to the lower rooms on the airshaft. Furthermore, the shafts quickly became garbage dumps, as families pitched their garbage and sanitary waste out of the windows. The population of a five story building based on this plan could reach 100–150 people and often did, since poor families sublet space to boarders to help with the rent. Still the Tenement House Act of 1879 did provide some improvements: cellars could not be rented out except by permission of the Board of Health; there had to be running water somewhere either in the house or yard; buildings were to contain one toilet for each two apartments. Backyard houses—buildings for multiple occupancy put up behind the original ones and having no direct access to the street (another ploy to exploit all available space)—were prohibited.

In 1901 a reformer named Lawrence Veiller, who began as a settlement worker, helped push through the state legislature a law forbidding further construction of dumbbell tenements. Instead of the narrow airshaft, the law required a light court at least $4\frac{1}{2}$ ft wide. It limited the height of non-fireproof tenements to five stories and required a toilet in each apartment. Windows had to be installed in all rooms. Unfortunately the 1901 law came rather late to help most tenement dwellers, since in the years since 1879 a vast blight of tenements had spread across the Lower East Side: in 1864 there were 534 tenements in the old Tenth Ward; by 1893, there were 1196.

At 14 Eldridge St is **Congregation Khal Adath Jeshurun with Anshe Lubz** (Community of the People of Israel with the People of Lubz), the first of a number of abandoned or derelict synagogues on this route. It is too grand for the scale of this small street, towering above the neighbouring tenements, richly ornamented with foliate figures, stars of David and bands of ornamentation whose intricacy increases as the eye travels upwards. Like other such buildings in this part of town, it has outlived the people who once used it, and now suffers the ravages of vandalism and of time. Built in 1886 in a predominantly Moorish Revival style (note the keyhole shaped door and window openings), it housed a congregation of Polish Jews formed in 1856, which had grown sufficiently wealthy thirty years later to hire the prestigious firm of Herter Brothers to design their house of worship. The upstairs sanctuary, not open to the public because of its state of deterioration, was once a showplace of synagogue decoration, with its great brass chandeliers (gaslit in early days) and Victorian glass shades, its large rose window in the W. wall; its towering Ark carved in walnut, its elaborately designed pews, galleries, and vaulted ceiling.

The future of this and similar buildings appears bleak; the congregations cannot support their maintenance and grow smaller and poorer with the passage of time; other organisations have shown little interest in rescuing them from oblivion, although the Jewish Museum has considered restoring this building as a synagogue museum. The Synagogue Rescue Project has dedicated itself to preserving the artifacts, if not the buildings themselves, from the ever dwindling number of Lower East Side synagogues.

Diversion. Continue down Eldridge St to the intersection of Division St. Turn left and walk a block to Allen St.

The warehouse at the corner of Allen and Pike Sts once held a power station of the Second Avenue El, which came down Allen St, turned W. into Division St, and continued on to Chatham Square and City Hall. Evidence of the original purpose of the building remains in the lettering on the wall, 'Manhattan Railway Company' and in the circular openings that once accommodated the power lines.

The extension of Allen St E. of Division St is called Pike St. Walk a block and a half S.E. on Pike St.

CONGREGATION SONS OF ISRAEL KALWARIE (15 Pike St) was built in 1903 for a congregation of Jews from the town on the Polish-Lithuanian border which gave its name to the synagogue. Now abandoned, it was once a fine, elegant building, and a favourite East Side meeting place. The facade is light coloured with tall stained glass windows in the central section and in the two projecting side sections. The stained glass at the top of the arches in the central windows contains eight-pointed rose designs, while the side windows bear Star of David motifs. Slender columns with Corinthian capitals separate the windows and the entranceways above the main stairways.

Return to the intersection of Canal and Eldridge Sts.

Walk three blocks W. on Canal St to the intersection of the Bowery.

The Manhattan Bridge Approach, Arch, and Colonnade, a Designated Landmark, were designed in 1912 by Carrère & Hastings. Gustav Lindenthal (1850–1935) engineered the bridge.

HISTORY: When the Brooklyn Bridge opened in 1883, it aroused enthusiasm both as a feat of engineering and as an object of beauty; the Williamsburg Bridge which followed it in 1903 was considered ugly. Consequently feelings ran high over the design for a third East River crossing, the Manhattan Bridge.

The two disputing parties were the 'engineers', whose interests were primarily technological, and the 'architects', whose goals were essentially aesthetic, who had too often been commissioned to apply superficial decoration to structurally graceless buildings. Because of these opposing interests and the political factions expressing them, plans for the bridge went through numerous modifications as architects and bridge Commissioners came and went.

An early plan was scrapped in about 1901 and the bridge redesigned by Henry Hornbostel, an architect whose belief in 'artistic' engineering resulted in a proposal which included the use of eye-bars instead of the usual cables to support the roadway. City officials, however, preferred the older suspension cable system, and Carrère & Hastings (also designers of the New York Public Library and Frick Museum) were hired to replace Hornbostel. The bridge, with its 1470-ft span, opened in 1909.

Meanwhile the World's Columbian Exposition in Chicago (1893) had awakened public interest in neo-classic architecture and had given birth to the City Beautiful movement, whose ideal metropolis was studded with great civic centers set in landscaped parks, linked by broad avenues, whose vistas were enhanced by sculpture, fountains, and other visual delights. From these enthusiasms sprang the plans for improving the approaches to the bridge, both on the Manhattan and Brooklyn sides. Carrère and Hastings, who had studied at the École des Beaux-Arts in Paris, the cradle of the neo-classical movement, were well-qualified for such an undertaking.

DESCRIPTION: The Manhattan approach originally featured an elliptical landscaped plaza which surrounded the actual roadway. Eight rail lines carried both subways and surface railroads while the paved roadways accommodated both vehicular and foot traffic. Nowadays the subways are carried on the lower deck of the bridge, and the landscaping has gone the way of too many city trees, replaced by a small parking area and considerable debris.

The approach ends in a monumental arch and colonnade, the arch modelled after the 17C Porte St. Denis in Paris, the colonnade after Bernini's colonnade at St. Peter's Square in Rome. The frieze over the arch opening by Charles Cary Rumsey (1879–1922) is said to have been inspired by the Panathenaic procession on the Parthenon frieze, suitably altered for American mythology. It depicts a group of four Indians on horseback hunting buffalo. The choice of such primitive subject matter may seem peculiar on a classical arch signalling the approach of a modern steel suspension bridge linking two boroughs of a vast urban center, but such frontier themes were popular when the arch was designed and Rumsey was already known for his portrayal of Indians and animals.

Flanking the arch opening are two large granite sculptural groups by Carl Augustus Heber: the *Spirit of Commerce* on the N. side and the *Spirit of Industries* on the S. Above these groups are decorations sculpted in low relief representing trophies and ships' prows. Above the arch opening (36 × 40 ft) is a cornice and a low attic story decorated with lions' heads. The interior of the arch is barrel-vaulted and coffered, and the opening is framed by a band of heraldic decoration.

The arch is set in the middle of a colonnade which reaches half the length of the plaza and consists of Tuscan columns (31 ft high) set on pedestals facing the plaza. Above the colonnade are cornices with balustrades which connect the columns to one another and to the arch.

Two monumental granite sculptural groups by Daniel Chester French originally enhanced the approach on the Brooklyn side; they are now displayed outside the Brooklyn Museum.

Preservation: In the 1960s a proposed expressway which was to cut through

Lower Manhattan threatened the existence of this fine bridge approach. Robert Moses, the Parks Commissioner and head of the Triborough Bridge and Tunnel Authority whose consuming interest in ever larger and wider highways led to some of New York's finer arteries and more blighted neighbourhoods, asked the city Art Commission for permission to demolish the bridge approaches claiming that the removal of the sculpture was necessary for bridge connections to the proposed roadway. Since it appeared that the road was inevitable and that the bridge approaches were doomed, the Commission sadly gave permission, under the condition that some of the sculpture be removed to other sites where the public might still enjoy it. The Brooklyn Museum then volunteered to take the groups by D.C. French and the Buffalo Hunt frieze. Unlike many urban preservation stories, this one had a happy outcome, since the roadway project was defeated in 1969 and the removal of the approaches became unnecessary. Traffic problems demanded reconstruction of the Brooklyn approach, and in 1963 the sculptures by French were removed to the Brooklyn Museum, cleaned, and set on new pedestals.

The jewellery stores on the Bowery and on Canal St in the blocks near the bridge approach remain from a time when diamond merchants carried on an active but informal sidewalk trade, often carrying their stock, perhaps a single diamond, in a vest pocket.

Walk back E. one block on Canal St to the intersection of Chrystie St; turn left and go one block N. to Hester St.

SARA DELANO ROOSEVELT PARK, named after the mother of Franklin D. Roosevelt, was created in 1934 by widening Chrystie and Forsyth Sts, tearing down the seven blocks of tenements between them, and installing benches and playground equipment. At the time the park was named, Mrs Roosevelt sent several telegrams to the Board of Aldermen requesting that the park be named after former Park Commissioner Charles Stover, who had devoted 40 years of his life to improving conditions on the Lower East Side, but the Board bowed to the wishes of the district alderman who favoured Mrs Roosevelt.

The park is surely an improvement over the tenements which once stood here, but like many others in the city suffers from an excess of pavement and a dearth of greenery.

Walk E. on Hester St. During the late 19C, HESTER STREET became synonymous with the Lower East Side. It was the home of the sweat shop, the tenement house, and the area's busiest street market, crowded with housewives, pedlars, and pushcarts offering all kinds of merchandise, bread, vegetables, dry goods, and fish sometimes the worse for the warm weather and the passage of time. Writers of the period found it the quintessential street of the ghetto, ringing with the shouts of vendors, the haggling and chattering of women, the cries of children who darted through the crowds playing games and making swift raids on the pushcarts. A sympathetic reporter from the 'Times' in 1898 found the street scene touching and attractive, the people intensely human, pious, and homeloving, worthy subjects of the student of human nature. Another reporter for the same journal with sterner standards of cleanliness and perhaps more interest in hygiene than humanity, described it as the filthiest place on the western continent and called its inhabitants slatternly, lawless (they had failed to empty their garbage cans at a specified hour) and indecent.

ORCHARD ST, which intersects Hester St three blocks E of the park, is now the main shopping street of the district, especially interesting to visit on Sundays when the streets are jammed with bargain hunters. Like Hester St, Orchard St was once a center of the pushcart market, which stretched a few blocks N. and S. from

Delancey St. The pushcarts may have been picturesque and productive of an occasional bargain, but they were unsanitary and the city outlawed them in the late 1930s. For the immigrants they represented one of the few ways a man without skills could eke out a living (in 1898 the daily rental of such a cart was 10¢), and so peddling from the carts became a chief occupation of the poor.

Walk N. (left) on Orchard St to Grand St; turn left and continue five blocks to the Bowery.

The Bowery, a name now redolent with associations of loneliness and poverty, alcoholism and tawdry vice, is one of Manhattan's oldest streets. It began as an Indian trail and got its name from the Dutch colonial period when it led to Peter Stuyvesant's farm or *bouwerie* (see p174). During the 18C, it formed part of the Boston Post Road and so figured in the Revolutionary War as an evacuation route for the retreating American troops. In the early 19C, it was still suburban, and the nearby side streets became the center of the abatoir district. There were slaughterhouses on Chrystie, Elizabeth, and Forsyth Sts as well as factories for the production of lard, soap fats, and candles.

In the mid 19C, the Bowery glittered with the lights of theatres; it saw the first blackface minstrel show in the city as well as the first stage version of 'Uncle Tom's Cabin', and toward the end of the century it hosted several Yiddish theatres. After about 1870, as the slums encroached on both sides, it began its famous and apparently irreversible plunge into the depths of vice and poverty. Its popular night life gave way to cheap saloons, either beer halls or distilleries which made their own raw whiskey and then sold it not infrequently adulterated with knockout drops. The Bowery had its rancid eateries and cheap lodgings. There were 25¢ establishments, advertising themselves as hotels, which offered private rooms to its clientele. For 15¢ a visitor could sleep in a dormitory bed with indifferently clean linen and a clothing locker. In the 10¢ lodgings the locker became unnecessary, as the patrons had nothing worth locking up, according to Jacob Riis, who knew the proprietor of three of these holes, who made enough from them to live swankly in Murray Hill. For 7¢ the lodger could rest his bones on a canvas strip stretched like a hammock between timber posts; and for 5¢ (in 1885) the lodger flopped on the floor, his space chalked out for him by the proprietor.

The Bowery has not yet recovered from this period in its history and still is one of the city's Skid Rows. Things are not as bad, perhaps, as they were during the Depression when its flophouses, doorways, and all night restaurants offered the army of the city's unemployed a place to spend the night, or wait until times got better. The Bowery Mission and the Salvation Army Hotel near Rivington St made sincere but futile efforts to diminish the sea of human misery by offering inexpensive food and lodging as well as spiritual nourishment for the downtrodden. At the present time, the area is still seedy and depressing, but not a dangerous place to visit. The bums still huddle in doorways or wander aimlessly down the sidewalks, occasionally begging or confronting the visitor with odd conversational remarks.

THE BOWERY SAVINGS BANK (130 Bowery at the corner of Grand St), built in 1894 by McKim, Mead & White, is now a Designated Landmark. With its imposing Roman Corinthian portico and handsome pediment sculpted with lions and seated classic figures, it embodies the spirit of the classic revival sweeping the country after the World's Columbian Exposition the previous year (see p144). A guidebook of 1893 condescendingly points out that while the bank is an 'afiduciary institution of the highest order', and its incorporators bear some of New York's finest names, it has traditionally taken care of the 'savings of the poorer classes and has earned for them all that their small accumulations could safely return.' The magnificent interior seems to express the affluence of the incorporators rather than the slender means of the depositors. The main banking room with its coffered ceiling, ornate metal and glass skylight, massive columns painted to resemble marble, and classically enframed windows must have dazzled those humble depositors.

The blocks N. of Grand St on the Bowery feature stores offering extravagant, even garish displays of electric lighting fixtures, a hangover from the time when the gas light trade was prominent in the neighbourhood. A few blocks to the N., the stores specialise in new and used restaurant supply equipment.

Walk N. on the Bowery to Delancey St, turn right. DELANCEY ST, now a rather shabby thoroughfare leading to the Williamsburg Bridge, is named after the De Lancey family, early settlers of French Huguenot origin. Etienne or Stephen De Lancey, the original owner of what is now the Fraunces Tavern, had a farm in this vicinity on the W. side of Division St (a street that got its name for marking the boundary between the De Lancey and Rutgers farms in the 18C). James De Lancey (1703–60), son of Etienne, who became chief justice of the New York supreme court and lieutenant governor of the colony, had a home at the corner of the present Chrystie and Delancey Sts.

When the street was widened to accommodate traffic to the bridge, it was renamed Schiff Parkway in honour of Jacob Schiff, financier and philanthropist, who contributed generously to the Henry Street Settlement and the Educational Alliance. The name never took root, however, and so the dubious honour reverted to the De Lancey family.

The blocks E. of the Bowery, originally called First, Second, Third St and so on, were renamed following the War of 1812 to honour several now very obscure heroes wounded or killed in the fighting. Lt-Col John Chrystie was killed on the Niagara frontier; Lt Forsyth died in Canada, as did Lt Eldridge, who seems to have been scalped; Lt William Allen was wounded during a naval battle between the 'Argus' and the 'Pelican'; and Lt Ludlow was slain aboard the 'Chesapeake', but not until he had received the famous dying command of Capt. William Lawrence: 'Don't give up the ship.'

The *Dominican Union Square Seventh Day Adventist Church* on the S.E. corner of Forsyth and Delancey Sts, one block E. of Chrystie St, was once one of the largest and most active congregations in the area. The Forsyth Street *shul* (synagogue), as it was known, was relatively wealthy; its activities included a burial society, as well as a nightly Talmud study group and a Ladies' Benevolent Society. The row of shops built into the Delancey St side of the building were intended to provide financial security for the synagogue.

Continue E. on Delancey St to Allen St. During the closing years of the 19C, Allen St, darkened and begrimed by the Second Avenue El, became a haven for prostitution (although there were brothels also on Houston, Delancey, Rivington, Forsyth, and Chrystie Sts). A local minister complained that the women openly solicited from the stoops of tenements adjoining his church, while writer Michael Gold in his classic novel of an East Side childhood, 'Jews without Money', recalls the time when prostitutes sat out on the sidewalks in chairs sunning themselves, their legs sprawled indolently in the way of anyone who wanted to pass by. After the street was widened in 1930 and the El torn down in 1942, the S. part near the Manhattan Bridge became a center for antiques, especially copper and brass ware. There was also a large center for bed linen run by the Romanian immigrants who settled chiefly around Allen St; a few of these shops still survive.

Turn N. (left) on Allen St. The vacant building at 133 Allen St with its white rather antiseptic-looking facade and sea horse motifs, was the last surviving *Municipal Bath House* built just after the turn of the century. It was one of a number provided by the city for people who didn't have bathing facilities, or perhaps even running water, at home. In 1893 there were more than 16 such facilities used by an estimated 4 million people annually.

Continue N. to Rivington St. RIVINGTON ST is named after James Rivington (1724–1803), who emigrated to Philadelphia from England in 1760. Eventually he moved to New York, where he continued in the bookselling business and became publisher of 'Rivington's New York Gazetteer', a Tory newspaper which attacked the American revolutionary movement. Rivington's sentiments, as well as his rather abrasive personality, earned him the hostility of a group of American patriots who mobbed his shop, destroyed his presses, and stole his fonts of type, an act of vandalism made more serious by the fact that no American foundries produced type of the same high quality as Rivington's imported English type. Undaunted he returned to England and got new equipment, came back to New York, and started another loyalist newspaper. In 1781, he seems to have had a change of heart, for he became a spy for General Washington and is credited with deciphering a British military code.

Diversion. A half block W. of the intersection of Rivington and Allen Sts stands the former *Erste Warshawer Congregation* (the First Warsaw Congregation), built by a Polish group in 1903 in an eclectic style that has been described as vaguely Byzantine. The great circular window with its Star of David motif is surrounded by a heavy frame with the name of the congregation embossed in Hebrew letters. Like other abandoned synagogues, this one has suffered from repeated acts of vandalism, and consequently much of the ornamentation of the lower part of the facade is now gone.

Return to the intersection of Allen and Rivington Sts.

Turn right on Rivington St. *The First Romanian-American Congregation, Shaarey Shamoyim* (Gates of Heaven) at 89 Rivington St bought this building in about 1890, although the congregation itself may have been organised as early as 1860. Like other congregations, this one did not construct its own synagogue, but remodelled a Christian church, since gentile groups fled as the Jewish immigrants poured into the Lower East Side. The building formerly belonged to the Allen Street Methodist Church, whose members apparently made a serious error in planning when they erected this large church, for they sold it and moved out only two years after it was finished. It is one of the few Romanesque Revival buildings in the area, with a simple brick facade, round arch windows, and a generally fortress-like appearance. The sanctuary holds 1600 seats, far too many for the present congregation, which although no longer Romanian is still active. In the days when cantors were lionised as opera stars are today, Shaarey Shamoyim was important as a place for a cantor to make his reputation, and two of America's famous operatic singers appeared here before they went on to secular work, Jan Peerce (then Jacob Pincus Perelmuth) and Richard Tucker (then Reuben Ticker).

Walk E. to Essex St.

Diversion: Continue E. on Rivington St and turn N. (left) on Norfolk St. Walk a block and a half.

Congregation Anshe Slonim (People of Slonim) at 172 Norfolk St has the honour of being the oldest surviving synagogue building in the city, though survival can barely be used to describe its present condition. Built in 1850 by Alexander Saeltzer (who also designed the Astor Library, now the New York Shakespeare Festival Public Theater), it belongs to the Gothic Revival tradition and once was resplendent with pointed arch windows, quatrefoil designs, pyramidal towers, and other Gothic trappings, most of which have been removed. Like other downtown synagogues, its ownership reflects the waves of Jewish immigration: it was first owned by a German congregation called Anshe Chesed (People of Kindness), followed by a Hungarian immigrant group, and eventually after several more changes of name and ownership it became Anshe Slonim, named after a fondly remembered native village in Poland.

The synagogue housed an active congregation until 1975 when the usual sad social facts forced its closure: shrinking membership, neighbourhood harassment, loss of economic base, vandalism. The exterior, originally of brick with stucco over it to provide a smooth surface, now bears layers of peeling pink paint. The windows, bereft of their stained glass, gape blindly at the street. Despite the barricaded doors, intruders have entered, smashed the Ark which formerly contained the Torah scrolls, ripped out the electrical and plumbing fixtures, and shredded the prayer books. Innumerable small depredations have reduced the building to a shambles, its interior a heap of rubble. At the present time the building has been declared unsafe and the courts have ordered it demolished unless a new, adaptive use can be found for it.

Return to Stanton St; go two blocks E. to Clinton St; turn left. *Chasam Sopher Synagogue* (Seal of the Scribe) at 8 Clinton St is the second oldest surviving synagogue in the city, built in 1853 for a German-Jewish congregation which moved uptown in 1886. A group from Poland purchased the property and renamed it Chasam Sopher to honour Moshe Sofer (or Schreiber, in the Germanicised form of the name), a religious leader, scholar, and rabbi, who was born in Frankfurt in 1762. Sofer devoted the later part of his life to fighting Reform Judaism, and founded numerous Hebrew charitable institutions and schools. This red brick building is constructed in the round-arch Romanesque Revival style, although its appearance has been altered by the loss of the original parapets topping off the flanking towers.

A block E. and two blocks S. at 87 Attorney St is another formerly fine synagogue, *Beth Haknesseth Mogen Avraham* (Synagogue of the Shield of Abraham). The building, dating from 1845, started out as a Methodist Church, but was soon sold to a black congregation who renamed it the Emmanuel African Methodist Episcopal Church and eventually sold it to a group from Poland called the Erste Galitsianer Chevra (First Galician Congregation). The Galician Jews later changed their name to Mogen Avraham. Although the building was adapted to Jewish worship, it was never really modernised, and retained its gas fired radiators and outdoor plumbing. The small brick building to the N. originally served as the parsonage for the Emmanuel African M.E. Church.

Return to Rivington St and go W. toward Essex St. *Streit's Matzoth Company* (150 Rivington St) is the sole remaining bakery in Manhattan producing matzoth, an unleavened bread used especially during Passover.

Schapiro's Wine Company (126 Rivington St) offers free wine tours on Sundays, hourly from 10 to 6 or as the crowd gathers. The company, now the only remaining kosher wine firm in Manhattan, was founded by the present owner's grandfather, who performed his own charitable work, giving new immigrants a free meal, a bottle of honey wine, and 50¢. The kosher wine is made from grapes grown in upstate New York and pressed there under the supervision of rabbis sent to see that the requirements of Jewish law are observed. The juice is then shipped to the city in tank trucks where it is handled only by staff members who are Jewish Sabbath observers.

Continue W. to Essex St.

On the N.W. corner of Essex and Rivington Sts (131 Essex St) is the *Economy Candy Shop*, whose proprietors offer their wares both on the street and inside the store. In the immigrant world candy stores such as this one became informal social centers or gathering places for people who had no privacy at home and nowhere else to go. Although the Lower East Side had its political clubs and educational centers where tenement dwellers could improve their minds or assert their beliefs, candy shops and delicatessens became important precisely because of their informality and closeness to the vitality of street life.

Bernstein-on-Essex a few doors to the N. (135 Essex St) is a kosher restaurant serving meat dishes, sandwiches, and, surprisingly, the city's only kosher Chinese food. The proprietors have adapted various dishes from the Chinese cuisine so that they might be enjoyed by Jews following the restrictions of traditional dietary laws.

Walk S. on Essex St. The building on the N.W. corner of Broome and Essex Sts (75 Essex St) once housed *the Eastern Dispensary*, one of several privately endowed clinics serving the poor with free or low cost medical care. The clinic was founded in 1832, and became the Good Samaritan Dispensary in 1891, at which time it treated about 160,000 patients annually.

Seward Park High School, a block to the S., occupies the site of the old ESSEX MARKET COURT HOUSE and the LUDLOW STREET JAIL. The jail held prisoners whose offences came under the jurisdiction of the Sheriff of the County of New York as well as violators of federal laws, for whom the federal government paid a stipulated daily allowance. Sheriff's prisoners with enough money could buy fancier accommodations in the jail, a system which naturally led to abuse. William M. Tweed (see p117), availed himself of these privileges while he was serving his sentence for defrauding the city; his cell had two rooms, flower pots on the window sills, even a piano to ease the tedium of prison life. Tweed died in the Ludlow Street jail in 1878.

Turn left on Broome St and walk a block to Norfolk St. Turn right. BETH HAMEDRASH HAGODOL SYNAGOGUE (Great House of Study) at 60 Norfolk St is one of the two synagogues on the Lower East Side to be Designated Landmarks. Built as the Norfolk Street Baptist Church in about 1852, this Gothic Revival building was sold in 1885 to the present owners, a Russian Orthodox congregation, and for a while enjoyed a fine reputation as a center of scholarship. Unlike many other synagogues in the area, this one is still well preserved and maintained, rising proudly from the rubble of the rest of the block. The stained glass in the W. window, the bands of quatrefoils on the two towers, and the mouldings framing the pointed window arches are all that remain of the original exterior decoration, but the interior still has artifacts from the time when the building was a Christian church: carved pews, a former altar rail, a vaulted ceiling, and an elaborate gallery. Murals with Biblical scenes now adorn the walls, and a reader's desk replaces the former pulpit.

Walk S. to Grand St and turn left (E.). At 466 Grand St between Pitt and Willett Sts is the *Arts for Living Center of the Henry Street Settlement* (1975; Prentice & Chan, Ohlhausen), a red brick building which has won awards for architectural excellence. Along with the adjoining Harry De Jur Henry Street Settlement Playhouse, it is the focal point of the arts programmes of the settlement and has changing exhibitions of contemporary artists, usually reflecting the ethnic interests of the Lower East Side (gallery open Tues–Sat, 12–6 and before evening performances. Admission free. Tel: 598–0400).

Continue to Willett St and turn left. Just N. of the intersection of Willett and Grand Sts. is the BIALYSTOKER SYNAGOGUE (1826; DL), originally the Willett Street Methodist Church, a severe building with random fieldstone masonry, trimmed with brownstone and whitestone. The name 'Bialystoker' refers to the city from which the members emigrated, Bialystok, formerly in Poland, now in the U.S.S.R.

The word 'Bialystoker' has found another niche in the language of New York as the name of a kind of onion roll (now abbreviated to 'bialy') said to have been perfected by the bakers of Bialystok.

Willett St is named after Marinus Willett (1740–1830), an American patriot who served with distinction during the Revolutionary War, went on in politics to become sheriff of the city and eventually mayor. Return along Willett St to Grand St and continue E. At the N.W. corner of Grand and Kazan Sts are the AMALGAMATED DWELLINGS (1930; Springsteen & Goldhammer), built as co-operative apartments and sponsored by the Amalgamated Clothing Workers of America. Though commended architecturally for their 'complete elimination of meaningless ornament' the apartments were said to be too expensive for most clothing workers with an average rent of $12·33 per room per month. They are now joined by a larger project called the *Hillman Houses* (1951; Springsteen & Goldhammer) on Grand St between Willett and Lewis Sts, named in honour of Sidney Hillman (1887–1946), a Lithuanian immigrant, union organiser, and prominent labour leader. Kazan St is named after Abraham Kazan, instrumental in the construction of the housing project; formerly it was called Sheriff St after Marinus Willet who served as city sheriff before he became mayor.

At the intersection of East Broadway and Grand St (311–13 E. Broadway) is the EAST SIDE MIKVAH, or ritularium, the last remaining public ritual bath in the area. Although individual synagogues often have their own *mikvahs*, public ones became necessary in a neighbourhood where synagogues were often converted from churches or from store fronts, and there were formerly several of these public baths.

Among Orthodox Jews it is customary for brides to take a ritual bath before marriage, and for women to use the *mikvah* monthly. The *mikvah* is also used for immersion of new vessels and utensils purchased from non-Jews, and as part of the ceremony of converting proselytes.

Turn right into Henry St just beyond the intersection of Grand and Kazan Sts.

At 290 Henry Street is SAINT AUGUSTINE'S CHAPEL, built between 1827–28, now a Designated Landmark. Originally the All Saints' Free Church, it is now part of Trinity Parish. According to tradition, the fieldstones for its masonry were dug from Mount Pitt, a hill located near the present intersection of Grand and Pitt Sts.

During the Revolution, Mount Pitt was fortified and was one of a chain of fortifications, most of them primitive and inadequate, running across Manhattan from the East to the Hudson River.

Details of the facade recall several other churches in Lower Manhattan dating from the same period (see the Sea and Land Church, and the Church of the Transfiguration). The windows are enframed with brick and have pointed Gothic arches. Stone lintels top the doors; the cornices are of wood. The central section below the single tower projects from the facade and has a small pediment enframed by the larger gabled end of the building.

The interior details of the church mirror the simplicity of the exterior. Particularly fine are the wineglass pulpit with a three feather Prince of Wales crest on the sounding board, and the organ by Henry Erban, both dating from 1830. The galleries, which once were used for slaves, rest on fluted cast iron columns.

The **Henry Street Settlement Houses** (263, 265, and 267 Henry St) are also a Designated Landmark. Architecturally they attract attention as typical late Federal residences, built in what was once a semi-rural setting at the edge of town. Although the three houses are roughly contemporary, only the center one, dated 1827, has escaped alteration; fortunately it survives with much of its original detail intact: the wrought-iron stoop railing with open box newel posts, the areaway fence with acorn finials (sometimes said to symbolise hospitality, an attribute also attached to the pineapple which appears as a finial on the newel post of 263 Henry St), and the louvred shutters on the first story windows. Also original is the fine doorway, divided into eight panels and flanked by slender fluted columns with Ionic capitals. The sidelights and transom once held leaded glass. The cornice above the doorway and the lintels above the windows are later alterations.

But more important than the doorways and the windowsills is the history of the buildings as the home of one of the nation's pioneer social agencies. Lillian Wald (1867–1940), who founded the Henry Street Settlement, remains one of New York's great figures, a compassionate, gentle, yet shrewd and worldly woman who devoted herself tirelessly to the poor. Trained as a nurse, Lillian Wald was teaching home nursing to a group of Lower East Side mothers in 1893 when by chance she was taken to visit a patient sick at home. The vision of the wretched two room apartment shared by a family of seven and their two boarders (who helped with the rent) awoke in her an immediate sense of vocation. She moved to a fifth floor walkup at 27 Jefferson St and began her unending rounds, fighting ignorance, typhoid, measles, malnutrition, rats, and bigotry. She persuaded other nurses to join her. She battled with hospital administrations to get the poor admitted to hospitals and then went along with her patients to help them overcome their terror of such institutions. She raised money, largely through the assistance of Jacob Schiff, the philanthropist who gave two of the Henry St buildings to the settlement. By 1898, her agency had nine nurses on its staff; by 1906 it had 27. Coming from a bourgeois German-Jewish family, of Rochester, New York, she gradually grew to accept these strange East European immigrants as her own people and became an important liaison between the 'uptown' and 'downtown' Jews who often found themselves at odds with one another.

After Lillian Wald retired in 1933, her work was carried on by Helen Hall, whose career was as distinguished as the founder's. The present director, Bertram M. Beck, is only the third to head the organisation, which continues its work in the original settlement house tradition. Programme workers may live in the settlement residence to share the problems of the neighbourhood and establish community relationships, part of the original settlement house ideal. The programmes of the agency adapted to reflect changing social conditions include a credit union (originally founded in 1937 to offer the needy an alternative to street-based loan sharks), a day care center for small children, a companions' programme for the elderly, programmes in the arts, in parent-child relationships, a school for students severely handicapped by social and emotional problems, and a programme of supported employment for adolescents in legal difficulties.

The settlement is a non-profit organisation, whose annual operating budget of $5·3 million comes from private contributions, foundation grants, and contracts with public agencies. Its present staff includes 800 employees, of whom 200 are full time workers.

Turn right at the intersection of Henry and Montgomery Sts and walk one block to East Broadway.

At one time EAST BROADWAY was the center of Orthodox Judaism in New York, and traces of this past still linger. The two blocks between Jefferson and Montgomery Sts contain a row of storefront synagogues housing small congregations which often share space because they cannot afford their own quarters. Most of these congregations are composed of countrymen from the same European locale, who are unwilling to merge with other groups and lose their particular national or ethnic identity, and so struggle on at the edge of extinction. Some of the groups are Hasidic, members of an extreme and fundamentalist sect which originated in 18C Poland and holds conservative views on social matters and ultra-Orthodox views on religious questions. As part of their emphasis on unworldliness, Hasidic men do not dress according to contemporary conventions, but maintain their beards and side curls, their black clothing and dark, wide brimmed hats.

The *Young Israel Synagogue*, however (225 E. Broadway), belongs to a group founded in the early 20C in New York City, to counteract what its young Orthodox members considered the triple threat of Reform Judaism, rising crime among second-generation Jews, and godless socialism. Although the founders were deeply committed to Orthodoxy, they also considered themselves Americanised, and so shaved their beards, accepted mixed social dancing, dressed in modern style, and listened to sermons in English. Today they continue their social programmes, promoting Orthodox styles of living and worship.

The building formerly belonged to the Hebrew Immigrant Aid and Sheltering Society, an organisation founded in 1892 to assist immigrants as they arrived in New York, by providing such services as interpreters, lawyers, and temporary shelter (see p192).

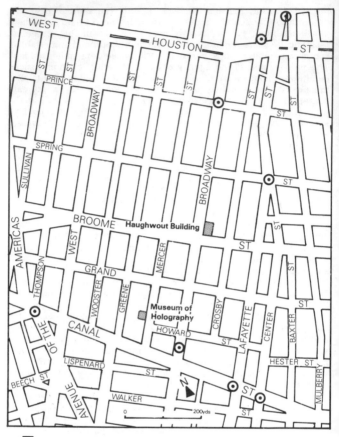

7 SoHo

SUBWAY: IRT Lexington Ave local (train 6) to Canal St. IND Eighth Ave local (AA, CC, E) to Canal St; walk 3 long blocks E. (counting on the S. side of the street) to Broadway. IND Sixth Ave (D, F) to W. 4th St; change to Eighth Ave local trains.

BUS: M6 (southbound via Sixth Ave) to Canal St and Broadway; M1 (southbound via Fifth Ave and Park Ave S.) to Canal St and Broadway.

CAR PARKING: Street parking on weekends only. Limited parking lots available, especially on Broadway.

WHEN TO VISIT: Saturday is the traditional day for browsing and visiting galleries, an activity that begins around noon and winds up at night in the bars, restaurants, and lofts. For a less crowded view, go Tues–Fri in the afternoon. Most galleries are closed in the mornings and on Sun–Mon; some are closed Tues.

For a fleeting moment in the late 1960s, SoHo—an acronym for SOuth of HOuston, with apologies to London's Soho—was an artist's

Eden, where rents were cheap, space was plentiful, and society was made up mostly of other artists, all searching for style, authenticity, identity, or whatever other goals separated them from the rest of the populace. Today SoHo is cleaner (though not much), slicker, more expensive, and, according to critics who should know, it is the center of contemporary art in the western world, successor to Greenwich Village in the 1920s and Paris between the wars.

Before its present heady revival SoHo endured its peaks and valleys. Its great farms were first subdivided and developed as a quiet residential suburb in the years after the Revolution, although the oldest remaining house dates only from c. 1806. By 1825 what is now SoHo was the most densely populated part of New York. By 1840 it was highly fashionable. By the 1850s retail stores of sterling reputation and expensive hotels lined Broadway while the side streets began sporting brothels, dance halls, and casinos, some of them elegant in their own way. As the carriage trade vanished uptown, industry came in to fill the vacuum. During the decades between 1860 and 1890, most of the cast-iron architecture so admired today was constructed, the buildings serving as factories or warehouses, often with shop fronts on the ground floor. Appealing as they may seem now with their Corinthian columns, Palladian windows, or French Second Empire dormers, many operated as sweatshops where the immigrants now arriving in droves from southern and eastern Europe endured twelve or more hours a day of exhausting labour in degrading surroundings for the sake of their offspring. SoHo and Little Italy still overlap and much of the present Italian population, especially visible in warm weather on the streets west of West Broadway, is descended from those overworked immigrants.

Although the sweatshops were legislated out of existence—in part by immigration quotas that staunched the flow of cheap, uneducated and hence acquiescent labour—SoHo remained industrial until recently. Gradually the cast-iron buildings became outmoded and inconvenient, and small industry—paper box companies, tool and die factories, wool remnant companies—began moving elsewhere. In 1959 the City Club of N.Y. published an influential report labelling the area, then known as Hell's Hundred Acres or as The Valley (a lowland between the architectural highs of the financial district and midtown), a dismal industrial slum with no architecture of note.

In the early 1960s artists attracted by those same empty commercial buildings began moving in, illegally converting them to apartments, surreptitiously installing such amenities as plumbing, household wiring, and adequate heating. To protect themselves from greedy landlords, artists' cooperatives began buying entire buildings and tenants' associations began lobbying for legalisation of the status quo.

By 1970 SoHo had become a boom town for real estate dealers, for art dealers (now headed downtown from the reaches of the East Side), and for artists themselves who, if not becoming rich were at least forming a coherent artistic community with its own aesthetics and codes of living. Film, video, and 'performance'—the avant-garde media of the 1960s—became staple commodities of SoHo artistic life. Experimental dance and drama flourished. Cooperative galleries opened.

Today SoHo is still exciting, though it has become fashionable and 'established'. Art and industry stand side by side, and a sense of mystery or seclusion emanates from behind the windowless metal doors and industrial fronts of the old buildings. Some of the lofts inside provide working space for SoHo's artists, most of them young and experimental; other buildings serve firms dealing in pinking shears, wool remnants, and electronic components. Commerce has established itself also in the form of the many small, cleverly arrayed shops offering clothing, foodstuffs, Tibetan jewellery—all the appointments necessary for a tasteful yet casual existence. Naturally the artists complain; the rents are too steep again. Newcomers (and hard-pressed earlier arrivals) head for cheaper territory in Hoboken and Brooklyn. Limousines discharge chic, stylish passengers at SoHo restaurants. But even though SoHo has changed, it has not entirely succumbed to the charms of the bourgeoisie; one can still observe the energy, the ambition, the youthful idealism involved in this community dominated at many levels by art.

SoHo's *cast-iron architecture, capable of arousing passionate emotions in the hearts of admirers, is only now emerging from a century of obscurity. Though these prefabricated buildings were a major architectural innovation and in their freshly painted prime a source of personal and civic pride, they have suffered the ravages of neglect—disfigured by ugly ground-floor modernisations, dimmed by layers of dull paint, or devastated by urban renewal. Since SoHo has been declared an Historic District (1973), we can be assured that the facades will not be wantonly destroyed; in many cases they are being tastefully restored. The Friends of Cast Iron Architecture, established in 1969, was instrumental in securing the landmark designation and still continues its educational function.

Early cast-iron architecture was designed to imitate stone, adorned with the familiar quoins, columns, and consoles of the classical tradition and painted tan, buff, or cream to resemble marble or limestone. Sometimes cast-iron plates were even grooved to resemble blocks of stone mortared together. Eventually iron founders, many of whom had previously dealt in stoves, safes, and lawn furniture, began offering catalogues of ornaments from which the client or architect could select whatever he liked, combining these elements in simple or lavish compositions. While the earliest cast-iron buildings hark back to Italy (Sansovino's Library in Venice and the Roman Colosseum were much admired), later examples were based on French Renaissance, Second Empire, or neo-Grec styles. In one sense cast-iron architecture was standardised: the ornaments were machine made, mass-produced, and as interchangeable as parts of a Winchester rifle. On the other hand, their deployment allowed the architect great scope and originality, as the general exuberance of these SoHo buildings testifies.

The route begins at Canal St and Broadway. CANAL ST owes both its name and its exceptional width to a canal proposed by the city fathers in 1805 to serve as a storm drain, a conduit siphoning off the waters of the Collect Pond near present Foley Square, and a household sewer. By the 1820s both the street and the canal had been paved over, a mixed blessing: while the covered sewer alleviated the mosquito problem, the stench it created depressed both property values and morale until adequate air traps were installed.

Walk a block E. along Canal St to Lafayette St. On the S.W. corner

of the intersection is an early cast-iron building (No. 254–60 Canal
St) dating from 1857. Its Italianate half-round window arches and the
Medusa head keystones over the 4th floor windows suggest that the
building may have been designed by James Bogardus (1800–74),
inventor of the cast-iron building, an impression strengthened by the
Venetian style of the structure, since it is known that Bogardus was
inspired by Venetian architecture in his development of the cast-iron
front.

Bogardus, who also invented a dry gas meter, a postage engraving machine,
and a mechanical pencil, is known to architectural students for developing and
mass-producing parts for prefabricated cast-iron buildings. Although he served
as contractor for erecting many of these innovative buildings, he does not seem
to have operated a large foundry of his own. The only existing New York
building which can be absolutely attributed to him is No. 85 Leonard St.

Return to Broadway. The **SoHo Historic District,** designated in 1973,
is bounded on the S. by Canal St, on the W. by West Broadway, on
the N. by Houston St, and on the E. by Crosby St. It encompasses 26
blocks with the largest concentration of cast-iron architecture in
America.

Walk W. on Canal St, which over the years has become a bazaar
for industrial wares: nuts, bolts, spare machine parts, plexiglass and
lucite, sheet metal, tools, and surplus office furniture. Recently it has
become also a source for more domesticated items: blue jeans and
military surplus clothing, household appliances of unfamiliar prov-
enance, mops and brooms, and novelties like rubber monsters and
flamingo ashtrays. An indoor flea market, the *SoHo Canal Flea
Market* (Wed–Mon, 11–6) is located at No. 369 Canal St, between
Wooster St and West Broadway.

On the N.E. corner of Canal and Mercer Sts at No. 307–311 Canal
St stands the former *Marble House* (1856–65; Griffith Thomas),
onetime home of the Arnold Constable department store, just one of
the elegant retail establishments this neighbourhood boasted during
the 1850s and 1860s. Lord & Taylor's, ultimately the victor in its
perennial rivalry with Arnold Constable's since it still survives, was
located a block N. at Broadway and Grand St, on the site of the
present parking lot

Turn right into Mercer St, where it becomes apparent that only the
Canal St facade of Marble House was faced with marble, though the
brickwork of the side and rear of the building is nonetheless
handsome. *Mercer St*, still paved with its 19C Belgian blocks, is
named after Hugh Mercer, a surgeon and brigadier general in the
Revolutionary War. At No. 11 Mercer St is the MUSEUM OF
HOLOGRAPHY (Wed–Sun, noon–6, Thurs eves until 9; tel: 925–
0526. Adults $2; children under 12 and senior citizens, $1).

Founded in 1976, this small museum features exhibitions of state-of-the-art
holograms (3-dimensional images produced by laser photography) and ex-
planatory displays of historic prototypes. Reference library and guided tours by
appointment.

The building itself (1870; F.E. Graef) was built as a warehouse for the
India Rubber Company. It has a fine vault cover, also known as an
illuminated sidewalk or light platform, with glass discs embedded in
the iron stoop to permit sunlight to illuminate the storage vault
below, a system invented in 1845 by one Thaddeus Hyatt.

At No 19 Mercer St is the *SoHo Repertory Theater* (weekends only;

tel: 925–2588) founded in 1975, one of the many dramatic groups that makes SoHo a focal point of theatrical activity.

In the next block across Grand St is a handsome cast-iron building at *No. 47 Mercer St* (1872; Joseph M. Dunn), now used by the Decter Wool Stock Company. With its unembellished cornices at each floor and smooth, round columns, it is appealing in its simplicity, although it is simpler now than when it was built, for the quoin blocks are missing from the left edge of the building and the decorations have been stripped from the columns.

Walk one block W. to Greene St, named after Revolutionary War general Nathanael Greene. A *flea market* (Sat–Sun, 11.30–4) is held during warm weather in the parking lot at the N.W. corner of Canal and Greene Sts. Turn right into Greene St.

The vista up this street, little changed since the 19C, delights cast-iron buffs as it reveals the city's longest continuous row of cast-iron architecture, Nos 8–34 Greene St, as well as several other superlative examples of the form. The row may be catalogued as follows: No. 8 (1883) and Nos 10–14 (1896) by John B. Snook; Nos 16–18 (1880) and Nos 20–26 (1880) by Samuel A. Warner; Nos 28–30 (1872) and No. 32 (1873) by J.F. Duckworth; No. 34 (1873) by Charles Wright. As the proximity of dates suggests, SoHo became industrial rapidly in the 1870s and 1880s. Many of these buildings were erected with retail space on the ground floor and lofts for warehouses or workshops (some of them sweatshops) above.

During the 1850s when Broadway sparkled with theatres, hotels, and casinos, Greene and Mercer Sts were notorious for their brothels. While the houses on the S. end of the streets near Canal St catered to sailors from the ships docked in the Hudson, the houses further N. appealed to a wealthier clientele. An 1859 'Directory to the Seraglios in New York' written by an anonymous Free Loveyer recommends a Miss Clara Gordon at No. 119 Mercer St, 'beautiful, entertaining and supremely seductive', who is patronised by Southern merchants and planters, and a Mrs Bailey of No. 76 Greene St, whose comfortable and quiet 'resort' is within a few moments' walk of Broadway and the principal hotels.

The *pièce de resistance* of the block, the 'Queen of Greene St', is No. 28–30 (1872; J.F. Duckworth), a grandly ornate Second Empire building crowned with a stupendous mansard roof and painted a startling blue. The tall broad windows flanked by half-round columns, the keystoned segmental arches, the central two-window bay rising the full height of the building to a broken pediment, and the elaborate dormers with balustrades, modillions, pediments, and finials offer a wealth of architectural ornament.

One of the attractions of cast-iron as a building material was the ease of achieving details of any architectural style. As long as patterns could be carved and moulds made, elaborate ornaments could be created and cheaply reproduced, allowing businessmen who could not afford the extravagance of stonecutting the prestige of fluted Corinthian columns (then painted to resemble stone).

The plants in the upper story windows reveal to the casual observer as they once did to the snooping city inspector that the loft space has been converted to living quarters.

Although a few independent spirits migrated to SoHo as early as the 1940s, many artists attracted by cheap rents and large open spaces began drifting here in the 1960s, filling the vacuum left as light industry began seeking better or cheaper facilities elsewhere. These pioneers settled illegally in industrial buildings whose wiring, plumbing, and fireproofing fell short of the city's residential code and then refurbished them to make them livable. But because such lofts were still illegal, the artists found themselves at the mercy of their landlords and were often evicted or subjected to exorbitant rents once they had restored the loft space. Hence a tenants association was formed to legalise these dwellings, and in 1970 the city declared that manufacturing buildings could be leased to qualified artists—painters, dancers, sculptors, and others whose work demanded space and light. During the first year of the programme a panel certified 3000 people as bona fide artists, making SoHo an official artists' society complete with requisite membership card.

Continue N. to Grand St and turn right (E.) to look at *Nos 91 and 93 Grand St* (1869; John B. Snook), two iron-fronted buildings resolutely imitating stone. The iron plates, cast in large sections and bolted through the brick front wall of the house are grooved to look like uniform blocks of stone mortared together. The houses, which originally cost $6000 apiece, were built in $4^{1}/_{2}$ months from a design offered in the catalogue of ironworker J.L. Jackson & Bros, whose foundry label is attached to the W. pier of No. 91. The columns at No. 89 Grand St (1885) are identical to those at Nos 31 and 72 Grand St, no doubt cast from the same mould. Return to Greene St and continue N.

The buildings at *Nos 44 and 46–50 Greene St* are masonry structures with cast-iron ornaments. The ground floor pilasters at No. 46–50 (1860) are decorated with scrollwork and ornate medallions bolted onto the long horizontal panels of the pilasters. Some of the acanthus leaves, cast separately and bolted to the capitals, have fallen off, demonstrating how the ironwork was installed.

Another advantage of cast-iron as an architectural material in a period of rapid industrial expansion was speed and convenience of construction. The pieces of a facade could be separately cast, the smaller pieces bolted together at the factory, the whole facade laid out with pieces numbered and tested for fit, and then shipped to the construction site where the front was assembled and permanently bolted into place.

Further up Greene St at the S.W. corner of Broome St (No. 469–475 Broome St) is the GUNTHER BUILDING (1871–72; Griffith Thomas), built as a warehouse for furrier William H. Gunther. The elegant corner turning, with its curved panes of glass, is a particularly notable feature of this handsome, restrained, cast-iron building. The structure houses a cooperative art gallery with studio space for its member artists.

During the 1950s a group of such cooperative galleries sprang up around 10th St, founded by artists who rejected the values of the uptown art establishment. Although the 10th St galleries faded in the 1960s, a second generation emerged in SoHo in the 1970s, undertaken by artists who have not found or do not wish to find, acceptance in private galleries. Co-op galleries, run by their members with or without a professional manager and financed by annual dues, may be politically or artistically exclusive, limiting membership to women, black artists, or such groups as realist painters, or they may accept a wide range of work. In general they are more informal and less polished than private galleries.

Continue N. on Greene St across Broome St. The building at *No. 66 Greene St* (1873; John B. Snook) was built as a store for the Lorillard tobacco company. The cocoa-coloured building at NO. 72–76 GREENE ST (1872; J.F. Duckworth), a redoubtable old pile known as 'the King of Greene St', is actually two structures designed as one, unified by a central pedimented portico which rises to a pedimented cornice. The monogram cast on the central pilaster between the doorways belongs to the Gardner Colby Company, who used the building as a warehouse. Most of the other buildings on the block, now used by firms dealing in wool clippings, wool rags, fabric remnants and rug clippings, were designed by Henry Fernbach and Jonathan B. Snook in the early 1870s.

Continue N. to Spring St, named after a spring tapped by Aaron Burr's Manhattan Water Company, whose ostensible purpose was to supply drinking water to the city but which quickly evolved into a banking company instead (see p100). Local legend asserts that a well at Broadway and Spring St became the grave of one Juliana (or Gulielma) Elmore Sands, whose body minus shoes, hat, and shawl was found floating there on 2 Jan 1800. Her fiance was acquitted of the crime but the victim apparently remained dissatisfied, for her ghost has been seen occasionally in the area; as recently as 1974 a resident of 535 Broadway at Spring St reported that a grey haired apparition wearing mossy garments emerged from his waterbed. But 1974 seems to have been a boom time for the spring anyhow, since that same year it burst its underground channel and flooded a basement on West Broadway.

Turn right (E.) on Spring St. The three cast-iron buildings on the N. side date from the late 1870s: No. 119 (1878; Robert Mook); Nos 115–17 and 113 (1878; Henry Fernbach).

Continue to the N.W. corner of Spring and Mercer Sts where the oldest house in SoHo stands (No. 107 Spring St), a brick Federal dwelling (now unfortunately slathered over with stucco) built c. 1806. Used as a physician's office, it bears the sign 'Dr. 107'. Return to Green St.

The handsomely renovated building at the S.E. corner of Spring and Greene Sts (No. 124 Spring St) was built in 1883 as a glass factory.

Turn right and continue N. on Greene St. On the left (W.) side are three cast-iron buildings (Nos 93–95, 97, and 99), all designed in the neo-Grec style by Henry Fernbach in 1881.

The term 'neo-Grec' refers not to an imitation of ancient classical models but to a style of incised ornament favoured during the 1870s in Paris and imported to New York. The designs, which may suggest classical ornamentation but may also be geometric—circles, diamonds, dots, bandings—are cut into smooth surfaces to a uniform depth so that they look drawn rather than carved. The style has been said to look machine-made, thereby expressing the nation's industrial development during the late 19C.

NO. 113 GREENE ST (1883; Henry Fernbach), built as a shop and warehouse for Lippman Toplitz, seller of caps and imported headgear, has a handsome cast-iron ground floor facade added to a masonry building. The unusual and restrained ornamentation includes an Art Nouveau moulding with entwined leaves below the architrave and incised ornament on the vertical supports flanking the central door and at the edges of the building. No. 114–20 across the street (1882; Henry Fernbach) was built as a branch of the Frederick Loeser Department Store, whose main facility was in Brooklyn.

At the S.W. corner of Prince and Greene Sts (No. 112 Prince St) is a famous trompe l'oeil *mural* (1973) by Richard Haas, sponsored by City Walls Inc., an organisation dedicated to enlivening such blank outdoor surfaces. With wit and precision the mural reproduces in paint on the brick E. wall of the building (1889; Richard Berger) the cast-iron detail of the N. Facade; the cast-iron in turn suggests masonry construction—banded corner pilasters resembling masonry blocks, colonnettes standing on pedestals and supporting impost blocks, protruding cornices ending in decorative blocks supported by consoles.

The building houses the *SoHo Center for Visual Artists* (Tues–Fri, noon–5; Sat, 11–5; tel: 226–1993), a tax-exempt center providing research facilities and exhibition space for fledgling artists. The reading room at Wooster and Prince Sts requires an artist's pass for entry.

The buildings on the N. side at *Nos 113–115, 117–119, and 121 Prince St* were built (1890; Cleverdon & Putzel) as warehouses but have now been converted to the kind of imaginative emporia that mark the current SoHo revival; they offer natural foods, herbal medicines, cookware, and imported edibles. Look at the wealth of ornament lavished on the warehouse facades, something different at every floor: geometric, floral, foliate, and heraldic motifs, egg and dart mouldings, and scrollwork.

Return to Greene St and turn N. At *No. 109 Prince St* (N.W. corner of the intersection) is a handsome cast-iron building with a chamfered entrance built (1882; Jarvis Morgan Slade) as a warehouse. Since 1943 it has been occupied by one of SoHo's more enduring businesses, the Industrial Electronic Hardware Company, a firm that now produces electronic components. The foundry label for 'Architectural Iron Works, Cheney & Hewlett' is visible on the base of the column at the corner of Greene St.

Continue N. on Greene St toward Houston St *No. 121–123 Greene St* (1883; Henry Fernbach) is a fine example of this prolific architect's work, elaborated with fluted pilasters, Corinthian columns, and an ornate cornice, all painted a smooth cream color. Note the granite sidewalks, some with their original self-curbing.

Look in the windows of *No. 142 Greene St.* Behind most cast-iron fronts are buildings of conventional internal structure with brick bearing walls, wooden beams, and joists supporting wooden floors, but occasional buildings, like this one (1871; Henry Fernbach) have a system of slender cast-iron columns supporting the floors, an arrangement which permits a very open interior (and hence a lot of rentable space). Such columns, usually painted white, were often fluted and embellished with elaborate Corinthian capitals.

Across the street at *No. 139 Greene St* is a brick Federal house dating from c. 1824 and still graced by its original dormers and brownstone lintels. One of the few buildings remaining from SoHo's early period of residential development, it was owned originally by one Anthony Arnoux; after various commercial transformations it is now being restored.

Continue N. to Houston St, the N. boundary of SoHo, widened when the IND subway tunnels were carved out in 1936. Many of the buildings on the S. side still present blank walls and truncated facades to the road. Turn left and walk two blocks along Houston St to West Broadway, SoHo's mecca of galleries, its widest street, and its western frontier (only the E. side of the street lies within the historic district so that building fronts on the W. side have been altered extensively).

Walk S. on West Broadway. While the architecture of W. Broadway is less impressive than that of the interior streets, the activity level is higher. Among the galleries on the block S. of Houston St are those noted for or specialising in the works of M.C. Escher, American decorative arts including Mission style furniture, neon art, and American Indian art. At No. 472–478 West Broadway is a brick warehouse whose first floor pilasters have been decorated with floral designs including cast-iron sunflowers. Next door at No. 468 is a brick Romanesque Revival building (c. 1885?), with strong arches relieved by cast-iron floral swags in the spandrels.

Continue S. Galleries and boutiques line the avenue, the latter offering such chic or trendy garb as cowboy boots, lamé aprons, Victorian underwear, and glitter handbags. At *No. 420 West Broadway* is a group of the most famous and influential galleries in SoHo. The four galleries—the Mary Boone Gallery, the Sonnabend Gallery, the John Weber Gallery, and the Leo Castelli Gallery—serve as the hub of SoHo activity and are frequented by museum people, artists, dealers, collectors, and anyone interested in the frontiers of American art. Leo Castelli, acknowledged as the single most important dealer in contemporary American art, became internationally recognised as an authority on Pop Art and still represents such luminaries as Warhol, Lichtenstein, and Oldenberg.

Continue S. on West Broadway. In the block between Spring and Broome Sts are more galleries known like other SoHo establishments for their innovative spirit, which have delighted or bewildered the public with a wide range of art: lifelike casts of tourists and 'shopping bag ladies', pictures of road signs and truck stop architecture, installations of tubes of fluorescent lighting. One work now permanently installed at 141 Wooster St (check for hours at the Heiner Friedrich Gallery, 393 West Broadway) is 'New York Earth Room', (1977) by Walter de Maria, which consists of 220,000 lbs or 222 cubic yards of dirt filling the gallery space to a depth of 21 inches.

Continue down West Broadway to Broome St, named in 1806 after John Broome, lieutenant governor of New York state (1804) and a prominent businessman who demonstrated his acuity by purchasing 2 million pounds of tea from China at the end of the Revolutionary War, thereby initiating the romantic and lucrative China trade.

Previously called Bayard Lane, the street led across the Bayard family farm to the Bowery Road past Bayard's Mount, once the highest point in the developed part of Manhattan. When the hill was levelled between 1807–11 and its earth dumped as landfill into the Collect Pond (see p123), Broome St became a major east–west access route, a function it still maintains, linking the Holland Tunnel with the Williamsburg Bridge. Its history as a crosstown artery made it the target of Robert Moses's missionary zeal; his projected Lower Manhattan Expressway, an elevated highway above Broome St, was to carry heavy traffic from tunnel to bridge, levelling a swathe of cast-iron buildings, bisecting, and hence destroying SoHo. Moses's plan, conceived of as early as World War II, was rejected by the Board of Estimates in 1968.

Walk E. on Broome St. The brick building on the S.E. corner of the intersection with West Broadway (No. 499 Broome St) dates from c. 1825 when it was owned by one Alfred Pell, who probably used it as a residence. Much of Broome St, however, early developed as one of the area's commercial streets, retains its industrial flavour better than some of the surrounding territory. At *No. 484–490 Broome St* on the corner of Wooster St (1890; Alfred Zucker) is a fine Romanesque Revival brick and rockface brownstone building once the warehouse and salesrooms of Fleitmann & Co., dealers in dry goods and tailors' trimmings. Note the carved sandstone decoration: writhing griffins, staring faces, assorted winged creatures. The arches are framed with stylised terracotta leaf forms, and the cast-iron window supports with entwined vines and leaves.

The building houses *The Kitchen* (second floor), an organisation established in 1971 to foster video art, which offers performances, contemporary music, exhibitions, and dance programmes (Tues–Sat, 1–6; tel: 925–3615). Across Broome St at No. 485 (1872; Elisha Sniffen) note the iron pillars with Romanesque furled-leaves on the capitals and the foundry labels (Atlantic Iron Works) on the bases.

Turn left (N.) on Wooster St. At No. 80 Wooster St is *Anthology Film Archives*, founded uptown in 1964 by filmmaker Jonas Mekas to provide a showcase for avant-garde films. The archives' collection of films contains both classic and contemporary works (admission $2; tel: 226–0010). The *Museum of Colored Glass and Light* (No. 70–72 Wooster St, 2nd floor; Tues–Sun, 1–6; admission $1; tel: 226–7258) displays, among other glass pieces, the works of its founder Raphael Nemeth. Return to Broome St.

Continue E. on Broome St across Greene St. At No. 464–466 Broome St on the N.E. corner of the intersection is a building (1861) constructed for Aaron Arnold of Arnold Constable's department store, who left it to his son and daughter. On the S. side of the street is a fine stretch of cast-iron facades, albeit somewhat shabby, including *No. 453–455 Broome St* (1873; Griffith Thomas), originally built as the Welcome G. Hitchcock silk and veilings firm. Hitchcock came as a poor boy from Montrose, Pennsylvania and according to a contemporary achieved success by 'industry, economy, ability, fidelity to each and every obligation, knowledge of his business, and proper consideration of his customers'. Among his partners were Aaron Arnold and James Constable.

Global Village at No. 454 Broome St (Mon–Fri, 12–6; tel: 966–7526) is a non-profit video center with facilities for teaching, production, and exhibition. The center emphasises documentary uses of video and has become a source of productions for national non-commercial television.

The former warehouse across the intersection of Mercer St at *No. 448 Broome St* (1875; Frederick Clarke Withers), with its unusual floral and filigree decoration, is the only known cast-iron building by the architect responsible for the reredos in Trinity Church, the Church of the Good Shepherd on Roosevelt Island, and the Jefferson Market Courthouse.

Continue E. along Broome St to Broadway and the supremely elegant ***Haughwout Building** (1857; John P. Gaynor; DL) at No. 488–492 Broadway. Designed in the Italianate palazzo style common to many early cast-iron buildings and perhaps even modelled on the Sansovino Library in Venice, the Haughwout Building (sometimes inappropriately called the Parthenon of Cast-Iron Architecture) was nonetheless a pioneering structure—one of the first New York buildings whose floor loads were carried by a cast-iron skeleton instead of walls and the very first to feature a passenger elevator with a safety device, a steam driven, cable and drum contraption invented by Elisha Otis. The economy of casting many forms from the same mould fostered the repetition of detail on cast-iron buildings such as this one whose basic motif—a round-arch window between slender Corinthian colonettes flanked by larger Corinthian columns—is repeated 92 times in four tiers on two facades. The horizontal elements too—a full entablature and balustrade course—are repeated at every floor. It is this repetition, the result of a practical and economic principle, that results in the frequently invoked harmony of the building, its subtle balance between horizontal and vertical, between planar and 3-dimensional elements. Originally the Haughwout Building, whose ironwork was cast by Daniel D. Badger & Co., was painted bright cream.

Eder V. Haughwout sold china, glassware, chandeliers, and silver (to the White House and elsewhere) from the groundfloor showroom. After he retired in 1869, the building became a loft, housing among its now lowly occupants M.H. Pulaski & Co., manufacturers of embroidery, whose monogram remains etched in the glass of the entrance. Today the Broadway Manufacturers Supply Co., a wholesale handler of cotton fabrics, occupies the building, which is adequately but not elegantly maintained.

Less than a half block S. of the Haughwout Building is the ROOSEVELT BUILDING (1874; Richard Morris Hunt) at No. 478–482 Broadway, one of two cast-iron buildings by the architect of society's Fifth Ave palaces. With its three wide bays, tracery arches at the fourth floor, outleaning fifth floor cornice, and neo-Grec ornamental motifs (note especially the ground floor pilasters), it is quite original, disdaining to imitate stonework as do so many cast-iron buildings. Roosevelt Hospital holds the building as an investment, having inherited the site from James H. Roosevelt who lived and practiced law here (1843–1861). The Roosevelt Building extends through the block to Crosby St where its narrow rear facade echoes the main one with unusual charm.

Turn around and walk N. on Broadway. At No. 514 Broadway is the 'SoHo Weekly News', a lively newspaper whose editorial boundaries stretch well beyond SoHo. Founded in 1973 when SoHo received Historic District status, the paper burgeoned during the 1978 newspaper strike which paralysed the city's three major dailies. It now has a reputation for extensive coverage of the arts and local issues and for energetic, sometimes experimental journalism.

The *'bishop's crook'* lampost in front of No. 515 Broadway dates from c. 1900 when it and others of its kind replaced the older gas lights which had been introduced in the 1860s. About 1880 arc lights, perfected by Charles Francis Brush, were installed at the intersections along Broadway and in Union and Madison Squares but in 1893 there were still 26,524 gas lamps and 1535 electric lights. In 1896 this classic lamppost—with its tendrils, scrollwork, and acanthus leaves—designed by Richard Rodgers Bowker began to appear on city streets. More than 30, documented for preservation, still remain.

At No. 521–523 Broadway are the bare remains of the *St. Nicholas Hotel* (opened 1853), an establishment of legendary luxury. All that survives of a white marble building that once ran about 275 ft S. from the corner of Spring St is this portion whose upper story windows, visible behind the fire escape, retain their original carved stone ornamentation.

The present shabby condition of the building makes it difficult to believe that at one time the hotel dazzled its clientele with tapestry carpets, magnificent chandeliers, Sheffield plate and a bridal suite, decorated in an excess of white satin and carved rosewood said by 'Putnam's Magazine' to make timid brides shrink and cower. This splendour was short-lived, for by 1870 these blocks of Broadway had fallen to commerce and the hotel, while remaining profitable for another decade, had lost its glamour. It closed in 1884 to be replaced in part by a loft building.

Cross Spring St. The restrained cast-iron facade at *No. 550 Broadway* was added in 1901 to modernise an older masonry building and is one of the last such facades erected, though the use of cast-iron to spruce up an old-fashioned masonry building or to convert a residence into a commercial building was common in earlier decades. The building itself (1854) housed Tiffany & Co., until 1870.

On the W. side of the street at No. 555 Broadway the handsomely maintained ROUSS BUILDING (1889; Alfred Zucker) still proclaims the aplomb of merchant Charles 'Broadway' Rouss, who came debt-ridden to New York from Maryland and so flourished that he took the street's name as his own and had it emblazoned on his storefront. In 1900 Rouss appended a 25-ft wing at the N. end of his department store, finishing the front with ironwork to match the original facade and topping off the whole with the present elaborate roof which in 1900 had, in addition to the dormered pyramids at each end and the central plaque bearing Rouss's name, a globe surmounted by an eagle.

On the S.W. corner of Prince St and Broadway, at No. 561–563 Broadway, is the former **'Little Singer Building'** (1904; Ernest Flagg), so called because there once existed a bigger Singer Building, demolished in 1967 for the undistinguished skyscraper at 1 Liberty Plaza. Despite ugly ground floor modifications, the building (now the Paul Building) is extremely handsome, with terracotta panels, delicate curls of wrought iron, large expanses of plate glass (albeit filthy) that forecast the curtain wall, and a great arch beneath the cornice. The building wraps around the corner of Prince St, enveloping No. 565 Broadway next door, (1859; John Kellum), whose carved marble Corinthian columns evoke the days when Ball, Black & Company purveyed jewellery to society.

This stretch of Broadway, now a rather drab street of small manufacturers and shops, glittered with the bright lights of theatres and music halls during the late 1850s and 1860s. The Empire Hall, the Palace of Mirrors, Heller's Salon Diabolique, and Willis' Gambling House all stood in this block as well as Niblo's Garden (1827) at No. 568–578 Broadway, known for its extravagant productions, its 75-ft stage, and its illuminated marquee with red gas jets.

Continue N. across Prince St. No. 583–587 Broadway (1896; Cleverdon & Putzel), built as a store and loft well after elegance had departed from this part of Broadway, nonetheless features elaborately carved stone columns above the defaced ground floor level.

The nearest public transportation is the IND Sixth Ave (B, D, or F train), at Broadway-Lafayette and Houston Sts; the IRT Lexington Ave local (train 6) at Bleecker and Lafayette Sts; or the IND Eighth Ave (AA, CC, or E train), at Spring St and Sixth Ave. Broadway buses M1 and M6 stop at Prince St; the Fifth Ave bus, M5, stops at W. Houston St.

8 Lafayette Historic Group, East Village, St. Mark's Historic District

SUBWAY: IRT Lexington Ave local (train 6) to Bleecker St. IND Sixth Ave (trains B, D, and F) to Broadway-Lafayette St.

BUS: M1, M5, M6 to Houston St.

This walking tour through the Astor Place district, the East Village, and the St. Mark's Historic District explores one of New York's more motley areas. Within its boundaries live the derelicts of the Bowery

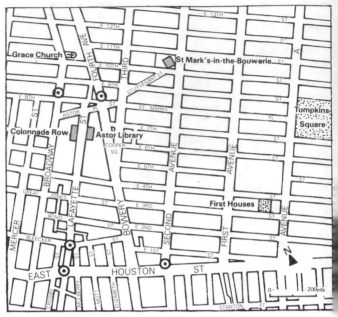

and the well-to-do residents of Renwick Triangle, the remnants of
19C Polish, Russian, and Ukrainian immigrant communities, the
middle class 'hippies' around St. Mark's Place, and a large black and
Puerto Rican population east of Tompkins Square. Culturally the
area includes such established institutions as Grace Church, Cooper
Union, and the New York Public Theater; as well as the more
experimental theatres of the East Village, and the ethnic shops,
restaurants, and cultural institutions around Second Avenue. Architecturally it offers a beautiful 18C church, several late-federal
residences—both shabby and restored—fine examples of 19C commercial cast-iron and masonry architecture, and Louis H. Sullivan's
only New York skyscraper. Because of historical circumstance—sudden and rapid development as a fine residential area followed by an
equally rapid decline precipitated by the invasion of commerce
along Broadway and the pressures of immigration around Tompkins
Square—the district preserves in strange juxtaposition traces of its
various stages of evolution. Here and there amidst grime and litter
arise gallant old buildings, some of them lovingly refurbished or
imaginatively recycled, others obscured by layers of paint and disfigured by clumsy 'improvements'. Yet the area also shows evidence of
renewal, in its neighbourhood action groups, its new businesses and
churches, and in its experimental theatres, ethnic festivals, and other
cultural expressions.

The tour, however, begins in one of the seedier parts of the
district, on E. Houston St where in a milieu of broken bottles and
trash, Bowery derelicts accost pedestrians or shamble into the street
to panhandle from cars stopped at the traffic lights. While not
actually dangerous, this part of the tour is grim and depressing. The

later part of the tour, beginning on Lafayette St with the New York Public Theater and Colonnade Row, is more pleasant.

Begin at Broadway and Houston St; on the N.W. corner of the intersection is the former *Cable Building* (1894; McKim, Mead & White), built as an office building and power station for the Broadway Cable Traction Company.

Cable cars or trolleys, popular in other American cities, had to compete in New York with horse cars and horse-drawn stages in which Boss Tweed (see p118) held considerable interests. Most of the city's cable cars ran on Broadway and Third Ave, where electricity supplanted horse power at the end of the 19C.

Across the street at *No. 620 Broadway* (1858; John B. Snook) is one of the city's earliest cast-iron buildings. Known as the *Little Cary Building*, because its facade was cast from the same moulds as the wider Cary Building on Chambers St, the iron work is designed to simulate masonry. Against walls with imitation rustication are paired Corinthian columns from which spring half-round arches decorated with grapevines and heraldic keystones. Next door at Nos 624–626 Broadway once stood Laura Keene's Varieties Theater, opened in 1856, gutted by fire in 1881. The original *New York Mercantile Exchange* at Nos 628–630 Broadway (1882; Herman J. Schwartzmann) still retains its charming cast-iron facade adorned with roses and lilies, slender colonnettes ridged to suggest bamboo, and oriental filigree arches below the cornice.

Continue N. on Broadway to Bleecker St and turn right (E.); walk a block to Crosby St, named after William Bedlow Crosby (1786–1865). Orphaned at the age of 2, Crosby had the good luck to be adopted by his great uncle Henry Rutgers, whose fortune he inherited and then devoted to good works.

The BAYARD-CONDICT BUILDING at No. 65 Bleecker St (1897–99; Louis H. Sullivan; DL), tucked away at the N. end of grimy Crosby St is one of Manhattan's hidden architectural treasures, the only example here of the work of Louis H. Sullivan, one of America's finest early 20C architects and a pioneer in skyscraper design. It is best seen from Crosby St near Houston St.

First called the Bayard Building in honour of one of the city's oldest families (though no Bayards were financially involved in the project), this 12-story office tower was undertaken by the United Loan and Investment Company, who hired Sullivan. Already known for his work in Chicago, Sullivan had also attracted attention for his radical theories on skyscraper design, theories which departed from the adaptation of classical and Renaissance models and stressed instead the importance of function as a determinant of form. Sullivan also recognised the importance of new building materials and their influence upon design.

His first plan for the building incorporated a vertical freestanding steel skeleton with uniform 14-inch structural columns and uniform 12-inch exterior brick walls clad with terracotta. Unfortunately the extreme conservatism of the New York City building code ruled against the steel column system and the walls and columns had to be greatly thickened on the lower floors, resulting in a loss of floor space and hence a loss of rental income for the owner. The United Loan and Investment Company, now unable to afford the building, sold it to Silas and Emmeline Condict.

The EXTERIOR reflects Sullivan's famous dictum that a skyscraper should be a proud and soaring thing. Slender, moulded piers rise above the base over the interior structural columns, ending in arches just below the frieze. Between the windows are narrow vertical columns also ending in arches. The sumptuous surface decoration of terracotta—a material that became practical as iron and steel framing techniques were developed—in leafy and geometric forms (designed by Sullivan and George Elmslie) culminates in an ornate cornice beneath which hover six angels with outspread wings, a motif Sullivan had used in his Transportation Building at the World's Columbian Exposition in 1893. Although legend asserts that Silas Condict insisted on the angels over Sullivan's objection, the angels appear in a drawing made before Condict purchased the building.

Unfortunately this magnificent office tower made little impression on other practicing architects, who continued working in more traditional styles.

Return to Broadway; turn right; walk a block N. to Bond St. The ornate building at No. 670 Broadway is a *former Brooks Brothers clothing store* (1874; George E. Harney). The ironwork (attrib. to Michael Grosz and Sons) is particularly interesting; note the geometrically designed bases and graceful leaf forms on the capitals of the street level columns.

Brooks Brothers Clothiers occupied this store from 1874–84. Founded in 1818 on Cherry and Catherine Sts, the store first moved in 1863 when it was looted during the Draft Riots. Like other fashionable retailers, Brooks Brothers began a pilgrimage uptown, moving first to Broadway and Grand St, later to this site, on to the 23rd St area, and finally to their present location at 44th St and Madison Ave in 1915.

Walk a short block E. on Bond St. to Jones Alley. The ornate, pale grey cast-iron building at NO. 1 BOND ST occupies the site of the home of Albert Gallatin, secretary of the treasury under Thomas Jefferson.

For a while in the 1830s and 1840s, the Bond St area was the cynosure of fashion, but the encroachment of commerce along Broadway put an end to its social eminence and its fine homes became boarding houses and offices. 'Leslie's Illustrated Magazine' pointed out in 1857 that 'the number of teeth that are pulled out or "filled" in Bond St in one day would afford a curious statistic.' By 1870 it was solidly commercial.

The building now occupying No. 1 Bond St (1871; S.D. Hatch), originally the home of publishing firm D.D. Appleton and Co., is a dramatic example of the French Second Empire style executed in cast iron. Note the elaborate mansard roof with three pavilions. The beribboned torches of learning in the spandrels above the main doorway are trademarks of the Appleton Co. Also noteworthy are the large expanses of plate glass, made possible by the strength of iron under compression so that a few widely spaced columns could support a sizable facade. With their gleaming plate windows and their light-coloured facades (cast-iron buildings were frequently painted off-white), buildings such as this one must have dazzled onlookers accustomed to the more sober Greek Revival streetscape.

Continue E. on Bond St. to the BOUWERIE LANE THEATRE (1874; Henry Engelbert; DL), at No. 330 Bowery, built as the Bond Street Savings Bank, later the German Exchange Bank, and converted to its present use in 1963. The architect, working with a standard 25 × 100-ft building lot, has managed to create the impression of massive grandeur associated with bank architecture an undertaking made even more difficult by the fact that the short side of the lot faces the Bowery, the more important thoroughfare. The Corinthian columns arrayed singly or in pairs, the cornices at every floor, the quoins and rusticated piers all masquerade as stone though they are executed in cast iron. The building is presently painted an attractive cream colour.

Cross the Bowery and continue E. to Second Ave. Turn left (N.). Half way up the block (W. side) between E. 2nd and E. 3rd Sts is small, gated (and locked) *New York Marble Cemetery* (DL) the city's first nonsectarian graveyard, built as a commercial venture in 1830 following passage of an ordinance outlawing burials below Canal St. The investors in this half acre constructed 156 underground vaults of Tuckahoe marble and sold them to nearby residents including surgeon Valentine Mott, pastor Gardiner Spring, publisher Uriah Scribner and tobacco magnate Peter Lorillard. Of this group only the Scribners are buried here, though they were joined by Beekmans, Howes, Varicks, and Hoyts.

The following year the same corporation constructed another cemetery (walk S. to 2nd St; turn left or E. and continue a half block) on 2nd St east of Second Ave. Called the NEW YORK *CITY* MARBLE CEMETERY (1831; DL) to distinguish it from its predecessor, it is laid out in rectilinear fashion and features handsome monuments and gravestones, which can be seen through the fence. John Ericsson and James Monroe were once interred here but later removed; still remaining are Marinus Willett, Revolutionary army officer and mayor (1807), and various members of the Roosevelt and Kip families. Here also rests Preserved Fish, member of a prominent family of lawyers and politicians, apparently the victim of his parents' fondness for punning.

Continue on to First Ave and turn left (N.); at E. 3rd St turn right (E.) and continue a quarter block to the **First Houses** (1935–36; N.Y.C. Housing Authority; Frederick L. Ackerman; DL). The first project of the New York City Housing Authority, created during the Depression, the First Houses are rebuilt from existing tenements using work relief labour and bricks salvaged from demolished buildings. The Housing Authority purchased many of the original tenements at a fraction of their value from Vincent Astor who had inherited them from his grandfather John Jacob Astor, real estate genius and slumlord. Every third house was demolished to create light and air space for the remaining tenements which had to be rebuilt and reinforced with structural steel after the removal of adjoining structures made them unsound.

The Housing Authority opened a rental office for the 122 units in mid-January, 1935 and was flooded with 3–4000 applications by March. Tenants were chosen by social workers with preference given to dwellers of the worst slums and those with small families. To the chosen, the new apartments, renting for $6·05 per room, were luxurious, each equipped with a refrigerator, a four-burner stove, and a bathroom. Though attacked as a boondoggle and an extravaganza, the First Houses remain a source of pride to the city and a residential haven for an ethnically mixed, predominantly elderly group of tenants.

On the S. side of E. 3rd St near the Bowery is the *Men's Shelter* run by the city Department of Social Services, where destitute and derelict men can get a meal and a voucher to sleep in a nearby flophouse. Nearly 1300 men visit the shelter each day, most of them patients released from the state's psychiatric hospitals. On the first floor is the 'Big Room' with rows of attached plastic chairs where as many as 250 men will sit all night if neighbourhood facilities are full, an increasingly common condition as flophouses are torn down or upgraded for more profitable uses.

Walk W. on E. 3rd St, which becomes Great Jones St W. of the

Bowery. The land for the street was ceded to the city by Samuel Jones, a prominent lawyer and the city's first comptroller (1796–99), with the stipulation that it be named after him. Unfortunately New York already had a Jones St; for a while it had two, until Samuel Jones suggested calling his street 'Great Jones St'.

Continue W. At No. 44 Great Jones St is the firehouse of ENGINE COMPANY 33 (1898; Ernest Flagg and W.B. Chambers; DL), a satisfyingly flamboyant Beaux-Arts building dominated by a monumental three-story arch rising to a handsome cartouche. Unlike most buildings in this neighbourhood, the firehouse is impeccably maintained, displaying to best advantage its elegant details: the deep cornice with scroll brackets, tall French windows, ornamental railings.

Continue W. to Lafayette St. *No. 376 Lafayette St* (N.W. corner of Great Jones St) is an imposing building (1888; Henry J. Hardenbergh; DL) designed by the architect of the Plaza Hotel and the Dakota Apartments. Built as a warehouse, this strong building displays Hardenbergh's interest in ornament and sculptural detail: note the ground level piers and the Gothic terracotta ornament on the upper stories.

Turn right and walk a block N. on Lafayette St to E. 4th St. On the N.E. corner of the intersection at No. 399 Lafayette St is the former **De Vinne Press Building** (1885; Babb, Cook & Willard; DL), a spare, powerful Romanesque Revival building constructed with masonry bearing-walls and executed in dark brick with terracotta trim. Massive and simple, the DeVinne Press Building is remarkable for its appearance of weight and strength: note the deeply recessed window arches which express the thickness of the masonry walls, and the restrained trim on the rounded corner turning.

Theodore De Vinne (1828–1914) was a successful printer and distinguished scholar of the history of printing. The De Vinne Press achieved prominence through its publication of 'Scribner's Monthly' and the 'Century' magazine, but DeVinne's more enduring achievements are his edition of the Book of Common Prayer, the 'Century Dictionary', and his scholarly contributions.

Turn right (E.) and walk a half block to the OLD MERCHANT'S HOUSE (1832; attrib. Minard Lafever; DL), at 29 E. 4th St between Lafayette St and Broadway. Known also as the Seabury Tredwell House, this three-story brick townhouse was built by hat merchant Joseph Brewster and was sold in 1835 to Tredwell. The house remained in the family until the last surviving direct descendant Gertrude Tredwell died in 1933. A distant relative purchased it and its furnishings and formed a non-profit corporation to preserve it as a museum (open Sun, 1–4; adults, $2, students and senior citizens, $1. Tel: 777–1089). Stylistically the house straddles the Federal and Greek Revival periods, and many of its external details—leaded glass fanlight, wrought-iron stoop railings, hollow urn newel posts— refer to the Federal period while the interior with its elegant ornamentation and more spacious proportions is generally classified as Greek Revival in style. The unusual doorway with its multiple splayed keystones and arched mouldings puzzles architectural historians who believe it may have been inspired by some of the great English houses of the late 17–early 18C.

Tredwell was a noted abolitionist and the house contains a hidden passageway to the East River, perhaps indicating that its owner used his home for sheltering runaway slaves on their way to freedom.

Nearby (No. 37 E. 4th St) is the SAMUEL TREDWELL SKIDMORE HOUSE (1844–45; DL) built by a distant Tredwell cousin, who made his living as a drug importer and served as a vestryman of Trinity Church. Most of its brownstone trim has succumbed to the pollutants in the city's atmosphere, but the panelled door flanked by Ionic columns is still handsome. Less impressive and smaller in scale than the Old Merchant's House, it was built as one of a row of speculative dwellings.

Return to Lafayette St; turn right (N.) and walk uptown to the *Durst Building* at Nos 409–411 Lafayette St (1891; Alfred Zucker), a cast-iron and brick building with terracotta trim, designed for Simon Goldenberg's haberdashery and workshops. On the ground floor are great iron-clad piers and freestanding iron columns ornamented with beaded rings.

Lafayette St (originally Lafayette Place) ran only from Great Jones St to Astor Place when opened in 1826 and was, for a single generation, the city's swankiest residential address, the home of Astors, Vanderbilts, and Delanos.

Jacob Sperry, a Swiss physician who immigrated in 1748, bought the land where Lafayette St now runs when it was still pasture and developed it as a garden for flowers and hothouse plants. In 1804 Sperry sold his garden to John Jacob Astor for $45,000; while waiting with his usual acumen for land values to rise, Astor leased it to a Frenchman named Delacroix who, in turn, created a pleasure ground called Vauxhall Gardens. He installed fountains, statuary, walks, and summer pavilions where people could buy light refreshments and remodelled the greenhouse as a saloon where those so inclined could indulge in heavier drinking. When Delacroix's lease ran out in 1825, Astor reclaimed the gardens, carved out Lafayette Place, and sold building lots facing the new street for more than $45,000 apiece, the price of the entire parcel only 20 years earlier.

John Jacob Astor himself never lived on Lafayette St, but his son William B. Astor did—opposite Colonnade Row at No. 34 Lafayette Pl, in a house described by a contemporary as a 'plain but substantial looking brick mansion.'

On the W. side of Lafayette St (Nos 428–34) stand the remains of **Colonnade Row** (1833; attrib. Alexander Jackson Davis; DL), an architectural masterpiece now suffering the indignities of neglect. First named La Grange Terrace after the country home of the Marquis de Lafayette, the row originally consisted of nine houses joined by a monumental two-story colonnade of Corinthian columns. The houses, built on speculation by Seth Geer and faced with white Westchester marble cut by Sing Sing prisoners, sold for upwards of $25,000 apiece—a high price for a row house at the time—and were purchased eagerly by such notables as Franklin Delano, grandfather of Franklin D. Roosevelt, and David Gardiner, whose daughter Julia married President John Tyler in 1844. So successful were the houses that other colonnaded rows were built on Brooklyn Heights, on Broadway, and on W. 23rd St, but none has survived. Colonnade Row itself enjoyed only a brief moment of social splendour, as commerce continued moving up Broadway, depressing residential land values in its path. By the 1860s the Astor mansion had become a restaurant, a neighbourhood church had been converted to a boxing ring, and the five southernmost houses of Colonnade Row opened as the Colonnade Hotel. When Lafayette St was extended S. to the City Hall area in the 1880s, the remaining houses on the street became tenements and rooming houses or were torn down to make way for warehouses and factories. In 1901 the Wanamaker warehouse replaced the Colonnade Hotel and the district became solidly commercial.

Directly opposite Colonnade Row is the **Public Theater** (at No. 425 Lafayette St), originally the **Astor Library,** a complicated building with a complicated pedigree (S. wing, 1849–53, Alexander Saeltzer; center wing, 1856–59, Griffith Thomas; N. wing, 1879–81, Thomas Stent; remodelled, 1966, Giorgio Cavaglieri; DL). Although handsome and well-proportioned, the building is remarkable not so much for its architectural style (it is a Victorian version of a Renaissance Italian palace), as for its rich historical associations. It opened in 1854 as the Astor Library, the only public benefaction of crusty, tightfisted John Jacob Astor, who ostensibly dedicated it to working people but kept it open only during the day when workers couldn't use it. When the Astor Library was merged with the Lenox and Tilden collections in 1912 to form the nucleus of the New York Public Library system, the Hebrew Immigrant Aid Society took over the building and used it from 1921–65 in its work of resettling the flood of immigrants arriving from Eastern Europe. In 1965, with the HIAS determined to move, impressario Joseph Papp convinced the city to buy the building and remodel the interior under the guidance of Giorgio Cavalgieri, whose work at the Jefferson Market Courthouse made him well-known as a renovator. The building is now the headquarters of the N.Y. Shakespeare Festival and contains seven different auditoriums where plays, films, jazz concerts, and other theatrical events are offered.

Continue N. on Lafayette St to Astor Place. On the traffic island on the right (E.) side of the intersection is a 15-ft weathering steel cube (1966) by Bernard (Tony) Rosenthal. Balanced on one apex so that it will revolve when pushed, the work is entitled '*Alamo*,' a name derived from a remark by the sculptor's wife that the piece had the strength and feeling of a fortress.

Across Lafayette St to the W. at No. 13 Astor Pl. is the *District 65 Building* (1890; George Harney), built on the site of the old Astor Place Opera House. The opera house is now remembered chiefly as the site of the Astor Place riot (10 May 1849), an uprising that stemmed from a bitter theatrical rivalry between English actor William Macready and his American counterpart Edwin Forrest and was fanned by the anti-British and anti-aristocratic sentiments of the working class and of the Native American political party. While the audience inside the theatre pelted Macready with garbage, a mob outside assaulted the building with bricks and paving stones. The militia was summoned from nearby Tompkins Market Armory and was eventually ordered to fire into the crowd. Estimates of casualties differ, but the number of dead is usually set at about 30 and the number of wounded at about 150.

Facing Broadway across E. 8th St (N. of the District 65 Building) is a 15-story structure (1903; Daniel H. Burnham & Co.) today used by the federal government but originally built as the annex of the famous Wanamaker Department Store.

Here begins a stretch of Broadway known during palmier days as LADIES' MILE, which reached its acme during the 1870s and 1880s when it hosted an impressive list of fine department stores. Ladies' Mile, which ran from 8th to 23rd Sts and spilled over to Fifth and Sixth Aves, became the city's most fashionable promenade, as women of taste and money shopped in James McCreery & Co., Arnold Constable, Lord and Taylor, B. Altman & Company, Best & Company, or Bonwit Teller. While none of these stores has survived in this location and some have not survived at all, several of the store buildings remain, and have been adapted to other uses.

Across E. 10th St where the Stewart House apartments presently stand was the old Wanamaker Store, a magnificent cast-iron building, constructed in 1862 as the A.T. Stewart store by architect John Kellum. Outside, it dazzled observers with its large, plate-glass Palladian windows and its gleaming white facade. Inside, it featured a central rotunda encircled by galleries like the balconies in an opera house and lit by a great glass dome. The Wanamaker store descended from A.T. Stewart's famous emporium which began to fail after Stewart's death in 1876 and was purchased in 1896 by John Wanamaker, the Philadelphia merchant, under whose care it first bloomed and then merely survived. In 1952 when the retail trade had moved far uptown the building was sold; while awaiting demolition, a spectacular fire ravaged it (15 July 1956).

Continue N. along Broadway to E. 10th St., where *Grace Church (Protestant Episcopal) lifts its delicate spire skyward (open daily 8 a.m. to 6 p.m.; Sunday during services). Praised as New York's finest Gothic Revival church (1846; James Renwick, Jr; DL), it was also once its most socially desirable, ministering to the city's finest families, famous for its society weddings. The EXTERIOR white marble, quarried by Sing Sing convicts as an economy measure, has been dimmed by grime and pollution, but the delicate stonework and fine proportions of the church remain undiminished. The octagonal steeple (1884) rising from the central tower replaces a wooden steeple—another economy measure instituted by the building committee; unfortunately the marble spire cost $2/3$ the original cost of the whole church. Despite early fears that the building would collapse beneath its weight, the steeple remains proudly upright. Above the main entrance is a handsome gable and a fine rose window.

The INTERIOR is especially beautiful, with Pre-Raphaelite stained glass windows by Henry Holiday in the N. and S. aisles and a beautiful mosaic floor. On the S. wall is a chantry added from Renwick's designs. In 1900 the chancel was enlarged to accommodate the boys' choir. In the N. transept is a bust of architect Renwick.

Renwick's wife, born Margaret A, Brevoort, belonged to the family that long held the land on which Grace Church stands. A relative, Henry Brevoort according to legend, so loved his gardens and orchards that he refused to let the city push Eleventh St through his property, thereby giving Grace Church its rather spacious plot.

The handsome pews were sold to prominent families at the time the church opened, with some going as high as $1400.

To the N. of the church is the **Rectory** (DL), designed by Renwick at the same time as the church, one of the city's earliest Gothic Revival dwellings, replete with pinnacles, gables, quatrefoil ornamentation, and traceried windows. Although the house actually has two symmetrical wings, Renwick has achieved the appearance of assymmetry by treating the two bay windows quite differently from one another, an effect highly admired by practitioners of Gothic Revival architecture. The large Roman urn in the Rectory Garden was brought to New York by William Reed Huntington (rector, 1883–1909).

Across the street from the Rectory on the N.W. corner of Broadway and E. 11th St. is a handsome building (67 E. 11th St) which formerly housed the James McCreery Dry Goods Store. Known as the CAST IRON BUILDING (1868; John Kellum; converted, 1971; Stephen P. Jacobs), it features a handsome colonnade along 11th St with $^3/_4$ round Corinthian columns on paneled pedestals. The first floor, 20 ft high, has broad glass windows whose light once flooded the sales counters. The unattractive 5th floor is an unfortunate addition.

Unlike other department stores, McCreery's long adhered to its original line, dry goods, and at the end of the 19C was known for its fabrics, especially its silks and woollens, its wedding and trousseau gowns and its ball dresses. James McCreery arrived as an Irish immigrant in 1845, began trade as a lace merchant, and rose to become a major merchandiser; he dedicated his fortune to the arts and eventually became a patron of the Metropolitan Museum of Art. McCreery's store moved uptown as fashion dictated, closing finally in 1954.

Walk around the S. side of the church on E. 10th St to Fourth Ave and turn left. GRACE MEMORIAL HOUSE (1882–83; James Renwick, Jr; DL) at Nos 94–96 Fourth Ave is now used as a gymnasium and classroom building for the Grace Church School.

By the late 1870s the parish served by Grace Church was no longer exclusively wealthy, and the church needed different facilities to serve its members. Levi P. Morton, Vice-President of the United States under Benjamin Harrison, donated money in memory of his wife for Grace Memorial House, which served first as a day nursery, then as a home for young women of modest means, and still later as a rehabilitation center for girls. Closed in 1957, it was threatened with demolition until it received landmark status in 1974. The building, originally two Greek Revival townhouses, was altered to its present appearance by Renwick, who added the facade, the gable, and other features. No. 96 was later duplicated by CLERGY HOUSE at No. 92 (1902; Heins & La Farge) to make No. 94 with its tall gable the center of a symmetrical group of buildings. Later NEIGHBORHOOD HOUSE at No. 98 (1907; Renwick, Aspinwall, & Tucker) was added in the same style.

The stretch of Fourth Ave between Cooper Square and Union Square on 14th St was once **Booksellers' Row,** a center for used and antiquarian books. But, as one book dealer noted recently, the antiquarian book business demands a site with low rent and high traffic, irreconcilable conditions in New York today, and the number of such stores is dwindling. Among the survivors are *The Strand* (828 Broadway), *The Pageant Book Company* (59 Fourth Ave) and *The Fourth Avenue Bookstore* (138 Fourth Ave). *Biblo and Tannen's* at No. 63 Fourth Ave, one of the most famous old stores, closed in 1979.

Return to E. 10th St and walk E. through **St. Mark's Historic District,** which includes much of E. 10th St between Third and Second Aves, Renwick Triangle, St. Mark's-in-the-Bowery, and No. 232 E. 11th St. The district once lay within the boundaries of Peter Stuyvesant's original farm or *bouwerie,* purchased in 1651 from the Dutch W. India Company and extending from the East River to Fourth Ave, from about present day 5th to 17th Sts.

The governor's great-grandson, Petrus Stuyvesant, decided to develop a part of the estate and in the late 1780s had his property mapped into building lots along a grid of streets oriented to the points of the compass, with the road that ran to the Bowery Road from the old Stuyvesant mansion (whose probable foundations were uncovered in 1854 during excavations at 129 E. 10th St) incorporated into the plan as Stuyvesant St. Building began c. 1800, but a few years later the city moved to impose its own scheme for development based on the Commissioners' Plan of 1811 which featured a street grid orientated according to the long axis of Manhattan Island. Although the city generally closed existing streets or tore down buildings that did not conform to its plan, the Stuyvesant St neighbourhood was allowed to remain, largely in deference to its wealthy families, including the Stuyvesants.

Nos 112–128 E. 10th St and the houses directly behind them (Nos 23–35 Stuyvesant St) comprise RENWICK TRIANGLE (1861; attrib. James Renwick, Jr), a group of 16 houses planned and built on land that once belonged to Hamilton Fish who sold it under the condition that no 'noxious or offensive establishments'—breweries, slaughter houses, soap or glue factories, tanneries, cattle yards, or blacksmith shops—be built there. Before restrictive zoning laws, such covenants were the sole means of ensuring residential tranquillity.

The houses, built in the Anglo-Italianate style with red Philadelphia pressed brick and brownstone trim, have rusticated ground floors, bold cornices, and fully enframed upper story windows. The dimensions of the houses conform to the triangular plot of land, with widths varying from 16–32 ft and depths from 16–48 ft.

Continue along E. 10th St to *St. Mark's-in-the-Bowery (Protestant Episcopal) at the N.W. corner of Second Ave (1799; DL). The church is the second oldest in the city after St. Paul's Chapel, and is built on the probable site of governor Stuyvesant's own chapel. The rubble-stone walls and simple triangular pediment of the body of the church date from its late-Georgian, rural beginnings. The lovely Greek Revival steeple was added in 1828, designed by Ithiel Town, and an Italianate cast-iron portico was built in 1854 keeping the church abreast of the latest architectural fashions and presumably satisfying the social aspirations of its then fashionable congregation.

The beautiful Georgian interior (now closed during restoration) was severely damaged in 1978 when a worker's acetylene torch ignited the wooden gallery on the second floor.

The idyllic graveyard contains the remains of Peter Stuyvesant and a statue (to the right of the porch) of the governor sculpted in the Netherlands (1911) by Toom Dupuis. Flanking the main doorway are two Florentine marble lions and, outside the portico, two granite statues of American Indians by Solon Borglum (1868–1922). The sculptor, brother of the more famous Gutzon Borglum, had been a rancher and adventurer before he took up art and is known for his frontier subjects. At the W. end of the porch is a *bust of Daniel Tompkins* (1774–1825) by O. Grymes, erected in 1939. Lawyer, judge, legislator and state governor, Tompkins was known for his liberal reforms in education, the criminal code, and human rights.

The graveyard, now paved with undulating rows of cobblestones, was the scene of a ghoulish kidnapping in 1878 when department store millionaire A.T. Stewart was exhumed and carted off for $20,000 ransom. His body was recovered 2 years later. Resting more peaceably here are Commodore Matthew Perry, Daniel Tompkins, Philip Hone, described in Moses King's 1893 Handbook as 'one of the most courtly and most distinguished New York mayors', and members of the Fish, Goelet, Schermerhorn, and Livingston families.

Second Avenue from Houston St to 14th St, once called the *Jewish Rialto*, was the home of a flourishing Yiddish theatre whose musical comedies and melodramas made the native American theatre pale by comparison. Between the turn of the century and the 1930s such stars as Jacob Adler, Boris Thomashefsky, David Kessler, and later Molly Picon, Menashe Skulnik, Muni Weisenfreund (Paul Muni), and Luther and Stella Adler delighted their audiences. The area also served as a restaurant center, with Russian, Polish, Hungarian, and Romanian restaurants serving native specialities to an immigrant clientele. Traces remain of the Jewish population, notably in such restaurants as the Second Avenue Delicatessen (Second Ave and E. 10th St) founded in 1954 and Hammer's Dairy Restaurant (No. 243 E. 14th St between Second and Third Aves).

Return westward along Stuyvesant St, the other long leg of Renwick Triangle. At No. 21 near Third Ave is the **Stuyvesant-Fish Residence** (1804; DL) which dates from the earliest period of development of the Stuyvesant property. Built by Petrus Stuyvesant as a wedding present for his daughter Elizabeth and her husband Nicholas Fish, the house is one of the city's grandest Federal residences, expressing the Stuyvesant wealth in its unusual height and width ($28^{3}/_{4}$ ft) and in its E. windows—indicating that it was built as a freestanding (not a row) house. Note the handsome dormers, splayed brownstone lintels, rectangular top and sidelights, and Flemish bond brickwork.

Hamilton Fish (1808–93), born in this house to Elizabeth and Nicholas Fish, inherited from a childless relative half a million dollars and went on to become governor of New York, U.S. senator, and secretary of state.

Continue S.W. along Stuyvesant St, across Third Ave to Cooper Sq. (intersection of E. 7th St, the Bowery, Astor Place, and Fourth Ave) and the **Cooper Union Foundation Building** (1859; Frederick A. Peterson; additions 1890s, Leopold Eidlitz; remodelling, 1973–74, John Hejduk; DL), which embodies the innovative genius of its founder both in its physical equipment and in the institution it houses.

Peter Cooper (1791–1883), a self-made, self-educated genius, designed the first American locomotive, promoted the Atlantic cable with Cyrus W. Field, and helped develop Morse's telegraph, but made his fortune largely through an ironworks in Trenton, N.J., and a glue factory in Baltimore. Unlike others of his breed, Cooper recognised that his wealth had come from the 'cooperation of multitudes', and turned his millions to philanthropy. By establishing the Cooper Union as a free educational institution to give students the equivalent of a college degree while stressing also the practical arts and trades, Cooper provided for others the education he would have wished for himself. Requiring no other credentials than a good moral character, Cooper Union opened its doors to women as well as men, to adults as well as young people.

Built of brownstone in an Italianate style, the building incorporates some of the first wrought-iron beams used anywhere, beams which Cooper developed from train rails and for which he built the necessary rolling machinery in his Trenton plant. Later Cooper's beams evolved into I-beams and when translated into steel became the backbone of the modern skyscraper. Other innovations included the installation of air vents under the seats in the auditorium and the construction of an elevator shaft, awaiting the installation of an elevator, an event which finally took place in 1975. The upper stories, added in the 1890s, once housed the collection of decorative arts that later became the nucleus of the Cooper-Hewitt Museum.

In 1973–74 the INTERIOR was gutted; a framework of steel towers and girders supported the building from outside while the interior beams and columns were exposed and encased in non-combustible materials. The new interior, painted stark white, bears little relation to the old one except in its general proportions. Toward the N. end of the lobby is an elaborate carved Victorian 'birthday card' from the Foundation, thanking its benefactor for a donation of $150,000 on the occasion of his 80th birthday. Cooper donated over $650,000 to the school, but didn't endow it, thinking that rentals from shops in the street level arcade (E. and W. sides of the building) and offices would provide adequate operating income. On the right side of the lobby a staircase leads down to the *Great Hall*, a fine auditorium with arcades of supporting granite arches. One of Cooper's aims in founding the Union was to establish a forum where great issues of the day could be freely discussed. Here Henry Ward Beecher, William Cullen Bryant, and William Lloyd Garrison spoke against slavery before the Civil War. Here Abraham Lincoln made his famous 'Might makes right' speech in 1860, winning the support of the N.Y. press and hence the presidential nomination. Later the auditorium housed the People's Institute, offering lectures to education-hungry Jews from the Lower East Side.

Just S. of the main entrance to Cooper Union is a *statue of Peter Cooper* (1897; Augustus Saint-Gaudens) by a sculptor who had received his early training as a night student at Cooper Union. The bronze statue sits enshrined beneath a marble canopy designed by Stanford White.

Across Third Ave to the E. (between E. 6th and E. 7th Sts) is the *Abram S. Hewitt Memorial Hall* of Cooper Union (1905; Clinton & Russell). Active in founding and managing Cooper Union, Hewitt established the first American open-hearth furnace with Cooper's son Edward; later he became a U.S. congressman and mayor of New York (1887–88). The building stands on the site of the former Tompkins Market Armory, home of the Seventh Regiment whose troops were called out to put down the Astor Place Riots.

Walk E. on 7th St through the city's small but active Ukrainian enclave numbering about 1600 inhabitants. On the S. side of the street at the intersection with Taras Sevchenko Place, renamed in 1978 for the 19C Ukrainian writer and political activist (it was formerly called Hall Pl. in memory of the man who ceded the land for the street), is the new building of St. George's Ukrainian Catholic Church (1977; Apollinare Osadca). On the N. side of the street is the Surma Book and Record Company (11 E. 7th St), which specialises in Ukrainian books, records, and crafts. McSORLEY'S OLD ALE HOUSE (formerly McSorley's Saloon) at No. 15 E. 7th St was founded by John McSorley in 1854 and has befriended the drinking man ever since. Peter Cooper was a customer, as was painter John Sloan who recorded its atmosphere in his painting 'A Mug of Ale at McSorley's' (1913); Joseph Mitchell wrote of it in the 'New Yorker' magazine and in a book, 'McSorley's Wonderful Saloon'. Only in 1970, when it became illegal to exclude women, did McSorley's befriend also the drinking woman.

Return to Third Ave. The grand marble edifice at the N.E. corner (59 Third Ave), once the Metropolitan Savings Bank (1868; Carl Pfeiffer; DL) is now the COOPER SQUARE UKRAINIAN ASSEMBLY OF GOD. This French Second Empire style building is—in marble—what the Bouwerie Lane Theatre (also formerly a bank) pretends to be in cast iron; massive and imposing, with quoins at the corners and cornices articulating every floor, it was built 7 years before the Bouwerie Lane Theatre and could have been its prototype.

Turn right (N.) and walk a block along Third Ave to St. Mark's Place, actually the section of E. 8th St between Third Ave and Avenue A. Turn right into St. Mark's Pl.

During the 1960s, **St. Mark's Place** became the Main St of the East Village (the neighbourhood east of the Bowery stretching from about

Houston St to 14th St) and the focus of New York's 'counterculture'. Before that period, the East Village had been considered simply a part of the Lower East Side, and as such had witnessed from the mid-19C onward the arrival of various ethnic groups: Germans, Poles, Ukrainians, Russians, and later Puerto Ricans and blacks, now mostly concentrated in the eastern section near Avenues A–D. Seen historically the influx of 'hippies' in the 1960s was one more wave of immigrants, seeking cheap rents and a place to establish a new life. Like the groups that preceded them, they put their stamp on the streetscape: the book and bead shops, the avant-garde theatrical establishments; and the layers of peeling pink and blue paint mark their presence as the ethnic churches, social clubs, and restaurants recall earlier arrivals.

When first developed in the early 19C, St. Mark's Pl. was a fashionable street, its houses set back from the sidewalks to give a street of standard width (60 ft) the impression of spacious elegance. The house at No. 4 (1831–32) with its rickety, lop-sided dormers, retains an ornamental stone moulding on its Federal style fanlight doorway. At No. 12 is the building (1885) of the *Deutsch-Ameri-kanische Schuetzen Gesellschaft*, the former social hall of a German shooting club. At No. 20 (1832; DL) is the original *Daniel LeRoy House*, its Federal doorway—ornamented with splayed triple key-stones—reminiscent of that gracing the Old Merchant's House four blocks S. Painted pink and grey, the building now houses a record shop upstairs and a tavern in the basement. On the other side of the street at No. 23 is a building that once housed the Dom, a Polish-American social club, and later as the home of the rock group, the Electric Circus, became a central institution of East Village culture. Now it features craft classes and experimental theatre.

Continue E. to Second Ave and turn left. On the W. side of the street at No. 135 Second Ave is the OTTENDORFER BRANCH OF THE NEW YORK PUBLIC LIBRARY (1884; William Schickel; DL), originally the Freie Bibliothek und Lesehalle, a handsome red brick building with terracotta ornament, donated by Oswald and Anna Ottendorfer to the large German immigrant community which settled in this neighbourhood.

Anna Ottendorfer immigrated to the U.S. in 1844 with her first husband Jacob Uhl, who purchased the 'New Yorker Staats Zeitung' and made it a thriving daily newspaper. Six years after Uhl's death in 1853, she married Oswald Ottendorfer, the paper's editor-in-chief, under whose directorship it further evolved into a respected, conservative journal. The Ottendorfers endowed both this library and the clinic next door, though the library seems to have been Mr Ottendorfer's special project, since he personally selected the original collection of books.

Next door at No. 137 Second Ave is the STUYVESANT POLYCLINIC HOSPITAL (1884; William Schickel; DL) founded by the Ottendor-fers as the German Dispensary. Designed in an energetic neo-Italian Renaissance style, the clinic is architecturally noteworthy for its terracotta ornament, which includes portrait busts of physicians and scientists: Celsius, Hippocrates, Aesculapius and Galen on the porch; Harvey, Linne, Humboldt, Lavoisier, and Hufeland on the frieze beneath the cornice. The facade of pressed Philadelphia brick is now painted an unfortunate white.

The dispensary, which provided free out-patient care to the poor, became (1866) a branch of the German Hospital at Park Ave and 77th St (now Lenox Hill Hospital). In 1906, the German Polyklinik, another charitable organisation which provided free care as well as observation sessions for medical students, bought the building. During World War I, because of intense anti-German sentiment, the clinic's name was changed to the Stuyvesant Polyclinic. Between the wars it reverted to its original name only to become the Stuyvesant Polyclinic again during World War II.

Across the street at No. 140–142 Second Ave is the *Ukrainian National Home*, with its Ukrainian restaurant offering East European dishes.

Other evidence of the vitality of the Ukrainian population appears in the Ukrainian American Soccer Association (122 Second Ave), the Ukrainian American Youth Association (136 Second Ave). the Ukrainian Publishing Company (48 E. 7th St), and the **Ukrainian Museum** (203 Second Ave). Located between 12th and 13th Sts, the museum is open Wed 1–5 p.m.; Fri 3–7 p.m.; and Sat and Sun 1–5 p.m. Adults $1; children 50¢. It contains over 900 items illustrating the range of Ukrainian crafts: embroidered and woven textiles, pysanky (Easter eggs), ceramics, woodwork and metalwork. Tel: 228–0110.

Turn around and walk S. on Second Ave to E. 7th St; turn left (E.) and walk two blocks to Avenue A and **Tompkins Square Park,** named after Daniel Tompkins whose remains lie at St. Mark's-in-the Bowery, a 16-acre park whose walks, greenery, and playground equipment provide relief from the dreary surrounding tenements. Originally part of a salt marsh known as Stuyvesant Swamp, the land was given to the city by the Stuyvesant family in 1833. It served as a recruiting camp during the Civil War and witnessed riots during the financial panic of 1873. Its present population reflects the ethnic and racial mix of the neighbourhood: members of the Russian, Ukrainian, and Polish community, most of them older people, enjoy the benches and tables for chess and checkers along the S. side; younger people, many of them black or Puerto Rican, use the ball courts, skate on the walkways, and listen to music on their large, semi-portable radios and tape players.

Near the S.W. entrance to the park is a statue of Samuel Sullivan Cox, 'the letter carrier's friend', who earned this appellation as an Ohio congressman by sponsoring legislation that gave postmen pay rises and salaried vacations. The statue (1891; Louise Lawson) was commissioned by the mailmen of America and erected in Cooper Square where it occasioned criticism that the figure resembled a floor walker beckoning an approaching customer. When Saint-Gaudens's figure of Peter Cooper was installed there, congressman Cox was moved here.

Return to Avenue A. At the N.W. corner of the avenue and E. 7th St is the Leshko Coffee Shop, one of the remaining Polish restaurants in the area. Walk N. along the park on Avenue A. On the S.W. corner of E. 10th St and Avenue A is *St. Nicholas Carpatho Russian Orthodox Greek Catholic Church*, founded (1884) by the Rutherford-Stuyvesant family as St. Mark's Chapel.

The interior is distinguished by tiled walls, stained glass, and carved wooden beams.

Along the N. side of the park is a row of handsome houses built in 1846 when the Tompkins Square neighbourhood was felt to have an auspicious future. The houses on the S. side, built just a year later, were described at the time of completion as 'new and desirable tenements' but their ground floors were designed as stores to be rented for $200 a year, an indication of the coming decline of the area. By the 1850s German immigrants had begun to displace the previous residents and the one- and two-family houses were sliced up into rooming houses or razed to make way for profitable tenements. By the 1860s the area was described as dirty, seedy, and dusty; Fourth St between Avenues A and B was called 'Ragpickers' Row', while Eleventh St from First Ave to Avenue B became 'Mackerelville'.

Enter the park along the N. walkway near E. 10th St. About halfway through the park along the walkway is a small monument whose eroded features once depicted a boy and girl looking at a steamboat, a memorial to the victims of the 'General Slocum', an excursion steamer that burned in the East River on 15 June 1904. Some 1200 people, most of them women and children from this predominantly German neighbourhood, burned or drowned in the tragedy. Many men, kept home from the outing by their jobs, lost their entire families; for the bereaved the Tompkins Square neighbourhood became too painful, and an exodus to other German communities within the city followed the disaster. As the Germans moved out, Jews moved in, changing the ethnic character of the area within a few years.

The nearest subway is the BMT 14th St Local (LL train) at 14th St and First Ave. The IRT Lexington Ave Local (train 6) stops at Astor Pl. (E. 8th St and Fourth Ave). Bus M15 runs uptown on First Ave and downtown on Second Ave.

9   Greenwich Village

When Washington Square was still marshland traversed by Minetta Brook, an Indian settlement called Sapokanican stood in the general area of Greenwich Village. The Dutch pushed out the Indians and divided the land into large farms one of which, the Bossen Bouwerie (Wooded Farm) belonged to Wouter Van Twiller, second governor-general of the colony, a maladroit administrator whose particular liabilities were greed and a fondness for wine. Under the British the area became known as Greenwich (Green Village), a name that first appeared in city records in 1713. A few large landholders dominated the rural fields—Trinity Church which held considerable property in the W. Village S. of Christopher St, Captain Peter Warren, who purchased 300 acres in 1744, and such established families as De Lanceys, Lispenards, and Van Cortlandts. By the 1790s, however, as the city spread northward, in part fleeing epidemics of yellow fever and other diseases, the large estates were being broken up and sold as building lots or rented as leaseholds.

Between 1825–50 the population of the Village quadrupled. Since its inhabitants were predominantly native born, the area became known as the 'American Ward', a title that lost its accuracy toward the end of the century. By 1870 the Village had become something of a backwater, as fashionable commerce sweeping ever north along Broadway first enveloped the area and then left it behind. The well-to-do and socially ambitious middle class moved north; the immigrants moved in. First came the Irish and a black population who settled south of Washington Square, displaced in turn by an influx of Italians in the 1890s and a second, poorer, wave of Irish who settled around Sheridan Square. Profitable tenements replaced row houses, while shops and hotels were converted to warehouses or manufacturing lofts suitable for exploiting immigrant labour. The scars and some of the odd architectural beauties of this period are visible today.

Around the turn of the century, the Village entered its halcyon period. Because of its relative isolation, its historic charm, and the indifference of a foreign population who adhered to the spiritual precepts of the Roman Catholic church and the political dictates of Tammany Hall, the Democratic party machine, the Village offered a haven for the radical, avantgarde element of American society. Here were cheap rents and freedom from the late-Victorian sexual and materialistic attitudes that dominated middle-class American culture. Soon the place swarmed with radical social and artistic activity: Max Eastman founded 'The Masses' (1910), a radical paper whose publication was suppressed in 1918 because it opposed the war; the 'Seven Arts' (founded 1916), whose columns integrated political and artistic ideas met a similar fate. Clubs like the 'A' Club and the Liberal Club became forums for such inflammatory topics as women's suffrage, birth control, anarchy, and 'free love'.

Among theatre groups flourishing in the opening decades of the 20C were the Provincetown Players whose plays, staged in a converted stable on MacDougal St, displayed the talents of such playwrights and performers as Eugene O'Neill, Edna St. Vincent Millay, Susan Glaspell, and Bette Davis. The Theater Guild, which started as the Washington Square Players, moved uptown in 1919 and became an innovative force in the American theatre, producing new plays and hiring unknown actors. Resident Village writers included Sherwood Anderson, Theodore Dreiser, John Dos Passos, and Van Wyck Brooks as well as poets e.e. cummings, Hart Crane, and Marianne Moore.

The isolation of the Village, however, was at an end. Seventh Ave South was cut through south of Greenwich Ave and W. 11th St in 1919. Sixth Ave was extended south of Carmine St in the 1920s, and in the 1930s the IND subway joined the old IRT (opened 1904) linking the Village to the rest of the city. Real estate developers began tearing down the old row houses and replacing them with high rise, high rent apartments, a process that accelerated distressingly after World War II.

Though its high rents exclude the struggling, unrecognised artist, an aura of bohemianism still clings to the Village. Handbills along the streets advertise saxophone recitals, karate lessons, instruction in macrobiotic cooking, film festivals, and symposia by women composers. Because of its longstanding tolerance, the Village has a significant homosexual community and has been a seedbed for such controversial ideas as feminism and gay liberation, but it also attracts middle class and professional people who, perhaps because of the traditional Village sense of community, have frequently and visibly exercised themselves in political and social causes. It is this social diversity and sense of identity, along with its architectural charm, that makes Greenwich Village one of the city's most attractive areas.

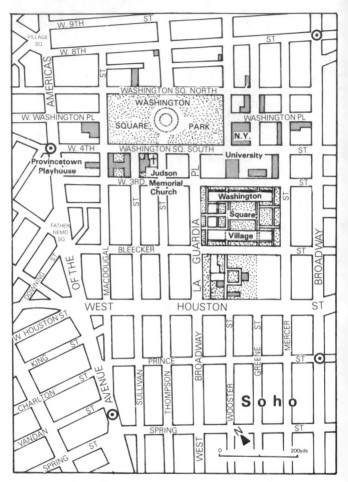

A. Washington Square, New York University, South Village, and the Charlton-King-Vandam Historic District

SUBWAY: IND Sixth and Eighth Ave lines (trains A, B, D, E, and F) to W. 4th St station.

BUS: M2, M3, M5, M6, M7. Culture Bus Loop II (weekends and holidays) to Stop 22 (Fifth Ave and 9th St) or Stop 23 (Sheridan Sq).

Begin at W. 8th St and Sixth Ave (Avenue of the Americas). Formerly the main shopping street of the Village, *W. 8th St* has become sleazy and rundown in recent years, its neighbourhood stores, art galleries, and studios giving way to fast food outlets, discount shoe shops, boutiques selling cheap clothing, and 'head shops' supplying the accessories of drug use. Concerned residents and business people are putting up a struggle, and the opening of a new bookshop and several neighbourhood restaurants may signal better times ahead.

Walk E. on W. 8th St. The *Eighth Street Playhouse* (52 W. 8th St), now an ordinary movie theatre, opened in 1928 as a showcase featuring the technological advances of architect Frederick J. Kiesler. Slide shows could be projected on the side walls and the main screen could be enlarged or reduced, innovations which failed to impress several successive owners who drastically altered Kiesler's work. Recently, however, the theatre has enjoyed something of a renaissance, both in its choice of films and in its physical condition.

Further along at No. 8 is the *New York Studio School of Drawing, Painting, and Sculpture*, occupying a peeling pink Art Deco building that once housed the collection of the Whitney Museum of Art, founded in 1931 by Gertrude Vanderbilt Whitney. Member of a well-to-do New York family and a sculptor herself, Mrs Whitney remodelled one of the stables in MacDougal Alley as a studio and gallery. From this beginning evolved the Studio Club and eventually the museum which remained here until 1949.
Return to the intersection of MacDougal St and W. 8th St.

Turn S. into MACDOUGAL ST, named after Alexander McDougall [*sic*], a successful merchant and political activist (died 1786). As a major general in the American Revolution, he succeeded Benedict Arnold commanding the defences at West Point; after the war he became first president of the Bank of New York.

The austere modern building on the W. side of the street (171 MacDougal St) is the *Tenth Church of Christ, Scientist* (1967; Victor Christ-Janer). Directly opposite the church is MACDOUGAL ALLEY, a private, dead-end street overhung by the bulky apartment building at No. 2 Fifth Ave. The houses, now remodelled in a variety of styles ranging from vaguely Federal to pseudo-Tudor, were built in the 1850s as stables for homes on W. 8th St and Washington Square and were converted to residences during the 1920s and 1930s. Gertrude Vanderbilt Whitney's studio was at No. 19.

Continue half a block S. on MacDougal St to Waverly Place, renamed in 1833, the year after Sir Walter Scott's death, from his famous novel. The house at 108 Waverly Place (half a block W. of MacDougal St) dates from 1826 but was altered to its present odd, crenellated form in 1906 by architect Charles C. Haight. War correspondent and novelist Richard Harding Davis (1864–1916) lived here during his early newspaper days.

Turn left and walk along the N. side of Washington Square Park. Throughout the 19C, attractive rowhouses faced the square on three sides, but now only **Washington Square North** suggests the former dignity and gentility of the neighbourhood. The row here, on the W. portion of the street, was developed (late 1820s–50s) by individual owners, and the houses reflect various styles—Federal, Greek Revival, and Italianate. Nos 21–23 are Greek Revival mansions (1835–36) with fine freestanding columned doorways, long parlour windows, and elegant ironwork. The parlour window balcony on No. 21 with anthemion and Greek key motifs combined on a wheel is especially handsome.

The earliest house on the square (No. 20) is one of the city's few remaining Federal mansions, constructed 1828–29 as a country residence for George P. Rogers and converted into apartments in 1880 by Henry Hardenbergh, architect of the Plaza Hotel. The keystone and blocks in the arched doorway and the panels in the lintels are decorated with a bold vermiform design. The building is owned by the Catholic church and houses a center for senior citizens in the basement and dormitories for nuns on the upper stories.

The original buildings from No. 18 east to Fifth Ave have been demolished, including two matching Rhinelander family mansions and Henry James's grandmother's Greek Revival house (No. 18), which provided the setting for his novel 'Washington Square'. In 1951 the entire site with adjoining property on Fifth Ave was sold for an apartment house to the dismay of Villagers who then waged an early territorial battle against wanton development of their neighbourhood. The only concession the developers made was to scale down the wing facing the park, but the result is bland mediocrity.

Cross Fifth Ave to the E. One of the architectural jewels of this part of the Village is the group of houses extending from Fifth Ave east to University Place, Nos 1–13 Washington Square North, known simply and snobbishly as *'**The Row.**' Built in 1831–33 on land belonging to Sailors' Snug Harbor, they form one of the city's first examples of controlled urban design.

Sailors' Snug Harbor, a foundation for the benefit of aged and decrepit seamen, came into existence under the will of Robert Richard Randall (died 1801). His father, Thomas Randall, a ship's captain and privateer, amassed a large fortune before leaving the seas for a sedate mercantile career. Among his assets was a large plot of land running N. and E. from the foot of Fifth Ave, a tract which his son enlarged and bequeathed to endow a home for impoverished sailors. In 1801 the land was valued at 25 thousand dollars, but by the beginning of the 20C it had appreciated to a value of 50 million dollars. The original sailors' home, supported by income from this land, is now a Designated Landmark on Staten Island, although the sailors themselves have moved to a new facility in North Carolina. Sailors' Snug Harbor headquarters remains nearby at 262 Greene St.

In 1831 builders James Boorman, John Johnston, and John Morrison leased the land for the row from Sailors' Snug Harbor with certain stipulations: that the houses be set back 12 ft from the front lot line, that they be brick or stone, that they be at least three stories high, and that stables or carriage houses be provided only if they were not used for slaughterhouses, tallow chandleries, forges, or other offensive businesses. Thus the row of fine Greek Revival houses (built 1831–33) forms one continuous, monumental streetscape.

The fronts are red brick; the basement stories and trim are marble, as are the freestanding porches and massive balustrades—a feature of only the most elegant houses. Along the street runs an iron fence with anthemia, lyres, and Greek key motifs. Yet even this fine row has not escaped alteration. The house at No. 3 is a Victorian replacement. In 1939 Sailors' Snug Harbor gutted the interiors of Nos 7–13 and converted them to apartments to increase the income from the property.

Among the famous residents of the row have been Edith Wharton, William Dean Howells, and John Dos Passos, who wrote 'Manhattan Transfer' at No. 3.

At the corner of Washington Square North and University Place, cross over to the park and walk back (S.W.) along the diagonal path.

Washington Square Park was once marshland through which Minetta Brook wandered on its way to the Hudson River. Its first inhabitants, after the Indians, were some black slaves, freed by the Dutch beginning in 1644 and granted land for farming in this vicinity. Toward the end of the 18C it became a potters' field and a hanging ground. In 1826 the field was converted to a parade ground and began to attract crowds more genteel than those who had enjoyed the public hangings of earlier times. In 1827 the park was laid out and shortly thereafter fashionable homes began rising along its borders. In 1837 New York University built its first building on the

E. side of the park, a handsome Gothic Revival building that added its own distinction to the neighbourhood.

In the early 1950s Robert Moses, city Parks' Commissioner, power broker, and highway advocate, decided to push a highway over, under, or through the park to ease the flow of traffic downtown on Fifth Ave, a project that Villagers fought for almost a decade, this time with a successful outcome. In 1958 the park was closed temporarily to traffic (before that time buses had used it as a turnaround), and later the traffic prohibition became permanent, making way for the present redesign of the park (1971; Robert Nichols, landscape architect; Edgar Tafel & Assocs, service buildings; Cityarts Workshop, mosaic plaza).

Today the park swarms with activity during good weather: parents and children, students, chess players, roller skaters (in defiance of posted notices), and the inevitable representatives of the city's distressed and derelict population all coexist in uneasy harmony.

Near the intersection of the diagonal walk and the central cross walk is a rather stiff *statue of Giuseppe Garibaldi* (1888; Giovanni Turini) presented to the city by its Italian-American citizens; between 1851–53, the Italian revolutionary lived in exile on Staten Island. Directly W. of the statue across the central plaza is a heroic *bust of Alexander L. Holley* (died 1882), metallurgist, inventor, and engineer, who established the Bessemer steel process in America. The bronze bust (1889) by John Quincy Adams Ward is one of the finer works of the sculptor who endowed the city with more pieces of public sculpture than any other artist.

Walk N. to **Washington Arch** (designed 1892, dedicated 1895; Stanford White), which dominates the entrance to the park. The present grand marble arch replaces a temporary wooden one erected (1889) to commemorate the centennial of George Washington's inauguration as the nation's first president. William Rhinelander Stewart, who lived at No. 17 Washington Square North, collected $2765 from friends and had a triumphal arch built a near the foot of Fifth Ave to enhance the centennial parade. Onlookers were so pleased that the structure was perpetuated in marble.

The arch is 77 ft high; the piers are 30 ft apart, the arch opening is 47 ft high. The frieze is carved with a design of 13 large stars, 42 small stars, and the initial 'W' repeated at intervals between emblems of war and peace; in the spandrels of the arch are figures of Victory. On the N. side of the E. pier is a sculpture, 'Washington in War' (1916; Hermon A. MacNeil) depicting the commander-in-chief flanked by Fame (right) and Valour. On the W. pier is 'Washington in Peace' (1918; Stirling A. Calder), showing the statesman with Justice and Wisdom, holding a book inscribed 'exitus acta probat' ('the end justifies the deed').

Like most of the city's outdoor sculpture, the arch has been defaced by spray paint—in this case by political, religious, feminist, and racial slogans in several languages.

Cross Washington Square North and walk N. on Fifth Ave. A half block N. on the E. side of the avenue is WASHINGTON MEWS, a charming private alley. The buildings on its N. side were stables, as the configuration of the doors suggests, while those on the S. were built in the 1930s on land formerly part of the back gardens of the houses facing Washington Square.

Continue N. on Fifth Ave to the corner of Eighth St. The apartment tower (NO. 1 FIFTH AVE) on the S.E. corner (1929; Helmle, Corbett & Harrison and Sugarman & Berger) is a handsome Art Deco building with such 'Gothic' touches as stylised gargoyles, pointed window arches over the balconies, and simulated vertical piers achieved by using different colours of brick. During the 1920s the 'A' Club met at One Fifth Ave claiming among its politically and socially avant-garde members Rose O'Neill, inventor of the Kewpie doll, and Frances Perkins, later secretary of labour during Franklin D. Roosevelt's presidency.

Across Eighth St on the N.E. corner of the intersection are the *Brevoort Apartments*, whose name is the only reminder in this vicinity of a family that once owned and later dominated the land surrounding lower Fifth Ave. The Brevoorts' holdings, which came into the family as early as 1701, stretched north and south from about 8th to 13th Sts and east and west between Fourth and Sixth Aves.

Henry Brevoort, one of New York's few millionaires in the 1840s, built an elegant Greek Revival mansion on the corner of Fifth Ave and 9th St, partly with the proceeds from real estate sales. The house became famous as the site of a scandalous masked ball during which two of the guests took advantage of their disguises to elope, circumventing parental disapproval. After this incident masked balls were forbidden for a while and the sponsors of such dangerous entertainments became liable for fines of up to $1000.

The famous Brevoort Hotel (opened 1854) later stood on the site of the present Brevoort Apartments, a quiet, aristocratic hotel noted for its cuisine and its appeal to English tourists. While the upstairs dining room catered to an expensively sedate uptown clientele, the basement café became a gathering place for the Village's Bohemian population and the site of various extravagant parties, climaxed on the eve of Prohibition when the hotel's liquor was sold at wholesale prices to an overflow crowd.

Walk E. on Eighth St. The unusual row of houses, Nos 6–26 E. Eighth St (best seen from the N. side), are apartments remodelled by Harvey Wiley Corbett in 1916. Corbett, remembered for the Criminal Courts Building (the old 'Tombs') and his work at Rockefeller Center, has here transformed a row of 19C Greek Revival houses in a picturesque, stagy manner, altering rooflines and window shapes, decorating the facades with brickwork, stucco, and wrought iron.

Continue E. to the corner of University Place. *The Cookery* (21 University Place) on the N.E. corner of the intersection is one of the Village's established jazz clubs. Turn S. and walk back to Washington Square. The remodelled row houses at the E. entrance to Washington Mews belong to N.Y.U. (as do several of the houses within the mews) and serve the French and German departments.

Continue S. on University Place across Waverly Place to the Main Building of *New York University*, founded in 1831 by a group of business and professional men including Albert Gallatin, secretary of the Treasury under Thomas Jefferson. The university—nonsectarian and modern—was to offer practical as well as classical courses to a middle class student body, providing an alternative to Episcopalian and conservative Columbia College. Among its early faculty members were John W. Draper, professor of chemistry and physiology, who is credited with making the first photographic portrait of the human face, and Samuel F.B. Morse, painter and sculptor, known now as the inventor of the telegraph and of Morse code.

The main building replaces a beautiful Gothic Revival structure built to resemble King's College Chapel in Cambridge, England, and torn down in

1894. Rooms in its tower were rented to students, including Winslow Homer, Walt Whitman, and inventor Samuel Colt, who worked there on the revolver ultimately named after him.

During the early 1960s, N.Y.U. gained an unsavoury reputation for its rampant territorial expansion and its disregard for existing Village architecture. In 1964 the university hired architects Philip Johnson and Richard Foster to produce a master plan that would unify the campus and put an end to its haphazard growth, but the plan the architects eventually submitted unfortunately resulted in a group of bulky, self-important buildings faced with bright red sandstone. It was planned to reface the buildings on the E. side of the square with the same stone, but the soaring building costs made the plan too costly and, happily, it has been scrapped.

Continue past the main building to Washington Place and turn left. The S.W. corner of the building (entrance at 33 Washington Pl.) has been refurbished as the *Grey Gallery*, and offers interesting, unusual art exhibitions (tel: 598–3479 for information).

The next building on Washington Place, now called the BROWN BUILDING of N.Y.U., was built in 1900 as a manufacturing loft, the Asch Building. Touted as fireproof, it proved tragically flammable for on 25 March 1911 a fire broke out in the upper stories where the Triangle Shirtwaist Company employed a large number of Italian and Jewish immigrant girls. Before the fire was brought under control, 146 workers perished, most of them jumping to their death on the street 10 stories below. Mass meetings held on the Lower East Side where most of the victims lived resulted in improved fire safety regulations and working conditions for sweatshop employees. A plaque on the S.E. corner of the building commemorates the victims.

The building at 10 Washington Pl., half a block E., demonstrates how attractive the cast iron and granite loft buildings must have been in their prime. This building (1891; Richard Berger) was restored in 1972 under direction of master-plan architects Johnson and Foster. The facade is pink granite; the decoration terracotta. Toward the end of the 19C, as the village waned in elegance, numerous manufacturing lofts were built to take advantage of the cheap labour pouring into the Lower East Side, several of which are evident in the blocks between Greene St and Broadway to the E.

Visible on the S.W. corner of Broadway and Washington Pl. is the André and Bella Meyer Physics Hall (1971; Philip Johnson and Richard Foster), one of the bright red sandstone towers of the master-plan.

Both Mercer and Greene Sts are named after Revolutionary War generals: Nathanael Greene from Rhode Island and Hugh Mercer, born in Scotland.

Turn S. (right) on Mercer St and walk to the intersection of W. 4th St. On the N.E. corner is the new home of *Hebrew Union College* (architects Abramovitz, Harris & Kingsland). *The Bottom Line*, across the street at 15 W. 4th St, is a popular cabaret theatre, offering jazz, rock, and folk music. Walk west on W. 4th St toward the park. Across from the Bottom Line is *Warren Weaver Hall*, housing the Courant Institute of Mathematical Sciences, an early N.Y.U. effort at contemporary architecture (1966; Warner, Burns, Toan & Lunde). Next to it is *Tisch Hall* (1972; Philip Johnson and Richard Foster), another product of the master plan. At the W. end of the plaza in front of it is a Gothic finial removed from the original N.Y.U. Gothic Revival building on Washington Square. Continue to the intersection of

Washington Square East. The third red sandstone tower is the *Elmer Holmes Bobst Library* (1973; Philip Johnson and Richard Foster).

Beyond the library is La Guardia Place, named after Fiorello Henry La Guardia, mayor between 1934–45, known for his fighting spirit and ferocious temper, his boundless energy and ambition, and his facility in seven languages. Born on Varick St in 1882 to a Jewish mother and an Italian father, married first to a Catholic and then a Lutheran, La Guardia was a living example of his city's ethnic diversity. He was a liberal, a reformer, and an irate opponent of graft; he died in 1947 of cancer, with only a small house in Queens and $8000 to show for his years in office.

N.Y.U. occupies most of Washington Square South. The *Loeb Student Center* (1959; Harrison & Abramovitz) at the intersection of La Guardia Pl. has aluminum sculptural forms by Reuben Nakian (born 1889) on the facade. The building stands on the site of Marie Blanchard's famous boarding house (demolished in 1948?) whose roster of famous occupants has been said to include Adelina Patti, Theodore Dreiser, Willa Cather, O. Henry, and Eugene O'Neill. John Reed, later the author of 'Ten Days that Shook the World', described the so-called 'house of genius' as sheltering 'inglorious Miltons by the score and Rodins ... one to every floor.' Next to the Loeb Center is the *Generoso Pope Catholic Center* (1964; Eggers & Higgins).

Cross Thompson St to the **Judson Memorial Church** (1892; McKim, Mead & White; DL), named by its founder Edward Judson after his father Adinoram Judson (1788–1850), first Baptist missionary to Burma and compiler of an English-Burmese dictionary. The younger Judson turned his missionary zeal to city dwellers and from its inception this church has involved itself in urban problems.

Designed by Stanford White, the building and adjoining square bell tower are generally Romanesque Revival in style, built of amber Roman brick with terracotta mouldings and panels of coloured marble. The auditorium (open weekdays, 9–5, restricted summer hours) bears evidence of its former splendour. The stained glass windows are by John La Farge (best seen during the middle of the day); the marble relief on the S. wall, executed by Herbert Adams, follows designs by Augustus Saint-Gaudens.

The bell tower once held a charitable house for children, supported in part by revenue from Judson Hall, the apartment building directly to the W. Both tower and hall are now residences for N.Y.U.

Next to Judson Hall is the *Hagop Kevorkian Center for Near Eastern Studies* (1973; Philip Johnson and Richard Foster). The quadrangle of bland red Neo-Georgian buildings across Sullivan St to the W. is the *Vanderbilt Law School of N.Y.U.* (1951; Eggers & Higgins).

Continue W. a block to MacDougal St and turn left (S.). Formerly a magnetic tourist attraction, full of boutiques, coffeehouses, small bars and restaurants, this stretch of MacDougal St has become seedy, although traces of happier times still linger. The *Provincetown Playhouse* (133 MacDougal St, S. of the intersection of Washington Square S.) is an American theatrical landmark.

In 1915 the Provincetown Players, a group of struggling actors and writers, formed a summer theatre on Cape Cod. The following year Eugene O'Neill joined them, bringing along a suitcaseful of plays. One of them, 'Bound East for Cardiff', achieved such success that the group opened a New York season in 1916 using the parlour floor of a house at 139 MacDougal St. In 1917 they remodelled a stable and bottling works at 133 MacDougal St into a theatre seating 182 people. Among the plays first produced here were Edna St. Vincent Millay's 'Aria da Capo', and 'The Emperor Jones', and 'The Hairy Ape', by O'Neill, whose work changed the shape of American drama.

Next door was the Liberal Club housed in rooms upstairs at 137 MacDougal St, organised as 'a meeting place for those interested in New Ideas'. Downstairs in the same building was Polly Holliday's restaurant, a famous eating and meeting place for artists and intellectuals. Polly's lover, anarchist Hippolyte Havel, who served as cook and waiter, gave the place its own cachet by shouting insults such as 'Bourgeois pigs' at the patrons, who nonetheless remained loyal; Polly later moved her restaurant around the corner to 147 West 4th St. Another popular watering place at the corner of West 4th St and Sixth Ave was the Golden Swan, known by its intimates as the Hell Hole, whose clientele included thugs and Bohemians, and which later provided the setting and characters for O'Neill's 'The Iceman Cometh'.

The small Federal houses at 127–131 MacDougal St, next to the theatre, their facades altered for commercial purposes, were built on speculation in 1829 for Aaron Burr, who invested heavily but with little success in Greenwich real estate. The original pineapple newel post, symbolic of hospitality, remains at No. 129.

Across the street and a half block S. (130–32 MacDougal St) is an unusual double house (1852; DL) with an ironwork portico.

Continue S. on MacDougal St. The next intersection on the right is *Minetta Lane*, named from the Minetta Brook which flowed from former hills near 23rd St to the Hudson near Charlton St. Once famous for its trout, the brook was called Mintje Kill ('little stream') by the Dutch and the name was later anglicised to its present form. Minetta St, which intersects Minetta Lane a half block W., follows the course of the brook.

On the S.W. corner of MacDougal St and Minetta Lane is the *Minetta Tavern* (113 MacDougal St), whose walls are covered with pictures of illustrious clients.

The tavern's most famous patron was Joe Gould, Bohemian poet and writer. Born to an old New England family and duly sent to Harvard (class of 1911), Gould lived in the Village by his wits and on the charity of friends for more than 30 years, gathering material for his ambitious work, 'An Oral History of Our Time' (sometimes called 'An Oral History of the World'). The work, consisting of innumerable conversations, some of them overheard, was reputed to have reached 11 million words when Gould died in a mental institution in 1957. Though it was rumoured that he carried on his person a will leaving $2/3$ of the MS to Harvard and $1/3$ to the Smithsonian Institution, neither the will nor the work was ever found. The Lions' Club of the Village paid for Gould's funeral to which Ernest Hemingway sent gladioli.

Continue S. to BLEECKER ST, named after Anthony Bleecker, an early 19C man of letters and owner of the land ceded to the city for the street. The Chinese restaurant on the N.W. corner of the intersection occupies the site of the old *San Remo Cafe*, a favourite literary hangout during the 1940s and 1950s. The *Café Borgia* (185 Bleecker St) and *Le Figaro* (186 Bleecker St) are among the Village's better known coffee houses, institutions that flourished during the 'beatnik' period of the 1950s when Jack Kerouac and Allen Ginsberg reigned as culture heroes and such entertainments as poetry reading with or without jazz accompaniment enlivened the premises. The coffee houses that have survived the waning of this culture still offer espresso, snacks, and a setting for conversation. Other examples of the genre include the Peacock Caffé (149 West 4th St), the Caffè Reggio (119 MacDougal St) and the Caffè Dante (81 MacDougal St).

Cross Bleecker St and walk a half block S. Here begins one of Greenwich Village's small Historic Districts, the *MacDougal-Sullivan Gardens Historic District* consisting of 24 houses (1844–50) sharing a common back garden. In the mid-19C this land, bounded by MacDougal, Bleecker, Houston, and Sullivan Sts, belonged to Nicholas Low, a banker, large scale land speculator, and legislator, who subdivided the property and built the houses as an investment. Although a large immigrant population altered the social makeup of the neighbourhood in the late 19C, the Low family resisted the temptation to tear down their houses and replace them with more profitable tenements. Then in 1920 William Sloane Coffin, scion of the W. & J. Sloane furniture company, hit upon the idea of modernising old row houses to provide moderate cost housing for professional people. He bought the block and converted the buildings to apartments, selling off the houses facing Bleecker and Houston Sts to finance the project.

Although the facades of the buildings have been significantly altered, the district remains interesting as an example of early urban renewal and for the creation of a single common garden from small individual plots.

Return to Bleecker St and turn right (E.).

Cross Sullivan St (named after Brigadier General John Sullivan, a commander in the Revolutionary War).

The *Circle in the Square* (159 Bleecker St) got its name from an earlier theatre in Sheridan Square where plays were presented in the round. It offers classic and contemporary plays and has grown to include an uptown branch on 50th St.

Across the street at 160 Bleecker St is the massive *Atrium* apartment building (1896; Ernest Flagg), designed by the architect of the much lamented Singer Tower and other elegant buildings. It opened as the Mills Hotel offering rooms for about 20¢ a day to 'gentlemen' of modest means, including Theodore Dreiser. Its 1500 small rooms faced either the streets or the open, grassy interior courts. Eventually the building deteriorated into the Greenwich Hotel, whose sad clientele stood around the sidewalks with wine bottles concealed in paper bags. In 1976 the building was converted into apartments and its interior courts reconstructed. The *Village Gate* cabaret-theatre in the basement opened in 1958 and has become a standby.

Continue E. on Bleecker St across Thompson St, named after another Revolutionary War general; William Thompson from Pennsylvania. The *Bleecker Street Playhouse,* (144 Bleecker St) now a movie theatre presenting foreign and classic films, owes its elegant facade to architect Raymond Hood, guiding spirit behind Rockefeller Center. The building once housed Mori's, a restaurant founded by Placido Mori in 1884. Hood converted two row houses in 1913 and added the present facade in 1919.

Continue E. along Bleecker St to the massive apartment complexes across La Guardia Place. Named *Washington Square Village* and *University Village* in utter disregard of their architectural and social realities, the buildings, most of them owned by N.Y.U., tower above the surrounding streets. The oldest group (1956–58; S.J. Kessler, Paul Lester Weiner) are institutional in feeling; the newer buildings (S. of Bleecker St, 1966; I.M. Pei & Partners) have been admired for their design and for the technological achievement of their cast-in-place concrete. In the center of the Pei group is a monumental sculpture after a design (1934) by Picasso, entitled 'Portrait of Sylvette'. The original, representing the profile of a girl wearing a ponytail, was only 2 ft high, painted on a piece of bent metal. The present adaptation (1968) by Carl Nesjar is 36 ft high and is made of concrete with black basalt aggregate revealed by sandblasting.

Walk S. to Houston St and turn right. The name *Houston* (its first syllable is pronounced 'house') is a corruption of *Houstoun*, after William Houstoun, a Georgia delegate to the Continental Congress (1784–86), who got a New York street named for him by marrying the daughter of Nicholas Bayard III, owner of the land where the W. part of the street now runs.

Walk W. to the intersection of Sullivan St. On the S. side of Houston St is the *Church of St. Anthony of Padua*. During the first two weeks of June this church sponsors the Feast of St. Anthony of Padua, beginning with a procession during which the saint's image is carried through the streets and followed by an open air fair in the evenings with rides, carnival games, and staggering quantities of Italian street food.

Continue W. on Houston St to Sixth Ave (Avenue of the Americas), slashed through the irregular network of village streets S. of Carmine St in the 1920s, creating a freeway for traffic and a free-for-all for pedestrians, and leaving a swath of mutilated buildings. The city has attempted to improve the situation (1976) by providing trees and benches, by converting some of the odd triangular spaces created by the avenue to vestpocket parks, and by repaving the street with asphalt and attractive concrete paving block.

Cross Sixth Ave and walk S. two blocks. In the area bounded on the N. by King St and on the S. by Vandam St is the second of the Village's small historic districts, the *Charlton-King-Vandam Historic District*, featuring Federal houses from the 1820s and 1830s.

History. In the 18C the district belonged to Abraham Mortier, who built (c. 1707) a fine mansion, Richmond Hill, on high ground overlooking the Hudson, Washington used it for his headquarters; John and Abigail Adams lived there while he was Vice-President in 1789; Aaron Burr bought it in 1793 to further his colossal social ambitions and entertained there lavishly. Never one to overlook his business interests, Burr had the estate mapped for development in 1797 and laid out the present Vandam, King, and Charlton Sts. In 1817, his political career long dead, he sold the property to John Jacob Astor who cut down the hill and rolled the mansion down to the S.E. corner of Charlton and Varick Sts. Astor sold off the land as 25 × 100-ft building lots to speculators who constructed the present houses. The first homeowners were lawyers, builders, and merchants whose livelihood was tied to the Hudson River wharves nearby. The mansion became a theatre, menagerie, and tavern, and was demolished in 1849.

The best preserved street in the district is *Charlton St* with the longest unbroken row of Federal houses in the city (N. side). Many are in pristine condition, retaining original details and features: brick facades laid in Flemish bond, doorway and window trim of modest brownstone, granite, or more refined marble, high stoops guarded by wrought iron railings sometimes with hollow cage newel posts, elegant panelled front doors surrounded by leaded top- and sidelights, steep roofs pierced by dormers. The rooflines were originally joined by a continuous cornice which, along with the similarities in scale, design, and materials, gave the row the unity and harmony typical of the best domestic architecture of the period.

Charlton, King, and Vandam Sts are all named after prominent early 19C New Yorkers. Dr John Charlton came from Britain with the troops in the Revolution, stayed after the war, and became president of the New York Medical Society. Rufus King was New York's first U.S. senator, a minister to Britain, and a candidate for the Vice-presidency. Anthony Van Dam was a 19C alderman.

The nearest subway stops are the IND at Sixth Ave and Spring St (uptown entrance in the S. side of the library building) and the IRT at W. Houston St and Varick St.

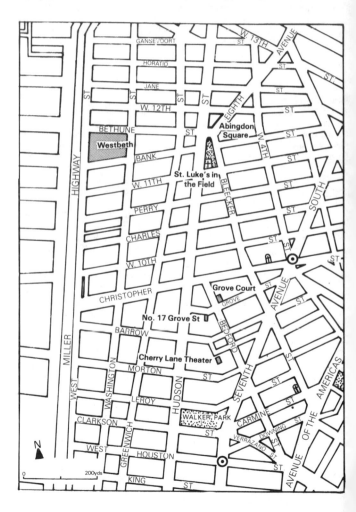

B. West Village from St. Luke's Place to Westbeth and Bank Street, Abingdon Square and Bleecker Street south to Carmine Street

SUBWAY: IRT Broadway–7th Ave local (train 1) to Christopher St-Sheridan Square or to W. Houston St.

BUS: M5, M6, or M10. Culture Bus (weekends and holidays), Loop II, Stop 24 (7th Ave S. and Barrow St).

The route begins at St. Luke's Place and Seventh Ave S.

ST. LUKE'S PLACE is one of New York's most beautiful streets, its finely maintained Italianate row houses breathing an aura of settled repose characteristic of much of the West Village.

Built in the early 1850s for prosperous merchants, many of whose livelihoods were tied to the Hudson River, the houses retain the red brick facades typical of the earlier Greek Revival style, but incorporate such fashionable Italianate details as brownstone trim, door hoods supported by carved consoles, bold cornices, tall stoops with rather elaborate cast iron railings, high rusticated basements, and deeply recessed doorways with double doors.

While the street has sheltered such people as Theodore Dreiser, Sherwood Anderson, Marianne Moore, and painter Paul Cadmus, its most famous resident was James J. ('Jimmy') Walker—popular, high-living mayor of New York from 1926 until his resignation under a cloud of fiscal scandal in 1932. Walker's home at No. 6 is still marked by two lanterns, a traditional way of indicating the mayor's residence. The playground across the gingko-lined street is *James J. Walker Park*, originally St. John's Burying Ground of Trinity Parish (which owned the W. Village up to Christopher St under a 1705 land grant from Queen Anne). In 1898, under the guidance of architects Carrère & Hastings, the deteriorating cemetery was dug up and landscaped as Hudson Park. During excavations, workers uncovered a stone marked 'Leroy' which romantic rumour claimed as the grave marker of Louis Charles, son of Louis XVI and Marie Antoinette, although the dauphin may have been smuggled out of prison after his parents' death, he surely did not die in Greenwich Village. Leroy St, of which St. Luke's Place is a segment, is named after Jacob Leroy, alderman and successful merchant.

Just inside the fence is an elaborate monument for Eugene Underhill and Frederick A. Ward, two firemen of Eagle Engine Company No. 13, who died in 1834 while performing their duties.

Visible across the park is the annex of the Food and Maritime Trades Vocational High School, which maintains the school ships moored at the Morton Street Pier (included later on this route).

Continue W. on St. Luke's Pl. to Hudson St and turn right (N.). One block N. is Morton St, named after Jacob Morton, a prominent early-19C lawyer. Turn right and walk E. on Morton St toward Bedford St.

Some of the houses on the W. end of Morton St, for example No. 68, remain from the early 19C, when the more modest houses of the West Village sheltered tradespeople and craftsmen, many of whom, like the sailmakers and building suppliers, were involved with the city's maritime trade. At No. 59 is a fine Federal doorway. Toward the E. end of the block, the smaller row houses give way to Old Law Tenements—bigger, bulkier, filling the entire building lot—constructed in the late 19C when the Village experienced the influx of a large Italian and Irish immigrant population.

Turn left at *Bedford St*, mapped before 1799 and named after its precursor in London. On the E. side of the block stands a row of early 19C houses (Nos 64–70) in fine condition, though suffering various alterations. James Vandenburgh, master mason of Trinity Church, lived at No. 68 in 1821, another reminder of Trinity's influence in the West Village. The house at No. 70 belonged first (c. 1807) to a sailmaker, John P. Roome. Across the street at 75^1/$_2$ Bedford St is a house only 9·5 ft wide, distinguished both as the narrowest house in the Village and as a residence of Edna St. Vincent Millay. Built in 1873, it was wedged into a former carriage alley; the ugly pink brick facing is a recent addition.

Edna St. Vincent Millay (1892–1950), poet, playwright, and actress, arrived in Greenwich Village in 1917, illuminating Bohemian society with her beauty and intoxicating personality. In 1923, when she won the Pulitzer prize, she married Eugen Boissevain and lived briefly in this house.

The *Isaacs-Hendricks House* next door (S.W. corner of Bedford and Commerce Sts) was built in 1799 by Joshua Isaacs and sold to his son-in-law Harmon Hendricks, a pioneer in the business of copper rolling and the New York agent for Paul Revere. Altered in 1836 and 1928, the house retains little of its original appearance, though the old clapboards are still visible from Commerce St. Both this building and the narrow house at 75^1/$_2$ Bedford St face the rear courtyard.

Turn left into Commerce St. Formerly called Cherry Lane, the street took its present name from the sudden arrival of many downtown business firms during the smallpox epidemic of 1822. The *Cherry Lane Theatre* (38 Commerce St) was founded in 1924 as an experimental theatre in what was a former brewery or malt house; it has evolved into an Off-Broadway house and still presents new and sometimes experimental plays. Around the sharp bend in the street (at *39 and 41 Commerce St*) are two remarkably elegant houses (built 1831 and 1832) facing one another across a central courtyard. Although local legend affirms that they were built by a sea captain for his two feuding daughters, land records attribute them to Peter Huyler, a milk seller. The mansard roofs were added in the 1870s.

At the intersection of Commerce and Barrow Sts turn right and walk back to Bedford St; turn left. The inhospitable looking building part way up the block (86 Bedford St) is *Chumley's* restaurant, a hangover from Prohibition days when, disguised as a garage, it operated as a speakeasy, catering to such notables as Edna St. Vincent Millay and John Dos Passos. In commemoration of those clandestine times, the restaurant does not advertise its presence with a sign, although the liquor license is visible through the barred window.

The attractive small apartment house diagonally opposite (95 Bedford St) was built in 1894 (Kurzer & Kohl) as a stable for J. Goebel & Co., dealers in wine. It was converted to a residence in 1927.

Continue to the corner of Bedford and Grove Sts. The clapboard house at 17 GROVE ST (N.E. corner of the intersection) was built in 1822 by William Hyde, a window sash maker. Although the house has been considerably altered—a Greek Revival doorway added in the 1830s or 1840s, a third story with ginger-bread cornice in 1870, and an obtrusive fire escape later—it is still the most intact of the Village's few wood frame houses. Behind it at 100 Bedford St stands Hyde's workshop (1833), a small, picturesque building erroneously rumoured to have been a slave quarters. Clifford Daily, whose greatest project stands next door, 'renovated' it in the 1920s using mouldings and other trim salvaged from demolished 19C houses.

The bizarre house known as 'TWIN PEAKS' (102 Bedford St) was built in 1830 as an ordinary frame house. Designer Clifford Daily, who felt that local artists were being 'herded into barracks . . . with the result that the Village is growing into a desert of mediocrity with nothing of inspiration to Villagers who depend a great deal on their surroundings for inspiration', persuaded financier Otto Kahn to undertake renovation of the house which would be turned over to artists, writers, and actors who could then live in inspirational surroundings free from financial pressures. The resulting house, said to be a replica of a house in Nuremberg, contains bricks from the old Madison Square Garden, the Brevoort Hotel, a Second Ave tenement and an upper West Side apartment. The opening ceremonies of this stuccoed, gabled, and half-timbered extravagance were held in 1926; Princess Amelia Troubetzky sat on one of the peaks making a burnt offering of acorns (presumably to the god Pan) while actress Mabel Normand sat atop the other peak christening the building with the customary bottle of champagne.

Return to the corner of Grove and Bedford Sts; walk W. toward the river. This block, between Bedford and Hudson Sts, is especially attractive, with a row of vine-covered Greek Revival houses (Nos 14–16 were built in 1840 by Samuel Winant and John Degraw), followed by a group of Federal houses (Nos 4–10 date from 1834; James N. Wells, builder), which retain many original features: hand-wrought ironwork including boot scrapers in the stoop fences at Nos 6 and 8, small dormers, and panelled doorways. Between Nos 10 and 12 is the entrance to one of the Village's hidden architectural enclaves, GROVE COURT, a group of shuttered brick houses built in 1853–54 as dwellings for workmen. Remarkable for its quiet and graciousness, the court has a more boisterous past, having been called at different times Mixed Ale Alley and Pig's Alley.

Follow Grove St to Hudson St. Directly across the intersection is *St. Luke's in the Fields* (1822; James N. Wells builder), formerly St. Luke's Chapel of Trinity Parish. In March 1981 the church was severly damaged by fire and is currently undergoing restoration. It is the city's third oldest church behind St. Paul's Chapel and St. Mark's-in-the-Bowery and reflects the austerity of the Federal style adapted for a rural setting. Built of brick rather than the more customary rubble stone, St. Luke's has a low, bulky square tower unadorned with a steeple, and its park-like setting, surviving from the builder's original plan, still gives it a pastoral atmosphere. In its early years, the church was flanked by 14 townhouses planned by Wells, of which six remain (Nos 473–477 and 487–491 Hudson St, all built in 1825) as does the handsome vicarage in the churchyard. The buildings and playground of St. Luke's School (founded 1894) now occupy much of the park.

The church was founded independently by local residents with financial aid from wealthy Trinity Parish, but when in the late 19C the neighbourhood was overwhelmed by immigrants, the fashionable congregation built a new church uptown on Convent Ave at W. 141st St, and Trinity Parish bought this one and reopened it in 1893.

St. Luke's was for a long time the source of Leake's Dole, a weekly gift of bread to poor parishioners who attended the 10 o'clock Saturday service, provided by a bequest in the will of John Leake (died 1792) who left a thousand pounds 'put out at interest to be laid out in the annual income in sixpenny wheaten loaves of bread and distributed . . . to such poor as shall appear most deserving.'

Walk N. on Hudson St. A plaque on No. 487, now the parish house of St. Luke's, marks the building as writer Bret Harte's boyhood home. Continue along Hudson St with its antique shops featuring 19C Americana and flea market curiosities. Just E. of the intersection with Christopher St is the *Theatre de Lys* (121 Christopher St), where Kurt Weill's 'Three-penny Opera' was revived with smashing success in the 1950s. Turn W. (left) on Christopher St and walk towards the river.

Because of its generally permissive attitudes, the Village has long had a visible homosexual community, now centered on Christopher St in the West Village, where a number of shops and boutiques cater to gay tastes. In 1969 a confrontation between gays and police in the now defunct Stonewall Inn near Sheridan Square is said to have sparked the drive for civil rights for homosexuals.

Continue W. on Christopher St. The 10-story dark brick building filling the block bounded by Washington, Greenwich, Christopher, and Barrow Sts was originally the **U.S. Appraiser's Stores** (1899; Willoughby J. Edbrooke and others; DL), a warehouse for goods passing through customs. Later it served as a federal archives building and a post office; at present it is slated for residential renovation. Imposing in scale and massive in appearance, it typifies the Romanesque Revival style at its best, with strong brick arches at ground level, rounded corner turnings, and successive bays of arched windows.

On the N. side of Christopher St between Greenwich and Washington Sts is *St. Veronica's Roman Catholic Church*, built c. 1900.

Continue walking W. on Christopher St straight ahead to the river. The *Morton Street pier*, at the foot of Christopher and Morton Sts, renovated and provided with benches and modest amounts of greenery, has become a favoured spot for strolling and sunbathing. The two ships, 'John W. Brown' and 'John W. Brown II', permanently moored here belong to the Board of Education and are used as training ships by the High School of Maritime Trades.

During the early 19C the New York State Prison was located on landfill just N. of Christopher Street and, oddly, was considered an ornament to the neighbourhood. In 1828–29, after serving as a terror to evil-doers for a full quarter of a century (according to Moses King's 1893 handbook), the prison was closed and its inmates moved up the river to Sing Sing in Ossining, New York.

Return to Christopher St and walk inland a half block. Weehawken St, one of the city's shortest, is named after the Weehawken Market, a former distribution point where New Jersey farmers (presumably including some from Weehawken) brought their produce. The curious old house at No. 6 dates, in part, back to the 18C.

Continue along Weehawken St to W. 10th St; turn right and walk E. to Washington St. The large apartment building on the N.E. corner of the intersection with its bold Romanesque Revival facade of brick and unfinished stone was originally *Everhard's Storage Warehouse* (built c. 1894), renovated as Shepherd House in 1978.

Walk N. along Washington St. The WEST VILLAGE HOUSES (1974; Perkins & Will), stretching along Washington St from W. 10th St to Bank St, represent the outcome of another territorial struggle between Village activists and the city bureaucracy. Led by Jane Jacobs, whose book 'The Life and Death of American Cities' has become a classic, local residents succeeded in having the scale of a proposed high rise development reduced, but the resulting walkups are grimly institutional and bleak, with windowless walls facing blankly out on Washington St.

Continue N. along Washington St.

Turn right at Charles St. The Gendarme Arms, a half block inland from Washington St (135 Charles St) occupies the *former Sixth Precinct Station House* (1895; John Du Fais) and offers another example of the conversion of older, commercial or public buildings to new, often residential uses. Continue E. on Charles St to the next intersection at Greenwich St. The *Sven Bernhard Residence* (121 Charles St) on the N.E. corner is an oddly rural house with wide clapboards, old double hung windows, and unexpected angles and proportions. Tucked away on a small triangular plot amidst larger commercial buildings, the house, which may date from the 18C, has been moved twice to its present location, most recently (1968) from York Ave and 71st St where it was a back house with no street frontage. When the building was threatened with demolition, the owner purchased this small piece of land and had the house trucked here through 5 miles of city streets. Return to Washington St.

Continue N. along Washington St to Bank St, once an important financial center. In 1798 the Wall Street Bank of New York established a branch bank on a nameless Greenwich Village lane to be used for emergencies (the downtown branch was threatened with quarantine for yellow fever); during the smallpox epidemic of 1822 other banks came for similar reasons.

The bulky industrial building filling the block between Bank and Bethune Sts is WESTBETH (1900; Cyrus L. W. Eidlitz), renovated in 1965 by Richard Meier, a pioneer in the reuse of old buildings. After the Bell Telephone Company moved its laboratories from this site to New Jersey, the building was converted to studios and artists' housing, an experiment so successful that similar conversions have opened up several new neighbourhoods in downtown Manhattan.

Along the N. side of Westbeth runs *Bethune Street*, named after Johanna Graham Bethune, a 19C educator and philanthropist whose charitable works included opening New York's first school for 'young ladies', and ceding to the city the land for Bethune St.

Gansevoort St, four blocks N. of Bethune St, forms the S. border of the GANSEVOORT MARKET, the city's wholesale meat district (bounded roughly on its other sides by 14th St, Ninth Ave, and the Hudson River). Hectic and noisy, crowded into a clutter of 19C buildings and small streets, the Gansevoort Market is descended from two major 19C markets: the West Washington Market at the foot of W. 12th St, through whose handsome buildings and piers arrived cargoes of produce from southern and Caribbean ports as well as the city's oyster supply; and the old Gansevoort Market across from it, a large paved area where New Jersey and Long Island farmers drove their market wagons to await the beginning of the 4 a.m. workday. Herman Melville, author of 'Moby Dick,' worked as a customs inspector on the former Gansevoort Dock for 19 years beginning in 1866, his literary career apparently in ruins.

Gansevoort St is named after Peter Gansevoort (1749–1812), officer in the American Revolution and later brigadier general in the U.S. army.

Walk inland (E.) on Bethune St. The block between Washington and

Greenwich Sts is lined with handsome Greek Revival houses. Nos 19–29 were built in 1837 by Henry S. Forman and Alexander Douglass. Those at Nos 24–34 date from 1845, (builder Alexander R. Holden). Note the unusual ironwork anthemion motifs on the door at No. 25.

Continue E. on Bethune St to *Abingdon Square* (intersection of Hudson, Greenwich and Bethune Sts and Eighth Ave), named after Charlotte Warren who married the Earl of Abingdon. Although many British place names were changed in 1794, after due consideration by the city council, Abingdon Square's name was allowed to remain because the earl and his wife had been sympathetic to the American revolution.

One of Greenwich's great 18C landholders was Charlotte's father, Admiral Sir Peter Warren, who owned some 300 acres and built a handsome mansion on the block now bounded by Charles, Perry, Bleecker, and Washington (?) Sts. A true adventurer, Warren went to sea as a 12 year old, rose to his own command at age 24, made a fortune as a privateer, and married Susannah De Lancey. Before the Revolution he returned to England where he became an MP, and acquitted himself brilliantly in society. He died in 1752 at the age of 49 and is buried in Westminster Abbey. His three daughters inherited his estate, later divided by the Commissioners' Map of 1811 into small 12- and 15-acre farms. The manor house was demolished in 1865.

The *Abingdon Square playground*, imaginative and well-used, was designed in 1966 by Arnold Vollmer with assistance from the local community. To the N. of the playground is Abingdon Square itself, with the *Greenwich Village War Memorial* (1921; Philip Martiny), a bronze figure of an American soldier carrying a flag.

Leave Abingdon Sq. on the W.; walk W. on Bank St where there is an especially attractive group of 19C houses. The small top story windows of No. 76 Bank St (1839–42; Andrew Lockwood) are surrounded by cast-iron wreaths, a Greek Revival ornament seldom found today. Return to Bleecker St.

Turn left and walk S. on Bleecker St, one of the Village's most attractive shopping streets, with antique shops, boutiques, small restaurants, and other attractive, generally expensive places to spend money. At the intersection of Bleecker and W. 11th Sts, look a block W. to the *White Horse Tavern* (567 Hudson St at the corner of W. 11th St), a pleasant, old-fashioned bar (founded 1880) made famous by Dylan Thomas, who frequented it in the early 1950s, before his untimely death (1953) in St. Vincent's Hospital. Continue down Bleecker St; at the intersection of Christopher St, four blocks to the S., is one of the Village's few Art Deco buildings (95 Christopher St), a massive apartment house (1931; H.I. Feldman) executed in two tones of amber brick. A half block E. on Christopher St (81 Christopher St) stands *St. John's Evangelical Lutheran Church*, built in 1821 as the Eighth Presbyterian Church, and later St. Matthew's Protestant Episcopal Church. Like its denomination, the building has been altered several times, and now retains a Federal cupola above its grey, painted brownstone and sheet metal body. The church housed America's first Lutheran seminary.

Continue N.E. on Christopher St to Sheridan Square where there is a stop of the IRT Seventh Ave subway.

Diversion. Continue S. on Bleecker St. Just W. of the next intersection at Grove St is the former Samuel Whittemore residence (45 Grove St), once a grand late Federal mansion (c. 1830) situated on spacious grounds with stables and a hothouse. Although mutilated, the house retains its original arched doorway and iron torchières flanking the stoop.

At No. 59 Grove St (on the block E. of Bleecker St) the name of *Marie's Crisis* restaurant memorialises, though obscurely, political theorist Thomas Paine who died in a house on this site in 1809, a victim of social ostracism and poverty. His periodical, 'Crisis', was published during the Revolutionary War to propagandise for the colonial cause.

Follow Bleecker St S. across Seventh Ave. Visible from this intersection is Greenwich House at 27 Barrow St, a large neo-Federal building (1917; Delano & Aldrich) significant for its history rather than its appearance. Founded in 1902 by social worker Mary Kingsbury Simkhovitch, Greenwich House originally directed its major efforts toward the children of the densely concentrated immigrant and black population in the area around Jones St (a block S. of Barrow St)—a population which reached an appalling 975 people per acre around the turn of the century. Today Greenwich House continues to address itself to social problems, offering drug counselling programmes, a day care center for children, adult education, and activities and programmes for the elderly.

Barrow St is named after Thomas Barrow, a prominent early 19C artist. Originally named Reason St to honour Thomas Paine's 'The Age of Reason', the name degenerated to 'Raisin St', and was changed at the request of Trinity Church.

The section of Bleecker St between Seventh and Sixth Aves reflects the Italian population of the Village and is an attractive, lively street for household shopping; its bakeries, butchers, and grocery stores retain a strong ethnic appeal.

At the intersection of Bleecker and Carmine Sts, a block W. of Sixth Ave, is the *Church of Our Lady of Pompeii* (1926), which replaces a church where St. Francesca Xavier Cabrini (born 1850), first American citizen to be canonised, once worshipped. Mayor Fiorello La Guardia named the nearby square for Father Antonio Demo (died 1936), who served this church for 35 years.

The nearest subway is the Seventh Ave IRT at W. Houston and Varick Sts (walk S.W. two blocks on Downing St).

C. Sheridan Square to W. 14th Street

SUBWAY: IRT Broadway–7th Ave local (train 1) to Christopher St–Sheridan Square. IND Sixth Ave (trains B, D, F) or Eighth Ave (trains A, E) to W. 4th St station (walk W. on W. 4th St to Seventh Ave and Sheridan Square).

BUS: M10 or Culture Bus Loop II (weekends or holidays) to Stop 23 (Christopher St–Sheridan Square).

The route begins at *Sheridan Square*, a bleak triangle of asphalt bounded by Washington Place, Barrow, Grove, and W. 4th Sts (cross Seventh Ave to the IRT subway stop and walk a few yards along W. 4th St). *Christopher Park*, around the corner to the N., is often mistaken for Sheridan Square, primarily because it contains a *statue* (1936) of *General Philip Sheridan* (1831–88) by Joseph Pollia (1893–1954). Sheridan, successful Union general during the Civil War, and exterminator of the American Indian afterwards, was the unfortunate author of the remark that 'the only good Indians I saw were dead'.

Follow Christopher St N.E. to Waverly Place. Except for City Hall, the NORTHERN DISPENSARY (1831; Henry Bayard, carpenter and John C. Tucker, mason) is the only remaining public building from the Federal period in the city. Constructed of red brick, this austere, triangular building with its well-proportioned rows of double-hung windows, was originally two stories high. The addition of a third story (1854) can be detected by a line in the brickwork; the

cap-moulded lintels and the cornice (sheet metal, not stone) are also later additions.

Chartered in 1827 to offer free medical care to the poor (its most famous patient was Edgar Allan Poe, treated for a cold in 1837), it still functions as a public clinic. The vagaries of Greenwich Village geography make it possible for the building to have two different sides facing a single street and one side facing two streets, since Waverly Place forks at its S.E. corner and Christopher St joins Grove St along its N. facade.

Follow Waverly Pl. along the S. side of the dispensary to *Gay St*, still graced by several small, dormered Federal houses. During the mid-19C, Scottish weavers lived on this crooked, block-long street; off and on until about 1920 it was a residential enclave for the Village's black population. During Prohibition it was enhanced by the Pirate's Den, a speakeasy where the waiters reputedly refused to give change. Novelist Ruth McKenney (born 1911) who lived at No. 14, made it famous, writing an account of her adventures in the bohemia of the 1930s entitled 'My Sister Eileen', later adapted as the musical comedy 'Wonderful Town'.

Continue E. along Waverly Place. At No. 138 is a brick and

brownstone Gothic Revival townhouse (1895: George H. Streeton), formerly the rectory of St. Joseph's church around the corner, now the home of the Graymore Friars. At Sixth Ave (Avenue of the Americas), turn right. Down the block is *St. Joseph's Church* (1833; John Doran), the city's oldest Roman Catholic Church and one of its earliest Greek Revival church buildings. The main facade belongs to the emerging Greek Revival tradition, with its smooth surface, two large Doric columns, low pediment and frieze. The rubble stone masonry on the side walls, bold corner quoins, and tall, round-headed windows hark back to the Federal period. John McCloskey (1810–85), an early rector, became America's first cardinal.

The interior (open during services) is elegantly classical and well-preserved but suffers from the unfortunate later addition of stained glass windows.

Turn around and walk N. on Sixth Ave. At the intersection with W. 10th St stands the remarkable **Jefferson Market Courthouse** (1877; Vaux & Withers), now, after a long struggle with the forces of demolition, a branch of the New York Public Library system. Turreted, towered, gabled, carved, and further embellished with stained glass and ironwork, the building exemplifies Victorian Gothic architecture at its most flamboyant. Voted the nation's fifth most beautiful building in 1855, it stood empty from 1945 until 1967, when Giorgio Cavaglieri handsomely remodelled it for its present use.

The courthouse stands on the site of the Jefferson Market, one of the city's main food markets in the 19C. The old market (founded 1833) had a tall wooden fire tower with a bell to alert volunteer fire fighters, the precursor of the present main tower originally used for the same purpose. Assembly rooms above the market sheds were used for holding court. When the present courthouse was built, it became part of a complex that included a brick jail (also Victorian Gothic in style) and a reconstructed market building. In 1877 the jail was demolished and replaced by the infamous *Women's House of Detention* (1931; Sloan & Robertson), a massive, Art Deco building, long a village landmark or eyesore depending on the beholder's point of view. The women's prison, originally intended for the temporary detention of women awaiting trial, was more successful architecturally than socially. Conditions within it became deplorable and its grim bulk was heavy with unpleasant associations for Villagers, especially since the inmates could often be heard shouting out of the windows. In 1973–74 it was demolished, lamented only by architectural historians and admirers of the Art Deco style. Its site has been converted to a garden officially called the Jefferson Market Greening, begun and maintained by volunteers with aid from the Vincent Astor Foundation.

Cross W. 10th St on the N. side of the courthouse and turn left. In the middle of the block W. of Sixth Ave is PATCHIN PLACE, a secluded mews with ten brick houses built in 1848 by Aaron D. Patchin. Theodore Dreiser lived here in 1895 while still an obscure journalist and e.e. cummings enjoyed its serenity for some 40 years as the occupant of No. 4. Walk back around the corner of Sixth Ave and half a block N. to the entrance of MILLIGAN PLACE, another enclave of 19C houses clustered around a tiny triangular courtyard. The street is named after Samuel Milligan, who purchased farmland here in 1799 and, according to a local legend, hired Aaron Patchin, later his son-in-law, to survey it. The houses, built c. 1852, are said to have housed Basque waiters from the Brevoort Hotel on nearby Fifth Ave and French feather workers who dealt in the ostrich and egret plumes necessary to elegant 19C millinery.

Walk S. to W. 9th St and turn left (E.) toward Fifth Ave. Lining this residential sidestreet are handsome row houses, especially Nos 54, 56, and 58 W. 9th St (1853; Reuben R. Wood, builder), and apartments—the Portsmouth, 38–44 W. 9th St (1882; Ralph Townsend) and its neighbour the Hampshire (1883; Ralph Townsend).

At No. 23 Fifth Ave, on the N.E. corner of Ninth St, stood a house where Mabel Dodge held her famous 'evenings'. In 1912 Mrs Dodge and her wealthy husband rented the second floor of the house which she had fitted up in white, including a white bearskin rug in front of a white marble fireplace. She invited anarchists, poets, artists, sculptors, and journalists and organised her evenings around a theme—psychoanalysis, birth control, or the labour movement. Featured speakers included A.A. Brill, Big Bill Heywood (head of the Wobblies or Industrial Workers of the World), and anarchist Emma Goldman. The evenings, covered by the press, sometimes degenerated into quarrels,.but were nonetheless considered symbolic of the Village's artistic and intellectual eminence.

Cross Fifth Ave and walk a block N. to 10th St. Just E. of the avenue at 7 E. 10th St stands a house that was originally the *Lockwood de Forest Residence* (1887; Van Campen Taylor) with an adjoining apartment building, No. 9 E. 10th St (1888; Renwick, Aspinwall & Russell). The house has unusual East Indian decorative detail, including an ornate teakwood bay window and a carved teakwood door frame. Lockwood de Forest designed the teakwood trim for the family library of the Carnegie Mansion (p338) and with his more prominent brother gave a room from an Indian Jain temple to the Metropolitan Museum of Art.

Return to Fifth Ave. On the N.W. corner of Fifth Ave and 10th St is the **Church of the Ascension** (1840–41; Richard Upjohn), a fine brownstone Gothic Revival church by the architect who later designed Trinity Church at the head of Wall St. In 1844 it witnessed the wedding of President John Tyler and Julia Gardiner, whom a contemporary diarist described as 'one of those large fleshly Miss Gardiners of Gardiners Island', a resident of Colonnade Row (see p171), and a woman who apparently knew the value of publicity since she had already allowed herself to appear in an advertisement for a nearby department store.

The church is noted for its interior (open daily 12–2 and 5–7) with stained glass windows and an *altar mural by John La Farge and a marble altar relief by Augustus Saint-Gaudens.

Walk W. on 10th St. Next to the church is the *Rectory* (1839–41), a $2^1/_2$ story Gothic Revival rowhouse, romantically picturesque and daringly innovative for its day, with assymetrical massing, drip mouldings, a steep roof, large chimney, pointed dormers, and a rough brownstone facade. Across the street at *12 W. 10th St* is a townhouse (1846, renovated 1895; Bruce Price) once owned by Bruce Price, the father of etiquette expert Emily Post. Next to it at *14 W. 10th St* (1855–56) is a beautiful and elegantly carved brownstone briefly inhabited by Mark Twain in the winter of 1900–01. The adjacent houses (Nos 16 and 18) have lost much of the original detail.

The row of houses at 20–38 W. 10th St is known as RENWICK TERRACE (1856–58; attrib. James Renwick, Jr) or as the English Terrace since it was influenced by rows or 'terraces' of townhouses in London. Stylistically these Anglo-Italianate or English basement houses differ from the more common Italianate brownstone because of their low stoops (three or four steps instead of ten or twelve) and their round-arched single windows and doorways on the ground floor. Like other brownstones of the mid-19C when architects could afford to develop a row of houses at one time, Renwick Terrace was designed as part of a planned streetscape, with cornices, rooflines, and window levels aligned to create an impressive architectural vista.

The house at *50 W. 10th St*, built shortly after the Civil War as a stable, has been handsomely converted to a residence. The small dormered house at *56 W. 10th St* (1832) dates back to the Federal period and is one of the oldest houses in this part of Greenwich Village. Next to it at No. 58 is another early house built c. 1836 and remodelled by Stanford White. Behind it stood a back house (now joined to the main building) where the Tile Club once met. This prestigious society of artists claimed such members as Augustus Saint-Gaudens, Daniel Chester French, and John Singer Sargent, and was a nationally important intellectual group. Across the street stood another indication of the Village's artistic and intellectual vitality during the late 19C, Richard Morris Hunt's Studio Building, (at No. 51 W. 10th St), whose clients included Winslow Homer, John La Farge, Albert Bierstadt, Frederick MacMonnies, Saint-Gaudens, and French.

Continue W. to Sixth Ave. Walk a block N. and turn E. into W. 11th St. About a quarter of a block along the S. side of the street is the small triangular remnant of the SECOND CEMETERY OF THE SPANISH AND PORTUGUESE SYNAGOGUE, once a larger, rectangular plot. When the first graveyard of the synagogue (also called Shearith Israel) at Chatham Square (see p121) was full, this one was opened (1805) and used until W. 11th St was cut through in 1830 obliterating most of it. The bodies were moved to W. 21st St where the congregation established its third graveyard, used until 1852 when the city passed a law prohibiting further burials within the city limits. The present Shearith Israel cemetery is in Long Island.

Continue E. along W. 11th St. The new town house (1978; Hardy Holzman Pfeiffer Assocs) at *18 W. 11th St* replaces one that belonged to lyricist Howard Dietz, destroyed by an explosion in 1970. Members of the Weathermen, one of the more violently radical sects of the strife torn 1960s, were concocting homemade bombs in the basement, and one went off killing three people and sending two young women into hiding in the radical underground. Architect Hugh Hardy proposed as his own house a contemporary replacement for the Greek Revival house, but although his design remained faithful to the scale, materials, cornice line, and stoop projection of neighbouring buildings, it elicited a free-for-all between architectural conservatives and modernists. While the Landmarks Commission debated its merits, construction costs sky-rocketed and the building became too expensive. Years later the design was salvaged for another client.

Continue E. to Fifth Ave. The **First Presbyterian Church** (1846; Joseph C. Wells; S. transept, 1893; McKim, Mead & White. Chancel added, 1919) on the W. side of the avenue between 11th and 12th Sts is one of three handsome Gothic Revival churches built in the Village in the mid-19C (the others are Grace Church and the Church of the Ascension). British architect Joseph C. Wells modelled the crenellated central tower on that of Magdalen College, Oxford. The *Church House* around the corner on W. 12th St was designed by Edgar Tafel (1960) in dark brown Roman brick to blend with the brownstone of the church itself; the Gothic quatrefoil motifs in the balcony railings repeat the design of the roof cresting of the church.

Across the avenue at 47 Fifth Ave is the SALMAGUNDI CLUB (1852–53; DL), the only survivor of the great mansions that once ennobled lower Fifth Ave. Built for Irad Hawley, president of the Pennsylvania Coal Company, it belongs to the Italianate tradition, with a boldly rusticated basement, a high stoop and grand balustrade, an ornate door hood supported on foliate consoles, and lavish cast iron work on the parlour window balconies. The Italianate brownstone came into style (late 1840s) when many New Yorkers, enjoying new wealth, were looking for an architectural vehicle for flaunting that wealth and the elaborate ornamentation of the style offered those so disposed unlimited opportunities for display.

The interior (open afternoons, 1–5) provides a glimpse into the pleasures of wealth in 19C New York. The ceilings are richly ornamented with plasterwork; doors are rosewood; the marble mantels are handsomely carved; Corinthian columns separate the front from the back first floor parlours, and elegant chandeliers glitter overhead. Oddly, this house was nothing spectacular in its day; contemporary guidebooks refer to the nearby Lenox, Schiff, Belmont, and Haight residences but are silent about this mansion.

The Salmagundi Club is the nation's oldest artists' club, founded in 1870 and numbering among its alumni John La Farge, Louis Tiffany, and Stanford White. The name 'Salmagundi' (whose origins cannot reliably be traced back beyond the Fr. *salmigondis*, a rather unlikely salad of minced veal, anchovies, onions, lemon juice, and oil) was adopted by Washington Irving and his collaborators as the title of a periodical whose pages satirised New York life.

On the W. side of Fifth Ave between W. 12th and W. 13th Sts are the *Dauber & Pine Bookshops*, a Village institution, cluttered, dusty, and grandly disorganised. In 1973 protests by publishers and booklovers averted demolition of this browser's paradise. At one time Albert and Charles Boni ran their publishing house in this building as did the Macmillan Company, which later moved next door to No. 60 Fifth Ave (1925; John Russell Pope), now the home of 'Forbes' magazine.

Walk S. to W. 12th St and turn west. The *Winfield Scott House* (1851) at 24 W. 12th St, now a cooperative apartment, became a national historic landmark in 1974 as the onetime home of General Winfield Scott (1786–1866), hero of the Mexican War and Whig candidate for President (1852). The iron railings date from the 1880s. Across the street at 31–33 W. 12th St are the *Ardea apartments* (1895 and 1901; John B. Snook & Sons), built for a department store baron. Next door at *35 W. 12th St* stands a narrow house (c. 1840), only 13 ft wide, with a basement and two stories plus an anachronistic mansard roof with a single dormer. In 1867 when the house, then 25 ft wide, was cut in half to widen its eastern neighbour, the mansard roof and dormer were added without altering the Federal lintels and doorway. During this period homeowners commonly topped off their Federal and Greek Revival houses with mansard roofs, partly to follow fashion and partly to gain additional space in a city where housing was already cramped. Next to this attractive little house is a highly lauded modern apartment, BUTTERFIELD HOUSE (1962; Mayer, Whittlesey & Glass) which sits agreeably alongside the older buildings of the street. On 12th St it rises only seven stories to conform to the existing 19C scale; on 13th St it rises to 13 stories in a more commercial block. At *45 W. 12th St* is another curious small house (c. 1846) whose side wall slants back to follow the former banks of Minetta Brook, now channelled underground.

At 66 W. 12th St is the main building of the NEW SCHOOL FOR SOCIAL RESEARCH (1930; Joseph Urban). Known for his stage sets and theatrical designs, Urban has exercised architectural sleight of hand to make the building as unobtrusive as possible on a street where most structures are smaller, using alternating courses of black and white brick and strip windows to emphasise the building's horizontal dimension, and recessing the upper stories.

The New School was founded (1919) as a small, informal intellectual center for adults and has evolved into a university whose major committment is still adult education. Through the years it has offered innovative courses including in the 1920s the first college level work on black culture (taught by W.E.B. DuBois) and on psychoanalysis. During the following decades it became a 'university in exile' for intellectuals fleeing Nazi Germany.

On the first floor is a small, handsome *auditorium* designed by Urban whose theatrical credits included sets for the Metropolitan Opera and the Ziegfeld Follies.

At the corner of Sixth Ave turn right (N.) and walk a block to W. 13th St. Continue W. to the **Village Community Church**, one of the best Greek Revival churches in the city. Built as the 13th Street Presbyterian Church (1846; attrib. Samuel Thompson), the church echoes the Hephaisteion in Athens, with six Doric columns, a frieze of triglyphs and metopes, a cornice and low triangular pediment of painted wood; the body of the building is brick. At various times the church has housed Presbyterian congregations, a Jewish synagogue, and a bilingual theatrical group; it was converted to condominiums in 1982.

Its first rector was Dr Samuel D. Burchard, for whom the row house next door at 146 W. 13th St was built in 1846. Burchard is best known for having undermined the presidential hopes of Republican James G. Blaine in 1884 by making an inflammatory speech in which he labelled the opposition, Grover Cleveland's Democratic Party, the party of 'rum, Romanism, and rebellion'. In the Catholic backlash that followed, Blaine lost New York City, New York state, and the nation.

Continue to Seventh Ave and turn left (S.). The complex of institutional buildings along the avenue belongs to ST. VINCENT'S HOSPITAL, the city's oldest and the nation's largest Catholic hospital. The modern white building with its two scalloped over-hangs (36 Seventh Ave) is the *Edward and Theresa O'Toole Medical Services Building* (1964; Albert C. Ledner & Assocs), built as the headquarters of the National Maritime Union of America. Union president Joseph Curran once described the ungainly building—a squared-off, inverted, stepped pyramid—as 'the box in which the Guggenheim Museum came'. The modern main hospital building rising on the N.E. corner of W. 11th St, Seventh, and Greenwich Aves (designed 1979; Ferrenz & Taylor) replaces a longtime Village landmark, a red brick and limestone structure (1899; Shickel & Ditmars) which local efforts could not save.

St. Vincent's Hospital, opened by the Sisters of Charity in 1849, has served the city well, counting among its patients battlefield casualties of the Civil War, survivors of the 'Titanic', and President Grover Cleveland; among its students, Georges Clemenceau, and among its grateful admirers the parents of Edna St. Vincent Millay, who gave the poet her middle name to honour the hospital whose staff had saved the life of a family member.

The *Seton Building* (1899; Schickel & Ditmars) on the N.E. corner of Seventh Ave and W. 11th St, scheduled for demolition as part of a major expansion programme, is named after Elizabeth Bayley Seton, first American canonised by the Roman Catholic Church, founder of the Sisters of Charity who established the hospital. On its N. flank the Coleman Pavilion (1982; Ferrenz & Taylor) is currently under construction. Continue N. along Seventh Ave to 14th St.

FOURTEENTH ST marks the N. boundary of Greenwich Village but seems miles away from its quaint and historic insularity. It is a broad, busy, rundown, and gritty commercial street, though some of the richly ornamental facades of bygone days still hover above street level.

The W. extreme of 14th St lies within the Gansevoort Market district. W. of Seventh Ave is an established Hispanic neighbourhood, whose restaurants, groceries, and shops cater to local tastes. Of particular interest are the Iglesia Catolica Guadalupe (229 W. 14th St between Seventh and Eighth Aves), founded in 1902 in a brownstone row house later converted to a church by the addition of a Spanish-style facade, and the *Casa Moneo* (210 W. 14th St), the city's best-known Spanish grocery and import store. The Little Spain Merchants Association, founded in 1975 to fight what its members considered the 'blight' spreading across W. 14th St, has banned the selling of merchandise on the sidewalks between Seventh Ave and the Hudson. East of that frontier, however, sleazy 'bargain' goods pour out from the interiors of numerous small shops. Between Seventh and Sixth Aves is the headquarters of the Salvation Army at 120 W. 14th St in *Centennial Memorial Temple* (1930; Voorhees, Gmelin & Walker), a grandiose Art Deco monument to a spiritual soldiery. Across the street at 125 W. 14th St is the *42nd Division Armory* of the N.Y. National Guard (1971; N.Y. State General Services Administration, Charles S. Kawecki, architect), a depressing example of modern secular military architecture.

The Seventh Ave IRT stop is at 14th St and Seventh Ave. IND stations are at Sixth and Eighth Aves.

10 Chelsea

SUBWAY: IRT Broadway–7th Ave Local (train 1) to 23rd St; IND Eighth Ave (train AA or E, train C during rush hours) to 23rd St.

BUS: M10 (via Seventh Ave) to 23rd St; M11 (via Ninth Ave) to 23rd St, walk E; M2 or M3 (via Fifth Ave) to 23rd St, walk W. to Seventh Ave; M6 or M7 (via Broadway) to 23rd St, walk W. to Seventh Ave. M26 crosstown bus on 23rd St. Culture Bus (weekends and holidays), Loop II, Stop 21.

Chelsea owes its name and approximate boundaries to Captain Thomas Clarke who bought (1750) a tract of land (present 14th–24th Sts, Eighth Ave to the Hudson River—though today Chelsea is considered to extend N. to about 30th St), and named the estate after the Chelsea Hospital in London. It owes its most attractive streets to his grandson, Clement Clarke Moore, who developed the area as a residential district, and its ethnic diversity and slums to the New York Central Railroad.

History. Moore (1779–1863), distinguished as the compiler of the first Hebrew lexicon published in the United States but remembered for his poem beginning 'Twas the night before Christmas', kept Chelsea for a summer home until it became clear that the pressures of the city's northward growth would engulf the rolling hills and meadows of his patrimony. He moved uptown from Greenwich Village, generously but astutely donated a block to the General

Theological Seminary, and began selling building lots with design and use controls attached—no alleys, no stables, no manufactures, and a 10-ft setback for all houses.

Chelsea's residential tranquillity was disrupted when the Hudson River Railroad, later absorbed by the New York Central, laid tracks down Eleventh Ave (c. 1847), attracting breweries, slaughterhouses, and glue factories which in turn attracted job-hungry immigrants including a large group of Irish fleeing the potato famines. The Ninth Ave El (1871) whose overhead rails plunged the avenue below into shadow, further depressed the area, and although the El was dismantled before World War II, the W. part of Chelsea has not recovered, still housing thousands of the city's poor either in decrepit tenements or in municipal housing projects like the Robert Fulton Houses, the Chelsea Houses, and the Elliott Houses.

The E. part has fared better. During the 1870s and 1880s a theatrical district flourished on W. 23rd St, home of Edwin Booth's Theater (1869–83), Proctor's (opened 1888), and Pike's Opera (1868). Although the theatre district inevitably moved uptown, Chelsea enjoyed a brief artistic revival around World War I as the center of early moviedom, before a better climate and more open space lured the industry to California. The Famous Players' Studio (221 W. 26th St) in an old armoury released some of Mary Pickford's early films and other studios like and the Reliance and the Majestic (both at 520 W. 21st St) and the Kalem Company (235 W. 23rd St) attracted such stars as Alice Joyce and Wallace Reid to Chelsea.

Chelsea has long embraced a wide range of ethnic groups, from the predominant Irish, to a French colony whose most important remaining trace is the R.C. Church of St. Vincent de Paul (127 W. 23rd St), to a Greek enclave on Eighth Ave, and a Spanish community extending N. from 14th St, one of the oldest in the city. Tolerance has been extended also to union activists, to artists and their followers recently overflowing Greenwich Village, and to a gay population visible in the 'leather bars' of Eleventh Ave.

Today Chelsea is in a state of flux. Its population which reached 60,000 in the mid-1960s is down to fewer than 44,000. To some extent the older immigrant groups have been replaced by Japanese, Chinese, and S. American, mostly Ecuadoran, residents but the number of families is still dwindling. The 1970 census showed that 81·6% of Chelsea households had only one or two members with an average per capita income of $9402. Real estate conversions—business offices into $400 a month studios, large-roomed tenements into $600 single bedroom apartments—threaten Chelsea's ethnic and social fabric by destroying low-income housing as do Westway, the 12-lane superhighway proposed as a replacement for the West Side Highway, and the New York Exhibition and Convention Center now rising on the old New York Central freight yards.

The **Chelsea Hotel** between Seventh and Eighth Aves on W. 23rd St (1884; Hubert, Pirsson & Co.; DL), now down at the heels, enjoys a reputation as a literary and architectural landmark. Replete with gables, chimneys, dormers, lancet and semi-elliptical windows, terracotta reliefs and bands of white stonework, it is most remarkable aesthetically for its cast-iron balconies, with their interlaced sunflowers, stretched row upon row across the long facade. Built as an apartment house, the Chelsea Hotel has earned a minor niche in the annals of New York as the first apartment building to reach 12 stories and the first to feature a penthouse. Writers William Dean Howells and O. Henry (William Sydney Porter) lived there in its early days, but its artistic heyday came after the 1930s when Thomas Wolfe, James T. Farrell, Mary McCarthy, Dylan Thomas, Arthur Miller, Brendan Behan, Vladimir Nabokov, Gregory Corso, John Sloan,

Sarah Bernhardt, and Yevgeni Yevtushenko all enjoyed its hospitality.

A painted papier-mâché sculpture (1969?; Eugenia Gershoy) in one of the front windows depicts a group of the hotel's famous residents: playwright Arthur Miller and his wife photographer Inga Morath, science-fiction writer Arthur C. Clarke, composer Virgil Thompson, and director Peter Brook.

Continue W. on 23rd St to the N.W. corner of Eighth Ave. Here stood Pike's Opera House (1868), bought a year later by financier Jay Gould and his partner Jim Fisk, directors of the Erie Railroad. Gould and Fisk renamed it the Grand Opera House and in addition to producing opera, revues, and plays in the theatre, installed the railroad offices upstairs and a printing press in the basement, a famous piece of apparatus used to increase greatly the capitalisation of the railroad. Attached to the theatre by a tunnel was a brownstone mansion where Fisk kept his buxom and beautiful mistress Josie Mansfield.

This remarkable complex of business, pleasure, and art came to an end in 1872 when Fisk, by now supplanted both on the board of the Erie Railroad and in the affections of Josie Mansfield, was murdered by her new lover Edward S. Stokes. Fisk's body lay in state in the foyer of the opera house, which shortly thereafter entered a period of decline, becoming a vaudeville house, and a movie theatre before its demise (1960).

Turn left and walk S. on Eighth Ave to 20th St. Turn W. At No. 346 W. 20th St, between Eighth and Ninth Aves, is ST. PETER'S CHURCH (Protestant Episcopal), a modest fieldstone church important as the earliest Gothic Revival church in America (1836–38; James W. Smith, builder, from designs by Clement Clarke Moore; DL). At the W. end of the group is the Rectory (1832) which first served as the church and is built in the Greek Revival style, though with engaged brick pilasters instead of the usual freestanding columns. According to legend, the foundations for the present church had already been laid when a vestryman returned from England, so enthralled with the Gothic parish churches there that he persuaded his colleagues to redesign the new church. The resulting structure, therefore, is Gothic more in its details than in its proportions and materials. The newest building, the brick Parish Hall, was started in 1854 and completed in 1871 when the churchlike front was added. Trinity Parish donated the wrought iron fence (1790), formerly used in front of St. Paul's Chapel.

The block bounded by Ninth and Tenth Aves, 20th And 21st Sts (Chelsea Square) is filled by the GENERAL THEOLOGICAL SEMINARY (Main Building, 1960; O' Connor and Kilham; West Building, 1836; other principal buildings, 1883–1900; Charles C. Haight). Clement Clarke Moore, who taught Hebrew and Greek here, donated the land on which the seminary (founded 1817) now stands.

Enter through the modern building on Ninth Ave. With the exception of the Gothic Revival West Building (1832), most of the college was built during the tenure of dean Eugene Augustus Hoffman, who hired Charles C. Haight to design the present Collegiate Gothic quadrangle. Especially attractive is the central Chapel of the Good Shepherd with its 161-ft tower and bronze doors by J. Massey Rhind.

Return to Ninth Ave. Just N. of the seminary on the N.W. corner of

21st St is a small Federal house (1831) with fine Flemish bond brickwork, now used as a store (183 Ninth Ave), its pitched roof, dormers, and simple cornice still intact. The three houses adjacent— No. 185 Ninth Ave (1856) and Nos 187 and 189 Ninth Ave (1868)—among the few wooden houses remaining in Manhattan, were built by James N. Wells, one of Chelsea's major 19C developers and the builder of St. Luke's in the Fields in Greenwich Village.

Return to W. 20th St with its gracious Greek Revival and Italianate row houses, now a little rundown. No. 402 W. 20th St (1897; Charles P.H. Gilbert) is a late 19C house remarkable primarily for the way it adapts to its neighbours, with a concave facade that makes the transition between the corner tenement and the 10-ft setback of the adjoining row of older houses. The letters DONAC above the door commemorate Don Alonzo Cushman, not a Spanish grandee but a dry goods merchant, friend of Clement Clarke Moore, parish leader, and land developer who made a fortune building in Chelsea. No. 404 W. 20th St (1830) is the earliest house in the area.

Stretching W. on 20th St (Nos 406–418 W. 20th St) is CUSHMAN ROW, named after Don Alonzo Cushman. Completed in 1840 (DL), these brick, brownstone-trimmed Greek Revival houses have retained much original detail: fine cast-iron wreathes around small attic windows, panelled doors, iron stoop railings and areaway fences, pilastered doorways with slender sidelights. Nos 416 and 418 still have their pineapple newel posts.

Nos 446–450 W. 20th St (1853) are exceptional Italianate houses with round-headed doorways and ground floor windows and unusual trim beneath the cornices. Arched windows and doorways, exemplifying the Italianate style's attraction to circular forms, appeared only on expensive houses, since they were relatively difficult to execute.

Turn right (N.) at Tenth Ave and walk a block to 21st St. At No. 193 Tenth Ave (N.W. corner) is the *Guardian Angel Roman Catholic Church* (1930; John Van Pelt), an elaborate red brick and limestone Romanesque style church with a tile roof. Before the Chelsea Piers closed (1968), the church served the large number of seamen and dockworkers residing in the neighbourhood, and in the 1930s its pastor was the port chaplain.

The Chelsea Piers (1902–07; Warren & Wetmore) once received ships from the United States, Panama Pacific, American Merchant, and Grace Lines. With the decay of New York as a port, due in part to its lack of facilities for handling containerised cargoes, this segment of Chelsea's economy has sagged (in the early 1970s the city lost 20,000 waterfront jobs), and many of the Irish-American dockworkers who once lived here have moved to New Jersey where the piers are still active.

Another group of fine Italianate houses (Nos 465–473 W. 21st St) stretches along the N side of 21st St just E. of Tenth Ave.

Continue up Tenth Ave to *Clement Clarke Moore Park* at the S.E. corner of 22nd St, a pleasant multi-level playground (1968; Coffey, Levine & Blumberg). Across the street on the N.E. corner of the intersection is the *Empire Diner* (1943, altered 1976; Carl Laanes), a relic of the period when these 'railroad car' eateries dotted the country; it has been refurbished in black and chrome appropriate to its Art Deco origins (open 24 hours).

Turn right (E.) on 22nd St. The double house (1835) at *No. 436–438 W. 22nd St*, now stripped down and converted to apartments, was once the residence of actor Edwin Forrest, remembered primarily as one of the dramatic antagonists involved in the Astor Place riots (see p172). *No. 414–416 W. 22nd St* is a once-elegant mansion (1835; James N. Wells), the only surviving five-bay Greek Revival house in Manhattan. Wells himself lived here briefly; in 1864–66 the building was remodelled and in 1870 began a tour of duty as the Samaritan Home for the Aged. Continue to Ninth Ave and walk N.

The original *Clarke family mansion* stood between Ninth and Tenth Aves, 22nd and 23rd Sts, until demolished in 1854.

Continue to 23rd St. Filling an entire block (23rd to 24th Sts, Ninth to Tenth Aves) are the LONDON TERRACE APARTMENTS, an early modern apartment project (1930; Farrar & Watmaugh), built in a vaguely Romanesque (or Gothic?) style around a central garden, which, along with such other amenities as a swimming pool, solarium, gymnasium, and doormen dressed as London bobbies, lured early tenants to its 1670 apartments. The original London Terrace, torn down for the present apartments, was a row of colonnaded townhouses (1845; Alexander Jackson Davis) with an extravagant 35-ft setback and handsome front gardens. Continue N. on Ninth Ave.

Diversion. The far W. of Chelsea, once dominated by the piers and railroads, still bears traces of that past, perhaps soon to be eradicated with the construction of a new convention center. Walk W. on 25th St to Eleventh Ave; turn N. and walk a block to the STARRETT-LEHIGH BUILDING (1931; Russell G. and Walter M. Cory with Yasuo Matsui, assoc. architect), between Eleventh and Twelfth Aves, 26th and 27th Sts, an imposing Art Deco industrial building often overlooked because of its bleak surroundings. Admirers praise its dramatic exterior—horizontal bands of glass, concrete, and brown brick wrapped around curved corners—and its innovative concrete column-and-slab construction. Built over a spur line of the Lehigh Valley Railroad, it was intended for freight handling, warehousing, and manufacturing and was equipped with powerful elevators that could lift loaded boxcars from the tracks to the warehouse above. The railroad tracks inside the building were never built and those at street level were torn out, but the elevators are still used, hoisting 15-ton trucks into the vast interior.

Across the street (block bounded by 27th and 28th Sts, Eleventh and Twelfth Aves) stand the *Central Stores of the Terminal Warehouse Company* (1891), 25 storage buildings (24 acres of warehousing space) walled into one massive fortress surmounted by a Tuscan tower. The great arched doorway at one time admitted locomotives on a spur line of the New York Central Railroad, while the W. facade opened onto the deepwater Hudson River piers. Cool cellars running beneath the entire structure were used to store wines, liquors, gums, and rubber.

Before the diesel truck supplanted the locomotive as America's prime freight hauler, this part of Chelsea was the hub of the city's freight distribution. The Thirtieth St Yards of the New York Central Railroad (30th–37th Sts between Eleventh and Twelfth Aves with two additional blocks, 30th–32nd Sts between Tenth and Eleventh Aves) received trains from a railroad that stretched far into the hinterlands. Additional yards at 60th St were connected to this facility by a freight line down Eleventh Ave, known grimly as Death Ave until the 1930s when the tracks were dropped beneath street level. S. of the yards an elevated rail viaduct (parts still visible) led to the St. John's Park Freight Terminal (1934) between Charlton and Clarkson Sts west of Washington St. After years of controversy, in governmental and financial circles, the N. section of the now-abandoned yards (34th to 39th Sts) has been designated as the site of the New York Exposition and Convention Center, a massive 5-square block complex designed by I.M. Pei & Partners and to be completed in 1984. Return to Ninth Ave on 28th St, past Chelsea Park and the rubble-strewn lot next to the Morgan Post Office.

On the S.E. corner of Ninth Ave and W. 28th St is the Protestant Episcopal CHURCH OF THE HOLY APOSTLES (1848; Minard

Lafever; transepts 1858; Richard Upjohn & Sons; DL), a small brick church with a copper-covered, slate-roofed spire and bracketed eaves, set in the midst of an overscaled modern housing project. Handsome stained-glass windows by William Jay Bolton, America's earliest and most famous stained-glass artist, enhance the interior (open during services, Sunday at 11). Composed of monochromatic central medallions surrounded by stylised roses, lilies, and foliate forms, the windows depict scenes from the life of Christ and from the Acts of the Apostles.

The nearest subways are the IND Eighth Ave at 23rd St and the IRT Seventh Ave at 28th St. The M10 bus runs uptown on Eighth Ave and downtown on Seventh Ave. The nearest crosstown bus is at 23rd St.

11   Union, Madison, and Stuyvesant Squares, Gramercy Park and the East Twenties

SUBWAY: IRT Lexington Ave Local or Express (trains 4, 5, 6) to 14th St-Union Square. BMT Broadway or Broadway Local (train N or RR) to 14th St-Union Square. BMT 14th St-Canarsie (train LL) to Union Square.

BUS: M1 (Fifth Ave-Park Ave S.) to Union Square. M2, M3, M5 (Fifth Ave) to 14th St; walk E. one long block to Union Square. M6, M7 (Broadway) to Union Square.

CAR PARKING: Difficult during the week. Metered parking N. of Union Square, on the E. side of Madison Square ($^1/_2$ hour), around Gramercy Park, and on Second Ave near Stuyvesant Square (2 hrs); occasional small parking lots.

Union Square, first named Union Place (1811) because it stood at the junction of the two main roads out of town has fallen on hard times. Surrounded by cheap stores and unimpressive buildings, frequented by a less than savoury crowd, Union Square has lost the repose and charm of its beginnings as a residential square, the glamour of its period as New York's theatrical district, and the fervour of its days as a political forum.

Part of the Brevoort farm in the 18C, Union Square was designated as a park in 1815 and laid out in 1831 when it was enjoyed by such prominent local families as Roosevelts and Goelets. In the decade before the Civil War the socially prominent flocked to its Academy of Music (14th St and Irving Place), Wallack's Theater (13th St and Broadway) and Irving Hall (later the Irving Place Theater at 15th St and Irving Pl.). During the later part of the century 14th St marked the midpoint of Ladies' Mile, a promenade of fashionable stores that stretched from Broadway and 8th St to 23rd St, but by 1900 both commerce and art had moved uptown to Madison Square, leaving Union Square stranded between the immigrant ghetto and the industrial area to the south and the fashionable district uptown. Needle trade workers moved in and during the early years of the 20C many old homes became tenements housing labourers and occasional artists. In the years before World War I, the square became a center of political dissidence, for anarchists, socialists, 'Wobblies', and Communists. Mass meetings sometimes developed into confrontations with the police: most famous were a gathering protesting the execution of anarchists Nicola Sacco and Bartolomeo Vanzetti (22 August 1927) and a Depression labour demonstration (6 March 1930) attended by 35,000 workers and sympathisers. Public outcry after police injured 100 demonstrators at this meeting secured the square as a place of assembly, and making it the heart of radical political activities in the

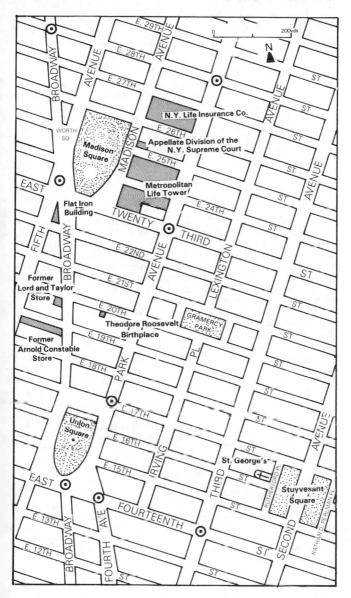

city. During the 1930s numerous radical, progressive, and labour groups made their headquarters in the area: the Socialist party and newspaper, the Communist party and newspaper, the American Civil Liberties Union, the Amalgamated Clothing Workers of America, and the International Ladies Garment Workers Union.

Union Square Park was landscaped in 1935–36 when the ground level was raised to accommodate the labyrinthine subway station beneath. While the park shelters its share of derelicts, 'shopping bag ladies', and drug dealers, it also contains some of the city's finest outdoor statuary. Near the S. entrance is an **equestrian statue of George Washington** (1856; Henry Kirke Brown with John Quincy Adams Ward), a 14-ft bronze work considered the sculptor's masterpiece. It commemorates Washington's entrance to the' city on Evacuation Day (25 Nov 1783), ending the British occupation during the Revolutionary War.

Walk around the outside of the park to the E. (counterclockwise). The remains of S. Klein, a store selling moderately priced women's apparel, loom across Park Ave South. In 1921, a low point in Union Square's past, Klein bought three derelict buildings and opened a discount apparel outlet, soon to be joined by Orbach's and Hearn's, thus making the neighbourhood a center for bargain hunters as well as dissidents. North of Klein's at No. 20 Union Sq. E. is the *United Mutual Savings Bank*, originally the Union Square Savings Bank (1907; Henry Bacon), whose handsome Corinthian colonnade belies its recently plasticised interior. Bacon also designed the Lincoln Memorial in Washington, D.C.

At the edge of the park near E. 15th St still on the Park Ave S. side is a bronze *statue of the Marquis de Lafayette* (1876; Frédéric Auguste Bartholdi) presented in gratitude for support during the Franco-Prussian War. Bartholdi, best known for that other monument of Franco-American friendship, the Statue of Liberty, shows Lafayette offering his sword to the cause of American independence. The *Guardian Life Insurance Co.* at No. 201 Park Ave S. on the N.E. corner of E. 17th St (1911; D'Oench & Yost) has a grand mansarded tower and a modern annex (1961; Skidmore, Owings & Merrill).

In the center of the park stands the *Independence Flagstaff* (1926; Anthony De Francisci) whose base (36 ft diam.; $9^1/_2$ ft high) has bronze reliefs which symbolise the forces of good and evil during the American struggle for independence. Formerly called the Charles F. Murphy Memorial after the Tammany Hall boss (1858–1924), the flagpole was financed by $80,000 of Tammany money collected on the 150th anniversary of the signing of the Declaration of Independence. The pedestal bears the text of the Declaration and a quotation by Thomas Jefferson. On the W. side of the park is a fountain with a figure of a woman and child by Adolph Dondorf. At the N. end of the park stands a *bronze figure of Abraham Lincoln* (1868) also by Henry Kirke Brown. Erected three years after Lincoln's assassination, the figure, draped in a cloak but dressed in a baggy suit, has been criticised for its uninspiring dowdiness.

North of the statue is a colonnaded pavilion dating from the 1930s, whose spray-painted slogans attest to the radical tradition of Union Square: Socialist Revolution is Inevitable; Don't fall for US Patriotism, a tool of capitalists.

Cross the parking lot N. of Union Square. The empty red brick building with its ornate terracotta decoration at *No. 33–37 E. 17th St* (1881; William Schickel) once housed the 'Century Illustrated' and

'St. Nicholas' magazines. Turn left and walk toward Broadway. Visible on the W. side of Broadway are two turn-of-the-century office buildings. At *No. 31 Union Sq. W.* (N.W. corner of E. 16th St) is the Bank of the Metropolis (1902; Bruce Price), a narrow graceful tower with an Ionic portico of dark granite columns and a large cornice. Next door at *No. 33 Union Sq. W.* is a small, wildly eclectic building (1893; Alfred Zucker), whose primary stylistic ancestors seem to have been Moors and Venetian Goths.

Walk N. on Broadway. Hectic and dirty today, it abounds with the glories of yesteryear when it was the home stretch of Ladies' Mile. Although its palatial department stores and robust office buildings grown shabby have been reduced to offering costume jewellery and imported party favours, they still survive, majestically occupying the prominent intersections of Broadway and Fifth Ave. The *MacIntyre Building* (1892; R.H. Robertson) at No. 874 Broadway on the N.E. corner of E. 18th St is a prime example, a slender office tower boldly adorned with Romanesque arches, finials, and a spectacular heraldic device. A block further along, on the S.W. corner of E. 19th St is No. 881–887 Broadway built as **the Arnold Constable Dry Goods Store** (1869, extended 1873 and 1877; Griffith Thomas), with one of the city's finest surviving mansard roofs, Thomas, architect of Marble House, the Arnold Constable store on Canal St, faced the original Broadway wing with marble—the only suitable material according to Aaron Arnold—and as the store expanded added the two-story mansard roof, pushed out along 19th St, and finally duplicated the Broadway facade—in cast iron—along Fifth Ave, wrapping the mansard roof around the entire building.

On the S.E. corner of the same intersection (No. 880–888 Broadway) is the *former W. & J. Sloane store* (1882; W. Wheeler Smith), a six-story brick building with cast-iron decoration, wide windows, and classical detailing. Originally dealers in carpets, oriental rugs, lace curtains and upholstery fabrics, W. & J. Sloane moved uptown in 1912.

On the N.W. corner (No. 889 Broadway) is the *former Gorham Manufacturing Co. building* (1883; Edward H. Kendall), a fussy brick structure with a chamfered corner turning that once rose to a tower. The building housed showrooms which displayed Gorham silver— tableware, urns, and a gleaming array of goblets, beakers, basins, amphorae, candelabra, and ecclesiastical metalwork.

Continue N. on Broadway. *No. 900 Broadway* (S.E. corner of E. 20th St) is an eclectic commercial building (1887; McKim, Mead & White), part Romanesque, part Renaissance, with fine brickwork. The **former Lord & Taylor store** (No. 901 Broadway, S.W. corner of the E. 20th St intersection) is best seen from the E. side of the street. The building (1869; James H. Giles), the fourth and grandest Lord & Taylor emporium, is a cast-iron French Second Empire extravaganza now sadly reduced in circumstances and mutilated both above and below. Although the two-story arched entranceway on Broadway and the fine corner turning with its tall display windows and marble columns are gone, the imposing corner tower and its high mansard roof remain, giving some idea of the splendour of the original. Known for its fine window displays and its modern equipment (including Otis elevators), Lord & Taylor's was a tourist attraction as well as one of the city's largest merchandisers of dry goods and ladies' wear.

Turn right (E.) on E. 20th St and walk a half block to No. 28, **the**

Theodore Roosevelt Birthplace (original building, 1848; replicated, 1923; Theodate Pope Riddle; DL).

Open Wed–Sun, 9–4.30, except Christmas, New Year's and Thanksgiving. Adults, 50¢; children under 16 and senior citizens free. Tel: 260–1616 for information about group tours.

At the time of Roosevelt's birth (1858), this four-story brownstone was an upper middle class home in a comfortable residential neighbourhood. Theodore's parents moved uptown in 1873 but the house remained in the family until 1896 when it was sold, altered for commercial use, and eventually demolished (1910). After Roosevelt's death (1919), his sisters bought the site and rebuilt their childhood home, a mirror image of their uncle's house still standing next door. The Roosevelt birthplace contains five rooms of period furniture, some of it originally in the family, and an excellent collection of Theodore Roosevelt memorabilia.

Return to Broadway and continue W. a short block to Fifth Ave. On the S.W. corner (No. 150 Fifth Ave) is the *former Methodist Book Concern* (1889; Edward H. Kendall), a Romanesque Revival building whose rockface granite lower stories and handsome brickwork arches survive above a boorishly modernised ground floor. Originally the building was the headquarters of the 'Christian Advocate', official organ of the Methodist Episcopal Church, a weekly journal which apprised its readers of the progress of humanity along religious and philanthropic lines and carried its moral principles into its business policies, refusing advertisements of products endorsed by bishops or ministers and financial opportunities offering investors interest rates greater than 8%.

Walk N. along Fifth Ave. At No. 153–157 is the first SCRIBNER'S STORE, a classically elegant little building designed by Ernest Flagg (1894; DL), favourite architect of the Scribner family, who also obliged them with a printing plant, the uptown Scribner's store, and the family mansion.

Continue up Fifth Ave past the Flatiron Building at E. 22nd St and the former Western Union Building (No. 186 Fifth Ave), both better seen from Madison Square Park. Cross 23rd St and enter the park from the S.W.

Look back at the *Flatiron Building (1902; D.H. Burnham & Co.; DL), filling the elongated triangle where Broadway joins Fifth Ave at 23rd St, the world's tallest building (300 ft) when completed and one of the first to be supported by a steel skeleton. Dramatically sited and radically constructed, the Flatiron Building is nonetheless conservatively garbed in limestone and terracotta moulded in ornate French Renaissance detail. The rounded corner turning (only 6 ft wide at the N. end), and the eight-story undulating bays in the midsection of the side walls soften the severity of this fine building.

First called the Fuller Building after its developer, the Flatiron Building has evoked strong responses from such diverse observers as H.G. Wells (1906) who admired its 'prow . . . ploughing up through the traffic of Broadway and Fifth Ave in the afternoon light', and Edward Steichen whose photos of it are justly famous. Because of the gusty winds often swirling around 23rd St and Broadway, the Flatiron Building was once a haunt of street corner Romeos who gathered to see a bit of ankle beneath a billowing skirt. Policemen, shooing these offenders, are said to have originated the expression '23 Skidoo'.

On the S.W. corner of 23rd St, just W. of the Flatiron Building is No. 186 Fifth Ave, the *former Western Union Telegraph Company*

Building (1884; Henry J. Hardenbergh). Small in scale, this red brick building with limestone trim, a gabled roof and dormers, and an odd, octagonal chimney tower at the N.W. corner, is an early work by the architect of the Dakota Apartments and the Plaza Hotel.

***Madison Square** has withstood the onslaughts of commercialism and urban decay better than Union Square, but the completion of the Flatiron Building spelled the end of an era when it was the city's most glamourous neighbourhood, a garden of pleasure for the socially elite.

On its west stood expensive hotels, including the white marble Fifth Avenue Hotel (opened 1859, between 23rd and 24th Sts), nicknamed Enos's Folly because Amos Enos had ventured to build so far uptown, and the Hoffman House (1865 Broadway between 24th and 25th Sts), famous for the racy Bouguereau painting of Nymphs and Satyrs above the bar in the gentlemen's cafe. Delmonico's Restaurant hastened uptown (1876) to the S. side of 26th St between Fifth Ave and Broadway to provide a place for the cream of society to dine and dance. At the N.E. corner of the square was Stanford White's old Madison Square Garden and on the E. side near 25th St his pillared and domed Madison Square Presbyterian Church. Nowadays these old buildings are all gone, but their replacements, with one exception, are graciously scaled and dignified. Dealers in insurance, giftwares, and toys have supplanted the social aristocracy, but the Madison Square district still retains the aura of its pleasant past.

MADISON SQUARE PARK was, successively, a marsh, a potter's field, and a parade ground before the Commissioners' Plan of 1811 designated the whole area bounded by 23rd and 34th Sts, Third and Seventh Aves as a park. In 1844 the city fathers reduced it to its present size (between 6–7 acres) and named it after President James Madison; it opened officially in 1847. Its earliest claim to fame came in 1845 when a group of men who had been playing the new game of baseball there since 1842 codified the rules and organised the Knickerbocker Club, ancestor of all American baseball teams.

At the S. end of the park is a *statue of William Henry Seward* (erected 1876; Randolph Rogers), U.S. senator and secretary of state under Lincoln and Andrew Johnson, best known for purchasing Alaska from Russia. The bronze figure, admired when first installed, drew scorn when it turned out that Rogers had recast the body from a figure of Lincoln made earlier for Fairmount Park in Philadelphia and simply attached Seward's head to Lincoln's neck.

Walk through the park toward the N.W. (toward Broadway). The flagpole near the sidewalk bears the *Eternal Light Memorial* (1924; Thomas Hastings and Paul Bartlett), commemorating American forces fallen in France during World War I. Visible on the traffic island between Fifth Ave and Broadway is a 51-ft granite obelisk, marking the grave of General William Jenkins Worth (1857; James Goodwin Batterson), hero of the Mexican War.

A half block W. of the park at No. 15 W. 25th St (between Broadway and Sixth Ave) is the SERBIAN EAST ORTHODOX CATHEDRAL OF ST SAVA (1855; Richard Upjohn; DL), originally built as an uptown outpost of Trinity parish, purchased by the present Serbo-Croatian congregation in 1943. Like other early Gothic Revival churches, it is a severe, simple brownstone, its somberness intesified by the darkening of the brownstone in the city's polluted atmosphere. Inside (open Sun at 11 during services) is a reredos (1892) and altar (1897) by Frederick Clarke Withers. The *Parish House* (1860; Jacob Wrey Mould; DL) just E. of the church is more fanciful, with polychromy, ornamental brickwork, and carved stonework in the Victorian Gothic manner. Between the buildings a walkway leads to *Clergy House*, built by Upjohn at the same time as the church and also designated as a landmark. Along the walkway a statue commemorates Michael Pupin (1858–1935), the noted Columbia University physicist who came to New York as a Serbian immigrant. Return to Madison Square park.

Continue clockwise through the park. At the N. end is the fine **Admiral Farragut Monument** (1881; Augustus Saint-Gaudens; base by Stanford White). The bronze figure of the admiral, whipped by an imaginary wind, gazes off at the horizon atop a pedestal (a replica of the original) on which two low relief female figures, Courage and Loyalty, emerge from a swirl of ocean currents. The monument was unveiled by John H. Knowles, the sailor who lashed Farragut to the mast of his ship during the historic Civil War battle of Mobile Bay.

In the N.E. corner of the park is a *statue of Chester A. Arthur* (1899; George E. Bissell), 21st President of the United States. Behind the statue (N.W. corner of Madison Ave and E. 26th St) is the *Child Study Association of America, Inc.* (50 Madison Ave), originally the American Society for the Prevention of Cruelty to Animals (1896; Renwick, Aspinwall & Owen), a limestone Italian Renaissance palazzo with an elaborately worked cornice. At one time this dignified and restrained building housed a dispensary and hospital for animals. Across Madison Ave (No. 51 Madison Ave) is the NEW YORK LIFE INSURANCE COMPANY (1928; Cass Gilbert), designed by the architect of the Woolworth Building. Its limestone Italian Renaissance base rises to a brightly gilded pyramidal tower, a favourite Gilbert motif (cf. the Woolworth Building and the Federal Courthouse at Foley Square). The building has a grandiose lobby, whose imposing scale, coffered ceiling, bronze appointments, and great staircase suggest the wealth of the institution that commissioned the building.

Unfortunately it replaces Stanford White's beautiful Madison Square Garden (1890; demolished 1925), the second of four successive buildings with that name. The first, converted from the abandoned railroad depot of the New York and Harlem Railroad, was leased by P.T. Barnum and known as the Hippodrome before it became Madison Square Garden in 1879. In 1883 the National Horse Show Association bought the site and built the second and most famous Madison Square Garden, which housed a restaurant, theatre, and roof garden as well as a sports arena. The walls were of yellow brick and white terracotta; the sidewalks were arcaded and the roof ornamented with six open cupolas, two small towers, and a large tower (249 ft to the base of the cupola) modelled after the Giralda in Seville. On top of the tower stood Augustus Saint-Gaudens's gilded statue of Diana, whose nudity distressed the city's more proper citizens, though since the goddess's head was 332 ft from the sidewalk, her anatomical charms could be glimpsed only remotely. Ironically this Madison Square Garden was the site of White's death. In June 1906 he was murdered, an unusual fate for an architect, shot to death in the roof garden by Pittsburgh millionaire Harry K. Thaw whose wife, the former showgirl Evelyn Nesbit, had in earlier days enjoyed a well-publicised affair with White.

Just S of the N.Y. Life Building is Madison Square's ugliest structure, the *Merchandise Mart* (1973; Emery Roth & Sons), a big, shiny black box, especially unfortunate since the Leonard Jerome mansion was sacrificed for it, the only Designated Landmark destroyed under a loophole in the law allowing demolition if no financially viable use can be found.

The *Jerome Mansion* (1859), built with the fortune Leonard Jerome reaped selling short in the Panic of 1857, featured a stables panelled in black walnut

The original Madison Square Garden in 1893. The controversial nude statue of Diana crowns the tower. On the right is the mansion of Leonard Jerome, grandfather of Winston Churchill. (The New-York Historical Society)

and a theatre seating 600, perhaps because Jerome was notably fond of actresses. When his wife moved to Paris (1868), he rented the house to the Union League Club. Later when the Manhattan Club took over the lease, it became the legendary site of the invention of the Manhattan cocktail. Jennie Jerome, Leonard's daughter who spent part of her childhood here, became Lady Randolph Churchill, mother of Winston Churchill.

Walk S. along Madison Ave on the park side to the N.E. corner of E. 25th St (No. 27 Madison Ave), the **Appellate Division of the New York State Supreme Court** (1900; James Brown Lord; DL), a small building remarkable for its sculpture and decoration. Built of white marble with a hexastyle Corinthian portico facing 25th St and four engaged columns along Madison Ave, the courthouse cost $633,768 of which more than one-third went for statuary and murals.

Along Madison Ave are (on the roof balustrade, N. to S.): Confucius (Philip Martiny); Peace flanked by Wisdom and Strength (Karl Bitter), and Moses (William Couper). The four caryatids below (Thomas Shields Clarke) represent the four seasons. Along the balustrade on 25th St are (W. to E.): Zoroaster

(Edward C. Potter); Alfred the Great (Jonathan Scott Hartley); Lycurgus (George Edwin Bissell); Solon (Herbert Adams); Justice flanked by Power and Study (Daniel Chester French); Louis IX (John Donoghue), Manu (Augustus Lukeman) and Justinian (Henry Kirke Bush-Brown). At one time a statue of Mohammed stood next to Zoroaster but was removed at the request of the city's Moslem community because Islamic law forbids images of the prophet. The pediment above the main doorway bears a sculptural group, the Triumph of Law (Charles H. Niehaus). Flanking the steps are Wisdom and Force (Frederick Wellington Ruckstuhl).

The interior of the building (open weekdays during working hours) is lavishly decorated, with murals, beaded chandeliers, and panelling. In the courtroom is a fine stained glass skylight bearing the names of famous American lawyers.

Directly across E. 25th St (No. 11–25 Madison Ave) is the **North Building** of the **Metropolitan Life Insurance Company** (1932; Harvey Wiley Corbett and D. Everett Waid), a massive limestone Art Deco building, best seen from the park. Note the high vaulted entrances and the elaborate, angled setbacks that lighten the apparent mass of the building while conforming to the zoning code. Here stood Stanford White's Madison Avenue Presbyterian Church (1906), a white marble, domed and colonnaded temple demolished in 1919.

Adjacent to the North Building is the **Metropolitan Life Tower** (1909; Napoleon Le Brun) on the S.E. corner of Madison Ave and 24th St, which took the title as world's tallest building from the Flatiron Building only to be topped by the Woolworth Building 4 years later. The tower (700 ft high, 75 ft wide on Madison Ave, 85 ft wide on 24th St) was inspired by the Campanile in St. Mark's Square in Venice and was considerably fancier before a remodelling in 1962. Its four dial clock, the world's largest, sounds a measure by Handel on the quarter hour. At the top of the pyramidal roof and choragic monument a gilded lantern emits flashes of red light to indicate the quarter hour and flashes of white to tell the hour.

Near the Madison Ave side of the park at its S. end is a bronze *statue of Roscoe Conkling* (1893; John Quincy Adams Ward), U.S. senator and presidential candidate, who died of exposure after trying to walk home from his downtown office in the Blizzard of 1888. The only modern work in the park is *Skagerrak* (1972; Antoni Milkowski), in the center of the park between Conkling and Seward. It consists of three rectangles (7 × 7 × 16 ft) of weathering steel and is named from a waterway separating Norway, Sweden and Denmark.

Return to E. 26th St and walk E. across Park Ave South to Lexington Ave. At No. 68 Lexington Ave between 25th and 26th Sts is the former 69TH REGIMENT ARMORY (1905; Hunt & Hunt), now used by the N.Y. National Guard, site of the famous 'Armory Show' (1913), where Marcel DuChamp's cubistic 'Nude Descending the Stairs' stunned the New York art world. Behind the Lexington Ave facade with its copper framed windows and mansard roof is a ribbed and buttressed drill hall.

Walk S. on Lexington Ave. On the N.W. corner of E. 22nd St is the Mabel Dean Bacon Vocational High School (1919; C.B.J. Snyder). Across the street on the N.E. corner is Baruch College of the City University of New York. On the S.W. corner is the former RUSSELL SAGE FOUNDATION (c. 1914; tower added 1919; Grosvenor Atterbury), converted to apartments in 1975. The building, a lavishly handsome Renaissance Revival palace, bears a frieze proclaiming its purpose—'For the Improvement of Social and Living Conditions'. Sage, who acquired millions on the stock market after a start as a grocery clerk, left his fortune, more than $10 million, to his philanthropic second wife who established the foundation.

Turn right and walk a block along E. 22nd St to Park Ave South, Fourth Ave prestigiously renamed. This stretch was once filled with charitable organisations, some of which still remain. On the N.E. corner is the *former United Charities Building* at No. 287 Park Ave S. (1891; R.H. Robertson and Rowe & Baker), once headquarters for some 45 social welfare agencies, still the home of the Children's Aid Society. On the S.E. corner is the Federation of Protestant Welfare Agencies at No. 281 Park Ave S. (1893; Robert W. Gibson and Edward J.N. Stent), formerly the CHURCH MISSIONS' HOUSE, headquarters of the Episcopal Church's missionary societies. Built of rockface granite and Indiana limestone over a steel skeleton, it is sometimes described as Flemish Renaissance and sometimes as Romanesque Revival. The tympanum above the entry shows St. Augustine preaching to the barbarians in England and Bishop Seabury preaching to the barbarians in America.

The *New York Bank for Savings* (1894, altered 1954; Cyrus L.W. Eidlitz) at No. 280 Park Ave S. is a handsome building marred by an unfortunate new corner entrance. *Calvary Church* (Protestant Episcopal) at No. 273 Park Ave S., on the N.E. corner of E. 21st St (1846; James Renwick, Jr) is not the best work of the architect of Grace Church and St. Patrick's Cathedral. Renwick also designed the Sunday School Building (1867).

Turn left and walk one block E. to **Gramercy Park,** New York's only private residential square. It was created by Samuel Bulkley Ruggles, a lawyer and small-scale urban planner, who bought a 20-acre farm in 1831 from the descendants of James Duane (mayor 1784–89), drained the marshland, and laid out a park because such an amenity would increase the value of his land. Around the park he designated 66 building lots and sold them with the stipulation that only lot owners could have access to the park. His wishes are still in force: except for a brief period during the Draft Riots of 1863 when troops camped inside the 8-ft iron fence, the park trustees have prevented all intrusions, including a proposed cable car line (1890) down Lexington Ave and an extension of the avenue (1912) through the park. Only residents facing the square who pay a yearly maintenance fee are granted keys.

The Gramercy Park Historic District, designated in 1966, includes the park, the streets facing it on the S., W., and E., and parts of 19th and 18th Sts.

Begin walking S. along Gramercy Park West, with its fine Greek Revival townhouses (numbered counterclockwise). Dr Valentine Mott (died 1865), a prominent surgeon and a founder of Bellevue Hospital, lived at No. 1. **Nos 3–4 Gramercy Park West** (c. 1840; attrib. Alexander Jackson Davis) are distinguished by beautiful cast-iron verandahs with profuse Greek Revival ornamentation—anthemions, meanders, and floral motifs. This lacy iron work, more familiar in southern cities like Charleston and New Orleans, was considered a rustic touch especially appropriate to houses facing parks or enjoying deep front yards. A pair of Mayor's Lamps stand at No. 4, once the home of James Harper, mayor (1844–45) and a founder of Harper & Brothers, publishers. At No. 15 on the S. side of the park is the **National Arts Club** (1845; remodelled 1874; Calvert Vaux; DL), a badly spalled brownstone built during the Gothic Revival period of the 1840s as two houses and remodelled for Samuel J. Tilden during the heyday of a more flamboyant Victorian Gothic style. Tilden, pursuer of the Tweed Ring, governor of New York, and disappointed presidential candidate (1876) seems to have doubted the public's good will for he had rolling steel doors installed behind the lower windows and an escape tunnel built to 19th St. Note the polychrome decoration, assymetric bays, heavy lancet windows, and the medallions portraying Goethe, Dante, Franklin, and Milton. The National Arts Club bought the building in 1906; occasionally it holds exhibitions open to the public (tel: GR5–3424).

Next door at No. 15 is **The Players** (1845; remodelled, 1888; Stanford White; DL) a simple Gothic Revival brownstone (note the drip mouldings on the upstairs windows) until actor Edwin Booth bought it and hired Stanford White to remodel it as an actors' club. The fine iron railings and lanterns and the two-story porch based on an Italian Renaissance prototype are known to be White's personal work.

Cross Gramercy Park South and look into the park for a view of the *statue of Edwin Booth* in the Character of Hamlet (1918; Edmond T. Quinn). The name Gramercy harks back to the Dutch colonial period when the area was called Krom Moerasje ('crooked little swamp') after a marshy brook that wandered from Madison Square to the East River near 18th St. Later the neighbourhood was called Crommashie Hill, and eventually Gramercy Park.

At *No. 19 Gramercy Park South* (S.E. corner of Irving Place) stands the former Benjamin Sonnenberg mansion, a five-story red brick house built in 1845 and updated with a mansard roof in 1860. Stuyvesant Fish, whose business interests included railroads, insurance, and banking, bought it in the 1880s and his wife here began her assault on society. After Fish moved uptown near the turn of the century the house declined until public relations counsel Benjamin Sonnenberg bought it in 1931 and restored it to its former glory, both as a house and as a center of the city's social life.

Continue E. past No. 21 Gramercy Park South, one of the city's worst restorations. At the S.E. corner (No. 144 E. 20th St) is the former FRIENDS' MEETING HOUSE (1859; King & Kellum; DL), an austere Italianate building whose severity is broken only by the arched pediment above the doorway. Saved in 1965 from a developer who wanted a 30-story apartment building, the meeting house was renovated in 1975 as the Brotherhood Synagogue by Stewart Polshek.

Two apartments on Gramercy Park East deserve brief note. No. 34 (1883; George DaConha), a red brick building with an octagonal turret and a lavish mosaic lobby floor, is probably the city's first cooperative apartment. No. 36 (1908; James Riley Gordon) has elaborate terracotta Gothic ornament and two cast stone armoured knights guarding the entrance. Return to Irving Pl.

Walk S. on Irving Pl., named (1831) by Samuel Ruggles after Washington Irving, writer and diplomat. The block of E. 19th St between Irving Pl. and Third Ave is known as '*The Block Beautiful*'. Remodelled in the 1920s, its little 19C houses and stables while individually undistinguished have unusual serenity and charm, though a few suffer from excessive cuteness. During the 1930s a small artists' colony flourished here, its residents including muckraker Ida Tarbell ('The History of Standard Oil') and painter George Bellows. *Pete's Tavern* on the N.E. corner of Irving Pl. and 18th St is one of the city's oldest taverns (opened 1864), having survived Prohibition as a speakeasy. Its most illustrious client, writer O. Henry (William Sydney Porter), lived at No. 55 Irving Pl., and described the café in a story, 'The Lost Blend'.

Continue S. to 17th St. The house at No. 40 Irving Pl. (S.W. corner of the intersection), bears a plaque identifying it as Washington Irving's home. It wasn't. Built c. 1845, its most famous residents were Elsie de Wolfe and Elisabeth Marbury (later, Lady Mendl), two ladies of taste and social ability who became famous as an interior decorator and a literary agent. During their stay in this house at the turn of the century the ladies ran a Sunday salon which, according to their own recollections, attracted so many foreign celebrities that it was known as the 'Immigrants' Home'. Across the street a bronze *bust of Washington Irving* (1885; Frederick Beer) stands in front of the high school bearing his name.

Turn left and walk E. on 17th St. At No. 190 Third Ave between 17th and 18th Sts is *Tuesday's*, now a singles' bar, formerly Joe King's Rathskeller (also known as the German-American), host to several generations of beer-drinking collegians. The building (1894; Weber & Drosser) owes its ornate baroque facade to its early days as Scheffel Hall, a *biergarten* serving the large 19C neighbourhood German population. Continue E. on 17th St past Second Ave to Stuyvesant Square. Its N. boundary is especially attractive, with the picturesque Victorian Gothic building housing a *Salvation Army Residence* at No. 231–235 E. 17th St (E. section, 1877; E.T. Littel; W. section, 1883; Charles C. Haight) and a house (1883) by Richard Morris Hunt at No. 245 E. 17th St.

The Stuyvesant Square Historic District, designated in 1975, includes the square, Rutherford Place, and partial frontages on E. 15th and E. 17th Sts.

Cross into STUYVESANT SQUARE, once part of Peter Stuyvesant's farm, later (1837) a Stuyvesant family gift to the city. The 4-acre park, which has always been bisected by Second Ave, was landscaped in 1936 with shade trees and small pools. The bronze statue of Peter Stuyvesant (1936, installed 1941) is by Gertrude Vanderbilt Whitney, founder of the Whitney Museum. Although the neighbourhood especially to the E. has deteriorated, the park, surrounded by medical and spiritual institutions, remains pleasant, despite its usual handful of derelicts and panhandlers.

To the E. are the buildings of Beth Israel Medical Center and the New York Infirmary. To the S.E. is St. Mary's Catholic Church of the Byzantine Rite (1964; Brother Cajetan J.B. Baumann), with its stained glass windows and bright mosaics.

West of Stuyvesant Square, across Rutherford Place is the FRIENDS' MEETING HOUSE AND SEMINARY (1860; Charles T. Bunting; DL), a red brick Greek Revival building with brownstone quoins, austere like all Quaker houses of worship. A 17C schism accounts for the presence of two contemporary meeting houses within a few blocks of one another.

Rutherford Pl. is named after Colonel John Rutherford, a member of the committee that laid out the city's streets beginning in 1807 and eventually issued the Commissioners' Plan of 1811 (see p174).

Across 16th St from the meeting house is ST. GEORGE'S CHURCH (Protestant Episcopal), a powerful Romanesque Revival brownstone (1856; Otto Blesch and Leopold Eidlitz; DL), remembered as J.P. Morgan's church because as an elder he ruled it with an iron hand. The first church (1847) burned in 1865 but was rebuilt according to the original plans, although at the time of the reconstruction the rector insisted on an evangelically simple interior without the customary altar and reredos. Originally the church had two tall spires, weakened by the fire and removed (1888). N. of the church is the *Chapel* (1911; Matthew Lansing Emery and Henry George

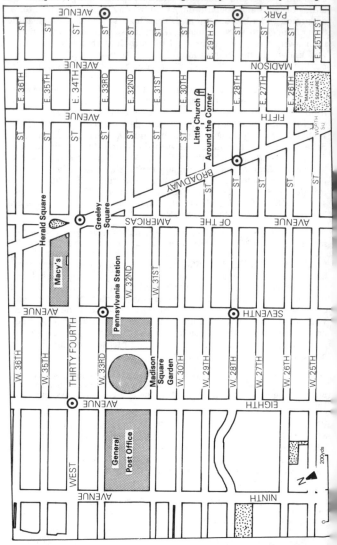

Emery), an overly elaborate Byzantine-Romanesque companion to the more somber church.

Walk W. on 16th St past the original *Rectory* at No. 209 E. 16th St, built in the early 1850s by Leopold Eidlitz. Because of neighbourhood population changes, St. George's is now combined with Calvary and the Church of the Holy Communion (W. 20th St and Sixth Ave) in a single parish.

Continue walking W. to Third Ave; turn left (S.) and walk to 14th St. At No. 145 E. 14th St near the corner of Third Ave is the *Consolidated Edison Energy Museum* (10–4, Tues–Sat; admission free), with displays of early electrical equipment, dioramas, and recorded narrations documenting the history of electricity in America. Especially interesting is the room-sized model of the subterranean energy distribution system in New York.

The *Consolidated Edison Company Building* (N.E. corner of Irving Pl. and E. 14th St) is Henry Hardenbergh's last large work (1915–29; Henry J. Hardenbergh; tower, 1926; Warren & Wetmore), and not one of his most successful. It occupies the site of the old Academy of Music, of Tammany Hall, and of Tony Pastor's Music Hall.

Tammany Hall, founded in 1789 as a fraternal society and political club, later grew into the Democratic party machine, long the most potent factor in city politics. By the mid 19C, Tammany had become synonymous with corruption and crooked elections (notably with bought immigrant votes), and its leaders were known as 'Bosses', e.g. Boss Tweed.

Continue W. on 14th St to Union Square. Until June 1982 Lüchow's restaurant at 110 E. 14th St opposite Irving Pl. remained as the last survivor of the former theatre district, moving uptown to the Broadway area one hundred years after opening.

12 Herald Square and the Garment District

SUBWAY: IRT Broadway–7th Ave Local or Express (trains 1, 2, 3) to 34th St–Penn. Station. IND Sixth Ave (trains B, D, F) or IND Eighth Ave (trains A, AA, CC, E) to 34th St–Penn Station or BMT (trains N, QB, RR) to 34th St.

BUS: M6 or M7 via Broadway–Seventh Ave or M10 via Seventh Ave to 34th St. M16 runs crosstown on 34th St. M4 via Fifth Ave to 34th St and Sixth Ave. Culture Bus (weekends and holidays) Loop I, Stop 22.

PARKING: Crosstown traffic in the Garment District during working hours is very slow. There are large parking facilities under 1 Penn Plaza and on the block of W. 31st St between Seventh and Eighth Aves as well as many smaller garages and lots in the Madison Square Garden area.

Begin at **Herald Square,** not really a square at all but two triangles (W. 32nd to W. 35th Sts) created by the intersection of Broadway and Sixth Ave. It owes its name to the 'New York Herald', which between 1895 and 1921 occupied a fine McKim, Mead & White Venetian-style palazzo just N. of 35th St. Both the palazzo and the paper are gone now, the former demolished in favour of an office building, the latter, after a number of mergers, finally succumbing in 1966. Only the bell and clock that once adorned the building remain, installed when the Sixth Ave El was torn down (1939) as a memorial to Herald publishers James Gordon Bennett and his son James Gordon Bennett, Jr (pedestal and redesign of square, 1940; Aymar Embury II). Two muscular bronze figures nicknamed Stuff and Guff or alternately Gog and Magog hammer out the hours on the Meneeley bell, while a bronze Minerva and her owl observe the proceedings (statuary, 1894; Antonin Jean Carles). The S. triangle between W. 32nd and W. 33rd Sts, properly called GREELEY SQ., contains a statue of 'New York Tribune' founder Horace Greeley (1890; Alexander Doyle).

Beneath Herald Sq. stretches a labyrinthine subway station, a maze of pedestrian access tunnels and transit lines—the BMT subway, the railroad tubes connecting lines in New Jersey and Long Island with Penn Station, and the Sixth Ave, IND subway which was threaded through the existing tangle (1939) about 52 ft below street level.

Herald Square also enjoys a reputation as a major retail shopping district, dominated by Macy's and Gimbels while W. 32nd St between Sixth and Seventh Aves offers a concentration of shops dealing in photographic equipment.

R.H. Macy & Co. (W. 34th to W. 35th St, Broadway to Seventh Ave) now occupies a square block containing 2·2 million sq. ft of selling space (original building facing Broadway, 1901; DeLemos & Cordes; Seventh Ave building, 1931; Robert D. Kohn).

It was founded by Rowland Hussey Macy, a Nantucket Quaker who went to sea at the age of 15 and returned four years later with $500 and a red star, now Macy's logo, tattooed on his hand. After six failures in merchandising and additional disappointments in real estate and the stock market, Macy founded (1858) his New York store on Sixth Ave near 14th St, an enterprise he developed to the point where he could bill it as 'the world's largest store'. Its 168 selling departments are overseen by a staff of 11,000 employees, who deal with 45 million business transactions annually. Despite the efforts of a security force that includes Doberman pinschers to guard the store after hours, Macy's loses about $10 million annually to thieves and shoplifters, about 2% of its $480 million yearly sales.

The store's longtime image as a conservative, middle-class store has resulted in part from its founder's business principles: sell at fixed prices, undersell all competitors, buy and sell only for cash (the last a throwback to Macy's Quaker heritage). In the late 1930s, however, Macy's began to extend credit to its customers, and recently the store has sought to exhibit a more daring, more fashionable image to attract customers from the suburbs, the Upper West Side, and the new, relatively affluent loft areas like SoHo lying S. of 34th St. At a cost of $10 million, the Herald Square store has been refurbished floor by floor to make it visually more dramatic, apparently a successful marketing strategy.

Macy's is also known for the variety of its merchandise, stocking almost half a million items, from furs and diamonds, caviar and raspberries, to all the more humble articles needful in this life. Among its more spectacular sales have been a cowboy costume for a show business chimpanzee, the plumbing fixtures for the presidential palace in Liberia, and a length of silk to outfit the members of a Saudi Arabian harem.

A decade after its founder's death the store passed (1887) to Isidor and Nathan Straus who had leased space in the basement (1874) to run a china and glassware department, and the Straus family has now been associated with Macy's for five generations. Isidor Straus and his wife Ida, who perished together during the sinking of the 'Titanic' (1912), are honoured by a plaque near the entrance.

Gimbels, a block downtown at Broadway and W. 33rd St (open Mon and Thurs, 9.45–8.30; Tues, Wed, Fri, 9.45–6; Sun and holidays, 12–5; tel: 564–3300) is famous as Macy's competitor, but is hardly an upstart in the field. Adam Gimbel, a Bavarian immigrant who began his career in this country as a pack peddler, began a line of department stores in the midwest in 1842 but Gimbels came to New York in 1910. The feud between Macy's and Gimbels which has given rise to such slogans as 'Nobody but Nobody undersells Gimbels', and 'Does Macy's tell Gimbels', a rivalry romanticised in the film 'Miracle on 34th St', has generally been profitable to both stores. Today Gimbels is known primarily for its sales and its bargain basement.

Walk W. to Seventh Ave. The street signs for Seventh Ave as it passes through the **Garment District** are subtitled 'Fashion Ave', a name imposed with some bravado on an area beset with serious economic problems. The American garment industry as a whole is shrinking in the face of cheap imported goods, and the New York sector is further threatened with transportation difficulties, high labour costs, and infiltration by organised crime. Nonetheless, the Garment District, bounded roughly by 25th and 41st Sts, Sixth and Ninth Aves, houses one of the city's most important industries which moved uptown from the sweat shops of the Lower East Side around the time of World War I.

The S. part of the district is dominated by the fur industry; the area around 34th St by children's wear firms, and the section N. of 36th St by women's apparel, though these geographical divisions are only general. On the fringe of the Garment District are allied industries and trades—firms dealing in millinery (a depressed industry because hats are out of style), in hosiery, and in buttons, thread, trimmings, and fabrics.

The Garment District is notorious for its congested traffic, and only the ignorant or leisured driver will try to negotiate the crosstown streets during working hours when double-parked trucks, wheeled clothing racks, and pushcarts clog both the roadway and the sidewalk. The lunchtime crowd, once famous for its density though it has thinned with the shrinking of the work force, still gathers in such traditional haunts as Dubrow's Cafeteria (515 Seventh Ave) or at Lou G. Siegel's (209 W. 38th St), an expensive Kosher restaurant that caters to buyers and bosses, the upper crust of the Garment District.

In this area of conglomerates and monopolies, the garment trade remains decentralised, composed mostly of small workshops hiring fewer than 100 employees. Because of the elusive nature of 'style', the business also remains highly speculative and competitive, offering the dream of windfall profits and the spectre of bankruptcy. Furthermore, the subdivision of labour all along the line—from the designer to the final presser—has resulted in a complex system of production that borders sometimes upon chaos and reaches seasonal peaks of frenzy.

Although the workshops and showrooms are not open to the public, it is sometimes possible to visit one by arranging with the Education Department of the International Ladies Garment Workers Union (tel: CO 5–7000), which offers a film about the union's development and a visit to a workroom with a union representative. In general workers within the industry are highly specialised—cutters, machine operators who sew the garments together, finishers who sew

Concourse of the former Pennsylvania Station in 1910. The demolition of this magnificent building and its replacement by the present non-entity mark one of the saddest episode's in the city's architectural history. (The New-York Historical Society)

on hooks and eyes, buttons, and belts, pleaters, pressers, and so on. Workshops are usually organised according to areas of work, and workers repeat these specialised operations over and over, paid either by the hour or by the piece. The manufacturer whose label adorns a finished garment may send out the cut work to contractors, who are then responsible for the actual sewing and finishing of the garments.

Workers in the industry were originally Italian or Jewish immigrants; nowadays while many still belong to these ethnic groups, black, Hispanic, and oriental workers dominate the work force, with women outnumbering men by a factor of three to one.

Walk S. on Seventh Ave. On the S.E. corner of W. 33rd St is the *Statler-Hilton Hotel* (1918; McKim, Mead & White), formerly the Hotel Pennsylvania, whose telephone number was immortalised by bandleader Glenn Miller, composer of a song called 'Pennsylvania 6–5000'; during the 1930s the hotel was a center for big bands as well as the gathering place for buyers who arrived in town to stock their stores from the offerings of the Garment District.

Pennsylvania Station is still across the street but it is now contained in a hole, underground. Until wantonly destroyed in 1963–66, **the former Pennsylvania Station** (1906–10) was McKim, Mead & White's masterpiece, a symbol of the power of the Pennsylvania Railroad, and a happy union of history and technology. The facade with its imposing Doric colonnade and the General Waiting Room with its vaulted ceiling were modelled on the Roman Baths of Caracalla while the steel and glass arches, domes, and vaults covering the Concourse belonged to the more recent tradition of crystal palaces and glass exhibition galleries. Not only did the station provide the visitor with a spectacular entrance to the city, but the tunnels leading to it allowed, for the first time, a convenient approach from either New Jersey via the Hudson River tubes or Long Island via a connecting crosstown tunnel and tubes beneath the East River.

When the station was destroyed in the interests of greater profits, the 'New York Times' declared (3 Oct 1963): 'Until the first blow fell, no one was convinced that Penn Station really would be demolished or that New York would permit this monumental act of vandalism. . .Any city gets what it admires, will pay for, and ultimately deserves.'

In its place arose the present utterly graceless and unappealing MADISON SQUARE GARDEN CENTER (1968; Charles Luckman Assocs). The complex includes Madison Square Garden, a 20,000 seat arena enclosed in a pre-cast concrete-clad drum, the Felt Forum (1000 seats), a movie theatre (500 seats), a bowling alley (48 lanes), an office building (29 stories), an exhibition gallery, and a shopping arcade. A hockey team, the New York Rangers, and a basketball team, the New York Knickerbockers, call the Garden home; other events are regularly scheduled: track meetings, ice shows, tennis tournaments, the Barnum and Bailey circus, rock concerts, and boxing matches. For ticket information call 563–8000.

Beneath the Garden is the present PENN STATION, still using the old tracks laid down when its predecessor was completed. About 650 trains use the station daily carrying c. 200,000 passengers; with additional access from the BMT, IRT, and IND subways and the PATH (Port Authority Trans-Hudson) system, the station receives a crowd of half a million people daily.

Walk W. to Eighth Ave. Between W. 31st and W. 33rd Sts on the W. side of the avenue is the GENERAL POST OFFICE (1913; McKim, Mead & White; DL), whose tall Corinthian colonnade once echoed that of the railroad station. Around the frieze marches a motto loosely adapted from Herodotus and only vaguely applicable to the workings of the present New York postal system: 'Neither snow nor rain nor heat nor gloom of night stays these couriers from the swift completion of their appointed rounds'.

Walk S. on Eighth Ave and turn left on W. 30th St. At 211 W. 30th St, between Seventh and Eighth Aves, is the small, handsome brownstone ST. JOHN THE BAPTIST CHURCH (Roman Catholic), designed (1872) by Napoleon LeBrun, architect of the Metropolitan Life Tower and a number of handsome firehouses.

Continue walking E. to Seventh Ave and turn right (S.). The **Fur District** stretches roughly from 27th to 30th Sts between Sixth and Eighth Aves. Like the rest of the garment industry, the fur trade is shrinking, with about 3000 workers today compared with some 8000 ten years ago and 15,000 in the 1930s. The rather dismal looking shops whose barred windows attest to the value of the merchandise within are protected by closed-circuit TV cameras, alarm systems, and buzzer-operated locked doors. Even though robbery is a threat it is still possible to see couriers walking casually through the streets with fur coats worth tens of thousands of dollars dangling from hangers or slung over their arms.

Continue S. on Seventh Ave. The FASHION INSTITUTE OF TECHNOLOGY (1958–77; DeYoung & Moscowitz), located along the avenue from W. 26th to W. 28th St, is a professional school for students seeking careers in the clothing industry. Three galleries in the Shirley Goodman Resource Center (between W. 26th and W. 27th Sts) offer changing exhibitions of interest to observers or historians of fashion. The F.I.T. library (tel: 760–7695) is open to the public for reference (9 a.m.–10 p.m. weekdays; noon to 5 p.m. weekends) and contains 50,000 books. The costume collection in the Design Laboratory (admission by membership only) contains 250,000 articles of clothing and a large collection of accessories including such items as a 52-lb black beaded gown formerly owned by movie star Joan Crawford.

Walk E. on 28th St to Sixth Ave. The **Flower Market**—not a centralised market building but a collection of wholesale and retail stores along Sixth Ave and the side streets near W. 28th St—delights the eye with a burst of colour in an otherwise undistinguished neighbourhood. The market awakens to a buzz of wholesale activity during the early morning hours, subsiding later in the day to more sedate retail selling, when one can browse at leisure among palm fronds, rubber plants, and masses of fragrant cut flowers. The market began about 1870, when Long Island growers brought their flowers daily to the foot of E. 34th St at the East River; gradually the district moved inland to be near what was then the center of retail selling.

In the 1880s a variety theatre, dance hall, and restaurant called the Haymarket stood at the S.E. corner of Sixth Ave and W. 30th St. It was the most notorious resort of a district known as the **Tenderloin,** which stretched from about 24th to 40th St between Fifth and Seventh Aves and was so famous for its brothels, saloons, and dance halls that Brooklyn reformer T. DeWitt Talmadge called it 'Satan's Circus'. Police Inspector Alexander Williams, transferred to this precinct from quieter streets, gave it its best-known name by remarking: 'I've had nothing but chuck steak for a long time, and now I'm going to get a little of the tenderloin.' Williams then began supplementing his modest salary with protection money extorted from the proprietors of saloons, gambling houses and brothels, eventually coming to possess a city home, a Connecticut estate, and a yacht. Through the efforts of reformers and the Lexow Committee (1894), the involvement of public officials in vice and crime became a source of general indignation; Williams was retired 'for the good of the force'.

Continue E. to Fifth Ave; turn left and walk N. At 272 Fifth Ave on the N.W. corner of 29th St is the *Marble Collegiate Reformed Church* (1854; Samuel A. Warner; DL), a Gothic Revival contemporary of Trinity Church. The Collegiate Dutch Reformed Church, the oldest denomination in the city dating from 1628, is so named because its ministers, serving as equals, are called colleagues. Norman Vincent Peale, prolific author, popular speaker, and master of public relations, made the church famous during his pastorate.

The Church of the Transfiguration (Protestant Episcopalian) at 1 E. 29th St in its quiet garden is better known as '**The Little Church Around the Corner**', a name it earned in 1870. Actor Joseph Jefferson, trying to arrange the funeral of George Holland, another actor, was told by the minister of a fashionable nearby church who declined to perform the service that 'the little church around the corner' might be willing to bury someone as socially disreputable as an actor. Jefferson replied, 'God bless the little church around the corner', a remark now enshrined in a stained glass window in the S. aisle.

The body of the church (architect unknown) dates from 1849; the Guild Hall and Rectory by Frederick C. Withers were added in 1861, while the Lich Gate, also designed by Withers, was donated (1896) by Mrs Franklin Delano, the former Laura Astor, aunt of President Franklin D. Roosevelt. The Lich Gate, unusual in American churchyards, provided a covered resting place for the coffin before burial. The church, rectory, Guild Hall, Lich Gate, Lady Chapel, and Mortuary Chapel are all Designated Landmarks.

Enter the church (open 8–6 daily; during the winter months the nave is closed except during services because of heating costs). To the left of the entrance is the Chantry or Chapel of the Holy Family, first used as a parish schoolroom. The altar, called the Brides' Altar because it was donated by couples married in the church, is surmounted by a reredos containing three Scottish carved oak panels more than 400 years old depicting aspects of the Crucifixion. Old copies of famous paintings adorn the N. wall. The Baptistry to the left of the altar contains a bronze marker commemorating actress Gertrude Lawrence (died 1952). The paintings (artist unknown) flanking the font are Flemish (17C). The LADY CHAPEL, separated from the chantry by three stained-glass doors was added in 1906. Its windows reproduce (left to right) Raphael's 'Madonna del Gran Duca', the high altar of this church, and Botticelli's 'Virgin and Child'. Enter the NAVE, which contains a number of memorials to actors. Begin in the N. aisle. Montague (Henry J. Mann), a handsome matinee idol (died 1878), is depicted in the first window wearing the robes of a pilgrim. The first clerestory window honours Mary Shaw (died 1929), actress and feminist. The window depicting St. John the Beloved Disciple is dedicated to American actor John Drew (died 1927). Other windows in the N. aisle honour St. Alban, first martyr of Britain, and St. Augustine, first Archbishop of Canterbury. The *St. Faith window* nearest the pulpit in the N. aisle is said to be the oldest church window in America, made of 14C Belgian glass saved from a church destroyed during the Napoleonic wars. The window depicts St. Faith on a mound of flowers beneath a canopy of early Renaissance design. In the S. aisle the *Joseph Jefferson Memorial Window* commemorates the incident which gave the church its nickname. Jefferson, clad in the rags of his role as Rip Van Winkle is shown leading enshrouded George Holland toward the Lich Gate. The bronze tablet next to the window honouring actor Otis Skinner is the work of Paul Manship.

The Peace Shrine near the S. TRANSEPT contains a wood statue of Christ designed after Thorwaldsen's 'Christus Consolator'. At the end of the transept is the Madonna Shrine dating from 1930. The *Actors' Memorial Window* in the transept clerestory honours members of the theatrical profession and depicts the Flight into Egypt. On the W. wall of the transept is the **Edwin Booth Memorial Window*, given to honour the tragedian, depicted in the garb of Hamlet, by the Players which he founded. Next to it is the '*Jewelled Window*', whose richly coloured pieces of glass are said to resemble rubies and sapphires, a memorial to Joseph W. Drexel, a communicant of this church. Both the Drexel and Booth windows are the work of John La Farge. The MORTUARY CHAPEL (1908) is dedicated to St. Joseph of Arimathea. The window above its altar depicting Raphael's Transfiguration was originally above the high altar.

The nearest subway is the IRT-Lexington Ave Local (train 6) at Lexington Ave and 33rd or 28th St. Uptown buses run on Madison Ave. Downtown buses run on Fifth Ave (as far as Madison Sq.) or Park Ave S. (all the way downtown).

13   East 42nd Street, Kips Bay, and Murray Hill

SUBWAY: IND Sixth Ave trains (B,D, or F) to 42nd St. IRT Flushing train (train 7) to Fifth Ave and 42nd St.

BUS: Downtown buses via Fifth Ave (M1, M2, M3, M4, M32); downtown from upper W. Side (M5 or M104). Uptown buses via Park Ave S. and Madison Aves (M1, M2, M3, M4, M32). Uptown buses via Sixth Ave (M5, M6). 42nd St crosstown (M106). Culture Bus Loop I, Stop 19 (42nd St and Fifth Ave); Loop II, Stop 18 (42nd St and Vanderbilt Ave), weekends and holidays only.

Since 1838 Fifth Avenue has been the dividing line between the East Side and the West Side, a division with social as well as geographical ramifications. The East Side has a reputation for being rich and chic while the West Side is known to be a little down at the heels. While this is true of 42nd St too, generally, with W. 42nd deserving its reputation for seediness and E. 42nd its acclaim as the site of such institutions as the Ford Foundation and the United Nations, the change is gradual rather than abrupt.

The block of W. 42nd St just before Fifth Ave has several interesting buildings. At 33 W. 42nd St (between Fifth and Sixth Aves) is the *Graduate Center of the City University of New York*, originally Aeolian Hall (1912), remodelled (1970; Carl J. Petrilli & Assocs) with a mid-block pedestrian arcade and gallery for changing exhibitions. The tenth floor cafeteria is open to the public. The *W.R. Grace Building* at 41 W. 42nd St (1974; Skidmore, Owings & Merrill) is a big white building with a swooping facade, maligned for its ostentation and for the architects' indifference to the existing streetscape.

Cross Fifth Ave and walk E. At 60 E. 42nd St is between Madison and Park Aves is the *Lincoln Building* (1939; J.E.R. Carpenter), a 53-story skyscraper with a striking series of setbacks. The lobby contains a smaller bronze version of Daniel Chester French's

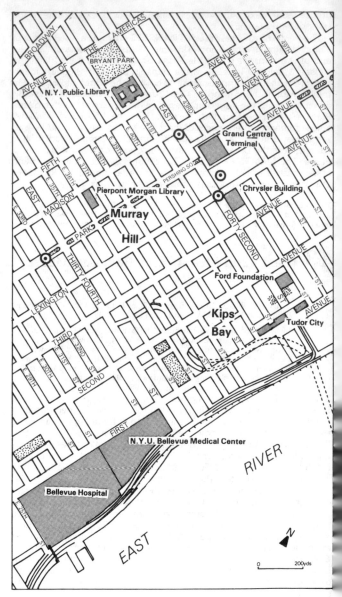

immense seated Lincoln in the Lincoln Memorial in Washington, D.C.

Across the street *Grand Central Terminal (1903–13; Reed & Stem and Warren & Wetmore; DL) looms into view, majestically straddling Park Ave. Though railroad travel has declined in scope and grandeur since the terminal was built, Grand Central Terminal remains one of the world's great railroad stations and an enduring symbol of the city. Visually less exciting than those other emblems of New York's pre-eminence—the Empire State Building, the Brooklyn Bridge, and the Statue of Liberty—it is still a fine building and a marvel of engineering and urban planning, bringing the railroad into the heart of the city while enhancing property around itself.

At one time Grand Central was the terminus for two major railroads, the New York Central which reached to the Mississippi River and the New York, New Haven and Hartford which served New England, but today it has become essentially a commuter station, through whose portals pass c. 140,000 passengers daily, mostly from towns N. and N.E. of the city.

The station covers three city blocks—42nd to 45th Sts between Vanderbilt Pl. and Madison Ave—and beneath it are luggage tunnels, electric power facilities, steam, water, sewage, and electric mains, and loops of track where trains can turn around without backing out of the station.

EXTERIOR: The best view of the terminal—albeit impaired by the presence of the bland yet obtrusive Pan Am Building—is from a few blocks S. on Park Ave. Whitney Warren, primarily responsible for the S. facade, saw the station as a gateway to the city and designed it with three great arched windows framed by pairs of columns to recall the triumphal arches of the cities of antiquity. Jules-Alexis Coutan created the sculptural group (1914) that crowns the facade. Entitled 'Transportation', it depicts Mercury (Commerce) flanked by Hercules (Physical Energy) and Minerva (Intellectual Energy). Directly beneath the clock (13 ft in diam.) stands an heroic bronze figure of Cornelius Vanderbilt, commissioned by the Commodore himself (1869; Albert De Groot) and moved here from the former Hudson River Freight station in 1929.

History. By 1869 Cornelius Vanderbilt, known as the Commodore because of his beginnings as a ferryboat entrepreneur, had seized control of all the railroads into New York by a series of bold financial manoeuvres. He determined to consolidate the lines physically by erecting at Fourth Ave and 42nd St a Grand Central Depot, magniloquently named in the manner of his breed since in 1896 42nd St was in the hinterlands. He then acquired sufficient land along Fourth Ave for storage and marshalling yards, land that constitutes practically all of the present Grand Central complex. A station designed by John B. Snook rose between 1869–71, a 'head house', whose trains either backed in or backed out. Never really adequate, the original station and its sheds and yards underwent almost constant enlargement and rearrangement, including a remodelling in 1898 in which a new waiting room for immigrants was created in the basement so that passengers in the main waiting room and rotunda might not have to mix with immigrants. Shortly after the original depot had been completed, the Vanderbilt interests began the process of lowering the tracks below street level, first in an open cut with a roofed tunnel provided with smoke vents, ultimately in the present subterranean system that includes a tunnel from 96th St to the station and fans out at 57th St to a width of 31 tracks on the upper level and 17 tracks on the lower level.

In 1903 when the city demanded that the railroad electrify its lines or move the terminal to the outskirts, William J. Wilgus, brilliant chief engineer, submitted a proposal for submerging the tracks, introducing the two present levels of trackage and electrifying the lines as far as Mott Haven in the Bronx. He further suggested building a new terminal while using the air rights over the tracks (Madison to Lexington Aves, 42nd to 50th Sts) for new, revenue-producing office and apartment buildings. A competition for the design of the station produced the innovative plan of architects Reed and Stem (Reed was Wilgus's brother-in-law) that wrapped Park Ave around the station on viaducts. Later the firm of Warren & Wetmore (Warren was a cousin of William K. Vanderbilt, then Chairman of the Board of the New York Central Railroad) was brought into the project. Though Warren & Wetmore seem to have triumphed in the power struggle between the two firms, the basic premises of the design are those of Reed & Stem: the elevated driveway around the station, the bridge across 42nd St with ramps down to street level at 40th St, and the placement of piers for future office buildings along Park Ave.

INTERIOR: Enter the terminal through the central doorway at Park Ave. Directly behind the Main Waiting Room is the MAIN CONCOURSE (120 ft wide; 375 ft long), sheathed in marble and simulated Caen stone, which rises to an elliptical vault (125 ft high), coloured cerulean and decorated with constellations designed by Warren with Paul Helleu and Charles Basing. Worked into the ornamentation throughout are clusters of oak leaves, chosen by the Vanderbilts as the family emblem. The concourse, with its elegant spaces and rich materials, has suffered various commercial depredations: the conversion of some of its bronze-grilled ticket windows into Off-Track Betting booths and the installation of a too large, too bright Kodak billboard on the E. wall. The shopping arcade (main level), long the site of dingy and unappealing enterprises, now offers several attractive shops. Among the concessions on the lower level (accessible from the Grand Staircase at the W. end of the concourse) is the *Oyster Bar*, architecturally interesting for the Guastavino tiles supporting its vaulted ceiling and gastronomically appealing for its many varieties (sometimes as many as 12) of oysters, of which some 12,000 are opened and served daily.

Beneath the lower level, whose tracks once served the lowly commuter while more glamorous long-distance arrivals and departures took place on the upper level, a vast network of tunnels carries mains and pipes for the steam, hot water, electricity and telephone cables that serve the station and several nearby buildings. It is possible, though hardly advisable, to walk from 43rd to 49th St in these dark, sometimes rat-infested service tunnels, which despite efforts of the management have become home for a population of derelicts to whom they become more attractive as the weather gets colder and inflation makes the cost of cheap rooms prohibitive.

PRESERVATION. It is not surprising that many assaults have been made on the architectural integrity of the terminal, sitting as it does on a prime midtown site. Fortunately most have come to naught, with the unhappy exception of the Pan Am building which towers above the terminal from the N. Among the more revolting of the unsuccessful schemes was a plan (1960) to divide the Main Waiting Room horizontally into four 15-ft stories, the upper three to contain bowling alleys. This proposal doubtless hastened designation of the terminal as a landmark (1965), a status the Penn Central Railroad, then operating it, soon came to resent, recognising the inflation in surrounding real estate generated by the station and wanting to cash in on the rising values itself. The railroad proposed a 54-story tower over the Waiting Room, a design rejected by the Landmarks Commission. After several other plans to circumvent the designation failed, the railroad sued to have the landmark status withdrawn on the grounds of economic hardship, but in 1978 the Supreme Court upheld the city's right to protect architecturally or historically valuable buildings by this means.

Return to 42nd St. The intersection of Park Ave and E. 42nd St, though not properly a square, is named *Pershing Square* in honour of General John Joseph Pershing, commander of the American forces in Europe during World War I. PARK AVE began as Fourth Ave on the 1811 grid, but was not developed because a granite ridge ran its entire length. When the New York and Harlem Railroad requested a right of way for its tracks and permission to run its steam engines above 14th St (1832), the city granted it Fourth Ave. The railroad then blasted out the granite and laid the tracks in a cut from which coal smoke and noise polluted the neighbourhood. In 1857 the city set 42nd St as the S. limit for steam engines and the trains were then pulled by horses downtown to their terminal. Fourth Ave was renamed in sections, with the final portion up to the Harlem River receiving the name Park Ave in 1888.

Go E. on 42nd St. Built on the steel skeleton of the old Commodore Hotel is the new GRAND HYATT HOTEL (1980; Gruzen & Partners with Der Scutt), a chunky 30-story building sheathed in grey mirrored glass that reflects its surroundings. Inside, the 1400-room luxury hotel exudes the swank and glitter once associated with the Grand Central district. The foyer is paved in Paradiso Italian marble; the round columns are covered with bronze; the hardware is brass. The 275-ft four-story atrium is resplendent with fountains, plants, and a 77-ft sculpture by Peter Lobello entitled 'Bronze Tracery'.

Return to E. 42nd St and look across it to the geometric and floral bas reliefs on the CHANIN BUILDING (1929; Sloan & Robertson) at 122 E. 42nd St. Cross to the S. side of the street and enter the lobby, a treasure of Art Deco design in bronze and marble. Note especially the grille work on the Lexington Ave side, with its elaborate motifs of the cosmos and of human labour interspersed with geometric patterns and swirls.

The BOWERY SAVINGS BANK just to the W. at 110 E. 42nd St (1923; York & Sawyer) is one of the master works of the city's finest bank architects, a grand Romanesque palace with a dramatic deep arched entrance. Inside, the banking room is imposing in its proportions and in the elaboration of detail: beamed and coffered ceiling (65 ft high, 165 ft long, 80 ft wide), varicoloured marble columns on whose capitals are carved human and animal forms suggesting qualities and aspirations associated with money (the squirrel for thrift, the rooster for punctuality, the lion for power, the bull and bear representing Wall St), intricate mosaic floor, and inspirational messages included above the large arches.

Walk E. to the intersection of Lexington Ave. At 150 E. 42nd St between Lexington and Third Aves is the *Mobil Building*, originally the Socony Mobil Building (1955; Harrison & Abramovitz), upon completion the holder of a number of records: the world's largest (1·6 million sq. ft) metal-clad office building with the city's largest office floor (the second, 75,000 sq. ft) and its largest central air-conditioning system. The facade, whose cost was underwritten by the steel industry, at the time threatened by the emerging potential of glass and aluminum as building materials, is practical if dull. The repeated stamped design prevents the sheet metal from warping and, scoured by the wind, stays clean. In this day of hermetically sealed environments, the windows actually open, pivoting vertically to allow the window cleaners to remain safely indoors while performing their rites.

Across the street (405 Lexington Ave, between 42nd and 43rd Sts) is the ***Chrysler Building** (1930; William Van Alen; DL), a beautiful skyscraper just emerging from a period of obscurity and neglect. Built by Walter P. Chrysler, the automobile magnate, it expresses both the luxury and the mechanical precision of that automobile in its Jazz Age incarnations.

History. Walter Chrysler's interest in his building was not purely speculative and financial, though the building was constructed as an investment. Like other ambitious men, whose ilk reaches back through Frank Woolworth to the builders of the Tower of Babel, Chrysler wanted to put up the world's tallest tower, a yearning that led to a secret contest between his architect William Van Alen and H. Craig Severance then at work on the company headquarters of the Bank of Manhattan (now 40 Wall St). Van Alen planned the Chrysler Building at 925 ft. Severance in 1929 topped off triumphantly at 927 ft. Meanwhile a secret team of steelworkers inside the crown of the Chrysler Building constructed its 123-ft spire and pushed it through a hole in the roof, bringing its height to 1048 ft, 64 ft higher than the Eiffel Tower, previously the world's tallest structure. In 1931, however, the Empire State Building soared above them all to 1250 ft.

EXTERIOR: The slender 1048-ft tower rises to a shining stainless-steel spire above concentric arches pierced by triangular windows. There is probably more stainless steel on the facade of the Chrysler Building than on any other building in New York, for although sleek, mirrorlike and hence vastly appealing to Art Deco designers stainless steel cost too much for all but the most lavish builders. Below the spire, winged gargoyles resembling hood ornaments stare off in four directions and a brickwork frieze of wheels studded with radiator caps encircles the building.

Enter the *lobby*, one of the city's most beautiful interiors. The walls are veneered with sensuously veined African marbles in warm tones of buff and red, and the elevator doors and walls are inlaid with African woods in intricate floral designs. Overhead a mural depicts two favourite Art Deco themes—transportation and human endeavour—themes appropriate also to the Chrysler interests. After a decade of neglect the most recent owners of the building, Massachusetts Life Insurance Co. (1978) and Jack Kent Cooke (1980), investor and ball club owner, have chosen to restore it to its former splendour. The Cloud Club on the 66th floor, with its magnificent Art Deco dining room is scheduled to re-open (1983).

The only surviving AUTOMAT (1958; Horn & Hardart Co.) in New York stands on the S.E. corner of E. 42nd St and Third Ave (200 E. 42nd St), a latecomer to a group of some three dozen dating back to 1912 but flourishing in the 1930s. Tourists and nostalgic New Yorkers come to drop their quarters and nickels in the slots and retrieve their food from behind little glass doors. While the Automats inspired composers and poets (David Amram wrote 'Horn & Hardart Succotash Blues', and P.D.Q. Bach, alias Peter Schickele, wrote a Concerto for Horn and Hardart), they also attracted vagrants who sat in them all day over a cup of coffee or over someone else's coffee cup; they even became the unwilling dispensers of a free soup made of ketchup, hot water, salt and pepper. Today Horn and Hardart holds the local franchise to Burger King, a fast-food chain, and the other former Automats have been retooled to dish up burgers and fries instead of baked beans, lemon meringue pie, and other former standbys.

Continue E. At 220 E. 42nd St between Third and Second Aves is the DAILY NEWS BUILDING (1930; Howells & Hood), a fine Art Deco skyscraper whose design emphasises its height. White vertical strips of brick alternate with dark strips of windows broken up by red and black brick spandrels. The water tower and other machinery atop the roof are concealed within a vertical extension of the building—a radical notion at a time when such fripperies as temples, flèches, and choragic monuments usually served as camouflage. Handsome brickwork and a bas relief around the entrance form the only decoration of this severe, cubistic building. Inside the lobby are meteorological displays including a revolving globe set into a floor recess. The extension of the building to Second Ave (1958; Harrison & Abramovitz) retains the style of the original.

Midway between Second and First Aves on the N. side of E. 42nd St (main entrance, 320 E. 43rd St) is the FORD FOUNDATION (1967; Kevin Roche & John Dinkeloo & Assocs), justly admired for its beautiful interior garden, a quiet lush landscape filled with plants, trees, and a small pond into which visitors throw coins. Surrounding the garden is the cube-shaped building, with piers of pinkish-grey granite, a facade of weathering Cor-Ten steel, and such large expanses of glass that it resembles a modern Crystal Palace, all suitably elegant for a foundation that disburses millions of dollars to the arts, the humanities, and science.

TUDOR CITY (E. 40th–E. 43rd Sts between First and Second Aves), an ambitious and successful private effort at urban renewal (1928; Fred F. French Co. and H. Douglas Ives), is a self-contained city with a hotel (the Tudor, 600 rooms) and apartments (3000 of them) rising on abutments over First Ave. Developer Fred French bought more than 100 crumbling brownstones and tenements and erected twelve high-rise buildings in the American Tudor style popular in the 1920s—that is, brick with an occasional stained glass window, Gothic doorway, and decorative lion or unicorn. Such former amenities as tennis courts and a miniature golf course are long gone, and the residents are presently locked in a 10-year struggle with developer-owner Harry Helmsley to retain the two remaining parks on which the Helmsley organisation wishes to build more apartment towers. Because the site of the United Nations was once occupied by slaughterhouses and breweries, the buildings of Tudor City face inward, with only occasional windows looking toward what is nowadays a splendid river view.

Walk S. on Tudor City Pl. to E. 40th St. The East Side from about 27th to 40th Sts, Second Ave to the East River, is known as **Kips Bay**. In 1655 one Jacobus Kip owned a farm around Second Ave and E. 35th St reaching to the East River which at the time curved inward forming a bay. Kips Bay later became a beachhead for British troops invading the city during the Revolutionary War and the site of an American rout that caused one of George Washington's uncontrolled outbreaks of temper. His forces, mostly ill-trained recruits exhausted from their defeat on Long Island, broke before broadsides from the British men-of-war in the bay and fled in panic. Washington, enraged, tried to turn them around, drew his sword and threatened both foot soldiers and officers, and even used his cane whip on a brigadier general. Kips Bay remained pastoral until the mid-19C when its country estates, subdivided around the time of the Civil War, gave way to rows of brownstone houses. The arrival of the Second and Third Ave Els hastened its decline, bringing about a period of residential and industrial squalour from which it is just recovering. The bay itself has long since disappeared under tons of fill.

At E. 40th St turn right (W.) and begin walking toward Park Ave. The entrance to the QUEENS-MIDTOWN TUNNEL cuts through the block between First and Second Aves. Operated by the Triborough Bridge and Tunnel Authority, it was completed in 1940, its two tubes (N., 6414 ft; S., 6272 ft) joining E. 37th St with Long Island City in Queens. At one time optimistic city planners hoped to bore a crosstown tunnel linking the Queens-Midtown with the Lincoln Tunnel.

West of Kips Bay is **Murray Hill,** bounded roughly by Madison and Third Aves, 34th and 42nd Sts, named after Robert Murray who had a country home there (present E. 37th St and Park Ave) during the Revolutionary War period. Legend, probably erroneously, asserts that after the British landing at Kips Bay, Mrs Murray detained General Howe and his chief officers at tea thereby allowing the American troops stationed in Lower Manhattan to escape up the West Side to Harlem Heights. In the mid-19C Murray Hill became fashionable and real estate values soared as the upper crust built brownstone mansions along Fifth, Madison, and Park Aves. Although most have been torn down or stripped of details, a few homes and carriage houses remain to suggest Murray Hill at its peak.

Continue W. on E. 40th St. At No. 148 (between Third and Lexington Aves) is a fine old carriage house (c. 1875) with Second Empire detailing.

Others survive at 157 and 159 E. 35th St (c. 1890; between Third and Lexington Aves), and at 149 E. 38th St (1902; also between Third and Lexington Aves) Two fine townhouses dating from c. 1900 remain at 19 and 21 E. 37th St (between Madison and Park Aves).

Ernest Flagg, architect to the Scribner family and the Singer Sewing Machine Co. built (1905) the mansion at 109 E. 40th St (between Lexington and Park Aves) as his own home; the *Chess and Athletic Club* now occupies this opulent residence.

Turn S. at Park Ave and walk to E. 38th St. On the S.W. corner at 38 E. 38th St is the *Union League Club*, organised in 1863 by Woolcott Gibbs and his conservative Republican allies who bolted the Union Club because it harboured Confederate symphathisers. The fittingly conservative neo-Georgian building was designed by Morris & O'Connor (1931).

Across from the Union League Club at the S.E. corner of Park Ave and E. 38th St is the Roman Catholic *Church of Our Saviour* (1959; Paul Reilly), a new church imitating its Gothic and Romanesque forbears.

Continue S. and turn right (W.) at E. 37th St. One block W., on the N.E. corner of E. 37th St (233 Madison Ave) is the CONSULATE GENERAL OF THE POLISH PEOPLE (1905; Charles P.H. Gilbert; DL), originally the DeLamar mansion, built for a sea captain of Dutch ancestry with interests in S. African gold mines and considerable acuity on Wall St. The interiors are as imposing as the lavish Second Empire facade implies.

Just across the street on the S.E. corner of E. 37th St and Madison Ave is a handsome brownstone (231 Madison Ave) built as the home of J.P. Morgan, Jr, since 1944 owned by the LUTHERAN CHURCH IN AMERICA. Built in 1852, it is one of the city's few freestanding Italianate brownstone houses. The church had a landmarks designation rescinded, claiming financial hardship (they wanted to put up a money-making high rise), but the house still survives.

Beyond it is the ***Pierpont Morgan Library** (1906; McKim, Mead & White; DL; extension to Madison Ave, Benjamin Wistar Morris,

1928), a monument to the finely honed acquisatory tastes of the great banker. Established as a museum in 1924, the library contains a priceless collection of manuscripts from the Middle Ages and the Renaissance, drawings by artists from before 1800, incunabula, autograph MSS and letters, musical MSS, early children's books, and ancient written records including Assyrian and Babylonian seals, cuneiform tablets, and papyri.

The library, main entrance at 33 E. 36th St, is open, Sept–June, Tues–Sat, 10.30–5.00; Sun, 1–5; July, Tues–Sat, 10.30–5.00. Closed Aug, Mondays, and holidays. Requested contribution, $1·50. Tel: 685–0008.

The present entrance is in the 1928 extension. Walk down E. 36th St toward Park Ave to the middle of the block to see the original library, a simple classical building with a Palladian porch flanked by two niches. Sculptured panels (Adolph A. Weinman) below the frieze represent (right to left), Truth with Literature, Philosophy, History, Oratory, and Astronomy; and Music Inspiring the Arts. The sphinx in the right panel wears McKim's profile and serves as the architect's signature on his work. It was McKim's idea to construct the library like the marvels of antiquity, without mortar, using marble blocks fitted together, tongue in groove, a procedure only possible where costs were no great object and where labour was plentiful. The total library cost $1,154,669 of which only about $50,000 went for the extra stone cutting. The marble lionesses guarding the doorway are by Alexander Phimister Proctor.

Enter the vestibule. To the left is the *Exhibition Hall* where rotating exhibitions are displayed. To the right is the *Reading Room*, open to scholars and other qualified readers by application and presentation of credentials at the entrance. Beyond, a corridor leads past the restrooms and the shop to the original library, two rooms connected by a vestibule.

WEST ROOM, Morgan's study, is preserved as it was during his lifetime, though fabrics and wall coverings have been renewed as necessary. The wall covering of red silk damask is a modern copy of the original armorial pattern that once hung on the walls of the Chigi Palace in Rome. The marble mantelpiece is ascribed to the studio of Desiderio da Settignano, the 16C polychromed carved ceiling is from a palace in Lucca. Displayed in the room are some of Morgan's favourite paintings and objets d'art including bronzes, faience, and metalwork. Clockwise from doorway: E. Wall: *Memling*, Kneeling Female Donor and her Patron, St. Anne; *Cima da Conegliano*, Mystic Marriage of St. Catherine (c. 1510); *Memling*, Kneeling Male Donor and his Patron, St. William of Maleval; workshop variant of Botticelli's Madonna of the Magnificat (c. 1485). S. Wall: *Francesco Francia*, Virgin and Child with Saints Dominic and Barbara (c. 1500); studio of Desiderio da Settignano, marble bust of Florentine Lady perhaps Marietta Strozzi; *Frank Holl*, Portrait of Pierpont Morgan (1888); *Perugino*, Virgin and Two Saints Adoring the Child; marble statue of St. John the Baptist (Florence, 16C). W. Wall: *Frank O. Salisbury*, Portrait of J.P. Morgan (1933); *Lucas Cranach the Elder*, Wedding Portraits of Martin Luther and his Wife (beneath the Morgan portrait). N. Wall: *attrib. Bellini*, Virgin and Child with Saints and a Kneeling Donor (c. 1505); four-panelled Altarpiece attrib. Master of St. Mark, Catalonia (1355–60); *Tintoretto*, Portrait of a Moor (c. 1570) E. Wall: *Memling*, Portrait of a Man with a Pink. On a table in the N.W. corner of the room: Court painter in the circle of Clouet, Portrait of a French Princess, probably Marguerite de Valois; attrib. *Antonio Rossellino*, Bust of the Christ Child (15C). On a table to the right of the fireplace, silver gilt, enamelled and jewelled book cover (second half of 16C). Case under the Tintoretto portrait, life mask of George Washington taken by *Houdon* (1785).

In the EAST ROOM, the actual library, are displayed tiers of rare books and changing exhibitions of MSS, letters, and other items of interest. Permanently on display are a *Gutenberg Bible* (Mainz, c. 1455), one of three in the Morgan collection, an Antiphonary made for Carlo Pallavicino, Bishop of Lodi (third quarter of the 15C), and the *Stavelot Triptych* (1156), a portable altar made by Godefroid de Claire with Byzantine enamels framing relics of wood and a nail from the True Cross.

Diversion. The densest concentration of converted carriage houses on Murray Hill is the Sniffen Court Historic District (150–158 E. 36th St between Lexington and Third Aves, a little over two blocks E. of the Pierpont Morgan Library). Named after builder John Sniffen, this group of ten small Romanesque Revival brick carriage houses (c. 1850–60) has been attractively preserved, though some of the large arched doors for carriages have been altered. Sculptor Malvina Hoffman had her studio at the S. end of the court and at one time the Comedy Club converted one of the stables to a theatre. Return to Madison Ave.

The *Anthroposophical Society in America* (211 Madison Ave between E. 35th and E. 36th Sts) occupies the original Pierpont Morgan carriage house. Adjacent to it (209 Madison Ave) is the *H. Percy Silver Parish House* (1868; Robert Mook; altered c. 1905, Edward P. Casey). At 205 Madison Ave on the N.E. corner of E. 35th St is the Protestant Episcopal CHURCH OF THE INCARNATION (1864; Emlen T. Little; rebuilt and enlarged after a fire in 1882). Founded as a mission of Grace Church, it is English Gothic in style with a brownstone front and a corner tower. The *interior* is noteworthy for stained glass windows by Tiffany, John La Farge and others.

S. Aisle: Henry Holiday (London), Resurrection and Ascension window; Heaton, Butler & Bayne (London), Old Testament window; Clayton & Bell (London), New Testament window depicting St. Paul preaching on Mars Hill; *John La Farge, Christian Discipleship window; Henry Holiday, Parental and Christian Nurture window; John La Farge, Grapevine window; Phillips Brooks Memorial, with marble, onyx and glass decoration by Tiffany Glass and Decorating Co.; *William Morris, two Angels' windows dedicated to infant children; Louis Comfort Tiffany, Christian Pilgrim window.

The carved oak angels on the altar rail are by Daniel Chester French; the large mural flanking the altar and depicting the Adoration of the Magi is by John La Farge.

N. Aisle (E. to W.): Burne-Jones, Window of Faith and Charity; Cottin & Co. (London), Window showing Christ Feeding the Multitudes; *Tiffany Glass Co.; Tomb of Lazarus window; *Tiffany Glass Co., the Twenty-third Psalm window. In the gallery: Guthrie & David, Samuel window; Tiffany Glass Co., Dignity of Labour window. The West Window, depicting the Adoration of Christ Enthroned in Heaven, is in the style of 15C English glass painters and was designed by C.E. Kempe (England).

Located between First Ave and the Franklin D. Roosevelt Drive, 25th–30th Sts is the **Bellevue Hospital Center** (1908–39; McKim, Mead & White; New Building between 27th–28th Sts, 1974; Katz, Waisman, Weber, Strauss; Joseph Blumenkranz; Pomerance & Breines; Feld & Timoney). North of the hospital is the *New York University-Bellevue Medical Center*, 30th–34th Sts, First Ave to Franklin D. Roosevelt Drive (1950; Skidmore, Owings & Merrill; later additions), a white-glazed brick building housing the teaching hospital associated with N.Y.U.

History. Bellevue began as an infirmary in New York's first alms house, erected 1736, and since then has become one of the city's principal municipal hospitals, serving all who need medical care, regardless of race, religion, or ability to pay costs. It became an important public facility as early as 1816 when it was known as the Bellevue Establishment and had also a penitentiary, soap factory, bake shop, and church school in addition to its facilities for the ill. In 1819, during an epidemic of yellow fever, a 'fever hospital' was built near the Bellevue Establishment and eventually took the name of Bellevue Hospital. Famous during the 19C, Bellevue was rebuilt after the turn of the century, with the first section opening in 1908. Later came a pathology building (1911), new Medical and Surgical Pavilions (1916 and 1927), and a Psychiatric Hospital (1939).

The hospital boasts of a number of pioneering achievements in the annals of medicine: the first recorded U.S. instruction in anatomy dissection (1750), the first lying-in wards in the city (1799), first appendectomy in the U.S. (1867), first hospital-based ambulance service in the world (1869), first hospital Caesarian section (1887), and first development of the method of heart catheterisation (1956). The Bellevue Hospital emergency service is one of the most famous in the nation, which cares for about 80,000 patients each year on a 24-hour basis. The hospital also maintains a special emergency vehicle known as the Manhattan Disaster Bus which responds from Bellevue to any disaster in the city involving multiple casualties—fires, subway derailments.

The nearest subway is the IRT Lexington Ave local (train 6) at E. 33rd St and Park Ave. Uptown buses run on Park Ave S. (M1, M2, M3) and on Madison Ave (M4). Downtown buses run on Park Ave S. (M1). There is a crosstown bus on 34th St (M16) and a Culture Bus stop at 34th St and Fifth Ave (Loop I, Stop 22).

14 West 42nd Street and the Times Square Theatre District

SUBWAY: IND Eighth Ave (A, AA, CC or E train) to 42nd St.

BUS: M11 uptown on 10th Ave or downtown on Ninth Ave to 42nd St. M106, 42nd St crosstown to Ninth Ave. M16, 34th St crosstown, makes a loop N. to 42nd St between 9th and 12th Aves.

CAR PARKING: The roof of the Port Authority Bus Terminal has an immense parking lot. For patrons of Theater Row there is a large parking lot in the Manhattan Plaza apartment building. The theatre district, particularly the side streets between Seventh and Eighth Aves, offers numerous commercial parking lots.

This route begins on W. 42nd St at Ninth Ave and proceeds E. to Times Square and the theatre district. The early part of the tour, while not dangerous, is not pleasant, passing through the neighbourhood of the Port Authority Bus Terminal with its resident population of derelicts and through the block of W. 42nd St between Eighth and Seventh Aves, with its dense concentration of pornographic activities. The section from Times Square north is more attractive.

The two 45-story brick towers of the MANHATTAN PLAZA apartment complex (1977; David Todd & Assocs) occupying the block between W. 42nd and W. 43rd Sts, Ninth and Tenth Aves, could be part of any upper middle class apartment complex. The majority of its 1688 apartments, however, are rented to performing artists who pay 25% of their annual gross income as rent, incomes which in the theatrical profession are usually both low and insecure.

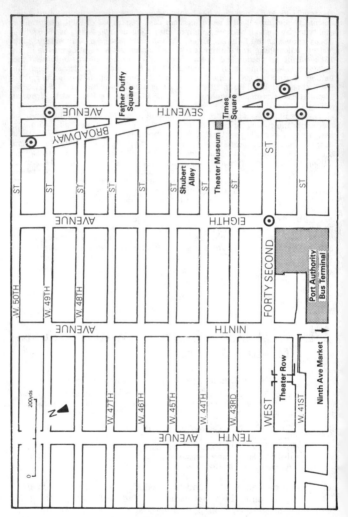

Manhattan Plaza was planned as a middle class development which would spur growth in the depressed Clinton area, but it nearly foundered in 1975 when the housing market collapsed and it became obvious that no member of the middle class who could afford the rent would want to live here so near the tenements of Ninth Ave and the flesh pots of Times Square. The city picked up the mortgage and was able to convert the buildings to federally subsidised housing for performers, who constitute the real strength of this neighbourhood and whose presence has already demonstrated a salutory effect.

THEATER ROW on the S. side of 42nd St between Ninth and Tenth Aves is one expression of the neighbourhood's new health.

This group of eight Off Off Broadway theatres and a restaurant opened officially in 1978, although three of the companies came here several years earlier. The row includes: the *Black Theater Alliance* (410 W. 42nd St), the *Actors and Directors Lab* (412 W. 42nd St), a central ticket agency (414 W. 42nd St; tel: 279–4280), *Playwrights Horizons* (416 W. 42nd St), the *Harlem Children's Theater and Intar* (International Arts Relations), a Hispanic cultural center (420 W. 42nd St), the *Lion Theater Company* (422 W. 42nd St), the *South Street Theater* (424 W. 42nd St) and the *Nat Horne Theater Company* across Dyer Ave (440 W. 42nd St) A group of tenements on the S.W. corner of Dyer Ave is presently undergoing rehabilitation as part of the theatre project.

Dyer Ave which exists primarily as part of the ramp system for the Lincoln Tunnel seems to have been named (with a variation in spelling) after William Dyre, mayor of the city in 1680, owner of Oyster Island (now Ellis Island), and customs collector. The LINCOLN TUNNEL, owned and operated by the Port Authority of New York and New Jersey, links midtown with Weehawken, New Jersey, and the interstate highway system. Its three tubes were opened in 1937 (center), 1945 (north) and 1957 (south) and now carry over 32,609,000 vehicles annually. The maximum depth from mean high water to the roadway is 97 ft, and the longest tube (center) is 8216 ft from portal to portal.

The New York Post Office Parking Lot is located on 42nd St between Eleventh and Twelfth Aves. Should you want a used postal truck, you can acquire one here at reasonable prices (open Tues and Wed except in Dec and on holidays; inspection 8–10 a.m., sale 10–4; tel: 971–5244).

Walk E. on 42nd St toward Ninth Ave.

The name **Hell's Kitchen** once designated a slum that stretched from about 30th St to 57th St west of Ninth Ave, whose housing included some of the city's worst tenements and whose industries, attracted by the tracks of the Hudson River (later the New York Central) Railroad down Eleventh Ave, included stables, slaughterhouses, gas plants, glue and soap factories. Supposedly two policemen watching a street fight on a muggy summer night gave the district its name. Said one, "This neighbourhood is hot as hell.' 'Hell is cool,' corrected the other. 'This here's Hell's Kitchen.' Its festering social conditions spawned gangs who played on the railroad yards and terrorised the neighbourhood so that policemen from the nearby 20th Precinct would venture out only in groups of three. Bearing such colourful names as the Hudson Dusters, the Gophers, the Gorillas and Battle Row Annie's Ladies' Social and Athletic Club, these organised mobs gave Hell's Kitchen a reputation as one of the most dangerous spots on the American continent. After 1910, however, things improved as the New York Central Railroad hired a strong arm squad who clubbed, shot, arrested, and otherwise incapacitated most of the old style gangsters. The elimination of the Ninth Ave El and the Eleventh Ave grade level railroad tracks as well as the demolition of many tenements that stood in the way of the ramps for the Lincoln Tunnel improved the district physically, paving the way for social changes that are now taking place. Nowadays residents prefer the neighbourhood to be called Clinton after a park of that name between W. 52nd and W. 54th Sts.

At Ninth Ave turn right (S.) and walk a block or so to look at the Ninth Ave market, a congregation of small, ethnic food shops whose roots go back to the turn of the century when a large pushcart market known as **Paddy's Market** flourished under the Ninth Ave El between about 35th and 42nd Sts. When the streets were being widened to construct the Lincoln Tunnel ramps in the late 1930s, the Port of New York Authority with the city Department of Markets had the pushcart operators evicted by means of a court order. For a while business slumped as the hucksters tried to move their carts to the side streets, but eventually the market re-established itself and has recently enjoyed a renaissance attracting not only local people but also knowledgeable consumers from all over the city. The ethnic orientation of the shops offers great variety to shoppers and reflects the immigrant groups who have passed through here: Puerto Rican, Italian, Greek, West Indian, Filipino, Polish.

FESTIVAL: Absolutely the best time to visit is during the annual Ninth Ave Street Festival (a weekend in mid-May), when the avenue is closed to traffic and an estimated half million people stroll from 37th to 57th St, glutting themselves on ethnic foods and buying handmade items and souvenirs. Jugglers, mimes, magicians, and puppeteers perform in the streets while more elaborate entertainment including steel bands, jazz combos, high school choruses, and folk dancers appear on temporary stages set up along the route. Return to 42nd St.

Along the S. side of 42nd St. between Eighth and Ninth Aves. (330 W. 42nd St) is the former **McGraw-Hill Building** (1931; Raymond Hood, Godley & Fouilhoux), one of New York's finest modern buildings, the only one to rate inclusion in Henry Russell-Hitchcock and Philip Johnson's 'The International Style' (1932). Because the building originally contained the printing presses of the McGraw-Hill publishing enterprises it was relegated to the fringes of midtown by the Zoning Resolution of 1916 which prohibited light industry further inland, a means of preventing the garment district from encroaching upon the theatres and restaurants of Times Square. Its owners nonetheless hoped that the fortunes of the neighbourhood would rise, a hope that was never fully realised, so the building remains an architectural gem in the midst of tenements and nondescript industrial buildings. It is much admired for its blue-green terracotta sheathing, its horizontal bands of strip windows, its energetic setbacks, and its lobby, whose blue, green, bronze, and chrome bands echo the exterior design. McGraw-Hill has long departed for more genteel surroundings uptown, but the present owners of the building are undertaking to restore its former splendour.

On the N. side of the street (333 W. 42nd St) is HOLY CROSS CHURCH (Roman Catholic), the oldest building on 42nd St, known primarily for its association with Father Francis Duffy (see p252) but interesting also for its architecture. Considered Byzantine in style when built (1870; Henry Engelbert), the church has a simple brick and limestone facade over which rises an octagonal drum, dome, lantern, and crucifix (148 ft to the top). The interior is noteworthy for its fine stained glass windows and marble work. The chancel windows were executed by Mayer and Co., in Munich, while Louis Comfort Tiffany designed the clerestory windows and the large circular windows of St. Peter and St. Paul in the transepts, the window of St. John in the Baptistry, and the mosaics at the base of the cupola and in the sanctuary.

Walk E. along 42nd St past the side of the PORT AUTHORITY BUS TERMINAL now filling two city blocks from 40th to 42nd Sts between Eighth and Ninth Aves (1950; decks added 1963; expansion to W. 42nd St 1982; Port Authority Design Staff). Vast, efficient, and depressing, this terminal is a way station for some 207,000 commuters delivered and received by some 7500 buses on an average weekday; it is 'home' for the usual group of derelicts and panhandlers who gravitate to the bus terminals of any major city. Commuter buses make up 80% of the traffic, but most of the long distance buses entering New York use it as well. Vehicular ramps feed directly into the Lincoln Tunnel without impeding traffic on the streets below and pedestrian passageways connect underground with the 42nd St stations of the Eighth Ave IND, the IRT, and the BMT subways. A mammoth parking lot on the roof and on decks along 42nd St holds more than 1000 cars.

On the N.W. corner of W. 42nd St and Eighth Ave (661 Eighth Ave) is the *Franklin Savings Bank* (1974; Poor, Swanke, Hayden & Connell), a small bank with an attractive interior of exposed concrete and warm-toned paving brick that provides relief from the swarming humanity outside.

The block of W. 42nd St between Eighth Ave and Broadway is probably the worst in the Times Square area, an unrelieved line-up of pornographic movies and bookshops, peep shows, live sex shows, topless bars, and massage parlours. The crowd that prowls this dazzingly illuminated block includes not only people drawn to its entertainments but derelicts, aggressive panhandlers, three-card monte players, and drug dealers. Since the area is the center of the theatre and tourist industries and is hence essential to New York's economy, the city has repeatedly sought to clean it up. In 1982 city and state agencies agreed to a 10-year, $1-billion **42nd Street Redevelopment Project** which will include four new office towers, a wholesale apparel market, a first class hotel, and the restoration or conversion of nine once-famous theatres: the Empire and Liberty Theatres (S. side of 42nd St), the New Amsterdam and Harris Theatres (also on the S. side of the block, flanking the Chandler Building), and the Victory, Selwyn, Lyric, Apollo, and Times Square theatres on the block between 42nd–43rd Sts.

Behind many of the marquees of the pornographic movie houses are the facades of the old theatres that once brought glitter to Times Square.

On the S. side of the street is the *Empire Theatre* (1912; Thomas A. Lamb) (240 W. 42nd St) formerly called the Eltinge after Julian Eltinge, a popular female impersonator during the first decade of the twentieth century. It opened in 1912 and housed a number of successful plays until it closed during the early years of the Depression; for a while it was leased for burlesque, but after Mayor La Guardia's crackdown it became a movie theatre. The *Liberty Theatre* next door (234 W. 42nd St), designed by architects Herts & Tallant (opened 1904), was originally part of the Klaw and Erlanger syndicate and achieved its most notable success with the great Negro musical, 'Blackbirds of 1928'. After 1932 it too began showing movies.

At 220 W. 42nd St, is the *Candler Building*, named after its builder Asa Candler, then president of the Coca Cola Company. Clad in white terracotta, the building (1914; Willauer, Shape & Bready) was recently cleaned and renovated. It has been called Spanish Renaissance in style and noted as perhaps the first office building in New York with a fireproof stairtower.

Across the street at 229 W. 42nd St is the *Selwyn Theatre* (1918; George Keister), built by Arch Selwyn, a Broadway producer who went to Hollywood; it is now a movie theatre which shows primarily X-rated films. The fate of the *Apollo Theatre* at 219 W. 42nd St is brighter. Built in 1910 (Eugene DeRosa) as a combination motion picture and vaudeville house, it became a legitimate theatre ten years later, its most famous production George White's 'Scandals' which ran yearly from 1924 to 1931. After a Depression stint showing motion pictures and burlesque (it was leased by the Minskys), and a period of showing pornographic films, it is again a legitimate theatre. The *Times Square Theatre*, joined by a common facade to the Apollo, was built by Arch and Edgar Selwyn in 1920 as a musical house; 'Gentlemen Prefer Blondes' opened here. It was converted to a movie theatre in 1933.

The *Lyric Theatre* (213 W. 42nd St) was built by the Shuberts to be the home of the American School of Opera and to feature a yearly engagement of actor Richard Mansfield and his company. It opened in 1903 (architect, V. Hugo Koehler) and enjoyed an impressive history booking such stars as Douglas Fairbanks, Otis Skinner, Fred Astaire, Flo Ziegfeld, Rudolf Friml, and the Marx Brothers before it became a movie theatre in 1933. Although the original stone portico has been torn off the 42nd St facade, and the two-story ornamented arch has been obscured by a metal sign, it is still possible to see something of the building's original grandeur by walking around to the back on W. 43rd St where progress has made fewer inroads. One of Koehler's innovations was designing the auditorium parallel to the street so that the audience could take their seats from the side aisles. Plans are underway to return this theatre to its original function as a legitimate playhouse.

The *Victory Theatre* at 207 W. 42nd St was built in 1900 (J.B. McElfatrick & Co.) by Oscar Hammerstein, who called it the Republic. It was 42nd St's first theatre, built by the man who brought theatre to Times Square. Hammerstein, however, was soon in financial distress and turned the house over to David Belasco who quickly renamed it after himself. In 1931 the theatre was taken over by burlesque and after 1942, when it received its present name, it became a movie house.

The heart of ***Times Square** is the area where Broadway and Seventh Ave intersect, bounded roughly by 42nd and 48th Sts. Once called the Crossroads of the World, Times Square is now known for its spectacular displays of neon, its theatres, its crowds, and its seediness. The area acquired its name in 1904 when the 'New York Times', just moving to its new building, succeeded in having its name appended to the subway stop also just opening here, a move the sedate newspaper may regret nowadays.

Before 1904 Times Square, then Longacre Square, was dominated by horse exchanges, carriage factories, stables, and blacksmiths' shops. On its E. side was the 12th Regiment Armory. The Astor family owned much of the W. part of the district as part of a tract that ran from 42nd to 46th Sts along Broadway and W. to the Hudson River, a parcel John Jacob Astor had picked up for an economical $25,000 in the early 19C.

The IRT reached Times Square in 1904, nine years after the area had been electrically lighted. O.J. Gude, an advertising man, is said to have coined the term 'Great White Way' in 1901, when he realised the advertising potential of electrical displays. The first electric sign (1891) in the city at Broadway and 23rd St had extolled the seaside pleasures of Long Island, but it was a pallid beginning to an art form that flowered in Times Square and produced such landmark extravaganzas as a gigantic smoker emitting real smoke rings, a shower of golden peanuts cascading from an illuminated bag, a waterfall whose spray doused passersby on windy days, and a figure of Little Lulu advising the use of Kleenex.

Times Square is always crowded, but particularly so in the evenings around theatre time, and on occasions of public celebration. Every New Year's Eve the square is choked with celebrants who have come to witness the descent of an illuminated apple from the top of the Times Tower on the stroke of midnight. The crowd that packed the square at the conclusion of World War II has become legendary both for its density and for the quantity of alcohol consumed during the festivities.

In the triangle created by the intersection of Seventh Ave and Broadway at 42nd St is ONE TIMES SQUARE, formerly the Allied Chemical Tower, originally the Times Tower (1904; Eidlitz & MacKenzie), once a world-famous building now in such sadly reduced circumstances that it has been proposed for demolition. When the 'New York Times' moved in on 31 Dec 1904, the building had a granite base, a fine marble lobby, and 25 floors sheathed in ornamented terracotta. The 'Times' has moved to W. 43rd St, and the terracotta and granite have been replaced by a slick marble facing (1966; Smith, Smith, Haines, Lunberg & Waehler), a remodelling that was supposed to have a catalytic effect on the neighbourhood but which only despoiled it of one of its finer buildings. In 1977 real estate developer Alex Parker announced plans to have the building sheathed in mirrored glass to reflect the famous Times Square outdoor light show. Nothing has come of these plans nor of a 1979 proposal to demolish it in favour of three major new office buildings on the west, south, and east blockfronts facing the present building. The city has yet to take action on this plan which, though it would provide considerably higher revenues than does the present group of buildings, will probably be rejected.

Wrapped around the building some three stories up is the Motogram, a moving sign 360 ft long with letters 5 ft tall, whose 14,800 light bulbs once informed the public of important events. Now dark, the sign has been replaced by a coloured electrically lighted billboard on the N. end of the building, whose messages include a heavy dose of advertising. On the S.E. side of the building is *Hotalings newsstand* and shop: the sidewalk stand carries newspapers from most major American cities while the shop indoors offers a large selection of foreign language newspapers and periodicals. Across 42nd St facing the S. side of One Times Square is a *mural by Richard Haas*, a mirror image of the Times Tower as it looked in 1904. At the foot of the mural (S. side of W. 42nd St between Broadway and Seventh Ave) is an *Information booth* maintained by the police department, where one may inquire about theatre tickets, public transportation, current attractions, etc. (tel: 221–9869).

On the eighth floor of One Times Square (take the elevator in the lobby) is the *Songwriters' Hall of Fame and Museum* (Mon–Sat, 11–3; free. Tel: 221–1252). This one-room museum contains memorabilia of American song writers and performers including such objects as George Gershwin's writing desk, Fats Waller's piano, and one of Elvis Presley's guitar picks, as well as displays of sheet music, a diorama of Tin Pan Alley at the turn of the century, and a selection of musical instruments ranging from a player saxophone with pre-recorded rolls (like a player piano), to synthesisers, electric guitars, and a rhythm machine (to produce rhumba, cha cha, waltz, and other rhythms) which the visitor may try out. A library and archive are available to students and researchers.

Return to street level. On the S.E. corner of Broadway and W. 42nd

St is the original *Knickerbocker Hotel* (1902; Marvin & Vavis, architects with Bruce Price, consultant), now converted to an office building. This massive pile of brick and limestone, crowned with a mansard roof, was commissioned by John Jacob Astor and once opened its doors to such notables as Enrico Caruso and George M. Cohan.

Walk N. along the W. side of Times Square on Broadway; turn left into W. 43rd St. At 229 W. 43rd St is the building, which houses the business and editorial *offices of the 'New York Times'* as well as the presses on which the paper is actually printed. Founded in 1851, the 'Times' rose to prominence under Adolph S. Ochs (publisher, 1896–1935) who increased its daily circulation from 19,000 to 490,000 and established it as the nation's most respected newspaper. It is still the 'newspaper of record', distinguished for its reliability, thorough coverage of foreign news, and editorial restraint.

On the S. side of W. 43rd St across from the 'Times' are the stage doors of the Lyric, Times Square, and Apollo theatres. Untouched by the sleazy alterations of 42nd St, the rear facades of these buildings suggest their former elegance.

Return to Broadway. The PARAMOUNT BUILDING (1927; Rapp & Rapp) at 1501 Broadway between W. 43rd and W. 44th Sts is a Times Square skyline landmark with its 14 setbacks converging on an illuminated bulb at the top. Although the palatial Paramount Theatre is no longer here, the lobby is still theatrical, with its heavily ornate gilded ceiling, black marble faced walls, opulent chandeliers, and panelled bronze elevator doors. A block N. on the same side of the street at 1515 Broadway is *One Astor Plaza* (1969; Kahn & Jacobs), a large, ill-named office building: the 'Astor' part comes from the Astor Hotel (1904) which once but unfortunately no longer stands here; the plaza is too small to merit naming the building after it. Architecturally the building is recognisable at some distance from Times Square by the concrete fins adorning its upper stories; historically it is significant as the first building in the specially designated Times Square Theatre District to take advantage of zoning bonuses that allow extra floor space to a building that includes a new legitimate theatre.

In the arcade of the Minskoff Theater in One Astor Plaza is the THEATER MUSEUM (open Tues–Sat, 12–8; Sun, 1–5; suggested donation; tel: 944–7161), a satellite of the Museum of the City of New York, whose exhibitions feature memorabilia—costumes, photographs, clippings, posters and paintings—pertaining to the history of the theatre in New York.

Cross Broadway to the E. The *Manhattan Church of the Nazarene* at 130 W. 44th St was originally the home of the Lambs Club (1904; McKim, Mead & White; DL), the city's oldest theatrical club founded in 1875. The club, still active, is now located at 3 W. 51st St. The *1–2–3 Hotel*, formerly the Hotel Girard, at 123 W. 44th St, a small hotel extravagantly adorned with dormers and gables, is typical of the many such hotels that once filled the side streets near Times Square.

The *Belasco Theatre* (1907; George Keister) at 111 W. 44th St was built by David Belasco as a showcase for his technical innovations; it included an elevator stage, a sophisticated lighting system, and a studio for developing special effects as well as a grandly furnished apartment for Belasco himself. Return to Broadway.

The city's largest, most concentrated **theatre district** developed around Times Square during the first three decades of this century. First came a few pioneers, creeping up Broadway from Herald Square: Charles Frohman's Empire Theatre (1893) on Broadway at 40th St and the former Metropolitan Opera House (1883) between 39th and 40th Sts. Oscar Hammerstein, however—opera impresario, composer, cigar maker, and onetime plasterer—was the first to forge N. of 42nd St, and while his Olympia Theatre (1895) on Broadway between 44th and 45th Sts lasted only two years, Hammerstein rebounded from bankruptcy and resiliently built three more theatres in Times Square—the Victoria, the Republic, and the Lew Fields—earning himself kudos as 'the man who created Times Square'.

As advances in transportation made the district widely accessible and investors began to realise the potential profits in theatres as real estate, Times Square began to flourish. Theatres were built either by speculators aware that a hit show could gross a million dollars in a single year, roughly the price it cost to build a theatre in the peak years of the 1920s, or by financial backers working with independent producers like Charles Frohman, David Belasco, and Harrison Grey Fiske. The theatre became a flourishing and complex industry and Times Square began attracting agents, producers, theatrical publications, restaurants, hotels, and theatrical clubs. New York's best season came in 1927–28 when 257 productions were mounted and 71 theatres were in operation.

The Depression devasted Broadway; tickets remained unsold; actors were unemployed; even the Shuberts went into receivership. The Federal Theater Project kept some actors and writers in work during these years, but the Times Square theatre district began a process of attrition that still continues, abetted by rising land values and the inroads of television and the movies. In 1967 the city passed a zoning ordinance that encourages the construction of legitimate theatres within office towers in the Times Square area.

Continue W. across Broadway. On the S. side of the street at 234 W. 44th St is *Sardi's restaurant*, venerable haunt of actors, writers, theatre people, and celebrity watchers. Across the street at 225 W. 44th St is the SHUBERT THEATRE (1913; Henry B. Herts), named after Sam S. Shubert, who with his brothers Lee and J.J. founded a theatrical empire that still survives.

The Shubert brothers, offspring of a Syracuse peddler, came to New York around the turn of the century. Beginning with a single theatre, they took on and survived the ruling monopoly of the day, the Klaw and Erlanger Syndicate, and emerged as the most powerful force in the American theatre. In their heyday the Shuberts controlled the production, booking, and presentation of shows; they dominated the try-out circuits through their ownership of theatres outside New York; and they forced producers to book exclusively through their organisation, while discriminating in favour of the shows they produced themselves. A decree issued against them in 1956 as the result of an antitrust action brought by the federal government required them to stop their restrictive booking practices and to sell 12 theatres in six cities. At the present time the Shubert Organization controls 16·5 Broadway theatres (Irving Berlin owns a half interest in the Music Box) or 48·5% of the 34 existing houses.

The Shubert Theatre, whose upper floors house the headquarters of the Shubert Organization, has had an uneventfully prosperous career, beginning with its opening production 'Hamlet', to 'A Chorus Line', which won the Pulitzer Prize in 1976.

To the E. of the theatre is SHUBERT ALLEY, now a promenade for theatregoers, formerly a gathering place for singers, actors, and dancers who hoped to be cast in Shubert-produced plays. Walk through Shubert Alley to the *Booth Theatre* (1913; Henry B. Herts) at 222 W. 45th St. Named after Edwin Booth and built by Lee Shubert and Winthrop Ames, the Booth is a small theatre (783 seats; the Shubert has 1483), perhaps because its developers had just emerged from the spectacular failure of the New Theatre on Central Park West, a palatial marble-faced edifice that was to enshrine theatrical art far above the hustle of Broadway but collapsed financially after two seasons.

Walk N. to W. 46th St and turn right. At 154 W. 46th St are the *offices of 'Variety'*, the trade magazine of show business, known to the general public for its snappy literary style, particularly its headlines. The all-time classic appeared above a story about the operator of a chain of midwestern theatres visiting Hollywood and reporting on his customers' taste in films (17 July 1935): 'Stix Nix Hick Pix'. Across the street at 149 W. 45th St is the LYCEUM THEATRE (1903; Herts & Tallant; DL), the oldest surviving New York legitimate theatre, now a part of the Shubert Organization whose archives occupy the one-time apartment of entrepreneur Daniel Frohman. The building stands out for its Baroque ornamentation: its undulating marquee, its elaborate columns decorated with flutings, foliated bands, and buttercups between the flutings, and its high mansard roof pierced with oval windows. On the S. side of the street at 120 W. 46th St is the *High School of Performing Arts*, a school within the city system geared to train students for professional careers. Return to Broadway.

Cross Broadway and continue W. on 46th St. Currently under construction along Broadway between 45th–46th Sts is the controversial *Times Square Hotel*, a 50-story tower undertaken by Portman Properties, Inc, of Atlanta. The luxury hotel will feature a dramatic atrium—an architectural trademark of the developer—2000 rooms for visitors, and an 1800-seat theatre. In October 1982, despite protests from actors, directors, producers, and preservationists, the historic Helen Hayes and Morosco theatres were demolished in favour of the hotel which, it is hoped, will upgrade the neighbourhood. Return to Broadway.

The N. end of Times Square is properly known as FATHER DUFFY SQUARE. Near the 46th St end is a *statue* (1959; Georg Lober) *of George M. Cohan* (1878–1942), the song-and-dance man best known for writing 'Give My Regards to Broadway', 'Over There', and 'I'm a Yankee Doodle Dandy'. The statue was unveiled in a ceremony with Oscar Hammerstein II presiding, George Jessel acting as master of ceremonies, and a crowd of 45,000 attending. At the conclusion, everyone broke into 'Give My Regards to Broadway'. N. of the debonair bronze figure of Cohan is another bronze statue (1937; Charles Keck), portraying *Father Francis P. Duffy* (1871–1932), the 'Fighting Chaplain' of the 69th Regiment during World War I. As pastor of Holy Cross Church, Father Duffy also served a parish that embraced the slums of Hell's Kitchen, the burlesque houses and dance halls of Times Square and the glittering theatres of Broadway. When the statue was unveiled, a crowd of 30,000 including prize fighters, political figures, and Broadway characters came to pay him tribute, joining the 69th Regiment and the military bands which struck up 'Onward Christian Soldiers'. Father Duffy is shown in his World War I uniform grasping a copy of the New Testament, his back to a granite Celtic cross.

Just N. of Father Duffy (W. 47th St between Seventh Ave and Broadway) is **tkts** (short for Times Square Ticket Center), a canvas and pipe structure where you can buy cheap theatre tickets shortly before curtain time.

The ticket service, run by the Theater Development Fund, often sells as many as 4000 tickets in the two-hour pre-show period. Tickets to Broadway and

Off-Broadway productions, music and dance events, are sent over from the theatres and sold at half-price plus a small service charge. Performances for which tickets are available are posted on the N. side of the structure. Open Mon–Sat, 3–8 (evening tickets), Wed and Sat, 12–2 (matinee tickets), and Sun, 12–3 (matinee and evening tickets). Tel: 354–5800.

Visitors with a burning interest in the history of Madison Square Garden may walk W. to the corner of Eighth Ave and 49th St, where the third Madison Square Garden stood in what is presently a large parking lot. At one time gymnasiums, fight managers' offices, and watering holes favoured by the sporting crowd lined the streets in this area. Designed with an undistinguished exterior by Thomas W. Lamb, a theatre architect, the third Garden was 'built'

Elevated lines at Pearl St and Hanover Square (1936). While the 'els' lessened surface traffic, they created dark grimy avenues beneath their clattering viaducts. The last el was demolished in 1956. (The Museum of the City of New York)

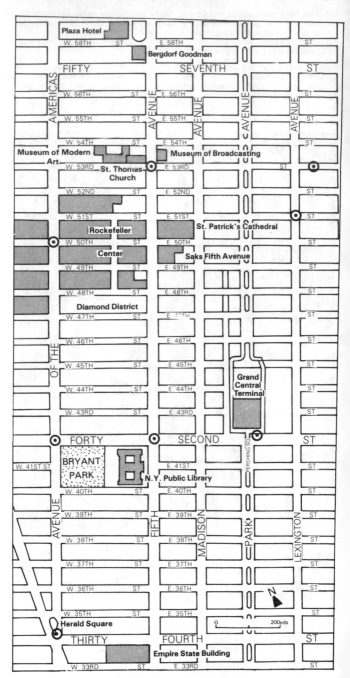

as an institution by John Ringling, a circus magnate, and Tex Rikard, sometime gambler, cattleman, and promoter of prizefights. Its staple offerings were boxing matches, as well as ice hockey and basketball games, track meetings, ice shows, the circus, rodeos and expositions including antiques shows, poultry, dog, and cat shows, political meetings, and benefits. Its social climax came with the annual horse show, for which a box cost $315 in 1939, its social nadir was probably the Six-day Bicycle Race for which in the same year a one-week admission cost a dollar, making the Garden a temporary home for drifters and those down on their luck during the Depression.

15 Fifth Avenue, 34th–59th Street

SUBWAY: IRT Lexington Ave local (train 6) to 33rd St. IND Sixth Ave local or express (D or F train, B train except during rush hours) to 34th St. BMT Broadway local (RR train or N train except during rush hours) to 34th St at Sixth Ave.

BUS: Downtown via Fifth Ave, M2, M3, M4, M5, M32. Downtown via Fifth Ave and Park Ave S., M1. Downtown via Seventh Ave, M10. Uptown via Madison Ave, M2, M3, M5, M32. Uptown via Sixth Ave, M10. 34th St crosstown, M16. Culture Bus (weekends and holidays) Loop I, Stop 22 or Loop II, Stop 20.

Among the streets of New York, Fifth Avenue is pre-eminent. It is 'the' avenue, the most famous, most glittering promenade in the city, known as the route of its grand processions, as the site of many of its most elegant shops, and as the best place to observe the chic and the famous on their daily rounds. During the closing years of the 19C and for a while at the beginning of the 20C, Fifth Ave was the city's most desirable place to live, the territory of the rich and the socially ambitious. Gradually commerce invaded, first with the old Waldorf-Astoria Hotel at 34th St, then with B. Altman & Co. a block further north, driving society uptown. Today urban decay follows the same route; the shops in the 30s and low 40s, with the monumental exceptions of B. Altman & Co., Lord & Taylor, W. & J. Sloane, and a few others, offer shoddy merchandise, pseudo-oriental rugs, electronic gadgetry, and garish bric-a-brac. Further N., however, Fifth Ave still glitters, with jewellers, international boutiques, and expensive apartment houses where (foreign) tenants have been known to spend $2 million redecorating their apartments. While the homes of Vanderbilts and Goulds are gone from this area, traces remain of the heady days before the income tax: grand hotels like the Plaza, the St. Regis-Sheraton, and the Pierre further north, St. Thomas' Episcopal Church where the cream of society married each other or sought to wed their wealth to the titles of Europe, the exclusive University Club, and the Morton Plant residence now remodelled as Cartier's.

As a ceremonial route, Fifth Ave is used by Norwegians, Israelis, Puerto Ricans, Germans, Poles, and Italians to honour their countries of origin, and by people in general to show off their finery after Easter services during the Easter Parade. Between Thanksgiving and Christmas the shops offer extravagant window displays (B. Altman & Co., Lord & Taylor, F.A.O. Schwartz, and Saks Fifth Avenue) with elaborately costumed dolls and mechanical figures. Members of the armed forces and the Salvation Army perform on brass instruments or bang on tambourines as they solicit money for charitable causes.

Finally, Fifth Ave is famous for its skyscrapers, most notably the

Empire State Building, but also the towers of Rockefeller Center (described in Rte 17), and several lesser buildings.

While some stores are open nowadays on Sunday, it is better to visit during the week. During the Christmas season it is especially beautiful but crowded and hectic.

The ****Empire State Building** (1931; Shreve, Lamb & Harmon) between 33rd and 34th Sts at 350 Fifth Ave, is no longer the world's tallest building, surpassed by the Sears Roebuck Building in Chicago and the two towers of the World Trade Center, but for many people it remains the quintessential skyscraper. It is 1250 ft to the 102nd floor observatory or 1472 ft to the top of the TV tower (installed 1951). It weighs 365,000 tons and occupies 37 million cubic ft on a site of about two acres. The structure includes 10 million bricks, 2·5 million ft of electrical wire, and enough steel to build a double-track railroad from New York to Baltimore (187 miles).

History. In 1827 a son of John Jacob Astor bought the site where, beginning in 1859, two younger Astors, John Jacob III and William Backhouse Astor, Jr, built adjoining mansions. William married Caroline Webster Schermerhorn, later the dowager queen of society, and after fathering four children spent a great deal of time elsewhere. The Astor mansions remained until Caroline's nephew, William Waldorf Astor, inheritor of the southern house, lost out in a social competition with his redoubtable aunt and determined to revenge himself by tearing down his mansion and putting up a hotel, which he named the Waldorf after the ancestral Astor home in Germany. Caroline, offended by the towering hotel, moved uptown, leaving her house to her son, John Jacob IV, who tore it down and built the Astoria part of the Waldorf-Astoria, named after a city in Oregon, part of the original John Jacob's fur empire.

The Waldorf-Astoria (opened 1893) flourished both financially and socially, its men's Bar the domain of Frick, Morgan, Guggeneim, et al., its dining room presided over by the legendary Oscar Tschirky, known better as Oscar of the Waldorf, a maître who understood the minutiae of social discrimination and deployed his knowledge imperiously. The hotel saw many splendid affairs, the most famous of which was the Bradley-Martin ball (1897) to which 1200 guests were invited to appear dressed as for the Versailles of Louis XV. In 1929 the hotel moved uptown to its present location.

The concept of the Empire State Building, a world's tallest skyscraper budgeted at $60 million, was a product of the optimistic 1920s, but the building itself was a child of the Depression, demolition beginning in 1929 just two months before the Stock Market Crash. Because of the Depression, actual costs came only to $40,948,900, but the economic climate also prevented full occupancy until almost the beginning of World War II, a period during which the building was nicknamed 'the Empty State Building'. Remarkably it was finished ahead of schedule, setting construction records still unrivalled, rising an average of 4^1/2 stories a week and 14^1/2 stories during the ten peak working days. Steel was set in place as little as 80 hours after leaving the furnaces of Pittsburgh, and the supply and delivery of other materials was superbly coordinated with the building schedule. Lewis Hine's photographs of the 'skyboys' at work on the high steel are a tribute to them and a landmark in American photography.

The Empire State Building opened with elaborate ceremonies in 1931. In 1933 Irma Eberhardt became the first successful suicide to leap from the top; 15 other jumpers have followed. In the same year Hollywood used the building for the climax of 'King Kong', showing the mythical giant ape atop the tower fighting off a squadron of army planes; although a later version of the movie used the towers of the World Trade Center instead, the 1933 version has become a classic and at the time was considered a masterpiece in composite motion picture photography. On a foggy 28 July in 1945, after threading its way among the pinnacles of midtown, an Army B-25 crashed into the 79th floor, killing 14 and doing $1 million of damage. A year later the elevator operators went on strike. A group of businessmen holding a conference on one of the upper stories telephoned down to a sandwich shop on the street for lunch; when the delivery man arrived with the sandwiches, the grateful executives tipped him $75.

Steelworkers on the Empire State Building. In the background are the Chrysler Building, Roosevelt (then Welfare) Island, and the Queensboro Bridge. (George Eastman House, Rochester, N.Y.)

Exterior. The facade consists of a limestone curtain wall, blonde in tone, pierced by windows set flush and trimmed with vertical strips of stainless steel running the height of the building, a design chosen after 15 discarded attempts, in part because it would facilitate speed of construction. Everything possible—windows, spandrels, steel strips, even slabs of stone—was fabricated at the site of origin and shipped in quantity to be installed as on an assembly line without further hand fitting or stone cutting. The setbacks, necessitated by zoning laws, were designed by taking the allowable volume, slicing away at the width and adding as much as possible on the top, a process that resulted in a single major setback with a 60-ft terrace at the fifth floor and a tower rising straight above that. Originally the building was to end at the 86th floor, but one of the backers determined that it needed a 'hat', a mast for mooring zeppelins, which added 150 ft to the projected height. Several attempts were made, but the mast never succeeded, though a Navy blimp managed to tie up long enough in 1931 to dump its ballast—water—on pedestrians several blocks away.

Interior. The lobby, three stories high, is lined with marble imported from France, Italy, Belgium, and Germany. In 1963 illuminated panels by Roy Sparkia and Renée Nemorov were installed depicting the eight wonders of the world—the traditional seven plus the Empire State Building.

The ticket office for the *observatories (86th and 102nd floors) is on the Concourse Level, one floor below the main lobby (open 9.30 a.m.–midnight; adults $2·25, children under twelve, $1·15). The view from the observatories is spectacular.

Also on the Concourse level is the *Guinness World Record Exhibit Hall* (Mon–Sun, 9.30–5.30; adults $2·50, children under twelve, $1·75), where the unusual records and record holders—tallest, fattest, smallest, fastest—are displayed in cleverly designed exhibitions, including video films of stunts and sports records.

Begin walking N. on Fifth Ave. Between 34th and 35th Sts on the E. side is B. ALTMAN & COMPANY (1906; Trowbridge & Livingston), the first department store to intrude on a previously residential area, modelled like a great palazzo perhaps to soften the blow to disgruntled neighbours. Founder Benjamin Altman, son of a Lower East Side milliner, opened his first shop on Third Ave near 9th St and worked his way uptown via a stylish store in Ladies' Mile (Sixth Ave and 19th St). When Altman died unmarried in 1913, he left his art collection to the Metropolitan Museum of Art and $20 million in Altman's stock to a foundation which owns the store today and has channelled millions to philanthropy. Today the store is known for its home furnishings, dishes, glassware, and imported Irish goods.

While the Altman palazzo has been handsomely maintained, two nearby stores have been less fortunate. The former Gorham Building at 390 Fifth Ave (1906; McKim, Mead & White) on the S.W. corner of 36th St, an Italian Renaissance palace built for the jeweller and silver company, and the former Tiffany's at 409 Fifth Ave (1906; McKim, Mead & White) on the S.E. corner of 37th St, modelled after the Venetian Palazzo Grimani, have suffered ugly alterations. In 1982 **W. & J. Sloane,** the well-known furniture store, left its Fifth Ave address (S.W. corner of 38th St) and moved around the corner to 8–16 W. 38th St. LORD & TAYLOR, however, still remains at the N.W. corner of the intersection of 38th St and Fifth Ave and is one of the city's famous department stores, whose founders moved up from humble Lower East Side beginnings to Fifth Ave elegance. Despite the deterioration of this part of the avenue, or perhaps to stem the tide, Lord & Taylor in 1977 elected to remodel their Fifth Ave Store (1914; Starrett & Van Vleck) at an estimated cost of $5 million, furnishing the ground floor with mirrored columns, marble floors, and greenery. The store is known for its women's sportswear.

Across the street on the N.E. corner of 39th St formerly stood Arnold Constable, traditional merchandising rival of Lord & Taylor's, now out of business, its space taken over by the New York Public Library. The **American Radiator Building** (1924; Hood & Fouilhoux; DL) at 40 W. 40th St between Fifth and Sixth Aves is a handsome black brick and gold terracotta tower with a grand Gothic top. The ground floor features a lobby clad in mirrors and black marble.

Continue N. The **Main Branch of the New York Public Library** on the W. side of Fifth Ave between 40th–42nd Sts (1911; Carrère & Hastings; DL) is one of the world's leading research institutions with some six million volumes of printed material and 17 million other documents. The building itself is a triumph of Beaux Arts design, an extravagant white marble temple lavishly decorated inside and out.

Open Mon–Wed, 10–6; Fri–Sat, 10–6; closed Thurs, Sun, holidays. Admission free. Hours vary for specific collections. Tours at 11 and 2 on Mon, Tues, Wed. Tel: 790–6161.

History. The research collections of the New York Public Library developed from the consolidation of two great privately endowed libraries, the Astor and Lenox Libraries, and the Tilden Trust, a bequest of $2 million and 15,000 books from Samuel J. Tilden, lawyer, governor, and unsuccessful presidential candidate. Immigrant John Jacob Astor, hardly a bookish man, was persuaded by Joseph Green Cogswell to establish a public library (see p172) as a fitting testimonial to his adopted country (Astor for a while favoured a huge monument to George Washington), and bequeathed $400,000 and a plot of land for its foundation. The books, largely chosen by Cogswell, provided a general reference service in the fields of greatest public interest including books on the 'mechanic arts and practical industry' and books on languages, since Cogswell saw the American nation coming 'into near relation with countries formerly the most remote'. James Lenox, on the other hand, was a scholar whose particular interests are reflected in the strengths of his collection: American literature and history, the Bible, Milton, Shakespeare, Bunyan and Renaissance literature of travel and discovery. Lenox built his own library (1875) on the site of the present Frick Collection (Fifth Ave between 70th–71st Sts) but at his death (1880) left his 85,000 peerless books and an endowment of $505,000 to the New York Public Library. The gift of bachelor Samuel J. Tilden, a bequest reduced from $4 million to $2 million by his relatives who contested the will, was sorely needed as by 1886 the Astor and Lenox libraries already needed funds for books and maintenance. In 1895 the three gifts were united as the New York Public Library, Astor, Lenox, and Tilden Foundations—the Central Research Library at its exists today. In 1901 Andrew Carnegie, made aware that the city had nothing comparable to the public circulating systems of Boston and other American cities, gave $52,000,000 for the building of branch libraries. Today the library has 80 branches including the Library and Museum of the Performing Arts at Lincoln Center and the Schomburg Center for Research in Black Culture in Harlem. The circulating collections are publicly supported while the research libraries depend upon endowment and contributions.

EXTERIOR. The building sits on a wide terrace running the length of the Fifth Ave facade. In the center a broad flight of steps leads to three deep entrance arches framed by Corinthian columns. Flanking the steps which have long been attractive to tourists, pigeons, footsore shoppers, and the usual urban eccentrics, are two famous couchant marble lions by Edward C. Potter (1911), originally criticised as tame, mealy-mouthed, complacent creatures but now fondly accepted by the public. The bronze flagstaff bases (1912) by Raffaele J. Menconi were cast in the Tiffany Studios. In niches behind the fountains against the facade are statues of Truth (right), a man leaning against a sphinx, and Beauty (left), a woman seated on the winged horse Pegasus, both by Frederick MacMonnies (1913). Above the entrance on the frieze are six allegorical figures (left to right) representing History, Romance, Religion, Poetry, Drama, and Philosophy by Paul Wayland Bartlett. The pediment figures at the ends of the facade are Art (S.) and History (N.) by George Grey Barnard (see p447). Architect Thomas Hastings was never totally happy with the facade on Fifth Ave, which early critics found too ornate, and undertook studies for improving it, even leaving money in his will for alterations, but today its extravagance is generally admired.

INTERIOR. The entrance hall (DL) finished in white Vermont marble, with an elaborate vaulted ceiling, marble canedlabra, and wide staircases, holds changing exhibitions from the collections. Take the elevator (end of the right corridor) to the third floor. The third floor corridor leading away from the elevator is used for

New York looking south from 42nd St in 1855. The Croton Distributing Reservoir and the Crystal Palace occupy the site of the library and Bryant Park, while surrounding blocks remain sparsely developed. (Museum of the City of New York)

changing exhibitions of prints, often prints of American cities. The central hall is decorated with murals depicting the History of the Book, and on the second floor landing is Munkacsy's Blind Milton Dictating 'Paradise Lost' to His Daughters. The *Public Catalogue* in Room 315 has more than 10 million cards. Beyond is the *Main Reading Room* with a shelf collection of 35,000 reference books.

SPECIAL COLLECTIONS. Room 318 is an exhibition room with treasures from the Berg Collection (Room 320) which contains some 85,000 items mostly in the fields of American and English literature: manuscripts from the 15–20C, authors' corrected proofs, family correspondence, and rare books. The library's major portraits hang here. The *Prints Division* (Room 308) has some 150,000 prints including the Phelps Stokes Collection of American Historical Prints, one of whose treasures is an engraving by Paul Revere of the British landing in Boston in 1768. The *Spencer Collection* (Room 308) has illuminated manuscripts from the 9–16C, and finely illustrated and bound books including a 14C Tickhill psalter. The *Arents Collection* (Room 324) consists of two sections, a collection of books published in serial form, acquired unbound as originally issued, and a collec-

tion of manuscripts, printed works, and other documents (1507–present) concerned directly or tangentially with tobacco, a resource for researches interested in the early history of America or such matters as taxation. The *Rare Book Division* (Room 303) has more than 91,000 volumes and 20,000 broadsides including such treasures as a Gutenberg Bible, the only known copy of the original folio edition (in Spanish) of Christopher Columbus's letter describing his discoveries (dated 1493), the first full folio of Shakespeare (1623), and a Bay Psalm Book (1640) from Cambridge, Mass, the first English book printed in the U.S.

Directly behind the library is **BRYANT PARK,** named after William Cullen Bryant (1794–1878), editor, writer, abolitionist, and proponent of such projects as Central Park and the Metropolitan Museum of Art. A *statue of Bryant* (1911; Herbert Adams) as an elderly sage, sits in the center of the park beneath an elaborate pillared architectural setting by Thomas Hastings, one of the designers of the library. At the S. end of the park near 40th St is a heroic bronze *bust of Goethe* (1932; Karl Fischer); towards 42nd St is a bronze *statue of William Earl Dodge* (1885; John Quincy Adams Ward), wealthy industrialist and supporter of virtuous causes (founder of the American Y.M.C.A., president of the National Temperance Society). Near the N.W. corner of the park is a bronze *statue of José Bonifacio de Andrada*, scholar, poet, and 'patriarch of Brazilian independence', by

José Lima, cast from an original (1889) and presented to the United States in 1954 as a gift from Brazil. The park's present formal design (1934; Lusby Simpson), essentially a grid raised 4 ft above street level and walled in by shrubbery has been criticised for attracting and sheltering drug pushers and a menacing group of drifters from the Times Square area. Since 1980 efforts have been made to clean up the park and to provide greater security for the public.

History. Before these 9·6 acres became Bryant Park (1884), the land was called Reservoir Park after the Croton Reservoir (1837–1900) which stood where the library is now, a walled and buttressed mass of grey granite with a wide promenade on top from which strollers could observe the sights of Manhattan. In June 1842 the first Croton water poured into the reservoir, flowing from artificially created Lake Croton (which rose behind a dam in the Croton River, a tributary flowing into the Hudson N. of Ossining), along 33 miles of aqueduct, across the Harlem River on High Bridge, through pipes in the Manhattanville Valley and into a tunnel that emptied into the reservoir. A jubilant crowd listened to speeches and a 38-gun salute as water filled the two basins within the aqueduct to a capacity of 150 million gallons, ending a period of more than 200 years when the city, dependent on shallow wells and springs, was subject to frequent outbreaks of cholera and the ravages of uncontrollable fires. The Croton system, enlarged, updated, and supplemented by the Catskill system still forms a significant part of the city's water supply.

In 1853 a world's fair, complete with Crystal Palace, opened in the park behind the reservoir, displaying pumps, hardware, sewing machines, and less utilitarian objects. On the N. side of 42nd St stood the Latting Tower, a 350-ft iron structure with an ice cream parlour at the bottom and a view at the top, reached via an unreliable steam-propelled elevator. Both the Latting Tower (1856) and the Crystal Palace (1858) burned, possibly so their owners might recover the insurance.

Across the street from the library is *Lane Bryant* (465 Fifth Ave), a store specialising in clothing for larger women. Lena Himmelstein Bryant, who founded the chain of stores (1904), was an immigrant from Lithuania, a widow without financial resources who pawned her wedding gift, a pair of diamond earrings, to make the down payment on a sewing machine. She introduced stylish maternity clothing to America (where newspapers refused to carry advertising for it until 1911) and with her second husband pioneered the merchandising of clothing for larger women. Insurance company statistics and on-the-spot measurements of 4500 customers confirmed that 40% of American women were larger than the standard size 36, considered ideal at the time.

Continue N. on Fifth Ave. The steel and glass box at the S.W. corner of W. 43rd St (510 Fifth Ave) is *Manufacturers Hanover Trust Co*. (1954; Skidmore, Owings & Merrill), rather ordinary today but innovative in 1954 when banks still resembled palazzos or ancient temples. At 7 W. 43rd St is the *Century Association* (1891; McKim, Mead & White; DL). Founded by William Cullen Bryant, the club has long been known for its intellectual and cultural orientation. Its membership included both Charles Follen McKim and Stanford White, who here designed one of their first neo-Italian Renaissance clubhouses. The building is faced with granite, terracotta and brick, and features above the main doorway a handsome Palladian window, once part of an open loggia. Return to Fifth Ave and continue north.

On W. 44th St between Fifth and Sixth Aves (27 W. 44th St) is the *Harvard Club* (1894; McKim, Mead & White, additions 1905 and 1915; DL), a handsome neo-Georgian clubhouse whose restrained brick and limestone facade recalls the early architecture of the college itself. The NEW YORK YACHT CLUB at 37 W. 44th St (1901; Warren & Wetmore) is a study in Beaux Arts exuberance, festooned with ropes and pulleys, anchors and hooks; truly astonishing, however, are the three windows fashioned like the sterns of ships ploughing through ossified seas whose stony waves overhang the sidewalk. The keystone above the main entrance appropriately represents Poseidon. Built on land donated by J. P. Morgan (commodore 1897–99), the club houses the America's Cup, given in 1851 by Queen Victoria and now considered the ultimate prize in yachting.

The ALGONQUIN HOTEL at 59 W. 44th St (1902; Goldwyn Starrett) first rose to fame as a literary hangout when H.L. Mencken stayed there in 1914; since then it has enrolled William Faulkner, Gertrude Stein, James Thurber, F. Scott Fitzgerald, Tennessee Williams, and Graham Greene on its guest register. Beginning in 1919 Robert Benchley and Dorothy Parker among others held forth at the Round Table, where the bar now is in the Rose Room, amusing one another with clever conversation, whose prize witticisms Franklin P. Adams reported in his column in the 'New York World'. Later the Round Table extended itself into the Thanatopsis Pleasure and Literary Club, which in turn evolved into the Thanatopsis Poker and Inside Straight Club. Harold Ross, founder of the 'New Yorker' magazine belonged to the coterie and created his magazine—less highminded in its beginnings than presently—partly to enshrine the sophisticated, incisive humour of his friends. While today's clientele may glitter less, the hotel still attracts literary and theatrical people. The lobby and dining rooms have been restored to their old, casual handsomeness.

The ROYALTON HOTEL across the street at 44 W. 44th St long enjoyed the presence of George Jean Nathan who maintained an apartment there from 1908 until his death in 1959. With Mencken, Nathan was editor (1914–1925) of the 'Smart Set', prime literary magazine of its day until it fizzled into triviality. Robert Benchley, writer and humourist, also maintained a suite here, furnished with the red draperies and coverings of the Victorian era and appointed with two portraits of the queen herself. The *Hippodrome Garage* at 50 W. 44th St marks the site of the Hippodrome Theatre (1905; Frederick Thompson and Elmer S. Dundy), which faced Sixth Ave and was the largest legitimate theatre in the world, seating a crowd of 5000 spectators. Because it was so large that the audience couldn't hear the lyrics, it was used for spectacles—elephants pulling automobiles, horses or girls plunging into the theatre's giant tank, ballets featuring its permanent company of 200 dancers who supplemented 400 chorus girls and 100 chorus boys.

Walk back toward Fifth Ave along the S. side of W. 44th St. The ponderous limestone building with massive Doric columns at ground level (42 W. 44th St) is the *Association of the Bar of the City of New York* (1895; Cyrus L.W. Eidlitz; DL). At 20 W. 44th St is a more humble institution, the *Mechanics' and Tradesmen's Institute* (1891; Lamb & Rich), originally the Berkeley Preparatory School, which still offers courses to technical students. Inside is a three-story drill hall now converted to a library and museum. The *John M. Mossman Collection of Locks* (Mon–Fri, 9–4; admission free; tel: 687–2490) offers a large collection of antique and modern locks, including such delights as a Very Complicated lock which more than justifies its name. The Mechanics' and Tradesmen's Institute library is open by membership to the public (tel: 840–1840), and includes a good collection of books on Gilbert and Sullivan as well as books appealing to a general readership.

Return to Fifth Ave and continue N. The FRED F. FRENCH BUILDING at 551 Fifth Ave (N.E. corner of 45th St) typifies the better skyscrapers of the 1920s (1927; Fred F. French & Co., Douglas Ives) with its ornate lobby, upper story setbacks, and ornamental work—unusual faience polychromy delineating the setbacks and the top of the building. The panels concealing the water tower on the roof are decorated with faience motifs chosen by architect Ives: N. and S., the rising sun (progress) amidst winged griffins (integrity and watchfulness) and golden beehives and bees (thrift and industry); E. and W., heads of Mercury, god of commerce.

Continue N. on Fifth Ave to 47th St; turn left (W.). At 41 W. 47th St between Fifth and Sixth Aves is the GOTHAM BOOK MART, established in 1920 by Frances Steloff, friend and supporter of such American writers as William Carlos Williams, Henry Miller, and T.S. Eliot. Thousands of books, including a wide selection of poetry and prose, literary magazines, and works on the dance, cram the shelves. The James Joyce Society organised in 1947 with T.S. Eliot purchasing the first membership, still meets here. Upstairs the gallery is sometimes rented by publishers to celebrate new releases or may offer exhibitions of a literary nature.

Return along 47th St toward Fifth Ave. Dingy though it may be, the block of W. 47th St between Fifth and Sixth Aves is the city's **Diamond District,** where daily about $400 million in gems is exchanged. The glittering shops at street level are for tourists, while the real business is transacted upstairs, in seedy buildings equipped with ultra-sensitive cameras and sophisticated alarm systems. Still, at least until 1977 when two traders were killed and $3 million in gems stolen, dealers handed over valuable stones to friends of friends on the sidewalk and consummated million-dollar agreements with handshakes. Virtually all the brokers and diamond cutters are Jewish, using skills passed down the generations from as far back as the 16C, when stone cutting was one of the few trades open to Jews. The community includes a group of Hasidic Jews, highly visible with their beards, long sidelocks, black, wide-brimmed hats, and dark clothing, drawn to the trade partly by tradition and partly because the flexible hours permit them to observe the rigours of their religion. The Diamond Dealers Club, a trading center for dealers in cut diamonds, is at 30 W. 47th St, while the Diamond Trade Association, a center for trading uncut stones, is at 15 W. 47th St. Neither is open to outsiders.

Continue up Fifth Ave. North of about 47th St Fifth Ave begins to live up to its reputation, though here and there even in this glittering shopping district cheap stores have begun to intrude. At 586 Fifth Ave between 47th and 48th Sts is *Brentano's* bookstore, one of several that make this portion of the avenue a delight for browsers. *Charles Scribner's Sons* bookstore at 597 Fifth Ave between 48th and 49th Sts is ensconced in a handsome building (1913; Ernest Flagg) with a black iron and glass storefront and an elegant two-story interior.

For Rockefeller Centre which begins at Fifth Ave and W. 49th St, see Route 17. SAKS FIFTH AVENUE, on the E. side of the avenue between 49th and 50th Sts, a department store known for high fashion boutiques and exquisite merchandise, was founded by Andrew Saks, who began as a peddler in Washington, D.C., and ended a wealthy man. In 1923 his son Horace sold a less exclusive store, Saks Thirty-fourth, to Gimbels for $8 million in order to follow the carriage trade uptown and the following year opened this store, whose windows featured a pigskin trunk ($3000), raccoon coats ($1000) and chauffeur's livery.

* *St. Patrick's Cathedral** (1879; towers, 1888; James Renwick, Jr; DL), filling the block between E. 50th and E. 51st St on Fifth Ave is the seat of the Roman Catholic Archdiocese of New York, one of the city's most famous landmarks, and a symbol of the success in New York of its immigrant Irish Catholic population. Designed by James Renwick with William Rodrique, whose contribution seems to have been minimal, it draws on the decorated Gothic style of the 13C and has been compared to French, German and English cathedrals of that period. It is the largest Catholic cathedral in the U.S. and the eleventh largest in the world.

History. In 1828 the two major Catholic churches of New York, St. Peter's and St. Patrick's—then at the corner of Prince and Mott Sts—bought the plot where the cathedral now sits, intending it as a burial ground. Unfortunately the buyers neglected to examine the land, which was far too rocky for its intended purpose. In 1850 Archbishop John Hughes announced his intention to build a new cathedral on the site, a church 'worthy of God, worthy of the Catholic religion, and an honor to this great city'—the last phrase remarkable at a time when upper class New York was largely Protestant, its Catholic population a rabble of immigrant outsiders from Ireland and later Germany, Italy, and Poland, whom the established Protestants kept isolated from the mainstream of American life, denying them all but the most menial, poorly paid jobs and levelling against them a deep-rooted prejudice. Hughes had arrived in America from Ireland in 1817, an uneducated twenty year old eager to become a priest. He arrived in New York in 1838 as bishop, a skilful administrator and flamboyant orator. Eight years after announcing his plan, Hughes solicited enough money to lay the cornerstone and begin construction (1858); in 1879 the cathedral was dedicated, having cost twice as much and taken four times as long to build (including an interruption during the Civil War) as estimates had predicted. It was consecrated, debt-free in 1910.

Measurements. Exterior: length, 332 ft; width 174 ft; base of towers, 32 sq. ft; height from street to top of spire, 330 ft; height of central gable, 156 ft. Interior: length, 306 ft; length of nave and transept, 144 ft; width of nave, 48 ft; height of nave, 108 ft.

Exterior. The general plan is a Latin cross with traditional east–west orientation. The facade is of marble, cleaned in 1978–79 to its original white. The two square towers facing Fifth Ave are topped by octagonal lanterns rising to spires. Because the interior vaulting is brick and plaster, not stone, flying buttresses were not necessary to support the upper walls, but the pinnacles of the buttresses exist, perhaps because Renwick originally called for stone interior vaulting supported by flying buttresses. The bronze doors (added 1949) at the W. entrance were designed by Charles Maginnis with figures by John Angel.

Figures represent (top to bottom, left to right): St. Joseph, patron of this church; St. Isaac Jogues, first Catholic priest in New York; St. Frances X. Cabrini, founder of the Missionary Sisters of the Sacred Heart and 'Mother of the Immigrant'; the Blessed Kateri Tekakwitha, an Indian maiden called 'the Lily of the Mohawks'; and St. Elizabeth Ann Seton, first American-born saint.

The 19 bells, commissioned in France, were installed in the N. tower in 1897, 160 ft above the ground. Originally worked by a mechanical keyboard in the spire, they are operated electrically today.

Interior. Enter the nave, defined by two rows of clustered columns.

Above the arches runs the triforium, divided into four sections by the arms of the cross. Above the triforia rise clerestory windows (14 × 26 ft in the nave, 28 × 58 ft in the transept). The ceiling is groined with (plaster) ribs with foliated bosses at the intersections.

Chapels and aisle windows in the **S. aisle** (near 50th St): (1) Window of St. Vincent de Paul over the book shop. (2) Altar of St. Anthony of Padua with window showing St. Elizabeth of Hungary, St. Andrew, and St. Catherine of Alexandria. (3) Altar of St. John the Evangelist with window of the Annunciation. (4) Shrine of St. Elizabeth Ann Seton (sculptor Frederick Shrady) which dates from 1975 and window dedicated to St. Henry, 11C Holy Roman Emperor. (5) Altar of St. Rose of Lima, patroness of S. America, with window depicting Pope Pius IX proclaiming the dogma of the Immaculate Conception.

S. Transept: (6) The stations of the cross were designed by Peter J. H. Cuypers in Holland and are carved in Caen stone (seven in S. transept, seven opposite them in N. transept). The windows above the stations of the cross are (S. transept) St. Luke (right of entrance) and St. John (left of entrance). Over the entrance is a window devoted to St. Patrick, depicting 18 scenes from his life. It was made in the atelier of Henry Ely in Nantes, France, and was given by Old St. Patrick's Cathedral. In the W. wall of the transept is another St. Patrick's window, given by architect Renwick, who appears in the lower panels. (7) Altar of the Blessed Sacrament, with a tabernacle containing the sacrament beneath a baldachin of oak with gold leaf, which once hung over the cardinal's throne.

S. Ambulatory: (8) Altar of St. Andrew with window of St. Agnes, virgin martyr of Rome. (9) Altar of St. Theresa of the Little Flower, with window of St. Alphonsus Liguori. (10) Archbishop's sacristy with window depicting the death of St. Joseph. Beyond the sacristy is (11) a marble Pietà (1906; William O. Partridge) based on Michelangelo's masterpiece. Next is (12) the altar of St. Elizabeth, mother of St. John the Baptist.

The **Lady Chapel,** begun in 1901 and completed in 1906, was designed by Charles T. Matthews and is patterned after 13C French Gothic architecture. Constructed of Vermont marble (but with plaster vaults), it is 56 ft long, 28 ft wide, and 56 ft high. The stained glass windows (Paul Woodroffe) over this altar and the two flanking it depict the mysteries of the rosary. The chapel pavement of polished marble contains a mosaic of the heraldic arms of Pope Leo XIII.

Directly behind the Lady Chapel is the entrance to the *Crypt* (13) in which are buried the remains of Archbishop Hughes, the other cardinals of New York, and several rectors of this church, as well as Archbishop Fulton J. Sheen. (Crypt not usually open to the public.)

N. Ambulatory: Adjacent to the Lady Chapel on the N. side is (13) the Altar of St. Michael and St. Louis, designed by Charles T. Matthews and executed by Tiffany & Co. Beyond the usher's office and bride's room is (14) the altar of St. Joseph. Further along is the chancel organ (1928), with its handsome case and 2520 pipes (15).

N. Transept: The altar of the Holy Family (16) stands against the E. wall of the transept, with the Baptistry (17) in front of it, the eight-sided font of Bottocino marble inscribed with traditional baptismal symbols. Like the S. transept, this one has stations of the cross, carved figures of doctors of the church and theologians flanking the door, and windows depicting evangelists: St. Matthew (right of door) and St. Mark (left of door). Above the door is a window depicting the life of Mary. Opposite the Holy Family altar is the St. Charles Borromeo window.

The focal point of the **sanctuary** is the high altar (18) with its baldachin or canopy designed by Charles D. Maginnis. Made of bronze and rising to a height of 57 ft, it is decorated with statuary (John Angel) telling the story of the redemption of mankind. The present altar (1942) replaces an earlier one designed by Renwick before the Lady Chapel was added. The altar frontal shows the bark of St. Peter, a symbol of the church.

Suspended from the ceiling of the sanctuary above the altar are the *galeros* or ceremonial hats of all the cardinals of New York. The clerestory windows surrounding the sanctuary depict (clockwise from N.): sacrifice of Abel, sacrifice of Noah, sacrifice of Melchisedech, apsidal windows illustrating parables of Christ and symbols of the evangelists, sacrifice of Calvary, sacrifice of the eating of the Paschal lamb, sacrifice of Abraham.

From the crossing is a good view of the **West or Rose Window**, 26 ft in diam. and filled with stained glass in geometric patterns. In the loft beneath it is the Great Organ (1930), with 9000 pipes ranging from a little over 3 inches to 32 ft

ST. PATRICK'S CATHEDRAL

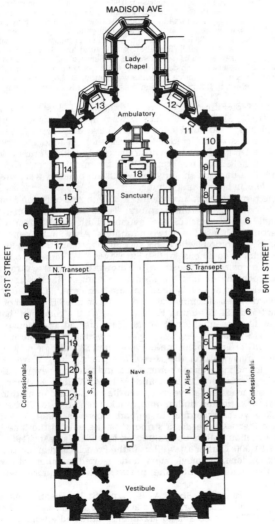

in length. The cathedral has a third organ, the echo organ, placed in the S. triforium near the American flag, which is used to enhance the chancel organ.

N. Aisle: The first altar (19) beyond the transept is the Altar of the Holy Face, formerly called the Chapel of St. Veronica and the Chapel of the Holy Relics because relics received by the archbishops of New York were kept here for veneration. Above the altar is a window depicting St. Bernard preaching the Second Crusade. To the right of the altar is a statue of St. Jude. The shrine of St. John Neumann (20) was erected in 1978 to honour this missionary in western New York state and bishop of Philadelphia, elevated to sainthood in 1977. The metal church depicted is Old St. Patrick's Cathedral where he was ordained. Above the shrine is a window depicting the martyrdom of St. Lawrence. The altar of St. Jean Baptiste de la Salle (21) stands below a window showing Pope Benedict XIII. The altar of St. Brigid and St. Bernard (22) is designed around a replica of a doorway of St. Bernard's Chapel in Mellifont, County Louth, Ireland, which dates from 1142. In front of the altar is a statue of the Infant of Prague, and above it a window depicting St. Columbanus, an Irish missionary, rebuking Burgundian King Thierry III for his scandalous life.

Continue N. on Fifth Ave. On the N.E. corner of E. 51st St is *Olympic Tower* (1976; Skidmore, Owings & Merrill), a luxurious multi-use building (shops at ground level, offices above, and apartments on the highest floors) constructed by a consortium headed by Aristotle Onassis. Olympic Place, a pedestrian arcade with a granite lobby and a waterfall, slices through the building midblock from E. 51st to E. 52nd St, a dubious amenity for which the builders were granted concessions in height and volume.

At the turn of the century the block of Fifth Ave between 51st and 52nd Sts was Vanderbilt territory. Three brownstone mansions occupied the W. side of the avenue, built by William Henry Vanderbilt for himself and two daughters. Alva Smith Vanderbilt, the socially ambitious wife of his second son, commissioned Richard Morris Hunt to do a house at 660 Fifth Ave (N.W. corner of 52nd St), a $3 million palace of limestone (not brownstone), whose turrets and Gothic traceries recalled the French château of Blois in the Loire Valley. Alva's husband, William Kissam Vanderbilt, alarmed by the northward sweep of commerce, sold the lot on the S.E. corner of Fifth Ave and 52nd St to Morton F. Plant, only on the condition that the site remain residential for 25 years. Plant erected a residence, now CARTIER'S (1905; Robert W. Gibson; remodelled as a store, 1917; DL), worthy of a man of his means (a reputed $32 million in 1919) and stature (Commodore of the New York Yacht Club). However, by 1916 he found the area too commercial and started a new mansion at the N.E. corner of Fifth Ave and 86th St. William K. Vanderbilt bought the mansion, a five-story neo-Italian palazzo of marble and granite, for a million dollars and quickly rented it to Cartier's for $50,000 a year. According to legend, however, Plant traded the house to Pierre Cartier for a string of pearls, said at the time to be worth a million dollars but valued on Mrs Plant's death (1956) at a mere $151,000. Cartier's, jewellers to the French court in the 18C and to later millionaires, movie stars, and assorted members of royalty, offers the general public the pleasure of its exquisite window displays.

Between Fifth and Sixth Aves, 52nd St has been designated **'Swing St'** to commemorate its place in the history of jazz. Known simply as 'The Street' among jazzmen, it attracted attention beginning in the late 1930s with its nightclubs, many of them former speakeasies, where most of the great innovators and performers of the period worked: Art Tatum, Dizzy Gillespie, Thelonius Monk, Lester Young, Kenny Clark, and of course Charlie Parker for whom the most famous jazz club of all, Birdland, would later be named. In particular the street has been identified with 'bop', a style which emerged from a series of jam sessions at Minton's Playhouse in Harlem between 1940–44 and came downtown as black musicians began working in the clubs of 52nd St. The best known were the Onyx, the Spotlight, the Three Deuces, the Famous Door, and on nearby Broadway, the Royal Roost and Bop City. The period was a golden age for jazz and for 52nd St, but by 1948, when heroin abuse was widespread among jazz musicians, the street had become the territory of prostitutes, strippers, and drug pushers.

Just W. of the avenue at 21 W. 52nd St is the Twenty-one Club, risen from its origins as a speakeasy to its present status as a celebrity haunt.

Continue N. on Fifth Ave past the *Tishman Building* (666 Fifth Ave, between W. 52nd and W. 53rd Sts), with its embossed aluminum facing typical of the skyscrapers of the 1950s (1957; Carson, Lundin & Shaw) and its pedestrian shopping arcade; the sculpted waterfall is by Isamu Noguchi. B. Dalton, Bookseller occupies the S. portion of the building.

On the N.W. corner of 53rd St and Fifth Ave (1 W. 53rd St) is Protestant Episcopal **St. Thomas' Church** (1914; Cram, Goodhue & Ferguson; DL), a picturesque asymmetric French Gothic church placed on a small corner plot. Originally it was built without steel, following the principles of Cram (also architect of St. John the Divine), who believed that if a church were Gothic in style it should be Gothic in construction, its columns supporting its weight. However, eleven years after completion the unbuttressed N. wall was bulging dangerously and steel beams were placed across the columns above the ceiling. Later, during blasting for the subway tunnel under 53rd St a steel beam was installed under the altar.

The EXTERIOR is of Kentucky limestone. Though architect Goodhue planned the facade, the sculptural figures were completed only in 1963 (sculpture, Theodore Barbarossa; stone carving, Rochette & Parzini). Above the double entrance doors a gilded relief shows the four different buildings in which the congregation has worshipped, two on Houston St and Broadway, two on the present site. The central figure on the facade is St. Thomas, shown having risen from his knees after recognising the risen Christ. Left of the main portal is the Bride's Entrance, decorated with a lover's knot. Next to it some have reported a dollar sign, a gesture of medieval origin when carpenters and stoneworkers regularly left tokens of social criticism in obscure parts of their cathedrals.

The INTERIOR is especially fine, culminating in the 80-ft **reredos** of ivory coloured Dunville stone (Ohio) pierced by three stained glass windows. Lee Lawrie, known for his work at Rockefeller Center, and architect Bertram G. Goodhue designed it, though the central portion showing the Cross and kneeling angels was copied from a smaller reredos by Augustus Saint-Gaudens in the previous church on this site (burned 1905).

Plan of the reredos. The central panel at the base shows St. Thomas and Christ. Above the heavy horizontal the empty Cross symbolises the Resurrection; above it is a Calvary group (the Virgin Mary, Christ, and St. John). Surrounding them are the apostles. The figures at the top of the reredos represent early saints and martyrs while the row of smaller figures just beneath the windows represents English church fathers and American bishops. The figures at the far right and left also represent men of importance in the spiritual history of England and America.

Also of interest are the tapestries in the nave and the wood carving of the chancel which was donated as a thanks offering after World War I.

The carved panels on the kneeling rail in front of the choir stalls represent the industries of mankind and important events in human history, including such motifs as (from the left) Christopher Columbus's ship, Theodore Roosevelt, Lee Lawrie, sculptor (between the steamship and the telephone), a radio, finance (with the initials of J. P. Morgan), and medicine.

The small carved heads above the choir stalls also represent contemporary personages including (S. side, second, third, and fourth figures from altar) President Woodrow Wilson, Premier Paderewski of Poland, and King Victor Emmanuel of Italy. The clerestory windows were made by Whitefriars in London and represent (N. side) the fruits of the spirit, substituting 'music' for 'longsuffering', and (S. side) sacraments of the church, St. Thomas, and builders of churches.

Visitors interested in iconography may purchase a book from the caretaker explaining the symbolism of the architecture and decoration in much greater detail.

Just off Fifth Ave at 1 E. 53rd St is the MUSEUM OF BROADCASTING, founded (1975) by William S. Paley, to document the history of American broadcasting. The collection, gathered from the major commercial networks, public television, and other sources, now includes more than 7000 radio and TV shows and televised events available to the public either in special exhibitions or in broadcast study centers.

Open Tues–Sat, noon–5. Mornings reserved for groups by appointment. Adults, $2; children under 14, $1. Tel: 752–7684. Daily programmes in the 63-seat theatre and the smaller Videotheque. Lectures and seminars (for information call 752–4682). The Library, 3rd floor, contains a catalogue of the collection, its 2400 rare scripts, and books and periodicals on broadcasting and related topics.

The earliest programme in the collection is a speech by Samuel Gompers, founder of the American Federation of Labor; other landmarks of history and entertainment include the Amos 'n' Andy show, Lord Haw Haw, Jack Benny, radio concerts by Toscanini, Edward R. Murrow's documentary on Senator Joseph McCarthy, the Beatles and Elvis Presley on the Ed Sullivan Show, and the funeral of John F. Kennedy.

PALEY PARK (1967; Zion & Breen, landscape architects; Albert Preston Moore, consulting architect) just E. of Fifth Ave (5 E. 53rd St) is the best vest-pocket park in the city. Measuring only 42 × 100 ft, graced by some ivy, a dozen honey locust trees, and a 'waterwall' whose splashing drowns out the clamour of traffic, it is a peaceful oasis in hectic midtown. Unusual for New York is the moveable furniture (which is secured at night). Before William S. Paley, chairman of the board of CBS, donated the park in memory of his father Samuel, the site was occupied by the Stork Club, a nightclub beloved of café society and gossip columnists.

Continue up Fifth Ave. On the N.W. corner of the next intersection at 1 W. 54th St is the UNIVERSITY CLUB (1899; McKim, Mead & White; DL), a grand neo-Italian palazzo built during the heyday of the club, when some clubmen, Cornelius Vanderbilt for example, belonged to as many as 16 and spent in dues when the average worker earned in a year. Even then the University Club was remarkable for its grandeur. The facade of pink Milford granite, quarried in Maine, is decorated with shields representing major American universities and is divided by cornices into three levels, each with round-arch windows finishing in keystones (grotesque animal heads on the top story keystones, human faces on the lower ones). Behind the small square windows are bedrooms; behind the arched windows, public rooms. Above the main door, flanked with marvellous reeded and foliated columns, is a head of Athena modelled after a statuette owned by Stanford White. The interior (not open to the public) is remarkable for its opulent decoration: hallways paved with marble, ceiling paintings by H. Siddons Mowbray, pilasters of Italian walnut.

Turn W. (left). At 7 W. 54th St is the *Philip Lehman residence* (1900; John H. Duncan), a handsome townhouse noteworthy for having once held the Robert Lehman collection of paintings now exhibited in the Metropolitan Museum of Art. Further along the same side of the street at 17 W. 54th St (between Fifth and Sixth Aves) are the ROCKEFELLER APARTMENTS (1936; Harrison & Fouilhoux), a project consisting of two buildings running back to back (the other faces W. 55th St) with a central garden between to admit light but not noise to the rear bedrooms. Because the cylindrical bays were designed as dining rooms, their windows face away from one another, insuring privacy. The land on which the apartments stand was acquired along with the land for Rockefeller Center, as was the land on which the Donnell Library and the Museum of Modern Art now stand.

Return to Fifth Ave and cross it. At 4 E. 54th St is another McKim, Mead & White building (1900; DL), originally the residence of William H. Moore, a Chicago industrialist and a founder of the United States Steel Corporation, the American Can Company, and the National Biscuit Company. The neo-Italian townhouse now belongs to the *America-Israel Cultural Foundation*, which fosters cultural exchange between the two countries.

Return to Fifth Ave and go N. On the S.E. corner of the next intersection (2 E. 55th St) is the ST. REGIS-SHERATON HOTEL (1904; Trowbridge & Livingston, with an addition to the E., 1925), a property venture of John Jacob Astor IV, who after his experience with the Waldorf-Astoria realised that elegant hotels in or near residential neighbourhoods attracted a clientele eager for proximity to social splendour. The exterior has stone garlands, a mansard roof with bull's-eye windows and copper cresting, and a brass and glass kiosk for the doormen on E. 55th St. Inside, Astor provided automatic thermostats in every room, a system for heating, cooling, moistening, or drying the air (in the days before air conditioning), 47 Steinway pianos, a service of gold-plated flatware, and other decorative touches that cost him $1·5 million. Once famous for its restaurants including a palm room where members of both sexes could smoke publicly at all hours, the St. Regis is now known for the King Cole Room, present home of Maxfield Parrish's mural originally commissioned for another Astor enterprise, the Knickerbocker Hotel in Times Square. Across the street on the S.W. corner of Fifth Ave (2 W. 55th St) is the *Gotham Hotel* (1905; Hiss & Weeks), also ornate and elite.

Continue N. On the N.W. corner of Fifth Ave and 55th St is the *Fifth Avenue Presbyterian Church* (1875). The *Rizzoli International*

Bookstore (712 Fifth Ave between 55th and 56th Sts) in the former Cartier Building (1907; A.S. Gottlieb) offers elegant browsing in a collection of foreign language and English books. *Harry Winston* (718 Fifth Ave, S.W. corner of 56th St) is a jeweller whose international reputation rests on the size, quality, and rarity of his gems. The block of W. 56th St between Fifth and Sixth Aves, called '*Eat Street*' by columnist Earl Wilson, is known for its dense concentration of restaurants—Italian, French, Korean, and Japanese, among others.

Across the street on the S.E. corner of Fifth Ave and 56th St (717 Fifth Ave) is the *Corning Glass Building* (1959; Harrison, Abramovitz & Abbe), a 28-story tower with greenish glass facing. On the ground floor are the showrooms of Steuben Glass, whose windows, convex to prevent glare, seem invisible.

Continue N. The construction project between 56th and 57th Sts was once occupied by Bonwit Teller, a department store selling expensive women's clothing. The project rising there now is a multi-use tower with stores, offices, and 300 condominiums on the upper floors. It is currently estimated that a one-bedroom apartment in the building will cost $700,000. Next to the construction site, at the S.E. corner of 57th St at 727 Fifth Ave is *Tiffany & Co.*, another of the avenue's famous jeweller, founded by Charles L. Tiffany, father of Louis Comfort Tiffany, who became famous as a designer of glass, stained glass, jewellery, enamels, and interiors. The firm moved to this modest granite palazzo (1940; Cross & Cross) from its fancier palace on 37th St and Fifth Ave.

Walk a block N. The *Solow Building* at 9 W. 57th St (1974; Skidmore, Owings & Merrill), with its glassy facade and swooping form is a more expensive though equally maligned version of the W.R. Grace Building on W. 42nd St.

Like so many of the city's other luxury stores, BERGDORF GOODMAN (W. side of Fifth Ave between 57th and 58th Sts) had humble beginnings. Herman Bergdorf, a tailor known for adapting men's suits to the female figure and also for his enjoyment of wine, founded it but Edwin Goodman, who bought out Bergdorf in 1901, raised the store to its present heights, moving it to this location in 1928. Before Bergdorf's arrived, the Cornelius Vanderbilt mansion stood here, a 137-room castle, filling the whole block with peaks, gables, dormers, and other Victorian architectural gingerbread.

Across the street at the N.E. corner of Fifth Ave and 58th St is *F.A. O. Schwartz*, a large, famous, and expensive toy store.

16 United Nations, Turtle Bay, and Beekman Hill

SUBWAY: IRT Lexington Ave local or express (train 4, 5, or 6) or Flushing IRT (train 7) to Grand Central Station-42nd St.

BUS: Uptown via First Ave, downtown via Second Ave: M15. Via Third and Lexington Aves: M101 or M102. Crosstown on 49th-50th Sts: M27. Crosstown on 42nd St: M104 or M106. Culture Bus (weekends and holidays): Loop I, stop 21 or Loop II, stop 17.

The neighbourhood in the east 40s today dominated by the United Nations is known as Turtle Bay, after a cove in the East River that reached from about 45th to 48th St. Whether the bay, long since

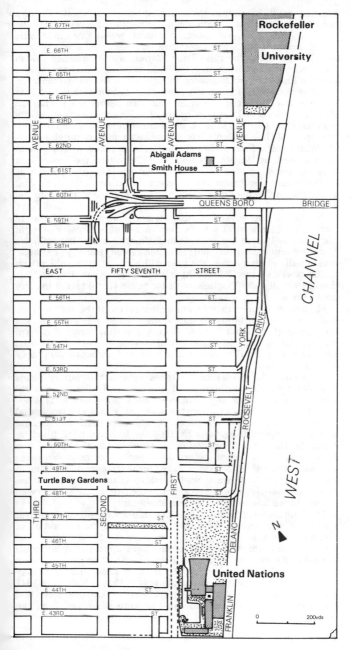

filled in, got its name from the abundant turtles in its waters or as a corruption of the Dutch word 'deutal' (a bent blade), referring to its shape, the land around it, 'Deutal Bay Farm', was granted in 1639 by Dutch governor William Kieft to two Englishmen, George Holmes and Thomas Hall. Later, Sir Peter Warren, a distinguished British naval officer who settled in New York, married a De Lancey, and enjoyed a mansion in Greenwich Village (see p198), owned the farm, while James Beekman owned a nearby parcel from 49th to 51st St in an area now known as Beekman Hill. Just before the Revolution (1775), the Sons of Liberty, a group of belligerent, radical, mostly working class patriots, sailed a sloop from Greenwich, Connecticut, through Hell Gate to Turtle Bay, and seized a military storehouse on the Warren farm from its British guards, taking its supplies back to Boston. Marinus Willett, after whom Willett St on the Lower East Side is named, led the foray. Later, Nathan Hale (see p112) was captured near the former Dove Tavern (Third Ave at 66th St) and sentenced in the Beekman greenhouse as a spy and traitor to the king.

In the mid-19C several notable literary figures sought refuge in Turtle Bay, then a rural suburb. Publisher Horace Greeley brought his wife here to ease her grief at the death of several of her children. Margaret Fuller, writer and reformer, spent some years here, occasionally rowing across the river with a friend to visit the prison on Blackwell's (now Roosevelt) Island. Edgar Allan Poe and his desparately ill wife, Virginia, rented a house (1846) facing the bay near 47th St.

At Third Ave and 46th St an enrollment office for the draft into the Union Army was established during the Civil War and became the focal point of the Draft Riots of 1863, a three-day binge of rioting, looting, and burning, in which 18 blacks were lynched, the Colored Orphan Asylum on Fifth Ave was burned, and perhaps 1000 people killed or injured.

In the later 19C, modest brownstones replaced the country homes and although the neighbourhood around the Beekman farm remained pleasant because of James W. Beekman's careful development of his property, elsewhere the area, unrestricted by residential covenants, deteriorated into slums. The shores of Turtle Bay became a smelly garbage dump, and by 1868 the bay had been filled in. When the Third Ave El opened in 1878 followed by the Second Ave El in 1880, the far East Side rapidly deteriorated, its brownstones converted to rooming houses or razed for tenements. In addition to Italian, German, Irish, and Jewish immigrants, the area attracted the city's night people: actors, musicians, stage hands, and waiters who worked in the fine restaurants near Broadway.

The resurgence of Turtle Bay began around the end of World War I with the development of Turtle Bay Gardens, the renovation of individual brownstones, and the greening of Sutton Place and Beekman Hill which began to attract such literary and theatrical people as Alfred Lunt and Lynn Fontanne, the Barrymores, Helen Hopkinson, Henry Luce, Irving Berlin, Billy Rose, and Humphrey Bogart. But it was not until the coming of the United Nations in 1947 that the cattle pens, slaughterhouses, breweries, and coal yards that had followed the opening of the Els were dislodged from the shoreline.

Begin at First Ave and 43rd St. **United Nations Headquarters** at

United Nations Plaza (First Ave) between 42nd and 48th Sts was built (1947–53) by an international committee of architects to house this organisation of sovereign nations whose primary purpose is maintaining world peace. Each year almost a million people visit the 18-acre site to see the buildings and gardens and to be instructed in the goals and workings of the institution.

Buildings open weekdays, 9–5.20; Sat, Sun, and holidays, 9.15–5.20. Children under 12 must be accompanied by an adult. No lunches or snacks allowed on the grounds inside the gate, though they are permitted in the park to the N. Coffee shop, telephones, post office, and restrooms in the basement of the General Assembly Building. Delegates' dining room on 2nd floor, open to the public; enquire at the Information Desk in the lobby of the General Assembly Building.

History. Soon after the signing of the United Nations Charter (1945), the General Assembly moved to locate the U.N. permanent headquarters in the United States. On 11 Dec 1946, John D. Rockefeller, Jr offered $8·5 million to buy a large parcel of land on the East River assembled by William Zeckendorf, a real estate operator who had obtained an option to buy it for private development. With unusual rapidity Congress accepted the gift and exempted it from the usual gift taxes while the city agreed to contribute adjacent properties. A plan by Zeckendorf to condemn everything E. of Third Ave between 46th–49th Sts, including Turtle Bay Gardens and other areas just emerging from urban squalour, was discarded in favour of a scheme sponsored by Robert Moses to widen 47th St between First and Second Aves and to route First Ave beneath United Nations Plaza in a tunnel.

The buildings were designed by an international committee of architects headed by Wallace K. Harrison, whose ties with the Rockefeller family went back to the building of Rockefeller Center. Other staff architects were: Max Abramovitz (U.S.A.), N.D. Bassov (U.S.S.R.), Gaston Brunfaut (Belgium), Le Corbusier (France), Ernest Cormier (Canada), Ssu-Ch'eng Liang (China), Sven Markelius (Sweden), Oscar Niemeyer (Brazil), Howard Robertson (U.K.), G.A. Souileux (Australia), and Julio Vilamajo (Uruguay). Construction costs, financed by an interest-free loan from the U.S., came to $67 million excluding the Dag Hammarskjöld Library (1961), a $6·7 million gift from the Ford Foundation.

Exterior. Begin at U.N. Plaza and 43rd St. On the W. side of the street a staircase leads down to RALPH J. BUNCHE PARK, a small park with a steel sculpture, *Peace Form One* by Daniel Larue Johnston, near which is inscribed a quotation from Bunche's acceptance of the Nobel Peace Prize. On the wall nearby is inscribed the verse from Isaiah 2:4 beginning 'They shall beat their swords into plough shares. . .'. Look across the avenue to the U.N. buildings prefaced by a row of flags representing the member nations (arranged in alphabetical order). From left to right (N. to S.) the buildings are: the General Assembly Building with a curving roof from which protrudes the dome covering the assembly hall, the Secretariat Building, and the Dag Hammarskjöld Library. Behind the General Assembly Building, but not visible from the street, is the Conference Building. In a circular pool in front of the Secretariat is a bronze sculptural abstraction, *Single Form*, 21 ft high, by Barbara Hepworth, placed there to honour Dag Hammarskjöld, secretary-general of the U.N. killed (1961) in a plane crash on a peace keeping mission in the Congo (now Zaire). Commissioned by the U.N. (1963) and funded by a grant from the Jacob and Hilda Blaustein Foundation (Blaustein was a U.S. delegate to the U.N. and a friend of Hammarskjöld), the work was cast in six sections whose outlines still remain and is by a sculptor whose art Hammarskjöld admired and collected.

When built, the **Secretariat Building** seemed a daring piece of architecture, a 544-ft slab (287 ft wide and 72 ft thick) with white marble end walls and side walls of green glass set in an aluminum grid. Its vast E.–W. exposure long created air-conditioning problems that led critic Henry Russell-Hitchcock to predict, erroneously, the demise of glass-walled skyscrapers unless their western facades were shielded from the sun. Le Corbusier established the original design of the complex: a tall slab with offices for the bureaucracy, a low horizontal building for conferences, and a functionally-shaped though imposing assembly building, all to be set on a landscaped site, a scheme, according to Lewis Mumford, that demonstrated architecturally that 'bureaucracy ruled the world'. When Le Corbusier withdrew after personal difficulties, Wallace K. Harrison became responsible for implementing the details of the project.

Enter the *Visitors' Entrance* along the N. side of the General Assembly Building near 46th St. The seven nickel-bronze entrance doors were donated by Canada and their bas relief panels symbolise peace, justice, truth, and fraternity.

Interior. At the left or E. end of the lobby is a mural, *Brotherhood* (1971) by Rufino Tamayo, the gift of Mexico. In front of it is a bronze cast of the famous 5C *Poseidon* of Artemision, gift (1952) of Greece: the original is in the National Museum of Athens. Overhead is a *replica of the first Sputnik*, launched in 1957, gift of the U.S.S.R.

In the center of the lobby is an *information desk*, where you may apply for tickets to any public sessions or for passes to the Delegates' Dining Room. On the W. wall of the lobby is the *United Nations Peace Rug*, worked by the American Needlework Guild, displaying the emblems of the member states at the time of donation (1976). Near the curve in the stairway is a *Foucault pendulum*, gift (1955) of the Netherlands. Beyond the stairway arch is a case containing a Moon Rock, gift of the U.S.A., collected on the Apollo 14 mission (1971), man's first landing on the moon. To the right is the DAG HAMMARSKJOLD MEMORIAL CHAPEL with a stained glass memorial window on themes of Man and Peace donated by the artist Marc Chagall. The chapel also honours other U.N. workers—soldiers, observers, and diplomats—who died in the performance of their duties. A door on the S. wall opens into the MEDITATION ROOM with an abstract fresco by Swedish artist Bo Beskow and a six-ton polished block of Swedish iron ore.

Walk through the lobby beyond the Information Desk to the *Tour Desk*.

The only way to visit other parts of the U.N. is on a guided tour. Given in 30 languages, tours leave about every 15 minutes 9.15–4.45 and last about an hour. Adults, $2·50; students with identification, $1·50; children under 12, $1. Children under five years not permitted. The following description reflects areas visited on the tours. Tel: 754–7710 (Mon–Fri).

In the garden along the W. wall of the Secretariat Building is the *Japanese Peace Bell*, cast from coins and metal donated by people from 60 nations. The Secretariat Building, 39 floors high, houses a working population of some 6000 people and is not open to the public except for its lobby where portraits of former secretaries-general are displayed: Trygve Lie (by Norwegian artist, Harald Dal), Dag Hammarskjöld (by Swedish artist, Bo Beskow), and U Thant (by American artist, James Whitney Fosburg).

The **Conference Building** houses technical installations, conference rooms, delegates lounges, chambers for the major councils, and the delegates' dining room.

The *SECURITY COUNCIL CHAMBER (designed by Arnstein Arneberg, Norway) is dominated by a mural (Per Krohg) showing a central figure of Peace, a phoenix rising from a foreground devastated by war, with side panels depicting themes of brotherhood, liberty, and equality.

The main function of the Security Council is to keep international peace and to do so it may undertake investigation and mediation, may impose economic sanctions, send a peace keeping force or undertake collective military action. Of the 15 member nations, five are permanent: China, France, the U.S.S.R., the U.K., and the U.S. Matters of procedure require a majority of nine votes, while matters of substance require this majority including the concurring votes of the five permanent members, a requirement for unanimity that gives these countries veto power.

The *ECONOMIC AND SOCIAL COUNCIL CHAMBER, finished in natural wood, with red geometric wall hangings and white marble flooring, donated by Sweden (designer, Sven Markelius), houses an organisation that coordinates social and economic agencies of the U.N.

Working under the assumption that conditions of well-being are necessary to world peace, UNESCO administers programmes to develop economic resources, improve health care, housing, education, transportation, and communications, principally in emerging nations.

The *TRUSTEESHIP COUNCIL CHAMBER, designed by Finn Juhl, was the gift of Denmark. The statue of a woman with upraised arms and a bluebird is said by artist Henrick Starcke to suggest man's hope for 'unlimited flight upward . . . [and] the appeal for compassion for the weak, the unfortunate, the oppressed'.

The Trusteeship Council was formed to administer territories placed under international trusteeship while they evolved toward self-government and independence. Of the 11 territories originally assigned only one, Micronesia, has not achieved self-government. When it does, the room will be assigned another function.

In the corridor between the council chambers and the General Assembly hall are works of art including a painting, *Christ Crucified*, by Georges Rouault, presented by Pope Paul VI when he visited in 1965, the only work not donated by a member nation. Also displayed is an astonishingly intricate *ivory carving made from eight elephant tusks, depicting the *Chengtu-Kunming Railroad* as it winds through forested mountains, a work that weighs c. 330 lbs and took 150 artists about $2^1/2$ years to make, the gift of China. In the Delegates' Entrance Hall are two murals depicting War and Peace by Brazilian Candido Portinari, as well as the largest tapestry ever woven, a work designed by Belgian Peter Colfe illustrating themes of peace, prosperity, and equality.

The GENERAL ASSEMBLY HALL was decorated by the 11 architects of the building committee in recognition of the equal representation of all member nations in the assembly. Measuring 165 ft long by 115 ft wide with a ceiling 75 ft high, the hall provides seats for more than 2000 people; 1400 seats for delegates, deputies and advisors; 160 seats for the press, and about 400 seats for the public. Booths for broadcasters, photographers, and simultaneous interpreters line the walls of the room. Through the earphones at the seats delegates may listen to speeches translated into one of the six official languages of the assembly: Chinese, English, French, Russian, and Spanish and Arabic, the last an official language of the General Assembly but not of the U.N. as a whole. The murals on the side walls are by Fernand Léger, executed by Bruce Gregory. At the green Italian marble podium are places for the president of the General Assembly, the Secretary-General of the U.N., and the Under-Secretary-General for General Assembly Affairs.

The General Assembly, the main deliberative body of the U.N. in which all member nations are represented, discusses and makes recommendations on all matters of the charter including issues of war and peace, economic, social, and environmental problems. The Assembly cannot compel action by any nation but its sanctions carry moral weight.

Leave the U.N. buildings and walk N. to the PUBLIC GARDENS, whose entrance is on U.N. Plaza opposite 46th St. (At 48th St is an entrance to the playground area; adults not admitted unless accompanied by a child.) On the E. side of the lawn is Evgeny Vuchetich's bronze *statue, Let Us Beat Our Swords Into Plowshares (1959), a gift of the U.S.S.R. Also on the lawn is a 16-ft bronze equestrian Monument to Peace (1954; Antun Augustinčić), given by Yugoslavia. The rose garden runs between the river promenade and the E. wall of the General Assembly building on which is an abstract sculpture by Ezio Martinelli. From the promenade are fine views of the decaying hospitals on the S. tip of Roosevelt Island, the Queensboro Bridge to the N., and the Williamsburg Bridge to the S. To the E. is the industrial architecture of Queens.

Walk N. along the promenade. In the wooded area just N. of the lawn is a *memorial to Eleanor Roosevelt*, a bronze statue entitled The Rising Man (1975; Fritz Cremer), gift of the German Democratic Republic, and a bronze bust of Francisco de Vitoria, 16C Spanish Dominican theologian, given by Juan Carlos I (1976) on the occasion of his visit to the U.N.

Cross U.N. Plaza to the N.W. corner of 44th St. Here stands ONE UNITED NATIONS PLAZA (1976; Kevin Roche, John Dinkeloo & Assocs), a 39-story, glass-walled building providing office space for the U.N. and a hotel for delegates and others. Because the U.N. Development Corporation which built it has a charter forbidding the construction of any building taller than the Secretariat, this one stops at 505 ft. The mirrored, greenish glass facade, which conceals floor divisions and the distinction between wall and window, has been much admired as has the decor of the hotel lobby (enter on 44th St), executed in chrome, mirrored glass, and marble. Those visitors fearing for their personal safety may bypass the lobby altogether by driving their limousines into an enclosed entranceway and alighting by the elevator banks.

The UNITED STATES MISSION TO THE UNITED NATIONS (1961; Kelly & Gruzen and Khan & Jacobs) faces U.N. Plaza on the S.W. corner of 45th St (799 U.N. Plaza). On the N. side of the building is a stabile entitled Object in Five Planes, by Alexander Calder who donated it (1965) in the interest of world peace.

Next door is *Uganda House* at 336 E. 45th St, built (1977) during the regime of Field Marshall Idi Amin. Its 14-story height was said to be a deliberate attempt to overshadow the U.S. Mission to the E. as an expression of Amin's outrage at American denunciations of his repressive policies. The U.S. retaliated architecturally by installing a flagpole atop the mission (the best view of the rooflines is from 46th St). When Amin fell, the new team of Ugandan delegates discovered an elaborate system of electronic listening devices in the walls and hidden behind curtains. Most recently (1980), when a neighbouring garage was razed in preparation for a 40-story tower at 2 United Nations Plaza, it appeared that Uganda House had no outside wall below the fifth floor on its W. side; its insulation was attached directly to the garage, a circumvention of the building code possible because Uganda as a foreign government was not required to have the city approve the building plans.

Continue N. on U.N. Plaza to the S.W. corner of 47th St (833 U.N. Plaza). The *African-American Institute* (open Mon–Fri, 9–5, Sat 11–5; tel: 949–5666) features special exhibitions of African arts and crafts. The widened section of 47th St, Hammarskjold Plaza, sometimes offers a small flower market. A little W., between U.N. Plaza and Second Ave is JAPAN HOUSE (1971; Junzo Yoshimura and Gruzen & Partners) at 333 E. 47th St. Designed by a Tokyo architect in a typically Japanese style, but using primarily American building materials, Japan House is the headquarters of the Japan Society, which seeks to promote better understanding between the United States and Japan primarily through cultural exchange. The second floor gallery offers beautiful exhibitions of Japanese art, while such activities as film shows, poetry readings, craft demonstrations, kabuki and No theatre, and discussions on economic and social problems common to the two countries are held in the first floor auditorium. (Open during exhibitions, daily 11–5; Fri, 11–7.30. Tel: 832–1155. Donations requested.)

Continue to Second Ave; walk N. to 49th St and turn left (W.). At 226–246 E. 49th St and 227–247 E. 48th St (between Second and Third Aves) is the **Turtle Bay Gardens Historic District** (remodelled 1920; Clarence Dean), two rows of ten houses each, back to back with a common garden inside the block. Mrs Walton Martin in 1919–20, inspired by houses with shared gardens in France and Italy, bought the houses, tore down the back fences, filled in the swampy areas, shaved 6 ft off each back yard to create a common garden, and redesigned the houses so that they faced inward to the garden where she placed a replica of the fountain at the entrance of the Villa Medici in Rome. The gardens have attracted such famous residents as Judge Learned Hand, Leopold Stokowski, Katharine Hepburn, Mary Martin, Tyrone Power, and Stephen Sondheim. E.B. White, one of the 'New Yorker' magazine's most famous writers, immortalised the willow tree in the garden in the closing paragraph of his classic essay, 'Here is New York':

A block or two west of the city of man in Turtle Bay there is an old willow tree that presides over an interior garden. It is a battered tree, long suffering and much climbed, held together by strands of bailing wire but beloved by those who know it. In a way it symbolizes the city: life under difficulties, growth against odds, sap-rise in the midst of concrete, and the steady reaching for the sun.

Across the street at 225–227 E. 49th St is the former *Efrem Zimbalist House* (1926), built for the violinist, his wife diva Alma Gluck, and her daughter novelist Marcia Davenport. The cartouche over the door bears a violin, a staff with some unidentified musical theme, and an open-mouthed cherub. Later Henry Luce of Time-Life Inc. lived here, but between 1957–60 the house became the 17th Precinct Police Station House, its panelling and artistic interiors ripped out in favour of institutional iron stairways and bilious green paint. Nowadays it has been divided into apartments.

AMSTER YARD at 211–215 E. 49th St. (1870; remodelled 1945; Harold Sterner) is another enclave, also almost entirely secluded from the street. Originally Amster Yard (enter through an arcade on 49th St) was a group of workshops and small houses built on the site of what may have been the terminal stop of the Boston–New York stage coach following the Boston Post Road. After the Second Ave El was demolished in 1942, James Amster, a designer, bought the property and developed it into an attractive group of shops, apartments, and offices, around a central courtyard.

A block S. is the former WILLIAM LESCAZE RESIDENCE at 211 E. 48th St between Second and Third Aves, which began as an ordinary 19C brownstone but was transformed (1934; William Lescaze; DL) into a home and studio for the architect. The facade is covered with smooth grey stucco (originally white), has industrial tubular railings instead of the familiar iron balustrades, and glass block panels instead of the usual Italianate window frames. Lescaze, an early practitioner of the International Style, believed that functionalism was one tenet of modernism, and so the interior of the house is designed to meet the needs of his home and office. The studio occupies the entire ground floor and is lit by a skylight in a rear extension. The library and living quarters are above, with the living room filling the entire top floor, also lit by a skylight. The whole house is centrally air-conditioned, a rarity in 1934; the top floor window of glass block admitted light but muffled noise at a time when the Els still ran up and down Second and Third Aves. The house caused such a stir that for a while Lescaze and his wife set aside an hour on Mondays for public visitation.

Return to First Ave and walk N. to *Mitchell Place* at 49th St on the E. side of the avenue. At the N.E. corner of the intersection stands the former Panhellenic Hotel (1928; John Mead Howells), once a residence for sorority women, now converted to the BEEKMAN TOWER APARTMENTS. William Mitchell, whose name this small street bears was a distinguished 19C jurist, who served as a member of the state Court of Appeals and as presiding justice on the State Supreme Court.

Walk along Mitchell Place to Beekman Place. The small park on the S. side of Mitchell Place is called *General Douglas MacArthur Plaza*, named after the controversial general who fought in Europe during World War I, led the allied forces in the Pacific during World War II, and finally commanded the U.N. forces in Korea, a post from which he was relieved by President Truman for disobeying (Truman's) orders.

Walk N. to 51st St along **Beekman Place.** Named after the Beekman family, the street runs only two blocks but its location on a high bluff overlooking the river and its history of controlled development (no slaughterhouses here) by the Beekmans have made it a socially desirable enclave since the 18C.

The Beekman mansion Mount Pleasant (built 1765) stood near the river at about 51st St, and for a while during the Revolution served as British headquarters. In 1783 James Beekman got his house back and here entertained the American officers and staff entering New York on Evacuation Day 'in the drawing room with punch made with lemons plucked from trees growing in the green-house'. A cholera epidemic eventually drove away the Beekman family who lived there until 1854, and in 1874 the house was demolished.

At 51st St descend the steps which lead to a footbridge across the Franklin D. Roosevelt Drive and go N. along the walkway next to the drive. One of the more imposing prominences overlooking the water is RIVER HOUSE (1931; Bottomley, Wagner & White) at 433–437 E. 52nd St (E. of First Ave). Completed the same year as the George Washington Bridge, the Empire State Building, and the Waldorf-Astoria, River House quickly became synonymous with privilege and wealth. The apartments in the tower were built on two or three floors with as many as 17 rooms, (one had nine bathrooms), while those in the body of the building were only slightly more modest. Tennis courts, a swimming pool, and a dock for yachts added to comfort and convenience of such tenants as Marshall Field and William Rhinelander Stewart.

The serenity of the setting was disturbed somewhat by the arrival of the FRANKLIN D. ROOSEVELT DRIVE, begun downtown in 1936 and completed after World War II as a major artery linking the city with outlying highways. Much of the landfill used for the roadbed is rubble from the London Blitz, brought back as ballast in returning American ships.

In 1821 someone named Youle built a shot tower near 53rd St at the river, which after falling down and being rebuilt served as a landmark for some 40 years. *Cannon Point* as the area was known is now only a few rocks in the river near 52nd St.

Cross back over the F.D.R. Drive to **Sutton Place,** formerly and less glamorously known as Avenue A. It was renamed after one Effingham B. Sutton, a dry goods merchant who developed the area around 1875 with a fortune he had made in the California gold rush of 1849, not striking the mother lode but selling picks, shovels, and provisions to prospectors who hoped to do so. His venture with Sutton Place was less profitable, the street remaining modest until Anne Morgan, daughter of J.P. Morgan, moved there in 1921. The S. part of the street, now lined with attractive apartment houses, was a later extension and is called Sutton Place South (53rd to 57th Sts). *No. 1 Sutton Place South* (1927; Cross & Cross, with Rosario Candela) vies with River House as one of the city's most luxurious apartments. SUTTON SQUARE, the block between 57th and 58th Sts, has a group of townhouses sharing a common back garden. At the foot of 57th St is a small park with a replica of the boar, 'Il Porcellino', standing in the Straw Market in Florence. The sculptor Pietro Tacca made three copies altogether—the one in Florence, this one, and another said to be in Country Club Plaza in Kansas City. The original for all three, itself a copy of a Hellenistic original, is in the Uffizi Gallery in Florence. On the N. side of 57th St abutting the park (No. 1 Sutton Place) is a neo-Georgian townhouse built for Anne Morgan. No. 3 Sutton Place is the residence of the secretary-general of the U.N. At 58th St toward the river is another small park and N. of it, parallel to the river, a small, cobbled, private street, RIVERVIEW TERRACE, with five 19C houses looking out from the top of the ridge.

From the end of 58th St is a fine view of the **Queensboro Bridge** (1909; Gustav Lindenthal, engineer; Palmer & Hornbostel, architects), which joins Long Island City in Queens to 59th St in Manhattan. As early as 1852 some of Long Island City's most powerful families—Steinways and Pratts—began agitating for a bridge, an enterprise furthered by Long Island Railroad tycoon

Austin Corbin and later by a Dr Thomas Rainey, who foresaw the
bridge as an aid to tourism, freight handling, and the funeral
business (there were 15 cemeteries on Long Island at the time).
Political and financial problems delayed its construction for some 40
years and the collapse of another partially built cantilever bridge,
the Quebec bridge, caused a furore as to the safety of this one. An
alleged engineer vouched for it saying that in his 20 years of
experience he had never seen so many birds gathering on a bridge
as on the Queensboro, a peculiar remark based on the superstition
that large numbers of birds will only roost on a soundly engineered
structure. Less whimsical was designer Lindenthal who reduced the
number of elevated tracks crossing it and removed some deadload,
which may have been added to pad the profits of the steel supplier.
This extra steel may also have accounted for architect Hornbostel's
outcry, 'My God—it's a blacksmith's shop' when he first saw the
completed superstructure. Today, however, the bridge is generally
admired for its intricate mesh of steelwork and its handsome
ornaments, including the finials on top.

The span is 1182 ft long and 135 ft above mean high water. About
50,000 tons of steel were used in construction at a cost of $20·8
million. Bicycle riders and pedestrians can still cross the bridge, but
can no longer descend to Roosevelt Island, though once a building
with an entrance lobby on the eighth floor and elevators down to the
ground provided access from Manhattan. Beneath the Manhattan
approach to the bridge are vaulted arches finished with Guastavino
tile, now used to house police department equipment, the wooden
barriers for crowd control and the trucks for hauling them around.
None of the various plans for this appealing space, including a
market and a cinematheque, has been implemented.

Walk N. on First Ave. At 421 E. 61st St, between First and York
Aves, is the **Abigail Adams Smith House** (open Mon–Fri, 10–4;
admission $1; tel: 838–6878), built as a coach house and stable (1799;
DL) for Colonel William S. Smith and his wife Abigail Adams,
daughter of President John Adams. The Colonial Dames of America
maintain the house as a museum with period rooms displaying
American furniture of the Federal period.

History. In 1795 Colonel Smith bought 23 acres where the house now stands
from the Van Zandt family, on which he planned a mansion suitable for a man
of his social position. He named the estate Mount Vernon in honour of George
Washington, his commander during the Revolutionary War, but because of rash
real estate speculations Smith lost his fortune, mortgaged and then sold his
property which became known locally as Smith's Folly. In 1798 William T.
Robinson bought it and completed the present house as a stable and coach
house. The mansion, also completed by Robinson, was converted first to a hotel,
famous for its turtle soup and facilities for fishing and salt water bathing, and
then a school. In 1826 it burned. The estate was purchased and broken up into
individual lots, while the stable became a country tavern, the Mount Vernon
Hotel. From 1833 to 1905 it belonged to the Towle family, who sold it to the
Standard Gas Company, who built three large gas tanks nearby and let the
house fall into disrepair. Subdivided into apartments, it reached its nadir as a
Salvation Army soup kitchen during World War I.

In 1919 Miss Jane Teller rented and restored it, displaying there her
collection of early American furniture, and five years later the Colonial Dames
of America bought the house, furnished it, and eventually opened it as a
museum.

On the ground floor is a *kitchen* with a cooking fireplace, utensils,
and an exposed beam showing the construction of the house. The

Music Room on the other side of the entrance hall is furnished to show French Empire and Greek Revival influences, with reproduction wallpaper, a Hepplewhite spinet (Thomas Tomkisen, London, 1790) and gilded French Empire harp. The pastel Aubusson rug dates from about 1840. In the *Dining Room* are 'American Fancy' painted chairs with woven straw seats, which predate Hitchcock chairs, as well as examples of Canton china, an American Sheraton table, a wine cooler, and sideboard. These two rooms were originally the stable and housed six horses.

On the second floor, once the carriage house, is a *Ballroom* with an American Sheraton eight-legged sofa and side chairs (c. 1795), portraits of Colonel William Stephen Smith and Abigail Adams Smith (copies by Pietro Pezzati of originals by Mather Brown), and a tall English late Chippendale clock made by Sam Clegg (c. 1780). In the *Library* are a Queen Anne table and chairs, a mantle clock by Eli Terry of Plymouth, Connecticut (c. 1760), Delft vases with covers (c. 1760) and a case with Adams family memorabilia. In the *bedroom* adjacent is an American Sheraton mahogany bedstead, and a mannequin wearing an embroidered muslin dress which Abigail Adams Smith made at the White House when her father was President.

On the other side of the ballroom is a *Drawing Room* with a fine Chinese black and gold lacquer desk (c. 1810), a table with the Adams family tea service, and an American Sheraton wing chair (c. 1800). The *Game Room* has a portrait of Abigail Adams as a young girl (a copy from a portrait by Copley), poker chips once belonging to John Adams, and the needlepoint sampler of a 10-year old girl. The third floor, originally the hayloft, is not open to the public. Behind the house is a small herb garden and plantings reminiscent of those popular in about 1800.

Walk N. on York Ave. Between 62nd and 68th Sts on the E. side of the avenue is **The Rockefeller University,** founded (1901) as The Rockefeller Institute for Medical Research (name changed in 1965). The campus occupies the site of the former Schermerhorn family summer estate which still had the original farmhouse when John D. Rockefeller, Sr bought the property. Today the university, small and prestigious, is dedicated to advanced education and research in the biomedical sciences.

University scientists have earned 16 Nobel Prizes, seven since 1972, and more than half of the full professors have been elected to membership in the National Academy of Sciences. The 40-bed hospital (established in 1910) was the first in the country devoted exclusively to clinical research. Today more than 30 diseases are under investigation, mainly those for which there are no satisfactory means of prevention or cure. Among the achievements by university scientists were the first demonstration that animal cancer can be caused by a virus, the first demonstration that DNA is the substance that transmits hereditary information, and the first isolation and successful tests of antibiotics. One of the most far-reaching innovations, though not recognised as such at the time, was the development of a way to preserve whole blood, making possible the blood banks of today. In addition, Rockefeller scientists have made basic discoveries and technical innovations that resulted in the development of the modern science of cell biology and pioneered studies on the role of cholesterol in the body's metabolism.

The entrance gate is opposite 66th St; ask the guard for permission to walk around. The complex includes the *Caspary Auditorium* to the left of the walkway (1957; Harrison & Abramovitz) with its domed roof once covered with blue tile. A work entitled Mouth of the River

(1966) sculpted in German marble by Minoru Nizuma stands E. of the hall. _Founder's Hall_ is at the end of the walkway, flanked by the hospital on the right and Flexner Hall on the left. The _President's House_ (1958; Harrison & Abramovitz) stands at the N.E. corner of the campus.

N. of Rockefeller University between 68th and 70th Sts is the **New York Hospital-Cornell University Medical College** (1932; Coolidge, Shepley, Bulfinch & Abbott), a 6·4 acre complex for patient care, research and teaching occupying 11 buildings and having 45 acres of floor space and five miles of corridors. The _Main Building_ of glazed white brick constructed in Art Deco Gothic has been much admired for its skilful massing and spartan use of detail. At the time of completion it was also widely admired for its technical advances— air conditioning, X-ray machines, and shadowless lights in the operating rooms—and for the humane quality of its interior design— the small wards subdivided by glass partitions into four-bed sections, lounges overlooking the East River, the non-institutional use of colour in corridors and pavilions, and the free crosstown bus service from Fifth Ave for patients and visitors.

History. The city's oldest hospital, New York Hospital was founded under a charter from King George III in 1771 as a hospital for the sick poor and, incidentally, as a medical school. During the Revolution it was used as an army hospital for British and Hessian soldiers but was not reopened to the public until 1791. In 1877 a new 200-bed hospital was built on W. 15th St near Fifth Ave with such modern amenities as steam heat and artificial ventilation. The present hospital (1350 beds) was built after the New York Hospital-Cornell Medical College Association was formed (1927) with donations of some $27 million by Payne Whitney, J. Pierpont Morgan, the Rockefellers, and others. In 1938 more than 100 anonymous donors gave an additional $1000 for removing from the 325-ft chimneys the swastika designs, which had acquired sinister connotations with the rise of Hitler, and replacing them with the present Greek crosses.

Today the New York Hospital-Cornell University Medical Center is also affiliated with the Hospital for Special Surgery (535 E. 70th St at York Ave), and the Memorial Sloan-Kettering Cancer Center (1275 York Ave at 68th St), as well as other institutions outside the immediate neighbourhood.

17 Rockefeller Center

SUBWAY: IRT Broadway-7th Ave Local (train 1) to 50th St. IRT Lexington Ave Local (train 6) to 51st St. IND Sixth Ave (B,D, or F trains) to 47th–50th Sts–Rockefeller Center. BMT Broadway Express (N train) or Broadway Local (RR train) to 49th St.

BUS: M1, M2, M3, M4, M5, M6, M7, M27, M32; Culture Bus (weekends and holidays), Loop 1, Stop 3 or 18.

CAR PARKING: The Rockefeller Center Garage, with entrances on 48th and 49th Sts between Fifth and Sixth Aves, is open 24 hours, but is often full.

TOURS: Guided tours of Rockefeller Center, the Radio City Music Hall including the backstage area, and the Observation Roof of the RCA Building leave the Guided Tour Office (N. corridor of the RCA Building, ground floor) at intervals from 20–45 min., depending on need, Mon–Sat from 9.45 a.m.–4.45 p.m. Adults, $2·50; children under 12, $1·50. Admission to the Observation Roof only (open Oct–March, 11 a.m.–7 p.m.; April–Sept, 10 a.m.–9 p.m.); adults, $1·75; children under 12, $0·90. For additional information telephone 489–2947.

Rockefeller Center is a complex of 19 commercial buildings, theatres, plazas, streets, underground pedestrian passageways, and shops located on almost 22 acres of land W. of Fifth Ave in midtown Manhattan. It is the world's largest privately owned business and entertainment center, the first architecturally coordinated development in New York City, a major tourist attraction, and a financially successful venture which maintains high aesthetic standards. More than 240,000 people—including visitors and workers—use it daily; about 240 million patrons have paid admission to Radio City Music Hall, the center's great theatre, recently renovated. John D. Rockefeller, Jr (1874–1960), one of America's richest men, built the center which remains in the hands of his heirs who control the stock of Rockefeller Center, Inc., the corporation that developed and still maintains the property.

History. In 1927 the Metropolitan Opera, seeking to replace its cramped and outmoded house on Broadway and 40th St became interested in some land owned by Columbia University. The land—about 12 acres between Fifth and Sixth Aves, 48th and 51st Sts—had blossomed briefly between 1801–11 as the Elgin Botanic Garden but now held only dingy speakeasies, roominghouses, and brothels. The opera company approached Rockefeller as a possible benefactor, hoping he might donate land for a plaza in front of the new opera house. Rockefeller in turn began exploring the possibilities of leasing the land himself, making the central portion available to the opera, and then subleasing the rest to commercial interests who would build their own buildings. Since property experts led him to believe that he could realise as much as $5·5 million dollars annually on the property, he entered into negotiations with the trustees of Columbia University, signing a contract in October 1928 leasing the property for a 24-year period with renewal options to 2019, now extended to 2069. When the stock market crashed in 1929, the Metropolitan Opera Company abruptly dropped its plans for a new house, leaving Rockefeller holding a lease under which he owed more than $3·8 million a year on property that brought in only about $300,000.

Rockefeller's only real choice, since even he could ill afford a $2 million annual deficit, was to develop the property without the opera house. He directed his planners to design a commercial center 'as beautiful as possible consistent with maximum income', and work began on the city's first integrated commercial center, where skyscrapers could be planned in relation to one another with due consideration of open space, light, and traffic control. Largely responsible for the early project were real estate developers Todd, Robertson & Todd, and three principal architectural firms, Reinhard & Hofmeister; Corbett, Harrison, and MacMurray; and Hood & Fouilhoux (before 1931 Hood, Godley & Fouilhoux), who worked under the name of The Associated Architects, making it impossible to assign specific credit for individual buildings in the original development.

Between 1931–40 14 buildings were constructed; 228 were demolished to make way for them; 4000 tenants were relocated; and 75,000 workers found jobs on the site during the depths of the Depression. Although Rockefeller drove the 'last' rivet in the United States Rubber Company Building in 1939, development continued after World War II, when the Warner Communications (formerly Esso) Building pushed the center beyond its original boundaries. During the 1950s and 1960s, Rockefeller Center expanded W. Sixth Avenue, replacing a neighbourhood of nondescript low buildings and small business tenants with a group of stiff, monotonous office towers which express the affluence of their corporate tenants at the expense of neighbourhood vitality.

The most dramatic approach to Rockefeller Center is from Fifth Ave between 49th–50th Sts. Flanking a central promenade are two low buildings, the BRITISH BUILDING (completed 1933) on the N. and LA MAISON FRANÇAISE (1933) on the S., buildings whose modest scale reflects an earlier and more gracious Fifth Ave. By placing these low structures on the avenue, the developers gained rights to build a large tower (the RCA Building) in the center of the block, simultaneously preserving neighbourhood property values by leaving the side streets unshadowed.

Over the main entrance of the British Building (formerly the British Empire Building) is a bronze panel (1933) by Carl Paul Jennewein (born 1890) whose figures represent nine major industries of the British Commonwealth; at the bottom is a bronze sun, symbolic of the empire on which the sun never set. Above the panel is a cartouche with the British coat of arms and the mottos of British royalty and the Order of the Garter.

Cross the Promenade to La Maison Française. A bronze strip in the sidewalk near the building line at the entrance to the Promenade marks the boundary of the property belonging to Columbia University. Over the main door of La Maison Française is another bronze panel (1934). Designed by Alfred Janniot (born 1889), it depicts Paris and New York joining hands above figures representing Poetry, Beauty, and Elegance. Inscribed on a ribbon behind the figure of Paris is that city's motto: 'Fluctuat nec mergitur' ('It is tossed by waves but does not sink'). Above the panel soars an Art Deco version of the traditional symbol of France, a woman holding the flaming torch of liberty; beneath her is the motto of the French Republic: 'Liberté, Égalité, Fraternité'.

Enter the Promenade, popularly known as the *Channel Gardens because it separates the British and French buildings; the walkway (60 ft wide and 200 ft long) is embellished with granite pools, seasonal floral displays, and fountains. The bronze fountain heads (1935), designed by René Chambellan, represent tritons and nereids riding dolphins; they symbolise (E. to W.): leadership, will, thought, imagination, energy, and alertness—qualities chosen as those contributing to human progress.

Most of the themes of the center's artwork were chosen by Prof. Hartley Burr Alexander of the University of Southern California, hired to impose thematic unity on the whole development. His original suggestion for an overall theme was 'Homo fabor' ('Man the Maker'), a subject that was modified to 'New Frontiers and the March of Civilisation'.

The Promenade opens into the LOWER PLAZA, dominated by an 18-ft figure of Prometheus, designed by Paul Manship (1885–1966) and installed in 1934. The 8-ton gilded bronze statue rests on a pedestal shaped like a mountain peak and encircled by a ring containing the signs of the zodiac. On the red granite wall behind is a quotation from Aeschylus: 'Prometheus, teacher in every art, brought the fire that hath proved to mortals a means to mighty ends.' Behind the statue during summer 50 jets of water form a backdrop for an electronically controlled lighting display (nightfall to 1 a.m.). During the Christmas season, a large tree is installed on the sidewalk behind the plaza and illuminated by thousands of lights, accounting in large part for the spectacular crowds who pack the area during the holidays. During the summer, the sunken plaza becomes an outdoor café; during the winter it is flooded and used as an ice rink.

At the top of the stairway leading to the lower level is a commemorative plaque inscribed with John D. Rockefeller, Jr's personal credo.

Cross ROCKEFELLER PLAZA, the street separating the Lower Plaza from the RCA Building. The idea of breaking up the long east–west block with a private street was one of the happy inspirations of the developers. Rockefeller Plaza remains one of the few private streets in the city and is closed to all traffic, vehicular and pedestrian, once a year—usually a Sunday in July—to preserve its private status.

The most famous and imposing building at Rockefeller Center is the **RCA Building**, directly W. of Rockefeller Plaza. Completed in 1933, the building (70 stories, 850 ft) once had the largest gross floor area of any commercial structure in the world, a dubious distinction. Roughly rectangular with its thin edge facing east–west and a broad, slab-like wall on the N. and S., it owes its disproportionate length to Rockefeller's desire to include within its perimeter some potentially unprofitable lots he owned on Sixth Ave, still darkened and begrimed by the El. Skilfully designed setbacks give the building the impression of soaring height. Receding wings flank the main rectangle and an 11-story wrap-around structure houses the National Broadcasting Company studios, constructed free from the rest of the building to minimise vibrations.

When the Metropolitan Opera decided not to build at Rockefeller Center, architect Raymond Hood proposed that the Radio Corporation of America (RCA), still prospering during the stagnation of the Depression, be invited to replace the opera company as the center's major tenant. For years most of the radio programmes of NBC, a subsidiary of RCA, were produced here, and Rockfeller Center was known popularly as Radio City.

At the present time few programmes originate in New York. For information about viewing television broadcasts, however, write to Guest Relations, NBC Ticket Division, 30 Rockefeller Plaza (zip code 10020) or telephone 664–3055.

EXTERIOR. Over the E. entrance is a stone relief by Lee Lawrie (1877–1963), whose subject is 'Genius, which Interprets to the Human Race the Laws and Cycles of the Cosmic Forces of the Universe, Making the Cycles of Light and Sound'. Genius, a giant with a remarkable Art Deco beard, spreads a compass above a glass screen made of 240 blocks of glass, cast in relief in 84 different molds. Only when the work was well underway did the art committee notice the embarrassing similarity between Lawrie's work and William Blake's frontispiece to 'Europe: A Prophecy' (1794).

Flanking the 49th St entrance are two limestone pylons with sculptures by Leo Friedländer (1890–1966) representing 'Transmission Receiving an Image of Dancers and Flashing It Through the Ether by Means of Television to Reception, Symbolized by Mother Earth and her Child, Man'. At the 50th St entrance two more pylons, also sculpted by Friedländer, represent 'Transmission Receiving Music and Flashing It through the Ether by Means of Radio to Reception'. Rockefeller found these works 'gross and unbeautiful', an opinion with which critics generally concur.

INTERIOR. Directly in front of the main entrance is a large mural by José Maria Sert (1876–1945), originally entitled 'Triumph of Man's Accomplishments through Physical and Mental Labor', now called 'American Progress'. Sert's ponderously moralistic painting (1937) is renowned primarily for what it replaces—the controversial Diego Rivera fresco destroyed by the Rockefellers.

Commissioned to paint a mural illustrating the theme 'man's new possibilities from his new understanding of material things', Rivera submitted a sketch acceptable to the patrons and then produced a fresco which included a portrait of Lenin, a crowd of workers carrying red flags near Lenin's tomb, and a scene of rich people playing cards with venereal disease germs hovering over them. When asked to substitute another face for Lenin's, Rivera replied that he would prefer the destruction of the painting, at least preserving its integrity. The fresco remained shrouded in canvas during opening ceremonies, but eventually the Rockefellers had it destroyed. In the recriminations that followed, cowboy humourist and sage Will Rogers made one of his most famous *bons mots*, advising Rivera that he 'should never try to fool a Rockefeller in oils'.

The ceiling painting, again by Sert, is entitled 'Time', while the murals against the elevator banks in the N. and S. corridors by Sert and Frank Brangwyn (1867–1956) illustrate themes of progress against such obstacles as disease, slavery, and crushing physical labour.

Continue down the N. corridor to the elevator banks, containing the first high speed elevators in New York City. The last row of cars contains the elevators to the **Observation Roof,** which offers fine views of midtown Manhattan as well as a glimpse of the roof gardens on the French, British, and International Buildings. The fibre-glass globe on top of the RCA Building houses the radar of the National Weather Service. The Gothic style fence around the observation platform is a concession to John D. Rockefeller, Jr's conservative tastes.

Return to the main corridor. Stairways behind the elevator banks lead down to the Concourse, with more than 2 miles of underground passageways lined with shops, services, and restaurants. Also underground are ten large trucking ramps and loading docks which, along with facilities located beneath the new office towers on Sixth Avenue, take an estimated 700–1000 trucks off the city streets daily.

Continue through the main ground floor corridor to Sixth Avenue entrance. Less opulently decorated than the E. facade, it features a glass mosaic by Barry Faulkner (1881–1966) made of about one million pieces of coloured glass and is entitled 'Intelligence Awakening Mankind'. Four limestone panels by Gaston Lachaise (1882–1935) on the W. facade depict: 'Genius Seizing the Light of the Sun', 'Conquest of Space', 'Gifts of Earth to Mankind', and 'Understanding—Spirit of Progress'.

Across Sixth Avenue from the RCA Building loom the four newest additions to the center. Architectural critics have found them sadly wanting in comparison to the original development, charging that they lack sympathetic human scale, that they have driven small businesses from the area, that their plazas—cold and ill-planned—compete with one another, and that their use of modern technology has allowed them to contain maximum permissible space at the expense of light, air, and human values.

The southernmost of these towers, the *Celanese Building* (1973; Harrison, Abramovitz & Harris) occupies the block between 47th–48th St. Like its companions, it is a slab building divided vertically into columns and vertical window strips. In the lobby is a white-on-crimson mosaic mural developed from a design by Josef Albers (1888–1976) entitled 'Reclining Figure'. To the W. of the building is a covered shopping plaza which enabled developers to exceed building limits according to the Zoning Resolution of 1961. At one time troubled by strong down-draughts from the neighbouring McGraw-Hill Building, the plaza is still cold and uninviting. In the center is Ibram Lassaw's (born 1913) welded bronze plate sculpture (1973), 'Pantheon'.

Just N. of the Celanese Building is the MCGRAW-HILL BUILDING (1972; Harrison, Abramovitz, & Harris).

The 'New York Experience', an attractive if noisy multi-screen movie with special effects (suitable for children) is shown in a theatre accessible from the Lower Plaza. Showings are hourly, Mon–Thur, 11–7; Fri & Sat, 11–8; Sun, 12–8.

Adults, $3·20; children under 12, $1·60. For additional information telephone 869–0346.

In the sunken plaza is a sculpture (1973) by Athelstan Spilhaus (born 1911) entitled 'Sun Triangle', made of steel with stainless steel cladding. The three sides of the triangle point to the sun's noon position at the equinoxes and solstices. In the nearby reflecting pool whose diameter represents that of the sun are nine stainless steel globes representing the planets, their diameters also accurately proportioned. To the W. of the building is an attractive little park with a waterfall and tunnel.

Cross 49th St to the EXXON BUILDING (1971; Harrison, Abramovitz, & Harris), a 54-story rectangular slab clad in limestone, with a 7-story wrap-around wing on the W. Like its neighbours, it has an austere facade of vertical columns alternating with vertical window strips. On the E. is a street-level plaza with a large fountain; on the W. is a small, unimaginative park. In the N. lobby are displayed a tapestry reproduction of a theatre curtain designed by Pablo Picasso for a 1924 production of 'Mercure', and a three-part gilded bronze sculpture, 'Moon and Stars', by Mary Callery (born 1903).

Cross 50th St to the TIME & LIFE BUILDING (1959; Harrison & Abramovitz), the earliest of the new buildings across Sixth Avenue. Along its E. facade is a plaza with a central pool and basin surrounded by a low wall that serves as a bench. The undulating grey and white pattern on the pavement is similar to one that architect Wallace K. Harrison admired in Rio de Janeiro. The blue-painted steel sculpture, 'Cubed Curve', on the S.E. corner of the lot, is by William Crovello (born 1929) and was installed in 1971. Inside the lobby are (W. end of elevator banks) a glass and metal mural (1961) by Josef Albers, entitled 'Portals', and (E. end of elevator banks) an oil-on-canvas mural (1960), 'Relational Painting #88' by Fritz Glarner (1899–1972).

Cross Sixth Avenue to **Radio City Music Hall** (1932; DL—interior), the nation's largest indoor theatre and a masterpiece of Art Deco Decoration.

The hall can be seen only by attending a performance or joining a Rockefeller Center Tour (see p284), which provides a cursory view of the auditorium and the backstage area or an hour-long backstage tour ($3·95; tel: 757–3100).

History. Samuel Lionel Rothafel (1882–1936), better known as Roxy, was a self-made man who began his career showing movies in the back room of a bar and rose to become a mogul of show business, producing radio programmes and stage shows, and managing a series of New York theatres including the opulent Roxy. Because he enjoyed the reputation of knowing infallibly what the public wanted, he was given broad powers by the RKO Corporation, a subsidiary of RCA, who hired him as director of the Music Hall. He contributed to the design of the theatre and shaped its general policies, intending to revive vaudeville and produce spectacular variety entertainment.

Unfortunately Roxy's variety shows lost $180,000 in the first two weeks of operation, and the format was changed. Until television began competing strenuously, the Music Hall successfully presented a long list of wholesome movies coupled with elaborate stage productions, drawing an average 5 million patrons yearly to the end of 1967. By 1977 attendance had fallen to less than 2 million and the theatre lost $2·3 million. In 1978 the closing of the Music Hall was announced but a wave of public support resulted in its interior being designated a landmark; in 1979 the parent company, Rockefeller Center Inc., renovated and reopened it with a new format of elaborately staged musical shows, concerts, and special events.

INTERIOR. The interior of the Music Hall, climaxed by the great auditorium, is one of the high points of American theatre design and one of the city's grandest and most sophisticated displays of Art Deco styling.

The ticket lobby, low and relatively dark, forms a deliberate contrast to the Grand Lobby beyond. Walls are of red marble above black marble wainscoting; the low ceiling, painted black, is illuminated by dramatic circular light fixtures. The Grand Lobby inside the doors measures 140 ft long, 45 ft wide, and 60 ft high. The carpet of red, brown, gold, and black features abstract forms of musical instruments and was designed by Ruth Reeves (born 1892).

The unity of the decorative features of the hall—carpets, wall coverings, statues, murals, and furniture—was coordinated by Donald Deskey (born 1894), who reputedly spent his last $5000 preparing his entry for the competition. Deskey had worked in Paris and attended (1925) the Exposition Internationale des Arts Decoratifs et Industriels Modernes, an exhibition generally credited with establishing the Art Deco style in the public taste.

Over the imposing staircase at the N. end is a mural by Ezra Winter (1886–1949), 'The Fountain of Youth', its subject suggested by Prof. Burr and drawn from a legend of the Oregon Indians. It depicts an old man gazing at a gleaming inaccessible mountain top on which bubbles the fountain of youth; across the sky marches a cloudy procession representing the vanities of life. Gold mirrored panels reflect the light from two 29-ft glass chandeliers (2 tons apiece).

Staircases at the ends of the Grand Lobby lead down to the *Main Lounge* and restrooms. The lounge is richly decorated in grey and black: Donald Deskey designed the plaid carpet; the nine piers are faced with black glass and edged with chrome trim; walls are covered with black Permatex, a novel material at the time of installation. Vignettes of famous theatrical figures decorate the walls; they are drawn from Louis Bouché's (1896–1969) mural, 'The Phantasmagoria of the Theater'. William Zorach's (1887–1966) cast aluminum nude, 'Spirit of the Dance', kneels in the center of the room.

Along with Gwen Lux's (born 1912) statue of 'Eve' (niche at top of S. stairway leading to Grand Lobby) and Robert Laurent's (1890–1970) 'Girl with Goose' (S. end of first mezzanine), this statue caused a scandal when installed, since Roxy declared the three nudes morally offensive. In view of his own racy reputation and the tameness of the statues, his outrage seems surprising. Nevertheless the nudes were removed, to be reinstated at the demand of art lovers.

Even the restrooms (E. side) are impressively decorated, though the mural, 'Men without Women', by Stuart Davis (1894–1964) has been removed from the men's smoking lounge to the Museum of Modern Art. The women's lounge has a mural by Witold Gordon, 'The History of Cosmetics'. Fixtures, mirrors, and tile work were all especially designed for the Music Hall.

Equal care has been lavished on the lounges and restrooms throughout the building, although fabrics and murals are by now faded with time. Especially attractive is the women's lounge on the first mezzanine, designed by Deskey himself.

Return to the Grand Lobby. Separating it from the auditorium are 11 double stainless steel doors with bronze bas-reliefs representing theatrical scenes, designed by René Chambellan. The most impressive space in the Music Hall is the *auditorium,* which seats 6200 people. The ceiling is egg-shaped, a form Roxy demanded for its supposed acoustic superiority. The great proscenium arch (60 ft high, 100 ft wide) dominates the room. Rising outward and forward from it are the successive overlapping bands of the ceiling, painted with perpendicular rays, whose effect has been compared to the aurora borealis, a sunburst, and the rays of dawn. Roxy liked to assert that a sunrise he had witnessed aboard ship had inspired the design for the ceiling, but the model of the auditorium, complete with ceiling, had been photographed six days before he embarked on the voyage in question.

The lighting system is installed between the bands and regulated by a large control board placed between the footlights and the audience. The stage machinery, designed by Peter Clark, includes sections that can be raised or lowered on elevators, a revolving central turntable, and a moveable orchestra pit. The stage can support twelve grand pianos, or three Roman chariots with horses, or six elephants. While animals frequently appear in the Christmas pageant, the most famous performers of the Music Hall stage are the Rockettes, a troupe of precision dancers founded in 1925 by Russell Markert, who brought them from St. Louis to New York.

Leave the Music Hall and walk E. on 50th St. Adjacent to the theatre is the *Associated Press Building* (1938). Above the main entrance (E. side of building, facing Rockefeller Plaza) is Isamu Noguchi's (born 1904) stainless steel panel (1940), 'News', depicting five men with the tools of the reporter's trade: pad and pencil, camera, telephone, teletype, and wirephoto.

Continue E. along 50th St to the INTERNATIONAL BUILDING (1935). Over the entrance at 25 W. 50th St is a massive limestone screen by Lee Lawrie symbolising the international purpose of the building.

The four figures in the central rectangle on the bottom row represent the four races of mankind; above them are: a trading ship; three figures representing art, science, and industry; and Mercury, messenger of trade. The upper side panels represent regions of the Earth (whale's fluke, palm trees, mosque, and Aztec temple), while the lower ones symbolise the old order (Norman tower and lion, symbol of kings) and the new industrial, republican age (smoke stacks and eagle). Panels at 19 and 9 W. 50th St, also by Lawrie, represent 'Swords into Ploughshares', and 'St. Francis of Assisi with Birds'.

The main entrance of the building is on Fifth Ave, where a central doorway is flanked by two projecting wings. The S. wing is known as the PALAZZO D'ITALIA, and like the British and French Buildings demonstrates a policy of the developers to attract foreign tenants at a time when American ones were not readily available. Two bronze reliefs by Giacomo Manzu (born 1908) adorn the main entrance: a high relief of entwined grapevines and wheat stalks symbolising fruitfulness and a smaller low relief depicting an immigrant mother and child. These works, installed in 1965, replace earlier decorations by Attilio Piccirilli removed in 1940 when the United States was on the brink of war with Italy. In front of the central entrance of the International Building is a statue of *Atlas* (1937) supporting an armillary globe studded with signs of the zodiac. Designed by Lee Lawrie, this bronze, muscle-bound giant (figure, 15 ft; diameter of sphere, 21 ft; weight 14,000 lbs) impresses by size rather than grandeur. The N. wing of the building, known as the International Building North, retains its original decoration. Above the door is a glass panel by Attilio Piccirilli (1868–1945) entitled 'Youth Leading Industry'. Made of 3 tons of cast pyrex, it depicts a charioteer reining in two plunging horses as a youth points out the road ahead. Above the panel is a limestone cartouche by Piccirilli with male and female figures representing Commerce and Industry.

INTERIOR. Enter the building through the main entrance. The lobby is tall and deep, with thin piers leading the eye to the central escalators which dominate the room like the grand staircases of 18–19C public buildings, but suggest the fondness of Art Deco designers for machinery as a stylistic motif. The ceiling is covered with copper leaf and illuminated by indirect lighting. Ride up the escalator to the blank wall at the top, decorated with a bust of the aviator Charles A. Lindbergh. The trip down the escalator offers a fine view through the rings of Atlas's sphere to the rose window and Gothic arches of St. Patrick's Cathedral across the street, an odd but appealing juxtaposition of old and new.

18 Fifth Avenue, 59th–79th Street

SUBWAY: IRT Lexington Ave (trains 4, 5, 6) to 59th St; IND Sixth or Eighth Ave (B or E train) to Fifth Ave. BMT Nassau or Broadway trains (N or RR) to Fifth Ave.

BUS: M1, M2, M3, M4, M5 (uptown on Madison Ave, downtown on Fifth Ave), M6, M7 (uptown on Sixth Ave), M28 (57th St crosstown), M30, M32.

History. Fifth Ave between 59th–79th Sts, one of the city's most attractive boulevards, remained undeveloped until the city purchased land for Central Park in 1856. Before then 59th St formed the frontier between the city's most exclusive residential section and a social and geographical wasteland called 'Squatters' Sovereignty' which stretched almost to 120th St and contained poverty-stricken people living in wooden shacks sometimes patched together with flattened tin cans. After the park was begun the area was purged of its humble human and animal population (pigs and goats) and began to receive many of the city's wealthiest and most powerful families. From the closing decades of the 19C to the years of World War I, the area displayed a formidable concentration of wealth and an imposing collection of monumental residences.

The period during which the great mansions were built coincided roughly with the Eclectic period in American architecture. As the new millionaires, many of whom had made their fortunes during the post-Civil War boom, arrived on the social scene desirous of building suitably impressive homes, they turned for advice to the city's influential architects, who thus dominated and controlled the canons of taste. What the established architects—notably Richard Morris Hunt, Charles Follen McKim, and Stanford White—offered was Eclecticism, a self-conscious selection of styles from the classical orders of the past. The development and spread of Eclecticism was made possible by the contemporaneous development of photography, for now designers who could not study at first hand the monuments of Europe had access to them through accurate photographic renderings. Architects, becoming more professional at this time, began to acquire libraries for historical research so that their buildings could be historically correct in the smallest details. The new classical architecture also depended on the availability of cheap, skilled labour, supplied by the influx of immigrants, many of whom were experienced in masonry, ironwork, stone carving, painting and gilding, and ornamental plaster work. Coupled with the low wages of the period, their skill made possible an elegance of detail no longer feasible. Eclecticism died after the end of World War I, when changing economic patterns and new building technology dictated the end of sumptuous masonry building and ushered in the era of the skyscraper and the high-rise apartment.

Although Eclectic buildings exist in other parts of the city, the greatest concentration of them in residential uses is here on Fifth Ave and its side

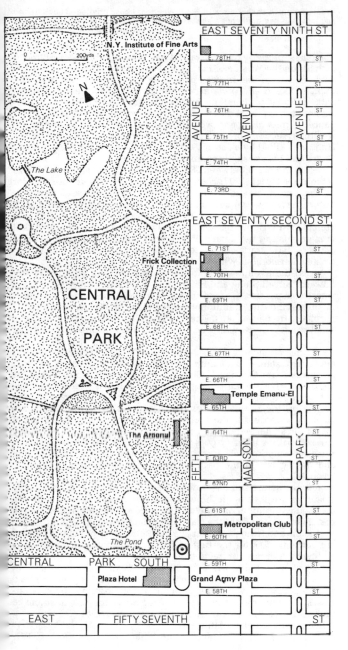

streets. So much so that novelist Edith Wharton, whose privileged background and judicious eye made her a keen commentator on social developments of the period, once described this wide-ranging selection of detail as a 'complete architectural meal'.

The Plaza, properly called **Grand Army Plaza,** lies between 58th and 60th Sts on the W. side of Fifth Ave. The open square, one of the few deviations from the gridiron plan of the city, provides a site for the *Pulitzer Memorial Fountain*, erected in 1916 (Carrère & Hastings) with a $50,000 donation from publisher Joseph Pulitzer. It is surmounted by Karl Bitter's *statue of Pomona*, goddess of abundance, a graceful young woman surely at home here in one of the wealthier sections of the city. Bitter, a protegé of Richard Morris Hunt, was killed by a car in 1915 as he was leaving the Metropolitan Opera and his assistants completed the statue.

Facing the plaza between 58th–59th Sts on the W. side of Fifth Ave is the **Plaza Hotel** (1907; Henry J. Hardenbergh; DL), remarkable for the beauty of its site with vistas in two directions and its social history, having witnessed many glittering events and attracted such visitors as Eleanor Roosevelt, Mark Twain, Groucho Marx, and Frank Lloyd Wright. Architectural critics admire Hardenbergh's skill in manipulating the details of its French Renaissance design, using dormers, balustrades, high roofs, and rounded corner turnings to create a harmonious whole.

Across the avenue is the former *General Motors Building* (1968; Edward Durrell Stone and Emery Roth & Co.), a 50-story skyscraper whose construction aroused controversy among observers interested in preserving the traditional organisation of the square and its hospitality to pedestrians. The building, clad in white marble, has a small sunken plaza with trees and bushes and a carpet of artificial turf.

On the W. side of Fifth Ave, N. of Central Park South is an equestrian *statue of General William Tecumseh Sherman* (1903; Augustus Saint-Gaudens), Civil War general best remembered for his destructive sweep through Georgia. Walking before the conqueror and waving an olive branch is a figure of Victory; the pine branch on the granite pedestal (Charles Follen McKim) signifies Georgia, according to the sculptor. The work, conceded to be one of the nation's finest equestrian statues, was at the time of its unveiling covered with a layer of gold leaf and its heroic appearance made some contemporary observers uneasy, remembering the devastation and misery left in the path of Sherman's march from Atlanta to Savannah.

Near the statue stands a row of horse-drawn cabs available to the visitor for a trot through the park or down the avenues. The horses are shod with rubber and the drivers, male and female, are attired in costumes ranging from the traditional black overcoat and top hat to blue jeans and fringed leather jackets. Rates per trip, not per person, are currently $17 for the first half hour or fraction and $5 for each additional half hour or fraction.

East of Fifth Ave. (5 E. 59th St) is the *Playboy Club*, New York branch of a chain of establishments devoted to drinking, eating, and nightlife, best known perhaps for the rabbit costumes of its waitresses. Around the corner (14 E. 60th St) is the *Copacabana*, a nightclub recalling an earlier style of American social life.

Begin walking N. on Fifth Ave.

On the N.E. corner of 60th St and Fifth Ave stands the METRO-

POLITAN CLUB, an imposing Italian Renaissance palazzo (1892–94; McKim, Mead & White; DL). The club was founded by J.P. Morgan and other discontented members of the Union Club after the board of governors had blackballed a candidate Morgan proposed for membership. One of the participants in the rejection remarked that Morgan's protegé had been voted down because, figuratively at least, he ate with his knife. The new club, whose membership boasted Vanderbilts and Goelets as well as the redoubtable Morgan, was soon nicknamed 'The Millionaires' Club'. The present approach to the building—a carriage entrance with a cobbled courtyard guarded- by an impressive wrought-iron fence and a colonnaded gateway—has become a controversial site as the club entertains proposals for a hotel tower on top of this handsome but under-used piece of real estate.

The *Hotel Pierre* (1928; Schultze & Weaver) at 2 E. 61st St, is another of the city's older, prestigious hotels, its towered top a skyline landmark. The apartment house at *800 Fifth Ave* (1978; Ulrich Franzen & Assocs) on the N.E. corner of 61st St replaces a plain brick and limestone townhouse which formerly belonged to Mrs Marcellus Hartley Dodge, a niece of John D. Rockefeller, Sr. Mrs Dodge was a great animal lover and toward the end of her life retired to an estate in New Jersey where her dogs ran up yearly meat bills of over $10,000. Her art collection included over 50 paintings by Rosa Bonheur, busts by the French 18C sculptor Houdon, and casts of hands that included Paderewski, Abraham Lincoln, and the Brownings (clasped). The construction of the apartment marks the passing of an era.

Although the majority of buildings in the Eclectic style like the Plaza Hotel and the Metropolitan Club reflect French, Italian, or Roman originals, the *Knickerbocker Club* (1914; Delano & Aldrich) at 2 E. 62nd St recalls a townhouse of the Federal period with its fine brickwork, marble lintels, and wrought-iron window gratings.

Diagonally across the intersection is the *Fifth Avenue Synagogue* (1959; Percival Goodman) at 5 E. 62nd St. Unlike many New York churches which are constructed as freestanding buildings and often located on the N.–S. avenues, this one standing on a cross street and attached to its neighbours on either side has been described as particularly urban. The limestone facade has pointed oval windows filled with abstract patterns of stained glass, the shape of which is reiterated in the design of the sanctuary.

The intersection of Fifth Ave with 63rd St is graced with two palatial apartment houses, *Nos 817 and 820 Fifth Ave* (both 1916; Starrett & Van Vleck). No. 820 has never been subdivided and each apartment occupies a full floor and includes five fireplaces, a kitchen-pantry with four sinks, six and a half bathrooms, servants' rooms, and a conservatory. The exterior details of the building—copper cornice with a frieze beneath, pedimented windows, balconies—were all used in the great townhouses of the period.

Turn right into E. 63rd St. *New India House* (1903; Warren & Wetmore), home of the Indian Consulate and headquarters for the Indian delegation to the U.N., stands at 3 E. 64th St, one of the few remaining buildings of modest scale designed by Warren & Wetmore, most famous for Grand Central Station. It originally belonged to Mrs Marshall Orme Wilson, daughter of the dowager Mrs Astor (see p296) and herself a prominent figure in society. The mansion of moulded limestone with a slate and copper roof, arched drawing room windows, and small oval dormers, exemplifies the Beaux-Arts style.

The S. corner of the intersection, 2 E. 64th St, is occupied by the *former Edward Berwind mansion* (1896; N.C. Mellon). At one time reputedly the largest owner of coal mining properties in the nation, Berwind was also for many years the chief executive officer of the IRT (Interborough Rapid Transit). Described as Prussian in appearance, and as dour, close-mouthed, and acquisitive in business dealings, he was apparently socially charming and belonged to about 40 clubs and societies. This brick and limestone house in the style of an Italian palazzo was his home in town; his country residence was 'The Elms' at Newport, Rhode Island.

Across Fifth Ave at E. 64th St is the **Arsenal** (1848; Martin E. Thompson; DL), a building of eccentric charm surmounted by eight crenellated octagonal towers which perhaps offer a sense of security to the present tenants, the administrators of the Parks Department. The newel posts of the central staircase represent cannon and the balusters supporting the railing resemble rifles; the door is guarded by a carved eagle, its wings outspread over two piles of cannon-balls.

History. Although it was constructed to replace an older ammunition depot downtown on Centre St whose decrepitude made it an easy mark for thieves, the remoteness of the present building (in 1848) rendered it only dubiously effective as a place for stockpiling arms and ammunition. One critic complained in an official report to the state that the cannon in the Arsenal, four and a half miles distant from the previous depot, would be utterly useless, since a mob bent on riot could accomplish its purpose before the troops could arm themselves and drag the artillery into action.

Before becoming the home of the Parks, Recreation, and Cultural Affairs Department in 1934, the building housed the Eleventh Police Precinct, the Municipal Weather Bureau, the American Museum of Natural History, and assorted animals of what is now the Central Park Zoo.

On the site of the present Temple Emanu-El (Fifth Ave at 65th St) stood the dwelling of Mrs Caroline Schermerhorn Astor (Mrs William Astor), the acknowledged leader of New York society in the closing years of the 19C. Mrs Astor had been forced to move uptown when her nephew William Waldorf Astor vengefully built the Waldorf Hotel next to her 34th St mansion as a reprisal against her social domination of his wife. Mrs Astor's uptown mansion, designed by Richard Morris Hunt, was styled like a French Renaissance château and featured a two-ton bathtub cut from a single block of marble, an elaborate picture gallery, and an immense ballroom. According to legend the capacity of the ballroom coincided precisely with the number of acceptable people in New York society, the 'Four Hundred'.

TEMPLE EMANU-EL at 1 E. 65th St, N.E. corner of Fifth Ave, is one of the largest churches in the city and has a greater seating capacity than St. Patrick's Cathedral. The building (1929; Robert D. Kohn, Charles Butler, and Clarence Stein) was constructed in an adaptation of Moorish and Romanesque styles to symbolise the mingling of Eastern and Western cultures.

INTERIOR (open Sun–Thurs, 10–5; Fri, 10–4; Sat, 12–5; organ recital Fri at 5 p.m. before the service). At the center of the altar on the E. wall is the Ark which contains the Torah, the scrolls of Mosaic law. Hanging in front of it is the perpetual light, the *ner tamid*, symbolising the Torah, God's law which the Jews are to keep alive in the world. The bronze grille of the Ark with its abbreviated versions of the Ten Commandments is flanked by two menorahs,

The Astor mansion at 65th St on Fifth Ave in 1898 and other homes of Millionaires' Row. The Mrs Astor, dowager queen of New York society, lived here until her death in 1903. (The Byron Collection, Museum of the City of New York)

or seven-branched candlesticks. In accordance with the Jewish restriction on visual images which might be considered idolatrous, the other decoration of the sanctuary is limited to a few traditional designs: the six-pointed Star of David seen in the mosaics and stained glass windows, the Lion of Judah, and the crown, a traditional Torah ornament. The mosaics are by Hildreth Meiere

The *Lotos Club*, 5 E. 66th St, formerly the William J. Schieffelin residence (1900; Richard Howland Hunt), is an extravagant Beaux-Arts townhouse; note especially the elaborate motifs above the fourth story dormer windows, the decoration of the window arches on the parlour floor, and the ornamental iron balcony. The Lotos Club was founded in 1870 as an organisation devoted to literature and the arts.

Next door at 3 E. 66th St a modest placard marks the site of a house where Ulysses S. Grant spent his final years (1881–85) and wrote his memoirs.

At 854 Fifth Ave between 66th and 67th Sts stands the elegant townhouse formerly belonging to R. Livingston Beekman, now the home of the *permanent Mission of Yugoslavia to the United Nations* (1905; Warren & Wetmore). Designed as a reflection of 18C classic French architecture of the period of Louis XV, the house crowned by a steep copper-covered mansard roof with two stories of dormers maintains an air of dignity and monumentality, despite being hemmed in by two large apartment buildings.

Across the avenue at the intersection of 67th St and the Park is the

Seventh Regiment Monument (1927; Karl Illava), a memorial to the men of the 107th Infantry who died in World War I.

Continue uptown. At the edge of the park between 70th–71st Sts is a *memorial to Richard Morris Hunt* (1898; Daniel Chester French) opposite the site of the former Lenox Library (torn down and replaced by the Frick mansion), one of Hunt's finest achievements.

Architect Bruce Price planned the granite monument on which rests a bust of Hunt flanked by two classically draped women symbolising his achievements: Sculpture and Painting (left) carries a mallet and a palette supporting the remains of a figure modelled on one from the Parthenon (now vandalised and amputated above the knee); the other, Architecture, bears a replica of Hunt's Administration Building at the World's Columbian Exposition, a fair in Chicago (1893) which contributed greatly to the development of the Eclectic style in architecture. The figures which weigh nearly 600 lbs apiece and are about 6 ft tall were abducted in 1962 and were nearly melted down in a belt buckle factory before they were recognised and recovered.

Across the street at 1 East 70th St is the ****Frick Collection,** housed in one of the most elegant remaining Fifth Ave mansions (1914; Carrère & Hastings. Renovated as a museum, 1935; John Russell Pope; DL. Addition to the E. 1977; Harry Van Dyke and John Barrington Bayley). The collection is a monument to that passion for acquiring European art harboured by so many millionaires and industrialists of Frick's generation. The museum contains a superb group of European paintings, mostly from the Renaissance to the end of the 19C, a fine collection of small Renaissance bronzes, antique furniture, enamels, prints and drawings, and porcelains.

Open Tues–Sat, 10–6; Sun, and minor holidays, 1–6; closed Mon, major holidays, and Tues during July and August. Adults, $1 on weekdays, $2 on weekends; students and senior citizens, $1. Children under 10 not admitted; children under 16 must be accompanied by an adult. Tel: 288–0700. Lectures, occasional chamber music concerts.

The Frick Art Reference Library, 10 E. 71st St, is open to scholars, advanced students, and readers with legitimate research projects; inquire about hours and dress code.

No eating facilities in the museum.

History. Henry Clay Frick (1849–1919), a pioneer in the development of the coke and steel industries and a self-made man, began collecting art seriously around 1895, indulging his taste for such French painters as Daubigny, Bouguereau, and the Barbizon school. As his taste matured, he sold earlier acquisitions and began buying the Flemish, Dutch, Italian, and Spanish paintings which presently ornament the collection, aided by such dealers and art historians as Roger Fry, Joseph Duveen, and Knoedler and Company. In 1905 he abandoned plans for a new house and gallery in Pittsburgh because he felt that pollution from the steel mills would be hazardous to his collection and commissioned Thomas Hastings of Carrère and Hastings to build (1913–14) this building as a dwelling and museum. Designed in an 18C French style, the mansion stands on the site of the former Lenox Library; after Frick's death both the house and the artworks were left in trust to establish a public gallery and in 1935 the house, enlarged and remodelled by John Russell Pope, was opened to the public.

ANTEROOM: This room is reserved for changing exhibitions of paintings and drawings from the part of the collection not on permanent display.

BOUCHER ROOM: The panels by *François Boucher* representing the Arts and Sciences are thought to have been commissioned by Mme de Pompadour, mistress of Louis XV and patroness of the arts, for a boudoir in the château at Crécy. The arts and sciences chosen may have borne some relationship to Mme de Pompadour's personal interests: Poetry and Music, Astronomy and Hydraulics, Comedy and Tragedy, Architecture and Chemistry, Fishing and Hunting, Fowling and Horticulture, Painting and Sculpture, Singing and Dancing. Among the pieces of period furniture are a writing table by *Jean-Henri Riesener*, a chest of drawers attrib. to *André-Louis Gilbert*, and a dressing table by *Martin Carlin*. The sculpture bust of a little girl was made in the 19C after a model of 1750 by *François-Jacques-Joseph Saly*.

In the DINING ROOM are 18C English portraits: *John Hoppner*, The Ladies Sarah and Catherine Bligh; *William Hogarth*, Miss Mary Edwards; *Sir Joshua Reynolds*, General John Burgoyne; *George Romney*, Henrietta, Countess of Warwick and her Children; *Thomas Gainsborough*, Richard Paul Jodrell, The Mall in St. James Park, and Grace Dalrymple, Mrs Elliott.

In the West Vestibule are four panels by *Boucher* representing The Four Seasons.

The *FRAGONARD ROOM, another lovely period room, demonstrates Frick's taste toward the end of his collecting career. The four

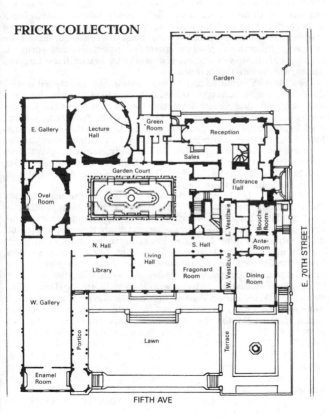

FRICK COLLECTION

largest panels depict The Progress of Love and were painted for Mme du Barry who succeeded Mme de Pompadour in Louis XV's affections. The paintings are entitled The Pursuit, The Meeting, Love Letters, and The Lover Crowned. Later Fragonard complemented them with Love Triumphant, Reverie, Love the Jester, Love the Sentinel, Love the Avenger, and Love Pursuing a Dove, as well as the Hollyhock panel also displayed here.

Sculpture includes *Jean-Antoine Houdon*, Comtesse du Cayla, and two terracotta groups by *Clodion*, Satyr with Two Bacchantes, and Zephyrus and Flora. Among the porcelains are a Sèvres vase in the form of a ship, and two pairs of Chinese jars from the famille rose period of the Ch'ing dynasty. Furniture includes a set of armchairs covered in Beauvais tapestry after designs by *Boucher* and *Jean-Baptiste Oudry*.

Paintings in the *LIVING HALL include: *Titian*, Man in a Red Cap; *Giovanni Bellini*, St. Francis in Ecstacy; *Titian*, Pietro Aretino; *Hans Holbein the Younger*, Sir Thomas More, Thomas Cromwell; *El Greco*, St. Jerome. Furniture is in the style of *André-Charles Boulle*, cabinetmaker to Louis XIV, and the pedestals between the court windows are probably from his workshop. In this room also are displayed examples of the small Renaissance bronzes which Frick began to collect toward the end of his life, purchasing some from the estate of J. P. Morgan (died 1914), who had purchased bronzes from European collections in great quantity. Especially noteworthy is *Antonio Pollaiuolo's* Hercules; also works by Masimiliano Soldani, Antico, and Severo da Ravenna.

The LIBRARY contains further examples of Frick's interest in 18C English portraits, Chinese porcelains, Renaissance bronzes, and some English side chairs from the Queen Anne period. *George Romney*, Lady Hamilton as 'Nature'; *Gilbert Stuart*, George Washington; *Sir Thomas Lawrence*, Julia, Lady Peel; *Romney*, Miss Mary Finch-Hatton; *Gainsborough*, Sarah, Lady Innes, Mrs Charles Hatchett; *Sir Joshua Reynolds*, Selina, Lady Skipwith; *John Constable*, Salisbury Cathedral from the Bishop's Garden; *Reynolds*, Elizabeth, Lady Taylor; *J.M.W. Turner*, Fishing Boats Entering Calais Harbour, Mortlake Terrace.

The *WEST GALLERY, planned as a setting for the major part of the collection, permits the kind of interesting juxtaposition of paintings Frick preferred, although the present arrangement was not made by him. Complementing the paintings are three imposing 16C Italian tables and other N. Italian Renaissance furniture. *Rembrandt*, Portrait of a Young Artist; *Anthony Van Dyck*, Frans Snyders, Margareta Snyders; *Jean-Baptiste-Camille Corot*, The Lake; *Turner*, The Harbour of Dieppe; *Henry Raeburn*, James Cruickshank, Mrs Cruikshank; *Hobbema*, Village with Watermill among Trees; *Constable*, The White Horse; *Agnolo Bronzino*, Lodovico Capponi; *Paolo Veronese*, Allegory of Wisdom and Strength, Allegory of Vice and Virtue; *Gerard David*, The Deposition; *Hals*, Portrait of a Painter; *Rembrandt*, The Polish Rider; *Hals*, Portrait of a Man; *Georges de la Tour*, The Education of the Virgin; *Turner*, Cologne: The Arrival of a Packet Boat; *Rembrandt*, Nicolaes Ruts; *Jacob van Ruisdael*, Landscape with a Footbridge; *Rembrandt*, Self-Portrait; *Vermeer*, Mistress and Maid; *Velasquez*, King Philip IV of Spain; *El Greco*, Vincenzo Anastagi; *Francisco de Goya*, The Forge.

Among the bronzes are *Riccio*, Naked Youth and *Francesco da Sangallo*, St. John Baptising.

The beautifully panelled ENAMEL ROOM, the smallest of the museum, contains Frick's collection of painted French enamels dating from the late 15C–17C. They were made in the workshops at Limoges and most were acquired from the J.P. Morgan collection after Morgan's death. Paintings include: *Gentile da Fabriano*, Madonna and Child with Saints Lawrence and Julian; *Duccio di Buoninsegna*, The Temptation of Christ on the Mountain; *Piero della Francesca*, St. Simon the Apostle; *Jan van Eyck*, Virgin and Child with Saints and Donor; *Hans Memling*, Portrait of a Man.

The OVAL ROOM at the other end of the West Gallery was added during the remodelling of 1935. It contains a terracotta statue of Diana the Huntress by *Houdon* and four elegant portraits by *Whistler*: Miss Rosa Corder; Valerie, Lady Meux; Mrs Frederick R. Leyland; and Robert, Comte de Montesquiou-Fezensac.

The EAST GALLERY. Paintings: *Van Dyck*, Paola Adorno, Marchesa di Brignole Sale; *Ruisdael*, Quay at Amsterdam; *Hobbema*, Village among Trees; *Goya*, An Officer, perhaps the Conde de Tepa; *Lorrain*, The Sermon on the Mount; *Goya*, Dona Maria Martinez de Puga; *Aelbert Cuyp*, Dordrecht: Sunrise, River Scene; *Goya*, Don Pedro, Duque de Osuna; *Van Dyck*, James, Seventh Earl of Derby, His Lady and Child; *El Greco*, Purification of the Temple; *Jacques-Louis David*, Comtesse Daru; *Degas*, The Rehearsal; *Jean-Baptiste Greuze*, The Wool Winder; *Gainsborough*, Mrs Peter William Baker, Frances Duncombe.

The GARDEN COURT, designed by John Russell Pope to occupy the site of the original carriage court, is an oasis of greenery and fountains. Around the outside of the room are portrait busts: *Danese Cattaneo*, Bust of a Jurist; *Antoine Coysevox*, Robert de Cotte, and (attrib. to Coysevox) The Maréchal de Turenne; *Jacques Jonghelinck*, The Duke of Alba; *Federico Brandani*, Antonio Galli. In the central part of the court is a bronze Angel by *Jean Barbet* dated 1475 on the left wing.

The NORTH HALL: *Jean-Auguste-Dominique Ingres*, Comtesse d'Haussonville; *Claude Monet*, Vétheuil in Winter; *Giovanni Battista Tiepolo*, Perseus and Andromeda; *Jean-Baptiste-Siméon Chardin*, Lady with a Bird-Organ; *Théodore Rousseau*, The Village of Becquigny. Also *Houdon*'s marble bust of Armand-Thomas Hué, the Marquis de Mironesnil.

Cross through the Living Hall to the SOUTH HALL. *Paolo and Giovanni Veneziano*, Coronation of the Virgin; *Corot*, The Boatman of Mortefontaine ; *Vermeer*, Officer and Laughing Girl, Girl Interrupted at her Music; *Boucher*, Portrait of Mme Boucher; *François-Hubert Drouais*, The Comte and Chevalier de Choiseul as Savoyards. The organ front was designed by Eugene Mason of Carrère and Hastings; the secretary and chest of drawers were made for Marie Antoinette by Riesener; the calendar clock is dated 1767 and tells the month and day as well as the hour and the barometric pressure. Behind the organ console is *Renoir*'s Mother and Children.

Continue N. on Fifth Ave. The LYCÉE FRANÇAIS occupies two Beaux-Arts townhouses just off Fifth Ave at 72nd St. *No. 7 E. 72nd St* (1899; Flagg & Chambers; DL) with its vermiculated stonework, began as the home of Oliver Gould Jennings. *No. 9 E. 72nd St* next door (1896; Carrère & Hastings; DL) was the home of Henry T. Sloane.

A block further N. and a little off Fifth Ave at 11 E. 73rd St is a Venetian palace (1903; McKim, Mead & White), formerly the Joseph Pulitzer residence. Modelled on the Ca'Rezzonico with a wide facade, arched windows and colonnades, the house stood empty much of the time Pulitzer owned it, because illness, near-blindness and his extreme sensitivity to sound made the house unattractive to him.

Continue up Fifth Ave. At 943 Fifth Ave between 74th–75th Sts is the *French Consulate* (1926; Walker & Gillette). Beyond it at 1 E. 75th St is the home of *The Commonwealth Fund*, the former Edward S. Harkness House (1909; Hale & Rogers), a remarkable example of the superb craftsmanship available to the very wealthy at the turn of the century. Protected by a spiked iron fence and a 'moat', the house, with its beautifully carved marble, is modelled after an Italian palazzo and elegantly detailed from the elaborate cornice to the iron ground floor gates. Harkness, a noted philanthropist, was the son of Stephen Harkness, one of the original partners in Standard Oil.

Further N. at 1 East 78th St is the former James B. Duke mansion (1912; Horace Trumbauer; DL; interior remodelled 1958; Robert Venturi, Cope & Lipincott), now preserved as the *New York University Institute of Fine Arts*. Built of white limestone so fine that it looks like marble, it was modelled after the late 18C Labottiere mansion in Bordeaux in the classical style of Louis XV. James B. Duke rose from humble beginnings on a North Carolina farm to dominate the tobacco industry, becoming president of the American Tobacco Co. in 1890 and maintaining his position of power even after the Supreme Court ruled his company in violation of the anti-trust laws. He lived in this mansion until his death in 1925; his daughter Doris Duke and his widow donated the property to N.Y.U. in 1957.

The *Cultural Services of the French Embassy*, on Fifth Ave between 78th–79th Sts. (972 Fifth Ave) are located in the former Payne Whitney House (1906; McKim, Mead & White; DL), one of the earliest Italian Renaissance mansions N. of 72nd St. It is especially interesting for its gracefully curved and elaborately carved facade of light grey granite, a material not generally favoured because of its extreme hardness. The carving includes a wave moulding above the ground floor, winged cherubs above the arched parlour-floor windows, and lions' heads on the ends of the roof brackets. The house belonged first to Payne Whitney, philanthropist, financier, and aficionado of horse racing who kept stables in Kentucky and on Long Island. His estate was calculated at a quarter of a billion dollars. His wife, Helen Hay Whitney, was a daughter of John Hay, secretary of state under presidents McKinley and Theodore Roosevelt. Their daughter Joan Whitney Payson was the principal owner of the New York Mets baseball team until her death in 1975 and their son John Hay (Jock) Whitney was publisher of the 'New York Herald Tribune' and ambassador to Great Britain.

The former Cook mansion next door at 973 Fifth Ave was built between 1902–05 by McKim, Mead & White and is visually continuous with the Payne Whitney House.

Looming up on the S.E. corner of Fifth Ave and 79th St is the home of the UKRAINIAN INSTITUTE OF AMERICA, the former mansion of Augustus Van Horn Stuyvesant, the last direct male descendant of the famous one-legged Dutch governor, Peter Stuyvesant. The house (1899; C.P.H. Gilbert; DL) is a picturesque French Gothic mansion, with high slate roofs, pinnacled dormers, gargoyles, and a 'moat' protected by an iron fence. Here Augustus Stuyvesant, a successful real estate dealer, spent his declining years, eventually becoming a complete recluse, limiting his social activities to meetings with the family lawyer and visits to the graves of his ancestors buried in the churchyard of St. Mark's-in-the-Bowery, where he was driven by his chauffeur in an old Rolls Royce.

The Ukrainian Institute (open Tues–Fri, 2–6, Sat and Sun by appointment; voluntary donation; tel: 288–8660) has a collection of paintings by contemporary Ukrainian painters, sculpture, religious relics, and folk costumes.

19 Museum of Modern Art and Vicinity

SUBWAY: IRT Broadway-7th Ave local (train 1) to 50th St and Broadway. IND Sixth Ave (B train) to 57th St. IND Sixth Ave (D train) or Eighth Ave (E train) to Seventh Ave and 53rd St.

BUS: Downtown on Fifth Ave or uptown on Madison Ave, M1, M2, M3, M4, M32. Downtown on Broadway and Fifth Ave, M5. Uptown on Sixth Ave, M5, M6, M7. Crosstown on 49th–50th Sts, M27.

The ****Museum of Modern Art** at 11 W. 53rd St offers an unrivalled collection of modern painting and sculpture spanning the years from about 1880 to the present. The collections also include films, photographs, prints and drawings, and embrace the arts of architecture and industrial design.

Open Mon–Sat, 11–6; Sun 12–6; Thurs until 9. Closed Wed and on Christmas Day. Adults $2·50; students with ID, $1·50; children under 16 and senior citizens, $0·75. Tues by voluntary contribution. Restaurant in Penthouse. Monthly calendar with film showings (included in price of admission) available at information desk in lobby. Gallery talks weekdays at 12.30 and Thurs evenings at 5.30 and 7. Tel: 956–7070. The gallery space of the museum is currently undergoing extensive re-arrangement.

The museum building (1939; Edward Durell Stone & Philip L. Goodwin), constructed on a street previously occupied by gracious 19C brownstones and townhouses, was as innovative as the collection it was to contain. It remains one of the city's best International Style buildings, with a flat facade of white marble and opaque glass, horizontal strip windows, and an overhang pierced with round holes. As the museum outgrew its quarters, Philip Johnson remodelled the sculpture garden and the gallery space, adding the W. wing (1951) and the E. wing (1964). At the present time, the museum is engaged on a massive expansion programme, having sold the air rights over its original building to developer Charles H. Shaw for $17 million. To the W. of the building is rising a tower which will have six museum floors (doubling the present gallery space) and 44 residential floors. This will generate financial support for the museum which is maintained largely by admission fees, dues, sales, and contributions. The architects for the project are Cesar Pelli & Assocs and Edward Durell Stone.

One of the most important collections of modern art in the world, the museum contains representatives of almost all of the significant movements in painting from the Impressionist period to the present,

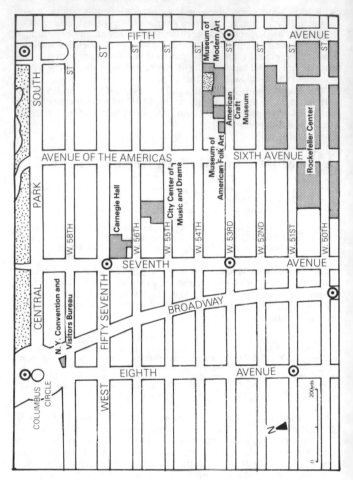

with about one third of the collection devoted to American artists working since 1945.

Among the most famous paintings are *Picasso*: Les Demoiselles d'Avignon, Girl Before a Mirror, Three Musicians; *Rousseau*: The Sleeping Gypsy, The Dream; *Van Gogh*: The Starry Night; *Matisse*: Dance, The Moroccans; *Braque*: Woman with a Mandolin; *Monet*: Water Lilies; *Jackson Pollock*: One (Number 31, 1950); *Cézanne*: The Bather. Other painters represented are Albers, Bacon, Balthus, Bearden, Beckman, Chagall, Dali, Degas, Duchamp, Ernst, Feininger, Gauguin, Gorky, Kandinsky, Klee, Léger, Lichtenstein, Louis, Magritte, Marin, Miró, Modigliani, Mondrian, Motherwell, Nolde, O'Keeffe, Oldenburg, Orozco, Picabia, Redon, Rivera, Rothko, Rouault, Schlemmer, Seurat, Severini, Shahn, Soutine, Stella, Tanguy, Tchelitchew, Tobey, Toulouse-Lautrec, Vuillard, and Andrew Wyeth. Sculptors represented include Constantin Brancusi, Alexander Calder, Gaston Lachaise, Lipchitz, Henry Moore, Rodin, Maillot, Picasso, and Giacometti.

The collection also includes architectural material, industrial objects, textiles, kitchenware, crafts, and furniture, especially chairs, with more than a thousand objects selected for their quality and historical importance. The museum has an important collection of prints and drawings and an archive of classic and American films.

The DONNELL LIBRARY CENTER, across the street at 20 W. 53rd St, a branch of the New York Public Library, is named after Ezekiel J. Donnell, a cotton merchant who in 1896 bequeathed money for a library 'in which young people can spend their evenings profitably away from demoralising influences'. The center, financed by the city, lends a million books each year and has the nation's best collection of children's literature. The Rare and Old Book Collection has English and American children's books of the 18 and 19C.

On the same side of the street is one of the two branches of the AMERICAN CRAFT MUSEUM (44 W. 53rd St; the other is at 77 W. 45th St. near Sixth Ave).

Museum I on 53rd St is open Tues–Sat, 10–6; Sun, 11–5; tel: 397–0630. Museum II on 45th St (sponsored by the International Paper Company) is open Mon–Fri, 11–7. Adults, $1·50; students with I.D., senior citizens, and children under 16, 75¢. Fee includes admission to both locations.

The museum offers about five shows yearly, each shared between the two locations, focusing on such crafts as ceramics, fiber art, metalwork, enamel, woven and printed textiles, and glass. Founded (1956) by the American Craft Council as the Museum of Contemporary Crafts, the museum also has a collection of American crafts since 1900, portions of which are sometimes on display.

Another crafts' museum, but with a different emphasis, is a little further west (49 W. 53rd St), the MUSEUM OF AMERICAN FOLK ART.

Open Tues 10.30–8; Wed–Sun, 10.30–5.30. Adults, $1. Students, children, and senior citizens, 50¢. Tel: 581–2474.

This small museum, housed in a brownstone row house, opened in 1963 for the purpose of showing the work of American folk artists. Four or five shows each year focus on such aspects of folk art as stuffed animals, toys and dolls, weather vanes, rubbings from gravestones, Shaker furnishings, and paintings

Continue W. to Sixth Ave and walk N. At 1335 Sixth Ave (between 53rd and 54th Sts) is the *New York Hilton Hotel* (1963; William B. Tabler), one of the first of New York's big (2200 rooms) convention hotels.

At 135 W. 55th St between Sixth and Seventh Aves is the CITY CENTER OF MUSIC AND DRAMA (1924; H.P. Knowles), a whimsical domed structure built as the Mecca Temple of the Ancient and Accepted Order of the Mystic Shrine (Masons). The city took it over during the tenure of Fiorello La Guardia and converted it to a theatre (3000 seats and no elevators to the balcony levels). The New York City Ballet and the New York City Opera resided here until their move to Lincoln Center but the Joffrey Ballet, the Alvin Ailey American Dance Theater, the Paul Taylor Dance Company, and the Dance Theater of Harlem regularly perform here still, as well as foreign groups (primarily in the summer months).

Burlington House (1970; Chermayeff & Geismar) at 1345 Sixth Ave on the N.W. corner of 54th St stands on the site of Joseph Urban's Ziegfeld Theater built in 1927 for the Ziegfeld Follies.

Walk W. to Seventh Ave and go N. **Carnegie Hall** at 154 W. 57th
St (S.E. corner of Seventh Ave) was built (1891; William B. Tuthill,
architect with Dankmar Adler and William Morris Hunt, consultants;
DL) by Andrew Carnegie as a home for the Oratorio Society of which
he was then president. He also hoped to make money on his $2
million investment. Architecturally the building is not outstanding—
a bulky brownish neo-Italian Renaissance hall with a high square
tower at one corner—but it is historically important as an early
example of mixed-use construction combining studios and offices (in
the tower) with shops on the ground floor and an auditorium (2760
seats) in the middle; musically it is a landmark. The superb acoustics
of the auditorium have long delighted both audiences and performers, beginning with Tchaikovsky who appeared as guest conductor
during opening week. Despite the popularity of the hall, it came
close to demolition in the early 1960s when its owners began
yearning for larger profits (Andrew Carnegie didn't make money on
it either), but a committee of preservationists headed by violinist
Isaac Stern saved it. Although the New York Philharmonic, which
first made Carnegie Hall its home and appeared here under the
batons of Toscanini and Stowkowski, now resides at Lincoln Center,
major orchestras and soloists are still booked into the hall. *Carnegie
Recital Hall* is a small but prestigious auditorium where less
well-known artists display their talents.

The presence of Carnegie Hall long made this part of 57th St a
center of musical activity, as shops dealing in music, musical
instruments new and used, and instrument repair gravitated to the
area. Still in evidence are the *Joseph Patelson Music House* behind
Carnegie Hall (at 160 W. 56th St), whose bulletin board offers
announcements of interest to musicians, and *Steinway Hall*, now the
Manhattan Life Insurance Building (1925; Warren & Wetmore) at 111
W. 57th St between Seventh and Sixth Aves. The showroom still
occupies the ground floor, but the upstairs concert hall is gone.

Diagonally across Seventh Ave from Carnegie Hall at 205 W. 57th
St are the *Osborne Apartments* (1885; James E. Ware), a fine early
apartment house ·with a facade of reddish stone. The lobby still
maintains its former splendour but the rest of the ground floor has
been converted into storefronts. The ART STUDENTS LEAGUE
(1892; Henry J. Hardenbergh; DL) at 215 W. 57th St between
Seventh Ave and Broadway, an art school, enjoys a handsome
French Renaissance building by the architect of the Plaza Hotel.

Go W. on 57th St. At 965 Eighth Ave on the S.W. corner of the
intersection is the bizarre, theatrical HEARST MAGAZINE BUILD-
ING (1928; Joseph Urban), worthy of both its designer and original
owner. Joseph Urban, famous as a set designer whose talents
encompassed the high seriousness of the Metropolitan Opera and
the large-scale frivolity of Florenz Ziegfeld's Follies, met William
Randolph Hearst through Marion Davies, a Ziegfeld showgirl who
became Hearst's wife. Urban designed sets for several of Marion
Davies' movies and then the Hearst Magazine Building, which, with
its oversized urns and fluted columns, its grand entrance way and
massive keystone, could be yet another movie set. Originally Hearst
planned to add another seven stories to the building's present six,
which would have altered its squat appearance in the direction of
greater conventionality. The statuary by Henry Kries depicts (left to
right): Sport and Industry, Comedy and Tragedy, Music and Art.

20 North of Grand Central: Park Avenue and Environs

SUBWAY: IRT Lexington Ave express or local (train 4, 5, or 6) to Grand Central. IRT Flushing line (train 7) to Grand Central. Shuttle (SS) from Times Square to Grand Central. IND Sixth Ave (train B, D, F) to 42nd St and Sixth Ave; walk E. to Vanderbilt Ave and N. to the Pan Am Building.

BUS: Downtown via Fifth Ave (M1, M2, M3, M4 M5, M32) or Lexington Ave (M101, M102) to 42nd St. Downtown via Broadway and crosstown on 42nd St (M104). Uptown via Madison Ave (M1, M2, M3, M4) to 42nd St. Uptown via Sixth Ave (M5) or Third Ave (M101, M102, M104) to 42nd St. Crosstown on 42nd St (M106). Culture Bus (weekends and holidays), Loop I, stop 20 or Loop II, stop 18 at 42nd St-Vanderbilt Ave.

Almost 20 years after its arrival the PAN AM BUILDING (1963; Emery Roth & Sons, Pietro Belluschi, and Walter Gropius) at 200 Park Ave just N. of Grand Central Station is still able to evoke hostility. It is big (59 stories or 2·4 million sq. ft of rentable space on a 3·5 acre site), unattractive (with a facade of precast concrete panels and windows relieved by two square-columned floors for machinery and equipment), and intrusive (spoiling the former vista down Park Ave and ignoring the scale of nearby buildings). A heliport on top once further disrupted the neighbourhood with noise and fumes, but after a fatal accident (1977) when a landing strut collapsed, it was closed.

History. Once this neighbourhood was the focal point of the New York Central Railroad's vast real estate empire. Handsome if staid hostelries rose around Grand Central Station—the Hotel Biltmore (1914; Warren & Wetmore), on Vanderbilt Ave, named after Cornelius Vanderbilt's château in North Carolina (designed by Richard Morris Hunt), the Commodore, named after the railroad's founder but now replaced by the Hyatt Regency Hotel on 42nd St at Lexington Ave, and the Yale Club at 50 Vanderbilt Ave (1915; James Gamble Rogers), still opening its doors to visiting alumni.

The NEW YORK CENTRAL BUILDING (1929; Warren & Wetmore), now the Helmsley Building at 230 Park Ave between 45th and 46th Sts served as headquarters for the railroad executives. Walk N. through the elegant lobby with its travertine, Jaspé oriental marble, and bronze fittings. From the N. the building, its trim regilded and dramatically floodlit at night, overlooks Park Ave, its facade pierced by two vehicular portals that carry traffic on ramps around the railroad terminal.

Park Avenue N. of the Helmsley Building is now in its third stage of urban development. Before 1900 when the railroad yards ran above ground, the street attracted modest dwellings and factories. The avenue began its upward surge when the Fourth Avenue Improvement Scheme (completed 1872–74) depressed the tracks below street level as far as 56th St, but the neighbourhood remained fairly humble until the tracks were completely covered during the construction of Grand Central Terminal (1903–13). By the 1920s all the air rights over the tracks had been taken over by apartments and hotels, and luxury dwellings began appearing along both sides of the avenue up to 96th St where the tracks still emerge from the tunnel. As Park Ave became prime residential territory, land values soared, increasing over 200% between 1914 and 1930. After World War II, however, the drop in passenger revenues led the railroad to

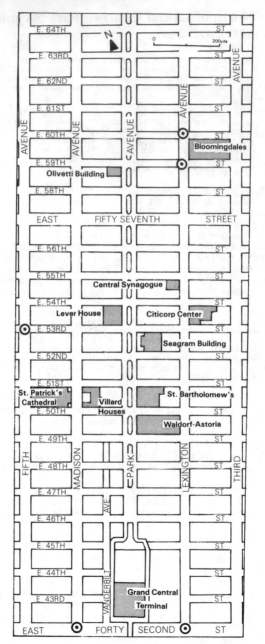

re-examine the potential of its real estate empire and to take advantage of the enormous inflation along Park Ave. Starting in the 1950s Park Ave began changing from a fine residential to a desirable commercial area, so much so that today city planners are worried about its becoming overbuilt, the home of nothing but enormous, often sterile, corporate towers.

No. 250 Park Ave (1925; Cross & Cross) above 46th St is one of only a handful of buildings remaining here from before World War II. At *270 Park Ave* between 47th and 48th Sts. is the former Union Carbide Building (1960; Skidmore, Owings & Merrill), 52 stories of matte black and stainless steel, with grey glass (707 ft). The boxy 12-story annex on Madison Ave and the 33-ft setback of the tower represent accommodations to the zoning law. Since 75% of the building stands over the railroad yards, the elevator machinery, normally installed in the basement, is above ground and the lobby on the second floor.

Walk N. The WALDORF-ASTORIA HOTEL (1931; Schultze & Weaver) at 301 Park Ave between 49th–50th Sts is still architecturally and socially one of the city's most appealing hotels. Faced in brick and limestone over a granite base, the hotel rises to two chrome-capped 625-ft towers, the Waldorf Towers, whose private apartments, reached from a separate entrance on 50th St, have attracted such notable tenants as the Duke of Windsor, President Hoover, and General MacArthur. Facing Park Ave above the main door is a figure by Nina Saemundsson symbolising the Spirit of Achievement, though it is uncertain whether this applies to the clientele or the hotel management.

Inside, the lobby is half a flight up, since like other Park Ave buildings the hotel (c. 1800 rooms) stands over the railroad yards and needs space above ground for mechanical equipment. While the tracks may have been inconvenient for the architects, they were a pleasure for former guests arriving in private railcoaches, who could be shunted onto a special siding, bypassing the inconvenience of passing through the station. When the hotel opened during the Depression, President Hoover lauded it as an 'exhibition of . . . confidence to the whole nation', and surely its former exquisite Art Deco interiors with marble, bronze, and matched woods suggested that the management foresaw better times. In the 1960s the hotel was redecorated in a gilded decor whose Edwardian overtones must be intended to evoke the original Waldorf-Astoria (1894), which stood on the site of the Empire State Building. Many of the present public rooms recall those bygone days: Peacock Alley, where society's grand dames once flaunted their plumage, the Empire Room, and the Palm Garden, the old hotel's most aristocratic restaurant. Oscar's Bar commemorates that legendary maître d'hôtel, Oscar Tschirky, whose command of the subtle points of social distinction raised him to the position of social arbiter.

Walk E. on 50th St. to Madison Ave and the HELMSLEY PALACE HOTEL (1980; Emery Roth & Sons). Not since the opening of the Waldorf-Astoria has such expectation and controversy surrounded the opening of a hotel as the clamour that greeted this one. The excitement came not from the tower with the private rooms, an uninspired 51-story dark brown boxy structure, but from the public rooms housed in part of the extraordinary **Villard Houses** (1886; McKim, Mead & White), a U-shaped grouping of six brownstone dwellings with sumptuous interiors built in a neo-Renaissance style for Henry Villard.

History. Villard, an Austrian immigrant and sometime railroad baron at the peak of his power in early 1883, began construction on a group of houses that would display the extent of his success to the most casual pedestrian. By Christmas, however, Villard had lost his fortune (perhaps $5 million), his presidency of the Northern Pacific Railroad, and his health. The unfinished houses were transferred to trustees to be completed and sold. Their buyers included Villard's lawyer Artemas Holmes, Harris C. Fahnestock and his son William who founded the brokerage firm Fahnestock & Co., and Mrs Whitelaw Reid, wife of the editor of the 'New York Tribune', who bought Villard's own house for $350,000 in 1886 with wedding money from her father, millionaire Darius Ogden Mills. The houses remained residential until after World War II, when social and economic changes destroyed the style of life implied by their grandeur. Random House, the publishing firm, Capital Cities Communications, and the Archdiocese of New York all used the buildings as offices, fortunately failing to do much remodelling. When the Archdiocese no longer wanted the property, exhaustive negotiations (75 official meetings and 15 public hearings) made possible the present project. One of the stipulations of the conversion of the houses to a hotel was the preservation of the most important interiors.

EXTERIOR. Finished in warm Belleville (New Jersey) brownstone, the facade is modelled after the Roman Palazzo Cancelleria (1489–96), and was designed by Joseph Morrill Wells, first assistant in the office of McKim, Mead & White, an architect known for his wit as well as his talent. Once when White boasted that one of his own drawings was as good 'in its way . . . as the Parthenon', Wells, eating breakfast, replied, 'Yes, and so too, in its way, is a boiled egg.' In the center of the complex is a courtyard, once used as a carriage turnaround. The two projecting wings with their rusticated ground floors were the Harris Fahnestock (N.) and Villard-Whitelaw Reid (S.) houses. Those in the central wing behind the graceful portico were smaller and less elaborate and have now been converted for use by the hotel.

INTERIOR. Under the guidance of architect James Rhodes, at a cost of $20 million, the interiors where possible have been restored to their original beauty. Enter the hotel from the courtyard. In the *Grand Lobby* is a red fireplace mantle with marble figures above it representing Joy, Hospitality, and Moderation, designed by Augustus Saint-Gaudens, who, with Stanford White, also designed the zodiac clock near the top of the stairs.

The present *Gold Room*, used for cocktails and afternoon tea, was the Villard-Reid Music Room, its barrel-vaulted ceiling (30 ft high) gilded according to instructions by Stanford White who completed the decor of the room left incomplete when Villard went bankrupt. In the lunettes at the ends of the vault are murals (completed 1888) by John La Farge representing Music and Drama. Beneath them are plaster casts of Luca della Robbia's marble Cantoria (1431–48) in Florence, perhaps suggested by Augustus Saint-Gaudens who had returned from study in Italy with casts of works by sculptors he admired. The *Madison Room* (nearest Madison Ave) was the drawing room which the Reids had enlarged and redecorated with painted panels and marble columns with bronze doré Corinthian capitals in the new 'French' taste. The small door right of the fireplace was concealed behind a hinged marble niche and allowed an unobtrusive escape from dull receptions. The *Hunt Room*, with its carved English oak panelling remains more or less as it was in Villard's day; the inlaid panels along the bottom of the frieze are mahogany and have sentimental mottos in Latin, French, English, and German—Villard's native language (he was baptised Ferdinand Heinrich Gustav Hilgard).

The grand new hotel was at first to be called simply The Palace, a name it unfortunately shared with a Bowery flophouse, which began receiving unexpected phone calls from major corporations and well-heeled visitors requesting reservations. When the Bowery establishment refused to change its name to suit the upstart newcomer, the latter became the Helmsley Palace.

The wing N. of the courtyard, originally owned by Harris Fahnestock but later joined with the adjacent house by his son William who inherited it, now serves the URBAN CENTER, a group of organisations dedicated to historic preservation, architecture, and urban planning: the Municipal Art Society, the Parks Council, the Architectural League, and the New York Chapter of the American Institute of Architects. Visitors may enjoy the Fahnestocks' reception rooms as they attend lectures, seminars, and exhibitions or browse in the bookstore specialising in architectural books.

The Municipal Art Society was founded (1892) during the City Beautiful movement by architect Richard Morris Hunt and others to embellish the city with sculpture, fountains, and other forms of public art. Today the organisation is concerned with the total urban environment, its design, preservation, and maintenance. Among the society's causes have been battles against gaudy advertising on Fifth Ave (1917), on river barges (1964), and on taxis (1973) as well as campaigns for the preservation of Pennsylvania Station (1963), Grand Central (1970), and Radio City Music Hall (1978).

Return to Park Ave. **St. Bartholomew's Church** (Protestant Episcopal) facing Park Ave between 50th-51st Sts (1919; Bertram G. Goodhue; DL) is one of the oldest buildings along the avenue, though its present situation is soon to be sadly altered. The congregation bought the site for $1·5 million in 1914 from the F. & M. Schaefer Brewing Company, which had been making beer by the railroad tracks since 1860.

EXTERIOR. The ornate carved portico comes from the previous St. Bartholomew's Church (1902) on Madison Ave, designed by Stanford White who styled it after a Romanesque church at St. Gilles in the South of France and hired Daniel Chester French and Philip Martiny, among others, to execute the figures. Connecting the three arches of the portal is a frieze depicting events from the Old and New Testaments. The tympanum over the center doors contains a representation of the Coronation of Christ.

INTERIOR. The mosaics on the ceiling of the narthex by Hildreth Meiere tell the story of the Creation. The narthex opens into the three aisles of the nave, built facing E. in the traditional cruciform shape with a barrel vaulted ceiling. The structural elements are stone and marble veneered over concrete and much of the wall surface has been covered with rough-textured Guastavino acoustic tiles. The *West Window* is made of stained glass given as memorials for the earlier Madison Ave church and has figures of evangelists and scenes from the New Testament. Along the N. aisle (toward 51st St) are six stained glass windows by John Gordon Guthrie illustrating the Te Deum. Dominating the interior is a mosaic of glass and gold leaf (also by Hildreth Meiere) filling the ceiling of the *apse*. It represents the Transfiguration with Christ in the center flanked by Elijah and Moses standing on the mountain and the disciples Peter (N. side), James and John (S. side). The five tall windows in the apse below are filled with thin sheets of amber onyx and covered with grilles of the same material. The *Baptistry* in the E. wall of the N. transept has a font by Danish sculptor Thorwaldsen, representing a kneeling angel holding a shell. Along the S. aisle is a chapel designed primarily for services for children but nowadays used frequently for baptisms and weddings. The ceiling of trussed timber is painted and gilded in the manner of the Romanesque church of San Miniato al Monte in Florence. Over the altar is a mural by Telford Paullin and his wife Ethel Parsons Paullin depicting the Adoration of the Magi, around which are scenes from the infancy and boyhood of Christ in small medallions.

Return to Park Ave. On the S. side of the church is the *Community House* (1927; Bertram G. Goodhue Assocs and Mayers, Murray & Philip; DL) added by Goodhue's successor firm after his death. The garden, the Sallie Franklin Cheatham Memorial Garden (1971), with the Community House converts the church into an L-shaped complex whose pleasing proportions and open space provide a rare moment of grace along an avenue that is becoming increasingly an unrelieved wall of skyscrapers. In 1981, however, the rector and vestry announced a plan to lease the land under the garden and Community House to the highest bidder for development of an office tower. The church will use much of the estimated $7 million annual income from the development for its ministry, since, according to a billboard now posted in the garden 'to do less would be blasphemous because it would be idolatrous'. Critics of the development, both inside and outside the congregation, point out that such large scale construction on the site will overwhelm and visually destroy the present church.

Raised on a platform as a security measure are three bronze figures of *The Four Generations* by Mexican sculptor Francisco Zuniga, which before the fourth figure, a 350-lb, 68-inch girl was stolen (March 1981) depicted four barefoot Mexican peasant women.

Providing a dramatic background to the church is the reddish-orange brick of the GENERAL ELECTRIC BUILDING (1931; Cross & Cross) at 570 Lexington Ave (S.W. corner of 51st St), whose spiked Art Deco crown is familiar on the skyline. Several skyscrapers of the period end in pinnacle forms suggestive of the fantasies of science fiction which in this case are as appropriate to the present tenant as to the original one, the R.C.A. Victor Company.

Walk N. on Park Ave from St. Bartholomew's Church. On the S. side of 345 Park Ave along 51st St is a large bronze sculpture *Dinoceras* (Robert Cook). On the next block between 52nd and 53rd Sts stands the ***Seagram Building** (1958; Ludwig Mies van der Rohe and Philip Johnson; Kahn & Jacobs), a classic, elegant metal and glass curtain-wall building that started the now dying fascination with unadorned glass boxes on plazas. Set back 90 ft from the building line, the Seagram tower rises on square columns to a height of about 500 ft (150 ft wide by 90 ft thick). All the materials—from the wall of the custom-made amber glass and bronze, to the green Italian marble seating around the fountain, to the brushed aluminum and stainless steel hardware—were chosen for their quality and deployed with meticulous care. The excellence of the building stems largely from the interest and sophistication of Phyllis Lambert, daughter of Seagram board chairman Samuel Bronfman, who persuaded her father to erect a monumental building, not just a serviceable one, and who chose Mies van der Rohe as architect and paid continued attention to the design and construction.

So spectacular was the success of the building that it paved the way for the 1961 revision of the zoning code encouraging tall buildings on plazas which then spawned a glut of imitations—less finely crafted and well-proportioned, indifferent to the streets upon which they intruded themselves. In 1979 the building was sold for $85·5 million to a teachers' retirement fund, but with an agreement that the buyer continue to call it the Seagram Building and to cooperate with the efforts of the Bronfman family to seek landmark status—an unusual action for a building owner.

When the Four Seasons restaurant opened (1959; Philip Johnson & Assocs) in the Seagram Building, its intentionally 'modern' decor created a stir which has since subsided into continued admiration. There is a sculpture of metal rods by Richard Lippold in the grill and a stage backdrop for 'Le Tricorne' (1929) by Picasso in the corridor between the two main dining rooms.

Across the street from the Seagram Building at 370 Park Ave between 52nd and 53rd Sts is the RACQUET AND TENNIS CLUB (1918; McKim, Mead & White), a large scale Tuscan palace modelled after the Palazzo Antinori in Florence. Behind the row of blind arched windows at the top are tennis and squash courts. Beneath the cornice is a terracotta frieze of tennis racquets and netting. The club was built for the enjoyment of the well-to-do and well-connected athlete who could disport himself on its especially constructed, slate-based tennis courts built at a time when indoor tennis was a rarity or indulge in court (real) tennis, the sport of kings (i.e. Louis XIV), still a rarity.

Like the Villard Houses and presumably St. Bartholomew's Church, the Racquet and Tennis Club has become a purveyor of air rights and now squats in front of a 575-ft office tower clad in aquamarine-tinted glass. In a complicated legal manoeuver the developer, Fisher Bros, got permission to build a tower called Park Avenue Plaza (1981; Skidmore, Owings & Merrill) that contains as much space as would be permitted on the site of the office building plus the site of the racquet club, thus 'shoehorning' a big building onto a small site and concurrently naming the structure from a street on which it does not sit. The building has an elegant high atrium with greenery, a sculptural waterfall, and no place to sit. In June 1981 the City Planning Commission proposed a new zoning law which will discourage midblock 'shoehorning' on the overbuilt East Side, seeking to limit the size of buildings and to decrease allowable floor area.

Continue up Park Ave. **Lever House** at 390 Park Ave between 53rd and 54th Sts (1952; Skidmore, Owings & Merrill; DL) by the same architectural firm seems modest today, though it did not when it appeared on Park Ave, the first commercial structure on a residential avenue and the first steel and glass building in a file of stolid masonry apartment houses. The building takes its form from two slabs, one stretched out horizontally along the street, the other rising vertically. On the ground floor is an open interior courtyard with a garden and a pedestrian arcade. Lever House, once thought of as the ultimate corporate headquarters, is impressive today partly because it is so small, smaller than it legally had to be, an act of restraint on the part of the builders which has since elicited proposals from developers to tear it down and replace it with something bigger.

Walk E. on 54th St to Lexington Ave. Here, filling the block between 53rd and 54th Sts is the **Citicorp Center** (1978; Hugh

Stubbins & Assocs), a midtown office tower as representative of recent architectural values as Lever House and the Seagram Building were of the values of the 1950s. The Citicorp Center is a mixed-use building with offices and shops. The tower, sheathed in gleaming white aluminum, rises 915 ft from the street, resting on four 127-ft columns which support it at the midpoints of the sides, not at the corners. The top of the building slants at a 45 degree angle, the large plane surface facing south originally intended but not completed as a solar collector, now a conspicuous form on the skyline among the domes, crowns, and spires of yesteryear and the flat tops of the last generation.

On the N.W. corner of the site, under the tower, is **St. Peter's Church** (Lutheran), founded in 1861, which has existed here since 1904 and allowed Citicorp to buy its old building with the understanding that it would erect a new one (1977; Hugh Stubbins & Assocs). The angular form of the church faced with Caledonia granite to some observers suggests a rock, to others a granite tent; inside are the sanctuary, acoustically isolated from the street and subway, a small theatre (seats 250), and the beautiful Erol Beker *Chapel of the Good Shepherd (open for meditation during the day), enhanced by permanent wall sculptures by Louise Nevelson. N. Wall: Cross of the Good Shepherd and three columns, Trinity. E. wall: Frieze of the Apostles. W. wall: Sky Vestment—Trinity. S. wall: Grapes & Wheat Lintel and S.W. wall: Cross of the Resurrection.

Enter the Citicorp Building either from Lexington Ave or from 54th St. (Public restrooms are located near the 54th St entrance.) Inside the atrium, lit by a skylight, are attractive shops and restaurants. Concerts and other events are sometimes held in the atrium; pick up a schedule near the S.W. entrance of the building (off the sunken plaza).

Return to Lexington Ave, and walk a block N. to the **Central Synagogue** (1872; Henry Fernbach; DL) at 652 Lexington Ave (S.W. corner of 55th St). It is the oldest synagogue in continual use in the state and was designed by the first Jew to practice architecture in New York, Henry Fernbach, known chiefly for his cast-iron work in SoHo. While Judaism has never had an architectural heritage similar to the Gothic tradition in Christianity, the Moorish style with its allusions to Judaic roots in the Middle East became the dominant style of synagogue architecture in the middle 19C, and the Central Synagogue is generally considered the finest example of Moorish Revival architecture in the city. The onion-shaped green copper domes rise to 122 ft. The interior is colourfully stencilled in red, blue, and ochre. The congregation was founded as Ahawath Chesed (Love of Mercy) in Coblenzer's Hotel on Ludlow St by 18 men, most of them immigrants from Bohemia. Following the uptown migration of the Jewish population, the congregation moved northward gradually, acquiring the present site in 1870.

Return to Park Ave and walk N. one block to 56th St. On the S.W. corner, jammed into the N. end of 430 Park Ave is the *Mercedes-Benz showroom*, remarkable mainly for being Frank Lloyd Wright's first (1955) New York work.

On the sixth floor of the Korean Consulate, 460 Park Ave at 57th St, is the gallery of the *Korean Cultural Service*, offering yearly about six loan exhibitions of Korean art.

Open Mon–Fri, 10–5. Admission free. Tel: 759–9550. Library, lectures and film series.

Three blocks N. at 59th St (500 Park Ave) is another fine small office building, the **Olivetti Building** (1960; Skidmore, Owings & Merrill). This elegant aluminum and glass box was built for the Pepsi Cola Company, which fled the city for the suburbs around 1970, tired of the taxes, traffic jams, and other harrassments. Its successor the Olivetti Corporation left in 1978 and now the building, smaller than it legally needs to be, is the target for another 'shoehorning' proposal.

Walk a block W. to Madison Ave. Two large corporate skyscrapers are presently under construction here: the new *American Telephone and Telegraph Building* between 55th and 56th Sts (Philip Johnson & John Burgee), which caused a furor when its design was announced in 1979, and the *IBM headquarters* between 57th and 58th Sts (Edward Larrabee Barnes). The AT & T building, projected at 654 ft, will stand on a 131-ft masonry base of rose-grey granite with ground floor arcades and will rise to a huge broken pediment—the cause of the furore—which has elicited jokes about New York's first Chippendale skyscraper and questions about the architect's seriousness. The IBM building will be a five-sided prism, with dark grey-green granite sheathing and a glass-enclosed 'park' along one side.

Begin walking E. on 57th St. At 45 E. 57th St (N.E. corner of Madison Ave) is the FULLER BUILDING (1929; Walker & Gillette), a slender Art Deco building with a clock and sculptural figures by Elie Nadelman. At 57th St and Park Ave (N.E. corner) is the RITZ TOWER (1925; Emery Roth and Carrère & Hastings), a vintage Park Ave masonry apartment building with all the trappings of its period—an elaborate top, swags, urns, cartouches, and balustrades marking the major setbacks. The legendary restaurant Le Pavillon (founded during the New York World's Fair of 1939) once stood where the *First Women's Bank* (1975; Stockman & Manners Assocs, designers) now stands. Nearby at 117 E. 57th St is *The Galleria* (1975; David Kenneth Specter & Philip Birnbaum), the second experiment after Olympic Tower to rise under the zoning law redistricting Fifth Ave and some surrounding territory for mixed residential and commercial uses. It contains luxury apartments, offices, and a health club. The elaborate penthouse on top (four stories) was built for millionaire Stewart Mott as an office, residence and vegetable garden, whose prospective 2000 tons of soil necessitated a frame of concrete, poured in place. Mott, however, decided the place was too expensive and did not buy it.

Continue E. to Lexington Ave and turn left (N.). On the E. side of the avenue between 57th and 58th Sts is ALEXANDER'S, one of the city's major department stores, vying with Macy's, Gimbel's, and Bloomingdale's in sales. Like other New York department stores, Alexander's began (1928) as a small shop—on Third Ave—specialising in dry goods; it is known as a discount store with an eye to fashion.

To its N. is **Bloomingdale's** (between 59th and 60th Sts on the E. side of Lexington Ave), which in the past decades has become associated with whatever is chic and trendy in women's fashion. Known to its habitués as 'Bloomies', it is one of the nation's most successful stores. In 1976 sales were calculated at $350 per sq. ft of

selling space, probably the highest ratio in America but far behind
Marks & Spencer's London record the same year of $575 per sq. ft.

History. Lyman Bloomingdale, who with his brother Joseph founded the store
in 1872, learned the retail business as a clerk in Bettlebeck & Co. Dry Goods in
Newark, New Jersey, a firm with an all-star sales staff that also included
Benjamin Altman and Abraham Abraham (later of Abraham and Straus).
Unlike the other 19C department stores which began downtown and followed
the middle class uptown, Bloomingdale's started at 938 Third Ave, only a few
blocks from its present location. In both its arrival and demise, the Third Ave El
was a blessing to Bloomingdale's, first bringing so many shoppers from
downtown when it opened (1879) that within seven years the store had to move
to larger quarters on the N.W. corner of Third Ave and 59th St, a block it now
completely occupies. When the El was torn down (1954), the upper East Side,
formerly depressed by the inconveniences attendant upon the El, began a swift
climb to respectability and affluence. Fortunately Bloomingdales' management
had already begun upgrading the inventory from its former good quality but
sensible merchandise to the present stuff of fashion and fantasy.

The exterior of the building is a conglomeration of styles, the section
at 740 Lexington Ave (1930; Starrett & Van Vleck), an Art Deco
addition, its most interesting part. The ground floor interior, redesigned (1979) by Barbara D'Arcy in black plastic, marble, and
mirrored glass is as chic and glittering as anything in New York.

The *Grolier Club* (founded 1884), at 47 E. 60th St between

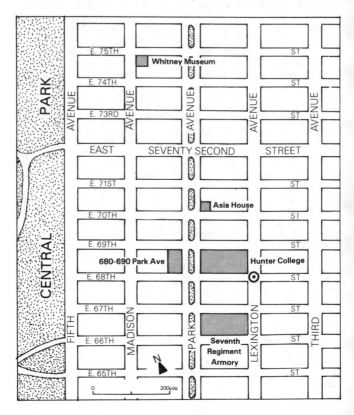

Madison and Park Aves (1917; Bertram G. Goodhue) takes its name from 16C French bibliophile Jean Grolier and is dedicated to the art of book production. In connection with this scholarly interest, the club presents (Oct–June) changing exhibitions featuring books, writers, manuscripts, and old prints.

Open Mon–Fri, 10–5; Sat, 10–3. Admission free. Tel: 838–6690.

The *Museum of American Illustration*, founded in 1980, at 128 E. 63rd St between Park and Lexington Aves, serves as an exhibition space for the Society of Illustrators and offers changing exhibitions designed to encourage interest in the art of illustration.

Open Mon–Fri, 10–5. Closed in August and on holidays. Admission free. Tel: 838–2560. Occasional lectures.

In addition to shows of individual artists and groups, historical and thematic exhibitions—Cream of Wheat Advertising, 1910–1940, the Chicago School in the 1940s—the society presents the Illustrators' Annual Exhibition with the best book, editorial, advertising, and institutional illustrations of the year.

21 The Whitney Museum and Environs

The *Whitney Museum of American Art (945 Madison Ave at 75th St) houses an outstanding collection of 20C American art in a handsome building (1966) designed by Marcel Breuer.

Open Tues, 11–8; Wed–Sat, 11–6; Sun and holidays, 12–6. Adults, $2; senior citizens 62 and older, college students with ID, and children under 12, free. Tues, 5–8, free. Restaurant. Tel: 570–3676.

History. In 1907 Gertrude Vanderbilt Whitney, an aspiring sculptor connected by birth and marriage to two of the city's pre-eminent families, opened a studio in Greenwich Village (see p183); she soon purchased the house adjoining it and began showing the work of young American artists, for whom she organized the Studio Club as an exhibition center and meeting place. Strongly believing that these artists needed recognition and encouragement, Mrs Whitney bought many of the paintings she exhibited, and using them as the nucleus of her collection opened the first Whitney Museum on Eighth St in 1931. In 1954 the museum moved uptown to 54th St next to the Museum of Modern Art, a move that boosted its attendance from 70,000 to 270,000 annually, soon necessitating a new building. Today the Whitney continues to support young artists with exhibitions and to publish works on American art. As the museum continues to expand it has elected to create branches: the Downtown Branch at the Federal Hall National Memorial (see p97), and one in suburban Stamford, Connecticut. Another is planned for the Philip Morris Building presently under construction on 42nd St opposite Grand Central Station, and will open in March 1983.

The building. Marcel Breuer, a member of the Bauhaus group, commissioned to design the new building, spoke of wanting the museum to have the vitality of the streets, the latitude of a bridge, and the weight of a skyscraper. What resulted is a building of three tiers of reinforced concrete clad in grey granite and cantilevered out like the steps of an inverted pyramid. The seven windows are randomly sized and placed; the entrance is reached by a concrete bridge over a sunken sculpture garden. The floors are slate and the walls are concrete with movable partitions making possible a variety of exhibition spaces.

The collections are shown in a changing series of exhibitions, many of which have attracted wide interest. Among the artists whose work is represented are Stuart Davis, John Sloan, Edward Hopper, Joseph Stella, William J. Glackens, Reuben Nakian, Reginald Marsh, Charles Demuth, Robert Rauschenberg, Frank Stella, Joseph Albers, Alexander Calder, Elie Nadelman and Mark di Suvero. Less traditional shows have been a retrospective of the work of Walt Disney and his animators and a show on 'Articulate Muscle—the Male Body in Art', which featured such famous body builders as Arnold Schwartzenegger and Frank Zane. On the third floor is a gallery with highlights from the permanent collection.

The Madison Ave corridor from about 57th St to 86th St has one of the city's two major concentrations of galleries (the other is in SoHo). The uptown galleries, generally older and more traditional than those in SoHo, offer works of virtually every period and movement in the history of art.

Both the Sunday 'New York Times' and the 'New Yorker' Magazine offer schedules of current gallery shows. Most galleries are closed Sun and Mon and many close for vacation during part of the summer.

Other nearby points of interest. The ARCHIVES OF AMERICAN ART at 41 East 65th St (at Madison Ave) offers changing exhibitions and is one of five national centers for scholars and researchers interested in the history of American visual arts. Available on microfilm are materials stored in the Smithsonian Institution in Washington, D.C.: letters, sketchbooks, photographs of artists at work, and every known art-auction catalogue from 1785–1963. (Open Mon–Fri, 9.30–5. Admission free. Tel: 826–5722). CHINA HOUSE at 125 E. 65th St. between Park and Lexington Aves mounts two exhibitions of classical Chinese art yearly and offers courses in Chinese culture, literature, and cooking. (Open Mon–Fri, 10–5; Sat, 11–5; Sun, 2–5. Admission free. Tel: 744–8181.) The CENTER FOR INTER-AMERICAN RELATIONS (680 Park Ave at 68th St), founded to increase understanding among the nations of the Western Hemisphere, offers exhibitions of the art of the Americas, from Canada to South America including the cultures of the Caribbean. (Open Tues–Sun, 12–6. Admission by voluntary contribution. Tel: 249–8950.) The building housing the center was originally the *Percy R. Pyne residence* (1911; McKim, Mead & White; DL) and is one of four landmark neo-Georgian and neo-Federal townhouses along the block. In 1965 a developer wanted to demolish them in favour of an apartment building but the Marquesa de Cuevas, a grand-daughter of John D. Rockefeller, bought them all and turned them over to their present owners. The others are: the *Spanish Institute* at 684 Park Ave (1926; McKim, Mead & White; DL), the *Italian Cultural Institute* at 686 Park Ave (1919; Delano and Aldrich; DL) and the *Consulate General of Italy* at 690 Park Ave (1917; Walker & Gillette; DL).

The **Asia Society,** 725 Park Ave at 70th St, was founded in 1956 to further American awareness of Asian culture, arts, politics, economics, and customs. On the Park Ave facade of the new building (1981;

Edward Larrabee Barnes), incised in the red Oklahoma granite is the society's logo, a lion adapted from an 18C bronze Nepalese guardian lion. The galleries host changing exhibitions and house a permanent collection of Asian art, given by Mr and Mrs John D. Rockefeller, III.

Open Tues–Sat, 10–5; Sun 1–5; Thurs, 10–8.30. Admission, $2 for adults. Guided and recorded tours; films, programmes of Asian music, dance, and theatre. Bookstore with a large selection of publications on Asian arts and culture. Tel: 288–6400.

The collection includes some 250 objects, not all on display, given to the society in 1979 by John D. Rockefeller, III, who began collecting Asian art in 1951. On the ground floor are monumental stone sculptures from India and Indonesia, 6–11C. The Ross Gallery at the top of the stairs features sculpture from Southeast Asia, notably Cambodia and Thailand. Inside the Rockefeller Gallery, the first room contains *Indian and Southeast Asian sculpture*: along the left (W.) wall are works from N. India including those from the Gupta period, Nepal, Tibet, and Kashmir. Along the N. wall is S. Indian sculpture from the Chola period, including a 12C bronze Shiva as Lord of the Dance (1979.29).

To the right is the *Chinese Room*, with bronzes, ceramics, and a hanging scroll from the Ming dynasty (1979.124). Notable are a large bronze basin from the Han dynasty (1979.108), a T'ang figure of a court lady with cymbals (1979.113), blue and white ware from the Ming dynasty, Sung dynasty celadons, and a pair of 12C Korean foliate bowls and saucers (1979.193.1–4) with celadon glaze.

The final room is devoted to *Japanese arts*. Displayed here are a 6–7C earthenware Haniwa figure (1979.199) of a man with a mitre-shaped hat, a kneeling woman (1979.200) from the Nara period (8C), wooden sculpture, and painting.

The EXPLORERS' CLUB (46 E. 70th St near Park Ave) is a scientific organisation founded in 1904 whose 3500 members from 58 countries include a number of famous explorers: Sir Edmund Hillary and Tenzing Norgay, several of the early astronauts, and Reinhold Messner. The club (not open to the public except for occasional lectures) owns rare books, manuscripts, and paintings of historical value as well as memorabilia of famous explorers. Named Lowell Thomas House after the broadcaster and world traveller who served as honorary club president, the building (1912; Frederick J. Sterner) originally was the home of Stephen C. Clark, younger son of Singer Sewing Machine magnate Edward Clark who built the Dakota Apartments.

To the E. between Park and Lexington Aves is the *Visiting Nurse Service of New York* (107 E. 70th St), formerly the Thomas W. Lamont residence (1921; Walker & Gillette), a Gothic style building built for a parson's son who rose to chair the board of J.P. Morgan & Co. Nearby is the *Paul Mellon House* (125 E. 70th St), one of the few townhouses built after World War II (1965; H. Page Cross), an anachronistic but appealing French Provincial style home.

22   Central Park

SUBWAY: IRT Lexington Ave local or express (train 4, 5, 6) to 59th St. BMT Broadway (N, QB, or RR train) to Fifth Ave.

BUS: Uptown on Madison Ave (M1, M2, M3, M4) and downtown on Fifth Ave (M1, M2, M3, M4). 72nd St crosstown bus (M30) goes E.–W. at 57th St. Crosstown buses on 59th–60th Sts (M103) and 57th St. Culture Bus weekends and holidays, Loop II, stop 17.

CAR PARKING: There is some metered parking along Fifth Ave. Parking lots are located within the park under the Metropolitan Museum of Art, near the Tavern-on-the-Green, near the 79th St Transverse, and near the Loeb Boathouse, but are likely to be filled.

GENERAL INFORMATION. The park is open from dawn to 1 a.m. though it is closed to motorised traffic on weekends and on major holidays. Information at the Dairy; tel: 397–3156; open Tues–Sun, 10–4.30.

CRIME. Central Park has a fearsome reputation for crime which it doesn't entirely deserve since the 22nd Precinct (i.e. Central Park) has the lowerst crime rate in the city. On the other hand, it is foolhardy and naive to wander around alone at night or in remote areas of the park. Company is the best security; either bring your own, join organised tours to isolated areas, or stay around other people. Precinct policemen, urban rangers, and special services men patrol the park and emergency call boxes are located throughout. The first two digits on the metal plate attached to most park lamp-posts (some have been ripped off) tell the approximate cross street: thus 06413 means 106th St and 70235 means 70th St.

ORGANISED TOURS are offered by the Central Park Historical Society, tel: 473–3754; the Central Park Task Force, 737–8810; the Friends of Central Park, 861–9696; and the Urban Park Rangers, 360–8194.

PARK ACTIVITIES. A seasonal schedule of events is available at the Dairy or the Arsenal. To obtain one by mail, send a stamped, self-addressed envelope to Rm 103, the Arsenal, 830 Fifth Ave, New York, N.Y. 10021. Specify season. For daily information call 397–3156.

SPORTS AND RECREATION. *Ball fields*: Permits required for organised athletic activities; tel: 397–3114. The Sheep Meadow is open for frisbee, walking, and picnicking.

Bicycling: On bike paths beside roadways or on roadways when park is closed to traffic.

Boating: For rowing, see Loeb Memorial Boathouse, p 326. For model yachting see Kerbs Memorial Boathouse, p325.

Carriage rides: Grand Army Plaza, Fifth Ave at 60th St. See p294 for rates.

Folk dancing (seasonal), Sat and Sun, 2–6, at King Jagiello statue, 80th St, E. of Belvedere Lake. Tel: 673–3930.

Horseback riding: Rentals at Claremont Stables, 175 W. 89th St, tel: 724–5100.

Ice skating: See Wollman Rink, p329 or Lasker Rink, p330.

Lawn bowling and croquet: Permit required, tel: 360–3430.

Roller skating: On closed road N.E. of Sheep Meadow. See p327.

Running: Jogging path around Reservoir, 1·58 miles. Jogging also on park roads when closed to traffic.

Swimming: See Lasker Pool, p330.

CULTURAL ACTIVITIES. Get seasonal schedule of events.

The Metropolitan Opera: Usually appears at least once during the summer; call 397–3156.

New York Philharmonic: Several summer concerts on Great Lawn. Call 397–3156.

Bandshell concerts: Naumberg Bandshell, include orchestral, jazz, rock, and ethnic programmes. Also performances of New York Grand Opera Co. Call 397–3156 or Department of Cultural Affairs, 360–8196.

Conservatory Garden Concerts: Jazz and popular music during summer months; call 360–8236.

Shakespeare In the Park: Performances Tues–Sun during summer months, except when Metropolitan Opera or New York Philharmonic is performing. See p326.

CHILDREN'S ACTIVITIES. *Puppets* at Swedish Cottage Marionette Theater (see p326) or at Heckscher Puppet House in the Heckscher Playground, 62nd St; call 988–9093 (Swedish Cottage) or 397–3089 (Heckscher Puppet House).

The *Zoo* at 64th St and Fifth Ave is closed for renovation; scheduled reopening, 1986.

Carousel, mid-park at 65th St. See p328.

Story telling at the Hans Christian Andersen statue, see p325.

**Central Park, bounded by 59th St (Central Park South), 110th St (Central Park North), Fifth Ave and Eighth Ave (Central Park West), is the heartland of Manhattan, 843 acres set aside for the recreation of all its citizens. Although the park seems 'natural', the largest surviving piece of Manhattan unencrusted with asphalt and masonry, its landscape and scenery are completely manmade, based on a design by Frederick Law Olmsted and Calvert Vaux.

History. In 1844 poet William Cullen Bryant among others began calling for a public park, noting that even then commerce was devouring every inch of Manhattan and the population sweeping over the land. Andrew Jackson Downing, architect and the pre-eminent landscape designer of the period, added his appeal as did several politicians, and in 1856 the city bought most of what is now the park for $5 million. The land was then desolate, covered with scrubby trees, rocky outcroppings and occasional fields where squatters grazed their pigs and goats; a garbage dump, bone-boiling works, and a rope walk added to the grim and fetid atmosphere. Egbert Viele was hired to survey the land and to supervise its clearing, aided by the police who forcibly ejected the squatters and their livestock.

The board of Park Commissioners (established 1857) decided to hold a competition for the park's design in part because Andrew Jackson Downing, who probably would have been chosen, had recently drowned at the age of 37 trying to rescue his mother-in-law during a steamboat accident. Among 33 entries the Greensward Plan submitted (1858) by Olmsted and Vaux was chosen, a plan, unlike the others, based on enhancing the existing land contours to create a more picturesque, more dramatic landscape.

During the initial 20 years of construction, 10 million cartloads of dirt were

Key to Statuary in Central Park

South

1	Alice in Wonderland	17	Shakespeare
2	Hans Christian Andersen	18	Robert Burns
3	Still Hunt	19	Indian Hunter
4	Angel of the Waters	20	Columbus
5	The Tempest	21	Balto
6	King Jagiello	22	Delacorte Clock
7	Obelisk	23	Dancing Bear
8	Daniel Webster	24	Dancing Goat
9	Schiller	25	Tigress and Cubs
10	Beethoven	26	Sophie Loeb Fountain
11	Victor Herbert	27	Maine Monument
12	Mother Goose		
13	Eagles and Prey	**North**	
14	Samuel F.B. Morse		
15	Fitz-Greene Halleck	1	Frances Hodgson Burnett Fountain
16	Sir Walter Scott	2	A.H. Green Memorial Bench
		3	Untermeyer Fountain

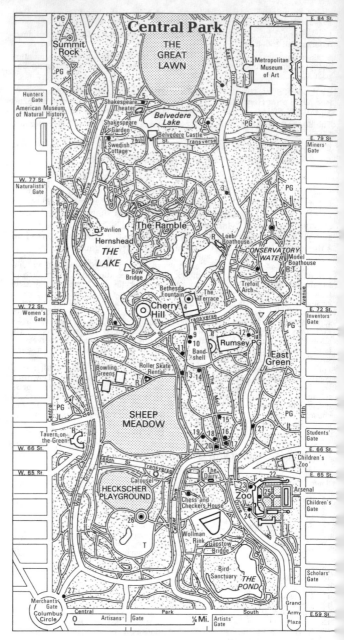

Central Park

THE GREAT LAWN

Summit Rock

PG

PG

E. 84 St.

Metropolitan Museum of Art

Hunters Gate
American Museum of Natural History

Shakespeare Theater
Shakespeare Garden
Swedish Cottage

5

Belvedere Lake

6

Belvedere Castle
79th St. Transverse

7

E. 79 St.
Miners' Gate

PG

W. 77 St.
Naturalists' Gate

3

PG

PG

Pavilion

Hernshead

THE LAKE

The Ramble

R Loeb Boathouse

CONSERVATORY WATER

Model Boathouse
B T

2

Bow Bridge

Trefoil Arch

Bethesda Fountain

Cherry Hill

4

The Terrace

W. 72 St.
Women's Gate

8

72nd St. Transverse

E. 72 St.
Inventors' Gate

9
10 Band-shell
11

12

Rumsey PG

PG

East Green

Bowling Greens

Roller Skate Rental

13 14

The Mall

SHEEP MEADOW

15

19 18 16
20

21

Fifth

PG

Tavern-on-the-Green
R

W. 66 St.

W. 65 St.

65th St. Transverse

Carousel

The Dairy

Students' Gate

E. 66 St.

Children's Zoo

E. 65 St.

22

T

23

Zoo

25

Arsenal

Children's Gate

HECKSCHER PLAYGROUND

Chess and Checkers House

24

26

T

Wollman Rink

Gapstow Bridge

Bird Sanctuary

THE POND

Scholars' Gate

27

Merchants' Gate
Columbus Circle

Central

Artisans'

Park

Gate

South

Grand Army Plaza

E. 59 St.

0

¼ Mi.

Artists' Gate

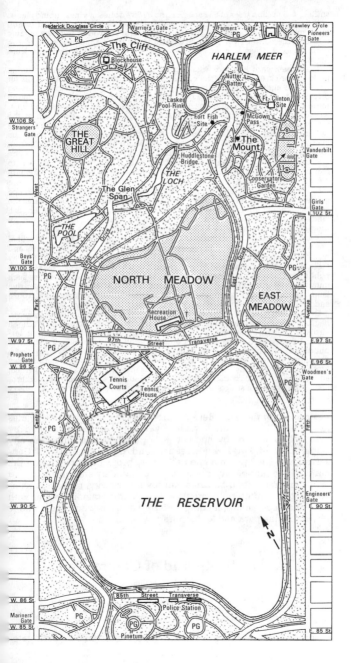

shifted, 4–5 million trees of 632 species and 815 varieties of vines, alpine plants, and hardy perennials were planted, and half a million cubic yards of topsoil were spread over the existing poor soil (some of it recovered from the organic refuse of the earlier swill mills). Sixty-two miles of ceramic pipe were laid to drain marshy areas and to supply water to lawns where hydrants were installed.

The Greensward Plan took into account two features already existing in the park, the brick Arsenal and the old reservoirs, rectangular receiving pools for the Croton aqueduct system that brought water from the Catskills. Curving drives, designed to avoid straightways for horse racing, carried traffic around these obstacles while straight transverse roads depressed below ground level would carry crosstown traffic unobtrusively through the park. North of the reservoir site (later filled in to become the Great Lawn as the present reservoir was created) the land was high and rocky, with good views and the designers chose to leave this area as wild as possible. South of the reservoir were long, rocky glacial ridges running north–south, which would be changed into open meadows, shady glens, and gently sloping hills. The formal element was to consist of a mall, an avenue of trees with a fountain at one end and statuary placed along its length.

In all of this Vaux and Olmsted were influenced by English landscape gardeners beginning with Lancelot 'Capability' Brown, who turned against the earlier preference for symmetrical flower beds and topiary; later the English landscape tradition proceeded from Brown's pastoral ideal to a love of more rugged, craggy scenery—the kind of landscape in the N. end of the park.

Socially the park was intended as a democratic experiment, for the delight of the working classes whose daily lives were often confined to tenements and grim labour as well as for the amusement of the wealthy who could display their clothing, carriages, and horses along the tree-lined drives. It was also a public works project employing a staff of several thousand labourers, as such unfortunately attracting corrupt politicians who saw in its labour-intensive landscape a golden opportunity for patronage (controlling immigrant votes) and for letting out lucrative contracts to cronies in the building trades.

Even before completion the park was a target for unwanted encroachments, beginning with a Racing Track for horses which Olmsted blocked. While an airplane field (1919), trenches (1918) to memorialise World War I, an underground garage for 30,000 cars (1921 and frequently thereafter), and a statue of Buddha (1925) have not materialised, paved playgrounds, skating rinks, swimming and wading pools, a theatre and a zoo have taken park land. Robert Moses, zealous Parks Commissioner from the La Guardia era to 1960, advocated organised sports, accepted various buildings donated by philanthropists, and tore down structures of Olmsted's vintage replacing them with boxy brick buildings.

Restoration of the park. Because the park is ever-popular (estimates range from 13–20 million visitors yearly), it is today ravaged by over-use as well as by neglect. Recognising its fragility, the city Department of Parks & Recreation and the Central Parks Conservancy in 1980 put in motion a 10-year project that will return the park to its former beauty, dredging lakes silted by erosion, resodding lawns and replanting hillsides, improving security, restoring monuments, redesigning buildings to make them harmonise better with the landscape, and planning programmes to encourage public respect for the park and to discourage vandalism.

A. The South End of Central Park

SUBWAY: IRT Lexington Ave local (train 6) to 68th St.

BUS: Uptown on Madison Ave (M1, M2, M3, M4) or downtown on Fifth Ave (same buses). 72nd St crosstown bus (M30). Culture Bus, weekends and holidays, Loop II, stop 15.

Begin at 72nd St and Fifth Ave. In 1862 the original 18 park gates were named, though only three of the gates are actually inscribed, and several others were named later. This is the *Inventors' Gate* (the others bearing inscriptions are the Mariners' and Engineers' Gates).

Clockwise from this point the other named gates are: *Miners' Gate* (79th St and Fifth Ave), *Engineers' Gate* (90th St and Fifth Ave), *Woodmen's Gate* (96th St and Fifth Ave), *Girls' Gate* (102nd St and Fifth Ave), *Vanderbilt Gate* (105th St and Fifth Ave, named later from the gates from the Vanderbilt mansion installed here, see p272), *Pioneers' Gate* (Frawley Circle), *Farmers' Gate* (Central Park North and Lenox Ave), *Warriors' Gate* (Central Park North and Powell Blvd), *Strangers' Gate* (Duke Ellington Blvd, i.e. 106th St and Central Park West), *Boys' Gate* (100th St and Central Park West), *Prophets' Gate* (96th St and Central Park West), *Mariners' Gate* (85th St and Central Park West), *Hunters' Gate* (81st St and Central Park West), *Naturalists' Gate* (77th St and Central Park West), *Women's Gate* (72nd St and Central Park West), *Merchants' Gate* (Columbus Circle), *Artisans' Gate* (Seventh Ave and Central Park South), *Artists' Gate* (Sixth Ave and Central Park South), *Scholars' Gate* (60th St and Fifth Ave), *Children's Gate* (64th St and Fifth Ave) and *Students' Gate* (67th St and Fifth Ave).

On the left side of the road is a playground (1970; Richard Dattner & Assocs), one of 19 along the park perimeter. Nearby, inside an iron fence, is a small-leaved Chinese elm (Ulmus parvifolia), one of the oldest trees in the park. Olmsted hired Ignaz Anton Pilat, an Austrian who had studied in the Imperial Botanical Gardens in Vienna, as nurseryman for the park; Pilat, who chose the varieties to be planted, emphasised native trees and shrubs, especially conifers to give colour during the winter.

Take the first right turn in the path on the N. side of the roadway, and walk to the **Conservatory Water,** named after a conservatory planned here but eventually erected at 104th St. On the east shore of the pond is the KERBS MODEL BOATHOUSE (1954; Aymar Embury II; refreshments and restrooms) where enthusiasts fit out sleek, radio-controlled model yachts. Regattas usually take place Sat mornings during summer months. Walk around to the N. end of the pond and José de Creeft's bronze 11-ft *statue of Alice in Wonderland*, (1960) sitting on a mushroom and surrounded by other characters from the story. Loved by children who clamber all over it, the statue is still an object of distaste to park purists who would prefer all sculpture restricted to the Mall as Vaux and Olmsted originally desired. Hideo Sasaki designed the granite platform, seats, and landscaping.

Continue around the pond to the W. shore (good view of the East Side skyline from here) to the 8-ft seated bronze *statue of Hans Christian Andersen* (1956; Georg Lober) with a 2-ft, 65-lb Ugly Duckling waddling in front.

Storytelling Sat mornings, 11–12, May–Sept. For information tel: 397–3156.

In 1973 a thief sawed the duckling off its base and stole it but it was recovered undamaged several weeks later in a paper bag near a Queens junkyard.

Take the path that leads under the TREFOIL ARCH to the Lake. The brownstone arch with its wooden ceiling, designed by Vaux who planned the original park architecture, is one of a series that revolutionised traffic planning by separating different modes of transportation within the park, an innovative notion in the 19C as were the sunken transverse roads across the park carrying city traffic.

Beyond the arch and to the right is the LOEB MEMORIAL BOATHOUSE (1954), donated by the banking family.

Refreshments and restrooms. Boats for hire during summer months, 9–5 every day. Deposit required. Tel: 288–7707. Behind the boathouse enclosed by an ugly chain-link fence is the bicycle rental concession, open 9–6 every day, Apr–Oct. Tel: 772–7020. $20 deposit required plus two pieces of identification.

N. of the boathouse and bicycle concession along East Drive is Edward Kemeys's *Still Hunt* (1907), a bronze mountain lion crouched on a natural rock. Return to the boathouse.

Continue S.W. around the Lake to the formal *Terrace. At the center is the BETHESDA FOUNTAIN and its statue, *Angel of the Waters* (1873) by Emma Stebbins, one of the few works especially commissioned for the park. It depicts the Biblical angel who descended to the Bethesda pool in Jerusalem giving it healing powers. On the column beneath the angel four plump cherubs represent the particularly 19C virtues of Temperance, Purity, Health, and Peace. The fountain has recently been refurbished and its waterworks engineered to recirculate the flow of water. Plans are underway for restoring the plaza, the eroded hillsides, and the ornamental stonework nearby.

Long side trip for energetic walkers. Follow the shore of the lake to the beautiful cast-iron *Bow Bridge* (1859; Calvert Vaux) which crosses the Lake to the *Ramble*, a heavily planted glen with intricately winding paths and carefully planned cascades in a meandering brook, the *Gill*. Among the trees planted here are Shagbark hickory, Siberian elm, Chinese Pagoda tree, and American cork tree. An artificial cave designed by Vaux and Olmsted as an expression of the reigning spirit of Romanticism has been walled up. N. of the Ramble, a favourite haunt of bird watchers, is *Vista Rock* (elev. 135 ft), site of the BELVEDERE CASTLE (1869), since 1919 used as a weather station and now home of the Central Park Rangers. N. of the castle is the Belvedere Lake and the DELACORTE SHAKESPEARE THEATER on its W. shore, with appropriate sculpture nearby, notably the bronze *Tempest* (1973; Milton Hebald) dedicated to Joseph Papp, theatrical producer who brought free Shakespeare to the park. (Free tickets distributed from 6.15 on the night of performance. Plays held during the summer Tues–Sun at 8 except when opera or Philharmonic concerts are scheduled. For information call the Dairy, 397–3156.)

The *Shakespeare Garden* (E. of West Drive, at the latitude of 80th St) contains plants mentioned in the dramatist's work. The Swedish Cottage, a replica of a Swedish school house made for the Philadelphia Centennial Exposition, houses the *Swedish Cottage Marionette Theater* (Tues–Fri during the academic year for school groups, general admission weekdays in summer and Sat all year; reservations required; tel: 988–9093 for prices and time schedule). BELVEDERE LAKE, formerly New Lake, is the last trace of the old Croton Receiving Reservoir (drained (1920) which once filled the site now occupied by the GREAT LAWN. During the Depression squatters built shanties on the dry reservoir bed from which they could easily see the towers of the El Dorado and other luxury apartments looming over the park. Today the lawn is a favourite place for ball games and during the summer the New York Philharmonic and Metropolitan Opera give free performances (tel: 360–8209 and 360–8196 for information).

To the S.E. of the lawn near Belvedere Lake is a bronze statue of *King Jagiello* (1946; Stanislaw Kazimierz Ostrowski), King of Poland and Grand Duke of Lithuania under whom Poland became a major power. N. of this statue behind the Metropolitan Museum of Art is the 71-ft, 224-ton *Obelisk*, built c. 1600 B.C. by Thotmes III at Heliopolis. It stood there a thousand years until some irate Persians toppled it and then lay on the ground until the Romans set it up on a beach in Alexandria in 16 B.C. near a temple built by Cleopatra, hence its nickname, Cleopatra's Needle. In 1877 the Khedive of Egypt gave it to the city; William H. Vanderbilt paid the $100,000 shipping bill; Cecil B. de Mille, the film producer, presented the plaques translating the heiroglyphs. Since its installation (1881), the pink granite has been attacked by the city's damp climate and air pollution.

Return to the Bethesda Fountain past the Shakespeare Theater, the Swedish Cottage, and the W. shore of the Lake. On the shore S. of 76th St is a promontory known as the *Hernshead* with the *Ladies' Pavilion* (1871; Vaux & Mould), originally a convenience for ladies awaiting streetcars at Columbus Circle, moved here when the Maine monument went up. At the intersection of West Drive and the 72nd St transverse is a 24-ft pedestal bearing a 14-ft *statue of Daniel Webster* (1876; George Ball). In 1863 Ball modelled for mass production a 2-ft statuette of the famous statesman and orator; the present work is a rather unsuccessful enlargement of that original. The area near Central Park West and the 72nd St entrance is being renamed *Strawberry Fields* to honour John Lennon, the songwriter and singer, who was assassinated in the courtyard of the nearby Dakota Apartments in 1980; among his contributions to popular music was a song called 'Strawberry Fields Forever'.

From here either go back to the Bethesda Fountain or continue S. to the Tavern-on-the-Green, an expensive restaurant open to the public (66th St at Central Park West), with a parking lot so conspicuous that critics call the place the Tavern-on-the-Parking Lot. Originally it was the Sheepfold (1870; Jacob Wrey Mould) and until 1934 sheltered a flock of white Southdowns that grazed during the day in the Sheep Meadow. When the sheep were exiled to Prospect Park commissioner Robert Moses converted the Sheepfold to an elegant restaurant, with doormen garbed in top hats, riding boots, and hunting coats, cigarette girls in court costumes, and a 12-piece orchestra on the terrace dressed in forest green. In 1956 Moses wanted to enlarge the parking lot, tearing down trees and paving over a playground to do so. A brigade of parents and conservationists fought for the playground in the courts and on the playground, wheeling baby carriages in front of Moses's bulldozers which had been stealthily brought in after midnight. Eventually the publicity made Moses relent and drop plans for the lot, but not before his previously impeccable reputation had been soiled.

Cut across the Sheep Meadow to the Bethesda Fountain area.

From the Bethesda Fountain, walk through the TERRACE BRIDGE ARCADE, with its fine Minton tile roof and ornamental stonework by Jacob Wrey Mould. On its S. side is the *Mall*, a formal avenue of trees (1212 ft long) set aside by Olmsted and Vaux for the park's statuary; the memorials deposited elsewhere result mainly from a passion for commemorative objects that gripped the city during the last half of the 19C. Near the beginning of the Mall is a *statue of J.C. Friedrich von Schiller* (1859; C.L. Richter), the first portrait statue erected in the park. Nearby are busts of *Beethoven* (1884; Henry Baerer) and *Victor Herbert* (1927; Edmond T. Quinn). On the E. side of the Mall is the NAUMBERG BANDSHELL (free concerts and dance events during the summer; call the Dairy at 397–3156).

Behind the bandstand is the *Pergola*, covered by Chinese wisteria, with the Mary Harriman Rumsey playground behind it, given (1936) by the sister of former governor Averell Harriman. Formerly the Casino, an expensive play spot for high-living adults, stood here, its clientele including mayor James J. Walker who entertained lavishly without always paying his bills. The *statue of Mother Goose* (1938) is by Frederick G.R. Roth.

Return to the Mall through the oak grove and cross over to the W. side. The roadway between the Mall and the Sheep Meadow has been closed to traffic and set aside for roller skating and during pleasant weather talented skaters swirl and dance to music from their own headsets or from the omnipresent large portable radio blaring out disco music for the general enjoyment. (Skates may be rented at Good Skates, N.W. corner of the Sheep Meadow at 69th St, 10–6, seven days a week; tel: 535–1080.) Nearby is Christian Fratin's *Eagles and Prey* (1863), a bronze group of two ferocious eagles sinking their claws into a dead goat. Facing the Mall is Byron M. Pickett's bronze statue (1871) of *Samuel F.B. Morse*, whose skill as a historical painter and miniaturist was eclipsed by his fame as the inventor of the telegraph and of Morse code.

Further down the Mall are (E. side) statues of minor 19C poet *Fitz-Greene Halleck* (1877; James Wilson MacDonald), who also served as John Jacob Astor's private secretary, *Sir Walter Scott* (1871; John Steell), and *Shakespeare* (1864; John Quincy Adams Ward). On the W. side are *Robert Burns* (1880; John Steell) and the **Indian Hunter* (1869; John Quincy Adams Ward), a realistic bronze portrait of an Indian brave grasping his bow and arrow, leaning forward to hold his dog; Ward spent months in the Dakotas sketching Indians to prepare for this work, one of the best in the park. Near the S. end of the Mall is a bronze statue of *Christopher Columbus* (1894; Jeronimo Suñol).

Walk back N. by Shakespeare and Sir Walter Scott to the WILLOWDELL BRIDGE; beyond it is a statue of **Balto* (1925; Frederick G.F. Roth), leader of a team of huskies that carried diphtheria serum across 600 miles of stormy Alaskan wasteland to Nome in 1925. Balto's back and tail have been worn shiny by affectionate petting.

From here a path leads S. to the Children's Zoo and the **Central Park Zoo**, both closed for major renovations and scheduled to re-open in 1986. Although park designers Olmsted and Vaux disapproved of caging animals in urban parks, the park commissioners were deluged with gifts of animals including white mice, cattle, and deer, and to provide shelter for them established a menagerie in the Arsenal which remained there until 1934. The Central Park Zoo, which opened in 1935, expressed the attitudes of the period and included large animals penned in small cages; the present renovation will make the exhibits more suitable to the small scale of the zoo and will feature a formal garden; an outdoor landscaped garden with ponds and islands for otters, snow monkeys, and red pandas; a polar circle for penguins, polar bears, and Arctic foxes, and a tropical building with a simulated rain forest, snakes, frogs, tropical fish, and giant insects. One of the early problems of the renovation has been the relocation of three hard-to-place animals: Tina, a mean-tempered elephant; Caroline, an aged gorilla; and Skandy, a polar bear who killed an apparently deranged man who climbed into his cage at night.

The **Arsenal** (see p296) is now the home of the city Department of Parks and Recreation and Cultural Affairs (open 9–5, weekdays, for general information and permits).

Continue W. of the zoo to the **Dairy** (1870; Calvert Vaux), built as a refreshment stand for mothers and children and now used as the principal information center of the park. At one time the facilities in this part of the park were planned for children, including a stable for the cows that provided the milk for the Dairy, and a play area on a little hill called the Kinderberg, where the CHESS AND CHECKERS HOUSE (1952) now stands. Cross under Center Drive via the PLAYMATES' ARCH just N. of the Chess and Checkers House to the Friedsam Memorial **Carousel** (open every day, weather permitting; 10.30–4.45 week days, and 10.30–5.45 weekends; 50¢).

The *Heckscher Playground* (1925) occupies 17 acres of what Vaux and Olmsted once called The Ball Ground. The concrete dates from 1936 as does the *Sophie Loeb Memorial Fountain* (Frederick G. R. Roth) with characters from 'Alice in Wonderland'.

Cross back under Center Drive via DRIPROCK ARCH (opposite

63rd St) and walk up the hill alongside the popular **Wollman Rink** (ice skating in season; tel: 360–8260). The meandering outline of the **Pond,** which begins at 59th St, was destroyed by the instrusion of the rink and the surrounding land further mutilated during the conversion (1966) of the rink into an amphitheatre for rock concerts, a function it no longer serves.

Continue up the hill past the chain link fence enclosing the Bird Sanctuary and cross the GAPSTOW BRIDGE spanning the Pond where once both swan boats and real swans plied the waters. A few of the latter remain; the boats disappeared in 1934. The Pond, about twice its present size before the advent of the skating rink, was fed by De Voor's Mill Stream which flowed through the park and continued S. and E. to Turtle Bay. Like other city streams it is now channelled underground but its waters can be tapped to fill the pools outside the Corning Glass Building (Fifth Ave at 56th St) during droughts.

From here the path leads S. to Grand Army Plaza at 59th St and Fifth Ave. Lined up along the sidewalk are horsedrawn carriages for hire, the horses shod with shock absorbent rubber shoes (official rate per trip; $17 for the first $1/2$ hour or fraction, $5 for each additional half hour).

B. The North End of Central Park

Note: Since this part of the park is less havily used and has some isolated, wooded areas, you may feel more comfortable taking the route with friends.

SUBWAY: IRT Lexington Ave local (train 6) to 103rd St.

BUS: M1, M2, M3, M4, northbound on Madison Ave. Limited street parking on Fifth Ave.

Begin at the VANDERBILT GATE, Fifth Ave and 105th St, formerly guarding the Cornelius Vanderbilt II mansion where Bergdorf Goodman now stands (58th St at Fifth Ave). Made in Paris (1894) by Bergrotte and Bauviller, the handsome wrought iron gates were donated to the city (1939) by Gertrude Vanderbilt Whitney. Inside the gate is the Conservatory Garden which once had greenhouses and later a fine Conservatory (1899; torn down, 1934) with impressive seasonal displays. The present garden (1936; Thomas D. Price), with its borders of flowering quince, yew hedges, and symmetrical rows of crabapples, is one of the few formal areas in the park. On the hillside is an old Chinese wisteria (Wisteria sinensis) on a wrought iron arbour. Two sculptural fountains adorn the garden. On the left (S.) beyond the trees is the *Frances Hodgson Burnett Memorial* (1936; Bessie Potter Vonnoh), which honours the author of 'Little Lord Fauntleroy'. To the right is the Untermeyer Fountain (1947; Walter Schott), with its three playful girls dancing in a circle. The pedestal contains granite from the Yonkers home of donor Samuel Untermeyer, a wealthy trial lawyer.

Continue past the Untermeyer Fountain and take the left fork of the path that leads up the hill toward McGown's Pass. On the right is the **Harlem Meer** (completed 1866) with its severely vandalised boathouse (scheduled for restoration). At McGown's Pass take the right fork to the remains of FORT CLINTON, built as part of a line of fortifications around the pass. The memorial cannon dates from 1905.

History. The Albany Post Road, built over an old Indian trail, once ran northward more or less along the course of East Drive from 103rd St to 106th St, threading its way between two jutting hills where the remains of Fort Clinton and Fort Fish now stand. During the Revolutionary War the pass became an escape route for Col William Smallwood's Marylanders covering the retreat of the colonial troops after the British invasion at Kip's Bay (15 Sept 1776) and for the rest of the war, British troops and German mercenaries were garrisoned there to protect the city from a northerly invasion. About 30 years later during the War of 1812 the pass again gained strategic importance as New Yorkers realised, following the bombardment of Stonington, Connecticut, that their city was vulnerable to attack by land from the N. A volunteer force that included gentlemanly Columbia College students as well as butchers, lawyers, Free Masons, and tallow chandlers worked by day and night to strengthen the old line of Revolutionary forts from Third Ave to the Hudson. In the McGown's Pass area were Fort Clinton, named after mayor De Witt Clinton, Fort Fish, named after Nicholas Fish, chairman of the defence committee, and NUTTER'S BATTERY.

Descend the hill and follow the path to **The Mount** where McGown's Tavern once stood, now a composting area. The early stone tavern bought from the Dyckman family was replaced in 1790 by a frame house which members of the McGown family ran as an inn until 1845. Two years later the Sisters of Charity of St. Vincent de Paul bought it and added other buildings for use as a convent, Mt Saint Vincent's. When the land was incorporated in the park, park commissioners used the convent buildings for administrative offices and Olmsted lived in one with his family for a while. Later it became a Civil War hospital, a restaurant with a sculpture gallery, and after burning in 1881, a restaurant again; it was finally torn down in 1917. The nearby bench (1928) is a *memorial to Andrew Haswell Green*, park commissioner, lawyer, preservationist (he helped save Niagara Falls from exploitation), and moving force behind the consolidation of the five boroughs into one city. The five American elms planted here to symbolise the boroughs have unfortunately succumbed to Dutch elm disease. Green himself was murdered at the age of 81 by a madman who mistook him for someone else.

Take the path under the East Drive past the site of Fort Fish, and continue to the Huddlestone Bridge. Through the arch you can see the LASKER POOL-RINK, aesthetically one of the most disastrous intrusions in the park, donated, or rather forced upon the park against the objections of the commissioner, by the Loula D. Lasker Foundation (swimming, May–Aug; ice skating and hockey, Oct–April; tel: 397–3142).

Near the bridge is a Cascade, actually a trickle except in wet weather, one of several along a watercourse that begins at **The Pool** near Central Park West and leads to the Harlem Meer. All the bodies of water in the park are artificially created and filled with water from the city system. **The Loch,** as this stream is called, flows through a wooded area which, despite its great natural beauty, suffers neglect and vandalism. Beer bottles, papers, and garbage litter the area; vandals have sprayed graffiti on rocks; bicycle riders in the woods have destroyed undergrowth. Follow The Loch to the W.

Side trip. The Springbanks Arch leads to the North Meadow and its ball fields. At the S.W. edge of the meadow across the 97th St Transverse are tennis courts and the tennis house. (Courts open during spring, summer, and early autumn. Permits required; available at the Arsenal Mon–Fri during working hours or Sat morning. For information call 360–8111.) Beyond the tennis courts is the Reservoir encircled by a running track (1·58 miles). Running clinics organised by the New York Road Runners every Sat during the summer at about 10 a.m.; also occasional races; call 860–4455 for information. Return to The Loch.

At the W. end of The Loch the rocky *Glen Span* leads through the Ravine to **The Pool,** formed by damming an old stream, Montayne's Rivulet (named after a Walloon family who farmed the area), that rose in high ground at Columbus Ave and 95th St and flowed into Harlem Creek at Fifth Ave and 107th St. Around the pond are tulip trees (Liriodendron tulipifera), weeping willows (Salix babylonica), and a handsome bald cypress (Taxodium distichum) with small leaves and fuzzy orange bark.

From here either leave the park by taking the left fork on the S. side of the lake or take the right fork and walk up **The Great Hill** (134 ft), third highest elevation in the park after Summit Rock (137 ft 6 in.) at 83rd St and Central Park West and Vista Rock (135 ft) at the Belvedere Castle. Workmen here in 1864 found evidence of a Revolutionary War encampment—bayonets, shot, and pot hooks. From the summit take a path on the N.W. side of the hill under the drive to the BLOCKHOUSE, built as part of the chain of fortifications for the War of 1812. At one time a cannon was mounted on the platform roof of the fort so that it could fire over the parapet in any direction. From here descend the Great Hill along its W. side to the Boys' Gate at Central Park West and 100th St.

The nearest subway is the IND Eighth Ave local (AA or CC train) or the IND Sixth Ave (B train) at Central Park West and 103rd St. Bus M10 runs N. and S. on Central Park West. There is a crosstown bus (M19) at 96th St.

23 Museum Mile: Fifth Avenue from 79th to 104th Street

SUBWAY: IRT Lexington Ave local (train 6) to 77th St.

BUS: M1, M2, M3 or M4, uptown on Madison Ave and downtown on Fifth Ave. M17 crosstown on 79th St. Culture Bus (weekends and holidays), Loop I; stop 14.

The section of Fifth Ave between 79th and 106th Sts surely has more museums, libraries, archives, and cultural exhibitions than any comparable stretch in the city. Dominating the group is the Metropolitan Museum of Art, but along the E. side of the avenue are nine other institutions, most of them housed in the former homes of millionaires since the sector of Fifth Ave renamed **Museum Mile** in 1981 was once, before the debilitations of the income tax, known as Millionaire's Row. In 1979 the ten institutions formed a consortium to encourage joint ventures and shared resources.

Walk N. to 79th St and W. to Fifth Ave. The palazzo-inspired house at *15 E. 79th St* now occupied by the Rudolf Steiner School was built (1918; McKim, Mead & White) for Thomas Newbold, a lawyer, state senator, and head of the New York State Department of Health. The uninspired brown and white brick 27-story apartment house at *980 Fifth Ave* (1968; Paul Resnick & Harry F. Green) replaces two townhouses known as the Brokaw mansions, built by Isaac Vail

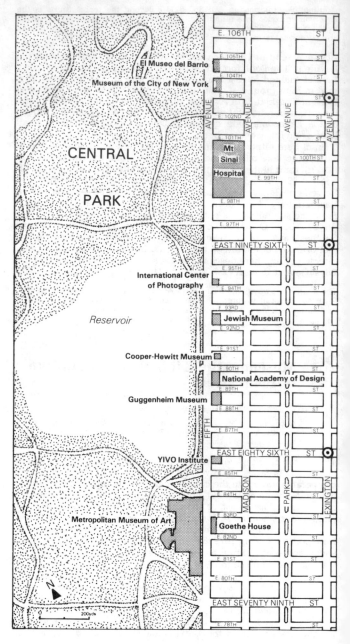

Brokaw, a real estate dealer and clothing manufacturer, for himself and his daughter. They were demolished in 1965 despite efforts of convervationists to save them, the first blows falling surreptitiously at the weekend. Although Brokaw's own mansion was a grand neo-French Renaissance château with turrets and dormers, its real contribution as a landmark was in its demise as public outrage pushed Mayor Robert B. Wagner to sign the Landmarks Preservation Law (1965). The glazed brick apartment at *985 Fifth Ave* (1970; Wechsler & Schimenti) stands where Brokaw built two more houses for his sons.

Cross 80th St. A few of the old townhouses remain. *No. 991 Fifth Ave* (1901; Turner & Killian), now the home of the American Irish Historical Society, was built as a speculative house and at one time was owned by William Ellis Corey, a president of U.S. Steel, who shocked society by marrying (1907) Mabelle Gilman, a musical comedy star. The house with its swell front, ornamental cartouches, and slate mansard roof is a fine example of the Beaux-Arts style. The 16-story apartment at 993 Fifth Ave (1930) exemplifies the work of Emery Roth père (see p421) who liked the classical mode; now his firm is known for its blander, boxier towers (e.g., the General Motors Building, the tower of the Helmsley Palace Hotel).

Continue uptown. On the S.E. corner of 81st St and Fifth Ave is the *Stanhope Hotel* (1926; Rosario Candela) with its pleasant outdoor café. *No. 998 Fifth Ave* (1910; McKim, Mead & White; DL) on the N.E. corner of 81st St has been called 'the finest Italian Renaissance style apartment house in New York City'. Although luxury apartments like the Dakota had been built earlier, only after the turn of the century did the city's elite families begin to succumb to the advantages of apartments. Among the first tenants here were Murry Guggenheim, Elihu Root, secretary of state and Nobel Peace Prize winner, and Levi P. Morton, banker and vice-president under Benjamin Harrison. The rental agent reputedly offered Root a cut-rate rent, hoping thus to lure his social equals into the building.

Another Beaux-Arts townhouse, handsomely ornamented with wrought iron and limestone, stands at the S.E. corner of 82nd St (1009 Fifth Ave). Built speculatively (1901; Welch, Smith & Provot), it was sold to Benjamin N. Duke, brother of James B. Duke (see p302) and has remained in the family ever since; it is one of the few Fifth Ave mansions surviving as single family residences.

Most of the block facing Fifth Ave between 82nd and 83rd Sts remained unbuilt until the 1920s. Today with its one early 20C townhouse squeezed in by newer, larger apartment buildings, it illustrates changing patterns of living in the second decade of the century as expensive, impractical townhouses gave way to more efficient apartments. The remaining townhouse at 1014 Fifth Ave (1907; Welch, Smith & Provot), a handsome Beaux-Arts building first owned by banker and broker James Francis Aloysius Clark, now belongs to the Federal Republic of Germany which operates it as **Goethe House New York.**

Open Tues and Thurs, 11–7; Wed, Fri, and Sat, 12–5. Gallery and library closed during summer. Admission free. Tel: 744–8310.

A branch of the Goethe Institute in Munich, Goethe House offers film programmes, lectures, exhibitions, musical and theatrical performances. The library has more than 16,000 volumes on German culture and history as well as current issues of German newspapers and periodicals and an extensive record collection.

The *Marymount School* on the S.E. corner of Fifth Ave and 84th St occupies a trio of townhouses (1026, 1027, and 1028 Fifth Ave) previously occupied by wealthy but unremarkable bankers, oil refiners, real estate dealers, leather manufacturers, and dairymen. The two southern houses were built (1903; Van Vleck & Goldsmith) as a pair; the corner house (1903; Charles Pierrepont H. Gilbert) first belonged to Jonathan Thorne, an art lover who spent the last two decades of his life collecting beautiful objects with which to adorn this elegant Beaux-Arts house.

Continue uptown. Only one early home survives in the block between 84th–85th Sts, *1033 Fifth Ave*, designed as a brownstone (1878; Stephen D. Hatch) but altered in 1912 to the then-fashionable Beaux-Arts style. The 17-story apartment at *1040 Fifth Ave* (between 85th and 86th Sts) is another work (1930) of Rosario Candela. Candela was born in Sicily, immigrated to the United States at the age of 19, and graduated from the Columbia School of Architecture (1915) three years later. In addition to building luxury apartments in the city's most elite precincts, he published two books on cryptography.

One of the finest mansions along the avenue is the *William Starr Miller mansion* (1914; Carrère & Hastings) on the S.E. corner of 86th St. Miller, who had investments in railroads and banking worth more than $3 million at the time of his death (1935), divided his time between this house and his Newport mansion, 'High Tide'. His daughter married an English baron. Later Grace Wilson Vanderbilt, widow of Cornelius Vanderbilt III, bought the house (1944); after her death (1953) the YIVO INSTITUTE FOR JEWISH RESEARCH took it over. Built of red brick and limestone, crowned with a slate mansard roof and embellished with Ionic pilasters, brackets, scrolls, balustrades, rosettes, and bullseye windows, the mansion is reminiscent of the 16C houses in the Place des Vosges in Paris, not surprising since both Carrère and Hastings had studied at the École des Beaux Arts and were known for their work in French classical styles.

The YIVO Institute houses 300,000 books, 100,000 photographs, ceremonial objects, and 22 million archival documents on the history of East European Jews and their descendants.

Open Mon–Fri, 9.30–5.30. Admission free. Tel: 535–6700.

The name YIVO is an acronym for Yidisher Visnshaftlekher Institut (Institute for Jewish Research), an institute founded in 1925 in Vilna for graduate students of Yiddish and East European Jewish history. Exhibitions focus on East European and American Jewish history and culture.

Facing Fifth Ave between 88th and 89th Sts is the ***Solomon R. Guggenheim Museum** (1071 Fifth Ave), Frank Lloyd Wright's only New York building (completed 1959), the repository of a collection of some 4000 paintings, sculptures, and works on paper from the Impressionist period to the present.

Open Wed–Sun and holidays, 11–5; Tues, 11–8; closed Mon except holidays; closed Christmas Day. Adults, $2; Students, senior citizens, $1.25. Tues evening 5–8, free. Tel: 860–1313. Restaurant, open 11–5. Taped tours of the museum building, special exhibitions, and the Justin K. Thannhauser wing available at admissions desk.

One of the city's most controversial and distinctive buildings, the museum in form is a spiral with a ramp cantilevered out from its interior walls sitting above a horizontal slab. The ramp, 1416 ft long (about a quarter of a mile) rises 1·75 inches per 10 ft to a domed skylight 92 ft above the ground. The ramp diameter at ground level is 100 ft; at the top, 128 ft. Wright called the building 'organic' architecture, imitating the forms and colours of nature, though his critics called it a bun, a snail, and an insult to art. Sixteen years elapsed between Wright's original design and the completion of the building, many of them spent in arguments with the city Department of Buildings whose ideas on construction differed from Wright's and in quarrels with former museum director James Johnson Sweeney, who argued that Wright's ideas would create serious problems storing and hanging the collection. Today the interior of the building is much admired as a work of art though not as a display space for paintings. The addition facing 89th St (1968) is by William Wesley Peters, Wright's son-in-law.

History. Solomon R. Guggenheim was the fourth of seven Guggenheim brothers whose father Meyer Guggenheim arrived from Switzerland in 1848. He began as an itinerant peddler and made a fortune based on mining and smelting. Like other American millionaires Solomon set out to collect art, concentrating at first on Old Masters, until in 1927 he met Baroness Hilla Rebay von Ehrenwiesen, an artist from whom he commissioned a portrait. She introduced him to her friends, painters like Delaunay, Gleizes, Léger, Chagall, Kandinsky, and Rudolf Bauer, the last two of whom she intensely admired. Guggenheim in turn admired Hilla Rebay and guided by her intensity and enthusiasm began collecting modern painters. At first he hung his collection on the walls of his apartment in the Plaza Hotel, relegating the Old Masters to his wife's bedroom; later he rented space in Carnegie Hall and installed Rebay as custodian. In 1939 the Solomon R. Guggenheim Collection of Non-Objective Painting was shown in rented quarters at 24 E. 54th St with the baroness in charge. The idea of building a splendid museum and of hiring Frank Lloyd Wright to design it apparently came from Hilla Rebay, who had long wanted to create a temple to art, rather in the manner of Wagner's Bayreuth, and to use it to display the work of her beloved Bauer. Solomon Guggenheim, however, died long before the museum could be built and the realisation of the building was left to Hilla Rebay and Harry Guggenheim, Solomon's successor. The relationship between them was always tense, exploding finally as Hilla insulted Harry Guggenheim with anti-Semitic remarks. James Johnson Sweeney succeeded her as museum director and under his guidance the Guggenheim Museum became less eccentric in its purchases; Sweeney added some 250 paintings to the collection including Picassos and Cézannus which Rebay would have outlawed on grounds that they were objective.

Take the elevator to the top ramp and walk down. The collection is shown through changing exhibitions and in two galleries with permanent installations. The gallery off the fourth ramp of the spiral emphasises works of 20C PIONEERS: *Klee*, The Red Balloon (48.1172 × 524); *Robert Delaunay*, Eiffel Tower (37.463), *Léger*, Woman Holding a Vase (58.1508), The Great Parade (62.1619); *Chagall*, Green Violinist (37.446), Paris through the Window (37.438); *Kandinsky*, Blue Mountain (41.505); *Mondrian*, Composition (49.1228); *Picasso*, Accordionist (37.537), and *František Kupka*, Large Nude (68.1860), among others. In the JUSTIN K. THANN-HAUSER WING are works primarily from the Impressionist and Post-Impressionist periods donated by the late Mr Thannhauser (1978) hung with selected paintings from the museum's original collection. In the first room are *Vuillard*, Place Vintimille (T74); *Renoir*, Woman with Parrot (T68) and Still Life: Flowers (T70); *Manet*, Before the Mirror (T27) and Woman in Evening Dress (T28);

Fifth Ave at 89th St in 1868. N.Y. artist Ralph Blakelock painted these squatters' hovels dotting the upper stretches of the avenue after the Civil War, displacing former country estates. (Museum of the City of New York)

Modigliani, Young Girl Seated (T31), Nude (41.535), Portrait of a Student (45.997). In the second room are paintings by Picasso and Braque, notably *Picasso*, Le Moulin de la Galette (T34), Woman Ironing (T41) and Woman with Yellow Hair (T59), and *Braque*, The Buffet (81.21.21). In the third room are Post-Impressionists and Fauves: *Cézanne*, Flask, Glass and Jug (T3), Plate of Peaches (T4), Man with Crossed Arms (54.1387), Mme Cézanne (T5) and Bibémus (T6); two Tahitian landscapes by *Gauguin*, Haere Mai (T16) and In the Vanilla Grove, Man and Horse (T15); *Van Gogh*, Mountains at Saint-Rémy (T24); *Rousseau*, Artillerymen (38.711) and The Football Players (60.1583); *Toulouse-Lautrec*, Au Salon (T73) and paintings by Seurat, Picabia, and Kees van Dongen.

The collection of Peggy Guggenheim and the Palazzo Venier dei Leoni in Venice where she housed it were donated to the museum in 1974 and legally transferred upon her death in 1979. Since she stipulated that the paintings should remain there unless Venice sank, the Solomon R. Guggenheim Foundation refurbished the palazzo and reinstalled the paintings including works by Braque, Picasso, Picabia, Pollock, Brancusi, Ernst, and Gorky.

A block N. between 89th and 90th Sts is the *National Academy of Design* (1083 Fifth Ave).

Academy open Tues–Sun, 12–5. Closed Mon. Admission $1. Tel: 369–4880.

The townhouse facing Fifth Ave (1914; Ogden Codman, Jr) where the academy holds its exhibitions was donated (1940) by Archer M. Huntington, whose wife Anna Hyatt Huntington was an academy member. The academy, as the name implies, is a conservative institution, its members drawn from the ranks of the nation's established painters, sculptors, and graphic artists. Founded in 1825 as a school and exhibition center by painters Samuel F.B. Morse and

Rembrandt Peale, architect Ithiel Town, sculptor John Frazee, and engraver Peter Maverick, the academy has a collection of more than 2000 paintings and 200 works of sculpture, in part the product of a ruling that elected members supply a representative sample of their work. The programme includes loan exhibitions, works drawn from the collection, and an annual juried show. The most famous of the academy's several homes was a fantastic Venetian Gothic building at 23rd St and Fourth Ave, now Park Ave South, whose facade is now incorporated in Our Lady of Lourdes Church (427. W. 142nd St; see p396). The academy maintains an art school around the corner at 3–5 E. 89th St. North of the academy on the S.E. corner of Fifth Ave at 90th St is the Protestant Episcopal CHURCH OF THE HEAVENLY REST (1929; Hardie Philip of Mayers, Murray & Philip), a Gothic church with external sculpture by Ulrich Ellerhausen and a pulpit madonna by Malvina Hoffman. The rose window is by J. Gordon Guthrie and the clerestory windows are by J.H. Hogan. Off the S aisle is the Chapel of the Beloved Disciple, originally a separate congregation.

Continue N. At 2 E. 91st St (S.E. corner of Fifth Ave) is the *Cooper-Hewitt Museum, the Smithsonian Institution's National Museum of Design, presiding over the neighbourhood in a mansion built for millionaire Andrew Carnegie (1901; Babb, Cook & Willard).

Open Tues, 10–9; Wed–Sat, 10–5; Sun, 12–5. Closed Mon and major holidays. Admission: $1·50; Tues. eve 5–9, free; children under 12, free; senior citizens and students, $1. Tel: 860–6868.

History. Andrew Carnegie, an immigrant from Scotland, began as a bobbin boy in a cotton factory and evolved into an industrial genius, amassing a fortune in iron, coal, steel, steamship and railroad lines. When he bought the land for his mansion, it was a rocky, semi-rural plot between Yorkville and Harlem, far N. of the dwellings of his financial equals, although developers had begun to erect brownstones nearby. As architects he chose Babb, Cook & Willard, a firm whose reputation was established with industrial buildings but which later moved on to grander schemes. What Carnegie asked for was 'the most modest, plainest, and roomiest house in New York', and what he got was this 64-room mansion, remarkably comfortable and technically advanced for its time, well-suited for his domestic needs and for the philanthropic projects he administered from his first floor library and office. The sub-basement was filled with pumps and boilers, the most advanced and sophisticated available, with two of each major piece so that a spare could be used should the primary piece malfunction. If city water or electricity were interrupted, an artesian well and generator would relieve the family and servants of any inconvenience. Up in the attic great fans pulled air through cheese-cloth filters over tanks of cool water in a primitive system of air-conditioning. The house was the first private residence in the city with a structural steel frame, an Otis passenger elevator, and central heating.

The Building. Enter from 91st St. An ornate copper and glass canopy shelters the door. The marble vestibule leads to the Great Hall panelled in Scottish oak, an indication of Carnegie's affection for his homeland, to which he returned yearly. At the E. end of the hall stood the organ, its pipes in a shaft now used for the elevator. On the W. end was Carnegie's study, now used as a gallery. Carnegie, like Fiorello La Guardia, was 5 ft 2 inches tall and the doorways leading into the library and office are appropriate in scale. Along the S. side of the first floor, facing the garden, were public rooms—the Music Room on the W. with a large crystal chandelier and musical motifs, including a Scottish bagpipe, in the ceiling mouldings. Next to the Music Room is the garden vestibule with leaded glass windows by Louis Tiffany. The formal dining room was E. of the vestibule and adjacent to it a breakfast room facing the garden and conservatory, which had an elevator to the potting shed below. All these are currently used for displays.

Upstairs were family bedrooms and a family library with elaborately carved teakwood trim designed by Lockwood de Forest who used the same material on his own townhouse near Greenwich Village (see p202). Across the garden facing 90th St is a townhouse that formerly belonged to Carnegie's daughter, Mrs Margaret Carnegie Miller, now used for museum administration.

The Museum. In 1897 the granddaughters of Peter Cooper (see p176), Sarah, Eleanor, and Amy Hewitt, impressed on their travels by the South Kensington Museum (now the Victoria and Albert Museum) in London and the Musée des Arts Décoratifs in Paris, opened the Cooper Union Museum for the Arts of Decoration. Early acquisitions included three European textile collections given by J.P. Morgan and Italian architectural and decorative drawings belonging to the Cavaliere Giovanni Piancastelli, curator of the Borghese collection. Although the collections increased over the years in size and quality, the museum could not continue its activities because of financial pressures and closed in 1963. A committee was formed to save it, its collections entrusted to the Smithsonian Institution, and the name changed to its present form. In 1972 the Carnegie Corporation deeded the mansion to the museum.

The collections are shown in a series of changing exhibitions with no permanent display. Holdings include more than 30,000 examples of drawings and prints, most of them restricted to architecture, design, and ornament, including Italian architectural designs, French textile designs, American wood engravings, N. European woodcuts, designs for theatre scenery and costumes, and a large selection of 19C American drawings. The collection of ceramics includes European and oriental porcelain, stoneware, and earthenware including faience and majolica, and 19C figurines. There is a growing collection of glass. Also furniture, architectural woodwork and hardware, wallpaper, bandboxes, goldsmiths' work, jewellery, work in minor metals, locks and keys, and a vast collection of fabrics and textiles including Egyptian, Near Eastern, and Mediterranean fabrics from the 3–15C. Among the more amusing trifles in the collection are valentines, Christmas tree ornaments, feather pictures, and sand toys. The library is the most comprehensive reference collection of design and decorative arts in the city and is open for research.

Across the street at 1 E. 91st St (N.E. corner of Fifth Ave) is the **Convent of the Sacred Heart** (1918; Charles Pierrepont H. Gilbert & J. Armstrong Stenhouse; DL), built as the mansion of Otto Kahn— financier, philanthropist, and patron of the arts. One of the largest and most restrained neo-Italian palazzi in the city, the house has unusual arched carriage entrances. Kahn, a member of the German-Jewish elite known as 'Our Crowd', was chairman of the board of the Metropolitan Opera which he saved from artistic indifference, bringing Giulio Gatti-Casazza as manager and Toscanini as conductor from La Scala in Milan; he also donated an estimated $2·5 million from his own pocket to save it from bankruptcy.

Next door are the neo-Renaissance mansions of two more eminently successful capitalists: No. 7 E. 91st St (1902; Warren & Wetmore; DL), now part of the convent, and the **Consulate of the U.S.S.R.** (1909; Carrère & Hastings; DL). The first was built for James A. Burden, scion of Henry Burden, whose iron works in Troy, New York, produced most of the horseshoes for the Union Army during the Civil War, at the rate of 3600 per hour. The present consulate started as the home of John Henry Hammond, whose daughter married Benny Goodman. The house became the Soviet consulate in 1942, and the driveway gate was added in 1976.

Continue N. on Fifth Ave. On the S.E. corner of 92nd St is **No. 1107 Fifth Ave** (1925; Rouse & Goldstone), a building remarkable for once having had the 54-room, three-story apartment of Marjorie Meriwether Post (whose fortune came from breakfast cereals) and her husband E.F. Hutton (the stock broker). The Palladian window two floors down from the cornice facing the park opened into her foyer; the port cochère on 92nd St led to the vestibule of her private elevator. The apartment has long since been subdivided.

At 1109 Fifth Ave on the N.E. corner of 92nd St is the *Jewish Museum, under the auspices of the Jewish Theological Seminary of America.

Open Mon–Thurs, 12–5; Sun 11–6; closed Fri, Sat, major Jewish holidays and some legal holidays. Adults $2; children under 16 and students, $1. Tel: 860–1888.

The Jewish Museum offers changing exhibitions from the most extensive collection of Judaica in the world, including an outstanding group of Jewish coins and medals, archaeological artifacts, and fine arts. The collection is housed in the former *Felix M. Warburg mansion* (1908; Charles Pierrepont H. Gilbert) which was donated by his widow Frieda Schiff Warburg in 1944; to this French Renaissance mansion has been annexed the Albert A. List wing (1962; Samuel Glazer), whose uninspired modern architecture detracts from the pleasure of the older building.

THE COLLECTIONS. On the ground floor are changing exhibitions in the Joe and Emily Lowe Gallery of the new wing.

Upstairs on the *Second Floor* (in the Warburg mansion) are ceremonial objects, fine arts, books, and manuscripts from the permanent collection. The Harry G. Friedman collection, gathered by the Wall St financier, includes ceremonial objects, folk art, drawings, and prints from Europe, N. Africa, Syria, Palestine, Persia, and India. The Benjamin and Rose Mintz collection purchased by the museum in 1947 includes 500 objects of Polish-Jewish culture: kiddush cups, Hannukah lamps, tefillin bags, Torah crowns and wrappers. In the Benguiat Collection is a Torah ark from the synagogue of Urbino dating from 1551. The Danzig Collection arrived in 10 crates in 1939, communal property sold by Jews of that city to raise funds for emigration.

On the *Third Floor* is a permanent archaeological exhibition focusing on Biblical archaeology and including photographs and maps illustrating Jewish biblical history. Objects, primarily from the Holy Land, date from the Bronze and Iron Ages and from periods of Persian, Hellenistic, and Roman domination. Also on the third floor is a permanent exhibition of coins and medals.

Continue N. There are several fine townhouses on 93rd St between Madison and Park Aves. The **Smithers Alcoholism Center of the Roosevelt Hospital** (1932; Walker and Gillette; DL) occupies a house built for William Goadby Loew—stockbroker and sportsman—and is one of the last great New York mansions, a fine example of the 'American Adam' style with Palladian and bull's-eye windows and an elegantly curved white limestone facade. Later the house belonged to Billy Rose, theatrical producer, art collector, and inventor of the Aquacade. The PERMANENT MISSION OF ROMANIA TO THE U.N. (1930; John Russell Pope; DL) occupies a house once owned by Virginia Graham Fair Vanderbilt. The SYNOD OF BISHOPS OF THE RUSSIAN ORTHODOX CHURCH OUTSIDE RUSSIA (75 E. 93rd St) has taken over the Francis F. Palmer House (1918; Delano & Aldrich; DL). While banker George F. Baker owned the house during the late 1920s, he added the garden courtyard and the wing to the W. with a ballroom. Beneath the house ran a spur from the New York Central line under Park Ave so that Baker could take his private railroad car all the way home.

Look S. down Park Ave to the Louise Nevelson sculpture at 92nd St, moved here from the entrance to Central Park at Fifth Ave and 60th St. *Night Presence IV* (1972), a work of Cor-Ten steel (22 ft high, 13 ft wide, 9 ft deep) was given to the city by the artist who said at the presentation ceremony that she felt it fitting since New York represented 'the whole of [her] conscious life'.

Return along 93rd St to Fifth Ave. Look uptown as you cross Madison Ave to the FACADE OF THE SQUADRON A ARMORY (1895; John Rochester Thomas; DL) along the E. side of the avenue between 94th–95th Sts. At one time this facade with its virtuoso brickwork and fanciful towers, machicolations, crenellations, and arched doorways, was part of a building that filled the block and housed Squadron A of the First New York Hussars, later reorganised as the 105th Machine Gun Battalion. Until 1966 when threatened with demolition it hosted horse shows and polo matches. Today it is the W. wall of a playground that serves *Hunter High School* (1971; Morris Ketchum, Jr), designed to complement the remains of the old armoury.

Return to Fifth Ave. At 1130 Fifth Ave (N.E. corner of 94th St) is the **International Center of Photography** (ICP), a museum with changing exhibitions of traditional, avant-garde, documentary, and land-scape photography.

Open Tues, 11–8; Wed–Sun, 11–5. Closed Mon. Adults, $1·50; students, 50¢; senior citizens and children under 8, free. Tues 5–8, free. Tel: 860–1777.

Founded (1974) by Cornell Capa, the museum has a growing permanent collection of photographs by 20C photographers including Henri Cartier-Bresson, Andreas Feininger, Ernst Haas and W. Eugene Smith. The Federal style house (1914; Delano & Aldrich; DL) now occupied by the museum was built for Willard Straight, diplomat, financier, and founder of the 'New Republic' magazine. Straight, who spent much of his adult life in the Far East, volunteered for service in World War I and died of pneumonia contracted in the line of duty four years after the house was completed.

Continue N. on Fifth Ave. The RUSSIAN ORTHODOX CATHEDRAL OF SAINT NICHOLAS (1902; DL) just E. of the avenue (15 E. 97th St), with its five onion domes, gold crosses, red, blue, and yellow majolica tiles, and ornate terracotta, is an exotic form in a staid neighbourhood. Between 98th and 101st Sts along Fifth Ave is MOUNT SINAI HOSPITAL, whose medical school is associated with the City University of New York. Originally known as 'Jews' Hospital', Mount Sinai was founded in 1852 by a group of Jews including Sampson Simson, one of the city's wealthiest citizens who donated land for the original buildings on 28th St. The older buildings of the present complex date from 1904; the newest addition, a large, dark, rusty tower (436 ft, sheathed in Cor-Ten steel) is the *Annenberg Building* (1976; Skidmore, Owings & Merrill). In the central plaza is a sculptural *Sphere* (1967) by Arnaldo Pomodoro.

Opposite 101st St at the edge of Central Park is a *memorial to Arthur Brisbane* (1939; Richard Barth), a journalist and editorial columnist for several Hearst newspapers.

The NEW YORK ACADEMY OF MEDICINE (1926; York & Sawyer) at 2 E. 103rd St (S.E. corner of Fifth Ave) is a picturesque eclectic (Byzantine, Italian, Romanesque) building whose library contains in addition to the expected scientific tomes an astonishing collection of cookery books, the gift of Dr Margaret Barclay Wilson, who donated (1930) 4000 volumes on food and nutrition to assist workers in dietetics. The rarest item in the collection is a manuscript on roast boar duplicated only at the Vatican. Dr Wilson also translated and edited the *De re coquinaria* of Apicius Caelius.

Library open to the public Mon 12.30–5; Tues–Fri 9–5. Abridged hours during summer.

At Fifth Ave and 103rd St is the *****Museum of the City of New York,** founded in 1923 to familiarise New Yorkers with the history and culture of their city.

Open Tues–Sat, 10–5.30; Sun and holidays, 1–5; closed Mon. Admission free; donations welcome. No restaurant. Tel: 534–1672.
The museum is particularly suitable for children and is visited by large numbers of school groups during the academic year.

On the GROUND FLOOR is the *Fire Gallery*, with antique fire engines, prints and paintings of famous New York fires, fire engine models, and memorabilia associated with fire fighting.

Left of the main entrance on the FIRST FLOOR is the *****Dutch*

Gallery with dioramas and models covering the rise of the Dutch nation in the 16C, the age of exploration, Dutch and Indian life in New Amsterdam. There is a large model of a Dutch fort and a detailed model of New Amsterdam in 1660 based on the Castello plan. The corridor beyond the rotunda, the *English and Revolutionary War Gallery* with furniture, prints, portraits (including two Gilbert Stuart portraits of George Washington), maps and views of the city, focuses on the history of New York after the British conquest in 1664. The BIG APPLE, a multimedia display, uses film and objects from the collection to dramatise the city's history.

On the SECOND FLOOR at the N. end of the corridor are six period rooms showing New York interiors from the late 17C Dutch period to the early 20C. At the W. end of the gallery is a stained glass window by Richard Morris Hunt (53.1.29) taken from the home of a financier, Henry G. Marquand. In the corridor outside the period rooms is the *Alexander Hamilton Collection,* including his desk and furniture and portraits of him and his wife by John Trumbull and Ralph Earl. Other portraits here are by John Durand, John Singleton Copley, and Gilbert Stuart. In the *J. Clarence Davies Gallery* are displayed paintings, prints, maps, and documents concerning the history of the city from Davies's remarkable collection started in 1892; at his death in 1934 it numbered 15,000 items. The *Silver Gallery* in the middle of the building includes work by Dutch, English, and early New York silversmiths and portraits of New Yorkers. In the *Stock Exchange Gallery* dioramas and a display of documents and memorabilia illustrate the history of Wall St and the New York Stock Exchange. At the end of the corridor an exhibit called the **Port of New York* offers outstanding ship models, figureheads, paintings, photographs, and maps to trace the history of New York as a maritime city from 1524 to the present.

On the THIRD FLOOR (N. end) is the *Communications Gallery* with dioramas and memorabilia beginning with early letters and postmarks and proceeding through the advent of electric communications, telegraph, telephone, radio, and television. In the **Toy Gallery* are changing exhibits from the museum's outstanding collection of dolls and toys. The permanent doll's house exhibition has period doll's houses and furniture from 1769 to the present including an architectural model of the library of the Frick mansion, the Goelet House (1845) modelled on the former brownstone at 890 Broadway (19th St) and the Stettheimer House (1925) with miniature reproductions of works of art by Marcel Duchamp, Gaston Lachaise, William Zorach, and others. The dolls represent leading figures in the arts at the time, including Gertrude Stein, Virgil Thompson and Edward Steichen. The *Costume Gallery* has changing exhibits of historical costumes. Paintings and furniture of the late 18C and early 19C are displayed in the corridor. At the S. end of the hall is a gallery for special exhibitions and a gallery for changing exhibits of material from the museum's fine theatre collection.

The Fourth Floor houses museum offices. On the FIFTH FLOOR are the *John D. Rockefeller Rooms,* the bedroom and dressing room from the Rockefeller home at 4 East 54th St decorated in the style of Charles Eastlake, removed *in toto* to the museum.

Between 104th–105th Sts along Fifth Ave is EL MUSEO DEL BARRIO (1230 Fifth Ave), the only museum in the nation devoted to the culture of Puerto Rico and Latin America. Founded in 1969 as a neighbourhood museum in a public school classroom in East Harlem, it is housed today in a building formerly used by the Heckscher Foundation for Children and the New York Society for the Prevention of Cruelty to Children.

Open Tues–Fri, 10.30–4.30; Sat and Sun 11–4. Closed Mon. Admission free but contributions welcome. Tel: 831–7272.

In addition to a handsomely mounted permanent exhibition of Santos de Palo, a folk religious art form, the museum offers four or five exhibitions of paintings and graphic arts yearly. The f: STOP Gallery has shows of photography. In the permanent collection are paintings, pre-Colombian objects, farm and household implements, sculpture, works on paper, and photographs.

The nearest subway is the IRT Lexington Ave local (train 6) at Lexington Ave and 103rd St. More pleasant are downtown buses on Fifth Ave or uptown buses on Madison Ave. There is a crosstown bus at 96th St (M 19).

24 The Metropolitan Museum of Art

SUBWAY: IRT Lexington Ave express or local (trains 4, 5, or 6) to 86th St.

BUS: M1, M2, M3, or M4 uptown on Madison Ave or downtown on Fifth Ave. M17 or M18 crosstown on 79th and 86th Sts.

CAR PARKING: Garage under the museum, enter from Fifth Ave at 80th St; garage open 24 hours; arrive early to avoid waiting.

Founded in 1870 by a group of civic leaders, art collectors, and philanthropists, the **METROPOLITAN MUSEUM OF ART** is now the largest art museum in the western hemisphere. Its collections include more than 3·3 million works from ancient, medieval, and modern times and from all over the world.

Open Tues, 10–8.45; Wed–Sat, 10–4.45; Sun and holidays, 11–4.45. Closed Mon, New Year's Day, Thanksgiving Day, and Christmas. Suggested donations: Adults, $4·00; children, students, and senior citizens, $2·00.
 Restaurant and snack bar. Gallery tours, lectures, concerts, and film showings. Recorded tours available at the Audio Desk in the Great Hall and at certain special exhibitions. Special programmes for senior citizens and the disabled. For information on libraries and study rooms, call 879–5500. Gift shops offer a large selection of books, children's publications, postcards, prints, posters, reproductions of sculpture, jewellery, and other works in the collections.
 Certain galleries may be closed for part of each day because of a shortage of guards. For current schedule, inquire at the main information desk in the Great Hall. For recorded information, call 535–7710. For recorded information on concerts and lectures, call 744–9120.

EXTERIOR: The building housing the museum has grown from its modest Ruskinian Gothic beginnings to encompass 1·4 million square feet and to reflect the reigning architectural styles of the past century.

The rear facade (1874–80; Calvert Vaux and Jacob Wrey Mould) originally faced Central Park and is partially visible from the Lehman wing. To it were added N. and S. wings (1894; Arthur L.T. Tuckerman and 1888; Theodore Weston) both largely covered or demolished by later expansion. The central Fifth Ave pavilion, the present facade of the museum, was designed by

Richard Morris Hunt (1902) and executed by his son Richard Howland Hunt, while the N. and S. wings facing the avenue (1911 and 1913) are the work of McKim, Mead & White. Recent expansion undertaken by Roche, Dinkeloo & Assocs has resulted in the redesign of the Fifth Ave stairs and the addition of three glass-walled wings on the other facades: the Lehman wing (1975) to the rear, the Sackler wing (1979) to the N., and the Rockefeller wing (1982) to the S. The entire building is a designated landmark.

The large uncarved blocks above the columns of Hunt's imposing neo-classical facade were to be carved into allegorical groups representing major periods in the history of art, but funds never became available. The recent building programme has aroused criticism among park conservationists, who resent the museum's intrusion into the park, and among architectural critics who have labelled the new additions banal and flashy.

The Fifth Ave entrance leads directly into the **Great Hall,** designed by Richard Morris Hunt and designated one of the city's few interior landmarks. Over the two-story hall are three domes with circular skylights and a balcony with imposing hemispherical arches. The floral exhibits, whose scale matches that of the hall, are changed weekly.

The **information desk** in the center of the room has floor plans, notices of special exhibitions and events, and information for disabled visitors. At the N. end of the hall is the desk for renting **recorded tours** of various exhibits. Two gift shops opening off the Great Hall offer museum reproductions and a large selection of books on art history, architecture and other subjects pertinent to museum exhibits.

On the left side of the hallway in an architectural niche near the Great Staircase is a blue and white glazed terracotta Madonna and Child (c. 1470–1475) by Andrea della Robbia, nephew of Luca della Robbia who first applied blue and white enamelled glazes to terracotta sculpture.

Greek and Roman Art.

The department is strong in Cypriot art, painted Greek vases, Attic sculpture, Roman portrait busts, ancient glass, and Greek, Etruscan, and Roman bronzes. Works date from the 3rd millennium B.C. to A.D. 313, the date of the emperor Constantine's conversion to Christianity. Geographically the objects have been gathered from the classical lands bordering the Mediterranean, though there is some overlapping with the departments of Ancient Near Eastern Art and Egyptian Art. Recorded tours of Greek sculpture, Greek vases, and Roman art available.

FIRST FLOOR GALLERIES. The first gallery on the W. side of the corridor near the entrance to the restaurants contains material representing **Cycladic and Greek bronze age cultures** (2nd–3rd millennia B.C.). Among the objects usually on display are the earliest pieces in the Cypriot collection, three small steatite figurines (51.11.5–7); Mycenaean pottery including a stirrup jar (53.11.6) decorated with fish and octopus; Cycladic statuettes including a *Seated Harp Player (47.100.1), and a female figure or idol (68.148), her arms crossed over her chest. Also, Cypriot tripods, Minoan and Helladic seals, and a wide range of archaic pottery types.

The second gallery contains Greek and Roman bronzes, the

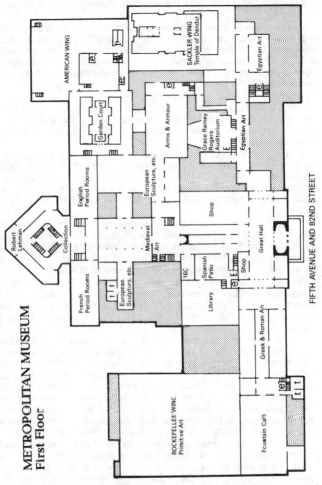

earliest dating from the Geometric period (8C B.C.). Note especially a small bronze horse (21.88.24) and a bronze group with a centaur and a standing male figure (17.190.2072), perhaps Zeus or Herakles. Later works include a *Sleeping Eros (43.11.4) from c. 200 B.C., probably one of the few surviving original bronzes of antiquity, as well as Roman portrait busts, Greek and Hellenistic figurines, ornaments, helmets, mirrors, wine jugs, and water jars.

The next gallery contains **Greek sculpture of the Classic period,** 6–4C B.C. Among the finer works in the collection are Wounded Warrior (25.116), a Roman copy of a Greek bronze original by Kresilas; Amazon (32.11.4), a Roman copy of a Greek original attrib. to Kresilas; Hermes (56.234.15), Roman Copy; relief of Dancing

Maenad (35.11.3), and a fragmentary relief of Demeter, Triptolemos, and Persephone (14.130.9), a Roman copy restored after the original in Athens.

Also on this side of the corridor is a gallery devoted to **Etruscan art,** including a bronze ceremonial *chariot (550–525 B.C.) with bronze repoussé reliefs illustrating episodes from the life of a hero, perhaps Achilles. The Etruscan collection also contains gems, bronze mirrors, tripods, cauldrons and pails, and examples of Etruscan pottery and bronzes from 4–6C B.C.

Directly in front of the entrance to the restaurant is the *Sardis column* (26.59.1), a gracefully scrolled Ionic capital and parts of a deeply fluted column from a temple of Artemis in Sardis (capital of ancient Lydia, near modern Smyrna in Turkey), found during excavations in 1911–14 and dating from the 4C B.C.

On the E. side of the corridor (nearest Fifth Ave) the first gallery contains **Greek sculpture of the archaic period** (7–6C B.C.). Outstanding are a fine marble *kouros (32.11.1) or nude male figure, and a gravestone with a relief boy and girl and a sphinx guardian on top (11.185); also a *grave relief of a girl with doves (27.45) from c. 450 B.C.

The next gallery contains **Greek marble grave sculpture from the 4–5C B.C.,** including fragments of stelae; marble stele of a warrior (40.11.123) attacking his fallen enemy; monuments in the shape of lekythoi or oil jars decorated with farewell scenes; gravestone of a woman (48.11.4); gravestone of a woman and child (44.11.2,3).

The last gallery along this side of the hall contains **Greek sculpture from the Hellenistic period,** 4–2C B.C. *Old Peasant Woman (09.39); *Aphrodite (52.11.5) in a Roman copy; Herakles (03.12.14), an enlarged Roman copy, and a group of marble portrait heads.

The long gallery in the central corridor (leading from the restaurant toward the Great Hall) contains **Cypriot sculpture,** notably an array of votive figures, grave reliefs, and sarcophagi, most dating from 550–500 B.C. and gathered by Luigi Palma di Cesnola, American consul in Cyprus and first paid director of the museum from 1879 until his death in 1904. Believing that Cyprus was the cradle of Greek civilisation, Cesnola devoted his energies to that area while other institutions, notably the Boston Museum, were buying up high quality Greek and Roman works from elsewhere.

The corridor opens into a gallery devoted to **Roman sculpture and wall paintings.** The *Boscoreale frescoes, removed from a villa at Boscoreale buried by the eruption of Vesuvius in A.D. 79, are the finest Roman paintings outside Italy. The room also contains the Badminton sarcophagus (55.11.5) dating from A.D. 220–230, named after Badminton House in England where it resided after its discovery in 1728; the piece shows Dionysos seated on a tiger or panther, surrounded by satyrs, maenads, and figures representing the Four Seasons. In the center of the room is a section of mosaic floor from a villa near Antioch. On the far wall is a marble portrait *bust of a young woman (30.11.11) from the early 3C. Also displayed are marble portrait busts from 1–2C A.D. and a large nude bronze portrait statue of Trebonius Gallus (05.30).

Just beyond this room at the edge of the Great Hall (E. side) is a **cubiculum** or Roman bedroom, from the villa near Boscoreale. Wall paintings depict architectural scenes perhaps drawn from stage settings; also displayed are a mosaic pavement from the 2C and a couch and footstool with bone carving and glass inlay.

Egyptian Art.

The new Egyptian galleries contain the finest and most comprehensive collection of Egyptian art in America. It numbers almost 45,000 objects dating from 3000 B.C. to A.D. 641, from prehistoric time to the Byzantine occupation during the reign of the emperor Justinian. Eventually all the objects will be displayed chronologically but at present some galleries are temporarily closed and others still under construction. Those now open include art of the Predynastic period, the Amarna to Coptic periods, and the Temple of Dendur in the Sackler wing. The final phase of the installation is scheduled for late 1983. Recorded tours are available.

Gallery 1, **Predynastic Period and Orientation.** The reconstruction of the mastaba (tomb) and chapel of Pernebi and the chapel of Rauemkai (both from c. 2415–2375 B.C.) dominate the room. Graphic orientation material includes an Egyptian time-line relating events in Egyptian history to other cultures. Along the Fifth Ave side of the gallery are predynastic objects (6000–3100 B.C.) including pottery, jewellery, and neolithic flint and basalt implements.

To continue viewing the collection in chronological order, go to the Amarna Room near the entrance to the Sackler Wing (Temple of Dendur). The outer of two galleries devoted to the **Amarna period** during which Akhenaton (Dynasty 18, before c. 1347 B.C.) reigned at Tell el Amarna, contains relief carvings from temple and palace walls depicting ceremonial occasions and aspects of daily life (on long term loan from the collection of Norbert Schimmel).

The inner room, known as the Amarna Room (late Dynasty 18) contains objects from the reigns of Akhenaton, Tutankhamun, Ay, and Haremhab. Sculptors' models and trial pieces found in an artist's workshop; two rare letters from the royal archives (24.2.11–12); ivory horse and gazelle (26.7 1292–3); shawabtys or servant figurines from the funerary equipment of Akhenaton. Relief blocks from temples to the god Aton (27.6.1, 21.9.8); fragments of plaster pavement from the royal palace (20.22, 23.2.33); head of Tutankhamun being crowned by the god Amun (50,56); colossal head of Amun (07.228.34). The E. wall is devoted to materials from the embalming of Tutankhamun and the remains of his funerary banquet from an 'embalmer's cache' found in 1907 by Theodore Davis, a wealthy American businessman; this discovery later helped Howard Carter to localise his excavations which resulted in the spectacular discovery of Tutankhamen's tomb in 1922. In the center of the room is a case devoted to the contents of Tomb 55 from the Valley of the Kings; included is a noteworthy alabaster canopic jar (09.226.1) whose lid has been carved as a portrait head of a royal lady.

In the **Architectural Hallway** are a fine life-sized statue of Haremhab portrayed as a scribe (23.10.1), two statues of Yuny (33.2.1 and 15.2.1), a royal scribe of the 19th Dynasty, and a huge granite doorjamb representing Ramesses II (13.183.2). Major sculpture in the **Ramesside Room,** Dynasties 19–20, includes a statue of Sety I (22.2.21), first king of Dynasty 19, a head of Amenmesse (34.2.2), and the stele of Ptahmose (67.3), a minor 19th Dynasty official. Among the decorative arts are polychrome faience tiles and a collection of Ramesside glass.

The **Third Intermediate Period Gallery** (Dynasties 21–25) includes a gold statuette of the god Amun (26.7.1412), faience amulets, and bronzes. Very little has survived from this period and the museum's holdings are exceptional, including purchased material shown here and material excavated on museum expeditions shown in the adjacent *Archaeological Room,* Dynasties 19–26. The display shows the development of burial customs in Thebes and includes painted and decorated coffins, canopic chests, shawabtys, Osiride figures, and mummies.

The **Late Period Gallery,** Dynasties 26–29, is dominated by a large section of relief decoration from the tomb of the 26th Dynasty official Nespakashuty at Thebes. Also shown are other objects from the tomb, sculpture from neighbouring tombs, and funerary material from other parts of Egypt including a fine set of canopic jars with tinted lids (12.183.1a–d), faience shawabtys and gold foil mummy amulets. Noteworthy are a framentary face from a large statue of superb quality (12.187.31); a silver statuette of a woman (30.8.93), and a display of miniature figurines, scarabs, and bijoux.

From the Late Period Gallery walk around the corner to the lounge near the elevators, Gallery 6: **Facsimiles of tomb and temple paintings,** many from Thebes, most from the 3rd–11th Dynasties. Made between 1907–29 by members of the museum's Egyptian Graphic Expedition, they provide an archive of Egyptian art and a source of information on daily life. Gallery 7, **Dynasty 30,** is dominated by the large stone sarcophagus of Wennefer (11.154.1a,b) displayed along with granite reliefs from temples of the delta and dark stone sculpture reflecting the renaissance of this dynasty. Galleries 8–9, **Ptolemaic period,** contain art from the time of Alexander's conquest of Egypt (332 B.C.) to the death of Cleopatra (30 B.C.) including stone sarcophagi, mummies, painted wood figures of canopic gods, Osiride figures, and two long papyri. Also noteworthy are a coffin for a sacred cat (56.16.1), a gilded bronze figure of a sacred ibis (56.18), and a limestone plaque, a sculptor's model of a ram-headed deity (18.9.1). Gallery 10, the lounge to the Grace Rainey Rogers Auditorium, contains more colour **facsimiles of tomb and temple paintings,** those on the W. wall from the 18th Dynasty, those on the E. wall from the 18th Dynasty through the Coptic period. Gallery 11, currently closed, is reserved for departmental temporary exhibitions.

Gallery 12, **Roman art from the time of Augustus to the 4C A.D.,** contains the museum's collection of 'Fayum Portraits', panel portraits found in Graeco-Roman cemeteries in Egypt, especially in the Fayum district. Also painted shrouds and mummy masks, jewellery, faience, and glass vessels. Gallery 13 (the W. area of Gallery 1), **Roman and Coptic periods** (30 B.C.–A.D. 641), contains about 40 of the museum's finest Coptic pieces, including textiles, jewellery, a linen and silk tunic (90.5.901), wood carvings, liturgical vessels, a carved *ivory relief showing the Ascension of Christ (17.190.46), painted wooden coffin with funerary mask, and architectural elements.

On the ground floor of the Sackler Wing, named after its donors Drs Arthur M., Mortimer, and Raymond R. Sackler, is the **Temple of Dendur** (recorded tour available), a small temple from Lower Nubia (S. of Aswan) built c. 23–10 B.C. and given to the United States in gratitude for contributions to save the monuments of Nubia submerged by the waters behind the Aswan High Dam. The Temple of

Dendur honours two brothers, Pedesi and Pihor, who drowned in the Nile during campaigns between Nubia and Ethiopia to the S. in 25 B.C. Though the circumstances of the drowning are unclear, it is reasonably certain that the body of one washed ashore at Dendur and was buried in a chamber cut into the hillside behind the original temple site, on the W. bank of the Nile.

DESCRIPTION. The temple consists of a *Gateway* of the usual Egyptian pattern, built of blocks of stone with a cavetto cornice and torus moulding below. A winged disk above the lintel represents the god Horus who flew up to the sky in this form. The gateway is decorated with reliefs showing the Pharoah (Augustus at this time) making offerings to the gods of the temple, a theme repeated both inside and outside the rest of the structure. Interior reliefs, seen in subdued light, are raised above their background while exterior ones illuminated by sunlight are carved in sunk relief. Beyond the gateway, the temple itself consists of three chambers (interior not open to the public): a Pronaos; a second, undecorated chamber probably used for storing offerings and vessels; and a Sanctuary where the image of the chief temple gods would normally be kept.

In the exterior rear wall a bevelled block can be removed to reveal a hidden chamber ($9^1/2 \times 6 \times 2$ ft), perhaps the tomb of the drowned brothers. Also on the exterior walls, in addition to the reliefs, are graffiti by visitors through the centuries—the earliest inscribed left by one Pakhom (10 B.C.), the later ones dating from the 19C.

Arms and Armour.

This Department contains the largest collection of arms and armour in the Western Hemisphere (about 15,000 objects) and one of the most comprehensive in the world. Besides European medieval armour and arms it also has holdings in Islamic, Indian, and Indonesian, Chinese, and Japanese arms, ranging chronologically from the Great Migration Period after the downfall of the Roman Empire up to the 19C, including important Colt revolvers but excluding purely military, mass-produced weapons.

At the present time (early 1982) the galleries are in a state of transition and the non-European material is not on exhibition. The following description attempts to suggest what is important in the collection until the galleries are rearranged. Recorded tour available.

In the center is the **Great Armor Hall** with an impressive group of mounted knights in 15–16C German and Italian armour. English armour displayed in the hall (left side) includes the earliest dated (1527) armour (19.131.1,2) from the Royal Court Workshop in Greenwich, a present from Henry VIII to the French ambassador, the Vicomte de Turenne, entirely covered with gilt-etching; a splendid black and gilt-etched armour (32.130.6) for George Clifford, personal champion of Queen Elizabeth; the field armour of Henry Herbert, Earl of Pembroke (32.130.5), and two armours (11.128.1,2) of Sir John Scudamore, who appears in Spenser's 'Faerie Queene'. Alongside this group is a lavishly embossed armour from the Royal French Workshop (c. 1555) made for Henry II of France (39.121) and a helmet (04.3.217) from the same workshop once owned by Cosimo II de Medici, Grand Duke of Tuscany. Near them is perhaps the finest single object in the collection, a *parade burgonet with mermaid crest (17.190.1720) signed by the Milanese master armourer Filippo Negrolo and dated 1543.

On the other side of the hall (right side) is a group of field and tilting armour made in S. Germany for the Spanish Court under Philip II (04.3.278, 26.234.3, 29.150.10) and nearby a huge

'Maximilian' armour, a fluted style named after the Emperor Maximilian, a patron of armourers, made c. 1535 for a Bavarian knight about six feet four inches tall. In wall cases are fine crossbows, one (25.42), dated 1489, once owned by Matthias Corvinus, King of Hungary, and another (04.3.36), dated 1460, owned by Ulrich V, Duke of Wüttemberg. Also, interesting early firearms, many of them of special constructions, including early breech-loading and multi-shot systems, combination weapons, swords, daggers, maces, and crossbows with pistol barrels.

Alcove galleries on the right are organized chronologically. Gallery 2 (first on right), **Medieval arms and armour before 1500:** Among the oldest objects are a gilded Germanic and a silver-covered Iranian spangelhelm (45.50.1 and 62.82) from the Great Migrations Period and a splendid Iranian sword with golden hilt and scabbard (65.28). A Viking sword with silver inlaid hilt (55.46.1) and a gorgeous parade helmet of c. 1460 in the shape of a lion's head (23.41) are in freestanding cases in the center. Along the walls, topped by panoplies of staff weapons, halberds, poleaxes, and boar spears, are cases with helmets of the 14–15C and 15C shields. Also, two full suits of armour, a series of knightly swords, and the sword pommel of Pierre de Dreux (38.60)—one of the few objects that can be credited with having been on a crusade—a bascinet (04.3.241) thought to have been the helmet of Joan of Arc, and a helmet for the baston course (04.3.274) owned by Sir Giles Capel, a companion of Henry VIII.

Gallery 3 (second on right), **German and Italian armour, 1475–1525:** Helmets, armour elements and riding equipment; one fine fluted 'Maximilian' armour (49.163.1). Several helmets with mask visors, and a manuscript record or Tournament Book of jousts held in Nuremberg between 1446 and 1561 with colourful watercolour illustrations. In the center is a cuirass etched with the images of saints for added protection (38.143).

Gallery 4 (third on the right), **Arms of the 17–19C:** Prominent among the firearms is a group of hunting rifles and fowling guns made in the workshop of Napoleon's master gunsmith, Nicolas Noël Boutet and his competitor, Pirmet. The earliest firearm in this room is a double-barreled wheellock pistol (14.25.1425) made c. 1540 for Emperor Charles V by Peter Peck in Munich. Impressive are the Italian—Brescian and Neapolitan—firearms with lacelike perforated or boldly sculpted mountings in cut steel. A very fine group of 18C courtswords, many of them with hilts of precious materials—gold silver, ivory, mother-of-pearl, tortoise-shell or porcelain—show the last refinement of a deadly weapon.

Gallery 5 (to the left near the entrance to the American Wing), **Edged weapons, 16–17C:** Freestanding cases display silver-mounted and cup-hilted rapiers; wallcases contain groups of Swiss daggers with gilt-bronze scabbards decorated in figural reliefs, Saxon silver-mounted rapiers and daggers, and two-handed swords including a Scottish claymore. Another freestanding case contains an outstanding firearm, the fowling gun of Louis XIII of France, c. 1615, one of the three earliest flintlocks known (1972.223).

The American Wing.

The new •American Wing (first phase, 1980) contains the finest collection of American art in existence. The floor plans are provided

METROPOLITAN MUSEUM: AMERICAN WING
First Floor, Old & New Wings

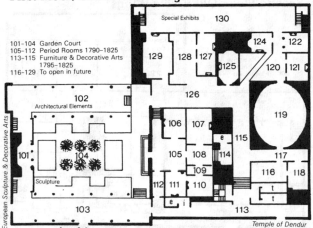

101-104 Garden Court
105-112 Period Rooms 1790-1825
113-115 Furniture & Decorative Arts
        1795-1825
116-129 To open in future

to unravel its complexities which arise because the new structure is wrapped around an older wing. Period rooms (recorded tour) are organised chronologically with the earliest displays on the top floor.

The *CHARLES ENGELHARD COURT (gallery 104 on the floor plan) contains 19C and early 20C sculpture and architectural elements (recorded tour available). At the N. end is the facade (1824) of the United States Branch Bank once located on Wall St. At the other end is a loggia with ceramic capitals, glass tiles, and lanterns (1978.10.1) by Louis Comfort Tiffany, cast-iron staircases by Louis H. Sullivan (1972.50.1–4), and *stained glass by Tiffany, John La Farge, and Frank Lloyd Wright. Sculpture (1850–1940) includes work by William Rimmer, George Grey Barnard, Gutzon Borglum, Frederick MacMonnies, Paul Manship, Gaston Lachaise, and William Zorach. The gilded statue of Diana (28.101) is a reduced replica of Augustus Saint-Gaudens's original (now in Philadelphia) that once adorned the first Madison Square Garden.

Period rooms in the FIRST FLOOR galleries contain furniture from the early Federal period, 1790–1820. The doorway of the United States Branch Bank leads from the garden courtyard into the *Federal Gallery* (105) with distinguished examples of furniture from Boston, New York, Philadelphia, and Baltimore. Furniture in the *Baltimore Room* (106) is unusual in its use of light-wood inlays and painted glass set into the wood. The *Benkard Room* (107) has elegant architectural elements salvaged from a derelict house (1811) in Petersburg, Virginia. Furniture in the *Neoclassical Gallery* (108) reflects the French Empire style in America; especially important is a marble-topped pier table (53.181) by Charles-Honoré Lannuier with gilt bronze and gilded terracotta ornamentation. Gallery 109, Orientation, has an exhibition on the reconstruction of the Richmond Room. Gallery 110, the *Richmond Room*, has later Federal work from

METROPOLITAN MUSEUM: AMERICAN WING
Second Floor, Old & New Wings

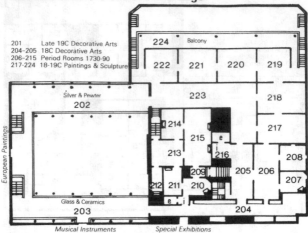

the Duncan Phyfe workshop including a sofa (60.4.1) and mahogany
chairs with 'Grecian Cross' legs. The wallpaper reproduces Dufour's
'Monuments of Paris' wallpaper (1814). The *Haverhill Room* (111)
from Massachusetts features a distinguished canopied bed
(18.110.64) while the Philadelphia Gallery (112) shows representative examples of the distinguished neoclassical tradition in that city.
Galleries 113 and 115 contain other examples of early and late
Federal furniture including a fine display of clocks.

Galleries on the BALCONY (see floor plan for second floor, below)
contain a survey of **American decorative arts** from the 17C to the
20C. Gallery 202: Pewter and silver including coins, Baroque pieces,
work of the late Colonial and Federal periods (several pieces by Paul
Revere). Especially well-known are a pair of silver candlesticks and
snuffer stand by Cornelius Kierstede (57.153.a,b, 64.83.a,b, 23.80.21),
and a silver cake basket by Myer Myers (54.167). Presentation and
exposition pieces show the extravagant taste of the later 19C
(Gallery 201), including the famous enamelled Magnolia Vase (99.2)
and the gold Adams Vase (04.1) by Tiffany and Company. Glass and
ceramics (Gallery 203) includes examples of export ware made for
the American market as well as American domestic wares beginning
with salt-glazed stoneware, red earthenware of the Pennsylvania
Germans, and other significant ceramics made up to 1924. Glassware includes examples from the earliest free-blown tableware to
the Favrile glass of Louis Comfort Tiffany. A replica of Daniel
Chester French's grave memorial, Mourning Victory (15.75) is
mounted against the S. wall.

Period rooms on the SECOND FLOOR are devoted to the late
Colonial period (1730–90). The orientation gallery (Old Wing, 209)

focuses on design books which provided colonial craftsmen with models for ornamentation. The Pennsylvania German Room (210) has work created by German-speaking immigrants from the Rhine Valley and the Palatinate who settled in S.E. Pennsylvania, notably a painted overmantel (34.27.1,2,10) from Lancaster, Pennsylvania. The carved and moulded decoration in the Powel Parlor (211) from Philadelphia, dates from c. 1765 and is derived from contemporary English pattern books while the furniture is made in the elegant Philadelphia version of the Chippendale style. In the New England Furniture Gallery (212–213) are exemplary desks, chairs, chests, and secretaries by master craftsmen. The Almodington Room (214), a gentleman's bedroom from Somerset County, Maryland, features a fine Boston-made four poster bed (10.125.336), while the Alexandria Ballroom (215), an assembly room from a tavern in Virginia, has a musicians' gallery, a mahogany spinet in the Queen Anne style (1976.229), and a group of mid-18C chairs.

Three more period rooms are installed in the NEW WING OF THE SECOND FLOOR. Galleries 204–205: 18C Furniture and Decorative Arts and Philadelphia Chippendale Furniture. The Van Rensselaer Hall (206) comes from a distinguished Georgian manor house in Albany, New York, built (c. 1765) by Stephen Van Rensselaer, the last patroon of that domain. Its remarkable scenic wallpaper was painted in England while the furniture was made by New York craftsmen in the Chippendale style. The furnishings of the Verplanck Room (208) belonged to Samuel and Judith Crommelin Verplank, who lived at 3 Wall St. The Marmion Room (207) from a Virginia plantation is remarkable for its woodwork, some painted to simulate marble, other panels decorated with urns, leaves, scrolls, and landscapes reminiscent of Dutch paintings.

The *Joan Whitney Payson galleries* contain a permanent display of *American paintings and sculpture* arranged chronologically. Gallery 217, 18C Paintings and Sculpture: *John Smibert*, Francis Brinley (62.79.1), *John Singleton Copley*, *Mrs John Winthrop (31.109), *Augustus Brine, Midshipman (43.86.4); *Charles Willson Peale*, George Washington (97.33). Gallery 218, late 18C–early 19C Painting and Sculpture: *Benjamin West*, the Triumph of Love (95.22.1); *John Trumbull*, *The Sortie Made by the Garrison of Gibraltar (1976.332). Among the paintings by *Gilbert Stuart* are an early portrait of George Washington (07.160), apparently done from life, and the Vicomte de Noailles (1970.262).

Gallery 219, 1812–40: *James Peale*, Balsam Apple and Vegetables (39.52); *George Caleb Bingham*, Fur Traders Descending the Missouri (33.61); *Samuel F.B. Morse*, The Muse: Susan Walker Morse (45.62.1). Gallery 220, Early Hudson River School: *Thomas Cole*, View from Mount Holyoke, Massachusetts, after a Thunderstorm— The Oxbow (08.228); *Asher B. Durand*, The Beeches (15.30.59). Gallery 221, Late Hudson River School: *Martin Johnson Heade*, The Coming Storm (1975.160); *Fitz Hugh Lane*, Stage Fort Across Gloucester Harbor (1978.203), *Albert Bierstadt*, The Rocky Mountains, Lander's Peak (07.123); and *Frederick Edwin Church*, The Heart of the Andes (09.95). In Gallery 222 is the work of *Winslow Homer:* *Northeaster (10.64.5), *The Gulf Stream (06.123.4) and scenes from the Civil War and rural New England. Sculpture by John Quincy Adams Ward and Augustus Saint-Gaudens. Paintings in Gallery 223 are shown on a rotating basis with the exception of *Emanuel Leutze*, *Washington Crossing the Delaware (97.34), a romantic reconstruction of history inaccurate in many details but nonetheless deeply imprinted on the American consciousness.

Gallery 224, Post-Civil War Realism, Trompe l'Oeil Painting, Western Art, and Visionary Painting. *Thomas Eakins*, Portrait of a Lady with a Setter Dog (23.139), The Thinker (17.172). Paintings and bronzes by *Frederic Remington*, definitive chronicler of cowboys, Indians, and army troopers. Paintings by Albert Pinkham Ryder, Ralph Albert Blakelock, and William Michael Harnett.

From this gallery a stairway leads down to the MEZZANINE in the new wing (Gallery M1) with Late 19C and Early 20C Realists: *Mary Cassatt*, Young Mother Sewing (29.100.48); *James A. MacNeill Whistler*, Arrangement in Flesh Colour and Black: Portrait of Theodore Duret (13.20); *John Singer Sargent*, Madame X (16.53); *William Merritt Chase*, At the Seaside (67.187.123); *John Twachtman*, Arques-La-Bataille (68.52); sculpture by Bessie Potter Vonnoh and Augustus Saint-Gaudens. All the members of The Eight are represented in the collection—Robert Henri, John Sloan, George Luks, Maurice Prendergast, Ernest Lawson, Everett Shinn, Arthur B. Davies, and William Glackens. Especially famous are Glacken's Central Park in Winter (21.164) and Davies's Unicorns (31.67.12). At the far end of the gallery are paintings which date from after 1913, the year the Armory Show brought European modern painting to the forefront of American consciousness. Included is work by Georgia O'Keeffe, Arthur Dove, and Milton Avery. Painters working in a more traditional vein are *Edward Hopper*, Office in a Small City (53.183) as well as such regionalists as Thomas Hart Benton, John Steuart Curry, and Grant Wood.

Period rooms on the THIRD FLOOR have exhibits from the early Colonial period (1630–1730). In Gallery 301 are 17C and 18C chairs,

METROPOLITAN MUSEUM: AMERICAN WING
Mezzanine, New Wing

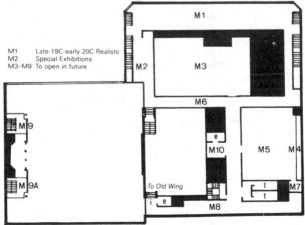

M1   Late 19C-early 20C Realists
M2   Special Exhibitions
M3–M9 To open in future

METROPOLITAN MUSEUM: AMERICAN WING
Third Floor, Old Wing

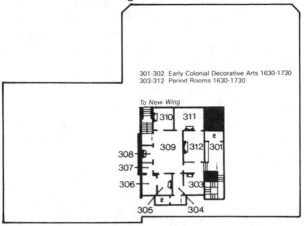

301-302 Early Colonial Decorative Arts 1630-1730
303-312 Period Rooms 1630-1730

To New Wing

310 311

309 312 301

308
307
306 303

305 304

including a Brewster chair (51.12.2), so-called because the elder William Brewster of Plymouth Plantation is said to have owned one, and a 'Turkeywork' chair (52.77.51), with needlepoint fabric over marsh-grass stuffing. Gallery 302, Orientation: Woodframe Construction. The Meetinghouse Gallery (309) in the center of the floor features chests—some with Tudor and Jacobean motifs—cupboards, and several pieces in the William and Mary style. The Hart Room (303), the earliest in the collection, comes from Ipswich, Massachusetts (before 1674) and is furnished with 17C oak and pine furniture.

Gallery 304: Chests from Massachusetts and Connecticut. The Newington Room (305) from a mid-18C Connecticut home, the Hampton Room (306) from a New Hampshire farmhouse, and the New York Alcove (308) with panelling from a stone house in Ulster County, show regional variations on colonial furniture. The Wentworth stair (307) is a rare survival (c. 1700) with unusual spiral-turned balusters. The Hewlett Room (310), from a house (c.1740) on Long Island, has Dutch tiles surrounding the fireplace opening and a painted Kas or chest (23.171) showing Dutch influence. The Bowler Room (311) from Portsmouth, Rhode Island near Newport (c.1763) recalls the formal elegance of Georgian England. In the Wentworth Room (312) from Portsmouth, New Hampshire (c.1700) are new designs of the William and Mary period and such imported luxuries as a Turkey 'carpitt' and tin-glazed pottery from Holland and England.

Medieval Art.

The collection of the Department of Medieval Art (main floor, adjacent to and behind the Grand Staircase) contains objects from

METROPOLITAN MUSEUM
First Floor, Medieval Art, etc.

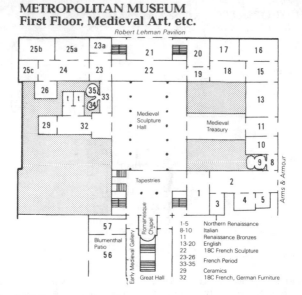

Robert Lehman Pavilion

25b	25a	23a
25c	24	23

21, 20, 17, 16
22, 19, 18, 15

26, 35, 33, 34
t t
13

Medieval Sculpture Hall

29, 32

Medieval Treasury, 11

10

9, 8

Tapestries

2

1

3, 4, 5

Arms & Armour

57

Blumenthal Patio 56

Romanesque Chapel

Early Medieval Gallery

Great Hall

1-5	Northern Renaissance
8-10	Italian
11	Renaissance Bronzes
13-20	English
22	18C French Sculpture
23-26 33-35	French Period
29	Ceramics
32	18C French, German Furniture

the 4–16C representing all the main aspects of medieval art: Early Christian, Byzantine, Barbarian, pre-Romanesque, Romanesque, and Gothic art.

GALLERY 1, **Early Christian Art** (S. side of staircase, just W. of Great Hall). Near the entrance are tomb reliefs and sarcophagus fragments including: a tomb relief (48.76.2) from 4C Rome showing Christ giving the law and a Syrian fragment (77.7) with Jonah swallowed and cast up by the whale. Displayed along the staircase wall (E. to W.) are: examples of early Christian plain and gold glass, gold jewellery, a marble bust of a lady of rank (66.25); objects from the Albanian treasure of Byzantine and Avaric jewellery from the 6–9C; Byzantine art from the 9–13C including ivory plaques, enamels, icons, lockets, earrings, and bracelets. Noteworthy among the ivories is a standing figure of the Virgin and Child (17.190.103) dating from the 10–11C. Cases on the other side of the hall (again from E. to W.) contain: articles from the second Cyprus treasure including five silver dishes (17.190.394–99) decorated with scenes from the early life of David, and a fine gold necklace (17.190.151); Byzantine bronze steelyard weights; silver from the 3–6C B.C.; Byzantine ivory plaques and caskets; and bronze lamps. Beyond the archway are three cases devoted to Barbarian metalwork and jewellery and Frankish glass from the 5–8C and an Italian doorway.

GALLERY 2, the **Romanesque Chapel** (on the E. wall of Gallery 3, the Tapestry Hall) contains Romanesque architectural elements including capitals, heads, and columnar statues. On the front wall are two wooden representations of the Virgin and Child from Auvergne (L.48.44 and 16.32.194) and a 13C stained glass window from the abbey of St. Germain-des-Près in Paris; on the altar, a 12C silver processional cross (17.190.1406) from N. Spain.

GALLERY 3, the **Medieval Tapestry Hall,** is dominated by a number of beautiful tapestries including (clockwise from door): a rare Annunciation Tapestry (45.76); two scenes from the Trojan War (52.69 and 39.74), one probably from a set made for Charles the Bold in Tournai; two of the so-called Rose Tapestries (09.137.1–2), showing courtiers in elegant dress against a background of stripes and rosebushes; and a fragment with the Crucifixion from Constance (16.90), the museum's earliest medieval tapestry. Around the walls are displayed pieces of furniture and examples of ceramics; near the entrance to the chapel is a 12C stone head of King David (38.180) from Notre Dame, Paris. Precious objects of ivory, metal, and enamel are displayed in small cases. Near the entrance to the Sculpture Hall is a monumental seated Virgin and Child (33.23) from Burgundy.

GALLERY 4, the **Medieval Sculpture Hall,** is dominated by an impressive 17C *choir screen (56.234.1) from Valladolid, Spain. The room contains numerous Gothic sculptural works in marble, alabaster, limestone, and wood, as well as furniture, majolica, Hispano-Moresque lustreware, paintings, and tapestries. Of particular interest among the statues are: (left of door) a small polychrome and gilt group representing the Visitation (17.190.724); and a Flemish St. Catherine (50.64), c. 1530. To the right of the entrance is a marble bust of Marie de France (41.100.132), daughter of Charles IV. Against the central pilasters (right side) is a Spanish 14C wooden statue of St. Peter as bishop of Rome (27.18.2); near the entrance to the Treasury is an Eagle lectern from Giovanni Pisano's pulpit in the cathedral of Pistoia (18.70.20) dating from c.1300, and near it three marble sculptures (c. 1308–10) that once decorated the pulpit of the cathedral of Pisa (10.203.1,2 and 23.101).

GALLERY 5, the **Medieval Treasury,** contains objects of gold, silver, ivory, enamel, and leather, as well as textiles. Between the two entrances doors an exceptionally important large 13C Limoges enamel shrine (17.190.735) dominates the room. Other noteworthy objects include: (left wall) a silver-gilt figure of St. Christopher and the Christ child (17.190.361); champlevé enamel plaques from the Mosan Valley in a pyramid case nearby; a 13C reliquary head of St. Yricix (17.190.352) in the center of the room, two limestone groups (facing each other) from the château of Biron in Perigord; ivory plaques and caskets, a Venetian altarpiece (17.190.489) of bone with scenes from the lives of Christ, St. John the Baptist, and St. John the Evangelist; secular silver gilt cups, flagons, and beakers; aquamanilia or pitchers in the form of animals. Along the right wall are a rare ivory situla (17.190.45) or Holy Water bucket; ivory plaques; enamel plaques and châsses or caskets; small ivory and wood figures; an English 14C exquisitely embroidered chasuble, stole and maniple (27.662.1–3).

European Sculpture and Decorative Arts.

The galleries of European Sculpture and Decorative Arts contain one of the largest collections in the museum including period rooms, furniture, a wide variety of decorative arts—silver, ceramics, metalwork—and some sculpture from the Renaissance to 1900. The galleries devoted to the arts of the Renaissance in northern Europe begin adjacent to the Medieval section, followed by the Italian and English galleries. English and French Period rooms are located along the W. side of the museum, with further examples of French and

German furniture and porcelain near the period rooms. The 16C Spanish patio and an adjacent gallery (changing exhibits from the collection) and the ground floor galleries of porcelain, silver, and minor decorative arts complete the installation.

Begin just next to the Tapestry Hall in the Medieval section. GALLERY 1 serves as an INTRODUCTORY GALLERY with late medieval and Renaissance objects including small sculptures, textiles, Renaissance bronzes, aquamanilia (brass pitchers in fanciful shapes), tools, and other domestic implements, many from the huge collection of Judge Irwin Untermeyer whose gift (especially strong in English arts) is one of the treasures of the museum. GALLERY 2 contains a display of 16–17C ENGLISH DECORATIVE ARTS including stoneware (tankards), silver, porcelain, and furniture, notably a fine oak table (64.101.1065) and a tester bed (53.1) from the late 16C. On the E. wall are two terracotta busts by Pietro Torrigiano formerly in the main room at Whitehall: John Fisher, Bishop of Rochester (1936.36.69) and Henry VIII (1944.44.92). On the E. side of this gallery are three period rooms. The *Chapel of the Château de la Bastie d'Urfé* (recorded tour available) near Lyons (GALLERY 3) has inlaid and carved woodwork designed by Vignola and commissioned from the workshop of Fra Damiano in Bologna. The walls are illuminated by a set of 16C stained glass windows from the Abbey of Flavigny-sur-Moselle.

GALLERY 4, the *Elizabethan Room*, has carved oak panelling from a house in Yarmouth, later commercially operated as the Star Hotel, and is furnished in the dark oak furniture of the period. The *Swiss Room* (GALLERY 5) from the mid-17C has elaborately carved and veneered panelling on ceiling and walls, and a stove of faience tiles painted with scenes from the Old Testament.

Galleries 8–11 are devoted to ITALIAN ARTS. Gallery 8, with minor Italian arts including two gondola prows from Venice, serves as an antechamber to the *bedroom from the 18C Venetian Palazzo Sagredo* (GALLERY 9), on the Grand Canal near the Rialto. Such niceties as the ceiling painting, Dawn, possibly by Gaspare Diziani, and the 32 fluttering stucco cupids were created for other eyes than those of the home owner, since it was customary at the time to receive formal visits in bed.

GALLERY 10 contains *18C Italian furniture* including two monumental carved oak and poplar bookcases (69.292.1,2) and a set of allegorical frescoes from the workshop of Giovanni Battista Tiepolo. RENAISSANCE BRONZES in GALLERY 11 include examples from 15–17C Italy, Germany, and the Netherlands, by such sculptors as *Tiziano Aspetti, Adriaen de Vries, Giovanni Bologna, Il Riccio* (Andrea Briosco) and *Antico* (Pier Jacopo Alari-Bonacolsi). Noteworthy is Antico's Seated Paris (55.93) with gilt hair.

Galleries 13–20 contain ENGLISH FURNITURE FROM THE LATE 17C–18C and the English period rooms. (To see the collection chronologically you must begin at Gallery 20 near the sculpture gallery.) GALLERY 13: Neo-classical English furniture, late 18C. Note especially the painted and gilded doorway (64.101.1213) with its Adam-style ornament, the white marble chimney piece (64.101.1215) made c. 1770 for the dining room of Gloucester House in London, and the large commode (64.101.1152) veneered with satinwood and painted with an oval scene of nymphs adorning a statue of Pan. Cases in the center hold changing exhibits of silver, crystal, and porcelain contemporary with the furniture. GALLERY 15 is furnished with groupings of mahogany furniture from the mid-18C, much of it showing Oriental exoticisms or French Rococo influence: mahogany china table (64.101.1099) with carved fretwork gallery stretcher and cabriole legs, large rococo firescreen (64.101.1155) with carpet pile panel based on a French Savonnerie design; also noteworthy is a pine doorway frame (64.101.1212) carved after a design by Piedmontese architect Giovanni Battista Borra with monkeys, fruit and flowers.

In this gallery is one entrance to the *DINING ROOM FROM LANSDOWNE HOUSE (1768), Berkeley Square, London (GALLERY 16), decorated by Robert Adam in neo-classical style. Joseph Rose executed the beautiful plasterwork on walls and ceilings with its vases, scrolls, rosettes, and garlands. The statues in the niches are cast from Roman originals in the museum's collection; the silver on the table is by *Paul Lamerie*. More 18C English silver including the work of the great Huguenot silversmiths active in London at the beginning of the century (*Simon Pantin, Paul Lamerie, Lewis Mettayer, Pierre Harache*) as well as Chelsea and Bow porcelains are shown in cases near the other doorway to the Lansdowne room (selections of porcelain and silver rotated occasionally).

GALLERY 17, the TAPESTRY ROOM FROM CROOME COURT (1760), shows the contemporary English fashion for rooms 'in the French taste', and is remarkable for the *Gobelins tapestries that cover the walls and the seating. Made to measure in Paris, the wall tapestries incorporate four medallions based on designs of François Boucher. Wood and plaster decoration is from designs by Robert Adam.

GALLERY 18 contains ENGLISH DECORATIVE ARTS FROM THE EARLIER 18C. Notable are an embroidered portrait of Queen Anne Crowned by Fame and Peace (64.101.1353), two armchairs from c. 1700 (55.8.2a,b and 64.101.1353) covered with contemporary English needlework, a tapestry portrait of George II (64.101.1331) in its original frame, and a fine mahogany commode (64.101.1142).

The focal point of GALLERY 19 is a **staircase** (32.152) **from Cassiobury Park** in Hertfordshire, a country house no longer standing. Carved c. 1674 by *Grinling Gibbons* or *Edward Pearce*, the staircase has oak leaf and acorn decoration referring to the 'Royal Oak' where Charles II hid during the Civil War. GALLERY 20 is a DINING ROOM FROM KIRTLINGTON PARK, N. of Oxford, c. 1748, notable for its carved wood doors and Rococo plaster decoration from designs by Thomas Roberts, a local master. The builder-owner, Sir James Dashwood, appears in a painting by *Enoch Seaman* on the N. wall. The room is now furnished as a drawing room with pieces of contemporary furniture.

GALLERY 22, The Josephine Bay Paul Gallery of **18C French sculpture**. The finest piece in the gallery is *Jean-Louis Lemoyne's* *The Fear of Cupid's Darts (67.197), made for Louis XV in c. 1740. Also displayed are *Antoine Coysevox*, bust of Michel le Tellier (68.79) and *Guillaume Coustou*, bust of Samuel Bernard (66.20), banker to Louis XIV. Jean-Baptiste Pigalle and Nicolas-Sebastien Adam designed the two immense marble vases for the gardens of Choisy, the king's country retreat. In the center are lead groups made for the gardens of the royal palace in Turin: attrib. *Lambert Sigisbert Adam*; Struggling Children on a Fish (1970.325.1–2) and; attrib. *François Ladatte*, Children Playing with Fruit and Children Playing with Birds (1970.8.1–2). On the other side of the W. wall in the lobby to the Lehman Collection (Gallery 21) are three stucco reliefs with Bacchanalian subjects (59.24.2a,b,c) by *Clodion*, modelled for the Hôtel de Bourbon-Condé in Paris. Toward the French period rooms are *Pierre-Étienne Monnot*'s Andromeda and the Monster (67.34) and Leda and the Swan (1970.140) by *Michel Anguier*.

The Wrightsman Galleries of *French 18C period rooms are superb. Turn left on entering the galleries and walk to GALLERY 33, Introductory Gallery and PARIS SHOPFRONT, the only Parisian shopfront (c. 1775) remaining from the reign of Louis XVI. In the windows are examples of Paris silver, rare survivals from a period when much was melted down on royal orders to finance royal wars. The display of gold boxes includes a double snuff box (1967.155.21) with miniature portraits of the French royal family and a snuff box (1976.155.22) with views of the Château de Chanteloup, country seat of the Duc de Choiseul. Two small panelled rooms open from the left side of the corridor. The ROOM FROM THE HÔTEL DE CRILLON (GALLERY 34) is a mirrored boudoir from the residence of the Duc d'Aumont in the present Place de la Concorde. Among the furnishings are a daybed and armchair that belonged to *Marie-Antoinette*. The BORDEAUX ROOM (GALLERY 35) is a circular salon with carved neo-classical panelling; a Beauvais tapestry carpet covers the floor and the table is set with pieces of black Sèvres porcelain.

Beyond the Bordeaux Room is (23) the LOUIS XV ROOM, with corner panels carved with trophies of the four seasons. *Hyacinthe Rigaud* painted the portrait of Louis XV as a Boy (60.6); the original silk and wool Beauvais tapestry covers the gilded beechwood settee. In the SÈVRES ALCOVE are superb examples of porcelains including part of a turquoise-blue *desert service ordered by Louis, Prince de Rohan (and later cardinal) as well as a rose vase (58.75.89a,b) in the form of a ship, considered a tour-de-force of Sèvres work. The *SÈVRES ROOM (23a) with polychromed panelling from the Hôtel de Lauzun on the Île Saint-Louis, Paris, houses a magnificent collection of furniture set with Sèvres plaques including pieces signed by *Martin Carlin* and *Bernard II Van Risen Burgh*. When the left earring of the Negress clock (58.75.127) on the mantel is pulled, the eyes recede and the hour appears in the right eye, the minutes in the left. The right ear originally activated a pipe organ in the base.

The LOUIS XVI GALLERY (24) is dominated by a double portrait of *Antoine-Laurent Lavoisier and His Wife (1977.10) by *Jacques-Louis David*. Furniture includes two secretaries and a commode by *Adam Weisweiler* with panels of Japanese lacquer. The first doorway on the right opens into (25a) a ROOM FROM THE HÔTEL DE VARENGEVILLE, the Paris townhouse of the Duchesse de Villars, wife of one of Louis XIV's great generals. Louis XV's own *writing table (1973.315.1) from the study at Versailles stands in the center on a Savonnerie carpet, one of 92 woven for the Grande Galerie at the Louvre. The carved, painted, and gilded oak panelling was commissioned in about 1735. Adjacent is the PAAR ROOM (25b) from the Palais Paar in Vienna, built in c. 1630 for the Baron Johann Christoph von Paar, postmaster of the Holy Roman Empire, and remodelled 1765–71. Among the furnishings are a writing table with marquetry of tulipwood, rosewood, ebony, and stained horn (1976.155.100) by *Bernard II Van Risen Burgh*, a gilded dog kennel (1971.65.45), and two terracotta statuettes by *Clodion*, Drunken Nymph and Satyr (14.40.687) and a Model for a monument to commemorate the invention of the Balloon (44.21).

The carved and gilded panelling in the CABRIS ROOM was executed in Paris (c. 1775–78) for a home in Grasse, some 12 miles from Cannes. In the center of the room is a travelling table whose upper section was fitted out as a bed table with a book rest and toilet accessories while the lower section served as an eating table, with drawers for cutlery and a Sèvres breakfast service for two. The final gallery (26) is the DE TESSÉ ROOM, the grand salon of a Paris townhouse still standing at No. 1 Quai Voltaire. Several pieces of furniture made by *Jean-Henri Riesener* for Marie-Antoinette include a Japanese lacquered secretary (20.155.11) on the chimneypiece wall and a mechanical table (33.12) of adjustable height used to serve the Queen her meals in bed after the birth of her first child.

GALLERY 32 contains **18C French and German furniture** from the Lesley and Emma Sheafer collection. Outstanding among the French pieces are japanned and lacquered commodes, a fine marquetry writing table (1974.356.186) by *Bernard II Van Risen Burgh*, and a pair of armchairs with Savonnerie covers (1974.356.191–2). German Rococo furniture includes carved, painted, and gilded commodes, armchairs, settees and sidechairs, as well as wall mirrors and lights. Among the paintings and drawings is an Architectural Fantasy by *Francesco Guardi* (1974.356.28).

The next gallery (29) contains **18C ceramics** from the Shaefer collection. Included among the Meissen porcelains are early examples showing Chinese influence, crinoline figures, animals, birds, and a royal hunting cup modelled by *J. J. Kändler* (1974.356.337a,b), and *Franz Anton Bustelli's* commedia dell'arte figure, Lucinda (1974.356.802). Also, porcelains from Fulda, examples of Vezzi porcelain (cup and saucer, 1974.356.546–7) produced near Venice and Doccia porcelain from the environs of Florence. German faience includes jugs and tankards; animals, birds, and vegetables, and other whimsical ware produced at Hoechst and Strasbourg. The gallery also has a small collection of 17–18C German silver.

The **Blumenthal Patio** (Gallery 56) from the castle of Los Vélez in S.E. Spain was donated by George Blumenthal, president of the museum 1933–41, who had previously installed it as the principal interior feature of his home on Park Ave and 70th St. The patio (1506–15) was decorated in part by Italian craftsmen who executed the marble work around the doorways and on the arcades. It now serves as a sculpture garden containing a group of Renaissance works, notably *Tullio Lombardo*, Adam (36.163).

The Robert Lehman Pavilion.

The ****Robert Lehman Pavilion** contains the collection of paintings, drawings, and decorative arts gathered by Robert Lehman and his father Philip and formerly housed largely in the Lehman townhouse on W. 54th St. The collection, with its superb Italian, Flemish, and 19C French paintings, ceramics, Renaissance bronzes, and drawings, was promised to the museum in 1969 with the stipulation that it remain permanently together and that seven period rooms from the Lehman townhouse be recreated within the museum. Recorded tour available.

The LEHMAN WING (1975; Roche, Dinkeloo & Assocs) is set against the original W. wall of the museum (1880; Calvert Vaux and Jacob Wrey Mould; DL), a bold surface of salmon-coloured brick, and buff and grey limestone pierced by five Victorian Gothic arches.

A high pyramidal glass roof shelters an interior courtyard around which are two rings of galleries. The lower ring is devoted to changing exhibitions from the more than 1600 drawings in the collection; the upper ring contains the period rooms where the paintings are hung.

The GRAND GALLERY, nearest the central courtyard, contains **19–20C French painting** arranged chronologically by painter.

Because of the special nature of the collection, paintings are not labelled with the usual museum accession numbers; page numbers on placards refer to the catalogue available at the desk inside the pavilion entrance. Audioguide tour available.

Among the paintings are: *Jean-Baptiste Camille Corot*: Diana and Actaeon. *Claude Monet*: Landscape near Zaandam. *Pierre-Auguste Renoir*: Two Young Girls at the Piano, Young Girl Bathing. *Vincent van Gogh*: Madame Roulin and Her Baby. *Paul Gauguin*: Tahitian Women Bathing. *Edgar Hilaire Germain Degas*: Landscape. *Albert Marquet*: Sergeant of the Colonial Regiment. *Suzanne Valadon*: Reclining Nude. *Maurice Utrillo*: 40 Rue Ravignan. *Balthus*: Figure in Front of a Mantle. Also paintings by Alfred Sisley, Camille Pisarro, Louis Valtat, Maurice de Vlaminck, and Pierre Bonnard.

In the FIRST ROOM (N.W. side of courtyard), arranged as in the Lehman townhouse, **Sienese and Italian Renaissance painting** is displayed along with period furniture and decorative arts. *Lippo Vanni*: St. Ansanus; Madonna and Child. *Ugolino da Nerio*: Madonna and Child. *Bartolo di Fredi*: *Adoration of the Magi. *Giovanni di Paolo*, Bishop Saint. *Roberto d'Odorisio*: Saints John and Mary Magdalen. *Avignon Master*: Adoration of the Magi. *Lorenzo Veneziano*: Madonna and Child.

The SECOND ROOM contains a number of small paintings, most from other schools of Italian painting. *Niccolo da Foligno*: St. Anne and the Madonna and Child Surrounded by Angels. *Bicci di Lorenzo*: Two Standing Saints. *Carlo Crivelli*: Apostle with Scroll. *Lorenzo Monaco*: Crucifixion; *Nativity. *Bernardo Daddi*: Virgin with Angels. A collection of fine majolica includes plates made in Deruta based on Pollaiuolo's 'Labours of Hercules', part of a service for Isabella d'Este and her husband Gian Francesco Gonzago, and a *bowl painted with the arms of Pope Julius II.

The DINING ROOM is dominated by a Flemish tapestry (c. 1510) depicting St. Veronica's Veil Curing the Emperor Vespasian. The 17C brass chandelier is from Holland. Objects on the table were commissioned by French patrons and include a footed dish of Venetian glass, majolica candlesticks, an enamel plate from Limoges, and a triangular faience salt cellar from St. Porchaire.

French paintings and furniture in the SPECIAL GALLERY have been assembled to suggest a sitting room in Lehman's Park Avenue apartment. Dominating the room is *Jean-Auguste-Dominique Ingres*: *Portrait of the Princesse de Broglie. Otherworks include: *Paul Cézanne*: House behind Trees on the Road to Tholonet. *Matisse*: L'Espagnol—Harmonie en bleu. *Dégas*: Dancing Peasant Girls. *Kees van Dongen*: Avenue du Bois. *André Derain*: Houses of Parliament at Night. *Edouard Vuillard*: Girl at the Piano. Paintings by Paul Signac, Pierre Bonnard, and Georges Seurat.

The *RED VELVET ROOM, closest in appearance to rooms in the Lehman Townhouse, contains paintings by the most important and influential masters and schools of **15C Italian painting** displayed against 18C French wall coverings. *Sassetta*: *The Annunciation, The Temptation of St. Anthony Abbot. Giovanni di Paolo*: Coronation of the Virgin, *Expulsion from Paradise. Giovanni Bellini*: *Madonna and Child. Sandro Botticelli*: *Annunciation. Jacometto Veneziano*: Portrait of Alvise Contarini and a companion portrait, Nun of San Secondo. *Lorenzo Costa*: Portraits of Alessandro di Bernardo Gozzadini and Donna Canonici. Alongside the paintings are notable pieces of Renaissance furniture including a large *bronze incense burner with a seated faun holding Panpipes on top by Andrea Briosco, known because of his curly hair as Il Riccio.

The STAIRCASE LANDING contains a large 16C Flemish tapestry representing the Last Supper and an altarpiece by Bartolommeo Vivarini. Beyond the landing is the SITTING ROOM with 16–18C Spanish and 17C Dutch painting. Pieter de Hooch, Gerard TerBorch, and Francisco de Goya are represented. *El Greco*: Saint Jerome as a Cardinal. *Rembrandt*: *Portrait of Gérard de Lairesse. Diego Velázquez*: Portrait of Maria Teresa.

The final room, the *FLEMISH ROOM, contains **15C northern European painting** and decorative arts. Paintings include: *Master of Moulins*: *Portrait of a Young Princess (Margaret of Austria). Hans Memling*: Annunciation. *Petrus Christus*: *St. Eligius. Gerard David*: two panels, one with *Christ Bearing the Cross and the Crucifixion and the other with *The Resurrection with Pilgrims of Emmaus (the outer sides depict the Archangel Gabriel and the Virgin of the Annunciation). *Lucas Cranach*: Nymph of the Spring, Venus and Cupid the Honey Thief. *Hans Holbein*: Portrait of Erasmus of Rotterdam.

Primitive Art.

The Michael C. Rockefeller Wing, 42,000 sq. ft of exhibition space devoted to the art of Africa, the Americas, and the Pacific Islands, contains more than 1500 objects spanning 3000 years and three continents. Within an architecturally dramatic setting (1982; Kevin Roche, John Dinkeloo & Assocs), millions of dollars worth of sophisticated technology have been lavished on the preservation of these 'primitive' objects, protecting them from vibration, sunlight, excess humidity or dryness.

History. Displayed here along with objects collected over the years by the museum is the collection of Nelson A. Rockefeller (donated 1978–79) formerly housed in the Museum of Primitive Art which he founded. The wing is named after his son, inheritor of his father's keen interest in primitive art and cultures, who died in 1961 on a collecting expedition in Papua New Guinea when his native boat overturned. The Asmat memorial poles in the largest exhibition room, collected by Michael Rockefeller, are prominently displayed and illuminated at night as a tribute to the young explorer.

The first of two galleries devoted to AFRICA is adjacent to the entrance from Greek and Roman Art and features artifacts from the Western Sudan and Guinea Coast. (Note: At the time of writing, the wing had just opened and all labels with accession numbers had not yet been attached.) Notable among the many wooden sculptures are a *7-ft male figure with upraised arms, Senufo helmet masks from the Ivory Coast in the form of animals, Bamana antelope headdresses from Mali, and (left side) a group of monumental bird figures carried on the heads of dancers.

The second African gallery opens to the left and is devoted to the arts of Central Africa, the Guinea Coast, and Equatorial Africa. In the Central African section are stools and chairs, including a rare *stool (1979.290) by the Buli master, Luba people (Zaire), a Songe mask (1979. 206.83) probably worn at ceremonies for the death of a king, a Kongo fetish of a man or spirit riding on a dog (1978.412.531), a Kongo figure of wood, nails, cloth, beads, and shell (1979.206.127) believed to have good and evil powers, and a Kongo mask (1979.206.27). Nearby in a freestanding case is an important Fang reliquary head (1979.206.229) from Gabon, once owned by sculptor Jacob Epstein. In the middle section devoted to the Guinea Coast are a Janus headdress (1976.329) of the Yoruba people of Nigeria, masks of the Guro people of the Ivory Coast including a monkey mask (1978.299) and an antelope mask (1979.206.105). Displayed prominently in a freestanding case is an important mid-16C *pendant mask of ivory (1978.412.323) from the court of Benin in Nigeria; it was worn on the belt of the ruler as part of his regalia. Among the fine collection of bronze and brass objects from the court of Benin are a leopard (1978.412.321), a group of memorial heads used to honour ancestors (i.e. 1979.206.86 and 1979.206.87), and also a plaque (1978.412.309) showing a ruler and his attendants supporting him and shielding him from the sun. A beautiful 16C ivory salt cellar (1972.63a,b) was found in Europe but carved in Nigeria according to Portuguese specifications. On the end wall is a Bangwa dancing figure (1978.412.576) from Cameroon and a Janus headdress from the Cross River area in Nigeria (1979.206. 299).

The galleries of THE AMERICAS lie behind the African galleries. Enter the first gallery, *Meso-America*, from the first African gallery. The collection of Aztec stone sculpture includes animals, female figures, perhaps agricultural or fertility goddesses, and a seated Standard Bearer (62.47) made in Veracruz in the 15C. Among the ceramics are examples from Huastec, Tlatilco, Colima, Nayarit, and Jalisco cultures. Olmec artifacts include an important *jade mask (1977.187.33) as well as pendants, ornaments, and 'baby' figures. Maya artifacts include ceramic vessels and a limestone lintel (1979.206.1047) depicting an enthroned ruler receiving gifts. From Veracruz (Remojadas) comes a rare 'smiling' figure (1979.206.1211) and a group of ornamented stone objects associated with a ritual ball game. In the center of the room are an Izapan rock altar (1978.412.22) carved in the shape of a jaguar, and a rare wooden *kneeling Maya priest or dignitary (1979.206.1063), remarkably surviving from the 6–9C.

The second gallery of the Americas opens from the first. Against the rear wall, *Central America*, are stone sculptures including metates or grinders, and ceramics from Ecuador and N. Peru, including vessels from the Chavin period. In the Treasury are ornaments and small objects of gold: Mohican ear spools (66.196.40,41) of gold with stone and shell inlay, a fine pendant (69.7.10) of a pugnacious figure with an elaborate headdress from the Tairona of Colombia, pectorals, an eagle pendant (1979.206.735), and other animal pendants resembling frogs, turtles, and sharks. Near the exit is a gold funerary mask (1974.271.35) of the Peruvian Chimu people. In the front area of the gallery are S. Peruvian ceramics including two fine Paracas storage jars (1974.123.1,2), feather hangings and ornaments.

From the second Americas gallery enter the third display area with a small section devoted to Eskimo and Northwest Coast Indian cultures of *N. America* (the Haida sea-bear mask of copper with inlaid shell eyes and teeth, 1979.206.830 is exceptional). The rest of the wing focuses on cultures of *the Pacific*. Adjacent to the N. American exhibit is a recreation of a ceremonial house with ceiling paintings on bark by the Kwoma people of New Guinea. Among the important objects in the Polynesian section are a temple drum with an elaborate openwork stand from the Austral Island (1978.412.720), a rare 18C ivory figure from Tonga, and an anthropomorphic pendant of a type known formerly only from the writings of the 18C explorer Captain Cook.

The main gallery in this area with its glass wall facing south contains objects from the Pacific islands, including large funerary festival carvings from N. New Ireland, standing slit gongs and figures from the New Hebrides, and an impressive collection of artifacts from New Guinea. The Michael C. Rockefeller collection of Asmat art includes *nine memorial poles from 12–21 ft tall facing the glass wall, reclining two-headed ancestor poles, costumes of straw and reed with woven masks, spears and shields, sago pounders, and canoe ornaments. On a low platform parallel to the window is a 25-ft crocodile effigy from the Karawari River region of New Guinea.

SECOND FLOOR.

The museum holds one of the world's great collections of **European Paintings,** which began with trustee William T. Blodgett's purchase of 174 paintings (c. 1870) when Old Masters were just becoming popular. It has since received major bequests from railroad financier H.B. Marquand, Benjamin Altman, J.P. Morgan, H.O. Havemeyer, and Michael Friedsam, as well as from Jacob S. Rogers, a locomotive manufacturer known as the meanest man in Paterson (New Jersey), who gave $5 million to the museum instead of to his relatives. With the exception of the Altman and the Lehman collections, gifts conditional upon specific arrangement within the museum, paintings are arranged chronologically and by school.

Audio tour available at the Audioguide desk in the Great Hall. Floor plan available at the main information desk. The Harry Payne Bingham Galleries to the right of Gallery 1 are used for special exhibitions. Because of the high quality of the collection as a whole, individual paintings have not been starred.

The collection of European paintings, one of the highlights of the museum, spans roughly the late 14–18C (19C paintings and sculpture arc displayed in the Andre Meyer Galleries).

GALLERY 1: *Giovanni Battista Tiepolo*: The Triumph of Marius, (65.183.1) The Capture of Carthage, (65.183.2). GALLERY 2: 18C English and Italian painting. *Sir Joshua Reynolds*: Lady Smith and her Children (25.100.10), Colonel George Coussmaker (20.153.3). *Thomas Gainsborough*: Mrs Grace Dalrymple Elliott (20.155.1), *Giovanni Paolo Panini*: Modern Rome (52.63.2); Ancient Rome (52.63.1).

Galleries 3–9 contain **Italian Painting.** GALLERY 3: *Berlinghiero*: Madonna and Child (60.173). *Giotto*: The Epiphany, (11.126.1). *Sassetta*: Madonna and Child with Angels (41.100.20), Journey of the Magi (43.98.1). *Giovanni di Paolo*: Madonna and Child with Saints (32.100.76). Works by Nardo di Cione, Maso di Banco, Lorenzo Monaco, and Segna di Buonaventura. GALLERY 4: Italian

METROPOLITAN MUSEUM
Second Floor, European Paintings

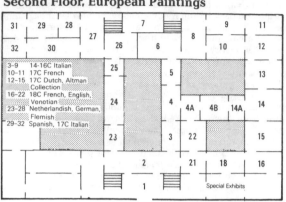

```
 31    29    28               7              9     11
           ┤  ├──── 27  ┤            8  ┤         ├──┤
 32    30                26      6            10    12

 3-9    14-16C Italian     25              5              13
 10-11  17C French
 12-15  17C Dutch, Altman                                 13
        Collection
 16-22  18C French, English,
        Venetian           24              4   4A 4B 14A 14
 23-28  Netherlandish, German,
        Flemish
 29-32  Spanish, 17C Italian
                           23          3   22        15

                            2             21   18    16

                            1                Special Exhibits
```

secular painting of the 15C. *Filippo Lippi*: Portrait of a Man and a Woman at a Casement (89.15.19). *Domenico Ghirlandaio*: Francesco Sassetti and his son Teodoro (49.7.7), Portrait of a Lady (32.100.71). GALLERY 4A: Ceiling panels from the Palazzo del Magnifico in Siena by Bernardo Pintoricchio; frescoes from the Villa Mattei in Rome by Baldassare Peruzzi. GALLERY 4B: Italian Renaissance paintings from the Altman Collection.

Benjamin Altman, founder of the department store and a bachelor who devoted himself totally to his work and his art collection, left a $15 million collection of paintings and porcelains to the museum on the condition that it be maintained intact in two suitable adjoining rooms, one for the paintings, statuary, Limoges enamels, and rock crystals, another for the Chinese porcelains.

Andrea Mantegna: The Holy Family with Saint Mary Magdalene (14.40.643). *Botticelli*: The Last Communion of St. Jerome (14.40.642). *Fra Angelico*: The Crucifixion (14.40.628). GALLERY 5: 15C **Venetian Painting.** *Carlo Crivelli*: ˙Madonna and Child (49.7.5). *Giovanni Bellini*: Madonna and Child (08.183.1), Madonna Adoring the Sleeping Child (30.95.256). *Vittore Carpaccio*: Meditation on the Passion (11.118). *Andrea Mantegna*: Madonna and Child with Seraphim (32.100.97). *Antonello da Messina*: Christ Crowned with Thorns (32.100.82). *Cosimo Tura*: Flight into Egypt (49.7.17).

GALLERY 6: 15C Italian Painting. Filippino Lippi: Madonna and Child (49.7.10). Domenico Ghirlandaio: St. Christopher with the Infant Christ (80.3.67). Luca Signorelli: Madonna and Child (49.7.13). Piero di Cosimo: Young St. John the Baptist (22.60.52). Paintings by Lorenzo di Credi, Cosimo Rosselli, and Perugino.

GALLERY 7: 16C Italian Painting. Bronzino: Portrait of a Young Man (29.100.16). Raphael: Madonna and Child Enthroned with the Young Baptist and Saints Peter, Catherine, Lucy, and Paul (16.30a,b). Andrea del Sarto: Holy Family with Infant St. John (22.75).

GALLERY 8: 16C Venetian Painting. *Titian*: Venus and the Lute Player (36.29), Venus and Adonis (49.7.16). *Paolo Veronese*: Mars and Venus United by Love (10.189), Alessandro Vittoria (46.31).

GALLERY 9: 16C Italian painting. *Correggio*: Saints Peter, Martha, Mary Magdalen, and Leonard (12.211). *Moretto da Brescia*: The Entombment (12.61). *Giovanni Battista Moroni*: Bartolommeo Bonghi (13.177). Work of Dosso Dossi, Andrea Solario, and Francesco Francia.

French Painting is displayed in galleries 10–11. GALLERY 10: 17C French painting. *Nicolas Poussin*: The Blind Orion Searching for the Rising Sun (24.45.1), The Rape of the Sabine Women (46.160). *Claude Lorrain*: View of La Crescenza (1978.205), Sunrise 47.12.

GALLERY 11: *Georges de la Tour*: The Penitent Magdalen (1978.517). *Philippe de Champaigne*: Jean Baptiste Colbert (51.38). Work of Paulus Bor, Hendrick Terrughen, Sebastien Bourdon.

The galleries of **17C Dutch Painting** occupy galleries 12–15. GALLERY 12: *Jan Steen*: Merry Company on a Terrace (58.89). *Johannes Vermeer*: Young Woman with a Water Jug (89.15.21), Portrait of a Young Woman (1979.396). Nicholas Maes: The Lacemaker (32.100.5).

GALLERY 13: 17C Dutch Landscape Painting. Salomon van Ruysdael, Jan van der Heyden, Aert van der Neer. *Meindert Hobbema*: A Woodland Road (50.145.22). *Aelbert Cuyp*: Starting for the Hunt (32.100.20). Young Herdsman with Cows (14.40.616). *Jan van Goyen*: Country House near the Water (32.100.6). *Jacob van Ruisdael*: Landscape (89.15.4).

GALLERY 14: 17C Dutch Painting from the **Benjamin Altman Collection**. *Frans Hals*: Young Man and Woman in an Inn (14.40.602), Merrymakers at Shrovetide (14.40.605). *Rembrandt*: Self-Portrait (14.40.618), Man with a Magnifying Glass (14.40.621), Lady with a Pink (14.40.622), Portrait of a Young Man (The Auctioneer) (14.40.624). *Vermeer*: A Girl Asleep (14.40.611). Also work by Maes, Cuyp, and Hobbema.

In GALLERY 14A are other Netherlandish and N. European Paintings from the Altman Collection. *Frans Hals*: Boy with a Lute (14.40.604). *Durer*: Virgin and Child with St. Anne (14.40.633). *Hans Memling*: Tommaso Portinari (14.40.626) and his wife, Maria Baroncelli (14.40.627). Also paintings by Dieric Bouts, Gerard Dou, Pieter de Hooch.

GALLERY 15: Dutch 17C Portraits. *Frans Hals*: Portrait of a Man (49.7.33). *Rembrandt*: Man in Oriental Costume—the Noble Slav (20.155.2), Aristotle with a Bust of Homer (61.198), The Standard Bearer (49.7.35), Flora (26.101.10).

GALLERY 16: **18C English Portraits.** *Sir Thomas Lawrence*: Elizabeth Farren (50.135.5). GALLERY 18: **18C French Painting.** *Jean-Baptiste Siméon Chardin*: Boy Blowing Bubbles (49.24). Paintings by Hubert Robert, Jean-Baptiste Greuze. GALLERY 21: French 18C Painting. *Jean Honoré Fragonard*: The Two Sisters (53.61.5), The Love Letter (49.7.49). *François Boucher*: The Toilet of Venus (20.155.9). *Antoine Watteau*: Mezzetin (34.138).

GALLERY 22: **18C Venetian painting.** *Francesco Guardi*: Venice: Piazza San Marco (50.145.21), Venice: Santa Maria della Salute (71.120), Fantastic Landscape (three canvases: 53.225.3, 41.80, and 53.225.4). Landscape painting by Pietro Longhi and Bernardo Belloto. *Gian Domenico Tiepolo*: A Dance in the Country (1980. 67).

In the other wing of galleries, opening to the left of Gallery 2 are

Renaissance paintings from northern Europe, Spanish paintings, and 18C Italian paintings.

GALLERY 23: **15C Netherlandish Painting** (recorded tour available). *Jan van Eyck*: The Crucifixion and The Last Judgment (33.92.a,b). *Petrus Christus*: Lamentation over the Dead Christ (91.26.12), Portrait of a Carthusian (49.7.19). Attrib. *Van Eyck, or Petrus Christus* Annunciation (32.100.35). *Rogier van der Weyden*: Christ Appearing to His Mother (22.60.58), Francesco d'Este (32.100.43). *Hugo van der Goes*: Portrait of a Man (29.100.15). *Gerard David*: Rest on the Flight into Egypt (49.7.21), triptych with the Adoration of the Shepherds, St. John the Baptist, St. Francis Receiving the Stigmata, (32.100.40a–c). GALLERY 24: *Gerard David*: Annunciation (50.145.9a,b). *Hieronymus Bosch*: The Adoration of the Magi (13.26). *Quentin Massys*: The Adoration of the Magi (11.143). *Joos van Cleve*: Virgin and Child (32.100.57).

GALLERY 25: **16C German Painting,** *Lucas Cranach*: John, Duke of Saxony (08.19). *Hans Holbein the Younger*: Edward VI when Duke of Cornwall (49.7.31), A Member of the Wedigh Family (50.135.3). *Jean Clouet*: Guillaume Budè (46.68). GALLERY 26: *Pieter Breughel the Elder*: The Harvesters (19.164). *Joachim Patinir*: The Penitence of St. Jerome (36.14.a–c). *Lucas Cranach*: The Judgment of Paris (28.221).

GALLERY 27: **17C Flemish Painting.** *Anthony van Dyck*: Portrait of a Genoese Lady, possibly the Marchesa Durazzo? (14.40.615), James Stuart, Duke of Richmond and Lennox (89.15.16). *Peter Paul Rubens*: Venus and Adonis (37.162). *Jacob Jordaens*: Holy Family with St. Anne and the Young Baptist and his Parents (71.11).

GALLERY 28: Van Dyck, Jordaens.

GALLERY 29: **El Greco.** Portrait of a Man (24.197.1). Cardinal Don Fernando Niño de Guevara (29.100.5), *View of Toledo (29.100.6), The Miracle of Christ Healing the Blind (1978.416). *Francisco de Zubarán*: The Young Virgin (27.137).

GALLERY 30: **17C Italian Painting.** *Caravaggio*: The Musicians (52.81). *Annibale Carraci*: The Coronation of the Virgin (1971.155). *Salvator Rosa*: The Dream of Aeneas (65.118). *Guido Reni*: Charity (1974.348). **17C Spanish Painting.**

GALLERY 31: *Diego Velázques.* Philip IV of Spain (14.40.639), Juan de Pareja (1971.86). GALLERY 32: *Bartolomé Esteban Murillo*, Virgin and Child (43.13). Also paintings by Luca Giordano and Zubarán.

The Department of **Twentieth Century Art** is located on the second floor adjacent to the galleries of European painting and is devoted to painting, works on paper, sculpture, and the decorative arts from 1900 to the present. Because the collection is shown in a succession of changing exhibitions, the visitor may see only a small portion at a given time; the department also mounts special exhibitions not drawn from the permanent collection. The particular strength of the collection is American painting, including the work of early 20C painters Joseph Stella and Max Weber; early American modernists Georgia O'Keeffe, Arthur Dove, Charles Demuth, Stuart Davis, and Arshile Gorky; Pacific Northwest painters Mark Tobey and Morris Graves; realist painters George Bellows, Edward Hopper, and Andrew Wyeth; regionalist painters Thomas Hart Benton, John Steuart Curry, Grant Wood, and Charles Burchfield; Josef Albers; abstract expressionists Jackson Pollock, Willem de Kooning, and Franz Kline; painters of the New York School; colour field painters

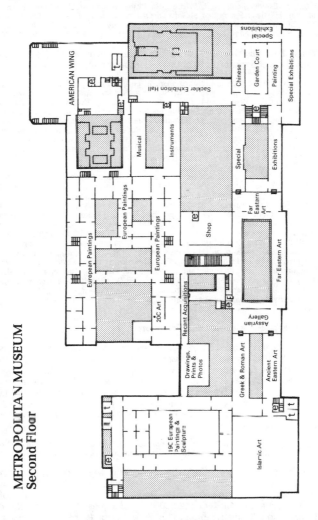

METROPOLITAN MUSEUM
Second Floor

AMERICAN WING

Special Exhibitions

Chinese

Garden Court Painting

Special Exhibitions

Sackler Exhibition Hall

Musical Instruments

Special Exhibitions

European Paintings

European Paintings

European Paintings

European Paintings

Far Eastern Art

Far Eastern Art

Shop

20C Art

Recent Acquisitions

Assyrian Gallery

Drawings, Prints & Photos

Greek & Roman Art

Ancient Eastern Art

19C European Paintings & Sculpture

Islamic Art

Ellsworth Kelly, Kenneth Noland, Barnett Newman, and Morris Lewis. Artists of the 60s and 70s represented in the collection are: Andy Warhol, Bruce Boice, Neil Welliver, Nancy Graves, Edward Avedisian, etc. In one of the galleries is a changing exhibition of decorative objects including examples in glass, ceramics, metalware, textiles, and furniture from the Art Nouveau and Art Deco periods with a good selection of Wiener Werkstätte pieces and more recent works.

Among the most important works in the collection are: *Pablo Picasso*: Portrait of Gertrude Stein; *Grant Wood*: Midnight Ride of Paul Revere; *Georgia*

O'Keeffe: Cow's Skull: Red, White, and Blue; *Joseph Stella*: Coney Island; Marsden Hartley, Portrait of a German Officer; *Edward Hopper*: The Lighthouse at Two Lights; *Jackson Pollock*: Autumn Rhythm; *David Smith*: Becca; *Kenneth Noland*: Magic Box; *Isamu Noguchi*: Kouros.

Prints, Drawings, and Photographs are shown in changing exhibitions in the galleries S. of the Recent Acquisitions gallery.

Drawings: The collection includes work in pen and ink, pencil, pastel, chalk, and watercolour, and is especially strong in Italian and French drawings, drawings by Rembrandt and Goya, and 18C Venetian drawings. The Alfred Stieglitz bequest focused on Post-Impressionist, Fauve, and Cubist draftsmen including Matisse and Picasso. Renaissance artists represented are Filippino Lippi, Leonardo da Vinci, Michelangelo, Raphael, Titian, Paolo Veronese, Dürer, and Jean Fouquet. 18C English drawings include the work of Gainsborough, Cozens, Hogarth, Rowlandson, and Blake. The American collection is noted for work by Winslow Homer, Thomas Eakins, John Singer Sargent, John Marin, and Charles Demuth.

The collection of the Department of **Prints and Photographs** includes also illustrated books, posters, silhouettes, trade cards, and certain kinds of drawings. Prints date from the early 15C and include the work of many major artists: Breuguel, Rubens, Michelangelo, Cranach, Goya, and Degas; it is especially rich in Rembrandt etchings. The poster collection includes examples by Léon Bakst, Toulouse-Lautrec, Bonnard, Vuillard, and Will Bradley. Among the printed books are a fine group of German and Italian 15C illustrated books, architectural books, fête books published to commemorate royal or state occasions, herbals, and pattern books for calligraphy, lace, and jewellery. At the core of the collection of photographs is the Alfred Stieglitz bequest, a survey of photography from its inception to about 1920. The department is especially strong in 19C photography, including the work of such pioneers as Julia Margaret Cameron and Adolphe Braun.

The study room is open to scholars by appointment only; tel: 879–5500, ext. 254.

19C European Paintings and Sculpture.

In 1980 the new André Meyer Galleries of ****19C European Paintings and Sculpture** opened allowing the public to see for the first time about 75% of the museum's outstanding collection from this period. The focus of the installation is the central gallery where the Impressionist and Post-Impressionist paintings are hung, while peripheral galleries contain minor painters, precursors of the period, and sculpture, with separate rooms devoted to Rodin, Degas, Courbet, and Corot.

Recorded tour available. Floor plan posted near entrance to galleries. The collection is of such quality that individual paintings have not been starred.

GALLERY 1 (enter from the galleries of Greek vases) contains works of the Neo-classical period. *Jacques-Louis David*: The Death of Socrates (31.4.5). *Jean-Auguste-Dominique Ingres*: Portraits of Joseph Antoine Moltedo (29.100.23), Jacques Louis Le Blanc (19.77.1), and Mme Le Blanc (19.77.2). Attrib. *Pierre Jeuffrain* (?): Portrait of Charlotte du Val d'Ognes (17.120.204).

GALLERY 2, the long gallery adjacent, is devoted to the origins of the 19C and contains works of influential Romantic painters. *Goya*: The Bullfight (22.181), José Costa y Bonells, called Pepito (61.259); Don Manuel Osorio Manrique de Zuniga (49.7.41); Majas on a Balcony (29.100.10). *Eugène Delacroix*: Basket of Flowers (67.178.60), The Abduction of Rebecca (03.30). *J.M.W. Turner*: The Whale Ship (96.29), The Grand Canal, Venice (99.31). *John Constable*: Salisbury Cathedral from the Bishop's Garden (50.145.8).

GALLERY 3 is devoted to **Gustave Courbet,** and the 22 paintings

METROPOLITAN MUSEUM
Andre Meyer Galleries

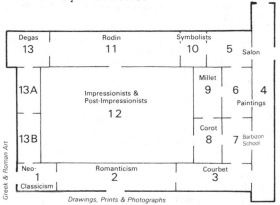

on display constitute one of the world's largest holdings of his work. Included are: Portrait of Jo (29.100.63), Young Ladies from the Village (40.175), Woman with a Parrot (29.100.57), Lady in a Riding Habit (29.100.59), and The Source of the Loue (29.100.122).

At the end of the Courbet gallery turn left into GALLERY 4, **Salon Paintings,** devoted to conservative painters who found favour with the Royal French Academy and the conservative public attracted to academy-sponsored salons. Included are a group of animal bronzes by *Antoine-Louis Barye* and paintings by such artists as *William Bouguereau, Adolf Schreyer,* and *Jean Léon Gérôme.* At the far end are paintings by Russian realists *Ilya Repin* and *Arkip Kuindji,* as well as the anon. City on a Rock (29.100.12), until recently attributed to Goya.

Turn left into GALLERY 5 devoted to **Second Empire Painters.** *Franz Winterhalter:* Countess Maria Ivanovna Lamsdorf (67.187.119), the Empress Eugenie (1978.403). Also, *Charles Marchal,* Penelope (17.138.2), and *Mihaly de Munkacsy,* The Music Room (08.136.11). Dominating the room is a marble group by *Jean-Baptiste Carpeaux,* Ugolino and His Sons (67.250), its subject drawn from Dante's Divine Comedy.

Turn left into GALLERY 6, also devoted to **Salon Paintings,** including such once popular works as: *Rosa Bonheur,* The Horse Fair (87.25); *Jules Bastien-Lepage,* Joan of Arc (89.21.2); *Pierre Auguste Cot,* The Storm (87.15.134); and *Henri-Alexandre-Georges Regnault,* Salome (16.95).

GALLERY 7, beyond, is the first of three devoted to the **Barbizon School.** Here are hung landscapes by Charles-François Daubigny and Théodore Rousseau, including his famous painting *The Forest in Winter at Sunset (11.4). To the right GALLERY 8 features the work of *Jean-Baptiste Camille Corot* and including figure paintings as well as the more familiar landscapes: Hagar in the Wilderness (38.64), The Ferryman (14.40.811), A Woman Gathering Faggots at

Ville d'Avray (17.120.225), Woman Reading (28.90). GALLERY 9 (straight ahead) contains the work of *Jean-François Millet* and *Honoré Daumier* along with lesser painters. Notable are Millet, Autumn Landscape with a Flock of Turkeys (17.120.209); Daumier, The Third Class Carriage (29.100.129); and *Arnold Böcklin*, Island of the Dead (26.90).

GALLERY 10, between the Second Empire Room and the gallery of Rodin sculpture contains paintings by **Symbolist Painters.** Included are *Gustave Moreau*, Oedipus and the Sphinx (21.134.1); *Frederick Leighton*, Lacrymae (96.28), *Edward Burne-Jones*, Le Chant d'Amour (47.26), and several allegorical paintings by *Pierre Puvis de Chavannes*.

GALLERY 11 has some 40 works by **Rodin** in bronze, marble, terracotta, and plaster. Included are a terracotta Head of Balzac (12.11.1), bronzes from his unfinished project The Gates of Hell, Adam (11.173.1) and Eve (11.173.2), a marble group of Cupid and Psyche (10.63.1), and several portrait busts. Also in this room are two works by *Aristide Maillol*, Night (50.100) and Summer (67.187.40).

GALLERY 12: Impressionist and Post-Impressionist Paintings. *Édouard Manet*: Woman with a Parrot (89.21.3); The Dead Christ with Angels (29.100.51); Mlle Victorine in the Costume of an Espada (29.100.53), The Spanish Singer (49.582), Boating (29.100.115). *Pierre-Auguste Renoir*: Mme Charpentier and Her Children (07.122), A Waitress at Duval's Restaurant (61.101.14), Tilla Durieux (61.101.13), By the Seashore (29.100.125). *Paul Cézanne*: Still Life (60.101.3), The Gulf of Marseilles Seen from L'Estaque (29.100.67), Dominique Aubert (53.140.1), The Cardplayers (61.101.1), Mont Sainte-Victoire (29.100.64), Mme Cézanne in a Red Dress (62.45), Still Life with a Ginger Jar and Eggplants (61.101.4). *Georges Seurat*: Invitation to the Sideshow (61.101.17), Study for a Sunday Afternoon on the Island of La Grande Jatte (51.112.6). *Paul Gauguin*: La Orana Maria (51.112.2), A Farm in Brittany (54.143.2), Two Tahitian Women (49.58.1). *Douannier Rousseau*: The Repast of the Lion (51.112.5).

Claude Monet: Rouen Cathedral (30.95.250), Bridge over a Pool of Water Lilies (29.100.113), Morning on the Seine near Giverny (56.135.5), Haystacks in the Snow (29.100.109), La Grenouillère (29.100.12), Terrace at Sainte-Adresse (67.24), The Park Monceau (59.206). *Camille Pissarro*: The Boulevard Montmartre on a Winter Morning (60.174), Two Young Peasant Women (1973.311.5). *Vincent van Gogh*: Cypresses (49.30), Sunflowers (49.41), The Potato Peeler (67.187.70b), Self-Portrait with a Straw Hat (67.187.70a), The Flowering Orchard (56.13), Mme Ginoux, also called L'Arlésienne (51.112.3), Irises (58.187).

GALLERY 13 (along with the two following galleries, 13a and 13b) contains the museum's outstanding collection of the work of **Edgar Degas,** much of it the bequest of Mrs H.O. Havemeyer, wife of the sugar tycoon, who, encouraged by Mary Cassatt, changed the focus of her husband's collection from oriental art to paintings. Woman with Chrysanthemums (29.100.128), Jacques-Joseph Tissot (39.161), Dancers in Rehearsal with Bass (29.100.127), The Collector of Prints (29.100.44), Sulking (29.100.43). In a case near the entrance is a bronze Fourteen Year Old Dancer (29.100.370). Nearby is a case of bronze casts of dancers; the museum owns an almost complete set of casts from the models of Degas and most of these are shown. In the next room are more small bronzes, paintings, and pastels: The

Dancing Class (29.100.184), Dancers Practicing at the Bar (29.100.34), and Woman Ironing (29.100.46). The last room contains pastels by Degas and contemporaries. Degas: Nude Combing her Hair (56.231); Woman Bathing in a Shallow Tub (29.100.41). *Mary Cassatt*: Mother Playing with her Child (22.16.23), Sara in a Green Coat (22.16.24), Margot in an Orange Dress (22.16.25). *Redon*: Bouquet of Flowers (56.50).

Islamic Art.

The museum's collection of Islamic art, the most comprehensive such collection in the world, is displayed in handsome galleries in the S. wing of the second floor and arranged chronologically and geographically to suggest the entire range of Islamic art—developing over a span of some 1300 years in countries as far apart as Spain and western China. Recorded tour available.

GALLERY 1, **Introductory Gallery,** presents exquisite objects suggesting the full sweep of the collection. From the left of the door (clockwise): inlaid wood and ivory doors from a 14C Cairo mosque (91.1.2064); bronze ewer from Iran, c. 1200 A.D. (44.15); glass bottle (41.150) from the Mamluk period, Syria, 14C; leaves from the Houghton *Shah Nameh*; jewelled dagger (36.25.664) from the Mughal period in India, 18C; fine silk carpet; bronze throne leg shaped like the forepart of a griffin (1971.143). In the center of the room a case contains a ceramic dish (65.106.2) from Iran or Transoxiana, 10C, with an underglaze slip-painted Arabic proverb.

GALLERY 2, to the right of the introductory gallery, contains objects found in the **Nishapur excavations** which the museum carried out from 1935–39 and again in 1947. Of particular interest are the central cases displaying a sampling of the great variety of ceramic types produced at Nishapur between the ninth and twelfth centuries; also tombstones, carvings, small vessels, tools, and utensils. A doorway on the far wall leads to a reconstruction of a small *ivan* or hall from the 10C with carved stucco panels once polychromed.

GALLERY 3 contains artifacts from the **Early Centuries of Islam** (7–12C A.D.) representing the cultures of the Umayyad dynasty (661–750 A.D.), whose capital was at Damascus, its offshoot the Spanish Umayyad dynasty (756–1031), the Egyptian Fatimid dynasty (969–1171), and its cultural children Islamic Sicily and S. Italy, as well as the Abbasid dynasty (750–1258) having as its capital city Baghdad and (836–889) Samarra on the Tigris River. Cases along the W. wall contain glassware, textiles, and ceramics. Cases along the E. wall contain a fine collection of glassware, delicately carved ivory plaques, and a collection of chess and gaming pieces. At the S. end of the E. wall are objects produced under a variety of Iranian dynasties of the 10–12C which paid nominal allegiance to the Abbasid caliphs but were in fact independent.

GALLERY 4A, directly beyond Gallery 3, is devoted to the **Seljuk** (11–13C) **and Mongol** (13–14C) **periods** and focuses on ceramics of the Seljuk period. Of special interest are the ceramic tabouret (69.225) and the large bronze incense burner in the form of a cat (51.56) in the S.W. case, the monumental stone tympanum (38.96) over the W. door, and the earliest known complete (except one pawn) •chess set (1971.193, a–ff) in the N.E. case, which dates from the 12C.

GALLERY 4B, to the W. also devoted to the **Seljuk and Mongol periods**, contains metalwork, painting, and sculpture as well as ceramics. On the left end wall near the entrance is a particularly fine *stucco head with Turkic features (42.25.17) and on the far left wall are fine ceramic pieces of the *mina'i* (i.e. overglaze enamelled) type. On the right wall are stone and tile niches and on the far right wall, a ceramic ewer with carved and pierced outer shell (32.52.1). Cases in the center of the room contain leaves from 14C manuscripts of the *Shah Nameh* of Ferdowsi, the Iranian national epic, as well as other 13–14C manuscript leaves.

GALLERY 4C contains objects which originally formed part of mosque settings including a historical progression of calligraphy styles as represented in Koran leaves, Koran stands, enamelled glass mosque lamps, and wood panels. The centerpiece of the room is a *Mihrab (39.20) or prayer niche that indicates the direction of Mecca, executed in small pieces of ceramic arranged to form floral and geometric patterns and Arabic inscriptions.

GALLERY 5, which opens off Gallery 4B, contains mainly works from the **Ayyubid** (1171–1250) and **Mamluk** (1250–1517) **periods** in Egypt and Syria and the **Nasrid period** (1230–1492) in Spain. In the center is a superb *Mamluk geometric carpet (1970.105); also displayed are examples of ceramics, textiles, brass, and architectural ornament including the monumental carved, painted, and gilded ceiling (56.234.35) from early 16C Spain.

GALLERY 6, **Timurid period** (1395–1501) **and Savafid period** (1501–1736) in Iran, contains a number of beautiful miniatures from such manuscripts as the *Mantiq at-Tayr* ('Language of the Birds') dated 1483, the *Haft Paikar* ('Seven Portraits'), from c. 1426, the Houghton *Shah Nameh*, executed over a period of years and consequently affording a picture of the development of Savafid painting over the second quarter of the 16C. The room also contains carpets, a jade signet ring (12.224.6), and dagger hilt (02.18.765) from the Timurid period.

GALLERY 7, **other arts of the Savafid period,** contains ceramics, carpets, metalwork, and book bindings. Of particular interest are (left wall, 5th case clockwise) a ceramic plate (65.109.2) following Chinese blue and white porcelain ware in its colour scheme and design of intertwined dragons; Timurid jug (91.1.607) in N.W. case, Tabriz carpet (10.61.3) with geometric star pattern filled with mythological creatures. There is also a changing exhibition of carpets on sliding rug racks.

GALLERY 8, **art of the Ottoman Empire,** mainly Turkey, (1281–1924), contains ceramics including many beautiful pieces of painted and glazed ware from Iznik (16–17C), carpets, and textile fragments.

GALLERY 9, **Mughal period in India** (1526–1858), has examples of carpets, miniature painting, jewellery, and jade carving. Opposite the entrance on a marble platform is a dramatic wool carpet (17.190.857 alternating with 17.190.858) from the period of Shah Jahan. On the right wall is a display of jade with colours ranging from green so dark as to appear almost black, through smokey green, to white.

GALLERY 10, adjacent to the introductory gallery, is the luxurious panelled *Nur ad-Din room (1707) from Damascus, a traditional reception room of a well-to-do gentleman of the Ottoman period. The floor is executed in richly coloured marble; the wall panels are gesso on wood with raised floral and geometric designs; the ceiling is sumptuously decorated.

The RAYMOND AND BEVERLY SACKLER GALLERY FOR **Assyrian Art** is dominated by 20 large reliefs and two imposing carvings from the palace of King Assurnasirpal II (883–859 B.C.) in Nimrud (northern Iraq). The reliefs were collected from a number of rooms in the palace but are here displayed set into the walls of one large gallery whose entrance is guarded by two immense carvings of human-headed mythical winged creatures, a bull and a lion. Supplementing the reliefs are objects from the excavations at Nimrud—bowls, clay figurines, ivories in Syrian, Assyrian, and Phoenician styles.

The other galleries of Ancient Near Eastern Art are undergoing reinstallation, although highlights (changed occasionally) of the collection are shown in a temporary gallery opposite the entrance to Islamic Art.

Greek and Roman Art.

Five rooms are devoted to the museum's fine collection of **Greek Vases**, arranged chronologically beginning in the elevator lobby adjacent to the department of Islamic art. Recorded tour available at the audio desk in the Great Hall.

In the lobby are displayed three large sepulchral vases from the Geometric period (8C B.C.) which served as tomb monuments (14.130.14; 14.130.16; and 31.11.2). Also, a four-handled jar with lid (64.51.965) from Cyprus (8C B.C.), decorated with horses, goats, and birds.

Enter ROOM 1 (room number above entrance door) with its displays of wares from the Protogeometric period (11–10C B.C.) to the Attic Black-Figured ware of the 6C B.C. Wall cases at the left of the entrance contain (cases 1–2) Attic Protogeometric and Geometric wares, Corinthian, Laconian, Boeotian, Euboean, Chalcidian, and Rhodian wares (cases 3–6) including (case 5, 63.11.3) a fine neck amphora with palmettes, sirens, and cocks. Among the black-figured vases are a column krater (case 8, 24.97.95) depicting the struggle between Zeus and the titans, another column krater (case 9, 31.11.11) showing Hephaistos brought back to Olympos, and a volute krater (case 10, 1977.11.2) with a bull and boars. The monumental neck amphora (case 11, 11.210.1) depicting Herakles battling a centaur, probably Nessos, is from the earlier orientalizing period (7C B.C.). Also noteworthy (case 13, 01.8.6) is a cup with a gorgon's head (interior) and Achilles pursuing Troilos and Polyxena (exterior).

ROOM 2 also contains Attic Black-Figured vases, including a group (cases 1–6) of prize amphorae of the type used at the Pan-Athenaic festival held in Athens. The vases when presented to the winner were filled with about 40 litres of olive oil and depict an armed Athena on one side and on the other a scene of the athletic event for which they were awarded. Especially famous is one depicting a foot race (case 2, 14.130.12). In case 7 is a fine hydria or water jar (56.171.29) showing Ajax and Achilles playing at draughts, and in case 9 a lekythos or oil jug (56.11.1) depicting a bridal procession.

ROOM 3, primarily devoted to Attic Black-Figured ware, contains central cases with selections of black-figured pottery and a study collection of interest to the specialist in cases against the walls. To the left of the exit door are several psykters or wine-coolers (for example, 10.210.18), which float upright in a larger vessel filled with ice water or snow, the stem serving as a keel. On the other side of the doorway is a red-figured amphora (63.11.6) depicting the struggle between Herakles and Apollo over the Delphic tripod. Painted by the Andokides Painter, it is one of the earliest red-figured vases in existence.

The next gallery (ROOM 4) devoted to Red-Figured ware contains (case 19) the *Euphronios vase (1972.11.10), the most famous piece in the collection.

In 1972 the museum purchased it legally in Switzerland, though many people, including officials of the Italian government, believe that it was dug up by tomb robbers not long before the sale and smuggled out of Italy. Dating from c. 515 B.C. this calyx krater (bowl for mixing wine and water) depicts an episode from the Trojan War, the death of Sarpedon, whose body is lifted by Sleep and Death as Hermes looks on. The other side of the vase shows a scene of soldiers donning their battle gear. Admired for the design of the individual compositions, for the virtuosity of the brushwork, and the skillful rendering of anatomical detail, the vase is considered by many to be Euphronios's masterpiece.

Also displayed in the room are (case 6) an exhibit illustrating the traditional shapes of Attic vases from 6–4C B.C., an amphora (case 3, 56.171.38) by the Berlin painter depicting a youth singing and playing the cithara, a stamnos or wine storage jar (case 7, 41.162.20) depicting Helen fleeing from Menelaos at the sack of Troy and another (case 7, 56.171.51) with Peleus wrestling with Thetis. Other noteworthy pieces include an oinochoe or wine jug (case 10, 23.160.55) depicting Ganymede with hoop and gamecock fleeing Zeus; a kylix or cup (case 15, 53.11.4 and 1970.46) depicting Theseus taking leave of his father Poseidon (exterior) and Theseus and Amphitrites at the bottom of the sea (interior); a lekythos (case 16, 54.11.7) by the Achilles Painter depicting a lady handing a bundle of clothes to her maid, executed in the white-ground technique; and (case 17, 07.286.84), a large volute krater depicting the battle between the Amazons and the Athenians, whose main composition is believed to have been taken from a famous contemporary painting no longer in existence.

ROOM 5 contains Attic and S. Italian Red-Figure ware from the late 5–4C B.C., by which time vase painting had declined as a major art. A study collection around the outside walls contains a collection of Apulian, Campanian, Lucanian, Gnathian, and Teano ware. Of interest are (case 16, 51.11.2) a rare calyx krater depicting a grotesque comic actor playing the role of a reveller, a fine column krater (case 18, 50.11.4) showing a painter colouring a marble statue of Herakles while Herakles and Zeus look on, and a polychromed vase from Sicily (case 7, 53.11.5) dating from the 3C B.C. Also displayed in this room is a small but choice collection of ANCIENT GLASS, ranging from early Mycenaean to late Roman times and including examples of both moulded and blown glass.

Far Eastern Art.

The collection of Far Eastern Art covers a time span from the 2nd millennium B.C. to the 19C A.D. with objects from China, Japan,

Korea, Southeast Asia, and a small but choice collection of Indian sculpture.

In 1981 the museum completed the first phase of installing its permanent collection of Far Eastern art. Open are the two Douglas Dillon galleries of Chinese paintings and the Chinese garden court. Cases around the Great Hall balcony contain Chinese ceramics and bronzes, Indian sculpture, and a small sampling of Japanese, and Southeast Asian art, all of which will be reinstalled in permanent galleries (Japanese galleries scheduled to open 1984–85).

The collection of **Chinese Ceramics and Bronzes** is arranged chronologically along the E. side of the Great Hall balcony. The cases on the S. end of the balcony have selected examples of Indian and S.E. Asian sculpture while those at the N. end have a small display of Japanese ceramics. Along the W. side of the balcony and around the Great Stairway are porcelains with enamelled decoration and monochrome glazes.

The earliest material is in the N.E. corner of the balcony. Among the pieces from the neolithic period and the Shang dynasty (14–11C B.C.) is a neolithic jar (1980.4.13) painted in black and red, an earthenware wine vessel (50.61.5) from the Shang dynasty whose shape and decoration reflect the influence of contemporary bronzes. In the next case are bronzes from the Shang and Chou dynasties including a three-legged vessel (49.136.5), an impressive ritual altar set (24.72.1–14), a wine vessel with bands of copper decoration (29.100.545) depicting birds, masks, and animals, and a ritual grain or wine vessel (43.24.5). Pottery from the Chou dynasty includes a beautifully shaped earthenware jar (50.61.10) and a bowl (50.61.9) with a foot and footed lid.

Among the noteworthy pieces from the Han dynasty (206 B.C.–A.D. 220) are an earthenware jar (26.292.83), an incense burner (65.74.2) decorated with a stylised landscape, and a gilt and polychromed horse (25.20.04) which served as a tomb figure.

Beyond the arches are bronzes from the T'ang, Wei, and Ch'i dynasties (6–7C) including an appealling lion (45.25.31). Tomb figures in the following case include a heavenly guardian or Lakapala (11.83.1) from the T'ang dynasty; also, T'ang stonewares including a flask (1972.274) with thick dark brown, grey, and bluish glazes.

The next case contains porcelaneous stoneware including a finely sculpted crouching animal (60.75.2) with pale olive glaze, an amphora (29.100.217) with white glaze, a celadon-glazed 'bowl (18.56.36) with carved dragons, one of the high points of the collection, and a ewer (26.292.73) with carved flying phoenixes. In the two remaining cases before the arch are a rare vase (26.292.61) with sgraffito decoration dating from the 11–12C, black and white painted pillow (60.73.2) and a black glazed bowl (60.81.3) with rust-colored splashes from the Northern Sung dynasty (12–13C); Sung porcelains include a greenish-white pillow (26.292.82) with a reclining lady underneath and a Kuan ware plate (24.172.1). with crackled blue glaze.

In a case under the next arch is a large blue and white Ming (1368–1644) dynasty porcelain jar (37.191.1) with a ferocious dragon. The remaining cases contain wares from the Yüan (1279–1368), Ming and Ch'ing (1644–1912) dynasties. In the first case are examples of Chün ware with blue glazes, an exceptional Ming bowl (18.56.35) with underglaze red copper oxide decoration, a pair of incense burners (34.113.2,3) in the shape of lions, a Yüan vase (26.271.1) with cobalt oxide decoration, and several examples of Ming blue and white wares. The superb Bodhidharma (63.176) is made of a type of porcelain known as blanc de chine. The next case contains early Ch'ing dynasty porcelains of the K'ang-hsi period (1662–1722) with coloured enamel decoration. In the last case on this side of the hall is a pair of seated figures, one (61.200.11) perhaps representing the God of Wealth in Civil Aspect, the other (61.200.12) showing him in Military Aspect.

Cases on the S. end of the hall contain a small selection of Indian, Pakistani, Nepali, Thai, Tibetan, Indonesian, and Cambodian sculpture. Notable among the Indian figures are a bronze standing *Buddha (69.222) from c. A.D. 600–650 and a bronze figure of Parvati (57.51.3).

On the W. side of the hall is a collection of porcelaneous stoneware and porcelain from the Ming dynasty and porcelains from the Ch'ing dynasty decorated with coloured enamels and exquisite monochrome glazes. The cases surrounding the staircase contain porcelains from the collection of Benjamin Altman, grouped together because of a stipulation in the bequest (see p366). In the center of the balcony stands *Antonio Canova*'s marble Perseus with the Head of Medusa (67.110).

Cases at the N. end of the hall display Japanese ceramics including early stoneware, tea ceremony objects and utensils, ceramics from the Momoyama period, and porcelains from the Edo period.

Adjacent to the balcony is the Arthur M. Sackler Gallery of **Chinese Stone Sculpture**, focusing on large scale works mostly from the 5–6C. Included are a Buddhist stele (65.29.3), a fine gilt bronze *standing Buddha (26.123), a large standing Bodhisattva (65.29.4), and a wall painting of a Buddhist Assembly (65.29.2) showing Buddha flanked by divine, mythological, or symbolic figures.

The galleries beyond, presently used for special exhibitions, will display early Chinese, Indian, Southeast Asian, and Korean art when the permanent installation is completed.

The galleries of **Chinese Paintings** are named in honour of Douglas Dillon, chairman of the museum's board of trustees. Inside the entrance is a room displaying **Chinese Sculpture:** a seated Bodhisattva (42.25.5) from the Sung (960–1279) or Ch'ing (1115–1254) dynasty, a Seated Bodhidharma (43.114) from the Sung dynasty, and a Standing Monk (52.41) from the Liao (907–1125) dynasty.

The galleries themselves are organized chronologically with the earlier material in the left or W. gallery. On view are some 80 works of Chinese painting from the Sung, Yüan, Ming, and Ch'ing dynasties, shown on a rotating basis along with sculpture and objects from comparable periods, important loans, and special exhibitions. In the right or E. gallery is a permanent display of jades from the Heber R. Bishop collection donated in 1902.

The Astor Court between the two galleries is a small *Chinese garden court* (recorded tour available) modelled on the Garden of the Master of the Fishing Nets in Suzhou, W. of Shanghai, first built in the 12C by Shi Zhengzhi, who retreated from the burdens of public administration to this garden-residence. A full-scale prototype erected in Suzhou remains there as a gift to the Chinese people while the present courtyard was constructed in China and assembled on site (1980) according to traditional methods by 27 engineers and craftsmen from the Suzhou Garden Administration.

Enter the courtyard through the circular moon gate in the S. wall. At the N. end lies the moon-viewing room and the Ming Room whose tall lattice doors can be opened completely. The bricks on the courtyard floor were fired in the imperial kiln at Lumu built between 1736–96 to make tiles and bricks for the palace at Peking. The pillars are of *nan* wood, a broadleafed evergreen of the cedar family known for its resistance to warping, insects, and deterioration. Once nearly extinct because of over-cutting, *nan* wood has been used since the establishment of the People's Republic (1949) for only a few select projects including this one and the Memorial Hall for Chairman Mao. Against the W. wall stands a half-pavilion with upturned eaves, named the Cold Spring Pavilion for the small spring that flows from the rocks into a pool on the left of the structure. The pavilion provides a fixed point from which to view the garden in contrast to the covered walkway on the other side which guides the visitor to the most pleasing views while offering shelter from rain and sun. On the S. and E. walls are latticed windows, each different to avoid the boredom of repetition, their patterns chosen from a garden manual of 1634. Against the S. wall stands a fantastically shaped Taihu rock, one of several in the courtyard harvested from the bottom of Lake Tai, whose waters and sands give these rocks their characteristic forms. To the connoisseur the proportions of the rock are significant—it should appear lean and bony, be broader at the top than at the base, have holes so that it rings when struck, and have 'walkable' passages through its surface where the mind may wander and climb. Another rock composition, this one of three peaks, stands to the right of the Cold Spring Pavilion.

At the N. end of the courtyard is the Ming Room with a collection of fine Chinese furniture. The early 16C rosewood side table and four red sandalwood chairs exemplify the peak of hardwood furniture design reached during the Ming period. The large clothes cupboard dates from 15–16C and is also of rosewood, while the table with drawers at one time was a family ancestral altar.

Musical Instruments.

The *Collection of Musical Instruments displayed in the André Mertens Galleries is outstanding for its scope and for the beauty of the individual instruments.

Recorded tour available at desk in Great Hall. The galleries are arranged in a rectangle with instruments from Europe and the United States on the W. (left) side, instruments from the Americas and the Pacific on the N., and Near Eastern, African, and Asian instruments on the E.

In the 1870s Mrs Mary Crosby Brown, wife of a New York banker, began collecting instruments from all over the world with the help of missionaries, foreign officers of her husband's bank, scholars, and diplomats. By 1914 she had gathered some 3000 instruments which now form the nucleus of the present collection of more than 4000 instruments.

The INTRODUCTORY GALLERY (cases 1–3) provides an overview of the collection and includes western and oriental brass instruments, a Javanese *saron* in the form of a dragon (89.4.1462), drums from Europe, Thailand, and Melanasia, and a group of unusual keyboard instruments.

EUROPEAN GALLERIES. The instruments are arranged by family or by material. Case 4: Ivory instruments including a baroque oboe, *cornetto (52.96.1) and recorder. Horns include post horns, hunting horns, a shofar, and falconer's horn, as well as serpent and bass horns (case 6). Among the reed instruments are saxophones and Sarrusophones (similar but with double reeds), shawms, oboes, and bassoons. Vitrine 2 has an amusing display of walking stick instruments including a violin, bow and all, built into a slender walking stick. Case 11 contains a variety of recorders and flutes of porcelain, ivory, ebony, glass, and tortoise shell. Among the keyboard instruments are a *piano (89.4.1219) by Bartolommeo Cristofori, a spinettino (53.6) made for Eleanora della Rovere, and a *double virginal (29.90) by Hans Ruckers. Among the stringed instruments are lutes, mandolins, citterns, guitars, and American folk instruments, as well as a freestanding case with *baroque violins by Stradivari and Amati. Case 18 holds instruments with sympathetic strings, *viols, arpeggione, baryton, and mute instruments.

GALLERIES OF THE AMERICAS, ASIA, AND AFRICA. Instruments from the Americas (cases 19–21) include pottery whistles, whistling jars, and rattles in human and animal forms. The next cases contain instruments of the S. Pacific (22–23), North Africa (24), the Near East (25), Iran and Turkey (26). African instruments (cases 27–31) include whistles, shrine drums, *Benin bells, rattles, thumb pianos, and a marimba with gourd resonators (89.4.492). Japanese instruments (cases 32–34) include fiddles, kotos, drums, bells, and gongs, as well as a startling *large bronze gong (89.4.2016) carried by demons with glass eyes. Chinese and Korean instruments (cases 35–37) include a beautiful sonorous stone (89.4.64), gong chimes, bronze bells, drums, a *jade flute (65.149), and a mouth organ (89.4.96) of bamboo pipes in a lacquered bowl. Cases 39–41 contain Tibetan instruments including trumpets made from the thigh bones of priests, and instruments of S.E. Asia. Indian instruments (cases 42–46) include sitars, tambura and vina, drums and trumpets, other bowed and plucked stringed instruments, and a large bronze temple gong (89.4.278).

GROUND FLOOR.

Located on the ground floor adjacent to the Grace Rainey Rogers Auditorium, the **Costume Institute** contains a collection of more than 35,000 articles of clothing including regional costumes and sophisticated articles of urban dress. The regional costumes, representing cultures of Asia, Africa, Europe and the Americas, include such diverse examples as bullfighters' costumes and capes, a bridal robe from Korea, and tribal headgear from Central Africa. Among the urban costumes are a collection of American and European dresses from the late 17C to the present time, lingerie, accessories, sport costumes (skating dresses, fencing costumes), and notable examples of elegant couturier clothing.

The collection is shown in special exhibitions changed approximately once a year and often mounted with great style. (Recorded tour available.) Past exhibitions have included The World of Balenciaga, American Women of Style, and The Glory of Russian Costume, viewed by some 830,000 visitors.

The institute has storerooms, private study rooms, a library, and a conservation room. The library, which contains reference works on costume design and history, fashion journals, pattern books, photographs, and fashion plates from the 19–20C, is open to students and researchers by appointment only; telephone 879–5500, ext. 628.

European Decorative Arts.

The galleries on the ground floor (go down the staircase from the Medieval Tapestry Hall) are devoted to European decorative arts, primarily ceramics, silver, and glass. Gallery 37 at the bottom of the stairs features **17–18C French Ceramics.** Among the earlier wares are late 16–early 17C tin-glazed faience from Nevers and Lyons, and lead-glazed earthenware. Other faience comes from such provincial centers as Rouen, Nevers, Luneville, and Strasbourg. Among the porcelains are examples from the factories at Vincennes and Sèvres including plaques used as inlays on furniture and figurines, along with vases and table wares. Galleries 52–53 beneath the stairs contain **German and Austrian Ceramics.** Noteworthy in the first gallery is a pair of large stove tiles, c. 1560, depicting the Execution of the Five Kings of the Amorites (68.81.2) and the Adoration of the Shepherds (68.81.1). Also: salt-glazed stoneware including cups, tankards, and jugs, faience from Fulda and Hoechst, 18C Swiss and German porcelain figurines (Nymphenburg, Ludwigsburg, Fulda, Hoechst, Frankenthal). In the last gallery in this row (54) is a wide range of Meissen wares including part of a Swan table service made (1737–41) for Count Brühl, director of the Meissen factory, a number of pieces showing the influence of oriental porcelains, and a family of large porcelain goats (69.192. 62.245) cast from models by J.J. Kändler.

Opening from the first room of German ceramics is GALLERY 48, devoted to other European ceramics including 17C Delft ware, Dutch and German tiles, 15–16C Italian majolica (examples from Florence, Siena, Deruta, Urbino, Faenza, and Castel Durante), and three examples of Medici porcelain. In the following gallery (47) is one of the earliest dated majolica works (1487), a Lamentation (04.26). GALLERY 46, to the left, contains an exhibit introducing various types of ceramic ware and the techniques of the silversmith. GALLERY 45, beyond, is devoted to **English Ceramics** and contains examples of salt-glazed wares, tin-enamelled earthenware, porcelains from Chelsea and Bow, Wedgewood jasper ware, Bristolware.

Return to Gallery 48 (European ceramics). GALLERY 49, opening from the middle of this room, contains a collection of China trade porcelain. GALLERY 50, beyond, has a collection of 16–19C **European Glass,** including Venetian, Dutch, German, Austrian, French, Spanish, and Bohemian examples.

Return to GALLERY 37 (French 17–18C ceramics) at the foot of the staircase. GALLERIES 38 and 39, adjacent, contain examples from the collection of French and English silver. The French collection contains over 500 pieces, Parisian and provincial, from the bequest of Catherine D. Wentworth. Also noteworthy in the collection (but not always on display) is a group of silver and silver gilt cups in the form of animals, English and Irish table silver, English silver by master

silversmith Paul Lamerie, and a collection of N. European spoons
from 16–19C, the initial gift to the collection.

The final room, GALLERY 40, contains watches and clocks,
examples of French and English enamelling and goldsmithing, and
pieces from the Morgan bequest of 1917 including snuff boxes,
Renaissance jewels, and enamelled jewelled cups. Outstanding are
the Rospiglioso Cup (14.40.667) now attrib. to Jacopo Bilivert, a
Flemish craftsman, but sold to Benjamin Altman as the work of

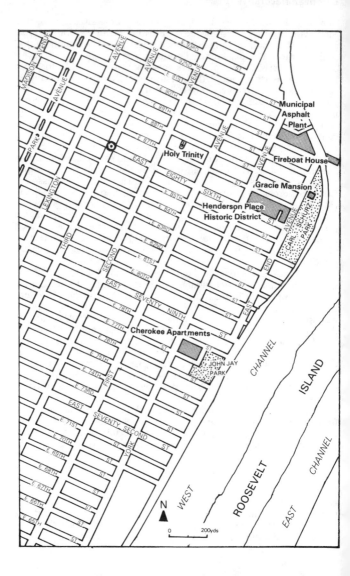

Benvenuto Cellini, an Astronomical tower clock (17.190.747), with dials to show the movement of the planets and signs of the zodiac, and an Automaton (17.190.746), Diana seated on a stag, which at one time moved when wound up.

25 Yorkville

SUBWAY: IRT Lexington Ave local or express (train 4, 5, or 6) to 86th St. Walk five blocks E. to East End Ave; enter Carl Schurz Park and walk N. along the promenade.

BUS: M15, uptown on First Ave or M18, uptown on York Ave (from 57th St) to 88th St; walk E. to Carl Schurz Park. M31, crosstown on 86th St; enter Carl Schurz Park at 86th St and East End Ave, walk N. along the promenade.

Yorkville, today not easily distinguishable from other middle class neighbourhoods, was once home to three major ethnic groups: Germans, Czechoslovakians, and Hungarians. Although most of the East European population has moved out to the suburbs and Yorkville itself with the spate of new luxury high rises has become suddenly chic and too expensive for many of the ageing survivors, traces of the old way of life still remain.

History. In the late 18C Yorkville was a small hamlet between New York and Harlem, its country estates attracting such wealthy families of Germanic origin as Schermerhorns, Rhinelanders, and Astors. When the New York and Harlem Railroad arrived in 1834, Yorkville quickly became a suburb attracting prosperous middle class Germans, among them people like the Rupperts who operated a brewery, but the main concentration of Germans remained on the Lower East Side, notably around Tompkins Square in a neighbourhood called 'Kleindeutschland'. By 1900 as waves of East European and Italian immigrants poured in, the downtown Germans began moving out, a migration hastened by the 'General Slocum' disaster (1904) when an excursion steamer jammed with holiday tourists, mostly women and children from 'Kleindeutschland', burned and sank in the East River, killing more than a thousand people. Many of the surviving husbands, prevented from attending the excursion by work, found their homes unbearable and moved to Yorkville to be with their countrymen.

Though Yorkville was never rich it remained a solid neighbourhood through the years of the Depression, a place where people worked close to home—either in small businesses or for the brewery—and enjoyed themselves at local restaurants, beer gardens of the Bavarian variety or cafés modelled after those in Vienna. At some restaurants, presumably those for tourists, the doormen wore lederhosen and plumed Tyrolean hats.

In the years before World War II, Yorkville was a center of both Nazi and anti-Nazi activity, the home of the Nazi-supported German-American Bund with its official paper, the 'Deutscher Weckruf und Beobachter' (at 178 E. 85th St) and the German-American Business League which published a list of Nazi-approved American business firms. The German Central Book Store (218 E. 84th St) carried books banned by Hitler, while the German Workers Club (1501 Third Ave) served as an anti-Nazi labour organisation.

After World War II, the area saw a last wave of German immigration and later an influx of Hungarians following the uprising of 1956. Since then newcomers have been largely Hispanics filtering down from Spanish Harlem on the N. edge of Yorkville or working couples and single people who rent the apartments in the luxury high rise buildings. Much of the remaining German population is believed to live in unrenovated, rent-controlled apartments above the neighbourhood's shops.

Begin at the N. end of Carl Schurz Park along the East River opposite 90th St. Visible to the N.W. (York Ave to Franklin D. Roosevelt Drive,

90th–91st Sts) is a strange parabolic structure of exposed concrete over an arched steel frame, formerly the **Municipal Asphalt Plant** (1944; Kahn & Jacobs; DL), used for making material for paving city streets until 1968 when larger facilities were needed. In 1972 a citizens' group argued that the plant and surrounding land should not be used for a housing project but for a public park and recreational facility, convinced the city to go along with the project, and tore up the former parking lot to create an athletic field, known as the Asphalt Green. The Neighborhood Committee for the Asphalt Green is now working to convert the asphalt plant itself to an arts and recreation center.

At the N. end of the park along the river is the **Fireboat House Environmental Center,** another work of community faith and dedication, today a center for studies on energy and the river environment where some 5000 schoolchildren come yearly. The boathouse was built c. 1930 as one of 22 fireboat stations around the city. When faster and more powerful diesel boats began replacing the earlier steam models in the 1950s, stations were gradually phased out and by 1976 when this one was abandoned only four remained. The Committee for the Asphalt Green was given control of the building by the Department of Ports and Teminals in February 1977 but in May 1978 four loaded sand barges coming through Hell Gate broke loose from their tug and smashed the pier. The following May a fire set by arsonists destroyed half the boathouse. Eventually with financial support from foundations, the state, and the community, the present boathouse was built, using active and passive solar heating devices and a small wind generator to demonstrate energy conservation measures available to the average homeowner.

Walk S. along the promenade by the river. **Carl Schurz Park** bears the name of the most notable German-American of the 19C—hero of the German revolutionary movement of 1848, immigrant (1852), supporter of Abraham Lincoln, brigadier general in the Civil War, U.S. senator, secretary of the interior, editor of the 'New York Evening Post' and the 'Nation', and, at the end of his life, resident of Yorkville. The park reaches from 90th St to Gracie Square at 84th St, offers fine river views, and is pleasantly landscaped (remodelled during construction of the F.D.R. Drive, 1938). The promenade, *John Finley Walk*, honours John Huston Finley (1863–1940), president of the City College of New York, editor of the 'New York Times', state commissioner of education, and unflagging pedestrian; more than once he walked the 32 miles around Manhattan island.

From the walkway look N. The small island N. of the Fireboat House at the confluence of the East and Harlem Rivers is Mill Rock, part of a group of islands and reefs in the Hell Gate section of the Harlem River. The East River, spanned by the Triborough Bridge with the curve of Hell Gate Arch behind it, runs along the E. side of Mill Rock and out into Long Island Sound.

Mill Rock, thought once to have been a pirate's refuge, got its name from a mill (c. 1701–07) that harnessed tidal currents. During the War of 1812 a blockhouse along with fortifications on both shores protected the N. entrance to New York harbour, but was destroyed by fire in 1821. In 1860 one Sandy Gibson bought it and moved there with his family and several cows. The U.S. government bought it in 1911 for $25,000 and used it as a base of operations for surveying the harbour and removing hazards until the city took it over in 1953, placing it under the jurisdiction of the Parks Department because commissioner Robert Moses was afraid that otherwise some commercial operator would buy it and adorn it with a giant billboard. In 1979 the Parks Department placed it under the care of the Neighborhood Committee for the Asphalt Green who plan to use it for environmental and nautical studies.

To the W. of Mill Rock runs the Harlem River along the shore of Manhattan. The large island just N. of Mill Rock is *Wards Island*, now joined by landfill to *Randalls Island* at its northern end.

These islands are of interest only to the extremely thorough visitor, and the following description is given to satisfy the curiosity of the average tourist who might wonder what is on them but not wish to visit. They are accessible either from the pedestrian footbridge at 103rd St or via the M35 bus which runs from 125th St and Lexington Ave across the Triborough Bridge to Wards and Randalls Islands and then across a second arm of the Triborough Bridge to Astoria in Queens.

Look N. along the Harlem River. The *Wards Island Pedestrian Bridge* (1951), painted purple and yellow (1976) joins 103rd St in Manhattan with Wards Island, now used for parks, mental hospitals, and a firemen's training center.

History. Wards Island, used by the British as a military base during the Revolution and called Buchanan's Island or Great Barn Island, a corruption of Great Barent Island, belonged to farmers Jasper and Bartholomew Ward after the war. Around 1810 a cotton mill stood there, but when the mill closed after the War of 1812, the island remained deserted until the city took it over for a potter's field, digging up 100,000 bodies on the present site of Bryant Park and moving them there. The state immigration service (1847) had a refuge for sick and destitute aliens there until 1860 when the island served as a back-up station for the immigration facilities in Battery Park. When Ellis Island opened in 1892 the abandoned immigration buildings were taken over by the New York City Asylum for the Insane and a few years later the state took control of the mental hospital, changing its name to *Manhattan State Hospital*. Once scheduled for demolition, the hospital is still there with new facilities, the *Rehabilitation Building of the Manhattan Psychiatric Center* (1970; Caudill Rowlett Scott), a 'half-way house', and the *Manhattan Children's Treatment Center* (1972; Richard G. Stein & Assocs), for teaching and treating retarded and disturbed children. On the N.E. part of Wards Island is a *Firemen's Training Center* (1975; Hardy Holzman Pfeiffer Assocs) which replaces an earlier one on Roosevelt Island. The center, not open to the public, includes a model city of vitrified tile block which can be set on fire and extinguished as a training exercise. The island also houses a Municipal Sewage Disposal Plant, 77·5 acres on the N.E. corner.

Randalls Island, the northernmost part of the island, once a separate body of land separated from Wards Island by Little Hell Gate but now joined to it with landfill, is the home of the headquarters of the Triborough Bridge and Tunnel Authority and holds also the junction of the three arms of the Triborough Bridge, the tracks of the old New York Connecting Railway, a park with athletic facilities, and Downing Stadium which is used for summer concerts, athletic events, and the San Juan Festival (last weekend in June) honouring the patron saint of Puerto Rico. With the exception of the railroad (see p385) all these facilities were constructed under the aegis of the Triborough Bridge project.

History. In 1668 British governor Richard Nicolls granted the island to Thomas Delavall, a tax collector; later (1772) one Captain James Montresor bought it and lived there, giving it his name until Jonathan Randel took possession in 1784. The city paid Randel (or Randal) $60,000 for it in 1835, misspelling his name on the deed, a mistake which has endured to the present. From then until the Triborough Bridge project (begun 1929), the island shared the dreary history of other East River islands: it held a potter's field (1843) with bodies exhumed from a graveyard at 50th St and Fourth (now Park) Ave, an almshouse (1845), a House of Refuge for the Society of the Reformation of Juvenile Delinquents (1851), and a state asylum for the feeble minded. The Bartholdi

Crèche founded in 1886 maintained a seaside cottage there at the end of the 19C for mothers with sick children who could not afford to leave the city.

The channel N.E. of Mill Rock is called **Hell Gate,** and leads to the sea via the protected waters of Long Island Sound. Ever since Adraien Block sailed the 'Tyger' through it in 1612, Hell Gate has had a reputation for treachery, but the name comes from the Dutch 'Hellegat' which means 'beautiful pass' and originally applied to the entire East River. Hell Gate is only 22·5 miles from the open sea via New York Bay and Sandy Hook (the southern route) but more than 100 miles via Long Island Sound (the northern route), a discrepancy which accounts for three hours' difference in the tides at the two ends of the East River. These conflicting tides along with reefs and rocky islets once made Hell Gate so tortuous that hundreds of wrecks are believed to lie beneath its waters including a Revolutionary frigate, 'Hussar', that went down in 1780 with a payroll estimated at more than $1 million in gold and silver coins for British troops in America. Blasting operations from 1851 to the mid-1920s have made the colourfully named rocks a thing of the past: Hen and Chickens, Negro's Head, Hog's Back, Frying Pan, Pot Rock, Bald Headed Billy, and Way's Reef.

Two bridges span Hell Gate. The southernmost is the **Triborough Bridge** (1936; Othmar Ammann, chief engineer), whose Y-shaped structure touches three boroughs—Manhattan, Queens, and the Bronx. The Bronx arm begins on a viaduct between East 132nd and East 134th Sts (Bronx) and with seven truss spans (1683 ft) over land and water crosses the Bronx Kills (span, 383 ft) to Randalls Island. The bridge has been designed so that it may be converted into a lift bridge if the Kills, now a ditch, is ever made navigable. The Manhattan arm crosses the Harlem River at 125th St to Randalls Island, with three truss spans (total length 772 ft) and a 310-ft vertical lift bridge over the river. Within each of the twin 215-ft towers is a thousand-ton cement counterweight and a 200-horsepower motor which lift the six-lane roadway and the span to a height of 135 ft above the river (closed, the span is 55 ft above mean high water). The Queens arm, above Hell Gate, is a 1380-ft suspension bridge joining Randalls Island and Astoria, Queens. The towers rise 315 ft and the roadway is 143 ft above mean high water. The three arms converge above Randalls Island in an intricate whorl of 22 lanes and ramps punctuated by two toll plazas, the most complex traffic sorter built up to then. All the roadways have footwalks and pedestrians as well as motorists may descend to Randalls Island from the bridge.

History. Construction began on Black Friday, 25 October 1929, when the stock market began its plunge, but when funds ran out in 1932 only a $3 million lump of cement on Wards Island, a future anchorage, remained to show three years' work. In 1933 the Triborough Bridge Authority was created to finance and build the stalled bridge and under Roosevelt's Public Works Administration got a $37 million construction loan. Robert Moses, soon the force impelling the TBA, pushed the bridge to completion despite political interference from a hostile Roosevelt and in addition built the stadium on Randalls Island, an extension of the East River Drive (later renamed after Roosevelt) past 96th St, a marina in Flushing Bay, and improvements in Astoria Park including a large pool used for the Olympic trials of 1936.

Hell Gate Arch (1917; Gustav Lindenthal, engineer and Henry Hornbostel, architect), visible beyond the Triborough Bridge, is a 1017-ft span carrying four railroad tracks across the East River from Wards Island to Queens. It stands as a monument to Lindenthal, structurally beautiful and imaginatively engineered, the high point of a career later mired in the frustrations of city politics, and to Alexander Cassatt, president of the Pennsylvania Railroad (1899–1907), who planned the New York Connecting Railroad, a direct rail link between New England and the rest of the Northeast Corridor (Philadelphia, Baltimore, and Washington) of which the bridge is the most prominent part.

The design of the arch is unusual in that the upper arc curves upward at the ends, a pleasing effect which also allows correct overhead clearance for locomotives and aids the bridge's rigidity by allowing deeper stiffening trusses. The handsome granite faced towers with their arched openings reminded early observers of the portico to a mammoth temple. Among Lindenthal's engineering achievements were the bridging of an underwater fissure in the bedrock beneath the Wards Island foundation and the discovery of a way to build the arch without using scaffolding to support the unfinished span which would have closed Hell Gate to navigation. When the final steel section was hoisted in place at the center, an adjustment of only $^5/16$ of an inch was needed to close the arch.

Begin walking S. along the promenade. Facing the river near the N. end of the park is **Gracie Mansion** (1799; additions, 1966; Mott B. Schmidt; DL), official residence of the mayor of New York. Built as the country home of merchant Archibald Gracie, whose offices were on Whitehall St and whose townhouse stood on State St where the Seamen's Institute is today, the house, with its 16 rooms and fine detailing (leaded glass sidelights and semicircular fanlight above the main doorway, elegant railings around the roof and above the main floor), exemplifies Federal domestic architecture at the upper end of the income scale. Louis Philippe, later King of France, the Marquis de Lafayette, Alexander Hamilton, John Quincy Adams, and Washington Irving all enjoyed Gracie's hospitality, but in the years preceeding the War of 1812, his shipping business suffered financial reverses and Gracie went bankrupt. He sold the mansion in 1819 and the city bought it in 1887, adding its grounds to Carl Schurz Park and allowing the house to deteriorate until the Museum of the City of New York took it over (1924–30). In 1942 it became the mayor's house after Fiorello La Guardia, then mayor, rejected another major contender, the Charles M. Schwab 75-room French château (Riverside Drive at 73rd St, now demolished). 'What,' said the 5 ft 2 inch fiery proletarian mayor, 'me in that?' In 1966 reception and conference rooms were added so skilfully that the observer must look carefully to see where the new wing begins. The mansion is not generally open to the public and during the summer is difficult to see from the park because of the picket fence and the leafy trees.

Walk S. along the Finley Walk in Schurz Park. Across the East River lies the N. tip of *Roosevelt Island* with its lighthouse, hospital buildings, and octagonal dome originally part of the New York City Lunatic Asylum. Opposite the lighthouse turn inland and walk down the curved double staircase to the walkway leading to 86th St, the main street of German Yorkville. On the N. side between York and East End Aves is the HENDERSON PLACE HISTORIC DISTRICT, once part of John Jacob Astor's country estate. It was purchased in 1881 by John C. Henderson, who, having made his fortune in furs and fur hats, decided to speculate on some row houses for people of moderate means. Some 20 of the original 32 houses (1882; Lamb & Rich) remain, small (typical lot size 18 × 46 ft) but charming Queen Anne style townhouses with turrets, paired entranceways, double stoops and carefully considered details. The houses facing East End Ave have been altered and those on the W. side of Henderson Place (a half block W.) exist in the shadow of a gargantuan apartment building which, while blighting the historic district, has usurped its name. There is also a good view of the houses from 87th St.

Walk N. to 88th St. At 312–316 E. 88th St between First and Second Aves, little known because of its location, is the (Protestant Episcopal) CHURCH OF THE HOLY TRINITY (1897; Barney & Chapman; DL), a neo-Francis I church with a fine belfry. The brown brick church ornamented with terracotta has a copper crested roof and red slate shingles and is part of a homogeneous group that includes a parsonage, the bell tower, and St. Christopher House, now the home of the Theater of the Open Eye. In 1897 Serena Rhinelander gave the diocese part of the Rhinelander farm (purchased by the family, 1798) in memory of her father and grandfather. The church and the *Rhinelander Children's Center of the Children's Aid Society* (1890; Vaux & Radford) next door (350 E. 88th St), its original brickwork now slathered over with mortar, are the fruits of her gift.

Two blocks N. and not really worth the walk *Yorkville Towers and Ruppert Towers* (1976; Davis, Brody & Assocs), two immense apartment houses, stand on part of the site where Jacob Ruppert's Brewery (90th–93rd Sts, Second–Third Aves) once dominated the neighbourhood, offering jobs to the Germanic populace and filling the streets with the aroma of roasting hops. Once the city had more than 100 breweries; today there is none.

Return to 86th St along Second Ave. The main residue of German small business is here along 86th St between Second and Third Aves, a few cafés and restaurants, butcher shops, pastry stores, and a candy store featuring marzipan animals and vegetables. In the midst of these shops is *Corso*, the city's most famous Puerto Rican nightclub (205 E. 86th St), whose bands dish up salsa, a polyglot music of Latin and African rhythms and American jazz that began in Cuba and has become the most popular form of urban Latin music.

On the S.E. corner of 85th St and Lexington Ave (a block W. of Third Ave) is the *New York Turnverein*, built c. 1900 in a Germanic Renaissance Revival style for a German sports club. Established on E. 4th St in 1849, the Turnverein still offers gymnastics and fencing instruction, though it no longer provides for members in case of illness or financial distress as it once did. Return to Second Ave and continue S.

The **Hungarian section** of Yorkville, around Second Ave in the upper 70s and low 80s, like the German and Czech sections, has a diminishing ethnic population. The abortive Hungarian Revolution (1848) touched off the first wave of Hungarian immigration which peaked just before World War I, but which increased again after the 1956 invasion of Hungary by the Soviet Union. Today an estimated 100,000 Hungarian-Americans including second and third generation families live in greater New York. The original center of the Hungarian population was, as with other groups, the Lower East Side, particularly Avenues A and B near Houston St with immigrants beginning to move uptown around 1905. The community still celebrates two Hungarian heroes: Louis Kossuth, who led the momentarily successful struggle for independence from Austria in 1848, is honoured by a parade (15 March) from Yorkville to his statue at Riverside Drive and 113th St, while the first king of Hungary is honoured on St. Stephen's Day (20 August) or the nearest Sunday to it by another parade and picnic.

Among the Hungarian institutions remaining are the *Balaton Club* (1586 Second Ave at 82nd St), a social club for members only, and *St. Stephen's Roman Catholic Church* (414 E. 82nd St between First and Second Aves), the largest house of worship for local Hungarians, though also nearby are churches for Hungarian Baptists, Jews, and those who follow the Byzantine Rites. Along Second Ave are butcher shops specialising in sausages, pork products, liverwurst, and paprika-coated bacon as well as pastry shops offering tortes and strudel. Two well-known East European shops that have remained in the same families for generations are *Paprikas Weiss* (1546 Second Ave, between 80th–81st Sts), whose founder got his start importing Hungarian paprika because his wife demanded it for cooking, and *Lekvar by the Barrel* (1577 First Ave at 82nd St), whose speciality, lekvar, is a kind of Hungarian prune butter. At 323 E. 79th St between First and Second Aves is the *First Hungarian Literary Society*, whose elderly members seem to prefer pinochle to literary chats.

At 79th St walk E. to *York Ave*, a block E. of First Ave and formerly called Avenue A. In 1928 the avenue was renamed to honour World War I hero Alvin C. York who singlehandedly (8 Oct 1918) killed 25 Germans and took 132 prisoners in a battle of the Meuse-Argonne campaign. The *City and Suburban Homes* (1900; Ernest Flagg) between 79th–78th Sts, York Ave and the F.D.R. Drive are an early attempt at middle class apartment housing.

Walk E. on 78th St to *Cherokee Place*, named after a branch of Tammany Hall (see p225), the Cherokee Club, which once stood on 79th St between First and Second Aves. *John Jay Park*, along the E. side of Cherokee Place between 78th–77th Sts, is a popular neighbourhood gathering spot with trees, a playground, and a swimming pool; it is named after the first Chief Justice of the U.S., drafter of the Constitution, and governor of New York state (1795–1801).

Across from the park (507–523 E. 77th St between York Ave and Cherokee Place) are the CHEROKEE APARTMENTS (1912; Henry Atterbury Smith), a six-story complex built as model housing for people of moderate income, whose high architectural standards are still admired though building maintenance is beginning to slip. Note the small balconies accessible from triple-hung windows, the ironwork, and the Guastavino-tiled tunnels leading to the central courtyards. In the courtyards corner stairways rise to the upper floors, roofed against the rain with iron and glass.

Walk back to First Ave. South of Little Hungary is the remnant of the **Czech quarter** centered around First Ave in the mid-60s to mid-70s, a section of the avenue once called Czech Broadway. Like other immigrant groups, the Czechs and Slovaks first settled on the Lower East Side, with the Slovak enclave E. of Avenue A between 4th and 7th Sts. New immigrants continued to arrive from the 1920s to the late 1940s, with the latest influx after the Russian invasion of Czechoslovakia in 1968. Today, however, the area has more high rises than tenements and is rapidly becoming more chic than Czech. Among the remaining institutions is the *Jan Hus Presbyterian Church* (351 E. 74th St between First and Second Aves), whose namesake was burned as a heretic for his efforts at religious reformation. Part of the building is used as a school for children of United Nations' employees, but the senior citizens' center still draws a Czech-speaking clientele. The church tower is said to be modelled on the old Powder Tower in Prague. A few Czech restaurants, butcher shops, and speciality shops can be found in the area, including the *Czechoslovak Store* (1363 First Ave between 74th–73rd Sts) which sells Czech newspapers and magazines and serves as a gathering place for older residents.

One block E. at 1334 York Ave, near 72nd St, is **Sotheby's,** legally Sotheby Parke Bernet Inc., the American branch of the world's oldest firm of fine arts auctioneers (founded 1744). The American firm, the Parke-Bernet Galleries, originated in 1883 as the American Art Association, an exhibition gallery, but was catapulted into the top ranks of auction houses when one George Seney, a bank president, got caught with his hand in the till and had the AAA auction off his possessions to pacify his creditors, a sale that brought $405,821. Otto Bernet began in 1896 at the age of 14 with the gallery, working by day and studying art appreciation at night. Hiram Haney Parke, one of the country's greatest auctioneers, came to the firm from Philadelphia, a gentleman in bearing though of humble background. In 1937 Parke and Bernet founded their own immediately successful firm whose auctions have included spectacular sales, among them Renoir's 'Les Filles de Durand-Ruel', a painting exhibited but not sold at the old AAA Impressionist Exhibition in 1886, knocked down for $225,000 in 1959, and Rembrandt's 'Aristotle with the Bust of Homer', sold to the Metropolitan Museum of Art for $2·3 million in 1960. Since the merger (1964) with Sotheby's of London, the firm has auctioned collections of Nelson Rockefeller, Helena Rubenstein, and Edgar William and Bernice Chrysler Garbisch, a collection of art and antiques that brought $20·3 million, a record in this country. The firm was moved to vacate its galleries at 980 Madison Ave, which it had occupied for 33 years, in June 1982 during a slump in the art market. Exhibition hours are Mon–Fri, 9.30–5. Tel: 472–3400.

Further downtown is the Roman Catholic *Church of St. John Nepomucene* (411 E. 66th St, N.E. corner of First Ave), whose interior (open during services) has folk designs and a mosaic above the altar with scenes from the lives of St. Cyril and his brother St. Methodius who brought Christianity to Moravia in the 9C. Cyril is said to have invented the Cyrillic alphabet and to have translated the gospel and liturgy into Old Slavonic.

The nearest subway is the Lexington Ave at 66th St, three blocks W. There are uptown buses on First Ave and downtown buses on Second Ave as well as crosstown buses on 72nd and 67th–68th Sts.

26 Harlem and Hamilton Heights

Geographically Harlem is defined by the East and Harlem Rivers, the cliffs of Morningside Heights and St. Nicholas Terrace, and by 110th and c. 168th Sts. The E. and S.E. section, which used to be predominantly Italian with a few Germans spilling over from the Yorkville area, today is predominantly Puerto Rican and is known as 'El Barrio' or Spanish Harlem. A small and dwindling Italian community still remains around Pleasant Ave and E. 116th St. Central Harlem, from 110th St to 145th St, is mostly poor and black with Puerto Rican enclaves and small neighbourhoods of relative affluence—Sugar Hill, Striver's Row, and the 'Gold Coast', a group of middle income developments along the Harlem River N. of 125th St.

As this may suggest, Harlem is not merely a homogenous slum of rat infested, rotten tenements, a jobless ghetto whose population is shaken by drug addiction and crime and whose streets are marked by burned out buildings and rubble-strewn lots. While all these things exist, there are also parks and wide boulevards, adequate public transportation, rows of fine brownstones, handsome churches, and evidence of flourishing artistic and educational institutions.

History. When Upper Manhattan still enjoyed its pristine topography, an Indian village stood on the banks of the Harlem River between about the location of 110th and 125th Sts. In 1658, attracted by the fertile soil and the strategic advantages of the terrain, Dutch farmers incorporated the village of Nieuw Haarlem and hired a contingent of soldiers to build and defend their settlement. In 1672 black slaves, originally brought to this country by the Dutch, built a wagon road from Nieuw Haarlem to New Amsterdam about 10 miles south at the tip of Manhattan. Increasingly this beautiful outlying land attracted gentlemen farmers or wealthy merchants who developed estates and built country mansions of which the only survivor is the Morris-Jumel Mansion.

In 1827 the state prohibited slavery, but its black population remained in a kind of civil limbo until the Emancipation Proclamation (1863) gave citizenship to all former slaves. At the close of the Civil War, New York's black population, estimated at 15,000, was concentrated in various ghettos in lower Manhattan, notably around Thompson St in Greenwich Village. By the end of the century the black population was centered around the Tenderloin (W. of Broadway between c. 32nd and 42nd Sts) and Hell's Kitchen districts (the 40s and 50s W. of Seventh Ave). As demolition for the construction of the old Penn Station displaced them, blacks moved up into the San Juan Hill neighbourhood, N. and W. of Columbus Circle.

Meanwhile, Harlem had begun its metamorphosis to a suburb as the New York and Harlem railroad opened a line along Park Ave from City Hall to the Harlem River (1837), opening the area for development, but simultaneously raising a barrier between the east and west sides of Harlem and creating a strip of blight where factories, squatters' shacks, and tenements quickly appeared.

East Harlem, further blighted by the arrival of the Third and Second Ave elevated railroads in 1879 and 1880, was soon established as a working class neighbourhood. Speculators erected rows of tenements along the avenues which became home to immigrants from Russia, Germany, Italy, Ireland, Hungary, Scandanavia, even England and Spain.

In western Harlem, however, encouraged by the opening of the IRT subway along Lenox Ave in 1901, speculators were putting up fine apartment buildings and handsome row houses, anticipating the arrival of the middle class from downtown in large numbers. Oscar Hammerstein had opened the Harlem Opera House at 205 W. 125th St in 1889 anticipating the same thing. When it didn't happen the real estate market collapsed, leaving landlords with unrentable buildings. Black realtor, Philip A. Payton, stepped into the gap, taking over building management and guaranteeing high rents to landlords who would accept black tenants, making decent housing available to them for the first time in New York.

Although rents were inflated because they could not get comparable housing elsewhere, black people poured into Harlem from other parts of the city, and also from the rural south and from the West Indies. During the 1920s the black population of Harlem increased from 83,248 to 203,894 with a density of 236 people per acre, twice that of the rest of the city. White business and property owners fought bitterly to keep Harlem white, but failed simply because it was too profitable to rent to blacks, although the arriving blacks were effectively barred from holding jobs in white-owned businesses. Since many of the new arrivals were either single or had small families, landlords began subdividing apartments, increasing their own profits but beginning a policy of overcrowding and poor building maintenance that continues today with appalling results.

The 1920s were years of optimism and great artistic activity as writers, artists,

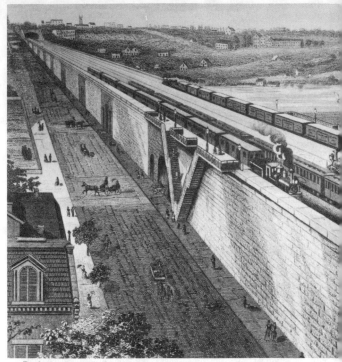

Park Avenue viaduct, 98th–112th Sts (1865–66). Speculators were already dotting the Harlem flatlands with rowhouses. In the background on McGown's Pass (right) rise the former buildings of Mount St Vincent's Convent. (Museum of the City of New York)

and intellectuals made the pilgrimage to Harlem, by then the capital of black America. According to poet Langston Hughes, it was a time when local and visiting royalty were not uncommon in Harlem, when every year a Broadway hit play had an all-black cast, when black authors were being published with greater frequency than ever before. Marcus Garvey awoke black self-respect and militancy with his back-to-Africa movement, and black and white intellectuals enjoyed cordial relations. Harlem was famous for its music, and whites flocked uptown to enjoy the jazz at its famous nightclubs—the Cotton Club, Connie's and Smalls' Paradise—many of which were white-owned and which had white-only audiences. Casinos, ballrooms, and cabarets, some catering to whites and some refusing entrance to them, provided a glittering nightlife.

With the Depression, the gaiety ended and the poverty behind the glittering surface became apparent. People marginally employed were the hardest hit, and blacks, excluded from virtually all but menial jobs, were among the first to suffer. The 1930s were the years of 'rent parties', where guests paid an entrance fee to hear the music, drink the bathtub gin, and help pay off the month's rent. Literary output dried up, housing deteriorated, racial tensions heightened, and Harlem became the ground for several unpleasant incidents and riots.

The physical and social scars of the Depression are still visible. During the period of civil rights activism of the 1960s, Harlem became the focus of both political and social activity. The Black Muslims founded the Temple of Islam at 116th St and Lenox Ave, and black civil rights leader Malcolm X worked

there until he broke with the Muslims and founded his own Organization of Afro-American Unity in 1964. In February 1965, he was assassinated at the Audubon Ballroom on W. 166th St between Broadway and St. Nicholas Ave at a political rally. After the riots of 1968 federal, state, and local money was channelled into Harlem in programmes of redevelopment, to improve housing, education, and to solve its social problems, but while some gains have been made, the programmes have not produced the results hoped for. Unemployment, crime, and drug addiction rates are still high; housing, education, and other public services are still below standard. Efforts are being made to bring Harlem back to the center of black cultural life, a position it lost in the late 1950s and early 1960s when black artists, actors, musicians, and dancers were drawn to the commercially more successful cultural scene in midtown or Greenwich Village.

Visiting Harlem. Because of its high crime rate and the attention it receives in the press, Harlem has a lurid reputation. Nevertheless it is certainly possible to walk around in Harlem and return unscathed, although hostility to whites is real and sometimes intense. A car is the best means of getting around.

The PENNY SIGHTSEEING COMPANY, black-owned and black-operated, offers a three-hour bus tour of Harlem: Mon and Thurs, 10 am, and Sat (March—Nov), 11 a.m. Reservations required; call 247–2860. Fee, $8. Tours leave from the fifth floor offices of 303 W. 42nd St, (between Eighth and Ninth Aves). The UPTOWN CHAMBER OF COMMERCE at 209 W. 125th St (between Seventh and Eighth Aves) also conducts group and individual tours on occasion and sells the 'Greater Harlem Informational Map & Guide'. Tel: 427–7200.

The following route, therefore, lists points of interest in reasonable geographical order but is not intended as a walking tour; the distances covered are quite great.

At the N.W. corner of Central Park is FREDERICK DOUGLASS CIRCLE, named after the escaped slave, journalist, orator, and crusader for abolition. Along the park are handsome brownstone and elevator buildings built at the turn of the century for middle- and upper-class families, for example the *Semiramis Apartments* (c. 1905) at 137 Central Park North. Playwright Arthur Miller was born at No. 45.

Go W. to Manhattan Ave and **Morningside Park,** designed by Frederick Law Olmsted and Calvert Vaux (preliminary plan, 1873; revised plan, 1887), whose sheer cliffs separate the poor in the Harlem Valley below from the university community on Morningside Heights above. The park is not safe, its natural wooded beauty providing concealment for muggers. It became a cause célèbre in 1968 when Columbia University, increasingly cramped on Morningside Heights, wanted two acres of park for a gymnasium; student riots saved the park land, of which ironically, only the outer edges are much used. The heroic bronze *statue of Washington and Lafayette* (executed 1890; unveiled 1900) at the intersection of Manhattan Ave and W. 114th St is by Frédéric Auguste Bartholdi.

Street names. The major avenues have been renamed as they pass through Central Harlem. Eighth Ave is Frederick Douglass Blvd and Seventh Ave was named Adam Clayton Powell, Jr Blvd, shortly after the black leader's death in 1972. The extension of Sixth Ave N. of Central Park is Lenox Ave, named after the family who established the Lenox Library, now part of the New York Public Library. For the sake of clarity and conciseness Frederick Douglass Blvd and Adam Clayton Powell, Jr Blvd, shall be referred to here by their old, numerical names.

Nearby reminders of bourgeois turn-of-the-century Harlem are the rusticated limestone *115th St Branch of the New York Public Library* (1908; McKim, Mead & White; DL) at 203 W. 115th St, between Seventh and Eighth Aves, and the theatre at 1910 Seventh Ave (S.W. corner of W. 116th St), built as the *Regent Theater* (1913; Thomas W. Lamb). Here Samuel Lionel Rothafel, later famous as 'Roxy', began the New York phase of his career as a movie theatre mogul, saving this 'Venetian' picture palace from financial failure. At 1923 Seventh Ave on the N.E. corner of the same intersection is *Graham Court Apts* (1901; Clinton & Russell), the most elegant of the early Harlem apartment houses.

Roman Catholic ST. THOMAS THE APOSTLE CHURCH at 260 W. 118th St, on the S.W. corner of St. Nicholas Ave (1907; T. H. Poole), now splattered with graffiti, is an unusual neo-Gothic building with an arcaded porch and grand entrance stairway.

Follow St. Nicholas Ave N. to Morningside Ave at W. 125th St. ST. NICHOLAS AVE was named in 1901 after the patron saint of New Amsterdam, whose image as figurehead graced the 'Nieu Nederlandt', the ship that brought the first settlers from the Netherlands. Just across 125th St, Morningside Ave becomes Convent Ave and rises steeply to Hamilton Heights. CONVENT AVE is named after the Convent of the Sacred Heart (established 1841) which stood between St. Nicholas Ave and Amsterdam Ave (then called Tenth Ave) until it burned in 1888.

Along Convent Ave between W. 130th and W. 135th Sts is the S.

campus of the *City University of New York, originally the City College of New York.

C.C.N.Y. was founded in 1849 after a bill (passed 1847) by the state legislature authorised the board of education to establish a free academy for students who had attended city schools and could pass the entrance exams. Because of its policy of free admissions to city residents, City College was long a step upward for immigrants. In 1903 more than 75% of the students were Jewish, and in 1910 almost 90%, of whom most came from eastern European families. Nowadays tuition is no longer free, and the student body is more black and Hispanic than Jewish, but C.U.N.Y. still provides an educational outlet to the city's aspiring young people.

The grounds are divided into a North and South Campus, the South Campus originally having belonged to the Academy and Convent of the Sacred Heart which moved to Westchester County as the Manhattanville College of the Sacred Heart in 1952. The *Finley Student Center* and *Goldmark Hall* (1847–90) were formerly the Main Building and chapel of the Catholic college. The President's House (1912) on the N.E. corner of Convent Ave and W. 133rd St served as the gatehouse of the college. The most impressive new building is *Aaron Davis Hall* (1978; Abraham W. Geller & Assocs and Ezra D. Ehrenkrantz & Assocs) for the performing arts, at the S.E. corner of Convent Ave and W. 135th St, which has three theatres inside and an outdoor amphitheatre.

At the S.W. corner of W. 135th St and Convent Ave between the two campuses is a GATEHOUSE (1890) for the Croton Aqueduct, a brownstone and granite structure that marks the end of the masonry aqueduct leading into Manhattan from High Bridge. Here the water enters a system of underground pipes that carry it to the next gatehouse at 119th St and Amsterdam Ave.

The academic complex now under construction between W. 135th and W. 138th Sts along the W. side of Convent Ave occupies the site of Lewisohn Stadium, given to the college in 1915 by Jewish philanthropist Adolph Lewisohn as an athletic field but more fondly remembered as the place the New York Philharmonic held summer outdoor concerts.

The **North Campus**, between W. 138th and W. 140th Sts was designed in 1905 by George B. Post in a neo-Gothic style and constructed of Manhattan schist dug out during the tunnelling for the Broadway-Seventh Ave IRT subway. Shepard Hall, just inside the archway, is the main building.

N. of the campus along Convent Ave between W. 141st and W. 145th Sts is the **Hamilton Heights Historic District** (designated 1974), an enclave of fine rowhouses built roughly between 1886 and 1906 that remains heroically unchanged by the fortunes of the neighbourhood. The centerpiece is Hamilton Grange, the country home of Alexander Hamilton (1801; John McComb, Jr; DL), now at 287 Convent Ave between W. 141st and W. 142nd Sts, where it was moved in 1889 from a location about 100 yards N. The Grange, one of the finest Federal houses of its day, has not fared well, stripped of the porches that once surrounded it and jammed between an apartment house and a church. Hamilton lived here at the end of his life, which ended (1804) when he was fatally wounded in a duel by Aaron Burr, his political enemy. The National Park Service now owns Hamilton Grange and is restoring it. The heroic bronze *statue of Hamilton* (1889) is by William O. Partridge.

On the N.E. corner of W. 141st St is ST. LUKE'S (PROTESTANT

EPISCOPAL) CHURCH (1892; R.H. Robertson), a handsome brown-stone Romanesque building, the uptown home of the congregation founded on Hudson St in Greenwich Village. The tower remains unfinished. Across the street at 280–298 Convent Ave (1902; Henri Foucheaux) is a row of limestone-faced Beaux-Arts houses.

Further up the street are Nos 311–339 (1890; Adolph Hoak), a picturesque Romanesque row, and Nos 320–328 (1890; Horace B. Hartwell) and Nos 330–336 (1892; Robert Dry), all constructed at about the same time.

A block E. of Convent Ave is Hamilton Terrace, running three blocks between W. 141st and W. 144th Sts.
    AUNT LEN'S DOLL AND TOY MUSEUM at 6 Hamilton Terrace, a private collection of more than 2500 dolls, miniatures, and toys, is housed in one of the row houses.

Open Tues–Sun by appointment. Adults, $1; children, 50¢. Tel: 926–4172.

Hamilton Terrace returns to Convent Ave at W. 144th St. A block W. is Hamilton Square (W. 144th St, Amsterdam Ave and Hamilton Pl.) where one of the city's early cast-iron street lights still survives. Hamilton Pl. cuts diagonally across the usual street grid because it follows the course of the old Bloomingdale Road that zig-zagged across upper Manhattan.

Just W. of Convent Ave at 467 W. 142nd St is OUR LADY OF LOURDES CHURCH (1904; O'Reilly Brothers), an astonishing exercise in architectural recycling, made up of the parts of three different, unrelated buildings. The National Academy of Design (1865; Peter B. Wright) which once stood at Park Ave South and E. 23rd St contributed its grey and white marble Ruskinian-Gothic facade. The apse and parts of the E. wall came from the Cathedral of St. John the Divine, when the E. wall there was altered to make way for the Lady Chapel. The pedestals flanking the main entrance were salvaged from department store millionaire A.T. Stewart's mansion (1867; John Kellum) on the N.W. corner of 34th St and Fifth Ave.
    The heights between St. Nicholas and Edgecombe Aves, from about 143rd to 155th Sts is known as **Sugar Hill,** a place where the poor of central Harlem could see the more affluent black bourgeoisie living the sweet life. Among the prominent figures, athletes, and show business people who have lived there are Duke Ellington, Count Basie, Sugar Ray Robinson, and Supreme Court Justice Thurgood Marshall.
    Go N. to W. 150th St and E. to St. Nicholas Pl. bordering Colonial Park. At 10 St. Nicholas Pl. on the N.E. corner of W. 150th St is the *M. Marshall Blake Funeral Home* (1888; Samuel B. Reed; DL), a rockface limestone gabled and towered mansion, built by circus entrepreneur James Anthony Bailey, partner of P.T. Barnum and co-founder of the Barnum & Bailey Circus, 'the greatest show on earth'.
    Go N. on St. Nicholas Ave (the left fork) to W. 162nd St; turn right (E.) and right again (S.) onto Jumel Terrace. (Street parking usually available.)
    Situated in small Roger Morris Park with a commanding view is the **•Morris-Jumel Mansion** (N.W. corner of W. 160th St and Edgecombe Ave). One of the city's few remaining pre-Revolutionary buildings (1765; remodelled with portico added, 1810; DL), it is now a museum.

Open Tues–Sun, 10–4; admission, 50¢. Knock on the door if the building appears to be closed. Visitors may picnic in the surrounding park. For information about special events, workshops, and crafts demonstrations, tel: 923–8008.

Built as the summer home of Lt-Col Roger Morris and his wife Mary Philipse, the house retains its original Georgian hipped roof, wooden corner quoins, and wide-board facade (though the rear of the house is shingled for economy). Morris served under Gen. Edward Braddock during the French and Indian War and was a friend of George Washington, who has been romantically linked to Mary Philipse before her marriage. When the war broke out, the family returned to England as did many wealthy loyalists. Washington used the house as his headquarters between Sept 14 and Oct 18 1776 during his vain defence of Manhattan. The house gradually deteriorated, becoming a tavern, until Stephen Jumel, a wealthy French wine merchant, and his wife bought it and had it restored, adding the portico and enlarging the doorway in the Federal style.

Mme Jumel, neé Betsy Bowen of Providence, Rhode Island, who had a reputation for an imperious tongue, a scandalous love-life, and boundless social ambition, became one of the richest women in America upon Jumel's death in 1832. About a year afterward 77-year old Aaron Burr married her (she was then about 60), apparently for her money but the marriage was stormy and unsuccessful. Mme Jumel lived on in the mansion after the separation and died there in 1865 at the age of 93. The city acquired the property (1903) then being offered for development and opened the museum (1907) under the custodianship of the Daughters of the American Revolution.

Interior. The furnishings include many original Jumel pieces as well as others chosen to illustrate the 100-year period in which the mansion served as a private residence. In the basement is the old kitchen with its fireplace for cooking. To the left of the hallway on the first floor is the Front Parlor where Mme Jumel and Burr were wed, furnished with original Jumel pieces and papered with a copy of the Jumel French wallpaper. The Dining Room across the hallway and the small Drawing Room behind the Front Parlor reflect the Federal Period around the turn of the century, while the Octagon Drawing Room at the rear of the house with its hand-painted Chinese wallpaper and American and English Chippendale furniture draws on the pre-Revolutionary period (c. 1765) when the Morrisons were still in residence.

Upstairs the Burr Bedroom contains Federal furniture from around 1830 including a four-poster bed with Scalamandre curtains. Mme Jumel's Bedroom has Empire furniture brought from France c. 1810. Behind it is a Nursery, originally a dressing room (currently screened from view). At the rear of the house is the Washington Study with pre-Revolutionary American furniture.

On the third floor (not always open) is a collection of Staffordshire ware, and a Candle-Dipping Room.

Across Jumel Terrace between W. 160th and W. 162nd Sts is **Sylvan Terrace,** once the carriage drive of the Morris-Jumel mansion. Two rows of modest wooden houses, built c. 1882 for workers, face one another across the street, all but one recently restored. Several fine townhouses remain on Jumel Terrace.

On the E. of the mansion lies Edgecombe Ave, whose name (from Saxon 'combe', hill) implies its situation on the side of a ridge or bluff. HIGHBRIDGE PARK (1888; Calvert Vaux & Samuel Parsons, Jr) which runs from W. 155th St to Dyckman St along the E. side of the escarpment, gets its name from High Bridge near W. 174th St, the oldest remaining bridge joining Manhattan to the

*High Bridge and the Harlem River in 1895. Originally an
aqueduct carrying Croton water, High Bridge is the oldest
link between Manhattan and the mainland. A single steel
span has replaced the five central masonry arches. (The
New-York Historical Society)*

mainland, in this case the Bronx. *High Bridge was originally called Aqueduct Bridge (1839–48; John B. Jervis; DL) and was part of the Croton system bringing water into the city from tributaries of the Hudson River in Westchester Country. Built of closely-spaced granite piers supporting 15 arches and resembling the aqueducts of the Roman *campagna*, the bridge once attracted tourists who enjoyed views from promenade across the top (closed many years ago because of vandalism and crime). In 1923, during construction of the Harlem Ship Canal, the Navy replaced several of the center spans with a steel arch to provide a wider ship channel. The campanile, **Highbridge Tower** (1872; attrib. John B. Jervis; DL), W. 173rd St in the park was once a water tower with a 47,000 gallon tank providing pressure to keep the water flowing in its regular 13 ft per mile downhill course to the reservoirs in Central Park.

Return down Edgecombe Ave along the E. side of the park to W. 155th St. Here the rocky spine of Harlem is known as *Coogan's Bluff*. W. 155th St sweeps down the E. flank of the bluff into the Harlem Valley. Across the Harlem River the top of Yankee Stadium rises into view. On its N. side between the W. branch of the Harlem River Drive and Eighth Ave are the POLO GROUNDS TOWERS (1968) occupying the site of the former ballpark once called home by the New York Giants. The stadium (1912) in turn took its name from actual polo grounds here, used in the 1880s when the area was still rural.

Turn right or S. on MACOMBS PL., which takes its name from Alexander Macomb, a hero of the War of 1812 who had his home nearby. The *Macombs Dam Bridge* across the Harlem River at W. 155th St (opened 1895) is the modern descendant of a toll bridge and dam built (c. 1813) by his son John, who thereby harnessed the river's power to run a mill but simultaneously obstructed shipping and turned much of the river upstream into a large millpond. In 1838 irate citizens bashed a hole in Macomb's dam with picks and shovels, restoring the river's navigability, an action later upheld by the courts.

Between W. 151st and W. 153rd Sts, Macombs Pl. and the Harlem River Drive is one of Harlem's oldest redevelopment projects and still one of the best, the **Harlem River Houses** (1937; Archibald M. Brown, Horace Ginsbern, Charles F. Fuller, Richard W. Buckley, John L. Wilson, Frank J. Forster, and Will R. Amon; DL). These four-story red brick walkups, grouped either around central open spaces or facing the river, represent a period of high hopes for public housing and redevelopment which were not later fulfilled. At a time when black families living in filthy Old and New Law tenements often paid 50% of their incomes for rent and 'rent parties' were a major social institution, the fortunate 574 black families in these houses paid from $19·28 to $31·42 for rent and enjoyed such amenities as playgrounds, steam heat, cross ventilation, and tiled bathrooms. Only blacks living in substandard housing with incomes less than five times the rent who could reasonably prove their ability to continue paying the rent were eligible and so relatively few families qualified. The houses remain handsomely maintained, quite free of graffiti and the scars of vandalism, the ultimate expression of their social and architectural success.

The **Dunbar Apartments** (1928; Andrew J. Thomas; DL), six well-designed low-rise buildings bounded by W. 149th and W. 150th Sts, Seventh and Eighth Aves, represent a private attempt to solve ghetto housing problems. John D. Rockefeller, Jr, had the project constructed as a housing cooperative for which tenant stockholders had to pay $150 down plus $50 a room and a monthly fee that amounted to some $14·50 per room. All the apartments sold quickly and the project succeeded until the Depression deprived most of the tenants of their jobs, causing them to default on their mortgages. Rockefeller foreclosed in 1936, returning the tenants' equity and thereafter offering the apartments on a rental basis. The handsome buildings, grouped around a central courtyard have attracted an illustrious clientele including poet Countee Cullen, A. Philip Randolph, dancer Bill 'Bojangles' Robinson, and arctic explorer Matt Henson. Like the Harlem River Houses they are still in fine condition.

Continue downtown on Eighth Ave to W. 139th St and the ST. NICHOLAS HISTORIC DISTRICT (The King Model Houses), an enclave of handsome row housing in depressed surroundings. In 1891 David H. King, Jr, prominent as the builder of Stanford White's original Madison Square Garden, decided to put up four rows of housing designed by different architects but on the same scale. McKim, Mead & White designed the neo-Italian Renaissance group on the N. side of 139th St between Eighth and Seventh Aves; facing it and on the N. side of W. 138th St is a neo-Georgian row by Bruce Price and Clarence S. Luce in lighter brick with profuse terracotta and limestone trim. The row by James Brown Lord on the S. side of W. 138th St is also neo-Georgian, but of red brick with brownstone trim. Built during the Harlem real estate boom, the houses were intended for upper middle class white families; beginning in 1919 they attracted upper middle class and presumably ambitious black families, hence their nickname, 'Striver's Row'. Among the strivers have been W.C. Handy, Noble Sissle, Eubie Blake, and a number of professional and civic leaders.

A little S. and E. at 132 W. 138th St between Seventh and Lenox Aves is the *Abyssinian Baptist Church* (1923; Charles W. Bolton), a neo-Gothic church built of New York bluestone (a fine-textured bluish grey sandstone) known more for its former preacher, Adam Clayton Powell, Jr, than for its architectural beauty. The church was founded downtown on Worth St in 1808 and gradually moved uptown along with the black centers of population, with former buildings on Thompson St, Spring St, and in the Hell's Kitchen area of W. 40th St between Seventh and Eighth Aves.

The present building was erected during the pastorate of Adam Clayton Powell, Sr. His son, Adam Clayton Powell, Jr, a charismatic preacher, began working for black civil rights during the Depression and became a U.S. Congressman in 1945. He sponsored legislation focusing on civil rights and education, the minimum wage, and segregation in the Armed Forces, and became a powerful figure both in Congress and in Harlem. Always a controversial man, Powell was censured by the House for financial irregularities in 1967 and stripped of his office, although the Supreme Court reinstated him in 1969. The church maintains a memorial room with memorabilia of his political career; tel: AU6–2626.

Go E. to Lenox Ave and turn S. Over the main doorway of HARLEM HOSPITAL on Lenox Ave between W. 137th and W. 135th Sts is a sculptural group of a black family by John W. Rhoden. Founded as a municipal hospital in 1887, Harlem Hospital is now the main facility serving the local populace; a strike of house physicians in 1981 pointed up its problems of overcrowding and inadequate care.

Diagonally across Lenox Ave between W. 135th and W. 136th Sts is **The Schomburg Center for Research in Black Culture** (1978; Bond Ryder Assocs), a branch of the New York Public Library.

Open autumn–spring Mon–Wed, 12–8; Thurs–Sat, 10–6. Summer hours slightly different; tel: 862–4000.

The Schomburg Collection, whose nucleus was gathered by a black Puerto Rican informed by a schoolteacher that blacks had no history, is the world's largest collection documenting the history and literature of all peoples of African descent. The library contains some 75,000 volumes, 50,000 photographs, 3000 prints and posters, personal papers, extensive holdings in West Indian history and literature, recordings of African folk music, jazz, Afro-American blues and spirituals, and an important collection of African and Afro-American artifacts.

Next door at 103 W. 135th St is the 135TH STREET BRANCH OF THE N.Y. PUBLIC LIBRARY (1905; McKim, Mead & White), where the Schomburg collection was first housed after the library acquired it (1926) with a grant from the Carnegie Corporation. An extension to the N. of this building, the COUNTEE CULLEN BRANCH OF THE N.Y. PUBLIC LIBRARY (1942; Louis Allen Abramson) at 104 W. 136th St (S.W. corner of Lenox Ave) is named after the poet, editor, and social critic, an important figure of the Harlem Renaissance. The extension stands on the site of a mansion built in 1913 by Mme C.J. Walker, a St. Louis laundress who discovered a hair-straightening process and reaped a fortune. Her daughter, A'Lelia Walker Robinson, was Harlem's outstanding hostess during the 1920s and for a time established one floor of the mansion as a café and gathering place for black poets and intellectuals. Another nearby literary landmark is the *Harlem Branch of the Y.M.C.A.* (1932; James C. Mackenzie) at 180 W. 135th St between Lenox and Seventh Aves. In 1945 the Harlem Writers' Workshop was founded at the Y, which also served as the temporary home of many aspiring blacks drawn to Harlem, including Langston Hughes and Ralph Ellison.

Continue W. to Seventh Ave and turn left (S.).

During the Roaring '20s, entrepreneurs taking advantage of white curiosity billed W. 133rd St between Lenox and Seventh Ave as 'Jungle Alley', a place where whites could see 'the primitive essence' of Harlem; of course it was a tourist trap whose nightclubs—Dickie Wells', the Nest, Mexico's, Pod's—were rigged to show the unsuspecting just what they wanted to see.

Harlem's most famous nightclub during the 1920s was the Cotton Club, located at Lenox Ave and 143rd St. Whites owned it and enjoyed its bands and revues. Blacks—preferably light-skinned ones, worked there: on the stage, backstage, and out front as bouncers to keep out other blacks. The chorus line of light-skinned black women (which Lena Horne joined for a while) was so famous that white women tried to 'pass' to get in. Cab Calloway performed here and Duke Ellington, whose band played here between 1927–31, achieved his first brilliant success both musically and commercially through his association with the club. The Depression killed the Cotton Club, which tried to reopen c. 1979 on the far W. side of 125th St (666 W. 125th St) with an elegant floorshow; after a few months, the club went disco. The only remaining old time club is Small's Paradise (2294 Seventh Ave between W. 134th–135th Sts), now owned by basketball star Wilt Chamberlain.

The WILLIAMS CHRISTIAN METHODIST CHURCH (2225 Seventh Ave, between W. 131st and W. 132nd Sts) began as the Lafayette Theater (c. 1910) which hit its stride offering black revues in the 1920s. While the shows, especially the midnight shows, were a local social event, some people perceived that black talent and a black audience were being exploited for the profit of the white outsiders who owned and operated the theatre. During the Depression the Lafayette housed the W.P.A. Federal Negro Theater among whose productions was a 1937 'Macbeth' directed by Orson Welles with an all-black cast.

Outside the theatre at Seventh Ave and W. 131st St once flourished the **'Tree of Hope'**, purported to bring good luck to black actors and actresses out of work. When a job came through the lucky performer kissed the tree in gratitude. Old age and pollution killed both the original and its replacement donated by Bill 'Bojangles' Robinson (1878–1949), the famous dancer. Now a sculptural tree of weathering steel (1972; Algernon Miller) marks the site.

Continue S. towards 125th St. Any visitor to Harlem notices its empty, derelict buildings and rubble-strewn vacant lots, the legacy of generations of landlord-tenant hostilities. The combination of uncorrected building violations, landlord neglect, tenant abuse, and tax delinquency has resulted in the stark abandonment of many buildings by landlords who find it cheaper to walk away from their property than to pay the taxes on it. The empty buildings then become havens for drug addicts or winos, and targets for criminals who rip out the plumbing, wiring and other things of value. Landlords have been known on more than a few occasions to hire arsonists to burn their buildings down, thereby collecting on the insurance. When the landlord defaults on taxes and abandons the building, the city becomes the *in rem* owner and by this depressing and vicious chain of events has become Harlem's largest landlord.

Continue down Seventh Ave to 125th St, Harlem's main commercial strip. On the N.E. corner of the intersection (163 W. 125th St) in a monumental plaza is the HARLEM STATE OFFICE BUILDING (1973; Ifill Johnson Hanchard), constructed to house administrative offices of the State of New York. The project has been controversial, as local residents debated its actual value to the neighbourhood. On the S.E. corner of the site formerly stood Lewis Michaux's National Memorial African Bookstore, long an informal center of black intellectual activity. The sidewalk outside used to be a kind of Hyde Park, where political activists, including Malcolm X, made speeches and organised rallies. Michaux began his shop with a collection of about a dozen books but by his death in 1976 his inventory had grown to some 200,000 titles.

Diagonally across the intersection at the S.W. corner (2090 Seventh Ave) is the THERESA TOWERS (c. 1910), now an office building (altered 1971) but originally the Theresa Hotel. The Theresa became famous most recently as the place Fidel Castro chose to stay when he visited the United Nations in 1960.

At 144 W. 125th St between Seventh and Lenox Aves is the **Studio Museum in Harlem** (open Wed–Fri, 10–5; Sat–Sun, 1–6; admission, $1 suggested donation; tel: 865–2420), founded in 1968 to collect, conserve, and exhibit the work of black artists. Changing exhibitions often feature emerging artists, and the museum also offers shows on historical or cultural themes of interest to blacks. The permanent collection includes works of Romare Bearden as well as historic photographs of Harlem and black life by James Van DerZee.

In the next block (253 W. 125th St) between Seventh and Eighth Aves is the APOLLO THEATER (1913) which opened as a burlesque house for whites only; in 1934 Leo Brecher and Frank Schiffman opened it to blacks and began presenting revues, singers, and bands. Bessie Smith and Billie Holiday, Duke Ellington, Count Basie, Charlie Parker and Dizzy Gillespie, as well as soul and rock stars Gladys Knight and Aretha Franklin all appeared here. In the mid-1970s the Apollo, pressurised by poor box office receipts, began showing films and eventually closed. In 1980 it reopened under black management (for the first time) with movies, jazz and rock groups, and other attractions, but the experiment was not successful. It is now a cable tv studio.

Turn around and go E. to Fifth Ave. Just W. of that avenue at 55 W. 125th St is the *CAV Building*, the largest black-owned office building in the nation.

There are several handsome churches in the vicinity. The EPHESUS SEVENTH DAY ADVENTIST CHURCH (1887; J.R. Thomas), originally the Reformed Low Dutch Church of Harlem at 267 Lenox Ave on the N.W. corner of W. 123rd St was the second church of that denomination to serve the burghers of Harlem; the first was established in 1660. On the S.E. corner of the same intersection at 36 W. 123rd St is the picturesque Romanesque Revival BETHEL GOSPEL PENTACOSTAL ASSEMBLY (1889; Lamb & Rich), built as the Harlem Club for businessmen and civic leaders. **St. Martin's Episcopal Church** (1888; William A. Potter; DL) on the S.E. corner of Lenox Ave and W. 122nd St, a handsome Romanesque church with a fine carillon of 40 bells, began as the Holy Trinity Episcopal Church. The parish was established 20 years earlier; five years after the church was built it had a communicant list of 1000 and enjoyed increasing prosperity. The MOUNT OLIVET BAPTIST CHURCH at 201 Lenox Ave on the N.W. corner of W. 120th St was built as Temple Israel (1907; Arnold W. Brunner) for a prestigious congregation of German Jews.

A little out of the way is the Roman Catholic ALL SAINTS' CHURCH on the N.E. corner of Madison Ave and E. 129th St, a splendid Gothic group of ecclesiastical buildings in the Renwick tradition (Church: 1894; Renwick, Aspinwall & Russell. Rectory at 47 E. 129th St: 1889; Renwick, Aspinwall & Russell. School at 52 E. 130th St: 1904; W.W. Renwick). Especially handsome is the 129th St facade and the row of rose windows in the clerestory along Madison Ave. Return to Fifth Ave and 125th St.

A little S., straddling Fifth Ave between 120th and 124th Sts is **Marcus Garvey Park,** originally called Mount Morris Park but renamed to honour the black leader in 1973. Garvey, flamboyant, fond of titles and prerogatives, a charismatic leader, arrived in Harlem from the W. Indies in 1914, dedicated to the improvement of his race. His major interest was in leading his people back to Africa, of which he dubbed himself Emperor and 'Sir Provisional President'. To this end he formed two steamship companies whose vessels also attempted to subvert Prohibition by carrying some $3 million worth of liquor from New York to Cuba, a voyage which ended in the confiscation of the liquor by the government. Later Garvey, convicted of mail fraud and imprisoned, was deported to Jamaica; he died an exile in London in 1940.

In 1839 the city established the park, mainly because its steep, rocky terrain was unsuitable for building. That it was unsuitable for recreation does not seem to have deterred the planners; but when the surrounding blocks were levelled and built upon, the central hill in the park (called Snake Hill by the Dutch) achieved a prominence that at least made the park visually dramatic. Its dominant man-made feature is a cast-iron fire *Watchtower* (1856; Julius Kroehl; DL), the sole survivor of many that once served as lookout and warning stations (even the bell remains). Two modern intrusions in the park are the Mount Morris Recreation Center and Amphitheater (1969; Lundquist & Stonehill) on the W. side near 122nd St, and the Mount Morris Park Swimming Pool and Bathhouse (1969; Ifill & Johnson) near Madison Ave and W. 124th St. Near the park, especially to the W., are fine rows of houses. Of especial interest are the row directly facing the park on its W. flank, the row on Lenox Ave between W.

120th and W. 121st Sts, and those on 122nd and 123rd Sts between the park and Lenox Ave.

Go S. on Fifth Ave to 116th St. A block W. (102 W. 116th St, S.W. corner of Lenox Ave) is the *Malcolm Shabazz Masjid*, originally the Lenox Casino, converted to temple (1965) by the addition of an aluminum onion-shaped dome. Elijah Muhammad established it as his Temple of Islam and Malcolm X preached there before his break with Muhammad and the Black Muslims.

Continue down Fifth Ave. At the N.E. corner of Central Park (110th St) is FRAWLEY CIRCLE, named (1926) after James J. Frawley, a Tammany politician, state senator, and public administrator. Before the coming of the Arthur A. Schomburg Plaza, Frawley Circle was as nondescript as the other Central Park circle in Harlem, Frederick Douglass Circle to the W. Nowadays the SCHOMBURG PLAZA (1975; Gruzen & Partners and Castro-Blanco, Piscioneri & Feder) with its two 35-story octagonal towers rising high above anything else in the neighbourhood, serves to demarcate the corner of the park. Constructed at about the same time (1976) by the same architects is the Fifth Avenue Lakeview apartment complex between 106th and 107th Sts.

Spanish Harlem, E. of Park Ave and N. of 96th St, no longer has the largest number of Hispanic residents in the city (the Bronx has), but it is still the cradle of Latin American culture here, known also as 'El Barrio', the neighbourhood, the district. Unlike central Harlem it was never elegant but from the time of its development housed poor immigrants—Italians, Scandanavians, Irish, Jews—in its long rows of tenements. Puerto Ricans, who form the largest group among the city's Hispanic population, began immigrating to mainland United States after 1917 when they became American citizens, but the largest influx came after World War II, peaking in the mid-1950s and fluctuating with economic conditions since that time. The neighbourhood around Pleasant Place and 114th St still has a dwindling number of Italians, most of whom originated in Sicily and S. Italy, and elsewhere in Spanish Harlem are enclaves of Cubans, Dominicans, and Asians.

Spanish Harlem has a fairly high incidence of crime. It is wiser to tour by day, by car, or in company.

The *Aguilar Branch of the New York Public Library* (174 E. 110th St between Third and Lexington Aves) was established in 1886 as a private library to satisfy the intellectual hunger of the predominantly Jewish immigrants who lived in the neighbourhood. Named after Grace Aguilar, an English novelist of Spanish Jewish parentage, the building (1899, expanded 1905; Herts & Tallant) now serves as part of the public system.

Among the large housing projects in East Harlem several stand out. One is the *1199 Plaza* apartment complex (between 107th and 110th Sts, First Ave and the Franklin D. Roosevelt Drive), a mix of brick towers (32 stories) and lower residential buildings (1975; The Hodne/Stageberg Partners, architects; Herb Baldwin, landscape architect) on a landscaped site that divides public and private spaces in the best traditions of city planning. The name refers to District 1199 of the National Union of Hospital and Health Care Employees, sponsors of the project.

One of the area's newer cultural institutions, the *East Harlem*

Music School, occupies two tenements along Lexington Ave (1679 Lexington Ave near 105th St and 1681 Lexington Ave near 106th St). Probably the only music school in the nation devoted to Latin music, it was founded by pop singer Johnny Colón, to train musicians and to teach those qualities of discipline and character that accompany the art.

One of the most colourful, boisterous spots in the neighbourhood, even the city, is LA MARQUETA, an enclosed market under the Park Ave railroad viaduct between 110th–116th Sts (open 8–6 every day except Sunday and major holidays). Merchants cater to local tastes offering plantains, coconuts, mangoes, chayotes, and banana leaves; in the fish stalls toward the N. end are eels, octopus, and salt cod along with the more familiar seafood staples; butchers offer whole pigs or virtually any of the parts thereof. Other merchants fill their stalls with religious items, plaster figurines of saintly or secular figures, herbal preparations, clothing, and jewellery. The market spills out onto the street where loudspeakers blare forth the latest in Latin hit tunes.

The Harlem Courthouse at 170 E. 121st St on the corner of Sylvan Place was erected during Harlem's more affluent days (1893; Thom & Wilson; DL) in the eclectic style then popular—here a mix of

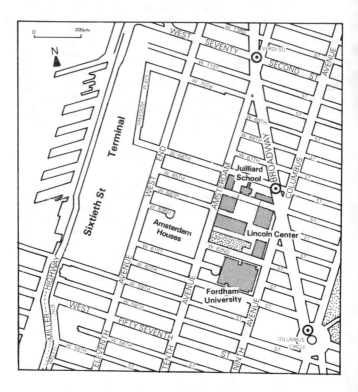

Victorian Gothic and Romanesque elements. It remained a court-house until 1961 when its functions were reduced to more menial governmental tasks. The second of East Harlem's most impressive slum clearance projects is *Taino Towers* (between 122nd and 123rd Sts, Second and Third Aves) which dates from 1977 (Silverman & Cika) and was sponsored by a group of local residents and community leaders. The name 'Taino' refers to the pre-Colombian natives of Puerto Rico, who, incidentally called their island Borinquén, a name also perpetuated in various Puerto Rican endeavours in the city.

27 Columbus Circle to Lincoln Center

SUBWAY: IRT Broadway–7th Ave express or local (trains 1, 2, 3), IND Eighth Ave express or local (trains A, AA, CC) or IND Sixth Ave express (D train), all to 59th St-Columbus Circle.

BUS: M5 or M7 uptown via Sixth Ave; M104 or M10 uptown via Eighth Ave; M103 crosstown on 59th St or M28 crosstown on 57th St. Culture Bus (weekends and holidays), Loop I, stop 6.

CAR PARKING: Large parking garages serve the Coliseum on W. 58th St between Eighth and Ninth Aves. The Lincoln Center Garage (enter from W. 62nd or W. 65th St) holds 720 cars; arrive at least one hour before performance time.

Begin at Columbus Circle, the intersection of Central Park South (59th St), Central Park West (Eighth Ave) and Broadway. In the triangle N. of the circle is GULF & WESTERN PLAZA (1970; Thomas E. Stanley), a white rectangular slab of an office building set down on a triangular site. On the Broadway side is the Paramount Theater, mostly underground, with a cylindrical 'hat box' sticking up through the pavement. The *New York Coliseum* (1965; Leon & Lionel Levy), an unremarkable light tan brick building, hosts the New York Boat Show, the New York Auto Show, and similar commercial attractions.

The Columbus Monument, the Maine Memorial, and the New York City Department of Cultural Affairs are covered in Rte 29.

Points of Interest W. of Columbus Circle. West of Columbus Circle on a slight rise near Ninth Ave and the upper W. 50s was a black neighbourhood known after the turn of the century as SAN JUAN HILL from the heroism of black soldiers in the Spanish-American War. ROOSEVELT HOSPITAL, along Ninth Ave between W. 57th and W. 59th Sts, was founded in 1871; the oldest building remaining is the *William J. Syms Operating Theater* (1892; W. Wheeler Smith) on the S.W. corner of W. 59th St. Between Eleventh and Twelfth Aves, W. 58th to W. 59th Sts, is the POWER PLANT OF CONSOLIDATED EDISON (1904; McKim, Mead & White), originally the main powerhouse for the first New York subway, the Interborough Rapid Transit which opened in 1904 and ran between City Hall and W. 145th St. The electricity was generated from furnaces (once there were six tall smokestacks on the building) fuelled by coal brought upriver on barges and transported to the powerhouse on electric conveyor belts. Today the city buys power for the subways from Consolidated Edison Co. Those who enjoy industrial architecture might walk to the N.E. corner of Twelfth Ave and W. 59th St to see the GARDNER WAREHOUSE CO., originally the *Rossiter Stores* of the New York Central and Hudson River Railroad (1889; Walter Katté, chief engineer), a block of masonry warehouses whose tiers of arched windows are protected by steel shutters.

On the W. side of Columbus Ave at 60th St is the (Roman Catholic) CHURCH OF ST. PAUL THE APOSTLE (1885; Jeremiah O'Rourke), the home of the Paulist Fathers or Missionary Society of St. Paul, founded (1858) by Father Isaac Thomas Hecker to spread Catholicism and an awareness of its thought and traditions in the essentially Protestant societies of Canada and the U.S. The Gothic exterior is unremarkable except for the bas-relief on the E. facade (Lumen Martin Winter), which contains 50 tons of travertine fixed against a mosaic background of Venetian glass tesserae in 15 shades of blue; it depicts the conversion of St. Paul.

Interior (described clockwise from entrance). The bronze panel on the S. wall depicting the Raising of the Daughter of Jairus is by Charles Keck. The baptismal font in the second bay, designed by John La Farge, is constructed of Tennessee, Numidian, and Colonna marble; the mural above it is a copy from Bellini. The Altar of the Blessed Virgin at the far end of the S. aisle was designed by Stanford White, as were the High Altar and the Altar of St. Joseph in the N. aisle. Frederick MacMonnies executed the bronze kneeling angels on top of the baldachin; the sanctuary lamp was designed by Stanford White and executed by Philip Martiny. The murals (dark and difficult to see) high on the walls of the Sanctuary representing the Angel of the Moon (S. wall) and the Angel of the Sun (N. wall) are by John La Farge and William Laurel Harris respectively. The altar of St. Patrick in the N. aisle (second bay from the main entrance), executed in Connemara marble, is also by John La Farge. Father Hecker's tomb is in the next bay. Bertram Goodhue designed the floor whose mosaics touch on the apostleship of St. Paul. The East Window was designed by John La Farge as were the two blue windows at the W. end of the church.

About a block E. and N. of the church at 1865 Broadway (N.W. corner of W. 61st St) is *Bible House* (1966; Skidmore, Owings & Merrill), headquarters of the American Bible Society, a white precast concrete building with huge exposed beams on the Broadway side.

Bible House offers changing exhibitions (Mon–Fri, 9–4.30, admission free) of rare and unusual Bibles—an 1849 Nu Testament in Fonetic Shorthand, Helen Keller's imposing stack of Braille volumes, a collection of miniature Bibles—as well as facsimile leaves from a Gutenberg Bible and the Dead Sea scrolls and a full-scale reproduction of the Gutenberg printing press.

Return to Columbus Ave, originally Ninth Ave, renamed above 59th St in 1890 (as were West End Ave, Amsterdam Ave, Central Park West, and Central Park South at various times) to enhance its prestige and the value of its real estate. Oddly, those who petitioned the city for the name change regarded it as second in importance only to the advantages of increased rapid transit in its beneficial effect on property values.

At 47 Columbus Ave, between W. 61st and W. 62nd Sts, is the storage WAREHOUSE OF SOFIA BROTHERS, INC. (1930; Jardine, Hill & Murdock), a much-admired Art Deco building, constructed as one of the city's first high-rise, 'automatic' (i.e. elevator-equipped) parking garages. Pressed up against the warehouse at 44 W. 62nd St is *Lincoln Plaza Tower* (1973; Horace Ginsbern & Assocs), an attractive 30-story apartment building with curved balconies, bay windows, and cylindrical columns—one of many residential buildings to arise after the construction of Lincoln Center set the neighbourhood on its present upward course.

The LINCOLN CENTER CAMPUS OF FORDHAM UNIVERSITY, a Jesuit institution founded in 1841 with its main campus in the west

Bronx, occupies the blocks bounded by Columbus and Amsterdam Aves, W. 60th and W. 62nd Sts. Built as part of the same urban renewal enterprise as Lincoln Center, the campus has two main buildings: the *Fordham Law School* (1962; Voorhees, Walker, Smith, Smith & Haines) on the S., and the *Leon Lowenstein Center* (1969; Slingerland & Booss) on the N. In the plaza of the Lowenstein Center is a 28-ft bronze statue of *Peter, Fisher of Men* (Frederick Shrady), casting a 14-ft bronze 'net' across the plaza's reflecting pool.

Walk N. on Columbus Ave. ****Lincoln Center for the Performing Arts,** bounded by Columbus and Amsterdam Aves, W. 62nd and W. 66th Sts, is a 14-acre, $185 million complex of six buildings devoted to drama, music, and dance. It is the home of the Metropolitan Opera, the New York Philharmonic, the New York City Ballet, the New York City Opera, and the Chamber Music and Film Societies of Lincoln Center, as well as the site of the Juilliard School and the New York Public Library at Lincoln Center, a branch specialising in the performing arts.

Visually the three largest halls—the Metropolitan Opera House, Avery Fisher Hall, and the New York State Theater—dominate the complex, facing on a central plaza adorned with a fountain (Philip Johnson) and a pavement design of travertine concentric circles and spokes against a background of dark aggregate. The three halls, classical in inspiration, are all faced with travertine, a creamy white marble available only from ancient quarries near Rome: all present large expanses of glass covered with colonnades of one sort or another to the plaza.

History. Three events in 1955 paved the way for Lincoln Center: the designation of Lincoln Square—the neighbourhood surrounding the intersection of Broadway and Amsterdam Ave at W. 65th St—as a target for urban renewal, the recognition by the Metropolitan Opera that Lincoln Square might be a site for a new and desperately needed opera house, and the impending homelessness of the New York Philharmonic, informed that Carnegie Hall was to be demolished. Heading the building committee was John D. Rockefeller, III, while Wallace K. Harrison, who had worked with the Metropolitan Opera for a quarter of a century and had participated in Rockefeller Center and the U.N. Headquarters, was chosen to head the board of architects. Construction began with groundbreaking in 1959 and ended with the opening of the Juilliard School in 1969.

From the outset Lincoln Center has aroused controversy. Urban planners objected to the burden placed on public transportation by the concentration of halls and theatres. Social critics saw a neighbourhood destroyed and rebuilt for the affluent at the expense of its former residents, the occupants of the 188 buildings demolished including 1647 families who had to find new homes.

Architectural critics have never liked Lincoln Center, at worst citing it for mediocre and slick classicism, at best faintly praising the scale and relationship of its plazas and open spaces. Artists have sometimes found it too institutional, too rich, too powerful. Nevertheless Lincoln Center, despite its plague of initial cost overruns and operating deficits, is a living and important cultural institution. An audience of about 5 million people attends yearly. A payroll of over $62 million supports over 6800 musicians, actors and dancers, stage hands, ushers and ticket takers, costume makers, set builders, office personnel, and other staff. Its fundraising campaign resulted in gifts of $141 million, a philanthropic breakthrough in the recognition of the arts. Its physical presence has inspired continuing renewal of the West Side, and its artistic programmes are vital to the cultural life of the city.

Tours, Visitors' Services, and Tickets. Two kinds of tours are offered, general tours of the buildings, which sometimes include glimpses of rehearsals, and backstage tours of the Metropolitan Opera House. The general tours leave from the Concourse Level (accessible from the foyer of the Metropolitan Opera House, down one flight) from 10.15 to 5. Adults, $2·95; children, $1·95. Backstage tours (1¹/₂ hours) leave from the entrance foyer of the Met, Mon–Fri at 3.30, Sat at 10.30. Advance reservations necessary. Adults, $5.00; students, $2.00. For reservations and information, tel: 582–3512.

BOX OFFICE HOURS vary slightly from house to house, but generally they are open between 10–11 a.m. and 6 p.m., or later if performances are scheduled. For box office information call:

Alice Tully Hall   362–1911
Avery Fisher Hall   874–2424
Juilliard School   799–5000
Metropolitan Opera   580–9830
N.Y. Public Library at Lincoln Center   870–1630
N.Y. State Theater   362–6000
Vivian Beaumont Theater   787–8080.
Tips for the physically handicapped are available at the Administrative Offices (140 W. 65th St); tel: 877–1800. Restaurants are located in the Avery Fisher Hall and the Metropolitan Opera House; times vary seasonally. Restrooms located on the Concourse level near the garage entrance.

The **Metropolitan Opera House,** the centerpiece of Lincoln Center (1966; Wallace K. Harrison), 10 stories high, faces Broadway from the W. side of the plaza. The main facade has five marble arches separated by columns, while the long side walls with their closely spaced mullions reach back the equivalent of 45 stories. Through the main facade two colourful murals by Marc Chagall can be seen, except when curtains are drawn to protect them on sunny mornings.

History. The Metropolitan Opera was founded by a group of 'new' capitalists— i.e., Goulds, Whitneys, J.P. Morgan, and several Vanderbilts—who were denied boxes at the Academy of Music on 14th St because the 'old' nobility already occupied them all. The new house (1883; J.C. Cady and Louis de Coppet Bergh) featured an auditorium whose deep Diamond Horseshoe gave box holders an unrivalled opportunity to look at one another and otherwise had disastrous sightlines with some 700 seats having partial or obstructed view of the stage. Backstage the house was cramped and outdated by the 1920s when the opera began searching for a new home. Nevertheless, the house enjoyed the affection of the public until it closed in 1966.
The new house opened on 16 Sept 1966 with the premier performance of Samuel Barber's 'Antony and Cleopatra', commissioned for the occasion, with the title roles sung by Leontyne Price and Justino Diaz.

The INTERIOR, finished in red plush, gold leaf, and marble, recalls the colour scheme of the old Met and attempts to reconcile the grandeur of traditional opera houses with a more contemporary approach, an attempt that critics generally feel has failed on the side of overdecoration and timidity. The crystal sunburst chandeliers were donated by the Austrian government. The concrete forms for the sweeping curves of the Grand Staircase were executed by boatbuilders.

The predominantly red Chagall mural on the S. side, *Le Triomphe de la Musique*, depicts singers, ballerinas, and musicians, along with references to opera, folk music, and jazz, and images of the New York skyline. Former Metropolitan general manager (1935–72) Sir Rudolph Bing appears in gypsy costume (central figure in the group of three on the left). The yellow mural, *Les Sources de la Musique*, shows a combined King David-Orpheus figure holding a lyre, a Tree of Life afloat in the Hudson River, and references to Wagner, Verdi, Bach, and the operas 'Fidelio' and 'The Magic Flute'.

Among the works of art in the foyers and corridors is a bronze (1911) by Wilhelm Lehmbruck, *Die Kniende* ('Kneeling Woman') at the top of the Grand Staircase. Two figures by Aristide Maillol, *Summer* (1910) and *Venus without Arms* (1920) are displayed on the S. and N. ends of the Grand Tier level. In the foyer of the Dress Circle is Maillol's *Kneeling Woman; Monument to Debussy* (1931). A gallery on the concourse level (one floor below the main foyer) contains paintings of Metropolitan stars and operatic composers. The heroic bronze *bust of Caruso* by Onorio Ruotolo and the marble *bust of Giulio Gatti-Casazzi*, general manager 1908–35, were familiar fixtures in the lobby of the old Met. The *portrait of Gluck* displayed in the N. passage (beyond the bust of Gatti-Casazza) is by Joseph Sifrede Duplessis (1725–1802) and is believed to be the original, the one in Vienna being a copy.

Backstage the building is superbly equipped, with a 110-ft fly loft above the main stage, three auxiliary stages as large as the main playing area, twenty rehearsal rooms—three of which are large enough to duplicate the main stage, and an orchestra pit which can hold 110 musicians. The stage equipment, including six 60-ft hydraulic lifts and a revolving stage, was a gift from the government of West Germany.

The *auditorium*, also decorated in red, has 3788 seats arranged in the traditional manner though with a widened horseshoe to improve sightlines. Immense by European standards (cf. Covent Garden's 2158 seats), it offers a single row of boxes with otherwise 'democratic' seating, in contrast to the old Met which provided segregated elevators and less comfortable seats for patrons of the cheaper levels of the house. The free form sculpture for the proscenium arch (1966) is by Mary Callery.

The Metropolitan Opera is known for the grandeur of its productions generally chosen from the traditional repertoire and for its star-studded casts. James Levine is the musical director.

On the S.W. corner of the Lincoln Center site is DAMROSCH PARK (1969; Eggers & Higgins) with the Guggenheim Bandshell, used for free outdoor concerts. The park is named in honour of Walter Damrosch, director of the New York Symphony Orchestra (1903–27), composer, and pioneer of orchestral radio concerts.

On the S. side of the plaza stands the **New York State Theater** (1964; Philip Johnson & Richard Foster), home of the New York City Opera and the New York City Ballet. Over the glass front wall rises a colonnade of paired square columns, interrupted by an outdoor balcony used as a promenade during intermissions.

INTERIOR. On the front wall of the ground level foyer are an *Untitled Relief* (1964; Lee Bontecou) and a painting entitled *Numbers* (1964) by Jasper Johns. On the stairway landings are two abstract sculptures of gold leaf on fibreglass by Kobashi entitled *Song* and *Dance*. Reuben Nakian's bronze *Voyage to Crete* (1963) stands inside the doors (left) leading to the orchestra level. Also displayed on the same level are Jacques Lipchitz's *Birth of the Muses* (1949) and an untitled *Sculpture* (1963) by Edward Higgins. One floor up is the Grand Promenade, with a marble floor, gold leaf-covered ceiling, beaded metallic curtains, and tiers of balconies for strolling. Since the state owns the building, the mayor and governor may use the foyer for receptions, as can private individuals—though for a fee. Two large, curvaceous statues at either end, one pair representing *Two Nudes*, the other, *Two Circus Women* (originals 1930 and 1931 by Elie Nadelman) were duplicated in Carrara marble at twice the original size by Italian artisans. Perhaps the most controversial objects in the theater, they have been called 'absolutely pneumatic' by detractors who also likened their polished whiteness to yogurt, while admirers have found them to combine 'high style, sly levity, and swelling monumentality'.

The *auditorium* (seats 2729), designed without a center aisle for better sightlines, is decorated in a garnet colour, with big jewel-like lights studding the tiers of balconies and a central chandelier that resembles a colossal, many-faceted diamond. The stage was engineered specifically to meet the demands of dancers and features a 'sprung' floor with air spaces between its layers, covered with dark grey linoleum.

The resident New York City Ballet (founded 1948), led by general director Lincoln Kirstein and artistic directors Jerome Robbins and George Balanchine, is especially famous for its performances of Balanchine's abstract, neo-classical ballets. The New York City Opera, under general manager Beverly Sills, is a company of predominantly young, predominantly American singers who perform an imaginative, adventurous repertoire as well as standard operatic favourites.

Facing the New York State Theater is **Avery Fisher Hall,** originally Philharmonic Hall (1962; Max Abramovitz), a glass box around which is wrapped a peristyle of 44 tapered travertine columns. Renamed (1973) after Avery Fisher, manufacturer of high-fidelity components and donor of $10 million to Lincoln Center, the hall is the professional home of the New York Philharmonic.

From the opening (23 Sept 1962) to its present redesign, the acoustics proved a nightmare to musicians, the audience, and the designers of the hall. Musicians complained of being unable to hear one another, while trained listeners in the auditorium were troubled by a lack of low frequency sounds, a strident quality in the upper registers, and an echo. When adjustment of the original 106 sound-reflecting 'clouds' hung over both the stage and the auditorium area failed to improve the acoustics, engineers resorted to increasingly radical measures, changing wall contours, replacing heavily upholstered seats with thinly padded, wooden-backed chairs, and filling in the space between the 'clouds' with plywood. Even so in 1974 the Boston and Philadelphia Orchestras, still dissatisfied, went back to Carnegie Hall for their New York appearances. Finally in 1976, using half of Avery Fisher's gift, architects Philip Johnson and John Burgee with acoustical guidance from Cyril Harris, consultant for the Metropolitan Opera House, had the hall completely gutted and rebuilt, to the acclaim of all concerned.

INTERIOR. In the main foyer is a two-part hanging work by Richard Lippold entitled *Orpheus and Apollo*, constructed of 190 strips of polished Muntz metal, a copper alloy, suspended from the ceiling by steel wires. Other works in the entrance foyer are (E. end) Seymour Lipton's *Archangel* (1964), an abstract sculptural work of bronze and Monel metal, and (W. end) Dimitri Hadzi's dark bronze *K458—The Hunt* (1964), whose title recalls a Mozart string quartet. At the S. end of the Grand Promenade is a bronze *Tragic Mask of Beethoven*, by Antoine Bourdelle, a *bronze head of Gustav Mahler*, made by Auguste Rodin in 1901 (W. side of Promenade level), and a set of *four Steuben glass panels* etched by Don Weir with figures representing opera, symphony, ballet, and drama (in the Green Room). In the penthouse garden terrace is a *bust of Antonin Dvorak* by Ian Mestrovic, presented in 1963 by the Czechoslovak National Council of America.

The *auditorium* (seats 2742) is used by the Philharmonic, now under the directorship of Zubin Mehta, about four times weekly during the season, and by soloists, other orchestras, jazz and popular groups for the rest of the time.

Between Avery Fisher Hall and the Vivian Beaumont Theater is a reflecting pool containing a two-piece bronze work by Henry Moore, *Lincoln Center Reclining Figure* (1965). Moore himself described the piece as 'a leg part and a head and arms part' and has expressed disappointment that the reflecting pool—because of leaks into the garage below—is frequently empty. Near the entrance to the library is Alexander Calder's *Le Guichet* (1965), a stabile of blackened steel (22 ft long, 14 ft high).

The **Vivian Beaumont Theater** (1965; Eero Saarinen), named after a generous donor, has been praised as the center's most successful building architecturally but has suffered financial and artistic difficulties that have resisted changes in leadership and in artistic direction. Joseph Papp, who headed it for several years, resigned in 1977, pronouncing it unworkable both physically and financially. After remaining dark for three years, it reopened in 1980 with Richmond Crinkley as executive director and a panel of directors including Woody Allen, Sarah Caldwell, Liviu Ciulei, Robbin Phillips, and Ellis Rabb.

Situated W. of the reflecting pool, the main facade appears as a horizontal slab of travertine projecting over a glass wall. Inside the entrance is a sculptural work, *Zig IV* (1961) by David Smith. The theatre itself, designed in consultation with Jo Mielziner at a time when thrust stages were in vogue, was conceived as a compromise between a traditional proscenium arch and a thrust stage with complex machinery for converting it from one form to the other. The stage area is much larger than that of any other legitimate theatre in the city and the auditorium is arranged as an amphitheater (seats 1089). Soon after the theatre opened it was discovered that the sightlines were poor, that members of the audience could not see action taking place at the rear of the deep stage; later the acoustics were found wanting. The lighting system, originally computerised, was changed to a conventional control system when the automatic system caused erratic and disrupting lighting changes. The theatre is currently scheduled for physical and acoustic renovation costing an estimated $4–5 million.

Also in the building is the *Mitzi E. Newhouse Theater*, a small house (seats 280) for experimental drama.

To the left of the theatre and wrapped around it is **The New York Public Library at Lincoln Center** (1965; Skidmore, Owings & Merrill), a library and museum of the performing arts, with a circulating library of some 50,000 volumes and 12,000 records, and a research library devoted to the performing arts.

Open Mon and Thurs, 10–8; Tues, Wed, 10–6; Fri and Sat, 12–6. Hours slightly different for access to research collections; tel: 799–2200.

Exhibitions pertaining to the performing arts are mounted in the *Main Gallery* and the *Vincent Astor Gallery*. The Heckscher Oval in the Children's Library often has special exhibitions of puppets, story theatres, and other memorabilia appealing to children. Free recitals are presented in the Bruno Walter Auditorium (apply for tickets in person after 3.00 on the day of the programme or Sat after noon at the Amsterdam Ave entrance).

The Juilliard School, founded in 1905 as the Institute of Musical Arts by Frank Damrosch and James Loeb and endowed in 1920 through a bequest from merchant and philanthropist Augustus D. Juilliard, lies on the N. side of W. 65th St. Of all the buildings in the center the Juilliard School (1969; Pietro Belluschi) is the most complex, housing ALICE TULLY HALL, home of the Chamber Music Society of Lincoln Center, and the school itself, which offers professional training for performance in music, dance, and drama. Facilities of the school include the JUILLIARD THEATER (seats 1026), with a moveable ceiling which can be raised or lowered to vary the reverberation time to suit spoken drama, instrumental, or vocal music, as well as a small recital hall (seats 278), a drama workshop theatre (seats 206), 82 soundproof practice rooms, three organ studios, 200 pianos, 35 teaching studios, and 16 two-story studios for dance, drama, or orchestral rehearsals.

Outside the building on the terrace facing Broadway stands a work of three tall zig-zag columns of polished stainless steel entitled *Three by Three Interplay* (1971; Jaacov Agam). In the foyer of Alice Tully Hall is Bourdelle's bronze *Beethoven à la Colonne* (1901). Louise Nevelson's wood construction, *Nightsphere-Light* (1969) covers the W. wall of the Juilliard Theater Lobby; an untitled abstraction of black Swedish granite by Masayuki Nagare stands on the landing of the main staircase in the 65th St lobby.

Just W. of Lincoln Center at 122 Amsterdam Ave (between W. 65th and W. 66th Sts) is MARTIN LUTHER KING, JR, HIGH SCHOOL (1975; Frost Assocs.) The memorial sculpture, by William Tarr, constructed of self-weathering steel, resembles a huge printer's block, with letters and numbers suggesting milestones in the career of the slain civil rights leader. Before the tenements of the Lincoln Square Urban Renewal Area were razed in the 1950s, Hollywood temporarily used the shabby streets for the set of its movie 'West Side Story'. Return to Broadway.

The S. triangle created by the intersection of Broadway and Columbus Ave (at 63rd St) has been designated Dante Park and contains a *bronze statue of Dante Alighieri* (1921; Ettore Ximemes) erected to commemorate the 600th anniversary of the poet's death. The family of tenor Richard Tucker placed a bronze bust of him in the N. triangle near 66th St not long after his untimely death in 1975; Tucker, who appeared in 499 performances in 21 seasons with the Met was, as a native New Yorker, one of the company's most popular singers.

On the E. side of Broadway between W. 65th and W. 66th Sts at 2 Lincoln Square, is the *Church of Christ of Latter-Day Saints and the Mormon Visitors' Center* (1975; Schuman, Lichtenstein & Claman). The visitors' center has a permanent exhibition introducing the beliefs of the Mormon church (10–8 daily, free admission) with dioramas, films, and speaking mannequins.

SUBWAY: IRT Broadway-7th Ave local (train 1) at 66th St-Broadway. IND Eighth Ave express (A train) or local (AA or CC train) at 59th St-Columbus Circle. IND Sixth Ave express (D train) or local (B train, southbound all times, northbound only during rush hours) at 59th St–Columbus Circle.

BUS: Uptown: M5 via Broadway and Riverside Drive; M7 via Broadway and Amsterdam Ave; M11 via Amsterdam Ave. M10 via Central Park West; M104 via Broadway. Downtown: M5 via Broadway and Fifth Ave; M7 via Columbus

Ave and Broadway; M11 via Columbus Ave and Ninth Ave. Culture Bus, Loop I, stop 7 (continues uptown). Crosstown bus, M29 65th (W.) and W. 66th (E.).

Other nearby points of interest. The triangle created by the intersection of Broadway and Amsterdam Ave at 72nd St is Sherman Square, named after General William Tecumseh Sherman (see p294). While no remembrance of Sherman marks the triangular traffic island, there is a fine *subway entrance* (1904; Heins & La Farge; DL) dating back to the original opening of the IRT, a little neo-Dutch colonial structure with limestone quoins and a Dutch gable, no doubt intended to recall the founding of the city by the Dutch. Three such 'control houses,' so-called because riders entering them passed into territory 'controlled' by the IRT, once stood along Broadway, but the other two at 103rd and 116th Sts have not survived.

The ANSONIA HOTEL (1904; Graves & Duboy; DL) at 2107 Broadway is a grand old dowager among West Side apartment houses, once the New York home of Caruso, Toscanini, Ziegfeld, Stravinsky, Pinza, and Pons, now the less splendid home of less famous residents, many of them musicians. Still the Ansonia, towering over Broadway from its commanding site where the avenue curves between W. 73rd and W. 74th Sts, delights the eye with its elaborate Beaux-Arts decoration, its rounded corner towers, high mansard roof, delicate iron balconies, cornices, and terracotta trim. The developer William Earl Dodge Stokes inherited his fortune from his father, a partner in the Phelps Dodge Corporation, parent company of the Ansonia Brass & Copper Company, whose main works were in Ansonia, Connecticut. The town, the company, and the apartment-hotel all got their names from industrialist Anson G. Phelps.

The triangle N. of 72nd St is known as Verdi Square, appropriately named in a neighbourhood that attracted musicians long before Lincoln Center was established nearby. The *Verdi Monument* (1906; Pasquale Civiletti) depicts the composer in Carrara marble on a granite pedestal against which stand life-sized figures of Aida, Otello, Falstaff, and Leonora (from 'La Forza del Destino').

At 2100 Broadway (N.E. corner of W. 73rd St) is the *Central Savings Bank* (1929; York & Sawyer; DL), founded as the German Savings Bank in 1859 but renamed in a period of anti-German feeling during World War I. York & Sawyer along with Samuel Yellin who is responsible for the decorative ironwork also designed the equally handsome Federal Reserve Bank in the Financial District.

SUBWAY. IRT Broadway-7th Ave local or express (train 1 or 2). IND Eighth Ave local (AA or CC) at Central Park West and W. 72nd St.

BUS. Uptown and downtown buses, the same as those serving Lincoln Center. Crosstown: M30 via 72nd St.

28 Columbus Circle to the American Museum of Natural History

SUBWAY: IRT Broadway-7th Ave express or local (trains 1, 2, 3) to 59th St-Columbus Circle. IND Eighth Ave express or local (trains A, AA, CC) to 59th St-Columbus Circle; IND Sixth Ave express (D train) to 59th St-Columbus Circle.

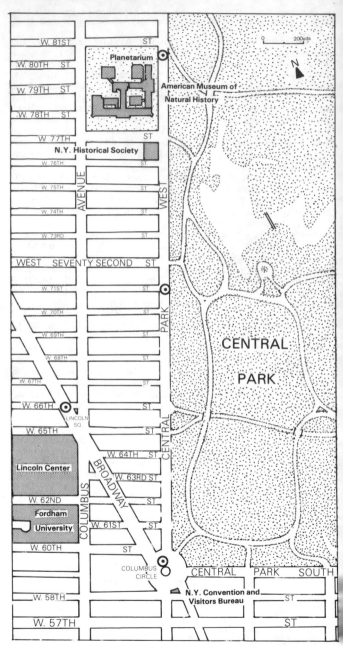

BUS: M5 or M7 uptown via Sixth Ave or M104 or M10 uptown via 8th Ave; M103 crosstown on 59th St or M28 crosstown on 57th St. Culture Bus (weekends and holidays) Loop I, Stop 6.

CAR PARKING: Limited space available at American Museum of Natural History, lot accessible from W. 81st St. Large garages serving the Coliseum on W. 58th St between Eighth and Ninth Aves.

At 59th St, Eighth Ave becomes Central Park West, renamed after the opening of the park in 1876 to boost land values. The ploy, or more likely the mere presence of Central Park, succeeded, for the street is now an elegant boulevard whose venerable institutions and stately apartment buildings serve the cultural and spiritual needs of many New Yorkers as well as the domestic needs of a select few. The older buildings date back to the last decade of the 19C, after the arrival of the Ninth Ave elevated railroad in 1879 made the Upper West Side accessible to the middle class. The newer ones date from before 1931 (with the exception of an apartment tower at 80 Central Park West and some additions to the New-York Historical Society), rather remarkable considering the city's penchant for tearing down and building up. Among the newer buildings are several splendid examples of Art Deco apartment architecture, among the older ones some fine masonry buildings, and along the side streets a glimpse at the brownstone row house architecture of the late 19C.

Begin at **Columbus Circle,** where W. 59th St, Broadway, and Eighth Ave merge in a snarl of traffic. Atop a 77-ft granite column decorated with ships' prows stands a *statue of Christopher Columbus* (1892; Gaetano Russo), given by the nation's Italian citizens to commemorate the quadricentennial of Columbus's discovery. At the base of the column a winged boy peruses a globe, while two bronze tablets depict the explorer's departure from Spain and his arrival in the New World.

Visible just inside the park is the recently refurbished *Maine Memorial* which commemorates the sinking of the U.S. battleship 'Maine' (15 February 1898), an incident that helped trigger the Spanish-American War. The memorial (1913; statuary by Attilio Piccirilli, pedestal by Harold Van Buren Magonigle) consists of a granite stele (43.5 ft) with bronze and marble sculptures. On the top 15-ft 'Columbia Triumphant' stands in a shell pulled by three hippocampi. At the base facing Broadway a boatload of marble figures includes Victory (a youth kneeling in the prow), accompanied by Courage (a male nude), and Fortitude (a mother comforting a weeping child). Behind them stands a robed figure representing Peace. Another group, facing the park, includes Justice, History, and a Warrior whose upraised hand once clenched a bronze sword. The reclining youth looking downtown represents the Atlantic, while the Pacific, facing uptown, appears as an aged man.

The Coliseum on the W. side of the intersection and the Gulf & Western Building on the triangle N. of the circle are discussed in Rte 28.

Look downtown to the headquarters of the NEW YORK CITY DEPARTMENT OF CULTURAL AFFAIRS (1965; Edward Durell Stone) at 2 Columbus Circle, housed in a white marble box on stilts pierced with rows of round holes and tall open arches. The building, whose vaguely Islamic appearance used to elicit jokes about Persian brothels, has suffered several reversals of fortune. A. & P. Supermarket heir Huntington Hartford built it as the Gallery of Modern Art to house his collection; when that didn't work out, the building became the New York Cultural Center offering exhibitions, concerts, and lectures. When that in turn failed, the owners, the Gulf & Western Company, gave it to the city for its present use.

On the ground floor is the **Visitors Information Center** of the New York Convention and Visitors Bureau, open Mon–Fri, 9–6; Sat–Sun, 10–6 (tel: 397–8222), with listings of hotels, restaurants, major attractions and shops, as well as information about transportation and sightseeing. On the second floor the *City Gallery* (Mon–Fri, 10–5.30; free; tel: 974–1150) offers exhibitions on the city and its artists.

Begin walking N. up Central Park West, preferably on the park side for the best view of the buildings. The CENTURY APARTMENTS (1931; Jacques Delamarre and the Irwin S. Chanin Construction Co.) at 25 Central Park West between 62nd and 63rd Sts is a handsome Art Deco building, with machine-like trim at the top, six rows of bay windows across the front, and cantilevered terraces at the base of the twin towers. The building is named after the Century Theater, a grandiose neo-classical fiasco (1909; Carrère & Hastings), planned as a national theatre which would be untainted by commerce. Unfortunately it was too large and too far uptown to make a profit, even when Florenz Ziegfeld tried offering spectaculars there.

The *West Side YMCA* at 5 W. 63rd St is housed in a massive building (1930; Dwight James Baum), within whose sombre brick walls are two swimming pools, handball and squash courts, and an indoor track. At 10 W. 64th St is the Frederick Henry Cossett Dormitory, offering rooms by the day and week. A plan evolved in 1966 to create a landscaped mall between Central Park and Lincoln Center to the W., which would have destroyed this and all its neighbours, a plan that fortunately died in the planning stages.

Filling the block front between W. 63rd and W. 64th Sts are two buildings of the ETHICAL CULTURE SOCIETY, founded in 1876 by Felix Adler to further morality without reference to particular religious creeds. The Ethical Culture school system began with the city's first free kindergarten (1878) and continued to educate working men and women as well as conventional students, early establishing itself as a force in experimental education and a pioneer in the use of education as a social tool. Today the society operates the Fieldston Schools in the Bronx as well as the Ethical Culture School here, all known for their progressive outlook. The more northerly of the two buildings at 2 W. 64th St (1910; Robert D. Kohn with Estelle Rumbold Kohn, sculptor; DL) is a formal limestone Art Nouveau structure, much admired at the time of completion.

The *Prasada Apartments* at 50 Central Park West on the S.W. corner of W. 65th St date from 1907 (Charles W. Romeyn & Henry R. Wynne) and are in the French Empire style, with a monumental entrance.

Holy Trinity Lutheran Church on the N.W. corner of W. 65th St dates from 1903. The apartment house at 55 CENTRAL PARK WEST (1940; Schwartz & Gross), another Art Deco-inspired building, has a fine ironwork canopy over the entrance and brickwork which shades from red at the bottom to tan at the top, to give the impression, it is said, of a ray of sunshine perpetually shining on the facade.

Walk down W. 66th St as far as No. 56, once the *First Battery Armory of the New York National Guard* (1901; Horgan & Slattery), now altered (1978) into television studios for the American Broadcasting Company. Across the street at 71 W. 66th St is another fanciful facade, originally housing the St. Nicholas Skating Rink (1896; Ernest Flagg and Walter B. Chambers), and later altered into an arena. Nowadays ABC uses it for broadcast engineering operations.

Return to Central Park West and continue N. W. 67th St is a charming anomaly, its housing consisting not of the usual brownstones but of studio buildings constructed expressly for the needs of working artists. The earliest such building here is 27 W. 67th St (1905), erected by ten artists who occupied half and rented out the rest, thereby realising a 23% profit on their investment. Most famous of the studio buildings is the HOTEL DES ARTISTES (1915; George Mort Pollard) at 1 W. 67th St, just off the park, with large two-story windows opening into the studios, and fanciful neo-Gothic statuary above the second story. Among its famous and/or artistic tenants have been Isadora Duncan, Noel Coward, Norman Rockwell, former mayor John V. Lindsay, and Howard Chandler Christy, whose murals still adorn the ground floor Café des Artistes. The new yellow brick building on the S. side of the street (30 W. 67th St) also houses studios and offices of ABC.

Return to Central Park West and keep walking uptown. The *Second Church of Christ, Scientist* on the S.W. corner of W. 68th St dates from 1900 (Frederick R. Comstock). Turn left and walk to 40 W. 68th St, originally the Free Synagogue (1923; S.B. Eisendrath and B. Horowitz) and now the JEWISH INSTITUTE OF RELIGION, a rabbinical training school. Under the leadership of its founder Stephen Wise, who was active in civic reform and an ardent Zionist, the Free Synagogue became a forum for both public and religious issues. In addition to founding the synagogue (1907), rabbi Wise organised the first section of the Federation of American Zionists and headed the delegation of the American Jewish Congress at the Paris Peace Conference following World War I. The present *Stephen B. Wise Synagogue* at 30 W. 68th St just E. of the original building was added in 1941 (Bloch & Hesse).

At the S.W. corner of W. 70th St (99 Central Park West) is the newest home (1897; Brunner & Tryon; DL) of CONGREGATION SHEARITH ISRAEL, the nation's oldest Jewish congregation, which dates back to 1654 when the first Jewish refugees arrived in New Amsterdam fleeing the Inquisition (see p85). Under Dutch rule the Jews had to worship in secret, but later, in 1682 under a more tolerant British governor, they founded Congregation Shearith Israel (Remnant of Israel) and held organised services, first in a rented room on Beaver St, then in the upper story of a flour mill on Mill Lane and S. William St. The first synagogue building (1730) at what is presently 26 S. William St is gone but some of its artifacts and two large millstones from the Dutch mill are preserved in the 'Little Synagogue' here (open during services, Fri evening and Sat morning; tel: 873–0300 for times), which reconstructs the original sanctuary. Congregation Shearith Israel maintains the three graveyards that mark its progress uptown (see pp121 and 203).

Turn W. into W. 71st St, whose BROWNSTONE ROW HOUSES, some of them a little seedy, bring delight to architectural historians.

'Brownstone' is a Triassic sandstone whose characteristic chocolate colour comes from the presence of iron ore. A 'brownstone' is a one-family row house faced with this material, usually dating from the late 19C, usually four or five stories high and two or three windows wide, featuring a tall stoop and a cornice at the top. Most brownstones were built by masons or builders, but the one at 20 W. 71st St, the best-preserved house on the block, enjoyed the talents of an architect (1889; Gilbert A. Schellenger), who designed a row of four houses here for the builders. Most brownstones were built in such small groups, and their widths became fractions of the standard city building lot (25 × 100 ft). The most elegant are 25 ft wide, while smaller varieties are 20 ft (a fifth of four lots), $18^{3}/_{4}$ ft (a quarter of three lots) or $16^{2}/_{3}$ ft (a third of two lots). Because these houses were built for prosperous middle class families, the interiors were executed in fine materials and the facades often elaborately decorated; note especially the cupids at the cornice of No. 24, the cartouches on Nos 26, 28, and 30, and the lions' heads on Nos 33–39.

Continue N. on Central Park West past the MAJESTIC APART-MENTS (115 Central Park West, between 71st and 72nd Sts), the

Italianate brownstone houses at 462 W. 23rd St in 1915. When built in the mid-late 19C, these fine single-family homes, often constructed in monumental rows, reflected the city's prosperity. (The New-York Historical Society)

second of four double-towered buildings that give the skyline along the park its distinctive character. Stylistically related to the Century Apartments nine blocks downtown, the Majestic was also built (1930) by the Irwin S. Chanin Co. with Jacques Delamarre, architect. René Chambellan, perhaps best known for the fountains at Radio City, designed the brickwork patterns. Note the corner windows, frequently used in Art Deco buildings, whose steel cage construction allowed corners to be opened up (unlike masonry construction where corners were load-bearing).

Across the street at 1 W. 72nd St are the **Dakota Apartments** (1884; Henry J. Hardenbergh; DL), architecturally one of the city's finest apartment buildings and socially the pre-eminent West Side address.

History. In 1884 apartments were just beginning to find favour with people who could afford private homes but didn't want them. Rutherfurd Stuyvesant had in 1869 remodelled some houses on E. 18th St near Irving Place as 'French flats', and had rented them all even before the renovation was completed. Other builders, alert to the potential profits in multi-family housing followed, so when Singer Sewing Machine heir Edward S. Clark undertook to build a magnificent apartment house on W. 72nd St, he was not acting without precedent. His choice of location, however, was daring—uptown, surrounded by shanties and vacant land, so far N. and W. of civilisation that detractors called it 'Clark's Folly' and one of the wittier among them remarked that the building might as well be in the Dakota territory. Clark liked the notion and instructed his architect to garnish the building with suitable motifs—ears of corn, arrowheads, and a bas relief of an Indian's head above the main gateway.

From the beginning the Dakota has been a luxury building, its apartments ranging from four to twenty rooms, originally fitted out with carved marble mantles, oak and mahogany panelling, inlaid marble floors, and hardware of solid brass. On the eighth and ninth floors, the least desirable in the days before the elevator, were rooms for servants, while the basement held boilders and generators to light the building, since the Edison Co. lines reached only as far as Spruce St. Not surprisingly the building has attracted a striking clientele, notably people involved in the arts. Among them have been Boris Karloff, Zachary Scott, Leonard Bernstein, Lauren Bacall, Roberta Flack, and scientist Michael Idvorsky Pupin. John Lennon, songwriter and former Beatle, was shot and killed in the courtyard by a deranged admirer on 8 Dec 1980. The Dakota also served as the setting for the horror movie, 'Rosemary's Baby'.

Built around an open central courtyard that provides light to interior rooms, the Dakota is finished in buff-coloured brick, decorated with terracotta and stone trim, and embellished with balconies, oriel windows, ledges, turrets, towers, gables, chimneys, finials, and flagpoles. The building has been likened to a great European château and its style characterised as an eclectic mix of German Renaissance and English Victorian styles. It is generally acknowledged to be a superb piece of work by an architect outstanding for his sense of composition.

Henry Hardenbergh also built some row houses and apartments on W. 73rd St behind the Dakota and further W. (15A–19 W. 73rd St, 41–65 W. 73rd St, and 101 and 103 W. 73rd St just beyond Columbus Ave).

Continue N. on Central Park West. At 145–146 Central Park West between W. 74th and W. 75th Sts is the third of the boulevard's twin towers, the SAN REMO APARTMENTS (1930; Emery Roth), finished in neo-classical garb with cartouches over the entrances and finialed temples on top.

The firm of Emery Roth & Sons has built more than 100 glass and steel skyscrapers since World War II, but Emery Roth himself, who worked in New

York between 1903 and the late 1930s, gave the city a series of masonry apartment buildings and hotels ornamented with neo-classical detail. He came to the U.S.A. in 1886 at the age of 13, and four years later began working as a draftsman on the Chicago's World's Columbian Exposition. Like other conservative architects, he was deeply impressed by the dignity of the Beaux-Arts buildings that dominated the exhibition, a style later reflected in his own work.

The San Remo is named after a hotel of that name which stood here before the turn of the century.

At the N.W. corner of W. 75th St (151 Central Park West) is another grand apartment building, *The Kenilworth* (1908; Townsend, Steinle & Haskell), remarkable for its elaborate stonework.

Continue to W. 76TH ST and turn left. The block between Central Park West and Columbus Ave has been designated a historic district, primarily because of its impressive row housing, built between 1889 and 1900. The earliest, Nos 31–37, (George M. Walgrove) have neo-Grec trim and a newly-fashionable rockface finish; Nos 8–10 were built by John H. Duncan (better known for Grant's Tomb) in a neo-Baroque style. Elsewhere on the block are neo-Italian Renaissance, Romanesque Revival, and neo-Gothic facades.

Return to Central Park West. Facing the park on the S.W. corner of W. 76th St is the *Universalist Church of New York* (1898; William A. Potter), formerly the Church of the Divine Paternity, and originally the Fourth Universalist Society. Andrew Carnegie worshipped here.

At 170 Central Park West, between W. 76th and W. 77th Sts is the *New-York Historical Society (1908; York & Sawyer; N. and S. wings, 1938; Walker & Gillette; DL), a neo-classical paragon of severity, faced in hard grey granite, and barely ornamented. Founded in 1804, the society retains the old hyphenated spelling of the city's name, and houses an intimate, elegant museum devoted to Americana and to New York City and state history.

Museum open, Tues–Fri, 11–5; Sat 10–5; Sun, 1–5. Suggested voluntary contribution, $1·50 for adults. Tel: 873–3400.

Among the high points of the collection are American paintings, including all but two of Audubon's 435 original illustrations for 'Birds of America', American silver and craftwares, early American toys, period rooms, and furniture. Special exhibitions frequently deal with some aspect of local history.

BASEMENT. The Fahnestock Carriage Collection contains 19C carriages, sleighs, stagecoaches, and fire engines, including the Beekman coach, a rare example of 18C coach making. On the FIRST FLOOR are the galleries of American silver, with a wide selection of 17 and 18C silver, as well as ornate Tiffany and other heavily decorated silver from the mid to late 19C. A gallery is devoted to the sculpture of John Rogers, whose genre scenes of American life made him the 'Norman Rockwell of American sculpture'.

On the SECOND FLOOR is the New York Gallery, with views and paintings of the city and its buildings. In the corridor and *Audubon Gallery are displayed a selection of the original illustrations for 'Birds of America' and memorabilia pertaining to Audubon's life and work. The glassware display includes a collection of paperweights of American, French, and English origin as well as examples of Boston, Sandwich, blown, and pressed American glass. Other galleries contain period rooms from the 17 and 18C centuries, and exhibitions of antique American toys. The *Library* (open to adults for research purposes, fee $1 per day) contains some 600,000 volumes, and is known for its collection of 18C New York newspapers, and its manuscripts including the papers of Horatio Gates, Rufus King, and Albert Gallatin, as well as many George Washington letters.

On the THIRD FLOOR are American crafts including pottery, household utensils, stoneware, flasks and bottles, and weathervanes. The Bella C. Landauer Advertising Collection displayed in the corridors offers early posters advertising such products as fire insurance, hair restorer, and patent medicine. The Print Room houses a large collection of prints and photographs of New York scenes, the Pach collection of photographs of distinguished New Yorkers (1867–1937), thousands of engraved portraits, and a group of political caricatures from the first half of the 19C.

The FOURTH FLOOR is devoted to painting and furniture. In the *Portrait Gallery* is Charles Wilson Peale's portrait of his family, along with many portraits of famous Americans: *John Trumbull,* Alexander Hamilton; *Charles Wilson Peale,* George Washington; *Rembrandt Peale,* Thomas Jefferson; *Gilbert Stuart,* George Washington; *Asher Brown Durand,* Self-Portrait, James Madison, James Monroe, John Quincy Adams, and Andrew Jackson; *John Vanderlyn,* Aaron and Theodosia Burr; *Rembrandt Peale,* a group of four naval portraits including Oliver Hazzard Perry and Stephen Decatur; *Gilbert Stuart,* Philip Jeremiah Schuyler, and Mrs Philip Jeremiah Schuyler; *John Singleton Copley,* Rev. John Ogilvie. Other portraits are by Ezra Ames, Abraham Tuthill, and John Paradise. The Landscape Gallery includes paintings, many of them of New York City or state locales, by Samuel Colmon, Asher B. Durand, Samuel F.B. Morse, and Albert Bierstadt.

The **•• American Museum of Natural History** along with the Hayden Planetarium, enjoyed by 2·8 million people yearly, should delight anyone—young or old—interested in biology, paleontology, anthropology, zoology, or mineralogy. The displays, conceived with imagination and painstaking accuracy, are world-famous, particularly the dioramas of animal habitat groups, the dinosaur exhibits, and the collection of gems and minerals. Besides serving as an exhibition center, the museum is an educational institution with 11 scientific departments, which sponsors research and publishes scientific literature geared both to the professional and the amateur,

Open daily 10–4 45; Wed until 8; Sun and holidays, 10 5. Closed Thanksgiving, Christmas and New Year's Day. Discretionary admission fee, adults $2, children $1; fixed admission fee at the planetarium serves as entrance fee to museum also.

Individual children under 18 not admitted without an adult between 10–2 when New York City Public Schools are in session. Large numbers of children visit the museum in groups (10–2 on school days), so that adult visitors wishing to enjoy the museum at its quietest might consider coming on weekday afternoons.

Cafeteria (no bag lunches) on ground floor. Guided tours of museum highlights are given free several times daily; inquire at the main information desk, second floor rotunda. For other information, call 873–4225. Library open to the public for research, Mon–Fri, 11–4.

History. The American Museum of Natural History was founded (1869) during a period of intense though usually private and undirected interest in the natural sciences, stimulated by the recent discoveries of Darwin, Thomas Huxley, Charles Lyell, and the other great Victorian scientists. Albert Smith Bickmore, a professor of natural history trained by Louis Agassiz, urged a group of philanthropic New Yorkers to get a state charter for a museum and to donate money for the original acquisition, some 3400 specimens, mostly stuffed birds, purchased from the estate of Parisian naturalist Edouard Verreaux. This purchase was soon outclassed by the acquisition of the collection of Prince Maximilian of Neuwied, a German explorer of Brazil, who had gathered some 4000 mounted birds, 600 mounted mammals, and 2000 mounted and pickled fishes and reptiles.

From these beginnings the museum has grown to its present stature: the collections include 34 million artifacts and specimens including 8 million insect specimens, 8·5 million fossil invertebrates, and more birds, spiders, fossil mammals, and whale skeletons than any other institution. The museum employs 150 scientists to work on more than 300 research projects. The library has a research collection of 325,000 volumes, making it the most comprehensive such resource in N. America.

The facilities have grown along with the collections, first housed in the Wall St banking house of Brown Brothers (James Brown was among the original charter incorporators). In 1871 the specimens were moved to the top two floors of the Arsenal in Central Park where the public could view them. On 2 June 1874, President U.S. Grant laid the cornerstone for the present building with a trowel purchased from Tiffany's. Both trowel and cornerstone disappeared, the first during the festivities, the second over the years as builders added a profusion of wings and auxiliary buildings to the original structure. During the centennial year (1969), however, the cornerstone was finally located at the N.E. corner of the Hall of Northwest Coast Indians.

Architecture. The museum occupies the equivalent of four city blocks (W. 77th to W. 81st Sts between Central Park West and Columbus Ave), an area called Manhattan Square and intended by the designers of Central Park as a park annex. The first museum building (1877) is now almost walled in by the wings and additions that have made the present museum an architectural hodge-podge of some 22 buildings.

First wing and general plan, 1872–77; Calvert Vaux and Jacob Wrey Mould. West 77th St wings, 1892–98; J. Cleveland Cady & Co. and 1899; Cady, Berg & See. Columbus Ave wing and powerhouse, 1908; Charles Volz. Additions, 1924, 1926, 1933; Trowbridge & Livingston. Theodore Roosevelt Memorial facing Central Park West, 1936; John Russell Pope. DL.

The oldest visible part of the facade (1892; J. Cleveland Cady & Co.; DL) faces W. 77th St and is architecturally the best. This wing (60 × 110 ft) is Romanesque in style, faced with pink granite from New Brunswick, with two round towers, an arcade of seven arches supported by Romanesque columns, and a central granite stairway sweeping up over what was once the carriage entrance. The facade facing Central Park West (1922; Trowbridge & Livingston) is faced with smooth ashlar blocks of the same granite. The central portion is the Theodore Roosevelt Memorial, its heroic arch framing a fine *equestrian statue of Theodore Roosevelt* (1940; James Earle Fraser), a 16-ft group depicting the 26th President as an explorer flanked by guides symbolising Africa and America.

Enter the barrel-vaulted lobby of the Roosevelt Memorial. Known as the Rotunda, it is finished in Renfrew marble from England containing fossils of colonial animals related to sponges (short end walls) and Portenelle marble, a limestone from Portugal with fossils of oyster-like bivalves (long side walls). The murals depict scenes from Roosevelt's life: the building of the Panama Canal, the signing of the treaty at the end of the Russo-Japanese War, and Roosevelt's explorations in Africa. The Rotunda is on the second floor of the museum.

First Floor. Hall 12, the Theodore Roosevelt Memorial, reflects the interests and background of this ardent naturalist, explorer, and conservationist. One diorama shows how the S. tip of Manhattan

MUSEUM OF NATURAL HISTORY
Basement

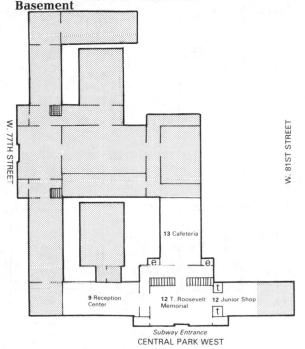

may have looked c. 1660 (Roosevelt's ancestors were early Dutch settlers).

Hall 19, BIOLOGY OF BIRDS. Facing the entrance is a diorama of marsh birds at evening; behind it skeletons of giant flightless birds, living and fossil. On the left wall hundreds of mounted specimens illustrate the major families of birds, including large birds (eagles, vultures, hornbills, penguins) and smaller ones (40 varieties of hummingbirds). At the far end of the room are three imposing colonies of nesting birds. On the right wall are displays on reproduction, migration, adaptation to environment, and distribution.

The *American Museum-Hayden Planetarium (Hall 18), named after investment banker Charles Hayden who donated the original equipment, is actually located in a separate building (1935; Trowbridge & Livingston) on the N.E. of the museum complex, but may be reached from the first floor corridor as well as from the street. Its focal point is the *Sky Theatre* (capacity 660), where a Zeiss Model VI Planetarium projector illuminates the interior of the dome (45 ft to apex, 75 ft in diameter) with celestial phenomena of the past, present, and future. Since its opening in 1935, more than 22 million visitors have visited the planetarium.

Sky Shows, changed about four times yearly, are scheduled twice each afternoon (1.30 and 3.30) on weekdays and more frequently on weekends; Wed

MUSEUM OF NATURAL HISTORY
First Floor

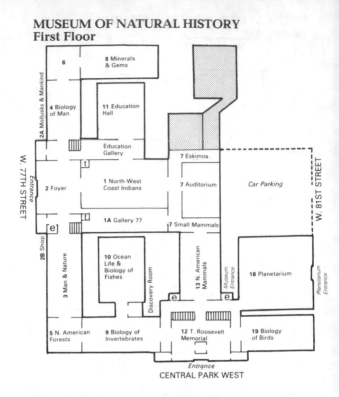

Entrance
CENTRAL PARK WEST

evening shows at 7.30 and Sat morning shows at 11. The planetarium is closed Thanksgiving and Christmas, and several other days during the year for installation of new shows. Call 873–8828 for information. Adults $2·75; students and Senior Citizens with ID cards $1·75; children under 13 $1·75.

On the first floor are the GUGGENHEIM SPACE THEATER, with 22 screens for panoramic slide shows, the Copernican orrery (a moving model of the solar system), the 14-ton Wilammette meteorite, a blacklit gallery with murals of astronomical subjects, and the Richard S. Perkin Library (9000 volumes) open to the public by appointment.

On the second floor, displays in the HALL OF THE SUN explore the relationships between the sun and the earth (energy, climate, time, eclipses) and the place of the sun among other stars. A short film offers dramatic photographs of the sun, taken from both the earth and space, while the 'Astronomia' exhibition presents an eclectic display of astronomical fact and fiction.

The planetarium also offers courses in astronomy, electronic and celestial navigation, meteorology, and science fiction (tel: 872–1300, ext 206).

In Hall 13, *NORTH AMERICAN MAMMALS, fine dioramas present major species in their native habitats, including musk oxen,

Osborn caribou, mountain goats, bison, Alaska brown bear, grizzly bear, and mountain lions. Smaller dioramas along the side walls contain wolves, coyotes, and lynxes, among others. The dioramas here are known for their background paintings, by such artists as Perry Wilson, C.S. Chapman, and B. Browne. The smaller dioramas of Hall 7, SMALL MAMMALS, portray habitat groups of such animals as the wolverine, armadillo, kit fox, and kangaroo rat.

Hall 9, BIOLOGY OF INVERTEBRATES. Overhead is a model of a giant squid (39 ft), the average of several found stranded in Newfoundland in the 1870s. Other giant invertebrates exhibited are a spider crab (spread of 11 ft), a Tridacna Gigas clam, largest bivalve mollusc, and a 34-lb. lobster. In the middle of the room are blown glass models of invertebrates and a display of bioluminescence. Wall cases contain displays elucidating invertebrate behaviour, reproduction, environments, and classification.

Hall 10, OCEAN LIFE AND THE BIOLOGY OF FISHES.

The *Discovery Room* near the entrance (open Sat–Sun, 12–4.30 except holidays) accommodates 25 children with accompanying adults who may experiment with a variety of scientific entertainments (admission by ticket, free at the information desk).

Dominating this hall is a 94-ft model of a blue whale, moulded from polyurethane, supported by steel, and coated with fibreglass. The upper level (clockwise from door) contains displays on the biology of fish (adaptation to environment, feeding, defence, etc.), and plaster and plastic casts of sharks. On the other side are cases devoted to the classification of fish beginning with fossil fish and including jawless and jawed fish, cartilaginous and bony fish. The lower level contains dioramas of fish and marine mammals: sharks, walrus, killer whale and giant squid, seals, polar bear, etc.

In the entrance corridor to Hall 5, NORTH AMERICAN FORESTS, is a display, enlarged 24 times, showing life on the forest floor, with gigantic earthworms, mycorhizae, and other specimens. Dioramas reproduce the primary N. American forest environments: giant cactus forest (Arizona), mixed deciduous forest (Tennessee), piñon-juniper pine forest (Colorado), and others.

The trees are made of wire frames with wood supports and covered with real bark. The leaves are crepe paper dipped in beeswax and individually put on wires which are tapered by immersing them in nitric acid and hanging them up to drip.

Between this hall and Hall 3, MAN AND NATURE, is a cross-section of a Giant Sequoia (harvested 1891), 16 ft 5 inches in diameter, cut from a tree that weighed 6000 tons. Displays in Hall 3 focus on such topics as soil use, the water cycle, glaciation, and the relation of plants to soil, with special reference to the geological history of New York State.

The 77th St foyer, originally intended as the main entrance to the museum, is now dominated by a $64^{1}/_{2}$ ft seagoing war canoe with figures of a Chilkat Indian chief and his followers on a ceremonial visit. Gallery 77 is a hall for changing, long-term exhibitions. To its left is the HALL OF NORTHWEST COAST INDIANS (Hall 1), offering an outstanding collection of artifacts of Indian tribes, living from S.E. Alaska to N. California but forming a single cultural group. Down the center of the room are two rows of imposing carved totem poles. Clockwise from the entrance are: wood sculpture, clothing, tools, and ceremonial objects of the Nootka and Kwakiutl Indians, Chilkat blankets and baskets, Tlingit wooden containers, armour masks, musical instruments, and carvings. At the far end are dioramas of a Tlingit potlatch and a Nootka ceremony with figures in animal masks and costumes. Along the other long wall are Haida tools, masks, and funeral objects, Tsimshian war regalia and ceremonial clothing, Bella Coola masks, hunting, and fishing gear, Lillooet and Thompson baskets, utensils, clothing and weaving, and Coast Salish objects of wood and horn.

Exhibited in Hall 7, ESKIMOS, are tools, weapons for hunting and fishing, masks, religious objects, a dog sled and skin-covered kayak, and domestic untensils. Dioramas and models show eskimo dwellings and illustrate the adaptive features of eskimo clothing.

Hall 2A, MOLLUSKS AND MANKIND, is devoted to the biology of mollusks (shell forms, formation of pearls, life cycles, distribution, and anatomy) and human uses of mollusks (collectors' shells, shells as objects of spiritual power, status or wealth, shells as form and material in art).

Hall 4, BIOLOGY OF MAN, uses plastic models, photographs, and other materials to explore such topics as man's place in the organic world, human evolution, major organ systems, genetics, and adaptation to environment. The display on reproduction and embryology includes five foetal specimens preserved in plastic, while the 'Visible Woman' includes a taped talk on human physiology and anatomy.

In Hall 8, the *HARRY FRANK GUGGENHEIM HALL OF MINERALS and the MORGAN MEMORIAL HALL OF GEMS (opened in 1976), directly beyond the Hall of Meteorites, some 6000 of the museum's 115,000 specimens of minerals are handsomely displayed. A cylindrical case near the entrance contains large specimens (as found) of fluorite, hematite, sulphur, etc., chosen to illustrate the nature of minerals. Along the left wall a display entitled Systematic Mineralogy classifies minerals by composition (native elements, halides, oxides, sulphates, etc.) and by structure (silicates). At the far end of the hall is a case of Esthetic Stones, whose form or colour makes them natural masterpieces. In the center of the room are two circular areas dominated by a $4^1/_2$ ton copper block with malachite and azurite crystals, in one, specimens are arranged according to mineral-forming environments; in the other, according to properties. Near these exhibits also appear (freestanding or in open circular cases): geodes, a giant topaz crystal (597 lbs or 1,330,040 carats), azurite and gold crystals, and agates from Brazil and Uruguay.

Near the entrance to the *J.P. MORGAN HALL OF GEMS stands a 4700-lb. slab of nephrite (from Poland), with one polished surface. In the hall, a cylindrical case opposite the door contains diamonds, star sapphires including the Star of India (563 carats, mined 300 years ago in Sri Lanka), rubies including the DeLong ruby (100 carats), emeralds including the Schettler engraved emerald (#2, right) and the Patricia emerald (#10, 632 carats), and 'fancy' (i.e. not blue) sapphires including (#1) the Padparadschah sapphire (100 carats), one of the finest on display anywhere. Around the walls are a reconstructed 'gem pocket', examples of precious metals, synthetic gemstones, semi-precious stones, examples of gem cutting with replicas of the world's famous diamonds, and a sculpture case containing *objets d'art* of fluorite, jadeite, malachite, etc.

Between the gem hall and the entrance are fine, large specimens of rock crystal, Labradorite, petrified wood, quartz, and beryl.

Older visitors may remember the jewel robbery (1964), in which three Florida beachboys, one picturesquely named Murph the Surf, stole the Star of India sapphire, the DeLong Star ruby and other gems. After reconnoitering the hall for a week, Murph the Surf and a companion climbed a fire escape to a fifth-floor ledge, dropped one story to a window left open two inches for ventilation, entered the former Morgan Memorial Hall, and cut holes in three glass cases. Fortunately for the intruders the burglar alarm, activated by lifting the Star of India, was out of order and they were able to escape undetected by the nightwatchman. Eventually, however, the thieves were apprehended and 85–90% of the jewels, in terms of cash value, were recovered. Naturally the security of the room has been strengthened and it is now considered impregnable.

Second Floor. Dioramas in Hall 19, the WHITNEY HALL OF OCEANIC BIRDS, display birds of the Pacific in a latitudinal sequence from Antarctica northward, including groups from New Zealand, Fiji, Australia, New Guinea, Hawaii, the Galapagos, the Peruvian guano islands, the Philippines, and islands in the Bering Strait. Harry Payne Whitney financed a series of expeditions (1920–40) during which museum representatives visited 1000 islands; after his death his widow, Gertrude Vanderbilt Whitney, and children gave this hall as well as the Rothschild Collection of 280,000 bird specimens. Francis Lee Jacques painted the ceiling and backgrounds.

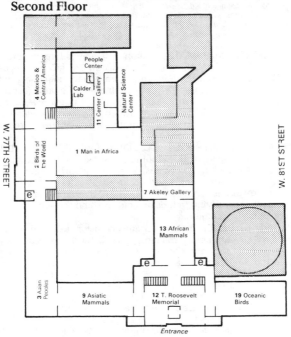

MUSEUM OF NATURAL HISTORY
Second Floor

Hall 13, the *AKELEY MEMORIAL HALL OF AFRICAN MAM-MALS is known for its beautiful and dramatic dioramas including habitat groups of such animals as gorilla, okapi, gemsbok, kudu, rhinoceros, lion, buffalo, giraffe, and zebra. As with all dioramas in the museum, settings are accurately recreated from photographs and sketches made on the site and vegetation is carefully simulated: a blackberry bush in the gorilla diorama has 75,000 artificial leaves and flowers, which took eight months to make and cost $2000 (in the 1930s). Special efforts have been made to present the animals in characteristic actions: hyenas and vultures devouring a dead zebra, giraffes browsing, wild dogs hunting in a pack. (The second floor of the gallery is reached from the third floor corridor.)

Carl Akeley (1864–1926), already famous for his innovations in taxidermy, began working for the museum in 1909, eventually becoming known also as a great field collector and explorer, an author and sculptor, and the inventor of a panoramic motion-picture camera and a cement gun. On an expedition to Africa in 1911 Akeley was nearly killed by an elephant which tried to gore him and, thwarted in that by the explorer's swinging up between its tusks, then attempted to crush him. Although the museum approved plans for the hall in 1912, it wasn't completed until 1936, ten years after Akeley's death on expedition in the Belgian Congo (now Zaire) where he was buried, near Mount Mikeno, the volcano seen furthest to the right in the gorilla diorama. When a Peace Corps worker recently found his grave ravaged the museum responded with funds to restore it.

Earlier taxidermists usually just skinned their specimens and stuffed them with some soft material, but Akeley pioneered a technique of mounting which began with observing the living animal in its habitat and photographing it in motion. Akeley then copied the skeleton of the specimen and filled out the muscles and tissues with clay; from this he made a plaster cast and from that a papier mâché mould onto which the skin—cleaned, softened, and deloused—was glued.

Hall 9, ASIATIC MAMMALS, contains specimens largely gathered by two English collectors, Arthur Vernay and Col J.C. Fanthorpe in the 1920s. Considered the best collection of such mammals in the world, the display includes a group of Indian elephants (center of room), and dioramas showing habitat groups of tigers, swamp deer, gibbons, wild boar, Sumatran and Indian rhinoceroses, water buffalo, Indian lions, and a dramatic diorama of a sambar attacked by a pack of wild dogs.

The *GARDNER D. STOUT HALL OF ASIAN PEOPLES (Hall 3), a fine new anthropological exhibition (opened 1980), documents traditional Asia, using costumes, artifacts, paintings and photographs, maps, models and charts. The display focuses on several anthropological themes: the relationship of the individual to family and society, the unifying beliefs of a culture, and the adaptation of a society to its environment.

The first part of the hall is organised historically and includes prehistoric development, archaeology, and the rise of civilisation. Clockwise from entrance: Cases 1–2, Early Man, contain a display of Peking and Neanderthal man, including skull casts, paleolithic tools, and the replica of a child's grave. Models in cases opposite show Koryak and Chukchee peoples of Siberia, living in the 19C very much as their Eurasian ancestors did during the last Ice Age. Cases 3–9, Man's Rise to Civilisation, illustrate the transition from hunting and gathering cultures to the beginnings of agriculture. The Rise of Civilisation in the Near East, documents the development of writing and codified law using a replica of the Code of Hammurabi.

Paintings, ceremonial objects, and stone reliefs in the displays on Early Religions show the rise of Judaism and Zoroastrianism, while a display of ship models and scale models of major trading centers document Asian Trade.

The rest of the hall is organised geographically. *Korea*: A diorama of a bride and older man in costumes illustrating their social status also includes examples of Korean celadon and moveable type, invented c. 200 years before the Gutenberg Bible. Beyond the entrance to the Japan section are cases devoted to four small-scale Asian cultures, chosen to illustrate cultural adaptation to environment: the Ainu, an island people of Japan; the Semai people of the Malaysian rain forests, the Kafir of the mountainous Hindu Kush, and the Tungus of arctic Siberia.

Japan: Atop the central case is an 18C wooden Buddha covered with gold leaf. An introductory case explores the concept of 'style' in Japanese life; other exhibits include objects from prehistoric Japan, models of a traditional Japanese home, a Mandala (1491 A.D.), objects of Shinto worship, a diorama of rural Japan, No theatre masks, carved ivory netsukes, wood blocks for printing, and a late 19C Buddhist shrine. A central display shows modern survivals of tradition and a 19C straw raincoat, the first costume acquired by the museum.

Proceed clockwise to the *China* display. On the left are cases devoted to ancestor worship and the gods of traditional China. A diorama shows a beautiful bridal chair of glass, copper, wire, gilt, and kingfisher feathers. Also shown are a collection of Taoist symbols, costumes and artifacts from the Chinese frontier, a display of traditional Chinese science and medicine, a large inkwash drawing of a tiger from the Ch'ing dynasty (18C), a rare carved white jade (also 18C), theatre masks and costumes, and musical instruments.

Southeast Asia is represented by clothing and artifacts of the Yao and Meo, two tribal societies, displays on Buddhism, and a Ravana costume from Thailand illustrating the Indian influence on theatrical and dance forms.

The galleries devoted to *India* focus on village life and include a fine diorama of an Indian village wedding, examples of crafts, theatre masks and costumes, a display on Hinduism, polychromed wooden horses and musicians from a W. Indian temple (19C) and wooden dancing figures (S. India, 17C).

The *Islamic World* exhibition is dominated by a painting of the Grand Mosque of Mecca. Along one wall are women's costumes from Kashmir, Afghanistan, Baluchistan, Yemen, Palestine, and Turkey illustrating the geographical spread of Islam. On the other wall are rugs, crafts, pots, musical instruments and paintings from various parts of the Islamic world.

Smaller sections are devoted to cultures of *Armenia, the Arabian peninsula, Caucasian Georgia,* and *Samarkand.* Included in a more extensive section on *Siberia* are carvings in wood, bone, and ivory, a diorama on Siberian shamanism, and artifacts of tribes who hunt, fish, and herd reindeer.

The cases in the long corridor between the Siberian and Tibetan exhibitions offer rugs, furniture, jewellery, crafts, and clothing of the *tribes of Central Asia*, including the tunic and purple coat of a Turkoman horseman and the gold-embroidered robes formerly belonging to a family member of the last Emir of Bukhara.

The religious aspect of the culture of *Tibet* appears in the collection of tangkas (religious paintings of deities and saints) and in Tantric ritual implements and religious sculptures. Harnesses, animal bells, and similar objects demonstrate the importance of nomadic herding and trading, while a group of masks and hats and a pair of long curved trumpets (overhead) represent Tibetan monastery life.

Hall 2, BIRDS OF THE WORLD, contains a small fraction of the museum's one million bird specimens representing 98% of the known bird species. The birds here are displayed in large dioramas organised by environment: Canadian tundra, New Forest in the S. of England, Alps, Gobi desert, Japan, East African plains, and S. Atlantic region near Antarctica.

Hall 1, MAN IN AFRICA, begins with two introductory rooms devoted to the origins of man and society in Africa and to river valley civilisations (the Nile, Niger, Zambesi, and Congo). The main part of the exhibition is organised environmentally, treating Grasslands, Forest-Woodland, and Desert cultures. In the *Grasslands* display (mostly E. and central Africa), exhibits focus on farming and herding, the principal means of livelihood. Included are tools, weapons, musical instruments, and other implements as well as a diorama of Pokot herders. Exhibits on government include objects indicating status; a display on women includes both beautiful crafts—Lozi baskets and beaded jewellery, Ndebele body ornaments, a beaded Zulu apron—and explorations of the role of women in African society. The *Forest-Woodland* section documents the cultures of the tropical rain forest in the Central Congo and the Guinea Coast. Exhibits focus on forest fishing (beautiful wooden and woven fish traps and other implements) and on forest farming. The central diorama shows Mbuti pygmies hunting. Other exhibits in this section include a group of fetishes and articles for divination and healing and fine ceremonial costumes and musical instruments.

The *Desert*, last of the major environments treated in this hall, includes models of irrigation, and displays pertaining to desert agriculture and hunting with articles and implements of skin, wood, and ostrich egg-shell. The diorama, accurate even to the position of the moon and stars in the sky, shows nomadic Berbers in the Atlas mountains. The final portion of the hall shows the power and influence of Islam in Africa.

In the corridor beyond the Hall of Birds of the World is an alcove devoted to *Gold of the Americas*, containing a dazzling array of gold objects from the pre-Columbian cultures of Peru, Ecuador, Colombia, Panama, Costa Rica, and Mexico.

Hall 4, MEXICO AND CENTRAL AMERICA, uses archaeological finds (primarily pottery and stone carvings) as well as full-sized replicas of large monuments still in Central America and architectural scale models to document the pre-Columbian cultures of Meso-America. At the right of the entrance a map and chronological chart gives an overview of these cultures. Exhibits begin (clockwise from entrance) with pottery, stone and clay figurines from a burial site in Sinaloa (1350 A.D.) in Western Mexico. Freestanding cases opposite hold human and animal clay figures from the Colima tombs (200 B.C.–600 A.D.) and Nayarit and Jalisco culpture of the same period. Ornate funerary urns, pottery, and a replica of a tomb in Monte Alban (c. 550 A.D.) represent the cultures of the Oaxaca area.

The rear of the room is devoted to Maya and Aztec cultures. Among the more spectacular objects are a cast of a large animal form and two 35-ft stelae, also casts, from the Maya site of Quirigua in eastern Guatemala, models of temples from the ruins at Palenque, Campeche, and Tikal, and casts of stelae and actual architectural elements from Uxmal brought back by John Lloyd Stephens, a principal discoverer of the ancient Maya ruins. Dominating the Aztec section is a full-sized replica of an Aztec stone of the sun, sometimes mistakenly thought to be a calendar.

Other objects on the same side of the hall are Toltec pottery, clay and stone sculpture from the Vera Cruz area, a tall terracotta figure (Toltec) of a man wearing the skin of a sacrificial victim, objects from the culture of Teotihuacan, a large Olmec head (reproduction) found in the Gulf Coast region, and objects from the pre-classic period (1500 B.C.–1 A.D.).

Third Floor. Exhibits in Hall 9, REPTILES AND AMPHIBIANS (opened 1977), include mounted skins, wax-impregnated specimens, and models and plastic casts of specimens from the collection of the Department of Herpetology. Directly in front of the entrance is a giant Galapagos tortoise, which died some decades ago in the Bronx Zoo. The cases devoted to reptiles (left side of room) include displays on growth, longevity, birth, parental care, defence, feeding, and locomotion. Among the specimens are a reticulated python (25 ft), a

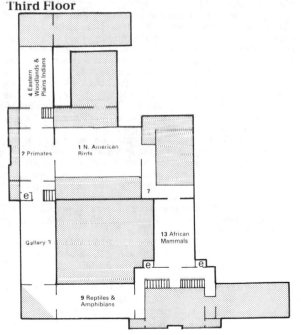

MUSEUM OF NATURAL HISTORY
Third Floor

4 Eastern Woodlands & Plains Indians

2 Primates

1 N. American Birds

e]

7

13 African Mammals

Gallery 3

e]   e]

9 Reptiles & Amphibians

rock python, a king cobra, egg-laying leatherback turtles, Komodo dragons (lizards), an alligator, and a crocodile.

Most of the displays on the other side of the aisle focus on amphibians and treat many of the same topics as the reptile exhibits. Included among the specimens are a Surinam toad, Panamanian egg brooding frog, Surinam poison frog, salamanders and wood frogs, pickerel frog, Goliath frog (up to 7·3 lbs), and Japanese giant salamander (up to 5 ft 2 inches).

Gallery 3 is used for special exhibitions.

Hall 2, the HALL OF PRIMATES, makes use of taxidermic specimens, skeletons, and diagrams to explore the distinctive characteristics and relationships of different groups of primates. Beginning with the lowly tree shrew (near the hall of Eastern Woodlands Indians), and proceeding through lemurs, lorises, languars, macaques, mangabeys, and baboons, the display leads up to the final case on man and the higher primates. In freestanding cases in the center of the hall are larger primates, including the lowland gorilla, orangutan, and chimpanzee.

Hall 4 documents the EASTERN WOODLANDS AND PLAINS INDIANS of the United States and Canada, from prehistoric times to the early 20C. An introductory foyer contains material on paleo-Indians. The Eastern Woodlands Hall is organised according to themes: clothing, houses, cooking, fishing, etc. On the left is an extensive display of beautiful *costumes from tribes of Canada, New England, and as far S. as Florida. Other exhibits include a birchbark canoe, examples of wampum and metal jewellery, pipes, ceremonial masks, and models of housing.

Behind this hall is the room devoted to the Plains Indians, nomadic or semi-nomadic tribes living W. of the Mississippi. Facing the entrance is a diorama depicting the interior of a Blackfoot teepee. Other exhibits include ceremonial smoking pipes, costumes and clothing, horse gear, tents and houses, and a diorama showing a bison hunt before the arrival of the horse.

The FRANK M. CHAPMAN MEMORIAL HALL OF NORTH AMERICAN BIRDS (Hall 1), completed in the late 1960s, is the successor of an earlier hall (1909), the first ever completely devoted to habitat groups. Clockwise from the entrance are groups of game birds, Canada geese, wood stork and limpkins (background painted by Ray DeLucia), western marsh birds, golden eagle, whooping crane, warblers, wading birds of the Everglades, boobies and frigate birds. The flamingo mural at the far end is by Louis Agassiz Fuertes. On the other walls are displays of hawks, California condor, great horned owl, American egret, bald eagle, wild turkey, and peregrine falcon.

A small corridor with birds and mammals of New York State leads to the upper level of the Akeley Hall of African Mammals (for a description, see Second Floor, Hall 13).

Fourth Floor. Hall 13, the *HALL OF EARLY DINOSAURS. The museum has the world's finest collection of fossil bones, about 5% of which are currently on display. On the central island stand three magnificent fossilized skeletons from the Jurassic period (180–120 million years ago): a Brontosaurus (66 ft long, probable live weight 35–40 tons), a Stegosaurus, and an Allosaurus. Museum paleontologist Barnum Brown found them in Wyoming in an area dubbed 'Bone Cabin Quarry' after a sheep herder's hut built with a foundation of dinosaur bones led him to the discovery of the excavation site. Elsewhere in the room are early reptiles of the Triassic period (225–180 million years ago), mammal-like reptiles of S. Africa, and Pelycosaur reptiles.

At the rear of the room is the gallery of *Fossil Fish*, its entrance framed by a 9¹/₂ ft jaw of a prehistoric shark (a cast, since cartilage does not fossilise well), with fossil teeth.

MUSEUM OF NATURAL HISTORY
Fourth Floor

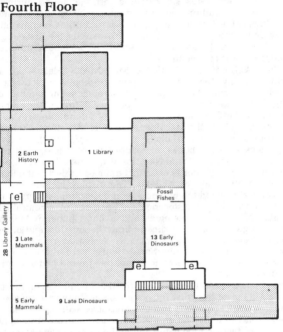

The corridor between this hall and the display of Late Dinosaurs contains marine reptiles—Ichthyosaurs, Plesiosaurs, and Mososaurs—and a fossil egg (Hypselosaurus) found in France.

Hall 9, *LATE DINOSAURS, contains fossil skeletons from the Cretaceous period (120–65 million years ago), the zenith of reptilian evolution. In a free-standing case left of the central aisle is a dinosaur 'mummy', a trachodont found in Wyoming with fossilized flesh between the ribs, webbing on the front feet, and a skin pattern of horny tubercles. The central island contains Trachodonts (web-footed, duck-billed dinosaurs), a Triceratops, and a spectacular **Tyrannosaurus rex* found (1902) in Montana. It is 50 ft long, 20 ft high, and weighed around 8–10 tons live. Its jaw could open a yard wide revealing teeth six inches long. The actual skull (750–1000 lbs) is in a case near the assembled skeleton. On the W. (right) wall are three *nests of dinosaur eggs*, found during a museum expedition to the Gobi Desert in 1923, a spectacular discovery since they were the first ever found in association with the dinosaur laying them.

The HALL OF EARLY FOSSIL MAMMALS (Hall 5) is organised to illustrate principles of vertebrate paleontology and early phases of mammalian differentiation. Included are a giant Australian marsupial and several Condylarths (early hoofed mammals), a Uintatherium (a rhinoceros-like mammal with five horns) and a fossil Edentate (ancestor of sloths, armadillos and anteaters). A large case contains a dramatically lit display of ground sloths and glyptodonts from S. America. Paleocene carnivores are represented by Creodonts. Among the insectivores are Zalambdalestidae, found during the Gobi Desert expeditions, an important discovery since mammal skulls during the Cretaceous period when reptiles dominated are usually fragmentary. Primates include Notharctus, the first complete primate skeleton found, and a Lemur, a prosimian antedating monkeys and apes in evolution.

In the HALL OF LATER FOSSIL MAMMALS (Hall 3), an older exhibition, many beautiful specimens are displayed showing the diversity of the collection. Albert Bickmore, museum founder, gave the Paleolithic skeleton of the 'Irish deer' just in front of the entrance. Along the S. (left) wall are fossil remains of Titanotheres (rhino-like animals) and behind the Irish deer stands the assembled skeleton of a Titanotherium. The bone block behind it ($5^{1}/_{2} \times$ 8ft), the largest single block of fossil bones on exhibition anywhere, is from the famous Agate Springs (Nebraska) fossil quarries. Beyond it is the *Asphalt Group*, with bones of extinct animals buried in the Rancho La Brea tar pits near Los Angeles. The display includes a sabre-toothed tiger mired in the pit and a wolf observing its trapped prey. On the right wall is a Pleistocene cave bear, and on a central island a display of mastodon skeletons and a huge Imperial Mammoth skeleton, organised chronologically from the smallest and oldest to the largest and most recent specimens. A display on the left wall shows the evolution of the horse, while across the room are prehistoric bison and a Miocene camel bedground (Agate Springs) with nine skeletons.

The HALL OF EARTH HISTORY (Hall 2) includes exhibits on the materials of the earth's crust and on the forces shaping it. Displays on various geological periods include dioramas with specimens and models arranged in habitat groups to illustrate marine environments from the Cambrian period to the end of the Cenozoic era and nearby cases offering related fossils. On one end wall is a demonstration of the geology of oil fields, while other exhibits include a display on the geology of New York City, a relief globe of the world, and cases of fossil invertebrates (coelenterates, arthropods, echinoderms, molluscs, sponges, etc.).

SUBWAY: IRT Broadway–7th Ave local (train 1) at 79th St and Broadway. IND Sixth Ave (B train) at 81st St or IND Eighth Ave local (AA or CC) at 81st St.

BUS: M7 or M11 downtown via Columbus Ave or uptown via Amsterdam Ave. M10 downtown via Central Park West and Seventh Ave. M17 crosstown via 79th St.

Other points of architectural interest on Central Park West. At 211 Central Park West (N.W. corner of 81st St) is the *Beresford* (1929; Emery Roth), a massive pile from which rise three towers topped with vaguely Baroque crowns, another skyline landmark along the park. The *Eldorado* (1931; Margon & Holder) between 91st and 92nd Sts at 300 Central Park West is the northernmost of the twin-towered apartment houses along the park. The *Ardsley* (1931; Emery Roth) at

No. 320 between on the S.W. corner of 92nd St is admired by
enthusiasts of Art Deco architecture for its elaborate brickwork and
the terrazzo reliefs at street level. The *First Church of Christ,
Scientist* (1903; Carrère & Hastings; DL) is a fine, Baroque-style
church often said to recall the London churches of Nicholas Hawks-
moor.

SUBWAY: IRT Broadway–7th Ave local (train 1) at 79th St and Broadway. IND
Sixth Ave (B train) at 81st St or IND Eighth Ave local (AA or CC) at 81st St.

BUS: M7 downtown via Columbus Ave or uptown via Amsterdam Ave. M10
downtown via Central Park West and Seventh Ave. M11 uptown via Amsterdam or downtown via Columbus Ave Culture Bus, Loop I (weekends and
holidays), Stop 8 (continues uptown).

29 Morningside Heights

SUBWAY: IRT Broadway–7th Ave local (train 1) to 110th St
(Cathedral Parkway).

BUS: M4, M5, M11, M104 to 110th St (Cathedral Parkway). Culture
Bus Loop I (weekends and holidays) to Stop 11.

Bounded by Cathedral Parkway (110th St) on the S. and the deep
valley of 125th St on the N., **Morningside Heights** sits on the rocky
ridge that runs the length of Manhattan. Harlem lies on low ground
to the E., and on the W. the terrain slopes down to the Hudson. The
area remained isolated, lacking adequate public transportation, until
the 9th Ave El opened in 1880; in its pastoral serenity dwelt the
owners of small farms and houses and the squires of country estates
as well as the orphans of the Leake & Watts Asylum and the inmates
of the Bloomingdale Insane Asylum. Riverside Drive opened in 1880,
touted as a new Fifth Ave, a prophecy that never quite materialised,
and Morningside Park, elegantly landscaped in the 19C but now too
dangerous to visit, was planned in 1887. By the end of the century it
seemed that the Heights would become a cultural, intellectual, and
spiritual center of the city, as Columbia University, the Cathedral of
St. John the Divine, and St. Luke's Hospital all moved there.

That promise has been only partially fulfilled and at considerable
social expense. It is true that major institutions—not only Columbia
but also Barnard College, Teachers College, St. John the Divine, St.
Luke's, the Riverside Church, Union Theological Seminary and the
Jewish Theological Seminary—dominate the social and economic
tone of the area. They boast beautiful and impressive buildings and
own an estimated 70% of the property. But shabby neighbourhoods
and abjectly poor slums impinge on the Heights from three sides.
The disparity between the wealth and power of the institutions and
the poverty of the surrounding communities has engendered hostility, especially during the 1960s when the institutions, seeking to
secure their frontiers and to expand, tried to encroach on nearby
park areas and residential space. Although the tensions have eased,
they are still evident in the locked churches and the visible security
measures taken in many public buildings.

The ****Cathedral Church of St. John the Divine,** cathedral of the
Episcopal Diocese of New York, rises in uncompleted splendour on
Amsterdam Ave at 112th St. The enormous stone arches erected to
support the unbuilt dome and tower of the crossing stand exposed to

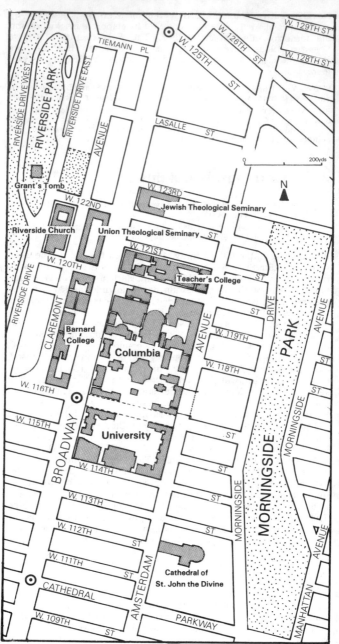

the eyes of the passerby who may never again see the inner structure of a masonry cathedral in construction. Begun in 1892, the church is about $^2/_3$ finished, and construction of the towers has started. Even in its unfinished state it is the largest Gothic church in the world.

ADMISSION AND SERVICES. The cathedral is open daily from 7–5, and visitors may wander at will except during services. Tours are offered at 11 and 2, except on Sunday when there is a single tour at 12.30. Sunday services are at 8, 9.30, (Spanish), 11, and 4. Weekday services are at 7.15 and 3.30, with an additional Wednesday service at 12.15. The gift shop inside the main doors offers excellent guidebooks on the history and iconography of the cathedral. There are restrooms near the entrance to and in the Museum of Religious Art on the site of the S. transept.

History. Although the idea of an American Episcopal cathedral in New York had been suggested as early as 1828, only after Bishop Horatio Potter proposed it to the diocesan convention in 1872 did it become a viable notion. Although the convention voted unanimously for the project, the financial panic of 1873 made fund raising impossible. Eventually (1887) a wooded plot of some 13 acres belonging to the Leake & Watts Orphan Asylum was purchased for the large sum of $885,000. The next year 60 entrants submitted designs in an architectural contest, from which the firm of Heins & La Farge emerged victorious. Like many of the other entries, the Heins & La Farge design, a Romanesque plan incorporating Byzantine elements, placed the long axis of the building along the spine of Morningside Heights, which would have given the church a spectacular flight of entrance stairs down to 110th St. The tradition of building cathedrals with the nave running E.–W. was so strong, however, that it eventually prevailed. In 1892 under Potter's nephew, Bishop Henry Codman Potter, the cornerstone was laid.

Excavations for such a heavy building proved difficult, and J.P. Morgan poured half a million dollars into an ever deeper hole before workers struck bedrock some 70 ft below the surface. In 1911, almost 20 years after the digging had begun, only the choir and the four stone arches to support the dome were in place. Five years later, in the wake of personal disputes and changing canons of taste, the Heins & La Farge Romanesque plan was discarded, and Ralph Adams Cram (of the firm of Cram & Ferguson) was hired to redesign the church on Gothic principles, solving somehow the problems created by the original plan, notably the width of the nave and the size of the crossing.

Cram added about 80 ft to the length of the nave, divided it into five aisles instead of the usual three, and proposed the use of alternate thick and slender piers to help in vaulting over its great width (146 ft; Westminster Abbey, 70 ft). He also made several proposals for covering the crossing, whose size presented aesthetic problems as well as difficulties in engineering. His ultimate solution involved reducing the 100-ft square to a 60-ft square by using intersecting arches and covering this smaller opening with a stepped-back 400-ft tower.

Ground was broken for the nave foundations in 1916; the nave itself was begun in 1925 and completed about 10 years later, but excavations for the N. transept encountered difficulties and the money raised for its construction ran out when the walls had reached a height of about 40 ft. In 1939 the Romanesque choir was bricked up and remodelled to conform to Cram's Gothic interiors. Seven new clerestory windows were installed but since the original Heins & La Farge roof still overhangs them, they are artificially lighted.

During World War II major construction was halted. In the 1960s a plan for completing the crossing in a contemporary style with an unattached 800-ft campanile (Washington Monument, 555 ft; Eiffel Tower, 984 ft) was submitted but not approved. Then in 1967 during an era of intense national social awareness, the bishop announced that the cathedral might never be completed but would devote its energies to the poverty in the community surrounding it. After more than a decade of social involvement, the trustees in 1978 announced a fund-raising campaign for completion of the crossing and the W. facade, including the two towers. Today some two dozen apprentice stonecutters, many from nearby neighbourhoods, are at work under the tutelage of English master mason James Bambridge in a shed adjacent to the cathedral cutting the 21,000 pieces of Indiana limestone needed for the S.W. tower, whose first stone was mortared into place in Sept. 1982.

MEASUREMENTS. Area of cathedral: 121.000 sq. ft. Length of nave, 248 ft, of

The Cathedral of St. John the Divine under construction. The columns, quarried in Maine, were shipped in barges and drawn by steam winches through the city streets, crushing every manhole cover in their path. (Byron Collection, Museum of the City of New York)

choir, 145 ft, total length, 601 ft. Width of W. front, 207 ft, of nave and aisles, 146 ft, of crossing, 100 ft. Height of nave roof, 177 ft, of nave vault, 124 ft. The W. towers, when completed, will be 291 ft tall.

EXTERIOR. The general appearance of the W. Front suggests medieval French influence, though no single direct antecedent exists. The doors of four of the five portals are Burmese teak, while those of the central portal are bronze. The bronze lights on the front steps, salvaged when Penn Station was demolished (1963–66), were installed in 1967. The *N. Tower Portal* is the only one whose statuary (sculptor John Angel) is complete.

Figures in the buttress niches (beginning with the rear buttress facing E.) are the apostles St. Peter, St. Andrew, St. James, St. John, and St. Philip. The figures flanking the doorway (left to right) are the martyrs St. Thomas Becket, St. Catherine of Alexandria, St. Stephen, St. Alban, St. Lawrence, St. Vincent of Saragossa, St. Joan of Arc, and St. Denis. On the central post is St. Peter. The pierced window in the arch above the door contains a Crucifixion; on the gable is a statue of the archangel Michael.

Central portal. The great bronze doors (sculptor Henry Wilson) were cast in Paris by M. Barbedienne. Their 60 panels depict scenes from the Old Testament (N. doors) and the New Testament (S. doors). The frieze above the doors shows the peoples of all nations standing before the Lamb. The figure on the central post, his eyes raised heavenward, is St. John the Divine. Directly above him in the tympanum is a Majestas, showing Christ in Glory surrounded by the seven lamps and the seven stars of St. John's revelation. The spandrels contain symbols of the four Evangelists. The central coat of arms in the gable belongs to the See of New York.

S. Portal. Only the figure of St. Paul on the central post and the portrayal of the Holy Family in the pierced window have been completed. Both are by John Angel.

INTERIOR. The W. doors open into the *Narthex.* Above the portals are carvings, again by John Angel, representing the Crusaders (N. doorway, partially obscured by the gift shop) and the Canterbury pilgrims (S. doorway). The stained glass window on the N. represents the Creation, while that on the S., called the Prototype window, presents scenes from the Old Testament which prefigure events in the gospels or attributes of Christ. Both windows are by Ernest W. Lakeman.

Just inside the Narthex are occasionally displayed some of the icons formerly mounted on the walls of St. Saviour's Chapel, one of the apsidal chapels. They are of Greek, Russian, and Byzantine origin, and date from the 15–18C.

The piers of the nave are alternately massive (16 ft) and slender (6 ft), an arrangement reflected both in the cathedral's exterior buttressing and in the design of the nave vaulting. The thick piers have an inner core of granite and are faced with limestone. The slender piers, made of solid granite, are constructed of 53 courses of single blocks each weighing about 4 tons, a method of construction necessitated by the city building engineer who would grant a permit only if each course was monolithic. The outer aisle on each side of the nave is divided by an arcade into seven bays, illuminated by stained glass windows—chapel windows 25·5 ft high and clerestory windows 44 ft high. The general theme of the windows is that of the religious spirit in human activity, and the iconography of the windows and other furnishings within each bay contributes to its individual theme. A general theme of the cathedral's iconography is that of internationalism, of the cathedral as a house of prayer for all nations. This theme is reflected especially in the windows, in the decoration of the apsidal chapels, and in the Pilgrim's Pavement.

In the pavement of the **Nave** (area 32,400 sq ft) are medallions commemorating important people and locations in Christian history. The medallions of the central aisle represent places identified with Christ's earthly life while those in the side aisles recall places and people venerated by pilgrims through the ages.

The *bays in the N. aisle* (from W. to E.) are the Sports' Bay, Arts' Bay, Crusaders' Bay, Education Bay, Lawyers' Bay (with a fine carved walnut reredos representing the themes of lawgiving and justice), Ecclesiastical Origins' Bay (tracing the growth of the Church of England and its translation to the New World), Historical and Patriotic Societies' Bay (which contains the tomb of Bishop William Thomas Manning, 1866–1949, with a recumbent marble figure of the bishop executed by Constantin Antonovici), and Fatherhood Window (this bay has only a clerestory window). Also displayed in the bays in the N. and S. aisles, are contemporary works of religious art and the Mortlake Tapestries, woven in England from a series of cartoons by Raphael and entitled The Acts of the Apostles.

CATHEDRAL OF ST. JOHN THE DIVINE

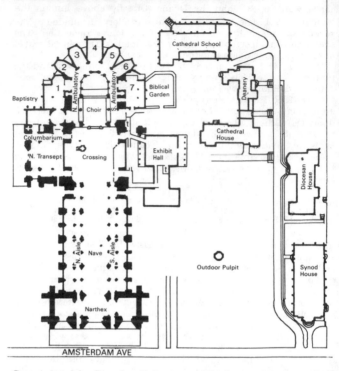

Commissioned by Pope Leo X in about 1513, the cartoons, from which numerous sets of tapestries were woven, were dispersed throughout Europe and eventually lost. Sir Francis Crane, manager of the Mortlake tapestry works, rediscovered them in Genoa in 1623 and had them sent to England to be woven for Prince Charles (later Charles I). Since some of the original borders depicted scenes from the life of Leo X, the Mortlake weavers added new borders with floral patterns, cherubs, and the arms of the Earldom of Winchelsea and Nottingham.

In the partially finished N. TRANSEPT is a small *museum of the construction of the cathedral*, containing interesting photographs and a large model of the cathedral as well as a rendering (1977) of plans for the next phase of construction. The museum is open during warm months since the transept is unheated.

In the **Crossing** the visitor can see the 'bones' of the cathedral, the great granite piers, the uncompleted arches, and the remarkable temporary dome of red-brown Guastavino tile hastily installed in the summer of 1909 as a cheap alternative to covering the crossing with a conventional flat wooden roof supported by steel beams. The pulpit (1916), carved of Tennessee marble, was designed by Henry Vaughan, a Boston architect influential in reawakening the Gothic taste of the period. Displayed in the Crossing are the cathedral's other important set of tapestries, the *Barberini Tapestries*, woven in the first half of the 17C on the papal looms founded by Cardinal

Barberini. They depict scenes from the life of Christ and a map of the Holy Land; the cartoons by Jean-François Romanelli are now in the Vatican.

The **Choir** shows both the work of Heins & La Farge and Ralph Adams Cram. The lower part up to the balustrade below the clerestory windows remains from the original Romanesque plan (completed 1911); the work above (altered 1939–41) is Cram's Gothic remodelling. Dominating the choir are eight granite columns from Vinalhaven, Maine, originally quarried as monoliths but cut in two after the first two columns cracked while being turned and polished on a special lathe (lower sections, 38 ft high, 90 tons; upper sections, 17 ft high, 40 tons). Because the land slopes sharply downhill at this end of the church, the foundations for the columns go down 135 ft. Although the choir is relatively short (145 ft), a kind of false perspective makes it seem longer: the arcades at the E. end are closer together and the floor slopes upward in that direction. The choir stalls were designed by Heins & La Farge after those in the Cathedral of San Domenico in Taormina, Sicily.

Among the interesting objects in the choir are the two menorahs (seven-branched candlesticks) near the altar. Designed after those in the Temple of Jerusalem as pictured on the Arch of Titus, they are the gift (1930) of former New York 'Times' publisher Adolph Ochs. The Magna Charta pedestal (S. side of main altar) was once part of the Altar of the Abbey of Bury St. Edmunds on which (20 November 1214), according to the inscription, 'the barons swore fealty to each other in wresting the Great Charter from King John'.

The original *organ* (Ernest M. Skinner, 1910) was remodelled and rebuilt in 1954 to achieve a better balance between the bass and treble. At that time a new stop, the State Trumpet, was added, whose 61 silver pipes are placed directly under the Rose Window in the W. Front. The *Rose Window* itself, best seen from the E. end of the nave, was designed by Charles Connick, is 40 ft in diameter, and contains more than 10,000 pieces of glass. From the central figure of Christ radiate symbols representing the gifts of the Holy Spirit, the Beatitudes, and the heavenly choir. The lesser Rose Window below it, also by Connick, develops the symbolism of the number seven: from a central monogram of Christ radiate seven fountains, seven growing vine forms, seven pairs of doves, and seven stars.

Enter the N. AMBULATORY from the archway in the Crossing. The first structure in the ambulatory is the *Baptistry* (1928; Frank Cleveland of Cram & Ferguson) donated by members of the Stuyvesant family whose Dutch origins are symbolised in the decoration of the room.

Over the entrance arch are the arms of the Netherlands with statues of St. Nicholas (right) and St. Catherine (left). On the E. wall of the entrance is a statue of Judith Bayard, wife of Peter Stuyvesant, last Dutch governor of New York; on the W. wall opposite is a figure of Louise de Coligny, wife of William of Orange. Inside the octagonal room a frieze of polychromed sculpture (John Angel) depicts the history of illustrious men associated with the Netherlands under whose flag New York was first settled. The coat of arms of the Stuyvesant family is in the spandrel of the ground level arcade in the N.E. wall. The baptismal font, also octagonal in form and about 15 ft high, is built of Champville marble and modelled on the font in the baptistry of the cathedral of Siena, Italy. The sculptured panels at its base depicting scenes from the life of John the Baptist are the work of Albert H. Atkins.

A doorway in the W. side of the Baptistry leads into the *Columbarium*, a repository for the ashes of the deceased.

Standing above a marble credenza in the N. ambulatory is a diptych of the *Annunciation, attributed to *Simone Martini* (1283?–1344). An opening on the right of the ambulatory leads into the *Presbytery*. The parapet at the ascent to the presbytery (in two sections at the S. and N. sides) is carved with figures representing outstanding men of the first 20 centuries of the Christian era. The block on the extreme left remains uncarved, awaiting the selection of a figure from the 20C.

The **Chapels** opening from the ambulatory are called the 'Chapels of Tongues', since each represents a different national or ethnic group, in keeping with the international ideal of the cathedral.

At the present time, for security reasons, the chapels are frequently locked. Ask at the information desk in the narthex.

The first chapel in the N. ambulatory is (1) *St. Ansgar's Chapel* (1918), named after the 9C Frankish missionary to Denmark, Sweden, and Germany. Designed by Henry Vaughan, it is stylistically reminiscent of 14C English Gothic. The windows are by C.E. Kempe of London. The crystal chandelier over the entrance is a gift of the government of Czechoslovakia (1927). The (2) *Chapel of St. Boniface* (1916), next along the ambulatory, is named after the Apostle of Germany (c. 680–755), martyred by a heathen mob while preaching in W. Friesland. The carved reredos and oak clergy stalls are particularly fine. Vaughan was again the architect, and Kempe designed the windows commemorating great missionaries. The 11-ft bronze statue of Michael the Archangel was made and donated in 1963 by Eleanor M. Mellon. *St. Columba's Chapel* (1911) next door (3) is named after the Irish saint (521–97) who founded the monastery of Iona and worked to convert the Celts. The statues by Gutzon Borglum flanking the entrance represent influential figures in English church history. The altarpiece is a 15C polyptych by Giovanni di Paolo. Architects Heins & La Farge designed this chapel in the Romanesque style they chose for the cathedral as a whole.

The Howard Thurman Listening Room in the chapel makes available a collection of taped meditations, sermons, and lectures. The hours when the chapel is open are posted outside the chapel entrance, or ask at the information desk in the narthex.

St. Saviour's Chapel, the central chapel (4) and the first one built (1904; Heins & La Farge), is dedicated to the Eastern Church, though its style is Gothic. The window depicting the Transfiguration is by Hardman, of Birmingham, England. The 20 figures flanking the entrance represent the heavenly choir and were designed by Gutzon Borglum, as were the figures of scholars, bishops, and saints of the Eastern Church on either side of the window. The heavenly choir occasioned controversy when installed, since the figures are all female. The icons, displayed behind the altar, on the side walls, and sometimes at the entrance to the nave of the cathedral, are Greek, Russian, and Byzantine, dating from the 15–18C. The shrine on the S. wall is dedicated to certain African saints while that on the N. wall opposite is dedicated to Athenagoras, the late Ecumenical Patriarch of the Orthodox Church. The large cloisonné vases usually displayed before the altar were a gift from the Emperor of Japan (1926); the King of Siam gave the teak cabinets flanking the altar in 1930; the altar frontal (1926) is the handwork of Zealous Orphans of War from the Kingdom of the Serbs, Croats, and Slovenes, as the Serbo-Croatian inscription proclaims.

In the ambulatory directly opposite the entrance to the chapel is the *tomb of Bishop Horatio Potter* (1802–87), designed after the tomb of Edward the Confessor in Westminster Abbey and occupying the spot behind the high altar traditionally reserved for a cathedral's founder.

The next chapel (open only for prayer and meditation) is the *Chapel of St. Martin of Tours* (5), the 4C Gallic bishop. Designed by Ralph Cram (1918) in a style reminiscent of 13C French Gothic, it is noteworthy for its beautiful windows (Charles Connick) depicting scenes from the lives of three French saints (left to right): St. Louis, St. Martin, and St. Joan of Arc. The statue of Joan of Arc (donated 1922) on the right wall is by Anna Hyatt Huntington, and stands above a stone taken from the saint's cell in Rouen. A small chip of Rhiems cathedral blasted away during World War I is embedded in the trefoil above the altar cross.

St. Ambrose' Chapel (6) is named after the 4C bishop of Milan and is designed (1914; Carrère & Hastings) in a style Cram called 'purely Renaissance'. The reredos of carved wood and gesso overlaid with gold leaf recalls Italian Renaissance examples. The choir stalls came from Spoleto; the marbles paving the floor are from Verona, Siena, and Cenere. Italian paintings include: The Annunciation by Andrea Sabbatini (1480?–1545); The Baptism of Christ, studio of the brother and sons of Paolo Veronese (16C); Virgin and Child, attributed to Perugino (1446–1523). The statue of St. Anthony is by Luca della Robbia (1400?–82).

Although the *Chapel of St. James* (1916), the last in the S. ambulatory, is dedicated to the people of Spain, it is decorated in a style recalling 14C English Gothic (architect Henry Vaughan). The Sacristy window (Henry W. Young) depicts figures in the history of Spain, particularly those associated with the discovery of the New World, including Christopher Columbus. In the central bay of the S. aisle is the tomb of Bishop Henry Codman Potter (1834–1908); behind the sarcophagus are three paintings depicting scenes from the life of St. Peter by Luca Giordano (1632–1705). The Ecce Homo is by Luis de Morales (1510?–86).

The glazed terracotta relief of the Annunciation in the S. ambulatory has been attributed to Luca della Robbia.

Continue along the S. ambulatory; a doorway in the S. wall of the crossing leads into the *Museum of Religious Art*, the only building remaining from the Leake and Watts Orphan Asylum.

Completely altered inside, this Greek Revival building dates from the 1830s and is now used for changing exhibitions of religious art; works of art from the cathedral are sometimes displayed here so that visitors may see them in better light.

Return to the crossing. In the display case on the S. wall are ecclesiastical garments.

The *Bays in the S. Aisle*, like those on the N. side of the nave, are devoted to religious aspects of various human activities. They are (E. to W.): Motherhood Window (only clerestory window), Armed Forces' Bay (with a 13C recumbent effigy of a knight in chain mail), Religious Life Bay (with an altar of Japanese cedar presented in 1975 by the Oomoto Foundation, a Japanese monotheistic community), Medical Bay (with an ornate carved oak reredos complementing that in the Lawyers' Bay opposite), Press or Communications Bay (with a marble statue of the Return of the Prodigal by William O. Partridge, 1861–1930), Labour Bay (with a memorial to N.Y. Firemen by Ralph Feldman, dedicated 1976), Missionary Bay, and All Souls' Bay.

Leave the cathedral by the W. doors and walk S. on Amsterdam Ave to 110th St to see the Auxiliary Buildings within the cathedral close. *Synod House*, at the corner of Amsterdam Ave and Cathedral Parkway-110th St, a Gothic structure (1913; Cram & Ferguson), houses the offices of the bishops of the diocese. Of particular interest is the W. entrance built like a medieval porch, its sculptural figures illustrating the progress of Christianity. In the center of the lawn is the *Outdoor Pulpit* (dedicated 1916), an open-work Gothic spire 40 ft high, designed by architects Howells & Stokes. Although outdoor services were once held on the lawn and enhanced by a small choir and brass band, the noise of traffic makes this impractical today.

Continue along the close road to *Diocesan House*, (1909–12; Heins & La Farge), once a training school for deaconesses. The building now contains the cathedral library (open Mon–Fri, 9–1 and 1.45–4.45) and archives. *Cathedral House*, across the road and E. of Diocesan House, was originally the *Bishop's House* (1914; Cram & Ferguson), built in the manner of a Gothic château with money donated by J.P. Morgan who defended its elegance by opining that bishops should live 'like everyone else'. Today the bishop occupies only the 3rd floor. Directly E. is the *Deanery* (1914; Cram & Ferguson), and beyond it to the left is the *Cathedral School* (1913; Walter Cook and Winthrop A. Welch), once a day school for choir boys, now a coeducational elementary and middle school from whose enrollment the choir still draws its treble voices. The lefthand branch of the road continues past the school to the *Biblical Garden*, whose plantings include only flora mentioned in the Bible (most of which spend the winter in nurseries). The close road now leads back to Amsterdam Ave.

Walk N. on Amsterdam Ave to the corner of 113th St. The small square building on the S.W. corner of the intersection is a *Gatehouse* (c. 1890) marking the end of a section of masonry aqueduct that runs beneath Amsterdam Ave. Most of the water supplied from the city's reservoirs is carried by pipes, but during the later years of the 19C when labour was relatively cheap and pipe was expensive, the city built a number of masonry aqueducts. A second gatehouse stands at 119th St, where the pipes end and the masonry begins.

Turn right at 113th St and walk E. Although much of *St. Luke's Hospital*, on the N. side of 113th St, is new, part of the original ˙central pavilion may still be seen, overshadowed by the modern wings.

The original hospital consisting of the central pavilion for administration and nine semi-detached outbuildings was designed in the Beaux-Arts style by Ernest Flagg and built in 1893–96. The hospital was founded in 1846 by the Episcopal Church; now administrators of the 780 bed facility are considering a merger with Roosevelt Hospital in an effort to streamline the city's patchwork system of private, voluntary, and municipal hospitals.

Walk E. on 113th St to Morningside Drive. Just across the drive is **Morningside Park,** a rocky cliff of Manhattan schist, which plunges steeply down to the Harlem plain.

In the mid-19C its precipitous slopes proved too steep for even the most ardent real estate developer, and so the area was handed over to landscape architects

Frederick Law Olmstead and Calvert Vaux to be converted to a park (final plan 1887). Realising that the most attractive feature of the area was the view to the E., now blighted by slums and overhung with air pollution, the designers planned a walkway on top of the cliff studded with balconies opening out toward the plains below. At the bottom of the hill, they laid out a secluded walk and a rambling ground; they proposed planting the cliff face with vines and creepers which could survive in its shallow soil, and they planned an alpine rock garden for the N. panhandle of the park at 123rd St.

Today Morningside Park has fallen on evil times. Its paths, choked with weeds, have become the haunts of urban predators and it is unsafe to walk there. Public School 36 has usurped the site of the alpine garden in the N. and concrete playgrounds have been built in the S. portion.

Continue N. on Morningside Drive. At the N.W. corner of 114th Street is the Roman Catholic ÉGLISE DE NOTRE DAME (apse 1909–10; Dans & Otto; remainder, 1914–28; Cross & Cross; DL). Originally built for a French-speaking congregation, the building recalls churches of Napoleonic France (the Church of the Madeleine in Paris has been mentioned). A handsome portico with four Corinthian columns faces Morningside Park. The interior (open for services, Sun, 8.30, 10, 11, 12.30, and 5; weekdays, 7, 8, 12.05, and 5.30) is remarkable for its replica of the grotto at Lourdes, donated by Mrs Geraldine Redmond, a parishioner whose son had been healed by its miraculous waters. Since plans for a large drum and dome over the crossing which would have brought natural light into the building never materialised, the interior is artificially lighted.

Two blocks N. at the intersection of 116th St and Morningside Drive is the *Carl Schurz Memorial* (sculptor, Karl Bitter; architect Henry Bacon, 1913). Forced to flee Germany because of his revolutionary political sentiments, Schurz (1829–1906) emigrated to the United States where he became a leader of the Republican party, a friend of Abraham Lincoln, a major-general in the Union Army during the Civil War, a senator, and an editor. Bitter's bronze statue depicts Schurz as a strong, idealistic man; the low relief panels on the monument, influenced by Bitter's admiration for archaic Greek sculpture, portray the liberation of oppressed peoples: American Indians, Asians, and blacks.

Directly across Morningside Drive are the outposts of ***Columbia University**, whose main campus lies just W. of Amsterdam Ave.

Free tours of the university are given Mon–Fri at 3 or by appointment, tel: 280–2845; they leave from the Office of Information and Visitors' Services, 201 Dodge Hall. During the academic year, non-residential buildings are generally open from 8 a.m. to 10 or 11 p.m. weekdays and until 5 or 6 p.m. on Saturdays. Most buildings are closed on Sundays. For further information, telephone the Security Office, 280–2796.

Columbia University, one of the oldest, wealthiest and most famous American universities, was founded as a gentlemen's college to 'instruct youth in the learned languages and in the liberal arts and sciences'. It is known for its professional schools—medicine, law, business, education, journalism, and architecture—and for the School of General Studies where adults, some in their 60s, can work toward degrees. Columbia College for men and Barnard, for women, are the undergraduate colleges.

The university has a student body of some 16,000 (10,200 men; 5800 women) and a faculty of 4000 members in teaching and research. The annual operating budget is $250 million and the market value of the endowment is $460 million. Columbia's motto is 'In lumine tuo videbimus lumen' (In thy light shall we see light).

History. By the mid 18C it became apparent to contemporary observers that while New York outstripped its American rivals commercially, it lagged behind culturally, its populace afflicted by ignorance, their lives dominated by a sordid thirst for money. Consequently a group of citizens set out to establish a center of learning that would lighten the intellectual gloom, simultaneously outshining Harvard, Yale, and the College of New Jersey (later Princeton). Among them were several vestrymen of Trinity Church who arranged a transfer of 5 acres of church property to the proposed college, a plot bounded by Church, Murray, and Barclay Sts and the Hudson River, then located at about West St. It was Columbia's first piece of valuable real estate. The college was chartered by King George II in 1754 and named King's College, the sixth such institution in the colonies. The first president was Dr Samuel Johnson, an Anglican pastor from Stratford, Connecticut, and the first class of eight men, who bore such resounding old New York names as Verplanck, Van Cortlandt, and Bayard, met in the schoolhouse of Trinity Church.

Among the early students were Alexander Hamilton (1755–1804), who enrolled in 1775 and stayed about a year, later first secretary of the U.S. treasury; John Jay (1745–1829), first chief justice of the U.S. supreme court; Gouverneur Morris (1752–1816), statesman and diplomat, minister to France; and Robert R. Livingston (1746–1813), first U.S. secretary of foreign affairs.

After the Revolution, the college, renamed Columbia, entered a period of intellectual dormancy which lasted well into the 19C. In 1814 the trustees appealed to the state for financial aid and received, instead of the share in the proceeds of a state lottery for which they had hoped, a plot of land between 47th and 51st Sts, W. of Fifth Ave, formerly the Elgin Botanic Garden. Appraised by the state at $75,000, it seemed worth much less to the trustees, since it was rocky, remote from the city, and overgrown with weeds. Today Columbia still owns most of this grant, now assessed at $146 million, and leases it to Rockefeller Center for an annual rental of $10 million.

In 1857 the college moved uptown, not to the Rockefeller Center site but to buildings formerly owned by an asylum for the deaf and dumb between Madison and Fourth (now Park) Aves, bounded by 49th and 50th Sts. The school remained here until its relocation on the Morningside Heights campus in 1897. In 1902 Nicholas Murray Butler became president and under his energetic guidance Columbia achieved its present high reputation. Its faculty has been illustrious, including such luminaries as John Dewey, Michael Pupin, Harold C. Urey, Isidore I. Rabi, Edward McDowell, and Franz Boas. Dwight D. Eisenhower resigned his presidency of the university (1948–53) to become President of the United States.

On the N.W. corner of Morningside Drive and 116th St is the house (1912; McKim, Mead & White) of the university president. Adjacent to it on 116th St is Johnson Hall, a residence principally for graduate women, named after the university's first president, Samuel Johnson.

Next to Johnson Hall on the N.E. corner of 116th St and Amsterdam Ave is the *Law School* (1961; Harrison & Abramovitz), a massive, white highrise building linked to the School of International Affairs on the N. (1971; Harrison & Abramovitz) by a wide bridge passing over Amsterdam Ave. In front of the Law School stands *Jacques Lipchitz's* Bellerophon Taming Pegasus (cast 1973, installed 1977), best seen from the W. side of Amsterdam Ave or the upper level plaza (take the stairway on 116th St). According to the sculptor, the monumental statue (30 ft high, 28 ft wide, 23 tons) symbolises the control by law over the forces of disorder in human society.

Cross Amsterdam Ave to the main campus. The MORNINGSIDE HEIGHTS CAMPUS of Columbia was designed (1893) by McKim, Mead & White, but is principally the work of Charles Follen McKim, who envisioned a densely developed area with small side courtyards and a narrow central quadrangle. McKim's original intentions can be seen in the brick and limestone classroom buildings with green copper roofs on the periphery of the main quadrangles, and in the placement of St. Paul's Chapel, Low Library, Earl Hall, and University Hall. The only side courtyard actually built is the one bounded by Schermerhorn, Avery, and Fayerweather Halls and St. Paul's Chapel (and it has been altered by the Avery Library extension), since after McKim's death (1909) the university elected to retain the central open space and expand instead into surrounding city streets, a policy that has not been without social repercussions in an area where the general populace is poor in comparison to the university). An attempt to build a gymnasium in Morningside Park was among the factors that sparked the student riots of 1968.

The university purchased the land from the Bloomingdale Insane Asylum in two parcels (1892 and 1903) for a total of $3·9 million. The original campus, built on the first parcel N. of 116th St, contains the college's finest buildings, Low Library and St. Paul's Chapel.

Continue along College Walk, the pedestrian extension of 116th St, to the center of the campus. The principal building in the lower or South Quadrangle is *Butler Hall* (formerly South Hall), the main university library (1934; James Gamble Rogers), distinguished more for the collection it houses than for its architectural attractions. Named after president Nicholas Murray Butler, the library can accommodate 4 million volumes. The present Columbia collection, housed in several smaller libraries as well as Butler Hall, numbers about 4,623,000 volumes and is one of the largest in the nation.

Dominating the Upper Quadrangle (N. of College Walk) is Low Library on whose broad steps sits Columbia's most famous piece of sculpture, **'Alma Mater'** (1903; Daniel Chester French). The statue, originally covered with gold leaf, was regilded in 1962 to the horror of students and faculty members who demanded the removal of the gaudy gold in favour of the familiar grey-green patina. In 1970 the statue was slightly damaged by a bomb set off during student uprisings. 'Alma Mater' sits in a curule chair flanked by torches implying enlightenment; her right hand holds a sceptre topped with a crown, an emblem referring to Columbia's beginnings as King's College. An owl peers from the folds of her robe near her left knee; a laurel garland wreathes her head; a book lies open on her lap.

A tablet set in the pavement a few yards in front of the statue bears a Latin inscription commemorating McKim: Desuper artificis spectant monumenta per annos (The monuments of the artist look down [upon us] through the years).

Low Memorial Library (1895–97; McKim, Mead & White, DL) dominates the quadrangle by virtue of its scale (dome, 136 ft above the terrace), its siting at the top of three flights of stairs, and its imposing classicism. Seth Low, president of Columbia from (1890–1901), gave the building to honour his father, Abiel Abbot Low (1811–93), the wealthy tea merchant and China trade pioneer whose warehouses still grace the South Street Seaport area. The younger Low resigned his office to become mayor of New York (1901–03), a position he won not because of special political acuity but because his opponents were outrageously corrupt. Low Library remained the main university library until 1934 when Butler Hall superceded it; now it houses administrative offices and the Columbiana Collection.

EXTERIOR. Low Library has its stylistic origins in the Roman Pantheon; its general plan is that of a Greek cross with an octagonal transition to a saucer dome. The outer dome of solid masonry covers an inner dome (diameter, 70 ft) of plaster on a steel frame, which forms the ceiling of the main reading room. At the S. end of the cross a portico of ten fluted Ionic columns enhances the principal entrance.

INTERIOR (open weekdays 9–4). The former Reading Room with its 16 polished granite columns capped by gilt bronze Ionic capitals, its galleries and heroic marble statuary, and its domed ceiling rising above semicircular clerestory windows exemplifies the work of McKim, Mead & White at their most elegant.

Room 210 on the first floor houses the COLUMBIANA COLLECTION (open Mon–Fri, 1–5), which contains books, portraits, and memorabilia relating to the history of the university. In the basement are restrooms. At one time the sub-basement contained a large canvas tank and a stationary rowing rack for the Columbia crew.

The picturesque three-story gabled brick building just E. of Low Library is *East Hall*, the only building remaining from the days of the Bloomingdale Asylum; it now houses the Foreign Student Center.

Just to the left or N. of East Hall is *St. Paul's Chapel (1904–07; Howells & Stokes; DL), one of the campus' most beautiful buildings. Originally affiliated with the Episcopal Church, the chapel is now used for diverse religious services, including a Roman Catholic Mass, a Taiwanese Prayer Meeting, and a Lutheran Service.

EXTERIOR. Constructed of brick and limestone, the building is shaped like a short Latin cross (140 ft long, 80 ft wide, 112 ft high) with a vaulted portico on the W. and a semi-circular apse on the east. A dome (interior diameter, 48 ft; height, 91 ft) covers the crossing. The capitals of the columns flanking the entrance are decorated with heads of cherubim by Gutzon Borglum.

The chapel is open Mon–Fri 12–4, Sat 10.30–1, and Sun 1–6. A schedule of services and musical events is posted outside the main entrance, or tel: 280–5113.

INTERIOR. The walls of the chapel are of tan brick and the fine vaulting is of Guastavino tile in warm tones of salmon and buff. The woodcarving and inlay of the pulpit, choir stalls, and organ front were executed in Florence from designs supplied by the architects but modelled on work in the cathedral of Santa Croce in Florence. In accordance with the educational aspirations of Columbia, the three apse windows (John La Farge) show St. Paul preaching to the Athenians on the Areopagus; the windows in the transepts show teachers of the Old Testament (N. transept) and the New Testament (S. transept).

Continue N. along the sidewalk from the chapel to *Avery Hall* (1912; McKim, Mead & White), one of the early classroom buildings in the style designated by McKim. It houses the School of Architecture and the nation's largest architectural library (not open to the public); the underground addition at the rear of the building was completed in 1977 (Alexander Kouzmanoff & Assocs).

Visible to the N. from the front of Avery Hall is the *Sherman Fairchild Center for the Life Sciences* (1977; Mitchell/Giurgola Assocs), the only building among recent additions to the campus to meet with approbation from the city's architectural critics.

Turn left in front of Avery Hall and walk west. In front of Uris Hall stands a 3-ton hollow, black painted steel sculpture (24 ft long, 11 ft wide, 12 ft high) by Clement Meadmore installed in 1968 and entitled 'Curl'. Meadmore, an Australian sculptor now living in New York, has left a similar work at the corner of Riverside Drive and 156th St.

Turn left again and walk S. along the side of Low Library toward College Walk. Between the library and Lewisohn Hall to the S.W. reclines a statue of 'The Great God Pan', by George Grey Barnard. Cast of bronze and weighing more than 3 tons, it was completed c. 1898.

Turn right at College Walk and continue toward Broadway. On the left is the *School of Journalism* (1912–13; McKim, Mead & White), founded by publisher Joseph Pulitzer in 1912, which comes into the public eye each spring when it announces the Pulitzer Prizes. On the S. side of the building is a statue (1914) of Thomas Jefferson by William Ordway Partridge (1861–1930), an alumnus of Columbia. Another of Partridge's statues (1908), 'Alexander Hamilton', stands in front of Hamilton Hall on the E. side of quadrangle.

On the N. side of College Walk, opposite the School of Journalism, is Dodge Hall, with the Office of Information and Visitors' Services. The walkway leads out to Broadway through a gate guarded by two classically draped figures representing 'Science' (1925) and 'Art' or 'Letters' (1916), both by Charles Keck.

Turn right (N.) on Broadway. The campus of **Barnard College** lies on the W. side of the street between 116th and 120th Sts. No tours are offered but visitors are welcome to explore.

History. Frederick A.P. Barnard (1809–89) became president of Columbia in 1864 after a string of men distinguished more for their piety than their administrative abilities. Among his liberal innovations was the institution of a women's course, which the trustees grudgingly accepted in 1883. Since women were not allowed to enter the classrooms and since faculty members were not allowed to counsel or advise women outside class, the course was not notably successful. Nevertheless it was due to Barnard's efforts that the women's college was founded in 1889.

The older buildings reflect the predominant style at Columbia, but two new buildings toward the N. end of the campus (at about 119th St) are attractive, imaginative additions: The Millicent McKintosh Center for student activities and the 14-story science building, Helen Goodhart Altschul Hall (both 1969; Vincent G. Kling & Assocs).

On the wall of the Mathematics Building on the E. side of Broadway at about 117th St is a large plaque *commemorating the Battle of Harlem Heights*, fought close to this site on 16 September 1776. It was Washington's only significant victory in the campaign for Manhattan, where his efforts resulted in a series of lost battles followed by spectacularly successful retreats.

On 15 September, the British army had landed at Kip's Bay (near the present site of 34th St on the East River) and had routed the defenders, nearly trapping the main body of American forces in lower Manhattan. The following day a force of American troops, encamped on Harlem Heights (roughly at 130th St, E of Broadway) moved S. to encounter a British force in a buckwheat field where the Barnard campus is presently located. The Americans hoped to lure some of the British down into the valley where 125th St lies, to outflank them, and eventually to cut them off, but the plan failed because the flanking party fired prematurely, making their whereabouts known. Nevertheless the Americans did hold off the British for several hours in the buckwheat field and forced them to retreat. While the battle had no great significance in the course of the war, it bolstered sagging American morale and demonstrated to Washington that his soldiers, despite several disastrous recent performances, were capable of standing up to the British.

Continue N. along Broadway, which now begins to slope downhill. Near the corner of 120th St is the side of the _Marcellus Hartley Dodge Physical Fitness Center_ (1974; Eggers Partnership), a gymnasium built after student and community hostility doomed the one proposed for Morningside Park.

Just N. of the gymnasium are the _Pupin Physics Laboratories_ (120th St and Broadway), built in 1925 but named 10 years later after Michael Idvorsky Pupin (1858–1935), a Serbian immigrant who became one of America's foremost inventors in the field of electricity and a revered professor of electrical engineering. In this building in the late 1930s and early 1940s, Harold C. Urey, Enrico Fermi, and I.I. Rabi did the work in nuclear fission and the release of atomic energy that eventually won them the Nobel Prize.

The row of red brick buildings on the E. side of Broadway between 120th and 121st Sts houses **Teachers College,** an affiliate of Columbia University. Founded in 1889 by Nicholas Murray Butler, the college grew from humble beginnings as the Kitchen Garden Club of the Church of St. Mark's-in-the-Bowerie, an organisation devoted to introducing manual training into the public school system and to teaching working class girls the elements of housekeeping and gardening. Since the days when John Dewey belonged to the faculty, Teachers College has earned a reputation for spearheading progressive causes in education.

Most of the buildings date from around the turn of the century and offer the charms of Victorian brick architecture. On the N.E. corner of the intersection is Horace Mann Hall (1901; Howells & Stokes and Edgar H. Josselyn), formerly the Horace Mann School, founded in 1887 and taken over by the college as an experimental school. Halfway down the block to the E. on 120th St is Main Hall (1892; William A. Potter), the campus' earliest building, an elaborate composition of dormers, gables, pointed-arch windows, porches, and turrets.

Cross Broadway to the W. side. **Union Theological Seminary** (1910; Allen & Collens, altered 1952 by Collens, Willis & Beckonert, DL) occupies the blocks between 120th and 122nd Sts. Founded in 1836 as a graduate school for Protestant ministers, the seminary has long enjoyed a reputation for liberal religious thought and involvement in social action. Its library (open to enrolled students and qualified scholars) is outstanding, containing the van Ess Collection, rich in manuscripts and incunabula, and the McAlpin Collection of British History and Theology. Among its faculty and graduates have been such luminaries as Reinhold Niebuhr, Norman Thomas, and Henry Sloane Coffin.

The classroom and residential buildings are organized in a quadrangle around a central courtyard dominated by the Brown Memorial Tower on Broadway and the James Memorial Tower on Claremont Avenue. Constructed of rockface granite with limestone trim, the buildings belong to an era when American universities imitated the Gothicism of Oxford and Cambridge, presumably in hopes of acquiring their academic tradition along with their appearance. The interior quadrangle and the James Chapel are especially attractive (for admission enquire weekdays, 9–5, at the Security Desk in the Rotunda near the Broadway–120th St entrance).

On the N.E. corner of 122nd St and Broadway is the **Jewish Theological Seminary** (1930; Gehron, Ross, Alley), a large but uninspired example of neo-Georgian architecture. Founded in 1886 to provide the Jewish population with American-trained rabbis and scholars, it has become a major center of Jewish education. Its library has the most comprehensive collection of Judaica and Hebraica in the Western Hemisphere and contains more than 250,000 volumes, including a fine collection of manuscripts from the repository of the Old Cairo Synagogue.

Tours of the buildings are available for organised groups by advance arrangement; tel: 749–8000.

An eternal light in memory of the Jews who died in the Holocaust burns upon the tower at Broadway and 122nd St. In 1966 a tragic library fire destroyed 70,000 books and damaged 120,000 more.

Walk W. on 122nd St. The building housing the MANHATTAN SCHOOL OF MUSIC (N. side of 122nd St, between Broadway and Claremont Ave) was built in 1910 (Donn Barber) for the Institute of Musical Art; later with substantial additions (1931; Shreve, Lamb & Harmon) it was the home of the Juilliard School of Music. The latest addition, the Mitzi Newhouse Pavilion (1970; MacFadyen & Knowles), was added by the present occupant.

Riverside Drive (opened 1880) and **Riverside Park** were planned by Frederick Law Olmsted at a time when it seemed that the Upper West Side might become one of the city's most desirable areas. Olmsted's plans implied elegance: he laid out a wide drive following the natural contours of the land (instead of the profitable perpendiculars of the 1811 grid); he divided the roadway into carriage and foot promenades; and he insisted that park and drive be unified, that the imaginary boundary between them be erased. Although fine homes did line the drive by the 1890s, the area lacked a tradition of fine old families and never did rival Fifth Ave in glitter and snob appeal.

Continue W. on 122nd to Claremont Ave. Up a flight of stairs in the park is a *statue of Daniel Butterfield*, designed by Gutzon Borglum and erected in 1918. Butterfield (1831–1901) was a Union general in the Civil War but achieved his greatest fame off the battlefield as the composer of 'Taps', the bugle call played as the flag is lowered at nightfall and at funerals. Visible across Sakura Park is *International House* (1924, Lindsay & Warren), a residence for graduate students from almost 100 countries built with funds provided by John D. Rockefeller, Jr.

Walk S. on Riverside Drive to the main entrance of ***Riverside Church.**

Open Mon–Sat, 9–4.30. Sunday services in the nave begin at 10.45. A guided tour is given on Sundays after the worship service. Visitors are welcome to have lunch in the cafeteria during the week and after the Sunday service.

The Riverside Church (1930; Allen & Collens and Henry C. Pelton. South wing, 1960; Collens, Willis & Beckonert) occupies a commanding site overlooking the Hudson River. Affiliated with the Baptist Church and the United Church of Christ, it has been known for its liberal appeal, for its community service, and for its historical connection with John D. Rockefeller, Jr, who was chairman of the building committee and a generous benefactor.

The church began as a small Baptist congregation meeting on Stanton Street on the Lower East Side. About 1850 the group moved to Norfolk St and occupied the landmark building now owned by Beth Hamedrash Hagodol (see p150). As the immigrant population overwhelmed the Lower East Side, the Baptists moved uptown, first to 46th St just W. of Fifth Ave, later to Park Ave, and finally to the present location.

Despite its Gothic inspiration and particular indebtedness to the cathedral of Chartres, the Riverside Church is a modern, steel-framed building, its Gothicism relegated to surface details. Although criticised at the time of completion for its disproportionately tall tower (392 ft), for its cultural servitude to Europe, and for its 'bewildered eclecticism', the church is nonetheless distinguished for its fine stained glass, stone carving, and wood work, which represent the finest materials and craftsmanship available.

MEASUREMENTS: Length (excluding S. wing), 265 ft; width, 100 ft; height of tower, 392 ft; length of nave, 215 ft; width of nave, 89 ft; height of nave, 100 ft; seating capacity of nave, c. 2500.

EXTERIOR. The building, faced with Indiana limestone, runs with its long axis parallel to Riverside Drive. The 22-story tower at the S. end contains classrooms and offices as well as the carillon. The principal entrance on the W. is elaborately carved and is clearly intended to recall the portals at Chartres. The tympanum depicts a seated Christ surrounded by emblems of the four Evangelists. Above the tympanum are five archivolts, the first and fifth depicting angels, the middle ones portraying scientists, philosophers, and religious leaders drawn from the whole sweep of human history—classical, Christian, and modern. The chapel door, just S. of the W. Portal, is thematically devoted to the Nativity.

Visitors may also enter the church through the Cloister entrance on Claremont Ave (E. side), near which is a bronze 'Madonna and Child' (1927) by Jacob Epstein, modelled on an Indian mother and child.

Inside the revolving door is the *Narthex*. In the E. wall are two windows of 16C Flemish glass, the only windows not made specifically for the church. A small chapel in the N.E. corner of the narthex contains Heinrich Hofmann's (1824–1902) painting, 'Christ in Gethsemane'. A door in the S. wall of the narthex leads into the *Chapel*, inspired by the 11C Romanesque nave of the Church of St. Nazaire at Carcassone, France.

The carved stone reredos portrays (bottom to top): the Last Supper, the Transfiguration, and Christ as Shepherd. The stained glass windows in the S. wall depict scenes from the life of Christ. The emblems of the apostles form the basis of the design in the rose window and the wrought iron rear doors.

Nave. On the N. of the narthex is the nave, finished in Indiana limestone and divided into three aisles by an arcade, above which is a triforium gallery and a clerestory. The clerestory windows are copies of the famous 12–13C windows at Chartres, while those on the aisle level present modern motifs as well as historical ones. There are 51 coloured stained glass windows in the church, made by firms in Boston, Chartres, and Rheims.

Aisle windows, W. wall (S. to N.): Agriculture, Reformers, Development of the Bible, State and Government, and Builders. Aisle windows, E. wall (S. to N.): International Character of Religion, Christ and Humanity, Scholars, Music, and Children. The capitals of the columns in the nave tell the prophecies of Jeremiah and the story of their fulfillment.

Continue along the nave to the *chancel*. The pulpit (weight, 9 tons) at the W. side of the chancel is carved from three blocks of limestone;

its niches (both upper and lower levels) contain figures of prophets; ten of the figures on the upper level stand beneath canopies representing the major cathedrals of France. The decoration of the carved oak choir stalls was inspired by Psalm 148, in which the psalmist calls upon all created things to praise the Lord. In the center of the chancel floor a marble maze has been adapted from the labyrinth at Chartres, whose route medieval penitents traced out on their knees. The communion table is carved from a block of Caen stone. Behind it is a baptismal pool. The *chancel screen portrays seven aspects of the life of Christ, shown in each panel surrounded by people who have fulfilled the divine ideal, including Pasteur, Savonarola, Florence Nightingale, and J.S. Bach. The panels represent (left to right): Physicians, Teachers, Prophets, Humanitarians, Missionaries, Reformers, and Lovers of Beauty.

On the S. wall of the nave, best seen from the chancel, is a work by Jacob Epstein, 'Christ in Majesty'; finished in gold leaf, it measures 19·5 by 6 ft.

Return to the narthex to ascend the *carillon tower (open daily 11–3, Sundays 12.30–4, admission 25¢). An elevator ascends 20 stories; stairs (147 steps) lead to the bell chamber and an open observation platform with fine views of upper Manhattan and the rivers. The Laura Spelman Rockefeller Memorial Carillon, gift of John D. Rockefeller, Jr, in memory of his mother, contains 74 bells, ranging from the 20-ton Bourdon (the largest tuned bell ever cast) to a 10-lb. treble bell. Cast in three stages (1925, 1930, and 1956; Gillet & Johnston Foundry, England and Van Bergen Foundry, Holland), it is the first carillon to exceed a range of five octaves. The Machine Room has equipment for operating the carillon automatically and the Clavier Cabin contains the keyboards for playing it manually. Peals may be rung on five of the largest bells, installed by means of wheels and electric motors.

The carillonneur plays recitals before and after the Sunday service, on Sat at noon, and on Sunday at 3.

Leave the church by the W. Portal and walk N. toward Grant's Tomb. On the N.W. corner of the church is the *Women's Porch*, with sculptured figures of four biblical women typifying ideal womanhood. Facing N. are Mary and Martha, the sisters of Lazarus, facing W. are Eunice and Lois, mother and grandmother of Timothy. On the ridgepole of the roof is an Angel of the Resurrection.

On the W. side of Riverside Drive at about 122nd St is **Grant's Tomb** (open Wed–Sun, 9–4.30, admission free), officially named the General Grant National Memorial (1891–97; John H. Duncan; DL), one of the city's most imposing formal monuments, a massive granite sepulchre containing the remains of Ulysses S. Grant (1822–85) and his wife, Julia Dent Grant. Intended to be unmistakably tomblike, despite objections that it would give a funeral tone to the neighbourhood, it was once a popular site of pilgrimage but is now rather sparsely visited.

History. Grant died after an illustrious career as commander-in-chief of the Union Armies in the Civil War and a scandal-ridden period as President (1868–76). He had requested burial in New York, at the U.S. Military Academy in West Point, or in Galena, Illinois. Because Galena seemed too remote and Mrs Grant could not be buried at West Point, New York was chosen. In 1885, Grant's body was temporarily interred in a brick structure at 123rd St, and five years later John H. Duncan won the architectural competition for a tomb to cost about half a million dollars (eventually 90,000 subscribers contributed about $600,000). Duncan's design was based largely on reconstructions of the Mausoleum at Halicarnassus (now in Turkey). Ground was broken in 1891 and the general's remains were quietly brought to the finished tomb in 1897. Despite the scandals that marred his administration, Grant himself remained a revered figure, and even while when the tomb was under construction two attempts were made to claim his remains for other locales.

EXTERIOR. The monument consists of a cubelike base topped by a drum supporting a stepped conical dome. A broad flight of steps flanked by two large eagles leads to the entrance enhanced by a hexastyle Doric portico. The raised stone blocks above the portico were originally intended to support equestrian statues of Union generals. Above the cornice a tablet contains Grant's words, 'Let us have peace', spoken upon accepting the presidential nomination of 1868; figures of two lamenting women recline against the tablet. The stepped cone, derived from reconstructions of Mausolus' tomb (died c. 532), was to have been crowned by a statue of Grant in a triumphal chariot.

INTERIOR. The austere interior, inspired by Napoleon's tomb at the Hôtel des Invalides in Paris, is cruciform in plan and dominated by the sunken crypt set directly below the dome. Amber coloured windows shed a golden light on the white marble walls. Above the windows mosaics (1966; Allyn Cox) depict Grant's victories at Vicksburg (E.) and Chattanooga (W.), and the surrender of Robert E. Lee at Appomattox (N.). The coffered dome rests on pendentives with sculptured women (by J. Massey Rhind) symbolising phases of Grant's life: birth and infancy (S.E.), military career (N.E.), civil career (N.W.), and death (S.W.). The two exhibition rooms on the N. wall are devoted to Grant's civil and military career. A double staircase in the N. arm (closed until a handrail is installed) leads down into the crypt containing the imposing polished red granite sarcophaghi of General and Mrs Grant. Niches in the wall at the crypt level contain bronze busts (1938) of Grant's generals, executed by William Mues (Generals Sherman and Sheridan) and Jens Juszko (Generals Thomas, Ord, and McPherson).

The park surrounding the monument, now known as *Grant Centennial Plaza* was established to commemorate Grant's establishment (1872) of Yellowstone, the first national park. The free-form, free-spirited mosaic benches (1972–74; Pedro Silva) depicting urban scenes, wildlife, the American flag, and other assorted subjects, were created as part of a community participation project.

Directly behind the tomb a fence encloses the *Commemoration Tree*, a ginkgo planted along with a Chinese cork tree in 1897 to honour Grant. The tree was the gift of China and was presented by Li Hung Chang (Guardian of the Prince and Grand Secretary of State) and Yang Yu (Envoy Extraordinary and Minister Plenipotetiary).

Until 1951 when it was burned and demolished by the city, the Claremont Inn stood at the N. end of the landscaped oval behind Grant's Tomb. Built in c. 1783 as a country manor by George Pollock, a successful linen merchant, it was named after Claremont in Surrey, England. The house became an inn before the Civil War, and among its illustrious tenants was Joseph Bonaparte.

Across Riverside Drive to the W. (about opposite the public restrooms in the park) a fence near the foot path encloses a small stone urn 'Effected to the Memory of an Amiable Child', St. Claire Pollock, aged 5, killed in a fall from the rocks on 15 July 1797. His uncle,

George Pollock, requested when he sold the property that the child's grave remain untouched.

SUBWAY: IRT Broadway–7th Ave local (train 1) from 116th St and Broadway.

BUS: M4 and M5 from Riverside Drive, M104 from Broadway. Culture Bus Loop I (weekends and holidays) from Stop 9, Riverside Drive and 120th St.

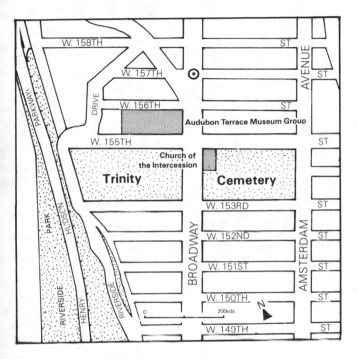

30 Washington Heights Museum Group (Audubon Terrace)

SUBWAY: IRT Broadway–7th Ave local (train 1) marked 242nd St to 157th St. IND Eighth Ave local (AA train) to 155th St and St. Nicholas Ave (walk two blocks west).

BUS: M4 or M5 to 155th St. Culture Bus, Loop I, stop 10 (weekends and holidays).

CAR PARKING: Metered parking on Broadway and some free street parking on 155th St along the S. side of the museum complex.

The **Washington Heights Museum Group,** which embraces the Museum of the American Indian, the Hispanic Society of America, the American Numismatic Society, and the American Academy of Arts and Letters, occupies a plot of land between W. 156th St, and W. 155th St along Broadway, once part of the estate of John James Audubon. The buildings, sometimes collectively referred to as

Audubon Terrace, were financed by Archer Milton Huntington, son of Collis P. Huntington, transcontinental railroad builder and steamship magnate. The interests of the younger Huntington, however, ran to poetry, and scholarship, not railroads, and he is remembered as the philanthropic donor of museums and libraries.

The museum buildings, grand and classical in the Beaux-Arts manner, appear incongruous in this mildly shabby neighbourhood remarkable more for its *bodegas* and active street life than for its intellectual tone, a location which has had unfortunate effects on museum attendance. The central feature of the museum group is a paved brick courtyard which opens on Broadway and is closed on the W. by the back of an apartment building. On the S. side are the Museum of the American Indian, Heye Foundation (1916), the Hispanic Society of America (1908)—founded by Archer M. Huntington—and the American Numismatic Society (1908), all designed by Charles Pratt Huntington, nephew of the donor, and the Administration Building (1923; William M. Kendall) of the American Academy of Arts and Letters. On the N. side of the courtyard are (E. to W.) the former headquarters of the American Geographical Society (1916; Charles Pratt Huntington), now occupied by Boricua College, the courtyard of the Hispanic Society, and the auditorium and gallery of the American Academy of Arts and Letters (1930; Cass Gilbert).

Dominating the plaza is a group of statues by Anna Hyatt Huntington, already well-known as a sculptor at the time of her marriage to the philanthropist. The largest is a bronze equestrian *statue of El Cid Campeador* (1927) surrounded by four seated warriors, a piece which celebrates the legendary medieval hero who defended Spain against the Moors and is a replica of Mrs Huntington's original erected the same year in Seville. The two limestone lions flanking the entrance of the Hispanic Society (1930), and the four limestone animal groups (bears, jaguars, boars, and vultures) on the terraces of the N. building (1936) are also her work as are the limestone equestrian reliefs of Don Quixote, Cervante's legendary knight of La Mancha, and Boabdil, the last Moslem king of Granada (1942 and 1944); the inscriptions beneath them are taken from the poetry of Archer M. Huntington.

The ***Museum of the American Indian,**** founded in 1916, by George C. Heye, is the largest Indian museum anywhere. Its fascinating and beautiful collections include objects belonging to aboriginal peoples ranging from the eskimos of the Arctic region to the inhabitants of Tierra del Fuego.

Open Tues–Sat, 10–5; Sun, 1–5. Closed Monday and major holidays. Tel: 283–2420. No restaurant facilities. Elevator service for handicapped visitors. Admission: adults, $1·50; students, 75¢. The Research Branch at 3401 Bruckner Boulevard in the Bronx (tel: 828–6969) may be visited by appointment only. The library at 9 Westchester Square in the Bronx (tel: 829–7770) has a non-circulating collection of more than 40,000 items on archaeology, ethnology, and history of native American peoples; visits by appointment only.

FIRST FLOOR displays focus on the ethnology of the eastern and midwestern United States. Clockwise from entrance: New England tribes including Huron, Lenni Lenape, Manhattan, and Pequot Indians. Iroquois False Face masks (case 2), the Van Cortlandt suit, earliest existing complete garment of lower Hudson origin (case 5); wampum including Treaty Belts given to William Penn in 1683 (case

5); costume of 'Old Solid Face', a forest deity (case 7). Displays on the Great Lakes tribes include material pertaining to Ojibwa, Kickapoo, Sauk, and Winnebago Indians and offer examples of clothing, farm implements, tools for gathering wild rice, toys and games. Displays on the Plains Indians—Sioux, Dakota, Crow, Blackfoot—include buffalo hide robes, a Medecine Society bonnet worn by Crazy Horse, a war club of Sitting Bull (case 16), photographs of Plains Indians made during the first quarter of the 20C, tomahawks and war clubs. Indians of the Basin-Plateau region of Idaho and Wyoming including Shawnee, Ute, Nez Percé and Paiute tribes are represented by clothing and artifacts as well as a display on peyote in Indian religion, a selection of tomahawks (case 25) and weapons belonging to famous warriors Tecumseh (case 31) and Joseph (case 29).

The exhibitions of the SECOND FLOOR are divided into two sections: archaeological displays (cases 48–80) and ethnographic materials from N. American Indians of the southwest and far west. Among the archaeological displays are a diorama of 16C Indian life in the Inwood section of Upper Manhattan; ceramic, shell, and stone objects from the Moundville excavation in Alabama (case 60); and objects of shell, fabric, stone, and wood from eight major mounds (c. 800–1400 A.D.) near Spiro, Oklahoma (case 64). The ethnographic displays include Navaho weaving (cases 83–84), costumes and basketry from tribes of California (cases 97–99), a diorama of a Kwakiutl potlatch (case 106), costumes of subarctic Indians and Eskimo masks.

On the THIRD FLOOR is a Special Exhibition Gallery and displays relating to the Indians of Central and S. America. Among the highlights are displays of pottery and sculpture from Colombia and Ecuador (500–1500 A.D.), Peruvian fabrics and clothing (case 204), Araucanian silver and weaving from Chile (cases 207–208), and, most bizarre, two shrunken figures and several shrunken heads from the Jivaro montañas Indians of Ecuador (case 211). Changing thematic exhibitions present such topics as games, wampum, personal adornment and aboriginal money.

The AMERICAN NUMISMATIC SOCIETY (founded 1858) contains one of the world's largest numismatic collections and its finest numismatic library, with some 70,000 items including books, periodicals, and auction catalogues.

Museum open Tues–Sat, 9–4.30; Sun, 1–4. Closed Mon and holidays. Library hours same as museum but closed also Sun. Admission free, but ring bell for entrance. Curatorial assistance and access to special sections of the collection upon request. Three public meetings with lectures yearly. Tel: 286–3030. No restaurant facilities.

The museum has two galleries. In the East Gallery is a long-term exhibition of Money in Early America. In the West Gallery is a handsome display of Medals and Decorations ranging from early Renaissance examples through contemporary medals and including the insignia of various orders of merit. The society's collection, estimated at some 800,000 pieces, was built around the nucleus of the bequest of Edward T. Newell, president of the society from 1916–1941, who gave some 87,000 coins, principally Greek, Roman, and Byzantine, and it is still recognised as having the world's finest group of Hellenistic coins as well as outstanding examples of Roman and Islamic coinage.

The *Hispanic Society of America* (founded 1904) houses a collection gathered mainly by Archer M. Huntington whose fascination with Spanish and Portuguese culture dated from his first visit to Spain at the age of 22, when he began collecting archaeological fragments from Italica, the earliest Roman colony in Spain. Today the collection ranges from the prehistoric period, through the periods of Roman and Moorish domination, to the present. The library contains over 100,000 volumes and manuscripts with an emphasis on Spanish and Portuguese history, literature and art.

Open Tues–Sat, 10–4.30; Sun, 1–4.30. Admission free. Closed Mon and major holidays. Library open Tues–Fri, 1 4.30, Sat, 10–4.30, but closed for several weeks at Christmas. No restaurant facilities. Tel: 926–2234.

The entrance hallway opens into the Main Court, two stories high and illuminated in part by skylights. Archways of deep red terracotta ornately worked in Spanish Renaissance style separate the center section of the room from a surrounding gallery. In the central part are two *Goya* portraits, *The Duchess of Alba and Manuel Lapena, Marquis of Bondad Real* as well as a 13C Mater Dolorosa of polychromed wood. Also displayed are pieces of antique furniture including several 17C varguenos and an Indo-Portuguese cabinet. Freestanding cases contain prints, drawings, and manuscripts. On the lower level of the gallery outside the arches are displayed panels from a 14C Catalan retablo, reliquaries of silver and silver gilt, architectural fragments, fabrics including Hispano-Moresque and Mudejar silk, and marble carvings from the tomb of the Duchess of Albuquerque (early 16C). Off the Main Court a small corridor contains a closet-like room with tiles and glazed 18–19C earthenware from Valencia and Toledo. The corridor opens into the *Sorolla Room*, decorated by a series of murals (commissioned 1911) by Joaquín Sorolla y Bastida, which depict street scenes and festivals of regional Spain.

The main stairway near the entrance to the building, decorated by a display of Hispano-Moresque tiles and mosaics, leads to the upper level of the main gallery. Here are displays of pottery and glass from prehistoric times onward as wall as paintings by Spanish artists, including *El Greco*: Pietà, St. Jerome, The Holy Family, and St. Luke; and *Velázquez*, *Portrait of a Little Girl*.

The AMERICAN ACADEMY OF ARTS AND LETTERS was founded in 1904 by the National Institute of Arts and Letters to recognise achievement in the arts. The parent organisation (founded 1898) elects 250 composers, architects, painters, writers, and poets of whom 50 are chosen for the even more elite American Academy. Among those so honoured have been Pearl S. Buck, Aaron Copland, Lillian Hellman, Edward Hopper, Walter Lippmann, John Steinbeck, Samuel L. Clemens (Mark Twain), and Andrew Wyeth. An annual art exhibition is held in the gallery on the N. side of the plaza and an annual literary exhibition in the building on the S. side. The library contains manuscripts and first editions, musical scores, notebooks, and other memorabilia pertaining to members and their work.

Museum open Tues–Sun, 1–4 during the spring and around the Christmas holiday season. Tel: 286–1480 for information and exact dates. Library open by appointment.

The bronze entrance doorways are decorated by symbolic reliefs by

Adolph Weinman. The female figures symbolise Throught and Inspiration, while the masculine figure above represents Spirit.

The building on the N.E. corner of the complex, now occupied by *Boricua College*, was constructed as the home of the American Geographical Society, which moved to the University of Wisconsin at Milwaukee for financial reasons, taking with it the largest map collection (some 325,000 maps) in the western hemisphere. Boricua College, a four-year liberal arts school, offers courses designed to meet the educational needs of Puerto Rican and Spanish-speaking students, and its offerings include bilingual courses, and a schedule of evening classes to accomodate a student body many of whose members work during the day.

Other nearby points of interest. TRINITY CEMETERY, occupying a plot of land from Riverside Drive to Amsterdam Ave, 153rd to 155th Sts (open 9–4.30 daily, entrance on 155th St near Riverside Drive), was established by Trinity parish in 1846 as land became scarce in lower Manhattan. It is the only cemetery in Manhattan still accepting burials, although in recent years the few burials annually have been those of Gallatins, Astors, Harsens, and others who purchased family plots many years ago. Its tranquil, hilly topography sloping toward the Hudson River suggests what Manhattan looked like before its inhabitants exercised their levelling effects. The grounds extend across Broadway to the present site of the Church of the Intercession and a suspension bridge (Vaux & Withers) at one time joined the two parcels, allowing visitors to wander freely without having to descend to the street. Although the bridge was demolished when the church was built, the high granite wall supporting its ornamental iron fence with gateways (1876) and the gatehouse and keeper's lodge (1883; Vaux & Radford) still remain. In the western part of the cemetery is the Astor plot containing the remains of John Jacob Astor and his wife. Elsewhere are Fernando Wood, mayor of the city during the Tweed era, Madame Jumel, whose mansion still stands further uptown (see p396), Alfred Tennyson Dickens, son of the novelist, Philip Livingston, a signer of the Declaration of Independence, and Clement Clarke Moore, writer of the verses beginning "I was the night before Christmas". At the W. end of the cemetery is a new mausoleum, built by the parish in part to help defray maintenance costs, some $200,000 annually.

Directly across Broadway on the S.E. corner of W. 155th St is the CHURCH OF THE INTERCESSION (1914; Cram, Goodhue & Ferguson; DL), another fine building by a pre-eminent ecclesiastical architect, Bertram Grosvenor Goodhue. The church complex, which includes a bell tower, cloister, parish house, and vicarage, has been praised for its site design which recalls the times when the neighbourhood was still rural and evokes the Gothic revival ideal of the country church. Noteworthy in the interior are the wooden ceiling supported by stone piers, the wood carving, the high altar inlaid with more than 1500 stones collected from the Holy Land and other shrines of early Christianity, and the wall tomb of architect Goodhue, decorated with reliefs of some of his buildings. Behind the church is part of the original graveyard including the burial plot of John James Audubon.

N. of Audubon Terrace at 264 W. 156th St is the *Church of Our Lady of Esperanza*, built in 1912 by Charles Pratt Huntington who

designed the museum group. Inside the entrance a stairway leads up
to the small sanctuary, decorated in gold and green, whose stained
glass windows, skylight, and hanging lamp were donated by the
King of Spain.

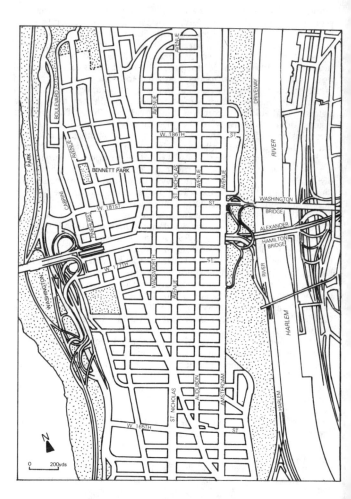

31 Washington Heights and Inwood. The Cloisters

SUBWAY: IRT Broadway–7th Ave local (train 1) to 168th St–Broadway; IND Eighth Ave express (A train) to 168th St.

BUS: M4 via Madison Ave or M5 via Broadway and Riverside Drive to the George Washington Bridge Bus Station.

Since the distances on this route are rather great and the traffic not too heavy, the route lends itself to car travel. The first portion passes through neighbourhoods that are quite run-down and visitors whose prime interest is in museums and architectural landmarks should start at Fort Tryon Park, for which separate directions are given.

Upper Manhattan, largely unknown to visitors except for the Cloisters, has some of the city's best scenery, several of its loveliest museums and oldest houses, as well as a population of about a quarter of a million people. The area from 155th St to Dyckman St is known as *Washington Heights*; north of that it is *Inwood*.

At the northern tip of Manhattan where the island narrows to a slender peninsula, the levelling effects of the city's developers are less evident than elsewhere in the city. Elevations rise to more than 200 ft, not precisely alpine but high enough to affect the street plan whose pleasant deviations from the downtown grid result from the existence of early roads built over Indian trails which in turn followed the contours of the land. Two ridges of Manhattan schist, the bedrock upon which the city's skyscrapers depend, run northward—the Fort Washington ridge on the W. and the Fort George ridge on the E., which ends at Dyckman St. Between them is a basin known as the Inwood lowlands, beneath whose architectural accretions and soil lies a base of Inwood marble, a stone more easily eroded than the schist. The Broadway valley between the ridges forms the natural roadbed for that avenue, formerly called the Boulevard in this part of town until in 1899 its full 15½ mile length from Bowling Green to Spuyten Duyvil was given one name.

As the names of the ridges suggest, the high ground had strategic importance during the Revolutionary War and was fortified with three outposts: Fort Washington overlooking the Hudson River, whose outlines are still recognisable in Bennett Park just W. of Fort Washington Ave at 183rd St, Fort Tryon a little to the N. in the park now bearing the same name, and Fort George on the E. ridge near the intersection of Fort George Ave and Fort George Hill (formerly an extension of St. Nicholas Ave, renamed in 1962). The area remained rural well into the 19C, attracting gentlemen farmers and others who located their country homes here including publisher James Gordon Bennett and naturalist John James Audubon.

C.K.G. Billings, heir to a Chicago gas fortune, owned the land where Fort Tryon Park now stands, and to celebrate the opening of a $200,000 stables completed in 1903, Billings, also known as the 'American Horse King', threw a dinner for 30 of his friends at Sherry's restaurant, an affair known in the annals of New York society as 'The Horseback Dinner'. The Horse King's companions enjoyed various courses served on little tables attached to the saddles of the horses (brought upstairs in the freight elevators) upon which they sat during the entire meal. Lest the guests be taken by the incongruity of it all, the walls of the restaurant were masked in painted woodland scenery, and the floor covered with grasses and other suitable materials.

The completion of the IRT subway in 1906, however, hastened the end of aristocratic exclusivity at the N. end of the island, and the process of urbanisation was essentially completed by the arrival of the IND in 1932. John D. Rockefeller, Jr had bought the Billings estate in 1917 and the city had begun purchasing large tracts of land, now parks, along the rivers around the turn of the century. Upper Manhattan was developed as a working class residential community and has remained one, though the population, once mainly Irish, is no longer predominantly white. Washington Heights, especially, is a warren of ethnic enclaves, whose residents are primarily black and Hispanic, but also Greek, Armenian, and even Japanese.

At 165th St and Broadway is the shell of the *Audubon Ballroom and the San Juan Theater*. Malcolm X, black activist and civil rights leader, was assassinated there in 1965. The ballroom and adjoining theatre, originally called the Audubon Theater, an elegant movie palace in its youth, were acquired by the city in the mid-1970s to construct a mental health facility on the site. Now private developers are considering the possibility of building a hotel there to serve the Columbia-Presbyterian Medical Center across the street. If the hotel is built, it will be the only major hotel N. of 96th St since the Theresa Hotel in Harlem closed in the late 1960s.

The COLUMBIA-PRESBYTERIAN MEDICAL CENTER, which fills the blocks between 165th–168th Sts, Broadway and Riverside Drive, is one of the largest and most prestigious medical centers in the nation. Although not architecturally distinguished (main complex 1928–47; James Gamble Rogers, Inc. 1947–64; Rogers & Butler. 1964–74; Rogers, Butler & Burgun), the center occupies a fine site along the hillside overlooking the Hudson River. Since 1911 it has embraced both the teaching and research facilities of Columbia University's College of Physicians and Surgeons and the clinics and facilities for patient care of the Presbyterian Hospital.

The Presbyterian Hospital was founded in 1868 by James Lenox and located downtown between Park and Madison Aves, 70th and 71st Sts. Now, with the corporate title of The Presbyterian Hospital in the City of New York, it has about 1400 beds and a staff of 1137 attending physicians and 384 interns and residents who care for about 150,000 patients annually. The hospital also includes Babies Hospital, whose old-fashioned name harks back to its foundation in 1887, the Dana W. Atchley Pavilion for ambulatory patient care, Harkness Pavilion for private patients, the Edward S. Harkness Eye Institute, the Neurological Institute, founded in 1909 as one of the first non-governmental hospitals in the nation treating diseases of the nervous system, and the New York Orthopaedic Hospital, founded 1866, one of whose founders was Theodore Roosevelt, father of the president of that same name, who was deeply interested in the problems of the crippled. The Vanderbilt family endowed the main outpatient facility (1888) which bears their name. The Sloane Hospital for Women, the Squier Urological Clinic, and the Radiotherapy Center also come under the corporate aegis of the Presbyterian Hospital. The Columbia University College of Physicians and Surgeons, along with its Schools of Public Health, Dental and Oral Surgery, and Nursing and the Institutes of Cancer Research and Human Nutrition are nationally recognised for the quality of their teaching and research.

Wadsworth Ave, which forks off Broadway to the right just above 173rd St, was named to honour the heroism of James Samuel Wadsworth, father of six and Republican candidate for governor in 1862, who rose to the rank of brigadier general in the Union Army despite a total lack of military training. Wadsworth died in the battle of Chancellorsville when, after two horses had been shot from under him, his third galloped in uncontrollable panic right at the Confederate lines.

The *Fort Washington Presbyterian Church* (21 Wadsworth Ave at the N.W. corner of 174th St) dates back to 1914 (Carrère & Hastings), although its portico, pediments, and the consoles, finials, and other details of its tower recall Christopher Wren's 17C London, a style Carrère and Hastings also used in the Christian Science Church at Central Park West and 96th St. Return to Broadway.

On the N.E. corner of Broadway and 175th St a sign on the marquee announces the building as the United Church where Rev. Ike (Frederick Eikerenkoetter) charismatically deals his brand of a religion that offers material rewards ('green power') as well as the usual less tangible ones. Once the church was *Loew's 175th St Theater* (1930; Thomas W. Lamb), but the luxurious trappings of the former movie palace—the tower and exotic, vaguely Egyptian or Mayan terracotta ornament on the S. and W. facades—seem appropriate to Rev. Ike's ministry.

The approaches to the *George Washington Bridge* (1931; O.H.

Steelwork of the George Washington Bridge in 1936. Le Corbusier called it the 'most beautiful bridge in the world ... the only seat of grace in a disordered city'. (Museum of the City of New York)

Ammann, engineer, and Cass Gilbert) cut across town between 179th and 180th Sts. Like the Brooklyn Bridge, the George Washington Bridge which crosses the Hudson River to Fort Lee, New Jersey, represented a step forward in technology while becoming also an object of beauty. Its 3500-ft span doubled the record for suspension bridges and its openwork steel towers and curving cables inspired Charles Edouard Jenneret (Le Corbusier) to call it 'the only seat of grace in the disordered city'.

History. A trans-Hudson bridge had been contemplated since 1868 when the state of New Jersey authorised one at the S. boundary of Union Township, a move which the State of New York ignored. Conflicting interests and difficulties in financing and engineering kept the agencies involved in constructing a bridge squabbling until the Port of New York Authority was formed in 1921 and brought the project to fruition. The man eventually chosen as chief engineer, Othmar H. Ammann, had emigrated from Switzerland in 1904 expressly to participate in American bridge projects, the most daring and advanced of that time, and had studied the political, financial, and structural problems surrounding previous attempts at a Hudson River crossing; it was he who proposed an automobile crossing, not a railroad bridge, thus cutting costs and anticipating America's romance with the internal combustion engine. The Port Authority funded the bridge ($60 million) by selling bonds, a difficult task in the years before 1929 when stock prices were booming. Groundbreaking ceremonies took place in 1927 and four years later 5000 people came to listen to speeches marking the completion of the project. The bridge was then opened to the public, the first of whom to cross were two boys from the Bronx on roller skates. Between 1958–62 a lower deck was constructed without disturbing traffic on the existing bridge, a feat accomplished by raising 76 steel sections from below, either from the shores or from barges. The lower deck, rather snidely called the Martha Washington Bridge, brought the total cost to $215·8 million and took longer to build than the original structure but increased its capacity 75% to its present level of about 40 million cars yearly (in the eastbound, toll, direction).

On the New York side the huge U-shaped anchorage in Fort Washington Park also serves as a roadway arch. To avoid placing such a bulky object on the New Jersey Palisades, Ammann had workers tunnel into the rock of the cliffs, place eye bar chains in the tunnels (which were large enough to accommodate four trolley tracks), attach the cables to the chains, and fill the tunnels with cement. The New Jersey tower stands 76 ft out in the river, but the New York tower is on land because a deep fissure runs beneath the river. The original plans called for clothing the towers in masonry and Cass Gilbert produced appropriate designs but by 1931 the Port Authority having just bought the Holland Tunnel was unwilling to spend money for cosmetic purposes.

Statistics. The bridge is 4760 ft between anchorages, with decks 115 ft and 212 ft above mean high water. The four steel cables (two on each side of the road) are composed of 26,474 wires apiece making the total length of steel wire in the cables 106,000 miles, almost half the distance to the moon. The towers rise to a height of 604 ft above the water. The bridge contains 113,000 tons of steel, 28,000 tons of cable wire and 200,000 cubic yards of masonry.

At the E. end of the George Washington Bridge, between Fort Washington and Wadsworth Aves, is the *George Washington Bridge Bus Station* (1963; Pier Luigi Nervi and the Port of New York Authority), the concrete wings of its butterfly-shaped roof rising to allow the fumes from the buses to escape from beneath. The station which connects with the Eighth Ave IND subway serves some 11 million commuters yearly. The *Bridge Apartments* (1964; Brown & Guenther) between 178th–179th Sts, Wadsworth and Audubon Aves, represent an early attempt to use the air rights over a highway for residential purposes. Unfortunately the roadway is not completely decked over and the noise, smell, and dirt from this major artery rise to assault the senses of those living above.

At 181st St and Pinehurst Ave a set of steps descends via a footbridge at Riverside Drive and an underpass at the Henry Hudson Parkway to Fort Washington Park along the river. Just under the tower of the bridge stands the **Little Red Lighthouse** (1921) which once warned river traffic of shoals off Jeffrey's Hook. When the navigational lights on the bridge took over that function, the lighthouse went up for auction (1951) but was saved by the pleas of admirers, many of whom had read Hildegarde Hoyt Swift's children's tale 'The Little Red Lighthouse and the Great Gray Bridge'. Today the lighthouse (not open to the public inside) is maintained by the Parks Department. (This section of the park tends to be quiet and isolated.) Return to Pinehurst Ave.

Rather out of the way unless you are traveling by car is YESHIVA UNIVERSITY between 183rd and 187th Sts along Amsterdam Ave (7 blocks E. of Fort Washington Ave) which evolved from the first Jewish parochial school (1886) in the nation and a theological seminary founded 10 years later. The *Main Building* (1928; Charles B. Meyers Assocs) on the S.W. corner of 186th St and Amsterdam Ave is an exotic Near Eastern conglommeration of minarets, towers, arches, domes, and buttresses executed in orange stone, ceramic tile, copper, and brass. The school provides undergraduate and graduate education in the arts, sciences, and Jewish studies, while the associated Rabbi Isaac Elchanan Theological Seminary trains rabbis and cantors.

Two bridges cross the Harlem River nearby: the Washington Bridge (1888) at 181st St and the Alexander Hamilton Bridge (1964) between 178th–179th Sts, which carries the Cross Bronx Expressway into Manhattan. The *WASHINGTON BRIDGE (best seen from the boat tour around the island or the Major Deegan Expressway across the Harlem River or, from Laurel Hill Terrace, a block E. of Amsterdam Ave between 183rd and 188th Sts) is one of the city's most handsome bridges, a double steel arch (each arch 510 ft across) spanning the river and the railroad tracks on its E. bank. The present design is a simplified version of a prize-winning plan submitted to the city by C.C. Schneider. Granite viaducts with masonry arches lead from high bluffs on both the Manhattan and Bronx sides, 151·6 ft above mean high water, making the bridge 16 ft higher than the Brooklyn Bridge and 6 inches higher than the Statue of Liberty. Return to Fort Washington Ave and 181st St.

BENNETT PARK, between 183rd and 185th Sts, Fort Washington and Pinehurst Aves, marks the site of Fort Washington, site of a rear guard action during the evacuation of the American troops from New York City after defeats on Long Island and in Manhattan.

Washington led his troops N. leaving behind a garrison at Fort Washington, a crudely fortified earthwork with five bastions, under the command of Col Robert Magaw. On 16 November 1776 the Americans were attacked by Hessians led by General von Knyphausen who scaled the outworks on Long Hill (the ridge in what is now Fort Tryon Park) from the N. and E. General Cornwallis invaded Manhattan across the Harlem River at what is now about 201st St; the 42nd Highlanders crossed the Harlem more or less where High Bridge now stands, and British troops led by Lord Percy marched up from downtown, while warships bombarded the fort from the Hudson. The defenders of the outworks were killed or pushed back into the fort, which quickly surrendered after it became clear that the American troops were hopelessly outnumbered. The loss of 54 lives and the capture of 2634 of Washington's best-equipped troops was a severe blow to the ragged, inexperienced American army.

Later the land where the fort stood came into the possession of James Gordon Bennett, founder of the New York 'Herald', whose son, an expatriot, gave the park to the city in 1903 in honour of his father. In the small park are paving stones marking the outlines of the fort and a rocky outcropping which is the highest natural elevation in Manhattan, 267·75 ft (some sources say 265·05 ft).

Pinehurst Ave running along the W. side of the park is named after the estate of one C. P. Bucking. Facing the park are the _Hudson View Gardens_ (116 Pinehurst Ave) built in 1925 (George F. Pelham) in the then-popular Collegiate Gothic style.

At 701 Fort Washington Ave, N. of 190th St and just S. of Fort Tryon Park, is _Mother Cabrini High School_, named after Saint Frances Xavier Cabrini (canonised 1946) the first American saint, founder of the Missionary Sisters of the Sacred Heart, known for her many charitable works including her assistance to immigrants. Her remains are buried in the chapel (open 9–4) beneath the altar.

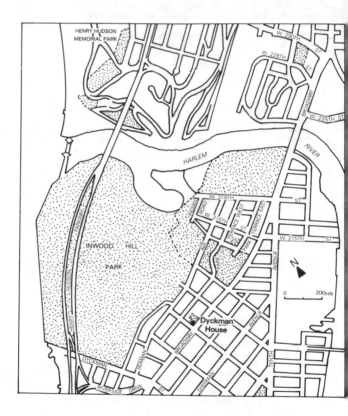

Fort Tryon Park

The 66 acres of ***Fort Tryon Park** contain not only the Cloisters but superb views of the Hudson River, landscaped terraces, lawns and gardens, and the reconstructed remains of the old fort. It is one of the city's best-maintained parks and at weekends one of its most popular.

SUBWAY: IND Eighth Ave express (A train) to 190th St.

BUS: M4 via Madison Ave. Culture Bus Loop I (weekends and holidays) to Stop 10 at 155th St; transfer to M4 or M100 (less convenient; enter the park at the N. end from Dyckman St and Riverside Drive).

CAR: N. on Riverside Drive, past George Washington Bridge to sign indicating park entrance. Cars come into the park beneath a dramatic masonry arch bridging a deep cut in the N.–S. ridge. Free parking, but usually crowded on pleasant weekends.

John D. Rockefeller, Jr, bought the park land—some of it from the C.K.G. Billings estate—in 1909 for $1·7 million and spent an additional $3·6 million to improve it before donating it to the city in 1930. The landscape architect was Frederick Law Olmsted, Jr, son of the designer of Central Park. Visible from Riverside Drive near the car entrance are the gate posts and part of the arcaded drive of the Billings estate.

From the plaza at Fort Washington Ave and Mother Cabrini Blvd a roadway and a footpath enter the park.

The roadway is named after Margaret Cochran Corbin, a 26-year-old Revolutionary War heroine who fought beside her husband John in the Battle of Fort Washington until he was killed; she took over his gun and continued firing until she herself was severely wounded. After the war, still known familiarly as 'Captain Molly', she became a domestic servant remarkable for her unbridled tongue and indifference to the niceties of dress. She died in 1800 and was buried in modest circumstances until the Daughters of the American Revolution had her body exhumed and reinterred in the Post Cemetery at West Point.

The footpath leads past flower gardens and the cafeteria (open all year, 10–5 with slight variations according to the weather) to the **site of the old fort.** Built in the summer of 1776 as an outwork to Fort Washington to the S., it fell on 16 November 1776 to an army of Hessian mercenaries. After the American defeat, the British renamed it Fort Tryon in honour of William Tryon, last British governor of New York (1771–78). From the site of the fort a path leads N. along the side of the hill to the Cloisters, offering beautiful views of the river and the New Jersey Palisades.

**The Cloisters, the only branch of the Metropolitan Museum of Art, is located at the N. end of Fort Tryon Park. Named after the medieval French cloisters recovered from ruined monasteries and incorporated within the building, it attracts visitors for its fine medieval collections—architectural elements, including the Fuentiduena chapel, examples of painting, sculpture, stained glass, furniture, metalwork, and weaving including the Unicorn tapestries—but also for its beautiful natural surroundings.

Open Tues–Sat, 10–4.45; Sun, 1–4.45 (May–Sept, 12–4.45 on Sun). Admission by voluntary contribution; suggested adult donation $4·00. Limited free car parking around museum. No restaurant facilities, but picnicking permitted in park; cafeteria in park S. of museum. Free museum tours Tues, Wed, Thurs at 3. Tel: 923–3700.

History. George Grey Barnard, well-known as a sculptor for his exhibits at two Paris Salons and for his heroic figures adorning the capitol building in Harrisburg, Pennsylvania, assembled the nucleus of the collection, particularly its architectural elements, before World War I. A self-taught medievalist and admirer of what he called 'the patient Gothic chisel', Barnard—also something of an eccentric—lived in France for years, scouring the countryside near abandoned monasteries and churches for examples of medieval art and architecture which he found secreted away unrecognised in barns, farmhouses, cellars, and even pigstys. Among the nearly 700 pieces he brought to New York

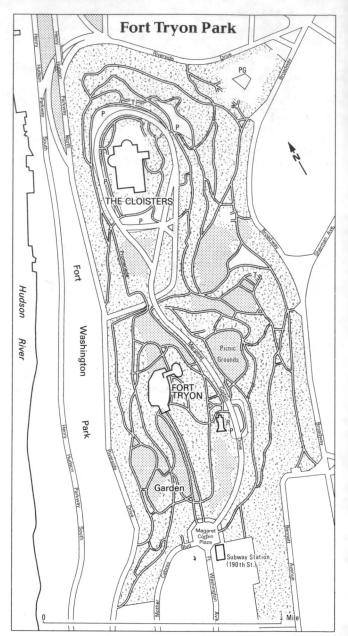

Fort Tryon Park

were large sections of the cloisters of four medieval monasteries—one Romanesque, three Gothic—and such treasures as the tomb effigy of Jean d'Alluye, and a Romanesque wood torso of Christ whose original polychromy was protected by layers of later gilding and gesso during the period when it served as a scarecrow.

In 1914 the Barnard collection was put on display in a building he designed and called the Cloisters, located on Fort Washington Ave. In 1925 with money provided by John D. Rockefeller, Jr, the Metropolitan Museum purchased the collection. Five years later Rockefeller, who had already donated 42 Gothic sculptures from his own collection and whose love of medieval art equalled Barnard's, gave the city the land for Fort Tryon Park, a trade for the city's conveying to him land on the East Side where the Rockefeller Institute now stands. He reserved space at the N. end of the park for the present museum building and to ensure an unspoilt view bought land across the river along the palisades and gave it to New Jersey for a park.

The Building. Although the Cloisters (1934–38; Charles Collens of Allen, Collens & Willis) is not copied from any medieval original, it is developed around medieval architectural elements with an effort to make modern additions as unobtrusive as possible. The exterior is of millstone granite quarried by hand near New London, Connecticut, according to the dimensions of building blocks in Romanesque churches, especially the church at Corneille-de-Conflent near Cuxa. The interior is finished principally in Doria limestone quarried near Genoa and hand-sawn to give the appearance of weathering. The courtyards and ramparts are paved with Belgian blocks taken from New York streets and the grounds are landscaped with trees—especially apple and crabapple trees—intended to recall, where New York's harsher climate permits, the plantings surrounding medieval monasteries. The gardens within the walls are based on medieval precedents known through manuscript illumination, paintings, and tapestries.

The Collection. The museum staff recommends seeing the displays, the first time at least, in chronological order, and the following itinerary follows that plan, beginning with the Romanesque Hall and ending with the Late Gothic Hall and Froville arcade. The accession numbers beginning 25.120 indicate works purchased from the original Barnard collection.

The ROMANESQUE HALL incorporates three portals exemplifying the evolution of the sculptured church doorway in the 12–13C: the 12C French *Entrance Doorway* (25.120.878), the late 12C *Reugny doorway* (34.120.1–120) from the Loire Valley, and a magnificent 13C *Gothic doorway* from Burgundy with figures of two kings sometimes identified as Clovis, first Christian king of France, and his son Clothar (32.147; 40.51. 1,2) known as the Moutiers-Saint-Jean doorway. The wooden *torso of Christ* from the Auvergne (25.120.221) is flanked by 13C Italian figures of the Virgin and St. John (25. 120. 214–215). Also displayed are frescos of a lion and winged dragon (31. 38. a,b) from Spain. In the center of the room is a *cross* (63.12) of walrus-tusk ivory carved with more than 100 figures showing scenes from the Passion of Christ and Old Testament events thought to have prefigured them. The cross is believed to have been made (c. 1180–90) for Samson of Tottington, abbot of the monastery of Bury St. Edmonds in Suffolk, England.

The FUENTIDUEÑA CHAPEL comes from the church of San Martin in Fuentidueña, about 100 miles N. of Madrid, and dates from c. 1160. The apse is decorated with limestone sculpture including

THE CLOISTERS
Main Floor

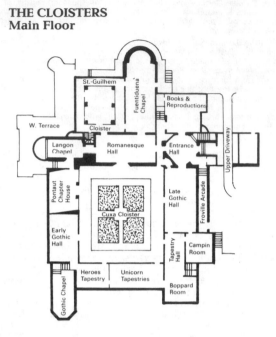

large pier figures of Saint Martin (left) and an Annunciation group (right). The two large capitals supporting the arch also have Biblical themes: the Adoration of the Magi (left) and Daniel in the Lions' Den (right). The *fresco depicting the Virgin and Child with the three magi and the archangels Michael and Gabriel (50.180.a–c) comes from the Pyrenees region, c. 1130–50, and is considered an exceptional work by the Pedret Master, one of the greatest Romanesque fresco painters. Other frescos represent the Temptation of Christ (61.248) and the Healing of the Blind Man and Raising of Lazarus (59.196). In the apse are a fine altar frontal (25.120.256) and a 12C carved wood Crucifix (35.36.2,b). Also displayed are a black calcite baptismal font (47.101.21) from the Meuse River area between France and Belgium and a mid-13C relief (16.43) showing Christ as the Lion of the Tribe of Judah.

The *SAINT-GUILHEM CLOISTER is built around a series of capitals, shafts, and columns (before 1206) from the Benedictine abbey of Saint-Guilhem-le-Désert (founded 804) near Montpellier. The capitals are decorated with various motifs including historical themes, acanthus leaves, and vines; several of the column shafts are handsomely carved. The ten grotesque corbels supporting the ribs and vaults are from the abbey of Notre-Dame-da-la-Grande-Sauve near Bordeaux. Also displayed are a relief from Reims of three clerics (47.101.22), a Florentine marble relief of the Annunciation (60.140); and two marble figures from Lucca (57.63 and 47.101. 79) representing an Old Testament prophet and a figure with a large water flask, perhaps Joseph on the Flight into Egypt. The fountain in the center was once a capital in the church of Saint-Sauveur in Figeac.

Incorporated in the walls of the LANGON CHAPEL is stonework from the 12C church of Notre-Dame-du-Bourg at Langon near Bordeaux. The two large crowned heads on the capital of the column nearest the altar on the right may represent Henry II of England and his wife Eleanor of Aquitaine who visited Langon in 1155. The ciborium (09.92.3) is from the church of Santo Stefano near Rome. The *Romanesque Virgin (47.101.15) is one of the few surviving wood sculptures from an artistically important area of 12C Burgundy; the *Autun angel (47.101.16) comes from the portal of the cathedral of Saint-Lazare at Autun in Burgundy. The massive iron-bound doors (25.120.291,292) are probably from the Pyrenees region and are unusual in size and in their state of preservation.

With the exception of the plaster vaults and the floor, the *CHAPTER HOUSE FROM PONTAUT is an architectural reconstruction, stone by stone and brick by brick, of the chapter house from the former abbey (12C) of Notre-Dame-de-Pontaut in Gascony. It served as a meeting room where the monks gathered to discuss monastery business and in its original setting had a dormitory above it. The windows in the W. wall were never glazed but have hinges for shutters and holes for iron bars. The carvings on capitals and keystone bosses of the vaults include stars, leaf forms, rosettes, birds, and basket patterns.

The *CUXA CLOISTER comes from the Benedictine monastery of Saint-Michel-de-Cuxa (founded 878), one of the most important abbeys in S. France during the 11–12C. The museum has erected 35 capitals, 19 abaci, seven arches, and part of the parapet coping from the original cloister as well as several additional capitals from other parts of the monastery (probably built between 1130 and 1145). The present reconstruction is about half the size of the original and is made according to evidence of fragments, excavations on the site, and notes and drawings from the 18–19C. The simplest and perhaps the earliest capitals are undecorated; more elaborate ones include a capital with rearing lions at the corners and a group with leaf forms and primitively designed men's heads.

The NINE HEROES TAPESTRY ROOM features the major part of a 14C set of French tapestries probably made for Jean, Duc de Berry, one of only two known existing sets from that period (the others are the Apocalypse tapestries in Angers). The Nine Heroes—Hector, Alexander, and Julius Caesar (pagan), David, Joshua, and Judas Maccabeus (Hebrew), and Arthur, Charlemagne, and Godfrey of Bouillon (Christian)—were a popular theme of medieval legend and frequently appear in 14C painting and sculpture. The set, cut up and dispersed over the centuries, has been reassembled from 95 fragments over a period of 20 years and now constitutes about $^2/_3$ of the original work. Around the doorway from the Cuxa Cloister is the largest section, with Joshua and David seated on Gothic thrones and dressed in medieval costumes (47.101.1; 32.130.3; 47.52). Clockwise from here the tapestries depict pagan heroes Hector or Alexander (47.101.2) and Julius Caesar (47.101.3), and King Arthur (32.130.3 and 47.101.4), the only Christian hero recovered.

In the EARLY GOTHIC HALL are statues from the 13–14C as well as architectural elements (ceiling beams and windows) and paintings. Among the sculptures are an early 14C Flemish statue of a Young King (52.82); a small English ivory *Enthroned Virgin and

Child (1979.402); a pair of Angels from Artois (52.33.1–2); a lime-stone *Virgin from the choir screen of Strasbourg cathedral (47.101.11); a Virgin and Child from the Île de France (37.159) and a seated *Virgin and Child (25.120.290) probably from the abbey of St. Denis. Also displayed are a reliquary of St. Margaret (17.190.813) and a painting, Adoration of the Shepherds (25.120.288), attributed to Bartolo di Fredi. A fresco over the entrance depicts Christ as the Man of Sorrows (25.120.241).

From this room a short stairway leads down to the GOTHIC CHAPEL and its tomb sculpture and stained glass. The *Tomb effigy of Jean d'Alluye (25.120.201), showing a young man fully armed, with his hands joined in prayer and his feet resting against a crouching lion, was one of Barnard's major acquisitions. Other important pieces in this room are the *tombs of the Spanish counts of Urgel: Armengol VII (28.95); the double tomb of Armengol X and Dona Dulcia (48.140.1 a–d; 48.140.3–4), and the tomb of Don Alvaro de Cabrera the Younger (48.140.2 a–d). Other sculpture includes an unidentified Spanish saint (47.101.12 a–b), a figure of St. Margaret (47.101.13 a–b), and a French bishop (47.101.14). Above the tomb slab of a monk (30.77.5) are French stained glass panels showing Isaiah and Mary Magdalene (28.107.1,2).

Next in chronological order is the *BONNEFONT CLOISTER, outside the Glass Gallery. The grey-white marble columns and capitals of this cloister come from the former Cistercian abbey of Bonnefont-en-Comminges near Toulouse. Founded in 1136, the convent was used as the burial place of the counts of Comminges until the mid-14C. The cloister, still standing in 1807, had virtually disappeared by 1813, plundered by local inhabitants, but Barnard still recovered some 50 double capitals and a few shafts from scattered locations including a stream where the grandfather of a farmer he questioned had used them to dam up a drinking pond for cattle. The capitals (first half of the 14C) over slender paired columns are carved to represent natural and imaginary plants. The garden in the cloister, from which there are lovely views of the river and George Washington Bridge, was suggested by medieval gardens depicted in paintings.

Next to the Bonnefont Cloister is the *TRIE CLOISTER from the Carmelite convent of Trie-en-Bigorre, S.W. of Toulouse, destroyed except for the church in 1571 by the Huguenots. Barnard purchased most of the present material from a family in Trie. The capitals, probably carved between 1484–90, show scenes from the Bible, saints' legends, and coats of arms of local families and are arranged where possible in chronological order of the scenes depicted, beginning at the N.W. corner near the entrance from the Bonnefont Cloister. In the S. arcade is a fine Nativity capital. The capitals in the N. arcade, against the main part of the building, are from the Bonnefont Cloister. The stations of the cross built into the S. and W. walls are from Lorraine (16C). The fountain in the garden, whose plants were selected from those shown in the Unicorn tapestries, is surmounted by a *cross with Christ between Mary and John on the front and St. Anne with the Child and Virgin among unidentified saints on the back. The octagonal fountainhead has seven apostles and John the Baptist in traceried niches (25.120.872 a,b).

The *Glass Gallery* is named from the 75 panels and roundels of stained glass in the S. windows (15–early 16C), usually found in

THE CLOISTERS
Ground Floor

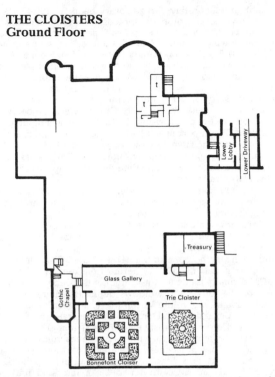

secular buildings but having sacred subjects. Among the sculpture displayed are a female saint holding a book (55.166), perhaps St. Catherine of Alexandria famed for her learning; St. Barbara (50.102.2) holding her attribute, a tower; a Virgin and Child from the Île de France (25.120.213) and two Angels playing musical instruments (47.89.1–2) in a free-standing case near the entrance. Another free-standing case contains reliquaries including a shoe reliquary of boiled leather, probably a case for a metal receptacle holding a foot bone of St. Margaret of Antioch. Beyond the doorway to the Trie Cloister is elaborately carved woodwork (13.138.1) from a house at Abbeville which once opened onto a spiral staircase. Opposite are two stained glass panels showing Wilhelm von Weitingen and his wife Barbara von Zimmern (30.113.5,6).

In the *TREASURY (three rooms) are smaller objects of exceptional quality and value used for religious and state ceremonies. The *Anteroom* contains an intricately carved Crucifixion from Freiburg im Breisgau (61.113), a painted altarpiece with the Nativity and related scenes (49.109) by a follower of Rogier van der Weyden, and 37 carved oak panels (50.147.1–37) with scenes from the lives of Christ and the Virgin.

In the *First Room* are ivory plaques, objects of champlevé enamel including a Eucharistic dove (47.101.34) and cruet (47.101.39), a cup depicting playful monkeys (52.50), covered beakers (50.7. 1a,b and

50.7.2 a,b), an elaborately carved rosary bead (17.190.475) a mitre (53.19.1), reliquaries; bronzes including several aquamanilia—vessels for pouring water over priests' hands—in the shape of a dragon swallowing a man (47.101.51) and a lion with a grotesque handle (47.101.52). Also a reliquary statuette of St. Stephen (55.165), a flabellum (47.101.32) used for keeping flies off the eucharistic vessels, an arm reliquary (47.101.33), chalices including the Bertinus chalice (47.101.30) and Books of Hours including the *Belles Heures of the Duc de Berry (54.1.1). In the center of the room is the *Chalice of Antioch (50.4), made in the early Christian era (probably 4–5C) and said to have been discovered in 1910 by Arabs digging a well near Antioch. The cup, consisting of an undecorated inner silver cup and an outer cup of silver openwork with grapevines and twelve male figures—ten apostles and two figures of Christ—has been the subject of much study and at one time the inner cup was conjectured to be the Holy Grail itself.

In the *Second Room* are embroidered roundels of silk and metal threads on linen depicting saints' legends, an embroidered hanging with scenes from the life of Christ (69.106) and other fine needlework. Paintings include Scenes from the Life of St. Augustine (61.199) and The Miracle of St. Giovanni Gualberto by Lorenzo di Nicolo Gerini (58.135).

Return to the main floor and the BOPPARD ROOM, containing six stained glass panels (37.52.1–6) dating from the second quarter of the 15C. Originally made for the church of the Carmelite convent at Boppard on the Rhine, the windows depict (left to right) a bishop saint trampling a dragon; the Virgin Mary; another bishop saint; St. Catherine of Alexandria; St. Dorothea of Caesarea; and St. Barbara. Also displayed are a *Rhenish Pietà (48.85) from 1350–75 and an alabaster retable from Spain (09.146) with scenes from the lives of St. Martin and St. Thecla. Above the retable is an altarpiece with the Virgin and Child and Sts Barbara, Catherine, Apollonia, and Lawrence (53.21) in the central panel. An imposing brass eagle lectern (68.8) and a 6-ft Paschal candlestick (44.631) stand before the altar.

The **HALL OF THE UNICORN TAPESTRIES contains a superb series of six late medieval tapestries along with fragments of another which depict **The Hunt of the Unicorn (37.80.1–6 and 38.51.1–2). The first five were probably made as a wedding gift for Anne of Brittany on the occasion of her marriage to Louis XII on 8 Jan 1499; the tapestries on the window wall were perhaps added when Anne's daughter was married to Francis I in 1514. The letters A and E (with the E reversed) form a cipher of the first and last letters of Anne's name and of her motto 'A ma vie'. According to medieval legend the unicorn could be caught only by a virgin whose presence made this normally wild, swift, and powerful creature tame and docile, a story interpreted both as an allegory of courtly love and as an allegory of the Incarnation (with the unicorn a symbol of Christ). The subjects of the tapestries include: the Start of the Hunt; the Unicorn at the Fountain; the Unicorn tries to Escape; the Unicorn Defends Himself; the Unicorn is Captured by the Maiden; the Unicorn is Killed and Brought to Louis XII of France and Anne of Brittany; and the Unicorn in Captivity—the last said to symbolise both the Resurrection and the consummation of the marriage. The tapestries are outstanding for the appeal of the subject matter, the naturalistically rendered animals and flowers and human figures, the range of colour, and the profusion of detail: over 100 different species of plants appear of which 85 are recognisable. Woven of wool and silk and dyed with vegetable dyes, they are works of such excellence that it is remarkable that their origin and the names of their designers should be unknown. John D. Rockefeller, Jr, donated them to the Cloisters.

The BURGOS TAPESTRY HALL is named after a Flemish tapestry (c. 1495) of the Nativity taken from the cathedral of Burgos in Spain and currently undergoing restoration. Dominating the hall now is a tapestry of the Glorification of King Charles VIII (41.100.24; 53.80; 53.81) which represents the French monarch during his youth in scenes iconographically related to the Old Testament story of Esther and Ahasuerus. The Armorial Tapestry (60.127.1) bears the arms of John, Lord of Dynham who in 1487 was made a Knight of the Order of the Garter. Also displayed here are a pair of Rhenish ewers (53.20.1–2) a Flemish reliquary bust of a female saint (1976.89); a carved and gilded Spanish *Lamentation (55.8.5); and statues of St. Germain with a Donor (47.101.18) and Saint Roch (25.120.239 a,b).

The SPANISH ROOM, so called because of the 15C painted Spanish ceiling (29.69) has been furnished as a room in a house. Among the furnishings are a bronze chandelier (47.101.50 a,b), a walnut armchair (57.144.2), and the only known 15C iron birdcage (52.121.1). However these pieces serve as a backdrop to the **Annunciation altarpiece by Robert Campin (c. 1425), an early Flemish masterpiece. The altarpiece has three panels: two kneeling donors on the left, the Annunciation, and St. Joseph in his workshop on the right. Campin is thought of as an early practitioner of realism in Flemish panel painting and as the first to place the mysteries of religion, such as the Annunciation, in bourgeois settings. Also exhibited here are two coloured and gilded paintings of the Lamentation and Crucifixion (61.100.1,2) by a Sienese artist working in Avignon (c. 1340–50).

The FROVILLE ARCADE, just outside the Late Gothic Hall, is built around nine pointed arches from the 15C Benedictine priory of Froville. The arches, grouped in threes and separated by buttresses as they were in their original setting, are typical of 14–15C cloisters which depended for effect on their proportions rather than on great skill in decoration or stonecutting as did earlier Gothic and Romanesque arcades.

From the Cloisters paths lead N. and E. to Broadway and Dyckman St. From this intersection walk N. along Broadway (three blocks) to **Dyckman House** (1783; DL) at the N.W. corner of 204th St (4881 Broadway), the only Dutch Colonial farmhouse remaining on Manhattan.

Open Tues–Sun, 1–5. Admission free. For information tel: the Morris-Jumel mansion, WA3–8008. To reach Dyckman House from midtown, take the IND Eighth Ave express (A train) to 207th St and Broadway; or the IRT Broadway–7th Ave local (train 1) to Dyckman St and walk N. three blocks. By bus, take the M104 to 125th St, transfer to the M5 to 168th St, transfer to M100, which goes past Dyckman House.

Situated in a neighbourhood of apartments, supermarkets, and shops providing services to the local populace, the house remains only through the determination of two Dyckman descendants who bought it in 1915, restored it, furnished it with family heirlooms, and donated it to the city, thereby rescuing it from the ambitions of an apartment developer.

The present house, once the center of the 300-acre Dyckman farm reaching to the Harlem River, was built to replace an earlier Dyckman homestead destroyed by the British during the Revolutionary war and is believed to contain materials from the original house. Constructed of brick and wood on a fieldstone foundation, the building has the overhanging eaves and porch typical of the Dutch Colonial style.

The Dyckman family was one of early Manhattan's most prominent, its first representative one Jan Dyckman who arrived from Germany via Holland in 1661. A book-keeper and woodcutter, Dyckman went into partnership with Jan Nagel (after whom nearby Nagel St is named) and began buying land for a farm. The two first acquired 74 acres which they leased in 1677 to tenant farmers for two hens a year for seven years, provided the tenant plant 50 fruit trees a year, a policy which eventually resulted in extensive peach, apple, and cherry orchards. Eventually the Dyckman farm became the largest in Manhattan and remained active for 200 years, until 1868.

Inside, the house is furnished with period furniture including clothing, toys, and cooking implements which suggest the manner of life in the 18C. Behind the house is a reconstructed smokehouse and a small military shed used by the British during the Revolutionary War as well as a slightly overgrown garden.

Like Dyckman and Nagel Sts, many of the place names in this neighbourhood commemorate early landowners. Vermilyea Ave is a corruption of the name of Isaac Vermeille who settled nearby in 1663. Post Ave is named after a family whose early settlers called themselves Postmael. John Seaman, a captain who arrived in 1630 and 20 years later owned 12,000 acres on Long Island, gave his name to Seaman Ave near which his descendants lived. Sherman Ave is named not after the famous Civil War general but after a humble family who lived along a little waterway called Shermans Creek, an indentation in the bank of the Harlem River; the Shermans seem to have settled along the creek in about 1807 and in 1815 occupied a fisherman's shack at the bottom of Fort George Hill. Sickeles St honours the family of that name whose American progenitor, Zacharias Sickels, followed Peter Stuyvesant here from Curacao in 1655. Arden St recalls Jacob Arden, patriot and butcher, whose land lay between 170th and 177th Sts. Arden probably died fighting in the Revolutionary war. The Francis Thayer who gave his name to Thayer St was an attorney active in local and civic affairs around 1911 when the street was mapped. Ellwood St was named also in 1911, but no one knows the honoree. When the street was being cut and graded, however, workers found the remains of crude military huts, presumably from Hessian soldiers during the Revolutionary War, a belief based on the fact that the British and their allies occupied this part of New York for most of the War but no British uniform buttons were found among the artifacts uncovered. Public School 52 which once stood on Academy St was razed in 1957. The namesakes of little Beak and Cumming Sts, both named in 1925, were probably early landowners.

As the date of these street names suggests, the Inwood section of Manhattan was developed relatively late. Many of its apartment buildings show the materials, brickwork patterns, typical setbacks, and window forms of the Art Deco architecture of the 1930s.

Two blocks N. of Dyckman House, Isham St crosses Broadway. The street is named after a prominent family who owned the surrounding land and in 1912 gave 20 acres to the city for ISHAM PARK. The main part of the park adjoins Inwood Hill Park and is indistinguishable from it, while the smaller sections to the E. lie S. of 214th St. The Isham residence, famous for its hospitality, once stood at the top of the terraced hill E. of Park Terrace West. (To get there, walk a block W. of Broadway along Isham St; turn right or N. onto

Park Terrace West and walk up the hill into the small park on the right side of the road.)

Park Terrace West reaches a dead-end at 218th St. To the N. lie the Columbia University athletic fields, including *Baker Field* the football stadium (a 54-year-old structure now undergoing major restoration), tennis courts, the field house, and the boat house (1930; Polyhemus & Coffin) which faces a small lagoon in the Harlem River. INDIAN ROAD, formerly Isham Ave, is a small street intersecting 218th St at its W. end along the border of the large park. It was renamed in 1911 when evidence of an Indian settlement was uncovered in the park lowlands. The Indians were Weequaesgeeks, a tribe that also inhabited much of what is now Westchester County, and the settlement was called 'Shora-Kap-Kok' (between the hills), a name reflected in modern Kappock St in the nearby Bronx. At the W. end of the ball fields near the beginning of the woods is a boulder in the pathway bearing a plaque marking the site as the place where Peter Minuit bought Manhattan Island from the Indians for $24, although historians generally believe that the famous transaction took place downtown in the vicinity of the Dutch settlements around the Battery.

The major part of the park is INWOOD HILL PARK, 196 acres stretching W. to the Hudson River, N. to the Harlem River, and S. to Dyckman St, Manhattan's only true wilderness, with a wide variety of trees and wild flowers, steep rocky slopes (which saved the park from development), and glacial potholes and caves where Indians once dwelt. Before the 1930s the park remained in its pristine state; when the Henry Hudson Parkway, which unfortunately cuts through part of the park, was developed some of the park was landscaped, but nowadays it is overgrown and wild again. The park is quite empty and isolated during the week, and it is probably wiser to use it on weekends when nearby residents are out in force.

Beyond the grassy fields of the park flows the HARLEM RIVER, where the Columbia boat crews train and race. It was not navigable to the Hudson River until 1895 when a channel was cut through a bulbous promontory that formerly extended N. of where Baker Field and Ninth Ave are presently located. Before then a narrow stream, Spuyten Duyvil Creek, flowed in a looping curve marked by the present boundary of Manhattan.

Some historians believe that Henry Hudson first anchored in Spuyten Duyvil Creek and was there received by a party of friendly Indians. Although no one really knows the origin of the creek's strange name, the most popular explanation is that advanced by Washington Irving in his 'Knickerbocker's History of New York': Anthony Van Corlaer, sent by Peter Stuyvesant to warn the settlers north of the creek of an imminent British attack, reached the waterway in the midst of such a storm that he could find no one to ferry him across. Emboldened by a few swigs from his flask, Van Corlaer swore he would swim across 'en spijt den Duyvil' (in spite of the Devil), threw himself into the wild waters, and drowned.

When the ship channel (400 ft wide and 15 ft deep) was finished, Spuyten Duyvil Creek was filled, making the area now known as Marble Hill physically a part of the Bronx; the residents petitioned successfully to remain politically a part of Manhattan.

To the W. can be seen the curve of the *Henry Hudson Bridge* (1936; D. Steinman), spanning the Harlem River with a fixed steel arch 2000 ft long and at its highest point 142.5 ft above the river. The bridge is part of the West Side Improvement project, conceived and brought to fruition by Robert Moses during the 1930s, and joins two sections of the Henry Hudson Parkway which links the West Side Highway with the Saw Mill Parkway to the N. The bridge was built originally as a single deck, four-lane structure, because the bankers underwriting the project would only authorise $3·1 million in bonds, unable to believe that commuters would choose a toll bridge when the nearby bridge crossing the Harlem River at Broadway was free. The bridge quickly proved itself financially viable, and the arches and steelwork were reinforced and the second deck added. The original structure (span 800 ft) opened on 12 December 1936.

To visit MARBLE HILL, a quiet neighbourhood whose apartment houses are relieved by occasional old frame buildings, take the M100 bus via Broadway across the Harlem River to 225th St. This 52-acre piece of Manhattan now geographically indistinguishable from the Bronx was given its name at the end of the 19C because of its terrain and its former quarries, although, as its street names indicate, it was settled early by the Dutch.

Jacobus St got its name from Jacobus Dyckman who ran a tavern until 1769; Teunissen Place recalls Tobias Teunissen who immigrated in 1636 and was killed in an Indian raid in 1655 during which more than a hundred settlers were taken captive. More fortunate was Adraien Van der Donck, the city's first lawyer, who in 1646 received a land grant that reached from Spuyten Duyvil to Yonkers. He left the area with several indications of his presence: Adrian St in Marble Hill is named after him and Leyden St honours his alma mater. Even the name Yonkers is a corruption of his title 'jonkheer' (young gentleman).

Today Marble Hill still is occasionally called Kingsbridge as is the surrounding part of the Bronx because a bridge named after William of Orange (King William III) crossed the Harlem River at its shallowest point near present 230th St and Broadway.

The Philipse family, landed Westchester aristocrats, received the franchise from the king (1693) and established one of the first toll bridges in America; 20 years later they replaced it with a wider span which endured until 1917 when traffic to the port during World War I made it obsolete. In 1758 irate citizens built a competing Free Bridge (also known as Dyckman's Bridge or Farmer's Bridge) at 225th St and Broadway which remained until 1911. Before its construction outlying farmers had had to pay the Philipses between six and fifteen pounds sterling yearly to bring their produce into city markets, annoying under normal circumstances but outrageous during the French and Indian war when the British requisitioned the crops and the farmers, generally apolitical, found themselves paying tolls to supply the British army. John Palmer began agitating for a free bridge, showing a lack of humility which aroused the influential Frederick Philipse to engineer his draft into the British army. Palmer paid a mercenary to fight for him; Philipse had him drafted again. Palmer hired another mercenary and got the bridge finished. One can imagine Palmer's jubilation when the fledgling American government confiscated the Philipse lands after the Revolution and made the bridge toll-free.

32 Roosevelt Island

ROOSEVELT ISLAND TRAM: Station at Second Ave and 60th St Open from 6 a.m. until 2 a.m.; weekends until 3.30 a.m. Tram leaves every 15 minutes on the quarter hour. Fare is one subway token. Tokens not for sale at tram station.

SUBWAY AND BUS: IND Sixth or Eighth Ave (train F or E) or Broadway (N train) to Queens Plaza. Transfer to Q102 bus to the island.

CAR: Take the upper level of the Queensboro Bridge (59th St) to

Queens; take a right turn on 21st St and a left turn on 36th Ave to the toll-free blue bridge. Parking at Motorgate Garage on the island. Car traffic restricted on Roosevelt Island but minibus service available from Motorgate.

Roosevelt Island, a $2^1/2$ mile strip of land in the East River, long used as a place of exile for madmen, criminals, and incurables, has recently emerged as 'Instant City', a planned community of some 5500 people of mixed economic background. Only 300 yards offshore, the island is quiet and remote in feeling, untouched by the frantic energy of Manhattan to which it belongs politically. In its midsection rise the towers of the new town where housing, schools, transport, even rubbish removal were all planned by urban strategists Down its midline runs a modern Main Street and around the shoreline is a promenade, planned for its beautiful views and ornamented with occasional pieces of sculpture. At the ends of the island, however, remain monuments of older, less orderly times—a decaying smallpox hospital, a lighthouse built by a lunatic.

History. In 1637 Dutch governor Wouter van Twiller bought the island from the Indians; because the Dutch used it to pasture swine, they called it Varcken (Hog) Island, a name the English corrupted to Perkins Island. The Blackwell family owned and farmed it from the late 1600s until 1828 when the city bought it for penal uses, a purpose for which according to one 19C clergyman, J.F. Richmond, it was more than suitable: 'separated on either side from the great world by a deep crystal current, [it] appears to have been divinely arranged as a home for the unfortunate and suffering, a place of quiet reformatory meditation for the vicious.' By the end of the 19C, its institutions included a workhouse, an almshouse, a madhouse, and the penitentiary where 'Boss' Tweed served time. By 1921 when its name was changed from Blackwells Island to Welfare Island, the place was notorious, the workhouse overcrowded and obsolete, the prison ruled by a bunch of hard core inmates who dealt in narcotics and lived well on the profits. In 1934 a new commissioner of corrections, Austin H. McCormick, raided the place and cleaned it up. The following year, when the Riker's Island Penitentiary opened, Welfare Island became a sanctuary for the aged and the ill, with a hospital for chronic diseases, a New York City Home for Dependents, a cancer hospital, and a charity hospital.

In the boom years of the late 1960s, city planners unwilling to have so much valuable real estate so under-used, began plans for redevelopment, renaming the island Roosevelt Island to polish its image (1973) and opening apartments for rental in 1975. Originally the master plan called for two 'towns' separated by a park with a combined population of 18,000, a number deemed adequate for supporting restaurants, stores, and cultural activities. With construction delays, rampant inflation, and the fiscal collapse of the Urban Development Corporation, the quasi-public agency undertaking development of the island, only Southtown has been built (2138 apartments).

The **Roosevelt Island Tramway** (1976; station by Prentice & Chan, Ohlhausen) crosses the river at 16 m.p.h., controlled automatically from the Roosevelt Island terminal, though the cabin attendant can override the automatic system. The tram has a rescue car with its own drive system and an emergency generator so that passengers won't dangle mid-river during a power failure. Despite these precautions, however, the Swiss-made tram which cost $7 million has suffered maintenance delays and breakdowns; in Dec 1980 a hauling cable fell on Second Ave snarling traffic, and later residents were infuriated when a film company leased the tram to make a thriller. Normally the ride takes three and a half minutes.

From the cablecar station, walk S. along the promenade. The low modern building near the terminal is a *Sports Park* (1977; Prentice & Chan, Ohlhausen), with a gymnasium and other facilities used by the island's schools. South of it is the *Goldwater Memorial Hospital* (1939; Isadore Rosenfield, senior architect of the New York Department of Hospitals; Butler & Kohn; York & Sawyer; addition, 1971), originally called the Welfare Hospital for Chronic Diseases. It has a central north–south corridor with short projecting wings to give patients, most of them chronically ill, maximal sunshine and river views. The *remains of the old City Hospital* (1859), originally called Island Hospital, and then Charity Hospital, stand S. of the Goldwater building, a remnant of the island's early institutional history. Built of granite quarried on the island by convicts, the hospital was first used for inmates of the penitentiary and later for the city's indigent sick. South and east of it are the *remains of the Strecker Memorial Laboratory* (1892; Withers & Dickson; DL). Romanesque Revival in style, the laboratory was the gift of a daughter of an otherwise unknown Mr Strecker; it housed on the first floor an autopsy room and a mortuary as well as a laboratory for the examination of specimens and on the second floor had facilities for pathological and bacteriological research.

Further S. still are the eerie ruins of the old *Smallpox Hospital* (1856; James Renwick, Jr; S. Wing added 1904; York & Sawyer; N. Wing added 1905; Renwick, Aspinwall & Owen; DL). The hospital replaced a group of wooden shacks on the riverbanks where smallpox sufferers were formerly quarantined. Although vaccination was common by the mid-19C, immigrants still brought the disease to New York and as late as 1871 it reached epidemic proportions. In 1886 a new hospital for quarantining smallpox victims was built on North Brother Island, lessening the danger of spreading the disease to the Blackwell's Island population which numbered some 7000 by the end of the century, and the hospital was converted to a nurses' home. When Blackwell's Island became Welfare Island (1921), many of the old institutional buildings were obsolete including the City Hospital whose functions were moved eventually (1950s) to new buildings in Queens. Both the hospital building and the nurses' residence (the former Smallpox Hospital) were abandoned and have deteriorated.

Proposed for the S. end of the island is *Landmark Park* which would incorporate these old buildings and include a memorial to Franklin Delano Roosevelt. At the S. tip of the island is the *Delacorte Fountain* (1969; Pomerance & Breines), given by George T. Delacorte, founder of Dell Publishing and donor of the Shakespeare Theater and musical clock in Central Park. The ill-fated geyser with a 250-ft plume has been smashed by a hit-and-run tugboat and has more than once been clogged by the polluted waters of the East River, sucking into its intake system all kinds of flotsam, including, according to Delacorte, 11 drowned bodies.

Return along the promenade to the tram station and either continue walking N. or take one of the free electric minibuses along Main St. North of the station, just before the main residential area, is the *Blackwell Farmhouse* (1796–1804; DL), a simple, clapboard country house used as headquarters of the Roosevelt Island Historical Society.

The society frequently offers weekend tours of the island's landmarks. Call 838–3681.

The Blackwell family came to the island through marriage. Captain

John Manning, the British officer who botched the defence of the fort at the Battery and then formally surrendered New York to the Dutch in 1673, an interlude that lasted from August 1673 to November 1674, retired in humiliation to the privacy of his island which he had bought five years earlier. His stepdaughter married Robert Blackwell and the house, built later for James Blackwell, remained in the family until the city bought the island for the penitentiary when it became the home of the warden.

On the right side of Main St are the *Eastwood Apartments* (1976; Sert, Jackson & Assocs), built for low and middle income tenants. The U-shaped buildings face industrial Long Island City in Queens and the smokestacks of a Consolidated Ediston generator, Big Allis, named for the Allis Chalmers company which built it. The richer tenants in the *Rivercross Apartments* (1975; Johansen & Bhavnani) across Main St to the W. look out on Manhattan's gilded East Side. Schools are divided by grades and distributed through different apartment buildings, with grades seven and eight in Rivercross. To the N. of this cooperative apartment are two more luxury complexes, *Island House* (1975; Johansen & Bhavnani) with a glassed-in swimming pool facing the river, and *Westview* (1976; Sert, Jackson & Assocs).

Between these last two is the CHAPEL OF THE GOOD SHEPHERD (1889; Frederick Clarke Withers; restored 1976, Giorgio Cavaglieri; DL), now used as a community center. The church bell (1888) stands on the plaza. Walk toward the East River through the apartment complex to the West Promenade, whose 3·6 mile loop around the island attracts joggers and strollers. Continue past Westview, dark brick with bright-red panels, and return to the main street. The modernistic parking garage, *Motorgate* (1974; Kallmann & McKinnell) holds a thousand cars and can be expanded to accommodate another 1500.

Keep walking N. past the *AVAC Building* (1975; Kallmann & McKinnell), an acronym for Automated Vacuum Collection, where garbage from the apartments arrives through underground tubes to be separated, shredded or compacted, packed into containers and shipped off the island by the Department of Sanitation.

Two more landmarks and a hospital stand at the N. end of the island. The OCTAGON TOWER, originally part of the New York City Lunatic Asylum (1839; Alexander Jackson Davis; DL) once stood as a central rotunda (dome added c. 1880; Joseph M. Dunn) at the intersection of two low granite wings demolished in 1970.

The asylum was founded to fill a desperate need for accommodating the insane who, up until then, were housed in overcrowded wards at Bellevue Hospital. Their early treatment in the asylum could hardly have been enlightened since they were supervised by inmates from the penitentiary. Physical activity and labour were considered therapeutic and so patients were put to work in vegetable gardens or building sea walls to reclaim land. At the end of the 19C the asylum had 10 wooden pavilions, a laundry and bath house (patients were bathed once a week), an Amusement Hall with a stage and piano, and a Catholic church. Later the asylum became Metropolitan Hospital for charity patients.

Today only the tower is left, along with hopes to restore it as the center of proposed Octagon Park.

Continue N. past the *Bird S. Coler Hospital* (1952), a city hospital for the chronically ill. At the very N. tip of the island is a rock lighthouse (1872; James Renwick, Jr; DL), with a curious inscription:

> This is the work
> Was done by
> John McCarthy
> Who built the light
> House from the bottom to the
> Top all ye who do pass by may
> Pray for his soul when he dies.

Local legend asserts that the warden of the asylum allowed McCarthy, a patient there, to build a small fort on the point of land where the lighthouse stands because he feared invasion by the British. When the lighthouse was planned, McCarthy was persuaded to demolish the fort and build the lighthouse in its place. The structure is 50 ft high and is built of granite (actually grey gneiss) quarried on the island, predominantly by convicts, and used for most of the older institutional buildings of the period.

II BOROUGH OF THE BRONX /
BRONX COUNTY

Home of the Bronx cheer (or raspberry), the Bronx Zoo, the Bronx Bombers (or New York Yankees), the Bronx has suffered a certain amount of ignominy at the hands of rhymester Ogden Nash. In 1931 he wrote, 'The Bronx? No thonx.' Later he changed his mind, 'The Bronx? God bless them.'

The Bronx is the only borough of New York City attached to the mainland of N. America and even so it is surrounded on three sides by water: the Hudson River on the W., the Harlem and East Rivers on the S., and Long Island Sound on the E. Its area of 43·1 square miles and population of 1,169,115 (a decrease of 20% in the last decade) make it the second smallest borough in both categories.

The eastern sector is largely flat land, some of it originally salt marsh, sliced into long peninsulas by inlets and tidal rivers. Tons of garbage, euphemistically known as landfill, have been dumped onto the marshes since World War II and the areas along Eastchester Bay including Throgs Neck, parts of Baychester, and Co-Op City are now densely populated residential areas. West of the flatlands are three north–south ridges which give the middle and western sections of the borough their hilly terrain. The westernmost runs through the Riverdale area near the Hudson and west of Broadway, with Broadway following the lowland valley. The second ridge crosses Van Cortlandt Park and runs S. to the Macombs Dam Bridge area with the Grand Concourse laid out along its spine. The third and lowest proceeds through the Bronx River Park and Crotona Park, falling away to the flatlands along the East River.

Most of the Bronx is residential, developed with apartment houses which range from one-time luxury Art Deco buildings along the Grand Concourse and the finely kept high rises overlooking the Hudson River to the big, ugly towers of Co-Op City and the crumbling five-story walk-ups of Crotona Park. A small part of the borough is industrial, mainly the strip along the East River which includes Mott Haven, Port Morris, and Hunts Point.

The Bronx is fortunate in having beautiful parks, 5861 acres of them or about 23% of its total area, most acquired by the city fathers in the years between 1880–1900. A plan to link them by wide, tree-lined boulevards has resulted in two attractive parkways, the Mosholu Parkway and the Bronx-Pelham Parkway. Unfortunately the city's straitened finances and changing government priorities have brought hardship to the parks, along with practically everything else in the outer boroughs, and they are deteriorating, though a $10–20 million plan to rehabilitate Van Cortlandt Park was proposed in 1981.

Long considered the stronghold of working class families—Jews, Italians, Irish, and others who had improved their lot sufficiently to escape the slums of the Lower East Side—the Bronx today shelters a population that is increasingly poor and mostly non-white and now has appalling slums of its own. Areas of the south, central and western sectors whose scarred, burned, and abandoned buildings

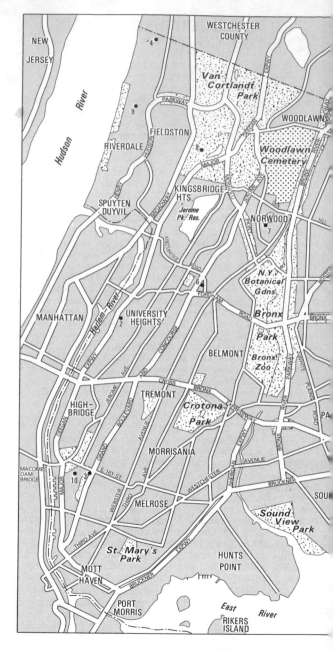

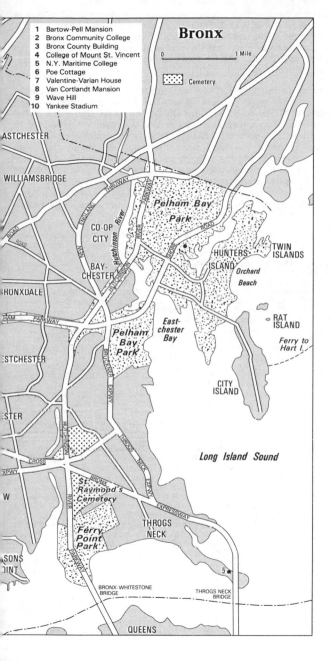

Bronx

1 Bartow-Pell Mansion
2 Bronx Community College
3 Bronx County Building
4 College of Mount St. Vincent
5 N.Y. Maritime College
6 Poe Cottage
7 Valentine-Varian House
8 Van Cortlandt Mansion
9 Wave Hill
10 Yankee Stadium

0 _____ 1 Mile

Cemetery

ASTCHESTER

WILLIAMSBRIDGE

THRUWAY

Pelham Bay Park

CO-OP
CITY

ENGLAND

MEN

Hutchinson River

RIVER

PARKWAY

BAY-
CHESTER

HUNTERS
ISLAND

TWIN
ISLANDS

SHORE ROAD

Orchard Beach

HUNXDALE

ROAD

ROAD

HAM PARKWAY

Pelham Bay Park

East-chester Bay

RAT
ISLAND

Ferry to
Hart I.

ESTCHESTER

BRUCKNER EXPWY

CITY
ISLAND

ESTER

HUTCHINSON

Long Island Sound

CROSS
XPWY

THROGS NECK FERRY

RIVER

BRONX
*St.
Raymond's
Cemetery*

W

EXPRESSWAY

THROGS
NECK

*Ferry
Point
Park*

PARKWAY

SONS
OINT

BRONX-WHITESTONE
BRIDGE

THROGS NECK
BRIDGE

5

QUEENS

rise from rubble-filled lots have evoked comparisons with Dresden at the end of World War II. The devastation which accelerated alarmingly in the 1970s still continues, though city officials and neighbourhood activists believe that the rate is slowing, if only because the downturn in the national economy makes moving elsewhere increasingly difficult.

Touring in the Bronx. There are sights in the Bronx that should appeal to the most hesitant visitor. The Bronx Zoo and New York Botanical Garden next to it are among the finest attractions in the city and are clean, well-kept, and secure; they can be reached easily by express bus, commuter train, or subway from midtown. For other sights a car is desirable since distances are great and some neighbourhoods are not safe for pedestrians. Riverdale offers fine views of the Hudson River, an assortment of educational institutions and examples of upper class domestic architecture including Wave Hill. Historic houses stand in Van Cortlandt Park and Pelham Park, near which is City Island, still untouched by the changes sweeping the rest of the borough.

History. In 1639 the Dutch West India Co. purchased from the Indians the land that now constitutes the Bronx, and in 1641 Jonas Bronck, a Dane who arrived in the New World by way of Amsterdam, purchased 500 acres along the river which soon was known as the Broncks' River. The borough today takes its name from the river. A few years later other early settlers arrived in the area, including religious dissenter Anne Hutchinson who, with her children and a band of followers, settled on the shores of what is now Pelham Bay in 1644, expelled as unfit for society by the theocrats of the Massachusetts Bay colony because of her liberal religious views and her quick tongue. John Throgmorton, an Anabaptist, arrived in the same year with 35 families who shared his religious views, unfortunately during a period of Indian uprisings. Indians attacked both colonies and though some of Throgmorton's followers were able to escape, Anne Hutchinson's colony was annihilated except for one of her daughters, Susannah, taken hostage by the Indians. After a two-year stay with her captors, she was returned, unwillingly, when the Dutch and the Indians made a treaty to settle their differences. The place names Throgs Neck and the Hutchinson River remain as evidence of these early sojourners.
Other British settlers including Thomas Pell and the Morris brothers arrived but endured difficulties with both the Dutch and the Indians and it was not until 1664 when the British took over New York that settlement of the Bronx began in earnest. From the end of the Revolution until the mid-19C, a rather remarkable span of three centuries, the Bronx remained quietly rural, its land divided between humble farmers and large landowners whose style of life imitated that of the English landed gentry. Villages evolved along the post roads to Albany and Boston—Mott Haven, Kingsbridge, Morrisania, East Chester, Pelham—later to become the commercial centers of borough neighbourhoods. The railroads following the general course of the roads also encouraged development in both the E. and W. sectors of the borough, and Riverdale became a fashionable country retreat for the wealthy, accessible not only by rail but also by steamboat. In the half century from 1790–1840, the population of the Bronx increased by less than 4000.
Thereafter, however, advances in transportation and technology resulted in the influx of a population that ended with the Depression in the early 1930s and created the Bronx so fondly remembered by those who grew up there in the first half of this century. The first newcomers to the territory were the Irish, who started to arrive in the 1840s to labour on the railroads and on the Croton Aqueduct. After 1848 Germans followed, most remaining farmers as they had been in their native land. The two decades from 1840–60 saw the population quadruple, from 5346 to 23,593. In 1888 the Third Ave Elevated Railway reached the hinterland of 169th St and a flood of newcomers began settling near it—more Irish and Germans, Jews, Italians, Poles, and Greeks—attracted to the Bronx because it seemed almost rural.
Politically the Bronx joined New York in two sections: first the western towns of Kingsbridge, West Farms, and Morrisania (1874), then (1894) the eastern

towns of Eastchester, Westchester, and part of Pelham voted to become part of the city. According to the provisions of the Greater New York charter in 1898, these two separately annexed areas officially became the borough of the Bronx, then with a population of 200,507.

The golden age of the Bronx lasted from about 1920 to the early 1950s. For these decades it was an area divided into tightly knit neighbourhoods, usually dominated by one ethnic group, which became the center of social life. City services—education, transportation, parks—made life comfortable and attractive. The arrival of the automobile, however, and the construction of superhighways, enabled the population, or at least the upwardly mobile part of it, a greater choice of where to live and the lure of Westchester and Long Island attracted many borough residents. Public transportation began to deteriorate; the last trolley ceased running in 1948. Jobs became less plentiful. As middle class whites left, areas of the S. and W. were taken over by a population increasingly dependent on public services that the city has been increasingly unwilling or unable to provide, setting in motion the cycle of urban blight that became so devastating in the 1970s.

33 The South Bronx

The **South Bronx** reaches geographically from the Harlem River on the W. to about White Plains Rd on the E., from the East River to a N. boundary presently put at Fordham Rd. It includes the old neighbourhoods of Mott Haven, Port Morris, Melrose, Morrisania, Hunts Point, and Soundview as well as Highbridge and University Heights near the Harlem River. The name, South Bronx, evokes images of looted, burned, abandoned housing standing in bleak open lots whose soil is invisible beneath tons of rubble, of street crime, of a populace whose feebler or more restrained members huddle in half-vacant, half-destroyed tenements while vandals from their own neighbourhoods strip vulnerable buildings or apartments of plumbing, wiring, and any kind of fixture that will bring money on a flourishing market. It has been called 'Fort Apache', and it connotes the end of the line. Despite the general accuracy of this picture, however, the South Bronx is not an area of uniform devastation; here and there are enclaves of hope—stable neighbourhoods, good new housing, rehabilitated older buildings whose renovation was undertaken by committed developers or local organisers, cultural organisations and religious groups active in promoting community pride.

Touring. Significant distances and the high crime rate of devastated neighbourhoods make a car desirable. Get a borough map as streets are laid out irregularly. The Urban Planning Department of Hunter College offers occasional bus tours of the Bronx as well as other parts of the city; well-informed guides focus on major issues of urban history and planning. Tel: 570–5594.

Mott Haven in the S.W. corner of the Bronx has been industrial since Jordan Mott, inventor of a cast-iron, coal-burning stove, built a factory (1828) on the Harlem River at 134th St. Mott purchased the land from Gouverneur Morris, scion of the aristocratic and powerful family (see p491). When asked if he would mind if the land, formerly part of Morrisania, were renamed Mott Haven, Morris allegedly snapped, 'I don't care what he calls it; while he is about it, he might as well change the name of the Harlem and call it the Jordan.' The Mott Iron Works flourished until 1906, attracting successive waves of immigrants, first Irish and German, to live in the tenements rapidly being built for them. In 1969 the area along Alexander Ave between

E. 137th–141st Sts was declared a historic district, cited for its handsome row housing (1870s and 1880s) and for two churches: *St. Jerome's Roman Catholic Church* (1898; Dehli & Howard) on Alexander Ave between E. 137th–138th Sts and the *Tercera Iglesia Bautista* (Third Baptist Church), originally the Alexander Ave Baptist Church (1902; Ward & Davis). Other important buildings on Alexander Ave include the *40th Precinct Police Station* (1924; Thomas E. O'Brien) between 138th–139th Sts and the *Mott Haven Branch of the New York Public Library* (1905; Babb, Cook & Willard) between 140th–141st Sts, which resembles a humble version of Andrew Carnegie's mansion and was designed by the same architects.

Indicative of new philosophies in renewal housing are the *Plaza Borinquen townhouses* on several sites (e.g., E. 137th St between Willis Ave and Brown Pl.), three-story red block houses (1974; Ciardullo-Ehmann), designed to keep residents close to the streets (as opposed to shutting them up in high towers surrounded with sterile open space).

Nearby is ST. ANN'S CHURCH (Protestant Episcopal) and grave-yard, 295 St. Ann's Ave between 139th–141st Sts; a modest field-stone church (1841; DL), the oldest in the Bronx. The hummocky churchyard of hard-packed dirt now denuded of grass, holds the graves of various members of the Morris family including Gouverneur Morris II, who sold Mott Haven to Jordan Mott. A railroad pioneer, a genius in the eyes of his acquaintances, and something of a rake, Morris built the little church to honour his mother, Anne Carey Randolph Morris, said to be a descendant of the Indian princess Pochahantas.

Hilly ST. MARY'S PARK, bounded by St. Ann's and Jackson Aves, St. Mary's and E. 149th Sts, takes its name from a modest Gothic style wooden Episcopal church that stood on Alexander Ave near 142nd St until 1959. The park, now in a neighbourhood populated largely by Puerto Ricans, has long served the children of working class families. Once the hill was called Janes' Hill after Adrian Janes whose iron works stood nearby. The amalgamated Janes, Kirtland & Co. Iron Works, formerly on Westchester Ave between Brook and St. Ann's Aves produced architectural ironwork, most notably (1863) the 8·9 million-lb dome of the U.S. Capitol Building in Washington, D.C.

ST. ANSELM'S CHURCH (Roman Catholic) at 673 Tinton Ave between E. 152nd St and Westchester Ave (1918; Gustave Steinback), an imposing neo-Byzantine brick church, was established by the Benedictine Order who founded the parish in 1892 and began the building in 1915. Long one of the leading parishes in the Bronx, St. Anselm's served German, Italian, and Irish working class families. After World War II blacks, Puerto Ricans and other Hispanic groups began replacing the older immigrants, and the Benedictines eventually gave up the church (1976). In 1979 under Cuban-born pastor Father Raul de Valle, the church, long in decline, was restored to its former beauty. Its rich interior appointments—marble columns, mosaics, bronze lamps, stained glass clerestory windows over which semi-circular arches sweep up to a great dome—come as a surprise in this deprived neighbourhood.

South of Mott Haven is **Port Morris,** developed by the Morris family in the 19C as a deep water port. Its main industry was long Richard Hoe & Co., Printing Machinery and Saws, a firm whose founder invented the rotary printing press. The Hoe factory was demolished in 1977 but Richard Hoe's Gothic Revival mansion (c. 1860) still stands at 812 Faile St on the N.E. corner of Lafayette St in the Hunts Point section. Formerly a synagogue (Temple Beth Elohim), it has been converted to the Bright Temple African Methodist Episcopal Church.

East of Port Morris and S. of the Bruckner Expressway is the neighbourhood of **Hunts Point,** now a grimy industrial area with economically depressed residential enclaves, once (before the Civil War) a fashionable place for waterside summer estates.

One Thomas Hunt had a house here in the late 17C, its site now incorporated in Hunts Point Park. Later the estate belonged to poet Joseph Rodman Drake (died 1820) who is buried in *Drake Park*, Hunts Point to Oak Point Aves, along with members of the Hunt family and other early elite Bronxites. Drake wrote of his borough in the early 19C, 'Yet I will look upon thy face again/My own romantic Bronx, and it will be/A face more pleasant than the face of men', a sentiment which he could hardly utter today. The streets around the park recall other American 19C poets: Whittier, Bryant, Longfellow, and Fitz-Greene Halleck.

The *American Banknote Co.*, Lafayette Ave N.E. corner of Tiffany St, has been in business on this site since 1911, turning out stock certificates, travellers' checks, bonds, and paper currency for such countries as Haiti, Ecuador, and Brazil, but the firm dates back much further having once printed paper money for the Continental Congress, an order issued by Paul Revere.

Hunts Point today is known as the site of the *New York City Terminal Market* (Halleck St between Lafayette and East Bay Aves), the city's primary fruit and vegetable wholesale market (1965; Skidmore, Owings & Merrill), and the *Hunts Point Cooperative Meat Market* (Hunts Point Ave, S. of East Bay Ave), which dates from 1976 (Brand & Moore). Other significant establishments in Hunts Point are a Consolidated Edison plant, a sewage treatment center, and the Spofford Juvenile Detention Center, on Spofford Ave at Tiffany St.

The neighbourhood of **Melrose** spreads out around the Hub, the intersection of E. 149th St, Third, Westchester, Melrose, and Willis Aves, long the commercial center of the South Bronx, with a branch of Alexander's department store and many other small businesses.

Morrisania, part of the S. Bronx centered around E. 170th St between Teller and Crotona Aves, was originally the town of Morrisania, incorporated in 1785.

The original American members of the Morris family, Richard and Lewis Morris, were born in Wales (presumably the place names Tinton Ave and Wales Ave reflect this fact) and made their way to the Bronx after successful careers as merchants and privateers in the Barbados. Their original holdings, purchased from Jonas Bronck's lands in c. 1670, were increased by a royal grant from William III, and the Morrises became one of the first families of New York, their descendants achieving national prominence. The first Gouverneur Morris, great-grandson of the first Richard Morris (there are many Richards, Lewises, and several Gouverneurs in the family), governor of New York, became one of the framers of the U.S. Constitution and also delivered the eulogy at George Washington's funeral.

The Lewis Morris who first owned Morrisania died in 1691. His grandson, the fourth Lewis Morris, also signed the Declaration of Independence and after the Revolution attempted to sell his estate as a site for the nation's capital. Eventually the neighbourhood became

German, and then Jewish, Irish and Italian. Today it is among the more depressed areas of the South Bronx.

Engine Company 82, Ladder Company 31 of the New York City Fire Department at 1213 Intervale Ave, N.W. corner of E. 169th St became famous in Dennis Smith's 'Report From Engine Co. 82', a 1972 documentary describing the horrors of firefighting in the South Bronx.

CROTONA PARK, bounded by Fulton, Third, Tremont, and Arthur Aves, and the perimeter roads Crotona Park, North, East and South, was laid out as a park by the city fathers in 1883 on land formerly belonging to the Bathgate family. A WPA swimming pool, the Crotona Play Center, was built in 1936, and other recreational facilities followed. None has survived unscathed.

Charlotte St, a short street running S.E. from the eastern border of Crotona Park, became a national symbol of urban despair after President Jimmy Carter's visit in 1978. Although Community School 61 on the street wears a new coat of paint, the area is utterly derelict, the last apartments torn down in the 1970s, the empty lots covered with rubble and garbage. Moved by the devastation of the area, President Carter promised a 732-unit, $32-million housing project on Charlotte St, to be the keystone of a larger redevelopment of the South Bronx, but in 1979 the city Board of Estimate turned down the housing. Today Charlotte St remains untouched, apparently forgotten by all except for occasional tourists who come to take photographs.

Near the intersection of E. 163rd St and Westchester Ave are two projects of renovated housing, modest in scale when compared to the behemoths constructed by the federal government and other agencies, but enthusiastically greeted by urban planners who see them, or other projects like them, as the best sign of health in the blighted South Bronx. On the block of Kelly St between Intervale Ave and E. 163rd St is the *Banana Kelly Project*, named after the bend or 'banana' in the street. Its several buildings were rehabilitated beginning in 1979 with private and public funds generated by local organisers who completed the renovations at an astonishingly low $26,000 per apartment (current estimates for gut rehabilitation—that is, rehabilitation including plumbing, wiring, heating, and other basic services—run at about $80–85,000 per apartment). Behind the apartments in lots cleared of rubble are park areas and even garden plots, created by the residents.

A block E. at 878 Tiffany St is *St. Athanasius Church*, the home of Father Louis Gigante, a charismatic community and parish leader who has had a significant impact on the South Bronx. In front of the church is a newly constructed plaza, its pink and white stucco ornament recalling Hispanic church architecture and reflecting the ethnic background of most of the parishioners. Through various secular activities (he ran once for City Council), Father Gigante has been able to fund and reconstruct some 1100 units of housing in the area.

Along the Harlem River, N. of Mott Haven lies the neighbourhood of **Highbridge,** taking its name from the aqueduct crossing the Harlem River (see p398) in the N. part of the district. Its most famous landmark, however, is YANKEE STADIUM, 'the house that Ruth built', at E. 161st St on the S.W. corner of River Ave.

It dates back to 1923 when former Yankee owner Jacob Ruppert (of brewery fame) had it tailored with a short right field fence to increase the percentages of his great left-handed home run hitter, Babe Ruth. Since then other stars—Joe DiMaggio and Mickey Mantle to name the most illustrious—have swung for its fences, though with less success. In 1976 (Praeger-Kavanagh-Waterbury), the city renovated the stadium (capacity 54,028), believing that its presence would bolster a failing neighbourhood. The rebuilding cost city taxpayers a staggering $100 million and three years later another million went toward patching up cracks that appeared in the structure.

Three blocks E. of the stadium is the GRAND CONCOURSE, laid out (1892) by Louis Risse who called it the 'Speedway Concourse' and provided separate lanes for carriages, cyclists, and pedestrians who used the thoroughfare as a route to Van Cortlandt Park. With the opening of public transportation, the avenue attracted large apartment buildings, many with grand facades, that make the street even now a showcase of Art Deco architecture. In the late 1920s and 1930s the avenue was the borough's finest residential boulevard, the Park Ave of the Bronx, its residents mostly well-to-do Jewish families drawn from the managerial and professional classes. Public buildings enhanced its monumentality: the *Bronx General Post Office*, 558 Grand Concourse, N.E. corner of 149th St (1935; Thomas Harlan Ellett), *Cardinal Hayes High School* (1941; Eggers & Higgins) at 650 Grand Concourse and E. 153rd St with its rear windows overlooking the railroad tracks running S. to Grand Central, and the *Bronx County Building*, 851 Grand Concourse, S.W. corner of E. 161st St (1934; Joseph H. Freedlander & Max Hausle), its severe Art Deco facade relieved by sculpture at the entrances (A.A. Weinman) and a frieze (Charles Keck). Inside is the *Bronx Museum of the Arts*, featuring changing exhibitions of modern art, painting, sculpture, and photography as well as shows of community interest.

Open Oct–June, Mon–Thurs, 9–5 and Sun, 12.30–4.30. Free. Tel: 681–6000.

N. of the Bronx County Building at Grand Concourse and E. 164th St is JOYCE KILMER PARK, named after the poet of 'Trees', at one time known to most American school children. The park contains the *Lorelei Fountain* (1899; Ernst Herter), a monument to Heinrich Heine, a better poet than Kilmer. Herter intended the fountain for Düsseldorf, Heine's birthplace, but it was rejected there and some New Yorkers of Germanic origin bought the work, hoping to install it where the Sherman statue now stands (Fifth Ave near the S.E. corner of Central Park), a site denied either because the statue lacked artistic value or because Heine was a German Jew. The main figure is that Teutonic siren, famous in one of Heine's lyrics, who with her beauty and song seduced careless sailors to a watery death. The fountain has been sadly vandalised.

Although the neighbourhoods east and west of the Grand Concourse began deteriorating rapidly during the mid-1960s, the middle class and working class white population moving out (many to Co-Op City), the Grand Concourse itself was able to withstand change to some degree, but in 1975 two well-known buildings, the Concourse Plaza Hotel at 161st St and Roosevelt Gardens at 170th St, both near abandonment, had to be taken over and sealed by the city. Happily both have been renovated and re-opened with city and federal funds. In 1982 a third premier Art Deco building, the Flatiron Building on the concourse at Tremont Ave, reopened with apartments for 43 low or moderate income families, chosen from 1200 applicants.

North of Highbridge lies the neighbourhood of **University Heights,** named after the University Heights campus of N.Y.U., on University Ave between W. 180th St and Sedgwick Ave, since 1973 taken over by the *Bronx Community College,* part of C.U.N.Y. The older buildings designed by the firm of McKim, Mead & White are believed to have been the work of Stanford White: *Gould Memorial Library, Cornelius Baker Hall of Philosophy,* and the *Hall of Languages* (all 1900; McKim, Mead & White; DL). Unfortunately the Hall of Fame for Great Americans (1901, 1914; McKim, Mead & White; DL), a classical arcade with bronze busts of famous Americans, has been closed for financial reasons.

The remains of the *Old Croton Aqueduct* are visible in University Heights, especially along University Ave north of W. Tremont Ave. A gatehouse (1890) from the second phase of aqueduct construction, the *New Croton Aqueduct* (1885–93), a system of tunnels, stands on W. Burnside Ave at the S.W. corner of Phelan Pl.

While surrounding neighbourhoods reel under a burden of crime, vandalism, arson, and poverty, **Belmont,** bounded by E. Fordham Rd, the Bronx Zoo, E. 187th St and Arthur Ave, is famous in large part for not experiencing those sorrows. Many of the people who live there, predominantly Italians but also Yugoslavians, Albanians, and some black and Hispanic families—have lived there for decades; their strong community committment and refusal to leave though surrounded with increasing urban decay has preserved the integrity of the society. Arthur Ave is an active commercial center and people from all over the city come there, especially on Saturdays, to buy Italian food from the open air fruit, vegetable, and seafood stalls or in the covered market (Arthur Ave near E. 186th St), established by mayor LaGuardia when he outlawed pushcarts. Others come to eat in the local restaurants and enjoy the gusto of the street life. Among the food emporia are importing companies displaying dried herbs, stacked tins of olive oil, and barrels of olives, as well as fish markets whose products include scungilli, calamari, baccalà, and other temptations for the Mediterranean palate.

34 Central Bronx

The main geographical and cultural feature of the **Central Bronx** is Bronx Park which includes the Bronx Zoo and the New York Botanical Garden. Nearby are the campus of Fordham University and the neighbourhood of Belmont, geographically part of the South Bronx since it lies S. of Fordham Rd, but psychologically part of the less battered Central Bronx. Formerly the Cross-Bronx Expressway was considered the S. boundary of the district, but its own deleterious effects on surrounding neighbourhoods and the wave of looting, burning, and abandonment of the 1970s have pushed the frontier N. to Fordham Rd.

A. The Bronx Zoo

SUBWAY: IRT Broadway-7th Ave express (train 2) or IRT Lexington Ave express (train 5) to Pelham Parkway. Walk W. to the Bronxdale entrance to the zoo.

EXPRESS BUS: Liberty Lines express service between midtown Manhattan and the zoo (BxM11 bus) on a regular schedule. Manhattan stops are on Madison Ave at 28th, 37th, 40th, 47th, 54th, 63rd, and 84th Sts. Return stops on Fifth Ave. Fare is $2·50; exact change required. For time schedule and more information tel: 881–1000.

CAR: The zoo is at Fordham Rd and Southern Blvd adjacent to the Bronx River Pkwy. From the East Side take the Bruckner Expwy east to Bronx River Pkwy north. Take exit marked 'Bronx Zoo' and turn left to Bronxdale parking lot. From the West Side, take West Side Highway to the Cross Bronx Expwy. Go E. to Bronx River Pkwy north. Take exit marked 'Bronx Zoo' and turn left to Bronxdale parking lot.

PARKING: Large lots along Bronx River Pkwy (Bronxdale) near exit 6 and on Southern Blvd at 182nd St (Crotona) Smaller lot at main gate (Fountain Circle) sometimes full. Parking fee, $2·50.

The New York Zoological Park, known popularly as the **Bronx Zoo**, is the largest urban zoo in the U.S., covering 262 acres and having 3600 animals of 600 species. It is clean, well-managed, attractively designed, and one of the city's major tourist attractions.

Open every day of the year (some exhibits closed in winter) 10–5 weekdays, 10–5.30 Sun and holidays, 10–4.30 every day in winter. General admission: Tues–Thurs, free; Fri–Mon, adults $2·50 and children, 75¢. Reduced admission rates during winter months. Additional fees for Bengali Express monorail (adults, $1·25; children, 75¢), Safari train (adults, $1·25; children, 75¢), Skyfari aerial tramway (adults, $1; children, 75¢), World of Darkness (10¢ Fri–Mon; 25¢ Tues–Thurs), and Children's Zoo (adults, 70¢; children, 80¢; tickets must be purchased one hour before closing time). Inquire at entrance gate about Zoo Pass (Fri–Mon, April–Oct) with reduced prices for entrance and rides.
  Cafeterias and snack bars (some closed in winter). Picnic tables at Wildfowl Terrace and Zoo Bar. Souvenir shops. Excellent official guide book. Zoo map included with entrance fee. Baby strollers for rent at Zoo Bar; wheelchairs may be reserved in advance (tel: 220–5188). For recorded announcement of hours, fees, special events tel: 367–1010; for other information tel: 220–5100.
  Feeding times: Pelicans, 11.30 a.m., crocodiles, 2 p.m. Mon and Thurs; penguins, 3 p.m.; sea lions, 3 p.m.; cats (Carnivore House) 3.30 p.m.

History. In the more than 80 years since its opening (1899), the zoo, established and operated by the N.Y. Zoological Society, has changed both physically and in its philosophy. During earlier decades administrators emphasised rarity and quantity and in 1910 the zoo had 5163 specimens of 1160 species. Today there are fewer animals and fewer kinds but larger numbers of many species, with herds and flocks replacing single animals where possible, a policy which has increased breeding potential (700–1000 live births each year). The zoo has also replaced most of the older cages with more natural habitats, an approach extended indoors in such exhibits as the Aquatic Birds Building, World of Darkness, and World of Birds.

The main entrance to the zoo at *Fountain Circle* is marked by the 36-ft bronze *Rainey Memorial Gate* (1934; Paul Manship, sculptor), whose stylised tree of life motif has 22 full-sized animals. In the center of the Fountain Circle parking lot stands a white limestone *fountain* (17–early 18C) from Como, Italy, adorned with sporting dolphins, sea horses, mermaids, and mermen, a gift (1902) from William Rockefeller. The stone jaguars near the stairs are the work of Anna Hyatt Huntington (1937) and were modelled after Señor Lopez, the first big cat in the Carnivore House (opened 1903).

Go left to the *Prairie Bison* (exhibit opened 1971), a species saved from extinction largely by the efforts of the N.Y. Zoological Society. In 1907 15 animals were shipped to Oklahoma as the nucleus of an independent national herd and other herds were formed later with animals from Bronx-bred bison. The 60 million beasts who had once roamed the plains had been hunted almost to extinction but today there are 20–30 thousand in parks and refuges, most of whom have Bronx Zoo blood. Try to see this exhibit at 10 a.m. when the animals come frolicking out of their night shelter.

*World of Birds (1972; building by Morris Ketchum, Jr & Assocs; c. 100 species) is a spectacular indoor display (c. 100 species) exploring the complexities of bird life, with exhibits on plumage, mating instinct, nests, etc, and many beautiful birds, especially tropical ones—toucans, tanagers, cocks-of-the-rock, hornbills, frogmouths, parrots, and peacock pheasants. An artificial waterfall plummets 40 ft from a 50-ft fibreglass cliff and at 2.00 p.m. a daily shower drenches the rain forest exhibit (but not the visitors).

Take the path S. to the ELK RANGE (1959) where more than 50 Roosevelt elk have been born since the herd was started. On the opposite side of the path is the WOLF WOOD (1966; enlarged in 1980). A pack of Alaskan tundra wolves live on the forested slopes, ringed by an 8-ft fence and a 15-ft wide water-filled moat. Turn left at the next intersection and pass the *Holarctic Tarn*, occupied by a variety of wild water fowl. Ahead are the *Polar Bears* in their pool. Snowcap, a cub, born in Dec 1981, is the fourth polar bear to be born and raised in the Bronx Zoo. The *Kodiak bears* in an adjacent exhibit have been provided with a rocky field and pools as well as an artificial honey tree which releases a dribble of honey at scheduled intervals.

Continue past the Kodiak bears to the **World of Darkness** (1969; building by Morris Ketchum, Jr and Assocs), another indoor exhibit (40 species) where low levels of white, blue, green, and red light turn day into night so that visitors may see nocturnal animals at their liveliest. Included are owls, foxes, herons, skunks, porcupines, sloths, and the world's largest captive breeding collection of bats. Vampire bats in a simulated cave are fed a daily ration of blood from a local slaughterhouse.

From the World of Darkness turn left and continue a short distance to **Africa,** a continental exhibit. The lions on LION ISLAND (1941) are usually visible from the N. edge of the display, confined to the island by a moat. In the AFRICAN PLAINS (1941; six species) are nyala antelope as well as ostriches, cranes, and geese. The rest of Africa is better seen from the far side of the exhibit.

Continue along the path toward the gnus to the entrance to **Wild Asia** (open May–Oct), the newest (1977; 14 species) of the zoo's geographic exhibits. The *Dragon Theater*, an open air arena in the Asian Plaza, features animal behaviour shows (check posted schedule). The Bengali Express, a monorail (25-minute guided tour) circles the 40 acres of Wild Asia and is the only way to see it. Monorail tours leave from the Asian Plaza beginning at 10.30 every morning in good weather. (*Jungle World*, now under construction near the plaza and scheduled for opening in 1984 will be an indoor exhibit featuring mammals, birds, and reptiles from tropical Asia.) The animals of Wild Asia include elephants, gaur (largest of the world's cattle), antelope, Siberian tigers, rhinoceroses, and many

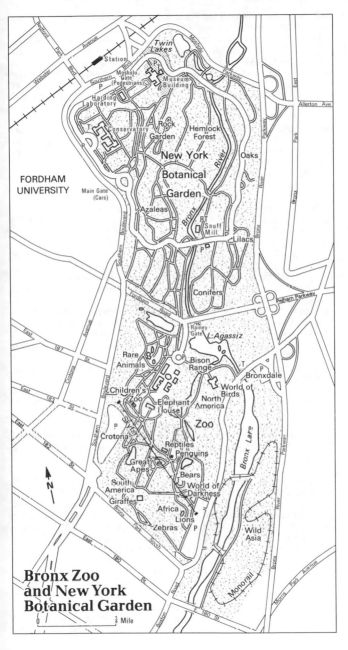

Twin
Lakes

Station

Mosholu
Gate
(Pedestrians)

Museum
Building

Harding
Laboratory

Conservatory

Rock
Garden

Hemlock
Forest

New York

Oaks

Bronx River

Botanical

Garden

FORDHAM
UNIVERSITY

Main Gate
(Cars)

Azaleas

RT
Snuff
Mill

Lilacs

Conifers

Pelham Parkway

Rainey
Gate

L. Agassiz

Rare
Animals

Bison
Range

Bronxdale

Children's
Zoo

Elephant
House

World of
Birds

North
America

Zoo

Crotona

Reptiles

Bronx Lane

Great
Apes

Penguins

Bears

South
America

World of
Darkness

Giraffes

Africa

Lions

Zebras

Wild
Asia

N

Bronx Zoo
and New York
Botanical Garden

0   ¼ Mile

Monorail

species of deer of which the Formosan sika deer is the rarest, having been declared extinct in nature in 1973.

From Wild Asia a path leads W. past the other side of the **Africa** exhibit with white-tailed gnus, blesbok, antelope, and Grevy's zebras. The GIRAFFE HOUSE at the top of the hill serves as a night shelter for the rare Grevy's zebras and as a winter exhibit area for the herd of Baringo giraffes, the zebras, and ostriches. In warmer weather the large exhibits around the building feature cheetahs and slender horned gazelles as well as the giraffes and ostriches.

The hillside in the S.W. corner of the zoo is devoted to wildlife of **South America** (1973; 10 species). The largest of the five exhibits, about an acre in size with a shallow central pool, features guanacos (wild relatives of llamas), tapirs, and rheas (large flightless birds). In smaller adjoining displays are giant anteaters, peccaries which resemble pigs but are not closely related to them, red brockets (deer) and Patagonian cavies (burrow-dwelling rodents).

Continue past the PHEASANT AVIARY and the WILDFOWL POND. Beyond is the Cafeteria (also picnic terrace, gift shops, restrooms, and first aid station). The ELEPHANT HOUSE (1908; Heins & La Farge) with its green-tinted dome and sculpted pachyderms awaits renovation. Around the outside are the Asian elephants used at the Riding Track, giant tortoises, and exhibits of social animals including prairie dogs and capybaras. The *Riding Track* N. of the Elephant House includes a ring used for animal behaviour demonstrations as well as elephant rides (open late spring–autumn; fee for rides).

Baird Court, once the main exhibit area of the zoo, consists of the Lion House (1903), the Primate House (1901, later renamed the Monkey House), the Administration Building (1910), the Main Bird House (1905), and the Heads and Horns Building (1922) in addition to the Elephant House. This formal area, named after Spencer Fullerton Baird, a 19C naturalist, is now used largely for administrative offices although the *Monkey House* and the *Carnivore House* still contain animals. In the former are 12 species of primates including langurs, mandrills, Barbary apes, and proboscis monkeys. Some of these animals will be moved to Jungle World in the Wild Asia exhibit when it is completed. Among the important carnivores are the snow leopards one of the largest breeding groups in captivity. The SEA LION POOL (renovated 1981) contains a group of sea lions who sport about in a pool which has small islands and a rocky beach.

Behind the Carnivore House the *Aquatic Bird House* (1964; 40 species) displays scarlet ibis, plovers, tufted puffins, and egrets in simulated natural habitats. The *Sea Bird Colony* has been renovated (1982) to resemble a coastal island in the S. Pacific and is home for penguins, cormorants, terns, and gulls. Pelicans live in Cope Lake, named after 19C paleontologist Edward Drinker Cope, while gibbons, who never willingly enter the water, swing in the willow trees on man-made islands. At the RARE ANIMALS RANGE EXHIBIT (1973) W. of the lake flourish three species that are no longer found in nature—the Mongolian wild horse (extinct c. 1969), the European bison (the last wild representative was shot in Poland in 1921) and the Père David deer (extinct in nature before 1863 but bred in the Imperial Hunting Park in Peking where they were discovered by Father Armand David, a French Jesuit missionary and naturalist). The imperial herds were destroyed during the Boxer Rebellion and all existing deer are descendants from 18 brought (1898) to Woburn Abbey in England by the eleventh Duke of Bedford.

Continue past the Rare Animals Range Exhibit to the EAGLES AND VULTURES AVIARY (1912) on the left with its hooded vultures, Andean condors, and other large birds of prey. Walk S. past the marsh garden and turn left to the delightful *Children's Zoo (1941; renovated 1981) which features imaginatively designed educational exhibits (giant spider web, prairie dog town, dioramas of insect life) as well as domestic animals for children to pet.

Continue back past the Elephant House and cafeteria to the display of *Wild Boars and Otters* whose playfulness has made them public favourites. In the SMALL MAMMALS HOUSE (1904; renovated 1961) are some 25 species of generally shy animals—squirrels, bush babies, mongooses, shrews, mouse deer, and hamsters—divided into daylight and nocturnal exhibit areas. In the nearby **Great Apes House** (1950; renovated 1971) are display areas for the arboreal gibbon of Asia and a simulated African forest for gorillas. Since 1972 the zoo has successfully bred gorillas, and the colony sometimes includes gorilla visitors from other cities brought in to broaden the genetic pool and to provide company for the Bronx-born residents.

The REPTILE HOUSE (1899; renovated in 1954 and 1969) is the oldest permanent indoor display at the zoo and offers amphibians—frogs, toads, salamanders—and reptiles—turtles, snakes, lizards, and crocodilians. The most imposing snakes are the venomous cobras, rattlesnakes, and vipers, shown in such a way that the visitor can meet them eye-to-eye with perfect equanimity. Anyone who can deliver a healthy snake of 30 ft or longer to the zoo will reap a $50,000 reward, an offer originally made by Theodore Roosevelt though with only a $5000 prize.

In the PENGUIN HOUSE (1950) visitors can watch penguins plunging and diving in their 24-ft long pool.

Continue straight ahead to the Kodiak bears. To leave the zoo turn left and continue past the Holarctic Tarn, the Wolf Wood, and the Elk Range to a fork in the path that leads left to the Fountain Circle area or right to the Bronxdale parking lot.

B. New York Botanical Garden

TRAIN: Conrail Harlem Line local from Grand Central Station to Botanical Garden station.

SUBWAY: IRT Lexington Ave express (train 4) to Bedford Park Boulevard. IND Sixth Ave (D train) to Bedford Park Boulevard. From the subway station walk E. eight blocks. If you cross Paul Ave you are going the wrong way.

BUS: From Manhattan take BxM 11 from Madison Ave to Pelham Parkway stop, walk ^{3}/10 of a mile; or to Gun Hill Road stop, then transfer to 55X to Bedford Park Boulevard and Webster Ave. Call 881–1000 for stops and schedule.

BY CAR: Take Pelham, Bronx River, or Mosholu parkways to Southern Boulevard exit. Follow signs to vehicular entrance. Ample car parking on grounds ($2·50 per car fee includes one adult entrance to conservatory).

The *New York Botanical Garden** with its 250 acres of garden and lawn, conservatory, arboretum, and wilderness, is also a major educational institution sponsoring biological and environmental research, expeditions, and scientific publications.

Open daily, dawn–dusk. Admission free to grounds. Conservatory closed Mon. Cafeteria in Snuff Mill open March–Dec, 9–4; Jan–Feb, seasonal hours, closed Mon. Picnic areas near Twin Lakes and at Snuff Mill. Restrooms in Conservatory, Snuff Mill, and Museum Building. Services: lectures, guided tours of grounds and conservatory, plant information, children's programmes: for information about educational programmes call 220–8747 or inquire at the Watson Building reception desk. Garden shop with plants, books, prints, and gardening items. Tel: 220–8700.

History. In 1884 the city bought 661 acres from the Lorillard family, tobacco dynasts, of which 250 became the site of the botanical garden. Urged by Nathaniel Lord Britton, a Columbia University botanist, the state legislature founded the garden (1891) and was happy to see such eminences as Andrew Carnegie, J.P. Morgan, and Cornelius Vanderbilt sit on the board of directors. The Lorillard mansion burned down in 1923, but in 1937 the city transferred other buildings from the estate to the Garden, including the Snuff Mill, the carriage house (now a maintenance center), and a stone cottage (used for private functions). Recently the conservatory, modelled after those at the Royal Botanic Gardens in Kew outside London, was restored and reopened, thanks to a $5 million gift from Enid A. Haupt.

Begin at the ****Enid A. Haupt Conservatory** (1902; William R. Cobb for Lord & Burnham, greenhouse manufacturers; altered in 1938 and 1953; restored, 1978; Edward Larrabee Barnes & Assocs; DL).

Open Tues–Sun, 10–5; closed Thanksgiving and Christmas. Adults, $2·50; children, students, and senior citizens, 75¢. Inquire about tours. Descriptive brochure available at Garden Shop in Museum Building. Conservatory cafe Wed and weekends, 10–4; outdoors in warm weather.

Enter Gallery 2, The _Orangery_, historically a forerunner of the modern greenhouse, displaying woody food plants of antiquity and changing seasonal displays. On one side is Greenmuse (Gallery 1), with an educational exhibition on food plants, directed at urban children. Gallery 3, on the other side, is the _Hanging Garden_, an orientation gallery with the information desk, and hanging baskets of plants with cascading foliage. In Gallery 4, _Lilies of the Field_ (see Matthew 6:28), are topiary boxwood animals and beautiful seasonal displays. Gallery 5, _Gardens from the Past_, has a medieval herb garden with wattle fence and turfed seat, Renaissance galleries or arbours, and a French parterre of geometrically arranged beds. The *_Palm Court_, Gallery 6, has an important collection of palms, more than 100 varieties, displayed under a glass dome 90 ft high and 100 ft in diameter. _Tropical Flora_, Gallery 7, includes a systematic arrangement of plants reflecting evolutionary development, with plant fossils next to such modern relatives as bananas, bromeliads, bird of paradise, and cycads. Gallery 8, the *_Fern Forest_, another spectacular exhibit, has a vast array of ferns from all over the world arranged in a forest with pool, waterfall, and simulated volcanic crater. Visitors can climb the skywalk to view plants from above. In Gallery 9, _Subtropical Flora_, are insectivorous plants and a sphagnum bog. Galleries 10 and 11 feature _Old World and New World Desert Flora_ including a 100-year old saguaro cactus and a 200-year old skeleton of the same variety. The beautiful displays in all the conservatories, a far cry from the former procedure of merely lining up plants on tables, were designed by Carlton F. Lees. Outside in the courtyard are pools with aquatic plants.

From the Conservatory pools walk around past the stand of fir trees and the perennial border to the **Rose Garden** (1972) behind the greenhouse with its 200 varieties of tea roses, (best season is June). Nearby are the SYSTEMATIC GARDEN, planted with flowering herbaceous and woody varieties arranged to show principles of classification, the CHEMURGIC GARDEN (plants with industrial uses), and the HERB GARDEN, with its traditional knot design.

From these specialised gardens walk through the PINETUM (20 species of pine as well as firs and spruces), past the *Harding Laboratory* (1956; Brown, Lawford & Forbes) where botanists and biochemists investigate plant structure and behaviour (not open to the public). An avenue of tulip trees (Liriodendron tulipefera) planted in 1903 leads to the now misnamed MUSEUM BUILDING (1902; Robert W. Gibson), which once held exhibits but now houses the garden shop and the herbarium, a systematic collection of some 4·3 million dried plant specimens, one of the largest in the nation. In front of the building stands a bronze *Fountain of Life* (1905; Carl Tefft), vitality in this case symbolised by plunging horses, nude figures, a mermaid and merman. The building also houses the *Harriet Barnes Pratt Library*, (open 9–4.30, Mon–Fri), whose 500,000 books, pamphlets, nursery and seed catalogues, make it the largest horticultural collection in the western hemisphere. The *Watson Building* (1973), an annex to the Museum Building, houses the educational services of the Botanical Garden.

From here walk E. (i.e., away from the parking lot), past *Rhododendron Valley* (late May–early June flowering) to the ROCK AND NATIVE PLANT GARDEN (open daily April–Oct, 9–4) enclosed within a fence. The THOMPSON MEMORIAL ROCK GARDEN (planted 1932–36) features plants from the mountainous areas of the world adapted to wind and poor soil (descriptive pamphlet available at Garden Shop). In the *Native Plant garden* with its overhead mist system grow plants normally found in the deep woods of the N.E. United States. A *Nature Trail* (descriptive pamphlet available at the Garden Shop) begins at the entrance to the Rock Garden. Behind the Rock Garden enclosure is the HEMLOCK FOREST, 40 acres of uncut woodland—the only virgin forest remaining in New York City. The forest is isolated and it is not advisable to wander there alone.

To visit the **Snuff Mill**, continue on the paved walking trail past the Rock Garden entrance; turn left at Azalea Way. Follow it past witch hazels, willows, and then azaleas and dogwoods to Snuff Mill Road (about ⅓ mile); turn left and follow the road to the mill.

Built by the Lorillard brothers Peter and George (1840; restored 1954; DL), the Snuff Mill harnassed the water-power of the Bronx River to grind tobacco with millstones instead of rubbing it over a grater, an innovation, devised by their father Pierre Lorillard which in part accounted for the success of the family business. When Pierre died (1843), diarist Philip Hone remarked: 'He led people by the nose for the best part of a century and made his enormous fortune giving them to chew that which they could not swallow.'

Walk N. of the fieldstone mill to the *High Bridge* to view the *Bronx River gorge*. The river originates near the Kensico Dam in Westchester County and empties into the East River near Hunts Point. Throughout the gorge the effects of the Wisconsin glacier are visible in the striation of the rocks, the scattered boulders and rocky outcrops. (The road over the bridge leads back to the edge of the Rock Garden and the conservatory area.) Trees in the outlying areas of the Garden are grouped by families.

The third major neighbourhood institution is **Fordham University,** E. of Webster Ave between E. Fordham Rd and Southern Blvd.

Founded in 1841 by the Right Reverend John Hughes, later the city's first Roman Catholic archbishop, it was headed in its early years by John McCloskey, later the nation's first cardinal. In 1846 it became a Jesuit institution as it is today.

The best of the campus buildings are the early ROSE HILL MANOR HOUSE (1838; DL), now used as an Administration Building, originally a wealthy merchant's home, and KEATING HALL (1936; Robert J. Reiley), Collegiate Gothic. The University Church, officially named *Our Lady, Mediatrix of All Graces* (1845; William Rodrigue; DL) was one of the original buildings; the transept, chancel, crossing, and latern were added in 1929.

35 Eastern Bronx: Throgs Neck, Parkchester, Westchester, Co-op City, Pelham Bay Park, and City Island

Throgs Neck, sometimes spelled Throggs Neck, is a peninsula stretching out at the S.E. extremity of the Bronx into Long Island Sound.

Its name honours John Throgmorton (or Throckmorton), who arrived here with a band of followers in 1643 only to be chased out by the Indians. In the 19C the wealthy, including Collis P. Huntington (railroads) and H.O. Havemeyer (sugar) had summer homes here. Nowadays it is a modest residential neighbourhood through the center of which cut the approaches to the Throgs Neck Bridge (1961; O.H. Ammann).

At the end of Pennyfield Ave beneath the bridge is FORT SCHUYLER, now the State University of New York Maritime College. The fort (1834–38; I.L. Smith; DL) dates from a period between the War of 1812 and the Civil War when the city, not in any immediate danger, was completing the system of coastal fortifications begun around 1812. Fort Schuyler, paired with Fort Totten on Willets Point in Queens, was designed to rake the lower part of Long Island Sound with cross fire. Before this period the waters of Hell Gate were considered sufficient protection for the East River, but with the development of steam propulsion, the military establishment saw fit to close this 'back door' into the city. (Fort Hamilton in Brooklyn and Fort Totten on Staten Island already guarded the mouth of the Upper Bay.) Although garrisoned during the Civil War, Fort Schuyler never saw action and was abandoned in 1870 to lie empty until the WPA restored it in 1934 and converted it to the Maritime College. In 1967, architect William A. Hall converted the gun galleries into a library.

Visitors may walk along the ramparts and enjoy a fine view of the N. shore of Long Island.

Parkchester, bounded by E. Tremont Ave, Purdy Ave, McGraw Ave, and White Plains Rd, was the first of the East Bronx's large scale housing projects (1938–42; Board of Design, Richmond H. Shreve, chairman) and remains one of the best, delighting city planners and residents with its curving roads and expanses of lawn. When it opened, a branch of Macy's, a movie theatre, 100 stores, and parking garages for 3000 cars made life pleasant for the projected population of 40,000. The land for the project, purchased by the Metropolitan Life Insurance Co. which administered it for some 30 years, formerly belonged to the New York Catholic Protectory, an institution for impoverished children, among whose wards was Hank Greenberg, now enshrined in baseball's Hall of Fame. Today the project belongs to the Helmsley-Spear & Co., the real estate giant that owns the Empire State building and other desirable properties.

Before the arrival of Parkchester, the eastern Bronx was sparsely developed, with small residential neighbourhoods, occasional business centers, and large expanses of marshland.

Westchester Square, at the intersection of Westchester Ave and E. Tremont Ave, was the village green of the colonial town of Westchester, earlier called Oostorp by the Dutch who founded it in 1653. Today it is an undistinguished commercial center. The area to the N., Westchester Heights, has in recent decades become home to several large state mental institutions and to the *Albert Einstein College of Medicine* of Yeshiva University (Morris Park Ave, S.W. corner of Eastchester Blvd). The *Bronx State Hospital Rehabilitation Center* (1971; Gruzen & Partners), the *Bronx Children's Psychiatric Hospital* (1969; Office of Max O. Urbahn), and the *Bronx Developmental Center* (1976; Richard Meier & Assocs) all occupy a tract of land bounded by the Hutchinson River Pkwy and Eastchester Rd. All have been praised for their design which minimises their institutional quality.

Looming up from the marshland near the Hutchinson River Parkway are the towers of **Co-Op City** (1968–70; Herman J. Jessor), the nation's largest housing development—35 bulky apartment towers, 236 clustered townhouses, eight parking garages, a firehouse, a heating plant, three shopping centers, and an educational park with five schools. The more than 15,000 apartments house more than 55,000 mostly working class and middle class people—bus drivers, construction and office workers, teachers, nurses—and a large population of elderly people, many of them Jewish, who fled here from decaying neighbourhoods elsewhere in the Bronx, ironically pushing the old neighbourhoods downward even faster. The sheer size of the project makes it appalling but it has had other problems too, garnering a reputation for corruption from well before the first spadeful of marsh muck was turned, and gaining notoriety (or fame) as the site of a successful tenants' rent strike in 1975–76. Despite its drawbacks, however, tenants still find it preferable to the neighbourhoods they left.

Pelham Bay Park, the largest of six tracts purchased by the city in 1883, consists of 2118 acres of salt marsh, lagoon, forest and upland, meadow, and sea shore. In addition to Orchard Beach, its most famous recreational facility, are two golf courses, bridle paths, and facilities for hiking, bicycling, tennis, boating, and running. The Police Shooting Range is not open to the public.

SUBWAY: IRT Lexington Ave (train 6) to Pelham Bay Park and then bus Bx 12 into the park itself. During the summer buses run hourly on the hour from the subway stop to the golf courses.

CAR: From Manhattan, Triborough Bridge to Bruckner Expressway and New England Thruway; take Orchard Beach exit.

History: Anne Hutchinson and her followers are believed to have settled somewhere near the park site (see p488). In 1654 an Englishman Thomas Pell bought more than 9000 acres from the Siwanoy Indians including the present park land but had to swear allegiance to the Dutch to keep his land.

Presumably he was relieved when the British took over the colony and he was granted (1666) a royal patent for the land.

The park is divided into two sections by the mouth of the Hutchinson River opening into Eastchester Bay. In the N. section are the golf courses, Orchard Beach, and the **Bartow-Pell Mansion,** which lies just E. of Shore Rd. near the golf courses.

Open Tues, Fri, and Sun, 1–5. Adults, 50¢; children accompanied by an adult, free. Tel: 885–1461.

> SUBWAY: As for Pelham Bay Park. At the subway stop, either take a taxi (about 2¹/2 miles) to the mansion or in summer take one of the hourly buses to the golf course. The regular Bx 12 bus runs into the park but continues on to City Island without passing the mansion during the off-season.

> CAR: As for Pelham Bay Park; follow Shore Rd in the park N. across the bridge to the golf course. The mansion is on the right just past the golf course clubhouse; parking available.

The present mansion, third on the site, is an unusually fine Greek Revival stone manor house, dating from 1836–42 (DL) and was built by Robert Bartow, a descendant of the Pell family. The city bought the house and grounds as part of a programme for developing parks in 1888 when the land still belonged to Westchester county, but let it stand vacant until in 1914 the International Garden Club took it over, restored it from its dilapidated state and planted its now lovely gardens. Behind the house, past the flower beds, herb garden, and immaculate lawn, a walkway leads to the family graveyard where the descendants of Thomas Pell are buried. Mayor La Guardia spent two summers in the house, no doubt enjoying the superb view of Long Island Sound and the clean, salt air.

The interior of the house has been restored and furnished with period pieces from private collections and from city museums including fine examples of American Empire furniture (c. 1810–40): canopied sleigh beds, Aubusson carpets, Sheraton mirrors. The elliptical stairway and elegant carved woodwork exemplify Greek Revival domestic architecture at its best.

On *Hunter's Island* E. of the Lagoon, now joined to the rest of the park by landfill, one John Hunter built a Georgian mansion (c. 1812) famous for lavish hospitality during his lifetime; later the house became an inn and after being abandoned and vandalised was finally demolished in the late 1930s. Traces of gardens and plantings (spruce groves particularly) and the foundations of the house are still visible. The mineral spring on the N. shore today attracts the runners who frequently work out in the park and other devotees of unchlorinated water who come with jugs to collect it.

Twin Islands, the point of land at the N.E. end of Orchard Beach now also joined to the park by landfill, has several glacial boulders including the Lion or Sphinx boulder (N.E. end of the point) revered by the Siwanoy Indians. The sweeping crescent of Orchard Beach is a Robert Moses artifact, its white sands dredged up at the Rockaways and carted here, and its colonnaded bath houses (1936; Aymar Embury II) reminiscent of his grander project at Jones Beach.

The dominant topographical feature of the southern sector of the park (take Shore Rd back across the Pelham Bay bridge) is known locally as *Garbage Mountain*, an imposing mound of trash closed to dumping in 1979 and seeded with grass. The *Pelham Bay War*

Memorial, a tall column (c. 1925; Belle Kinney, sculptor) crowned by a winged figure lies S. of the road which leads to *Isaac L. Rice Stadium* (1916; Herts & Robinson), built with a $1 million gift by the widow of the editor, lawyer, inventor and industrialist (electric storage batteries for cars and submarines), musician, and chess master (he devised Rice's gambit, an opening). In honour of Rice's gift to the city, some of the streets S. of the park reflect his interests: Watt Ave, Ohm Ave, Ampere Ave, and presumably also Stadium Ave, Research Ave, and Library Ave.

City Island Ave in the midsection of the park leads across a bridge to ***City Island,** a small community (4–4·5 thousand people) with a long maritime history.

In 1761 the local inhabitants put forth a plan to develop a port rivalling New York, a scheme that clearly failed, but the island has been economically healthy for several centuries. The first industry, a solar salt works (c. 1830), gave way to a profitable oystering industry in mid-century, and to a profitable shipbuilding industry thereafter. Vincent Astor's 'Nourmahal', Jules Bache's 'Colmena', J.P. Morgan's 'Corsair', and other pleasure boats slid down the ways at City Island. In 1902 Ratsey & Lapthorn Inc., the American branch of the famous English sailmaker, opened a sail loft on Scholfield St and still turns out suits of sails though business has dwindled from its former peak. Many of the famous America's Cup defenders have been built by boatyards on City Island.

Along the main street, City Island Ave, which runs from the bridge to Belden Point at the S. tip, stand numerous seafood restaurants, ranging from the fairly elegant to the small and humble. The modest CITY ISLAND HISTORICAL NAUTICAL MUSEUM in an old school building at 190 Fordham St (turn left from City Island Ave) has paintings, photographs, and memorabilia documenting the history and importance of the island, its shipbuilders, and sailmakers.

Open Sun, 2–4; closed holidays and during severe winter weather. Free. Tel: 855–1292. Mailing address: c/o 91 Pell Pl., City Island, Bronx, N.Y. 10464.

From the foot of Fordham St a ferry departs for *Hart Island*, where the city potter's field (not open to the public) has been since 1869 when Louisa Van Slyke, an orphan who died in the city Charity Hospital, was the first of some 700,000 unclaimed or unknown men and women and stillborn babies buried there. At one time inmates from the Reformatory Prison on the island buried the dead, but today, with the reformatory long since closed, prisoners from the Rikers Island Penitentiary perform the job assisted by bulldozers. A granite cross at the N. end of the island is said to bear the reassuring inscription, 'He calleth His children by Name'.

N. of the ferry slip is the *Pelham Cemetery* with some Pell family gravestones dating back to the mid-18C. *Rat Island*, a two-acre rocky islet visible offshore, has at various times sheltered yellow fever victims from Pelham, convicts escaping from the Hart's Island Reformatory, and an artists' colony.

36 Northwest Bronx: Riverdale and Fieldston

Riverdale is the Gold Coast of the Bronx, so much so that residents are said to be loath to append the borough's lowly appellation to their addresses. It stretches along the E. bank of the Hudson River from Spuyten Duyvil to the Westchester County line and is bounded on the E. by Van Cortlandt Park. The Henry Hudson Parkway slices through it lengthwise and along that roadway have arisen numerous high rise apartment buildings (mostly in the years since World War II) which have lessened the exclusivity of the neighbourhood. From the parkway, Riverdale looks like any comfortable upper middle class neighbourhood, but its handsome old estates and turn-of-the-century mansions, further W. by the river, testify to its wealthy past.

Although Riverdale would certainly be safe walking territory (except for dangers imposed by residents' watchdogs), distances are so great and the terrain so hilly that a car is necessary. Wave Hill may be reached using public transportation with a reasonable hike. The roads are scarred by potholes and frost heaves, whose existence in such an expensive neighbourhood suggests that the residents prefer to discourage casual sightseers. The streets are confusing and a map, while not necessarily accurate, is useful.

> CAR: Take the Henry Hudson Parkway across the bridge to the Kappock St exit. Follow Kappock St past Knolls Crescent to Johnson St which then becomes Palisades Ave.

Palisades Ave skirts the river and offers a superb view of the undeveloped (thanks to early conservationists) New Jersey palisades whose remarkable beauty T.H. Huxley found equal to that of some of the finest Himalayan landscapes. Go N. on Palisades Ave. *Henry Hudson Park*, bounded by Kappock St, Independence Ave and Palisades Ave, has as its outstanding feature a 100 ft column on which rests a statue of *Henry Hudson* (1938; Karl Bitter and Karl Gruppe) looking out to the river he discovered. Gruppe, Bitter's student, made the statue from a plaster model the sculptor had made some years earlier. (He was hit by a car and killed in 1915.)

Continue N. on Palisades Ave. Along the road toward the river are expensive houses built during the decades following World War I and further inland a number of tall apartment houses, most dating from a later period.

Turn inland at W. 247th St. At the S.W. corner of Independence Ave (690 W. 247th St) sits the *Greyston Conference Center of Teachers College*, (1864; James Renwick, Jr; DL) originally the residence of William E. Dodge and one of the earliest houses in Riverdale.

Dodge, whose money came from copper and metals, asked James Renwick to design him a little Gothic Revival summer cottage on the site to which he later added enough gables, dormers, and wings to make it a mansion. His daughter, Grace Dodge, became one of the moving forces behind the formation of Columbia Teachers' College and bequeathed both her interest in education and the mansion to her nephew who eventually willed the latter to Teachers' College for a conference center.

Return to Palisades Ave and continue N.; turn W. again into W. 248th St. On the left is part of the campus of the Riverdale Country School, formerly the property of George W. Perkins, benefactor of Wave Hill (see p507). On the left, 4715 Independence Ave, just S. of W. 248th St, is 'Alderbrook' (c. 1880), a brooding Gothic Revival mansion, formerly home of sculptor Elie Nadelman (died 1946) and, earlier, of Percy Pyne whose townhouse on Park Ave (see p318) is now a landmark.

Continue to Independence Ave and turn left. The *former Count*

Anthony Campagna Residence, 640 W. 249th St, S.E. corner of Independence Ave (1922; Dwight James Baum), with a grand cobblestone drive and red-tile roof, is one of the more theatrical houses in Riverdale.

On the other side of Independence Ave stands the **Wave Hill Center for Environmental Studies** (675 W. 252nd St, entrance on Independence Ave at W. 249th St) whose mansions and lawns enjoy a beautiful view of the Hudson River and a rich history.

Open daily 9.30–4.30; greenhouses open daily 10–12 and 2–4. Free during the week; Sat, Sun, and holidays, adults $2; senior citizens, $1. Tel: 549–2055.

> SUBWAY AND BUS: IRT Broadway–7th Ave (train 1) to 231st St station. Change to bus M10 (doesn't run weekends or holidays) or M100 city line bus at the N.W. corner of 231st St and Broadway. Leave bus at 252nd St and walk across parkway bridge; continue two long blocks on 252nd St to Independence Ave. Turn left to Wave Hill gate at 249th St. Or, IND Eighth Ave (A train) to last stop, 207th St. Change to the M10 (except weekends and holidays) or M100 bus and proceed as above.
>
> EXPRESS BUS: Liberty Lines runs Mid-Manhattan Riverdale Express via East Side and West Side routes. Tel: 881–1000 for information and schedule.
>
> CAR: From Manhattan take Henry Hudson Parkway to 246th St exit. Continue on service road to 252nd St. At 252nd St turn left over the parkway and turn left again. Turn right at 249th St and continue straight to Wave Hill gate. From points north, take Henry Hudson Parkway to 245th St exit and turn left immediately at stop sign. Turn left again at traffic light. Proceed south, turning right at 249th St, straight to Wave Hill gate.

The oldest building on the 28-acre estate is *Wave Hill manor* (central wing, 1844 with additions in the late 19C, 1928, 1933; DL), a handsome fieldstone mansion built by William Lewis Morris which passed (1903) into the hands of George F. Perkins, whose interests in conservation led him to purchase also two nearby estates, now part of the campus of Riverdale Country Day School. Perkins, a J.P. Morgan partner, added greenhouses, gardens, stables, an underground recreation building with a bowling alley and a neo-Georgian mansion called Glyndor. He worked personally with Albert Millard, previously a royal landscape gardener in Vienna, to lay out gardens emphasising the beauties of the site. Orchards and vegetable gardens planted on the lower slopes of the estate (now wooded) and greenhouses used for cultivation of both flowers and vegetables made the estate relatively self-sufficient. Such guests and tenants as Theodore Roosevelt, William Makepeace Thackeray, and T.H. Huxley enjoyed its hospitality at one time or another, and for a while Toscanini lived there as did the ambassadors of Britain to the U.S. In 1928 Bashford Dean, curator of arms and armour at the Metropolitan Museum (and also of reptiles and fishes at the Museum of Natural History), rented the house and had eminent Riverdale architect Dwight James Baum design him an Armor Hall, now used for lectures and chamber music. In 1960 Perkins's daughter gave the estate to the city for an environmental centre.

Activities include art exhibitions, outdoor sculpture shows, concerts, horticultural exhibitions and programmes for school children. The Greenhouses include a palm house, tropical house, and exhibitions of cacti and succulents as well as flowers. The Herb Garden behind the greenhouses contains 150 varieties. Near it a historical exhibition illustrates the history of Wave Hill and

Riverdale. The Wild Garden offers plants in a natural setting, and the Aquatic Garden features a Lily Pond.

Return to Independence Ave and continue N. to W. 252nd St; turn left into Sycamore Ave which then curves around to the right (N.). STONEHURST, 5225 Sycamore Ave (1861; DL), screened in summer by foliage, another Bronx fieldstone manor, first belonged to Robert Colgate, 19C paint and lead manufacturer; later Nicholas de B. Katzenbach, U.S. attorney general under President Johnson, lived there. Continue up Sycamore Ave. The *Salanter Akiba Riverdale Academy*, cut into the hillside at 655 W. 254th St between Independence and Palisade Aves (1974; Caudill Rowlett Scott Assocs) is an Orthodox Jewish school, the merger of three Hebrew day schools in the East Bronx from which Jews began migrating in the 1950s. Turn left to Palisade Ave and follow it around the campus. The neo-Tudor Administration Building (1905), originally the mansion of Henry W. Boettger, was Toscanini's last Riverdale home.

Follow Palisade Ave past Ladd Rd with its modern houses, past the Monastery and Retreat of the Passionist Fathers and Brothers to W. 261st St. Near the intersection is the *Hebrew Home for the Aged* (5901 Palisade Ave) with handsome new additions (1968; Kelly and Gruzen; additions, 1975). The Jewish population of Riverdale in the 1970s has been estimated to be somewhere between 40–60,000 out of a total population of 92,000.

At 261st St turn right. There is a side entrance (unmarked) to the COLLEGE OF MOUNT ST. VINCENT along 261st St (turn right) but the main gate is on Riverdale Ave at 263rd St. The college, founded as the Convent and Academy of Mount St. Vincent by the Sisters of Charity, moved here from its former quarters in Central Park from which the sisters were ousted when the park was developed. They took over Fonthill actor Edwin Forrest's picturesque Gothic Revival home (1846; DL) modelled after its English predecessor, Fonthill Abbey. The house, now used as a library, is dominated by six octagonal, machicolated towers upon which the eccentric Forrest bestowed individual names. The original college building (1857–59 with later additions; Henry Engelbert), a handsome brick building with Victorian charm, has a 180ft tower overlooking the river. The best view of these buildings is from the most westerly campus road, closest to the river. (Although the college is officially open only to those connected with it and parking is controlled, innocuous-looking visitors are usually allowed to view the campus; check with the gate keepers.)

To return to the parkway, take 261st St inland (E.) to Riverdale Ave and turn right; follow Riverdale Ave to exit 16 of the parkway.

Between the Henry Hudson Parkway and Broadway is the neighbourhood of **Fieldston,** known for its educational institutions and fine houses. Among the former are *Horace Mann High School* (231 W. 246th St, corner of Tibbett Ave), *the Fieldston Schools* (Manhattan College Pkwy at Fieldston Rd), run by the Ethical Culture Society, and *Manhattan College* (Manhattan College Pkwy, Tibbett Ave, and W. 242nd St), a Catholic college founded as an academy in 1849.

The main street, Fieldston Rd, shaded by an umbrella of venerable trees, is lined with handsome, rather formal suburban houses from the 1920s and 1930s in a variety of then-popular styles—Spanish colonial, Georgian, etc.

There is an entrance to the parkway at W. 246th St; turn right from Fieldston Ave.

37 Northern Bronx: Van Cortlandt Park, Woodlawn Cemetery, Kingsbridge Heights, Norwood

SUBWAY: IRT Broadway–7th Ave (train 1) to 242nd St/ Van Cortlandt Park.

BUS: M100 up Broadway to Isham St in the Inwood section of Manhattan; change to the Bronx bus, Bx 20 to Van Cortlandt Park.

CAR: From the West Side, take the Henry Hudson Parkway to the 246th St exit; go right to Broadway. From the East Side, take the F.D.R. Drive to the Willis Ave Bridge and then follow the Major Deegan Expressway N. to Van Cortlandt Park South; follow it W. to Broadway and go N. to the park entrance at 246th St. Street parking along Broadway.

Van Cortlandt Park, bounded by Broadway, the city line, Van Cortlandt Park South, Jerome Ave, and Van Cortlandt Park East, occupies about two square miles in the N. Central part of the Bronx and has facilities for tennis, swimming, golf, running, and other sports. On weekends and holidays the *Parade Ground* near Broadway attracts baseball and soccer players as well as devotees of cricket and rugby, mostly West Indians. The *old Croton Aqueduct*, (1837–42) runs north–south through the E. part of the park, punctuated with red brick service towers and the acqueduct trail has become a favourite path for park runners. Also slicing through the park are the tracks of Conrail's Putnam division and the Henry Hudson Parkway, part of Robert Moses's West Side Improvement scheme of the 1930s, and the Major Deegan Expressway, another Moses-sponsored highway.

The **Van Cortlandt Mansion** (c. 1748; DL) stands in the S. part of the park, not far from Broadway.

Open Tues–Sat, 10–4.45, Sun, 2–4.45. Adults, $1. Tel: 546–3323. Walk around the house to the main entrance which faces S. and ring the handbell to alert the guard.

History. In 1646 the Dutch West India Co. granted Adriaen Van der Donck, the first lawyer in the colony, a large tract of land which included the present park site. After his death some of the land passed to Frederick Philipse whose adopted daughter Eve or Eva married Jacobus Van Cortlandt. He bought 50 acres of what is now the park from his father-in-law and later added other parcels in the area which remained in the possession of the Van Cortlandt family until 1889. The first American Van Cortlandt, Oloff Stevensen Van Cortlandt, came as a soldier in the Dutch West Indies Co. (1638) and stayed, amassing one of the four biggest fortunes in the colony by the time of his death (1684). His descendants—merchants, shipbuilders, and frequent holders of city office—married into the Jay, Philipse, Van Rensselaer, Schuyler, and Livingston families, increasing their wealth and influence. Frederick Van Cortlandt, who built the mansion, was the grandson of Oloff Stevensen Van Cortlandt.

The house is built of rubble stone masonry with brick around the windows above which are keystones with grotesque carved faces, unique in colonial architecture but not uncommon in Holland.

INTERIOR. English, Dutch, and colonial furniture and utensils, many of which belonged to the Van Cortlandt family, are displayed in the house. In the East Parlor (right of the main hall) is a fine Georgian mantle, a portrait of Augustus Van Cortlandt by John Wesley Jarvis, and a blockfront secretary of Massachusetts origin. The West Parlor across the hall, used briefly by George Washington as his headquarters, contains a Dutch kas painted in grisaille, a fine piece from the Hudson River Valley; blue and white tiles around the fireplace opening depict biblical scenes. The Dining Room, where George Washington and Rochambeau dined on 23 July 1781, contains a portrait by Gilbert Stuart of John Jacob Astor, related to the Van Cortlandts by marriage; the large mahogany dining table has Chinese export place settings, mahogany knife boxes, and silver mounted wine bottles that belonged to the Van Cortlandt family. The large teakwood vultures standing on either side of the fireplace were given to Augustus Van Cortlandt by William Henry, Duke of Clarence, later King William IV, who dined here with Rear Admiral Robert Digby of the British Navy. Downstairs in the Kitchen are cauldrons, grazing kettles, and long handled peels for taking pans of bread from the Dutch oven. The green glass bowls for setting milk are rare.

On the second floor are the Munro Room, so called because Eve Van Cortlandt's daughter, Margaret, married Peter Jay Munro and the Washington Room, where George Washington slept during his peripatetic conduct of the Revolution. The chest at the left of the bed is a rare Connecticut Valley piece, and the Newport walnut chair of the transitional period, Queen Anne-Chippendale, is one of the most valuable in the museum. The remaining second floor bedroom, the Dutch Room, has a cupboard bed, enclosed for warmth, and an elaborately carved Dutch kas.

On the third floor are the Nursery, with an early American dollhouse, toys, a sled, and high chairs, and a room displaying spinning wheels, tools, ivory fans, articles of clothing, and other artifacts.

In front of the manor once grew a formal garden in the area below the terrace. Today some of that land has been taken over by a swimming pool, built as part of a crash programme in 1970 and a decade later cracked and scheduled for renovation. In the rear is the *Sugar House Window*, taken from the old warehouse on Duane Street, built by the Rhinelanders to store sugar from the West Indies. In 1776 the British used it as a prison for American soldiers and when it was torn down a section of wall and window, with iron bars, was rebuilt here. Also in the rear of the house is a statue of lawyer and soldier Josiah Porter (1902; William Clark Noble).

About a half mile N. of the mansion is VAULT HILL, site of the family burial ground; here Augustus Van Cortlandt, city clerk during the Revolution, secreted the municipal records in a strongbox on display within the mansion. (Several of the vault markers have been brought inside also, loosened from their original fastenings by vandals.)

Woodlawn Cemetery, first called Wood-Lawn, bounded by Jerome Ave, E. 233rd St, Webster Ave, Bainbridge, Ave, and E. 211th St, lies on the Fordham ridge, near the N. border of the borough.

Open daily, 9–4.30. Free admission. Tel: 547–5400. A free map with grave locations is available at the gate.

> SUBWAY: IRT Broadway–7th Ave (train 2) to Gun Hill Rd/White Plains Rd. IRT Lexington Ave (train 5) to Gun Hill Rd/White Plains Rd. IRT Lexington Ave (train 4) to Woodlawn/Jerome Ave.

> TRAIN: Take the Harlem Division train from Grand Central Station to the Woodlawn stop. The main entrance to the cemetery is just W. of the tracks at E. 233rd St and Webster Ave.

> CAR: Bronx River Parkway to E. 233rd St exit. Major Deegan Expressway to E. 233rd St or Jerome Ave to intersection of Bainbridge Ave. Car parking inside gates.

In 1863 the Rev. Absalom Peters and the cemetery trustees bought 313 acres of farmland for a rural cemetery which mourners from New York could reach by special Harlem River Railroad train in 35 minutes. Pleasantly landscaped in the manner of Green-Wood in Brooklyn, the park saw its first burial in 1865 and since then has become the final resting place of more than 250,000 people.

The cemetery is less noteworthy for the landscaping (though it is sufficiently unspoiled to have become a favourite haunt of bird-watchers) or for the Victorian excesses of its mausoleums, than for the prominence of those buried therein. Oliver Hazard Perry Belmont, financier and horse lover, lies in a mausoleum (1905; R.H. Hunt) modelled after the chapel at the Château d'Amboise in France along with his wife, Alva Vanderbilt Belmont (formerly married to William Kissam Vanderbilt), suffragette and tyrannical mother of Consuelo Vanderbilt whom she married off unwillingly to the Duke of Marlborough. Others interred here are: Jules S. Bache, head of the brokerage, whose mausoleum recalls the temple of Isis at Phylae; F.W. Woolworth and J.C. Penney, 5- and-10¢ millionaires; Herman Armour, meatpacker whose pinkish mausoleum (by James Renwick whose larger works include St. Patrick's Cathedral) has reminded some observers of ham; financier Jay Gould, whose railroads included the Erie and the Union Pacific; John 'Bet a Million' Gates, whose interests included Texaco oil, American Steel and Wire, and who made his mark introducing barbed wire to Texas, and Roland H. Macy, department store founder.

The list also includes Ralph Bunche, Fiorello La Guardia, William 'Bat' Masterson, sheriff and U.S. marshall, gambler, Indian scout, and sports writer, suffragette Elizabeth Cady Stanton, Joseph Pulitzer, Elizabeth Cochrane (Nellie Bly), journalist who went around the world in 80 days, Herman Melville, Victor Herbert, Fritz Kreisler, Admiral David Glasgow Farragut, Diana Barrymore, Vernon and Irene Castle, ballroom dancers who introduced the Castle Walk and the Castle Waltz, and William C. Handy, composer of 'The St. Louis Blues', and Duke Ellington. Perhaps the strangest epitaph in the cemetery is that of George Spenser (1894–1909), 'Lost life by stab in falling on ink eraser, evading six young women trying to give him birthday kisses in office of Metropolitan Life Building'.

Also near Van Cortlandt Park: In the middle class neighbourhood of **Kingsbridge Heights** perched on the hills and ridges S. of Van Cortlandt Park is the *Jerome Park Reservoir*, occupying part of the site of a racetrack built by Leonard W. Jerome. Known best as the father of Jennie Jerome (see p219), he was extremely fond of both horses and women, a founder of the American Jockey Club, and the moving force behind the racetrack, where he and his well-to-do colleagues raced their thoroughbreds from 1876–1890. In 1905 the reservoir was built as part of the Croton system, covering 94 acres and holding 773 million gallons of water. A second basin to the E. (which extended to Jerome Ave) has now been filled and its land given over to DeWitt Clinton High School, the Bronx High School of Science—probably the city's most prestigious public school and alma mater of several Nobel Prize winners—and Herbert H. Lehman College, until 1968 the uptown campus of Hunter College. Filling the rest of the site are subway yards and the imposing *Kingsbridge Armory* (1912; Pilcher & Tachau; DL), at 29 W. Kingsbridge Rd between Jerome and Reservoir Aves, reputedly the largest in the world.

Poe Park, a small green space on the E. side of the Grand Concourse at Kingsbridge Rd, contains the POE COTTAGE (1812; DL), a humble white frame farmhouse now rather forlornly preserved amid the apartments and commercial buildings of this borderline neighbourhood.

> SUBWAY: IRT Lexington Ave (train 4) to Kingsbridge Rd/Jerome Ave; walk three blocks E. to the Grand Concourse. IND Sixth Ave (D train) to Kingsbridge Rd/Grand Concourse.
>
> CAR: Major Deegan Expressway to Fordham Rd. Go E. to the Grand Concourse and turn left (N.) to Kingsbridge Rd.

For details about the Bronx Heritage Trail and public transportation between the Poe Cottage and other historic Bronx sites, see p513.

Open Wed–Fri, Sun, 1–5; Sat, 10–4. Adults, 75¢; children under 12 free. Tel: 881–8900.

Edgar Allan Poe came to this little house in 1846 hoping that the country air would cure his dying wife's tuberculosis. Already famous but still hounded by poverty and his own bleak disposition, the poet watched his wife die during the first winter, but stayed on to write 'Ulalume', and 'The Bells' as well as perhaps part of 'Annabel Lee', a eulogy to his bride whom he had married when she was just 13 years old. Poe left in 1849 and went south, dying in Baltimore in October of that year. The house has been converted to a simple museum, with a few period furnishings, memorabilia, and an audio-visual exhibit that evokes Poe's tragic life and literary achievement.

In the neighbourhood of **Norwood** just S. of Gunhill Rd is the third of the Bronx's historic houses, the VALENTINE-VARIAN HOUSE, now converted to the *Museum of Bronx History* (3266 Bainbridge Ave between Van Cortlandt Ave and E. 208th St).

> SUBWAY: IND Sixth Ave (D train) to 205th St Bainbridge Ave or IRT Lexington Ave (train 4) to Mosholu Pkway; walk E. on 208th St.
>
> CAR: Major Deegan Expressway to Van Cortlandt Park exit. Follow Van Cortlandt Park South and Gun Hill Rd to Bainbridge Ave; turn right and follow Bainbridge Ave to the museum. Street parking.

Open Sat, 10–4 and Sun, 1–5. Adults, $1. Children under 12, free. Tel: 881–8900. It is wise to telephone ahead to be sure that the museum is open scheduled hours.

About 1775 Isaac Valentine, a well-to-do farmer, built this sturdy fieldstone farmhouse (DL) on land purchased from the Dutch Reformed Church. During the Revolution the family fled, endangered by skirmishes nearby, and for a while the house was occupied by British and Hessian soldiers. In 1791 Isaac Varian bought it along with some 260 acres of land and the house remained in the family until 1964 when the owner wished to sell it to a developer eager to construct apartments. Fortunately a clause in the will under which the owner had taken title to the property stipulated that while the land could be divided, the house had to be preserved. In 1965 it was moved across the street to its present site and has since served as a museum with prints, paintings, photographs, and other artifacts of Bronx history. The research collection is the outstanding source of documents relating to the Bronx.

The **Bronx Heritage Trail** consists of tours of the Valentine-Varian House, the Poe Cottage, and the Van Cortlandt mansion which the visitor can reach by public transportation. Begin by taking the Sixth Ave IND (D train) to Bainbridge Ave/205th St and the Valentine-Varian House. Across the street from the house is the stop for bus Bx 20 which goes to the Poe Cottage. From there continue by bus Bx 20 to Broadway and 246th St, near the Van Cortlandt Mansion. The IRT Broadway–7th Ave (station at 242nd St) goes downtown on the West Side.

Behind the Valentine-Varian House an earthen embankment curves around a large playground on the site of the former (1888–1923) Williamsbridge Reservoir, part of the city water system. When the reservoir was abandoned, tunnels were cut through the dam and playground equipment installed. The former *Keeper's House* (c. 1890) still remains on Reservoir Oval East at the intersection of Putnam Pl.

The startling upswept roof of *St. Brendan's Church* (Roman Catholic), Perry Ave between E. 206th and E. 207th Sts, looks like the prow of a ship, understandable since St. Brendan is the patron saint of navigators. The church (1966; Belfatto & Pavarini) also has fine stained glass windows (open during services).

Montefiore Hospital and Medical Center, E. Gun Hill Rd between Kossuth and Tryon Aves, was founded in 1884 on the centenary of the birth of Sir Moses Montefiore, Anglo-Jewish leader and philanthropist. The earliest buildings on the present site date from 1913 (Arnold W. Brunner). Originally a home for incurable invalids, the hospital has become a major medical center. The most dramatic of the newer buildings is the *Montefiore II Apartments*, 3450 Wayne Ave between E. Gun Hill Rd and E. 210th St (1972; Schuman, Lichtenstein & Claman), a tall red-brown brick tower.

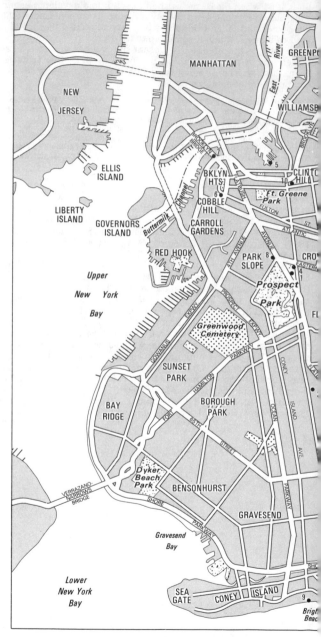

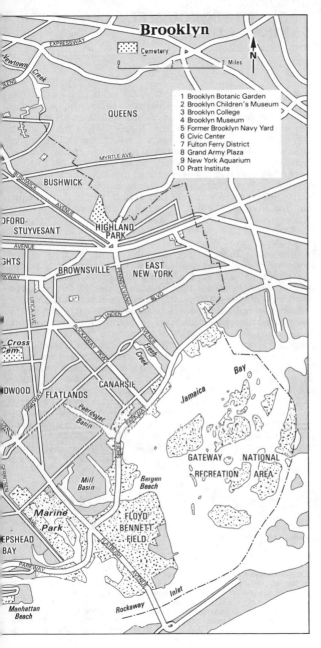

Brooklyn

···· Cemetery

0   1   2 Miles

N

1 Brooklyn Botanic Garden
2 Brooklyn Children's Museum
3 Brooklyn College
4 Brooklyn Museum
5 Former Brooklyn Navy Yard
6 Civic Center
7 Fulton Ferry District
8 Grand Army Plaza
9 New York Aquarium
10 Pratt Institute

EXPRESSWAY

Newtown Creek

QUEENS

MYRTLE AVE.

BUSHWICK

BUSHWICK AVENUE

OFORD-
STUYVESANT

AVENUE

HIGHLAND
PARK

GHTS

RKWAY

BROWNSVILLE

EAST
NEW YORK

PENNSYLVANIA

UTICA AVE.

LINDEN

ROCKAWAY PKWY.

Fresh Creek

AVENUE

BLVD.

Cross
Cem.

DWOOD   FLATLANDS

CANARSIE

Jamaica

Bay

Paerdegat
Basin

SHORE

PARKWAY

GATEWAY   NATIONAL
RECREATION   AREA

Mill
Basin

Bergen
Beach

GERRITSEN

Marine
Park

FLOYD
BENNETT
FIELD

EPSHEAD
BAY

PARKWAY

FLATBUSH AVENUE

Inlet

Rockaway

Manhattan
Beach

III THE BOROUGH OF BROOKLYN/ KINGS COUNTY

Once a separate city, Brooklyn today still holds on to a separate identity. In the popular mind its natives speak a unique, comic dialect, and its past gleams with such institutions as the departed Brooklyn Dodgers and the Brooklyn 'Eagle', while the Brooklyn Bridge is still praised as the world's most beautiful. Brooklyn conjures up images of endless blocks of rowhouses and apartments, some habitable and even handsome, others gutted and in the final throes of urban decay, and of beleaguered industry. There also exists a stereotypical Brooklynite, aggressive, humorous, street wise and ambitious, whose actual existence may account for the many famous people who were born or lived in Brooklyn: Mickey Rooney, Mae West, Beverly Sills, Sol Hurok, Isaac B. Singer, S.J. Perelman, Richard Wright, Floyd Patterson, John Steinbeck, Clara Bow and Aaron Copland.

Geographically Brooklyn occupies the E. tip of Long Island, bounded by the East River, the Narrows, and upper New York Bay on the W. and N. and by the Atlantic Ocean on the S. and the borough of Queens on the E. Rocky ridges created by the Wisconsin glacier run E.–W. through its central and western portions, while the S. and E. part of the borough is largely coastal plain. Many neighbourhood names describe local geography: Brooklyn Heights, Park Slope, Stuyvesant Heights (now part of the conglomerate Bedford-Stuyvesant), Crown Heights, Bay Ridge, Flatbush, Flatlands, and Midwood. Even the name 'Brooklyn', first applied to the 17C village near the present intersection of Fulton and Smith Sts, refers to a topographically similar Dutch town Breuckelen ('Broken Land'). Expectedly the waterfront has attracted industry and shipping; the downtown area is focused around Fulton St and the rest of Brooklyn is largely residential, the patterns of its settlement influenced by transit lines—first horse cars, then elevated railways and eventually subways—fanning outward through the borough. Its area of 78·5 sq. miles makes it the second largest borough geographically, while its 2,230,936 inhabitants (a loss of 14·3% since 1970) make it the largest in population.

History. The Dutch first settled Brooklyn in the 17C, buying land from the Canarsie Indians and chartering five of its six original villages: Breukelen (1657), 't Vlacke Bos, now Flatbush (1652), Nieuw Utrecht (1662), Nieuw Amersfoort, now Flatlands (1666), and Boswijck, now Bushwick (1660). The sixth charter for 's Gravensande, now Gravesend, went to Lady Deborah Moody in 1645, an Englishwoman. Dutch culture, agrarian and conservative, endured in Brooklyn long after the Revolution, especially inland, although New Yorkers, many of them of British origin, were attracted to the waterfront and northern districts. Brooklyn rejected overtures to join New York politically in 1833, accepting General Jeremiah Johnson's opinion that the two cities had 'nothing in common, either in object, interest, or feeling—nothing that even apparently tends to their connection unless it be the waters that flow between them', and in the following year (1834) became an independent city, covering 12 square miles and boasting a population of some 30,000 inhabitants. As the century progressed Brooklyn gradually absorbed outlying towns: New Lots, Flatbush, Gravesend, New Utrecht, and Flatlands, and in 1898, its destiny dictated by geography, Brooklyn voted by a slim majority to join Greater New York.

The late years of the 19C and the early ones of the 20th were a halcyon period for Brooklyn, its cultural institutions—the Brooklyn Museum, the Brooklyn Academy of Music, the Brooklyn Botanic Garden, the Long Island Historical Society—finding fertile soil in which to flourish, its major industries—oil and sugar refining, brewing and distilling, publishing, glass and ceramics, cast iron—providing jobs for its large resident population. Major public works projects—Prospect Park, the Brooklyn Bridge, the development of the Atlantic Basin—as well as the construction of sound housing along burgeoning rapid transit lines testified to its economic health.

After the turn of the century Brooklyn's demography began changing as immigrants poured in from Europe and after the 1930s from the American South. By 1930 half Brooklyn's adults were foreign born, most gravitating to ethnic neighbourhoods like Bushwick, Brownsville, Bensonhurst, and Greenpoint, and by the mid-1930s some of these areas had become slums. Established middle-class 'American' families moved further out to suburban neighbourhoods in Flatbush, Flatlands, or Canarsie. Despite the setbacks of the Depression, however, Brooklyn remained economically sound through World War II when the exodus to the suburbs of much of the remaining middle class, government policies favouring other regions of the country, and changes in the structure of capitalism eroded Brooklyn's economic base. In the past two decades the port has lost more than 10,000 jobs, the breweries of Bushwick have been largely abandoned, the Navy Yard was closed by the Defense Department, and large neighbourhoods have become derelict, bombed-out slums, most poignantly Brownsville, long a working-class Jewish area noted for its social and intellectual vitality. On the positive side, individual efforts—by cultural groups, by individual families undertaking the renovation of brownstones, by businesses like the Brooklyn Union Gas Co. which disseminates information on restoration, and by civic organisations like the Bedford-Stuyvesant Restoration Corporation—have made some progress confronting Brooklyn's massive urban problems.

Touring in Brooklyn. Where distances are short and neighbourhoods are safe, walking tours have been suggested and subway stops indicated. Loop II of the Culture Bus (weekends and holidays) makes 13 stops in Brooklyn. For outlying areas a car is ideal, even necessary. Several agencies offer tours for a fee in Brooklyn.

Brownstone tours: Spring and autumn; call the Brownstone Information Center for information, 636–4947 or 643–4293.

Greenwood Cemetery tours: Sundays, April–June and Sept–Nov. Tel: 439–8828.

Lou Singer: Tours by minibus for groups of about ten people (groups or individuals) to brownstone neighbourhoods and ethnically interesting areas. Tel: 873–9084 between 6–9 p.m.

Municipal Art Society: Discover New York walking tours cover parts of Brooklyn as well as other boroughs. Tel: 935–3960.

Planners' New York: Bus tours to 12 different neighbourhoods in New York emphasise current developments. Spring and autumn. Tel: 734–1366.

Prospect Park and surrounding areas: Tours by Urban Park Rangers, Tel: 856–4210. Or call the Prospect Park Environmental Center, Tel: 622–7686.

38 Fulton Ferry

SUBWAY: IND Eighth Ave (A train) to High St/Brooklyn Bridge. Follow Cadman Plaza West toward the bridge.

TO WALK ACROSS THE BROOKLYN BRIDGE: IRT Lexington Ave (train 4,5) to Worth St/Brooklyn Bridge or the BMT Nassau St (J or M train) to Chambers/Centre Sts in Manhattan and walk across the bridge. The stairs to the pedestrian promenade are under the bridge opposite the William St extension. To walk across from the Brooklyn

end, follow Cadman Plaza West beneath the Brooklyn-Queens
Expressway to Front St and the stairs to the promenade.

The *Fulton Ferry district (now a designated Historic District) lies on
low ground N. of Brooklyn Heights that before the advent of bridges
and tunnels offered the easiest access to Manhattan.

As early as 1642 one Cornelis Dircksen operated a regular rowboat service and
during the pre-Revolutionary period The Ferry, as it was known, became the
focus of industry and business, with slaughterhouses, taverns, a brewery, and a
distillery. After the disastrous Battle of Long Island in August 1776, Washington's forces, narrowly escaping annihilation, were ferried across the river from
here in rowboats manned by Massachusetts fishermen serving in the army.
When a new ferry was established at the foot of Main St in 1796, the district
became known as 'Old Ferry' until it was renamed after Robert Fulton who
introduced steam service in 1814 to supplement his other ferries, which
included boats powered by horses on treadmills. The area thrived until the
Brooklyn Bridge destroyed its economy; thereafter it degenerated into a slum.
By the time the last ferry crossed in 1924 the district was the haunt of derelicts
who patronised its flophouses and greasy restaurants. Today Fulton Ferry is
enjoying a renaissance with the development of a park, a museum, and several
thriving restaurants.

Begin at *No. 1 Front St* (corner of Cadman Plaza West), a cast-iron
palazzo (1869; William Mundell), built as a bank, the Long Island
Safe Deposit Company, during the high tide of prosperity following
the Civil War, now revitalised as a restaurant. Across the street at 28
Cadman Plaza West (S.E. corner of Elizabeth St) is the EAGLE
WAREHOUSE AND STORAGE CO. (1893, additions, 1910; Frank
Freeman), a monumental brick warehouse with a machicolated top,
standing on the site of the original offices of the Brooklyn 'Eagle'.
The newspaper's logo, a zinc eagle is bracketed to the facade.

History. The 'Eagle' was founded (1841) as an organ of the Brooklyn
Democratic party and its first editor was Henry C. Murphy, elected mayor of
Brooklyn in 1842. Walt Whitman edited it between 1846–48 but was relieved of
his job either because of his strong anti-slavery position or because he was
'slow, indolent, heavy, discourteous, and without steady principles', as his
publisher stated. The paper was directed at a stable, business-oriented,
Protestant readership and thrived as long as this population dominated
Brooklyn, reaching its peak between 1890–1930. In 1950 the 'Eagle' won a
Pulitzer Prize for a series of articles uncovering crime, gambling, and police
corruption, but on 16 March 1955 during a labour strike the paper died, in large
part because it had become an economic anachronism.

The low buildings leading down the N.E. side of the block toward
the river date from the 1830s; the one at 1 Cadman Plaza West,
corner of Water St, was a hotel and now has a small restaurant.
Across the street (8 Cadman Plaza West, S.E. corner of Furman St) is
the former *Brooklyn City Railroad Company* (1861; remodelled 1975;
David Morton; DL), originally headquarters for a horsecar, i.e.
railroad, firm whose tracks fanned out into the city of Brooklyn. After
the demise of the horsecars, a toilet seat manufacturer used it, but a
recent remodelling has converted it to apartments.

Behind this building (block bounded by Doughty, Vine, and
Furman Sts and Columbia Heights) is the former Squibb Building,
once home of a pharmaceutical plant, now used by the Watchtower
Bible and Tract Society of Jehovah's Witnesses.

On the waterfront itself at the foot of Cadman Plaza West the
NATIONAL MARITIME HISTORICAL SOCIETY MUSEUM occu-
pies a fireboat house built in 1926 for Marine Company 7 of the city

fire department, two years after the ferry stopped running and the former Victorian ferry house was demolished.

Open daily 12–6; admission free. It is wise to telephone ahead on weekends in the winter. The museum has a small permanent collection and offers about four exhibitions yearly on themes relating to the sea, shipping, the history of the waterfront and harbour, and the Fulton Ferry neighbourhood. During warm months the museum offers walking tours of the waterfront, craft programmes, and holiday celebrations. Tel: 858–1348.

Fulton Ferry Park, created in 1976, offers *spectacular views of the Brooklyn Bridge, which makes it a favourite with photographers. The guard rails in the park were salvaged (1970) from the grassy center islands on Park Ave; a plaque near the museum commemorates the evacuation of the American forces after the Battle of Brooklyn Heights.

The ****Brooklyn Bridge,** still thought by many to be the world's most beautiful bridge (1883; John A. Roebling and Washington Roebling; reconstruction, 1955; David B. Steinman, consulting engineer; DL), was the world's first steel suspension bridge, a triumph of engineering (in 1883 only Trinity Church was higher) and a product largely of immigrant labour. The view from the pedestrian promenade is spectacular, both down to the river and city and up to the cables and granite arches. (Enter at Cadman Plaza East near Prospect St; the promenade descends into Manhattan near City Hall Park.)

History. John A. Roebling, an immigrant from Prussia in 1831, began his American career as a farmer but soon began working on canal systems where he developed the wire rope that later would make the bridge possible. His plans (1869) for an East River Bridge included the towers with their pointed openings, the iron trusses that stiffen the roadway, and the system of inclined stays that run diagonally from the towers giving the bridge its particular beauty and, he contended, making it so stable that if all the cables snapped the bridge would sag but not fall. Only a week after the plans gained final approval, a boat docking at Fulton Ferry crushed the toes of his right foot and he died of tetanus three weeks later, before construction began. His son Washington A. Roebling took over actual supervision of the work which went slowly, hampered by blowouts of the compressed air in the caissons, fire, the dangers of 'caisson disease,' or the bends, whose cause was not yet understood, fraud, a taxpayers' suit against the bridge, and lack of funds. During the last decade of construction (it took 14 years), Emily Roebling became the liason between her husband, invalided by the bends, and the bridge workers, while Roebling himself watched the project from his window with a telescope.

The bridge opened 24 May 1883 amidst triumphal celebrations. Since then it has inspired artists—watercolourist John Marin, abstractionist Joseph Stella—and writers—Walt Whitman, Hart Crane, Thomas Wolfe, Vladimir Mayakovsky. Folklore surrounds it, beginning with the tragedies in the Roebling family and the death of twenty workers during its construction. The week after it opened 12 pedestrians died, crushed by a panic-stricken mob who believed the bridge was collapsing. In 1884 P.T. Barnum took 21 elephants over it, declaring himself satisfied thereafter as to its stability. In 1885 Robert Odlum, a swimming instructor, jumped to his death wearing a bright red swimming shirt and trunks. Steve Brodie, a personable but unemployed Irishman, claimed to have survived a jump in 1886; to prove it he opened a tavern featuring an oil painting of the event and an affidavit from the barge captain who allegedly picked him out of the river. In the Manhattan abutment are underground vaults which were used for many years to store wine, though they were sealed during prohibition; an alternative use for them is presently being sought.

STATISTICS. Length of river span, 1595·5 ft. Total length of bridge, 5989 ft. Width of bridge floor, 85 ft. The bridge is supported by four cables each 15·75 inches in diameter and 3578·5 ft long; each contains 5434 wires or a total wire length of 3515 miles per cable. The Brooklyn foundations reach a depth of 44 ft

6 inches below high water and the Manhattan foundations, 78 ft 6 inches. The towers are 276 ft 6 inches above high water while the roadway is 119 ft above the water at the towers. The total weight of the bridge exclusive of masonry is 14,680 tons.

Walk E. to the *Empire Stores* at 53–58 Water St between Dock and Main Sts. (To get there follow Front St under the bridge approach and turn left at Dock St and right at Water St.) Now owned by Consolidated Edison, these brick warehouses date from the years after the Civil War (W. group, 1870; E. group, 1885), when they were used to store goods brought to the waterfront by railroad cars which were then loaded aboard barges.

The nearest subway stop is the IND High St/Brooklyn Bridge stop (Eighth Ave A and CC trains, express and local) at Cadman Plaza West opposite the park.

39 Brooklyn Heights

SUBWAY: The nearest stops are the IRT Broadway-7th Ave (trains, 2, 3) at Clark St (rather deserted during off hours; access to street via an elevator) and the IND Eighth Ave (A train) at High St/Brooklyn Bridge. The IRT stop at Borough Hall serves both the B'way-7th Ave (trains 2,3) and the Lexington Ave (trains 4,5) and is more heavily used.

BUS: Culture Bus (weekends and holidays), Loop II, stop 1.

Brooklyn Heights, bounded by the East River, Fulton St, Atlantic Ave, and Court St, is an old residential neighbourhood distinguished by its tree shaded streets and its many well-preserved 19C houses of brick, brownstone, and even wood. New York's first suburb, it also became (1965) its first designated Historic District, a classification that preserves the facades of its buildings from wanton change. The Canarsie Indians had a settlement along its highlands facing the river and the defeated American troops after the Battle of Long Island fled here to be evacuated across the river from Fulton Ferry, but Brooklyn Heights began to burgeon only after 1814 when Robert Fulton's steam ferry began scheduled crossings to New York. Shortly thereafter prominent landowners whose names are commemorated in local streets divided their property into standard 25 × 100 ft lots for development, a process largely completed by 1890.

Victorian Brooklyn Heights was known for its fine families, its churches, and its clergymen. When the subway arrived (1908) the neighbourhood became less patrician and in the early 20C many of the private homes had deteriorated and been converted to rooming houses; a few had even become seamen's clubs or missions. The Heights remained in social limbo until the 1950s when the borough's first brownstone revival began, led primarily by young married couples willing to put labour and money into preserving the old houses. Today, however, taxation and strictures on landmark buildings have made single-family houses increasingly expensive and the trend is once more toward the subdivision of houses into apartments.

Begin in front of the Clark St entrance to the *St. George Hotel* (between Hicks and Henry Sts), named after a nearby 18C tavern. This blockbuster of a hotel, built in various stages (1885; Augustus Hatfield; additions 1890–1923; tower, 1930; Emery Roth) is now undergoing conversion in various stages to cooperative apartments. For a while it was the city's largest hotel, famous during the 1920s for its mirrored swimming pool and Art Deco ballroom; later it slipped into seediness (witness the portion around the subway station).

Walk E. along Clark St to Henry St and turn right (S.). In the long block of Henry St running S. of Clark St are two modest Gothic style churches among the many that gave 19C Brooklyn the name

'Borough of Churches': the *First Presbyterian Church*, 124 Henry St (1846; W.B. Olmsted. Memorial doorway, 1921; James Gamble Rogers) and the *German Lutheran Church* (1887) at 125 Henry St.

Turn around and walk N. on Henry St. On the right (E.) is a long block with urban renewal housing. The S. part of the project, *Cadman Towers* (bounded by Clark and Henry Sts and Cadman Plaza West with additional row housing along Clark St, Monroe Pl, and Cadman Plaza) is one of Brooklyn's more successful public housing efforts (1973; Glass & Glass and Conklin & Rossant), combing high- and low-rise buildings, shopping, parking, a community center, and even greenery atop the garages. The section of the project to the N., opposite Orange, Cranberry, and Middagh Sts, an apartment complex called Cadman Plaza North and townhouses and apartments on Whitman Close, is older (1967–68; Morris Lapidus & Assocs) and less successful.

From Henry St turn left into Orange St. The **Plymouth Church of the Pilgrims,** on Orange St between Henry and Hicks Sts, a red-brick Italianate barn of a church (1849; Joseph C. Wells), is best known as the church of Henry Ward Beecher, who used its pulpit for 40 years (1847–87) to address the great issues of the day—slavery, war, temperance, and morality.

At the height of his popularity 'Beecher boats' ferried throngs of New Yorkers across the river to hear him and policemen had to patrol the crowds who lined up hours before the service. Always theatrical, Beecher once brought a beautiful mulatto slave girl to the church with the avowed intention of selling her to the highest bidder; roused to furious indignation by the preacher's imitation of a slave auctioneer, the congregation purchased her freedom, putting Beecher in the front ranks of the nation's abolitionists, also occupied by his sister Harriet Beecher Stowe, author of 'Uncle Tom's Cabin'.

Return to Henry St and keep going N.

As you pass Cranberry St look E. toward the housing project. Until 1964 the Rome Brothers' Printshop stood a block E. at 170 Fulton St on the S.W. corner of Cranberry St (now part of the renewal project). Here in 1855 Walt Whitman set type for his 'Leaves of Grass'. The *Henry Street Studios*, 20 Henry St at the N.W. corner of Middagh St, occupy a former candy factory (1885; Theobald Engelhardt; reconstructed, 1975), whose products are still advertised at the top of the S. wall, thanks to a coat of paint that postdates the factory.

Walk N. a block to Poplar St and turn left. The dour and derelict Victorian pile at 57 Poplar St between Hicks and Henry Sts was built in 1883 as an orphanage for homeless newsboys by the Brooklyn Children's Aid Society.

Turn left on Hicks St and walk one block S. John and Jacob Middagh Hicks, early developers of Brooklyn Heights, named Hicks St after themselves and their ancestors. After years of decrepitude, Nos 38 and 40 Hicks St (c. 1830 and c. 1831) between Poplar and Middagh Sts were recently restored, a late but laudatory act of the Brooklyn Heights revival movement; once confined to row houses; the movement has spread to larger buildings, now being revitalised as cooperative apartments.

At Middagh St, also named after 19C landowners, turn right and walk a block W. to Willow St.

The house on the S.E. corner of Willow and Middagh Sts, *NO. 24 MIDDAGH ST, is one of the treasures of Brooklyn Heights, a well-preserved clapboarded house (1824) with fine carved Federal detailing around the door, dormer windows, and quarter-round attic windows visible from Willow St. The cottage behind it, now joined to it by a wall, was originally the carriage house. In 1848 Henry Ward Beecher lived at 22 Willow St across the intersection.

While many Brooklyn Heights streets are named after prominent 19C families, five—Pineapple, Orange, Cranberry, Poplar, and Willow—have botanical names, testimony to the ire of one Miss Middagh who allegedly tore down street markers bearing the names of neighbours she disliked and substituted the present names. In fact, however, the street names seem to have been bestowed by the developers of the area.

Continue walking S. on Willow St to Cranberry St. *No 19 Cranberry St*, on the N.W. corner, has a fine Federal fan-style doorway; the mansard roof was added later. NO. 57 WILLOW ST (c. 1824) on the N.E. corner of Orange St, is a good example of the Federal style, with dormers, pitched roofs, Flemish bond brickwork, tooled stone lintels, and a parapet between the chimneys concealing the roof gable. A merchant, Robert White, first owned it.

Turn right on Orange St and walk a block to Columbia Heights. The Hotel Margaret (1889; Frank Freeman), long a Brooklyn landmark, until recently occupied the vacant lot at the N.E. corner of the intersection; in 1980 it burned and was demolished.

Walk S. on Columbia Heights past the facilities of the Jehovah's Witnesses, a fundamentalist religious sect. To the N. can be seen the former Squibb factory now used as a home for its publication, the 'Watchtower'. The *Jehovah's Witnesses residence hall* at 124 Columbia Heights stands on the site of a house (110 Columbia Heights) where Washington Roebling lived and watched the construction of the Brooklyn Bridge. On the E. side of the street at 107 Columbia Heights (1960; Frederick G. Frost, Jr & Assocs) is a high-rise dormitory, also a residence hall for Jehovah's Witnesses. A little to the S. (119 Columbia Heights) is a newer *Jehovah's Witnesses Library and Dormitory* (1970; Ulrich Franzen & Assocs), hailed as a triumph of the landmarks law, since though contemporary in style the facility respects the scale and proportions of the existing 19C buildings, its architectural accommodation the fruit of long negotiations and several efforts at redesign.

Turn left at Clark St and walk a block inland. The former *Towers Hotel* (1928; Starrett & Van Vleck) at 25 Clark St on the N.E. corner of Willow St, which once glittered as one of Brooklyn's bright social spots, belongs also to the Jehovah's Witnesses, and serves as yet another residence hall. The territorial expansion of the sect and its members' efforts at proselytising in the neighbourhood have made it sometimes an unwelcome presence on the Heights.

Walk a block E. to Hicks St and turn right. Among Brooklyn's best Gothic Revival rowhouses are two (c. 1848) at 131 and 135 Hicks St (between Clark and Pierrepont Sts). Note the dark brownstone facades, the Tudor arches above the doors, the small-panelled casement windows with horizontal hoods and moulds. Return to Willow St and walk S.

Three houses (c. 1880) on Willow St (*Nos 108–112*) between Clark and Pierrepont Sts best exemplify in Brooklyn the offbeat architectural style known as Queen Anne that flourished between 1880–1900, after its introduction to this country from England at the Philadelphia Centennial Exposition (1876).

The style combines medieval and Renaissance elements in a free-handed, non-academic manner. These houses, treated by the designer as a unit, display an amusing variety of forms—gables, bay windows, chimneys, dormers, round, square, and elliptical openings—and materials—brick, stone, terracotta, ironwork, shingles.

Continue S. on Willow St past a trio of pristine small Federal row houses (c. 1829), Nos 155–159, between Clark and Pierrepont Sts. The panelled front doors with flanking colonettes, sidelights, and leaded transoms are especially handsome.

At Pierrepont St turn right and walk toward the water. *No. 6 Pierrepont St* (c. 1890) between Willow St and Pierrepont Pl. is an unusual Romanesque Revival townhouse with a rockface entrance stairway and posts carved with flourishing stone plant forms. Continue W. to Columbia Heights. Outstanding among the many fine Italianate townhouses in the area are *Nos 210–220 Columbia Heights* (1852–60) on the N.W. corner of Pierrepont St, amply proportioned with wide doorways and elaborate door hoods carved with acanthus leaves.

Turn around and walk back E. on Pierrepont St; cross Willow and Hicks Sts. The former *Herman Behr mansion* (1890; Frank Freeman) stands at 82 Pierrepont St on the S.W. corner of Henry St. With an addition in 1919 this handsome Romanesque Revival mansion became the Palm Hotel whose unsavoury reputation in its twilight days was later redeemed by the Franciscans of nearby St. Francis College who took it over as a residence for novitiates. It has now been converted to apartments. Continue walking E.

In the block between Henry and Clinton Sts are several fine townhouses. *No. 104 Pierrepont St* (c. 1857), a four-story brownstone with elaborately carved console brackets on the first and second stories, was first owned by one Thomas Clark, listed in an 1858 city directory as proprietor of a 'fancy store'. *No. 108–114 Pierrepont St* (1840) was once a Greek Revival double house with a central cupola; drastic remodelling has made it a strange hybrid, half Greek Revival, half Romanesque Revival. The doorway pediment and corner quoins on No. 108 remain from the original facade. The half at No. 114 was given its present Romanesque Revival form for publisher Alfred Barnes, by adding brownstone facing, terracotta ornament, a turret and a rounded bay.

MONROE PL., short, wide, and quiet, is named after James Monroe, fifth President of the nation, who finished his life in straitened circumstances in New York. On the N.W. corner of Monroe Pl. and Pierrepont St is the *Appellate Division of the New York State Supreme Court* (1938; Slee & Bryson). Minard Lafever's (1844) *Church of the Saviour*, also called the First Unitarian Church, stands on the N.E. corner. *No. 46 Monroe Pl.* has Brooklyn Heights's only remaining ironwork basket urn, topped with the traditional pineapple for hospitality.

Return to Pierrepont St. A block E. is the **Long Island Historical Society** (1878; George B. Post), at 128 Pierrepont St, S.W. corner of Clinton St, a grand building housing a grand collection of materials on local history.

Open Tues–Sat, 9–5. Library closed in Aug. Free admission to building but $1 fee for non-members using the research library. Tel: 624–0890.

The facade of this eclectic, asymmetrical building with its slate-roofed tower is ornamented with terracotta reliefs including busts of historical worthies peering out from between the window arches (sculptor Olin Levi Warner), and a Viking and an Indian overlooking the main door. Inside, the society has 125,000 volumes, as well as maps, manuscripts, diaries, legal documents, drawings and photographs, church histories, and other historical materials relating to Brooklyn and Long Island. Its genealogical collection is outstanding.

From the turn of the century until 1944 when the club closed, members of the Crescent Athletic Club (1906; Frank Freeman) swam, played squash, and exercised in the gymnasium of what is now *St. Ann's Episcopal School* across the street on the N.W. corner of Clinton St at 129 Pierrepont St.

Continue to Cadman Plaza; turn right and walk S. to MONTAGUE ST, the main commercial street of Brooklyn Heights. Here are restaurants, boutiques, book and record stores, groceries, and delicatessens serving the everyday needs of the neighbourhood.

On the N.W. corner of Clinton and Montague Sts is Protestant Episcopal *Holy Trinity Church* (1847; Minard Lafever), a brownstone Gothic Revival church now undergoing restoration. Cast terracotta ornament, windows by William Jay Bolton, a reredos by Frank Freeman, and a bust of pastor John Howard Melish (N. side of the entrance vestibule) by William Zorach adorn the interior.

Walk W. on Montague St. At Henry St turn left and walk S. to the N.E. corner of Remsen St. *Our Lady of Lebanon Church* (1846; Richard Upjohn), originally the Congregational Church of the Pilgrims, has since 1944 served a community of Middle Eastern Catholics practicing the Maronite rite. Simple and bold in form, faced with ashlar stonework instead of the usual brownstone, the church represents a brief departure from Upjohn's more familiar Gothic Revival style. The doors in the W. and S. portals come from the luxury liner 'Normandie' which burned (1942) and sank at its Hudson River berth; a projecting chunk of stone, inside near the corner tower, comes from Plymouth Rock, where the first pilgrim settlers safely disembarked in 1620. The steeple has been removed.

Return to Montague St and keep walking W. The *Hotel Bossert*, 98 Montague St on the S.E. corner of Hicks St (1909; with addition on the S., 1912; Helmle and Huberty) got its name from founder Louis Bossert, a Bushwick millwork manufacturer. In the 1920s and 1930s the Marine Roof, decorated by theatrical designer Joseph Urban, afforded visitors a vista of the Manhattan skyline while they dined and danced. Today the hotel is less glamorous.

Along the waterfront at the foot of Montague St runs the ***Esplanade,** known locally as the Promenade (1951; Andrews and Clark, engineers; Clarke & Rapuano, landscape architects), a five-block walkway between Remsen and Orange Sts cantilevered over the Brooklyn-Queens Expressway. The superb views of the Manhattan skyline compensate for the fumes rising from the road below. A plaque at the entrance recalls the original Pierpont mansion Four Chimneys which stood nearby.

*NOS 2–3 PIERREPONT PL. at the entrance to the Promenade, two superb Renaissance Revival brownstones (1857; Frederick A. Peterson) by the architect of Cooper Union, belonged originally to Abiel Abbot Low (teas) and Alexander M. White (furs), as an 1858 city directory lists them. Low, a Yankee from Salem, Massachusetts, got into the China trade early, made a fortune, and settled here with his family including son Seth, later mayor of Brooklyn and of New York City. From his opulent home, four stories elaborated with quoins, a heavy cornice, Corinthian pilasters at the entrance, and a conservatory added later on the S. end, Low could watch his ships setting out to sea. Alfred Tredway White lived at No. 2 from 1868–80. A children's playground stands on the site of Henry E. Pierrepont's mansion at No. 1.

PIERREPONT PL., like Pierrepont St, takes its name from Hezekiah Beers Pierpont, landowner and gin distiller, who early saw the advantages of opening Brooklyn Heights for suburban development. He backed the Fulton Ferry (1814) and by 1823 was offering 25 × 100 ft lots to 'gentlemen whose duties require their daily attendance in the city'. His estate faced the harbour and ran N.–S. from Remsen St to Love Lane, and westward to a point beyond Clinton St. Hezekiah spelled his last name with one 'r' but his children reverted to an earlier, fancier spelling.

Walk S. on Montague Terrace, like Montague St named after Lady Mary Wortley Montagu, née Pierrepoint, the English writer. The final 'e' is a misspelling. Turn left into Remsen St, named after Henry Remsen, a landowner. *Nos 18 and 16 Remsen St* have handsome scroll pediments above the doorways. Turn right on Hicks St and walk a short block to the S.W. corner of Grace Court. Richard Upjohn designed GRACE CHURCH (1847), a year after his experiment with the Church of the Pilgrims (see p524), retreating to his usual Gothic Revival manner. A glorious old elm tree shades the courtyard S. of the church; three Tiffany windows adorn the sanctuary.

GRACE COURT ALLEY, running E. of Hicks St, originally a mews for the horses and carriages of Remsen and Joralemon Sts, now houses the gentry itself in stables converted to apartments. Continue S. to Joralemon St, named after Teunis Joralemon, a 19C landowner.

Turn right on Joralemon St and walk toward the harbour. On the sloping W. end of the street, between Hicks and Furman Sts, stands a row of 24 modest Greek Revival houses, *Nos 29–75 Joralemon St,* many with their original iron railings and doorway trim. *No. 58,* across the street, shuttered with steel, its windows rimmed with soot, has become a ventilator for the IRT subway whose Battery-Joralemon St tunnel runs deep below. The RIVERSIDE BUILDINGS (4–30 Columbia Pl., S.W. corner of Joralemon St), accurately named until the Brooklyn-Queens Expressway usurped the shoreline, are another stand of model tenements built by Alfred Tredway White (1890; William Field & Son), whose good works also enhance Cobble Hill (see p529).

Return to Willow Pl., turn right and walk S. Gothic Revival townhouses were never as common in New York as other styles. *Nos 2–8 Willow Pl.* are unusual survivals (c. 1847), their Gothicism expressed mainly in the clustered colonnettes and pointed arches of the porches and the recessed decorative panels above. *Nos 43–49 Willow Pl.* are Brooklyn's sole remaining colonnade row, four Greek Revival houses (1847)—two battered, two restored—joined by a wooden colonnade. Unlike the city's other such rows intended for the wealthy, this one housed more humble folk, accountants and merchants.

Turn left on State St; walk E. past Hicks St, Garden Pl., and Henry St to Sidney Pl.; turn left.

Sidney Pl., originally called Monroe Pl. after the fifth President, was given its present name after 1831 by borough attorney George Wood, who wished for obscure reasons to honour Sir Philip Sidney,

16C English statesman and man of letters. Turn left into Sidney Pl. and walk N. past a handsome row (Nos 31–49) of Greek Revival houses, built together in 1845 with unusually generous front gardens. Roman Catholic *St. Charles Borromeo Church* (1869; P.C. Keely) a Gothic Revival, red-painted brick church, stands on the N.E. corner of Aitken Pl., recently renamed after pastor Ambrose S. Aitken.

Look N. to *135 Joralemon St*, a clapboarded frame house in the Federal style similar to No. 24 Middagh St. The cast-iron porch was added in the mid-19C when the first floor windows were elongated.

Follow Aitken Pl to Clinton St, named after De Witt Clinton, governor of New York State, mayor of New York City, builder of the Erie Canal. Rows of 19C houses line the block down to State St. Across Clinton St at the N.E. corner of Livingston St is the former **St. Ann's Church** (Protestant Episcopal), now the Auditorium of Packer Collegiate Institute. An exuberant Ruskinian Gothic building (1869; James Renwick, Jr), its brownstone facade banded with white limestone and topped with spires and traceried openings, the church is smaller but more flamboyant than Renwick's famous Manhattan churches—Grace Church on Broadway and St. Patrick's Cathedral.

The congregation, since 1966 merged with Holy Trinity Church nearby, dates back to 1784, and the zeal of its members in organising new parishes, six of them, gave it the title 'Mother of Brooklyn Churches'.

Go N. to Joralemon St and turn right. The PACKER COLLEGIATE INSTITUTE at 170 Joralemon St between Clinton and Court Sts with its Gothic Revival campus (1854; Minard Lafever) started out as a girls' school but is now a private secondary school.

The nearest subways are the BMT Court St/Montague St station next to Holy Trinity Church (Nassau St M train or Broadway local RR train) and the IRT Borough Hall/Court St station (Broadway–7th Ave train 2 or 3; Lexington Ave train 4 or 5). If the entrances on Joralemon St are closed, take the stairway in front of the Brooklyn Municipal Building.

40 The Civic Center and Downtown Brooklyn

SUBWAY: IRT Broadway–7th Ave (trains 2, 3) or IRT Lexington Ave (trains 4, 5) to Borough Hall. IND Eighth Ave (A train) or Sixth Ave (F train) to Jay St/Borough Hall.

BUS: Culture Bus (weekends and holidays), Loop II, stop I.

The **Civic Center,** today devoted to borough affairs, was formerly the seat of government of the independent City of Brooklyn established in 1834, the descendent of the town of Brooklyn or Breukelen, chartered by the Dutch in 1658. Long the focal point of Brooklyn's far-flung system of elevated railways, the Civic Center got a facelift in the 1950s when the trestles were torn down and the streets widened during the construction of Cadman Plaza. The main shopping street, once the main shopping street of all Brooklyn, is Fulton St.

Points of interest: •BOROUGH HALL, originally the City Hall of the independent city of Brooklyn (1846–51; Gamaliel King; cupola, 1898; Stoughton & Stoughton; DL) at 209 Joralemon St, intersection of Fulton and Court Sts, like certain other things in Brooklyn, began as a copy of its counterpart in New York across the river. Indecision and bureaucratic bungling resulted in three subsequent sets of plans, and today its stark Greek Revival mass—with an imposing stairway and entrance colonnade—supports a Victorian cupola, an afterthought. Across the street (210 Joralemon St) is the **Brooklyn Municipal Building** (1926; McKenzie, Voorhes, & Gmelin), home of many borough offices.

Cadman Plaza, officially S. Parkes Cadman Plaza, named after a noted Brooklyn Congregationalist minister and radio preacher, is bounded by Cadman Plaza West, Joralemon, Adams, and Court Sts, and the viaducts to the Brooklyn Bridge. The *New York State Supreme Court* (1957; Shreve, Lamb & Harmon) is at 360 Adams St in the S. part of the plaza. The verdigris lamp standards at the S. end were saved from the former (1905) Kings County Hall of Records. Near the entrance to the Supreme Court Building is a plaque honouring Washington A. Roebling, engineer and supervisor of the Brooklyn Bridge. To the W. is a bust of assassinated senator Robert F. Kennedy (1972; Anneta Duveen).

The best piece of sculpture in the plaza is John Quincy Adams Ward's 8-ft bronze *statue of Henry Ward Beecher* (1891). It stands on a granite pedestal, by Richard Morris Hunt, with figures of children bringing floral tributes.

The **Brooklyn General Post Office,** 271 Cadman Plaza East, N.E. corner of Johnson St (1885–91; Mifflin E. Bell, first designer; William A. Freret, successor; addition to the N., 1933; James Wetmore, supervising architect; DL), is a grand example of Romanesque Revival architecture, with a steep slatecovered roof, dormers, turrets, and a massive arcade at ground level. At the N. end of the plaza is the *Brooklyn War Memorial* (1951; Eggers & Higgins, architects; Charles Keck, sculptor).

A few blocks away is *St. James Cathedral,* formerly St. James' Pro Cathedral (1903; George H. Streeton), on Jay St between Cathedral Pl. and Chapel St, the first Roman Catholic church built in Long Island. The Georgian style brick church with a verdigris copper steeple became Brooklyn's cathedral more or less by default in 1972 when an imposing cathedral planned for the Fort Greene area was never built.

The *former City of Brooklyn Fire Headquarters,* 365–367 Jay St, between Willoughby St and Myrtle Ave (1892; Frank Freeman; DL), a Romanesque Revival masterpiece, is rated the best work of Brooklyn's best architect. Built of rock-face granite, dark brown brick, and red sandstone with terracotta ornament and a red tile roof, the firehouse has a large archway for the fire engines (and horses in the old days) and a tall tower for spotting fires.

Gage & Tollner's restaurant, 374 Fulton St between Smith St and Boerum Pl (1889; DL), is a Brooklyn gustatory landmark, known also for its dark panelled dining room and crystal light fixtures once illuminated by gas.

The NEW YORK CITY TRANSIT AUTHORITY MUSEUM, downstairs in the former IND Court Street subway station at the N.W. corner of Boerum Pl. and Schermerhorn St, offers subway devotees the chance to explore the history of the world's second largest mass transit system.

Open daily 9.30–4.00. Admission, adults 75¢ (a token); children 35¢. Guided tours, movies and slide shows, snack stand. Merchandise includes photos, books, t-shirts, transit articles. On Sat and Sun in season a train of restored subway cars, the Nostalgia Special, makes a four-hour excursion to the Jamaica Wildlife Refuge and the Rockaways. Tel. 330–3060.

The exhibits include classic subway cars, a model of the entire subway system as it exists today (263 miles of track in four boroughs, excluding Staten Island), historical photographs, examples of turnstiles and collection boxes, and displays of the mosaics from IRT and BMT Stations intended partly as decoration, partly as visual aids for immigrants who could not read English.

The piece of Fulton St between the Flatbush Ave Extension and Adams St is the hub of Brooklyn's commercial life. And the *Abraham & Straus department store* (known as A & S) occupying eight assorted buildings along Fulton St between Gallatin Pl. and Hoyt St is its largest and grandest institution.

Founded in 1865 by Abraham Abraham, who clerked in Newark with Benjamin Altman and Lyman Bloomingdale, his later rivals in business, the small dry goods business moved to Fulton St in 1883, the year the Brooklyn Bridge opened. Though others thought the location too far from the center of things, Abraham's vision of the significance of the bridge proved correct, as did his belief that the subway from New York would help trade. Joseph Wechsler, Abraham's original partner, sold his interest in 1893 to three Macy's partners including Isidor and Nathan Straus though A & S did not become part of Macy's.

The oldest part of the bulding is at the N.E. corner of Livingston St and Gallatin Pl. and dates from 1895; the Art Deco Main Building (Starrett & Van Vleck) dates from 1929 and 1935. *Fulton St* itself between Adams St and the Flatbush Ave Extension has been converted to a pedestrian mall—buses are the only vehicles allowed—with widened sidewalks and improved lighting.

The *Albee Square Mall* (1978; Gruen Associates), on DeKalb Ave at Albee Square West, stands on the site of the former RKO Albee movie theatre, demolished in 1977, the last of a group that included the Brooklyn Strand, the Brooklyn Paramount, the Loew's Metropolitan, the Fox, the Orpheum, and a number of burlesque houses. Only the Albee Square Mall, an indoor shopping mall named for Edward F. Albee, grandfather of the playwright, and the name of Fox Square (intersection of Flatbush Ave, Fulton and Nevins Sts) remain to commemorate the heyday of the silver screen in Brooklyn, though the Brooklyn Paramount Theater and its offices (1928) have been converted to Founder's Hall and Tristram W. Metcalf Hall of Long Island University, Brooklyn Center along the E. side of the Flatbush Ave Extension.

The nearest subway stops are the IRT Broadway–7th Ave and Lexington Ave (trains 2, 3, 4, 5) at Nevins St/Flatbush Ave. Also the IND Sixth Ave (B, D, trains) and the BMT Broadway and Nassau St lines (M, N, RR trains) all at DeKalb Ave/Flatbush Ave.

41   Cobble Hill and Carroll Gardens

The nearest SUBWAY stops are the Broadway–7th Ave IRT (trains 2, 3) stop at Borough Hall or the IND Sixth Ave (F train) stop at Bergen St.

N. of Red Hook and S. of Brooklyn Heights are two historic districts,

Cobble Hill and **Carroll Gardens,** formerly considered part of Red Hook but renamed to cleanse them of unpleasant associations as they undergo 'gentrification', the process of rehabilitation associated with the restoration of the old housing and the influx of the middle class.

The name Cobble Hill dates back to the Revolutionary War when 'Cobleshill' rose where Court St now intersects Atlantic Ave and Pacific St. The Cobble Hill Historic District extends from Atlantic Ave to DeGraw St, Hicks to Court St, except for the N.W. corner occupied by Long Island College Hospital. It contains numerous late-19C brick and brownstone townhouses built mostly by property speculators.

Atlantic Ave between Court and Hicks St is the center of Brooklyn's Arab population, whose members include Syrians, Palestinians, Yemenis, Iraqis, Jordanians, and Egyptians. Most New York Arabs are Christian, except for the Yemenis who are Moslem. The Brooklyn colony began after Little Syria (N. of Battery Park around Washington St in Manhattan) was destroyed by the excavations for the Brooklyn-Battery Tunnel, and many of the present residents had parents or grandparents in Manhattan. Merchants on Atlantic Ave offer an exotic variety of fruits, nuts, coffee, dates, and olives while other importers display brass water pipes, belly dancing costumes, backgammon sets, and records of Middle Eastern music. There are Arab bakeries, falafel stands, and pastry shops, as well as more formal restaurants, many of them Lebanese. On the third Sunday in September the Arab community holds the Atlantic Antic, a street fair whose attractions have included belly dancing and camel rides.

Begin at Henry St and Atlantic Ave; walk S. Visible at the S.E. corner of Hicks St and Atlantic Ave is the large red brick Atlantic Ave building of *Long Island College Hospital* (1974; Ferrenz & Taylor), newest addition to an institution founded in the 19C by German immigrants. The next block S. used to be devoted to the ministry of St. Peter's Church a block W., and the present *Congress Nursing Home*, 274 Henry St, served as St. Peter's Hospital (1888; William Schickel & Co.).

Turn the corner to the right on Warren St. Half way down the block on the S. side is **Warren Pl.** lined with handsome cottages constructed for working people (1879) by Alfred Tredway White as part of a large project that also includes the **Tower Buildings** (1879) filling the W. half of the block between Warren and Baltic Sts and the **Home Buildings** (1877) along Hicks and Baltic Sts (439–445 Hicks St and 134–140 Baltic St). The complex, designed by William Field & Son, included 226 tenement apartments and 34 cottages on which White, who disclaimed philanthropy, sought a modest 5% return. The apartments had stairwells entered from outdoor balconies as a fire safety provision, good light and ventilation, and bathing facilities in the basement. The cottages had indoor toilets, unusual in low income housing of the period, and rented for $18 a month.

Just N. of the Tower Buildings is *St. Peter's (Roman Catholic) Church* (1860; P.C. Keely), at Hicks St on the N.E. corner of Warren St, now called St. Paul's, St. Peter's, Our Lady of Pilar Church. Nearby is St. Peter's Academy (1866).

Return to Henry St and continue S. The houses at 412–420 Henry St (1888; George B. Chappell) once belonged to F.A.O. Schwarz, the toy seller.

Continue S. to DeGraw St and turn left. On the N.W. corner of

DeGraw St and Strong Pl. is the *St. Frances Cabrini (Roman Catholic) Chapel*, originally the Strong Place Baptist Church (1852; Minard Lafever), a stone church with a buttressed square tower designed by one of the city's eminent architects. The earlier *Strong Place Baptist Church Chapel*, 56 Strong Pl. (1849; Minard Lafever), is now a day care center.

Walk N. on Clinton St. CHRIST CHURCH (Protestant Episcopal) at 320 Clinton St, N.W. corner of Kane St, was designed (1842) by Richard Upjohn, architect of Trinity Church on Wall St, and has furnishings designed by Louis Comfort Tiffany including an altar and altar railings, the reredos, pulpit, lectern, and chairs. The Upjohns lived a block away at 296 Clinton St, N.W. corner of Baltic St, in a house (1843) designed by the father and enlarged by the son.

Continue N. *Verandah Place*, which runs S. of Congress St between Henry St and Clinton St has stables and small townhouses. Thomas Wolfe lived at No. 40 for a while, in the basement. Handsome Italianate townhouses line Congress St between Clinton and Henry Sts. Abraham J.S. DeGraw originally lived at 219 Clinton St (S.E. corner of Amity St), built for him in 1845, but Ralph L. Cutter, a dry-goods merchant, altered the mansion (1891; D'Oench & Simon), adding the tower for viewing the harbour and installing Brooklyn's first residential elevator. Turn right on Amity St *No. 197 Amity St*, between Clinton and Court Sts, now faced with motley permastone, is distinguished only by being the birthplace in 1854 of Jennie Jerome, mother of Winston Churchill. A few years thereafter her father Leonard Jerome moved the family to a new mansion on Madison Square. *St. Paul's Church* (Roman Catholic) at the S.W. corner of Court St and Congress Ave, half a block E. and a block S., is the second Catholic church built in Brooklyn (1838; Gamaliel King), once a brick Greek Revival building, now much altered and expanded, veneered with brownstone and topped with a steeple (c. 1860).

To reach the **Carroll Gardens Historic District,** follow Court St eight blocks S. (counting on the W. side) to Carroll St. Turn right for a detour to **No. 440 Clinton St** on the S.W. corner of Carroll St, now Guido & Sons Funeral Home, originally the Rankin Residence (c. 1840; DL), a freestanding masonry Greek Revival town house touted as the finest in the city. Its brickwork and grey granite trim are handsomely preserved.

Turn around and walk E. on Carroll St to the historic district centered around President and Carroll Sts between Smith and Hoyt Sts. Here are rows of brownstone row houses with deep front gardens developed between 1859 and 1884 by a group of enlightened real-estate entrepreneurs who planned both the self-contained quality of the district and the careful relationship of each house to its neighbour.

The nearest subway stop is the IND station at Carroll and Smith Sts (Sixth Ave F train and Brooklyn crosstown local GG train).

42 Red Hook

Red Hook, named 'Roode Hoek' by the Dutch—'hoek' meaning a point of land and 'roode' describing either the soil colour or the onetime cranberry bogs—originally referred to all the land below Atlantic Ave from the Gowanus Canal to the Buttermilk Channel. Today, however, as Cobble Hill and Carroll Gardens now undergoing 'gentrification' have been renamed to erase from memory former unpleasant associations, the term Red Hook refers only to the section S. of the Gowanus Expressway. It has long been a commercial area dependent on its piers and waterfront industry, having received its initial impetus from the opening of the Erie Canal in 1825.

The pier and terminal facilities in the *Atlantic Basin area* were developed in the early 1840s by the Atlantic Dock Company and the *Erie Basin* with its rocky breakwater in 1864 by William Beard, a railroad contractor. During the Civil War the warehouses served as a supply base for the Union Army and also as military prisons and hospitals. After the turn of the century the Brooklyn docks became one of the world's great grain ports, and the *former Port of New York Grain Elevator Terminal*, part of the New York State Barge Canal System, still stands between the Henry St Basin and lower Columbia St.

Built in 1922 and unused since 1955, the terminal served during the 1930s as a winter home for hundreds of families who spent their summers carrying cargoes on the Erie and Champlain Canals. Since World War II with the dramatic rise of containerised cargoes, the Brooklyn piers have diminished in importance, lacking sufficient upland space for the handling of containers, and most port activity takes place across the Hudson River in New Jersey.

The residential communities of Red Hook, mostly Italian and Irish in the opening decades of the 20C, were debilitated by the arrival of the Brooklyn-Queens Expressway which cut off the shopping area around Columbia St, throwing blocks of housing into shadow and polluting the air, while the recent loss of jobs on the docks has further depressed the area. Early slum clearance projects like the *Red Hook Houses* (1939), stretching from Clinton St to Dwight St, and such community improvements as the *Red Hook Play Center* (1936), S. of Bay St, a swimming pool and park, attempted to improve conditions but today reflect rather than relieve the surrounding squalour. Newer housing attempts (1972; Ciardullo Assocs) on Visitation Pl., Verona St, and Dwight St are on a more humane scale than the earlier blockbusters. Optimists hope that the recently opened (1981) Port Authority shipping terminal in the Atlantic Basin area and the brownstone revival to the N. may bring better times.

43 Fort Greene, Clinton Hill, and the Navy Yard

SUBWAY: The stop nearest the first point of interest listed below is the Atlantic Ave/ Long Island Railroad station stop, reached via the IND Sixth Ave (D train) or BMT Nassau St (M train); or the IRT Broadway-Seventh Ave (trains 2, 3) or the IRT Lexington Ave (trains 4, 5).

CAR: Follow the Flatbush Ave Extension and Flatbush Ave to Hanson Pl. and turn left.

Fort Greene, the neighbourhood bounded roughly by the Navy Yard on the N., Atlantic Ave on the S., the Flatbush Ave Extension and

Clinton Ave on the W. and E., is another neighbourhood built for the upper middle class in the late 19C, left to deteriorate, and then rediscovered by the middle class of another generation and revived, though its renaissance seems more tentative than those of Park Slope, Cobble Hill, and Brooklyn Heights.

Distances are quite short between points of interest, and the area is pleasant S. and E. of the park, making it attractive for a walking tour. The park itself is fairly safe, though one shouldn't walk there alone.

The neighbourhood has two distinct parts. North of the park are massive public housing projects. Notable among them are the Walt Whitman Houses and the Raymond V. Ingersoll Houses, originally called the Fort Greene Houses (1944), in the area bounded by Myrtle and Park Aves, Carlton Ave and Prince St, part of a crash housing programme for World War II industrial workers employed in the Navy Yard.

South of the park and E. of it are handsome brownstones, many being renovated. Near Atlantic Ave is the Atlantic Avenue Terminal area, dominated by the old passenger terminal of the Brooklyn spur of the Long Island Railroad. A renewal project from the mid-1970s to rehabilitate the terminal, build a campus for Baruch College, the business school of CUNY, and provide moderate- and low-income housing has not proceeded beyond the construction of some dwellings.

Points of interest (listed from S. to N. and from W. to E.): The *Hanson Place Seventh Day Adventist Church*, originally the Hanson Place Baptist Church, 88 Hanson Pl., S.E. corner of S. Portland Ave (1860; DL), is a handsome Greek Revival Church now painted a startling red.

SOUTH PORTLAND AVE and SOUTH OXFORD ST, especially the former, between Lafayette and DeKalb Aves exemplify the spirit of neighbourhood renewal, their tree-shaded brownstones dating from the 1860s. The N.–S. streets in Fort Greene bear the names of fashionable London streets: Adelphi, Carlton, Portland, Oxford, Cumberland, Waverly. The avenues running E.–W. bear the names of American Revolutionary war heroes: Gates, DeKalb, Greene, Willoughby, Lafayette.

Fort Greene Park, bounded by DeKalb and Myrtle Aves, St. Edwards St and Washington Park, was designed by Frederick Law Olmsted and Calvert Vaux (1860). Stanford White (1908) designed the granite column (148 ft 8 in.) whose crowning bronze brazier (by A.A. Weinman) was intended to shelter an eternal flame. A crypt below, not open to the public, contains the remains of some of the 12,000 American soldiers who died on British prison ships in Wallabout Bay between 1780–83. The bodies of the dead who had succumbed to starvation, disease, flogging, and exposure, were first buried in shallow graves along the water by their companions; later the bones were moved to a private estate in Brooklyn and in 1873 to the present crypt. During the Revolution Fort Putnam occupied the park site, renamed Fort Greene after Nathanael Greene during the War of 1812.

From the summit of the hill (100 ft) there is a fine view across to Manhattan, and W. to *Brooklyn Hospital*. The old building dates from 1920 (J.M. Hewlett) and the new part from 1967 (Rogers, Butler

& Burgun). Also new is the *Staff Residence*, (1976; Walker O. Cain & Assocs) on the S.W. corner of Saint Edwards St and Willoughby St.

The street E. of the park, known as WASHINGTON PARK, actually a section of Cumberland St, was once Fort Greene's grandest address, its Italianate brownstones housing such notable figures as publisher Alfred C. Barnes (No. 182), William C. Kingsley (No. 176), political force behind the Brooklyn Bridge, and Abner Keeney (No. 175), his partner in a contracting business. Together Kingsley and Keeney paved Brooklyn's streets, laid its sewers, built a reservoir at Hempstead, and did considerable work in Prospect Park.

Clinton Hill, E. of Fort Greene, formerly the home of Brooklyn's oil king Charles Pratt and other families of wealth, who referred to the neighbourhood simply as 'The Hill', is now the home of the Pratt Institute, St. Joseph's College, the Roman Catholic Bishop of Brooklyn, and a generally middle-class population.

Points of interest. At the N.W. corner of Lafayette and Vanderbilt Aves is *Our Lady Queen of All Saints Church* (1913; Gustave Steinback), built by George Mundelein, pastor of this parish and later Bishop of Chicago. Twenty-four saints adorn the church. Diagonally across the intersection (200 Lafayette Ave) is the *Skinner residence* (1812; DL), originally the Joseph Steele home, a Greek Revival yellow clapboard house with Italianate details probably added later.

The *site of the Roman Catholic Cathedral* for the Diocese of Brooklyn, never built, is in the block of Clermont St between Greene and Lafayette Aves. The diocese bought the land in 1860 and hired Patrick Charles Keely to design a church to be called the Church of the Immaculate Conception; construction began, and by 1887 the walls had reached 10 or 12 ft, and the bishop's residence (now the Chancery) still standing at 367 Clermont Ave had been completed. Funds ran out, construction stopped, new plans were drawn and then discarded, and in 1931 the walls, long a playground for children, were torn down and Bishop Loughlin Memorial High School (1933) built instead, its name commemorating the founder of the ill-fated cathedral.

The block of *CLINTON AVE BETWEEN DEKALB AND WIL-LOUGHBY AVES is the neighbourhood's finest, former home of the oil-rich Pratts. On the W. side (232 Clinton Ave) stands the *Charles Pratt mansion* (c. 1875), home of the founder of the Pratt Astral Oil Works in Greenpoint which he merged secretly and advantageously with John D. Rockefeller's Standard Oil Company in 1874. Ranged along the other side of the street are the homes Pratt built for three of his five sons, the youngest following fashion put his on Park Ave at 68th St (the fifth house has been demolished). The *George DuPont Pratt house*, 245 Clinton Ave (1901; Babb, Cook & Willard, later extensions to the S.), built by the architects of the Andrew Carnegie mansion, now belongs to St. Joseph's College as does the Charles Pratt mansion. Next door is the *Charles Millard Pratt Home*, now the residence of the Roman Catholic Bishop of Brooklyn (241 Clinton Ave), built in 1893 by architect William B. Tubby, a Romanesque Revival brick house with a tile roof and an arched port-cochère on one side balanced by a semicircular conservatory on the other. The *Caroline Ladd Pratt house*, 229 Clinton Ave, now a residence of the Pratt Institute, first belonged (1898; Babb, Cook, & Willard) to Frederick B. Pratt. The columned arbour on its N. serves as an entranceway to the grey and white Georgian Revival house.

Three blocks E. lies the campus of **Pratt Institute**, filling the blocks between Willoughby and DeKalb Aves, Hall St and Classon Ave.

Charles Pratt, a self-made man, founded the Pratt Institute as a trade school for young people situated as he had been. It opened with a drawing class in 1887 and soon expanded to include courses in engineering and science, training programmes for kindergarten teachers, a school for librarians, and courses in home economics, all of which are reflected in the present curriculum.

Ryerson Walk, once Ryerson St, bisects the campus. On its E. side are MEMORIAL HALL (1927; John Mead Howells) and the two original college buildings, the MAIN BUILDING (1887; Lamb & Rich), a sturdy Romanesque Revival, and the EAST BUILDING (1887; William Windrim). In the Main Building is the *Pratt Institute Gallery* which mounts eight or nine shows yearly, presenting sculpture, graphics, painting, book art, photography, and works in other media.

Open Sept–June, Mon–Fri, 9–5. Call for summer hours. Admission free. Occasional lectures, tours, performances. Tel: 636–3517.

The East Building, originally called the Mechanical Arts Building, contains the engine room and boiler for the original plant designed in such a way that Pratt could convert his educational experiment to a shoe factory if it failed. Across the lawn on the W. side of Ryerson Walk is the LIBRARY (1896; William B. Tubby), now being expanded, another of Pratt's philanthropies, founded as Brooklyn's first free public library and annexed to the college only in 1940. THRIFT HALL, now containing offices, on the E. side of Ryerson Walk at DeKalb Ave (1916; Shampan & Shampan), opened as a savings and loan company (in a building where Memorial Hall now stands) organised by the philanthropic Pratt to make low-cost mortgages avialable to workers.

Nearby (half a block S. and two blocks W. of Thrift Hall) is the former *Graham Home for Old Ladies* (1851) at 320 Washington Ave between DeKalb and Lafayette Aves, once a shelter for elderly females too genteel for the public poorhouse.

Underwood Park on Lafayette Ave between Waverly and Washington Aves stands on the site of the John T. Underwood mansion, home of the typewriter manufacturer. The *Apostolic Faith Mission*, 265 Lafayette Ave on the N.E. corner of Washington Ave (1868), now brightly painted, was surely more sombre when it served as the Orthodox Friends Meeting House. At the next corner, 279 Lafayette Ave, N.W. corner of St. James Pl. (1887; Francis H. Kimball; DL) is the *Emmanuel Baptist Church*, looking like a French 13C Gothic church with Romanesque influence, a mix chosen to suggest that the church was constructed over a period of time like its European predecessors.

The nearest subway stop is the IND Brooklyn-Queens Crosstown local (GG train) Clinton/Washington stop on Lafayette Ave. To get to Manhattan from here, take the GG train two stops W. to the Hoyt/Schermerhorn stop and change to the IND. Eighth Ave (A train).

The former **Brooklyn Navy Yard,** today an industrial park (closed to the public), stretches from the East River inland to Flushing Ave, from Kent Ave to Navy and Hudson Sts.

History. In 1781 John Jackson and William Sheffield started a small shipyard on the shores of Wallabout Bay, whose facilities included a sawmill and a pond for seasoning ship timbers. During the War of 1812, the yard, purchased from Jackson by the U.S. Navy for $40,000 in 1801, became an important base for servicing ships, though the first warship built there, the 74-gun ship-of-the-line 'Ohio', was launched only in 1820. Among the long line of distinguished ships produced in the yard are the battleship 'Maine', blown up in Havana harbour (1898), the 'Arizona', sunk at Pearl Harbor, and the battleship 'Missouri', on whose decks Japan signed the surrender ending World War II. Activity peaked in the Navy Yard during World War II, when 70,000 workers on continuous shifts turned out battleships and destroyers and overhauled some 5000 vessels. After the war, however it fell victim to Defense Department cutbacks and policies favouring other parts of the country and closed in 1966 with the loss of thousands of jobs. In 1969 the city took it over and leased it to a quasi-governmental agency given the name CLICK, during a period of acronymic enthusiasm, for Commerce, Labor, Industry of the County of Kings.

Visible from Flushing Ave between Ryerson St and Williamsburgh Pl. is the *former U.S. Naval Hospital*, originally the U.S. Marine Hospital (1838; Martin E. Thompson; DL), austerely constructed of Sing Sing marble, now closed and boarded up. Nearby stands the brick Second Empire style home of the hospital's chief of surgery (1863; True W. Rollins and Charles Hastings, builders; DL) officially known as the *Surgeon's House, Quarters R-1, Third Naval District*.

The oldest structure in the yard is the former COMMANDANT'S HOUSE also known as Quarters A (1806; attrib. to Charles Bulfinch associated with John McComb, Jr; DL) S. of Evans and Little Sts in the W. part of the yard, barely visible through the gates. The three-story white clapboarded house with narrow dormers, handsome porches, and elegant details—leaded glass fan- and sidelights at the main entrance, hewn oak floor beams 32 ft long, interior wood trim of carved mahogany—is one of the city's finest Federal structures. Abandoned in 1976, its fate is uncertain. Also designated as a landmark is DRY DOCK #1 of the shipyard, on Dock St at the foot of 3rd St (1851; William J. McAlpine, engineer and Thornton MacNess Niven, architect and master of masonry; DL), the oldest granite-walled dry dock in the nation, still quite usable.

44 Southwestern Brooklyn: Sunset Park and Bay Bridge

The neighbourhood of **Sunset Park,** named after its park, lies along Gowanus Bay between the Gowanus Expressway to the N., Bay Ridge to the S., and about 5th St to the E. Long a Scandinavian and Finnish quarter whose residents were attracted by the waterfront economy, the district deteriorated rapidly following the construction of the expressway in 1941, and is now largely Hispanic.

Points of interest. *Green-Wood Cemetery, Fifth to McDonald Ave, 20th–37th Sts, has more than 20 miles of paths winding through its 478 acres and includes the highest elevation in Brooklyn (216·5 ft). The cemetery (opened 1840), whose landscaped hills and winding roads offer fine views of the harbour, broke with earlier burial traditions—family plots, church yards—and soon became a popular outing spot for Victorian strollers who liked taking fresh air in a funereal atmosphere. The *MAIN GATE, Fifth Ave at 25th St, designed (1861; Richard Upjohn & Son; DL) by the architect of

Trinity Church, represents the full flowering of the Gothic Revival style. Built of brownstone with multi-coloured slate roofs on the flanking gatekeeper's lodge and office, the gate bristles with spires, turrets, finials, and crockets, its portals covered by tall traceried gables. *Other gatehouses*: Gate and Gatehouse at 20th St opposite Prospect Park West (1920; Warren & Wetmore); Gate and Gatehouse at 37th St and Fort Hamilton Pkwy (1875; Richard M. Upjohn).

Only the main gate is open for visiting hours daily 8–4. For information, tel. 768–7300. On weekdays a map is available at the office inside the main gate. Privately sponsored tours Sun in spring and autumn; tel: 439–8828.

Buried there, among a half million others, are Lola Montez, James Gordon Bennett, Samuel F.B. Morse, Boss Tweed, Henry Ward Beecher, and Peter Cooper.

High, sloping SUNSET PARK, Fifth to Seventh Aves, 41st–44th Sts, also has fine views of the harbour and the Bush Terminal docks but is not one of the city's best cared-for parks.

Finntown, one of two major Finnish settlements in New York (the other was in Harlem), in the early decades of the 20C centered around the N. and E. sides of Sunset Park and had a vital neighbourhood culture with half a dozen public saunas, many small restaurants and 'Mama and Papa' stores, ethnic celebrations, and clean, neat sidewalks swept by housewives who also scrubbed their stoops. A few traces remain today. The *Alku Toinen Finnish Cooperative Apts* (816–826 43rd St between 8th–9th Aves) date from 1916 and are said to be the city's first co-operative apartments. 'Alku' means 'beginning' in Finnish; other Finnish apartment houses were given such names as 'Poorhouse', 'Old Maids' Home', and 'Drop of Sweat'. Other survivals are a Finnish cooperative grocery store at 41st St and Seventh Ave, several Finnish churches, *Imatra Hall* (740 40th St between 7th–8th Aves), home of an organisation descended from the Finnish Aid Society Imatra, (founded 1890), named after a Finnish waterfall, and a weekly Finnish newspaper, the 'New Yorkin Utiset'.

The *Bush Terminal* district along the waterfront between about 28th–50th Sts is one of the major port facilities in Brooklyn, founded in 1890 by Irving T. Bush on land his father used for an oil business. At its peak the terminal employed some 30,000 workers, but container shipping has rendered some of its facilities obsolete. South of the Bush Terminal is the former *Brooklyn Army Terminal* or New York Port of Embarkation and Army Supply Base (Second Ave between 58th–65th Sts), built at the end of World War I to relieve the strain on the city's port facilities. The base, awaiting redevelopment, has two eight-story warehouses (1918; Cass Gilbert) and four piers on 50 acres of upland.

Today **Bay Ridge,** bounded by the Gowanus Expressway, the Narrows and Gravesend Bay, is a quiet residential community with fine waterfront property. The Dutch settled the area as the town of Nieuw Utrecht (1662) which also included Borough Park, Bath Beach, and part of Bensonhurst. Bay Ridge remained rural until late into the 19C, attracting only an occasional rich industrialist to the high ground overlooking the Narrows, and a population of Scandinavians, mostly Norwegian sailors and shipbuilders, to its more modest areas inland. The Scandinavian community remained essentially stable until after World War II, when it was replaced by Greeks, Italians, Asians, and Hispanics. In 1964 the Verrazano Bridge arrived. Most recently fame has come to Bay Ridge as the setting for the 1978 movie 'Saturday Night Fever', whose dance scenes were filmed in a discotheque at Eighth Ave and 64th St.

Points of interest. *Owl's Head Park* at Colonial Rd and Wakeman Pl. used to be part of the estate of Democratic politician Henry C. Murphy, first editor of the Brooklyn 'Eagle', supporter of the Brooklyn Bridge. S. of the park at the foot of Bay Ridge Ave remains an old pier where ferries departed for Staten Island before the advent of the Verrazano Bridge. Along Shore Road overlooking the Narrows and Staten Island are well-kept, well-to-do houses and apartments that have replaced the mansions. Bay Ridge's oddest house is a block inland from Shore Rd at 8220 Narrows Ave and 83rd St, an immense cottage with an extravagant fieldstone chimney. Another house, remarkable for its survival, is the *James F. Farrell residence* (119 95th St, N. side of block between Marine Ave and Shore Rd), a wooden Greek Revival dwelling (c. 1845), with wooden clapboards, shutters, trim, and cornice still intact.

At the S. end of Shore Rd is FORT HAMILTON PARK, a small triangular park between Fourth Ave and the bridge approach, containing a granite obelisk (1931) commemorating the service of the U.S. Navy in World War I.

W. of the bridge approach at 9818 Fort Hamilton Pkwy is *St. John's (Protestant Episcopal) Church* (1834), a modest country church that became known as the 'church of the generals' because of its proximity to neighbouring Fort Hamilton. Robert E. Lee served as vestryman and Stonewall Jackson was baptised here at the age of 30.

Overhead soars the **Verrazano-Narrows Bridge** (1964; Othmar H. Ammann, engineer), a 4260-ft span linking Staten Island and Brooklyn, the world's longest suspension bridge, 60 ft longer than the former record holder, the Golden Gate Bridge in San Francisco.

Proposed as early as 1926, the bridge became mired in politics, and bridge commissioner Robert Moses spent almost 20 years subverting and crushing opposition to the project. Ground was broken in 1959 and as a consolation to the Italian community of Bay Ridge, some of whose homes were destroyed for the approaches, the bridge was named after Giovanni da Verrazano, the Florentine explorer who discovered New York Bay in 1524.

STATISTICS: Length of span, 4260 ft; length of bridge including approaches, 13,700 ft. Height of roadway above mean high water, 228 ft. Height of towers, 693 ft. Weight of each tower, 27,000 tons.

Fort Hamilton, named after Alexander Hamilton, was built facing Fort Wadsworth on Staten Island in 1825–31 to protect the entrance to New York harbour. The 155-acre government reservation includes the *Fort Hamilton Veterans' Hospital* (1950; Skidmore, Owings & Merrill), and the *Fort Hamilton Officers' Club*, originally Casemate Fort (1825–31; DL), one of the city's earliest granite fortifications (not open to the public). The HARBOR DEFENSE MUSEUM (enter through the 101st St gate) offers changing exhibitions on military history and the coastal defence of New York.

Open Mon, Thurs, Fri, 1–4. Sat, 10–5; Sun, 1–5. Closed holidays. Free admission. Tours by appointment. Tel: 836–4100, ext. 4149.

On Fifth Ave between Bay Ridge Pkwy and about 82nd St and on Eighth Ave between about 59th and 55th Sts are the remnants of the Scandinavian communities of Bay Ridge. Delicatessens carry authentic Scandinavian sausages as well as fish (salt herring, dried cod, canned sardines), bread, cheese, and even canned reindeer meat. The delectable products of several Scandinavian bakeries suggest why that breakfast pastry known as a sweet roll elsewhere in the nation is called a Danish in New York. At 8104 Fifth Ave the 'Nordisk Tidende' or 'Norwegian News', (founded 1891) is still published.

45 Park Slope

SUBWAY: IRT Broadway–7th Ave (train 2, 3) to Grand Army Plaza. IND Sixth Ave (D train) to 7th Ave/Flatbush Ave. BMT Nassau St (M train) to 7th Ave/Flatbush Ave.

BUS: Culture Bus, Loop II (weekends and holidays), Stops 4 and 9.

Park Slope, a district rising from the lowlands around the Gowanus Canal to the hilltops of Prospect Park, can be divided into three separate neighbourhoods. The North Slope, between the park and Sixth Ave, has one of the nation's highest concentrations of Victorian architecture, fine brownstones developed after the Civil War for wealthy families seeking an alternative to Manhattan's Fifth Ave. West of about Fifth Ave is a neighbourhood known locally as 'no man's land', a dilapidated semi-industrial area with abandoned housing and a flourishing drug trade. The South Slope, beginning around Third St, has been a working-class district since it was developed for workers on the Brooklyn docks in the 19C. Until the 1940s it was also home of a small enclave of Newfoundlanders known locally as 'blue noses' who earned their livelihood on the fishing boats out of Sheepshead Bay. The following walking tour focuses on the Victorian residential architecture of the North Slope.

Begin at Grand Army Plaza (see p541 for description of the plaza). THE MONTAUK CLUB, 25 Eighth Ave, N.E. corner of Lincoln Pl. (1891; Francis H. Kimball), served Brooklyn's social, business, and political elite during its heyday before World War I and now opens its doors to a less illustrious membership. The building, an eclectic composition of Venetian Gothic and American Indian motifs, pays tribute to the Ca d'Oro in Venice and the Montauk Indians of eastern Long Island whose history appears in the terracotta frieze.

  Walk S. along the W. side of the plaza. *No. 276 Berkeley Pl.* (1891; Lamb & Rich), a sturdy Romanesque Revival house, belonged originally to George P. Tangeman, whose fortune was derived from the Royal and Cleveland Baking Powder Companies. Unlike the millionaires of New York's Fifth Ave, who dealt in railroads, real estate, and oil, Park Slope's industrialists generally owed their wealth to more homely commodities—chewing gum, hot dogs, cleansing powder.

  Walk W. (away from the park) to Eighth Ave; turn left and go S. a block to Union St. Among the attractive late 19C houses lining the block of Union St between Eighth and Seventh Aves are Nos 889–903 (1889; Albert E. White) and Nos 905–913 (1895; Thomas McMahon).

Continue S. along Eighth Ave to President St and turn right. The *former Stuart L. Woodford residence*, 869 President St between Eighth and Seventh Aves (1865; Henry Ogden Avery), remarkable for its oriel windows and the radial ornament over the ground floor windows and door, formerly belonged to the U.S. ambassador to Spain and now serves the Missionary Servants of the Most Holy Trinity. Return to Eighth Ave and continue S. a block to Carroll St.

On the N.E. corner of the intersection stands the *former Thomas Adams, Jr residence*, 115 Eighth Ave (1888; C.P.H. Gilbert), a brownstone Romanesque Revival mansion with an elaborately carved entrance arch on Carroll St, home of the inventor of Chiclets chewing gum, now apartments. On the S.W. corner of the same intersection stood the mansion (demolished 1950) of Charles Feltman, alleged inventor of the hot dog, whose Coney Island restaurant earned him fame and fortune.

Enthusiasts of row house architecture will find an interesting group on *Fiske Pl.* a half block W. of Eighth Ave between Carroll St and Garfield Pl. Nos 12, 14, and 16 (1896) were designed by an unknown architect apparently experimenting with triangular, semicircular, and rectangular window forms, an experiment whose results so pleased him that he repeated it a block W. at Nos 11, 15, and 17 Polhemus Pl.

Another architecturally interesting block is that of *Montgomery Pl. between Eighth Ave and Prospect Park West.* Developer Harvey Murdock, who apparently had an eye for the picturesque, chose C.P.H. Gilbert to design most of the houses on the street (Nos 11, 17, 19, 14–18, 21, 25, 36–46, 48–50, and 54–60). Murdock himself lived at No. 11. Return to Carroll St and Eighth Ave.

The block of CARROLL ST BETWEEN EIGHTH AVE AND PROSPECT PARK WEST is architecturally one of Park Slope's most interesting, developed by eminent 19C architects. Noteworthy are Nos 838–846 (1887; C.P.H. Gilbert), three houses each an imposing 40 ft wide; Nos 864–872 (1887; William B. Tubby), picturesque brick and shingled Queen Anne houses; Nos 855–861 (1892; Stanley M. Holden), Romanesque Revival houses with carved leaf forms and faces ornamenting the windows; and No. 863 (1890; Napoleon Le Brun & Sons), by a firm known for its fire houses.

On the S.W. corner of Prospect Park West and Carroll St are two limestone Renaissance Revival apartments, formerly houses, Nos 18 and 19 Prospect Park West (1898; Montrose W. Morris), the former retaining its glass canopy.

Continue down Prospect Park West. The *Woodward Park School,* 49 Prospect Park West between 1st and 2nd Sts (1892; Montrose W. Morris), belonged first to Henry J. Hulbert, whose financial interests included paper, Pullman cars, and life insurance. Long the biggest building around, the mansion was provided with towers which allowed Hulbert a fine view of the harbour. His next door neighbour at 53 Prospect Park West was William H. Childs, inventor of Bon Ami, precursor of the modern battery of cleansing powders. Today the red brick and limestone mansion (1901; William B. Tubby) serves as the *Brooklyn Ethical Culture Society Meeting House.* (For the nearby Litchfield Villa in Prospect Park about opposite 4th St, see p544.)

The nearest subway stops are those at Grand Army Plaza.

46 Prospect Park

SUBWAY: IRT Lexington Ave express (train 4) or IRT
Broadway-Seventh Ave express (train 2 or 3) to Grand Army Plaza.

BUS: Culture Bus Loop II, stops 4 and 9 to Grand Army Plaza.

CAR: From Manhattan take the Manhattan Bridge to Flatbush Ave
and follow it S. to Grand Army Plaza. From points E. take the
Brooklyn-Queens Expressway and get off at the Tillary St exit; turn
left onto Flatbush Ave Extension and follow it to Grand Army Plaza.
Parking on Prospect Park West, or in Brooklyn Museum parking lot
(fee).

**Prospect Park, 526 acres of meadows, woods, and lakes designed
by Frederick Law Olmsted and Calvert Vaux, is one of the chief
ornaments of Brooklyn. Laid out by its designers (1866–67) after
Central Park when they could profit from earlier mistakes, the park
is thought by many to be their masterpiece. Today, in addition to the
beautifully enhanced landscape, there are recreational facilities
such as picnic grounds, baseball diamonds, a zoo, and a skating rink,
but fortunately the park has by and large escaped the attention of
self-memorialising philanthropists.

CRIME: Prospect Park has an unsavoury reputation but is not the urban jungle
many people believe it to be. Use common sense. Do not wander in its more
isolated areas alone, and don't go there at night. As elsewhere, company is the
best security.

TOURS: The Urban Park Rangers offer guided tours to different attractions in
the park on weekends; call 856–4210.

RECREATIONAL FACILITIES: Ice skating at Wollman Rink, opens around 15
November. For information call 965–6561. Horses to ride on the bridle path can
be rented at Culmit Stables, 51 Caton Place at E. 8th St; lessons available. Call
438–8849. Roller skate rental at Park Slope Skates, 123A Seventh Ave (between
President and Carroll Sts); call 783–2550. Bicycle rental at Dixon's Bicycle
Shop, 792 Union St (near Seventh Ave), call 636–0067, or Prospect Park Bicycle
Shop, 494 Flatbush Ave (near Empire Blvd.); call 284–6936.

WEEKLY INFORMATION ABOUT PARK EVENTS: Call 788–0055. PPEC
(Prospect Park Environmental Center) sponsors frequent weekend events; call
622–7686.

History. In 1859, aroused by the success of Central Park across the river,
Brooklyn civic leaders headed by James S.T. Stranahan, moved to purchase a
\$4-million parcel of land for a pleasure ground. Egbert Viele, formerly the chief
engineer of Central Park, designed one ground which included much of the
present park as well as the area now occupied by the Brooklyn Museum and
the Botanic Garden. Fortunately the Civil War halted construction, giving the
commissioners time to reconsider Viele's plan. Unhappy with it, they hired
Calvert Vaux who convinced them to change the site to its present form,
eliminating Flatbush Ave which would have cut a swath down the middle, and
adding land for a large lake. Vaux brought in Frederick Law Olmsted and the
two worked on Prospect Park from 1866 to 1873, authorising some \$5 million in
improvements, enhancing the natural contours of the land, providing rustic
park shelters, building archways and roads, planting and replanting trees and
shrubs.
  At the end of the century the firm of McKim, Mead & White designed the
Peristyle and a number of handsome park entrances, and oversaw the formal
placement of statuary in the Concert Grove, all in their usual grand Renaissance manner, but these additions are peripheral and do not destroy the
integrity of the Olmsted-Vaux plan. Later and less happy intrusions have been
fenced ballfields on the Long Meadow, the zoo, and the skating rink, enjoyed
by their users but unloved by those who cherish the original design.
  Today Prospect Park, recognised as a masterpiece, is in a state of precarious

balance. A master plan for restoration has been developed and several structures—the Boathouse and the arch in Grand Army Plaza—have been refurbished. At the same time the park suffers from vandalism: graffiti are sprayed over many monuments; plaques and even statues are stolen for the value of the metals in them; animals at the zoo have been harrassed at night by intruders and recently a protective fence has been erected to close off the zoo at night.

Begin at *Grand Army Plaza (1870; Frederick Law Olmsted and Calvert Vaux), Flatbush Ave, at the intersection of Prospect Park West, Eastern Pkwy, and Vanderbilt Ave, a monumental oval plaza with a triumphal arch honouring the Union forces in the Civil War, Brooklyn's answer to the Parisian Place de l'Étoile. John H. Duncan designed the 80-ft arch (1892) on top of which rides a bronze Victory (1898; Frederick W. MacMonnies) in a four-horse chariot accompanied by trumpeters. On the S. pedestal two monumental groups also by MacMonnies (both 1901) represent the * Army and the Navy, while inside the arch are bas-reliefs of Lincoln and Ulysses S. Grant (1894; Thomas Eakins and William R. O'Donovan).

North of the arch is an ellipse surrounded by formally planted plane trees around the central Mary Louise Bailey Fountain (1932; Eugene F. Savage, sculptor; Edgerton Swartwout, architect), with a grotesque open-mouthed Neptune and sportive Tritons. North of it stands the city's sole official monument to John F. Kennedy, a modest marble tablet with a small bronze bust (1965; Neil Estern); still further N. across the road is a bust of Alexander Skene (1905; J. Massey Rhind), one time dean and president of Long Island College Hospital.

Walk back toward the park. On the W., across the road, is Henry Baerer's (1896) bronze statue of Gouverneur Kemble Warren, Civil War engineer and soldier, defender of Little Round Top in the Battle of Gettysburg, some of whose boulders have been incorporated in the statue's base. In the same position on the other side of the arch is a bronze statue of Henry Warner Slocum (1905; Frederick W. MacMonnies), a Civil War general who hailed from Brooklyn.

Enter the park through its most formal approach whose eagle-topped Doric columns and 12-sided classic temples (1894; Stanford White) express the rampant classicism of the period. Just inside the park entrance stands a statue of James S.T. Stranahan (1891; Frederick W. MacMonnies), park commissioner, public servant, and originator of Brooklyn's boulevard systems.

Take the right pathway (nearest Prospect Park West). A berm or earth mound girds the entire park, designed by Olmsted and Vaux as a visual and acoustic barrier distancing the park from its raucous urban surroundings. Take the left fork of the path and cross under the roadway (noticing how here as in Central Park Vaux and Olmsted have separated vehicular and pedestrian traffic); walk through the Meadowport Arch (1872; Calvert Vaux) and into the Long Meadow.

Almost a mile in length, the **Long Meadow** provides 75 acres of gently rolling grassland whose pastoral serenity Olmsted felt to be essential to an urban park, so essential that he had workers remove a narrow glacial ridge to enlarge the sweep of the land. He planted trees either singly (and some have grown to wonderful proportions) or in selected groups, using in many cases a tree-moving machine he and Vaux invented in 1867. Workmen with pick and shovel scooped out and packed into place the dips and rises that seem so natural.

1   Bailey Fountain
2   Kennedy Monument
3   Skene Monument
4   Warren Monument
5   Slocum Monument
6   Stranahan Monument
7   Meadowport Arch
8   Lafayette Memorial
9   Nethermead Arches
10 Maryland Monument
11 Mozart Monument
12 Beethoven Monument
13 Moore Monument
14 Grieg Monument
15 von Weber Monument
16 Lincoln Monument
17 World War I Monument
18 Horse Tamers
19 Cleft Ridge Span
20 Camperdown Elm
21 Endale Arch

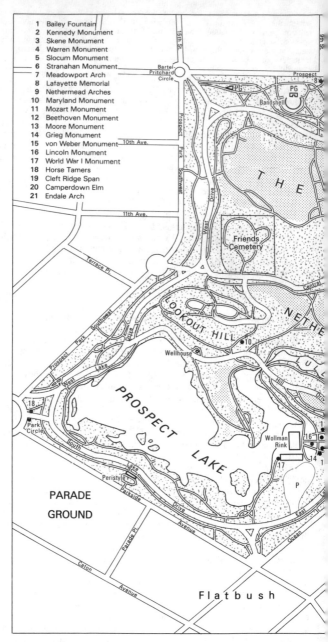

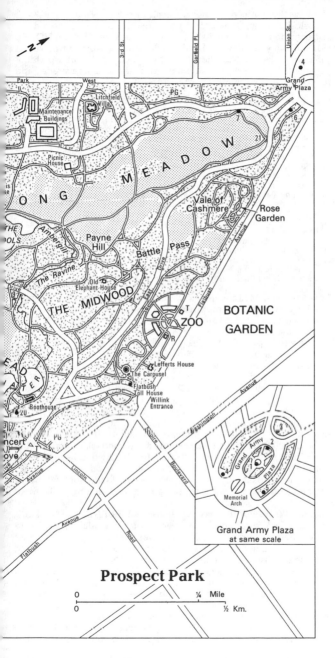

Prospect Park

0 ¼ Mile

0 ½ Km.

Grand Army Plaza
at same scale

Follow the path past the uninspired *Picnic House* (1927; J. Sarsfield Kennedy), now used as a recreation center for the elderly (restrooms in basement). Visible to the right is the TENNIS HOUSE (1910; Helmle & Huberty), of brick and limestone with open Palladian arches built in the days when lawn tennis was a portable sport played on lawns; vandals have ripped out its balustrades and sprayed the arched tile interior with graffiti.

Side trip. Take the path along the road and cross under it to the paved Ninth St playground, a place for roller hockey after school or for jazz and classical concerts (summer) in the nearby bandshell. At the Ninth St entrance is Daniel Chester French's (1917) *Lafayette Memorial*, a 10-ft bronze tablet with a high relief of Lafayette in the uniform of an American Revolutionary soldier. The park maintenance buildings between Eighth and Seventh Sts (inside the park) used to be the stables of the Litchfield estate. The LITCHFIELD VILLA itself, now the headquarters of the Park Department (in the park opposite about Fourth St) was built (1857; Alexander Jackson Davis; DL) as a home for Edwin C. Litchfield, a lawyer who made a fortune developing midwestern railroads. In 1853 he hired Davis to design this Italianate mansion, romantic, asymmetrical, towered, turreted, and balconied. Davis called it Ridgewood; the Litchfields called it Grace Hill after Mrs Litchfield, neé Grace Hill Hubbard. After the Civil War Litchfield donated 24 acres of his land to Prospect Park, but, according to the Brooklyn 'Eagle', the park commissioners lusted after Litchfield's castle with a craving like that of David for Naboth's vineyard, and appropriated his estate and home, allowing the family to rent it back for $2500 a year. The columns on the porches have bunches of corn and wheat on the capitals instead of the classic acanthus leaves, perhaps a reminder of the midwest where Litchfield achieved financial success. Return to the Long Meadow.

Cross the Long Meadow to the POOLS, two artificial ponds separated by cascades and supplied by a waterfall joined to the city system whose waters fill all the ponds and brooks in the park. Take the path along the shore to the *Ambergill*, a small stream flowing into the woods past *Payne Hill* (on the left as you enter the woods). Once a bronze bust of John Howard Payne (1873; Henry Baerer), composer of 'Home Sweet Home', graced the top of the hill but thieves took it and vandals have defaced the pedestal.

Follow the Ambergill into the RAVINE, keeping the brook on your right; the steep hills and plantings here were designed to satisfy the 19C taste for wild, romantic scenery and to complement the gentler landscape of the Long Meadow. Continue along the stream past the stone staircase to the *Nethermead Arches* (1870; Calvert Vaux), whose three spans accommodate walkers, horseback riders, and the brook. Inside the arches are vaults with fine brickwork. Beyond is the **Nethermead** or lower meadow, surrounded by woods and seemingly isolated from the city. Continue along the path to the right, following it along Central Drive to an unused paved road leading up Lookout Hill.

On the W. side of the drive is the fenced FRIENDS' CEMETERY (generally locked; apply to the keeper if he is available), a 15-acre Quaker burial ground established (1846) before the park was built and still in immaculate condition. Actor Montgomery Clift is buried here about halfway up the hill near the right (N.) fence.

Take the unused carriage drive up LOOKOUT HILL, the highest elevation (170 ft) in the park, planned as a gathering place with separate concourses for carriages and pedestrians. Today the hilltop, abandoned and overgrown, offers views of the city and harbour during the winter months when the trees are bare.

Walk down the E. stairway. Near the bottom of the hill, not far from the bridge, is the *Maryland Monument* (1895; Stanford White), a memorial to the heroism of a Maryland regiment whose holding action allowed the main body of Washington's troops to escape encirclement by the British during the Revolutionary War. Continue downhill to the lake. Off to the right (as you face the water), hugging the hillside is the abandoned *Well House* (1869) whose pumps once raised water to a reservoir on top of Lookout Hill. From here it flowed down into the Pools and thence through the Ravine into the Lullwater and Prospect Lake. City water came into the park at the turn of the century and the well was covered over.

From the foot of the hill cross the Terrace Bridge and continue straight on to the **Concert Grove,** laid out as a formal garden with avenues of trees and statues of musicians. At the edge of the lake stands the *Wollman Rink and Skating Shelter* (1960; Hopf & Adler), replacing a small cove and an offshore island that once served as a natural bandstand. In the grove today are *busts of composers: Mozart* (1897; Augustus Mueller), *Beethoven* (1894; Henry Baerer), *Thomas Moore* (1879; John G. Draddy), *Grieg* (1914; Sigvald Absjornsen), and *von Weber* (1909; Chester Beach). Directly behind the rink is Henry Kirke Brown's *statue* (1869) *of Abraham Lincoln,* formerly in Grand Army Plaza. Once the statue held a copy of the Emancipation Proclamation, but like many other metal objects in the park this has disappeared. Walk around the rink past the parking lot to the *World War I Memorial* (1921; Augustus Lukeman, sculptor; Daniel Chester French, architect), a shrouded bronze angel sheltering a soldier.

Nearby along the shore stands a rustic log shelter, similar to those designed by Vaux and Olmsted as part of the original park furniture. From here either follow the lake shore S. to the Park Circle exit or return to Grand Army Plaza past the zoo, the Lefferts Homestead, and the Vale of Cashmere.

To Park Circle: Continue along the shoreline and cross left under the drive, following the path to the PERISTYLE, sometimes called the Grecian Shelter (1906; McKim, Mead & White; DL), its limestone columns finished off with terracotta Corinthian capitals. Further along is the Park Circle entrance (1897; McKim, Mead & White) adorned with Frederick MacMonnies' wonderful, athletic *'Horse Tamers* (1897), two bronze groups flanking the roadway.

To Grand Army Plaza: Walk back to the Concert Grove. Along its main axis, furthest from the rink are the remnants of the Oriental Pavilion (1874; Calvert Vaux), now a charred wreck, once a fine example of Victorian exotic tastes in architecture, its hipped roof and posts modelled on a medieval Hindu temple.

At the ruined pavilion turn left and walk under the CLEFT RIDGE SPAN (1872; Calvert Vaux), its vaulted inside finished with polychrome blocks of moulded concrete. Beyond on the left is a Himalayan pine and (on the right) the park's most famous tree, a gnarled and twisted **'Camperdown elm,** planted in 1872.

Marianne Moore wrote a poem about it; its devotees raised money to fill its hollows and truss its branches, and the Friends of Prospect Park still hold benefit road races to maintain it and its fellows. Created by grafting a prostrate Scotch elm onto an upright elm trunk, the tree is descended from a crawling elm that grew (c. 1850) near Camperdown House in Dundee, Scotland.

Continue straight ahead to the BOATHOUSE (1905; Helmle & Huberty; DL) faced with white terracotta, formerly the site of a boating office and a soda fountain. Renovated in the mid-1970s, it has since been closed again. The *Lullwater Bridge* (1869), a single steel arch, crosses the pond.

Past the boathouse take the right fork of the path under the East Wood Arch toward the zoo. On the left is the *Carousel* (open weekends, 10–4; 50¢), on which prance horses salvaged from the McCullough Brothers' merry-go-round at Coney Island. Nearby is the octagonal *Flatbush Toll House* (c. 1855) which formerly stood on the boundary between the independent towns of Brooklyn and Flatbush. On the right is the LEFFERTS HOMESTEAD (1783; DL), a clapboard Dutch farmhouse burned by the British during the Revolution and rebuilt afterwards.

Open Wed, Fri, Sat, and Sun, 1–5; except the second Sat of each month Nov–May; admission free; tel: 965–6560.

The overhanging Dutch roof and six colonettes supporting it are typical Dutch details while the front door with its leaded transom and side lights was added later. Inside are examples of 18–early 19C American furniture and homely objects (a quilting frame, spinning wheels, bedwarmers, dolls and toys) to suggest the life of the Lefferts family, one of the most prominent in Flatbush.

Between the Carousel and the Zoo is the *Farm in the Zoo* with domestic animals and a pony track. The **Prospect Park Zoo** (open April–Nov, 8–5; Dec–March, 8–4.30; admission free; cafeteria and restrooms; tel: 965–6560) is a small urban zoo (1903) with elephants, bears, deer, camels, and other animals, its brick buildings (1935; Aymar Embury II) decorated during the Depression by federally supported artists with reliefs and murals illustrating Kipling's 'Jungle Books'. Park designer Olmsted would not have liked it; he couldn't reconcile caged animals in parks for people seeking escape.

Continue N. toward Grand Army Plaza. East Drive follows the course of a colonial road that passed through a narrow rocky defile in the hills left by the glacial moraine. Known today as BATTLE PASS after a Revolutionary War skirmish, an outnumbered American force led by General John Sullivan tried here to hold off Hessian mercenaries attacking from the south. The colonials got off only one volley before they were overrun, captured or killed. The *Battle Pass Marker* (1923; F.W. Ruckstull) with its bronze eagle, marks the site. Beyond Battle Pass on the right of the road is a meadow with a path leading to the *Vale of Cashmere* (c. 1894), a secluded hollow planted with azaleas and rhododendrons, once ornamented with rustic arbours and pedestals bearing Grecian urns. At its N. end a flight of stairs leads up to the Rose Garden (1894), now a stretch of lawn with empty lily pools. From the garden continue N. past the *Endale Arch* (1867) to the park exit.

47 Institute Park: The Brooklyn Public Library, the Brooklyn Museum, and the Brooklyn Botanic Garden.

SUBWAY: IRT Broadway–7th Ave (trains 2, 3) to Eastern Pkwy/Brooklyn Museum station.

BUS: Culture Bus (weekends and holidays), Loop II, stop 9.

CAR: Flatbush Ave to Grand Army Plaza; follow Eastern Pkwy signs around the traffic circle. For museum and botanic garden, follow Eastern Pkwy to Washington Ave and turn right. Metered street parking. Large enclosed parking lot (fee) behind the museum adjacent to the gardens.

The triangle of land bounded by Flatbush Ave, Eastern Pkwy, and Washington Ave is known as **Institute Park,** and contains three of Brooklyn's major cultural institutions: the Brooklyn Museum, the Brooklyn Botanic Garden, and the Central Library of the Brooklyn Public Library.

The MAIN BRANCH (INGERSOLL MEMORIAL) OF THE BROOK-LYN PUBLIC LIBRARY, Grand Army Plaza at Flatbush and Eastern Pkwys, (1941; Githens & Keally) is a handsome, streamlined, Art Deco building, the largest of 53 Brooklyn branches. C. Paul Jennewein sculpted the bas-reliefs and Thomas H. James the screen above the entrance.

Open Mon–Thurs, 9–8; Fri–Sat, 10–6. Sun, 1–5. Closed Sundays during the summer. Tel: 636–1378.

Highlights of its holdings include the morgue of the Brooklyn 'Eagle', which ceased publication in 1955, and the Brooklyn Photography Collection with more than 25,000 photos of Brooklyn and its people dating back to 1870.

Between the library and the Brooklyn Museum along Eastern Pkwy is a playground on the site of a 19C reservoir. Frederick Law Olmsted and Calvert Vaux designed *Eastern Parkway* in 1868, coining the word, and laying out the roadway with its side service roads and islands of trees and greenery. It was intended along with Ocean Parkway as part of a system of residential arteries which never came into being.

Located on Eastern Parkway at Washington Ave, the *****Brooklyn Museum** is one of the borough's major cultural resources, famous for its Egyptian collection and its educational programmes.

Open Wed–Sat, 10–5; Sun and holidays 1–5. Admission by voluntary contribution; suggested donation $2. Cafeteria. Film and dance programmes, art classes, craft demonstrations, lectures. Brooklyn Museum Art School. Museum shop with handcrafted gifts, reproductions.

Exterior. The Brooklyn Museum (1897; McKim, Mead & White, additions and alterations to 1978; DL), a neo-classical pile complete with Ionic portico and an imposing pediment, represents only a quarter of the architects' original grand plan. The *statues of Manhattan and Brooklyn* (1916; Daniel Chester French) flanking the main entrance on Eastern Parkway formerly stood near the Manhattan Bridge, but were placed here (1963) when the bridge ramps were widened. Manhattan wears a breastplate symbolising defence and holds a winged globe (dominion and progress) while the strongbox under her foot and the peacock at her side symbolise her wealth and pride. Brooklyn, less materialistic and more pensive, holds a book on her lap and sits between a reading child and emblems of art and religion. On the frieze are heroic sculptures of great thinkers and artists including four Chinese figures (*Karl Bitter*) representing Law, Art, Religion, and Philosophy (beginning at the far left of the facade), Mohammed (*Charles Keck*) left of the pediment, and (right of the pediment) Homer, Pindar, and Minerva by *Daniel Chester French*

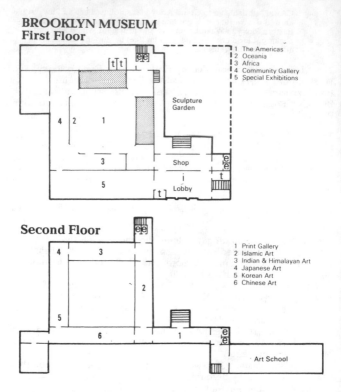

BROOKLYN MUSEUM
First Floor

1 The Americas
2 Oceania
3 Africa
4 Community Gallery
5 Special Exhibitions

Second Floor

1 Print Gallery
2 Islamic Art
3 Indian & Himalayan Art
4 Japanese Art
5 Korean Art
6 Chinese Art

and Plato, Phidias, Praxiteles, and Demosthenes by *Herbert Adams*. On the pediment itself eight heroic figures by *Adolph Weinman* and *Daniel Chester French* represent (left to right) Sculpture, Painting, Architecture, Art and Science, Geography, Astronomy, and Biology. Until 1936 a broad flight of stairs led to the third floor level (remodelling under WPA sponsorship; William Lescaze, architect); today the main entrance is on the first floor.

History. The museum began in 1823 as a library 'to shield young men from evil associations and to encourage improvement during leisure hours by reading and conversation', and still has an active educational programme. The Apprentices' Library, as it was called, had 724 books and 150 pamphlets donated by well-meaning citizens who carted them in wheelbarrows to the reading room on Fulton St. In 1843 the library became the Brooklyn Institute of Arts and Sciences and was endowed by Augustus Graham, a Brooklyn distiller; today it is funded both privately and by the city.

The main exhibition area on the FIRST FLOOR is the *Hall of the Americas** surrounded by other ethnographic displays. In the central gallery are artifacts from Indian cultures of the *Far North* (eskimo clothing, tools, boat models) and the *Northwest Coast* (wood carvings, rattles with bird and animal forms, masks including a talking man with a moveable jaw and one with moveable eyes, and several imposing totem poles). The art of the *Southwest Indians* includes a large collection of Kachina dolls of the Hopi and Zuni tribes which represent spirits and were used to teach children the names and qualities of these supernatural beings. The display on *Plains Indians* has carved pipes, decorated leather clothing, pipe stems, war clubs, and other objects, many of which were collected by Nathan Sturges Jarvis, an army surgeon at Fort Snelling, Minnesota from 1833–36. Jarvis, unlike many of his contemporaries, had the foresight to document what he found, giving the collection special importance. *Indians of Meso-America* are represented largely by pottery: ritual vessels, vases and bowls, ceramic figures and figurines representing gods. The arts of *Eastern South America* include feather arts, headdresses and body ornaments from the Amazon region, and shrunken heads from the Jivaro Indians of Ecuador. In a large case nearby are beautiful woven and painted fabrics and silver from the cultures of the *Central Andes*. Along the outside walls of two sides of the gallery is an imposing display of wood sculpture representing the **Cultures of Oceania**: New Zealand, Polynesia, New Guinea, Indonesia, and Melanesia.

A doorway near the totem poles leads into the **African Hall** with spears, ceremonial masks, body ornaments, shields, dolls and figurines, fabrics, and musical instruments crafted from traditional and modern materials.

The *Community Gallery* and the *Robert E. Blum Gallery* are used for special exhibitions. The other principal exhibition area on this level is the outdoor **Frieda Schiff Warburg Sculpture Garden** (1966; Ian White, designer) on whose lawn sit fragments of demolished New York buildings preserved by the Anonymous Art Recovery Society. Included among the gargoyles, masks, and columns are bits of famous buildings: McKim, Mead & White's Pennsylvania Station (a column capital and a heroic statue that once held up a clock), Steeplechase Park at Coney Island (a lion's head), Louis Sullivan's Bayard-Condict Building (first floor columns taken from the remodelled part of the facade; see p167). Also present are architectural ornaments from anonymous Lower East Side tenements.

The SECOND FLOOR has the museum's collection of prints and drawings and oriental art. In the W wing is the Brooklyn Museum Art School with its two associated galleries, the Little Gallery and the Art School Gallery. The Art Reference Library is open Wed–Fri, 1–5 except in July and Aug.

In the **Print Gallery** appear changing exhibitions from the museum's more than 20,000 prints and drawings (14C to the present) housed in the William A. Putnam Memorial Print Room (open by appointment), a collection especially strong in works of the German expressionists. In the recently refurbished galleries of **Islamic art** are displays of ceramics, textiles, rugs, illustrated manuscripts, and calligraphy. The **Indian gallery** contains sculpture from the 8–9C in stone and bronze, illustrated manuscripts, and work from the Himalayan region and Southeast Asia. The **Japanese gallery** offers examples of Japanese ceramic ware ranging from the 13C to the present, and painted screens, netsuke, scrolls, and furniture. The **Korean gallery** offers ceramics, painted screens, and a small exhibition of 19C chests with elaborate metalwork. In the **Chinese gallery**, carved jade, cloisonné and bronze ceremonial vessels are displayed along with a wide range of ceramics, beginning with pottery from the Han dynasty (1C A.D.) and proceeding through the T'ang dynasty (earthenware tomb figures including horses), and pottery of the Yuan, Sung, Ming, and Ch'ing dynasties illustrating various glazes, decorative techniques, and traditional shapes.

THIRD FLOOR galleries are devoted to ancient civilisations and include the *Egyptian collection. To view it chronologically begin with (1) the *gallery of Predynastic Egypt*, displaying tools, pottery, and other ancient artifacts. In (2) the *Old Kingdom gallery* is a large stone sarcophagus (48·110), limestone reliefs, alabaster storage jars, and a figure of the royal official Methethy in his old age (51·1). The adjacent *gallery of Old and Middle Kingdoms* (3) has two more wooden sculptures of the same official (53·222 and 50·77) as well as royal sculptures, stelae, and tomb fragments. The (4) *gallery of Minor Arts* contains silver and gold work, ceramics, glass, small ivories, ornaments, mirrors, utensils, etc. *Middle Kingdom and Dynasty 18* (5): Closed for renovation. In the *gallery of Funerary Arts* (6) are mummy cartonnages, anthropoid coffins, mummy masks, burial objects, a sarcophagus for an ibis (49·48), amulets, faience hearts, scarabs, and pectorals. The *gallery of Egyptian Deities* (7) has representations in wood, bronze, faience, and other media of the major Egyptian gods. *Egyptian Art from Dynasty 19 to the Roman Conquest* includes a late Ptolemaic portrait sculpture of an Egyptian official (58·30), a wooden chair (37·40), and a display of papyri as well as other large sculptural pieces. The *Wilbour Library of Egyptology* (13), open by appointment, is named after C.E. Wilbour whose collection gathered c. 1880 forms the nucleus of the museum's holdings.

In the **Hagop Kevorkian Gallery of the Ancient Middle East** are twelve Assyrian reliefs of gypseous alabaster from the palace of Ashurnasirpal II (9C B.C.) in Kalhu (Nimrud), as well as examples of weapons, tools, jewellery, and pottery. The galleries around the auditorium-court have **Greek, Roman, Coptic, and Nubian art,** including Coptic (3–6C Christianised Egyptian) ceremonial objects, pottery, sculpture, an alabaster Egyptian bust of Alexander the Great (54·162) from the 2C B.C., Hellenistic art from Egypt, examples of Greek black- and red-figured pottery, small Egyptian sculptures, and a 4C treasure of 180 pieces of Hellenistic gold.

The FOURTH FLOOR is devoted to **decorative arts.** The two-room *Jan Martense Schenck House* (c. 1675) which originally stood in the Flatlands section of Brooklyn has been reconstructed and filled with period furniture. Near it are the *Costume and Textiles Gallery* (changing exhibits) and the *Costume Theater* where clothing from the American and European collections is displayed on moving mannequins. The *18C American period rooms* include rooms from merchants' homes, plantation manors and other houses from New England to South Carolina. The *Galleries of Metalwares, Glassware, and Ceramics*, include pewter, Tole ware American and European silver, Jewish ritual silver, American and European ceramics, glass, and wrought iron as well as examples of decorative arts made in Brooklyn. Among the *19C American period rooms* are a Civil War dressing room, a drawing room from Saratoga Springs, and the *Moorish Room from the John D. Rockefeller townhouse in W. 54th St in Manhattan, with Moorish tiles, brocaded walls, and wood panelling. The galleries of *19C Decorative Arts* offer such articles as Thonet bentwood furniture, Tiffany and Art Nouveau glass, and elaborate examples of cabinetry including a Martin piano (61·231)

BROOKLYN MUSEUM
Third Floor

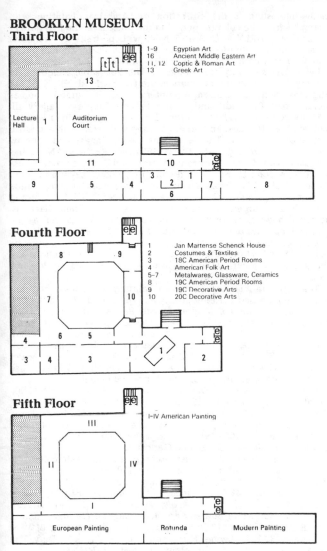

Third Floor

1–9 Egyptian Art
16 Ancient Middle Eastern Art
11, 12 Coptic & Roman Art
13 Greek Art

13

Lecture Hall | 1 | Auditorium Court

11 | 10

9 | 5 | 4 | 3 | 2 | 1 | 7 | 8
| | | 6

Fourth Floor

8 | 9

7 | 10

6 | 5

4
3 | 4 | 3 | 1 | 2

1 Jan Martense Schenck House
2 Costumes & Textiles
3 18C American Period Rooms
4 American Folk Art
5–7 Metalwares, Glassware, Ceramics
8 19C American Period Rooms
9 19C Decorative Arts
10 20C Decorative Arts

Fifth Floor

III

II | IV

I

I–IV American Painting

European Painting | Rotunda | Modern Painting

embellished with sphinxes and a relief of Odysseus's faithful Penelope, and the carved John Henry Belter rosewood bed (39·30). The *Worgelt Study (1928–30) shows the Art Deco style at its most elegant. In the *20C Decorative Arts gallery* are American and European furniture, glass, and textiles.

The FIFTH FLOOR is devoted to painting and sculpture. Especially interesting is the **collection of *American Painting** with examples from the colonial period to the present. In the first gallery (I) are 18C–EARLY 19C PAINTINGS with portraits by Benjamin West, John Singleton Copley, Charles Wilson Peale, Thomas Sully, and Gilbert Stuart, as well as early landscapes including one of Edward Hicks's many treatments of The Peaceable Kingdom. In Gallery II are works by members of the HUDSON RIVER SCHOOL and other romantic landscape painters: Asher B. Durand, Thomas Cole, Albert Bierstadt, and Jasper Francis Cropsey. Gallery III, AMERICAN ECLECTICISM, offers 19C paintings by Elihu Vedder, William Merritt Chase and others dealing with exotic subjects. Also displayed are works of Thomas Eakins, George Inness, and Winslow Homer. The corner gallery, the AMERICAN RENAISSANCE, has Augustus Saint-Gaudens's bronze Victory and Death, a stained glass window by John La Farge, and work by Abbott Thayer and Elihu Vedder. Gallery IV displays works of John Singer Sargent, Childe Hassam, and painters of New York's 'ASHCAN SCHOOL', including John Sloan, George Bellows, George Luks, and William Glackens, so-called because these painters depicted the grim as well as the pleasant moments of city life. Reginald Marsh's The Bowl represents patrons of an old Coney Island amusement whirling in a gigantic polished wooden bowl. The *Rotunda* offers changing exhibitions and the two small galleries flanking it have watercolours by Winslow Homer and John Singer Sargent.

The newly re-installed **European Paintings** galleries of the museum are organised chronologically and geographically. In the first room: *Maso di Banco*, Madonna with Saints and Scenes of the Annunciation (34·838); *Lorenzo d'Alessandro da San Severino*, Crucifixion (41·894); *Giovanni Bellini*, Portrait of a Young Man (32·864); *Gerard Dou*, Burgomaster Hasselaar and his Wife (32·783); *Franz Hals*, Portrait of a Man (32·821); *Carlo Crivelli*, St. James Major (78·151·10): *Lorenzo Monaco*, Madonna of Humility (34·442). Also works by Hobbema, Fragonard, Raeburn, and Panini.

The second room is devoted primarily to FRENCH PAINTING. *Corot*, The Albanian Girl (42·196); *Degas*, Mlle Fiocre in the Ballet 'La Source' (21·111); *Millet*, Shepherd Tending his Flock; *Corot*, Landscape, Ville d'Avray (51·10): *Giovanni Boldini*, Portrait of James McNeill Whistler (09·849). Paintings by Daubigny, Harpignies, Gérôme, Bouguereau, Delacroix, Gericault.

Beyond the Blue Gallery reserved for pastels and watercolours, is the third gallery, with IMPRESSIONIST AND POST-IMPRESSIONIST PAINTINGS: *Pisarro*, The Climbing Path (22·60); *Monet*, Rising Tide à Pourville (41·48·2), Houses of Parliament (64·48·1), Ducal Palace at Venice (20·634); *Renoir*, Vineyards at Cagnes (51·219); *Berthe Morisot*, Mme Boursier and her Daughter (29·30); *Bonnard*, The Breakfast Room (43·202); *Kees van Dongen*, Portrait of W.S. Davenport (32·117); *Lyonel Feininger*, Zirchow V (54·62); *Dufy*, The Regatta (64·91); *Matisse*, Carrefour de Malabai (67·24·16).

The ***Brooklyn Botanic Garden,** 50 carefully tended and intensively planted acres hedged around by asphalt and apartment houses, is an unexpected Eden.

SUBWAY: IRT Broadway–7th Ave express (trains 2, 3) to Eastern Parkway-Brooklyn Museum. IND Sixth Ave (D train) to Prospect Park. BMT Broadway line (M train) or Nassau St line (QB train) to Prospect Park.

BUS: Culture Bus Loop II, stop 8 (weekends and holidays).

CAR: From Manhattan take the Triborough Bridge to the Brooklyn-Queens Expwy (Route 278). Exit 27 to Atlantic Ave, turn right onto Washington Ave.

CAR PARKING: Enclosed parking lot (fee) on Washington Ave between the Garden and the Brooklyn Museum.

Open April–Oct, Tues–Fri, 8–6; weekends and holidays, 10–6. Nov–March, Tues–Fri, 8–4.30, weekends and holidays, 10–4.30. Conservatory open Tues–Fri, 10–4; weekends and holidays, 11–4. Admission free but nominal entrance fee on weekends and holidays for Ryoanji Garden complex, Japanese Garden, and Conservatory. Restrooms in Administration Building. No lunch facilities; picnicking prohibited (snack bars and picnicking facilities in nearby Prospect Park). No radios or tape players. Public tours Sun at 2; meet in front of the Garden Shop in the Administration Building. Extensive educational programmes; research facilities. Tel: 622–4433.

History: The Botanic Garden was founded (1910) as a department of the Brooklyn Institute of Arts and Sciences for the education and enjoyment of the public, a remarkable goal at a time when botanic gardens were still primarily attached to universities. Initially funded with a donation from Brooklyn philanthropist Alfred Tredway White and a matching sum from the City of New York, the Garden, waste land at first, was enriched in its early years with the by-products of nearby breweries and stables. Its plant collections have since been expanded to include more than 13,000 species of plants in 13 specialised gardens and groupings of generically related types.

Begin at the *Administration and Classroom Building* (completed 1918; McKim, Mead & White). Outside the main entrance is *Magnolia Plaza* where 80 magnolia trees of 11 species bloom beginning in early April along with daffodils planted on Boulder Hill (to the right). The figures on the armillary sphere representing signs of the zodiac are by Rhys Caparn, daughter of Harold Caparn, landscape architect for much of the Garden.

Continue past the brook to *Cherry Walk* and the *Cherry Esplanade* (on the right), famous for its deep pink Kwanzan cherry trees, spectacular in early May against a backdrop of red foliage provided by Schwedler maples planted on Armistice Day, 1918.

Diagonally across from the Rose Arc (on the left) is the *Cranford Rose Garden* (1927) with over 900 varieties of roses (more than 5000 plants) including many of the All-America rose selections.

Continue toward the hillside. On the left is the lilac collection arranged, like much of the Botanic Garden, as an arboretum with permanent plantings showing botanic relationships between species. Behind the fence on the left is the *Local Flora Section* featuring wild flowers, shrubs, and trees normally found within a 100-mile radius of the Botanic Garden. In the *Osborne Memorial Section* (1939) are rhododendrons, flowering crabapples, cherries, viburnums, and hollies. At the top of the stairs the *Overlook*, bordered by fastigiate gingkos, leads E. past the Rose Garden to the *Herb Garden* (1938), whose formally planted Elizabethan Knots were intended to be seen from above, presumably from one's castle window. The garden contains over 300 different herbaceous plants with culinary and medicinal uses.

Follow the path along to the *Japanese Garden*, designed and constructed in the traditional Hall-and-Pond style (1914–15) by Takeo Shiota and considered by its maker to be his masterpiece.

Open Apr–Oct, 10.30–4.30. Nominal entrance fee weekends and holidays.

The Viewing Pavilion with its circular window represents the home of the host and the shelter across the lake a Waiting House where in an actual Japanese tea garden guests would wait to be received by the host. In the lake, its flowing shape derived from the Japanese character for 'heart' or 'mind', stands a vermilion *torii* or gateway indicating the presence of a shrine, here a Shinto shrine to a harvest god on the hillside beyond. On the hillside five small cascades with echo caverns beneath them splash downward in a landscape of dwarfed trees and shrubs. During World War II the Japanese Garden was neglected, even vandalised, but since 1953 it has been restored and is now maintained by gardeners trained in oriental techniques of horticulture.

Outside it is a 3-ton Komatsu stone lantern (1652) given to the City by Japan (1980). A path near the lantern leads to the *Shakespeare Garden*, with some 80 varieties of plants mentioned in his works. In the nearby *Fragrance Garden for the Blind* (1955) grow plants chosen for touch, taste, and smell, labelled in Braille and planted in raised beds.

Beyond are the Administration Building and CONSERVATORY.

Open Tues–Fri, 10–4. Admission free. Weekends and holidays, 11–4; nominal admission fee. Guide book available at Garden Shop in Administration Building.

In the Main Tropical House are plants that flourish under warm, humid conditions: screw pines, sugar cane, bamboo, bananas, avocados, and others. The greenhouse on the right near the entrance normally contains warm temperate plants and seasonal floral displays. One of the conservatories on the left side of the Tropical House has desert plants and cycads. The other has a professionally robust collection of houseplants, ferns, and bromeliads including a spectacular display of epiphytic or tree-perching bromeliads, non-parasitic plants that use trees merely for support. The Bonsai display in the last room of this house offers a variety of styles (informal upright, formal upright, cascade, forest, etc).

Outside the conservatories two pools feature hardy and tropical waterlily varieties; nearby is a floral display area with annual and perennial borders. Follow the path to the RYOANJI STONE GARDEN, a replica of a 500-year-old Zen temple garden in Kyoto, Japan.

Open May–Oct, 11–1 and 2–4. Nominal entrance fee, weekends and holidays.

Not a garden at all by western standards, the Ryoanji garden has stones and raked gravel instead of plants, enclosed within a temple wall and arranged in a non-representational pattern for meditative purposes. The *Roji* or Dewy Path garden in the same complex recreates a garden type established in 16C Japan: bordering a path leading to a tea house the Roji aimed to create in the mind the feeling of a remote mountain wilderness, using mosses, plants, and ferns that thrive in moist conditions. Adjacent to the Roji is the *Tallman Dwarf Plant Collection*.

Return to the pathway and continue past the *Children's Garden*, a cherished local institution where 300–400 children annually learn to grow vegetables and flowers and absorb the human virtues associated with gardening. The pathway next leads past dogwoods, azaleas, forsythia, and the iris garden (late May–early June) to the

Rock Garden, featuring plants normally found on mountain slopes, whose low growth protects them from wind. The *Monocot bed*, on the other side of the path, is a display border of plants with parallel-veined leaves and includes irises, daylilies, and narcissi as well as more exotic grasses, cannas, and yuccas. The *Hedge Wheel* has 18 rows of evergreen and deciduous shrubs planted like spokes to show their use in hedges.

48 East Central Brooklyn: Crown Heights, Bedford-Stuyvesant, Brownsville, and East New York

Crown Heights, formerly considered part of Bedford, is bounded roughly by Atlantic Ave on the N., East New York Ave and Empire Boulevard on the S. and S.E., and Washington Ave on the W. The name seems to be a corruption of the 19C place name 'Crow Hill', which described a range of hills S. of Eastern Pkwy and may also have referred to the black settlements of Weeksville and Carrsville begun in the 1830s and 1840s. For most of the 20C Crown Heights existed as a lower middle class Jewish neighbourhood but today is predominantly black, its population including West Indians and a significant group of French-speaking Haitians as well as Jamaicans, Trinidadians, Barbadians, and Grenadians, all of whom spill over into surrounding areas.

On the main commercial strips near Nostrand and Utica Aves are West Indian restaurants, bakeries, grocery stores, and record shops. Climaxing the year is Carnival weekend over the Labor Day holiday (early September) when revellers celebrate for three days with steel bands, masquerades, street dancing, and a final chaotic parade down Eastern Parkway. (For carnival information, call the Brooklyn Arts & Cultural Assoc., tel: 783–9469)

Points of interest. The area around Grant Square (Dean St and Bedford Ave) when considered part of Bedford in the 19C was highly respectable, the *Union League Club* (Bedford Ave, S.E. corner of Dean St) its premier institution. Founded in 1888 as a social and political organisation for Republicans of high social standing, the club built this headquarters four years later (1892; Lauritzen & Voss), a brownstone Victorian pile adorned with medallions of Ulysses S. Grant and Abraham Lincoln and garnished with stone lions and American eagles. The club commissioned William Ordway Partridge (1896) to design the *equestrian statue of Ulysses S. Grant* that now stands in the square. A block N. stand the *Imperial Apartments* (1198 Pacific St, S.E. corner of Bedford Ave) which date from the same period (c. 1892; Montrose W. Morris) and same social milieu as the Union League Club. In addition to fine apartments Bedford also had a number of mansions (Frank W. Woolworth lived here before he moved to Fifth Ave, as did Abraham Abraham, a partner in the Wechsler and Abraham department store, precursor of Abraham and Straus).

The *Twenty-Third Regiment Armory of the New York National Guard* (1322 Bedford Ave, between Atlantic Ave and Pacific St) with its imposing crenellated tower, slit windows, and arched entry (1892; Fowler & Hough; DL) dates from the same period of prosperity, as does the *Medical Society of the County of Kings* across the street at 1313 Bedford Ave (1903; D. Everett Waid and R.M. Cranford), and *St. Bartholomew's Episcopal Church* (c.1893; George B. Chappell) a little to the E. (1227 Pacific St, between Bedford and Nostrand Aves.

The NEW MUSE COMMUNITY MUSEUM (founded in 1973), 1530 Bedford Ave at Lincoln Place (near Eastern Pkwy), is dedicated to black culture, and has a permanent exhibition on The Black Contribution to the Development of Brooklyn as well as changing exhibitions of art and history, a planetarium, and a small menagerie.

Open Tues–Fri, 2–6; Sat, 10–6; Sun, 2–6. Admission free. Children's programmes, jazz concerts, lectures. Tel: 774–2900.

In the block bounded by Montgomery St, McKeever Pl., Sullivan Pl., and Bedford Ave is the *site of Ebbets Field*, home of the former Brooklyn Dodgers, now, sadly, the Los Angeles Dodgers.

Built by Charles Ebbets and the McKeever Brothers in 1913, Ebbets Field held 32,111 fans while its parking lot accommodated 700 cars, a pittance by modern standards, and the inadequacy of the stadium and facilities eventually resulted in the departure of the team from Brooklyn. Although owner Walter O'Malley negotiated with the city between 1954–57 for a new stadium, opposition of key city officials, offers from the city of Los Angeles, and the general appeal of the far west which seemed free from the problems of crime, housing, and race that afflict Brooklyn persuaded O'Malley to go west. The loss of the team, which had distinguished itself by the ardour of its fans and by signing the first major league black player, the legendary Jackie Robinson, did not harm Brooklyn so much economically as sentimentally. but it was a loss that cut across social, racial, and economic boundaries.

The **Brooklyn Children's Museum,** in Brower Park at the intersection of Brooklyn and St. Marks Aves, was the first museum (1899) anywhere devoted solely to the education and delight of children. Formerly housed in two Victorian mansions belonging to L.C. Smith, typewriter manufacturer, and historian James Truslow Adams, it now occupies new quarters (1976; Hardy, Holzman, Pfeiffer).

Open Mon, Wed, Thurs, Fri, 1–5; weekends and holidays, 10–5. Admission free. Children's resource library, workshops, films, special events. Gift shop with crafts, posters, books. Tel: 735–4400.

> SUBWAY: IRT Broadway–7th Ave (train 2) to Kingston Ave; walk W. to Brooklyn Ave, right six blocks to St. Mark's Ave; IND Eighth Ave (A train) to Kingston/Throop; walk W. to Brooklyn Ave, left six blocks to St. Marks Ave.
>
> BUS: B47 to St. Marks Ave.
>
> CAR: Atlantic Ave to Brooklyn Ave; turn S. on Brooklyn Ave and continue four blocks to St. Marks Ave. Street parking.

Visitors enter through a 1907 trolley kiosk and a sewer culvert with a stream whose waterpower children can harness with sluices, gates, and waterwheels. The innards of the museum are gaily painted while ladders and catwalks convert the main hall to a high tech playground whose exhibits focus on natural science and human culture. Children can climb in a molecular maze of clear plastic modules, watch a liquid light show, a steam engine, a working windmill, a greenhouse, and enjoy other participatory and visual exhibits chosen from a collection of 50,000 artifacts.

The *Hunterfly Road houses*, best seen from Bergen St between

Rochester and Buffalo Aves, four modest houses (c. 1830; DL) undergoing restoration, once stood along Hunterfly Road, a colonial highway joining Bedford and Canarsie, and were part of Brooklyn's first black community, Weeksville, named after James Weeks, an early landowner.

Of the town little is known: it seems to have been settled by outsiders rather than slaves freed by state law in the 1820s; it had a school and churches; it took up arms for self-defence during the Draft Riots (1863) as white mobs attacked and murdered blacks in Manhattan; it was swallowed up by burgeoning white communities as new streets opened toward the end of the 19C. Of Carrsville to the S., another early 19C black community, no physical trace remains.

Bedford-Stuyvesant, today the city's largest black ghetto, used to be two neighbourhoods, Bedford on the W., settled by the Dutch in the 17C and the Stuyvesant Heights district to the E., settled later. Its boundaries, difficult to define precisely, are Flushing Ave on the N., Broadway and Saratoga Ave on the E., Atlantic Ave on the S., and Classon Ave on the W.

Like other outlying Brooklyn areas, Bedford-Stuyvesant went through several stages of development, first as farmland, later as a suburb with freestanding frame houses, then as an urban neighbourhood with prosperous middle-class brick and brownstone row houses, and finally as a black ghetto. Unlike other neighbourhoods, however, Bedford (the origin of the name is obscure) had a significant black population long ago, slave labourers on Dutch farms making up 25% of the population in 1790. Between the two world wars Jews, Italians, Irish, and West Indians began settling in the now aging yet still attractive neighbourhood, and after World War II the dramatic increase of black arrivals made Bedford-Stuyvesant the nation's second largest black community after Chicago's South Side.

Points of interest. It is advisable to tour by car.

The *former Boys' High School,* 823 Marcy Ave between Putnam Ave and Madison St (1891; James W. Naughton, DL), built by the long-time Superintendent for Buildings of the Brooklyn Public School system, is a grand Romanesque Revival building with a history of distinguished graduates.

On the N. side of *Tompkins Park,* between Marcy and Tompkins Aves is the only tree in New York that has been designated a landmark (c. 1880; DL), a *Magnolia grandiflora* that qualifies as Brooklyn's second most famous botanical specimen after the Camperdown elm in Prospect Park. Vaux and Olmsted designed the park, but probably wouldn't recognise it today. The painted concrete recreation center (Hoberman & Wasserman) dates from 1971.

In the E.-central part of the district N. of Fulton St is the STUYVESANT HEIGHTS HISTORIC DISTRICT, an L-shaped area bounded partially by Chauncey and Macon Sts, Stuyvesant and Tompkins Aves, built up during the last decades of the 19C with handsome row housing. Local street names, bestowed during a period of patriotic fervour, recall historic naval figures: Thomas MacDonough, Stephen Decatur, William Bainbridge, Isaac Chauncey; the avenues commemorate New York governors: Morgan Lewis, Enos T. Throop, Daniel D. Tompkins, and Peter Stuyvesant. Sumner Ave used to be Yates Ave after governor Joseph C. Yates, but was changed to avoid confusion with Gates Ave. Noteworthy blocks in the historic district are the block of Bainbridge St between

Lewis and Stuyvesant Aves dating from the 1890s, and the W. side of Stuyvesant Ave between Bainbridge and Decatur Sts.

The BEDFORD-STUYVESANT RESTORATION CENTER, 1360 Fulton St, S.E. corner of New York Ave (1976; Arthur Cotton Moore), is a $6-million complex of stores, offices, and a theatre, named after Billie Holiday, the great jazz singer. The project, utilising derelict industrial and commercial buildings, is a major achievement of the Bedford-Stuyvesant Restoration Corporation, founded (1967) after a widely publicised visit of Senator Robert F. Kennedy focused attention on the area.

In eastern Brooklyn are three principal neighbourhoods: Highland Park, Brownsville, and East New York, carved out of the old Dutch settlement of New Lots. New Lots itself, settled around 1670 by a group of Dutch farmers from the Old Lots section of present-day Flatbush, remained part of Flatbush until 1852, and joined the city of Brooklyn in 1886. None of these neighbourhoods is of particular interest to visitors though Brownsville is of historical importance.

The northern section, N. of Atlantic Ave, is called either **Highland Park,** after the park of that name, a steep hill rising from Jamaica Ave, or **Cypress Hills,** after the cemetery of that name, most of which lies in Queens (as does part of Highland Park).

Brownsville, today synonymous with urban squalour, is named after Charles S. Brown who subdivided the existing farmland for housing in 1865, it was long known as one of the city's centres of Jewish population. In 1887 a group of realtors put up cheap housing and encouraged Jews to move out from the Lower East Side, an exodus hastened by the construction of the Fulton St elevated line in 1889, and some of the early Jewish fortunes including that of the Chanin brothers come from this boom period. By 1900 Brownsville, home to 15,000 sweatshop workers, was a slum without sidewalks or sewers, with unpaved streets and only one public bath house. Between the 1920s and World War II, however, things improved remarkably as the population prospered by dint of individual effort. The main shopping street was Pitkin Ave, named after John R. Pitkin, founder of East New York. A pushcart market sprang up on Belmont Ave between Christopher St and Rockaway Ave, selling leftovers from the nearby produce market at Junius St by the railroad siding; it survives today catering to a Hispanic clientele. Loew's Pitkin Theatre (1501 Pitkin Ave at Saratoga St) now converted to the Hudson Temple Cathedral, was built in 1925 (Thomas Lamb), one among many movie palaces of the era.

From the Brownsville ghetto came a generation of eminent actors, writers, businessmen, and politicians, including Danny Kaye, sculptor Max Weber, Aaron Copland, Joseph Hirshhorn, whose art collection was financed by uranium, and Sol Hurok who launched his career as an impresario by persuading violinist Efrem Zimbalist to play for a local cultural society. After World War II, the Jews, drawn by the suburbs or by pleasanter parts of the city, began leaving, replaced by a poorer mostly non-white population. During the 1970s efforts at slum clearance eradicated some of the worst housing without really making a dent in the profound depression of the area. Among the better projects are Rutland Plaza (E. New York Ave and Rutland Rd, E. 92nd to E. 94th Sts) which dates from 1976 (Donald Stull and Assocs) and Marcus Garvey Village (1976; Institute for Architecture and Urban Studies, David Todd & Assocs), a community of low-rise apartments.

East New York, between Jamaica Ave and Jamaica Bay, E. of about Junius St, was founded as a commercial venture by one John R. Pitkin, a Connecticut businessman whose schemes for a town rivalling New York were dashed by the panic of 1837. It was developed later as a working-class neighbourhood and attracted Jews, Russians, Germans, and Italians, many arriving from Browns-ville. During the 1960s and early 1970s most of the former Jewish residents, pressured by unscrupulous real estate dealers, sold their property and moved away and today the area is mostly black.

Points of interest: The determined local historian might wish to visit two relics from the period when Dutch influence was still strong: the *Christian Duryea House* (c. 1787; DL), 562 Jerome St between Dumont and Livonia Aves, a Dutch-style farmhouse, and the *New Lots Reformed Dutch Church* (1823; DL), 630 New Lots Ave, S.E. corner of Schenck Ave, built by local farmers tired of the weekly trek to the Flatbush Reformed Church. The simple wooden building with pointed arch windows is surrounded by an old graveyard.

49 Northern Brooklyn: Greenpoint, Williamsburg, and Bushwick

Greenpoint, the neck of land N. of the Brooklyn-Queens Expressway between Newtown Creek and McCarren Park, was undoubtedly verdant in 1630 when the Dutch bought it from the Indians. After 1832, however, when Eliphalet Nott and Neziah Bliss surveyed the land and laid out streets and lots for development, Greenpoint gradually became industrial, attracting shipbuilding to its shoreline and the five 'black arts'—publishing, porcelain, glass, iron, and oil refining—to inland areas.

The birthplace of Mae West, Greenpoint in popular legend is also the cradle of Brooklynese, a dialect of American English that substitutes 'd' for 'th' as in 'dem Bums' and interchanges 'oi' and 'er', as in 'Hoiman hersted to 'Hoist', meaning that Dodger batter Babe Herman lifted a short fly ball to fielder Don Hurst. Linguists have shown in scholarly studies, however, that no dialect peculiar to Brooklyn exists, though they do identify 'metropolitan New York City speech' which is spoken in Long Island and nearby New Jersey as well.

Points of interest in Greenpoint include remnants of the old industrial era, several blocks of remarkably attractive and well-kept homes, and the commercial institutions of a middle class Polish-American community along Manhattan Ave.

Not far from the river at 184 Franklin St between Java and India Sts are the now dilapidated ASTRAL APARTMENTS (1886; Lamb & Rich), built by Charles Pratt for the workers in his oil refinery. Designed after the Peabody Apartments in London, they were a milestone in the tenement reform movement, giving every room daylight and fresh air. Pratt's Astral Oil works were located nearby on the East River at Bushwick Creek from Kent Ave to N. 12th St; in 1870 the refinery could process 1500 barrels of petroleum daily, yielding 1100 barrels of Astral Oil, Pratt's high quality kerosene which replaced whale oil and other fuels as an illuminating oil.

The street names here—Java, India—recall the 19C spice trade that flourished along the waterfront.

One of Greenpoint's most attractive blocks is MILTON ST between Franklin and Manhattan Aves, with well-tended late 19C rowhouses and several churches. Noteworthy among the houses are Nos 118–120 (c. 1880), small and mansarded, and Nos 122–124, a brick and brownstone Queen Anne pair with attractive ironwork (c.

1880). The *Greenpoint Reformed Church* (c. 1880), 138 Milton St, an Italianate Greek Revival church, and *St. John's Lutheran Church* (1892), 155 Milton St, both served earlier immigrant industrial populations. Closing off the end of Milton St is the red brick *St. Anthony of Padua Church* (1874; P.C. Keely), 862 Manhattan Ave, serving Roman Catholics.

Along Manhattan Ave, the commercial center for the nearby Polish population, are Polish restaurants, butcher shops and grocery stores, the Chopin Theater, and a trading company selling Polish and East European clothing and souvenirs.

During the Civil War period the Continental Ironworks stood on West St between Oak and Calyer Sts and several 19C industrial buildings now used for warehousing still remain from that period. In 1861 the works began production of the hull of the 'Monitor', and on 30 Jan 1862 the ironclad ship (see p81) slid down the ways into the East River. In MONSIGNOR MCGOLDRICK PARK (between Driggs and Nassau Aves, Russell and Monitor Sts) is *the Monitor monument* (1938; Antonio de Filippo), a bronze sailor straining at a bronze hawser. The park also contains a landmark *shelter* (1910; Helmle & Huberty) inspired by the Trianon at Versailles, but now in shabby condition.

Near the S. edge of Greenpoint stands the ***Russian Orthodox Cathedral of the Transfiguration** (1921; Louis Allmendinger; DL), 228 N. 12th St at Driggs Ave, its five verdigris onion domes hovering above the neighbouring low industrial and residential buildings. Outside, the building, finished in yellow brick, is modest; inside (entrance on Driggs Ave) services Sun at 11) it is richly decorated in bright colours with wall paintings of saints, stained glass windows, columns painted to simulate marble supporting a high, sky blue dome. During services the lighted crystal chandeliers, ornately vested priests, the incense and music, seem doubly exotic in this drab neighbourhood.

Williamsburg begins at the bridge of that name and stretches E. to Bushwick Ave and S. to Flushing Ave. Once part of the town of Bushwick, it became independent about 1810 and was named after Col Jonathan Williams who surveyed it.

A ferry to Corlear's Hook on Manhattan gave inland farmers a market for produce, but Williamsburgh (spelled with an 'h' until it became part of the City of Brooklyn in 1855) remained isolated until the opening of the bridge (1903). A distillery (c. 1819) later superceded by a brewery, was its first industrial plant, but in the mid-19C it still attracted sportsmen—Commodore Vanderbilt, William C. Whitney, Jim Fisk—to its resort hotels, while affluent businessmen built mansions along its avenues. The opening of the bridge, dubbed 'the Jews' Highway' by the press, brought a flood of the poor from the Lower East Side and sealed its fate as a slum.

Points of interest. Williamsburg was the first American home of the Satmarer Hasidic Community, an ultra-orthodox Jewish sect (Hasidim means 'pious ones') founded in 18C Poland and now including groups from Hungary as well. Sect members are highly visible because of their clothing: men wear black garments with wide-brimmed or sable hats, full beards and sidelocks, while the women, modestly garbed in dark, long sleeved dresses, if married have shaven heads covered with wigs and scarves. The boys wear sidelocks and skull caps (yarmulkes).

Along Lee Ave, advertised by signs in Hebrew and Yiddish, are kosher butchers, clothing stores selling Hasidic garments and wigs. Along Bedford Ave Jewish institutions and schools have taken over several former mansions and clubs from pre-bridge days: *Young Israel of Brooklyn* (561 Bedford Ave at the S.E. corner of Rodney St) occupies the original Hawley mansion (c. 1875), later the Hanover Club; the *Yeshiva Yesoda Hatora of K'hal Adas Yereim* (505 Bedford Ave, N.E. corner of Taylor St) once belonged to Frederick Mollenhauer (1896), a sugar refiner. Rebbe Joel Teitelbaum, who established the Hasidic community here around 1940, lived in the building (500 Bedford Ave at the N.W. corner of Clymer St) now used by the *National Committee to Aid New Immigrants*.

Near the foot of the Williamsburg Bridge stand two venerable landmarks in a desolate neighbourhood. The *Williamsburgh Savings Bank* (1875; George B. Post; additions 1906, 1925; Helmle, Huberty & Hudswell; DL), 175 Broadway, N.W. corner of Driggs Ave, has a grand dome and monumental entrance appropriate to some past era. Up the street is the *United Mutual Savings Bank*, 135 Broadway, N.E. corner of Bedford Ave (1868; King & Wilcox, William H. Wilcox; DL), a Second Empire masterpiece, once the Kings County Savings Bank, its ornate Victorian interior still intact. The *Peter Luger Steak House*, 178 Broadway, a 95-year old restaurant, still attracts a well-heeled clientele; inside ornate pressed tin ceilings and dark wood panelled walls suggest its beginnings as a cafe and billiard parlor.

Washington Plaza, S. 4th St to Broadway between New and Havemeyer Sts is the formal Brooklyn entrance to the bridge, once the hub of the borough's trolley network, now a dilapidated turnaround for buses. Henry M. Shrady's (1906) equestrian *statue of George Washington at Valley Forge*, predictably slathered with graffiti, needs a better home.

The *Williamsburg Houses*, between Maujer and Scholes Sts, Leonard St and Bushwick Ave (1937; Board of Design with Richmond H. Shreve, chief architect) have been lauded as the city's best public housing project, ever. Their cost, $12·8 million in 1939, adjusted for inflation, also makes them the costliest. The small buildings with private entries, outdoor courtyards for recreation, floor plans admitting generous amounts of air and light caused a critic of the period to remark that in many ways the houses were better than the average Park Ave luxury building.

Bushwick, famous for breweries, was one of Brooklyn's original six towns, chartered in 1660 as 'Boswijck', meaning 'town of the woods'. The neighbourhood stretches N.E. of Broadway to the Queens border and the Brooklyn-Queens Expressway and is industrial toward the N. and residential further S.

Bushwick long had a German population, beginning after the Revolution when some of the Hessian mercenaries billeted there chose to remain, mostly as farmers, but beer came to Bushwick in the 19C with the arrival of a new wave of immigrants fleeing Germany after the abortive 1848–49 uprisings; brewers like Otto Huber, Caspar Illig, Joseph Fallert, Ernest Ochs, and Samuel Liebermann, founder of the modern Rheingold Breweries, established factories on Brewers' Row (Scholes and Meserole Sts, Bushwick Pl. and Lorimer St), and many of these men lived in Bushwick, giving it its staid Germanic atmosphere. Peter Cooper in the 1840s had a glue factory on the site of the housing project named after him, while other industries thrived along Maspeth Creek. A few buildings from former breweries remain E. of Bushwick Ave, between Forrest and Jefferson Sts. Most have been demolished as the area awaits redevelopment.

Points of interest. On Bushwick Ave S. of Myrtle Ave remain occasional sobre mansions left behind by departing brewers, manufacturers, and other prosperous families. The *William Ulmer residence*, 670 Bushwick Ave on the S.W. corner of Willoughby Ave, built by a brewer, later owned by Arctic explorer Frederick A. Cook, is now a medical building. The *Catherine Lipsius residence*, 680 Bushwick Ave on the S.E. corner of the same intersection (c. 1886; Theobald Engelhardt), built by a brewer's widow, was once an elegant Italianate home, but is now barely recognisable as such.

Across the street along Bushwick Ave between Suydam and Hart Sts is the Ansaru Abdulla Black Muslim community, with a bookstore, restaurant, and mosque. The corner lot, occupied by a falafel stand, is the site of the former Bushwick Democratic Club (1892; Frank Freeman; DL) destroyed in a fire (c. 1978).

The SOUTH BUSHWICK REFORMED CHURCH (1853; DL) stands on the N.W. corner of Bushwick Ave and Himrod St, a white frame Greek Revival survivor of the days when Dutch influence was still strong in Brooklyn. The scale of the building, its grand Ionic columns and high tower suggest the affluence of the mid-19C congregation. Himrod St is named after its first minister.

Further S. are former homes of other affluent men: the *Gustav Doerschuck residence* (c. 1890) at 999 Bushwick Ave (N.W. corner of Grove St) and the *Louis Bossert residence*, 1002 Bushwick Ave, S.E. corner of Grove St, which dates from 1890 and has been converted to a church. Bossert, a millwork manufacturer, built the once-elegant Bossert Hotel in Brooklyn Heights.

ST. BARBARA'S CHURCH (Roman Catholic) on Central Ave, N.E. corner of Bleecker St (1910; Helmle & Huberty), a Spanish baroque church of buff brick with wedding cake terracotta ornamentation, rises like an apparition from the rubble of surrounding lots. Its present congregation is largely Hispanic; earlier parishioners were Italian and before that German.

50 South Central Brooklyn: Flatbush, Borough Park, and Bensonhurst

Flatbush is a quiet, residential area, stretching S. of Prospect Park to Kings Highway, bounded on the E. and W. by Nostrand and McDonald Aves. Its southern portion is often called *Midwood*, from the Dutch 'Midwout', a name that described vegetation no longer in evidence.

The Dutch settled Flatbush in 1634, chartering the town in 1652 and calling it 't Vlacke Bos or 'wooded plain'. Annexed to the city of Brooklyn in 1894, Flatbush remained rural and isolated until steam railways—the Brooklyn, Flatbush, and Coney Island Railroad later electrified as the Brighton Line of the BMT and IND—made rapid transportation possible. Thereafter it evolved into a well-to-do suburb which still maintains elements of gentility.

Points of interest. The *Flatbush Reformed Dutch Church* (1793–98; Thomas Fardon; DL), 890 Flatbush Ave, S.W. corner of Church Ave, was established by Peter Stuyvesant in 1654, and the present fieldstone building, its third home, has stained glass windows depicting the homes of old Flatbush families. The tower contains a Dutch bell, donated in 1796, which tolled the death of George Washington (1799) and every President since then. The nearby *Parsonage*, on Kenmore Terrace at the N.E. corner of E. 21st St, is a Greek Revival house (1853) with a colonnaded verandah.

Erasmus Hall Academy, the original building of the school that has evolved into Erasmus Hall High School at Flatbush Ave, S.E. corner of Church Ave, dates back to 1786. Funded by Alexander Hamilton, Aaron Burr, and John Jay among others, the academy opened in 1787 with a student body of 26 boys, and is now part of the city public school system. Among its illustrious students is chess champion Bobby Fischer who dropped out to work on his game. The original white clapboard Federal building (1787; DL) is now surrounded by a Gothic quadrangle dating from 1905–25; a statue of Dutch philosopher Desiderius Erasmus (copied from a 1622 Dutch original) stands in the courtyard.

The *Flatbush Town Hall*, 35 Snyder Ave near Flatbush Ave (1876; John Y. Cuyler; DL), was built by the citizens of Flatbush two years after they voted down a proposal to join the city of Brooklyn. The red brick and stone Victorian Gothic building now serves the Flatbush Historical Society and other community groups.

Prospect Park South, a designated historic district, is Flatbush's most elegant neighbourhood, bounded by Church Ave, Beverley Rd, Coney Island Ave, and the BMT/IND Brighton Line. The community consists of large houses dating from around the turn of the century set on streets planted with stately maples. The developer Dean Alvord, who planted the trees, put in the utilities, paved the roads, and established building restrictions that defined the community, presumably was an anglophile since the streets are named Stratford, Argyle, Westminster, Rugby, Marlborough, and Buckingham. Especially fine houses line Buckingham Rd between Church Ave and Albermarle Rd.

BROOKLYN COLLEGE, between Flatbush and Ocean Aves around Avenue H, was founded in 1930 as a co-educational liberal arts college and today enrolls about 16,000 undergraduates and 2000 graduates. The 26-acre campus opened in 1937 on a former golf course sometimes also used for tent shows of the Barnum and Bailey circus. The *Brooklyn Center for the Performing Arts at Brooklyn College* (BCBC) offers concerts, dance programmes, and theatrical events in the George Gershwin Theater and Walt Whitman Hall (for information call 780–5291 or 434–1900).

Borough Park like Bensonhurst to its S. was developed during the 1920s following the extension of the subway system from Manhattan and attracted a predominantly Jewish population. Its boundaries, difficult to define, may be considered 39th St and 65th St on the N. and S., Seventh Ave on the W. and McDonald Ave on the E.

During the 1960s as more prosperous Jews moved on to the suburbs, poorer families began moving to Borough Park from elsewhere in Brooklyn, notably from Williamsburg and Brownsville, and in contrast to earlier immigrants who had adopted American culture, the new residents resolutely maintain their old world customs including their style of dress. Many are orthodox Jews and Hasidim (see p560). The process of population displacement continues and today the Borough Park Jews who formerly shared the territory with Italians are increasingly surrounded by blacks and Hispanics. The neighbourhood is primarily residential and lower middle class, divided by the street grid into monotonously regular blocks of small one- and two-family houses and apartments.

Bensonhurst, S. of Borough Park, takes its name from Charles Benson, an 18C landowner, but settlement dates back to 1652 when Cornelis van Werckhoven, a member of the Dutch West India Company, bartered the land from the Canarsee Indians, and established a homestead. The town which grew up around the present intersection of New York Ave and 18th Ave was chartered in 1657 and named Nieuw Utrecht after van Werckhoven's home town. Today it is a lower middle-class residential neighbourhood.

Points of interest. *The New Utrecht Reformed Church* (1828; DL) on 18th Ave between 83rd–84th Sts, with its rubblestone walls, pointed windows, and square central tower, recalls St Augustine's Chapel on the Lower East Side, built at about the same time. On the grounds stands a Liberty Pole whose ancestors date back to the celebrations of Nov 1783, when the British army departed after the Revolution. The original Liberty Poles, actually flagpoles for flying dissident banners, were erected by patriotic colonists seeking to antagonise the British garrisons. The *Parsonage* (c. 1885) on 83rd St and the *Parish House* (1892) on 84th St, both between 18th–19th Aves date from the end of the century when Bensonhurst was said to be one of the most beautiful residential communities in the city.

Bath Beach, along the shore E. of the Verrazano-Narrows Bridge, has been effectively obliterated by the Belt Parkway, though at the turn of the century it was a fashionable seaside resort.

51 Southern Brooklyn: Gravesend, Coney Island, Brighton Beach, Manhattan Beach, and Sheepshead Bay

Gravesend (center at the intersection of McDonald Ave and Gravesend Neck Rd), originally called 's Gravensande, the only one of Brooklyn's original six towns not settled by the Dutch, was established by an English woman, Lady Deborah Moody, who in 1643 with her Anabaptist followers fled the puritan intolerance of the Massachusetts Bay Colony.

In 1645 the town was granted a charter and enjoyed both religious freedom and a degree of self-government. Unlike the other early settlements which grew up haphazardly Gravesend was formally planned in the manner of English colonial towns in Massachusetts or Connecticut with a central green. Along with the original cemetery where Lady Deborah Moody is buried (though the precise location of her grave is not known), the square remains the only trace of the original town plan.

Points of interest. The GRAVESEND CEMETERY (1650; DL) is at the S.W. corner of the square (between McDonald Ave and Van Sicklen St) but is kept locked. Nearby (27 Gravesend Neck Rd) is the *Hicks-Platt House* which dates from the mid-17C (considerable alteration) and in the 1890s was passed off by real estate entre-

preneur William Platt as Lady Moody's house. A little further out
Gravesend Neck Road (N.W. corner of E. 1st St) is the present
Gravesend Reform Church (1894), successor of the congregation's
earlier buildings at Neck Road and McDonald Ave.

*Coney Island, joined to the mainland by the filling of part of Coney
Island Creek, is no longer the 'world's largest playground' as it once
billed itself, but still survives as an archetype of American honky
tonk. The $2^{1}/_{2}$ mile Boardwalk remains, now frequented by joggers,
gangs of teenagers, and elderly strollers, as does the Cyclone, once
the ultimate terror of roller coasters. The rusting steelwork of the
parachute jump still lifts itself skyward, though the parachutes are
long gone. During the season (late May through early Sept), people
still crowd the wide, sandy beach, but nowadays the waters are not
remarkable for their purity nor the crowds for their gentility.

> SUBWAY: IND Sixth Ave express or local (B, D, F trains). The D
> train goes to Coney Island weekends and at night. The B train goes
> at all times as does the F train. BMT Broadway Express (N train) at
> all times. BMT Nassau St local (M train) to Coney Island during the
> day on weekdays.

> CAR: Take the Belt System around the shoreline (good views of the
> Verrazano Bridge, Narrows, and lower harbour) to the Coney
> Island/Ocean Parkway exit (# 7) and go S. Or take the
> Brooklyn-Queens Expressway to the Prospect Expressway and
> follow Ocean Parkway through Brooklyn to Coney Island. Large
> parking lot (fee) at the Aquarium (Surf Ave at W. 8th St).

At the eastern tip of the peninsula the *Kingsborough Community
College* (master plan 1968; Katz, Waisman, Weber, Strauss and
others) occupies the site of a World War II Naval training station in
an area once called Orient Beach. To its W. are Manhattan Beach
and Brighton Beach, both residential communities with public
bathing beaches. Coney Island proper is a relatively poor community
with the highest concentration of old people in the city, most housed
in high-rise urban renewal apartments. On the western edge of the
peninsula is Sea Gate, a private community whose guards keep out
the rest of the world.

History. The Dutch called the island *Konijn Eiland* (Rabbit Island), presumably
because of the local fauna. Its history as a resort began with the Coney Island
Hotel (1829) at Sea Gate, soon followed by other establishments whose
restaurants and bathing pavilions attracted a genteel clientele. By 1870,
however, Coney Island had declined and under the corrupt administration of
Gravesend political boss John Y. McKane, gambling and prostitution flourished. Around the turn of the century Coney Island was still a recognised
hangout for mobsters, but the construction of three spectacular amusement
areas ushered in its golden age: George C. Tilyou's Steeplechase Park (1897),
Luna Park (1903), the most ambitious, and Dreamland (1904). Technological
advances permitted new and thrilling rides, notably the ferris wheel and the
roller coaster. In 1910 a reform administration swept away the worst of the vice
and with the arrival of the subway (1920) Coney Island became the playground
of the common man, the 'empire of the nickel'. During the 1920s and 1930s
huge crowds thronged the boardwalk (opened 1921) or lay thigh to thigh on the
sand, although by this time the amusement areas were beginning to deteriorate. Dreamland burned in 1911 and Luna Park succumbed to a series of fires in
the 1940s, but had been losing money for decades. After World War II the rise
of the automobile and a preference for the more wholesome atmosphere of
Disneyland and its imitators hastened the decline of Coney Island. In 1966
Steeplechase Park closed; the city now owns the land and for 15 years has had

plans for making it a public park, but no visible action has been taken. Rumour has it that Coney Island is slated for casino gambling, presently illegal in New York State, and citizens' groups express concern about its effects on the community.

Begin at the *New York Aquarium, Surf Ave at W. 8th St, clean, attractive, and often nearly empty because of its remoteness from the city (the attendance is about a fifth of the 7000 visitors who daily went to the Aquarium when it was in Battery Park).

Open 10–5 weekdays, 10–6 weekends and holidays. Adults, $2; children 12 and under, 75¢. Cafeteria and snack bar. Picnic tables. Merchandise: souvenirs. Services: Educational programmes. Tel: 266–8500.

Feeding schedule: Penguins, 11.30 and 4.15. Seals, 10.45 and 3.30. Whales, 10.15 and 2.30. Sharks, 1.45.

The oldest public aquarium in the United States (1902), the facility was moved to its new building (1955; Harrison & Abramovitz) fourteen years after the old building closed. In the main exhibition hall are beluga whales (which can also be seen from an outdoor terrace), electric eels (eel shows daily), primitive fish, fish of the coral reef, and exhibits organised around feeding, coloration, body form, etc. Sea lions and seals sport about in outdoor tanks, along with dolphins, penguins, and a baby whale, Nyci, born (1981) in the aquarium with a birth weight of 147 lb. Smaller exhibition buildings offer sharks displayed along with huge skates and other ominous varieties, fish of the Bermuda Triangle, and North Atlantic fish including such dietary staples as striped bass and flounder. An outdoor exhibition for children allows them to handle horseshoe crabs and starfish. In the summer (May–Sept) dolphin and sea lion shows are held daily, weather permitting.

From the aquarium walk W. along the *Boardwalk. The amusement area stretches from about W. 8th to W. 16th St, dominated by Astroland and the Wonderwheel, a large ferris wheel with enclosed cabins, and an array of rides, many of them decked out as rockets or futuristic devices.

Inland, between W. 8th and W. 12th St, N. of Surf Ave and the subway tracks (elevated here) the *Luna Park Houses*, (not worth the detour) occupy the site of one of the major amusement parks. The drab renewal project is a sad contrast to the former fantasy architecture created by Frederick Thompson and Skip Dundy, entrepreneurs of Luna Park, who embellished their wonderland with a Venetian lagoon, a Chinese theatre, an Electric Tower, and a multitude of turrets, towers, onion-shaped domes, and minarets all illuminated with strings of lightbulbs.

Continue along the Boardwalk to Stillwell Ave and walk inland. *The Bowery*, a block off the beach between W. 12th and W. 16th Sts, once Coney Island's sin strip, lined with peepshows and entertainments that shocked turn-of-the-century moralists, today features an autoscooter speedway and other carnival amusements. A block further inland at Surf Ave and Stillwell Ave is *Nathan's Famous*, a stand-up eatery founded in 1916 as Nathan's and soon famous for its hot dogs—still available but not for a nickel.

Most of the old Coney Island restaurants have closed. The other outstanding survivor is Gargiulo's (founded 1907) at 2911 W. 15th St, Italian, palatial (and expensive).

SURF AVE separates the boardwalk area from the rest of the community, a seedy street with garishly illuminated discos and bars, a few small businesses, and a flea market under the tracks of the elevated railway.

Return to the Boardwalk and continue W. Jutting out into the ocean at 17th St is STEEPLECHASE PIER, being rebuilt by the city after one of Coney Island's many fires. Fisherman angle for bluefish, flounder, and striped bass in the surf. Opposite the pier is the *site of Steeplechase Park*, named after an outdoor horse race with wooden horses on a scaled-down roller coaster track. At the W. edge of the site is the abandoned *Parachute Jump* which first appeared at the 1939 World's Fair, its 11 coloured parachutes with double seats giving riders 'all the thrills of bailing out without any of the usual hazards or discomforts'.

Along the Boardwalk opposite 19th St is the *Abe Stark Center* (1969; Daniel Chait), an ice-skating rink operated by the city Department of Parks and Recreation. The rink opens in November and closes in April (tel: 965–6507). At the W. end of the peninsula are a number of *urban renewal projects* undertaken by the state Urban Development Corporation in the 1970s.

Redevelopment of Coney Island in the 1960s concentrated on placing high-rise apartments with subsidised rents in an area whose housing stock formerly consisted of summer cottages and small row houses. Although the new apartments were attractive and comfortable they existed in a wasteland, surrounded by parking lots, lacking community facilities. The Urban Development Corporation tried to soften their impact by mixing in a few low-rise structures, but even so the plan could not overcome the basic problems created by placing thousands of apartments in an area largely devoid of neighbourhood amenities.

Brighton Beach lies E. of Coney Island and can be reached by walking E. along the boardwalk past the Aquarium.

In the past decade the neighbourhood has seen the influx of a group of Russian immigrants, mostly Jews, and today it is estimated that of the 25,000 recent Soviet emigrés living in the city, about half live around the Brooklyn shore and about 8000 in Brighton Beach which has thus earned the nickname 'Little Odessa by the Sea'. Along Brighton Beach Ave are several food stores offering the staples of the Russian diet, including black bread, herrings, kasha and even such delicacies as sturgeon and caviar. Souvenir shops display amber necklaces, needlework, and nested dolls, while several cafés, including one on the boardwalk near Brighton 6th St, attract a Russian-speaking clientele who can be seen taking tea or vodka to refresh themselves after a stroll.

Manhattan Beach to the E. between Ocean Ave and MacKenzie St is the most pleasant of the city's subway beaches (toilets and changing rooms at Oriental Blvd) and is open in season from sunrise to midnight, with swimming from 10–6.30 (lifeguards on duty; for information tel: 965–6589).

Sheepshead Bay, a modest residential community of about 2 square miles E. of Coney Island on the S. edge of Brooklyn, has long been home to a population of New Yorkers of Italian and Irish extraction, though today there is an enclave of West Indians and Haitians. Moored along the waterfront (Emmons Ave between Ocean Ave and 27th St) is a small fleet of fishing boats, many for hire, which depart early in the morning and return in the late afternoon when fishermen offer their catch along the pier.

The bay which juts inward from the E. got its name either because its shape resembled a sheep's head or because sheepsheads, black banded fish with sheeplike teeth, once abounded in its waters. A quiet fishing village existed here until the land boom of 1877 followed by the opening of a race track in 1890 began attracting the city's celebrities like Diamond Jim Brady and Lillian Russell.

Points of interest. The enthusiast of Brooklyn history or colonial architecture might wish to seek out the *Wyckoff-Bennett House* (c. 1766; DL) at 1669 E. 22nd St, S.E. corner of Kings Highway, considered the finest Dutch colonial farmhouse still standing in Brooklyn. The house, built for Henry and Abraham Wyckoff and sold to the Bennett family four generations ago, has the overhanging eaves and columned porch typical of the style. During the Revolutionary War Hessian soldiers quartered here scratched their names on two panes of glass: 'Toepfer Capt of Reg de Ditfurth' and 'MBach Lieutenant v Hessen Hanau Artilerie'.

The *Elias Hubbard Ryder House*, 1926 E. 28th St between Avenues S and T, was built c. 1834 (DL) and is a late survival of the Dutch colonial style, evidence that rural vernacular architecture changes slowly.

Gerritsen Ave, the major N.–S. road E. of the Ryder House, runs S. to *Gerritsen*, a small, tidy community of bungalows and narrow streets crowded onto a neck of land between Shell Bank Creek and Marine Park.

Marine Park, lying W. of Flatbush Ave and S. of Avenue U along the shore, consists of some 2000 acres donated mostly by the Whitney family during the 1920s but still largely undeveloped.

Along the other (E.) side of Flatbush Ave, S. of the Shore Parkway, is **Floyd Bennett Field,** now part of the Gateway National Recreation Area, but originally developed as New York's first municipal airport (1931), and named to honour the pilot who flew Admiral Byrd over the North Pole in 1926.

It failed as a commercial airport because it was too far from central New York, although during the days before World War II when aviators competed for long-distance flight records, the field served as the take off point for Wiley Post (1933) who flew solo around the world (7 days, 18 hours, 49 minutes, 30 seconds) and for Howard Hughes and companions who halved that record five years later.

Today there are Coast Guard and Naval Reserve stations on the peninsula, and the Gateway Environmental Study Center, run by the National Park Service (seasonal walks and nature programmes; tel: 630–0126).

Flatbush Ave leads S. across the *Gil Hodges Bridge, formerly the Marine Parkway Bridge* (toll) built across Rockaway Inlet (1937) to Jacob Riis Park in Queens (see p589). The bridge has three spans totaling 4022 ft and a 540 ft central lift span. Gil Hodges was the first baseman for the Dodgers during its final years in Brooklyn and later managed the New York Mets baseball club.

52 Southeastern Brooklyn: Flatlands and Canarsie

Flatlands, one of the original Dutch towns in Brooklyn, also called Nieuw Amersfoort, was chartered in 1666, and took its name from its terrain, low coastal plains adjoining the salt marshes to the south. During the 17C a small Dutch town centered on what is now the junction of Flatbush Ave and Kings Highway. Today the area is primarily residential with some industrial development. Some landmark houses and a church remain of interest primarily to the local historian.

Points of interest. The *Flatlands Dutch Reformed Church*, 3931 Kings Highway between Flatbush Ave and E. 40th St, is one of three in Brooklyn established (1654) by Peter Stuyvesant and is the third church building on this site (1848; DL), a simple white clapboard Greek Revival building with a cemetery whose markers bear prominent old Brooklyn names: Lott, Kouwenhoven, Wyckoff. The earliest church on the site had stocks and a whipping post. Pieter Claessen Wyckoff arrived as an indentured servant (c. 1637) and rose to such prominence that he is buried beneath the pulpit. His home, the *Pieter Claessen Wyckoff House*, 5902 Clarendon Rd at Ralph and Ditmas Aves (c. 1641; DL), the oldest building in the state, is a low, wood-shingled farmhouse, currently undergoing restoration (not worth a detour).

Two other landmark houses in the vicinity are the *Hendrick I. Lott House*, 1940 E. 36th St between Fillmore Ave and Avenue S. (small wing 1676; larger wing 1800; DL), a Dutch colonial with overhanging eaves supported with round pillars in the front and square ones in back; and the *Stoothof-Baxter-Kouwenhoven House* (c. 1747; new wing 1811; DL), 1640 E. 48th St, whose three names belong to three prominent and related Brooklyn families who owned it for a century and a half.

Canarsie, which reaches from Foster Ave to Jamaica Bay between Paerdegat and Fresh Creek Basins, is named after its first inhabitants, the Canarsee Indians, a tribe of the Leni Lenape or Delawares of the Algonkian linguistic group. Both the Indians and the Dutch who bought the land from them cultivated maize, squash, and beans on the fertile plains, both fished the bay for shellfish, and the Dutch cut the salt hay from the marshes for fodder. Canarsie remained rural well into the 20C when it became a suburb reached primarily by automobile, built up with two-family row houses. Most recently it has become home to a Jewish community fleeing Brownsville and East Flatbush. The *Canarsie Pier*, part of the Gateway National Recreation Area (foot of Rockaway Pkwy), attracts fishermen and strollers.

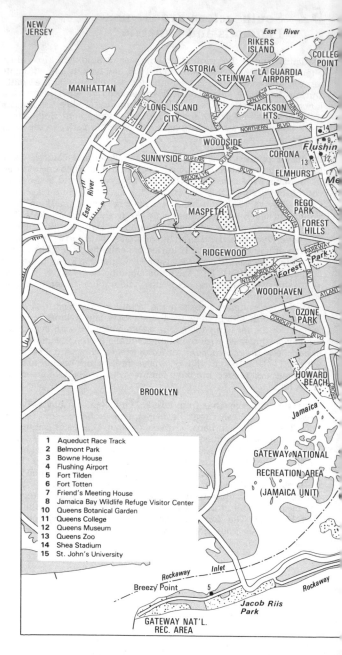

NEW
JERSEY

East River

RIKERS
ISLAND

COLLEGE
POINT

ASTORIA

STEINWAY

LA GUARDIA
AIRPORT

MANHATTAN

LONG ISLAND
CITY

JACKSON
HTS.

GRAND

CENTRAL

PARKWAY

NORTHERN BLVD.

●14

8

WOODSIDE

CORONA

Flushin

SUNNYSIDE

QUEENS

QUEENS

13

12

BROOKLYN

BLVD.

ELMHURST

Me

East River

MASPETH

REGO
PARK

WOODHAVEN

FOREST
HILLS

RIDGEWOOD

PARKWAY

Park

INTERBOROUGH

Forest

BLVD

WOODHAVEN

ATLANT

OZONE
PARK

CONDUIT

BLVD

CROSS

HOWARD
BEACH

BROOKLYN

Jamaica

GATEWAY NATIONAL

RECREATION AREA

(JAMAICA UNIT)

1 Aqueduct Race Track
2 Belmont Park
3 Bowne House
4 Flushing Airport
5 Fort Tilden
6 Fort Totten
7 Friend's Meeting House
8 Jamaica Bay Wildlife Refuge Visitor Center
9 Queens Botanical Garden
10 Queens Botanical Garden
11 Queens College
12 Queens Museum
13 Queens Zoo
14 Shea Stadium
15 St. John's University

Rockaway Inlet

Breezy Point

5

Rockaway

Jacob Riis
Park

GATEWAY NAT'L.
REC. AREA

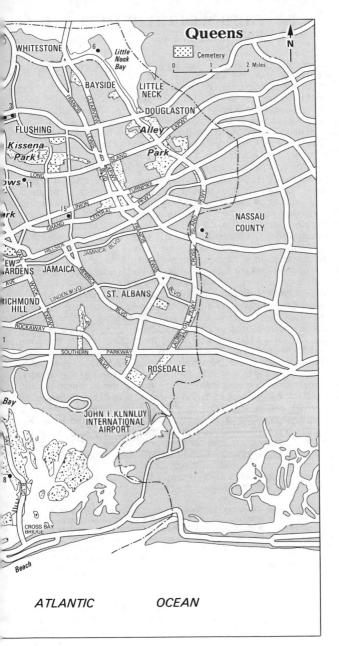

Queens

Cemetery

0   1   2 Miles

WHITESTONE

6

Little
Neck
Bay

BAYSIDE

LITTLE
NECK

DOUGLASTON

FLUSHING

Alley

*Kissena
Park*

Park

ws 11

15 UNION

NASSAU
COUNTY

2

EW
ARDENS

JAMAICA

RICHMOND
HILL

ST. ALBANS

ROCKAWAY

SOUTHERN   PARKWAY

ROSEDALE

Bay

JOHN F. KLNNLDY
INTERNATIONAL
AIRPORT

8

CROSS BAY
BRIDGE

Beach

ATLANTIC   OCEAN

IV THE BOROUGH OF QUEENS / QUEENS COUNTY

The borough of Queens, the largest in the city, covers 118·6 square miles (37·2% of the city's total area) in the W. portion of Long Island. It is bounded by Brooklyn on the W., with Newtown Creek forming part of the border, by the East River on the N., by the Atlantic Ocean on the S., and by Nassau County on the E. Topographically it resembles the rest of Long Island with a chain of hills created by glacial deposits running across the N. and a low outwash plain in the S. The N. shore is indented by Flushing and Little Neck Bays while the Rockaway peninsula juts westward across the mouth of Jamaica Bay in the S. to form a 10-mile ocean-front Atlantic Beach.

Home to 1,891,325 people (a decrease of 4·8% since the 1970 census), Queens is the second largest borough in population, surpassed only by Brooklyn. It is largely residential with more than 300,000 one- and two-family houses as well as apartment towers of various heights, but lacks the concentration of 19C brownstones and tenements that characterise Brooklyn and the Bronx. Some of its neighbourhoods—Douglaston, Forest Hills, Kew Gardens—are almost suburban in character with detached houses, attractive gardens, and garages for that definitive suburban vehicle, the family car. At the other end of the economic scale are slums in S. Jamaica, in the Rockaways, and in surrounding older industrial areas.

While Queens has earned its reputation as a bedroom community in the past half century, those areas developed earlier became industrial, with concentrations of factories in the vicinity of Long Island City and Maspeth, and along the right-of-way of the Long Island Railroad (LIRR). As elsewhere in the city, ageing physical plants, problems of transportation, taxation, and labour have made Queens less attractive to industry than other areas of the country. Commercial centers are scattered thoughout the borough, usually located at the crossroads of earlier towns, established independently before the creation of Greater New York in 1898: the most important ones are Astoria, Corona, Flushing, Jackson Heights, and Jamaica.

Queens has the highest median income of any borough and in the late 1970s before the current downturn in the national economy, a 92% rate of employment . Among its suburban amenities are 6474 acres of parkland, almost as much as in the other four boroughs combined, two racetracks, two major tennis centers, several golf courses, and a wildlife refuge.

Because of its spaciousness, Queens has also become the resting place of uncounted souls whose remains lie buried in the belt of cemeteries that begins on the Brooklyn-Queens border and stretches eastward along the Interborough Pkwy, an area known by the waggish as the 'terminal moraine' and which includes such cemeteries as Union Field, Bethel, Mt Carmel, Mt Neboh, Cypress Hills, Mt Lebanon, and Mt Judah. Other large graveyards in the borough, which also owe their impetus to an 1851 law which prohibited further burials in Manhattan, are St. John's, Mt Olivet, Lutheran, St. John's, Mt Zion, Calvary, and New Calvary.

More than any other borough, Queens bears the stamp of Robert Moses who as parks commissioner preserved acres and acres of land—forests, meadow, beaches, marshes—while as master road-builder (and head of various public authorities) he blighted equally large areas by lacing the borough with highways: Grand Central Pkwy, Interborough Pkwy, the Clearview Expwy, the Cross Island Pkwy, Laurelton Pkwy, the Long Island Expwy, the Brooklyn-Queens Expwy, and the Whitestone Expwy.

History. The first inhabitants of Queens were the Rockaway Indians whose name lives on in the peninsula stretching across Jamaica Bay, and the first settlers were the Dutch who arrived in c. 1635. Governor Kieft purchased title to the land from the Indians in 1639 and shortly thereafter the first towns were chartered Mespat (now Maspeth) in 1642, and Vlissingen (Flushing) in 1643. Middleburg, which became Newtowne in 1655, was founded in 1652 between the two earlier settlements, its first residents immigrants from France and England as well as Holland. Indeed, as settlement continued, the Dutch staked out their claims in the W. part of Long Island while the English colonised the E. portion including the towns of Hempstead and Jamaica (1650).

In 1683, nineteen years after the British took title to the former Dutch colony of New Amsterdam, these towns were organised as Queens County, one of 12 making up the British province of New York. The name honours Catherine of Braganza, queen of Charles II. During the Revolution most residents of Queens were British sympathisers and after the war many loyalists emigrated to Newfoundland.

Although a few industries established plants in Queens during the 19C, notably the Steinway piano factory and the Edward Smith & Co. paint factory, the borough remained rural and agricultural until almost the turn of the century. As the railroads began pushing E. across Long Island the beaches of both the N. and S. shores began attracting summer residents: at the turn of the century the land La Guardia airport now occupies held an amusement park and the Rockaways, whose remoteness is enshrined in the place name of its most E. settlement, Far Rockaway, attracted the well-to-do who enjoyed the facilities of grand hotels or the privacy of their own mansions. The major roads were used by farmers taking their produce to New York markets or by residents in outlying communities seeking the amenities of the commercial districts closer to the city.

In 1898 Queens voted to become part of Greater New York, although several of the eastern towns chose to remain independent—Hempstead, N. Hempstead, and Oyster Bay, and were then absorbed into Nassau County. At the time (1900) the population of the borough was only 152,999, a figure which tripled in the next 20 years and doubled again between 1920–30, as bridges, tunnels, and rapid transit opened Queens to development. In 1910 the Queensboro Bridge and the East River tunnel of the Pennsylvania Railroad allowed direct access to Manhattan, while the subways came during the next decades with the BMT and IRT both reaching the outer areas of the borough and the IND going all the way to Jamaica in 1937. The Triborough Bridge (1936), the Bronx-Whitestone Bridge (1939), the Queens-Midtown Tunnel (1939), and most recently the Throgs Neck Bridge (1961) made Queens readily accessible by car.

In 1939–40 the first of two world's fairs was held in Flushing Meadows and several of these public works projects along with the development of La Guardia Airport were undertaken to coincide with its opening. After World War II, when the populations of the other boroughs (except Staten Island) were either remaining stable or shrinking, Queens experienced its second great boom, one that took the form of suburban development as builders grabbed whatever open space remained and erected acre after acre of tract housing, small homes on small lots, monotonously repeated row upon row, block upon block. Despite the blandness of much of Queen's suburban development, its very newness has saved the borough from some of the problems of urban blight that afflict Manhattan, Brooklyn, and the Bronx.

Touring in Queens. Although security is not such a problem in Queens as in parts of Manhattan, Brooklyn and the Bronx, distances are such that a car is certainly convenient and probably necessary. The orientation of most museums and other attractions in Queens is toward the community in which they are located, and most of the sights of the borough are of interest primarily to the avid tourist, or the visitor intent on seeing the city as a whole. While a casual glance at a roadmap may make it appear that Queens is laid out in a recognisable rectilinear pattern, it is deceptively difficult to find one's way around in the borough. Numbered avenues generally run east and west, but they are sometimes interspersed with roads, drives, and even an occasional court bearing the same number; streets run generally north and south and seem to be more regular than avenues in their numbering. The pattern is further complicated by the vestiges of old roads—dating from the colonial period and themselves often following Indian paths—wandering across the modern grid according to topographical variations long erased by landfill or levelling. New highways have been rammed through old neighbourhoods, disrupting the continuity of street layouts as well as the social fabric of the neighbourhoods themselves. Finally developers have created special patterns, arcs or crescents for example, in communities like Forest Hills Gardens, Rego Park, or Kew Gardens that were developed all at once as planned communities or for real estate speculation.

53 Northwestern Queens: Long Island City, Sunnyside, Woodside, Astoria and Steinway

Long Island City, manufacturing center of the borough, raises its bleak, industrial skyline just across the East River from midtown Manhattan and Roosevelt Island, the stacks of the Con Ed generator, known as Big Allis, familiar on both sides of the river. Long Island City owes its name to a period of political independence (1870–98) after it broke away from the town of Newtown and before it joined Queens in 1898 as part of the consolidation of Greater New York. Although Long Island City like the rest of the metropolis has suffered a loss in manufacturing jobs, its factories still turn out perfume, surgical instruments, cookies, pianos, clothing, and chewing gum. It is also a hub of transportation: the IRT and BMT elevateds, the Long Island Railroad (now part of the Metropolitan Transit Authority), and the tracks of Conrail (formerly the Penn Central Railroad) converge here before making the river crossing to Manhattan.

Hunter's Point, in the S.W. corner of Long Island City and just across Newtown Creek from the Greenpoint section of Brooklyn, is a mixed industrial-residential district and one block, 45th Ave between 21st–23rd Sts, has been declared the *Hunter's Point Historic District*, mainly on the strength of a fine group of Italianate rowhouses. They date from the early 1870s and owe their good condition to their building material, Westchester stone, harder and less friable than the usual brownstone.

Hunter's Point takes its name from British sea captain George Hunter who owned land in the vicinity during the colonial period, but its development dates from about 1860 when the first steam ferry made regular crossings to Manhattan. Around the landing at 34th St a prosperous community arose, with inns and hotels for travellers and comfortable homes for commuters. This pleasant state of affairs lasted until 1909 when the opening of the Queensboro Bridge led to the rapid industrialisation of Hunter's Point and the development of more attractive residential areas further east.

Nearby, at 46–01 21st St between 46th Rd and 46th Ave, the *Institute for Art and Urban Resources: P.S. 1* occupies the former Ward 1 School (1892), now refurbished (1976; Shael Shapiro) as an experimental art center with exhibition space and artists' housing (open Thurs–Sat, 1–6; free; tel: 784–2084). Past exhibitions have included video art, photography, architecture, and environmental sculpture.

The IRT Flushing line of the subway crosses the East River to and from Hunter's Point in the Steinway Tunnels, named after piano manufacturer William Steinway who backed a subterranean trolley car connection to Manhattan in 1892. After the test run, a franchise dispute interrupted service and the tunnels, though completed in 1907, sat empty until 1913 when they were converted to subway use and opened (1915) for regular public service.

The **Queensboro Bridge** (1909; Gustav Lindenthal, engineer) sweeps overhead at 41st Rd, linking Queens to 59th–60th Sts in Manhattan (see p281). Just N. of it, (Vernon Blvd to 21st St, 40th Ave to Bridge Plaza) are the *Queensbridge Houses* (1939; William F.R. Ballard, chief architect), once the largest public housing project in the nation (3161 apartments in 26 buildings on 62·5 acres) and still considered one of the best. North of the bridge is the neighbourhood of Ravenswood, with housing projects, industry, and the Con Ed generator.

Until 1938 the *Brewster Building*, 27–01 Bridge Plaza North, between 27th–28th Sts (1910; Stephenson & Wheeler), with its bulky clock tower, housed a company that first produced fine carriages and later became the N. American assembler of Rolls Royce cars.

In the days before Hollywood became the nexus of the American film industry the *Astoria Studios*, (1919) 34th–38th Sts along 35th Ave, employed the talents of such stars as Gloria Swanson, the Marx Brothers, and Rudolf Valentino. Originally owned by the Famous Players Corp. which became a part of Paramount Pictures, the 13-building complex was first used to produce feature films; as the Eastern Service Studios its facilities were devoted to educational and comic shorts, and during World War II became the U.S. Army Pictorial Center, turning out training films. Recently the studios have been reopened comercially and produced several major films.

Sunnyside, a modest residential community centering around the intersection of Roosevelt Ave and Queens Blvd, is hemmed in by cemeteries, industrial zones, and the former *Sunnyside Yards of the Pennsylvania Railroad* (between Skillman and Jackson Aves). The yards opened in 1910 along with the tunnel beneath the East River to Pennsylvania Station, which allowed direct train travel from New England to New York for the first time. Today lines leading into the yards accommodate the trains of Conrail, a commuter and freight line to points N. and E., the Long Island Railroad, and Amtrak, the long-distance national railroad.

SUNNYSIDE GARDENS, bounded by Skillman and 39th Aves, 43rd–50th Sts (1924; Henry Wright, Clarence Stein, and Frederick Ackerman), is a community of detached homes and small apartment buildings, an early and successful experiment in urban planning, undertaken by a limited-profit agency which developed these 70 acres of unpromising land during the boom years of the 1920s. More notable for its site planning than its architecture, the development has houses facing both the street and the back gardens and also includes park and recreational areas. During the Depression many homeowners unable to pay their mortgages took collective action against the sheriffs serving eviction notices, sandbagging their doors, installing barbed wire, and physically harassing law enforcement officers, but more than 60% of the original owners lost their homes through foreclosure.

Woodside, N.E. of Sunnyside and geographically indistinguishable from it, is a lower middle class residential community developed after 1917 when the Flushing line of the IRT put it within minutes of Manhattan.

North of Long Island City and just across the East River from Wards and Randalls Islands is **Astoria.** Originally called Hallett's Cove after William Hallett to whom governor Peter Stuyvesant granted a patent for 1500 acres in 1654, Astoria got its present name in 1839 when it was incorporated as a town, a name accepted despite the bitter opposition of John Jacob Astor's detractors. The town grew as a suburb after a steam ferry began crossings to Manhattan and during the 1840s became the center of a thriving shipping business, some of whose entrepreneurs traded in exotic woods. Successful shippers built their mansions along the waterfront, though none has survived. Today Astoria has a huge Con Edison plant occupying 383 acres along the East River, a peninsula whose outer edge is still called Berrian's Island though it is no longer separated from Long Island.

Astoria Park, bounded by Shore Blvd, 19th St, Astoria Park South, and Ditmars Blvd, was developed in the 1930s during the construction of the Triborough Bridge (see p386). The Astoria Play Center and Swimming Pool (1936; J.M. Hatton), a WPA project with a large bath house, still serves the local population.

The *Remsen House*, 9–26 27th Ave, S.W. corner of 12th St (c. 1835; DL) survives from the period when the bulbous peninsula of Hallett's Point protruding into the East River just S. of Astoria Park had a fashionable summer colony and grand houses. Most of the homes have been demolished but this formerly handsome Greek Revival house with its pilastered doorway, tall parlour-floor windows, and iron fence survives from those genteel times. Across the street is the *Doctor Wayt House*, 9–29 27th Ave, N.W. corner of 12th St, an Italianate mansion now badly dilapidated. In healthier condition is a grand two-story colonnaded mansion at 25–37 14th St between

Astoria Park South and 26th Ave, partially hidden behind a spreading beech and looking as if it belonged in Georgia instead of Astoria.

Astoria is known today as the city's largest Greek enclave, a clean, safe neighbourhood where an estimated 75% of the Greek-Americans own their own homes and run their own businesses. Before the relaxation of immigration laws in 1965 allowed more arrivals from southern Europe, the population of Astoria consisted mainly of Italians who had previously lived elsewhere in New York, though a small group of Greeks did settle in the area before World War II. Unlike some other city ethnic neighbourhoods, Astoria is burgeoning as new immigrants come from Greece.

> SUBWAY: BMT Broadway local (RR train) to Astoria Blvd/Hoyt Ave.
>
> CAR: Queensboro Bridge to Northern Blvd; turn left (N.) at 31st St in Queens and follow it N. to Ditmars Blvd. Or Triborough Bridge to 31st St and turn left (N.) to Ditmars Blvd.
>
> PARKING: Difficult, especially on weekends, though there is a municipal lot on 33rd St, S. of Ditmars Blvd.

For a short walking tour, begin at Astoria Blvd and Hoyt Ave South on 31st St and follow 31st St north (street numbers will decrease) to Ditmars Blvd; turn right (E.) and continue to Steinway St. Along 31st St, the main commercial thoroughfare, are Greek orientated shops with icons, decorated candles, records, and books, as well as several restaurants and pastry shops. Butchers, whose staple is lamb, sometimes arrange rather startling displays of sheeps' heads in the show windows, while fish markets offer prickly sea urchins and squid, along with more familiar fare. The Ditmars Theater, 31st St between 23rd Ave and Ditmars Blvd, shows only Greek films. Restaurants and coffee shops stay open late and nightclubs get lively around 11 p.m. with Greek music and dancing, by the patrons or by professional belly dancers (though belly dancing is more a Near Eastern than a Greek speciality). Some of the clubs have recently emigrated from the old belly dance center on Eighth Ave around 28th St in Manhattan, following the exodus of the Greek population.

East of Astoria lies **Steinway**, developed by piano manufacturer William Steinway who moved his factory from Manhattan to a 400-acre site along Bowery Bay in 1872, surrounding it with a company town that had a park, library, ball fields, a kindergarten, and some row housing that still stands. Steinway was attracted by the availability of land and lumber in Queens, but he also chose this rather isolated spot to remove his workers from the influence of union organisers.

The *Steinway Mansion* still stands at 18–33 41st St between Berrian Blvd and 19th Ave (1850s; DL), on a hill overlooking the East River. Benjamin Pike, an optician, built the Italianate villa for himself, with rough stonework, romantically assymetric bays, arcades, and towers. Once graced by lawns, tennis courts, orchards, and stables, it now stands obscured by trees in a rather sinister neighbourhood whose tone is established by a sewage treatment plant, some junkyards, and ferocious guard dogs. The Steinway factory is at the N.W. corner of 19th Ave and 39th St and the *Steinway Company Housing* (c. 1880) on the S. side of 20th Ave between Steinway St and 41st Ave.

Nearby but rather difficult to find and worthwhile only for the avid local historian is the *Lawrence family graveyard* (20th Rd, S.E. corner of 35th St). This private cemetery (1703; DL) belongs to a distinguished Long Island family whose earliest members arrived during the Dutch colonial period; the graves span the years 1703–1956.

The *Lent Homestead*, 78–03 19th Rd at 78th St (c. 1729; DL) is the second oldest dwelling in Queens, a Dutch style farmhouse of fieldstone with hewn timbers and shingles built by Abraham Lent, grandson of Abraham Riker whose family once owned Rikers Island. It has been handsomely modernised so that only the shingles and original timbers at one end and the shape of the large, dormered, overhanging Dutch roof remain to testify to its antiquity.

Nearby at the intersection of 19th Ave and Hazen St is the bridge to **Rikers Island,** politically part of the Bronx but joined to Queens by a bridge (not accessible to the public). On the island are several city penal institutions, the most noteworthy being the Men's House of Detention, with about 5000 prisoners. Built in 1935 to replace the old Welfare (now Roosevelt) Island prison, it was heralded as a model penitentiary, but today is obsolete and the object of controversy. Other facilities on the island are the Correctional Institution for Men, the Correctional Institution for Women, the Adolescent Detention Center, the Rikers Island Hospital, and the Anna Kross Center. The island at low tide lies only about 100 ft from the runways of La Guardia Airport, and has long relied for security on the currents and tides of the river, today, according to prison employees, less treacherous than in the past.

Rikers Island is named after Abraham Rycken (later spelled Riker) and his descendants who owned it for generations after 1664.

Near Rikers Island is *North Brother Island*, site of the former Riverside Hospital for communicable diseases, whose most famous resident was 'Typhoid Mary' Mallon, a cook who unknowingly communicated the disease to New Yorkers and probably started several epidemics. The burning excursion steamer, the 'Genral Slocum', beached here in 1904, but not before more than a thousand passengers had lost their lives, most of them women and children on an outing from the Tompkins Square neighbourhood of the Lower East Side. *South Brother Island*, also part of the Bronx, is about seven acres of wasteland.

54 Central Queens

The first settlement in central Queens was the Dutch town (1642) of Middleburg between Maspeth and Flushing, renamed Newtowne (1655) by the English. Its boundaries encompass the contemporary communities of Jackson Heights, Corona, Elmhurst, Forest Hills, Maspeth, Ridgewood, and Rego Park, which range economically from the exclusivity of Forest Hills Gardens to the industrial blight and economic depression of parts of Ridgewood and Maspeth.

LA GUARDIA AIRPORT on the Grand Central Parkway bordering Flushing Bay and Bowery Bay in the **Jackson Heights** section was developed before World War II along with the neighbourhood surrounding it and is the city's second municipal air field after the economically unsuccessful Floyd Bennett Field.

Originally the Gala Amusement Park occupied the site, converted in 1929 to a private flying field, named first the Glenn H. Curtiss Airport and later the North Beach Airport. Taken over by the city, it was enlarged by purchase and landfill and opened to commercial traffic in 1939. In 1947 the airport was leased to the Port Authority and named La Guardia Airport, and in the 1960s was modernised and expanded. Today the facility occupies 650 acres, employs 8400 workers, has nine large hangars and a fuel storage facility fed by pipeline from Linden, New Jersey, with a capacity of 5·1 million gallons.

Passenger terminals are the *Central Terminal Building* (1965; Harrison & Abramovitz), which handles most scheduled airlines, the *Marine Air Terminal* (1939; Delano & Aldrich), the original terminal placed near the water to serve the flying boats of the period and now used by commuter airlines, air taxis, private aircraft, and the U.S. Weather Service, and the *Eastern Airlines/Shuttle Terminal* (1981), from which hourly shuttles are flown between New York, Boston, and Washington. The Parking Garage (1976; Staff of Port Authority) holds 2800 cars.

In 1967 the two main runways were extended over water to a length of 7000 ft on an L-shaped pier. The general aviation runway, 2000 ft long, is available for departures only to the N.W. and is used by light aircraft. In 1980 there were 316,811 plane movements at La Guardia, serving 17,459,336 passengers.

Maspeth, bounded by Newtown Creek, an oily tidal arm of the East River, is now heavily industrial though it has had a surprisingly stable population of ethnically mixed European residents—Poles, Italians, Lithuanians, and Germans. The town was settled early (1642) and named after an Indian village, called Maspaetches (spelled various ways) which meant 'bad water place' and referred to the swamps around Maspeth Creek. **Ridgewood** joins the neighbourhood of Bushwick in Brooklyn, and is similar to it in economic and social make-up.

In the 19C **Corona,** now a densely populated but undistinguished community bordering the Grand Central Parkway and Roosevelt Ave, was called West Flushing and in 1856 became the site of the Fashion Race Track, named after a race horse. It was subdivided for development in 1870 and took the name Corona, apparently expressing aspirations for eminence. For a long time, however, it was known chiefly as the site of the Corona Dump, but today in the aftermath of two Worlds' Fairs in Flushing Meadows it has become the site of major sporting facilities, a museum, and a large park.

FLUSHING MEADOWS PARK, sometimes called Flushing Meadows-Corona Park, occupies 1316 acres running north-south along what was once the Flushing River, a navigable waterway to the old town of Flushing, and is girded by the Grand Central Pkwy and the Van Wyck Expwy.

Originally the land was salt marsh, inundated daily by the tides and therefore useless to developers. Saved thus from becoming a subdivision, Flushing Meadows became the Corona Dump and the river an open sewer. By the 1920s trainloads of trash and garbage which arrived daily from Brooklyn smouldered nightly as they were burned, giving the place a Dantesque aura and inspiring novelist F. Scott Fitzgerald to name it the Valley of Ashes. The marsh disappeared beneath tons of filth, one mound rising high enough to earn the name Mt Corona. It took about 30 years to convert the dump to the present park, a project which involved channelling part of the Flushing River into a conduit as large as a tube of the Holland Tunnel, building sewage plants to decontaminate Flushing Bay, and removing hundreds of thousands of tons of garbage.

N. of Flushing Meadows Park and across the tracks of the Port Washington branch of the LIRR is *Shea Stadium* (1964; Praeger-Kavanagh-Waterbury), home turf of the New York Mets (baseball) and the New York Jets (football). The infield tiers of the baseball stadium rotate to accommodate a seating plan more amenable to football. The stadium holds 55,300 spectators for baseball and 60,000 for football.

The *National Tennis Center* lies just S. of the railroad tracks and has been the site of the U.S. Open Championships since the tournament moved here in 1978 from Forest Hills. The facility, with

27 outdoor courts and nine indoor courts, is open to the public when not in use for tournament play (tel: 592–8000 for rates and schedule).

The widest section of the park between the Long Island Expressway and the railroad tracks was the site of the 1964–65 World's Fair. The grounds, on which stand several monumental relics of the fair, have been reused for recreational facilities, a museum, and a zoo.

The mall of the fair begins near the E. edge not far from the Van Wyck Expressway. Its first artifact is Donald De Lue's 45-ft statue, *the Rocket Thrower*, a modestly draped, heavily muscular bronze athlete hurling a missle through a circle of stars. On the lawn to the right is a *statue of George Washington* (1959) by the same sculptor. Straight down the mall, beyond the now empty reflecting pools, is the fair's most imposing artifact, the *Unisphere* constructed by the U.S. Steel Corporation (140 ft high, 120 ft in diameter, and weighing 700,000 lbs), whose meridians and continents challenge local youngsters to climb upon it, and whose empty pool and fountain form a smooth surface for roller skating.

Off to the left, forlorn and derelict, is the *New York State Pavilion* (1964; Philip Johnson & Richard Foster), hailed for structural innovations two decades ago. The concrete tubular columns originally supported two roofs, one above the other, sheathed in coloured transparent plastic.

To the right of the mall near the New York City Building stands José de Rivera's *Free Form*, a curved scythe of polished metal, similar to others by this sculptor. During the fair it slowly revolved but the motor gave up in 1972.

The QUEENS MUSEUM stands at the head of the mall in the building that once held New York City's exhibition at the 1939–40 World's Fair.

Open Tues–Sat, 10–5; Sun, 1–5; suggested donation, adults, $1; children under 12, free; students and senior citizens, 50¢; tel: 592–5555.

This small museum has changing exhibitions on art and local history including major traveling shows. Its *pièce de résistance*, however, is a 15,000 square ft *panorama of New York City executed for the fair and regularly updated; from a glass-enclosed balcony visitors may admire its bridges, rivers, parks, streets, and 835,000 buildings.

Two overpasses lead to the W. section of the park beyond the Grand Central Pkwy. Near the road is the *Queens Zoo*, a small but attractive zoo renovated in 1981 after efforts to close it aroused public hostility (open daily, 10–4; free; cafeteria and restrooms). The zoo has bears, raccoons, bison, sea lions, wolves, deer, and a geodesic aviary dome with netting to keep the birds inside. Outside the zoo is a carousel (seasonal) and a *Children's Farm* (open daily, 10–3.45; free), where urban children may examine goats, sheep, rabbits, ducks, and ponies. Beyond the Terrace on the Park, a catering service, is the *New York Hall of Science*, now closed for renovation (scheduled to re-open in 1983; tel: 699–9400).

Elmhurst lies W. of the park around Queens Blvd and Grand Ave, near the center of the old town of Newtowne. Although its dense development today masks its rural antecedents, Elmhurst while still part of Newtowne boasted fine apple orchards, from which 'Newtown Pippins' were exported to England for cider. Of interest to the local historian are the *Reformed Dutch Church of Newtown* and its

Fellowship Hall, 85–15 Broadway at Corona Ave (church, 1831; hall, 1858; DL), both white clapboarded structures with Victorian stained glass, and the *St. James Fellowship Hall*, originally the St. James Episcopal Church, Broadway at the S.W. corner of 51st Ave (1734), the original church of a parish established in 1704. The original steeple is gone and the building was updated with carpenter-gothic ornament. The church which replaced this one as the house of worship for the parish was built in 1849 at the N.E. corner of Broadway and Corona Ave but later burned.

More expressive of contemporary life in Elmhurst are Lefrak City, between Junction Blvd and 99th St, 57th Ave and the Long Island Expwy, a huge brick housing development built (1962–67; Jack Brown) by real estate entrepreneur Sam Lefrak, and Queens Center, on Queens Blvd at the N.E. corner of 59th Ave, a shopping mall (1973; Guren Assocs) with branches of Orbach's and Abraham & Straus.

Forest Hills, bounded by Yellowstone Blvd, Metropolitan Ave, and Queens Blvd, is famous for tennis and for city planning. The *West Side Tennis Club*, bounded by 69th Ave, Burns St, Dartmouth St, and Tennis Pl, with its lawns, clay courts, and neo-Tudor club house, was the scene of the U.S. Open Championships until 1978 when heightened interest in tennis made the stadium (c. 13,500 spectators) less profitable than a larger one.

Forest Hills Gardens, 71st Ave to Union Turnpike, LIRR tracks to Greenway South, is today a pleasant upper class community with winding, tree-lined streets, many of whose houses imitate English rural prototypes. Originally the project (begun 1913; Grosvenor Atterbury, architect; Frederick Law Olmsted, Jr, landscape architect) was to be an experiment in middle-income housing for commuters and was sponsored by the Russell Sage Foundation. When it was about half finished, a residents' organisation took over, imposed restrictive covenants, and turned Forest Hills Gardens into what it is today.

In front of the *Queens Borough Hall* (1941; William Gehron & A. Thomas) on Queens Blvd between Union Turnpike and 82nd Ave stands Frederick MacMonnies's marble statue *Civic Virtue* (1922), a late and unsuccessful work by a fine sculptor, originally placed in front of City Hall in Manhattan.

When installed there the statue raised cries of protest in part for the near-nudity of its central figure, a muscular athletic male whose modesty is protected by wisps of seaweed and bubbles of foam, and in part for the symbolism of the two writhing female forms (Civic Vice?) on whom the hero appears to be trampling. MacMonnies defended himself by pointing out the Virtue's foot does not actually tread upon the women, but since feminist groups, the Women's Christian Temperance Union, and the president of Harvard all objected, the statue was moved to Queens where it would be less conspicuous.

In the S. part of Forest Hills is *Forest Park*, a 538-acre reserve with woods, walking trails, and a golf course, whose rocky terrain was created by the terminal moraine which forms the spine of Long Island.

Kew Gardens, E. of Forest Park, is similar to nearby Forest Hills, though less wealthy. **Rego Park,** with its curved streets, was laid out and developed by the Real Good Construction Co, whose acronym accounts for the community's name.

55   Northeastern Queens: College Point, Whitestone, Bayside, Little Neck, Douglaston, and Flushing

College Point lies along the shore of Long Island Sound N. of Flushing and owes its name to an Episcopalian divinity school founded (1836) by Rev. William A. Muhlenberg, but never completed. In the 17C William Lawrence had an estate here; his descendants sold off part of the land to one Eliphalet Stratton who developed it and named the community Strattonsport. During and after the Civil War era it was a busy industrial community whose rubber factories, ribbon mills, and breweries employed a population of Swiss and German immigrants. Its picnic grounds and beer gardens attracted New Yorkers (from Manhattan) of Germanic descent who came on the excursion steamers that plied Long Island Sound. Today College Point is still residential with a surprisingly small-town atmosphere, perhaps the result of its former physical isolation, when it was connected to Flushing by a causeway (now College Point Blvd) over the marshes. *Flushing Airport*, a private facility, occupies 300 acres near the Whitestone Pkwy.

The *Poppenhusen Institute*, 114–04 14th Rd, S.E. corner of 114th St (1868; Mundell & Teckritz; DL), now abandoned, was built primarily as an adult evening school by German-born Conrad Poppenhusen, who pioneered the hard-rubber industry in this country. Along with a trade school, a language school, and a free kindergarten for the children of working mothers, the institute once had a library, savings bank, youth center, and jail whose cells, according to local tradition, not infrequently held those visiting New Yorkers who had drunk too deeply in the nearby beer gardens. Adolph Poppenhusen later became a major stockholder in the Long Island Railroad.

The *First Reformed Church of College Point and Parish House*, 14th Ave at the N.W. corner of 119th St (1872), are fine examples of the carpenter-gothic tradition, worth seeking out for anyone interested in vernacular architecture.

E. of College Point along the N. shore of Long Island lies the community of **Whitestone,** its boundaries marked by the footings of the Bronx-Whitestone and Throgs Neck Bridges. Settled in 1645 by Dutch farmers who paid the Indians an axe for every 50 acres of land, the community took its name from a large, white boulder that once stood at the landing place but called itself Clintonville during the governorship of DeWitt Clinton, reverting to its old name in 1845. Today Whitestone has pleasant residential neighbourhoods, the private upper-class community of Malba on the W. almost beneath the Bronx-Whitestone bridge, Beechhurst in the N. along Powell's Cove Blvd between the bridges, and the Le Havre Houses, formerly known as the Levitt Houses, along 166th St and Utopia Pkwy, an apartment complex built by Alfred Levitt (1958; George G. Miller), brother of the founder of Levittown.

Bayside, Douglaston, and **Little Neck** are residential areas whose small apartment buildings and detached houses give them a distinctly suburban character. In the N.E. corner of Bayside, the *Fort Totten Battery* (1846; William Petit Trowbridge, engineer; DL), named after military engineer Joseph Totten, faces Fort Schuyler in the Throgs Neck section of the Bronx and at one time protected the N.E. entrance to New York harbour (see p502). The *Officers' Club* on Fort Totten Rd, a picturesque crenellated building (c. 1870, enlarged 1887; DL), made surprisingly of wood, is now abandoned. The post is used for the army reserve and is not open to the public except on Armed Forces Day (a Sat in mid-May) and on special occasions.

Flushing, first settled in 1642 and chartered in 1645, lies E. of the Flushing River. The name is a corruption of the Dutch Vlissingen, a town in Holland from which some of its early settlers emigrated. It has been associated with the development of religious freedom in the United States ever since the 17C struggles between Peter Stuyvesant and the Quakers whom he wished to suppress. During the 19C Flushing was a summer colony and remained a quiet residential town until the highways constructed for the first New York World's Fair led to its rapid development. Today it is still residential though not particularly quiet, intersected by major avenues and girded by expressways. It has a busy if not elegant commercial strip whose stores reflect the ethnic diversity of the population, and a number of historic sites sufficiently close together to be visited on foot.

> SUBWAY: IRT Flushing line (train 7) to Main St, the last stop.
>
> CAR: Take either the Long Island Expressway to exit 23 and go N. on Main St; or Northern Blvd to Main St.
>
> TRAIN: LIRR Port Washington Line to Flushing Main St.

Begin at Main St and Roosevelt Ave and walk N. (street numbers will decrease). *St. George's Episcopal Church* (1854; Wills & Dudley; DL), built of brownstone and Manhattan schist with a wooden steeple added later, replaces an earlier church of 1761, where Francis Lewis, signer of the Declaration of Independence, served as vestryman.

Continue N. to Northern Blvd. A famous 18C nursery flourished on the site of the RKO Keith Theater (Northern Blvd at Prince St); here William Prince planted the first specimen around 1737 and by 1750 the eight-acre tract, then called the *Linnaean Botanic Garden*, was a major commercial supplier. Though the gardens are gone, the offspring of Mr Prince's industry account for many of the 140 genera and 2000 species of trees and shrubs that beautify Flushing.

Turn right. At 137–16 Northern Blvd, between Main St and Union St, is the FRIENDS' MEETING HOUSE (1694; enlarged 1716–19; DL), a simple wooden building with a steep hipped roof and very small windows (open first and third Sun of every month except Aug, 2–4; free; tel: 762–9743). The rear faces Northern Blvd while the front opens onto a small graveyard whose stones were unmarked until 1848 in accordance with the Quaker belief that death equalises everyone. The two doors were once used as separate men's and women's entrances. Except for a period during the British occupation (1776–83) when it served as a prison, hay barn, and hospital, the Meeting House has been used continuously for religious services since its construction, though it must have been very uncomfortable during its first 50 winters as iron stoves were not installed until 1760; central heating followed two centuries later (1965).

Across Northern Blvd is the most imposing 19C structure in town,

the FLUSHING TOWN HALL, 137–35 Northern Blvd, N.E. corner of
Linden Pl. (1862; Cornelius Howard, builder; DL), a tan brick
building with chocolate brown trim, described as Romanesque
Revival but overlaid with Victorian detail—heavy cornice, gables,
turrets, and a porch. Once it held a court room, bank offices, a
library, a meeting hall, and a jail and during its heyday hosted
Flushing's most important events—town meetings, opera performances, firemen's balls—and its most illustrious visitors—Theodore
Roosevelt, U.S. Grant, Tom Thumb, P.T. Barnum, and Jenny Lind.
After a period of disuse, the building is being reclaimed as a medical
center.

Continue down Northern Blvd past the Flushing Armory (1905),
137–58 Northern Blvd, and the high school to Bowne St; turn right
and walk a block to 37th Ave. The boulder about 100 yards down the
street on the right, *Fox Oaks Rock*, gets its name from George Fox,
English founder of the Religious Society of Friends (i.e. Quakers)
who came to N. America in 1672 and preached here under a stand of
oaks.

On the S.E. corner of Bowne St and 37th Ave (37–01 Bowne St) is
the oldest dwelling in Queens, the BOWNE HOUSE (1661, with later
additions; DL), built by John Bowne and inhabited by nine generations of his family until 1945 when it was opened as a museum.

Open Tues, Sat, Sun, 2.30–4.30; adults, $1, children, 25¢. Tel: 359–0528.

The oldest part of the house contains a kitchen with a very large
fireplace and beehive oven fitted out with cranes, kettles, and other
utensils. Here John Bowne, a convert to Quakerism, allowed illegal
meetings of the sect whose fanaticism and frenzied habits of worship
(hence the name 'Quakers') along with their heretical beliefs drew
the wrath of conforming Christians. Peter Stuyvesant, who particularly abhorred the sect, fined Bowne and banished him to Holland.
There Bowne pleaded his cause with the Dutch West India Co.,
whose administrators found increased immigration to an underpopu-
lated colony more important than religious conformity and therefore
advised Stuyvesant to shut his eyes to what he saw as the outrages of
Quakerism.

In the garden is a plaque inscribed with the *Flushing Remon-
strance*, a reply by the people of the town to Peter Stuyvesant's edict
(1657) that the Dutch Reformed Church was the only permitted
religion in the colony.

Walk out through the garden to 37th Ave and past the playground
to the *Kingsland House*, once the William K. Murray House (1774;
DL), at 143–35 37th Ave (actually on 37th St W. of Parsons Blvd).

It was built by Charles Doughty, a Quaker farmer reputed to have been the first
person in the area to free a slave, his servant Sarah. Doughty's son-in-law
Joseph King inherited the house and settled down to a comfortable life in
Queens after a career as a sea captain, whose most harrowing moments came
during the French Revolution when he was captured by privateers, imprisoned
in Paris, and eventually smuggled out by an unidentified American. King's
daughter Mary married Lindley Murray of the Murray Hill family (see p240)
and their descendants owned the house until it was sold to a developer, rescued
by conservationists, and moved to its present location (from Northern Blvd and
55th St).

The Queens Historical Society opened it as a museum in 1968 with
a small collection of memorabilia from Joseph King, historical
photographs, maps, etc of Queens and neighbouring Nassau County,

a Victorian period room, and special exhibitions on local history and decorative arts (open Tues, Sat, Sun, 2.30–4.30; voluntary donation; tel: 939–0647).

Next to the house is Queens's most famous tree, a **weeping beech** (1847; DL) which now flourishes in mournful splendour in its own small park. Legend asserts that a Belgian Baron de Man, noticing a droopy seedling along his newly planted avenue of beeches, commanded his gardener to destroy it, but instead the gardener put it in a secluded spot where the little tree flourished, apparently assuming its unusual form through spontaneous mutation. The cutting from which this tree grew came from Belgium, brought back in a flower pot by nurseryman Samuel B. Parsons who supplied trees and shrubs for Central and Prospect Parks. Today the tree is more than 60 ft tall with a spread of about 85 ft and a trunk circumference of 14 ft.

QUEENS COLLEGE, its campus bounded by Reeves and Melbourne Aves, Main St, and Kissena Blvd, opened in 1937 and is part of CUNY. The college offers degrees in science and liberal arts. In the Paul Klapper Library (Mattis Room) is the *Frances Godwin and Joseph Ternbach Museum at Queens College*, with a small permanent collection of European art, ancient and antique glass, prints by American artists commissioned by the WPA, and a few examples of oriental, primitive, and Egyptian art. The museum also offers changing exhibitions of painting, sculpture, and drawing.

Open Mon, Wed, 9–8; Tues, Thurs, 9–6, and Fri, 9–5. Free. Tel: 520–7049.

The QUEENS BOTANICAL GARDEN, 43–50 Main St at Dahlia Ave (open 9 a.m.–dusk daily; free; tel: 886–3800), a 39-acre plot, includes along with its 22-acre arboretum of maples, magnolias, dogwoods, and other specimens, a large rose garden, several demonstration backyard gardens, seasonal plantings, and specialised gardens for birds and bees.

Kissena Park (bounded by Kissena Blvd, Booth Memorial Ave, Rose and Oak Aves, and Fresh Meadow Lane) is a 219-acre park with a small spring-fed lake on the site of Samuel Parsons's Nurseries, founded 1838, whose proprietor brought Flushing its famous weeping beech (see above).

56 Southern Queens: Jamaica, Richmond Hill, Woodhaven, Ozone Park, St. Albans, and Howard Beach.

Most of what is now southern Queens was contained within the original boundaries of the town of Jamaica (called Rustdorp by the Dutch), settled by the English in 1656 and chartered in 1660. The community today called Jamaica is a busy commercial center, with deteriorating economic conditions and slums in S. Jamaica. The outlying districts—Ozone Park, Richmond Hill, Woodhaven, St. Albans, Queens Village, and Howard Beach—are primarily residential. Richmond Hill is known for its shingle style Victorian houses, and its development dates back to the years after the Civil War (1868) when a banker, Albon P. Man, bought part of the Lefferts family farm and undertook to subdivide it. Woodhaven, also quiet and residential, was founded by the same John R. Pitkin who tried to build a rival to Manhattan in East New York, today a battered Brooklyn slum. Pitkin called his town Woodville and it began to prosper after two companies established factories for metal stamping on Atlantic Ave. Ozone Park and Howard Beach to the S. were farming and fishing communities until the 20C and Howard Beach enjoyed a period of popularity as a resort community before Jamaica Bay became polluted. **Ozone Park,** with its rows and rows of small houses is noted for its proximity to John F. Kennedy Airport, and the roar of planes overhead must surely depress the property values and the residents alike.

The main shopping strip of **Jamaica** lies along Jamaica Ave between Sutphin Blvd and 171st St. The KING MANSION, 150–03 Jamaica Ave in King Park at 153rd St (N. section 1730; W. section, 1755; E. section 1806; DL), is a large white-shingled house once owned by Rufus King, Federalist statesman, member of the Continental Congress, and father of a New York governor. Open as a museum (Thurs, 1–4; other times by appointment; donation requested; tel: 523–1653), it is of interest primarily to the local historian, and has period rooms, King family memorabilia, and changing exhibitions.

Nearby on Jamaica Ave between 153rd St and Parsons Blvd is *Grace Episcopal Church* (1862; Dudley Field; additions 1901–02; Cady, Berg & See; DL), a Gothic Revival brownstone church with an 18C graveyard (c. 1734) among whose residents is Rufus King. The *Jamaica Arts Center* occupies the landmark Jamaica Register Building (1898; DL), at 161–06 Jamaica Ave between 161st–162nd Sts, which once held the city office of the Register and today has an active programme of changing exhibitions (fine arts, local history) with a Community Gallery for the work of local artists or students enrolled in the center's classes and workshops (open Tues–Sat, 10–5; free; tel: 658–7400).

The *Prospect Cemetery*, established before 1669 (DL) at 159th St and the S.W. corner of Beaver Rd, is the oldest public burial ground in Queens; among lesser known people it contains members of the Van Wyck and Sutphin families who have given their names to an expressway and a local boulevard. The *Store Front Museum*, located in a former auto warehouse at 162–02 Liberty Ave, is a community museum oriented toward black culture (open 9.30–4.30, Tues–Fri; free; tel: 523–5199). Recent exhibitions have featured the work of local artists, traditional African art, and contemporary work by black artists; the museum has a small collection of memorabilia relating to black history and offers performances of music, dance, and drama in the Paul Robeson Theater.

Southeast of Jamaica is **St. Albans,** a residential community of middle class black families. To its W. are **Ozone Park** and **S. Ozone Park** whose chief ornaments are a racetrack and an airport.

AQUEDUCT RACE TRACK, bounded by Rockaway Blvd, Southern Pkwy, the IND Rockaway Line right-of-way, and 114th St, dates back to 1894 (reconstructed, 1959; Arthur Froehlich & Assocs). The track is named after an aqueduct that runs along Conduit Ave, the service road S. of the Southern Pkwy, bringing water from sources further E. on Long Island to the Ridgewood Reservoir near the Brooklyn-Queens border. Known as 'the Big A' to its fans, Aqueduct is the only raceway remaining within the city limits, real estate values having made racetracks less profitable than developments. *Rochedale Village*, for example, occupies the turf once belonging to the Jamaica Race Track near Baisley Pond Park.

John F. Kennedy International Airport at the S. end of the Van Wyck Expressway, bounded by Southern Blvd, Rockaway Blvd, and Jamaica Bay, is New York's largest airport, covering 4930 acres, an area equivalent to all of Manhattan from the Battery to 42nd St.

Construction began in 1942 when the first landfill was dumped onto the salt marshes bordering Jamaica Bay in preparation for a planned 100-acre New York International Airport on the site of the Idlewild golf course. Commercial flights began in 1948, and since then the facility has become the city's most important airport, serving primarily long-distance domestic and international flights. In 1980 it witnessed 307,500 take-offs and landings that involved 26,796,000 passengers.

The airport has two pairs of parallel runways aligned at right angles and a fifth general aviation runway for private, business, and commuter planes, a total of nine miles of runways served by 22 miles of taxiways. In addition to the terminal facilities there are 13 hangars for servicing aircraft, an air cargo center, a police building, a telephone office building, a medical building, a hotel, a bus garage, a federal office building, a post office, and seven food production centers.

Traffic approaches the airport from the Van Wyck Expressway in a counterclockwise direction. The *International Hotel* on the Van Wyck Expressway at Southern Pkwy (1961; William B. Tabler) and the *Federal Office Building* (1949; Reinhard, Hofmeister & Walquist) just beyond it on the W. side of the traffic circle form an architecturally undistinguished introduction to the airport. The access road leads past the *First National City Bank Building* (1959; Skidmore, Owings & Merrill), a glass box raised on stilts, to TERMINAL CITY, an 840-acre complex of parking lots, terminals, and service buildings. The first architecturally notable terminal is the *Pan American Airways Building* (1961; Tippetts-Abbett-McCarthy-Stratton, and Ives, Turano & Gardner, associated architects), originally a low pavilion with a disclike roof resembling some alien spacecraft settling to rest; the facility has now been expanded.

The access road continues past the *International Arrivals Building* (1957; Skidmore, Owings & Merrill), host to a number of foreign-based carriers. The scene within the terminal is usually hectic, even chaotic, and recent expansions have removed some of the former lounges and amenities.

Beyond is the sweeping concrete form of the *Trans World Airlines International Building* (1962; Eero Saarinen & Assocs), architecturally the most controversial of the terminals. Trans World Airlines now uses the former *National Airlines Sundrome* (1972; I.M. Pei & Partners) for its domestic flights.

Further along the access road are the *British Airways Terminal* (1970; Gollins Melvin Ward & Partners), and the *American Airlines Terminal* (1960; Kahn & Jacobs) with the world's largest stained glass wall (designer, Robert Sowers). Unfortunately only employees of the airline can admire its coloured light from the inside since it opens on offices and private rooms. The curved *United Airlines Building* (1961; Skidmore, Owings & Merrill) has also received the approbation of architectural critics for its skillful handling of detail.

In the center of the parking lots are three CHAPELS (all 1966) for the major faiths of the country: Roman Catholic *Our Lady of the Skies* (George J. Sole), the *Protestant chapel* (Edgar Tafel & Assocs), and the *Jewish chapel* (Bloch & Hesse).

The Jewish chapel contains the Ferkauf Museum of International Synagogue with a collection of Judaica, maps, Torahs, and gifts from several Israeli prime ministers (open Sun–Fri, 9–5; free; tel: 656–5044.).

57 Jamaica Bay and the Rockaways

Jamaica Bay, a shallow bay of about 20 square miles spotted with marshy islands, lies S.W. of Kennedy Airport. Today it is part of the Gateway National Recreation Area which maintains a wildlife refuge there on its largest land mass, an island known in its various parts as Black Bank Marsh, Rulers Bar Hassock, Big Egg Marsh, and Broad Channel.

Broad Channel, the only settlement in Jamaica Bay, dates back to the 1880s when it began as a fishing village. After 1915 the area was modernised, streets laid out, houses electrified, and water plants constructed. During Prohibition it became known as 'Little Cuba' and its visitors enjoyed the consumption of bootleg liquor in its yacht clubs and speakeasies. Railroads had come in the 1860s and 1870s, passing through the bay to the Rockaways, and in 1925 the Cross Bay Boulevard made Broad Channel accessible to motorists. Today the island has perhaps a thousand families, many of them of Irish descent, living in small houses or shacks on pilings which give the community a curiously archaic appearance.

About a mile N.W. of the subway station of the IND Rockaway line (A and CC trains), which took over the trestles and right-of-way of the LIRR, is the *Visitor Center of the Jamaica Bay Wildlife Refuge*, whose ponds and marshlands form a full-time or seasonal habitat for more than 300 species of birds. Located on the Atlantic flyway, the refuge is most interesting during the autumn and spring migrations when thousands of ducks and geese stop over in its wetlands. The refuge is under the jurisdiction of the National Park Service and park rangers offer hikes and nature walks, gardening demonstrations, and educational programmes for school children (tel: 630–0216 for schedule of events).

The southernmost portion of Queens is the **Rockaway peninsula,** a narrow spit of land reaching westward from the mainland of Long Island across the mouth of Jamaica Bay. The earliest settlement in the area was that of Hempstead (Heemstede in Dutch), settled and chartered in 1664 by the British. The remoteness and inaccessability of the area made it an exclusive summer resort until, beginning in 1868, the railroads put it within reach of the common man, thereby driving the more aristocratic visitors east to the Hamptons and other areas further out on Long Island. For a while the Rockaways enjoyed a period as a middle-class resort, and today much of the W. part of the peninsula has become public park, absorbed into the Gateway National Recreation Area. East of the Cross Bay Bridge are the communities of Hammels and Arverne, depressing slums with a few large-scale housing projects that seem utterly foreign on this low windswept land.

West of the Cross Bay Bridge are **Belle Harbor** and **Neponsit,** which retain traces of former gentility, and **Jacob Riis Park,** named after the 19C journalist who crusaded for better housing and parks for the poor. The mile-long sandy beach of Jacob Riis Park is one of the finest ocean beaches in the metropolitan area and is understandably mobbed in summer. Its cleanliness and well-maintained facilities may be the result of its being administered by the National Parks Service as part of the Gateway National Recreation Area. In addition to the beach are athletic fields and facilities for handball and paddleball. In cooler weather people stroll on the boardwalk (or run on it), fly model airplanes in the parking lot, and fish in the surf.

SUBWAY: IND Eighth Ave (A train) to Rockaway Park/Beach 116th St and walk W. along Rockaway Beach Blvd to the park (almost 2 miles to the center of the park).

CAR: Gil Hodges (formerly Marine Pkwy) Bridge (toll) to the parking field (fee).

At the W. end of Jacob Riis Park is the *site of Fort Tilden*, built in 1917 as part of the city's outer coastal defences and paired with Fort Hancock at Sandy Hook, N.J. It is named after Samuel J. Tilden, New York State governor and unsuccessful presidential candidate (1876), who left much of his money to the New York Public Library. At the far W. end of the peninsula is *Breezy Point*, with a private community joined by ferry to Sheepshead Bay in Brooklyn.

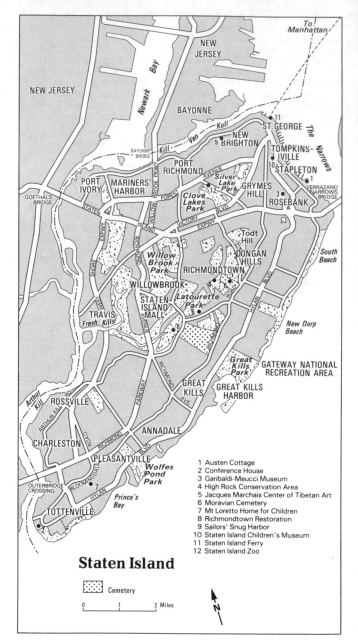

1 Austen Cottage
2 Conference House
3 Garibaldi-Meucci Museum
4 High Rock Conservation Area
5 Jacques Marchais Center of Tibetan Art
6 Moravian Cemetery
7 Mt Loretto Home for Children
8 Richmondtown Restoration
9 Sailors' Snug Harbor
10 Staten Island Children's Museum
11 Staten Island Ferry
12 Staten Island Zoo

Staten Island

Cemetery

0   1   2 Miles

N

V BOROUGH OF STATEN ISLAND/COUNTY OF RICHMOND

To the world at large Staten Island is simply the end point of one of the greatest, cheapest rides in the repertoire of tourism, the Staten Island ferry. It is 13·9 miles long and 7·3 miles wide in its largest dimensions, and separated from Manhattan by Upper New York Bay, from Brooklyn by Lower New York Bay and the Narrows, and from New Jersey by the Kill Van Kull and the Arthur Kill (the word 'kill' is a Dutch term for 'channel'). It is the third largest borough in area (60·9 square miles) but the smallest in population, 352,121, though it is the only one still growing, having experienced an increase of 19·2% since the 1970 census.

Down the center of the island as far as Latourette Park runs a spine of rocky hills whose highest point, Todt Hill (409·2 ft) is also the highest point in the city and the highest point on the Atlantic seaboard south of Maine. Along the crest of these hills during the years before and after the turn of the century, the wealthy built mansions and today many still survive along Howard Ave in Grymes Hill and in the neighbourhoods of Emerson Hills and Dongan Hills, though some have been adapted to use as schools or charitable institutions and others have surrendered part of their land to newer, often less imposing, homes. East of the central ridge lie low coastal plains which have been densely developed with back to back rows of tract housing and continuous commercial strips. The S. of Staten Island, once dominated by the sea, still retains some of its former charm though the fishing villages and oystering communities no longer exist. The W., fronting the Arthur Kill, is lowland, much of it salt meadow: some has been filled and used for more tracts of housing, some has been put to commercial and industrial uses, some befouled with the city's largest garbage dump. The far N., site of several of the oldest settlements on the island, has industrial areas and housing, much of it old and battered, looking across the Kill Van Kull at the oil tanks in New Jersey.

Joining the island to its neighbours are four major bridges whose construction spans 36 years but which were all engineered by Othmar H. Ammann. The Outerbridge Crossing (1928), a 750 ft span, joins the Charleston section of Staten Island with Perth Amboy in New Jersey and is named after Eugenius Outerbridge, the first chairman of the New York Port Authority. The Goethals Bridge (1928) a cantilever structure (span 672 ft) reaches from Howlands Hook to the Bayway section of Elizabeth, N.J. The Bayonne Bridge (1931) is a graceful steel arch (span 1675 ft) linking Port Richmond with Bayonne, N.J., and the most recent arrival, the beautiful Verrazano-Narrow Bridge (1964) crosses the Lower Bay (span 4260 ft) from Ft Wadsworth to Bay Ridge in Brooklyn. Its arrival triggered the present land boom.

Most of the industry of Staten Island remains confined to its outer margins. In the N.W. is Howland Hook with a major truck terminal along with Port Ivory, whose rather exotic name is derived from its use by Proctor & Gamble, producer of soaps, detergents, and similar household products. Along the N. shore are commercial and industrial areas, most of which have seen better days, while the W. coast is occupied by tank ports, Consolidated Edison plants, and a 3000 acre dump, the Fresh Kills Landfill, where 10,000 tons of garbage daily find their final resting place. Inland are separate towns or neighbourhoods, mostly built up with small, single-family houses, but as development continues apace the former separate communities are beginning to merge into one giant tract of suburban sprawl.

History. Both Giovanni da Verrazano (1524) and Henry Hudson (1609) made note of Staten Island during their explorations of the New World. The former stopped off at a spring to refill his water casks (the location is thought to be in present-day Tompkinsville) and the latter gave the borough its name, Staaten Eylandt, after the States General, governing body of the Netherlands. In the years that followed the Dutch attempted at least three times to colonise the island but hostile Indians, roused to anger by the provocative actions of the colonists, attacked the settlements. It wasn't until 1661 that a group of French and Dutch farmers were able to establish the first permanent settlement, Oude Dorp (Old Town) near present Fort Wadsworth. When the British took over New Amsterdam, Staten Island took the name of Richmond after the Duke of Richmond, illegitimate son of Charles II.

During the British colonial period, Staten Island continued to develop as an agricultural community with its less fertile areas devoted to raising stock, while its long coastline and protected waters made fishing, oystering, and shipbuilding also important factors in the economy. Along the kills several tidal mills were built for grinding grist and sawing lumber.

In the early summer of 1776 the arrival of some 30,000 British soldiers and Hessian mercenaries disrupted the agrarian quiet of the island which soon became a vast military camp from which the British would stage operations on Long Island. Although the population was largely loyalist and welcomed the arrival of the British forces, the billeting of so many soldiers strained the resources of the 3000 islanders and tensions inevitably developed. At the end of August the British attacked and took the W. end of Long Island, using barges built on Staten Island, and in September the Billopp House in present-day Tottenville became the site of abortive negotiations to end the war. Throughout the rest of the fighting the British maintained a strong point at Fort Hill in St. George, and Staten Island is said to have been the site of the last shot fired in the war, a derisive blast from an unknown soldier departing down the bay aimed at the crowds lining the shore and jeering a farewell.

After the war Staten Islanders continued farming and fishing, largely unaffected by the heady changes across the bay, although the federal government did see the strategic importance of the island and fortified it during the War of 1812. In 1829 teen-aged Cornelius Vanderbilt, born near Stapleton, started a regular ferry service to Manhattan, the first step in a business empire that would eventually make him the borough's wealthiest and most famous son. Soon Staten Island burgeoned as a seaside resort, especially New Brighton where such hotels as the Pavilion attracted prominent New Yorkers and a large clientele from the South. A literary circle formed around eye surgeon Samuel MacKenzie Elliott whose practice was located in Manhattan. Dr Elliott treated historian Francis Parkman (who later claimed that he had been nearly blinded by the doctor), James Russell Lowell, Henry Wadsworth Longfellow, and Richard Henry Dana. (The Samuel MacKenzie Elliott Residence dating from 1850 still stands at 69 Delafield Pl. between Bard and Davis Aves, a designated landmark.) Judge William Emerson had a summer house called 'The Snuggery' on what is now Emerson Hill where he entertained his brother Ralph Waldo Emerson and hired Henry David Thoreau for a short time in 1843 to tutor his son. Enthusiasts of sport as well as literature were attracted to the island and it is the home of the first American canoe club and the site of the first lawn tennis court (1880).

Less leisured visitors were Giuseppe Garibaldi who remained here for three years during his exile from Italy, Herman Melville who frequently visited his brother Tom, governor of Sailors' Snug Harbor from 1867–84, and Frederick Law Olmsted who tried his hand at farming before finding his life's work as a landscape architect.

During the Civil War the island again became a training ground and assembly point for troops who set up camps in the open fields and apple orchards and whose presence provoked hostility in a population with strong Confederate sympathies. Many southerners sent their families to the safety of hotels they had formerly visited for pleasure. During the Draft Riots (July 1863) abolitionist Horace Greeley came here and was hidden from angry mobs by his friend George W. Curtis, whose house still stands in the West Brighton section (234 Bard Ave, N.W. corner of Henderson Ave). In Stapleton, Factoryville (now West New Brighton), and New Brighton, mobs burned and pillaged buildings and attacked those blacks who had not escaped into the woods or across the Kill to New Jersey.

Toward the end of the 19C, Staten Island became less rural, but again changed more slowly than the other boroughs. Industries began to dot the N. and W. parts of the shoreline—brick and linoleum factories, breweries, dye works, chemical plants—but the Atlantic seacoast still attracted summer visitors. South Beach on the Lower Bay and Midland Beach, just S. of it, became popular resort areas, the latter offering an amusement park with rides and pavilions. The first railroad (1860) was extended along both sides of the island linking formerly isolated communities, and charitable institutions aware of the growing shortages of land in Manhattan began buying sites for hospitals, orphanages, and schools. Nevertheless, in 1898 when Staten Island became part of Greater New York it had only about 67,000 inhabitants, a population slightly larger than that of Manhattan in 1800.

Today Staten Island is struggling to maintain its heritage and preserve what natural beauty remains, while growing in some orderly fashion. Fortunately the National Park Service controls some of the ocean front through the Gateway National Recreation Area, including Great Kills Park and Miller Field, and recent laws have been enacted to preserve wetlands from indiscriminate use. Since the opening of the Verrazano Bridge which brought the growth spurt long desired by some the borough has seen a tenfold increase in crime and a fivefold increase in the number of people on welfare. Parts of Stapleton are covered with big housing projects and New Brighton has been described as Staten Island's only ghetto. Port Richmond, once a thriving commercial area for the north shore, is pocked by empty stores and abandoned buildings. Pollution is also a problem though some of it comes from the industrial plants of New Jersey, ironically nicknamed the Garden State. In 1977 a safety valve on an oil distillation unit in Linden, N.J., malfunctioned and oil drops splattered over 10 miles of Staten Island. When the wind is from the west (which it almost always is) the residents of Tottenville can sniff the fumes of Perth Amboy. Rural and small-town Staten

Island are virtually gone; it is a safe guess that what is replacing them will be less pleasant.

Touring in Staten Island. Unless you have considerable determination, a car is necessary though the Richmondtown Restoration, probably the most appealling of the island's tourist attractions, is readily accessible by public transportation. Also essential is a map, since the development of the island has been haphazard and the street plan has no particular pattern. Most of the sights are pleasant but small-scale, of interest either to the visitor with particular historical interests or a desire to see the city as a whole, far from the beaten path.

58 Northern Staten Island: St. George, New Brighton, West Brighton, Tompkinsville, Stapleton, Grymes Hill, and Rosebank

The *Staten Island Ferry, plying the waters between the Battery in Manhattan and St. George on Staten Island, makes a five-mile, half-hour, 25¢-trip with a view guaranteed to quicken the pulses of the most blasé passenger: Governors Island off one side, and Ellis Island, the Statue of Liberty, and the Verrazano-Narrows bridge off the other: the skyline of Lower Manhattan at one end and the steep hills of Staten Island with the spires and towers of St. George at the other. Inside the cavernous St. George ferry terminal is a small museum documenting the history of the service (open Mon–Fri, 8–2.45): Ferries leave frequently during daylight hours; for schedule call 566–8633.

St. George is the seat of borough government, a busy, urban area, which serves as the gateway to Staten Island and a nexus of its bus and train lines. Just S. of the ferry terminal at 1 Bay St is a *U.S. Coast Guard station* with the roof of the original Chief Physician's House (1815) visible above the wall enclosing it. On the S. side of Richmond Terrace facing the terminal is the *Staten Island Borough Hall* (1906; Carrère & Hastings), and adjacent to it, the *County Court House* (1919; Carrère & Hastings). The Family Court House, 100 Richmond Terrace between Wall St and Hamilton Ave, dates from 1930 (Sibley & Fetherston).

The *Staten Island Museum*, up the hill and to the right at 75 Stuyvesant Pl., N.E. corner of Wall St (open Tues–Sat, 10–5; Sun, 2–5; voluntary donation; tel: 727–1135), is sponsored by the Staten Island Institute of Arts and Sciences and offers changing exhibitions of fine arts, photography, natural history, decorative arts, etc.

Along Richmond Terrace which borders the shoreline to the N., ten Greek Revival mansions looked out over the Kill Van Kull enjoying the formerly pleasant vista, now replaced by a view of oil tanks. Nine of the mansions have departed along with the bucolic scenery, and the lone survivor is now a catering firm, well-maintained but painted bright pink, the Pavilion on the Terrace (1835) at 404 Richmond Terrace, between St. Peter's Pl. and Westervelt Ave; in happier times it was the residence of one William J. Taylor. Six blocks beyond at 806 Richmond Terrace between Clinton Ave and Tysen St is another former mansion, once the home of sea captain John Neville (c. 1770; DL) with a verandah facing the Kill. Later the house became the Old Stone Jug Tavern, whose hospitality was enjoyed by the sailors ensconced nearby in Sailors' Snug Harbor.

Today the beautiful 19C buildings of ***Sailors' Snug Harbor** (Richmond Terrace between Tysen St and Snug Harbor Rd), and its grounds have become the Snug Harbor Cultural Center, an immense restoration project still in its early stages.

Grounds open daily, noon to dusk. Exhibitions, Wed–Sat, 1–5. Closed most major holidays. Confirm hours during winter months for specific events. On-site parking usually available, enter West Gate on Kissel Ave off Delafield Pl. Admission to grounds, free; fee for performance events; most visual arts exhibitions free. Guided tours, March–Oct: Sun, 2 p.m.; tours depart from Building H near parking lot by West Lawn; tour fee, $2. Restaurant. Tel: 448–2500.

The center offers changing exhibitions of sculpture, painting, photography, and other arts, including the work of local artists and students enrolled in the center's art school.

History. Sailors' Snug Harbor was established by the will of Robert Richard Randall whose father had made a fortune at sea in activities described variously as 'profitable commerce' or 'privateering'. The son died in 1801 leaving the income from that fortune whose capital was invested mostly in Manhattan real estate (see p184) to found a home for 'aged and decrepit sailors'. After litigation during which disappointed relatives sought the income for themselves, trustees of the will bought a Staten Island farm (1831) and erected the row of Greek Revival temples facing the water. The iron fence surrounding the property (1842; Frederick Diaper) was put up not so much to bar intruders as to keep the old salts from making easy forays to neighbouring watering holes. The earliest building, the central one, dates from 1831–33 and is attributed to Minard Lafever and Samuel Thompson & Son, with the flanking buildings coming in the 1840s and 1880s. After almost a century of serenity, these lovely buildings were threatened with demolition since the trustees of the Harbor needed more modern facilities for the geriatric patients and were suffering financial hardship in retaining the old structures. After protracted negotiations the city brought the land and buildings and the few remaining sailors were moved to a new home in North Carolina. Today Snug Harbor is the home of several independent arts organisations and is operated on a non-profit basis on behalf of the city Department of Parks.

The buildings are now undergoing a $4·5 million restoration. Of particular architectural interest are Building C, the central building facing Richmond Terrace (1831; Minard Lafever; DL), the Gatehouse on Richmond Terrace (c. 1874; DL), and the Chapel (1856; James Salmon, builder; DL). The beautiful grounds with their mature trees and plantings have been enhanced with outdoor sculpture and the greenhouse is becoming the site of the Staten Island Botanical Garden.

The *Staten Island Zoo*, in eight-acre Barrett Park, 614 Broadway near Colonial Court (rear entrance on Clove Rd at Martling Ave) is a small urban zoo famous for its snakes (open daily, 10–4.45; adults, 75¢, children 50¢; snack bar; tel: 442–3100). The reptile house contains such fearsome delights as boa constrictors, a blood python, puff adders, a black mamba, cobras, and more than 30 varieties of rattlesnakes, the largest collection in the world. Also on view are mammals including a tiger and lioness, birds, a colony of vampire bats, and, for the children, farm animals in a petting zoo.

WAGNER COLLEGE, bounded by Howard Ave, Campus Rd,

Pleasant Valley Ave, and a network of small streets on the E., sits atop **Grymes Hill** enjoying a fine view of the harbour. It was founded in 1883 in Rochester, N.Y. as Wagner Memorial Lutheran College and moved to Staten Island in 1918, its campus the former Cunard Estate. No longer a sectarian school, the college enrolls 2539 students. The *Sir Edward Cunard Residence*, 'Bellevue' (c. 1851) in the East Campus on Howard Ave (c. 1851) has become Cunard Hall, the administration building of the college.

Howard Ave, originally called Serpentine Rd—after serpentinite, a local greenish, striated building stone, or perhaps after the winding course of the road—has one of the island's fine residential neighbourhoods, the old mansions interspersed with schools and newer homes.

Tompkinsville and **Stapleton,** next to one another along the N.E. shore of Staten Island, are rundown residential-industrial communities. At one time the deep water piers extending into the bay were municipal piers built (1921–23) by Mayor John Hylan to bring trade to the waterfront. Dubbed Hylan's Folly (along with another ill-fated project, the Bronx Terminal Market), they were designated (1937) a free port where foreign cargoes could be unloaded and stored for transshipment without payment of duty. When this, too, failed, the piers were converted (mid-1970s) to a facility for container shipping.

The *Edgewater Village Hall* (1889; DL) in Tappen Park (Bay St to Wright St, Water St to Canal St) is the only vestige of a 19C village which preceded modern Stapleton, birthplace of the 'Commodore', Cornelius Vanderbilt. Nearby is the *Staten Island Children's Museum*, 15 Beach St at the corner of Union Pl. (open Sept–June: Tues–Fri, 3–5; Sat and Sun, 1–5; July–Aug: Mon–Thurs, 1–4; adults, $1; children, 50¢; tel: 273–2060). This community-oriented children's museum mounts changing participatory exhibitions on the arts and sciences.

Avid fans of local architecture might seek out *Nos 364 and 390 Van Duzer St* (both 1835; DL), unusual 19C Dutch Colonial houses, now housing antique shops. *St. Paul's Memorial Church* (1870; Edward Tuckerman Potter; DL) is a fine country church with traprock walls in a pleasant suburban area.

Further S. on Bay St (N.W. corner of Vanderbilt Ave) is the *Bayley Seton Hospital*, recently decommissioned as a U.S. Public Health Service Hospital, whose earliest buildings (hidden by trees but visible from the Bay St driveway) date from 1834–37 when the hospital opened as the Seamen's Fund and Retreat. During the 1930s as the U.S. Marine Hospital, the facility was expanded (1933–36; James A. Wetmore, Louis A. Simon, supervising architects), assuming its present appearance. The National Institutes of Health, now located in Bethesda, Maryland, began as a small research facility in the laboratories here. Originally the Marine hospital was on Bedloes Island but was moved here in 1883 to make room for the Statue of Liberty. Behind it (119 Tompkins Ave, between Vanderbilt Ave and Tompkins St) is the *Mariners' Family Asylum of the Port of New York*, built by a charitable organisation called the Female Bethel Society of New York in 1855 as a refuge for the aged wives, widows, sisters, and daughters of seamen of the port. It is now abandoned and for sale.

In the middle of **Rosebank,** a neighbourhood long populated by Italians, stands the *Garibaldi-Meucci Museum,* at 420 Tompkins Ave on the S.W. corner of Chestnut St, a simple farmhouse (1840; DL) in a weedy lot. Between 1851–53 Giuseppe Garibaldi lived here with his friend Antonio Meucci, impoverished and anxious to return to his homeland from which he had been exiled after the collapse of the Republic in 1845. Meucci, inventor of a prototype of the telephone, and Garibaldi supported themselves making candles in a factory nearby. In 1891 the house and its contents were sold at auction and seventeen candles made by Garibaldi brought $6·75. The museum (open Tues–Fri, 10–5; Sat, Sun, and holidays, 1–5; free; tel: 442–1608) has letters and photos, documenting the life of the great Italian patriot.

The *Austen Cottage,* 'Clear Comfort' (1691–1710; alterations, 1844; DL) at 2 Hylan Blvd between Bay St and the water, now obscured by trees in the summer, was begun by a Dutch merchant in the late 17C but is famous as the home of photographer Alice Austen who went to live there at the age of two and stayed until she was 70 when poverty and illness forced her to leave. Only when she was near death were her unique contributions to the art of photography recognised and she was able to leave the public poorhouse for the last months of her life on the proceeds of an article about her remarkable career published in 'Life' magazine (1951). The Staten Island Historical Society has some 7000 glass negatives in which she depicted the world around her from 1880–1930.

St. John's Protestant Episcopal Church at 1331 Bay St, S.E. corner of New Lane (1871; Arthur D. Gilman; DL), a granite Victorian Gothic church, replaces an earlier frame building in which Cornelius Vanderbilt (born 1794) was the first baby baptised.

Just S. of the church (Bay St at the N.E. corner of Nautilus St) is the *Rosebank U.S. Government Quarantine Station* where persons from foreign ports suspected of carrying communicable diseases are kept under observation. About a quarter mile offshore are Hoffman and Swinburne Islands, constructed artificially in 1872 for a quarantine station but abandoned in the 1920s when laws restricted immigration. Now deserted and undeveloped, they are part of the Gateway National Recreation Area.

The original Quarantine Station had been established in 1799 at Tompkinsville but by the mid-19C had aroused the ire of nearby residents because disease was spreading to them. Further angered by the unwillingness of politicians to move the Quarantine Station, a group of citizens took matters into their own hands in 1858 and burned down the station, first removing the few patients to the grounds where they lay on beds reportedly enjoying the fire.

Von Briesen Park (Bay St at School Rd), once the estate of Arthur Von Briesen, offers superb views of the harbour, the Verrazano-Narrows Bridge, and the fortifications to its S. (Climb to the top of the hill.) Jutting out into the bay beneath the Verrazano-Narrows Bridge are the stern granite walls of BATTERY WEED (1847–61; DL) of the Fort Wadsworth Military Reservation, built just before the Civil War and later named after Stephen H. Weed, killed in the Battle of Gettysburg.

The Dutch fortified the site against Indian attacks as early as 1663 with a blockhouse and the British later elaborated the facilities. In 1812 the U.S. government erected Fort Richmond facing Fort Hamilton in Brooklyn across the Lower Bay and armed it with 30 cannon. Inside is a central courtyard and three tiers of arched galleries looking out over the harbour in three directions. Long the oldest continuously staffed military reservation in the nation, Fort Wadsworth is scheduled to become part of the Gateway National Recreational Area, but is not now open to the public.

59 Central Staten Island: Dongan Hills and Richmondtown

Dongan Hills, bounded by Richmond Rd and Todt Hill Rd, is one of the most affluent residential areas on the island, its large houses supplanting former grand estates. During the 17C a mining town sprang up to exploit the lodes of hematite and was named in honour of Thomas Dongan, 17C governor of the province of New York.

The *Billiou-Stillwell-Perine House* at 1476 Richmond Rd, between Delaware and Cromwell Aves began (1662–1830;DL) as a one-room stone farmhouse whose big Dutch fireplace was large enough to roast an ox. Pierre Billiou, leader of the Oude Dorp settlement (1661) built the oldest part (note the medievally steep roof) and the Stillwells and Perines added onto it later (now undergoing restoration).

During the 17C when the Dutch worked the iron deposits in the vicinity, **Todt Hill** was known as Yserberg ('Iron Hill'); the origin of its present somber name (i.e. 'Death Hill') is unknown.

The *Moravian Cemetery* at Todt Hill Rd and Richmond Rd contains the *Vanderbilt Family Mausoleum* (1886; Richard Morris Hunt), an ornate granite tomb containing the remains of the first Cornelius Vanderbilt and some of his descendants. The *Old New Dorp Moravian Church* (1763) in the cemetery, with its overhanging Dutch eaves, has been replaced by the New Dorp Moravian Church at 1265 Todt Hill Rd, N. of Richmond Rd, a Classical Revival church (1844) given by the Commodore's son William H. Vanderbilt. The Vanderbilt family association with the Moravian sect dates back to the conversion of Jacob Van Der Bilt in the 18C.

The *Ernest Flagg Residence* with its Gate and Gatehouse (1898; Ernest Flagg; DL) at 209 Flagg Pl., off Todt Hill Rd, for many years the home of the Scribner family's personal architect, is now the St. Charles Seminary. The 32-room mansion with its colonnaded verandah, imposing twin chimneys, white clapboarded upper stories and walls of painted serpentinite—a striated local stone—has been compared architecturally to the homes of wealthy Dutch colonists in the Caribbean. A swimming pool, orchards, gardens, and a stone water tower once graced the estate.

At the N. end Altamont St (but more easily seen from Beacon Ave and Boyle St) stands a little wooden lighthouse, called either the *New Dorp Lighthouse* or the Moravian Light (c. 1854; DL), actually a white clapboard house topped by a short square tower which once held a beacon.

The *High Rock Park Conservation Center*, 200 Nevada Ave at the top of the hill, is located in the greenbelt adjacent to the Moravian Cemetery. Marked trails meander through this 94-acre forest and bird refuge, which has ponds, a loosestrife swamp, and a garden for the blind. The Visitor Center offers a reading room and reference library, changing environmental exhibitions, lectures, and workshops.

Open daily, 9–5; free; tel: 987–6233. To reach the center, follow Richmond Rd to Rockland Ave; turn right to Nevada Ave; turn right on Nevada Ave to park entrance. Parking lot on Summit Ave.

The *Staten Island Light House* (1912; DL) on Edinboro Rd is visible from Lighthouse Ave, a right turn from Richmond Ave near Latourette Park. Surrounded by houses and parks, the beacon in its octagonal yellow brick tower shines out from its 231-ft elevation across the harbour, working in conjunction with the Ambrose Light Tower in the bay.

Further up Lighthouse Ave (338 Lighthouse Ave near Windsor Ave) is one of the curiosities of the island, the *Jacques Marchais Center of Tibetan Art* (open Sept–May: Sat and Sun, 1–5; June–Aug: Fri–Sun, 1–5; adults, $1; children, 50¢; tel: 987–3478), the largest private collection of Tibetan art outside Tibet, gathered by Jacques Marchais, the professional name of Mrs Harry Klauber, a dealer in oriental art. Her interest in oriental art began with twelve bronze figures collected by her grandfather, a merchant sea captain who had travelled to Darjeeling where he became acquainted with Tibetan lamas. The artworks, which include also examples from Nepal, Japan, China, and India, are housed in two stone buildings designed to resemble a Tibetan monastery and set in a terraced garden landscaped with pieces of oriental sculpture to provide a meditative retreat.

The ***Richmondtown Restoration,**** a 96-acre area in Latourette Park at Richmond Hill Rd begun in 1936, is an ambitious project of the Staten Island Historical Society and consists of more than 30 historic buildings in various stages of restoration which illustrate the evolution of village life from the 17th through the 19th centuries.

Open Sept–June: Sat, 10–5; Sun, 12–5; July–Aug: Tues–Sat, 10–5 and Sun, 12–5. Closed Thanksgiving, Christmas, New Year's Day. Adults, $3; students and senior citizens, $1·50; children, $1. Food concession open all year. Special programmes during the Christmas season; craft demonstrations. Maps and schedules available at the Visitors' Center. Tel: 351–9414.

TRANSPORTATION: Bus S113 from the St. George terminal of the Staten Island ferry to the restoration.

History. The village dates back to around 1700 when it was called 'Cocclestown', probably because of the oysters and clams found nearby, a name that degenerated to 'Cuckoldstown' and was prudently changed to Richmondtown by the end of the Revolution. It became the seat of the county government in 1729 and retained this position until 1898 when St. George superceded it, diminishing its importance and curtailing its development, but making it an attractive site for restoration. Since 1939 the Staten Island Historical Society has been restoring its historic buildings and moving to Richmondtown others on the island threatened with demolition. During the next few years the society plans to remove the roads and overhead power lines and to open the New Dorp train station as a food service building.

Just beyond the parking lot is the Visitors' Center in the *Third County Court House* (1837; DL), a Greek Revival courthouse with a central section of local traprock. To its left near Tysen Court is the *Reseau-Van Pelt Cemetery*, a small graveyard originally set aside on a remote part of a farm and used for family burials. Across Center St from the Third Court House is the *Second County Clerk's and Surrogate's Office* (1848; DL) which served in an official capacity until 1919. It is now undergoing restoration and is scheduled to re-open in 1983.

Across Court Pl. is the *Stephens House* (c. 1837; DL) and *Store* (c.

1840; DL), a modified Greek Revival home (period rooms) on its original site and a general store outfitted with the original coffee grinder, iron stove, and cracker barrel. Next to it is the small *Colon Store* (c. 1860; DL), now used as a tinsmith shop but built as a general store in the Pleasant Plains area of the island (N. of Tottenville). Just beyond it is the *Transportation Museum* (1966), whose collection includes carriages, firefighting equipment, and antique commercial vehicles, shown in changing exhibitions.

Walk up Court Pl past the Stephens House and Store to the *Grocery Store* (c. 1870; DL), originally a one-room frame country store now fitted out as a Print Shop with an 1820 press (undergoing restoration). Equally small is the adjacent *Carpenter Shop* (c. 1830; DL), once part of a farmhouse on the island, with exhibits of early hand tools. On the same side of the street at the corner of Richmond Rd is the *Bennett House* (1839; DL), on its original site. The large brick oven in the basement suggests that the house had an early bakeshop, which will be used for demonstrations of the 19C baking trade while the upper floors are to be used for doll and toy exhibits.

Facing the Bennett House on the other side of Richmond Rd is the *Guyon-Lake-Tysen* House (c. 1740; DL), one of the best surviving examples of Dutch Colonial architecture in the city with a characteristic gambrel roof and springing eaves. The house has a large kitchen with fireplace and beehive oven, Georgian panelling and furnishings in the West Rooms and Adams period panelling and furnishings in the East Rooms. In the basement a potter sometimes demonstrates his trade.

Next door is the *Britton Cottage* (c. 1670, with additions in c. 1755 and 1760; DL; not open), whose oldest section is believed to have been the Town House where public meetings were held. Facing the Britton Cottage across Richmond Rd are the *Barton House* (1866; DL), a Gothic Revival house on its original site scheduled to be decorated to be decorated with Victorian furnishings, and the *Guyon-Swaim Store* (c. 1815; DL; not open), also on its original site, used as a barter market until 1835 when it was converted into a house.

Turn right at Richmond Hill Rd and walk toward the Creek and Mill Pond. The *Cooper's Shop and Home* (c. 1790, with additions c. 1830 and c. 1860) was originally used as a dwelling and workplace for a barrelmaker but today houses a Leatherworker's Shop. In the center of the lot is the *Basketmaker's House* (c. 1810; DL) and next to the pond, the *Saw Mill* (c. 1800; DL) which when completed will have a wooden water wheel and gears.

Turn around and walk back up Richmond Hill Rd toward the center of town. On the right near the intersection of Richmond Rd is the *Treasure House* (c. 1700; DL; not open), so called because years ago $5000 worth of gold coins were discovered hidden within the walls. Samuel Grasset, a tanner and shoemaker from France, built it. Set back from the road is the *Christopher House* (c. 1696; DL; not open). The *Boehm-Frost House* (c. 1770, with additions, c. 1840; DL; not open), actually the Boehm House on the Frost foundation, preserves the homes of Henry Boehm, an educator, and Dr Thomas Frost, a physician whose original house burned down in 1883. The oldest part is faced with wide boards in contrast to the narrow, sawn clapboards of the later section.

One of the most important structures in Richmondtown, though not for its architecture, is the little frame *Voorlezer's House* (c. 1696; DL), built by the Dutch Reformed congregation for its 'voorlezer' or lay reader, who lived and also taught school there, making it the oldest elementary school building still standing in the nation.

The *Parsonage* (c. 1855; DL) on Arthur Kill Rd at Clarke Ave, a gabled, two-story Gothic Revival house on its original site, is now a private residence.

Near the restoration stand two churches of interest primarily to enthusiasts of local church architecture. *St. Andrew's (Protestant Episcopal) Church*, 4 Arthur Kill Rd, S.E. corner of Old Mill Rd (1872; William H. Mersereau; DL), at the marshy edge of Latourette Park, is a picturesque church that looks as if it had been transplanted from rural England with its random-fieldstone walls, bulls' eye windows, asymmetrical massing, and steep gables, all intact. *St. Patrick's (Roman Catholic) Church* (1862; DL), at 53 St. Patrick's Pl. between Center St and Clarke Ave, is a white brick Romanesque Revival church whose unusually narrow round-headed windows suggest the Gothic Revival style.

David Latourette once farmed the land now devoted to LATOURETTE PARK, and his masonry Greek Revival mansion (1836; DL) in the park E. of Richmond Hill Rd has become the clubhouse for the public golf course which occupies the N.E. part of the park.

The *Sylvanus Decker Farmhouse*, 435 Richmond Hill Rd between Forest Hill Rd and Bridgetown St (c. 1880; DL), a white clapboarded farmhouse, was left to the Staten Island Historical Society in 1955 by Richard Decker and is now a private dwelling.

60 Southern Staten Island: Pleasantville and Tottenville

At the S. tip of the island are **Pleasantville** and **Tottenville,** founded as fishing villages. The streets of Tottenville were once paved with oyster shells, and even now Main St is a throwback to an earlier, quieter time—tree-shaded, lined with 19C houses whose ginger-bread ornament recalls the skill of local craftsmen.

North of Tottenville in Pleasantville is the *Mount Loretto Home for Children* on Hylan Blvd between Sharrott and Richmond Aves, occupying a 650-acre estate run by the Mission of the Immaculate Virgin for children from broken homes. Father John C. Drumgoole founded the mission (1870) in Manhattan as a refuge for homeless newsboys and moved here 10 years later. The *Residence for the Mission of the Immaculate Virgin* was originally (c. 1868) the Prince's Bay Lighthouse and Keeper's House, (off Hylan Blvd W. of Sharrott Ave), its beacon now replaced by a statue of the Virgin Mary. The *Church of St. Joachim and St. Anne*, on the W. side of Hylan Blvd, first built in 1882, was reconstructed in 1976 after a fire three years earlier.

The indentation in the coast at the foot of Sharrott Ave is *Prince's Bay* in whose now-polluted waters once flourished oysters so fine the menus of fancy New York restaurants designated them by name.

At the foot of Hylan Blvd is Conference House Park whose westernmost tip is Wards Point where the Arthur Kill meets Raritan Bay. Overlooking the water is the stone **Billopp House,** also called the Conference House (c. 1680; DL), at 7445 Hyland Blvd, scene of an unsuccessful peace conference during the Revolutionary War.

Open Wed–Sun, 1–5; adults, 50¢; children under 12, free; tel: 984–2086.

PUBLIC TRANSPORTATION: Bus S103 from the St. George ferry terminal to the last stop on Craig Ave near the park. Or Staten Island Rapid Transit train from St. George to Tottenville Station; follow Bentley St to Craig Ave; turn right and continue to Hylan Ave; follow Hylan Ave a block to the park (about 1 mile altogether).

Set in an idyllic spot, its lawns sloping gently to the water's edge, the house has been restored and appointed with 18C furniture. The 17C basement kitchen, floored with Holland bricks made for the restoration, is especially interesting.

History. At some time around 1680 British sea captain Christopher Billopp built the manor which he called Bentley on land granted by governor Thomas Dongan. According to legend Billopp is responsible for Staten Island's belonging to New York instead of New Jersey. In 1664 when the British took over New Amsterdam the proprietors of New Jersey, the Lords of Berkeley and Carteret, claimed the island as theirs. To settle the dispute the Duke of York said he would award it to that province whose citizen could circumnavigate the island in less than 24 hours, a contest won for New York by Christopher Billopp. The manor house remained in the hands of his descendants and during the Revolution (11 Sept 1776) witnessed a conference between Admiral Lord Richard Howe, Benjamin Franklin, Edward Rutledge, and John Adams. Howe, who commanded the fleet anchored offshore, offered amnesty to any Americans who would lay down their arms and return to allegiance to the king, while the American representatives declined any offer of pardon that would not acknowledge the independence of the colonies. Later the house fell into disrepair and in the early years of the 20C was used as a factory for making rat poison, an activity that ended in 1918 when the explosion of a powder plant across the river blew out all its windows. Although plans for saving the manor house had been bandied about since 1846, work was not begun until 1926 when the Conference House Association was formed to rehabilitate and maintain it.

61 Western Staten Island: Charleston, Rossville, and Travis

Western Staten Island, mostly lowland, encompasses the communities of Charleston and Rossville and, N. of Fresh Kills, Travis, once called Linoleumville. Because no-one until recently found the salt marshes worth protecting, much of the S.W. part of the island has been used either for dumping or storing things. There are gas and oil storage areas, a graveyard for ships near St. Lukes Ave where rusting barges wallow on the tidal flats of the Arthur Kill, a huge garbage dump N. of Rossville, a city sewage disposal plant, railroad yards, and an industrial park.

In the 19C **Charleston,** then called Kreischerville, was a brickmaking town, its industry founded by Balthazar Kreischer who in 1854 discovered extensive clay deposits and started a factory. His home, the *Kreischer House*, (c. 1885; DL), a rural Victorian Gothic mansion with a trim of 'stickwork' like wooden lace applied decoratively to the irregular forms of its facade, stands in rapidly deteriorating condition at 4500 Arthur Kill Rd near Englewood Ave.

Further N. are the *Clay Pits*, E. of Arthur Kill Rd on both sides of Clay Pit Rd, a remote and strangely beautiful area known to conservationists for its pine barrens, forested with stunted trees and low bushes.

N. of Bloomingdale Rd along Arthur Kill Rd is tiny St. Luke's Cemetery (near Zebra Pl) over which loom the liquid-gas tanks of the

INDEX

Statues and monuments are indexed under personal names. Buildings without names are indexed under street addresses. Numbered streets designated at 'East' and 'West' are indexed according to those designations in numerical order. Names beginning with Saint (St.) are indexed under that heading.

Public Service Electric and Gas Company of New Jersey. Further N. at Rossville Ave is the Sleight Family graveyard, also known as the Blazing Star Burial Ground (after the Blazing Star ferry that once made regular crossings to New Jersey). Buried in it are members of families whose names are associated with the early years of Staten Island history: Winant, Seguine, Poillon, and Sleight, families also enshrined in local place names. The earliest grave dates from 1750.

The *Staten Island Mall*, Richmond Ave at the S.E. corner of Richmond Hill Rd (1973; Welton Becket & Assocs) is a big indoor shopping development erected for the area's burgeoning population. Many of the stores stand empty, however, since local Staten Islanders rather perversely choose to shop in New Jersey, ignoring the amount of pollution wafted their way from New Jersey industry and lured by lower taxes on gasoline and certain merchandise.

Typeset by Coats Dataprint Limited, Inverness, Scotland.
Printed by Fletcher & Son Limited, Norwich, England.